4th International Workshop on Semantic Evaluations 2007

(SemEval 2007)

Held in conjunction with ACL 2007

Prague, Czech Republic
23-24 June 2007

ISBN: 978-1-61738-517-9

Printed from e-media with permission by:

Curran Associates, Inc.
57 Morehouse Lane
Red Hook, NY 12571
www.proceedings.com

Some format issues inherent in the e-media version may also appear in this print version.

Printed by Curran Associates, Inc. (2010)

Association for Computational Linguistics
209 N. Eighth Street
Stroudsburg, Pennsylvania 18360

Phone: 1-570-476-8006
Fax: 1-570-476-0860

acl@aclweb.org

Preface

This volume contains papers describing the tasks and participating systems in SemEval-2007 — the Fourth International Workshop on Semantic Evaluations. The SemEval-2007 workshop was held in conjunction with the Association for Computational Linguistics meeting on June 23-24, 2007 in Prague, Czech Republic.

The ACL Special Interest Group on the Lexicon (SIGLEX) is the umbrella organization for SemEval-2007. SIGLEX previously ran three highly successful evaluation exercises for word sense disambiguation under the name Senseval. As the nature of the tasks in Senseval has evolved to include semantic analysis tasks outside of word sense disambiguation, the Senseval Committee changed the name of the evaluation exercises to SemEval.

SemEval-2007 was very successful. Our call for tasks solicited 27 task proposals. After a careful review process and a call for interest in participation, we selected 18 tasks to be part of the evaluation. Over 100 teams participated with over 125 unique systems. As a comparison, Senseval-3 (2004) organized 14 tasks with 55 teams.

Some tasks were updated versions of tasks found in Senseval-3, including lexical-sample word sense disambiguation tasks in Catalan, English, Spanish and Turkish, two all-words English word sense disambiguation tasks, and two multilingual lexical sample tasks (Chinese-English). The updates included using coarse-sense inventories, or combining word sense disambiguation and semantic role classification. The rest of the tasks were novel to this evaluation exercises, and some have been organized for the first time. Below is the full list of tasks. Note that Task 3 was withdrawn before the competition started.

- *Task 01: Evaluating WSD on Cross-Language Information Retrieval*
- *Task 02: Evaluating Word Sense Induction and Discrimination Systems*
- *Task 04: Classification of Semantic Relations between Nominals*
- *Task 05: Multilingual Chinese-English Lexical Sample*
- *Task 06: Word-Sense Disambiguation of Prepositions*
- *Task 07: Coarse-Grained English All-Words Task*
- *Task 08: Metonymy Resolution at SemEval-2007*
- *Task 09: Multilevel Semantic Annotation of Catalan and Spanish*
- *Task 10: English Lexical Substitution Task*
- *Task 11: English Lexical Sample Task via English-Chinese Parallel Text*
- *Task 12: Turkish Lexical Sample Task*
- *Task 13: Web People Search*

- *Task 14: Affective Text*
- *Task 15: TempEval Temporal Relation Identification*
- *Task 16: Evaluation of Wide Coverage Knowledge Resources*
- *Task-17: English Lexical Sample, SRL and All Words*
- *Task 18: Arabic Semantic Labeling*
- *Task 19: Frame Semantic Structure Extraction*

These proceedings include the descriptions of all tasks and most of the participating systems. The papers in these proceedings represent a wide variety of state-of-the-art methods for semantic analysis. The proceedings are organized as follows: we first present the task description papers, ordered by task number. System papers follow, with papers ordered according to system name. In addition to the usual author index we also include a task-system index in the back, for easier browsing.

All of the papers were peer-reviewed by the program committee, task organizers and fellow participants. We are truly grateful for everyone's careful and insightful reviews. The papers in this proceedings have benefited from this feedback.

We thank Ed Hovy for his invited talk, and we also thank the members of the two panels for providing discussion and insights on 1) inference with semantics, led by Bernarndo Magnini and 2) the future of SemEval, led by Rada Mihalcea.

The evaluation really comes down to the organization of the tasks. The task organizers did an extraordinary job of task design, data creation, and administration, under tight time constraints. We are grateful to the ACL 2007 conference organizers for local organization and the forum. We most gratefully acknowledge the support of our sponsor, the ACL Special Interest Group on the Lexicon (SIGLEX). Finally, the organizers wish to express their gratitude for the invaluable guidance provided by Rada Mihalcea and Phil Edmonds.

Eneko Agirre, Lluís Màrquez and Richard Wicentowski
June 2007

Organizers

Chairs:

Eneko Agirre, University of the Basque Country
Lluís Màrquez, Technical University of Catalonia
Richard Wicentowski, Swarthmore College

Task Organizers:

Eneko Agirre, University of the Basque Country
Javier Artiles, Universidad Nacional de Educación a Distancia
Collin Baker, International Computer Science Institute, Berkeley
Yee Seng Chan, National University of Singapore
Montse Cuadros, Technical University of Catalonia
Mona Diab, Columbia University
Michael Ellsworth, International Computer Science Institute, Berkeley
Katrin Erk, University of Texas at Austin
Christiane Fellbaum, Princeton University
Robert Gaizauskas, University of Sheffield
Roxana Girju, University of Illinois at Urbana-Champaign
Julio Gonzalo, Universidad Nacional de Educación a Distancia
Marti Hearst, University of California, Berkeley
Mark Hepple, University of Sheffield
Peng Jin, Peking University
Graham Katz, University of Osnabrück
Kenneth Litkowski, CL Research
Edward Loper, University of Pennsylvania
Oier Lopez de Lacalle, University of the Basque Country
Mohamed Maamouri, University of Pennsylvania
Bernardo Magnini, FBK/IRST
Katja Markert, University of Leeds
Lluís Màrquez, Technical University of Catalonia
M. Antònia Martí, University of Barcelona
Diana McCarthy, University of Sussex
Rada Mihalcea University of North Texas
Preslav Nakov, University of California, Berkeley
Vivi Nastase, European Media Laboratory
Roberto Navigli, University of Rome "La Sapienza"
Hwee Tou Ng, National University of Singapore
Malvina Nissim, University of Bologna and Institute for Cognitive Science and Technology
Zeynep Orhan, Fatih University
Arantxa Otegi, University of the Basque Country
Martha Palmer, University of Colorado at Boulder
Sameer Pradhan, BBN Technologies

James Pustejovsky, Brandeis University
German Rigau, University of the Basque Country
Satoshi Sekine, New York University
Frank Schilder, Thomson Legal & Regulatory
Aitor Soroa, University of the Basque Country
Carlo Strapparava, FBK/IRST
Stan Szpakowicz, University of Ottawa
Mariona Taulé, University of Barcelona
Peter Turney, National Research Council of Canada
Marc Verhagen, Brandeis University
Luis Villarejo, Technical University of Catalonia
Piek Vossen, Irion BV
Yunfang Wu, Peking University
Shiwen Yu, Peking University
Deniz Yuret, Koc University

Program Committee:

Collin Baker, University of California, Berkeley
Nicoletta Calzolari, Istituto di Linguistica Computazionale - CNR
Xavier Carreras, Massachusetts Institute of Technology
Walter Daelemans, University of Antwerp
Phil Edmonds, Sharp Laboratories of Europe
Julio Gonzalo, Universidad Nacional de Educación a Distancia
Veronique Hoste, University of Antwerp
Eduard Hovy, Information Science Institute
Nancy Ide, Vassar College
Adam Kilgarriff, The Lexicography Masterclass Ltd.
Dimitrios Kokkinakis, Goteborg University
Sadao Kurohashi, The University of Kyoto
Kenneth Litkowski, CL Research
Bernardo Magnini, FBK/IRST
David Martinez, University of Melbourne
Diana McCarthy, University of Sussex
Paola Merlo, University of Geneva
Rada Mihalcea University of North Texas
Hwee Tou Ng, National University of Singapore
German Rigau, University of the Basque Country
Mark Stevenson, University of Sheffield
Suzanne Stevenson, University of Toronto
Carlo Strapparava, FBK/IRST
Yorick Wilks, University of Sheffield
Dekai Wu, The Hong Kong University of Science & Technology
Deniz Yuret, Koc University

Additional Reviewers:

Task organizers and participant teams helped with the reviewing process. We also thank Marine Carpuat, Lluís Padró, and Horacio Rodríguez for serving as additional reviewers.

Invited Speaker:

Eduard Hovy, ISI - University of Southern California

Panel moderators:

Bernardo Magnini, FBK/IRST
Rada Mihalcea, University of North Texas

Sponsors:

ACL Special Interest Group on the Lexicon (SIGLEX)

Website:

`http://nlp.cs.swarthmore.edu/semeval/`

Table of Contents

Task description papers

System description papers

Indices

Conference Program

Saturday, June 23, 2007

9:00–9:15 Welcome

9:15–9:30 *SemEval-2007 Task 01: Evaluating WSD on Cross-Language Information Retrieval*
Eneko Agirre, Bernardo Magnini, Oier Lopez de Lacalle, Arantxa Otegi, German Rigau and Piek Vossen

9:30–9:45 *SemEval-2007 Task 02: Evaluating Word Sense Induction and Discrimination Systems*
Eneko Agirre and Aitor Soroa

9:45–10:00 *SemEval-2007 Task 04: Classification of Semantic Relations between Nominals*
Roxana Girju, Preslav Nakov, Vivi Nastase, Stan Szpakowicz, Peter Turney and Deniz Yuret

10:00–10:15 *UIUC: A Knowledge-rich Approach to Identifying Semantic Relations between Nominals*
Brandon Beamer, Suma Bhat, Brant Chee, Andrew Fister, Alla Rozovskaya and Roxana Girju

10:15–10:30 *FBK-IRST: Kernel Methods for Semantic Relation Extraction*
Claudio Giuliano, Alberto Lavelli, Daniele Pighin and Lorenza Romano

10:30–10:45 *SemEval-2007 Task 07: Coarse-Grained English All-Words Task*
Roberto Navigli, Kenneth C. Litkowski and Orin Hargraves

10:45–11:15 coffee break

11:15–11:30 *SemEval-2007 Task 08: Metonymy Resolution at SemEval-2007*
Katja Markert and Malvina Nissim

11:30–12:30 Invited Talk by Eduard Hovy: The OntoNotes project

12:30–14:30 lunch

Poster session 1

14:30–15:45 *SemEval-2007 Task 05: Multilingual Chinese-English Lexical Sample*
Peng Jin, Yunfang Wu and Shiwen Yu

SemEval-2007 Task 06: Word-Sense Disambiguation of Prepositions
Kenneth C. Litkowski and Orin Hargraves

CMU-AT: Semantic Distance and Background Knowledge for Identifying Semantic Relations
Alicia Tribble and Scott E. Fahlman

FUH (FernUniversität in Hagen): Metonymy Recognition Using Different Kinds of Context for a Memory-Based Learner
Johannes Leveling

GPLSI: Word Coarse-grained Disambiguation aided by Basic Level Concepts
Rubén Izquierdo, Armando Suárez and German Rigau

GYDER: Maxent Metonymy Resolution
Richárd Farkas, Eszter Simon, György Szarvas and Dániel Varga

HIT-WSD: Using Search Engine for Multilingual Chinese-English Lexical Sample Task
PengYuan Liu, TieJun Zhao and MuYun Yang

ILK: Machine learning of semantic relations with shallow features and almost no data
Iris Hendrickx, Roser Morante, Caroline Sporleder and Antal van den Bosch

IRST-BP: Preposition Disambiguation based on Chain Clarifying Relationships Contexts
Octavian Popescu, Sara Tonelli and Emanuele Pianta

LCC-SRN: LCC's SRN System for SemEval 2007 Task 4
Adriana Badulescu and Munirathnam Srikanth

LCC-WSD: System Description for English Coarse Grained All Words Task at SemEval 2007
Adrian Novischi, Muirathnam Srikanth and Andrew Bennett

MELB-KB: Nominal Classification as Noun Compound Interpretation
Su Nam Kim and Timothy Baldwin

Saturday, June 23, 2007 (continued)

MELB-YB: Preposition Sense Disambiguation Using Rich Semantic Features
Patrick Ye and Timothy Baldwin

SRCB-WSD: Supervised Chinese Word Sense Disambiguation with Key Features
Yun Xing

Sussx: WSD using Automatically Acquired Predominant Senses
Rob Koeling and Diana McCarthy

UCB: System Description for SemEval Task #4
Preslav Nakov and Marti Hearst

UCD-FC: Deducing semantic relations using WordNet senses that occur frequently in a database of noun-noun compounds
Fintan J. Costello

UCD-PN: Classification of Semantic Relations Between Nominals using WordNet and Web Counts
Paul Nulty

UCD-S1: A hybrid model for detecting semantic relations between noun pairs in text
Cristina Butnariu and Tony Veale

UCM3: Classification of Semantic Relations between Nominals using Sequential Minimal Optimization
Isabel Segura Bedmar, Doaa Samy and Jose L. Martinez

UMND2 : SenseClusters Applied to the Sense Induction Task of Senseval-4
Ted Pedersen

UNIBA: JIGSAW algorithm for Word Sense Disambiguation
Pierpaolo Basile, Marco de Gemmis, Anna Lisa Gentile, Pasquale Lops and Giovanni Semeraro

UOY: A Hypergraph Model For Word Sense Induction & Disambiguation
Ioannis Klapaftis and Suresh Manandhar

UP13: Knowledge-poor Methods (Sometimes) Perform Poorly
Thierry Poibeau

UPV-SI: Word Sense Induction using Self Term Expansion
David Pinto, Paolo Rosso and Héctor Jiménez-Salazar

UTD-HLT-CG: Semantic Architecture for Metonymy Resolution and Classification of Nominal Relations
Cristina Nicolae, Gabriel Nicolae and Sanda Harabagiu

UTH: SVM-based Semantic Relation Classification using Physical Sizes
Eiji Aramaki, Takeshi Imai, Kengo Miyo and Kazuhiko Ohe

UVAVU: WordNet Similarity and Lexical Patterns for Semantic Relation Classification
Willem Robert van Hage and Sophia Katrenko

UofL: Word Sense Disambiguation Using Lexical Cohesion
Yllias Chali and Shafiq R. Joty

XRCE-M: A Hybrid System for Named Entity Metonymy Resolution
Brun Caroline, Ehrmann Maud and Jacquet Guillaume

15:45–16:15 coffee break

16:15–16:30 *SemEval-2007 Task 10: English Lexical Substitution Task*
Diana McCarthy and Roberto Navigli

16:30–16:45 *SemEval-2007 Task 11: English Lexical Sample Task via English-Chinese Parallel Text*
Hwee Tou Ng and Yee Seng Chan

16:45–17:00 *The SemEval-2007 WePS Evaluation: Establishing a benchmark for the Web People Search Task*
Javier Artiles, Julio Gonzalo and Satoshi Sekine

17:00–17:15 *PSNUS: Web People Name Disambiguation by Simple Clustering with Rich Features*
Ergin Elmacioglu, Yee Fan Tan, Su Yan, Min-Yen Kan and Dongwon Lee

17:15–18:15 Panel: Inference with semantics: tasks and applications

Sunday, June 24, 2007

8:45–9:00	*SemEval-2007 Task 14: Affective Text* Carlo Strapparava and Rada Mihalcea
9:00–9:15	*CLaC and CLaC-NB: Knowledge-based and corpus-based approaches to sentiment tagging* Alina Andreevskaia and Sabine Bergler
9:15–9:30	*SemEval-2007 Task 15: TempEval Temporal Relation Identification* Marc Verhagen, Robert Gaizauskas, Frank Schilder, Mark Hepple, Graham Katz and James Pustejovsky
9:30–9:45	*WVALI: Temporal Relation Identification by Syntactico-Semantic Analysis* Georgiana Puşcaşu
9:45–10:00	*SemEval-2007 Task-17: English Lexical Sample, SRL and All Words* Sameer Pradhan, Edward Loper, Dmitriy Dligach and Martha Palmer
10:00–10:15	*I2R: Three Systems for Word Sense Discrimination, Chinese Word Sense Disambiguation, and English Word Sense Disambiguation* Zheng-Yu Niu, Dong-Hong Ji and Chew-Lim Tan
10:15–10:30	*NUS-PT: Exploiting Parallel Texts for Word Sense Disambiguation in the English All-Words Tasks* Yee Seng Chan, Hwee Tou Ng and Zhi Zhong
10:30–10:45	*UNT: SubFinder: Combining Knowledge Sources for Automatic Lexical Substitution* Samer Hassan, Andras Csomai, Carmen Banea, Ravi Sinha and Rada Mihalcea
10:45–11:15	coffee break

Sunday, June 24, 2007 (continued)

Poster session 2

Sunday, June 24, 2007 (continued)

HIT-IR-WSD: A WSD System for English Lexical Sample Task
Yuhang Guo, Wanxiang Che, Yuxuan Hu, Wei Zhang and Ting Liu

HIT: Web based Scoring Method for English Lexical Substitution
Shiqi Zhao, Lin Zhao, Yu Zhang, Ting Liu and Sheng Li

ILK2: Semantic Role Labeling of Catalan and Spanish using TiMBL
Roser Morante and Bertjan Busser

IRST-BP: Web People Search Using Name Entities
Octavian Popescu and Bernardo Magnini

JHU1 : An Unsupervised Approach to Person Name Disambiguation using Web Snippets
Delip Rao, Nikesh Garera and David Yarowsky

JU-SKNSB: Extended WordNet Based WSD on the English All-Words Task at SemEval-1
Sudip Kumar Naskar and Sivaji Bandyopadhyay

KU: Word Sense Disambiguation by Substitution
Deniz Yuret

LCC-TE: A Hybrid Approach to Temporal Relation Identification in News Text
Congmin Min, Munirathnam Srikanth and Abraham Fowler

MELB-MKB: Lexical Substitution system based on Relatives in Context
David Martinez, Su Nam Kim and Timothy Baldwin

NAIST.Japan: Temporal Relation Identification Using Dependency Parsed Tree
Yuchang Cheng, Masayuki Asahara and Yuji Matsumoto

NUS-ML:Improving Word Sense Disambiguation Using Topic Features
Jun Fu Cai, Wee Sun Lee and Yee Whye Teh

OE: WSD Using Optimal Ensembling (OE) Method
Harri M. T. Saarikoski

Sunday, June 24, 2007 (continued)

PKU: Combining Supervised Classifiers with Features Selection
Peng Jin, Danqing Zhu, Fuxin Li and Yunfang Wu

PNNL: A Supervised Maximum Entropy Approach to Word Sense Disambiguation
Stephen Tratz, Antonio Sanfilippo, Michelle Gregory, Alan Chappell, Christian Posse and Paul Whitney

PU-BCD: Exponential Family Models for the Coarse- and Fine-Grained All-Words Tasks
Jonathan Chang, Miroslav Dudik and David Blei

PUTOP: Turning Predominant Senses into a Topic Model for Word Sense Disambiguation
Jordan Boyd-Graber and David Blei

RACAI: Meaning Affinity Models
Radu Ion and Dan Tufiş

12:30–14:30 lunch

Poster session 3

14:30–15:45 *CLR: Integration of FrameNet in a Text Representation System*
Kenneth C. Litkowski

RTV: Tree Kernels for Thematic Role Classification
Daniele Pighin, Alessandro Moschitti and Roberto Basili

SHEF: Semantic Tagging and Summarization Techniques Applied to Cross-document Coreference
Horacio Saggion

SICS: Valence annotation based on seeds in word space
Magnus Sahlgren, Jussi Karlgren and Gunnar Eriksson

SW-AG: Local Context Matching for English Lexical Substitution
George Dahl, Anne-Marie Frassica and Richard Wicentowski

SWAT-MP:The SemEval-2007 Systems for Task 5 and Task 14
Phil Katz, Matt Singleton and Richard Wicentowski

Sunday, June 24, 2007 (continued)

Sunday, June 24, 2007 (continued)

UNN-WePS: Web Person Search using co-Present Names and Lexical Chains
Jeremy Ellman and Gary Emery

UNT-Yahoo: SuperSenseLearner: Combining SenseLearner with SuperSense and other Coarse Semantic Features
Rada Mihalcea, Andras Csomai and Massimiliano Ciaramita

UPAR7: A knowledge-based system for headline sentiment tagging
François-Régis Chaumartin

UPV-WSD : Combining different WSD Methods by means of Fuzzy Borda Voting
Davide Buscaldi and Paolo Rosso

USFD: Preliminary Exploration of Features and Classifiers for the TempEval-2007 Task
Mark Hepple, Andrea Setzer and Robert Gaizauskas

USP-IBM-1 and USP-IBM-2: The ILP-based Systems for Lexical Sample WSD in SemEval-2007
Lucia Specia, Maria das Graças, Volpe Nunes, Ashwin Srinivasan and Ganesh Ramakrishnan

USYD: WSD and Lexical Substitution using the Web1T corpus
Tobias Hawker

UTD-SRL: A Pipeline Architecture for Extracting Frame Semantic Structures
Cosmin Adrian Bejan and Chris Hathaway

UVA: Language Modeling Techniques for Web People Search
Krisztian Balog, Leif Azzopardi and Maarten de Rijke

WIT: Web People Search Disambiguation using Random Walks
José Iria, Lei Xia and Ziqi Zhang

XRCE-T: XIP Temporal Module for TempEval campaign.
Caroline Hagège and Xavier Tannier

15:45–16:15 coffee break

16:15–16:30 *UPC: Experiments with Joint Learning within SemEval Task 9*
Lluís Màrquez, Lluís Padró, Mihai Surdeanu and Luis Villarejo

Sunday, June 24, 2007 (continued)

16:30–16:45 *SemEval-2007 Task 19: Frame Semantic Structure Extraction*
Collin Baker, Michael Ellsworth and Katrin Erk

16:45–17:00 *LTH: Semantic Structure Extraction using Nonprojective Dependency Trees*
Richard Johansson and Pierre Nugues

17:00–18:00 Panel: Planning the future of SemEval

18:00 Closing

SemEval-2007 Task 01: Evaluating WSD on Cross-Language Information Retrieval

Eneko Agirre
IXA NLP group
University of the Basque Country
Donostia, Basque Counntry
e.agirre@ehu.es

Bernardo Magnini
ITC-IRST
Trento, Italy
magnini@itc.it

Oier Lopez de Lacalle
IXA NLP group
University of the Basque Country
Donostia, Basque Country
jibloleo@ehu.es

Arantxa Otegi
IXA NLP group
University of the Basque Country
Donostia, Basque Country
jibotusa@ehu.es

German Rigau
IXA NLP group
University of the Basque Country
Donostia, Basque Country
german.rigau@ehu.es

Piek Vossen
Irion Technologies
Delftechpark 26
2628XH Delft, Netherlands
Piek.Vossen@irion.nl

Abstract

This paper presents a first attempt of an application-driven evaluation exercise of WSD. We used a CLIR testbed from the Cross Lingual Evaluation Forum. The expansion, indexing and retrieval strategies where fixed by the organizers. The participants had to return both the topics and documents tagged with WordNet 1.6 word senses. The organization provided training data in the form of a pre-processed Semcor which could be readily used by participants. The task had two participants, and the organizer also provide an in-house WSD system for comparison.

1 Introduction

Since the start of Senseval, the evaluation of Word Sense Disambiguation (WSD) as a separate task is a mature field, with both lexical-sample and all-words tasks. In the first case the participants need to tag the occurrences of a few words, for which hand-tagged data has already been provided. In the all-words task all the occurrences of open-class words occurring in two or three documents (a few thousand words) need to be disambiguated.

The community has long mentioned the necessity of evaluating WSD in an application, in order to check which WSD strategy is best, and more important, to try to show that WSD can make a difference in applications. The use of WSD in Machine Translation has been the subject of some recent papers, but less attention has been paid to Information Retrieval (IR).

With this proposal we want to make a first try to define a task where WSD is evaluated with respect to an Information Retrieval and Cross-Lingual Information Retrieval (CLIR) exercise. From the WSD perspective, this task will evaluate all-words WSD systems indirectly on a real task. From the CLIR perspective, this task will evaluate which WSD systems and strategies work best.

We are conscious that the number of possible configurations for such an exercise is very large (including sense inventory choice, using word sense induction instead of disambiguation, query expansion, WSD strategies, IR strategies, etc.), so this first edition focuses on the following:

- The IR/CLIR system is fixed.
- The expansion / translation strategy is fixed.
- The participants can choose the best WSD strategy.

Proceedings of the 4th International Workshop on Semantic Evaluations (SemEval-2007), pages 1–6,
Prague, June 2007.

- The IR system is used as the upperbound for the CLIR systems.

We think that it is important to start doing this kind of application-driven evaluations, which might shed light to the intricacies in the interaction between WSD and IR strategies. We see this as the first of a series of exercises, and one outcome of this task should be that both WSD and CLIR communities discuss together future evaluation possibilities.

This task has been organized in collaboration with the Cross-Language Evaluation Forum (CLEF[1]). The results will be analyzed in the CLEF-2007 workshop, and a special track will be proposed for CLEF-2008, where CLIR systems will have the opportunity to use the annotated data produced as a result of the Semeval-2007 task. The task has a webpage with all the details at `http://ixa2.si.ehu.es/semeval-clir`.

This paper is organized as follows. Section 2 describes the task with all the details regarding datasets, expansion/translation, the IR/CLIR system used, and steps for participation. Section 3 presents the evaluation performed and the results obtained by the participants. Finally, Section 4 draws the conclusions and mention the future work.

2 Description of the task

This is an application-driven task, where the application is a fixed CLIR system. Participants disambiguate text by assigning WordNet 1.6 synsets and the system will do the expansion to other languages, index the expanded documents and run the retrieval for all the languages in batch. The retrieval results are taken as the measure for fitness of the disambiguation. The modules and rules for the expansion and the retrieval will be exactly the same for all participants.

We proposed two specific subtasks:

1. Participants disambiguate the corpus, the corpus is expanded to synonyms/translations and we measure the effects on IR/CLIR. Topics[2] are not processed.
2. Participants disambiguate the topics per language, we expand the queries to synonyms/translations and we measure the effects on IR/CLIR. Documents are not processed

The corpora and topics were obtained from the ad-hoc CLEF tasks. The supported languages in the topics are English and Spanish, but in order to limit the scope of the exercise we decided to only use English documents. The participants only had to disambiguate the English topics and documents. Note that most WSD systems only run on English text.

Due to these limitations, we had the following evaluation settings:

IR with WSD of topics , where the participants disambiguate the documents, the disambiguated documents are expanded to synonyms, and the original topics are used for querying. All documents and topics are in English.

IR with WSD of documents , where the participants disambiguate the topics, the disambiguated topics are expanded and used for querying the original documents. All documents and topics are in English.

CLIR with WSD of documents , where the participants disambiguate the documents, the disambiguated documents are translated, and the original topics in Spanish are used for querying. The documents are in English and the topics are in Spanish.

We decided to focus on CLIR for evaluation, given the difficulty of improving IR. The IR results are given as illustration, and as an upperbound of the CLIR task. This use of IR results as a reference for CLIR systems is customary in the CLIR community (Harman, 2005).

2.1 Datasets

The English CLEF data from years 2000-2005 comprises corpora from 'Los Angeles Times' (year 1994) and 'Glasgow Herald' (year 1995) amounting to 169,477 documents (579 MB of raw text, 4.8GB in the XML format provided to participants, see Section 2.3) and 300 topics in English and Spanish (the topics are human translations of each other). The relevance judgments were taken from CLEF. This

[1]`http://www.clef-campaign.org`

[2]In IR topics are the short texts which are used by the systems to produce the queries. They usually provide extensive information about the text to be searched, which can be used both by the search engine and the human evaluators.

might have the disadvantage of having been produced by pooling the results of CLEF participants, and might bias the results towards systems not using WSD, specially for monolingual English retrieval. We are considering the realization of a post-hoc analysis of the participants results in order to analyze the effect on the lack of pooling.

Due to the size of the document collection, we decided that the limited time available in the competition was too short to disambiguate the whole collection. We thus chose to take a sixth part of the corpus at random, comprising 29,375 documents (874MB in the XML format distributed to participants). Not all topics had relevant documents in this 17% sample, and therefore only 201 topics were effectively used for evaluation. All in all, we reused 21,797 relevance judgements that contained one of the documents in the 17% sample, from which 923 are positive[3]. For the future we would like to use the whole collection.

2.2 Expansion and translation

For expansion and translation we used the publicly available Multilingual Central Repository (MCR) from the MEANING project (Atserias et al., 2004). The MCR follows the EuroWordNet design, and currently includes English, Spanish, Italian, Basque and Catalan wordnets tightly connected through the Interlingual Index (based on WordNet 1.6, but linked to all other WordNet versions).

We only expanded (translated) the senses returned by the WSD systems. That is, given a word like 'car', it will be expanded to 'automobile' or 'railcar' (and translated to 'auto' or 'vagón' respectively) depending on the sense in WN 1.6. If the systems returns more than one sense, we choose the sense with maximum weight. In case of ties, we expand (translate) all. The participants could thus implicitly affect the expansion results, for instance, when no sense could be selected for a target noun, the participants could either return nothing (or NOSENSE, which would be equivalent), or all senses with 0 score. In the first case no expansion would be performed, in the second all senses would be expanded, which is equivalent to full expansion. This fact will be mentioned again in Section 3.5.

[3]The overall figures are 125,556 relevance judgements for the 300 topics, from which 5700 are positive

Note that in all cases we never delete any of the words in the original text.

In addition to the expansion strategy used with the participants, we tested other expansion strategies as baselines:

noexp no expansion, original text
fullexp expansion (translation in the case of English to Spanish expansion) to all synonyms of all senses
wsd50 expansion to the best 50% senses as returned by the WSD system. This expansion was tried over the in-house WSD system of the organizer only.

2.3 IR/CLIR system

The retrieval engine is an adaptation of the Twenty-One search system (Hiemstra and Kraaij, 1998) that was developed during the 90's by the TNO research institute at Delft (The Netherlands) getting good results on IR and CLIR exercises in TREC (Harman, 2005). It is now further developed by Irion technologies as a cross-lingual retrieval system (Vossen et al.,). For indexing, the TwentyOne system takes Noun Phrases as an input. Noun Phases (NPs) are detected using a chunker and a word form with POS lexicon. Phrases outside the NPs are not indexed, as well as non-content words (determiners, prepositions, etc.) within the phrase.

The Irion TwentyOne system uses a two-stage retrieval process where relevant documents are first extracted using a vector space matching and secondly phrases are matched with specific queries. Likewise, the system is optimized for high-precision phrase retrieval with short queries (1 up 5 words with a phrasal structure as well). The system can be stripped down to a basic vector space retrieval system with an tf.idf metrics that returns documents for topics up to a length of 30 words. The stripped-down version was used for this task to make the retrieval results compatible with the TREC/CLEF system.

The Irion system was also used for pre-processing. The CLEF corpus and topics were converted to the TwentyOne XML format, normalized, and named-entities and phrasal structured detected. Each of the target tokens was identified by an unique identifier.

2.4 Participation

The participants were provided with the following:

1. the document collection in Irion XML format
2. the topics in Irion XML format

In addition, the organizers also provided some of the widely used WSD features in a word-to-word fashion[4] (Agirre et al., 2006) in order to make participation easier. These features were available for both topics and documents as well as for all the words with frequency above 10 in SemCor 1.6 (which can be taken as the training data for supervised WSD systems). The Semcor data is publicly available [5]. For the rest of the data, participants had to sign and end user agreement.

The participants had to return the input files enriched with WordNet 1.6 sense tags in the required XML format:

1. for all the documents in the collection
2. for all the topics

Scripts to produce the desired output from word-to-word files and the input files were provided by organizers, as well as DTD's and software to check that the results were conformant to the respective DTD's.

3 Evaluation and results

For each of the settings presented in Section 2 we present the results of the participants, as well as those of an in-house system presented by the organizers. Please refer to the system description papers for a more complete description. We also provide some baselines and alternative expansion (translation) strategies. All systems are evaluated according to their Mean Average Precision [6] (MAP) as computed by the `trec_eval` software on the pre-existing CLEF relevance-assessments.

3.1 Participants

The two systems that registered sent the results on time.

PUTOP They extend on McCarthy's predominant sense method to create an unsupervised method of word sense disambiguation that uses automatically derived topics using Latent Dirichlet Allocation. Using topic-specific synset similarity measures, they create predictions for each word in each document using only word frequency information. The disambiguation process took aprox. 12 hours on a cluster of 48 machines (dual Xeons with 4GB of RAM). Note that contrary to the specifications, this team returned WordNet 2.1 senses, so we had to map automatically to 1.6 senses (Daude et al., 2000).

UNIBA This team uses a a knowledge-based WSD system that attempts to disambiguate all words in a text by exploiting WordNet relations. The main assumption is that a specific strategy for each Part-Of-Speech (POS) is better than a single strategy. Nouns are disambiguated basically using hypernymy links. Verbs are disambiguated according to the nouns surrounding them, and adjectives and adverbs use glosses.

ORGANIZERS In addition to the regular participants, and out of the competition, the organizers run a regular supervised WSD system trained on Semcor. The system is based on a single k-NN classifier using the features described in (Agirre et al., 2006) and made available at the task website (cf. Section 2.4).

In addition to those we also present some common IR/CLIR baselines, baseline WSD systems, and an alternative expansion:

noexp a non-expansion IR/CLIR baseline of the documents or topics.

fullexp a full-expansion IR/CLIR baseline of the documents or topics.

wsdrand a WSD baseline system which chooses a sense at random. The usual expansion is applied.

1st a WSD baseline system which returns the sense numbered as 1 in WordNet. The usual expansion is applied.

wsd50 the organizer's WSD system, where the 50% senses of the word ranking according to the WSD system are expanded. That is, instead of expanding the single best sense, it expands the best 50% senses.

3.2 IR Results

This section present the results obtained by the participants and baselines in the two IR settings. The

[4]Each target word gets a file with all the occurrences, and each occurrence gets the occurrence identifier, the sense tag (if in training), and the list of features that apply to the occurrence.

[5]`http://ixa2.si.ehu.es/semeval-clir/`

[6]`http://en.wikipedia.org/wiki/Information_retrieval`

	IRtops	IRdocs	CLIR
no expansion	0.3599	0.3599	0.1446
full expansion	0.1610	0.1410	0.2676
UNIBA	0.3030	0.1521	0.1373
PUTOP	0.3036	0.1482	0.1734
wsdrand	0.2673	0.1482	0.2617
1st sense	0.2862	0.1172	0.2637
ORGANIZERS	0.2886	0.1587	0.2664
wsd50	0.2651	0.1479	0.2640

Table 1: Retrieval results given as MAP. IRtops stands for English IR with topic expansion. IRdocs stands for English IR with document expansion. CLIR stands for CLIR results for translated documents.

Senseval-2 all words			
	precision	recall	coverage
ORGANIZERS	0.584	0.577	93.61%
UNIBA	0.498	0.375	75.39%
PUTOP	0.388	0.240	61.92%
Senseval-3 all words			
	precision	recall	coverage
ORGANIZERS	0.591	0.566	95.76%
UNIBA	0.484	0.338	69.98%
PUTOP	0.334	0.186	55.68%

Table 2: English WSD results in the Senseval-2 and Senseval-3 all-words datasets.

second and third columns of Table 1 present the results when disambiguating the topics and the documents respectively. Non of the expansion techniques improves over the baseline (no expansion).

Note that due to the limitation of the search engine, long queries were truncated at 50 words, which might explain the very low results of the full expansion.

3.3 CLIR results

The last column of Table 1 shows the CLIR results when expanding (translating) the disambiguated documents. None of the WSD systems attains the performance of full expansion, which would be the baseline CLIR system, but the WSD of the organizer gets close.

3.4 WSD results

In addition to the IR and CLIR results we also provide the WSD performance of the participants on the Senseval 2 and 3 all-words task. The documents from those tasks were included alongside the CLEF documents, in the same formats, so they are treated as any other document. In order to evaluate, we had to map automatically all WSD results to the respective WordNet version (using the mappings in (Daude et al., 2000) which are publicly available).

The results are presented in Table 2, where we can see that the best results are attained by the organizers WSD system.

3.5 Discussion

First of all, we would like to mention that the WSD and expansion strategy, which is very simplistic, degrades the IR performance. This was rather expected, as the IR experiments had an illustration goal, and are used for comparison with the CLIR experiments. In monolingual IR, expanding the topics is much less harmful than expanding the documents. Unfortunately the limitation to 50 words in the queries might have limited the expansion of the topics, which make the results rather unreliable. We plan to fix this for future evaluations.

Regarding CLIR results, even if none of the WSD systems were able to beat the full-expansion baseline, the organizers system was very close, which is quite encouraging due to the very simplistic expansion, indexing and retrieval strategies used.

In order to better interpret the results, Table 3 shows the amount of words after the expansion in each case. This data is very important in order to understand the behavior of each of the systems. Note that UNIBA returns 3 synsets at most, and therefore the wsd50 strategy (select the 50% senses with best score) leaves a single synset, which is the same as taking the single best system (wsdbest). Regarding PUTOP, this system returned a single synset, and therefore the wsd50 figures are the same as the wsdbest figures.

Comparing the amount of words for the two participant systems, we see that UNIBA has the least words, closely followed by PUTOP. The organizers WSD system gets far more expanded words. The explanation is that when the synsets returned by a WSD system all have 0 weights, the wsdbest expansion strategy expands them all. This was not explicit in the rules for participation, and might have affected the results.

A cross analysis of the result tables and the number of words is interesting. For instance, in the IR exercise, when we expand documents, the results in

		English	Spanish
No WSD	noexp	9,900,818	9,900,818
	fullexp	93,551,450	58,491,767
UNIBA	wsdbest	19,436,374	17,226,104
	wsd50	19,436,374	17,226,104
PUTOP	wsdbest	20,101,627	16,591,485
	wsd50	20,101,627	16,591,485
Baseline	1st	24,842,800	20,261,081
WSD	wsdrand	24,904,717	19,137,981
ORG.	wsdbest	26,403,913	21,086,649
	wsd50	36,128,121	27,528,723

Table 3: Number of words in the document collection after expansion for the WSD system and all baselines. wsdbest stands for the expansion strategy used with participants.

the third column of Table 1 show that the ranking for the non-informed baselines is the following: best for no expansion, second for random WSD, and third for full expansion. These results can be explained because of the amount of expansion: the more expansion the worst results. When more informed WSD is performed, documents with more expansion can get better results, and in fact the WSD system of the organizers is the second best result from all system and baselines, and has more words than the rest (with exception of wsd50 and full expansion). Still, the no expansion baseline is far from the WSD results.

Regarding the CLIR result, the situation is inverted, with the best results for the most productive expansions (full expansion, random WSD and no expansion, in this order). For the more informed WSD methods, the best results are again for the organizers WSD system, which is very close to the full expansion baseline. Even if wsd50 has more expanded words wsdbest is more effective. Note the very high results attained by random. These high results can be explained by the fact that many senses get the same translation, and thus for many words with few translation, the random translation might be valid. Still the wsdbest, 1st sense and wsd50 results get better results.

4 Conclusions and future work

This paper presents the results of a preliminary attempt of an application-driven evaluation exercise of WSD in CLIR. The expansion, indexing and retrieval strategies proved too simplistic, and none of the two participant systems and the organizers system were able to beat the full-expansion baseline. Due to efficiency reasons, the IRION system had some of its features turned off. Still the results are encouraging, as the organizers system was able to get very close to the full expansion strategy with much less expansion (translation).

For the future, a special track of CLEF-2008 will leave the avenue open for more sophisticated CLIR techniques. We plan to extend the WSD annotation to all words in the CLEF English document collection, and we also plan to contact the best performing systems of the SemEval all-words tasks to have better quality annotations.

Acknowledgements

We wish to thank CLEF for allowing us to use their data, and the CLEF coordinator, Carol Peters, for her help and collaboration. This work has been partially funded by the Spanish education ministry (project KNOW)

References

E. Agirre, O. Lopez de Lacalle, and D. Martinez. 2006. Exploring feature set combinations for WSD. In *Proc. of the SEPLN.*

J. Atserias, L. Villarejo, G. Rigau, E. Agirre, J. Carroll, B. Magnini, and P. Vossen. 2004. The MEANING Multilingual Central Repository. In *Proceedings of the 2.nd Global WordNet Conference, GWC 2004*, pages 23–30. Masaryk University, Brno, Czech Republic.

J. Daude, L. Padro, and G. Rigau. 2000. Mapping WordNets Using Structural Information. In *Proc. of ACL*, Hong Kong.

D. Harman. 2005. Beyond English. In E. M. Voorhees and D. Harman, editors, *TREC: Experiment and Evaluation in Information Retrieval*, pages 153–181. MIT press.

D. Hiemstra and W. Kraaij. 1998. Twenty-One in ad-hoc and CLIR. In E.M. Voorhees and D. K. Harman, editors, *Proc. of TREC-7*, pages 500–540. NIST Special Publication.

P. Vossen, G. Rigau, I. Alegria, E. Agirre, D. Farwell, and M. Fuentes. Meaningful results for Information Retrieval in the MEANING project. In *Proc. of the 3rd Global Wordnet Conference*.

Semeval-2007 Task 02: Evaluating Word Sense Induction and Discrimination Systems

Eneko Agirre
IXA NLP Group
Univ. of the Basque Country
Donostia, Basque Country
e.agirre@ehu.es

Aitor Soroa
IXA NLP Group
Univ. of the Basque Country
Donostia, Basque Country
a.soroa@ehu.es

Abstract

The goal of this task is to allow for comparison across sense-induction and discrimination systems, and also to compare these systems to other supervised and knowledge-based systems. In total there were 6 participating systems. We reused the SemEval-2007 English lexical sample subtask of task 17, and set up both clustering-style unsupervised evaluation (using OntoNotes senses as gold-standard) and a supervised evaluation (using the part of the dataset for mapping). We provide a comparison to the results of the systems participating in the lexical sample subtask of task 17.

1 Introduction

Word Sense Disambiguation (WSD) is a key enabling-technology. Supervised WSD techniques are the best performing in public evaluations, but need large amounts of hand-tagging data. Existing hand-annotated corpora like SemCor (Miller et al., 1993), which is annotated with WordNet senses (Fellbaum, 1998) allow for a small improvement over the simple most frequent sense heuristic, as attested in the all-words track of the last Senseval competition (Snyder and Palmer, 2004). In theory, larger amounts of training data (SemCor has approx. 500M words) would improve the performance of supervised WSD, but no current project exists to provide such an expensive resource. Another problem of the supervised approach is that the inventory and distribution of senses changes dramatically from one domain to the other, requiring additional hand-tagging of corpora (Martínez and Agirre, 2000; Koeling et al., 2005).

Supervised WSD is based on the "fixed-list of senses" paradigm, where the senses for a target word are a closed list coming from a dictionary or lexicon. Lexicographers and semanticists have long warned about the problems of such an approach, where senses are listed separately as discrete entities, and have argued in favor of more complex representations, where, for instance, senses are dense regions in a continuum (Cruse, 2000).

Unsupervised Word Sense Induction and Discrimination (WSID, also known as corpus-based unsupervised systems) has followed this line of thinking, and tries to induce word senses directly from the corpus. Typical WSID systems involve clustering techniques, which group together similar examples. Given a set of induced clusters (which represent word *uses* or senses[1]), each new occurrence of the target word will be compared to the clusters and the most similar cluster will be selected as its sense.

One of the problems of unsupervised systems is that of managing to do a fair evaluation. Most of current unsupervised systems are evaluated in-house, with a brief comparison to a re-implementation of a former system, leading to a proliferation of unsupervised systems with little ground to compare among them. The goal of this task is to allow for comparison across sense-induction and discrimination systems, and also to compare these systems to other supervised and knowledge-based systems.

The paper is organized as follows. Section 2 presents the evaluation framework used in this task. Section 3 presents the systems that participated in

[1]WSID approaches prefer the term 'word uses' to 'word senses'. In this paper we use them interchangeably to refer to both the induced clusters, and to the word senses from some reference lexicon.

Proceedings of the 4th International Workshop on Semantic Evaluations (SemEval-2007), pages 7–12,
Prague, June 2007.

the task, and the official results. Finally, Section 5 draws the conclusions.

2 Evaluating WSID systems

All WSID algorithms need some addition in order to be evaluated. One alternative is to manually decide the correctness of the clusters assigned to each occurrence of the words. This approach has two main disadvantages. First, it is expensive to manually verify each occurrence of the word, and different runs of the algorithm need to be evaluated in turn. Second, it is not an easy task to manually decide if an occurrence of a word effectively corresponds with the use of the word the assigned cluster refers to, especially considering that the person is given a short list of words linked to the cluster. We also think that instead of judging whether the cluster returned by the algorithm is correct, the person should have independently tagged the occurrence with his own senses, which should have been then compared to the cluster returned by the system. This is paramount to compare a corpus which has been hand-tagged with some reference senses (also known as the gold-standard) with the clustering result. The gold standard tags are taken to be the definition of the classes, and standard measures from the clustering literature can be used to evaluate the clusters against the classes.

A second alternative would be to devise a method to map the clusters returned by the systems to the senses in a lexicon. Pantel and Lin (2002) automatically map the senses to WordNet, and then measure the quality of the mapping. More recently, the mapping has been used to test the system on publicly available benchmarks (Purandare and Pedersen, 2004; Niu et al., 2005).

A third alternative is to evaluate the systems according to some performance in an application, e.g. information retrieval (Schütze, 1998). This is a very attractive idea, but requires expensive system development and it is sometimes difficult to separate the reasons for the good (or bad) performance.

In this task we decided to adopt the first two alternatives, since they allow for comparison over publicly available systems of any kind. With this goal on mind we gave all the participants an unlabeled corpus, and asked them to induce the senses and create a clustering solution on it. We evaluate the results according to the following types of evaluation:

1. Evaluate the induced senses as clusters of examples. The induced clusters are compared to the sets of examples tagged with the given gold standard word senses (classes), and evaluated using the FScore measure for clusters. We will call this evaluation *unsupervised*.
2. Map the induced senses to gold standard senses, and use the mapping to tag the test corpus with gold standard tags. The mapping is automatically produced by the organizers, and the resulting results evaluated according to the usual precision and recall measures for supervised word sense disambiguation systems. We call this evaluation *supervised*.

We will see each of them in turn.

2.1 Unsupervised evaluation

In this setting the results of the systems are treated as clusters of examples and gold standard senses are classes. In order to compare the clusters with the classes, hand annotated corpora is needed. The test set is first tagged with the induced senses. A perfect clustering solution will be the one where each cluster has exactly the same examples as one of the classes, and vice versa.

Following standard cluster evaluation practice (Zhao and Karypis, 2005), we consider the FScore measure for measuring the performance of the systems. The FScore is used in a similar fashion to Information Retrieval exercises, with precision and recall defined as the percentage of correctly "retrieved" examples for a cluster (divided by total cluster size), and recall as the percentage of correctly "retrieved" examples for a cluster (divided by total class size).

Given a particular class s_r of size n_r and a cluster h_i of size n_i, suppose n_r^i examples in the class s_r belong to h_i. The F value of this class and cluster is defined to be:

$$f(s_r, h_i) = \frac{2P(s_r, h_i)R(s_r, h_i)}{P(s_r, h_i) + R(s_r, h_i)}$$

where $P(s_r, h_i) = \frac{n_r^i}{n_r}$ is the precision value and $R(s_r, h_i) = \frac{n_r^i}{n_i}$ is the recall value defined for class s_r and cluster h_i. The FScore of class s_r is the maximum F value attained at any cluster, that is,

$$F(s_r) = \max_{h_i} f(s_r, h_i)$$

and the FScore of the entire clustering solution is:

$$\text{FScore} = \sum_{r=1}^{c} \frac{n_r}{n} F(s_r)$$

where q is the number of classes and n is the size of the clustering solution. If the clustering is the identical to the original classes in the datasets, FScore will be equal to one which means that the higher the FScore, the better the clustering is.

For the sake of completeness we also include the standard entropy and purity measures in the unsupervised evaluation. The entropy measure considers how the various classes of objects are distributed within each cluster. In general, the smaller the entropy value, the better the clustering algorithm performs. The purity measure considers the extent to which each cluster contained objects from primarily one class. The larger the values of purity, the better the clustering algorithm performs. For a formal definition refer to (Zhao and Karypis, 2005).

2.2 Supervised evaluation

We have followed the supervised evaluation framework for evaluating WSID systems as described in (Agirre et al., 2006). First, we split the corpus into a train/test part. Using the hand-annotated sense information in the train part, we compute a mapping matrix M that relates clusters and senses in the following way. Suppose there are m clusters and n senses for the target word. Then, $M = \{m_{ij}\}$ $1 \leq i \leq m, 1 \leq j \leq n$, and each $m_{ij} = P(s_j|h_i)$, that is, m_{ij} is the probability of a word having sense j given that it has been assigned cluster i. This probability can be computed counting the times an occurrence with sense s_j has been assigned cluster h_i in the train corpus.

The mapping matrix is used to transform any cluster score vector $\bar{h} = (h_1, \ldots, h_m)$ returned by the WSID algorithm into a sense score vector $\bar{s} = (s_1, \ldots, s_n)$. It suffices to multiply the score vector by M, i.e., $\bar{s} = \bar{h}M$.

We use the M mapping matrix in order to convert the cluster score vector of each test corpus instance into a sense score vector, and assign the sense with maximum score to that instance. Finally, the resulting test corpus is evaluated according to the usual precision and recall measures for supervised word sense disambiguation systems.

	All	Nouns	Verbs
train	22281	14746	9773
test	4851	2903	2427
all	27132	17649	12200

Table 1: Number of occurrences for the 100 target words in the corpus following the train/test split.

3 Results

In this section we will introduce the gold standard and corpus used, the description of the systems and the results obtained. Finally we provide some material for discussion.

Gold Standard

The data used for the actual evaluation was borrowed from the SemEval-2007 “English lexical sample subtask” of task 17. The texts come from the Wall Street Journal corpus, and were hand-annotated with OntoNotes senses (Hovy et al., 2006). Note that OntoNotes senses are coarser than WordNet senses, and thus the number of senses to be induced is smaller in this case.

Participants were provided with information about 100 target words (65 verbs and 35 nouns), each target word having a set of contexts where the word appears. After removing the sense tags from the train corpus, the train and test parts were joined into the official corpus and given to the participants. Participants had to tag with the induced senses all the examples in this corpus. Table 1 summarizes the size of the corpus.

Participant systems

In total there were 6 participant systems. One of them (UoFL) was not a sense induction system, but rather a knowledge-based WSD system. We include their data in the results section below for coherence with the official results submitted to participants, but we will not mention it here.

I2R: This team used a cluster validation method to estimate the number of senses of a target word in untagged data, and then grouped the instances of this target word into the estimated number of clusters using the sequential Information Bottleneck algorithm.

UBC-AS: A two stage graph-based clustering where a co-occurrence graph is used to compute similarities against contexts. The context similarity matrix is pruned and the resulting associated graph is clustered by means of a random-walk type algorithm. The parameters of the system are tuned against the Senseval-3 lexical sample dataset, and some manual tuning is performed in order to reduce the overall number of induced senses. Note that this system was submitted by the organizers. The organizers took great care in order to participate under the same conditions as the rest of participants.

UMND2: A system which clusters the second order co-occurrence vectors associated with each word in a context. Clustering is done using k-means and the number of clusters was automatically discovered using the Adapted Gap Statistic. No parameter tuning is performed.

upv_si: A self-term expansion method based on co-ocurrence, where the terms of the corpus are expanded by its best co-ocurrence terms in the same corpus. The clustering is done using one implementation of the KStar method where the stop criterion has been modified. The trial data was used for determining the corpus structure. No further tuning is performed.

UOY: A graph based system which creates a co-occurrence hypergraph model. The hypergraph is filtered and weighted according to some association rules. The clustering is performed by selecting the nodes of higher degree until a stop criterion is reached. WSD is performed by assigning to each induced cluster a score equal to the sum of weights of hyperedges found in the local context of the target word. The system was tested and tuned on 10 nouns of Senseval-3 lexical-sample.

Official Results

Participants were required to induce the senses of the target words and cluster all target word contexts accordingly[2]. Table 2 summarizes the average number of induced senses as well as the real senses in the gold standard.

[2]They were allowed to label each context with a weighted score vector, assigning a weight to each induced sense. In the unsupervised evaluation only the sense with maximum weight was considered, but for the supervised one the whole score vector was used. However, none of the participating systems labeled any instance with more than one sense.

system	All	nouns	verbs
I2R	3.08	3.11	3.06
*UBC-AS**	1.32	1.63	1.15
UMND2	1.36	1.71	1.17
upv_si	5.57	7.2	4.69
UOY	9.28	11.28	8.2
Gold standard			
test	2.87	2.86	2.86
train	3.6	3.91	3.43
all	3.68	3.94	3.54

Table 2: Average number of clusters as returned by the participants, and number of classes in the gold standard. Note that *UBC-AS** is the system submitted by the organizers of the task.

System	R.	All			Nouns	Verbs
		FSc.	Pur.	Entr.	FSc.	FSc.
1c1word	1	**78.9**	79.8	45.4	80.7	76.8
*UBC-AS**	2	**78.7**	80.5	43.8	80.8	76.3
upv_si	3	**66.3**	83.8	33.2	69.9	62.2
UMND2	4	**66.1**	81.7	40.5	67.1	65.0
I2R	5	**63.9**	84.0	32.8	68.0	59.3
*UofL***	6	**61.5**	82.2	37.8	62.3	60.5
UOY	7	**56.1**	86.1	27.1	65.8	45.1
Random	8	**37.9**	86.1	27.7	38.1	37.7
1c1inst	9	**9.5**	100	0	6.6	12.7

Table 3: Unsupervised evaluation on the test corpus (FScore), including 3 baselines. Purity and entropy are also provided. *UBC-AS** was submitted by the organizers. *UofL*** is not a sense induction system.

System	Rank	Supervised evaluation		
		All	Nouns	Verbs
I2R	1	**81.6**	86.8	75.7
UMND2	2	**80.6**	84.5	76.2
upv_si	3	**79.1**	82.5	75.3
MFS	4	**78.7**	80.9	76.2
*UBC-AS**	5	**78.5**	80.7	76.0
UOY	6	**77.7**	81.6	73.3
*UofL***	7	**77.1**	80.5	73.3

Table 4: Supervised evaluation as recall. *UBC-AS** was submitted by the organizers. *UofL*** is not a sense induction system.

Table 3 shows the unsupervised evaluation of the systems on the test corpus. We also include three baselines: the "one cluster per word" baseline (*1c1word*), which groups all instances of a word into a single cluster, the "one cluster per instance" baseline (*1c1inst*), where each instance is a distinct cluster, and a random baseline, where the induced word senses and their associated weights have been randomly produced. The random baseline figures in this paper are averages over 10 runs.

As shown in Table 3, no system outperforms the *1c1word* baseline, which indicates that this baseline is quite strong, perhaps due the relatively small number of classes in the gold standard. However, all systems outperform by far the *random* and *1c1inst* baselines, meaning that the systems are able to induce correct senses. Note that the purity and entropy measures are not very indicative in this setting. For completeness, we also computed the FScore using the complete corpus (both train and test). The results are similar and the ranking is the same. We omit them for brevity.

The results of the supervised evaluation can be seen in Table 4. The evaluation is also performed over the test corpus. Apart from participants, we also show the most frequent sense (MFS), which tags every test instance with the sense that occurred most often in the training part. Note that the supervised evaluation combines the information in the clustering solution implicitly with the MFS information via the mapping in the training part. Previous Senseval evaluation exercises have shown that the MFS baseline is very hard to beat by unsupervised systems. In fact, only three of the participant systems are above the MFS baseline, which shows that the clustering information carries over the mapping successfully for these systems. Note that the *1c1word* baseline is equivalent to MFS in this setting. We will review the random baseline in the discussion section below.

Further Results

Table 5 shows the results of the best systems from the lexical sample subtask of task 17. The best sense induction system is only 6.9 percentage points below the best supervised, and 3.5 percentage points below the best (and only) semi-supervised system. If the sense induction system had participated, it would be deemed as semi-supervised, as it uses, albeit in a shallow way, the training data for mapping the clusters into senses. In this sense, our supervised evaluation does not seek to optimize the available training data.

After the official evaluation, we realized that contrary to previous lexical sample evaluation exercises task 17 organizers did not follow a random train/test split. We decided to produce a random train/test split following the same 82/18 proportion as the official split, and re-evaluated the systems. The results are presented in Table 6, where we can see that all

System	Supervised evaluation
best supervised	**88.7**
best semi-supervised	**85.1**
best induction (semi-sup.)	**81.6**
MFS	**78.7**
best unsupervised	**53.8**

Table 5: Comparing the best induction system in this task with those of task 17.

System	Supervised evaluation
I2R	**82.2**
UOY	**81.3**
UMND2	**80.1**
upv_si	**79.9**
UBC-AS	**79.0**
MFS	**78.4**

Table 6: Supervised evaluation as recall using a random train/test split.

participants are above the MFS baseline, showing that all of them learned useful clustering information. Note that UOY was specially affected by the original split. The distribution of senses in this split did not vary (cf. Table 2).

Finally, we also studied the supervised evaluation of several random clustering algorithms, which can attain performances close to MFS, thanks to the mapping information. This is due to the fact that the random clusters would be mapped to the most frequent senses. Table 7 shows the results of random solutions using varying numbers of clusters (e.g. random2 is a random choice between two clusters). Random2 is only 0.1 below MFS, but as the number of clusters increases some clusters don't get mapped, and the recall of the random baselines decrease.

4 Discussion

The evaluation of clustering solutions is not straightforward. All measures have some bias towards certain clustering strategy, and this is one of the reasons of adding the supervised evaluation as a complementary information to the more standard unsupervised evaluation.

In our case, we noticed that the FScore penalized the systems with a high number of clusters, and favored those that induce less senses. Given the fact that FScore tries to balance precision (higher for large numbers of clusters) and recall (higher for small numbers of clusters), this was not expected. We were also surprised to see that no system could

System	Supervised evaluation
random2	**78.6**
random10	**77.6**
ramdom100	**64.2**
random1000	**31.8**

Table 7: Supervised evaluation of several random baselines.

beat the "one cluster one word" baseline. An explanation might lay in that the gold-standard was based on the coarse-grained OntoNotes senses. We also noticed that some words had hundreds of instances and only a single sense. We suspect that the participating systems would have beaten all baselines if a fine-grained sense inventory like WordNet had been used, as was customary in previous WSD evaluation exercises.

Supervised evaluation seems to be more neutral regarding the number of clusters, as the ranking of systems according to this measure include diverse cluster averages. Each of the induced clusters is mapped into a weighted vector of senses, and thus inducing a number of clusters similar to the number of senses is not a requirement for good results. With this measure some of the systems[3] are able to beat all baselines.

5 Conclusions

We have presented the design and results of the SemEval-2007 task 02 on evaluating word sense induction and discrimination systems. 6 systems participated, but one of them was not a sense induction system. We reused the data from the SemEval-2007 English lexical sample subtask of task 17, and set up both clustering-style unsupervised evaluation (using OntoNotes senses as gold-standard) and a supervised evaluation (using the training part of the dataset for mapping). We also provide a comparison to the results of the systems participating in the lexical sample subtask of task 17.

Evaluating clustering solutions is not straightforward. The unsupervised evaluation seems to be sensitive to the number of senses in the gold standard, and the coarse grained sense inventory used in the gold standard had a great impact in the results. The supervised evaluation introduces a mapping step which interacts with the clustering solution. In fact, the ranking of the participating systems varies according to the evaluation method used. We think the two evaluation results should be taken to be complementary regarding the information learned by the clustering systems, and that the evaluation of word sense induction and discrimination systems needs further developments, perhaps linked to a certain application or purpose.

[3] All systems in the case of a random train/test split

Acknowledgments

We want too thank the organizers of SemEval-2007 task 17 for kindly letting us use their corpus. We are also grateful to Ted Pedersen for his comments on the evaluation results. This work has been partially funded by the Spanish education ministry (project KNOW) and by the regional government of Gipuzkoa (project DAHAD).

References

E. Agirre, D. Martínez, O. López de Lacalle, and A. Soroa. 2006. Evaluating and optimizing the parameters of an unsupervised graph-based wsd algorithm. In *Proceedings of the NAACL TextGraphs workshop*, pages 89–96, New York City, June.

D. A. Cruse, 2000. *Polysemy: Theoretical and Computational Approaches*, chapter Aspects of the Microstructure of Word Meanings, pages 31–51. OUP.

C. Fellbaum. 1998. *WordNet: An Electronic Lexical Database*. MIT Press.

E. Hovy, M. Marcus, M. Palmer, L. Ramshaw, and R. Weischedel. 2006. Ontonotes: The 90% solution. In *Proceedings of HLT/NAACL*.

R. Koeling, D. McCarthy, and J.D. Carroll. 2005. Domain-specific sense distributions and predominant sense acquisition.

D. Martínez and E. Agirre. 2000. One sense per collocation and genre/topic variations.

G.A. Miller, C. Leacock, R. Tengi, and R.Bunker. 1993. A semantic concordance. In *Proc. of the ARPA HLT workshop*.

C. Niu, W. Li, R. K. Srihari, and H. Li. 2005. Word independent context pair classification model for word sense disambiguation. In *Proc. of CoNLL-2005*.

P. Pantel and D. Lin. 2002. Discovering word senses from text. In *Proc. of KDD02*.

A. Purandare and T. Pedersen. 2004. Word sense discrimination by clustering contexts in vector and similarity spaces. In *Proc. of CoNLL-2004*, pages 41–48.

H. Schütze. 1998. Automatic word sense discrimination. *Computational Linguistics*, 24(1):97–123.

B. Snyder and M. Palmer. 2004. The english all-words task. In *Proc. of SENSEVAL*.

Y Zhao and G Karypis. 2005. Hierarchical clustering algorithms for document datasets. *Data Mining and Knowledge Discovery*, 10(2):141–168.

SemEval-2007 Task 04: Classification of Semantic Relations between Nominals

Roxana Girju
Univ. of Illinois
at Urbana-Champaign
Urbana, IL 61801
girju@uiuc.edu

Preslav Nakov
Univ. of California at Berkeley
Berkeley, CA 94720
nakov@cs.berkeley.edu

Vivi Nastase
EML Research gGmbH
Heidelberg, Germany 69118
nastase@eml-research.de

Stan Szpakowicz
University of Ottawa
Ottawa, ON K1N 6N5
szpak@site.uottawa.ca

Peter Turney
National Research Council of Canada
Ottawa, ON K1A 0R6
peter.turney@nrc-cnrc.gc.ca

Deniz Yuret
Koç University
Istanbul, Turkey 34450
dyuret@ku.edu.tr

Abstract

The NLP community has shown a renewed interest in deeper semantic analyses, among them automatic recognition of relations between pairs of words in a text. We present an evaluation task designed to provide a framework for comparing different approaches to classifying semantic relations between nominals in a sentence. This is part of SemEval, the 4th edition of the semantic evaluation event previously known as SensEval. We define the task, describe the training/test data and their creation, list the participating systems and discuss their results. There were 14 teams who submitted 15 systems.

1 Task Description and Related Work

The theme of Task 4 is the classification of semantic relations between simple nominals (nouns or base noun phrases) other than named entities – *honey bee*, for example, shows an instance of the Product-Producer relation. The classification occurs in the context of a sentence in a written English text. Algorithms for classifying semantic relations can be applied in information retrieval, information extraction, text summarization, question answering and so on. The recognition of textual entailment (Tatu and Moldovan, 2005) is an example of successful use of this type of deeper analysis in high-end NLP applications.

The literature shows a wide variety of methods of nominal relation classification. They depend as much on the training data as on the domain of application and the available resources. Rosario and Hearst (2001) classify noun compounds from the domain of medicine, using 13 classes that describe the semantic relation between the head noun and the modifier in a given noun compound. Rosario et al. (2002) classify noun compounds using the MeSH hierarchy and a multi-level hierarchy of semantic relations, with 15 classes at the top level. Nastase and Szpakowicz (2003) present a two-level hierarchy for classifying noun-modifier relations in base noun phrases from general text, with 5 classes at the top and 30 classes at the bottom; other researchers (Turney and Littman, 2005; Turney, 2005; Nastase et al., 2006) have used their class scheme and data set. Moldovan et al. (2004) propose a 35-class scheme to classify relations in various phrases; the same scheme has been applied to noun compounds and other noun phrases (Girju et al., 2005). Chklovski and Pantel (2004) introduce a 5-class set, designed specifically for characterizing verb-verb semantic relations. Stephens et al. (2001) propose 17 classes targeted to relations between genes. Lapata (2002) presents a binary classification of relations in nominalizations.

There is little consensus on the relation sets and algorithms for analyzing semantic relations, and it seems unlikely that any single scheme could work for all applications. For example, the gene-gene relation scheme of Stephens et al. (2001), with relations like *X phosphorylates Y*, is unlikely to be transferred easily to general text.

We have created a benchmark data set to allow the evaluation of different semantic relation classification algorithms. We do not presume to propose a single classification scheme, however alluring it would

Proceedings of the 4th International Workshop on Semantic Evaluations (SemEval-2007), pages 13–18,
Prague, June 2007.

Relation	Training data positive	set size	Test data positive	set size	Agreement (independent tagging)	Example
Cause-Effect	52.1%	140	51.3%	80	86.1%	laugh (cause) wrinkles (effect)
Instrument-Agency	50.7%	140	48.7%	78	69.6%	laser (instrument) printer (agency)
Product-Producer	60.7%	140	66.7%	93	68.5%	honey (product) bee (producer)
Origin-Entity	38.6%	140	44.4%	81	77.8%	message (entity) from outer-space (origin)
Theme-Tool	41.4%	140	40.8%	71	47.8%	news (theme) conference(tool)
Part-Whole	46.4%	140	36.1%	72	73.2%	the door (part) of the car (whole)
Content-Container	46.4%	140	51.4%	74	69.1%	the apples (content) in the basket (container)

Table 1: Data set statistics

be to try to design a unified standard – it would be likely to have shortcomings just as any of the others we have just reviewed. Instead, we have decided to focus on separate semantic relations that many researchers list in their relation sets. We have built annotated data sets for seven such relations. Every data set supports a separate binary classification task.

2 Building the Annotated Data Sets

Ours is a new evaluation task, so we began with data set creation and annotation guidelines. The data set that Nastase and Szpakowicz (2003) created had relation labels *and* part-of-speech and WordNet sense annotations, to facilitate classification. (Moldovan et al., 2004; Girju et al., 2005) gave the annotators an example of each phrase in a sentence along with WordNet senses and position of arguments. Our annotations include all these, to support a variety of methods (since we work with relations between nominals, the part of speech is always *noun*). We have used WordNet 3.0 on the Web and sense index tags.

We chose the following semantic relations: Cause-Effect, Content-Container, Instrument-Agency, Origin-Entity, Part-Whole, Product-Producer and Theme-Tool. We wrote seven detailed definitions, including restrictions and conventions, plus prototypical positive and near-miss negative examples. For each relation separately, we based data collection on wild-card search patterns that Google allows. We built the patterns manually, following Hearst (1992) and Nakov and Hearst (2006). Instances of the relation Content-Container, for example, come up in response to queries such as "* contains *", "* holds *", "the * in the *". Following the model of the Senseval-3 English Lexical Sample Task, we set out to collect 140 training and at least 70 test examples per relation, so we had a number of different patterns to ensure variety. We also aimed to collect a balanced number of positive and negative examples. The use of heuristic patterns to search for both positive and negative examples should naturally result in negative examples that are near misses. We believe that near misses are more useful for supervised learning than negative examples that are generated randomly.

"Among the contents of the <e1>vessel</e1> were a set of carpenter's <e2>tools</e2>, several large storage jars, ceramic utensils, ropes and remnants of food, as well as a heavy load of ballast stones."

WordNet(e1) = "vessel%1:06:00::",
WordNet(e2) = "tool%1:06:00::",
Content-Container(e2, e1) = "true",
Query = "contents of the * were a"

Figure 1: Annotations illustrated

Figure 1 illustrates the annotations. We tag the nominals, so parsing or chunking is not necessary. For Task 4, we define a nominal as a noun or base noun phrase, excluding names entities. A base noun phrase, e.g., *lawn* or *lawn mower*, is a noun with premodifiers. We also exclude complex noun phrases (e.g., with attached prepositional phrases – *the engine of the lawn mower*).

The procedure was the same for each relation. One person gathered the sample sentences (aiming approximately for a similar number of positive and negative examples) and tagged the entities; two other people annotated the sentences with WordNet senses and classified the relations. The detailed relation definitions and the preliminary discussions of positive and negative examples served to maximize the agreement between the annotators. They first classified the data independently, then discussed every disagreement and looked for consensus. Only the agreed-upon examples went into the data sets. Next, we split each data set into 140 training and no fewer than 70 test examples. (We published the training set for the Content-Container relation as development data two months before the test set.) Table 1 shows the number of positive and negative examples for each relation.[1]

The average inter-annotator agreement on relations (true/false) after the independent annotation step was 70.3%, and the average agreement on WordNet sense labels was 71.9%. In the process of arriving at a consensus between annotators, the definition of each relation was revised to cover explicitly cases where there had been disagreement. We expect that these revised definitions would lead to much higher levels of agreement than the original definitions did.

3 The Participants

The task of classifying semantic relations between nominals has attracted the participation of 14 teams who submitted 15 systems. Table 4 lists the systems, the authors and their affiliations, and brief descriptions. The systems' performance information in terms of precision, recall, F-measure and accuracy, macroaveraged over all relations, appears in Table 3. We computed these measures as described in Lewis (1991).

We distinguish four categories of systems based on the type of information used – WordNet senses and/or Google queries:

A – WordNet = NO & Query = NO;
B – WordNet = YES & Query = NO;
C – WordNet = NO & Query = YES;
D – WordNet = YES & Query = YES.

WordNet = "YES" or WordNet = "NO" tells us only whether a system uses the WordNet sense labels in the data sets. A system may use WordNet internally for varied purposes, but ignore our sense labels; such a system would be in category A or C. Based on the input variation, each submitted system may have up to 4 variations – A,B,C,D.

Table 2 presents three baselines for a relation. *Majority* always guesses either "true" or "false", whichever is the majority in the test set (maximizes accuracy). *Alltrue* always guesses "true" (maximizes recall). *Probmatch* randomly guesses "true" ("false") with the probability matching the distribution of "true" ("false") in the test dataset (balances precision and recall).

We present the results in Table 3 grouped by category, to facilitate system comparison.

[1] As this paper serves also as a documentation of the data set, the order of relations in the table is the same as in the data set.

Type	P	R	F	Acc
majority	81.3	42.9	30.8	57.0
alltrue	48.5	100.0	64.8	48.5
probmatch	48.5	48.5	48.5	51.7

Table 2: Baselines: precision, recall, F-measure and accuracy averaged over the 7 binary classifications.

Team	P	R	F	Acc
A – WordNet = NO & Query = NO				
UCD-FC	66.1	66.7	64.8	66.0
ILK	60.5	69.5	63.8	63.5
UCB†	62.7	63.0	62.7	65.4
UMELB-B	61.5	55.7	57.8	62.7
UTH	56.1	57.1	55.9	58.8
UC3M	48.2	40.3	43.1	49.9
avg±stdev	59.2±6.3	58.7±10.5	58.0±8.1	61.1±6.0
B – WordNet = YES & Query = NO				
UIUC†	79.7	69.8	72.4	76.3
FBK-IRST	70.9	73.4	71.8	72.9
ILK	72.8	70.6	71.5	73.2
UCD-S1	69.9	64.6	66.8	71.4
UCD-PN	62.0	71.7	65.4	67.0
UC3M	66.7	62.8	64.3	67.2
CMU-AT	55.7	66.7	60.4	59.1
UCD-FC	66.4	58.1	60.3	63.6
UMELB-A	61.7	56.8	58.7	62.5
UVAVU	56.8	56.3	56.1	57.7
LCC-SRN	55.9	57.8	51.4	53.7
avg ± stdev	65.3±7.7	64.4±6.5	63.6±6.9	65.9±7.2
C – WordNet = NO & Query = YES				
UCB†	64.2	66.5	65.1	67.0
UCD-FC	66.1	66.7	64.8	66.0
UC3M	49.4	43.9	45.3	50.1
avg±stdev	59.9±9.1	59.0±13.1	58.4±11.3	61.0±9.5
D – WordNet = YES & Query = YES				
UTD-HLT-CG	67.3	65.3	62.6	67.2
UCD-FC	66.4	58.1	60.3	63.6
UC3M	60.9	57.8	58.8	62.3
avg±stdev	64.9±3.5	60.4±4.2	60.6±1.9	64.4±2.5

Systems tagged with † have a Task 4 organizer as part of the team.

Table 3: System performance grouped by category. Precision, recall, F-measure and accuracy macro-averaged over each system's performance on all 7 relations.

4 Discussion

The highest average accuracy on Task 4 was 76.3%. Therefore, the average initial agreement between annotators (70.3%), before revising the definitions, is not an upper bound on the accuracy that can be achieved. That the initial agreement between annotators is not a good indicator of the accuracy that can be achieved is also supported by the low correlation

System	Institution	Team	Description	System Type
UVAVU	Univ. of Amsterdam TNO Science & Industry Free Univ. Amsterdam	Sophia Katrenko Willem Robert van Hage	similarity measures in WordNet; syntactic dependencies; lexical patterns; logical combination of attributes	B
CMU -AT	Carnegie Mellon Univ.	Alicia Tribble Scott E. Fahlman	WordNet; manually-built ontologies; Scone Knowledge Representation Language; semantic distance	B
ILK	Tilburg University	Caroline Sporleder Roser Morante Antal van den Bosch	semantic clusters based on noun similarity; WordNet supersenses; grammatical relation between entities; head of sentence; WEKA	A, B
FBK-IRST	Fondazione Bruno Kessler - IRST	Claudio Giuliano Alberto Lavelli Daniele Pighin Lorenza Romano	shallow and deep syntactic information; WordNet synsets and hypernyms; kernel methods; SVM	B
LCC-SRN	Language Computer Corp.	Adriana Badulescu	named entity recognition; lexical, semantic, syntactic features; decision tree and semantic scattering	B
UMELB-A	Univ. of Melbourne	Su Kim Timothy Baldwin	sense collocations; similarity of constituents; extending training and testing data using similar words	B
UMELB-B	Univ. of Melbourne	Su Kim Timothy Baldwin	similarity of nearest-neighbor matching over the union of senses for the two nominals; cascaded tagging with decreasing thresholds	A
UCB†	Univ. of California at Berkeley	Preslav Nakov Marti Hearst	VSM; joining terms; KNN-1	A, C
UC3M	Univ. Carlos III of Madrid	Isabel Segura Bedmar Doaa Sammy José Luis Martínez Fernández	WordNet path; syntactic features; SVM	A, B, C, D
UCD-S1	Univ. College Dublin	Cristina Butnariu Tony Veale	lexical-semantic categories from WordNet; syntactic patterns from corpora, SVM	B
UCD-FC	Univ. College Dublin	Fintan Costello	WordNet; additional noun compounds tagged corpus; Naive Bayes	A, B, C, D
UCD-PN	Univ. College Dublin	Paul Nulty	WordNet supersenses; web-based frequency counts for specific joining terms; WEKA (SMO)	B
UIUC†	Univ. of Illinois at Urbana Champaign	Roxana Girju Brandon Beamer Suma Bhat Brant Chee Andrew Fister Alla Rozovskaya	features based on WordNet, NomLex-PLUS, grammatical roles, lexico-syntactic patterns, semantic parses	B
UTD-HLT-CG	Univ. of Texas at Dallas	Cristina Nicolae Garbiel Nicolae Sanda Harabagiu	lexico-semantic features from WordNet, VerbNet; semantic features from a PropBank parser; dependency features	D
UTH	Univ. of Tokio	Eiji Aramaki Takeshi Imai Kengo Miyo Kazuhiko Ohe	joining phrases; physical size for entities; web-mining; SVM	A

Systems tagged with † have a Task 4 organizer as part of the team.

Table 4: Short description of the teams and the participating systems.

Relation	Team	Type	P	R	F	Acc	Test size	Base-F	Base-Acc	Avg. rank
Cause-Effect	UIUC	B_4	69.5	100.0	82.0	77.5	80	67.8	51.2	3.4
Instrument-Agency	FBK-IRST	B_4	76.9	78.9	77.9	78.2	78	65.5	51.3	3.4
Product-Producer	UCD-S1	B_4	80.6	87.1	83.7	77.4	93	80.0	66.7	1.7
Origin-Entity	ILK	B_3	70.6	66.7	68.6	72.8	81	61.5	55.6	6.0
Theme-Tool	ILK	B_4	69.0	69.0	69.0	74.6	71	58.0	59.2	6.0
Part-Whole	UC3M	B_4	72.4	80.8	76.4	81.9	72	53.1	63.9	4.5
Content-Container	UIUC	B_4	93.1	71.1	80.6	82.4	74	67.9	51.4	3.1

Table 5: The best results per relation. Precision, recall, F-measure and accuracy macro-averaged over each system's performance on all 7 relations. Base-F shows the baseline F-measure (alltrue), Base-Acc – the baseline accuracy score (majority). The last column shows the average rank for each relation.

of 0.15 between the Acc column in Table 5 and the Agreement column in Table 1.

We performed various analyses of the results, which we summarize here in four questions. We write X_i to refer to four possible system categories (A_i, B_i, C_i, and D_i) with four possible amounts of training data (X_1 for training examples 1 to 35, X_2 for 1 to 70, X_3 for 1 to 105, and X_4 for 1 to 140).

Does more training data help?
Overall, the results suggest that more training data improves the performance. There were 17 cases in which we had results for all four possible amounts of training data. All average F-measure differences, $F(X_4)–F(X_i)$ where $X = A$ to D, $i = 1$ to 3, for these 17 sets of results are statistically significant:

$F(X_4)–F(X_1)$: N = 17, avg = 8.3, std = 5.8, min = 1.1, max = 19.6, t-value = −5.9, p-value = 0.00001.

$F(X_4)–F(X_2)$: N = 17, avg = 4.0, std = 3.7, min = −3.5, max = 10.5, t-value = 4.5, p-value = 0.0002.

$F(X_4)–F(X_3)$: N = 17, avg = 0.9, std = 1.7, min = −2.6, max = 4.7, t-value = 2.1, p-value = 0.03.

Does WordNet help?
The statistics show that WordNet is important, although the contribution varies across systems. Three teams submitted altogether 12 results both for A_1–A_4 and B_1–B_4. The average F-measure difference, $F(B_i)–F(A_i)$, $i = 1$ to 4, is significant:

$F(B_i)–F(A_i)$: N = 12, avg = 6.1, std = 8.4, min = −4.5, max = 21.2, t-value = −2.5, p-value = 0.01.

The results of the UCD-FC system actually went down when WordNet was used. The statistics for the remaining two teams, however, are a bit better:

$F(B_i)–F(A_i)$: N = 8, avg = 10.4, std = 6.7, min = −1.0, max = 21.2, t-value = −4.4, p-value = 0.002.

Does knowing the query help?
Overall, knowing the query did not seem to improve the results. Three teams submitted 12 results both for A_1–A_4 and C_1–C_4. The average F-measure difference, $F(C_i)–F(A_i)$, $i = 1$ to 4, is not significant:

$F(C_i)–F(A_i)$: N = 12, avg = 0.9, std = 1.8, min = −2.0, max = 5.0, t-value = −1.6, p-value = 0.06.

Again, the UCD-FC system differed from the other systems in that the A and C scores were identical, but even averaging over the remaining two systems and 8 cases does not show a statistically significant advantage:

$F(C_i)–F(A_i)$: N = 8, avg = 1.3, std = 2.2, min = −2.0, max = 5.0, t-value = −1.7, p-value = 0.07.

Are some relations harder to classify?
Table 5 shows the best results for each relation in terms of precision, recall, and F-measure, per team and system category. Column *Base-F* presents the baseline F-measure (alltrue), while *Base-Acc* the baseline accuracy score (majority). For all seven relations, the best team significantly outperforms the baseline. The category of the best-scoring system in almost every case is B_4 (only the ILK B_4 system scored second on the Origin-Entity relation).

Table 5 suggests that some relations are more difficult to classify than others. The best F-measure ranges from 83.7 for *Product–Producer* to 68.6 for *Origin–Entity*. The difference between the best F-measure and the baseline F-measure ranges from 23.3 for *Part-Whole* to 3.7 for *Product-Producer*. The difference between the best accuracy and the baseline accuracy ranges from 31.0 for *Content-Container* to 10.7 for *Product-Producer*.

The F column shows the best result for each relation, but similar differences among the relations may be observed when all results are pooled. The *Avg. rank* column computes the average rank of each relation in the ordered list of relations generated by each system. For example, *Product–Producer* is often listed as the first or the second easiest relation (with an average rank of 1.7), while *Origin–Entity* and *Theme–Tool* are identified as the most difficult relations to classify (with average ranks of 6.0).

5 Conclusion

This paper describes a new semantic evaluation task, *Classification of Semantic Relations between Nominals*. We have accomplished our goal of providing a framework and a benchmark data set to allow for comparisons of methods for this task. The data included different types of information – lexical semantic information, context, query used – meant to facilitate the analysis of useful sources of information for determining the semantic relation between nominals. The results that the participating systems have reported show successful approaches to this difficult task, and the advantages of using lexical semantic information.

The success of the task – measured in the interest of the community and the results of the participating systems – shows that the framework and the data are useful resources. By making this collection freely accessible, we encourage further research into this domain and integration of semantic relation algorithms in high-end applications.

Acknowledgments

We thank Eneko Agirre, Lluís Màrquez and Richard Wicentowski, the organizers of SemEval 2007, for their guidance and prompt support in all organizational matters. We thank Marti Hearst for valuable advice throughout the task description and debates on semantic relation definitions. We thank the anonymous reviewers for their helpful comments.

References

T. Chklovski and P. Pantel. 2004. Verbocean: Mining the web for fine-grained semantic verb relations. In *Proc. Conf. on Empirical Methods in Natural Language Processing, EMNLP-04*, pages 33–40, Barcelona, Spain.

R. Girju, D. Moldovan, M. Tatu, and D. Antohe. 2005. On the semantics of noun compounds. *Computer Speech and Language*, 19:479–496.

M. Hearst. 1992. Automatic acquisition of hyponyms from large text corpora. In *Proc. 14th International Conf. on Computational Linguistics (COLING-92)*, pages 539–545.

M. Lapata. 2002. The disambiguation of nominalizations. *Computational Linguistics*, 28(3):357–388.

D.D. Lewis. 1991. Evaluating text categorization. In *Proceedings of the Speech and Natural Language Workshop*, pages 312–318, Asilomar.

D. Moldovan, A. Badulescu, M. Tatu, D. Antohe, and R. Girju. 2004. Models for the semantic classification of noun phrases. In *Proc. Computational Lexical Semantics Workshop at HLT-NAACL 2004*, pages 60–67, Boston, MA.

P. Nakov and M. Hearst. 2006. Using verbs to characterize noun-noun relations. In *Proc. Twelfth International Conf. in Artificial Intelligence (AIMSA-06)*, pages 233–244, Varna,Bulgaria.

V. Nastase and S. Szpakowicz. 2003. Exploring noun-modifier semantic relations. In *Fifth International Workshop on Computational Semantics (IWCS-5)*, pages 285–301, Tilburg, The Netherlands.

V. Nastase, J. Sayyad-Shirabad, M. Sokolova, and S. Szpakowicz. 2006. Learning noun-modifier semantic relations with corpus-based and WordNet-based features. In *Proc. 21st National Conf. on Artificial Intelligence (AAAI 2006)*, pages 781–787, Boston, MA.

B. Rosario and M. Hearst. 2001. Classifying the semantic relations in noun-compounds via domain-specific lexical hierarchy. In *Proc. 2001 Conf. on Empirical Methods in Natural Language Processing (EMNLP-01)*, pages 82–90.

B. Rosario, M. Hearst, and C. Fillmore. 2002. The descent of hierarchy, and selection in relational semantics. In *Proc. 40th Annual Meeting of the Association for Computational Linguistics (ACL-02)*, pages 417–424, Philadelphia, PA.

M. Stephens, M. Palakal, S. Mukhopadhyay, and R. Raje. 2001. Detecting gene relations from MEDLINE abstracts. In *Proc. Sixth Annual Pacific Symposium on Biocomputing*, pages 483–496.

M. Tatu and D. Moldovan. 2005. A semantic approach to recognizing textual entailment. In *Proc. Human Language Technology Conf. and Conf. on Empirical Methods in Natural Language Processing (HLT/EMNLP 2005)*, pages 371–378, Vancouver, Canada.

P.D. Turney and M.L. Littman. 2005. Corpus-based learning of analogies and semantic relations. *Machine Learning*, 60(1-3):251–278.

P.D. Turney. 2005. Measuring semantic similarity by latent relational analysis. In *Proc. Nineteenth International Joint Conf. on Artificial Intelligence (IJCAI-05)*, pages 1136–1141, Edinburgh, Scotland.

SemEval-2007 Task 5: Multilingual Chinese-English Lexical Sample

Peng Jin, Yunfang Wu and Shiwen Yu
Institute of Computational Linguistics
Peking University, Beijing China
{jandp, wuyf, yusw}@pku.edu.cn

Abstract

The Multilingual Chinese-English lexical sample task at SemEval-2007 provides a framework to evaluate Chinese word sense disambiguation and to promote research. This paper reports on the task preparation and the results of six participants.

1 Introduction

The Multilingual Chinese-English lexical sample task is designed following the leading ideas of the Senseval-3 Multilingual English-Hindi lexical sample task (Chklovski et al., 2004). The "sense tags" for the ambiguous Chinese target words are given in the form of their English translations.

The data preparation is introduced in the second section. And then the participating systems are briefly described and their scores are listed.

In the conclusions we bring forward some suggestion for the next campaign.

2 Chinese Word Sense Annotated Corpus

All the training and test data come from the People's Daily in January, February and March of 2000. The People's Daily is the most popular newspaper in China and is open domain. Before manually sense annotating, the texts have been word-segmented and part of speech (PoS) tagged according to the PoS tagging scheme of Institute of Computational Linguistics in Peking University (ICL/PKU). The corpus had been used as one of the gold-standard data set for the second international Chinese word segmentation bakeoff in 2005.[1]

2.1 Manual Annotation

The sense annotated corpus is manually constructed with the help of a word sense annotating interface developed in Java. Three native annotators, two major in Chinese linguistics and one major in computer science took part in the construction of the sense-annotated corpus. A text generally is first annotated by one annotator and then verified by two checkers. Checking is of course a necessary procedure to keep the consistency. Inspired by the observation that checking all the instances of a word in a specific time frame will greatly improve the precision and accelerate the speed, a software tool is designed in Java to gather all the occurrences of a word in the corpus into a checking file with the sense KWIC (Key Word in Context) format in sense tags order. The inter-annotator agreement gets to 84.8% according to Wu. et al. (2006).

The sense entries are specified in the Chinese Semantic Dictionary (CSD) developed by ICL/PKU. The sense distinctions are made mainly according to the Contemporary Chinese Dictionary, the most widely used dictionary in mandarin Chinese, with necessary adjustment and improvement is implemented according to words usage in real texts. Word senses are described using the feature-based formalism. The features, which appear in the form "Attribute =Value", can incorporate extensive distributional information about a word sense. The feature set constitutes the representation of a sense, while the verbal definitions of meaning

[1] http://sighan.cs.uchicago.edu/bakeoff2005/

Proceedings of the 4th International Workshop on Semantic Evaluations (SemEval-2007), pages 19–23,
Prague, June 2007. ©2007 Association for Computational Linguistics

serve only as references for human use. The English translation is assigned to each sense in the attribute "English translation" in CSD.

Based on the sense-annotated corpus, a sense is replaced by its English translation, which might group different senses together under the same English word.

2.2 Instances selection

In this task together 40 Chinese ambiguous words: 19 nouns and 21 verbs are selected for the evaluation. Each sense of one word is provided at least 15 instances and at most 40 instances, in which around 2/3 is used as the training data and 1/3 as the test data. Table 1 presents the number of words under each part of speech, the average number of senses for each PoS and the number of instances respectively in the training and test set.

	# Average senses	# training instances	# test instances
19 nouns	2.58	1019	364
21 verbs	3.57	1667	571

Table 1: Summary of the sense inventory and number of training data and test set

In order to escape from the sense-skewed distribution that really exists in the corpus of People's Daily, many instances of some senses have been removed from the sense annotated corpus. So the sense distribution of the ambiguous words in this task does not reflect the usages in real texts.

3 Participating Systems

In order to facilitate participators to select the features, we gave a specification for the PoS-tag set. Both word-segmented and un-segmented context are provided.

Two kinds of precisions are evaluated. One is micro-average:

$$P_{mir} = \sum_{i=1}^{N} m_i / \sum_{i=1}^{N} n_i$$

N is the number of all target word-types. m_i is the number of labeled correctly to one specific target word-type and n_i is the number of all test instances for this word-type.

The other is macro-average:

$$P_{mar} = \sum_{i=1}^{N} p_i / N, \quad p_i = m_i / n_i$$

All teams attempted all test instances. So the recall is the same with the precision. The precision baseline is obtained by the most frequent sense. Because the corpus is not reflected the real usage, the precision is very low.

Six teams participated in this word sense disambiguation task. Four of them used supervised learning algorithms and two used un-supervised method. For each team two kinds of precision are given as in table 2.

Team	Micro-average	Macro-average
SRCB-WSD	0.716578	0.749236
I2R	0.712299	0.746824
CITYU-HIF	0.710160	0.748761
SWAT	0.657754	0.692487
TorMd	0.375401	0.431243
HIT	0.336898	0.395993
baseline	0.4053	0.4618

Table 2: The scores of all participating systems

As follow the participating systems are briefly introduced.

SRCB-WSD system exploited maximum entropy model as the classifier from OpenNLP[2] The following features are used in this WSD system:

- All the verbs and nouns in the context, that is, the words with tags "n, nr, ns, nt, nz, v, vd, vn"
- PoS of the left word and the right word
- noun phrase, verb phrase, adjective phrase, time phrase, place phrase and quantity phrase.

These phrases are considered as constituents of context, as well as words and punctuations which do not belong to any phrase.

- the type of these phrases which are around the target phrases

[2] http:// maxent.sourceforge.net/

- word category information comes from Chinese thesaurus

I2R system used a semi-supervised classification algorithm (label propagation algorithm) (Niu, et al., 2005). They used three types of features: PoS of neighboring words with position information, unordered single words in topical context, and local collocations.

In the label propagation algorithm (LP) (Zhu and Ghahramani, 2002), label information of any vertex in a graph is propagated to nearby vertices through weighted edges until a global stable stage is achieved. Larger edge weights allow labels to travel through easier. Thus the closer the examples, the more likely they have similar labels (the global consistency assumption). In label propagation process, the soft label of each initial labeled example is clamped in each iteration to replenish label sources from these labeled data. Thus the labeled data act like sources to push out labels through unlabeled data. With this push from labeled examples, the class boundaries will be pushed through edges with large weights and settle in gaps along edges with small weights. If the data structure fits the classification goal, then LP algorithm can use these unlabeled data to help learning classification plane.

CITYU-HIF system was a fully supervised one based on a Naïve Bayes classifier with simple feature selection for each target word. The features used are as follows:

- Local features at specified positions:
  PoS of word at w_{-2}, w_{-1}, w_1, w_2
  Word at w_{-2}, w_{-1}, w_1, w_2
- Topical features within a given window:
  Content words appearing within w_{-10} to w_{10}
- Syntactic features:
  PoS bi-gram at $w_{-2}w_0$, $w_{-1}w_0$, w_0w_1 , w_0w_2
  PoS tri-gram at w_{-2} $w_{-1}w_0$ and $w_0w_1w_2$

One characteristic of this system is the incorporation of the intrinsic nature of each target word in disambiguation. It is assumed that WSD is highly lexically sensitive and each word is best characterized by different lexical information. Human judged to consider for each target word the type of disambiguation information if they found useful. During disambiguation, they run two Naïve Bayes classifiers, one on all features above, and the other only on the type of information deemed useful by the human judges. When the probability of the best guess from the former is under a certain threshold, the best guess from the latter was used instead.

SWAT system uses a weighted vote from three different classifiers to make the prediction. The three systems are: a Naïve Bayes classifier that compares similarities based on Bayes' Rule, a classifier that creates a decision list of context features, and a classifier that compares the angles between vectors of the features found most commonly with each sense. The features include bigrams, and trigrams, and unigrams are weighted by distance from the ambiguous word.

TorMd used an unsupervised naive Bayes classifier. They combine Chinese text and an English thesaurus to create a `Chinese word'--`English category' co-occurrence matrix. This system generated the prior-probabilities and likelihoods of a Naïve Bayes word sense classifier not from sense-annotated (in this case English translation annotated) data, but from this word--category co-occurrence matrix. They used the Macquarie Thesaurus as very coarse sense inventory.

They asked a native speaker of Chinese to map the English translations of the target words to appropriate thesaurus categories. Once the Naïve Bayes classifier identifies a particular category as the intended sense, the mapping file is used to label the target word with the corresponding English translation. They rely simply on the bag of words that co-occur with the target word (window size of 5 words on either side).

HIT is a fully unsupervised WSD system, which puts bag of words of Chinese sentences and the English translations of target ambiguous word to search engine (Google and Baidu). Then they could get all kinds of statistic data. The correct translation was found through comparing their cross entropy.

4 Conclusion

The goal of this task is to create a framework to evaluate Chinese word sense disambiguation and to promote research.

Target Word	Sen se #	Train ing #	Test #	Base-line	Scores					
					SRCB -WSD	I2R	CITY U-HIF	SWA T-MP	TOR MD	HIT
补	3	63	20	.50	.70	.80	.75	.75	.55	.55
成立	3	73	27	.370	.778	.815	.741	.778	.481	.407
吃	4	69	23	.435	.696	.609	.696	.696	.174	.174
出	9	222	77	.130	.506	.506	.481	.532	.169	.091
带	8	197	67	.150	.567	.552	.537	.433	.119	.104
动	4	58	20	.50	.60	.50	.55	.60	.30	.30
动摇	2	47	16	.625	.875	.875	.875	.563	.50	.438
发	5	105	36	.278	.694	.667	.611	.889	.25	.139
赶	3	56	18	.50	.667	.722	.667	.667	.389	.333
叫	4	106	39	.256	.718	.615	.641	.538	.256	.256
进	5	132	44	.227	.659	.75	.727	.568	.25	.114
开通	2	56	20	.50	.90	.95	.95	.60	.50	.50
看	4	103	34	.294	.765	.706	.765	.559	.294	.294
平息	2	20	8	.50	.75	.75	.75	.625	.375	.50
使	2	46	16	.625	.938	.813	.813	.875	.563	.438
说明	2	60	18	.556	.667	.722	.778	.722	.444	.556
挑	2	40	14	.429	.571	.643	.571	.571	.143	.286
推翻	2	29	10	.60	.80	.70	.90	.80	.30	.30
望	2	37	13	.769	.769	.769	.769	.769	.462	.462
想	4	110	37	.270	.730	.676	.676	.541	.216	.216
震惊	2	38	14	.714	.930	1.0	.929	.786	.714	.571
Ave.	3.57	1667	571	.342/.44	.685/.728	.676/.721	.671/.723	.618/.66	.30/.355	.263/.335

Table 3: Performance on verbs. Micro / macro average precisions are spitted by "/" at the last row.

Together six teams participate in this WSD task, four of them adopt supervised learning methods and two of them used unsupervised algorithms. All of the four supervised learning systems exceed obviously the baseline obtained by the most frequent sense. It is noted that the performances of the first three systems are very close. Two unsupervised methods' scores are below the baseline. More unlabeled data maybe improve their performance.

Although the SRCB-WSD system got the highest scores among the six participants, it does not perform always better than other system from table 2 and table 3. But to each word, the four supervised systems always predict correctly more instances than the two un-supervised systems.

Besides the corpus, we provide a specification of the PoS tag set. Only SRCB-WSD system utilized this knowledge in feature selection. We will provide more instances in the next campaign.

Target Word	Sense #	Training #	Test #	Base-line	Scores					
					SRCB-WSD	I2R	CITYU-HIF	SWAT-MP	TORMD	HIT
本	3	68	25	.40	.88	.84	.88	.76	.72	.32
表面	2	53	18	.611	.611	.722	.722	.833	.556	.333
菜	2	56	19	.526	.842	.842	.684	.789	.474	.632
长城	3	48	21	.476	.571	.591	.619	.619	.429	.619
单位	2	50	17	.588	.824	.824	.824	.647	.706	.529
道	3	53	18	.50	.778	.722	.778	.611	.50	.222
队伍	3	64	22	.455	.591	.591	.636	.545	.318	.364
儿女	2	60	20	.50	1.0	.95	1.0	1.0	.50	.50
机组	2	38	14	.714	1.0	1.0	1.0	1.0	.643	.571
镜头	2	45	15	.533	.733	.733	.60	.467	.467	.467
面	3	67	23	.435	.783	.783	.739	.696	.348	.696
牌子	2	44	17	.353	.529	.589	.588	.588	.353	.529
旗帜	3	50	18	.556	.611	.611	.722	.722	.50	.111
气息	2	39	14	.714	.929	.786	.714	.786	.857	.571
气象	2	47	16	.625	.813	.813	.938	1.0	.438	.563
日子	3	88	32	.313	.656	.563	.625	.656	.281	.344
天地	3	65	25	.40	.88	1.0	.92	.60	.56	.44
眼光	2	41	14	.714	.786	.714	.786	.643	.714	.50
中医	2	43	16	.625	.875	.938	1.0	.875	.438	.50
Ave.	2.45	1019	364	.506/.528	.766/.773	.761/.769	.772/.778	.72/.728	.50/.516	.456/.464

Table 4: Performance on nouns. Micro / macro average precisions are spitted by "/" at the last row.

5 Acknowledgements

This research is supported by Humanity and Social Science Research Project of China State Education Ministry (No. 06JC740001) and National Basic Research Program of China (No. 2004CB318102).

We would like to thank Tao Guo and Yulai Pei for their hard work to guarantee the quality of the corpus. Huiming Duan provides us the corpus which has been word-segmented and PoS-tagged and gives some suggestions during the manual annotation.

References

Rada Mihalcea, Timothy Chklovski and Adam Kilgarriff. 2004. The Senseval-3 English lexical sample task. *Proceedings of SENSEVAL-3*. 25-28.

Timothy Chklovski, Rada Mihalcea, Ted Pedersen and Amruta Purandare. 2004. The Senseval-3 Multilingual English-Hindi lexical sample task. *Proceedings of SENSEVAL-3*. 5-8.

Xiaojin Zhu, Zoubin Ghahramani. 2002. Learning from Labeled and Unlabeled Data with Label Propagation. *CMU CALD tech report CMU-CALD-02-107.*

Yunfang Wu, Peng Jin, Yangsen Zhang, and Shiwen Yu. 2006. A Chinese Corpus with Word Sense Annotation. *Proceedings of ICCPOL*, Singapore, 414-421.

Zhen-Yu Niu, Dong-Hong Ji and Chew-Lim Tan. 2005. Word Sense Disambiguation Using Label Propagation Based Semi Supervised Learning. *Proceedings of the 43rd Annual Meeting of the Association for Computational Linguistics.*395-402

SemEval-2007 Task 06: Word-Sense Disambiguation of Prepositions

Ken Litkowski
CL Research
9208 Gue Road
Damascus, MD 20872
ken@clres.com

Orin Hargraves
5130 Band Hall Hill Road
Westminster, MD 21158
orinhargraves@googlemail.com

Abstract

The SemEval-2007 task to disambiguate prepositions was designed as a lexical sample task. A set of over 25,000 instances was developed, covering 34 of the most frequent English prepositions, with two-thirds of the instances for training and one-third as the test set. Each instance identified a preposition to be tagged in a full sentence taken from the FrameNet corpus (mostly from the British National Corpus). Definitions from the Oxford Dictionary of English formed the sense inventories. Three teams participated, with all achieving supervised results significantly better than baselines, with a high fine-grained precision of 0.693. This level is somewhat similar to results on lexical sample tasks with open class words, indicating that significant progress has been made. The data generated in the task provides ample opportunitites for further investigations of preposition behavior.

1 Introduction

The SemEval-2007 task to disambiguate prepositions was designed as a lexical sample task to investigate the extent to which an important closed class of words could be disambiguated. In addition, because they are a closed class, with stable senses, the requisite datasets for this task are enduring and can be used as long as the problem of preposition disambiguation remains. The data used in this task was developed in The Preposition Project (TPP, Litkowski & Hargraves (2005) and Litkowski & Hargraves (2006)),[1] with further refinements to fit the requirements of a SemEval task.

In the following sections, we first describe the motivations for a preposition disambiguation task. Next, we describe the development of the datasets used for the task, i.e., the instance sets and the sense inventories. We describe how the task was performed and how it was evaluated (essentially using the same scoring methods as previous Senseval lexical sample tasks). We present the results obtained from the participating teams and provide an initial analysis of these results. Finally, we identify several further types of analyses that will provide further insights into the characterization of preposition behavior.

2 Motivation

Prepositions are a closed class, meaning that the number of prepositions remains relatively constant and that their meanings are relatively stable. Despite this, their treatment in computational linguistics has been somewhat limited. In the Penn Treebank, only two types of prepositions are recognized (IN (locative, temporal, and manner) and TO (direction)) (O'Hara, 2005). Prepositions are viewed as function words that occur with high frequency and therefore carry little meaning. A task to disambiguate prepositions would, in the first place, allow this limited treatment to be confronted more fully.

Preposition behavior has been the subject of much research, too voluminous to cite here. Three recent workshops on prepositions have been sponsored by the ACL-SIGSEM: Toulouse in 2003, Colchester in 2005, and Trento in 2006. For the most part, these workshops have focused on individual prepositions, with various investigations of more generalized behavior. The SemEval preposition disambiguation task provides a vehicle to examine whether these behaviors are substantiated with a well-defined set of corpus instances.

Prepositions assume more importance when they

[1] http://www.clres.com/prepositions.html.

Proceedings of the 4th International Workshop on Semantic Evaluations (SemEval-2007), pages 24–29,
Prague, June 2007. ©2007 Association for Computational Linguistics

are considered in relation to verbs. While linguistic theory focuses on subjects and objects as important verb arguments, quite frequently there is an additional oblique argument realized in a prepositional phrase. But with the focus on the verbs, the prepositional phrases do not emerge as having more than incidental importance. However, within frame semantics (Fillmore, 1976), prepositions rise to a greater prominence; frequently, two or three prepositional phrases are identified as constituting frame elements. In addition, frame semantic analyses indicate the possibility of a greater number of prepositional phrases acting as adjuncts (particularly identifying time and location frame elements). While linguistic theories may identify only one or two prepositions associated with an argument of a verb, frame semantic analyses bring in the possibility of a greater variety of prepositions introducing the same type of frame element. The preposition disambiguation task provides an opportunity to examine this type of variation.

The question of prepositional phrase attachment is another important issue. Merlo & Esteve Ferrer (2006) suggest that this problem is a four-way disambiguation task, depending on the properties of nouns and verbs and whether the prepositional phrases are arguments or adjuncts. Their analysis relied on Penn Treebank data. Further insights may be available from the finer-grained data available in the preposition disambiguation task.

Another important thread of investigation concerning preposition behavior is the task of semantic role (and perhaps semantic relation) labeling (Gildea & Jurafsky, 2002). This task has been the subject of a previous Senseval task (Automatic Semantic Role Labeling, Litkowski (2004)) and two shared tasks on semantic role labeling in the Conference on Natural Language Learning (Carreras & Marquez (2004) and Carreras & Marquez (2005)). In addition, three other tasks in SemEval-2007 (semantic relations between nominals, task 4; temporal relation labeling, task 15; and frame semantic structure extraction, task 19) address issues of semantic role labeling. Since a great proportion of these semantic roles are realized in prepositional phrases, this gives greater urgency to understanding preposition behavior.

Despite the predominant view of prepositions as function words carrying little meaning, this view is not borne out in dictionary treatment of their definitions. To all appearances, prepositions exhibit definitional behavior similar to that of open class words. There is a reasonably large number of distinct prepositions and they show a range of polysemous senses. Thus, with a suitable set of instances, they may be amenable to the same types of analyses as open class words.

3 Preparation of Datasets

The development of the datasets for the preposition disambiguation task grew directly out of TPP. This project essentially articulates the corpus selection, the lexicon choice, and the production of the gold standard. The primary objective of TPP is to characterize each of 847 preposition senses for 373 prepositions (including 220 phrasal prepositions with 309 senses)[2] with a semantic role name and the syntactic and semantic properties of its complement and attachment point. The preposition sense inventory is taken from the *Oxford Dictionary of English* (ODE, 2004).[3]

3.1 Corpus Development

For a particular preposition, a set of instances is extracted from the FrameNet database.[4] FrameNet was chosen since it provides well-studied sentences drawn from the British National Corpus (as well as a limited set of sentences from other sources). Since the sentences to be selected for frame analysis were generally chosen for some open class verb or noun, these sentences would be expected to provide no bias with respect to prepositions. In addition, the use of this resource makes available considerable information for each sentence in its identification of

[2]The number of prepositions and the number of senses is not fixed, but has changed during the course of the project, as will become clear.

[3]TPP does not include particle senses of such words as *in* or *over* (or any other particles) used with verbs to make phrasal verbs. In this context, phrasal verbs are to be distinguished from verbs that select a preposition (such as *on* in *rely on*), which may be characterized as a collocation.

[4]http://framenet.icsi.berkeley.edu/

frame elements, their phrase type, and their grammatical function. The FrameNet data was also made accessible in a form (FrameNet Explorer)[5] to facilitate a lexicographer's examination of preposition instances.

Each sentence in the FrameNet data is labeled with a subcorpus name. This name is generally intended only to capture some property of a set of instances. In particular, many of these subcorpus names include a string **pp*prep*** and this identification was used for the selection of instances. Thus, searching the FrameNet corpus for subcorpora labeled **ppof** or **ppafter** would yield sentences containing a prepositional phrase with a desired preposition. This technique was used for many common prepositions, yielding 300 to 4500 instances. The technique was modified for prepositions with fewer instances. Instead, all sentences having a phrase beginning with a desired preposition were selected.

The number of sentences eventually used in the SemEval task is shown in Table 1. More than 25,000 instances for 34 prepositions were tagged in TPP and used for the SemEval-2007 task.

3.2 Lexicon Development

As mentioned above, ODE (and its predecessor, the *New Oxford Dictionary of English* (NODE, 1997)) was used as the sense inventory for the prepositions. ODE is a corpus-based, lexicographically-drawn sense inventory, with a two-level hierarchy, consisting of a set of core senses and a set of subsenses (if any) that are semantically related to the core sense. The full set of information, both printed and in electronic form, containing additional lexicographic information, was made publicly available for TPP, and hence, the SemEval disambiguation task.

The sense inventory was not used as absolute and further information was added during TPP. The lexicographer (Hargraves) was free to add senses, particularly as the corpus evidence provided by the FrameNet data suggested. The process of refining the sense inventory was performed as the lexicographer assigned a sense to each instance. While engaged in this sense assignment, the lexicographer accumulated an understanding of the behavior of the preposition, assigning a name to each sense (characterizing its semantic type), and characterizing the syntactic and semantic properties of the preposition complement and its point of attachment or head. Each sense was also characterized by its syntactic function and its meaning, identifying the relevant paragraph(s) where it is discussed in Quirk et al (1985).

After sense assignments were completed, the set of instances for each preposition was analyzed against the FrameNet database. In particular, the FrameNet frames and frame elements associated with each sense was identified. The set of sentences was provided in SemEval format in an XML file with the preposition tagged as **<head>**, along with an answer key (also identifying the FrameNet frame and frame element). Finally, using the FrameNet frame and frame element of the tagged instances, syntactic alternation patterns (other syntactic forms in which the semantic role may be realized) are provided for each FrameNet target word for each sense.

All of the above information was combined into a preposition database.[6] For SemEval-2007, entries for the target prepositions were combined into an XML file as the "Definitions" to be used as the sense inventory, where each sense was given a unique identifier. All prepositions for which a set of instances had been analyzed in TPP were included. These 34 prepositions are shown in Table 1 (*below*, *beyond*, and *near* were used in the trial set).

3.3 Gold Standard Production

Unlike previous Senseval lexical sample tasks, tagging was not performed as a separate step. Rather, sense tagging was completed as an integral part of TPP. Funding was unavailable to perform additional tagging with other lexicographers and the appropriate interannotator agreement studies have not yet been completed. At this time, only qualitative assessments of the tagging can be given.

As indicated, the sense inventory for each preposition evolved as the lexicographer examined

[5]Available for the Windows operating system at http://www.clres.com for those with access to the FrameNet data.

[6]The full database is viewable in the Online TPP (http://www.clres.com/cgi-bin/onlineTPP/find_prep.cgi).

the set of FrameNet instances. Multiple sources (such as Quirk et al.) and lexicographic experience were important components of the sense tagging. The tagging was performed without any deadlines and with full adherence to standard lexicographic principles. Importantly, the availability of the FrameNet corpora facilitated the sense assignment, since many similar instances were frequently contiguous in the instance set (e.g., associated with the same target word and frame).

Another important factor suggesting higher quality in the sense assignment is the quality of the sense inventory. Unlike previous Senseval lexical sample tasks, the sense inventory was developed using lexicographic principles and was quite stable. In arriving at the sense inventory, the lexicographer was able to compare ODE with its predecessor NODE, noting in most cases that the senses had not changed or had changed in only minor ways.

Finally, the lexicographer had little difficulty in making sense assignments. The sense distinctions were well enough drawn that there was relatively little ambiguity given a sentence context. The lexicographer was not constrained to selecting one sense, but could tag a preposition with multiple senses as deemed necessary. Out of 25,000 instances, only 350 instances received multiple senses.

4 Task Organization and Evaluation

The organization followed standard SemEval (Senseval) procedures. The data were prepared in XML, using Senseval DTDs. That is, each instance was labeled with an instance identifier as an XML attribute. Within the **<instance>** tag, the FrameNet sentence was labeled as the **<context>** and included one item, the target preposition, in the **<head>** tag. The FrameNet sentence identifier was used as the instance identifier, enabling participants to make use of other FrameNet data. Unlike lexical sample tasks for open class words, only one sentence was provided as the context. Although no examination of whether this is sufficient context for prepositions, it seems likely that all information necessary for preposition disambiguation is contained in the local context.

A trial set of three prepositions was provided (the three smallest instance sets that had been developed). For each of the remaining 34 prepositions, the data was split in a ratio of two to one between training and test data. The training data included the sense identifier. Table 1 shows the total number of instances for each preposition, along with the number in the training and the test sets.

Answers were submitted in the standard Senseval format, consisting of the lexical item name, the instance identifier, the system sense assignments, and optional comments. Although participants were not restricted to selecting only one sense, all did so and did not provide either multiple senses or weighting of different senses. Because of this, a simple Perl script was used to score the results, giving precision, recall, and F-score.[7] The answers were also scored using the standard Senseval scoring program, which records a result for "attempted" rather than F-score, with precision interpreted as percent of attempted instances that are correct and recall as percent of total instances that are correct.[8] Table 1 reports the standard SemEval recall, while Tables 2 and 3 use the standard notions of precision and recall.

5 Results

Tables 2 and 3 present the overall fine-grained and coarse-grained results, respectively, for the three participating teams (University of Melbourne, Koç University, and Instituto Trentino di Cultura, IRST). The tables show the team designator, and the results over all prepositions, giving the precision, the recall, and the F-score. The table also shows the results for two baselines. The **FirstSense** baseline selects the first sense of each preposition as the answer (under the assumption that the senses are organized somewhat according to prominence). The **FreqSense** baseline selects the most frequent sense from the training set. Table 1 shows the fine-grained recall scores for each team for each preposition. Table 1 also shows the entropy and perplexity for each preposition, based on the data from the training sets.

[7]Precision is the percent of total correct instances and recall is the percent of instances attempted, so that an F-score can be computed.

[8]The standard SemEval (Senseval) scoring program, **scorer2**, does not work to compute a coarse-grained score for the preposition instances, since senses are numbers such as "4(2a)" and not alphabetic.

Table 2. Fine-Grained Scores (All Prepositions - 8096 Instances)			
Team	Prec	Rec	F
MELB-YB	0.693	1.000	0.818
KU	0.547	1.000	0.707
IRST-BP	0.496	0.864	0.630
FirstSense	0.289	1.000	0.449
FreqSense	0.396	1.000	0.568

Table 3. Coarse-Grained Scores (All Prepositions - 8096 Instances)			
Team	Prec	Rec	F
MELB-YB	0.755	1.000	0.861
KU	0.642	1.000	0.782
IRST-BP	0.610	0.864	0.715
FirstSense	0.441	1.000	0.612
FreqSense	0.480	1.000	0.649

As can be seen, all participating teams performed significantly better than the baselines. Additional improvements occurred at the coarse grain, although the differences are not dramatically higher.

All participating teams used supervised systems, using the training data for their submissions. The University of Melbourne used a maximum entropy system using a wide variety of syntactic and semantic features. Koç University used a statistical language model (based on Google ngram data) to measure the likelihood of various substitutes for various senses. IRST-BP used Chain Clarifying Relationships, in which contextual lexical and syntactic features of representative contexts are used for learning sense discriminative patterns. Further details on their methods are available in their respective papers.

6 Discussion

Examination of the detailed results by preposition in Table 1 shows that performance is inversely related to polysemy. The greater number of senses leads to reduced performance. The first sense heuristic has a correlation of -0.64; the most frequent sense heuristic has a correlation of -0.67. the correlations for MELB, KU, and IRST are -0.40, -0.70, and -0.56, respectively. The scores are also negatively correlated with the number of test instances. The correlations are -0.34 and -0.44 for the first sense and the most frequent sense heuristics. For the systems, the scores are -0.17, -0.48, and -0.39 for Melb, KU, and IRST.

The scores for each preposition are strongly negatively correlated with entropy and perplexity, as frequently observed in lexical sample disambiguation. For MELB-YB and IRST-BP, the correlation with entropy is about -0.67, while for KU, the correlation is -0.885. For perplexity, the correlation is -0.55 for MELB-YB, -0.62 for IRST-ESP, and -0.82 for KU.

More detailed analysis is required to examine the performance for each preposition, particularly for the most frequent prepositions (*of*, *in*, *from*, *with*, *to*, *for*, *on*, *at*, *into*, and *by*). Performance on these prepositions ranged from fairly good to mediocre to relatively poor. In addition, a comparison of the various attributes of the TPP sense information with the different performances might be fruitful. Little of this information was used by the various systems.

7 Conclusions

The SemEval-2007 preposition disambiguation task can be considered successful, with results that can be exploited in general NLP tasks. In addition, the task has generated considerable information for further examination of preposition behavior.

References

Xavier Carreras and Lluis Marquez. 2004. Introduction to the CoNLL-2004 Shared Task: Semantic Role Labeling. In: *Proceedings of CoNLL-2004*.

Xavier Carreras and Lluis Marquez. 2005. Introduction to the CoNLL-2005 Shared Task: Semantic Role Labeling. In: *Proceedings of CoNLL-2005*.

Charles Fillmore. 1976. Frame Semantics and the Nature of Language. *Annals of the New York Academy of Sciences*, 280: 20-32.

Daniel Gildea and Daniel Jurafsky. 2002. Automatic Labeling of Semantic Roles. *Computational Linguistics, 28* (3), 245-288.

Kenneth C. Litkowski. 2004. Senseval-3 Task: Automatic Labeling of Semantic Roles. In *Senseval-3: Third International Workshop on the Evaluation of Systems for the Semantic Analysis of Text*. ACL. 9-12.

Kenneth C. Litkowski & Orin Hargraves. 2005. The Preposition Project. In: *ACL-SIGSEM Workshop on the Linguistic Dimensions of Prepositions and their Use in Computational Linguistic Formalisms and Applications*, University of Essex - Colchester, United Kingdom. 171-179.

Kenneth C. Litkowski.& Orin Hargraves. 2006. Coverage and Inheritance in The Preposition Project. In: *Proceedings of the Third ACL-SIGSEM Workshop on Prepositions*. Trento, Italy. ACL. 89-94.

Paola Merlo and Eva Esteve Ferrer. 2006. The Notion of Argument in Prepositional Phrase Attachment. *Computational Linguistics, 32* (3), 341-377.

The New Oxford Dictionary of English. 1998. (J. Pearsall, Ed.). Oxford: Clarendon Press.

Thomas P. O'Hara. 2005. Empirical Acquisition of Conceptual Distinctions via Dictionary Definitions. Ph.D. Thesis. New Mexico State .

The Oxford Dictionary of English. 2003. (A. Stevension and C. Soanes, Eds.). Oxford: Clarendon Press.

Randolph Quirk, Sidney Greenbaum, Geoffrey Leech, & Jan Svartik. (1985). *A comprehensive grammar of the English language.* London: Longman.

Table 1. SemEval-2007 Preposition Disambiguation

							Fine-Grained Recall				
				Number of Instances			Participating Teams			Baselines	
Prepostition	Senses	Ent	Perp	Total	Training	Test	Melb	KU	IRST	First Sense	Freq Sense
about	6	0.63	1.54	1074	710	364	0.885	0.934	0.780	0.885	0.885
above	9	1.80	3.49	71	48	23	0.652	0.522	0.565	0.043	0.609
across	3	0.23	1.17	470	319	151	0.960	0.960	0.914	0.960	0.960
after	11	2.15	4.44	156	103	53	0.472	0.585	0.585	0.434	0.434
against	10	1.89	3.69	287	195	92	0.880	0.793	0.826	0.446	0.435
along	4	0.30	1.23	538	365	173	0.954	0.954	0.936	0.954	0.954
among	4	1.55	2.93	150	100	50	0.660	0.680	0.620	0.300	0.300
around	6	2.05	4.13	490	335	155	0.561	0.535	0.381	0.155	0.452
as	2	0.00	1.00	258	174	84	1.000	1.000	0.988	1.000	1.000
at	12	2.38	5.21	1082	715	367	0.790	0.662	0.646	0.425	0.425
before	4	1.33	2.51	67	47	20	0.600	0.850	0.800	0.450	0.450
behind	9	1.31	2.47	206	138	68	0.662	0.676	0.471	0.662	0.662
beneath	6	1.22	2.33	85	57	28	0.714	0.679	0.750	0.571	0.571
beside	3	0.00	1.00	91	62	29	1.000	1.000	1.000	1.000	1.000
between	9	2.11	4.31	313	211	102	0.814	0.765	0.892	0.422	0.422
by	22	2.53	5.77	758	510	248	0.730	0.556	0.391	0.000	0.371
down	5	1.18	2.26	485	332	153	0.654	0.647	0.680	0.438	0.438
during	2	1.00	2.00	120	81	39	0.769	0.564	0.667	0.615	0.385
for	15	2.84	7.17	1429	951	478	0.573	0.395	0.456	0.036	0.238
from	16	2.85	7.21	1784	1206	578	0.642	0.415	0.512	0.279	0.279
in	15	2.81	7.01	2085	1397	688	0.561	0.436	0.494	0.362	0.362
inside	5	1.63	3.10	105	67	38	0.579	0.579	0.605	0.368	0.526
into	10	2.14	4.41	901	604	297	0.616	0.539	0.586	0.290	0.451
like	7	1.26	2.40	391	266	125	0.856	0.808	0.592	0.120	0.768
of	20	3.14	8.80	4482	3004	1478	0.681	0.374	0.144	0.000	0.205
off	7	1.16	2.23	237	161	76	0.658	0.776	0.408	0.171	0.763
on	25	3.42	10.68	1313	872	441	0.624	0.469	0.351	0.218	0.206
onto	3	0.60	1.52	175	117	58	0.879	0.879	0.776	0.879	0.879
over	17	2.52	5.73	298	200	98	0.510	0.510	0.480	0.010	0.327
round	8	2.31	4.95	263	181	82	0.610	0.512	0.000	0.037	0.378
through	16	2.71	6.54	649	441	208	0.524	0.538	0.481	0.322	0.495
to	17	2.43	5.38	1755	1183	572	0.745	0.579	0.558	0.322	0.322
towards	6	0.71	1.63	316	214	102	0.931	0.873	0.833	0.873	0.873
with	18	3.05	8.27	1769	1191	578	0.699	0.455	0.635	0.149	0.249
Total	332			24653	16557	8096	0.693	0.547	0.496	0.289	0.396

SemEval-2007 Task 07: Coarse-Grained English All-Words Task

Roberto Navigli
Università di Roma "La Sapienza"
Dipartimento di Informatica
Via Salaria, 00198 - Roma Italy
navigli@di.uniroma1.it

Kenneth C. Litkowski
CL Research
9208 Gue Road
Damascus MD 20872
ken@clres.com

Orin Hargraves
Lexicographer
orinhargraves
@googlemail.com

Abstract

This paper presents the coarse-grained English all-words task at SemEval-2007. We describe our experience in producing a coarse version of the WordNet sense inventory and preparing the sense-tagged corpus for the task. We present the results of participating systems and discuss future directions.

1 Introduction

It is commonly thought that one of the major obstacles to high-performance Word Sense Disambiguation (WSD) is the fine granularity of sense inventories. State-of-the-art systems attained a disambiguation accuracy around 65% in the Senseval-3 all-words task (Snyder and Palmer, 2004), where WordNet (Fellbaum, 1998) was adopted as a reference sense inventory. Unfortunately, WordNet is a fine-grained resource, encoding sense distinctions that are difficult to recognize even for human annotators (Edmonds and Kilgarriff, 2002). Making WSD an enabling technique for end-to-end applications clearly depends on the ability to deal with reasonable sense distinctions.

The aim of this task was to explicitly tackle the granularity issue and study the performance of WSD systems on an all-words basis when a coarser set of senses is provided for the target words. Given the need of the NLP community to work on freely available resources, the solution of adopting a different computational lexicon is not viable. On the other hand, the production of a coarse-grained sense inventory is not a simple task. The main issue is certainly the subjectivity of sense clusters. To overcome this problem, different strategies can be adopted. For instance, in the OntoNotes project (Hovy et al., 2006) senses are grouped until a 90% inter-annotator agreement is achieved. In contrast, as we describe in this paper, our approach is based on a mapping to a previously existing inventory which encodes sense distinctions at different levels of granularity, thus allowing to induce a sense clustering for the mapped senses.

We would like to mention that another SemEval-2007 task dealt with the issue of sense granularity for WSD, namely Task 17 (subtask #1): Coarse-grained English Lexical Sample WSD. In this paper, we report our experience in organizing Task 07.

2 Task Setup

The task required participating systems to annotate open-class words (i.e. nouns, verbs, adjectives, and adverbs) in a test corpus with the most appropriate sense from a coarse-grained version of the WordNet sense inventory.

2.1 Test Corpus

The test data set consisted of 5,377 words of running text from five different articles: the first three (in common with Task 17) were obtained from the WSJ corpus, the fourth was the Wikipedia entry for *computer programming*[1], the fifth was an excerpt of Amy Steedman's *Knights of the Art*, biographies of Italian painters[2]. We decided to add the last two

[1] http://en.wikipedia.org/wiki/Computer_programming
[2] http://www.gutenberg.org/etext/529

Proceedings of the 4th International Workshop on Semantic Evaluations (SemEval-2007), pages 30–35,
Prague, June 2007.

article	domain	words	annotated
d001	JOURNALISM	951	368
d002	BOOK REVIEW	987	379
d003	TRAVEL	1311	500
d004	COMPUTER SCIENCE	1326	677
d005	BIOGRAPHY	802	345
total		5377	2269

Table 1: Statistics about the five articles in the test data set.

texts to the initial dataset as we wanted the corpus to have a size comparable to that of previous editions of all-words tasks.

In Table 1 we report the domain, number of running words, and number of annotated words for the five articles. We observe that articles d003 and d004 are the largest in the corpus (they constitute 51.87% of it).

2.2 Creation of a Coarse-Grained Sense Inventory

To tackle the granularity issue, we produced a coarser-grained version of the WordNet sense inventory[3] based on the procedure described by Navigli (2006). The method consists of automatically mapping WordNet senses to top level, numbered entries in the Oxford Dictionary of English (ODE, (Soanes and Stevenson, 2003)). The semantic mapping between WordNet and ODE entries was obtained in two steps: first, we disambiguated with the SSI algorithm (Navigli and Velardi, 2005) the definitions of the two dictionaries, together with additional information (hypernyms and domain labels); second, for each WordNet sense, we determined the best matching ODE coarse entry. As a result, WordNet senses mapped to the same ODE entry were assigned to the same sense cluster. WordNet senses with no match were associated with a singleton sense.

In contrast to the automatic method above, the sense mappings for all the words in our test corpus were manually produced by the third author, an expert lexicographer, with the aid of a mapping interface. Not all the words in the corpus could be mapped directly for several reasons: lacking entries in ODE (e.g. adjectives underlying and shivering), different spellings (e.g. after-effect vs. aftereffect, halfhearted vs. half-hearted, etc.), derivatives (e.g. procedural, gambler, etc.). In most of the cases, we asked the lexicographer to map senses of the original word to senses of lexically-related words (e.g. WordNet senses of procedural were mapped to ODE senses of procedure, etc.). When this mapping was not straightforward, we just adopted the WordNet sense inventory for that word.

We released the entire sense groupings (those induced from the manual mapping for words in the test set plus those automatically derived on the other words) and made them available to the participants.

2.3 Sense Annotation

All open-class words (i.e. nouns, verbs, adjectives, and adverbs) with an existing sense in the WordNet inventory were manually annotated by the third author. Multi-word expressions were explicitly identified in the test set and annotated as such (this was made to allow a fair comparison among systems independent of their ability to identify multi-word expressions).

We excluded auxiliary verbs, uncovered phrasal and idiomatic verbs, exclamatory uses, etc. The annotator was allowed to tag words with multiple coarse senses, but was asked to make a single sense assignment whenever possible.

The lexicographer annotated an overall number of 2,316 content words. 47 (2%) of them were excluded because no WordNet sense was deemed appropriate. The remaining 2,269 content words thus constituted the test data set. Only 8 of them were assigned more than one sense: specifically, two coarse senses were assigned to a single word instance[4] and two distinct fine-grained senses were assigned to 7 word instances. This was a clear hint that the sense clusters were not ambiguous for the vast majority of words.

In Table 2 we report information about the polysemy of the word instances in the test set. Overall, 29.88% (678/2269) of the word instances were monosemous (according to our coarse sense inventory). The average polysemy of the test set with the coarse-grained sense inventory was 3.06 compared to an average polysemy with the WordNet inventory

[3]We adopted WordNet 2.1, available from: http://wordnet.princeton.edu

[4]d005.s004.t015

polysemy	N	V	A	R	all
monosemous	358	86	141	93	678
polysemous	750	505	221	115	1591
total	1108	591	362	208	2269

Table 2: Statistics about the test set polysemy (N = nouns, V = verbs, A = adjectives, R = adverbs).

of 6.18.

2.4 Inter-Annotator Agreement

Recent estimations of the inter-annotator agreement when using the WordNet inventory report figures of 72.5% agreement in the preparation of the English all-words test set at Senseval-3 (Snyder and Palmer, 2004) and 67.3% on the Open Mind Word Expert annotation exercise (Chklovski and Mihalcea, 2002).

As the inter-annotator agreement is often considered an upper bound for WSD systems, it was desirable to have a much higher number for our task, given its coarse-grained nature. To this end, beside the expert lexicographer, a second author independently performed part of the manual sense mapping (590 word senses) described in Section 2.2. The pairwise agreement was 86.44%.

We repeated the same agreement evaluation on the sense annotation task of the test corpus. A second author independently annotated part of the test set (710 word instances). The pairwise agreement between the two authors was 93.80%. This figure, compared to those in the literature for fine-grained human annotations, gives us a clear indication that the agreement of human annotators strictly depends on the granularity of the adopted sense inventory.

3 Baselines

We calculated two baselines for the test corpus: a *random baseline*, in which senses are chosen at random, and the *most frequent baseline* (MFS), in which we assign the first WordNet sense to each word in the dataset.

Formally, the accuracy of the random baseline was calculated as follows:

$$BL_{Rand} = \frac{1}{|T|}\sum_{i=1}^{|T|}\frac{1}{|CoarseSenses(w_i)|}$$

where T is our test corpus, w_i is the i-th word instance in T, and $CoarseSenses(w_i)$ is the set of coarse senses for w_i according to the sense clustering we produced as described in Section 2.2.

The accuracy of the MFS baseline was calculated as:

$$BL_{MFS} = \frac{1}{|T|}\sum_{i=1}^{|T|}\delta(w_i, 1)$$

where $\delta(w_i, k)$ equals 1 when the k-th sense of word w_i belongs to the cluster(s) manually associated by the lexicographer to word w_i (0 otherwise). Notice that our calculation of the MFS is based on the frequencies in the SemCor corpus (Miller et al., 1993), as we exploit WordNet sense rankings.

4 Results

12 teams submitted 14 systems overall (plus two systems from a 13th withdrawn team that we will not report). According to the SemEval policy for task organizers, we remark that the system labelled as UoR-SSI was submitted by the first author (the system is based on the Structural Semantic Interconnections algorithm (Navigli and Velardi, 2005) with a lexical knowledge base composed by WordNet and approximately 70,000 relatedness edges). Even though we did not specifically enrich the algorithm's knowledge base on the task at hand, we list the system separately from the overall ranking.

The results are shown in Table 3. We calculated a MFS baseline of 78.89% and a random baseline of 52.43%. In Table 4 we report the F1 measures for all systems where we used the MFS as a backoff strategy when no sense assignment was attempted (this possibly reranked 6 systems - marked in bold in the table - which did not assign a sense to all word instances in the test set). Compared to previous results on fine-grained evaluation exercises (Edmonds and Kilgarriff, 2002; Snyder and Palmer, 2004), the systems' results are much higher. On the other hand, the difference in performance between the MFS baseline and state-of-the-art systems (around 5%) on coarse-grained disambiguation is comparable to that of the Senseval-3 all-words exercise. However, given the novelty of the task we believe that systems can achieve even better perfor-

System	A	P	R	F1
NUS-PT	100.0	82.50	82.50	82.50
NUS-ML	100.0	81.58	81.58	81.58
LCC-WSD	100.0	81.45	81.45	81.45
GPLSI	100.0	79.55	79.55	79.55
BL_{MFS}	100.0	78.89	78.89	78.89
UPV-WSD	100.0	78.63	78.63	78.63
TKB-UO	100.0	70.21	70.21	70.21
PU-BCD	90.1	69.72	62.80	66.08
RACAI-SYNWSD	100.0	65.71	65.71	65.71
SUSSX-FR	72.8	71.73	52.23	60.44
USYD	95.3	58.79	56.02	57.37
UOFL	92.7	52.59	48.74	50.60
SUSSX-C-WD	72.8	54.54	39.71	45.96
SUSSX-CR	72.8	54.30	39.53	45.75
UOR-SSI†	100.0	83.21	83.21	83.21

Table 3: System scores sorted by F1 measure (A = attempted, P = precision, R = recall, F1 = F1 measure, †: system from one of the task organizers).

System	F1
NUS-PT	82.50
NUS-ML	81.58
LCC-WSD	81.45
GPLSI	79.55
BL_{MFS}	78.89
UPV-WSD	78.63
SUSSX-FR	77.04
TKB-UO	70.21
PU-BCD	69.72
RACAI-SYNWSD	65.71
SUSSX-C-WD	64.52
SUSSX-CR	64.35
USYD	58.79
UOFL	54.61
UOR-SSI†	83.21

Table 4: System scores sorted by F1 measure with MFS adopted as a backoff strategy when no sense assignment is attempted (†: system from one of the task organizers). Systems affected are marked in bold.

mance by heavily exploiting the coarse nature of the sense inventory.

In Table 5 we report the results for each of the five articles. The interesting aspect of the table is that documents from some domains seem to have predominant senses different from those in SemCor. Specifically, the MFS baseline performs more poorly on documents d004 and d005, from the COMPUTER SCIENCE and BIOGRAPHY domains respectively. We believe this is due to the fact that these documents have specific predominant senses, which correspond less often to the most frequent sense in SemCor than for the other three documents. It is also interesting to observe that different systems perform differently on the five documents (we highlight in bold the best performing systems on each article).

Finally, we calculated the systems' performance by part of speech. The results are shown in Table 6. Again, we note that different systems show different performance depending on the part-of-speech tag. Another interesting aspect is that the performance of the MFS baseline is very close to state-of-the-art systems for adjectives and adverbs, whereas it is more than 3 points below for verbs, and around 5 for nouns.

System	N	V	A	R
NUS-PT	**82.31**	**78.51**	**85.64**	89.42
NUS-ML	81.41	78.17	82.60	**90.38**
LCC-WSD	80.69	78.17	85.36	87.98
GPLSI	80.05	74.45	82.32	86.54
BL_{MFS}	77.44	75.30	84.25	87.50
UPV-WSD	79.33	72.76	84.53	81.25
TKB-UO	70.76	62.61	78.73	74.04
PU-BCD	71.41	59.69	66.57	55.67
RACAI-SYNWSD	64.02	62.10	71.55	75.00
SUSSX-FR	68.09	51.02	57.38	49.38
USYD	56.06	60.43	58.00	54.31
UOFL	57.65	48.82	25.87	60.80
SUSSX-C-WD	52.18	35.64	42.95	46.30
SUSSX-CR	51.87	35.44	42.95	46.30
UOR-SSI†	84.12	78.34	85.36	88.46

Table 6: System scores by part-of-speech tag (N = nouns, V = verbs, A = adjectives, R = adverbs) sorted by overall F1 measure (best scores are marked in bold, †: system from one of the task organizers).

System	d001 P	d001 R	d002 P	d002 R	d003 P	d003 R	d004 P	d004 R	d005 P	d005 R
NUS-PT	**88.32**	**88.32**	88.13	88.13	**83.40**	**83.40**	76.07	76.07	**81.45**	**81.45**
NUS-ML	86.14	86.14	**88.39**	**88.39**	81.40	81.40	**76.66**	**76.66**	79.13	79.13
LCC-WSD	87.50	87.50	87.60	87.60	81.40	81.40	75.48	75.48	80.00	80.00
GPLSI	83.42	83.42	86.54	86.54	80.40	80.40	73.71	73.71	77.97	77.97
BL_{MFS}	85.60	85.60	84.70	84.70	77.80	77.80	75.19	75.19	74.20	74.20
UPV-WSD	84.24	84.24	80.74	80.74	76.00	76.00	77.11	77.11	77.10	77.10
TKB-UO	78.80	78.80	72.56	72.56	69.40	69.40	70.75	70.75	58.55	58.55
PU-BCD	77.16	67.94	75.52	67.55	64.96	58.20	68.86	61.74	64.42	60.87
RACAI-SYNWSD	71.47	71.47	72.82	72.82	66.80	66.80	60.86	60.86	59.71	59.71
SUSSX-FR	79.10	57.61	73.72	53.30	74.86	52.40	67.97	48.89	65.20	51.59
USYD	62.53	61.69	59.78	57.26	60.97	57.80	60.57	56.28	47.15	45.51
UOFL	61.41	59.24	55.93	52.24	48.00	45.60	53.42	47.27	44.38	41.16
SUSSX-C-WD	66.42	48.37	61.31	44.33	55.14	38.60	50.72	36.48	42.13	33.33
SUSSX-CR	66.05	48.10	60.58	43.80	59.14	41.40	48.67	35.01	40.29	31.88
UOR-SSI†	86.14	86.14	85.49	85.49	79.60	79.60	86.85	86.85	75.65	75.65

Table 5: System scores by article (best scores are marked in bold, †: system from one of the task organizers).

5 Systems Description

In order to allow for a critical and comparative inspection of the system results, we asked the participants to answer some questions about their systems. These included information about whether:

1. the system used semantically-annotated and unannotated resources;
2. the system used the MFS as a backoff strategy;
3. the system used the coarse senses provided by the organizers;
4. the system was trained on some corpus.

We believe that this gives interesting information to provide a deeper understanding of the results. We summarize the participants' answers to the questionnaires in Table 7. We report about the use of semantic resources as well as semantically annotated corpora (SC = SemCor, DSO = Defence Science Organisation Corpus, SE = Senseval corpora, OMWE = Open Mind Word Expert, XWN = eXtended WordNet, WN = WordNet glosses and/or relations, WND = WordNet Domains), as well as information about the use of unannotated corpora (UC), training (TR), MFS (based on the SemCor sense frequencies), and the coarse senses provided by the organizers (CS). As expected, several systems used lexico-semantic information from the WordNet semantic network and/or were trained on the SemCor semantically-annotated corpus.

Finally, we point out that all the systems performing better than the MFS baseline adopted it as a backoff strategy when they were not able to output a sense assignment.

6 Conclusions and Future Directions

It is commonly agreed that Word Sense Disambiguation needs emerge and show its usefulness in end-to-end applications: after decades of research in the field it is still unclear whether WSD can provide a relevant contribution to real-world applications, such as Information Retrieval, Question Answering, etc. In previous Senseval evaluation exercises, state-of-the-art systems achieved performance far below 70% and even the agreement between human annotators was discouraging. As a result of the discussion at the Senseval-3 workshop in 2004, one of the aims of SemEval-2007 was to tackle the problems at the roots of WSD. In this task, we dealt with the granularity issue which is a major obstacle to both system and human annotators. In the hope of overcoming the current performance upper bounds, we

System	SC	DSO	SE	OMWE	XWN	WN	WND	OTHER	UC	TR	MFS	CS
GPLSI	√	×	√	×	×	√	×	×	×	√	√	√
LCC-WSD	√	×	√	√	√	√	×	×	×	√	√	√
NUS-ML	√	×	×	×	×	×	×	×	√	√	√	×
NUS-PT	√	√	×	×	×	×	×	Parallel corpus	×	√	√	√
PU-BCD	√	×	×	×	×	×	×	×	×	√	×	√
RACAI-SynWSD	×	×	×	×	×	√	√	×	√	×	×	√
SUSSX-C-WD	×	×	×	×	×	×	×	×	√	×	×	×
SUSSX-CR	×	×	×	×	×	×	×	×	√	×	×	×
SUSSX-FR	×	×	×	×	×	×	×	×	√	×	×	√
TKB-UO	×	×	×	×	×	√	×	×	×	×	×	×
UofL	×	×	×	×	√	√	×	×	×	×	×	×
UoR-SSI†	×	×	×	×	×	√	×	SSI LKB	×	×	√	×
UPV-WSD	×	×	×	×	×	√	√	×	×	×	√	×
USYD	√	×	√	×	×	√	×	×	√	√	√	√

Table 7: Information about participating systems (SC = SemCor, DSO = Defence Science Organisation Corpus, SE = Senseval corpora, OMWE = Open Mind Word Expert, XWN = eXtended WordNet, WN = WordNet glosses and/or relations, WND = WordNet Domains, UC = use of unannotated corpora, TR = use of training, MFS = most frequent sense backoff strategy, CS = use of coarse senses from the organizers, †: system from one of the task organizers).

proposed the adoption of a coarse-grained sense inventory. We found the results of participating systems interesting and stimulating. However, some questions arise. First, it is unclear whether, given the novelty of the task, systems really achieved the state of the art or can still improve their performance based on a heavier exploitation of coarse- and fine-grained information from the adopted sense inventory. We observe that, on a technical domain such as computer science, most supervised systems performed worse due to the nature of their training set. Second, we still need to show that coarse senses can be useful in real applications. Third, a full coarse sense inventory is not yet available: this is a major obstacle to large-scale *in vivo* evaluations. We believe that these aspects deserve further investigation in the years to come.

Acknowledgments

This work was partially funded by the Interop NoE (508011), 6th European Union FP. We would like to thank Martha Palmer for providing us the first three texts of the test corpus.

References

Tim Chklovski and Rada Mihalcea. 2002. Building a sense tagged corpus with open mind word expert. In *Proc. of ACL 2002 Workshop on WSD: Recent Successes and Future Directions*. Philadelphia, PA.

Philip Edmonds and Adam Kilgarriff. 2002. Introduction to the special issue on evaluating word sense disambiguation systems. *Journal of Natural Language Engineering*, 8(4):279–291.

Christiane Fellbaum, editor. 1998. *WordNet: an Electronic Lexical Database*. MIT Press.

Eduard Hovy, Mitchell Marcus, Martha Palmer, Lance Ramshaw, and Ralph Weischedel. 2006. Ontonotes: The 90% solution. In *Proceedings of the Human Language Technology Conference of the NAACL, Comp. Volume*, pages 57–60, New York City, USA.

George A. Miller, Claudia Leacock, Randee Tengi, and Ross T. Bunker. 1993. A semantic concordance. In *Proceedings of the ARPA Workshop on Human Language Technology*, pages 303–308, Princeton, NJ, USA.

Roberto Navigli and Paola Velardi. 2005. Structural semantic interconnections: a knowledge-based approach to word sense disambiguation. *IEEE Transactions on Pattern Analysis and Machine Intelligence (PAMI)*, 27(7):1063–1074.

Roberto Navigli. 2006. Meaningful clustering of senses helps boost word sense disambiguation performance. In *Proc. of the 44th Annual Meeting of the Association for Computational Linguistics joint with the 21st International Conference on Computational Linguistics (COLING-ACL 2006)*, pages 105–112. Sydney, Australia.

Benjamin Snyder and Martha Palmer. 2004. The english all-words task. In *Proc. of ACL 2004 SENSEVAL-3 Workshop*, pages 41–43. Barcelona, Spain.

Catherine Soanes and Angus Stevenson, editors. 2003. *Oxford Dictionary of English*. Oxford University Press.

SemEval-2007 Task 08: Metonymy Resolution at SemEval-2007

Katja Markert
School of Computing
University of Leeds, UK
markert@comp.leeds.ac.uk

Malvina Nissim
Dept. of Linguistics and Oriental Studies
University of Bologna, Italy
malvina.nissim@unibo.it

Abstract

We provide an overview of the metonymy resolution shared task organised within SemEval-2007. We describe the problem, the data provided to participants, and the evaluation measures we used to assess performance. We also give an overview of the systems that have taken part in the task, and discuss possible directions for future work.

1 Introduction

Both word sense disambiguation and named entity recognition have benefited enormously from shared task evaluations, for example in the Senseval, MUC and CoNLL frameworks. Similar campaigns have not been developed for the resolution of figurative language, such as metaphor, metonymy, idioms and irony. However, resolution of figurative language is an important complement to and extension of word sense disambiguation as it often deals with word senses that are not listed in the lexicon. For example, the meaning of *stopover* in the sentence *He saw teaching as a stopover on his way to bigger things* is a metaphorical sense of the sense "stopping place in a physical journey", with the literal sense listed in WordNet 2.0 but the metaphorical one not being listed.[1] The same holds for the metonymic reading of *rattlesnake* (for the animal's meat) in *Roast rattlesnake tastes like chicken*.[2] Again, the meat reading of *rattlesnake* is not listed in WordNet whereas the meat reading for *chicken* is.

As there is no common framework or corpus for figurative language resolution, previous computational works (Fass, 1997; Hobbs et al., 1993; Barnden et al., 2003, among others) carry out only small-scale evaluations. In recent years, there has been growing interest in metaphor and metonymy resolution that is either corpus-based or evaluated on larger datasets (Martin, 1994; Nissim and Markert, 2003; Mason, 2004; Peirsman, 2006; Birke and Sarkaar, 2006; Krishnakamuran and Zhu, 2007). Still, apart from (Nissim and Markert, 2003; Peirsman, 2006) who evaluate their work on the same dataset, results are hardly comparable as they all operate within different frameworks.

This situation motivated us to organise the first shared task for figurative language, concentrating on metonymy. In metonymy one expression is used to refer to the referent of a related one, like the use of an animal name for its meat. Similarly, in Ex. 1, *Vietnam*, the name of a location, refers to an event (a war) that happened there.

(1) Sex, drugs, and **Vietnam** have haunted Bill Clinton's campaign.

In Ex. 2 and 3, *BMW*, the name of a company, stands for its index on the stock market, or a vehicle manufactured by BMW, respectively.

(2) **BMW** slipped 4p to 31p

(3) His **BMW** went on to race at Le Mans

The importance of resolving metonymies has been shown for a variety of NLP tasks, such as ma-

[1] This example was taken from the Berkely Master Metaphor list (Lakoff and Johnson, 1980) .

[2] From now on, all examples in this paper are taken from the British National Corpus (BNC) (Burnard, 1995), but Ex. 23.

Proceedings of the 4th International Workshop on Semantic Evaluations (SemEval-2007), pages 36–41,
Prague, June 2007.

chine translation (Kamei and Wakao, 1992), question answering (Stallard, 1993), anaphora resolution (Harabagiu, 1998; Markert and Hahn, 2002) and geographical information retrieval (Leveling and Hartrumpf, 2006).

Although metonymic readings are, like all figurative readings, potentially open ended and can be innovative, the regularity of usage for word groups helps in establishing a common evaluation framework. Many other location names, for instance, can be used in the same fashion as *Vietnam* in Ex. 1. Thus, given a semantic class (e.g. location), one can specify several regular metonymic patterns (e.g. place-for-event) that instances of the class are likely to undergo. In addition to literal readings, regular metonymic patterns and innovative metonymic readings, there can also be so-called mixed readings, similar to zeugma, where both a literal and a metonymic reading are evoked (Nunberg, 1995).

The metonymy task is a lexical sample task for English, consisting of two subtasks, one concentrating on the semantic class *location*, exemplified by country names, and another one concentrating on *organisation*, exemplified by company names. Participants had to automatically classify preselected country/company names as having a literal or non-literal meaning, given a four-sentence context. Additionally, participants could attempt finer-grained interpretations, further specifying readings into prespecified metonymic patterns (such as place-for-event) and recognising innovative readings.

2 Annotation Categories

We distinguish between literal, metonymic, and mixed readings for locations and organisations. In the case of a metonymic reading, we also specify the actual patterns. The annotation categories were motivated by prior linguistic research by ourselves (Markert and Nissim, 2006), and others (Fass, 1997; Lakoff and Johnson, 1980).

2.1 Locations

Literal readings for locations comprise *locative* (Ex. 4) and *political* entity interpretations (Ex. 5).

(4) coral coast of **Papua New Guinea**.

(5) **Britain**'s current account deficit.

Metonymic readings encompass four types:

- place-for-people a place stands for any persons/organisations associated with it. These can be governments (Ex. 6), affiliated organisations, incl. sports teams (Ex. 7), or the whole population (Ex. 8). Often, the referent is underspecified (Ex. 9).

(6) **America** did once try to ban alcohol.

(7) **England** lost in the semi-final.

(8) [...] the incarnation was to fulfil the promise to **Israel** and to reconcile the world with God.

(9) The G-24 group expressed readiness to provide **Albania** with food aid.

- place-for-event a location name stands for an event that happened in the location (see Ex. 1).

- place-for-product a place stands for a product manufactured in the place, as *Bordeaux* in Ex. 10.

(10) a smooth **Bordeaux** that was gutsy enough to cope with our food

- othermet a metonymy that does not fall into any of the prespecified patterns, as in Ex. 11, where *New Jersey* refers to typical local tunes.

(11) The thing about the record is the influences of the music. The bottom end is very New York/**New Jersey** and the top is very melodic.

When two predicates are involved, triggering a different reading each (Nunberg, 1995), the annotation category is **mixed**. In Ex. 12, both a literal and a place-for-people reading are involved.

(12) they arrived in **Nigeria**, hitherto a leading critic of [...]

2.2 Organisations

The **literal** reading for organisation names describes references to the organisation in general, where an organisation is seen as a legal entity, which consists of organisation members that speak with a collective voice, and which has a charter, statute or defined aims. Examples of literal readings include (among others) descriptions of the structure of an organisation (see Ex. 13), associations between organisations (see Ex. 14) or relations between organisations and products/services they offer (see Ex. 15).

(13) **NATO** countries

(14) **Sun** acquired that part of Eastman-Kodak Cos Unix subsidary

(15) **Intel**'s Indeo video compression hardware

Metonymic readings include six types:

- org-for-members an organisation stands for its members, such as a spokesperson or official (Ex. 16), or all its employees, as in Ex. 17.

(16) Last February **IBM** announced [...]

(17) It's customary to go to work in black or white suits. [...] **Woolworths** wear them

- org-for-event an organisation name is used to refer to an event associated with the organisation (e.g. a scandal or bankruptcy), as in Ex. 18.

(18) the resignation of Leon Brittan from Trade and Industry in the aftermath of **Westland**.

- org-for-product the name of a commercial organisation can refer to its products, as in Ex. 3.

- org-for-facility organisations can also stand for the facility that houses the organisation or one of its branches, as in the following example.

(19) The opening of a **McDonald's** is a major event

- org-for-index an organisation name can be used for an index that indicates its value (see Ex. 2).

- othermet a metonymy that does not fall into any of the prespecified patterns, as in Ex. 20, where *Barclays Bank* stands for an account at the bank.

(20) funds [...] had been paid into **Barclays Bank**.

Mixed readings exist for organisations as well. In Ex. 21, both an org-for-index and an org-for-members pattern are invoked.

(21) **Barclays** slipped 4p to 351p after confirming 3,000 more job losses.

2.3 Class-independent categories

Apart from class-specific metonymic readings, some patterns seem to apply across classes to all names. In the SemEval dataset, we annotated two of them.

object-for-name all names can be used as mere signifiers, instead of referring to an object or set of objects. In Ex. 22, both *Chevrolet* and *Ford* are used as strings, rather than referring to the companies.

(22) **Chevrolet** is feminine because of its sound (it's a longer word than **Ford**, has an open vowel at the end, connotes Frenchness).

object-for-representation a name can refer to a representation (such as a photo or painting) of the referent of its literal reading. In Ex. 23, *Malta* refers to a drawing of the island when pointing to a map.

(23) This is **Malta**

3 Data Collection and Annotation

We used the CIA Factbook[3] and the Fortune 500 list as sampling frames for country and company names respectively. All occurrences (including plural forms) of all names in the sampling frames were extracted in context from all texts of the BNC, Version 1.0. All samples extracted are coded in XML and contain up to four sentences: the sentence in which the country/company name occurs, two before, and one after. If the name occurs at the beginning or end of a text the samples may contain less than four sentences.

For both the location and the organisation subtask, two random subsets of the extracted samples were selected as training and test set, respectively. Before metonymy annotation, samples that were not understood by the annotators because of insufficient context were removed from the datsets. In addition, a sample was also removed if the name extracted was a homonym not in the desired semantic class (for example *Mr. Greenland* when annotating locations).[4]

For those names that do have the semantic class `location` or `organisation`, metonymy annotation was performed, using the categories described in Section 2. All training set annotation was carried out independently by both organisers. Annotation was highly reliable with a *kappa* (Carletta, 1996) of

[3] `https://www.cia.gov/cia/publications/factbook/index.html`

[4] Given that the task is not about standard Named Entity Recognition, we assume that the general semantic class of the name is already known.

Table 1: Reading distribution for locations

reading	train	test
literal	737	721
mixed	15	20
othermet	9	11
obj-for-name	0	4
obj-for-representation	0	0
place-for-people	161	141
place-for-event	3	10
place-for-product	0	1
total	925	908

Table 2: Reading distribution for organisations

reading	train	test
literal	690	520
mixed	59	60
othermet	14	8
obj-for-name	8	6
obj-for-representation	1	0
org-for-members	220	161
org-for-event	2	1
org-for-product	74	67
org-for-facility	15	16
org-for-index	7	3
total	1090	842

.88/.89 for locations/organisations.[5] As agreement was established, annotation of the test set was carried out by the first organiser. All cases which were not entirely straightforward were then independently checked by the second organiser. Samples whose readings could not be agreed on (after a reconciliation phase) were excluded from both training and test set. The reading distributions of training and test sets for both subtasks are shown in Tables 1 and 2.

In addition to a simple text format including only the metonymy annotation, we provided participants with several linguistic annotations of both training and testset. This included the original BNC tokenisation and part-of-speech tags as well as manually annotated dependency relations for each annotated name (e.g. *BMW subj-of-slip* for Ex. 2).

4 Submission and Evaluation

Teams were allowed to participate in the location or organisation task or both. We encouraged supervised, semi-supervised or unsupervised approaches.

Systems could be tailored to recognise metonymies at three different levels of granularity: *coarse*, *medium*, or *fine*, with an increasing number and specification of target classification categories, and thus difficulty. At the *coarse* level, only a distinction between literal and non-literal was asked for; *medium* asked for a distinction between literal, metonymic and mixed readings; *fine* needed a classification into literal readings, mixed readings, any of the class-dependent and class-independent metonymic patterns (Section 2) or an innovative metonymic reading (category `othermet`).

Systems were evaluated via accuracy (acc) and coverage (cov), allowing for partial submissions.

$$acc = \frac{\#\ correct\ predictions}{\#\ predictions} \quad cov = \frac{\#\ predictions}{\#\ samples}$$

For each target category c we also measured:

$$precision_c = \frac{\#\ correct\ assignments\ of\ c}{\#\ assignments\ of\ c}$$
$$recall_c = \frac{\#\ correct\ assignments\ of\ c}{\#\ dataset\ instances\ of\ c}$$
$$fscore_c = \frac{2precision_c recall_c}{precision_c + recall_c}$$

A baseline, consisting of the assignment of the most frequent category (always literal), was used for each task and granularity level.

5 Systems and Results

We received five submissions (`FUH`, `GYDER`, `up13`, `UTD-HLT-CG`, `XRCE-M`). All tackled the location task; three (`GYDER`, `UTD-HLT-CG`, `XRCE-M`) also participated in the organisation task. All systems were full submissions (coverage of 1) and participated at all granularity levels.

5.1 Methods and Features

Out of five teams, four (`FUH`, `GYDER`, `up13`, `UTD-HLT-CG`) used supervised machine learning, including single (`FUH`, `GYDER`, `up13`) as well as multiple classifiers (`UTD-HLT-CG`). A range of learning paradigms was represented (including instance-based learning, maximum entropy, decision trees, etc.). One participant (`XRCE-M`) built a hybrid system, combining a symbolic, supervised approach based on deep parsing with an unsupervised distributional approach exploiting lexical information obtained from large corpora.

Systems `up13` and `FUH` used mostly shallow features extracted directly from the training data (including parts-of-speech, co-occurrences and collo-

[5] The training sets are part of the already available Mascara corpus for metonymy (Markert and Nissim, 2006). The test sets were newly created for SemEval.

cations). The other systems made also use of syntactic/grammatical features (syntactic roles, determination, morphology etc.). Two of them (GYDER and UTD-HLT-CG) exploited the manually annotated grammatical roles provided by the organisers.

All systems apart from up13 made use of external knowledge resources such as lexical databases for feature generalisation (WordNet, FrameNet, VerbNet, Levin verb classes) as well as other corpora (the Mascara corpus for additional training material, the BNC, and the Web).

5.2 Performance

Tables 3 and 4 report accuracy for all systems.[6] Table 5 provides a summary of the results with lowest, highest, and average accuracy and f-scores for each subtask and granularity level.[7]

The task seemed extremely difficult, with 2 of the 5 systems (up13, FUH) participating in the location task not beating the baseline. These two systems relied mainly on shallow features with limited or no use of external resources, thus suggesting that these features might only be of limited use for identifying metonymic shifts. The organisers themselves have come to similar conclusions in their own experiments (Markert and Nissim, 2002). The systems using syntactic/grammatical features (GYDER, UTD-HLT-CG, XRCE-M) could improve over the baseline whether using manual annotation or parsing. These systems also made heavy use of feature generalisation. Classification granularity had only a small effect on system performance.

Only few of the fine-grained categories could be distinguished with reasonable success (see the f-scores in Table 5). These include literal readings, and place-for-people, org-for-members, and org-for-product metonymies, which are the most frequent categories (see Tables 1 and 2). Rarer metonymic targets were either not assigned by the systems at all ("undef" in Table 5) or assigned wrongly (low f-scores). An exception is the object-for-name pattern, which XRCE-M and UTD-HLT-CG could distinguish with good success. Mixed readings also proved problematic since more than one pattern is involved, thus limiting the possibilities of learning from a single training instance. Only GYDER succeeded in correctly identifiying a variety of mixed readings in the organisation subtask. No systems could identify unconventional metonymies correctly. Such poor performance is due to the non-regularity of the reading by definition, so that approaches based on learning from similar examples alone cannot work too well.

Table 5: Overview of scores

	base	min	max	ave
LOCATION-coarse				
accuracy	0.794	0.754	0.852	0.815
literal-f		0.849	0.912	0.888
non-literal-f		0.344	0.576	0.472
LOCATION-medium				
accuracy	0.794	0.750	0.848	0.812
literal-f		0.849	0.912	0.889
metonymic-f		0.331	0.580	0.476
mixed-f		0.000	0.083	0.017
LOCATION-fine				
accuracy	0.794	0.741	0.844	0.801
literal-f		0.849	0.912	0.887
place-for-people-f		0.308	0.589	0.456
place-for-event-f		0.000	0.167	0.033
place-for-product-f		0.000	undef	0.000
obj-for-name-f		0.000	0.667	0.133
obj-for-rep-f		undef	undef	undef
othermet-f		0.000	undef	0.000
mixed-f		0.000	0.083	0.017
ORGANISATION-coarse				
accuracy	0.618	0.732	0.767	0.746
literal-f		0.800	0.825	0.810
non-literal-f		0.572	0.652	0.615
ORGANISATION-medium				
accuracy	0.618	0.711	0.733	0.718
literal-f		0.804	0.825	0.814
metonymic-f		0.553	0.604	0.577
mixed-f		0.000	0.308	0.163
ORGANISATION-fine				
accuracy	0.618	0.700	0.728	0.713
literal-f		0.808	0.826	0.817
org-for-members-f		0.568	0.630	0.608
org-for-event-f		0.000	undef	0.000
org-for-product-f		0.400	0.500	0.458
org-for-facility-f		0.000	0.222	0.141
org-for-index-f		0.000	undef	0.000
obj-for-name-f		0.250	0.800	0.592
obj-for-rep-f		undef	undef	undef
othermet-f		0.000	undef	0.000
mixed-f		0.000	0.343	0.135

[6] Due to space limitations we do not report precision, recall, and f-score per class and refer the reader to each system description provided within this volume.

[7] The value "undef" is used for cases where the system did not attempt any assignment for a given class, whereas the value "0" signals that assignments were done, but were not correct.

[8] Please note that results for the FUH system are slightly different than those presented in the FUH system description paper. This is due to a preprocessing problem in the FUH system that was fixed only after the run submission deadline.

Table 3: Accuracy scores for all systems for all the location tasks.[8]

task ↓ / system →	baseline	FUH	UTD-HLT-CG	XRCE-M	GYDER	up13
LOCATION-coarse	0.794	0.778	0.841	0.851	0.852	0.754
LOCATION-medium	0.794	0.772	0.840	0.848	0.848	0.750
LOCATION-fine	0.794	0.759	0.822	0.841	0.844	0.741

Table 4: Accuracy scores for all systems for all the organisation tasks

task ↓ / system →	baseline	UTD-HLT-CG	XRCE-M	GYDER
ORGANISATION-coarse	0.618	0.739	0.732	0.767
ORGANISATION-medium	0.618	0.711	0.711	0.733
ORGANISATION-fine	0.618	0.711	0.700	0.728

6 Concluding Remarks

There is a wide range of opportunities for future figurative language resolution tasks. In the SemEval corpus the reading distribution mirrored the actual distribution in the original corpus (BNC). Although realistic, this led to little training data for several phenomena. A future option, geared entirely towards system improvement, would be to use a stratified corpus, built with different acquisition strategies like active learning or specialised search procedures. There are also several options for expanding the scope of the task, for example to a wider range of semantic classes, from proper names to common nouns, and from lexical samples to an all-words task. In addition, our task currently covers only metonymies and could be extended to other kinds of figurative language.

Acknowledgements

We are very grateful to the BNC Consortium for letting us use and distribute samples from the British National Corpus, version 1.0.

References

J.A. Barnden, S.R. Glasbey, M.G. Lee, and A.M. Wallington. 2003. Domain-transcending mappings in a system for metaphorical reasoning. In *Proc. of EACL-2003*, 57-61.

J. Birke and A Sarkaar. 2006. A clustering approach for the nearly unsupervised recognition of nonliteral language. In *Proc. of EACL-2006*.

L. Burnard, 1995. *Users' Reference Guide, British National Corpus*. BNC Consortium, Oxford, England.

J. Carletta. 1996. Assessing agreement on classification tasks: The kappa statistic. *Computational Linguistics*, 22:249-254.

D. Fass. 1997. *Processing Metaphor and Metonymy*. Ablex, Stanford, CA.

S. Harabagiu. 1998. Deriving metonymic coercions from WordNet. In *Workshop on the Usage of WordNet in Natural Language Processing Systems, COLING-ACL '98*, 142-148, Montreal, Canada.

J.R. Hobbs, M.E. Stickel, D.E. Appelt, and P. Martin. 1993. Interpretation as abduction. *Artificial Intelligence*, 63:69-142.

S. Kamei and T. Wakao. 1992. Metonymy: Reassessment, survey of acceptability and its treatment in machine translation systems. In *Proc. of ACL-92*, 309-311.

S. Krishnakamuran and X. Zhu. 2007. Hunting elusive metaphors using lexical resources. In *NAACL 2007 Workshop on Computational Approaches to Figurative Language*.

G. Lakoff and M. Johnson. 1980. *Metaphors We Live By*. Chicago University Press, Chicago, Ill.

J. Leveling and S. Hartrumpf. 2006. On metonymy recognition for gir. In *Proceedings of GIR-2006: 3rd Workshop on Geographical Information Retrieval*.

K. Markert and U. Hahn. 2002. Understanding metonymies in discourse. *Artificial Intelligence*, 135(1/2):145–198.

K. Markert and M. Nissim. 2002. Metonymy resolution as a classification task. In *Proc. of EMNLP-2002*, 204-213.

K. Markert and M. Nissim. 2006. Metonymic proper names: A corpus-based account. In A. Stefanowitsch, editor, *Corpora in Cognitive Linguistics. Vol. 1: Metaphor and Metonymy*. Mouton de Gruyter, 2006.

J. Martin. 1994. Metabank: a knowledge base of metaphoric language conventions. *Computational Intelligence*, 10(2):134-149.

Z. Mason. 2004. Cormet: A computational corpus-based conventional metaphor extraction system. *Computational Linguistics*, 30(1):23-44.

M. Nissim and K. Markert. 2003. Syntactic features and word similarity for supervised metonymy resolution. In *Proc. of ACL-2003*, 56-63.

G. Nunberg. 1995. Transfers of meaning. *Journal of Semantics*, 12:109-132.

Y Peirsman. 2006. Example-based metonymy recognition for proper nouns. In *Student Session of EACL 2006*.

D. Stallard. 1993. Two kinds of metonymy. In *Proc. of ACL-93*, 87-94.

SemEval-2007 Task 09: Multilevel Semantic Annotation of Catalan and Spanish

Lluís Màrquez and Luis Villarejo
TALP Research Center
Technical University of Catalonia
{lluism,luisv}@lsi.upc.edu

M. A. Martí and Mariona Taulé
Centre de Llenguatge i Computació, CLiC
Universitat de Barcelona
{amarti,mtaule}@ub.edu

Abstract

In this paper we describe SemEval-2007 task number 9 (*Multilevel Semantic Annotation of Catalan and Spanish*). In this task, we aim at evaluating and comparing automatic systems for the annotation of several semantic linguistic levels for Catalan and Spanish. Three semantic levels are considered: noun sense disambiguation, named entity recognition, and semantic role labeling.

1 Introduction

The Multilevel Semantic Annotation of Catalan and Spanish task is split into the following three subtasks:

Noun Sense Disambiguation (NSD): Disambiguation of all frequent nouns ("all words" style).

Named Entity Recognition (NER): The annotation of (possibly embedding) named entities with basic entity types.

Semantic Role Labeling (SRL): Including also two subtasks, i.e., the annotation of verbal predicates with semantic roles (SR), and verb tagging with semantic–class labels (SC).

All semantic annotation tasks are performed on exactly the same corpora for each language. We presented all the annotation levels together as a complex global task, since we were interested in approaches which address these problems jointly, possibly taking into account cross-dependencies among them. However, we were also accepting systems approaching the annotation in a pipeline style, or addressing any of the particular subtasks in any of the languages.

In Section 2 we describe the methodology followed to develop the linguistic corpora for the task. Sections 3 and 4 summarize the task setting and the participant systems, respectively. Finally, Section 5 presents a comparative analysis of the results. For any additional information on corpora, resources, formats, tagsets, annotation manuals, etc. we refer the reader to the official website of the task[1].

2 Linguistic corpora

The corpora used in this SemEval task are a subset of CESS-ECE, a multilingual Treebank, composed of a Spanish (CESS-ESP) and a Catalan (CESS-CAT) corpus of 500K words each (Martí et al., 2007b). These corpora were enriched with different kinds of semantic information: argument structure, thematic roles, semantic class, named entities, and WordNet synsets for the 150 most frequent nouns. The annotation process was carried out in a semiautomatic way, with a posterior manual revision of all automatic processes.

A sequential approach was adopted for the annotation of the corpus, beginning with the basic levels of analysis, i.e., POS tagging and chunking (automatically performed) and followed by the more complex levels: syntactic constituents and functions (manually tagged) and semantic annotation (manual and semiautomatic processes with manual completion and posterior revision). Furthermore, some experiments concerning inter-annotator agreement

[1] www.lsi.upc.edu/~nlp/semeval/msacs.html

Proceedings of the 4th International Workshop on Semantic Evaluations (SemEval-2007), pages 42–47,
Prague, June 2007.

were carried out at the syntactic (Civit et al., 2003) and semantic levels (Màrquez et al., 2004) in order to evaluate the quality of the results.

2.1 Syntactic Annotation

The syntactic annotation consists of the labeling of constituents, including elliptical subjects, and syntactic functions. The surface order was maintained and only those constituents directly attached to any kind of 'Sentence' root node were considered ('S', 'S.NF', 'S.F', 'S*'). The syntactic functions are: subject (SUJ), direct object (OD), indirect object (OI), attribute (ATR), predicative (CPRED), agent complement (CAG), and adjunct (CC). Other functions such as textual element (ET), sentence adjunct (AO), negation (NEG), vocative (VOC) and verb modifiers (MOD) were tagged, but did not receive any thematic role.

2.2 Lexical Semantic Information: WordNet

We selected the 150 most frequent nouns in the whole corpus and annotated their occurrences with WordNet synsets. No other word categories were treated (verbs, adjectives and adverbs). We used a steady version of Catalan and Spanish WordNets, linked to WordNet 1.6. Each noun either matched a WordNet synset or a special label indicating a specific circumstance (for instance, the tag C2S indicates that the word does not appear in the dictionary). All this process was carried out manually.

2.3 Named Entities

The corpora were annotated with both *strong* and *weak* Named Entities. Strong NEs correspond to single lexical tokens (e.g., "[U.S.]$_{LOC}$"), while weak NEs include, by definition, some strong entities (e.g., "The [president of [US]$_{LOC}$]$_{PER}$"). (Arévalo et al., 2004). Thus, NEs may embed. Six basic semantic categories were distinguished: Person, Organization, Location, Date, Numerical expression, and Others (Borrega et al., 2007).

Two golden rules underlie the definition of NEs in Spanish and Catalan. On the one hand, only a noun phrase can be a NE. On the other hand, its referent must be unique and unambiguous. Finally, another hard rule (although not 100% reliable) is that only a definite singular noun phrase might be a NE.

2.4 Thematic Role Labeling / Semantic Class

Basic syntactic functions were tagged with both arguments and thematic roles, taking into account the semantic class related to the verbal predicate (Taulé et al., 2006b). We characterized predicates by means of a limited number of Semantic Classes based on Event Structure Patterns, according to four basic event classes: *states*, *activities*, *accomplishments*, and *achievements*. These general classes were split into 17 subclasses, depending on thematic roles and diathesis alternations.

Similar to PropBank, the set of arguments selected by the verb are incrementally numbered expressing the degree of proximity of an argument in relation to the verb (Arg0, Arg1, Arg2, Arg3, Arg4). In our proposal, each argument includes the thematic role in its label (e.g., Arg1-PAT). Thus, we have two different levels of semantic description: the argument position and the specific thematic role. This information was previously stored in a verbal lexicon for each language. In these lexicons, a semantic class was established for each verbal sense, and the mapping between their syntactic functions with the corresponding argument structure and thematic roles was declared. These classes resulted from the analysis of 1,555 verbs from the Spanish corpus and 1,077 from the Catalan. The annotation process was performed in two steps: firstly, we annotated automatically the unambiguous correspondences between syntactic functions and thematic roles (Martí et al., 2007a); secondly, we manually checked the outcome of the previous process and completed the rest of thematic role assignments.

2.5 Subset for SemEval-2007

The corpora extracted from CESS-ECE to conform SemEval-2007 datasets are: (a) SemEval-CESS-ESP (Spanish), made of 101,136 words (3,611 sentences), with 29% of the corpus coming from the Spanish EFE News Agency and 71% coming from Lexesp, a Spanish balanced corpus; (b) SemEval-CESS-CAT (Catalan), consisting of 108,207 words (3,202 sentences), with 71% of the corpus consistinf of Catalan news from EFE News Agency and 29% coming from the Catalan News Agency (ACN).

These corpora were split into training and test subsets following a a 90%–10% proportion. Each test set was also partitioned into two subsets: 'in-domain' and 'out-of-domain' test corpora. The first is intended to be homogeneous with respect to the training corpus and the second was extracted from a part of the CESS-ECE corpus annotated later and not involved in the development of the resources (e.g., verbal dictionaries).[2]

3 Task setting

Data formats are similar to those of CoNLL-2004/2005 shared tasks on SRL (column style presentation of levels of annotation), in order to be able to share evaluation tools and already developed scripts for format conversion.

In Figure 1 you can find an example of a fully annotated sentence in the column-based format. There is one line for each token, and a blank line after the last token of each sentence. The columns, separated by blank spaces, represent different annotations of the sentence with a tagging along words. For structured annotations (parse trees, named entities, and arguments), we use the Start-End format. Columns 1–6 correspond to the input information; columns 7 and above contain the information to be predicted. We can group annotations in five main categories:

BASIC_INPUT_INFO (columns 1–3). The basic input information, including: (a) **WORD** (column 1) words of the sentence; (b) **TN** (column 2) target nouns of the sentence, marked with '*' (those that are to be assigned WordNet synsets); (c) **TV** (column 3) target verbs of the sentence, marked with '*' (those that are to be annotated with semantic roles).

EXTRA_INPUT_INFO (columns 4–6). The extra input information, including: (a) **LEMMA** (column 4) lemmas of the words; (b) **POS** (column 5) part-of-speech tags; (c) **SYNTAX** (column 6) Full syntactic tree.

NE (column 7). Named Entities.

NS (column 8). WordNet sense of target nouns.

SR (columns 9 and above). Information on semantic roles, including: (a) **SC** (column 9). Semantic class of the verb; (b) **PROPS** (columns 10 and above). For each target verb, a column representing the argument structure. Core numbered arguments include the thematic role labels. ArgM's are the adjuncts. Columns are ordered according to the textual order of the predicates.

All these annotations in column format are extracted automatically from the syntactic-semantic trees from the CESS-ECE corpora, which were distributed with the datasets. Participants were also provided with the whole Catalan and Spanish WordNets (v1.6), the verbal lexicons used in the role labeling annotation, the annotation guidelines as well as the annotated corpora.

4 Participant systems

About a dozen teams expressed their interest in the task. From those, only 5 registered and downloaded datasets, and finally, only two teams met the deadline and submitted results. ILK2 (Tilburg University) presented a system addressing Semantic Role Labeling, and UPC* (Technical University of Catalonia) presented a system addressing all subtasks independently[3]. The ILK2 SRL system is based on memory-based classification of syntactic constituents using a rich feature set. UPC* used several machine learning algorithms for addressing the different subtasks (AdaBoost, SVM, Perceptron). For SRL, the system implements a re-ranking strategy using global features. The candidates are generated using a state–of–the–art SRL base system.

Although the task targeted at systems addressing all subtasks jointly none of the participants did it.[4] We believe that the high complexity of the whole task together with the short period of time available were the main reasons for this failure. From this point of view, the conclusions are somehow disappointing. However, we think that we have contributed with a very valuable resource for the future research and, although not complete, the current systems provide also valuable insights about the task and are very good baselines for the systems to come.

5 Evaluation

In the following subsections we present an analysis of the results obtained by participant systems in the

[2]For historical reasons we referred to these splits as '3LB' and 'CESS-ECE', respectively. Participants in the task are actually using these names, but we opted for using a more simple notation in this paper (see Section 5).

[3]Some members of this team are also task organizers. This is why we mark the team name with an asterisk.

[4]The UPC* team tried some inter-task features to improve SRL but initial results were not successful.

```
INPUT--------------------------------------------------------------> OUTPUT----------------------------------
BASIC_INPUT_INFO-----> EXTRA_INPUT_INFO----------------------------> NE NS-------> SR------------------------>
WORD              TN TV LEMMA        POS                 SYNTAX       NE  NS          SC          PROPS----------->
---------------------------------------------------------------------------------------------------------------

Las               -  -  el           da0fp0    (S(sn-SUJ(espec.fp*)     *  -           -            *  (Arg1-TEM*
conclusiones      *  -  conclusion   ncfp000        (grup.nom.fp*       *  05059980n   -            *           *
de                -  -  de           sps00              (sp(prep*)      *  -           -            *           *
la                -  -  el           da0fs0         (sn(espec.fs*)  (ORG*  -           -            *           *
comision          *  -  comision     ncfs000        (grup.nom.fs*       *  06172564n   -            *           *
Zapatero          -  -  Zapatero     np00000           (grup.nom*)  (PER*) -           -            *           *
,                 -  -  ,            Fc                   (S.F.R*       *  -           -            *           *
que               -  -  que          pr0cn00        (relatiu-SUJ*)      *  -           -  (Arg0-CAU*)           *
ampliara          -  *  ampliar      vmif3s0                  (gv*)     *  -           a1        (V*)           *
el                -  -  el           da0ms0     (sn-CD(espec.ms*)       *  -           -  (Arg1-PAT*            *
plazo             *  -  plazo        ncms000        (grup.nom.ms*       *  10935385n   -            *           *
de                -  -  de           sps00              (sp(prep*)      *  -           -            *           *
trabajo           *  -  trabajo      ncms000    (sn(grup.nom.ms*)))))   *  00377835n   -           *)           *
,                 -  -  ,            Fc                   *))))))      *)  -           -            *          *)
quedan            -  *  quedar       vmip3p0                  (gv*)     *  -           b3           *        (V*)
para              -  -  para         sps00            (sp-CC(prep*)     *  -           -            *  (ArgM-TMP*
despues_del       -  -  despues_del  spcms              (sp(prep*)      *  -           -            *           *
verano            *  -  verano       ncms000    (sn(grup.nom.ms*))))    *  10946199n   -            *          *)
.                 -  -  .            Fp                         *)      *  -           -            *           *
```

Figure 1: An example of an annotated sentence.

three subtasks. Results on the test set are presented along 2 dimensions: (a) *language* ('ca'=Catalan; 'es'=Spanish); (b) *corpus source* ('in'=in–domain corpus; 'out'=out–of–domain corpus). We will use a *language.source* pair to denote a particular test set. Finally, '*' will denote the addition of the two subcorpora, either in the language or source dimensions.

5.1 NSD

Results on the NSD subtask are presented in Table 1. BSL stands for a baseline system consisting of assigning to each word occurrence the most frequent sense in the training set. For new nouns the first sense in the corresponding WordNet is selected. The UPC* team trained a SVM classifier for each word in a pre-selected subset and applied the baseline in the rest of cases. The selected words are frequent words (more than 15 occurrences in the training corpus) showing a not too skewed distribution of senses in the training set (the most predominant sense covers less than 90% of the cases). No other teams presented results for this task.

Test	All words		Selected words	
	BSL	UPC*	BSL	UPC*
ca.*	85.49%	86.47%	70.06%	72.75%
es.*	84.22%	85.10%	61.80%	65.17%
*.in	84.84%	86.49%	67.30%	72.24%
*.out	85.02%	85.33%	67.07%	67.87%
.	84.94%	85.87%	67.19%	70.12%

Table 1: Overall accuracy on the NSD subtask

The left part of the table ("all words") contains results on the complete test sets, while the right part ("selected words") contains the results restricted to the set of words with trained SVM classifiers. This set covers 31.0% of the word occurrences in the training set and 28.2% in the complete test set.

The main observation is that training/test corpora contain few sense variations. Sense distributions are very skewed and, thus, the simple baseline shows a very high accuracy (almost 85%). The UPC* system only improves BSL accuracy by one point. This can be partly explained by the small size of the word-based training corpora. Also, this improvement is diminished because UPC* only treated a subset of words. However, looking at the right–hand side of the table, the improvement over the baseline is still modest (~3 points) when focusing only on the treated words. As a final observation, no significant differences are observed across languages and corpora sources.

5.2 NER

Results on the NER subtask are presented in Table 2. This time, BSL stands for a baseline system consisting of collecting a gazetteer with the strong NEs appearing in the training set and assigning the longest matches of these NEs in the test set. Weak entities are simply ignored by BSL. UPC* presented a system which treats strong and weak NEs in a pipeline of two processors. Classifiers trained with multiclass

AdaBoost are used to predict the strong and weak NEs. See authors' paper for details.

Test	BSL			UPC*		
	Prec.	Recall	F_1	Prec.	Recall	F_1
ca.*	75.85	15.45	25.68	80.94	77.96	79.42
es.*	71.88	12.07	20.66	70.65	65.69	68.08
*.in	83.06	17.43	28.82	78.21	74.04	76.09
*.out	68.63	12.20	20.72	76.21	72.51	74.31
.	74.45	14.11	23.72	76.93	73.08	74.96

Table 2: Overall results on the NER subtask

UPC* system largely overcomes the baseline, mainly due to the low recall of the latter. By languages, results on Catalan are significantly better than those on Spanish. We think this is attributable mainly to corpora variations across languages. By corpus source, "in-domain" results are slightly better, but the difference is small (1.78 points). Overall, the results for the NER task are in the mid seventies, a remarkable result given the small training set and the complexity of predicting embedded NEs.

Detailed results on concrete entity types are presented in Table 3 (sorted by decreasing F_1). As expected, DAT and NUM are the easiest entities to recognize since they can be easily detected by simple patterns and POS tags. On the contrary, entity types requiring more semantic information present fairly lower results. ORG PER and LOC are in the seventies, while OTH is by far the most difficult class, showing a very low recall. This is not surprising since OTH agglutinates a wide variety of entity cases which are difficult to characterize as a whole.

	Prec.	Recall	F_1
DAT	97.38%	96.88%	97.13
NUM	98.05%	89.68%	93.68
ORG	75.72%	75.36%	75.54
PER	70.48%	75.97%	73.13
LOC	73.41%	68.29%	70.76
OTH	56.90%	37.79%	45.41

Table 3: Detailed results on the NER subtask: UPC* team; Test corpus *.*

Another interesting analysis is to study the differences between strong and weak entities (see Table 4) . Contrary to our first expectations, results on weak entities are much better (up to 11 F_1 points higher). Weak NEs are simpler for two reasons: (a) there exist simple patters to characterize them, without the need of fully recognizing their internal strong NEs; (b) there is some redundancy in the corpus when tagging many equivalent weak NEs in embedded noun phrases. It is worth noting that the low results for strong NEs come from classification rather than recognition (recognition is almost 100% given the "proper noun" PoS tag), thus the recall for weak entities is not diminished by the errors in strong entity classification.

	Prec.	Recall	F_1
Strong NEs	73.04%	63.36%	67.85
Weak NEs	78.96%	78.91%	78.93

Table 4: Results on strong vs. weak named entities: UPC* team; Test corpus *.*

5.3 SRL

SRL is the most complex and interesting problem in the task. We had two participants ILK2 and UPC*, which participated in both subproblems, i.e., labeling arguments of verbal predicates with thematic roles (SR), and assigning semantic class labels to target verbs (SC). Detailed results of the two systems are presented in Tables 5 and 6.

Test	UPC*			ILK2		
	Prec.	Recall	F_1	Prec.	Recall	F_1
ca.*	84.49	77.97	81.10	84.72	82.12	83.40
es.*	83.88	78.49	81.10	84.30	83.98	84.14
*.in	84.17	82.90	83.53	84.71	84.12	84.41
*.out	84.19	72.77	78.06	84.26	81.84	83.03
.	84.18	78.24	81.10	84.50	83.07	83.78

Table 5: Overall results on the SRL subtask: semantic role labeling (SR)

The ILK2 system outperforms UPC* in both SR and SC. For SR, both systems use a traditional architecture of labeling syntactic tree nodes with thematic roles using supervised classifiers. We would attribute the overall F_1 difference (2.68 points) to a better feature engineering by ILK2, rather than to differences in the Machine Learning techniques used. Overall results in the eighties are remarkably high given the training set size and the granularity of the thematic roles (though we have to take into account that systems work with gold parse trees). Again, the results are comparable across languages and slightly better in the "in-domain" test set.

Test	UPC*			ILK2		
	Prec.	Recall	F_1	Prec.	Recall	F_1
ca.*	86.57	86.57	86.57	90.25	88.50	89.37
es.*	81.05	81.05	81.05	84.30	83.63	83.83
*.in	81.17	81.17	81.17	84.68	83.11	83.89
*.out	86.72	86.72	86.72	90.04	89.08	89.56
.	83.86	83.86	83.86	87.12	85.81	86.46

Table 6: Overall results on the SRL subtask: semantic class tagging (SC)

In the SC subproblem, the differences are similar (2.60 points). In this case, ILK2 trained specialized classifiers for the task, while UPC* used heuristics based on the SR outcomes. As a reference, the baseline consisting of tagging each verb with its most frequent semantic class achieves F_1 values of 64.01, 63.97, 41.00, and 57.42 on ca.in, ca.out, es.in, es.out, respectively. Now, the results are significantly better in Catalan, and, surprisingly, the 'out' test corpora makes F_1 to raise. The latter is an anomalous situation provoked by the 'es.in' tset.[5]

Table 7 shows the global SR results by numbered arguments and adjuncts Interestingly, tagging adjuncts is far more difficult than tagging core arguments (this result was also observed for English in previous works). Moreover, the global difference between ILK2 and UPC* systems is explained by their ability to tag adjuncts (70.22 vs. 58.37). In the core arguments both systems are tied. Also in the same table we can see the overall results on a simplified SR setting, in which the thematic roles are eliminated from the SR labels keeping only the argument number (like other evaluations on PropBank). The results are only ~2 points higher in this setting.

Test	UPC*			ILK2		
	Prec.	Recall	F_1	Prec.	Recall	F_1
Arg	90.41	87.73	89.05	89.42	88.58	88.99
Adj	64.72	53.16	58.37	72.54	68.04	70.22
A-TR	92.91	90.15	91.51	91.31	90.45	90.88

Table 7: Global results on numbered arguments (Arg), adjuncts (Adj), and numbered arguments without thematic role tag (A-TR). Test corpus *.*

Finally, Table 8 compares overall SR results on known vs. new predicates. As expected, the results on the verbs not appearing in the training set are lower, but the performance decrease is not dramatic (3–6 F_1 points) indicating that generalization to new predicates is fairly good.

[5]By chance, the genre of this part of corpus is mainly literary. We are currently studying how this is affecting performance results on all subtasks and, particularly, semantic class tagging.

Test	UPC*			ILK2		
	Prec.	Recall	F_1	Prec.	Recall	F_1
Known	84.39	78.43	81.30	84.88	83.46	84.16
New	81.31	75.56	78.33	79.34	77.81	78.57

Table 8: Global results on semantic role labeling for known versus new predicates. Test corpus *.*

Acknowledgements The organizers would like to thank the following people for their hard work on the corpora used in the task: Juan Aparicio, Manu Bertran, Oriol Borrega, Núria Bufí, Joan Castellví, Maria Jesús Díaz, Marina Lloberes, Difda Monterde, Aina Peris, Lourdes Puiggrós, Marta Recasens, Santi Reig, and Bàrbara Soriano. This research has been partially funded by the Spanish government: Lang2World (TIN2006-15265-C06-06) and CESS-ECE (HUM-2004-21127-E) projects.

References

Arévalo, M., M. Civit and M. A. Martí. 2004. MICE: a Module for Named-Entities Recognition and Classification. *International Journal of Corpus Linguistics*, 9(1). John Benjamins, Amsterdam.

Borrega, O., M. Taulé, M. A. Martí. 2007. What do we mean when we speak about Named Entities? In *Proceedings of Corpus Linguistics* (forthcoming). Birmingham, UK.

Civit, M., A. Ageno, B. Navarro, N. Bufí and M. A. Martí. 2003. Qualitative and Quantitative Analysis of Annotatotrs: Agreement in the Development of Cast3LB. In *Proceedings of 2nd Workshop on Treebanks and Linguistics Theories (TLT-2003)*, 33–45. Vaxjo, Sweden.

Màrquez, L., M. Taulé, L. Padró, L. Villarejo and M. A. Martí. 2004. On the Quality of Lexical Resources for Word Sense Disambiguation. In *Proceedings of the 4th EsTAL Conference, Advances in natural Language Processing*, LNCS, vol. 3230, 209–221. Alicante, Spain.

Martí, M. A., M. Taulé, L. Màrquez, and M. Bertran. 2007a. Anotación semiautomática con papeles temáticos de los corpus CESS-ECE. In *Revista de la SEPLN - Monografía TIMM* (forthcoming).

Martí, M. A., M. Taulé, L. Màrquez, and M. Bertran. 2007b. *CESS-ECE: A multilingual and Multilevel Annotated Corpus*. E-pub., http://www.lsi.upc.edu/~mbertran/cess-ece

Taulé, M., J. Castellví and M. A. Martí. 2006. Semantic Classes in CESS-LEX: Semantic Annotation of CESS-ECE. In *Proceedings of the Fifth Workshop on Treebanks and Linguistic Theories (TLT-2006)*. Prague, Czech Republic.

SemEval-2007 Task 10: English Lexical Substitution Task

Diana McCarthy
University of Sussex
Falmer, East Sussex
BN1 9QH, UK
dianam@sussex.ac.uk

Roberto Navigli
University of Rome "La Sapienza"
Via Salaria, 113
00198 Roma, Italy
navigli@di.uniroma1.it

Abstract

In this paper we describe the English Lexical Substitution task for SemEval. In the task, annotators and systems find an alternative substitute word or phrase for a target word in context. The task involves both finding the synonyms and disambiguating the context. Participating systems are free to use any lexical resource. There is a subtask which requires identifying cases where the word is functioning as part of a multiword in the sentence and detecting what that multiword is.

1 Introduction

Word sense disambiguation (WSD) has been described as a task in need of an application. Whilst researchers believe that it will ultimately prove useful for applications which need some degree of semantic interpretation, the jury is still out on this point. One problem is that WSD systems have been tested on fine-grained inventories, rendering the task harder than it need be for many applications (Ide and Wilks, 2006). Another significant problem is that there is no clear choice of inventory for any given task (other than the use of a parallel corpus for a specific language pair for a machine translation application).

The lexical substitution task follows on from some previous ideas (McCarthy, 2002) to examine the capabilities of WSD systems built by researchers on a task which has potential for NLP applications. Finding alternative words that can occur in given contexts would potentially be useful to many applications such as question answering, summarisation, paraphrase acquisition (Dagan et al., 2006), text simplification and lexical acquisition (McCarthy, 2002). Crucially this task does not specify the inventory for use beforehand to avoid bias to one predefined inventory and makes it easier for those using automatically acquired resources to enter the arena. Indeed, since the systems in SemEval did not know the candidate substitutes for a word before hand, the lexical resource is evaluated as much as the context based disambiguation component.

2 Task set up

The task involves a lexical sample of nouns, verbs, adjectives and adverbs. Both annotators and systems select one or more substitutes for the target word in the context of a sentence. The data was selected from the English Internet Corpus of English produced by Sharoff (2006) from the Internet (http://corpus.leeds.ac.uk/internet.html). This is a balanced corpus similar in flavour to the BNC, though with less bias to British English, obtained by sampling data from the web. Annotators are not provided with the PoS (noun, verb, adjective or adverb) but the systems are. Annotators can provide up to three substitutes but all should be equally as good. They are instructed that they can provide a phrase if they can't think of a good single word substitute. They can also use a slightly more general word if that is close in meaning. There is a "NAME" response if the target is part of a proper name and "NIL" response if annotators cannot think of a good substitute. The subjects are also asked to identify

Proceedings of the 4th International Workshop on Semantic Evaluations (SemEval-2007), pages 48–53,
Prague, June 2007. ©2007 Association for Computational Linguistics

if they feel the target word is an integral part of a phrase, and what that phrase was. This option was envisaged for evaluation of multiword detection. Annotators did sometimes use it for paraphrasing a phrase with another phrase. However, for an item to be considered a constituent of a multiword, a majority of at least 2 annotators had to identify the same multiword.[1]

The annotators were 5 native English speakers from the UK. They each annotated the entire dataset. All annotations were semi-automatically lemmatised (substitutes and identified multiwords) unless the lemmatised version would change the meaning of the substitute or if it was not obvious what the canonical version of the multiword should be.

2.1 Data Selection

The data set comprises 2010 sentences, 201 target words each with 10 sentences. We released 300 for the trial data and kept the remaining 1710 for the test release. 298 of the trial, and 1696 of the test release remained after filtering items with less than 2 non NIL and non NAME responses and a few with erroneous PoS tags. The words included were selected either manually (70 words) from examination of a variety of lexical resources and corpora or automatically (131) using information in these lexical resources. Words were selected from those having a number of different meanings, each with at least one synonym. Since typically the distribution of meanings of a word is strongly skewed (Kilgarriff, 2004), for the test set we randomly selected 20 words in each PoS for which we manually selected the sentences [2] (we refer to these words as MAN) whilst for the remaining words (RAND) the sentences were selected randomly.

2.2 Inter Annotator Agreement

Since we have sets of substitutes for each item and annotator, pairwise agreement was calculated between each pair of sets $(p1, p2 \in P)$ from each possible pairing (P) as $\frac{\sum_{p_1,p_2 \in P} \frac{p_1 \cap p_2}{p_1 \cup p_2}}{|P|}$

Pairwise inter-annotator agreement was 27.75%. 73.93% had modes, and pairwise agreement with the mode was 50.67%. Agreement is increased if we remove one annotator who typically gave 2 or 3 substitutes for each item, which increased coverage but reduced agreement. Without this annotator, inter-annotator agreement was 31.13% and 64.7% with mode.

Multiword detection pairwise agreement was 92.30% and agreement on the identification of the exact form of the actual multiword was 44.13%.

3 Scoring

We have 3 separate subtasks 1) **best** 2) **oot** and 3) **mw** which we describe below. [3] In the equations and results tables that follow we use P for precision, R for recall, and $Mode\ P$ and $Mode\ R$ where we calculate precision and recall against the substitute chosen by the majority of annotators, provided that there is a majority.

Let H be the set of annotators, T be the set of test items with 2 or more responses (non NIL or NAME) and h_i be the set of responses for an item $i \in T$ for annotator $h \in H$.

For each $i \in T$ we calculate the mode (m_i) i.e. the most frequent response provided that there is a response more frequent than the others. The set of items where there is such a mode is referred to as TM. Let A (and AM) be the set of items from T (or TM) where the system provides at least one substitute. Let $a_i : i \in A$ (or $a_i : i \in AM$) be the set of guesses from the system for item i. For each i we calculate the multiset union (H_i) for all h_i for all $h \in H$ and for each unique type (res) in H_i will have an associated frequency ($freq_{res}$) for the number of times it appears in H_i.

For example: Given an item (id 9999) for *happy;a* supposing the annotators had supplied answers as follows:

annotator	responses
1	glad merry
2	glad
3	cheerful glad
4	merry
5	jovial

[1] Full instructions given to the annotators are posted at http://www.informatics.susx.ac.uk/research/nlp/mccarthy/files/instructions.pdf.

[2] There were only 19 verbs due to an error in automatic selection of one of the verbs picked for manual selection of sentences.

[3] The scoring measures are as described in the document at http://nlp.cs.swarthmore.edu/semeval/tasks/task10/task10documentation.pdf released with our trial data.

then H_i would be *glad glad glad merry merry cheerful jovial*. The res with associated frequencies would be *glad 3 merry 2 cheerful 1* and *jovial 1*.

best measures This requires the **best** file produced by the system which gives as many guesses as the system believes are fitting, but where the credit for each correct guess is divided by the number of guesses. The first guess in the list is taken as the best guess (bg).

$$P = \frac{\sum_{a_i:i \in A} \frac{\frac{\sum_{res \in a_i} freq_{res}}{|a_i|}}{|H_i|}}{|A|} \quad (1)$$

$$R = \frac{\sum_{a_i:i \in T} \frac{\frac{\sum_{res \in a_i} freq_{res}}{|a_i|}}{|H_i|}}{|T|} \quad (2)$$

$$Mode\ P = \frac{\sum_{bg_i \in AM} 1\ if\ bg = m_i}{|AM|} \quad (3)$$

$$Mode\ R = \frac{\sum_{bg_i \in TM} 1\ if\ bg = m_i}{|TM|} \quad (4)$$

A system is permitted to provide more than one response, just as the annotators were. They can do this if they are not sure which response is better, however systems will maximise the score if they guess the most frequent response from the annotators. For P and R the credit is divided by the number of guesses that a system makes to prevent a system simply hedging its bets by providing many responses. The credit is also divided by the number of responses from annotators. This gives higher scores to items with less variation. We want to emphasise test items with better agreement.

Using the example for *happy;a* id 9999 above, if the system's responses for this item was *glad; cheerful* the credit for a_{9999} in the numerator of P and R would be $\frac{\frac{3+1}{2}}{7} = .286$

For $Mode\ P$ and $Mode\ R$ we use the system's first guess and compare this to the mode of the annotators responses on items where there was a response more frequent than the others.

oot measures This allows a system to make up to 10 guesses. The credit for each correct guess is not divided by the number of guesses. This allows for the fact that there is a lot of variation for the task and we only have 5 annotators. With 10 guesses there is a better chance that the systems find the responses of these 5 annotators. There is no ordering of the guesses and the $Mode$ scores give credit where the mode was found in one of the system's 10 guesses.

$$P = \frac{\sum_{a_i:i \in A} \frac{\sum_{res \in a_i} freq_{res}}{|H_i|}}{|A|} \quad (5)$$

$$R = \frac{\sum_{a_i:i \in T} \frac{\sum_{res \in a_i} freq_{res}}{|H_i|}}{|T|} \quad (6)$$

$$Mode\ P = \frac{\sum_{a_i:i \in AM} 1\ if\ any\ guess \in a_i = m_i}{|AM|} \quad (7)$$

$$Mode\ R = \frac{\sum_{a_i:i \in TM} 1\ if\ any\ guess \in a_i = m_i}{|TM|} \quad (8)$$

mw measures For this measure, a system must identify items where the target is part of a multiword and what the multiword is. The annotators do not all have linguistics background, they are simply asked if the target is an integral part of a phrase, and if so what the phrase is. Sometimes this option is used by the subjects for paraphrasing a phrase of the sentence, but typically it is used when there is a multiword. For scoring, a multiword item is one with a majority vote for the same multiword with more than 1 annotator identifying the multiword.

Let MW be the subset of T for which there is such a multiword response from a majority of at least 2 annotators. Let $mw_i \in MW$ be the multiword identified by majority vote for item i. Let $MWsys$ be the subset of T for which there is a multiword response from the system and $mwsys_i$ be a multiword specified by the system for item i.

$$detection\ P = \frac{\sum_{mwsys_i \in MWsys} 1\ if\ mw_i\ exists\ at\ i}{|MWsys|} \quad (9)$$

$$detection\ R = \frac{\sum_{mwsys_i \in MW} 1\ if\ mw_i\ exists\ at\ i}{|MW|} \quad (10)$$

$$identification\ P = \frac{\sum_{mwsys_i \in MWsys} 1\ if\ mwsys_i = mw_i}{|MWsys|} \quad (11)$$

$$identification\ R = \frac{\sum_{mwsys_i \in MW} 1\ if\ mwsys_i = mw_i}{|MW|} \quad (12)$$

3.1 Baselines

We produced baselines using WordNet 2.1 (Miller et al., 1993a) and a number of distributional similarity measures. For the WordNet **best** baseline we found the best ranked synonym using the criteria 1 to 4 below in order. For WordNet **oot** we found up to 10 synonyms using criteria 1 to 4 in order until 10 were found:

1. Synonyms from the first synset of the target word, and ranked with frequency data obtained from the BNC (Leech, 1992).
2. synonyms from the hypernyms (verbs and nouns) or closely related classes (adjectives) of that first synset, ranked with the frequency data.
3. Synonyms from all synsets of the target word, and ranked using the BNC frequency data.
4. synonyms from the hypernyms (verbs and nouns) or closely related classes (adjectives) of all synsets of the target, ranked with the BNC frequency data.

We also produced **best** and **oot** baselines using the distributional similarity measures l1, jaccard, cosine, lin (Lin, 1998) and αSD (Lee, 1999) [4]. We took the word with the largest similarity (or smallest distance for αSD and l1) for **best** and the top 10 for **oot**.

For **mw** detection and identification we used WordNet to detect if a multiword in WordNet which includes the target word occurs within a window of 2 words before and 2 words after the target word.

4 Systems

9 teams registered and 8 participated, and two of these teams (SWAG and IRST) each entered two systems, we distinguish the first and second systems with a 1 and 2 suffix respectively.

The systems all used 1 or more predefined inventories. Most used web queries (HIT, MELB, UNT) or web data (Brants and Franz, 2006) (IRST2, KU, SWAG1, SWAG2, USYD, UNT) to obtain counts for disambiguation, with some using algorithms to derive domain (IRST1) or co-occurrence (TOR) information from the BNC. Most systems did not use sense tagged data for disambiguation though MELB did use SemCor (Miller et al., 1993b) for filtering infrequent synonyms and UNT used a semi-supervised word sense disambiguation combined with a host of other techniques, including machine translation engines.

5 Results

In tables 1 to 3 we have ordered systems according to R on the **best** task, and in tables 4 to 6 according to R on **oot**. We show all scores as percentages i.e. we multiply the scores in section 3 by 100. In tables 3 and 6 we show results using the subset of items which were i) NOT identified as multiwords (NMWT) ii) scored only on non multiword substitutes from both annotators and systems (i.e. no spaces) (NMWS). Unfortunately we do not have space to show the analysis for the MAN and RAND subsets here. Please refer to the task website for these results. [5] We retain the same ordering for the further analysis tables when we look at subsets of the data. Although there are further differences in the systems which would warrant reranking on an individual analysis, since we combined the subanalyses in one table we keep the order as for 1 and 4 respectively for ease of comparison.

There is some variation in rank order of the systems depending on which measures are used. [6] KU is highest ranking on R for **best**. UNT is best at finding the mode, particularly on **oot**, though it is the most complicated system exploiting a great many knowledge sources and components. IRST2 does well at finding the mode in **best**. The IRST2 **best** R score is lower because it supplied many answers for each item however it achieves the best R score on the **oot** task. The baselines are outperformed by most systems. The WordNet baseline outperforms those derived from distributional methods. The distributional methods, especially lin, show promising results given that these methods are automatic and

[4] We used 0.99 as the parameter for α for this measure.

[5] The task website is at http://www.informatics.sussex.ac.uk/research/nlp/mccarthy/task10index.html.

[6] There is not a big difference between P and R because systems typically supplied answers for most items.

Systems	P	R	$Mode\ P$	$Mode\ R$
KU	12.90	12.90	20.65	20.65
UNT	12.77	12.77	20.73	20.73
MELB	12.68	12.68	20.41	20.41
HIT	11.35	11.35	18.86	18.86
USYD	11.23	10.88	18.22	17.64
IRST1	8.06	8.06	13.09	13.09
IRST2	6.95	6.94	20.33	20.33
TOR	2.98	2.98	4.72	4.72

Table 1: **best** results

Systems	P	R	$Mode\ P$	$Mode\ R$
WordNet	9.95	9.95	15.28	15.28
lin	8.84	8.53	14.69	14.23
l1	8.11	7.82	13.35	12.93
lee	6.99	6.74	11.34	10.98
jaccard	6.84	6.60	11.17	10.81
cos	5.07	4.89	7.64	7.40

Table 2: **best** baseline results

don't require hand-crafted inventories. As yet we haven't combined the baselines with disambiguation methods.

Only HIT attempted the **mw** task. It outperforms all baselines from WordNet.

5.1 Post Hoc Analysis

Choosing a lexical substitute for a given word is not clear cut and there is inherently variation in the task. Since it is quite likely that there will be synonyms that the five annotators do not think of we conducted a post hoc analysis to see if the synonyms selected by the original annotators were better, on the whole, than those in the systems responses. We randomly selected 100 sentences from the subset of items which had more than 2 single word substitutes, no NAME responses, and where the target word was

	NMWT		NMWS	
Systems	P	R	P	R
KU	13.39	13.39	14.33	13.98
UNT	13.46	13.46	13.79	13.79
MELB	13.35	13.35	14.19	13.82
HIT	11.97	11.97	12.55	12.38
USYD	11.68	11.34	12.48	12.10
IRST1	8.44	8.44	8.98	8.92
IRST2	7.25	7.24	7.67	7.66
TOR	3.22	3.22	3.32	3.32

Table 3: Further analysis for **best**

Systems	P	R	$Mode\ P$	$Mode\ R$
IRST2	69.03	68.90	58.54	58.54
UNT	49.19	49.19	66.26	66.26
KU	46.15	46.15	61.30	61.30
IRST1	41.23	41.20	55.28	55.28
USYD	36.07	34.96	43.66	42.28
SWAG2	37.80	34.66	50.18	46.02
HIT	33.88	33.88	46.91	46.91
SWAG1	35.53	32.83	47.41	43.82
TOR	11.19	11.19	14.63	14.63

Table 4: **oot** results

Systems	P	R	$Mode\ P$	$Mode\ R$
WordNet	29.70	29.35	40.57	40.57
lin	27.70	26.72	40.47	39.19
l1	24.09	23.23	36.10	34.96
lee	20.09	19.38	29.81	28.86
jaccard	18.23	17.58	26.87	26.02
cos	14.07	13.58	20.82	20.16

Table 5: **oot** baseline results

	NMWT		NMWS	
Systems	P	R	P	R
IRST2	72.04	71.90	76.19	76.06
UNT	51.13	51.13	54.01	54.01
KU	48.43	48.43	49.72	49.72
IRST1	43.11	43.08	45.13	45.11
USYD	37.26	36.17	40.13	38.89
SWAG2	39.95	36.51	40.97	37.75
HIT	35.60	35.60	36.63	36.63
SWAG1	37.49	34.64	38.36	35.67
TOR	11.77	11.77	12.22	12.22

Table 6: Further analysis for **oot**

	HIT		WordNet BL	
	P	R	P	R
detection	45.34	56.15	43.64	36.92
identification	41.61	51.54	40.00	33.85

Table 7: MW results

	good	reasonable	bad
sys	9.07	19.08	71.85
origA	37.36	41.01	21.63

Table 8: post hoc results

not one of those identified as a multiword (i.e. a majority vote by 2 or more annotators for the same multiword as described in section 2). We then mixed the substitutes from the human annotators with those of the systems. Three fresh annotators[7] were given the test sentence and asked to categorise the randomly ordered substitutes as good, reasonable or bad. We take the majority verdict for each substitute, but if there is one reasonable and one good verdict, then we categorise the substitute as reasonable. The percentage of substitutes for systems (sys) and original annotators (origA) categorised as good, reasonable and bad by the post hoc annotators are shown in table 8. We see the substitutes from the humans have a higher proportion of good or reasonable responses by the post hoc annotators compared to the substitutes from the systems.

6 Conclusions and Future Directions

We think this task is an interesting one in which to evaluate automatic approaches of capturing lexical meaning. There is an inherent variation in the task because several substitutes may be possible for a given context. This makes the task hard and scoring is less straightforward than a task which has fixed choices. On the other hand, we believe the task taps into human understanding of word meaning and we hope that computers that perform well on this task will have potential in NLP applications. Since a pre-defined inventory is not used, the task allows us to compare lexical resources as well as disambiguation techniques without a bias to any predefined inventory. It is possible for those interested in disambiguation to focus on this, rather than the choice of substitutes, by using the union of responses from the annotators in future experiments.

7 Acknowledgements

We acknowledge support from the Royal Society UK for funding the annotation for the project, and for a Dorothy Hodgkin Fellowship to the first author. We also acknowledge support to the second author from INTEROP NoE (508011, 6th EU FP). We thank the annotators for their hard work. We thank Serge Sharoff for the use of his Internet corpus, Julie Weeds for the software we used for producing the distributional similarity baselines and Suzanne Stevenson for suggesting the **oot** task .

[7] Again, these were native English speakers from the UK.

References

Thorsten Brants and Alex Franz. 2006. Web 1T 5-gram corpus version 1.1. Technical Report.

Ido Dagan, Oren Glickman, Alfio Gliozzo, Efrat Marmorshtein, and Carlo Strapparava. 2006. Direct word sense matching for lexical substitution. In *Proceedings of the 21st International Conference on Computational Linguistics and 44th Annual Meeting of the Association for Computational Linguistics*, Sydney, Australia, July. Association for Computational Linguistics.

Nancy Ide and Yorick Wilks. 2006. Making sense about sense. In Eneko Agirre and Phil Edmonds, editors, *Word Sense Disambiguation, Algorithms and Applications*, pages 47–73. Springer.

Adam Kilgarriff. 2004. How dominant is the commonest sense of a word? In *Proceedings of Text, Speech, Dialogue*, Brno, Czech Republic.

Lillian Lee. 1999. Measures of distributional similarity. In *Proceedings of the 37th Annual Meeting of the Association for Computational Linguistics*, pages 25–32.

Geoffrey Leech. 1992. 100 million words of English: the British National Corpus. *Language Research*, 28(1):1–13.

Dekang Lin. 1998. An information-theoretic definition of similarity. In *Proceedings of the 15th International Conference on Machine Learning*, Madison, WI.

Diana McCarthy. 2002. Lexical substitution as a task for wsd evaluation. In *Proceedings of the ACL Workshop on Word Sense Disambiguation: Recent Successes and Future Directions*, pages 109–115, Philadelphia, USA.

George Miller, Richard Beckwith, Christine Fellbaum, David Gross, and Katherine Miller, 1993a. *Introduction to WordNet: an On-Line Lexical Database*. ftp://clarity.princeton.edu/pub/WordNet/5papers.ps.

George A. Miller, Claudia Leacock, Randee Tengi, and Ross T Bunker. 1993b. A semantic concordance. In *Proceedings of the ARPA Workshop on Human Language Technology*, pages 303–308. Morgan Kaufman.

Serge Sharoff. 2006. Open-source corpora: Using the net to fish for linguistic data. *International Journal of Corpus Linguistics*, 11(4):435–462.

SemEval-2007 Task 11: English Lexical Sample Task via English-Chinese Parallel Text

Hwee Tou Ng and **Yee Seng Chan**
Department of Computer Science
National University of Singapore
3 Science Drive 2, Singapore 117543
{nght, chanys}@comp.nus.edu.sg

Abstract

We made use of parallel texts to gather training and test examples for the English lexical sample task. Two tracks were organized for our task. The first track used examples gathered from an LDC corpus, while the second track used examples gathered from a Web corpus. In this paper, we describe the process of gathering examples from the parallel corpora, the differences with similar tasks in previous SENSEVAL evaluations, and present the results of participating systems.

1 Introduction

As part of the SemEval-2007 evaluation exercise, we organized an English lexical sample task for word sense disambiguation (WSD), where the sense-annotated examples were semi-automatically gathered from word-aligned English-Chinese parallel texts. Two tracks were organized for this task, each gathering data from a different corpus. In this paper, we describe our motivation for organizing the task, our task framework, and the results of participants.

Past research has shown that supervised learning is one of the most successful approaches to WSD. However, this approach involves the collection of a large text corpus in which each ambiguous word has been annotated with the correct sense to serve as training data. Due to the expensive annotation process, only a handful of manually sense-tagged corpora are available.

An effort to alleviate the training data bottleneck is the Open Mind Word Expert (OMWE) project (Chklovski and Mihalcea, 2002) to collect sense-tagged data from Internet users. Data gathered through the OMWE project were used in the SENSEVAL-3 English lexical sample task. In that task, WordNet-1.7.1 was used as the sense inventory for nouns and adjectives, while Wordsmyth[1] was used as the sense inventory for verbs.

Another source of potential training data is parallel texts. Our past research in (Ng et al., 2003; Chan and Ng, 2005) has shown that examples gathered from parallel texts are useful for WSD. Briefly, after manually assigning appropriate Chinese translations to each sense of an English word, the English side of a word-aligned parallel text can then serve as the training data, as they are considered to have been disambiguated and "sense-tagged" by the appropriate Chinese translations.

Using the above approach, we gathered the training and test examples for our task from parallel texts. Note that our examples are collected without manually annotating each individual ambiguous word occurrence, allowing us to gather our examples in a much shorter time. This contrasts with the setting of the English lexical sample task in previous SENSEVAL evaluations. In the English lexical sample task of SENSEVAL-2, the sense tagged data were created through manual annotation by trained lexicographers. In SENSEVAL-3, the data were gathered through manual sense annotation by Internet users.

In the next section, we describe in more detail the process of gathering examples from parallel texts and the two different parallel corpora we used. We then give a brief description of each of the partici-

[1] http://www.wordsmyth.net

Proceedings of the 4th International Workshop on Semantic Evaluations (SemEval-2007), pages 54–58,
Prague, June 2007.

pating systems. In Section 4, we present the results obtained by the participants, before concluding in Section 5.

2 Gathering Examples from Parallel Corpora

To gather examples from parallel corpora, we followed the approach in (Ng et al., 2003). Briefly, after ensuring the corpora were sentence-aligned, we tokenized the English texts and performed word segmentation on the Chinese texts (Low et al., 2005). We then made use of the GIZA++ software (Och and Ney, 2000) to perform word alignment on the parallel corpora. Then, we assigned some possible Chinese translations to each sense of an English word *w*. From the word alignment output of GIZA++, we selected those occurrences of *w* which were aligned to one of the Chinese translations chosen. The English side of these occurrences served as training data for *w*, as they were considered to have been disambiguated and "sense-tagged" by the appropriate Chinese translations. The English half of the parallel texts (each ambiguous English word and its 3-sentence context) were used as the training and test material to set up our English lexical sample task.

Note that in our approach, the sense distinction is decided by the different Chinese translations assigned to each sense of a word. This is thus similar to the multilingual lexical sample task in SENSEVAL-3 (Chklovski et al., 2004), except that our training and test examples are collected *without* manually annotating each individual ambiguous word occurrence. The average time needed to assign Chinese translations for one noun and one adjective is 20 minutes and 25 minutes respectively. This is a relatively short time, compared to the effort otherwise needed to manually sense annotate individual word occurrences. Also, once the Chinese translations are assigned, more examples can be automatically gathered as more parallel texts become available.

We note that frequently occurring words are usually highly polysemous and hard to disambiguate. To maximize the benefits of our work, we gathered training data from parallel texts for a set of most frequently occurring noun and adjective types in the Brown Corpus. Also, similar to the SENSEVAL-3 English lexical sample task, we used WordNet-1.7.1 as our sense inventory.

Dataset	Avg. no. of senses	Avg. no. of examples	
		Training	Test
LDC noun	5.2	197.6	98.5
LDC adjective	3.9	125.6	62.9
Web noun	3.5	182.0	91.3
Web adjective	2.8	88.8	44.6

Table 1: Average number of senses, training examples, and test examples per word.

2.1 LDC Corpus

We have two tracks for this task, each track using a different corpus. The first corpus is the Chinese English News Magazine Parallel Text (LDC2005T10), which is an English-Chinese parallel corpus available from the Linguistic Data Consortium (LDC).

From this parallel corpus, we gathered examples for 50 English words (25 nouns and 25 adjectives) using the method described above. From the gathered examples of each word, we randomly selected training and test examples, where the number of training examples is about twice the number of test examples.

The rows *LDC noun* and *LDC adjective* in Table 1 give some statistics about the examples. For instance, each noun has an average of 197.6 training and 98.5 test examples and these examples represent an average of 5.2 senses per noun.[2] Participants taking part in this track need to have access to this LDC corpus in order to access the training and test material in this track.

2.2 Web Corpus

Since not all interested participants may have access to the LDC corpus described in the previous subsection, the second track of this task makes use of English-Chinese documents gathered from the URL pairs given by the STRAND Bilingual Databases.[3] STRAND (Resnik and Smith, 2003) is a system that acquires document pairs in parallel translation automatically from the Web. Using this corpus, we gathered examples for 40 English words (20 nouns and

[2] Only senses present in the examples are counted.

[3] http://www.umiacs.umd.edu/~resnik/strand

20 adjectives).

The rows *Web noun* and *Web adjective* in Table 1 show that we selected an average of 182.0 training and 91.3 test examples for each noun and these examples represent an average of 3.5 senses per noun. We note that the average number of senses per word for the Web corpus is slightly lower than that of the LDC corpus.

2.3 Annotation Accuracy

To measure the annotation accuracy of examples gathered from the LDC corpus, we examined a random selection of 100 examples each from 5 nouns and 5 adjectives. From these 1,000 examples, we measured a sense annotation accuracy of 84.7%. These 10 words have an average of 8.6 senses per word in the WordNet-1.7.1 sense inventory. As described in (Ng et al., 2003), when several senses of an English word are translated by the same Chinese word, we can collapse these senses to obtain a coarser-grained, lumped sense inventory. If we do this and measure the sense annotation accuracy with respect to a coarser-grained, lumped sense inventory, these 10 words will have an average of 6.5 senses per word and an annotation accuracy of 94.7%.

For the Web corpus, we similarly examined a random selection of 100 examples each from 5 nouns and 5 adjectives. These 10 words have an average of 6.5 senses per word in WordNet-1.7.1 and the 1,000 examples have an average sense annotation accuracy of 85.0%. After sense collapsing, annotation accuracy is 95.3% with an average of 4.8 senses per word.

2.4 Training and Test Data from Different Documents

In our previous work (Ng et al., 2003), we conducted experiments on the nouns of SENSEVAL-2 English lexical sample task. We found that there were cases where the same document contributed both training and test examples and this inflated the WSD accuracy figures. To avoid this, during our preparation of the LDC and Web data, we made sure that a document contributed only either training or test examples, but not both.

3 Participating Systems

Three teams participated in the Web corpus track of our task, with each team employing one system. There were no participants in the LDC corpus track, possibly due to the licensing issues involved. All participating systems employed supervised learning and only used the training examples provided by us.

3.1 CITYU-HIF

The CITYU-HIF team from the City University of Hong Kong trained a naive Bayes (NB) classifier for each target word to be disambiguated, using knowledge sources such as parts-of-speech (POS) of neighboring words and single words in the surrounding context. They also experimented with using different sets of features for each target word.

3.2 HIT-IR-WSD

The system submitted by the HIT-IR-WSD team from Harbin Institute of Technology used Support Vector Machines (SVM) with a linear kernel function as the learning algorithm. Knowledge sources used included POS of surrounding words, local collocations, single words in the surrounding context, and syntactic relations.

3.3 PKU

The system submitted by the PKU team from Peking University used a combination of SVM and maximum entropy classifiers. Knowledge sources used included POS of surrounding words, local collocations, and single words in the surrounding context. Feature selection was done by ignoring word features with certain associated POS tags and by selecting the subset of features based on their entropy values.

4 Results

As all participating systems gave only one answer for each test example, recall equals precision and we will only report micro-average recall on the Web corpus track in this section.

Table 2 gives the overall results obtained by each of the systems when evaluated on all the test examples of the Web corpus. We note that all the participants obtained scores which exceed the baseline heuristic of tagging all test examples with the most

System ID	Contact author	Learning algorithm	Score
HIT-IR-WSD	Yuhang Guo, <astronaut@ir.hit.edu.cn>	SVM	0.819
PKU	Peng Jin, <jandp@pku.edu.cn>	SVM and maximum entropy	0.815
CITYU-HIF	Oi Yee Kwong, <rlolivia@cityu.edu.hk>	NB	0.753
MFS	–	Most frequent sense baseline	0.689

Table 2: Overall micro-average scores of the participants and the most frequent sense (MFS) baseline.

Noun	MFS	CITYU-HIF	HIT-IR-WSD	PKU
age	0.486	0.643	0.743	0.700
area	0.480	0.693	0.773	0.773
body	0.872	0.897	0.910	0.923
change	0.411	0.400	0.578	0.611
director	0.580	0.890	0.960	0.960
experience	0.830	0.830	0.880	0.840
future	0.889	0.889	0.990	0.990
interest	0.308	0.165	0.813	0.780
issue	0.651	0.711	0.892	0.855
life	0.820	0.830	0.860	0.740
material	0.719	0.719	0.781	0.641
need	0.907	0.907	0.918	0.918
performance	0.410	0.570	0.690	0.700
program	0.590	0.590	0.730	0.690
report	0.870	0.840	0.880	0.870
system	0.510	0.700	0.610	0.730
time	0.455	0.673	0.733	0.693
today	0.800	0.750	0.800	0.780
water	0.882	0.921	0.868	0.895
work	0.644	0.743	0.842	0.891
Micro-avg	0.656	0.719	0.813	0.802

Table 3: Micro-average scores of the most frequent sense baseline and the various participants on each noun.

Adjective	MFS	CITYU-HIF	HIT-IR-WSD	PKU
ancient	0.778	0.667	0.778	0.741
bad	0.857	0.857	0.905	0.905
common	0.533	0.567	0.533	0.633
early	0.769	0.846	0.769	0.769
educational	0.911	0.911	0.911	0.911
free	0.760	0.792	0.854	0.917
high	0.630	0.926	0.815	0.852
human	0.872	0.987	0.962	0.962
little	0.450	0.750	0.650	0.650
long	0.667	0.690	0.786	0.714
major	0.870	0.902	0.880	0.913
medical	0.738	0.787	0.800	0.725
national	0.267	0.467	0.667	0.700
new	0.441	0.441	0.529	0.559
present	0.875	0.917	0.875	0.875
rare	0.727	0.818	0.727	0.909
serious	0.879	0.879	0.879	0.879
simple	0.795	0.818	0.864	0.864
small	0.714	0.929	0.893	0.929
third	0.888	0.988	0.963	0.963
Micro-avg	0.757	0.823	0.831	0.842

Table 4: Micro-average scores of the most frequent sense baseline and the various participants on each adjective.

frequent sense (MFS) in the training data. This suggests that the Chinese translations assigned to senses of the ambiguous words are appropriate and provide sense distinctions which are clear enough for effective classifiers to be learned.

In Table 3 and Table 4, we show the scores obtained by each system on each of the 20 nouns and 20 adjectives. For comparison purposes, we also show the corresponding MFS score of each word. Paired t-test on the results of the top two systems show no significant difference between them.

5 Conclusion

We organized an English lexical sample task using examples gathered from parallel texts. Unlike the English lexical task of previous SENSEVAL evaluations where each example is manually annotated, we only need to assign appropriate Chinese translations to each sense of a word. Once this is done, we automatically gather training and test examples from the parallel texts. All the participating systems of our task obtain results that are significantly better than the most frequent sense baseline.

6 Acknowledgements

Yee Seng Chan is supported by a Singapore Millennium Foundation Scholarship (ref no. SMF-2004-1076).

References

Yee Seng Chan and Hwee Tou Ng. 2005. Scaling up word sense disambiguation via parallel texts. In *Proceedings of AAAI05*, pages 1037–1042, Pittsburgh, Pennsylvania, USA.

Timothy Chklovski and Rada Mihalcea. 2002. Building a sense tagged corpus with Open Mind Word Expert. In *Proceedings of ACL02 Workshop on Word Sense Disambiguation: Recent Successes and Future Directions*, pages 116–122, Philadelphia, USA.

Timothy Chklovski, Rada Mihalcea, Ted Pedersen, and Amruta Purandare. 2004. The SENSEVAL-3 multilingual English-Hindi lexical sample task. In *Proceedings of SENSEVAL-3*, pages 5–8, Barcelona, Spain.

Jin Kiat Low, Hwee Tou Ng, and Wenyuan Guo. 2005. A maximum entropy approach to Chinese word segmentation. In *Proceedings of the Fourth SIGHAN Workshop on Chinese Language Processing*, pages 161–164, Jeju Island, Korea.

Hwee Tou Ng, Bin Wang, and Yee Seng Chan. 2003. Exploiting parallel texts for word sense disambiguation: An empirical study. In *Proceedings of ACL03*, pages 455–462, Sapporo, Japan.

Franz Josef Och and Hermann Ney. 2000. Improved statistical alignment models. In *Proceeedings of ACL00*, pages 440–447, Hong Kong.

Philip Resnik and Noah A. Smith. 2003. The web as a parallel corpus. *Computational Linguistics*, 29(3):349–380.

SemEval-2007 Task 12: Turkish Lexical Sample Task

Zeynep Orhan
Department of
Computer Engineering,
Fatih University 34500,
Büyükçekmece,
Istanbul, Turkey
zorhan@fatih.edu.tr

Emine Çelik
Department of
Computer Engineering,
Fatih University 34500,
Büyükçekmece,
Istanbul, Turkey
eminemm@gmail.com

Neslihan Demirgüç
Department of
Computer Engineering,
Fatih University 34500,
Büyükçekmece,
Istanbul, Turkey
nesli_han@hotmail.com

Abstract

This paper presents the task definition, resources, and the single participant system for Task 12: Turkish Lexical Sample Task (TLST), which was organized in the SemEval-2007 evaluation exercise. The methodology followed for developing the specific linguistic resources necessary for the task has been described in this context. A language-specific feature set was defined for Turkish. TLST consists of three pieces of data: The dictionary, the training data, and the evaluation data. Finally, a single system that utilizes a simple statistical method was submitted for the task and evaluated.

1 Introduction

Effective parameters for word sense disambiguation (WSD) may vary for different languages and word types. Although, some parameters are common in many languages, some others may be language specific. Turkish is an interesting language that deserves being examined semantically. Turkish is based upon suffixation, which differentiates it sharply from the majority of European languages, and many others. Like all Turkic languages, Turkish is agglutinative, that is, grammatical functions are indicated by adding various suffixes to stems. Turkish has a SOV (Subject-Object-Verb) sentence structure but other orders are possible under certain discourse situations. As a SOV language where objects precede the verb, Turkish has postpositions rather than prepositions, and relative clauses that precede the verb. Turkish, as a widely-spoken language, is appropriate for semantic researches.

TLST utilizes some resources that are explained in Section 2-5. In Section 6 evaluation of the system is provided. In section 7 some concluding remarks and future work are discussed.

2 Corpus

Lesser studied languages, such as Turkish suffer from the lack of wide coverage electronic resources or other language processing tools like ontologies, dictionaries, morphological analyzers, parsers etc. There are some projects for providing data for NLP applications in Turkish like METU Corpus Project (Oflazer et al., 2003). It has two parts, the main corpus and the treebank that consists of parsed, morphologically analyzed and disambiguated sentences selected from the main corpus, respectively. The sentences are given in XML format and provide many syntactic features that can be helpful for WSD. This corpus and treebank can be used for academic purposes by contract.

The texts in main corpus have been taken from different types of Turkish written texts published in 1990 and afterwards. It has about two million words. It includes 999 written texts taken from 201 books, 87 papers and news from 3 different Turkish daily newspapers. XML and Text Encoding Initiative (TEI) style annotation have been used. The distribution of the texts in the Treebank is similar to the main corpus. There are 6930 sentences in this Treebank. These sentences have been parsed, morphologically analyzed and disambiguated. In Turkish, a word can have more than one analysis, so having disambiguated texts is very important.

Proceedings of the 4th International Workshop on Semantic Evaluations (SemEval-2007), pages 59–63,
Prague, June 2007.

```
<?xml version="1.0" encoding="windows-1254" ?>
 - <Set sentences="1">
  - <S No="1">
     <W IX="1" LEM="" MORPH="" IG="[(1,"soğuk+Adj")(2,"Adv+Ly")]"
        REL="[2,1,(MODIFIER)]">Soğukça</W>
     <W IX="2" LEM="" MORPH="" IG="[(1,"yanıtla+Verb+Pos+Past+A1sg")]"
        REL="[3,1,(SENTENCE)]">yanıtladım</W>
     <W IX="3" LEM="" MORPH="" IG="[(1,".+Punc")]" REL="[,( )]">.</W>
    </S>
   </Set>
```

Figure 1: XML file structure of the Treebank

Words	Main English translation	# Senses	MFS	Train size	Test size	Total #of instances
Nouns						
ara	distance, break, interval, look for	7	53	192	63	255
baş	head, leader, beginning, top, main, principal	5	34	68	22	90
el	hand, stranger, country	3	75	113	38	151
göz	eye, glance, division, drawer	3	48	92	27	119
kız	girl, virgin, daughter, get hot, get angry	2	72	96	21	117
ön	front, foreground, face, breast, prior, preliminary anterior	5	21	72	23	95
sıra	queue, order, sequence, turn, regularity, occasion desk	7	30	85	28	113
üst	upper side, outside, clothing	7	20	69	23	92
yan	side, direction, auxiliary, askew, burn, be on fire be alight	5	21	65	31	96
yol	way, road, path, method, manner, means	6	17	68	29	97
Average		**5**	**39**	**92**	**31**	**123**
Verbs						
al	take, get, red	24	180	963	125	1088
bak	look, fac, examine	4	136	207	85	292
çalış	work, study, start	4	33	103	61	164
çık	climb, leave, increase	6	45	138	87	225
geç	pass,happen, late	11	51	164	90	254
gel	come, arrive, fit, seem	20	154	346	215	561
gir	enter, fit, begin, penetrate	6	88	163	84	247
git	go, leave, last, be over, pass	13	130	214	120	334
gör	see, understand, consider	5	155	206	68	274
konuş	talk, speak	6	42	129	63	192
Average		**9.9**	**101.4**	**263.3**	**99.8**	**363.1**
Others						
büyük	big, extensive, important, chief, great, elder	6	34	97	26	123
doğru	straight, true, accurate, proper, fair, line towards, around	6	29	81	38	119
küçük	little, small, young, insignificant, kid	4	14	45	14	59
öyle	such, so, that	4	20	51	23	74
son	last, recent, final	2	76	86	18	104
tek	single, unique, alone	2	38	40	10	50
Average		**4**	**35.2**	**66.7**	**21.5**	**88.2**

Table 1: Target words in the SEMEVAL-1 Turkish Lexical Sample task

Frequencies of the words have been found as it is necessary to select appropriate ambiguous words for WSD. There are 5356 different root words and 627 of these words have 15 or more occurrences, and the rest have less.

The XML files contains tagging information in the word (morphological analysis) and sentence level as a parse tree as shown in Figure 1. In the word level, inflectional forms are provided. And in the sentence level relations among words are given. The S tag is for sentence and W tag is for the word. IX is used for index of the word in the sentence, LEM is left as blank and lemma is given in the MORPH tag as a part of it with the morphological analysis of the word. REL is for parsing information. It consists of three parts, two numbers and a relation. For example REL="[2, 1, (MODIFIER)]" means this word is modifying the first inflectional group of the second word in the sentence. The structure of the treebank data was designed by METU. Initially lemmas were decided to be provided as a tag by itself, however, lemmas are left as blank. This does not mean that lemmas are not available in the treebank; the lemmas are given as a part of "IG" tag. Programs are available for extracting this information for the time being. All participants can get these programs and thereby the lemmas easily and instantly.

The sense tags were not included in the treebank and had to be added manually. Sense tagging has been checked in order to obtain gold standard data. Initial tagging process has been finished by a single tagger and controlled. Two other native speaker in the team tagged and controlled the examples. That is, this step was completed by three taggers. Problematic cases were handled by a commission and the decision was finalized when about 90% agreement has been reached.

3 Dictionary

The dictionary is the one that is published by TDK[1] (Turkish Language Foundation) and it is open to public via internet. This dictionary lists the senses along with their definitions and example sentences that are provided for some senses. The dictionary is used only for sense tagging and enumeration of the senses for standardization. No specific information other than the sense numbers is taken from the dictionary; therefore there is no need for linguistic processing of the dictionary.

4 Training and Evaluation Data

In Table 1 statistical information about the final training and testing sets of TLST is summarized. The data have been provided for 3 words in the trial set and 26 words in the final training and testing sets (10 nouns, 10 verbs and 6 other POS for the rest of POS including adjectives and adverbs). It has been tagged about 100 examples per word, but the number of samples is incremented or decremented depending on the number of senses that specific word has. For a few words, however, fewer examples exist due to the sparse distribution of the data. Some ambiguous words had fewer examples in the corpus, therefore they were either eliminated or some other examples drawn from external resources were added in the same format. On the average, the selected words have 6.7 senses, verbs, however, have more. Approximately 70% of the examples for each word were delivered as training data, whereas approximately 30% was reserved as evaluation data. The distribution of the senses in training and evaluation data has been kept proportional. The sets are given as plain text files for each word under each POS. The samples for the words that can belong to more than one POS are listed under the majority class. POS is provided for each sample.

We have extracted example sentences of the target word(s) and some features from the XML files. Then tab delimited text files including structural and sense tag information are obtained. In these files each line has contextual information that are thought to be effective (Orhan and Altan, 2006; Orhan and Altan, 2005) in Turkish WSD about the target words. In the upper level for each of them XML file id, sentence number and the order of the ambiguous word are kept as a unique key for that specific target. In the sentence level, three categories of information, namely the features related to the previous words, target word itself and the subsequent words in the context are provided.

[1] http://tdk.org.tr/tdksozluk/sozara.htm

Feature	Example
File id	00002213148.xml
Sentence number	9
Order	0
Previous related word root/lemma	tap
Previous related word POS(corrected)	verb
Previous related word onthology level1	abstraction
Previous related word onthology level2	attribute
Previous related word onthology level3	emotion
Previous related word POS	verb
Previous related word POS(derivation)	adv
Previous related word case marker	?
Previous related word possessor	fl
Previous related word-target word relation	modıfıer
Target word root/lemma	sev
Target word POS	verb
Target word POS(derivation)	noun
Target word case marker	abl
Target word possessor	tr
Target word-subsequent word relation	object
Subsequent related word root/lemma	sıkıl
Subsequent related word POS(corrected)	verb
Subsequent related word onthology level1	abstraction
Subsequent related word onthology level2	attribute
Subsequent related word onthology level3	emotion
Subsequent related word POS	verb
Subsequent related word POS(derivation)	verb
Subsequent related word case marker	?
Subsequent related word possessor	fl
Subsequent related word-target word relation	sentence
Fine-grained sense number	2
Coarse-grained sense number	2
Sentence	#ne tuhaf şey ; değil mi ? iyi olmamdan ; onu taparcasına sevmemden sıkıldı .#

Table 2: Features and example

In the treebank relational structure, there can be more than one word in the previous context related to the target, however there is only a single word in the subsequent one. Therefore the data for all words in the previous context is provided separately. The features that are employed for previous and the subsequent words are the same and they are the root word, POS(corrected), tags for ontology level 1, level 2 and level 3, POS, inflected POS, case marker, possessor and relation. However for the target word only the root word, POS, inflected POS, case marker, possessor and relation are taken into consideration. Fine and coarse-grained (FG and CG respectively) sense numbers and the sentence that has the ambiguous word have been added as the last three feature. FG senses are the ones that are decided to be the exact senses. CG senses are given as a set that are thought to be possible alternatives in addition to the FG sense. Table 2 demonstrates the whole list of features provided in a single line of data files along with an example. The "?" in the features shows the missing values. This is actually corresponding to the features that do not exist or can not be obtained from the treebank due to some problematic cases. The line that corresponds to this entry will be the following line (as tab delimited):

00002213148.xml 9 0 tap verb abstraction attribute emotion verb adv ? fl modıfıer sev verb noun abl tr object sıkıl verb abstraction attribute emotion verb verb ? fl sentence 2 2 #ne tuhaf şey ; değil mi ?iyi olmamdan ; onu taparcasına sevmemden sıkıldı .#

5 Ontology

A small scale ontology for the target words and their context was constructed. The Turkish WordNet developed at Sabancı University[2] is somehow insufficient. Only the verbs have some levels of relations similar to English WordNet. The nouns, adjectives, adverbs and other words that are frequently used in Turkish and in the context of the ambiguous words were not included. This is not a suitable resource for fulfilling the requirements of TLST and an ontology specific to this task was required. The ontology covers the examples that are selected and has three levels of relations that are supposed to be effective in the disambiguation process. We tried to be consistent with the WordNet tags; additionally we constructed the ontology not only for nouns and verbs but for all the words that are in the context of the ambiguous words selected. Additionally we tried to strengthen the relation among the context words by using the same tags for all POS in the ontology. This is somehow deviating from WordNet methodology, since each word category has its own set of classification in it.

6 Evaluation

WSD is a new area of research in Turkish. The sense tagged data provided in TLST are the first resources for this specific domain in Turkish. Due to the limited and brand new resources available and the time restrictions the participation was less. We submitted a very simple system that utilizes statistical information. It is similar to the Naïve Bayes approach. The features in the training data was used individually and the probababilities of the senses are calculated. Then in the test phase the probabilities of each sense is calculated with the given features and the three highest-scored senses are selected as the answer. The average precision and recall values for each word category are given in Table 3. The values are not so high, as it can be expected. The size of the training data is limited, but the size is the highest possible under these circumstances, but it should be incremented in the near future. The number of senses is high and providing enough instances is difficult. The data and the methodology for WSD will be improved by the experience obtained in SemEval evaluation exercise.

The evaluation is done only for FG and CG senses. For FG senses no partial points are assigned and 1 point is assigned for a correct match. On the other hand, the CG senses are evaluated partially. If the answer tags are matching with any of the answer tags they are given points.

Words	FG		CG	
	P	R	P	R
Nouns	0,15	0,50	0,65	0,43
Verbs	0,10	0,38	0,56	0,50
Others	0,13	0,50	0,57	0,44
Average	**0,13**	**0,46**	**0,59**	**0,46**

Table 3: Average Precision and Recall values

7 Conclusion

In TLST we have prepared the first resources for WSD researches in Turkish. Therefore it has significance in Turkish WSD studies. Although the resources and methodology have some deficiencies, a valuable effort was invested during the development of them. The resources and the methodology for Turkish WSD will be improved by the experience obtained in SemEval and will be open to public in the very near future from http://www.fatih.edu.tr/~zorhan/senseval/senseval.htm.

References

Orhan, Z. and Altan, Z. 2006. *Impact of Feature Selection for Corpus-Based WSD in Turkish*, LNAI, Springer-Verlag, Vol. 4293: 868-878

Orhan Z. and Altan Z. 2005. *Effective Features for Disambiguation of Turkish Verbs*, IEC'05, Prague, Czech Republic: 182-186

Oflazer, K., Say, B., Tur, D. Z. H. and Tur, G. 2003. *Building A Turkish Treebank*, Invited Chapter In Building And Exploiting Syntactically-Annotated Corpora, Anne Abeille Editor, Kluwer Academic Publishers.

[2] http://www.hlst.sabanciuniv.edu/TL/

The SemEval-2007 WePS Evaluation: Establishing a benchmark for the Web People Search Task

Javier Artiles
UNED NLP & IR group
Madrid, Spain
javart@bec.uned.es
nlp.uned.es/~javier

Julio Gonzalo
UNED NLP & IR group
Madrid, Spain
julio@lsi.uned.es
nlp.uned.es/~julio

Satoshi Sekine
Computer Science Department
New York University, USA
sekine@cs.nyu.edu
nlp.cs.nyu.edu/sekine

Abstract

This paper presents the task definition, resources, participation, and comparative results for the Web People Search task, which was organized as part of the SemEval-2007 evaluation exercise. This task consists of clustering a set of documents that mention an ambiguous person name according to the actual entities referred to using that name.

1 Introduction

Finding information about people in the World Wide Web is one of the most common activities of Internet users. Person names, however, are highly ambiguous. In most cases, the results for a person name search are a mix of pages about different people sharing the same name. The user is then forced either to add terms to the query (probably losing recall and focusing on one single aspect of the person), or to browse every document in order to filter the information about the person he is actually looking for.

In an ideal system the user would simply type a person name, and receive search results clustered according to the different people sharing that name. And this is, in essence, the WePS (Web People Search) task we have proposed to SemEval-2007 participants: systems receive a set of web pages (which are the result of a web search for a person name), and they have to cluster them in as many sets as entities sharing the name. This task has close links with Word Sense Disambiguation (WSD), which is generally formulated as the task of deciding which sense a word has in a given context. In both cases, the problem addressed is the resolution of the ambiguity in a natural language expression. A couple of differences make our problem different. WSD is usually focused on open-class words (common nouns, adjectives, verbs and adverbs). The first difference is that boundaries between word senses in a dictionary are often subtle or even conflicting, making binary decisions harder and sometimes even useless depending on the application. In contrast, distinctions between people should be easier to establish. The second difference is that WSD usually operates with a dictionary containing a relatively small number of senses that can be assigned to each word. Our task is rather a case of Word Sense Discrimination, because the number of "senses" (actual people) is unknown *a priori*, and it is in average much higher than in the WSD task (there are 90,000 different names shared by 100 million people according to the U.S. Census Bureau).

There is also a strong relation of our proposed task with the Co-reference Resolution problem, focused on linking mentions (including pronouns) in a text. Our task can be seen as a co-reference resolution problem where the focus is on solving inter-document co-reference, disregarding the linking of all the mentions of an entity inside each document.

An early work in name disambiguation (Bagga and Baldwin, 1998) uses the similarity between documents in a Vector Space using a "bag of words" representation. An alternative approach by Mann and Yarowsky (2003) is based on a rich feature space of automatically extracted biographic information. Fleischman and Hovy (2004) propose a Maximum Entropy model trained to give the probability that

Proceedings of the 4th International Workshop on Semantic Evaluations (SemEval-2007), pages 64–69,
Prague, June 2007.

two names refer to the same individual [1].

The paper is organized as follows. Section 2 provides a description of the experimental methodology, the training and test data provided to the participants, the evaluation measures, baseline systems and the campaign design. Section 3 gives a description of the participant systems and provides the evaluation results. Finally, Section 4 presents some conclusions.

2 Experimental Methodology

2.1 Data

Following the general SemEval guidelines, we have prepared trial, training and test data sets for the task, which are described below.

2.1.1 Trial data

For this evaluation campaign we initially delivered a trial corpus for the potential participants. The trial data consisted of an adapted version of the WePS corpus described in (Artiles et al., 2006). The predominant feature of this corpus is a high number of entities in each document set, due to the fact that the ambiguous names were extracted from the most common names in the US Census. This corpus did not completely match task specifications because it did not consider documents with internal ambiguity, nor it did consider non-person entities; but it was, however, a cost-effective way of releasing data to play around with. During the first weeks after releasing this trial data to potential participants, some annotation mistakes were noticed. We preferred, however, to leave the corpus "as is" and concentrate our efforts in producing clean training and test datasets, rather than investing time in improving trial data.

2.1.2 Training data

In order to provide different ambiguity scenarios, we selected person names from different sources:

US Census. We reused the Web03 corpus (Mann, 2006), which contains 32 names randomly picked from the US Census, and was well suited for the task.

Wikipedia. Another seven names were sampled from a list of ambiguous person names in the English Wikipedia. These were expected to have a few predominant entities (popular or historical), and therefore a lower ambiguity than the previous set.

ECDL. Finally, ten additional names were randomly selected from the Program Committee listing of a Computer Science conference (ECDL 2006). This set offers a scenario of potentially low ambiguity (computer science scholars usually have a stronger Internet presence than other professional fields) with the added value of the *a priori* knowledge of a domain specific type of entity (scholar) present in the data.

All datasets consist of collections of web pages obtained from the 100 top results for a person name query to an Internet search engine [2]. Note that 100 is an upper bound, because in some occasions the URL returned by the search engine no longer exists.

The second and third datasets (developed explicitly for our task) consist of 17 person names and 1685 associated documents in total (99 documents per name in average). Each web page was downloaded and stored for off-line processing. We also stored the basic metadata associated to each search result, including the original URL, title, position in the results ranking and the corresponding snippet generated by the search engine.

In the process of generating the corpus, the selection of the names plays an important role, potentially conditioning the degree of ambiguity that will be found later in the Web search results. The reasons for this variability in the ambiguity of names are diverse and do not always correlate with the straightforward census frequency. A much more decisive feature is, for instance, the presence of famous entities sharing the ambiguous name with less popular people. As we are considering top search results, these can easily be monopolized by a single entity that is popular in the Internet.

After the annotation of this data (see section 2.1.4.) we found our predictions about the average ambiguity of each dataset not to be completely accurate. In Table 1 we see that the ECDL-06 average ambiguity is indeed relatively low (except for the documents for "Thomas Baker" standing as the most ambiguous name in the whole training). Wikipedia names have an average ambiguity of 23,14 entities

[1] For a comprehensive bibliography on person name disambiguation refer to http://nlp.uned.es/weps

[2] We used the Yahoo! API from Yahoo! Search Web Services (http://developer.yahoo.com/search/web/).

Name	entities	documents	discarded
	Wikipedia names		
John Kennedy	27	99	6
George Clinton	27	99	6
Michael Howard	32	99	8
Paul Collins	37	98	6
Tony Abbott	7	98	9
Alexander Macomb	21	100	14
David Lodge	11	100	9
Average	23,14	99,00	8,29
	ECDL-06 Names		
Edward Fox	16	100	36
Allan Hanbury	2	100	32
Donna Harman	7	98	6
Andrew Powell	19	98	48
Gregory Crane	4	99	17
Jane Hunter	15	99	59
Paul Clough	14	100	35
Thomas Baker	60	100	31
Christine Borgman	7	99	11
Anita Coleman	9	99	28
Average	15,30	99,20	30,30
	WEB03 Corpus		
Tim Whisler	10	33	8
Roy Tamashiro	5	23	6
Cynthia Voigt	1	405	314
Miranda Bollinger	2	2	0
Guy Dunbar	4	51	34
Todd Platts	2	239	144
Stacey Doughty	1	2	0
Young Dawkins	4	61	35
Luke Choi	13	20	6
Gregory Brennan	32	96	38
Ione Westover	1	4	0
Patrick Karlsson	10	24	8
Celeste Paquette	2	17	2
Elmo Hardy	3	55	15
Louis Sidoti	2	6	3
Alexander Markham	9	32	16
Helen Cawthorne	3	46	13
Dan Rhone	2	4	2
Maile Doyle	1	13	1
Alice Gilbreath	8	74	30
Sidney Shorter	3	4	0
Alfred Schroeder	35	112	58
Cathie Ely	1	2	0
Martin Nagel	14	55	31
Abby Watkins	13	124	35
Mary Lemanski	2	152	78
Gillian Symons	3	30	6
Pam Tetu	1	4	2
Guy Crider	2	2	0
Armando Valencia	16	79	20
Hannah Bassham	2	3	0
Charlotte Bergeron	5	21	8
Average	5,90	47,20	18,00
Global average	10,76	71,02	26,00

Table 1: Training Data

per name, which is higher than for the ECDL set. The WEB03 Corpus has the lowest ambiguity (5,9 entities per name), for two reasons: first, randomly picked names belong predominantly to the long tail of unfrequent person names which, *per se*, have low ambiguity. Being rare names implies that in average there are fewer documents returned by the search engine (47,20 per name), which also reduces the possibilities to find ambiguity.

2.1.3 Test data

For the test data we followed the same process described for the training. In the name selection we tried to maintain a similar distribution of ambiguity degrees and scenario. For that reason we randomly extracted 10 person names from the English Wikipedia and another 10 names from participants in the ACL-06 conference. In the case of the US census names, we decided to focus on relatively common names, to avoid the problems explained above.

Unfortunately, after the annotation was finished (once the submission deadline had expired), we found a major increase in the ambiguity degrees (Table 2) of all data sets. While we expected a raise in the case of the US census names, the other two cases just show that there is a high (and unpredictable) variability, which would require much larger data sets to have reliable population samples.

This has made the task particularly challenging for participants, because naive learning strategies (such as empirical adjustment of distance thresholds to optimize standard clustering algorithms) might be misleaded by the training set.

2.1.4 Annotation

The annotation of the data was performed separately in each set of documents related to an ambiguous name. Given this set of approximately 100 documents that mention the ambiguous name, the annotation consisted in the manual clustering of each document according to the actual entity that is referred on it.

When non person entities were found (for instance, organization or places named after a person) the annotation was performed without any special rule. Generally, the annotator browses documents following the original ranking in the search results; after reading a document he will decide whether the mentions of the ambiguous name refer to a new entity or to a entity previously identified. We asked the annotators to concentrate first on mentions that strictly contained the search string, and then to pay attention to the co-referent variations of the name. For instance "John Edward Fox" or "Edward Fox Smith" would be valid mentions. "Edward J. Fox", however, breaks the original search string, and we do not get into name variation detection, so it will be considered valid only if it is co-referent to a valid

Name	entities	documents	discarded
	Wikipedia names		
Arthur Morgan	19	100	52
James Morehead	48	100	11
James Davidson	59	98	16
Patrick Killen	25	96	4
William Dickson	91	100	8
George Foster	42	99	11
James Hamilton	81	100	15
John Nelson	55	100	25
Thomas Fraser	73	100	13
Thomas Kirk	72	100	20
Average	56,50	99,30	17,50
	ACL06 Names		
Dekang Lin	1	99	0
Chris Brockett	19	98	5
James Curran	63	99	9
Mark Johnson	70	99	7
Jerry Hobbs	15	99	7
Frank Keller	28	100	20
Leon Barrett	33	98	9
Robert Moore	38	98	28
Sharon Goldwater	2	97	4
Stephen Clark	41	97	39
Average	31,00	98,40	12,80
	US Census Names		
Alvin Cooper	43	99	9
Harry Hughes	39	98	9
Jonathan Brooks	83	97	8
Jude Brown	32	100	39
Karen Peterson	64	100	16
Marcy Jackson	51	100	5
Martha Edwards	82	100	9
Neil Clark	21	99	7
Stephan Johnson	36	100	20
Violet Howard	52	98	27
Average	50,30	99,10	14,90
Global average	45,93	98,93	15,07

Table 2: Test Data

mention.

In order to perform the clustering, the annotator was asked to pay attention to objective facts (biographical dates, related names, occupations, etc.) and to be conservative when making decisions. The final result is a complete clustering of the documents, where each cluster contains the documents that refer to a particular entity. Following the previous example, in documents for the name "Edward Fox" the annotator found 16 different entities with that name. Note that there is no *a priori* knowledge about the number of entities that will be discovered in a document set. This makes the task specially difficult when there are many different entities and a high volume of scattered biographical information to take into account.

In cases where the document does not offer enough information to decide whether it belongs to a cluster or is a new entity, it is discarded from the evaluation process (not from the dataset). Another common reason for discarding documents was the absence of the person name in the document, usually due to a mismatch between the search engine cache and the downloaded URL.

We found that, in many cases, different entities were mentioned using the ambiguous name within a single document. This was the case when a document mentions relatives with names that contain the ambiguous string (for instance "Edward Fox" and "Edward Fox Jr."). Another common case of intra-document ambiguity is that of pages containing database search results, such as book lists from Amazon, actors from IMDB, etc. A similar case is that of pages that explicitly analyze the ambiguity of a person name (Wikipedia "disambiguation" pages). The way this situation was handled, in terms of the annotation, was to assign each document to as many clusters as entities were referred to on it with the ambiguous name.

2.2 Evaluation measures

Evaluation was performed in each document set (web pages mentioning an ambiguous person name) of the data distributed as test. The human annotation was used as the gold standard for the evaluation.

Each system was evaluated using the standard *purity* and *inverse purity* clustering measures Purity is related to the *precision* measure, well known in Information Retrieval. This measure focuses on the frequency of the most common category in each cluster, and rewards the clustering solutions that introduce less noise in each cluster. Being C the set of clusters to be evaluated, L the set of categories (manually annotated) and n the number of clustered elements, purity is computed by taking the weighted average of maximal precision values:

$$\text{Purity} = \sum_i \frac{|C_i|}{n} \max \text{Precision}(C_i, L_j)$$

where the precision of a cluster C_i for a given category L_j is defined as:

$$\text{Precision}(C_i, L_j) = \frac{|C_i \bigcap L_j|}{|C_i|}$$

Inverse Purity focuses on the cluster with maximum recall for each category, rewarding the clustering solutions that gathers more elements of each category in a corresponding single cluster. Inverse Purity is defined as:

$$\text{Inverse Purity} = \sum_i \frac{|L_i|}{n} \max \text{Precision}(L_i, C_j)$$

For the final ranking of systems we used the harmonic mean of purity and inverse purity $F_{\alpha=0,5}$. The F measure is defined as follows:

$$\text{F} = \frac{1}{\alpha \frac{1}{\text{Purity}} + (1 - \alpha) \frac{1}{\text{Inverse Purity}}}$$

$F_{\alpha=0,2}$ is included as an additional measure giving more importance to the inverse purity aspect. The rationale is that, for a search engine user, it should be easier to discard a few incorrect web pages in a cluster containing all the information needed, than having to collect the relevant information across many different clusters. Therefore, achieving a high inverse purity should be rewarded more than having high purity.

2.3 Baselines

Two simple baseline approaches were applied to the test data. The *ALL-IN-ONE* baseline provides a clustering solution where all the documents are assigned to a single cluster. This has the effect of always achieving the highest score in the *inverse purity* measure, because all classes have their documents in a single cluster. On the other hand, the *purity* measure will be equal to the *precision* of the predominant class in that single cluster. The *ONE-IN-ONE* baseline gives another extreme clustering solution, where every document is assigned to a different cluster. In this case *purity* always gives its maximum value, while *inverse purity* will decrease with larger classes.

2.4 Campaign design

The schedule for the evaluation campaign was set by the SemEval organisation as follows: (i) release task description and trial data set; (ii) release of training and test; (iii) participants send their answers to the task organizers; (iv) the task organizers evaluate the answers and send the results.

The task description and the initial trial data set were publicly released before the start of the official evaluation.

The official evaluation period started with the simultaneous release of both training and test data, together with a scoring script with the main evaluation measures to be used. This period spanned five weeks in which teams were allowed to register and download the data. During that period, results for a given task had to be submitted no later than 21 days after downloading the training data and no later than 7 days after downloading the test data. Only one submission per team was allowed.

Training data included the downloaded web pages, their associated metadata and the human clustering of each document set, providing a development test-bed for the participant's systems. We also specified the source of each ambiguous name in the training data (Wikipedia, ECDL conference and US Census). Test data only included the downloaded web pages and their metadata. This section of the corpus was used for the systems evaluation. Participants were required to send a clustering for each test document set.

Finally, after the evaluation period was finished and all the participants sent their data, the task organizers sent the evaluation for the test data.

3 Results of the evaluation campaign

29 teams expressed their interest in the task; this number exceeded our expectations for this pilot experience, and confirms the potential interest of the research community in this highly practical problem. Out of them, 16 teams submitted results within the deadline; their results are reported below.

3.1 Results and discussion

Table 3 presents the macro-averaged results obtained by the sixteen systems plus the two baselines on the test data. We found macro-average [3] preferable to micro-average [4] because it has a clear interpretation: if the evaluation measure is F, then we should calculate F for every test case (person name) and then average over all trials. The interpretation of micro-average F is less clear.

The systems are ranked according to the scores obtained with the harmonic mean measure $F_{\alpha=0,5}$ of

[3]Macro-average F consists of computing F for every test set (person name) and then averaging over all test sets.

[4]Micro-average F consists of computing the average P and IP (over all test sets) and then calculating F with these figures.

		Macro-averaged Scores			
		F-measures			
rank	team-id	$\alpha = ,5$	$\alpha = ,2$	Pur	Inv_Pur
1	CU_COMSEM	,78	,83	,72	,88
2	IRST-BP	,75	,77	,75	,80
3	PSNUS	,75	,78	,73	,82
4	UVA	,67	,62	,81	,60
5	SHEF	,66	,73	,60	,82
6	FICO	,64	,76	,53	,90
7	UNN	,62	,67	,60	,73
8	*ONE-IN-ONE*	*,61*	*,52*	*1,00*	*,47*
9	AUG	,60	,73	,50	,88
10	SWAT-IV	,58	,64	,55	,71
11	UA-ZSA	,58	,60	,58	,64
12	TITPI	,57	,71	,45	,89
13	JHU1-13	,53	,65	,45	,82
14	DFKI2	,50	,63	,39	,83
15	WIT	,49	,66	,36	,93
16	UC3M_13	,48	,66	,35	,95
17	UBC-AS	,40	,55	,30	,91
18	*ALL-IN-ONE*	*,40*	*,58*	*,29*	*1,00*

Table 3: Team ranking

purity and inverse purity. Considering only the participant systems, the average value for the ranking measure was $0,60$ and its standard deviation $0,11$.

Results with $F_{\alpha=0,2}$ are not substantially different (except for the two baselines, which roughly swap positions). There are some ranking swaps, but generally only within close pairs.

The good performance of the *ONE-IN-ONE* baseline system is indicative of the abundance of singleton entities (entities represented by only one document). This situation increases the inverse purity score for this system giving a harmonic measure higher than the expected.

4 Conclusions

The WEPS task ended with considerable success in terms of participation, and we believe that a careful analysis of the contributions made by participants (which is not possible at the time of writing this report) will be an interesting reference for future research. In addition, all the collected and annotated dataset will be publicly available [5] as a benchmark for Web People Search systems.

At the same time, it is clear that building a reliable test-bed for the task is not simple. First of all, the variability across test cases is large and unpredictable, and a system that works well with the names in our test bed may not be reliable in practical, open search situations. Partly because of that, our test-bed happened to be unintentionally challenging for systems, with a large difference between the average ambiguity in the training and test datasets. Secondly, it is probably necessary to think about specific evaluation measures beyond standard clustering metrics such as purity and inverse purity, which are not tailored to the task and do not behave well when multiple classification is allowed. We hope to address these problems in a forthcoming edition of the WEPS task.

[5] `http://nlp.uned.es/weps`

5 Acknowledgements

This research was supported in part by the National Science Foundation of United States under Grant IIS-00325657 and by a grant from the Spanish government under project Text-Mess (TIN2006-15265-C06). This paper does not necessarily reflect the position of the U.S. Government.

References

Javier Artiles, Julio Gonzalo, and Felisa Verdejo. 2005. A Testbed for People Searching Strategies in the WWW In *Proceedings of the 28th annual International ACM SIGIR conference on Research and Development in Information Retrieval (SIGIR'05)*, pages 569-570.

Amit Bagga and Breck Baldwin. 1998. Entity-Based Cross-Document Coreferencing Using the Vector Space Model In *Proceedings of the 36th Annual Meeting of the Association for Computational Linguistics and the 17th International Conference on Computational Linguistics (COLING-ACL'98)*, pages 79-85.

Michael B. Fleischman and Eduard Hovy 2004. Multi-document person name resolution. In *Proceedings of ACL-42, Reference Resolution Workshop*.

Gideon S. Mann. 2006. *Multi-Document Statistical Fact Extraction and Fusion* Ph.D. Thesis.

Gideon S. Mann and David Yarowsky 2003. Unsupervised Personal Name Disambiguation In *Proceedings of the seventh conference on Natural language learning at HLT-NAACL*, pages 33-40.

SemEval-2007 Task 14: Affective Text

Carlo Strapparava
FBK – irst
Istituto per la Ricerca Scientifica e Tecnologica
I-38050, Povo, Trento, Italy
strappa@itc.it

Rada Mihalcea
Department of Computer Science
University of North Texas
Denton, TX, 76203, USA
rada@cs.unt.edu

Abstract

The "Affective Text" task focuses on the classification of emotions and valence (positive/negative polarity) in news headlines, and is meant as an exploration of the connection between emotions and lexical semantics. In this paper, we describe the data set used in the evaluation and the results obtained by the participating systems.

1 Introduction

All words can potentially convey affective meaning. Every word, even those apparently neutral, can evoke pleasant or painful experiences due to their semantic relation with emotional concepts or categories. Some words have emotional meaning with respect to an individual story, while for many others the affective power is part of the collective imagination (e.g., words such as "mum", "ghost", "war").

The automatic detection of emotion in texts is becoming increasingly important from an applicative point of view. Consider for example the tasks of opinion mining and market analysis, affective computing, or natural language interfaces such as e-learning environments or educational/edutainment games. Possible beneficial effects of emotions on memory and attention of the users, and in general on fostering their creativity are also well-known in the field of psychology.

For instance, the following represent examples of applicative scenarios in which affective analysis would give valuable and interesting contributions:

Sentiment Analysis. Text categorization according to affective relevance, opinion exploration for market analysis, etc. are just some examples of application of these techniques. While positive/negative valence annotation is an active field of sentiment analysis, we believe that a fine-grained emotion annotation would increase the effectiveness of these applications.

Computer Assisted Creativity. The automated generation of evaluative expressions with a bias on some polarity orientation are a key component for automatic personalized advertisement and persuasive communication.

Verbal Expressivity in Human Computer Interaction. Future human-computer interaction, according to a widespread view, will emphasize naturalness and effectiveness and hence the incorporation of models of possibly many human cognitive capabilities, including affective analysis and generation. For example, emotion expression by synthetic characters (e.g., embodied conversational agents) is considered now a key element for their believability. Affective words selection and understanding is crucial for realizing appropriate and expressive conversations.

The "Affective Text" task was intended as an exploration of the connection between lexical semantics and emotions, and an evaluation of various automatic approaches to emotion recognition.

The task is not easy. Indeed, as (Ortony et al., 1987) indicates, besides words directly referring to emotional states (e.g., "fear", "cheerful") and for which an appropriate lexicon would help, there are words that act only as an indirect reference to

Proceedings of the 4th International Workshop on Semantic Evaluations (SemEval-2007), pages 70–74,
Prague, June 2007.

emotions depending on the context (e.g. "monster", "ghost"). We can call the former *direct affective words* and the latter *indirect affective words* (Strapparava et al., 2006).

2 Task Definition

We proposed to focus on the emotion classification of news headlines extracted from news web sites. Headlines typically consist of a few words and are often written by creative people with the intention to "provoke" emotions, and consequently to attract the readers' attention. These characteristics make this type of text particularly suitable for use in an automatic emotion recognition setting, as the affective/emotional features (if present) are guaranteed to appear in these short sentences.

The structure of the task was as follows:

Corpus: News titles, extracted from news web sites (such as Google news, CNN) and/or newspapers. In the case of web sites, we can easily collect a few thousand titles in a short amount of time.

Objective: Provided a set of predefined six emotion labels (i.e., Anger, Disgust, Fear, Joy, Sadness, Surprise), classify the titles with the appropriate emotion label and/or with a valence indication (positive/negative).

The emotion labeling and valence classification were seen as independent tasks, and thus a team was able to participate in one or both tasks. The task was carried out in an unsupervised setting, and consequently no training was provided. The reason behind this decision is that we wanted to emphasize the study of emotion lexical semantics, and avoid biasing the participants toward simple "text categorization" approaches. Nonetheless supervised systems were not precluded from participation, and in such cases the teams were allowed to create their own supervised training sets.

Participants were free to use any resources they wanted. We provided a set words extracted from WordNet Affect (Strapparava and Valitutti, 2004), relevant to the six emotions of interest. However, the use of this list was entirely optional.

2.1 Data Set

The data set consisted of news headlines drawn from major newspapers such as New York Times, CNN, and BBC News, as well as from the Google News search engine. We decided to focus our attention on headlines for two main reasons. First, news have typically a high load of emotional content, as they describe major national or worldwide events, and are written in a style meant to attract the attention of the readers. Second, the structure of headlines was appropriate for our goal of conducting sentence-level annotations of emotions.

Two data sets were made available: a development data set consisting of 250 annotated headlines, and a test data set with 1,000 annotated headlines.

2.2 Data Annotation

To perform the annotations, we developed a Web-based annotation interface that displayed one headline at a time, together with six slide bars for emotions and one slide bar for valence. The interval for the emotion annotations was set to $[0, 100]$, where 0 means the emotion is missing from the given headline, and 100 represents maximum emotional load. The interval for the valence annotations was set to $[-100, 100]$, where 0 represents a neutral headline, -100 represents a highly negative headline, and 100 corresponds to a highly positive headline.

Unlike previous annotations of sentiment or subjectivity (Wiebe et al., 2005; Pang and Lee, 2004), which typically relied on binary $0/1$ annotations, we decided to use a finer-grained scale, hence allowing the annotators to select different degrees of emotional load.

The test data set was independently labeled by six annotators. The annotators were instructed to select the appropriate emotions for each headline based on the presence of words or phrases with emotional content, as well as the overall feeling invoked by the headline. Annotation examples were also provided, including examples of headlines bearing two or more emotions to illustrate the case where several emotions were jointly applicable. Finally, the annotators were encouraged to follow their "first intuition," and to use the full-range of the annotation scale bars.

2.3 Inter-Annotator Agreement

We conducted inter-tagger agreement studies for each of the six emotions and for the valence annotations. The agreement evaluations were carried out using the Pearson correlation measure, and are shown in Table 1. To measure the agreement among the six annotators, we first measured the agreement between each annotator and the average of the remaining five annotators, followed by an average over the six resulting agreement figures.

EMOTIONS	
Anger	49.55
Disgust	44.51
Fear	63.81
Joy	59.91
Sadness	68.19
Surprise	36.07
VALENCE	
Valence	78.01

Table 1: Pearson correlation for inter-annotator agreement

2.4 Fine-grained and Coarse-grained Evaluations

Fine-grained evaluations were conducted using the Pearson measure of correlation between the system scores and the gold standard scores, averaged over all the headlines in the data set.

We have also run a coarse-grained evaluation, where each emotion was mapped to a 0/1 classification (0 = [0,50), 1 = [50,100]), and each valence was mapped to a -1/0/1 classification (-1 = [-100,-50], 0 = (-50,50), 1 = [50,100]). For the coarse-grained evaluations, we calculated accuracy, precision, and recall. Note that the accuracy is calculated with respect to all the possible classes, and thus it can be artificially high in the case of unbalanced datasets (as some of the emotions are, due to the high number of neutral headlines). Instead, the precision and recall figures exclude the neutral annotations.

3 Participating Systems

Five teams have participated in the task, with five systems for valence classification and three systems for emotion labeling. The following represents a short description of the systems.

UPAR7: This is a rule-based system using a linguistic approach. A first pass through the data "uncapitalizes" common words in the news title. The system then used the Stanford syntactic parser on the modified title, and tried to identify what is being said about the main subject by exploiting the dependency graph obtained from the parser.

Each word was first rated separately for each emotion (the six emotions plus Compassion) and for valence. Next, the main subject rating was boosted. Contrasts and accentuations between "good" or "bad" were detected, making it possible to identify surprising good or bad news. The system also takes into account: human will (as opposed to illness or natural disasters); negation and modals; high-tech context; celebrities.

The lexical resource used was a combination of SentiWordNet (Esuli and Sebastiani, 2006) and WordNetAffect (Strapparava and Valitutti, 2004), which were semi-automatically enriched on the basis of the original trial data.

SICS: The SICS team used a very simple approach for valence annotation based on a word-space model and a set of seed words. The idea was to create two points in a high-dimensional word space - one representing positive valence, the other representing negative valence - and then projecting each headline into this space, choosing the valence whose point was closer to the headline.

The word space was produced from a lemmatized and stop list filtered version of the LA times corpus (consisting of documents from 1994, released for experimentation in the Cross Language Evaluation Forum (CLEF)) using documents as contexts and standard TFIDF weighting of frequencies. No dimensionality reduction was used, resulting in a 220,220-dimensional word space containing predominantly syntagmatic relations between words. Valence vectors were created in this space by summing the context vectors of a set of manually selected seed words (8 positive and 8 negative words).

For each headline in the test data, stop words and words with frequency above 10,000 in the LA times corpus were removed. The context vectors of the remaining words were then summed, and the cosine of the angles between the summed vector and each of the valence vectors were computed, and the headline was ascribed the valence value (computed as [cosine * 100 + 50]) of the closest valence vector (headlines that were closer to the negative valence vector were assigned a negative valence value). In 11 cases, a value of -0.0 was ascribed either because no words were left in the headline after frequency and stop word filtering, or because none of the remaining words occurred in the LA times corpus and thus did not have any context vector.

CLaC: This team submitted two systems to the competition: an unsupervised knowledge-based system (ClaC) and a supervised corpus-based system (CLaC-NB). Both systems were used for assigning positive/negative and neutral valence to headlines on the scale [-100,100].

CLaC: The CLaC system relies on a knowledge-based domain-independent unsupervised approach to headline valence detection and scoring. The system uses three main kinds of knowledge: a list of sentiment-bearing words, a list of valence shifters and a set of rules that define the scope and the result of the combination of sentiment-bearing words and valence shifters. The unigrams used for sentence/headline classification were learned from WordNet dictionary entries. In order to take advantage of the special properties of WordNet glosses and relations, we developed a system that used the list of human-annotated adjectives from (Hatzivassiloglou and McKeown, 1997) as a seed list and learned additional unigrams from WordNet synsets and glosses. The list was then expanded by adding to it all the words annotated with Positive or Negative tags in the General Inquirer. Each unigram in the resulting list had the degree of membership in the category of positive or negative sentiment assigned to it using the fuzzy Net Overlap Score method described in the team's earlier work (Andreevskaia and Bergler, 2006). Only words with fuzzy membership score not equal to zero were retained in the list. The resulting list contained 10,809 sentiment-bearing words of different parts of speech.

The fuzzy Net Overlap Score counts were complemented with the capability to discern and take into account some relevant elements of syntactic structure of the sentences. Two components were added to the system to enable this capability: (1) valence shifter handling rules and (2) parse tree analysis. The list of valence shifters was a combination of a list of common English negations and a subset of the list of automatically obtained words with increase/decrease semantics, complemented with manual annotation. The full list consists of 450 words and expressions. Each entry in the list of valence shifters has an action and scope associated with it, which are used by special handling rules that enable the system to identify such words and phrases in the text and take them into account in sentence sentiment determination. In order to correctly determine the scope of valence shifters in a sentence, the system used a parse tree analysis using MiniPar.

As a result of this processing, every headline received a system score assigned based on the combined fuzzy Net Overlap Score of its constituents. This score was then mapped into the [-100 to 100] scale as required by the task.

CLaC-NB: In order to assess the performance of basic Machine Learning techniques on headlines, a second system ClaC-NB was also implemented. This system used a Naïve Bayes classifier in order to assign valence to headlines. It was trained on a small corpus composed of the development corpus of 250 headlines provided for this competition, plus an additional 200 headlines manually annotated and 400 positive and negative news sentences. The probabilities assigned by the classifier were mapped to the [-100, 100] scale as follows: all negative headlines received the score of -100, all positive headlines were assigned the score of +100, and the neutral headlines obtained the score of 0.

UA: In order to determine the kind and the amount of emotions in a headline, statistics were gathered from three different web Search Engines: MyWay, AlltheWeb and Yahoo. This information was used to observe the distribution of the nouns, the verbs, the adverbs and the adjectives extracted from the headline and the different emotions.

The emotion scores were obtained through Pointwise Mutual Information (PMI). First, the number of documents obtained from the three web search engines using a query that contains all the headline words and an emotion (the words occur in an independent proximity across the web documents) was divided by the number of documents containing only an emotion and the number of documents containing all the headline words. Second, an associative score between each content word and an emotion was estimated and used to weight the final PMI score. The obtained results were normalized in the 0-100 range.

SWAT: SWAT is a supervised system using an unigram model trained to annotate emotional content. Synonym expansion on the emotion label words was also performed, using the Roget Thesaurus. In addition to the development data provided by the task organizers, the SWAT team annotated an additional set of 1000 headlines, which was used for training.

	Fine	Coarse			
	r	Acc.	Prec.	Rec.	F1
CLaC	**47.70**	**55.10**	**61.42**	9.20	16.00
UPAR7	36.96	55.00	57.54	8.78	15.24
SWAT	35.25	53.20	45.71	3.42	6.36
CLaC-NB	25.41	31.20	31.18	**66.38**	**42.43**
SICS	20.68	29.00	28.41	60.17	38.60

Table 2: System results for valence annotations

	Fine	Coarse			
	r	Acc.	Prec.	Rec.	F1
		Anger			
SWAT	24.51	92.10	12.00	5.00	7.06
UA	23.20	86.40	12.74	**21.6**	**16.03**
UPAR7	**32.33**	**93.60**	**16.67**	1.66	3.02
		Disgust			
SWAT	**18.55**	97.20	0.00	0.00	-
UA	16.21	**97.30**	0.00	0.00	-
UPAR7	12.85	95.30	0.00	0.00	-
		Fear			
SWAT	32.52	84.80	25.00	14.40	18.27
UA	23.15	75.30	16.23	**26.27**	**20.06**
UPAR7	**44.92**	**87.90**	**33.33**	2.54	4.72
		Joy			
SWAT	**26.11**	80.60	35.41	**9.44**	**14.91**
UA	2.35	81.80	40.00	2.22	4.21
UPAR7	22.49	**82.20**	**54.54**	6.66	11.87
		Sadness			
SWAT	38.98	87.70	32.50	11.92	17.44
UA	12.28	88.90	25.00	0.91	1.76
UPAR7	**40.98**	**89.00**	**48.97**	**22.02**	**30.38**
		Surprise			
SWAT	11.82	**89.10**	11.86	10.93	11.78
UA	7.75	84.60	**13.70**	**16.56**	**15.00**
UPAR7	**16.71**	88.60	12.12	1.25	2.27

Table 3: System results for emotion annotations

4 Results

Tables 2 and 3 show the results obtained by the participating systems. The tables show both the fine-grained Pearson correlation measure and the coarse-grained accuracy, precision and recall figures.

While further analysis is still needed, the results indicate that the task of emotion annotation is difficult. Although the Pearson correlation for the inter-tagger agreement is not particularly high, the gap between the results obtained by the systems and the upper bound represented by the annotator agreement suggests that there is room for future improvements.

Acknowledgments

Carlo Strapparava was partially supported by the HUMAINE Network of Excellence.

References

A. Andreevskaia and S. Bergler. 2006. Senses and sentiments: Sentiment tagging of adjectives at the meaning level. In *Proceedings of the 19th Canadian Conference on Artificial Intelligence, AI'06*, Quebec, Canada.

A. Esuli and F. Sebastiani. 2006. SentiWordNet: A publicly available lexical resource for opinion mining. In *Proceedings of the Fifth International Conference on Language Resources and Evaluation (LREC 2006)*, Genoa, Italy, May.

V. Hatzivassiloglou and K. McKeown. 1997. Predicting the semantic orientation of adjectives. In *Proceedings of the 35th Annual Meeting of the ACL*, Madrid, Spain, July.

A. Ortony, G. L. Clore, and M. A. Foss. 1987. The referential structure of the affective lexicon. *Cognitive Science*, (11).

B. Pang and L. Lee. 2004. A sentimental education: Sentiment analysis using subjectivity summarization based on minimum cuts. In *Proceedings of the 42nd Meeting of the Association for Computational Linguistics*, Barcelona, Spain, July.

C. Strapparava and A. Valitutti. 2004. Wordnet-affect: an affective extension of wordnet. In *Proceedings of the 4th International Conference on Language Resources and Evaluation*, Lisbon.

C. Strapparava, A. Valitutti, and O. Stock. 2006. The affective weight of lexicon. In *Proceedings of the Fifth International Conference on Language Resources and Evaluation*.

J. Wiebe, T. Wilson, and C. Cardie. 2005. Annotating expressions of opinions and emotions in language. *Language Resources and Evaluation*, 39(2-3):165–210.

SemEval-2007 Task 15: TempEval Temporal Relation Identification

Marc Verhagen[†], **Robert Gaizauskas**[‡], **Frank Schilder**[⋆], **Mark Hepple**[‡], **Graham Katz**[*] **and James Pustejovsky**[†]

[†] Brandeis University, {marc, jamesp}@cs.brandeis.edu
[‡] University of Sheffield, {r.gaizauskas,m.hepple}@dcs.shef.ac.uk
[⋆] Thomson Legal & Regulatory, frank.schilder@thomson.com,
[*] Stanford University, egkatz@stanford.edu

Abstract

The TempEval task proposes a simple way to evaluate automatic extraction of temporal relations. It avoids the pitfalls of evaluating a graph of inter-related labels by defining three sub tasks that allow pairwise evaluation of temporal relations. The task not only allows straightforward evaluation, it also avoids the complexities of full temporal parsing.

1 Introduction

Newspaper texts, narratives and other texts describe events that occur in time and specify the temporal location and order of these events. Text comprehension, amongst other capabilities, clearly requires the capability to identify the events described in a text and locate these in time. This capability is crucial to a wide range of NLP applications, from document summarization and question answering to machine translation.

Recent work on the annotation of events and temporal relations has resulted in both a de-facto standard for expressing these relations and a hand-built gold standard of annotated texts. TimeML (Pustejovsky et al., 2003a) is an emerging ISO standard for annotation of events, temporal expressions and the anchoring and ordering relations between them. TimeBank (Pustejovsky et al., 2003b; Boguraev et al., forthcoming) was originally conceived of as a proof of concept that illustrates the TimeML language, but has since gone through several rounds of revisions and can now be considered a gold standard for temporal information. TimeML and TimeBank have already been used as the basis for automatic time, event and temporal relation annotation tasks in a number of research projects in recent years (Mani et al., 2006; Boguraev et al., forthcoming).

An open evaluation challenge in the area of temporal annotation should serve to drive research forward, as it has in other areas of NLP. The automatic identification of all temporal referring expressions, events and temporal relations within a text is the ultimate aim of research in this area. However, addressing this aim in a first evaluation challenge was judged to be too difficult, both for organizers and participants, and a staged approach was deemed more effective. Thus we here present an initial evaluation exercise based on three limited tasks that we believe are realistic both from the perspective of assembling resources for development and testing and from the perspective of developing systems capable of addressing the tasks. They are also tasks, which should they be performable automatically, have application potential.

2 Task Description

The tasks as originally proposed were modified slightly during the course of resource development for the evaluation exercise due to constraints on data and annotator availability. In the following we describe the tasks as they were ultimately realized in the evaluation.

There were three tasks – A, B and C. For all three tasks the data provided for testing and training includes annotations identifying: (1) sentence boundaries; (2) all temporal referring expression as

Proceedings of the 4th International Workshop on Semantic Evaluations (SemEval-2007), pages 75–80,
Prague, June 2007.

specified by TIMEX3; (3) all events as specified in TimeML; (4) selected instances of temporal relations, as relevant to the given task. For tasks A and B a restricted set of event terms were identified – those whose stems occurred twenty times or more in TimeBank. This set is referred to as the Event Target List or ETL.

TASK A This task addresses only the temporal relations holding between time and event expressions that occur within the same sentence. Furthermore only event expressions that occur within the ETL are considered. In the training and test data, TLINK annotations for these temporal relations are provided, the difference being that in the test data the relation type is withheld. The task is to supply this label.

TASK B This task addresses only the temporal relations holding between the Document Creation Time (DCT) and event expressions. Again only event expressions that occur within the ETL are considered. As in Task A, TLINK annotations for these temporal relations are provided in both training and test data, and again the relation type is withheld in the test data and the task is to supply this label.

TASK C Task C relies upon the idea of their being a main event within a sentence, typically the syntactically dominant verb. The aim is to assign the temporal relation between the main events of adjacent sentences. In both training and test data the main events are identified (via an attribute in the event annotation) and TLINKs between these main events are supplied. As for Tasks A and B, the task here is to supply the correct relation label for these TLINKs.

3 Data Description and Data Preparation

The TempEval annotation language is a simplified version of TimeML [1]. For TempEval, we use the following five tags: `TempEval`, `s`, `TIMEX3`, `EVENT`, and `TLINK`. `TempEval` is the document root and `s` marks sentence boundaries. All sentence tags in the TempEval data are automatically created using the Alembic Natural Language processing tools. The other three tags are discussed here in more detail:

- `TIMEX3`. Tags the time expressions in the text. It is identical to the `TIMEX3` tag in TimeML. See the TimeML specifications and guidelines for further details on this tag and its attributes. Each document has one special `TIMEX3` tag, the Document Creation Time, which is interpreted as an interval that spans a whole day.
- `EVENT`. Tags the event expressions in the text. The interpretation of what an event is is taken from TimeML where an event is a cover term for predicates describing situations that happen or occur as well as some, but not all, stative predicates. Events can be denoted by verbs, nouns or adjectives. The TempEval event annotation scheme is somewhat simpler than that used in TimeML, whose complexity was designed to handle event expressions that introduced multiple event instances (consider, e.g. *He taught on Wednesday and Friday*). This complication was not necessary for the TempEval data. The most salient attributes encode tense, aspect, modality and polarity information. For TempEval task C, one extra attribute is added: `mainevent`, with possible values YES and NO.
- `TLINK`. This is a simplified version of the TimeML `TLINK` tag. The relation types for the TimeML version form a fine-grained set based on James Allen's interval logic (Allen, 1983). For TempEval, we use only six relation types including the three core relations BEFORE, AFTER, and OVERLAP, the two less specific relations BEFORE-OR-OVERLAP and OVERLAP-OR-AFTER for ambiguous cases, and finally the relation VAGUE for those cases where no particular relation can be established.

As stated above the `TLINK`s of concern for each task are explicitly included in the training and in the test data. However, in the latter the `relType` attribute of each `TLINK` is set to `UNKNOWN`. For each task the system must replace the `UNKNOWN` values with one of the six allowed values listed above.

The `EVENT` and `TIMEX3` annotations were taken verbatim from TimeBank version 1.2.[2] The annota-

[1] See `http://www.timeml.org` for language specifications and annotation guidelines

[2] TimeBank 1.2 is available for free through the Linguistic Data Consortium, see `http://www.timeml.org` for more

tion procedure for TLINK tags involved dual annotation by seven annotators using a web-based annotation interface. After this phase, three experienced annotators looked at all occurrences where two annotators differed as to what relation type to select and decided on the best option. For task C, there was an extra annotation phase where the main events were marked up. Main events are those events that are syntactically dominant in the sentences.

It should be noted that annotation of temporal relations is not an easy task for humans due to rampant temporal vagueness in natural language. As a result, inter-annotator agreement scores are well below the often kicked-around threshold of 90%, both for the TimeML relation set as well as the TempEval relation set. For TimeML temporal links, an inter-annotator agreement of 0.77 was reported, where agreement was measured by the average of precision and recall. The numbers for TempEval are even lower, with an agreement of 0.72 for anchorings of events to times (tasks A and B) and an agreement of 0.65 for event orderings (task C). Obviously, numbers like this temper the expectations for automatic temporal linking.

The lower number for TempEval came a bit as a surprise because, after all, there were fewer relations to choose form. However, the TempEval annotation task is different in the sense that it did not give the annotator the option to ignore certain pairs of events and made it therefore impossible to skip hard-to-classify temporal relations.

4 Evaluating Temporal Relations

In full temporal annotation, evaluation of temporal annotation runs into the same issues as evaluation of anaphora chains: simple pairwise comparisons may not be the best way to evaluate. In temporal annotation, for example, one may wonder how the response in (1) should be evaluated given the key in (2).

(1) {A before B, A before C, B equals C}
(2) {A after B, A after C, B equals C}

Scoring (1) at 0.33 precision misses the interdependence between the temporal relations. What we need to compare is not individual judgements but two partial orders.

details.

For TempEval however, the tasks are defined in a such a way that a simple pairwise comparison is possible since we do not aim to create a full temporal graph and judgements are made in isolation.

Recall that there are three basic temporal relations (BEFORE, OVERLAP, and AFTER) as well as three disjunctions over this set (BEFORE-OR-OVERLAP, OVERLAP-OR-AFTER and VAGUE). The addition of these disjunctions raises the question of how to score a response of, for example, BEFORE given a key of BEFORE-OR-OVERLAP. We use two scoring schemes: strict and relaxed. The *strict scoring scheme* only counts exact matches as success. For example, if the key is OVERLAP and the response BEFORE-OR-OVERLAP than this is counted as failure. We can use standard definitions of precision and recall

$$Precision = R_c/R$$
$$Recall = R_c/K$$

where R_c is number of correct answers in the response, R the total number of answers in the response, and K the total number of answers in the key. For the *relaxed scoring scheme*, precision and recall are defined as

$$Precision = R_c w/R$$
$$Recall = R_c w/K$$

where $R_c w$ reflects the weighted number of correct answers. A response is not simply counted as 1 (correct) or 0 (incorrect), but is assigned one of the values in table 1.

	B	O	A	B-O	O-A	V
B	1	0	0	0.5	0	0.33
O	0	1	0	0.5	0.5	0.33
A	0	0	1	0	0.5	0.33
B-O	0.5	0.5	0	1	0.5	0.67
O-A	0	0.5	0.5	0.5	1	0.67
V	0.33	0.33	0.33	0.67	0.67	1

Table 1: Evaluation weights

This scheme gives partial credit for disjunctions, but not so much that non-commitment edges out precise assignments. For example, assigning VAGUE as the relation type for every temporal relation results in a precision of 0.33.

5 Participants

Six teams participated in the TempEval tasks. Three of the teams used statistics exclusively, one used a rule-based system and the other two employed a hybrid approach. This section gives a short description of the participating systems.

CU-TMP trained three support vector machine (SVM) models, one for each task. All models used the gold-standard TimeBank features for events and times as well as syntactic features derived from the text. Additionally, the relation types obtained by running the task B system on the training data for Task A and Task C, were added as a feature to the two latter systems. A subset of features was selected using cross-validations on the training data, discarding features whose removal improved the cross-validation F-score. When applied to the test data, the Task B system was run first in order to supply the necessary features to the Task A and Task C systems.

LCC-TE automatically identifies temporal referring expressions, events and temporal relations in text using a hybrid approach, leveraging various NLP tools and linguistic resources at LCC. For temporal expression labeling and normalization, they used a syntactic pattern matching tool that deploys a large set of hand-crafted finite state rules. For event detection, they used a small set of heuristics as well as a lexicon to determine whether or not a token is an event, based on the lemma, part of speech and WordNet senses. For temporal relation discovery, LCC-TE used a large set of syntactic and semantic features as input to a machine learning components.

NAIST-japan defined the temporal relation identification task as a sequence labeling model, in which the target pairs – a `TIMEX3` and an `EVENT` – are linearly ordered in the document. For analyzing the relative positions, they used features from dependency trees which are obtained from a dependency parser. The relative position between the target `EVENT` and a word in the target `TIMEX3` is used as a feature for a machine learning based relation identifier. The relative positions between a word in the target entities and another word are also introduced.

The **USFD** system uses an off-the-shelf Machine Learning suite(WEKA), treating the assignment of temporal relations as a simple classification task. The features used were the ones provided in the TempEval data annotation together with a few features straightforwardly computed from the document without any deeper NLP analysis.

WVALI's approach for discovering intra-sentence temporal relations relies on sentence-level syntactic tree generation, bottom-up propagation of the temporal relations between syntactic constituents, a temporal reasoning mechanism that relates the two targeted temporal entities to their closest ancestor and then to each other, and on conflict resolution heuristics. In establishing the temporal relation between an event and the Document Creation Time (DCT), the temporal expressions directly or indirectly linked to that event are first analyzed and, if no relation is detected, the temporal relation with the DCT is propagated top-down in the syntactic tree. Inter-sentence temporal relations are discovered by applying several heuristics and by using statistical data extracted from the training corpus.

XRCE-T used a rule-based system that relies on a deep syntactic analyzer that was extended to treat temporal expressions. Temporal processing is integrated into a more generic tool, a general purpose linguistic analyzer, and is thus a complement for a better general purpose text understanding system. Temporal analysis is intertwined with syntactico-semantic text processing like deep syntactic analysis and determination of thematic roles. TempEval-specific treatment is performed in a post-processing stage.

6 Results

The results for the six teams are presented in tables 2, 3, and 4.

team	strict			relaxed		
	P	R	F	P	R	F
CU-TMP	0.61	0.61	0.61	0.63	0.63	0.63
LCC-TE	0.59	0.57	0.58	0.61	0.60	0.60
NAIST	0.61	0.61	0.61	0.63	0.63	0.63
USFD*	0.59	0.59	0.59	0.60	0.60	0.60
WVALI	0.62	0.62	0.62	0.64	0.64	0.64
XRCE-T	0.53	0.25	0.34	0.63	0.30	0.41
average	0.59	0.54	0.56	0.62	0.57	0.59
stddev	0.03	0.13	0.10	0.01	0.12	0.08

Table 2: Results for Task A

team	strict			relaxed		
	P	R	F	P	R	F
CU-TMP	0.75	0.75	0.75	0.76	0.76	0.76
LCC-TE	0.75	0.71	0.73	0.76	0.72	0.74
NAIST	0.75	0.75	0.75	0.76	0.76	0.76
USFD*	0.73	0.73	0.73	0.74	0.74	0.74
WVALI	0.80	0.80	0.80	0.81	0.81	0.81
XRCE-T	0.78	0.57	0.66	0.84	0.62	0.71
average	0.76	0.72	0.74	0.78	0.74	0.75
stddev	0.03	0.08	0.05	0.03	0.06	0.03

Table 3: Results for Task B

team	strict			relaxed		
	P	R	F	P	R	F
CU-TMP	0.54	0.54	0.54	0.58	0.58	0.58
LCC-TE	0.55	0.55	0.55	0.58	0.58	0.58
NAIST	0.49	0.49	0.49	0.53	0.53	0.53
USFD*	0.54	0.54	0.54	0.57	0.57	0.57
WVALI	0.54	0.54	0.54	0.64	0.64	0.64
XRCE-T	0.42	0.42	0.42	0.58	0.58	0.58
average	0.51	0.51	0.51	0.58	0.58	0.58
stddev	0.05	0.05	0.05	0.04	0.04	0.04

Table 4: Results for Task C

All tables give precision, recall and f-measure for both the strict and the relaxed scoring scheme, as well as averages and standard deviation on the precision, recall and f-measure numbers. The entry for USFD is starred because the system developers are co-organizers of the TempEval task.[3]

For task A, the f-measure scores range from 0.34 to 0.62 for the strict scheme and from 0.41 to 0.63 for the relaxed scheme. For task B, the scores range from 0.66 to 0.80 (strict) and 0.71 to 0.81 (relaxed). Finally, task C scores range from 0.42 to 0.55 (strict) and from 0.56 to 0.66 (relaxed).

The differences between the systems is not spectacular. WVALI's hybrid approach outperforms the other systems in task B and, using relaxed scoring, in task C as well. But for task A, the winners barely edge out the rest of the field. Similarly, for task C using strict scoring, there is no system that clearly separates itself from the field.

It should be noted that for task A, and in lesser extent for task B, the XRCE-T system has recall scores that are far below all other systems. This seems mostly due to a choice by the developers to not assign a temporal relation if the syntactic analyzer did not find a clear syntactic relation between the two elements that needed to be linked for the TempEval task.

[3]There was a strict separation between people assisting in the annotation of the evaluation corpus and people involved in system development.

7 Conclusion: the Future of Temporal Evaluation

The evaluation approach of TempEval avoids the interdependencies that are inherent to a network of temporal relations, where relations in one part of the network may constrain relations in any other part of the network. To accomplish that, TempEval deliberately focused on subtasks of the larger problem of automatic temporal annotation.

One thing we may want to change to the present TempEval is the definition of task A. Currently, it instructs to temporally link all events in a sentence to all time expressions in the same sentence. In the future we may consider splitting this into two tasks, where one subtask focuses on those anchorings that are very local, like *"...White House spokesman Marlin Fitzwater [said] [late yesterday] that..."*. We expect both inter-annotator agreement and system performance to be higher on this subtask.

There are two research avenues that loom beyond the current TempEval: (1) definition of other subtasks with the ultimate goal of establishing a hierarchy of subtasks ranked on performance of automatic taggers, and (2) an approach to evaluate entire timelines.

Some other temporal linking tasks that can be considered are ordering of consecutive events in a sentence, ordering of events that occur in syntactic subordination relations, ordering events in coordinations, and temporal linking of reporting events to the document creation time. Once enough temporal links from all these subtasks are added to the entire temporal graph, it becomes possible to let confidence scores from the separate subtasks drive a constraint propagation algorithm as proposed in (Allen, 1983), in effect using high-precision relations to constrain lower-precision relations elsewhere in the graph.

With this more complete temporal annotation it is no longer possible to simply evaluate the entire graph by scoring pairwise comparisons. Instead the entire timeline must be evaluated. Initial ideas regarding this focus on transforming the temporal graph of a document into a set of partial orders built around precedence and inclusion relations and then evaluating each of these partial orders using some kind of edit distance measure.[4]

We hope to have taken the first baby steps with the three TempEval tasks.

8 Acknowledgements

We would like to thank all the people who helped prepare the data for TempEval, listed here in no particular order: Amber Stubbs, Jessica Littman, Hongyuan Qiu, Emin Mimaroglu, Emma Barker, Catherine Havasi, Yonit Boussany, Roser Saurí, and Anna Rumshisky.

Thanks also to all participants to this new task: Steven Bethard and James Martin (University of Colorado at Boulder), Congmin Min, Munirathnam Srikanth and Abraham Fowler (Language Computer Corporation), Yuchang Cheng, Masayuki Asahara and Yuji Matsumoto (Nara Institute of Science and Technology), Mark Hepple, Andrea Setzer and Rob Gaizauskas (University of Sheffield), Caroline Hagège and Xavier Tannier (XEROX Research Centre Europe), and Georgiana Puşcaşu (University of Wolverhampton and University of Alicante).

Part of the work in this paper was funded by the DTO/AQUAINT program under grant number N61339-06-C-0140 and part funded by the EU VIKEF project (IST- 2002-507173).

References

James Allen. 1983. Maintaining knowledge about temporal intervals. *Communications of the ACM*, 26(11):832–843.

Bran Boguraev, James Pustejovsky, Rie Ando, and Marc Verhagen. forthcoming. Timebank evolution as a community resource for timeml parsing. *Language Resources and Evaluation*.

Inderjeet Mani, Ben Wellner, Marc Verhagen, Chong Min Lee, and James Pustejovsky. 2006. Machine learning of temporal relations. In *Proceedings of the 44th Annual Meeting of the Association for Computational Linguistics*, Sydney, Australia. ACL.

James Pustejovsky, José Castaño, Robert Ingria, Roser Saurí, Robert Gaizauskas, Andrea Setzer, and Graham Katz. 2003a. TimeML: Robust specification of event and temporal expressions in text. In *Proceedings of the Fifth International Workshop on Computational Semantics (IWCS-5)*, Tilburg, January.

James Pustejovsky, Patrick Hanks, Roser Saurí, Andrew See, Robert Gaizauskas, Andrea Setzer, Dragomir Radev, Beth Sundheim, David Day, Lisa Ferro, and Marcia Lazo. 2003b. The TIMEBANK corpus. In *Proceedings of Corpus Linguistics 2003*, pages 647–656, Lancaster, March.

[4]Edit distance was proposed by Ben Wellner as a way to evaluate partial orders of precedence relations (personal communication).

SemEval-2007 Task 16: Evaluation of Wide Coverage Knowledge Resources

Montse Cuadros
TALP Research Center
Universitat Politécnica de Catalunya
Barcelona, Spain
cuadros@lsi.upc.edu

German Rigau
IXA NLP Group
Euskal Herriko Unibersitatea
Donostia, Spain
german.rigau@ehu.es

Abstract

This task tries to establish the relative quality of available semantic resources (derived by manual or automatic means). The quality of each large-scale knowledge resource is indirectly evaluated on a Word Sense Disambiguation task. In particular, we use Senseval-3 and SemEval-2007 English Lexical Sample tasks as evaluation bechmarks to evaluate the relative quality of each resource. Furthermore, trying to be as neutral as possible with respect the knowledge bases studied, we apply systematically the same disambiguation method to all the resources. A completely different behaviour is observed on both lexical data sets (Senseval-3 and SemEval-2007).

1 Introduction

Using large-scale knowledge bases, such as WordNet (Fellbaum, 1998), has become a usual, often necessary, practice for most current Natural Language Processing (NLP) systems. Even now, building large and rich enough knowledge bases for broad–coverage semantic processing takes a great deal of expensive manual effort involving large research groups during long periods of development. In fact, dozens of person-years have been invested in the development of wordnets for various languages (Vossen, 1998). For example, in more than ten years of manual construction (from version 1.5 to 2.1), WordNet passed from 103,445 semantic relations to 245,509 semantic relations[1]. That is, around one thousand new relations per month. But this data does not seems to be rich enough to support advanced concept-based NLP applications directly. It seems that applications will not scale up to working in open domains without more detailed and rich general-purpose (and also domain-specific) semantic knowledge built by automatic means.

Fortunately, during the last years, the research community has devised a large set of innovative methods and tools for large-scale automatic acquisition of lexical knowledge from structured and unstructured corpora. Among others we can mention eXtended WordNet (Mihalcea and Moldovan, 2001), large collections of semantic preferences acquired from SemCor (Agirre and Martinez, 2001; Agirre and Martinez, 2002) or acquired from British National Corpus (BNC) (McCarthy, 2001), large-scale Topic Signatures for each synset acquired from the web (Agirre and de la Calle, 2004) or acquired from the BNC (Cuadros et al., 2005). Obviously, these semantic resources have been acquired using a very different set of methods, tools and corpora, resulting on a different set of new semantic relations between synsets (or between synsets and words).

Many international research groups are working on knowledge-based WSD using a wide range of approaches (Mihalcea, 2006). However, less attention has been devoted on analysing the quality of each semantic resource. In fact, each resource presents different volume and accuracy figures (Cuadros et al., 2006).

In this paper, we evaluate those resources on the

[1]Symmetric relations are counted only once.

Proceedings of the 4th International Workshop on Semantic Evaluations (SemEval-2007), pages 81–86,
Prague, June 2007.

SemEval-2007 English Lexical Sample task. For comparison purposes, we also include the results of the same resources on the Senseval-3 English Lexical sample task. In both cases, we used only the nominal part of both data sets and we also included some basic baselines.

2 Evaluation Framework

In order to compare the knowledge resources, all the resources are evaluated as Topic Signatures (TS). That is, word vectors with weights associated to a particular synset. Normally, these word vectors are obtained by collecting from the resource under study the word senses appearing as direct relatives. This simple representation tries to be as neutral as possible with respect to the resources studied.

A common WSD method has been applied to all knowledge resources on the test examples of Senseval-3 and SemEval-2007 English lexical sample tasks. A simple word overlapping counting is performed between the Topic Signature and the test example. The synset having higher overlapping word counts is selected. In fact, this is a very simple WSD method which only considers the topical information around the word to be disambiguated. Finally, we should remark that the results are not skewed (for instance, for resolving ties) by the most frequent sense in WN or any other statistically predicted knowledge.

As an example, table 1 shows a test example of SemEval-2007 corresponding to the first sense of the noun capital. In bold there are the words that appear in its corresponding Topic Signature acquired from the web.

Note that although there are several important related words, the WSD process implements exact word form matching (no preprocessing is performed).

2.1 Basic Baselines

We have designed a number of basic baselines in order to establish a complete evaluation framework for comparing the performance of each semantic resource on the English WSD tasks.

RANDOM: For each target word, this method selects a random sense. This baseline can be considered as a lower-bound.

Baselines	P	R	F1
TRAIN	65.1	65.1	65.1
TRAIN-MFS	54.5	54.5	54.5
WN-MFS	53.0	53.0	53.0
SEMCOR-MFS	49.0	49.1	49.0
RANDOM	19.1	19.1	19.1

Table 2: P, R and F1 results for English Lexical Sample Baselines of Senseval-3

SemCor MFS (SEMCOR-MFS): This method selects the most frequent sense of the target word in SemCor.

WordNet MFS (WN-MFS): This method selects the first sense in WN1.6 of the target word.

TRAIN-MFS: This method selects the most frequent sense in the training corpus of the target word.

Train Topic Signatures (TRAIN): This baseline uses the training corpus to directly build a Topic Signature using TFIDF measure for each word sense. Note that this baseline can be considered as an upper-bound of our evaluation.

Table 2 presents the precision (P), recall (R) and F1 measure (harmonic mean of recall and precision) of the different baselines in the English Lexical Sample exercise of Senseval-3. In this table, TRAIN has been calculated with a vector size of at maximum 450 words. As expected, RANDOM baseline obtains the poorest result. The most frequent senses obtained from SemCor (SEMCOR-MFS) and WN (WN-MFS) are both below the most frequent sense of the training corpus (TRAIN-MFS). However, all of them are far below the Topic Signatures acquired using the training corpus (TRAIN).

Table 3 presents the precision (P), recall (R) and F1 measure (harmonic mean of recall and precision) of the different baselines in the English Lexical Sample exercise of SemEval-2007. Again, TRAIN has been calculated with a vector size of at maximum 450 words. As before, RANDOM baseline obtains the poorest result. The most frequent senses obtained from SemCor (SEMCOR-MFS) and WN (WN-MFS) are both far below the most frequent sense of the training corpus (TRAIN-MFS), and all of them are below the Topic Signatures acquired using the training corpus (TRAIN).

Comparing both lexical sample sets, SemEval-2007 data appears to be more skewed and simple for WSD systems than the data set from Senseval-3: less

<instance id="19:0@11@wsj/01/wsj_0128@wsj@en@on" docsrc="wsj"> <context>
" A sweeping restructuring of the industry is possible . " Standard & Poor 's Corp. says First Boston , Shearson and Drexel Burnham Lambert Inc. , in particular , are likely to have difficulty shoring up their **credit** standing in months ahead . What worries credit-rating concerns the most is that Wall Street firms are taking long-term **risks** with their own <head> **capital** </head> via leveraged buy-out and junk bond financings . That 's a departure from their traditional practice of transferring almost all **financing** risks to **investors** . Whereas conventional securities financings are structured to be sold quickly , Wall Street 's new penchant for leveraged buy-outs and junk bonds is resulting in long-term lending commitments that stretch out for months or years .
</context> </instance>

Table 1: Example of test id for capital#n which its correct sense is 1

Baselines	P	R	F1
TRAIN	87.6	87.6	87.6
TRAIN-MFS	81.2	79.6	80.4
WN-MFS	66.2	59.9	62.9
SEMCOR-MFS	42.4	38.4	40.3
RANDOM	27.4	27.4	27.4

Table 3: P, R and F1 results for English Lexical Sample Baselines of SemEval-2007

polysemous (as shown by the RANDOM baseline), less similar than SemCor word sense frequency distributions (as shown by SemCor-MFS), more similar to the first sense of WN (as shown by WN-MFS), much more skewed to the first sense of the training corpus (as shown by TRAIN-MFS), and much more easy to be learned (as shown by TRAIN).

3 Large scale knowledge Resources

The evaluation presented here covers a wide range of large-scale semantic resources: WordNet (WN) (Fellbaum, 1998), eXtended WordNet (Mihalcea and Moldovan, 2001), large collections of semantic preferences acquired from SemCor (Agirre and Martinez, 2001; Agirre and Martinez, 2002) or acquired from the BNC (McCarthy, 2001), large-scale Topic Signatures for each synset acquired from the web (Agirre and de la Calle, 2004) or SemCor (Landes et al., 2006).

Although these resources have been derived using different WN versions, using the technology for the automatic alignment of wordnets (Daudé et al., 2003), most of these resources have been integrated into a common resource called Multilingual Central Repository (MCR) (Atserias et al., 2004) maintaining the compatibility among all the knowledge resources which use a particular WN version as a sense repository. Furthermore, these mappings allow to port the knowledge associated to a particular WN version to the rest of WN versions.

The current version of the MCR contains 934,771 semantic relations between synsets, most of them acquired by automatic means. This represents almost four times larger than the Princeton WordNet (245,509 unique semantic relations in WordNet 2.1).

Hereinafter we will refer to each semantic resource as follows:

WN (Fellbaum, 1998): This resource uses the direct relations encoded in WN1.6 or WN2.0 (for instance, tree#n#1–hyponym–>teak#n#2). We also tested WN^2 (using relations at distances 1 and 2), WN^3 (using relations at distances 1 to 3) and WN^4 (using relations at distances 1 to 4).

XWN (Mihalcea and Moldovan, 2001): This resource uses the direct relations encoded in eXtended WN (for instance, teak#n#2–gloss–>wood#n#1).

WN+XWN: This resource uses the direct relations included in WN and XWN. We also tested $(WN+XWN)^2$ (using either WN or XWN relations at distances 1 and 2, for instance, tree#n#1–related–>wood#n#1).

spBNC (McCarthy, 2001): This resource contains 707,618 selectional preferences acquired for subjects and objects from BNC.

spSemCor (Agirre and Martinez, 2002): This resource contains the selectional preferences acquired for subjects and objects from SemCor (for instance, read#v#1–tobj–>book#n#1).

MCR (Atserias et al., 2004): This resource uses the direct relations included in MCR but excluding spBNC because of its poor performance. Thus, MCR contains the direct relations from WN (as tree#n#1–hyponym–>teak#n#2), XWN (as teak#n#2–gloss–>wood#n#1), and spSemCor (as read#v#1–tobj–>book#n#1) but not the indi-

Source	#relations
Princeton WN1.6	138,091
Selectional Preferences from SemCor	203,546
New relations from Princeton WN2.0	42,212
Gold relations from eXtended WN	17,185
Silver relations from eXtended WN	239,249
Normal relations from eXtended WN	294,488
Total	934,771

Table 4: Semantic relations uploaded in the MCR

rect relations of $(WN+XWN)^2$ (tree#n#1–related–>wood#n#1). We also tested MCR^2 (using relations at distances 1 and 2), which also integrates $(WN+XWN)^2$ relations.

Table 4 shows the number of semantic relations between synset pairs in the MCR.

3.1 Topic Signatures

Topic Signatures (TS) are word vectors related to a particular topic (Lin and Hovy, 2000). Topic Signatures are built by retrieving context words of a target topic from large corpora. In our case, we consider word senses as topics.

For this study, we use two different large-scale Topic Signatures. The first constitutes one of the largest available semantic resource with around 100 million relations (between synsets and words) acquired from the web (Agirre and de la Calle, 2004). The second has been derived directly from SemCor.

TSWEB[2]: Inspired by the work of (Leacock et al., 1998), these Topic Signatures were constructed using monosemous relatives from WordNet (synonyms, hypernyms, direct and indirect hyponyms, and siblings), querying Google and retrieving up to one thousand snippets per query (that is, a word sense), extracting the words with distinctive frequency using TFIDF. For these experiments, we used at maximum the first 700 words of each TS.

TSSEM: These Topic Signatures have been constructed using the part of SemCor having all words tagged by PoS, lemmatized and sense tagged according to WN1.6 totalizing 192,639 words. For each word-sense appearing in SemCor, we gather all sentences for that word sense, building a TS using TFIDF for all word-senses co-occurring in those sentences.

[2] `http://ixa.si.ehu.es/Ixa/resources/sensecorpus`

political_party#n#1	2.3219
party#n#1	2.3219
election#n#1	1.0926
nominee#n#1	0.4780
candidate#n#1	0.4780
campaigner#n#1	0.4780
regime#n#1	0.3414
identification#n#1	0.3414
government#n#1	0.3414
designation#n#3	0.3414
authorities#n#1	0.3414

Table 5: Topic Signatures for party#n#1 obtained from Semcor (11 out of 719 total word senses)

In table 5, there is an example of the first word-senses we calculate from party#n#1.

The total number of relations between WN synsets acquired from SemCor is 932,008.

4 Evaluating each resource

Table 6 presents ordered by F1 measure, the performance of each knowledge resource on Senseval-3 and the average size of the TS per word-sense. The average size of the TS per word-sense is the number of words associated to a synset on average. Obviously, the best resources would be those obtaining better performances with a smaller number of associated words per synset. The best results for precision, recall and F1 measures are shown in bold. We also mark in italics those resources using non-direct relations.

Surprisingly, the best results are obtained by TSSEM (with F1 of 52.4). The lowest result is obtained by the knowledge directly gathered from WN mainly because of its poor coverage (R of 18.4 and F1 of 26.1). Also interesting, is that the knowledge integrated in the MCR although partly derived by automatic means performs much better in terms of precision, recall and F1 measures than using them separately (F1 with 18.4 points higher than WN, 9.1 than XWN and 3.7 than spSemCor).

Despite its small size, the resources derived from SemCor obtain better results than its counterparts using much larger corpora (TSSEM vs. TSWEB and spSemCor vs. spBNC).

Regarding the basic baselines, all knowledge resources surpass RANDOM, but none achieves neither WN-MFS, TRAIN-MFS nor TRAIN. Only

KB	P	R	F1	Av. Size
TSSEM	**52.5**	**52.4**	**52.4**	103
MCR^2	45.1	45.1	45.1	26,429
MCR	45.3	43.7	44.5	129
spSemCor	43.1	38.7	40.8	56
(WN+XWN)^2	38.5	38.0	38.3	5,730
WN+XWN	40.0	34.2	36.8	74
TSWEB	36.1	35.9	36.0	1,721
XWN	38.8	32.5	35.4	69
WN^3	35.0	34.7	34.8	503
WN^4	33.2	33.1	33.2	2,346
WN^2	33.1	27.5	30.0	105
spBNC	36.3	25.4	29.9	128
WN	44.9	18.4	26.1	14

Table 6: P, R and F1 fine-grained results for the resources evaluated individually at Senseval-03 English Lexical Sample Task.

TSSEM obtains better results than SEMCOR-MFS and is very close to the most frequent sense of WN (WN-MFS) and the training (TRAIN-MFS).

Table 7 presents ordered by F1 measure, the performance of each knowledge resource on SemEval-2007 and its average size of the TS per word-sense[3]. The best results for precision, recall and F1 measures are shown in bold. We also mark in italics those resources using non-direct relations.

Interestingly, on SemEval-2007, all the knowledge resources behave differently. Now, the best results are obtained by (WN+XWN)^2 (with F1 of 52.9), followed by TSWEB (with F1 of 51.0). The lowest result is obtained by the knowledge encoded in spBNC mainly because of its poor precision (P of 24.4 and F1 of 20.8).

Regarding the basic baselines, spBNC, WN (and also WN^2 and WN^4) and spSemCor do not surpass RANDOM, and none achieves neither WN-MFS, TRAIN-MFS nor TRAIN. Now, WN+XWN, XWN, TSWEB and (WN+XWN)^2 obtain better results than SEMCOR-MFS but far below the most frequent sense of WN (WN-MFS) and the training (TRAIN-MFS).

5 Combination of Knowledge Resources

In order to evaluate deeply the contribution of each knowledge resource, we also provide some results of the combined outcomes of several resources. The

[3]The average size is different with respect Senseval-3 because the words selected for this task are different

KB	P	R	F1	Av. Size
(WN+XWN)^2	**54.9**	**51.1**	**52.9**	5,153
TSWEB	54.8	47.8	51.0	700
XWN	50.1	39.8	44.4	96
WN+XWN	45.4	36.8	40.7	101
MCR	40.2	35.5	37.7	149
TSSEM	35.1	32.7	33.9	428
MCR^2	32.4	29.5	30.9	24,896
WN^3	29.3	26.3	27.7	584
WN^2	25.9	27.4	26.6	72
spSemCor	31.4	23.0	26.5	51.0
WN^4	26.1	23.9	24.9	2,710
WN	36.8	16.1	22.4	13
spBNC	24.4	18.1	20.8	290

Table 7: P, R and F1 fine-grained results for the resources evaluated individually at SemEval-2007, English Lexical Sample Task .

KB	Rank
MCR+(WN+XWN)^2+TSWEB+TSSEM	**55.5**

Table 8: F1 fine-grained results for the 4 system-combinations on Senseval-3

combinations are performed following a very basic strategy (Brody et al., 2006).

Rank-Based Combination (Rank): Each semantic resource provides a ranking of senses of the word to be disambiguated. For each sense, its placements according to each of the methods are summed and the sense with the lowest total placement (closest to first place) is selected.

Table 8 presents the F1 measure result with respect this method when combining four different semantic resources on the Senseval-3 test set.

Regarding the basic baselines, this combination outperforms the most frequent sense of SemCor (SEMCOR-MFS with F1 of 49.1), WN (WN-MFS with F1 of 53.0) and, the training data (TRAIN-MFS with F1 of 54.5).

Table 9 presents the F1 measure result with respect the rank mthod when combining the same four different semantic resources on the SemEval-2007 test set.

KB	Rank
MCR+(WN+XWN)^2+TSWEB+TSSEM	38.9

Table 9: F1 fine-grained results for the 4 system-combinations on SemEval-2007

In this case, the combination of the four resources obtains much lower result. Regarding the baselines, this combination performs lower than the most frequent senses from SEMCOR, WN or the training data. This could be due to the poor individual performance of the knowledge derived from SemCor (spSemCor, TSSEM and MCR, which integrates spSemCor). Possibly, in this case, the knowledge comming from SemCor is counterproductive. Interestingly, the knowledge derived from other sources (XWN from WN glosses and TSWEB from the web) seems to be more robust with respect corpus changes.

6 Conclusions

Although this task had no participants, we provide the performances of a large set of knowledge resources on two different test sets: Senseval-3 and SemEval-2007 English Lexical Sample task. We also provide the results of a system combination of four large-scale semantic resources. When evaluated on Senseval-3, the combination of knowledge sources surpass the most-frequent classifiers. However, a completely different behaviour is observed on SemEval-2007 data test. In fact, both corpora present very different characteristics. The results show that some resources seems to be less dependant than others to corpus changes.

Obviously, these results suggest that much more research on acquiring, evaluating and using large-scale semantic resources should be addressed.

7 Acknowledgements

We want to thank the valuable comments of the anonymous reviewers. This work has been partially supported by the projects KNOW (TIN2006-15049-C03-01) and ADIMEN (EHU06/113).

References

E. Agirre and O. Lopez de la Calle. 2004. Publicly available topic signatures for all wordnet nominal senses. In *Proceedings of LREC*, Lisbon, Portugal.

E. Agirre and D. Martinez. 2001. Learning class-to-class selectional preferences. In *Proceedings of CoNLL*, Toulouse, France.

E. Agirre and D. Martinez. 2002. Integrating selectional preferences in wordnet. In *Proceedings of GWC*, Mysore, India.

J. Atserias, L. Villarejo, G. Rigau, E. Agirre, J. Carroll, B. Magnini, and Piek Vossen. 2004. The meaning multilingual central repository. In *Proceedings of GWC*, Brno, Czech Republic.

S. Brody, R. Navigli, and M. Lapata. 2006. Ensemble methods for unsupervised wsd. In *Proceedings of COLING-ACL*, pages 97–104.

M. Cuadros, L. Padró, and G. Rigau. 2005. Comparing methods for automatic acquisition of topic signatures. In *Proceedings of RANLP*, Borovets, Bulgaria.

M. Cuadros, L. Padró, and G. Rigau. 2006. An empirical study for automatic acquisition of topic signatures. In *Proceedings of GWC*, pages 51–59.

J. Daudé, L. Padró, and G. Rigau. 2003. Validation and Tuning of Wordnet Mapping Techniques. In *Proceedings of RANLP*, Borovets, Bulgaria.

C. Fellbaum, editor. 1998. *WordNet. An Electronic Lexical Database*. The MIT Press.

S. Landes, C. Leacock, and R. Tengi. 2006. Building a semantic concordance of english. In *WordNet: An electronic lexical database and some applications. MIT Press, Cambridge,MA., 1998*, pages 97–104.

C. Leacock, M. Chodorow, and G. Miller. 1998. Using Corpus Statistics and WordNet Relations for Sense Identification. *Computational Linguistics*, 24(1):147–166.

C. Lin and E. Hovy. 2000. The automated acquisition of topic signatures for text summarization. In *Proceedings of COLING*. Strasbourg, France.

D. McCarthy. 2001. *Lexical Acquisition at the Syntax-Semantics Interface: Diathesis Aternations, Subcategorization Frames and Selectional Preferences*. Ph.D. thesis, University of Sussex.

R. Mihalcea and D. Moldovan. 2001. extended wordnet: Progress report. In *Proceedings of NAACL Workshop on WordNet and Other Lexical Resources*, Pittsburgh, PA.

R. Mihalcea. 2006. Knowledge based methods for word sense disambiguation. In *E. Agirre and P. Edmonds (Eds.) Word Sense Disambiguation: Algorithms and applications.*, volume 33 of *Text, Speech and Language Technology*. Springer.

P. Vossen, editor. 1998. *EuroWordNet: A Multilingual Database with Lexical Semantic Networks* . Kluwer Academic Publishers .

SemEval-2007 Task 17: English Lexical Sample, SRL and All Words

Sameer S. Pradhan
BBN Technologies,
Cambridge, MA 02138

Edward Loper
University of Pennsylvania,
Philadelphia, PA 19104

Dmitriy Dligach and Martha Palmer
University of Colorado,
Boulder, CO 80303

Abstract

This paper describes our experience in preparing the data and evaluating the results for three subtasks of SemEval-2007 Task-17 – Lexical Sample, Semantic Role Labeling (SRL) and All-Words respectively. We tabulate and analyze the results of participating systems.

1 Introduction

Correctly disambiguating words (WSD), and correctly identifying the semantic relationships between those words (SRL), is an important step for building successful natural language processing applications, such as text summarization, question answering, and machine translation. SemEval-2007 Task-17 (*English Lexical Sample, SRL and All-Words*) focuses on both of these challenges, WSD and SRL, using annotated English text taken from the Wall Street Journal and the Brown Corpus. It includes three subtasks: i) the traditional All-Words task comprising fine-grained word sense disambiguation using a 3,500 word section of the Wall Street Journal, annotated with WordNet 2.1 sense tags, ii) a Lexical Sample task for coarse-grained word sense disambiguation on a selected set of lexemes, and iii) Semantic Role Labeling, using two different types of arguments, on the same subset of lexemes.

2 Word Sense Disambiguation

2.1 English fine-grained All-Words

In this task we measure the ability of systems to identify the correct fine-grained WordNet 2.1 word sense for all the verbs and head words of their arguments.

2.1.1 Data Preparation

We began by selecting three articles `wsj_0105.mrg` (on homelessness), `wsj_0186.mrg` (about a book on corruption), and `wsj_0239.mrg` (about hot-air ballooning) from a section of the WSJ corpus that has been Treebanked and PropBanked. All instances of verbs were identified using the Treebank part-of-speech tags, and also the headwords of their noun arguments (using the PropBank and standard headword rules). The locations of the sentences containing them as well as the locations of the verbs and the nouns within these sentences were recorded for subsequent sense-annotation. A total of 465 lemmas were selected from about 3500 words of text.

We use a tool called `STAMP` written by Benjamin Snyder for sense-annotation of these instances. `STAMP` accepts a list of pointers to the instances that need to be annotated. These pointers consist of the name of the file where the instance is located, the sentence number of the instance, and finally, the word number of the ambiguous word within that sentence. These pointers were obtained as described in the previous paragraph. `STAMP` also requires a sense inventory, which must be stored in XML format. This sense inventory was obtained by querying WordNet 2.1 and storing the output as a

Proceedings of the 4th International Workshop on Semantic Evaluations (SemEval-2007), pages 87–92,
Prague, June 2007. ©2007 Association for Computational Linguistics

set of XML files (one for each word to be annotated) prior to tagging. STAMP works by displaying to the user the sentence to be annotated with the target word highlighted along with the previous and the following sentences and the senses from the sense inventory. The user can select one of the senses and move on to the next instance.

Two linguistics students annotated the words with WordNet 2.1 senses. Our annotators examined each instance upon which they disagreed and resolved their disagreements. Finally, we converted the resulting data to the Senseval format. For this dataset, we got an inter-annotator agreement (ITA) of 72% on verbs and 86% for nouns.

2.1.2 Results

A total of 14 systems were evaluated on the All Words task. These results are shown in Table 1. We used the standard Senseval scorer – `scorer2`[1] to score the systems. All the F-scores[2] in this table as well as other tables in this paper are accompanied by a 95% confidence interval calculated using the bootstrap resampling procedure.

2.2 OntoNotes English Lexical Sample WSD

It is quite well accepted at this point that it is difficult to achieve high inter-annotator agreement on the fine-grained WordNet style senses, and without a corpus with high annotator agreement, automatic learning methods cannot perform at a level that would be acceptable for a downstream application. OntoNotes (Hovy et al., 2006) is a project that has annotated several layers of semantic information – including word senses, at a high inter-annotator agreement of over 90%. Therefore we decided to use this data for the lexical sample task.

2.2.1 Data

All the data for this task comes from the 1M word WSJ Treebank. For the convenience of the participants who wanted to use syntactic parse information as features using an off-the-shelf syntactic parser, we decided to compose the training data of Sections 02-21. For the test sets, we use data from Sections 01, 22, 23 and 24. Fortunately, the distribution of words was amenable to an acceptable number of instances for each lemma in the test set. We selected a total of 100 lemmas (65 verbs and 35 nouns) considering the degree of polysemy and total instances that were annotated. The average ITA for these is over 90%.

	Train	Test	Total
Verb	8988	2292	11280
Noun	13293	2559	15852
Total	22281	4851	

Table 2: The number of instances for Verbs and Nouns in the Train and Test sets for the Lexical Sample WSD task.

The training and test set composition is described in Table 2. The distribution across all the verbs and nouns is displayed in Table 4

2.2.2 Results

A total of 13 systems were evaluated on the Lexical Sample task. Table 3 shows the Precision/Recall for all these systems. The same scoring software was used to score this task as well.

2.2.3 Discussion

For the all words task, the baseline performance using the most frequent WordNet sense for the lemmas is 51.4. The top-performing system was a supervised system that used a Maximum Entropy classifier, and got a Precision/Recall of 59.1% – about 8 points higher than the baseline. Since the coarse and fine-grained disambiguation tasks have been part of the two previous Senseval competitions, and we happen to have access to that data, we can take this opportunity to look at the disambiguation performance trend. Although different test sets were used for every evaluation, we can get a rough indication of the trend. For the fine-grained All Words sense tagging task, which has always used WordNet, the system performance has ranged from our 59% to 65.2 (Senseval3, (Decadt et al., 2004)) to 69% (Seneval2, (Chklovski and Mihalcea, 2002)). Because of time constraints on the data preparation, this year's task has proportionally more verbs and fewer nouns than previous All-Words English tasks, which may account for the lower scores.

As expected, the Lexical Sample task using coarse

[1] http://www.cse.unt.edu/~rada/senseval/senseval3/scoring/

[2] scorer2 reports Precision and Recall scores for each system. For a system that attempts all the words, both Precision and Recall are the same. Since a few systems had missing answers, they got different Precision and Recall scores. Therefore, for ranking purposes, we consolidated them into an F-score.

Rank	Participant	System ID	Classifier	F
1	Stephen Tratz <stephen.tratz@pnl.gov>	PNNL	MaxEnt	59.1±4.5
2	Hwee Tou Ng <nght@comp.nus.edu.sg>	NUS-PT	SVM	58.7±4.5
3	Rada Mihalcea <rada@cs.unt.edu>	UNT-Yahoo	Memory-based	58.3±4.5
4	Cai Junfu <caijunfu@gmail.com>	NUS-ML	naive Bayes	57.6±4.5
5	Oier Lopez de Lacalle <jibloleo@si.ehu.es>	UBC-ALM	kNN	54.4±4.5
6	David Martinez <davidm@csse.unimelb.edu.au>	UBC-UMB-2	kNN	54.0±4.5
7	Jonathan Chang <jcone@princeton.edu>	PU-BCD	Exponential Model	53.9±4.5
8	Radu ION <radu@racai.ro>	RACAI	Unsupervised	52.7±4.5
9	*Most Frequent WordNet Sense*	Baseline	N/A	51.4±4.5
10	Davide Buscaldi <dbuscaldi@dsic.upv.es>	UPV-WSD	Unsupervised	46.9±4.5
11	Sudip Kumar Naskar <sudip.naskar@gmail.com>	JU-SKNSB	Unsupervised	40.2±4.5
12	David Martinez <davidm@csse.unimelb.edu.au>	UBC-UMB-1	Unsupervised	39.9±4.5
14	Rafael Berlanga <berlanga@uji.es>	tkb-uo	Unsupervised	32.5±4.5
15	Jordan Boyd-Graber <jbg@princeton.edu>	PUTOP	Unsupervised	13.2±4.5

Table 1: System Performance for the All-Words task.

Rank	Participant	System	Classifier	F
1	Cai Junfu <caijunfu@gmail.com>	NUS-ML	SVM	88.7±1.2
2	Oier Lopez de Lacalle <jibloleo@si.ehu.es>	UBC-ALM	SVD+kNN	86.9±1.2
3	Zheng-Yu Niu <niu_zy@hotmail.com>	I2R	Supervised	86.4±1.2
4	Lucia Specia <lspecia@gmail.com>	USP-IBM-2	SVM	85.7±1.2
5	Lucia Specia <lspecia@gmail.com>	USP-IBM-1	ILP	85.1±1.2
5	Deniz Yuret <dyuret@ku.edu.tr>	KU	Semi-supervised	85.1±1.2
6	Saarikoski <harri.saarikoski@helsinki.fi>	OE	naive Bayes, SVM	83.8±1.2
7	University of Technology Brno	VUTBR	naive Bayes	80.3±1.2
8	Ana Zelaia <ana.zelaia@ehu.es>	UBC-ZAS	SVD+kNN	79.9±1.2
9	Carlo Strapparava <strappa@itc.it>	ITC-irst	SVM	79.6±1.2
10	*Most frequent sense in training*	Baseline	N/A	78.0±1.2
11	Toby Hawker <toby@it.usyd.edu.au>	USYD	SVM	74.3±1.2
12	Siddharth Patwardhan <sidd@cs.utah.edu>	UMND1	Unsupervised	53.8±1.2
13	Saif Mohammad <smm@cs.toronto.edu>	Tor	Unsupervised	52.1±1.2
-	Toby Hawker <toby@it.usyd.edu.au>	USYD*	SVM	89.1±1.2
-	Carlo Strapparava <strappa@itc.it>	ITC*	SVM	89.1±1.2

Table 3: System Performance for the OntoNotes Lexical Sample task. Systems marked with an * were post-competition bug-fix submissions.

grained senses provides consistently higher performance than previous more fine-grained Lexical Sample Tasks. The high scores here were foreshadowed in an evaluation involving a subset of the data last summer (Chen et al., 2006). Note that the best system performance is now closely approaching the ITA for this data of over 90%. Table 4 shows the performance of the top 8 systems on all the individual verbs and nouns in the test set. Owing to space constraints we have removed some lemmas that have perfect or almost perfect accuracies. At the right are mentioned the average, minimum and maximum performances of the teams per lemma, and at the bottom are the average scores per lemma (without considering the lemma frequencies) and broken down by verbs and nouns. A gap of about 10 points between the verb and noun performance seems to indicate that in general the verbs were more difficult than the nouns. However, this might just be owing to this particular test sample having more verbs with higher perplexities, and maybe even ones that are indeed difficult to disambiguate – in spite of high human agreement. The hope is that better knowledge sources can overcome the gap still existing between the system performance and human agreement. Overall, however, this data indicates that the approach suggested by (Palmer, 2000) and that is being adopted in the ongoing OntoNotes project (Hovy et al., 2006) does result in higher system performance. Whether or not the more coarse-grained senses are effective in improving natural language processing applications remains to be seen.

Lemma	S	s	T	t	1	2	3	4	5	6	7	8	Average	Min	Max
turn.v	13	8	340	62	58	**61**	40	55	52	53	27	44	49	27	61
go.v	12	6	244	61	64	**69**	38	66	43	46	31	39	49	31	69
come.v	10	9	186	43	49	46	56	**60**	37	23	23	49	43	23	60
set.v	9	5	174	42	**62**	50	52	57	50	57	36	50	52	36	62
hold.v	8	7	129	24	58	46	50	54	54	38	50	**67**	52	38	67
raise.v	7	6	147	34	**50**	44	29	26	44	26	24	12	32	12	50
work.v	7	5	230	43	**74**	65	65	65	72	67	46	65	65	46	74
keep.v	7	6	260	80	56	54	52	**64**	56	52	48	51	54	48	64
start.v	6	4	214	38	53	50	47	**55**	45	42	37	45	47	37	55
lead.v	6	6	165	39	69	69	**85**	69	51	69	36	46	62	36	85
see.v	6	5	158	54	56	54	46	54	**57**	52	48	48	52	46	57
ask.v	6	3	348	58	**84**	72	72	78	76	52	67	66	71	52	84
find.v	5	3	174	28	**93**	**93**	86	89	82	82	75	86	86	75	93
fix.v	5	3	32	2	**50**	**50**	**50**	**50**	**50**	0	0	**50**	38	0	50
buy.v	5	3	164	46	**83**	80	80	**83**	78	76	70	76	78	70	83
begin.v	4	2	114	48	**83**	65	75	69	79	56	50	56	67	50	83
kill.v	4	1	111	16	**88**	**88**	**88**	**88**	**88**	**88**	**88**	81	87	81	88
join.v	4	4	68	18	44	50	50	39	56	**57**	39	44	47	39	57
end.v	4	3	135	21	**90**	86	86	**90**	62	87	86	67	82	62	90
do.v	4	2	207	61	92	90	90	**93**	**93**	90	85	84	90	84	93
examine.v	3	2	26	3	**100**	**100**	67	**100**	**100**	67	**100**	33	83	33	100
report.v	3	2	128	35	89	**91**	**91**	**91**	**91**	**91**	**91**	86	90	86	91
regard.v	3	3	40	14	**93**	**93**	86	86	64	86	57	**93**	82	57	93
recall.v	3	1	49	15	**100**	**100**	87	87	93	87	87	87	91	87	100
prove.v	3	2	49	22	**90**	88	82	80	**90**	86	70	74	82	70	90
claim.v	3	2	54	15	67	73	80	80	80	80	80	**87**	78	67	87
build.v	3	3	119	46	**74**	67	**74**	61	54	**74**	61	72	67	54	74
feel.v	3	3	347	51	71	69	69	74	**76**	69	61	71	70	61	76
care.v	3	3	69	7	43	43	43	43	**100**	29	57	57	52	29	100
contribute.v	2	2	35	18	67	**72**	**72**	67	50	61	50	67	63	50	72
maintain.v	2	2	61	10	80	80	70	**100**	80	90	90	80	84	70	100
complain.v	2	1	32	14	**93**	86	86	86	86	86	86	79	86	79	93
propose.v	2	2	34	14	**100**	86	**100**	86	**100**	93	79	79	90	79	100
promise.v	2	2	50	8	**88**	**88**	75	**88**	75	75	62	**88**	80	62	88
produce.v	2	2	115	44	**82**	**82**	77	73	75	75	77	80	78	73	82
prepare.v	2	2	54	18	**94**	83	89	89	83	86	83	83	86	83	94
explain.v	2	2	85	18	**94**	89	**94**	89	**94**	89	89	**94**	92	89	94
believe.v	2	2	202	55	**87**	78	78	86	84	78	74	80	81	74	87
occur.v	2	2	47	22	86	73	91	**96**	86	**96**	86	82	87	73	96
grant.v	2	2	19	5	**100**	80	80	80	40	80	60	80	75	40	100
enjoy.v	2	2	56	14	50	57	57	50	**64**	57	50	57	55	50	64
need.v	2	2	195	56	**89**	82	86	**89**	86	78	70	70	81	70	89
disclose.v	1	1	55	14	**93**	**93**	**93**	**93**	**93**	**93**	**93**	**93**	93	93	93
point.n	9	6	469	150	91	91	89	91	**92**	87	84	79	88	79	92
position.n	7	6	268	45	**78**	**78**	**78**	53	56	65	58	64	66	53	78
defense.n	7	7	120	21	**57**	48	52	43	48	29	48	48	46	29	57
carrier.n	7	3	111	21	**71**	**71**	**71**	**71**	67	**71**	**71**	62	70	62	71
order.n	7	4	346	57	93	**95**	93	91	93	92	90	91	92	90	95
exchange.n	5	3	363	61	**92**	90	**92**	85	90	88	82	79	87	79	92
system.n	5	3	450	70	**79**	73	66	67	59	63	63	61	66	59	79
source.n	5	5	152	35	**86**	80	80	63	83	68	60	29	69	29	86
space.n	5	2	67	14	93	**100**	93	93	93	86	86	71	89	71	100
base.n	5	4	92	20	75	**80**	75	50	65	40	50	75	64	40	80
authority.n	4	3	90	21	**86**	**86**	81	62	71	33	71	81	71	33	86
people.n	4	4	754	115	**96**	96	95	96	95	90	91	91	94	90	96
chance.n	4	3	91	15	60	67	60	60	67	**73**	20	**73**	60	20	73
part.n	4	3	481	71	90	90	92	**97**	90	74	66	66	83	66	97
hour.n	4	2	187	48	83	85	**92**	83	77	90	58	**92**	83	58	92
development.n	3	3	180	29	**100**	79	86	79	76	62	79	62	78	62	100
president.n	3	3	879	177	**98**	97	**98**	97	93	96	97	85	95	85	98
network.n	3	3	152	55	91	87	**98**	89	84	88	87	82	88	82	98
future.n	3	3	350	146	97	96	94	97	83	**98**	89	85	92	83	98
effect.n	3	2	178	30	**97**	93	80	93	80	90	77	83	87	77	97
state.n	3	3	617	72	85	**86**	**86**	83	82	79	83	82	83	79	86
power.n	3	3	251	47	**92**	87	87	81	77	77	77	74	81	74	92
bill.n	3	3	404	102	98	**99**	98	96	90	96	96	22	87	22	99
area.n	3	3	326	37	**89**	73	65	68	84	70	68	65	73	65	89
job.n	3	3	188	39	85	80	77	**90**	80	82	69	82	80	69	90
management.n	2	2	284	45	89	78	87	73	**98**	76	67	64	79	64	98
condition.n	2	2	132	34	**91**	82	82	56	76	78	74	76	77	56	91
policy.n	2	2	331	39	95	**97**	**97**	87	95	**97**	90	64	90	64	97
rate.n	2	2	1009	145	90	88	**92**	81	92	89	88	91	89	81	92
drug.n	2	2	205	46	94	94	**96**	78	94	94	87	78	89	78	96
			Average	Overall	86	83	83	82	82	79	76	77			
				Verbs	78	75	73	76	73	70	65	70			
				Nouns	89	87	86	81	83	80	77	76			

Table 4: All Supervised system performance per predicate. (Column legend – S=number of senses in training; s=number senses appearing more than 3 times; T=instances in training; t=instances in test.; The numbers indicate system ranks.)

3 Semantic Role Labeling

Subtask 2 evaluates Semantic Role Labeling (SRL) systems, where the goal is to locate the constituents which are arguments of a given verb, and to assign them appropriate semantic roles that describe how they relate to the verb. SRL systems are an important building block for many larger semantic systems. For example, in order to determine that question (1a) is answered by sentence (1b), but not by sentence (1c), we must determine the relationships between the relevant verbs (*eat* and *feed*) and their arguments.

(1) a. What do lobsters like to eat?

b. Recent studies have shown that lobsters primarily feed on live fish, dig for clams, sea urchins, and feed on algae and eel-grass.

c. In the early 20th century, Mainers would only eat lobsters because the fish they caught was too valuable to eat themselves.

Traditionally, SRL systems have been trained on either the PropBank corpus (Palmer et al., 2005) – for two years, the CoNLL workshop (Carreras and Màrquez, 2004; Carreras and Màrquez, 2005) has made this their shared task, or the FrameNet corpus – Senseval-3 used this for their shared task (Litkowski, 2004). However, there is still little consensus in the linguistics and NLP communities about what set of role labels are most appropriate. The PropBank corpus avoids this issue by using theory-agnostic labels (ARG0, ARG1, ..., ARG5), and by defining those labels to have only verb-specific meanings. Under this scheme, PropBank can avoid making any claims about how any one verb's arguments relate to other verbs' arguments, or about general distinctions between verb arguments and adjuncts.

However, there are several limitations to this approach. The first is that it can be difficult to make inferences and generalizations based on role labels that are only meaningful with respect to a single verb. Since each role label is verb-specific, we can not confidently determine when two different verbs' arguments have the same role; and since no encoded meaning is associated with each tag, we can not make generalizations across verb classes. In contrast, the use of a shared set of role labels, such as VerbNet roles, would facilitate both inferencing and generalization. VerbNet has more traditional labels such as Agent, Patient, Theme, Beneficiary, etc. (Kipper et al., 2006).

System	Type	Precision	Recall	F
UBC-UPC	Open	84.51	82.24	83.36±0.5
UBC-UPC	Closed	85.04	82.07	83.52±0.5
RTV	Closed	81.82	70.37	75.66±0.6
Without "say"				
UBC-UPC	Open	78.57	74.70	76.60±0.8
UBC-UPC	Closed	78.67	73.94	76.23±0.8
RTV	Closed	74.15	57.85	65.00±0.9

Table 5: System performance on PropBank arguments.

Therefore, we chose to annotate the corpus using two different role label sets: the PropBank role set and the VerbNet role set. VerbNet roles were generated using the SemLink mapping (Loper et al., 2007), which provides a mapping between PropBank and VerbNet role labels. In a small number of cases, no VerbNet role was available (e.g., because VerbNet did not contain the appropriate sense of the verb). In those cases, the PropBank role label was used instead.

We proposed two levels of participation in this task: i) Closed – the systems could use only the annotated data provided and nothing else. ii) Open – where systems could use PropBank data from Sections 02-21, as well as any other resource for training their labelers.

3.1 Data

We selected 50 verbs from the 65 in the lexical sample task for the SRL task. The partitioning into train and test set was done in the same fashion as for the lexical sample task. Since PropBank does not tag any noun predicates, none of the 35 nouns from the lexical sample task were part of this data.

3.2 Results

For each system, we calculated the precision, recall, and F-measure for both role label sets. Scores were calculated using the `srl-eval.pl` script from the CoNLL-2005 scoring package (Carreras and Màrquez, 2005). Only two teams chose to perform the SRL subtask. The performance of these two teams is shown in Table 5 and Table 6.

System	Type	Precision	Recall	F
UBC-UPC	Open	85.31	82.08	83.66±0.5
UBC-UPC	Closed	85.31	82.08	83.66±0.5
RTV	Closed	81.58	70.16	75.44±0.6
Without "say"				
UBC-UPC	Open	79.23	73.88	76.46±0.8
UBC-UPC	Closed	79.23	73.88	76.46±0.8
RTV	Closed	73.63	57.44	64.53±0.9

Table 6: System performance on VerbNet roles.

3.3 Discussion

Given that only two systems participated in the task, it is difficult to form any strong conclusions. It should be noted that since there was no additional VerbNet role data to be used by the Open system, the performance of that on PropBank arguments as well as VerbNet roles is exactly identical. It can be seen that there is almost no difference between the performance of the Open and Closed systems for tagging PropBank arguments. The reason for this is the fact that all the instances of the lemma under consideration was selected from the Propbank corpus, and probably the number of training instances for each lemma as well as the fact that the predicate is such an important feature combine to make the difference negligible. We also realized that more than half of the test instances were contributed by the predicate "say" – the performance over whose arguments is in the high 90s. To remove the effect of "say" we also computed the performances after excluding examples of "say" from the test set. These numbers are shown in the bottom half of the two tables. These results are not directly comparable to the CoNLL-2005 shared task since: i) this test set comprises Sections 01, 22, 23 and 24 as opposed to just Section 23, and ii) this test set comprises data for only 50 predicates as opposed to all the verb predicates in the CoNLL-2005 shared task.

4 Conclusions

The results in the previous discussion seem to confirm the hypothesis that there is a predictable correlation between human annotator agreement and system performance. Given high enough ITA rates we can can hope to build sense disambiguation systems that perform at a level that might be of use to a consuming natural language processing application. It is also encouraging that the more informative VerbNet roles which have better/direct applicability in downstream systems, can also be predicted with almost the same degree of accuracy as the PropBank arguments from which they are mapped.

5 Acknowledgments

We gratefully acknowledge the support of the Defense Advanced Research Projects Agency (DARPA/IPTO) under the GALE program, DARPA/CMO Contract No. HR0011-06-C-0022; National Science Foundation Grant NSF-0415923, Word Sense Disambiguation; the DTO-AQUAINT NBCHC040036 grant under the University of Illinois subcontract to University of Pennsylvania 2003-07911-01; and NSF-ITR-0325646: Domain-Independent Semantic Interpretation.

References

Xavier Carreras and Lluís Màrquez. 2004. Introduction to the CoNLL-2004 shared task: Semantic role labeling. In *Proceedings of CoNLL-2004.*

Xavier Carreras and Lluís Màrquez. 2005. Introduction to the CoNLL-2005 Shared Task: Semantic Role Labeling. In *Proceedings of CoNLL-2005.*

Jinying Chen, Andrew Schein, Lyle Ungar, and Martha Palmer. 2006. An empirical study of the behavior of active learning for word sense disambiguation. In *Proceedings of HLT/NAACL.*

Timothy Chklovski and Rada Mihalcea. 2002. Building a sense tagged corpus with open mind word expert. In *Proceedings of ACL-02 Workshop on WSD.*

Bart Decadt, Véronique Hoste, Walter Daelemans, and Antal Van den Bosch. 2004. GAMBL, genetic algorithm optimization of memory-based wsd. In *Senseval-3.*

Eduard Hovy, Mitchell Marcus, Martha Palmer, Lance Ramshaw, and Ralph Weischedel. 2006. Ontonotes: The 90% solution. In *Proceedings of HLT/NAACL*, June.

Karin Kipper, Anna Korhonen, Neville Ryant, and Martha Palmer. 2006. Extending VerbNet with novel verb classes. In *LREC-06.*

Ken Litkowski. 2004. Senseval-3 task: Automatic labeling of semantic roles. In *Proceedings of Senseval-3.*

Edward Loper, Szu ting Yi, and Martha Palmer. 2007. Combining lexical resources: Mapping between propbank and verbnet. In *Proceedings of the IWCS-7.*

Martha Palmer, Daniel Gildea, and Paul Kingsbury. 2005. The proposition bank: A corpus annotated with semantic roles. *Computational Linguistics*, 31(1):71–106.

Martha Palmer. 2000. Consistent criteria for sense distinctions. *Computers and the Humanities*, 34(1-1):217–222.

Semeval 2007 Task 18: Arabic Semantic Labeling

Mona Diab
Columbia University
mdiab@cs.columbia.edu

Musa Alkhalifa
University of Barcelona
musa@thera-clic.com

Sabri Elkateb
University of Manchester
Sabri.Elkateb@manchester.ac.uk

Christiane Fellbaum
Princeton University
fellbaum@clarity.princeton.edu

Aous Mansouri
University of Colorado, Boulder
aous.mansouri@colorado.edu

Martha Palmer
University of Colorado, Boulder
martha.palmer@colorado.edu

Abstract

In this paper, we present the details of the Arabic Semantic Labeling task. We describe some of the features of Arabic that are relevant for the task. The task comprises two subtasks: Arabic word sense disambiguation and Arabic semantic role labeling. The task focuses on modern standard Arabic.

1 Introduction

Recent years have witnessed a surge in available resources for the Arabic language.[1] The computational linguistics community is just about starting to exploit these resources toward several interesting scientific and engineering goals. The Arabic language is interesting from a computational linguistic perspective. It is significantly different from English hence creating a challenge for existing technology to be easily portable to Arabic. The Arabic language is inherently complex due to its rich morphology and relative free word order. Moreover, with the existence of several interesting varieties, the spoken vernaculars, we are witnessing the emergence of written dialectal Arabic everyday on the web, however there are no set standards for these varieties.

We have seen many successful strides towards functional systems for Arabic enabling technologies, but we are yet to read about large Arabic NLP applications such as Machine Translation and Information Extraction that are on par with performance on the English language. The problem is not the existence of data, but rather the existence of data annotated with the relevant level of information that is useful for NLP. This task attempts a step towards the goal of creating resources that could be useful for such applications.

In this task, we presented practitioners in the field with challenge of labeling Arabic text with semantic labels. The labels constitute two levels of granularity: sense labels and semantic role labels. We specifically chose data that overlapped such that we would have the same data annotated for different types of semantics, lexical and structural. The overall task of Arabic Semantic Labeling was subdivided into 4 sub-tasks: Arabic word sense disambiguation (AWSD), English to Arabic WSD task (EAWSD), argument detection within the context of semantic role labeling, and argument semantic role classification.

Such a set of tasks would not have been feasible without the existence of several crucial resources: the `Arabic Treebank` (ATB) (Maamouri et al., 2004), the `Arabic WordNet` (AWN) (Elkateb et al., 2006), and the `Pilot Arabic Propbank` (APB).[2]

This paper is laid out as follows: Section 2 will describe some facts about the Arabic language; Section 3 will present the overall description of the tasks; Section 4 describes the word sense disambiguation task; Section 5 describes the semantic role labeling task.

2 The Arabic Language

In the context of our tasks, we only deal with MSA.[3]

Arabic is a Semitic language. It is known for its templatic morphology where words are made up of

[1]Author 1 is supported by DARPA contract Contract No. HR0011-06-C-0023. Authors 2, 3 and 4 are supported by the US Central Intelligence Service.

[2]Funded by DARPA subcontract to BBN Inc. to University of Colorado, LDC-UPenn and Columbia University.

[3]In this paper we use MSA and Arabic interchangeably.

Proceedings of the 4th International Workshop on Semantic Evaluations (SemEval-2007), pages 93–98,
Prague, June 2007.

roots and affixes. Clitics agglutinate to words. For instance, the surface word وبحسناتهم *wbHsnAthm*[4] 'and by their virtues[fem.]', can be split into the conjunction *w* 'and', preposition *b* 'by', the stem *HsnAt* 'virtues [fem.]', and possessive pronoun *hm* 'their'. Arabic is different from English from both the morphological and syntactic perspectives which make it a challenging language to the existing NLP technology that is too tailored to the English language.

From the morphological standpoint, Arabic exhibits rich morphology. Similar to English, Arabic verbs are marked explicitly for tense, voice and person, however in addition, Arabic marks verbs with mood (subjunctive, indicative and jussive) information. For nominals (nouns, adjectives, proper names), Arabic marks case (accusative, genitive and nominative), number, gender and definiteness features. Depending on the genre of the text at hand, not all of those features are explicitly marked on naturally occurring text.

Arabic writing is known for being underspecified for short vowels. Some of the case, mood and voice features are marked only using short vowels. Hence, if the genre of the text were religious such as the Quran or the Bible, or pedagogical such as children's books in Arabic, it would be fully specified for all the short vowels to enhance readability and disambiguation.

From the syntactic standpoint, Arabic, different from English, is considered a pro-drop language, where the subject of a verb may be implicitly encoded in the verb morphology. Hence, we observe sentences such as اكل البرتقال *Akl AlbrtqAl* 'ate-[he] the-oranges', where the verb *Akl* encodes that the subject is a 3rd person masculine singular. This sentence is exactly equivalent to هو اكل البرتقال *hw Akl AlbrtqAl* 'he ate the-oranges'. In the `Arabic Treebank` (ATB), we observe that 30% of all sentences are pro-dropped for subject.

Also Arabic is different from English in that it exhibits a larger degree of free word order. For example, Arabic allows for subject-verb-object (SVO) and verb-subject-object (VSO) argument orders, as well as, OSV and OVS. In the ATB, we observe an equal distribution of both VSO and SVO orders each equally 35% of the time. An example of an SVO sentence is الرجال اكلوا البرتقال *AlrjAl AklwA AlbrtqAl* 'the-men ate-them the-oranges', this is contrasted with اكل الرجال البرتقال *Akl AlrjAl AlbrtqAl* 'ate the-men the-oranges'.

Arabic exhibits more complex noun phrases than English mainly to express possession. These constructions are known as *idafa* constructions. In these complex structures an indefinite noun is followed by a definite noun. For example, رجل البيت *rjl Albyt* 'man the-house' meaning 'man of the house'. Accordingly, MSA does not have a special prepositional use to express possession in a manner similar to English.

3 Overall Tasks Description

Given the differences between English and Arabic, we anticipate that the process of automatically tagging text with semantic information might take more than just applying an English semantic labeler to Arabic. With this in mind, we decided to design a set of tasks that target different types of semantic annotations. We designed an all-words style word sense disambiguation (WSD) task for all the nouns and verbs in Arabic running text. Moreover, we designed another task where the participants are asked to detect and classify semantic role labels (SRL) for a large portion of newswire text. The WSD texts are chosen from the same set used for SRL. All the data is from the `Arabic Treebank III ver. 2` (ATB). The ATB consists of MSA newswire data from `Annhar` newspaper, from the months of July through November of 2002. The ATB is fully annotated with morphological information as well syntactic structural information. The released data for the subtasks is unvowelized and romanized using the Buckwalter transliteration scheme. The part of speech (POS) tag set used in the released data for both the WSD and the SRL sub-tasks is the reduced tag set that is officially released with the ATB.

4 Task: WSD

In the context of this task, word sense disambiguation is the process by which words in context are tagged with their specific meaning definitions from a predefined lexical resource such as a dictionary or taxonomy. The NLP field has gone through a very

[4]We use the Buckwalter transliteration scheme to show romanized Arabic (Buckwalter, 2002).

long tradition of algorithms designed for solving this problem (Ide and Veronis, 1998). Most of the systems however target English since it is the language with most resources. In fact a big push forward dawned on English WSD with the wide release of significant resources such as WordNet.

Arabic poses some interesting challenges for WSD since it has an inherent complexity in its writing system. As mentioned earlier, written MSA is underspecified for short vowels and diacritics. These short vowels and diacritics convey both lexical and inflectional information. For example, كلية *klyp* could mean three different things, 'all', 'kidney' and 'college'. Due to the undiacritized, unvowelized writing system, the three meanings are conflated. If diacritics are explicitly present, we would observe a better distinction made between كلّية *kly~p* 'all' or 'college', and كُلْيَة *klyp* 'kidney'. Hence, full diacritization may be viewed as a level of WSD. But crucially, naturally occurring Arabic text conflates more words due to the writing system.

To date, very little work has been published on Arabic WSD. This is mainly attributed to the lack in lexical resources for the Arabic language. But this picture is about to change with the new release of an Arabic WordNet (AWN).

Arabic WordNet Arabic WordNet (AWN) is a lexical resource for modern standard Arabic. AWN is based on the design and contents of Princeton WordNet (PWN)(Fellbaum, 1998) and can be mapped onto PWN as well as a number of other wordnets, enabling translation on the lexical level to and from dozens of other languages.

AWN focuses on the the Common Base Concepts (Tufis, 2004), as well as extensions specific to Arabic and Named Entities. The Base Concepts are translated manually by authors 2 and 3 into Arabic. Encoding is bi-directional: Arabic concepts for all senses are determined in PWN and encoded in AWN; when a new Arabic verb is added, extensions are made from verbal entries, including verbal derivations, nominalizations, verbal nouns, etc.

To date, the database comprises over 8,000 synsets with over 15,000 words; about 1,400 synsets refer to Named Entities.

Task design With the release of the AWN, we set out to design a sub-task on Arabic WSD. The task had only trial and test data released in an XML compliant format marking instance, sentence and document boundaries. The relevant words are marked with their gross part of speech and underlying lemma and English gloss information.

The participants are required to annotate the chosen instances with the synset information from AWN. Many of the entries in AWN are directly mapped to PWN 2.0 via the byte offset for the synsets.

The two subtasks data comprised 1176 verb and noun instances: 256 verbs and 920 nouns. The annotators were only able to annotate 888 instances for both English and Arabic due to gaps in the AWN. Hence, the final data set comprised 677 nouns and 211 verbs. The gold standard data is annotated authors 2 and 3 of Arabic (the annotators who created the AWN). There was always an overlap in the data of around 300 instances. In the English Arabic WSD task, participants are provided with a specific English word in translation to an Arabic instance. They are also given the full English translation of the Arabic document. Unfortunately, there were no participants in the task.

5 Task: Semantic Role Labeling (SRL)

Shallow approaches to text processing have been garnering a lot of attention recently. Specifically, shallow approaches to semantic processing are making large strides in the direction of efficiently and effectively deriving tacit semantic information from text. Semantic Role Labeling (SRL) is one such approach. With the advent of faster and powerful computers, more effective machine learning algorithms, and importantly, large data resources annotated with relevant levels of semantic information `FrameNet` (Baker et al., 1998) and `ProbBank` corpora (Palmer et al., 2005), we are seeing a surge in efficient approaches to SRL (Carreras and Màrquez, 2005).

SRL is the process by which predicates and their arguments are identified and their roles defined in a sentence.

To date, most of the reported SRL systems are for English. We do see some headway for other languages such as German and Chinese. The systems for the other languages follow the successful models devised for English, (Gildea and Jurafsky, 2002;

Xue and Palmer, 2004; Pradhan et al., 2003). However, no SRL systems exist for Arabic.

Challenges of Arabic for SRL Given the deep difference between such languages, this method may not be straightforward.

To clarify this point, let us consider Figure 1.

It illustrates a sample Arabic syntactic tree with the relevant part of speech tags and arguments defined. The sentence is مشروع الامم المتحدة فرض مهلة نهائية ل إتاحة الفرصة امام قبرص *m$rwE AlAmm AlmtHdp frD mhlp nhAyp l AtAHp AlfrSp AmAm qbrS.* meaning 'The United Nations' project imposed a final grace period as an opportunity for Cyprus'. As we see in the figure, the predicate is *frD* 'imposed' and it has two numbered arguments: ARG0 is the subject of the sentence which is *m$rwE AlAmm AlmtHdp* 'United Nations project'; ARG1, in the object position, namely, *mhlp nhAyp* 'final grace period'. The predicate has an ARGM-PRP (purpose argument) in *l AtAHp AlfrSp AmAm qbrS* 'as an opportunity for Cyprus'.

As exemplified earlier in Section 2, there are several crucial structural differences between English and Arabic. These differences can make the SRL task much harder to resolve than it is for English.

Pro-drop could cause a problem for Arabic SRL systems that do not annotate traces.

Passivization is marked with a short vowel that hardly ever appears on unvocalized text.

The structural word order could create problems. For instance for a sentence such as بلغ الرجل الولد 'the man reached—told the boy', *Alrjl* 'the man' could be an ARG0 for the VSO, or ARG1 for an VOS. Or for the following structure الولد بلغ الرجل *Alwld blg Alrjl* 'the boy reached the man', *Alwld* 'the boy' could be an ARG0 if it were a SVO sentence, or could be an ARG1 if it were an OVS sentence.

Idafa constructions may cause problems for argument boundary detection systems unless the underlying parser is sensitive to these constructions. For example, in the sentence illustrated in Figure 1, the NP *m$rwE AlAmm AlmtHdp* 'the United Nations' project' is an *idafa* construction, so the scope of the NP has to cover all three words and then assign the ARG boundary to the correct NP.

Arabic Propbank Taking into consideration the possible challenges, an `Arabic Propbank` (APB) was created. APB comprises 200K words from ATB 3 version 2 annotating the proposition for each verb. The chosen verbs occur at least 12 times in the corpus covering 80% of the data. It provides semantic role annotations for 454 verbal predicates. The predicates are fully specified for diacritization hence no two lexically variant verbs are conflated. APB defines an overall 26 argument types. We have excluded here 4 of these argument types, three of which were absent from the training data and ARGM-TER which marks ATB errors. Once the verbs are chosen, the framers come up with frames based on a combination of syntactic and semantic behaviors expressed by the verb and its core arguments. The framers use their native intuition, look at a sample occurrence in the data, and use external sources to aid them in the frame-creating process. If the verb has more than one sense, it is divided into more than one frame depending on how it relates to its arguments. The arguments themselves are chosen based not only on what is deemed semantically necessary, but on frequency of usage, as well. Figure 1 shows an example predicate and its arguments annotated with semantic role labels.

Task Design The Arabic SRL task is split into an argument boundary detection task and an argument classification task. We released data for the 95 most frequent verbs. An important characteristic of the data-set is the use of unvowelized Arabic in the Buckwalter transliteration scheme. We released the gold standard parses in the ATB as a source for syntactic parses for the data. The data is annotated with the reduced Bies POS tag set (in the LDC ATB distribution). The data comprises a development set of 886 sentences, a test set of 902 sentences, and a training set of 8,402 sentences. The development set comprises 1710 argument instances, the test data comprises 1657 argument instances, and training data comprises 21,194 argument instances. For evaluation we use the official CoNLL evaluator (Carreras and Màrquez, 2005). The evaluation software produces accuracy, precision, recall and $F_{\beta=1}$ metrics.

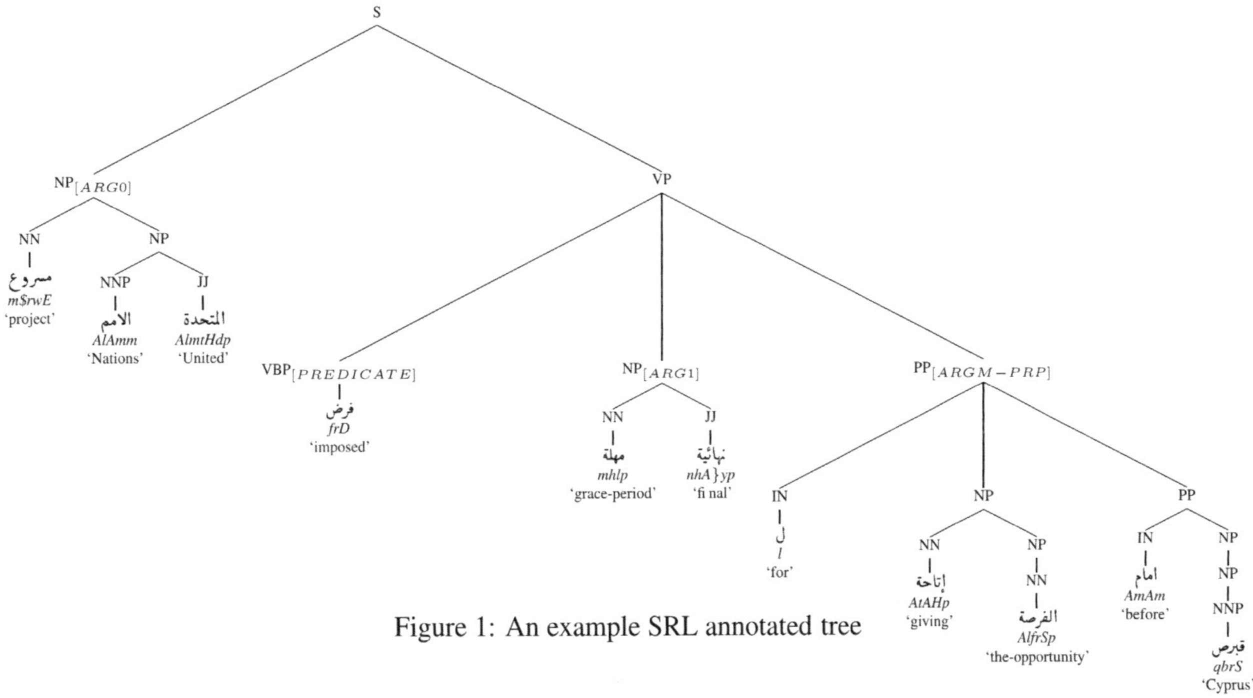

Figure 1: An example SRL annotated tree

5.1 Subtask : Argument Boundary Detection

In this task, the participating systems are expected to detect the boundaries of arguments associated with designated predicates. The systems are expected to identify the arguments with the correct level of scoping. For instance, in our running example sentence, the argument boundaries for the verb فرض *frD* 'imposed' are illustrated as follows: *[m$rwE AlAmm AlmtHdp]*$_{ARG}$ *[frD]*$_{Lemma:faroD}$ *[mhlp nhA}yp]*$_{ARG}$ *[l AtAHp AlfrSp AmAm qbrS]*$_{ARG}$. The three relevant arguments are *m$rwE AlAmm AlmtHdp* 'the United Nations Project', *mhlp nhA}yp* 'final grace-period', and *l AtAHp AlfrSp AmAm qbrS* 'as an opportunity for Cyprus'.

Only one system (CUNIT) participated in the subtask. CUNIT is an SVM based discriminative classification system based on different degrees polynomial kernels. The best CUNIT system (with degree 2 kernel) achieves an $F_{\beta=1}$ argument boundary detection score of 93.68% on the development data and 94.06% on the test data. We note that the results on the test data are higher than on the development data indicating that the test data is relatively easier.

5.2 Subtask: Argument Classification

In this task, the participating systems are expected to identify the class of the arguments detected in the previous step of argument boundary detection. In this sub task we have 22 argument types. Table 1 illustrates the different argument types and their distributions between the dev, train and test sets.

The most frequent arguments are ARG0, ARG1, ARG2 and ARGM-TMP. This is similar to what we see in the English Propbank. We note the additional ARG types with the extension STR. These are for stranded arguments. The tag STR is used when one constituent cannot be selected and an argument has two or more concatenated constituents. An example of this type of ARG is استقر في نيو يورك في بروكلين *{stqr fy nyw ywrk fy brwklyn* 'he settled in New York, in Brooklyn'. In this case, *fy nyw ywrk* 'in New York' is labeled ARG1 and *fy brwklyn* 'in Brooklyn' is labeled ARG1-STR.

Only one system (CUNIT) participated in the SRL subtask. CUNIT is an SVM based discriminative classification system based on different degrees polynomial kernels. The best CUNIT system (with degree 2 kernel) achieves an overall $F_{\beta=1}$ score for all arguments classification of 77.84% on the development data and 81.43% on the test data. It is worth noting that these results are run with the automatic argument boundary detection as an initial step. In both the test and the development results, the precision is significantly higher than the recall. For the development set precision is 81.31% and the recall

	#train	#dev	#test
ARG0	6,328	227	256
ARG0-STR	70	8	5
ARG1	7,858	702	699
ARG1-PRD	38	2	3
ARG1-STR	172	23	13
ARG2	1,843	191	180
ARG2-STR	32	5	4
ARG3	164	13	12
ARG4	15	0	4
ARGM	79	6	1
ARGM-ADV	994	103	115
ARGM-BNF	53	5	7
ARGM-CAU	89	12	11
ARGM-CND	38	6	3
ARGM-DIR	25	3	1
ARGM-DIS	56	8	5
ARGM-EXT	21	0	1
ARGM-LOC	711	82	61
ARGM-MNR	623	85	55
ARGM-NEG	529	76	39
ARGM-PRD	77	14	12
ARGM-PRP	343	42	27
ARGM-TMP	1,347	96	107
Total	21,194	1,710	1,657

Table 1: Distribution of training, development and test instances on the different role types.

is 74.67%. For the test set, the precision is 84.71% and the recall is 78.39%. We note that, similar to the boundary detection sub-task, the results on the test data are significantly higher than on the development data which suggests that the test data is relatively easier.

6 Conclusion

In this paper, we presented a description of Task 18 on Arabic Semantic labeling. Our goal was to rally interest in Arabic Semantic labeling. On the word sense disambiguation front, we have successfully created an all-words sense annotated set of Arabic nouns and verbs in running text. The set is annotated with both Arabic WordNet synset labels and their corresponding English WordNet 2.0 synset labels. Unfortunately, no systems participated in the WSD sub-tasks, however, we have prepared the data for future endeavors and hopefully this will motivate researchers in NLP to start experimenting with Arabic WSD.

On the task of Semantic Role Labeling, we have created a test, training and development set that has been successfully validated through being employed for building the first Arabic SRL system. Hopefully, this data will help propel research in Arabic SRL. It is also worth noting that we currently have effectively created a data set that is annotated for word senses, lexical information such as full morphological specifications, syntactic and semantic parses as well as English glosses and translations.

References

Collin F. Baker, Charles J. Fillmore, and John B. Lowe. 1998. The berkeley FrameNet project. In *COLING-ACL '98: Proceedings of the Conference, held at the University of Montréal*, pages 86–90.

Tim Buckwalter. 2002. Buckwalter Arabic Morphological Analyzer Version 1.0. Linguistic Data Consortium, University of Pennsylvania, 2002. LDC Catalog No.: LDC2002L49.

Xavier Carreras and Lluís M`arquez. 2005. Introduction to the CoNLL-2005 shared task: Semantic role labeling. In *Proceedings of CoNLL-2005*, Ann Arbor, Michigan.

S. Elkateb, H. Rodriguez, M. Alkhalifa, P. Vossen, A. Pease, M. Bertran, W. Black, and C. Fellbaum. 2006. The arabic wordnet project. In *Proceedings of the Conference on Lexical Resources in the European Community*, Genoa, Italy, May.

Christiane Fellbaum. 1998. *WordNet: An Electronic Lexical Database*. MIT Press. http://www.cogsci.princeton.edu/˜wn [2000, September 7].

Daniel Gildea and Daniel Jurafsky. 2002. Automatic labeling of semantic roles. *Computational Linguistics*, 28(3):245–288.

Nancy Ide and Jean Veronis. 1998. Word sense disambiguation: State of the art. In *Computational Linguistics*, number 24, pages 1–40.

Mohamed Maamouri, Ann Bies, Tim Buckwalter, and Wig dan Mekki. 2004. The penn arabic treebank : Building a large-scale annota ted arabic corpus.

Martha Palmer, Dan Gildea, and Paul Kingsbury. 2005. The proposition bank: A corpus anotated with semantic roles. In *Computational Linguistics Journal*, number 31:1.

Sameer Pradhan, Kadri Hacioglu, Wayne Ward, James H. Martin, and Daniel Jurafsky. 2003. Semantic role parsing: Adding semantic structure to unstructured text. In *Proceedings of ICDM-2003*, Melbourne, USA.

Dan Tufi s. 2004. The balkanet project. In *Special Issue of The Romanian Journal of Information Science and Technology*, number 7, pages 1–248.

Nianwen Xue and Martha Palmer. 2004. Calibrating features for semantic role labeling. In Dekang Lin and Dekai Wu, editors, *Proceedings of EMNLP 2004*, pages 88–94, Barcelona, Spain, July. Association for Computational Linguistics.

SemEval'07 Task 19: Frame Semantic Structure Extraction

Collin Baker, Michael Ellsworth
International Computer Science Institute
Berkeley, California
{collinb,infinity}
@icsi.berkeley.edu

Katrin Erk
Computer Science Dept.
University of Texas
Austin
katrin.erk@mail.utexas.edu

Abstract

This task consists of recognizing words and phrases that evoke semantic **frames** as defined in the FrameNet project (http://framenet.icsi.berkeley.edu), and their semantic dependents, which are usually, but not always, their syntactic dependents (including subjects). The training data was FN annotated sentences. In testing, participants automatically annotated three previously unseen texts to match gold standard (human) annotation, including predicting previously unseen frames and roles. Precision and recall were measured both for matching of labels of frames and FEs and for matching of semantic dependency trees based on the annotation.

1 Introduction

The task of labeling frame-evoking words with appropriate frames is similar to WSD, while the task of assigning frame elements is called **Semantic Role Labeling** (**SRL**), and has been the subject of several shared tasks at ACL and CoNLL. For example, in the sentence "Matilde said, 'I rarely eat rutabaga,'" *said* evokes the Statement frame, and *eat* evokes the Ingestion frame. The role of SPEAKER in the Statement frame is filled by *Matilda*, and the role of MESSAGE, by the whole quotation. In the Ingestion frame, *I* is the INGESTOR and *rutabaga* fills the INGESTIBLES role. Since the ingestion event is contained within the MESSAGE of the Statement event, we can represent the fact that the message conveyed was about ingestion, just by annotating the sentence with respect to these two frames.

After training on FN annotations, the participants' systems labeled three new texts automatically. The evaluation measured precision and recall for frames and frame elements, with partial credit for incorrect but closely related frames. Two types of evaluation were carried out: **Label matching evaluation**, in which the participant's labeled data was compared directly with the gold standard labeled data, and **Semantic dependency evaluation**, in which both the gold standard and the submitted data were first converted to semantic dependency graphs in XML format, and then these graphs were compared.

There are three points that make this task harder and more interesting than earlier SRL tasks: (1) while previous tasks focused on role assignment, the current task also comprises the identification of the appropriate FrameNet frame, similar to WSD, (2) the task comprises not only the labeling of individual predicates and their arguments, but also the integration of all labels into an overall **semantic dependency graph**, a partial semantic representation of the overall sentence meaning based on frames and roles, and (3) the test data includes occurrences of frames that are not seen in the training data. For these cases, participant systems have to identify the closest known frame. This is a very realistic scenario, encouraging the development of robust systems showing graceful degradation in the face of unknown events.

Proceedings of the 4th International Workshop on Semantic Evaluations (SemEval-2007), pages 99–104,
Prague, June 2007.

2 Frame semantics and FrameNet

The basic concept of Frame Semantics is that many words are best understood as part of a group of terms that are related to a particular type of event and the participants and "props" involved in it (Fillmore, 1976; Fillmore, 1982). The classes of events are the semantic **frames** of the **lexical units** (**LU**s) that evoke them, and the roles associated with the event are referred to as **frame elements** (**FE**s). The same type of analysis applies not only to events but also to relations and states; the frame-evoking expressions may be single words or multi-word expressions, which may be of any syntactic category. Note that these FE names are quite frame-specific; generalizations over them are expressed via explicit FE-FE relations.

The Berkeley FrameNet project (hereafter FN) (Fillmore et al., 2003) is creating a computer- and human-readable lexical resource for English, based on the theory of frame semantics and supported by corpus evidence. The current release (1.3) of the FrameNet data, which has been freely available for instructional and research purposes since the fall of 2006, includes roughly 780 frames with roughly 10,000 word senses (lexical units). It also contains roughly 150,000 annotation sets, of which 139,000 are lexicographic examples, with each sentence annotated for a single predicator. The remainder are from full-text annotation in which each sentence is annotated for all predicators; 1,700 sentences are annotated in the full-text portion of the database, accounting for roughly 11,700 annotation sets, or 6.8 predicators (=annotation sets) per sentence. Nearly all of the frames are connected into a single graph by frame-to-frame relations, almost all of which have associated FE-to-FE relations (Fillmore et al., 2004a)

2.1 Frame Semantics of texts

The ultimate goal is to represent the lexical semantics of all the sentences in a text, based on the relations between predicators and their dependents, including both phrases and clauses, which may, in turn, include other predicators; although this has been a long-standing goal of FN (Fillmore and Baker, 2001), automatic means of doing this are only now becoming available.

Consider a sentence from one of the testing texts:

(1) This geography is important in understanding Dublin.

In the frame semantic analysis of this sentence, there are two predicators which FN has analyzed: *important* and *understanding*, as well as one which we have not yet analyzed, *geography*. In addition, *Dublin* is recognized by the NER system as a location. In the gold standard annotation, we have the annotation shown in (2) for the Importance frame, evoked by the target *important*, and the annotation shown in (3) for the Grasp frame, evoked by *understanding*.

(2) [$_{\text{FACTOR}}$ This geography] [$_{\text{COP}}$ is] IMPORTANT [$_{\text{UNDERTAKING}}$ in understanding Dublin]. [$_{\text{INTERESTED\_PARTY}}$ INI]

(3) This geography is important in UNDERSTANDING [$_{\text{PHENOMENON}}$ Dublin]. [$_{\text{COGNIZER}}$ CNI]

The definitions of the two frames begin like this:

Importance: A FACTOR affects the outcome of an UNDERTAKING, which can be a goal-oriented activity or the maintenance of a desirable state, the work in a FIELD, or something portrayed as affecting an INTERESTED_PARTY...

Grasp: A COGNIZER possesses knowledge about the workings, significance, or meaning of an idea or object, which we call PHENOMENON, and is able to make predictions about the behavior or occurrence of the PHENOMENON...

Using these definitions and the labels, and the fact that the target and FEs of one frame are subsumed by an FE of the other, we can compose the meanings of the two frames to produce a detailed paraphrase of the meaning of the sentence: Something denoted by *this geography* is a factor which affects the outcome of the undertaking of understanding the location called "Dublin" by any interested party. We have not dealt with *geography* as a frame-evoking expression, although we would eventually like to. (The preposition *in* serves only as a marker of the frame element UNDERTAKING.)

In (2), the INTERESTED_PARTY is not a label on any part of the text; rather, it is marked INI, for "indefinite null instantiation", meaning that it is conceptually required as part of the frame definition, absent from the sentence, and not recoverable from the context as being a particular individual–meaning that *this geography* is important for anyone in general's understanding of Dublin. In (3), the COGNIZER is "constructionally null instantiated", as the gerund *understanding* licenses omission of its subject. The marking of null instantiations is important in handling text coherence and was part of the gold standard, but as far as we know, none of the participants attempted it, and it was ignored in the evaluation.

Note that we have collapsed the two null instantiated FEs, the INTERESTED_PARTY of the importance frame and the COGNIZER in the Grasp frame, since they are not constrained to be distinct.

2.2 Semantic dependency graphs

Since the role fillers are dependents (broadly speaking) of the predicators, the full FrameNet annotation of a sentence is roughly equivalent to a dependency parse, in which some of the arcs are labeled with role names; and a dependency graph can be derived algorithmically from FrameNet annotation; an early version of this was proposed by (Fillmore et al., 2004b)

Fig. 1 shows the semantic dependency graph derived from sentence (1); this graphical representation was derived from a semantic dependency XML file (see Sec. 5). It shows that the top frame in this sentence is evoked by the word *important*, although the syntactic head is the copula *is* (here given the more general label "Support"). The labels on the arcs are either the names of frame elements or indications of which of the daughter nodes are semantic heads, which is important in some versions of the evaluation. The labels on nodes are either frame names (also colored gray), syntactic phrases types (e.g. NP), or the names of certain other syntactic "connectors", in this case, Marker and Support.

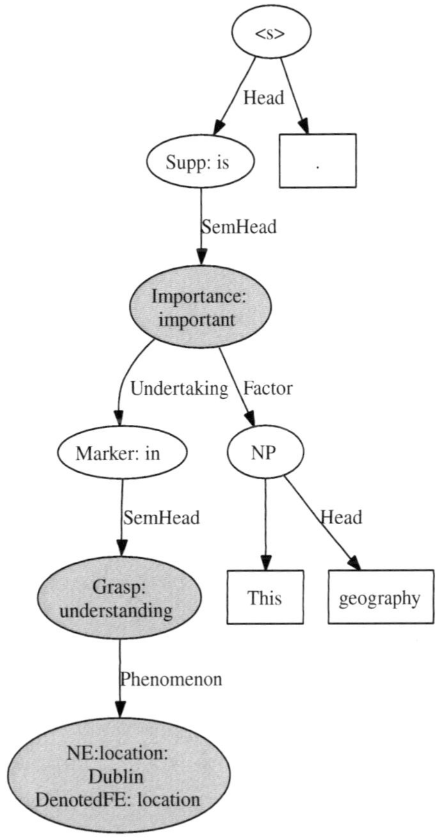

Figure 1: Sample Semantic Dependency Graph

3 Definition of the task

3.1 Training data

The major part of the training data for the task consisted of the current data release from FrameNet (Release 1.3), described in Sec.2 This was supplemented by additional training data made available through SemEval to participants in this task. In addition to updated versions of some of the full-text annotation from Release 1.3, three files from the ANC were included: from Slate.com, "Stephanopoulos Crimes" and "Entrepreneur as Madonna", and from the Berlitz travel guides, "History of Jerusalem".

3.2 Testing data

The testing data was made up of three texts, none of which had been seen before; the gold standard consisted of manual annotations (by the FrameNet team) of these texts for all frame evoking expressions and the fillers of the associated frame elements. All annotation of the testing data was carefully reviewed by the FN staff to insure its correctness. Since most of the texts annotated in the FN database are from the NTI website (`www.nti.org`), we decided to take two of the three testing texts from there also. One, "China Overview", was very similar to other annotated texts such as "Taiwan Introduction", "Russia Overview", etc. available in Release 1.3. The other NTI text, "Work Advances", while in the same domain, was shorter and closer to newspaper style than the rest of the NTI texts. Finally, the "Introduction to

	Sents	NEs	Frames	
			Tokens	Types
Work	14	31	174	77
China	39	90	405	125
Dublin	67	86	480	165
Totals	120	207	1059	272

Table 1: Summary of Testing Data

Dublin", taken from the American National Corpus (ANC, `www.americannationalcorpus.org`) Berlitz travel guides, is of quite a different genre, although the "History of Jerusalem" text in the training data was somewhat similar. Table 1 gives some statistics on the three testing files. To give a flavor of the texts, here are two sentences; frame evoking words are in boldface:

From "Work Advances": "The **Iranians** are **now willing** to **accept** the **installation** of cameras only **outside** the **cascade halls**, which will not enable the IAEA to **monitor** the **entire uranium enrichment process**," the **diplomat said**.

From "Introduction to Dublin": And **in** this **city**, **where literature** and **theater** have **historically dominated** the scene, visual **arts** are **finally** coming into their own with the **new Museum** of Modern **Art** and the **many galleries** that display the work of **modern Irish artists**.

4 Participants

A number of groups downloaded the training or testing data, but in the end, only three groups submitted results: the UTD-SRL group and the LTH group, who submitted full results, and the CLR group who submitted results for frames only. It should also be noted that the LTH group had the testing data for longer than the 10 days allowed by the rules of the exercise, which means that the results of the two teams are not exactly comparable. Also, the results from the CLR group were initially formatted slightly differently from the gold standard with regard to character spacing; a later reformatting allowed their results to be scored with the other groups'.

The LTH system used only SVM classifiers, while the UTD-SRL system used a combination of SVM and ME classifiers, determined experimentally. The CLR system did not use classifiers, but hand-written symbolic rules. Please consult the separate system papers for details about the features used.

5 Evaluation

The labels-only matching was similar to previous shared tasks, but the dependency structure evaluation deserves further explanation: The XML semantic dependency structure was produced by a program called fttosem, implemented in Perl, which goes sentence by sentence through a FrameNet full-text XML file, taking LU, FE, and other labels and using them to structure a syntactically unparsed piece of a sentence into a syntactic-semantic tree. Two basic principles allow us to produce this tree: (1) LUs are the sole syntactic head of a phrase whose semantics is expressed by their frame and (2) each label span is interpreted as the boundaries of a syntactic phrase, so that when a larger label span subsumes a smaller one, the larger span can be interpreted as a the higher node in a hierarchical tree. There are a fair number of complications, largely involving identifying mismatches between syntactic and semantic headedness. Some of these (support verbs, copulas, modifiers, transparent nouns, relative clauses) are annotated in the data with their own labels, while others (syntactic markers, e.g. prepositions, and auxiliary verbs) must be identified using simple syntactic heuristics and part-of-speech tags.

For this evaluation, a non-frame node counts as matching provided that it includes the head of the gold standard, whether or not non-head children of that node are included. For frame nodes, the participants got full credit if the frame of the node matched the gold standard.

5.1 Partial credit for related frames

One of the problems inherent in testing against unseen data is that it will inevitably contain lexical units that have not previously been annotated in FrameNet, so that systems which do not generalize well cannot get them right. In principle, the decision as to what frame to add a new LU to should be helped by the same criteria that are used to assign polysemous lemmas to existing frames. However, in practice this assignment is difficult, precisely because, unlike WSD, there is no assumption that all the senses of each lemma are defined in advance; if the system can't be sure that a new use of a lemma is in one of the frames listed for that lemma, then it must consider all the 800+ frames as possibilities. This amounts to the automatic induction of fine-grained semantic similarity from corpus data, a notoriously difficult problem (Stevenson and Joanis, 2003; Schulte im Walde, 2003).

For LUs which clearly do not fit into any existing frames, the problem is still more difficult. In the course of creating the gold standard annotation of the three testing texts, the FN team created almost 40 new frames. We cannot ask that participants hit upon the new frame name, but the new frames are not created in a vacuum; as mentioned above, they are almost always added to the existing structure of frame-to-frame relations; this allows us to give credit for assignment to frames which are not the precise one in the gold standard, but are close in terms of frame-to-frame relations. Whenever participants' proposed frames were wrong but connected to the right frame by frame relations, partial credit was given, decreasing by 20% for each link in the frame-frame relation graph between the proposed frame and the gold standard. For FEs, each frame element had to match the gold standard frame element and contain at least the same head word in order to gain full credit; again, partial credit was given for frame elements related via FE-to-FE relations.

6 Results

Text	Group	Recall	Prec.	F1
Dublin	UTD-SRL	0.4188	0.7716	0.5430
China	UTD-SRL	0.5498	0.8009	0.6520
Work	UTD-SRL	0.5251	0.8382	0.6457
Dublin	LTH	0.5184	0.7156	0.6012
China	LTH	0.6261	0.7731	0.6918
Work	LTH	0.6606	0.8642	0.7488
Dublin	CLR	0.3984	0.6469	0.4931
China	CLR	0.4621	0.6302	0.5332
Work	CLR	0.5054	0.7452	0.6023

Table 2: Frame Recognition only

The strictness of the requirement of exact boundary matching (which depends on an accurate syntactic parse) is compounded by the cascading effect of semantic classification errors, as seen by comparing the F-scores in Table 3 with those in Table 2. The difficulty of the task is reflected in the F-scores of around 35% for the most difficult text in the most difficult condition, but participants still managed to reach F-scores as high as 75% for the more limited task of Frame Identification (Table 2), which more closely matches traditional Senseval tasks, despite the lack of a full sense inventory. The difficulty posed by having such an unconstrained task led to understandably low recall scores in all participants (between 25 and 50%). The systems submitted by the teams differed in their sensitivity to differences in the texts: UTD-SRL's system varied by around 10% across texts, while LTH's varied by 15%.

Text	Group	Recall	Prec.	F1
Label matching only				
Dublin	UTD-SRL	0.27699	0.55663	0.36991
China	UTD-SRL	0.31639	0.51715	0.39260
Work	UTD-SRL	0.31098	0.62408	0.41511
Dublin	LTH	0.36536	0.55065	0.43926
China	LTH	0.39370	0.54958	0.45876
Work	LTH	0.41521	0.61069	0.49433
Semantic dependency matching				
Dublin	UTD-SRL	0.26238	0.53432	0.35194
China	UTD-SRL	0.31489	0.53145	0.39546
Work	UTD-SRL	0.30641	0.61842	0.40978
Dublin	LTH	0.36345	0.54857	0.43722
China	LTH	0.40995	0.57410	0.47833
Work	LTH	0.45970	0.67352	0.54644

Table 3: Results for combined Frame and FE recognition

There are some rather encouraging results also. The participants rather consistently performed better with our more complex, but also more useful and realistic scoring, including partial credit and grading on semantic dependency rather than exact span match (compare the top and bottom halves of Table 3). The participants all performed relatively well on the frame-recognition task, with precision scores averaging 63% and topping 85%.

7 Discussion

The testing data for this task turned out to be especially challenging with regard to new frames, since, in an effort to annotate especially thoroughly, almost

40 new frames were created in the process of annotating these three specific passages. One result of this was that the test passages had more unseen frames than a random unseen passage, which probably lowered the recall on frames. It appears that this was not entirely compensated by giving partial credit for related frames.

This task is a more advanced and realistic version of the Automatic Semantic Role Labeling task of Senseval-3 (Litkowski, 2004). Unlike that task, the testing data was previously unseen, participants had to determine the correct frames as a first step, and participants also had to determine FE boundaries, which were given in the Senseval-3.

A crucial difference from similar approaches, such as SRL with PropBank roles (Pradhan et al., 2004) is that by identifying relations as part of a frame, you have identified a gestalt of relations that enables far more inference, and sentences from the same passage that use other words from the same frame will be easier to link together. Thus, the FN SRL results are translatable fairly directly into formal representations which can be used for reasoning, question answering, etc. (Scheffczyk et al., 2006; Frank and Semecky, 2004; Sinha and Narayanan, 2005).

Despite the problems with recall, the participants have expressed a determination to work to improve these results, and the FN staff are eager to collaborate in this effort. A project is now underway at ICSI to speed up frame and LU definition, and another to speed up the training of SRL systems is just beginning, so the prospects for improvement seem good.

This material is based in part upon work supported by the National Science Foundation under Grant No. IIS-0535297.

References

Charles J. Fillmore and Collin F. Baker. 2001. Frame semantics for text understanding. In *Proceedings of WordNet and Other Lexical Resources Workshop*, Pittsburgh, June. NAACL.

Charles J. Fillmore, Christopher R. Johnson, and Miriam R.L Petruck. 2003. Background to FrameNet. *International Journal of Lexicography*, 16.3:235–250.

Charles J. Fillmore, Collin F. Baker, and Hiroaki Sato. 2004a. FrameNet as a "Net". In *Proceedings of LREC*, volume 4, pages 1091–1094, Lisbon. ELRA.

Charles J. Fillmore, Josef Ruppenhofer, and Collin F. Baker. 2004b. FrameNet and representing the link between semantic and syntactic relations. In Churen Huang and Winfried Lenders, editors, *Frontiers in Linguistics*, volume I of *Language and Linguisitcs Monograph Series B*, pages 19–59. Inst. of Linguistics, Acadmia Sinica, Taipei.

Charles J. Fillmore. 1976. Frame semantics and the nature of language. *Annals of the New York Academy of Sciences*, 280:20–32.

Charles J. Fillmore. 1982. Frame semantics. In *Linguistics in the Morning Calm*, pages 111–137. Hanshin Publishing Co., Seoul, South Korea.

Anette Frank and Jiri Semecky. 2004. Corpus-based induction of an LFG syntax-semantics interface for frame semantic processing. In *Proceedings of the 5th International Workshop on Linguistically Interpreted Corpora (LINC 2004)*, Geneva, Switzerland.

Ken Litkowski. 2004. Senseval-3 task: Automatic labeling of semantic roles. In Rada Mihalcea and Phil Edmonds, editors, *Senseval-3: Third International Workshop on the Evaluation of Systems for the Semantic Analysis of Text*, pages 9–12, Barcelona, Spain, July. Association for Computational Linguistics.

Sameer S. Pradhan, Wayne H. Ward, Kadri Hacioglu, James H. Martin, and Dan Jurafsky. 2004. Shallow semantic parsing using support vector machines. In Daniel Marcu Susan Dumais and Salim Roukos, editors, *HLT-NAACL 2004: Main Proceedings*, pages 233–240, Boston, Massachusetts, USA, May 2 - May 7. Association for Computational Linguistics.

Jan Scheffczyk, Collin F. Baker, and Srini Narayanan. 2006. Ontology-based reasoning about lexical resources. In Alessandro Oltramari, editor, *Proceedings of ONTOLEX 2006*, pages 1–8, Genoa. LREC.

Sabine Schulte im Walde. 2003. Experiments on the choice of features for learning verb classes. In *Proceedings of the 10th Conference of the EACL (EACL-03)*.

Steve Sinha and Srini Narayanan. 2005. Model based answer selection. In *Proceedings of the Workshop on Textual Inference, 18th National Conference on Artificial Intelligence*, PA, Pittsburgh. AAAI.

Suzanne Stevenson and Eric Joanis. 2003. Semi-supervised verb class discovery using noisy features. In *Proceedings of the 7th Conference on Natural Language Learning (CoNLL-03)*, pages 71–78.

AUG: A combined classification and clustering approach for web people disambiguation

Els Lefever and **Véronique Hoste**
LT3 Language and Translation Technology
Ghent University Association
Groot-Brittanniëlaan 45, 9000 Gent
els.lefever@hogent.be
veronique.hoste@hogent.be

Timur Fayruzov
Computational Web Intelligence
Ghent University Association
Krijgslaan 281, 9000 Gent
Timur.Fayruzov@UGent.be

Abstract

This paper presents a combined supervised and unsupervised approach for multi-document person name disambiguation. Based on feature vectors reflecting pairwise comparisons between web pages, a classification algorithm provides linking information about document pairs, which leads to initial clusters. In addition, two different clustering algorithms are fed with matrices of weighted keywords. In a final step the "seed" clusters are combined with the results of the clustering algorithms. Results on the validation data show that a combined classification and clustering approach doesn't always compare favorably to those obtained by the different algorithms separately.

1 Introduction

Finding information about people on the World Wide Web is one of the most popular activities of Internet users. Given the high ambiguity of person names and the increasing amount of information on the web, it becomes very important to organize this large amount of information into meaningful clusters referring each to one single individual.

The problem of resolving name ambiguity on the Internet has been approached from different angles. Mann and Yarowsky (2003) have proposed a Web based clustering technique relying on a feature space combining biographic facts and associated names, whereas Bagga and Baldwin (1998) have looked for coreference chains within each document, take the context of these chains for creating summaries about each entity and convert these summaries into a bag of words. Documents get clustered using the standard vector space model. Other researchers have taken this search for distinctive keywords one step further and tried to come up with "concepts" describing the documents. Fleischman and Hovy (2004) introduce the "maximum entropy model": a binary classifier determines whether two concept-instance pairs refer to the same individual. Pedersen (2006) presented an unsupervised approach using bigrams in the contexts to be clustered, thus aiming at a concept level semantic space instead of a word level feature space.

For the semeval contest, we approached the task from a double supervised and unsupervised perspective. For the supervised classification, the task was redefined in the form of feature vectors containing disambiguating information on pairs of documents. In addition to this, different clustering approaches were applied on matrices of keywords. These results were then merged by taking the classification output as basic "seed" clusters, which were then enhanced by the results from the clustering experiments.

In the remainder of this paper, Section 2 introduces the data sets and describes the construction of the feature vectors and the keyword matrices. The classification and clustering experiments, and the final combination of the different outputs are discussed in Section 3. Section 4 gives an overview of the results on the test data and Section 5 summarizes the main findings of the paper.

Proceedings of the 4th International Workshop on Semantic Evaluations (SemEval-2007), pages 105–108,
Prague, June 2007.

2 Data sets and feature construction

The data we have used for training our system were made available in the framework of the SemEval (task 13: Web People Search) competition (Artiles et al., 2007). As preliminary training corpus (referred to as "trial data" in our article), we used the WePS corpus (Web People Search corpus), available at http://nlp.uned.es/weps. For the real training set, this trial set was expanded in order to cover different degrees of ambiguity (very common names, uncommon names and celebrity names which tend to monopolize search results). The training corpus is composed of 40 sets of 100 web pages, each set corresponding to the first 100 results for a person name query. The documents were manually clustered. Documents that couldn't be clustered properly have been put in a "discarded" section. Test data have been constructed in a similar way (30 sets of 100 web pages).

The content of the web pages has been preprocessed by means of a memory-based shallow parser (MBSP) (Daelemans and van den Bosch, 2005). From the MBSP, we used the regular expression based tokenizer, the part-of-speech tagger and text chunker using the memory-based tagger MBT. On the basis of the preprocessed data we construct a rich feature space that combines biographic facts and distinctive characteristics for a given person, a list of weighted keywords and meta data information about the web page.

2.1 Feature vector construction

The following biographic facts and related named entities were extracted from the preprocessed data. Information on date and place of birth, and on date and place of death were extracted by means of a rule-based component. Furthermore, three named entity features were extracted on the basis of the shallow syntactic information provided by the memory-based shallow parser and additional gazetteer information. Furthermore, a "name" feature was aimed at the extraction of further interesting name information (E.g other surnames, family names) on the person in focus, leading to the extraction of for example "Ann Hill Carter Lee" and "Jo Ann Hill" for the document collection on "Ann Hill". The "location" feature informs on the overlap between all locations named in the different documents. In a similar way, the "NE" feature returns the inter-document overlap between all other named entities.

Starting with the assumption that overlapping URL and email addresses usually point to the same individual, we have also extracted URL, email and domain addresses from the web pages. Therefore we have combined pattern matching rules and markup information (HTML <href> tag). The link of the document itself has been added to the set of URL links. Some filtering on the list has been performed concerning length (to exclude garbage) and content (to exclude non-distinctive URL addresses such as index.html). Pair-wise comparison of documents with respect to overlapping URL, email and domain names resulted in 3 binary features.

Another binary feature we have extracted is the location, based on our simple supposition that if two documents are hosted in the same city, they most probably refer to the same person (but not vice versa). For converting IP-addresses to city locations, we have used MaxMind GeoIP(tm) open source database[2], which was sufficient for our needs.

2.2 A bag of weighted keywords

The input source for extracting our distinctive keywords is double: both the entire (preprocessed) content of the web pages as well as snippets and titles of documents are used. Keywords extracted from snippets and titles get a predefined -rather high- score, as we consider them quite important. For determining the keyword relevance of the words extracted from the content of the web pages, we have applied Term Frequency Inverse Document Frequency (TF-IDF) (Berger et al., 2000).

Once all scores are calculated, all weighted keywords get stored in a matrix, which serve as input for the clustering experiments. The calculated keyword weight is also used, in case of overlapping keywords, as a feature in our pairwise comparison vector. In case two keywords occurring in two different documents are identical or recognized as synonyms (information we obtain by using WordNet[3]), we sum up the different weights of these keywords and store this value in the feature vector.

[2] http://www.maxmind.com/app/geolitecity

[3] http://wordnet.princeton.edu/

3 Classification and Clustering algorithms

3.1 Classification

For the classification experiments, we used the eager RIPPER rule learner (Cohen, 1995) which induces a set of easily understandable if-then classification rules for the minority class and a default rule for the remaining class. The ruler learner was trained and validated on the trial and training data. Given the completely different class distribution of the trial and training data, viz. 10.6% positive instances in the trial data versus 66.7% in the training data, we decided to omit the trial data and optimize the learner on the basis of the more balanced training data set. There was an optimization of the class ordering parameter, the two-valued negative tests parameter, the hypothesis simplification parameter, the example coverage parameter, the parameter expressing the number of optimization passes and the loss ratio parameter. The predicted positive pairwise classifications were then combined using a for coreference resolution developed counting mechanism (Hoste, 2005).

3.2 Clustering Algorithms

We experimented with several clustering algorithms and settings on the trial and training data to decide on our list of parameter settings. We validated the following three clustering algorithms. First, we compared output from k-means and hierarchical clustering algorithms. Next to that, we have run experiments for agglomerative clustering[4]. with different parameter combinations (2 similarity measures and 5 clustering functions). All clustering experiments take the weighted keywords matrix as input. Based on the validation experiments, hierarchical and agglomerative clustering were further evaluated to find out the optimal parameter settings. For hierarchical clustering, this led to the choice of the cosine distance metric, single-link hierarchical clustering and a 50% cluster size. For agglomerative clustering, clustering accuracy was very dependent on the structure of the document set. This has made us use different strategies for clustering sets containing "famous" and "non famous" people. As a distinction criterion we have chosen the presence/non-presence of the person in Wikipedia. We started with the assumption that sets containing famous people (found in Wikipedia) most probably contain a small amount of bigger clusters than sets describing "ordinary" persons. According to this assumption, two different parameter sets were used for clustering. For Wikipedia people we have used the correlation coefficient and g1 clustering type, for ordinary people we have used the cosine similarity measure and single link clustering. For both categories the number of target output clusters equals (number of RIPPER output clusters + the number of documents*0.2).

Although the clustering results with the best settings for hierarchical and agglomerative clustering were very close with regard to F-score (combining purity and inverse purity, see (Artiles et al., 2007) for a more detailed description), manual inspection of the content of the clusters has revealed big differences between the two approaches. Clusters that are output by our hierarchical algorithm look more homogeneous (higher purity), whereas inverse purity seems better for the agglomerative clustering. Therefor we have decided to take the best of two worlds and combined resulting clusters of both algorithms.

3.3 Merging of clustering results

Classification and clustering with optimal settings resulted in three sets of clusters, one based on pairwise similarity vectors and two based on keyword matrices. Since the former set tends to have better precision, which seems logical because more evident features are used for classification, we used this set as "seed" clusters. The two remaining sets were used to improve recall.

Merging was done in the following way: first we compare the initial set with the result of the agglomerative clustering by trying to find the biggest intersection. We remove the intersection from the smallest cluster and add both clusters to the final set. The resulting set of clusters is further improved by using the result of the hierarchical clustering. Here we apply another combining strategy: if two documents form one cluster in the initial set, but are in separate clusters in the other set, we merge these two clusters. Table 1 lists all results of the separate clustering algorithms as well as the final clustering results for the Wikipedia person names. Second half of the ta-

[4]http://glaros.dtc.umn.edu/gkhome/views/cluto

Person Name Wikipedia	Ripper	agglom.	hierarch.	merged
Alexander Macomb	.69/.63	.64/.56	.57/.47	.79/.80
David Lodge	.69/.65	.69/.64	.43/.33	.79/.85
George Clinton	.65/.62	.64/.59	.54/.45	.75/.80
John Kennedy	.67/.62	.70/.66	.49/.39	.76/.80
Michael Howard	.56/.54	.63/.62	.65/.58	.62/.75
Paul Collins	.54/.57	.64/.62	.63/.56	.55/.62
Tony Abbott	.63/.59	.67/.63	.62/.54	.77/.83
Average Scores all Training Data	.73/.76	.67/.72	.62/.60	.66/.75

Table 1: Results on Training Data

ble shows the average results for the separate and combined algorithms. The first score always refers to $F_\alpha = 0.5$, the second score refers to $F_\alpha = 0.2$.

The average scores, that were calculated on the complete training set, show that RIPPER outperforms the combined clusters.

4 Results on the test data

4.1 Final settings

For our classification algorithm, we have finally not kept the best settings for the training data, as this led to an alarming over-assignment of the positive class, thus linking nearly every document to each other. Therefore, we were forced to define a more strict rule set. For the clustering algorithms, we have used the optimal parameter settings as described in Section 3.

4.2 Test results

Table 2 lists the results for the separate and merged clustering for SET 1 in the test data (participants in the ACL conference) and the average for all algorithms. The average score, that has been calculated on the complete test set, shows that the combined clusters outperform the separate algorithms for $F_\alpha = 0.2$, but the hierarchical algorithm outperforms the others for $F_\alpha = 0.5$. Table 3 lists the average results for purity, inverse purity and the F-measures.

5 Conclusions

We proposed and validated a combined classification and clustering approach for resolving web people ambiguity. In future work we plan to experiment with clustering algorithms that don't require a predefined number of clusters, as our tests revealed a big impact of the cluster size on our results. We will also

Person Name ACL	Ripper	agglom.	hierarch.	merged
Chris Brockett	.49/.39	.74/.69	.70/.61	.79/.80
Dekang Lin	.69/.58	.76/.67	.59/.47	.93/.89
Frank Keller	.48/.41	.68/.75	.64/.62	.56/.71
James Curran	.53/.50	.64/.77	.75/.78	.54/.72
Jerry Hobbs	.50/.39	.02/.01	.58/.47	.74/.70
Leon Barrett	.47/.40	.67/.74	.65/.66	.57/.73
Mark Johnson	.45/.42	.55/.70	.65/.77	.44/.65
Robert Moore	.39/.37	.60/.71	.66/.68	.46/.65
Sharon Goldwater	.60/.49	.72/.61	.40/.29	.91/.86
Stephen Clark	.41/.42	.53/.67	.68/.75	.46/.67
Average Scores all Test Data	.49/.45	.58/.63	.69/.69	.61/.74

Table 2: Results on Test Data

Test set	Purity	Inverse Purity	$F = \alpha = 0.5$	$F = \alpha = 0.2$
Set1	.57	.85	.64	.73
Set2	.45	.91	.58	.73
Set3	.48	.89	.60	.73
Global	.50	.88	.60	.73

Table 3: Purity/Inverse Purity Results on Test Data

experiment with meta-learning, other merging techniques and evaluation metrics. Furthermore, we will investigate the impact of intra-document and inter-document coreference resolution on web people disambiguation.

6 References

J. Artiles and J. Gonzalo and S. Sekine. 2007. *The SemEval-2007 WePS Evaluation: Establishing a benchmark for the Web People Search Task, Proceedings of Semeval 2007, Association for Computational Linguistics.*

A. Bagga and B. Baldwin. 1998. *Entity-based cross-document co-referencing using the vector space model, Proceedings of the 17th international conference on Computational linguistics*, 75–85.

A. Berger and R. Caruana and D. Cohn and D. Freitag and V. Mittal. 2000. *Bridging the Lexical Chasm: Statistical Approaches to Answer Finding, Proc. Int. Conf. Reasearch and Development in Information Retrieval*, 192–199.

William W. Cohen. 1995. *Fast Effective Rule Induction, Proceedings of the 12th International Conference on Machine Learning*, 115–123. Tahoe City, CA.

Walter Daelemans and Antal van den Bosch. 2005. *Memory-Based Language Processing.* Cambridge University Press.

Veronique Hoste. 2005. *Optimization Issues in Machine Learning of Coreference Resolution.* Phd dissertation, Antwerp University.

M.B. Fleischman and E. Hovy. 2004. *Multi-document person name resolution, Proceedings of 42nd Annual Meeting of the Association for Computational Linguistics (ACL), Reference Resolution Workshop.*

G. Mann and D. Yarowsky. 2003. *Unsupervised personal name disambiguation, Proceedings of CoNLL-2003*, 33–40. Edmonton, Canada.

T. Pedersen and A. Purandare and A. Kulkarni. 2006. *Name Discrimination by Clustering Similar Contexts, Proceedings of the World Wide Web Conference (WWW).*

CITYU-HIF: WSD with Human-Informed Feature Preference

Oi Yee Kwong
Language Information Sciences Research Centre
City University of Hong Kong
Tat Chee Avenue, Kowloon, Hong Kong
rlolivia@cityu.edu.hk

Abstract

This paper describes our word sense disambiguation (WSD) system participating in the SemEval-2007 tasks. The core system is a fully supervised system based on a Naïve Bayes classifier using multiple knowledge sources. Toward a larger goal of incorporating the intrinsic nature of individual target words in disambiguation, thus introducing a cognitive element in automatic WSD, we tried to fine-tune the results obtained from the core system with human-informed feature preference, and compared it with automatic feature selection as commonly practised in statistical WSD. Despite the insignificant improvement observed in this preliminary attempt, more systematic analysis remains to be done for a cognitively plausible account of the factors underlying the lexical sensitivity of WSD, which would inform and enhance the development of WSD systems in return.

1 Introduction

In recent years, many research teams all over the world have gained rich experience on word sense disambiguation (WSD) from the shared tasks of the SENSEVAL workshops. The need for multiple knowledge sources has become a golden rule, and the "lexical sensitivity" once remarked by Resnik and Yarowsky (1997) is addressed by various means in statistical classifiers, such as learning an optimal combination of the various knowledge sources for individual target words (e.g. Mihalcea, 2002; Escudero *et al.*, 2004). Another common practice is to use an ensemble of classifiers. As pointed out by Mihalcea *et al.* (2004), among the participating systems in the SENSEVAL-3 English lexical sample task, "several of the top performance systems are based on combination of multiple classifiers, which shows once again that voting scheme that combine several learning algorithms outperform the accuracy of individual classifiers". However, the advancement in WSD is rarely accompanied by any extensive account on the cognitive aspects of the task or qualitative analysis of the relation between the disambiguation results and the nature of individual target words underlying the apparent lexical sensitivity of the task.

Given that humans apparently use different strategies in making sense of words, it might be beneficial to have such cognitive aspects, including the type and strength of various kinds of semantic association, realised in NLP systems explicitly. Thus in addition to an optimal combination of classifiers alone, to better understand the contribution of different information types for different types of target words, it is important to look at WSD in relation to the very intrinsic nature of individual target words, which could comprise many factors such as frequency, abstractness, sense relatedness and parts-of-speech (POS). We thus use the concept *Information Susceptibility* (Kwong, 2005) to refer to the relationship between the intrinsic features of a target word and its senses, and the effectiveness of various lexical information to characterise them.

Our current participation in SemEval-2007 is thus intended as a means toward a larger goal, i.e., to incorporate a cognitive element into automatic WSD systems. In particular, we tried to fine-tune the results obtained from the core system with human-informed feature preference.

In Section 2, we will briefly describe the implementation of our disambiguation system and the features used. In Section 3 we will discuss the

Proceedings of the 4th International Workshop on Semantic Evaluations (SemEval-2007), pages 109–112,
Prague, June 2007.

human input on the target nature and the informativeness of various features. The experiments and results are presented in Section 4, followed by a conclusion in Section 5.

2 System Description

2.1 Core Classifier

The core system is a fully supervised one based on a Naïve Bayes classifier. We made use of the Weka API (Witten and Frank, 2005) in our implementation. According to Yarowsky and Radu (2002), Bayesian classifiers belong to one of the aggregative models which depend heavily on the multiple reinforcing feature clues obtainable from wide context. Thus we use all features described in Section 2.2 below for our core system.

2.2 Knowledge Sources

Only the training data provided by the task organisers was used to train the system. We used four major types of contextual features, which could be classified into *Target features*, *Local features*, *Topical features* and *Syntactic features*, as described in Table 1. All features were converted to binary features.

2.3 Feature Selection

On top of the core system, we tested two value-added steps to accommodate for the lexical sensitivity of WSD. One is automatic feature selection (AFS), for which we used CfsSubsetEval (correlation-based feature selection) as implemented in Weka, based on the training samples of each target word. The other is human-informed feature preference (HIF), for which we ran another Naïve Bayes classifier in parallel with a feature subset deemed informative by human judges to fine-tune the disambiguation results obtained from the core system (see Sections 3 and 4 below).

3 Intrinsic Nature of Target Words

Leacock *et al.* (1998), for example, observed that "the benefits of adding topical to local context alone depend on syntactic category as well as on the characteristics of the individual word". In other words, some target words happen to be more "topical" than others and might therefore be more susceptible to topical contextual features during disambiguation. Others, however, might only be optimally disambiguated with other types of information.

	Target Features
W_0	Word form of the target word
P_0	POS of the target word
	Local Features
P_{-2} P_{-1} P_{+1} P_{+2}	POS of words at fixed positions from the target word, including the first and second word on its left and the first and second word on its right
W_{-2} W_{-1} W_{+1} W_{+2}	Word forms of the words at fixed positions from the target word, including the first and second word on its left and the first and second word on its right
	Topical Features
$W_{-10} \ldots W_{+10}$	Content words appearing within the window of ten words on each side of the target word
	Syntactic Features
$P_{-2} P_0$ $P_{-1} P_0$ $P_0 P_{+1}$ $P_0 P_{+2}$	POS bigrams composed of the target word and its neighbouring words, the non-immediate $P_{-2}\ P_0$ and $P_0\ P_{+2}$ are included to accommodate for some flexibility
$P_{-2} P_{-1} P_0$ $P_0 P_{+1} P_{+2}$	POS trigrams composed of the target word and its neighbouring words

Table 1 Features Used in the Naïve Bayes Classifer

While statistical WSD has more or less reached its ceiling, it is assumed that a more thorough understanding of the effectiveness of different types of lexical information for characterising a word sense and distinguishing it from others should be able to further inform and enhance the development of WSD systems. To this end, three undergraduate linguistics students in the City University of Hong Kong were asked to go through the training data for the Chinese lexical sample task in SENSEVAL-3 and that for the multilingual Chinese-English lexical sample task (Task 5) in SemEval-2007. For each sense of a given target word, they were asked to rate the *difficulty*, *abstractness*, and *topicality* of the sense on a 3-point scale. At the same time, they were asked to indicate the type of information, among local POS, local words, and contextual words (i.e. the topical features in Table 1), which they reckon to be most useful for disambiguating a given sample of the target word.[1]

While the information collected from the human judges is pending in-depth analysis, the feature preference indicated by them was used to fine-tune the results obtained from our core system. During disambiguation, we run two Naïve Bayes classifiers in parallel, the core one on all features above, and the other only on the type of information deemed most useful by two or more of the human judges, and use the latter to adjust the results from the former, as further discussed in Section 4.2.

4 Experiment and Results

4.1 Datasets

We participated in the Multilingual Chinese-English Lexical Sample Task (Task 5) and the English Lexical Sample Task via English-Chinese Parallel Text (Task 11).

Task 5 consists of 40 Chinese target words, 19 nouns and 21 verbs. The number of senses for the target words ranges from 2 to 8, with an average of 3. There are altogether 2,680 training samples, i.e. on average about 22 for each sense. A total of 935 testing instances were to be tagged, i.e. on average about 23 for each target word. The data were from People's Daily. The sense tags are given in the form of their English translations in the Chinese Semantic Dictionary developed by the Institute of Computational Linguistics of Peking University. The task organiser has provided the data with word segmentation and POS for each segmented word.

Task 11 consists of 40 English target words, including 20 nouns and 20 adjectives. The average number of training samples for each sense is about 42. The number of senses for the target words ranges from 2 to 6, with an average of 3.125. The average number of testing samples for each target word is 68. The data were gathered from word-aligned English-Chinese parallel texts.

In addition, we also used the SENSEVAL-3 Chinese lexical sample data during evaluation, which contains 20 target words.

[1] To simplify the task for the human judges, we did not distinguish between fixed-position local POS and n-gram syntactic features, and only used the former.

4.2 Evaluation

For Task 5, we made use of the segmentation and POS information provided by the task organiser. For Task 11, we first ran the data through the Brill tagger (Brill, 1994) to obtain the POS, from which we then extracted the feature values.

On top of the core system, we also tested two value-added conditions, namely automatic feature selection (AFS) and human-informed feature preference (HIF). For the latter, we run a separate Naïve Bayes classifier in parallel to the core system, using the knowledge source deemed most useful for a given target word by two or more human judges. When the probability of the best guess from the core classifier is under a certain threshold, the best guess from the other is used instead. For the current experiment, the probability of the best guess from the core classifier must at least double that for the next best guess.

For evaluation, we ran a 10-fold cross validation on the SemEval-2007 Task 5 training data, with the core system and AFS. In addition, we tested with the Senseval-3 Chinese lexical sample data. We trained the classifier with the Senseval-3 training data, with the core classifier, AFS, and HIF. The results are discussed below.

4.3 Results

Table 2 shows the evaluation results of the various conditions described above.

Condition	Ave. Precision
SemEval-2007 training data (10-fold CV)	
Core classifier	77.33%
Core classifier + AFS	85.51%
Senseval-3 testing data	
Core classifier	60.2%
Core classifier + AFS	61.7%
Core classifier + HIF	60.7%

Table 2 Evaluation Results

Apparently, and as known and expected, feature selection is useful for choosing an optimal set of features for each target word. How this compares and works together with human intuition and the nature of the individual target words and senses is what we would like to further investigate. In the above experiment, fine-tuning with human-informed feature preference did not improve the performance as significantly as one would like to see, and the effect varied with individual target words. One possibility is that Naïve Bayes classifiers favour aggregative features, so it might not be most appropriate to do the fine-tuning with a separate classifier. Rather, we could explore the feasibility of adjusting the weights of individual features based on the feature preference.

Our next step is to perform in-depth and systematic analysis on the difficulty, abstractness and topicality of the target words and senses, with the information gathered from the human judges and the confusion matrices generated from the experiment, in association with psychological evidence like semantic activation and the organisation of the mental lexicon (e.g. Kwong, 2007).

4.4 Official Scores in SemEval-2007

The official scores for our system are shown in Table 3.

Task	System	MicroAvg	MacroAvg	Rank
5	HIF	71.0%	74.9%	3 / 6
11	AFS	75.3%[2]	-	3 / 3

Table 3 Official Scores for CITYU in SemEval-2007

Our scores are comparable to the state-of-the-art results. Although the HIF step did not increase the performance significantly, in view of the limitation of state-of-the-art statistical WSD systems, every minor improvement counts. It therefore remains for us to further investigate the cognitive aspects of WSD in relation to target nature and have them systematically realised in WSD systems.

5 Conclusion

In this paper, we have described our system participating in the SemEval-2007 multilingual Chinese-English lexical sample task and English lexical sample task via English-Chinese parallel text. Toward a larger goal of supplementing statistical methods with some cognitive elements of WSD, more systematic analysis of the intrinsic nature of target words underlying the lexical sensitivity of WSD is underway.

[2] A post-hoc analysis reveals a technical problem for six of the target words in Task 11 (educational.a, change.n, future.n, interest.n, need.n, program.n) which were not properly processed by the system in one of the steps, and the most frequent sense was used by default. Ignoring these cases, a precision of 78.3% was obtained using the task organiser's key and scoring program.

Acknowledgements

The work described in this paper was supported by a grant from the Research Grants Council of the Hong Kong Special Administrative Region, China (Project No. CityU 1508/06H).

References

Brill, E. (1994) Some advances in transformation-based part of speech tagging. In *Proceedings of the 12th National Conference on Artificial Intelligence (AAAI-94)*, pp.722-727.

Escudero, G., Màrquez, L. and Rigau, G. (2004) TALP System for the English Lexical Sample Task. In *Proceedings of SENSEVAL-3*, Barcelona, Spain.

Kwong, O.Y. (2005) Word Sense Classification Based on Information Susceptibility. In A. Lenci, S. Montemagni and V. Pirrelli (Eds.), *Acquisition and Representation of Word Meaning*. Linguistica Computazionale, pp.89-115.

Kwong, O.Y. (2007) Sense Abstractness, Semantic Activation and Word Sense Disambiguation: Implications from Word Association Norms. To appear in *Proceedings of NLPCS-2007*, Madeira, Portugal.

Leacock, C., Miller, G.A. and Chodorow, M. (1998) Using Corpus Statistics and WordNet Relations for Sense Identification. *Computational Linguistics, 24(1)*:147-166.

Mihalcea, R.F. (2002) Word sense disambiguation with pattern learning and automatic feature selection. *Natural Language Engineering, 8(4)*:343-358.

Mihalcea, R., Chklovski, T. and Kilgarriff, A. (2004) The SENSEVAL-3 English Lexical Sample Task. In *Proceedings of SENSEVAL-3*, Barcelona, Spain.

Resnik, P. and Yarowsky, D. (1997) A perspective on word sense disambiguation methods and their evaluation. In *Proceedings of SIGLEX'97 Workshop: Tagging Text with Lexical Semantics: Why, What, and How?*, Washington, D.C., pp.79-86.

Witten, I.H. and Frank, E. (2005) *Data Mining: Practical Machine Learning Tools and Techniques with Java Implementations*. Morgan Kaufmann.

Yarowsky, D. and Radu, F. (2002) Evaluating sense disambiguation across diverse parameter spaces. *Natural Language Engineering, 8(4)*:293-310.

CLR: Integration of FrameNet in a Text Representation System

Ken. Litkowski
CL Research
9208 Gue Road
Damascus, MD 20872
ken@clres.com

Abstract

In SemEval-2007, CL Research participated in the task for Frame Semantic Structure Extraction. Participation in this task was used as the vehicle for efforts to integrate and exploit FrameNet in a comprehensive text processing system. In particular, this involved steps to build a FrameNet dictionary with CL Research's DIMAP dictionary software and to use this dictionary (along with its semantic network processing capabilities) in processing text into XML representations. Implementation of the entire integrated package is only in its initial stages and was used to make only a bare submission of frame identification. On this task, over all texts, a recall of 0.372, a precision of 0.553, and an F-score of 0.445 were achieved. Considering only targets included in the DIMAP FrameNet dictionary, the overall F-score is 0.605. These results, competitive with the top scoring system, support continued attempts at a dictionary-based approach to frame structure extraction.

1 Introduction

CL Research participated in the SemEval-2007 task for Frame Semantic Structure Extraction. In participating in this task, we integrated the use of FrameNet in the Text Parser component of the CL Research Knowledge Management System (KMS). In particular, we created a FrameNet dictionary from the FrameNet databases with the CL Research DIMAP dictionary software and used this dictionary as a lexical resource. This new lexical resource was integrated in the same manner as other lexical resources (including WordNet and the *Oxford Dictionary of English* (ODE, 2004)). As such, the FrameNet dictionary was available as the basis for sense disambiguation. In the CL Research Text Parser, this integration was seamless, in which disambiguation can be performed against several lexical resources. This work attempts to expand on semantic role labeling experiments in Senseval-3 (Litkowski, 2004a, and Litkowski, 2004b).

In the following sections, we first describe the overall structure of the CL Research Knowledge Management System and Text Parser, describing their general parsing and text analysis routines. Next, we describe the creation of the FrameNet dictionary, particularly identifying design considerations to exploit the richness of the FrameNet data. In section 4, we describe our submission for the SemEval task. In section 5, we describe our results. Finally, we identify next steps that can be taken within the CL Research KMS and DIMAP environments to extend the FrameNet data.

2 CL Research Text Processing

The CL Research Knowledge Management System (KMS) is an integrated environment for performing several higher level applications, particularly question answering and summarization. The underlying architecture of KMS relies on an XML representation of texts that captures discourse structure and discourse elements, particularly noun phrases, verbs, and semantic roles (predominantly as reified in prepositions). The texts that are represented include primarily full texts as they may appear in several forms, but also include questions, topic specifications for which summaries are desired, and keyword search expressions.

Text processing is an integrated component of KMS, but for large-scale processing, a separate system, the CL Research Text Parser is frequently used. The same modules are used for both, with different interfaces. Text processing is performed in two stages: (1) syntactic parsing, generating a parse

Proceedings of the 4th International Workshop on Semantic Evaluations (SemEval-2007), pages 113–116,
Prague, June 2007. ©2007 Association for Computational Linguistics

tree as output; and (2) discourse analysis, analyzing the parse tree and building sets of data used to record information about discourse segments (i.e., clauses), discourse entities (primarily noun phrases, but also including predicate adjective and adverb phrases), verbs, and semantic relations (prepositions). After the data structures are completed for an entire text during the discourse analysis phase, they are used to create a nested XML representation showing all the elements and providing attributes of each component.

The parser is grammar-based and produces a constituent structure, with non-terminals representing syntactic components and leaves corresponding to the words of the sentence. The parser generates some dependency relationships by using dynamic grammar rules added during parsing, particularly through sets of subcategorization patterns associated with verbs (and some other words in the dictionary). This allows the identification of such things as sentence subjects, preposition phrase attachments, and clause attachments. Syntactic ambiguity is handled by carrying forward a variable number of possible parses (usually 40, but user adjustable for any number), eliminating parses that are less well-formed.

The discourse analysis phase includes an anaphora resolution component and detailed semantic analyses of each sentence element. Many dependency relationships are identified during this phase. The semantic analysis includes a disambiguation component for all words (using one or more of the integrated dictionaries). The semantic analysis also identifies (for later use in the XML representation) relations between various sentence elements, particularly identifying the complement and attachment point for prepositions.[1]

To make use of the FrameNet data, it is first necessary to put it into a form that can be used effectively. For this purpose, a DIMAP dictionary is used. Such dictionaries are accessible using btree lookup, so rapid access is ensured during large-scale text processing. Syntactic parsing proceeds at about eight or nine hundred sentences per minute; the discourse analysis phase is roughly the same complexity. The result is that sentences are normally processed at 300 to 500 sentences per minute.

3 A FrameNet Dictionary

The integration of FrameNet into KMS and Text Parser is generally handled in the same way that other dictionaries are used. Specifically, there is a call to a disambiguation component to identify the applicable sense. After this, FrameNet data are used in a slightly different way. Disambiguation proceeds sequentially through the words in a sentence, but the labeling of components with frame elements is performed only after a sentence has been fully discourse-analyzed. This is necessary because the location of frame elements requires full knowledge of all components in a sentence, not just those which precede a given target (i.e., in left-to-right parsing and discourse analysis).

The main issue is the design of a FrameNet dictionary; DIMAP provides sufficient capability to capture all aspects of the FrameNet data (Ruppenhofer, et al., 2006) in various types of built-in data structures. First, it is necessary to capture each lexical unit and to create a distinct sense for each frame in which a lexeme is used. The current FrameNet DIMAP dictionary contains 7575 entries, with many entries having multiple senses.[2] For each sense, the FrameNet part of speech, the definition, the frame name, the ID number, and the definition source (identified as FN or COD, the Concise Oxford Dictionary) are captured from the FrameNet files.[3]

If there is an associated FrameNet lexical entry file that contains frame element realizations, this information is also captured in the appropriate sense. In DIMAP, this is done in an attribute-value feature structure. Each non-empty feature element realization in the FrameNet data is captured. A DIMAP feature attribute is constructed as a conflation of the phrase type and the grammatical function, e.g. "NP (Dep)". The feature value is a conflation of the valence unit

[1]At present, the analysis of the complement and attachment points examines only the highest ranked attachment point, rather than examining other possibilities (which are frequently identified in parsing).

[2]We unwittingly used an August 2006 version of FrameNet, not the latest version that incorporated frames developed in connection with full-text annotation. This affects our results, as described below.

[3]The FrameNet dictionary data is captured using FrameNet Explorer, a Windows interface for exploring FrameNet frames, available for free download at CL Research (http://www.clres.com).

frame element name and the number of annotations in the FrameNet corpus, e.g., "Cognizer (28)". This manner of capturing FrameNet information is done to facilitate processing; the DIMAP feature structure is frequently used to access information about lexical items. Further experience will assess the utility of this format.

Frames and frame elements are captured in the same dictionary. However, they are not treated as lexical units, but rather as "meta-entries". In the DIMAP dictionary, frame names are entered as dictionary entries beginning with the symbol "#" and frame elements are entered beginning with the symbol "@". In these entries, different data structures of a DIMAP entry are used to capture the different kinds of relations between frames and frame elements (i.e., the frame-to-frame relations) that are found in the FrameNet data. Thus, a frame will have a "frame-element" link to each of its frame elements. It will also have attribute-value features listing its frame elements and their type (core, peripheral, or extra-thematic).

With a dictionary structured as described, it is possible not only to look up a lexical unit, but also to traverse the various links that are reachable from a given entry. Specifically, when a lexical unit is recognized in processing the text, the first step is to retrieve the entry for that item and to use the frame element realization patterns to disambiguate among the senses (if more than one of the same part of speech). After a sentence has been completely processed (as described above), the meta-entries associated with each lexical unit can be examined (and appropriate traversals to other meta-entries can be followed) in order to identify which sentence constituents fill the frame elements.

Specific routines for traversing the various FrameNet links have not yet been developed. However, this is primarily a matter of assessing which traversals would be useful. Similar traversals are used with other lexical resources, such as WordNet, where, for example, inheritance hierarchies and other WordNet relation links are routinely traversed.

4 The SemEval FrameNet Submission

To participate in the SemEval FrameNet task, the three test texts were wrapped into a standard XML representation used in processing texts. This wrapper consists only of an overall **<DOCS>** tag, a subtag **<DOC>** for each document, and a **<TEXT>** tag surrounding the actual text. The text was included with some minor changes. Since Text Parser includes a sentence splitter, we had to make sure that the texts would split into the identifiable sentences as given on each line of the texts. Thus, for headers in the text, we added a period at the end. Once we were sure that the same number of sentences would be recognized, we processed the texts using Text Parser, as described in section 2.[4]

As mentioned above, the FrameNet dictionary lookup occurred in a separate traversal of the parse tree after the discourse analysis phase. During this traversal, the base form of each noun, verb, adjective, or adverb content word was looked up in the FrameNet dictionary. If there was no entry for the word, no further FrameNet processing was performed. When an entry was found, each sense of the appropriate part of speech is examined in order to disambiguate among multiple senses. A score is computed for each sense and the score with the highest sense was selected.[5]

Having identified a sense in the FrameNet dictionary, this was interpreted as finding a FrameNet target, with the FrameNet frame as identified in the lexical entry. Since the character positions of each word in the source sentence are included in the parse tree information, this information was captured for inclusion in the output. (Further implementation to identify the frame elements associated with the target has not been completed at this time. As a result, our submission was only a partial completion of the FrameNet task.)

After completing the processing of each sentence,

[4] To make a submission for the FrameNet task, it was necessary to initialize an XML object into which the results could be inserted after processing each sentence. This is not a usual component of Text Parser, but was implemented solely for the purpose of participating in this task.

[5] At this time, all senses receive an identical score. The first sense is selected. Senses are unsystematically ordered as they were encountered in creating the FrameNet dictionary. This will be extended to compute a score based on the various frame element realization patterns associated with each sense.

all FrameNet frame information that had been identified was processed for inclusion in the XML submission for this task. In particular, the annotation sets required were incorporated into the XML object that had been initialized. (Our annotation sets included only the "Target" layer.) After all sentences had been completed, the XML object was printed to a file for submission.

5 Results

Our results are shown in Table 1, giving the recall, precision, and F-score for each text and over all texts. As indicated, these results are for only the target identification subtask.[6]

Table 1. Target Identification Scores

Text	Recall	Precision	F-Score
Dublin	0.33403	0.53572	0.41237
China	0.51148	0.52525	0.51827
Iran	0.44828	0.66102	0.53425
All	0.37240	0.55337	0.44520

As indicated above, we used an early version of the FrameNet databases that did not include all the lexical units in the training and test texts. As a result, we did not have FrameNet entries for 30 percent of the words identified as targets in the test texts. Table 2 shows an estimate of the adjusted scores that would result if those lexical items were included..

Table 2. Adjusted Target Identification Scores

Text	Recall	Precision	F-Score
Dublin	0.53445	0.65140	0.58716
China	0.57037	0.62097	0.59459
Iran	0.61494	0.72789	0.66667
All	0.56144	0.65132	0.60305

The results in Table 1 rank third of the four teams participating in this subtask. With the results in Table 2, our performance would improve to first for two of the texts and just below the top team for the other text.

[6]Corresponding to the "-e -n -t' options of the scoring program. In these tables, "Dublin" refers to **IntroOfDublin**, "China" to **ChinaOverview**, and "Iran" to **workAdvances**.

6 Future Steps

Participation in the FrameNet frame structure extraction task has demonstrated the basic viability of our approach. Many of the frames have been recognized successfully. We have not yet examined the extent to which the disambiguation among frames is significant, particularly since there are not many entries that have several senses. We have yet to develop specific techniques for making use of the frame element realization patterns. However, we believe that a reasonable performance can be expected since KMS and Text Parser produce output that breaks sentences down into the types of components that should be included as frame elements.

The architecture of KMS, Text Parser, and DIMAP provide significant opportunities for extending our performance. In particular, since these systems include the *Oxford Dictionary of English*, a superset of the *Concise Oxford Dictionary*, there is an opportunity for extending the FrameNet datasets. The COD definitions in FrameNet can be mapped to those in ODE and can be exploited to extend FrameNet frames to lexical items not yet covered in FrameNet.

References

Kenneth C. Litkowski. 2004a. Senseval-3 Task: Automatic Labeling of Semantic Roles. In *Senseval-3: Third International Workshop on the Evaluation of Systems for the Semantic Analysis of Text.* Association for Computational Linguistics. 9-12.

Kenneth C. Litkowski. 2004b. Explorations in Disambiguation Using XML Text Representation. In *Senseval-3: Third International Workshop on the Evaluation of Systems for the Semantic Analysis of Text.* Association for Computational Linguistics. 141-146.

The Oxford Dictionary of English. 2003. (A. Stevension and C. Soanes, Eds.). Oxford: Clarendon Press.

Josef Ruppenhofer, Michael Ellsworth, Miriam Petruck, Christopher Johnson, and Jan Scheffxzyk. 2006. FrameNet II: Extended Theory and Practice. International Computer Science Institute, University of California at Berkeley.

CLaC and CLaC-NB: Knowledge-based and corpus-based approaches to sentiment tagging

Alina Andreevskaia
Concordia University
1455 de Maisonneuve Blvd.
Montreal, Canada
andreev@cs.concordia.ca

Sabine Bergler
Concordia University
1455 de Maisonneuve Blvd.
Montreal, Canada
bergler@cs.concordia.ca

Abstract

For the Affective Text task at Semeval-1/Senseval-4, the CLaC team compared a knowledge-based, domain-independent approach and a standard, statistical machine learning approach to ternary sentiment annotation of news headlines. In this paper we describe the two systems submitted to the competition and evaluate their results. We show that the knowledge-based unsupervised method achieves high accuracy and precision but low recall, while supervised statistical approach trained on small amount of in-domain data provides relatively high recall at the cost of low precision.

1 Introduction

Sentiment tagging of short text spans — sentences, headlines, or clauses — poses considerable challenges for automatic systems due to the scarcity of sentiment clues in these units: sometimes, the decision about the text span sentiment has to be based on just a single sentiment clue and the cost of every error is high. This is particularly true for headlines, which are typically very short. Therefore, an ideal system for sentiment tagging of headlines has to use a large set of features with dependable sentiment annotations and to be able to reliably deduce the sentiment of the headline from the sentiment of its components.

The valence labeling subtask of the Affective Text task requires ternary — positive vs. negative vs. neutral — classification of headlines. While such categorization at the sentence level remains relatively unexplored[1], the two related sentence-level, binary classification tasks — positive vs. negative and subjective vs. objective — have attracted considerable attention in the recent years (Hu and Liu, 2004; Kim and Hovy, 2005; Riloff et al., 2006; Turney and Littman, 2003; Yu and Hatzivassiloglou, 2003). Unsupervised knowledge-based methods are the preferred approach to classification of sentences into positive and negative, mostly due to the lack of adequate amounts of labeled training data (Gamon and Aue, 2005). These approaches rely on presence and scores of sentiment-bearing words that have been acquired from dictionaries (Kim and Hovy, 2005) or corpora (Yu and Hatzivassiloglou, 2003). Their accuracy on news sentences is between 65 and 68%.

Sentence-level subjectivity detection, where training data is easier to obtain than for positive vs. negative classification, has been successfully performed using supervised statistical methods alone (Pang and Lee, 2004) or in combination with a knowledge-based approach (Riloff et al., 2006).

Since the extant literature does not provide clear evidence for the choice between supervised machine learning methods and unsupervised knowledge-based approaches for the task of ternary sentiment classification of sentences or headlines, we developed two systems for the Affective Text task at SemEval-2007. The first system (CLaC) relies on the knowledge-rich approach that takes into consid-

[1]To our knowledge, the only work that attempted such classification at the sentence level is (Gamon and Aue, 2005) that classified product reviews.

Proceedings of the 4th International Workshop on Semantic Evaluations (SemEval-2007), pages 117–120,
Prague, June 2007.

eration multiple clues, such as a list of sentiment-bearing unigrams and valence shifters, and makes use of sentence structure in order to combine these clues into an overall sentiment of the headline. The second system (CLaC-NB) explores the potential of a statistical method trained on a small amount of manually labeled news headlines and sentences.

2 CLaC System: Syntax-Aware Dictionary-Based Approach

The CLaC system relies on a knowledge-based, domain-independent, unsupervised approach to headline sentiment detection and scoring. The system uses three main knowledge inputs: a list of sentiment-bearing unigrams, a list of valence shifters (Polanyi and Zaenen, 2006), and a set of rules that define the scope and results of combination of sentiment-bearing words with valence shifters.

2.1 List of sentiment-bearing words

The unigrams used for sentence/headline classification were learned from WordNet (Fellbaum, 1998) dictionary entries using the STEP system described in (Andreevskaia and Bergler, 2006b). In order to take advantage of the special properties of WordNet glosses and relations, we developed a system that used the human-annotated adjectives from (Hatzivassiloglou and McKeown, 1997) as a seed list and learned additional unigrams from WordNet synsets and glosses. The STEP algorithm starts with a small set of manually annotated seed words that is expanded using synonymy and antonymy relations in WordNet. Then the system searches all WordNet glosses and selects the synsets that contain sentiment-bearing words from the expanded seed list in their glosses. In order to eliminate errors produced by part-of-speech ambiguity of some of the seed words, the glosses are processed by Brill's part-of-speech tagger (Brill, 1995) and only the seed words with matching part-of-speech tags are considered. Headwords with sentiment-bearing seed words in their definitions are then added to the positive or negative categories depending on the seed-word sentiment. Finally, words that were assigned contradicting — positive and negative — sentiment within the same run were eliminated. The average accuracy of 60 runs with non-intersecting seed lists when compared to General Inquirer (Stone et al., 1966) was 74%. In order to improve the list coverage, the words annotated as "Positiv" or "Negativ" in the General Inquirer that were not picked up by STEP were added to the final list.

Since sentiment-bearing words in English have different degree of centrality to the category of sentiment, we have constructed a measure of word centrality to the category of positive or negative sentiment described in our earlier work (Andreevskaia and Bergler, 2006a). The measure, termed Net Overlap Score (NOS), is based on the number of ties that connect a given word to other words in the category. The number of such ties is reflected in the number of times each word was retrieved from WordNet by multiple independent STEP runs with non-intersecting seed lists. This approach allowed us to assign NOSs to each unigram captured by multiple STEP runs. Only words with fuzzy membership score not equal to zero were retained in the list. The resulting list contained 10,809 sentiment-bearing words of different parts of speech.

2.2 Valence Shifters

The brevity of the headlines compared to typical news sentences[2] requires that the system is able to make a correct decision based on very few sentiment clues. Due to the scarcity of sentiment clues, the additional factors, such as presence of valence shifters, have a greater impact on the system performance on headlines than on sentences or texts, where impact of a single error can often be compensated by a number of other, correctly identified sentiment clues. For this reason, we complemented the system based on fuzzy score counts with the capability to discern and take into account some relevant elements of syntactic structure of sentences. We added to the system two components in order to enable this capability: (1) valence shifter handling rules and (2) parse tree analysis.

Valence shifters can be defined as words that modify the sentiment expressed by a sentiment-bearing word (Polanyi and Zaenen, 2006). The list of valence shifters used in our experiments was a com-

[2] An average length of a sentence in a news corpus is over 20 words, while the average length of headlines in the test corpus was only 7 words.

bination of (1) a list of common English negations, (2) a subset of the list of automatically obtained words with increase/decrease semantics, and (3) words picked up in manual annotation conducted for other research projects by two trained linguists. The full list consists of 490 words and expressions. Each entry in the list of valence shifters has an action and scope associated with it. The action and scope tags are used by special handling rules that enable our system to identify such words and phrases in the text and take them into account in sentence sentiment determination. In order to correctly determine the scope of valence shifters in a sentence, we introduced into the system the analysis of the parse trees produced by MiniPar (Lin, 1998).

As a result of this processing, every headline received a score according to the combined fuzzy NOS of its constituents. We then mapped this score, which ranged between -1.2 and 0.99, into the [-100, 100] scale as required by the competition organizers.

3 CLaC-NB System: Naïve Bayes

Supervised statistical methods have been very successful in sentiment tagging of texts and in subjectivity detection at sentence level: on movie review texts they reach an accuracy of 85-90% (Aue and Gamon, 2005; Pang and Lee, 2004) and up to 92% accuracy on classifying movie review snippets into subjective and objective using both Nave Bayes and SVM (Pang and Lee, 2004). These methods perform particularly well when a large volume of labeled data from the same domain as the test set is available for training (Aue and Gamon, 2005). The lack of sufficient data for training appears to be the main reason for the virtual absence of experiments with statistical classifiers in sentiment tagging at the sentence level.

In order to explore the potential of statistical approaches on sentiment classification of headlines, we implemented a basic Naïve Bayes classifier with smoothing using Lidstone's law of succession (with λ=0.1). No feature selection was performed.

The development set for the Affective Text task consisted of only 250 headlines, which is not sufficient for training of a statistical classifier. In order to increase the size of the training corpus, we augmented it with a balanced set of 900 manually annotated news sentences on a variety of topics extracted from the Canadian NewsStand database[3] and 200 headlines from different domains collected from Google News in January 2007[4].

The probabilities assigned by the classifier were mapped to [-100, 100] as follows: all negative headlines received a score of -100, all positive headlines +100, and neutral headlines 0.

4 Results and Discussion

Table 1 shows the results of the two CLaC systems for valence labeling subtask of Affective Text task compared to all participating systems average. The best subtask scores are highlighted in bold.

System	Pearson correl.	Acc.	Prec.	Rec.	F1
CLaC	**47.7**	**55.1**	**61.4**	9.2	16
CLaC-NB	25.4	31.2	31.2	**66.4**	**42**
Task average	33.2	44.7	44.85	29.6	23.7

Table 1: System results

The comparison between the two CLaC systems clearly demonstrates the relative advantages of the two approaches. The knowledge-based unsupervised system performed well above average on three main measures: the Pearson correlation between fine-grained sentiment assigned by CLaC system and the human annotation; the accuracy for ternary classification; and the precision of binary (positive vs. negative) classification. These results demonstrate that an accurately annotated list of sentiment-bearing words combined with sophisticated valence shifter handling produces acceptably accurate sentiment labels even for such difficult data as news headlines. This system, however, was not able to provide good recall.

On the contrary, supervised machine learning has very good recall, but low accuracy relative to the results of the unsupervised knowledge-based approach. This shortcoming could be in part reduced if more uniformly labeled headlines were available

[3]http://www.il.proquest.com/products_pq/descriptions/Canadian_newsstand.shtml

[4]The interannotator agreement for this data, as measured by Kappa, was 0.74.

for training. However, we can hardly expect large amounts of such manually annotated data to be handy in real-life situations.

5 Conclusions

The two CLaC systems that we submitted to the Affective Text task have tested the applicability of two main sentiment tagging approaches to news headlines annotation. The results of the two systems indicate that the knowledge-based unsupervised approach that relies on an automatically acquired list of sentiment-bearing unigrams and takes into account the combinatorial properties of valence shifters, can produce high quality sentiment annotations, but may miss many sentiment-laden headlines. On the other hand, supervised machine learning has good recall even with a relatively small training set, but its precision and accuracy are low. In our future work we will explore the potential of combining the two approaches in a single system in order to improve both recall and precision of sentiment annotation.

References

Alina Andreevskaia and Sabine Bergler. 2006a. Mining wordnet for a fuzzy sentiment: Sentiment tag extraction from wordnet glosses. In *Proceedings EACL-06, the 11rd Conference of the European Chapter of the Association for Computational Linguistics*, Trento, IT.

Alina Andreevskaia and Sabine Bergler. 2006b. Semantic tag extraction from wordnet glosses. In *Proceedings of LREC-06, the 5th Conference on Language Resources and Evaluation*, Genova, IT.

Anthony Aue and Michael Gamon. 2005. Customizing sentiment classifiers to new domains: a case study. In *RANLP-05, the International Conference on Recent Advances in Natural Language Processing*, Borovets, Bulgaria.

Eric Brill. 1995. Transformation-Based Error-Driven Learning and Natural Language Processing: A Case Study in Part-of-Speech Tagging. *Computational Linguistics*, 21(4).

Christiane Fellbaum, editor. 1998. *WordNet: An Electronic Lexical Database*. MIT Press, Cambridge, MA.

Michael Gamon and Anthony Aue. 2005. Automatic identification of sentiment vocabulary: exploiting low association with known sentiment terms. In *Proceedings of the ACL-05 Workshop on Feature Engineering for Machine Learning in Natural Language Processing*, Ann Arbor, MI.

Vasileios Hatzivassiloglou and Kathleen B. McKeown. 1997. Predicting the Semantic Orientation of Adjectives. In *Proceedings of ACL-97, 35nd Meeting of the Association for Computational Linguistics*, pages 174–181, Madrid, Spain. ACL.

Minqing Hu and Bing Liu. 2004. Mining and summarizing customer reviews. In *Tenth ACM SIGKDD Conference on Knowledge Discovery and Data Mining (KDD-04)*, pages 168–177.

Soo-Min Kim and Eduard Hovy. 2005. Automatic detection of opinion bearing words and sentences. In *Companion Volume to the Proceedings of IJCNLP-05, the Second International Joint Conference on Natural Language Processing*, pages 61–66, Jeju Island, KR.

Dekang Lin. 1998. Dependency-based Evaluation of MINIPAR. In *Proceedings of the Workshop on the Evaluation of Parsing Systems*, pages 768–774, Granada, Spain.

Bo Pang and Lilian Lee. 2004. A sentiment education: Sentiment analysis using subjectivity summarization based on minimum cuts. In *Proceedings of ACL-04, 42nd Meeting of the Association for Computational Linguistics*, pages 271–278.

Livia Polanyi and Annie Zaenen. 2006. Contextual Valence Shifters. In James G. Shanahan, Yan Qu, and Janyce Wiebe, editors, *Computing Attitude and Affect in Text: Theory and Application*. Springer Verlag.

Ellen Riloff, Siddharth Patwardhan, and Janyce Wiebe. 2006. Feature subsumption for opinion analysis. In *Proceedings of EMNLP-06, the Conference on Empirical Methods in Natural Language Processing*, pages 440–448, Sydney, AUS.

P. J. Stone, D.C. Dumphy, M.S. Smith, and D.M. Ogilvie. 1966. *The General Inquirer: a computer approach to content analysis*. M.I.T. studies in comparative politics. M.I.T. Press, Cambridge, MA.

Peter Turney and Michael Littman. 2003. Measuring praise and criticism: inference of semantic orientation from association. *ACM Transactions on Information Systems (TOIS)*, 21:315–346.

Hong Yu and Vasileios Hatzivassiloglou. 2003. Towards answering opinion questions: Separating facts from opinions and identifying the polarity of opinion sentences. In Michael Collins and Mark Steedman, editors, *Proceedings of EMNLP-03, 8th Conference on Empirical Methods in Natural Language Processing*, pages 129–136, Sapporo, Japan.

CMU-AT: Semantic Distance and Background Knowledge for Identifying Semantic Relations

Alicia Tribble
Language Technologies Institute
Carnegie Mellon University
Pittsburgh, PA, USA
atribble@cs.cmu.edu

Scott E. Fahlman
Language Technologies Institute
Carnegie Mellon University
Pittsburgh, PA, USA
sef@cs.cmu.edu

Abstract

This system uses a background knowledge base to identify semantic relations between base noun phrases in English text, as evaluated in SemEval 2007, Task 4. Training data for each relation is converted to statements in the Scone Knowledge Representation Language. At testing time a new Scone statement is created for the sentence under scrutiny, and presence or absence of a relation is calculated by comparing the total semantic distance between the new statement and all positive examples to the total distance between the new statement and all negative examples.

1 Introduction

This paper introduces a knowledge-based approach to the task of semantic relation classification, as evaluated in SemEval 2007, Task 4: "Classifying Relations Between Nominals". In Task 4, a full sentence is presented to the system, along with the WordNet sense keys for two noun phrases which appear there and the name of a semantic relation (e.g. "cause-effect"). The system should return "true" if a person reading the sentence would conclude that the relation holds between the two labeled noun phrases.

Our system represents a test sentence with a semantic graph, including the relation being tested and both of its proposed arguments. Semantic distance is calculated between this graph and a set of graphs representing the training examples relevant to the test sentence. A near-match between a test sentence and a positive training example is evidence that the same relation which holds in the example also holds in the test. We compute semantic distances to negative training examples as well, comparing the total positive and negative scores in order to decide whether a relation is true or false in the test sentence.

2 Motivation

Many systems which perform well on related tasks use syntactic features of the input sentence, coupled with classification by machine learning. This approach has been applied to problems like compound noun interpretation (Rosario and Hearst 2001) and semantic role labeling (Gildea and Jurafsky 2002).

In preparing our system for Task 4, we started by applying a similar syntax-based feature analysis to the trial data: 140 labeled examples of the relation "content-container". In 10-fold cross-validation with this data we achieved an average f-score of 70.6, based on features similar to the subset trees used for semantic role labeling in (Moschitti 2004). For classification we applied the updated tree-kernel package (Moschitti 2006), distributed with the svm-light tool (Joachims 1999) for learning Support Vector Machines (SVMs).

Training data for Task 4 is small, compared to other tasks where machine learning is commonly applied. We had difficulty finding a combination of features which gave good performance in cross-validation, but which did not result in a separate support vector being stored for every training sentence – a possible indicator of overfitting. As an example, the ratio of support vectors to training

Proceedings of the 4th International Workshop on Semantic Evaluations (SemEval-2007), pages 121–124,
Prague, June 2007.

examples for the experiment described above was .97, nearly 1-to-1.

As a result of this analysis we started work on our knowledge-based system, with the goal of using the two approaches together. We were also motivated by an interest in using relation definitions and background knowledge from WordNet to greater advantage. The algorithm we used in our final submission is similar to recent systems which discover textual entailment relationships (Haghighi, Ng et al. 2005; Zanzotto and Moschitti 2006). It gives us a way to encode information from the relation definitions directly, in the form of statements in a knowledge representation language. The inference rules that are learned by this system from training examples are also easier to interpret than the models generated by an SVM. In small-data applications this can be an advantage.

3 System Description: A Walk-Through

The example sentence below is taken (in abbreviated form) from the training data for Task 4, Relation 7 "Content-Container" (Girju, Hearst et al. 2007):

The *kitchen* holds a *cooker*.

We convert this positive example into a semantic graph by creating a new instance of the relation Contains and linking that instance to the WordNet term for each labeled argument ("kitchen%1:06:00::", "cooker%1:06:00::"). The result is shown in Figure 1. WordNet sense keys (Fellbaum 1998) have been mapped to a term, a part of speech (pos), and a sense number.

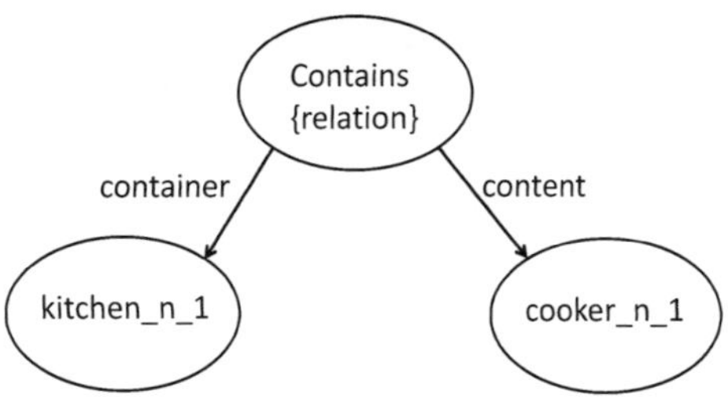

Figure 1. Semantic graph for the training example "The *kitchen* holds a *cooker*". Arguments are represented by a WordNet term, part of speech, and sense number.

This graph is instantiated as a statement using the Scone Knowledge Representation System, or

```
(new-statement {kitchen_n_1} {contains} {cooker_n_1})
(new-statement {artifact_n_1} {contains} {artifact_n_1})
(new-statement {whole_n_1} {contains} {whole_n_1})
```

Figure 2. Statements in Scone KR syntax, based on generalizing the training example "The *kitchen* holds a *cooker*".

"Scone" (Fahlman 2005). Scone gives us a way to store, search, and perform inference on graphs like the one shown above. After instantiating the graph we generalize it using hypernym information from WordNet. This generates additional Scone statements which are stored in a knowledge base (KB), shown in Figure 2. The first statement in the figure was generated verbatim from our training sentence. The remaining statements contain hypernyms of the original arguments.

For each argument seen in training, we also extract hypernyms and siblings from WordNet. For the argument kitchen, we extract 101 ancestors (artifact, whole, object, etc.) and siblings (structure, excavation, facility, etc.). A similar set of WordNet entities is extracted for the argument cooker. These entities, with repetitions removed, are encoded in a second Scone knowledge base, preserving the hierarchical (IS-A) links that come from WordNet. The hierarchy is manually linked at the top level into an existing background Scone KB where entities like animate, inanimate, person, location, and quantity are already defined.

After using the training data to create these two KBs, the system is ready for a test sentence. The following example is also adapted from SemEval Task 4 training data:

Equipment was carried in a *box*.

First we convert the sentence to a semantic graph, using the same technique as the one described above. The graph is implemented as a new Scone statement which includes the WordNet pos and sense number for each of the arguments: "box_n_1 contains equipment_n_1".

Next, using inference operations in Scone, the system verifies that the statement conforms to high-level constraints imposed by the relation definition. If it does, we calculate semantic distances between the argument nodes of our test statement and the analogous nodes in relevant training statements. A training statement is relevant if both of its arguments are ancestors of the appropriate arguments of the test sentence. In our example, only two of the three KB statements from Figure 2 are relevant to the test statement "box contains equipment": "whole contains whole" and "artifact contains artifact". The first statement, "kitchen contains cooker" fails to apply because kitchen is not an ancestor of box, and also because cooker is not an ancestor of equipment.

Figure 3 illustrates the distance from "*box* contains *equipment*" to "*whole* contains *whole*", calculated as the sum of the distances between *box-whole* and *equipment-whole*.

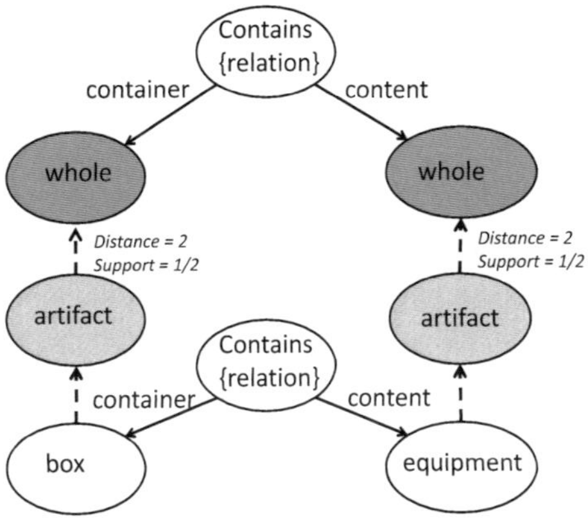

Figure 3. Calculating the distance through the knowledge base between "*equipment* contains *box*" and "*whole* contains *whole*". Dashed lines indicate IS-A links in the knowledge base.

The total number of these relevant, positive training statements is an indicator of "support" for the test sentence throughout the training data. The distance between one such statement and the test sentence is a measure of the strength of support. To reach a verdict, we sum over the inverse distances to all arguments from positive relevant examples: in Figure 3, the test statement "box contains equipment" receives a support score of (½ + ½ + 1 + 1), or 3.

Counter-evidence for a test sentence can be calculated in the same way, using relevant negative statements. In our example there are no negative training statements, so the total positive support score (3) is greater than the counter-evidence score (0), and the system verdict is "true".

4 System Components in Detail

As the detailed example above shows, this system is designed around its knowledge bases. The KBs provide a consistent framework for representing knowledge from a variety of sources as well as for calculating semantic distance.

4.1 Background knowledge

WordNet-extracted knowledge bases of the type described in Section 3 are generated separately for each relation. Average depth of these hierarchies is 4; we store only hypernyms of WordNet depth 7 and above, based on experiments in the literature by Nastase, et al. (2003; 2006).

Relation-specific and task-specific knowledge is encoded by hand. For each relation, we examine the relation definition and create a set of constraints in Scone formalism. For example, the definition of "container-contains" includes the following restriction (taken from training data for Task 4): *There is strong preference against treating legal entities (people and institutions) as content.*

In Scone, we encode this preference as a type restriction on the container role of any Contains relation: (new-is-not-a {container} {potential agent})

During testing, before calculating semantic distances, the system checks whether the test statement conforms to all such constraints.

4.2 Calculating semantic distance

Semantic distances are calculated between concepts in the knowledge base, rather than through WordNet directly. Distance between two KB entites is calculated by counting the edges along the shortest path between them, as illustrated in Figure 3. In the current implementation, only ancestors in the IS-A hierarchy are considered relevant, so this calculation amounts to counting the number of ancestors between an argument from the test sentence and an argument from a training example. Quick type-checking features which are built into Scone allow us to skip the distance calculation for non-relevant training examples.

5 Results & Conclusions

This system performed reasonably well for relation 3, Product-Producer, outperforming the baseline (baseline guesses "true" for every test sentence). Performance for this relation was also higher than the average F-score for all comparable groups in Task 4 (all groups in class "B4"). Average recall for this system over all relations was mid-range, compared to other participating groups. Average precision and average f-score fell below the baseline and below the average for all comparable groups. These scores are given in Table 1.

Relation	R	P	F
1. Cause-Effect	73.2	54.5	62.5
2. Instrument-Agency	76.3	50.9	61.1
3. Product-Producer	79.0	71.0	74.8
4. Origin-Entity	63.9	54.8	59.0
5. Theme-Tool	48.3	53.8	50.9
6. Part-Whole	57.7	45.5	50.8
7. Content-Container	68.4	59.1	63.4
Whole test set, not divided by relation	57.1	68.9	62.4
Average for CMU-AT	66.7	55.7	60.4
Average for all B4 systems	64.4	65.3	63.6
Baseline: "alltrue"	100.0	48.5	64.8

Table 1. Recall, Precision, and F-scores, separated by relation type. Baseline score is calculated by guessing "true" for all test setences.

Analysis of the training data reveals that relation 3 is the class where target nouns occur most often together in nominal compounds and base NPs, with little additional syntax to connect them. While other relations included sentences where the targets were covered by a single VP, Product-Producer did not. It seems that background knowledge plays a larger role in identifying the Producer-Produces relationship than it does for other relations. However this conclusion is softened by the fact that we also spent more time in development and cross-evaluation for relations 3 and 7, our two best performing relations.

This system demonstrates a knowledge-based framework that performs very well for certain relations. Importantly, the system we submitted for evaluation did not make use of syntactic features, which are almost certainly relevant to this task. We are already exploring methods for combining the knowledge-based decision process with one that uses syntactic evidence as well as corpus statistics, described in Section 2.

Acknowledgement

This work was supported by a generous research grant from Cisco Systems, and by the Defense Advanced Research Projects Agency (DARPA) under contract number NBCHD030010.

References

Fahlman, S. E. (2005). Scone User's Manual.

Fellbaum, C. (1998). WordNet An Electronic Lexical Database, Bradford Books.

Gildea, D. and D. Jurafsky (2002). "Automatic labeling of semantic roles." Computational Linguistics 28(3): 245-288.

Girju, R., M. Hearst, et al. (2007). Classification of Semantic Relations between Nominals: Dataset for Task 4. SemEval 2007, 4th International Workshop on Semantic Evaluations, Prague, Czech Republic.

Haghighi, A., A. Ng, et al. (2005). Robust Textual Inference via Graph Matching. Human Language Technology Conference and Conference on Empirical Methods in Natural Language Processing, Vancouver, British Columbia, Canada.

Joachims, T. (1999). Making large-scale SVM learning practical. Advances in Kernel Methods - Support Vector Learning. B. Schölkopf, C. Burges and A. Smola.

Moschitti, A. (2004). A study on Convolution Kernel for Shallow Semantic Parsing. proceedings of the 42nd Conference of the Association for Computational Linguistics (ACL-2004). Barcelona, Spain.

Moschitti, A. (2006). Making tree kernels practical for natural language learning. Eleventh International Conference on European Association for Computational Linguistics, Trento, Italy.

Nastase, V., J. S. Shirabad, et al. (2006). Learning noun-modifier semantic relations with corpus-based and Wordnet-based features. 21st National Conference on Artificial Intelligence (AAAI-06), Boston, Massachusetts.

Nastase, V. and S. Szpakowicz (2003). Exploring noun-modifier semantic relations. IWCS 2003.

Rosario, B. and M. Hearst (2001). Classifying the semantic relations in Noun Compounds. 2001 Conference on Empirical Methods in Natural Language Processing.

Zanzotto, F. M. and A. Moschitti (2006). Automatic Learning of Textual Entailments with Cross-Pair Similarities. the 21st International Conference on Computational Linguistics and 44th Annual Meeting of the Association for Computational Linguistics (ACL), Sydney, Austrailia.

CU-COMSEM: Exploring Rich Features for Unsupervised Web Personal Name Disambiguation

Ying Chen
Center for Spoken Language Research
University of Colorado at Boulder
yc@colorado.edu

James Martin
Department of Computer Science
University of Colorado at Boulder
James.Martin@colorado.edu

Abstract

The increasing number of web sources is exacerbating the named-entity ambiguity problem. This paper explores the use of various token-based and phrase-based features in unsupervised clustering of web pages containing personal names. From these experiments, we find that the use of rich features can significantly improve the disambiguation performance for web personal names.

1 Introduction

As the sheer amount of web information expands at an ever more rapid pace, the named-entity ambiguity problem becomes more and more serious in many fields, such as information integration, cross-document co-reference, and question answering. Individuals are so glutted with information that searching for data presents real problems. It is therefore crucial to develop methodologies that can efficiently disambiguate the ambiguous names from any given set of data.

In the paper, we present an approach that combines unsupervised clustering methods with rich feature extractions to automatically cluster returned web pages according to which named entity in reality the ambiguous personal name in a web page refers to. We make two contributions to approaches to web personal name disambiguation. First, we seek to go beyond the kind of bag-of-words features employed in earlier systems (Bagga & Baldwin, 1998; Gooi & Allan, 2004; Pedersen et al., 2005), and attempt to exploit deep semantic features beyond the work of Mann & Yarowsky (2003). Second, we exploit some features that are available only in a web corpus, such as URL information and related web pages.

The paper is organized as follows. Section 2 introduces our rich feature extractions along with their corresponding similarity matrix learning. In Section 3, we analyze the performance of our system. Finally, we draw some conclusions.

2 Methodology

Our approach follows a common architecture for named-entity disambiguation: the detection of ambiguous objects, feature extractions and their corresponding similarity matrix learning, and finally clustering.

Given a webpage, we first run a modified Beautiful Soup[1] (a HTML parser) to extract a clean text document for that webpage. In a clean text document, noisy tokens, such as HTML tags and java codes, are removed as much as possible, and sentence segmentation is partially done by following the indications of some special HTML tags. For example, a sentence should finish when it meets a "<table>" tag. Then each clean document continues to be preprocessed with MXTERMINATOR (a sentence segmenter),[2] the Penn Treebank tokenization,[3] a syntactic phrase chunker (Hacioglu, 2004), and a named-entity detection and coreference system for the ACE project[4] called EX-

[1] http://www.crummy.com/software/BeautifulSoup
[2] http://www.id.cbs.dk/~dh/corpus/tools/MXTERMINATOR.html
[3] http://www.cis.upenn.edu/~treebank/tokenization.html
[4] http://www.nist.gov/speech/tests/ace

Proceedings of the 4th International Workshop on Semantic Evaluations (SemEval-2007), pages 125–128,
Prague, June 2007. ©2007 Association for Computational Linguistics

ERT[5] (Hacioglu et al. 2005; Chen & Hacioglu, 2006).

2.1 The detection of ambiguous objects

For a given ambiguous personal name, for each web page, we try to extract all mentions of the ambiguous personal name, using three possible varieties of the personal name. For example, the three regular expression patterns for "Alexander Markham" are "Alexander Markham," "Markham, Alexander," and "Alexander .\. Markham" (".\." can match a middle name). Web pages without any mention of the ambiguous personal name of interest are discarded and receive no further processing.

Since it is common for a single document to contain one or more mentions of the ambiguous personal name of interest, there is a need to define the object to be disambiguated. Here, we adopt the policy of "one person per document" (all mentions of the ambiguous personal name in one web page are assumed to refer to the same personal entity in reality) as in Bagga & Baldwin (1998), Mann & Yarowsky (2003) and Gooi & Allan (2004). We therefore define an object as a single entity with the ambiguous personal name in a given web page. This definition of the object (document-level object) might be mistaken, because the mentions of the ambiguous personal name in a web page may refer to multiple entities, but we found that this is a rare case (most of those cases occur in genealogy web pages). On the other hand, a document-level object can include much information derived from that web page, so that it can be represented by rich features.

Given this definition of an object, we define a target entity as an entity (outputted from the EXERT system) that includes a mention of the ambiguous personal name. Then, we define a local sentence as a sentence that contains a mention of any target entity.

2.2 Feature extraction and similarity matrix learning

Most of the previous work (Bagga & Baldwin, 1998; Gooi & Allan; 2004; Pedersen et al., 2005) uses token information in the given documents. In this paper, we follow and extend their work especially for a web corpus. On the other hand, compared to a token, a phrase contains more information for named-entity disambiguation. Therefore, we explore some phrase-based information in this paper. Finally, there are two kinds of feature vectors developed in our system: token-based and phrase-based. A token-based feature vector is composed of tokens, and a phrase-based feature vector is composed of phrases.

2.2.1 Token-based features

There is a lot of token information available in a web page: the tokens occurring in that web page, the URL for that web page, and so on. Here, for each web page, we tried to extract tokens according to the following schemes.

Local tokens (Local): the tokens occurring in the local sentences in a given webpage;

Full tokens (Full): the tokens occurring in a given webpage;

URL tokens (URL): the tokens occurring in the URL of a given webpage. URL tokenization works as follows: split a URL at ":" and ".", and then filter out stop words that are very common in URLs, such as "com," "http," and so on;

Title tokens in root page (TTRP): the title tokens occurring in the root page of a given webpage. Here, we define the root page of a given webpage as the page whose URL is the first slash-demarcated element (non-http) of the URL of the given webpage. For example, the root page of "http://www.leeds.ac.uk/calendar/court.htm" is "www.leeds.ac.uk". We do not use all tokens in the root page because there may be a lot of noisy information.

Although Local tokens and Full tokens often provide enough information for name disambiguation, there are some ambiguity cases that can be solved only with the help of information beyond the given web page, such as URL tokens and TTRP tokens. For example, in the web page "Alexander Markham 009," there is not sufficient information to identify the "Alexander Markham." But from its URL tokens ("leeds ac uk calendar court") and the title tokens in its root page ("University of Leeds"), it is easy to infer that this "Alexander Markham" is from the University of Leeds, which can totally solve the name ambiguity.

Because of the noisy information in URL tokens and TTRP tokens, here we combine them with Local tokens, using the following policy: for

[5] http://sds.colorado.edu/EXERT

each URL token and TTRP token, if the token is also one of the Local tokens of other web pages, add this token into the Local token list of the current webpage. We do the same thing with Full tokens.

Except URL tokens, the other three kinds of tokens—Local tokens, Full tokens and TTRP tokens—are outputted from the Penn Treebank tokenization, filtered by a stop-word dictionary, and represented in their morphological root form. But tokens in web pages have special characteristics and need more post-processing. In particular, a token may be an email address or a URL that may contain some useful information. For example, "charlotte@la-par.org" indicates the "Charlotte Bergeron" who works for PAR (the Public Affairs Research Council) in LA (Los Angeles). To capture the fine-grained information in an email address or a URL, we do deep tokenization on these two kinds of tokens. For a URL, we do deep tokenization as URL tokenization; for an email address, we split the email address at "@" and ".", then filter out the stop words as in URL tokenization.

So far, we have developed two token-based feature vectors: a Local token feature vector and a Full token feature vector. Both of them may contain URL and TTRP tokens. Given feature vectors, we need to find a way to learn the similarity matrix. Here, we choose the standard TF-IDF method to calculate the similarity matrix.

2.2.2 Phrase-based features

Since considerable information related to the ambiguous object resides in the noun phrases in a web page, such as the person's job and the person's location, we attempt to capture this noun phrase information. The following section briefly describes how to extract and use the noun phrase information. For more detail, see Chen & Martin (2007).

Contextual base noun phrase feature: With the syntactic phrase chunker, we extract all base noun phrases (non-overlapping syntactic phrases) occurring in the local sentences, which usually include some useful information about the ambiguous object. A base noun phrase of interest serves as an element in the feature vector.

Document named-entity feature: Given the EXERT system, a direct and simple way to use the semantic information is to extract all named entities in a web page. Since a given entity can be represented by many mentions in a document, we choose a single representative mention to represent each entity. The representative mention is selected according to the following ordered preference list: longest NAME mention, longest NOMINAL mention. A representative mention phrase serves as an element in a feature vector.

Given a pair of feature vectors consisting of phrase-based features, we need to choose a similarity scheme to calculate the similarity matrix. Because of the word-space delimiter in English, the feature vector comprises phrases, so that a similarity scheme for phrase-based feature vectors is required. Chen & Martin (2007) introduced one of those similarity schemes, "two-level SoftTFIDF". First, a token-based similarity scheme, the standard SoftTFIDF (Cohen et al., 2003), is used to calculate the similarity between phrases in the pair of feature vectors; in the second phase, the standard SoftTFIDF is reformulated to calculate the similarity for the pair of phrased-based feature vectors.

First, we introduce the standard SoftTFIDF. In a pair of feature vectors S and T, $S = (s_1, \ldots, s_n)$ and $T = (t_1, \ldots, t_m)$. Here, s_i ($i = 1 \ldots n$) and t_j ($j = 1 \ldots m$) are substrings (tokens). Let $CLOSE(\theta; S;T)$ be the set of substrings $w \in S$ such that there is some $v \in T$ satisfying $dist(w; v) > \theta$. The Jaro-Winkler distance function (Winkler, 1999) is $dist(;)$. For $w \in CLOSE(\theta; S;T)$, let $D(w; T) = \max_{v \in T} dist(w;v)$. Then the standard SoftTFIDF is computed as

$$\text{SoftTFIDF}(S,T) = \sum_{w \in CLOSE(\theta;S;T)} \text{V}(w, S) \times \text{V}(w, T) \times \text{D}(w, T)$$

$$\text{V}'(w, S) = \log(\text{TF}_{w,S} + 1) \times \log(\text{IDF}_w)$$

$$\text{V}(w, S) = \frac{\text{V}\ (w, S)}{\sqrt{\sum_{w \in S} \text{V}\ (w, S)^2}},$$

where $\text{TF}_{w,S}$ is the frequency of substrings w in S, and IDF_w is the inverse of the fraction of documents in the corpus that contain w. To compute the similarity for the phrase-based feature vectors, in the second step of "two-level SoftTFIDF," the substring w is a phrase and *dist* is the standard SoftTFIDF.

So far, we have developed several feature models and learned the corresponding similarity matrices, but clustering usually needs only one unique similarity matrix. In the results reported here, we simply combine the similarity matrices, assigning equal weight to each one.

2.3 Clustering

Although clustering is a well-studied area, a remaining research problem is to determine the optimal parameter settings during clustering, such as the number of clusters or the stop-threshold, a problem that is important for real tasks and that is not at all trivial. Because currently we focus only on feature development, we choose agglomerative clustering with a single linkage, and simply use a fixed stop-threshold acquired from the training data.

3 Performance

Our system performs very well for the Semeval Web People corpus, and Table 1 shows the performances. There are two results in Table 1: One is gotten from the evaluation of Semeval Web People Track (SemEval), and the other is evaluated with B-cubed evaluation (Bagga and Baldwin, 1998). Both scores indicate that web personal name disambiguation needs more effort.

	Purity	Inverse Purity	F (α=0.5)	F (α=0.2)
SemEval	0.72	0.88	0.78	0.83
	Precision	Recall	F (α=0.5)	F (α=0.2)
B-cubed	0.61	0.83	0.70	0.77

Table 1 *The performances of the test data*

4 Conclusion

Our experiments in web personal name disambiguation extend token-based information to a web corpus, and also include some noun phrase-based information. From our experiment, we first find that it is not easy to extract a clean text document from a webpage because of much noisy information in it. Second, some common tools need to be adapted to a web corpus, such as sentence segmentation and tokenization. Many NLP tools are developed for a news corpus, whereas a web corpus is noisier and often needs some specific processing. Third, in this paper, we use some URL information and noun phrase information in a rather simple way; more exploration is needed in the future. Besides the rich feature extraction, we also need more work on similarity combination and clustering.

Acknowledgements

Special thanks are extended to Praful Mangalath and Kirill Kireyev.

References

J. Artiles, J. Gonzalo. and S. Sekine. 2007. *The SemEval-2007 WePS Evaluation: Establishing a benchmark for the Web People Search Task.* In Proceedings of Semeval 2007, Association for Computational Linguistics.

A. Bagga and B. Baldwin. 1998. *Entity–based Cross–document Co–referencing Using the Vector Space Model.* In 17th COLING.

Y. Chen and K. Hacioglu. 2006. *Exploration of Coreference Resolution: The ACE Entity Detection and Recognition Task.* In 9th International Conference on TEXT, SPEECH and DIALOGUE.

Y. Chen and J. Martin. 2007. *Towards Robust Unsupervised Personal Name Disambiguation.* EMNLP.

W. Cohen, P. Ravikumar, S. Fienberg. 2003. *A Comparison of String Metrics for Name-Matching Tasks.* In IJCAI-03 II-Web Workshop.

C. H. Gooi and J. Allan. 2004. *Cross-Document Coreference on a Large Scale Corpus.* NAACL

K. Hacioglu, B. Douglas and Y. Chen. 2005. *Detection of Entity Mentions Occurring in English and Chinese Text.* Computational Linguistics.

K. Hacioglu. 2004. *A Lightweight Semantic Chunking Model Based On Tagging.* In HLT/NAACL.

B. Malin. 2005. *Unsupervised Name Disambiguation via Social Network Similarity.* SIAM.

G. Mann and D. Yarowsky. 2003. *Unsupervised Personal Name Disambiguation.* In Proc. of CoNLL-2003, Edmonton, Canada.

T. Pedersen, A. Purandare and A. Kulkarni. 2005. *Name Discrimination by Clustering Similar Contexts.* In Proc. of the Sixth International Conference on Intelligent Text Processing and Computational Linguistics, pages 226-237. Mexico City, Mexico.

W. E. Winkler. 1999. *The state of record linkage and current research problems. Statistics of Income Division*, Internal Revenue Service Publication R99/04.

CU-TMP: Temporal Relation Classification Using Syntactic and Semantic Features

Steven Bethard and **James H. Martin**
Department of Computer Science
University of Colorado at Boulder
430 UCB, Boulder, CO 80309, USA
{bethard,martin}@colorado.edu

Abstract

We approached the temporal relation identification tasks of TempEval 2007 as pair-wise classification tasks. We introduced a variety of syntactically and semantically motivated features, including temporal-logic-based features derived from running our Task B system on the Task A and C data. We trained support vector machine models and achieved the second highest accuracies on the tasks: 61% on Task A, 75% on Task B and 54% on Task C.

1 Introduction

In recent years, the temporal structure of text has become a popular area of natural language processing research. Consider a sentence like:

(1) The top commander of a Cambodian resistance force said Thursday he has sent a team to recover the remains of a British mine removal expert kidnapped and presumed killed by Khmer Rouge guerrillas almost two years ago.

English speakers immediately recognize that *kidnapping* came first, then *sending*, and finally *saying*, even though *before* and *after* never appeared in the text. How can machines learn to do the same?

The 2007 TempEval competition tries to address this question by establishing a common corpus on which research systems can compete to find temporal relations (Verhagen et al., 2007). TempEval considers the following types of event-time temporal relations:

Task A Events[1] and times within the same sentence
Task B Events[1] and document times
Task C Matrix verb events in adjacent sentences

In each of these tasks, systems attempt to annotate pairs with one of the following relations: BEFORE, BEFORE-OR-OVERLAP, OVERLAP, OVERLAP-OF-AFTER, AFTER or VAGUE. Competing systems are instructed to find all temporal relations of these types in a corpus of newswire documents.

We approach these tasks as pair-wise classification problems, where each event/time pair is assigned one of the TempEval relation classes (BEFORE, AFTER, etc.). Event/time pairs are encoded using syntactically and semantically motivated features, and then used to train support vector machine (SVM) classifiers.

The remainder of this paper is structured as follows. Section 2 describes the features used to characterize event/time relations. Section 3 explains how we used these features to train SVM models for each task. Section 4 discusses the performance of our models on the TempEval data, and Section 5 summarizes the lessons learned and future directions.

2 Features

We used a variety of lexical, syntactic and semantic features to characterize the different types of temporal relations. In each task, the events and times were characterized using the features:

word The text of the event or time words

[1] TempEval only considers events that occurred at least 20 times in the TimeBank (Pustejovsky et al., 2003) corpus for these tasks

Proceedings of the 4th International Workshop on Semantic Evaluations (SemEval-2007), pages 129–132,
Prague, June 2007.

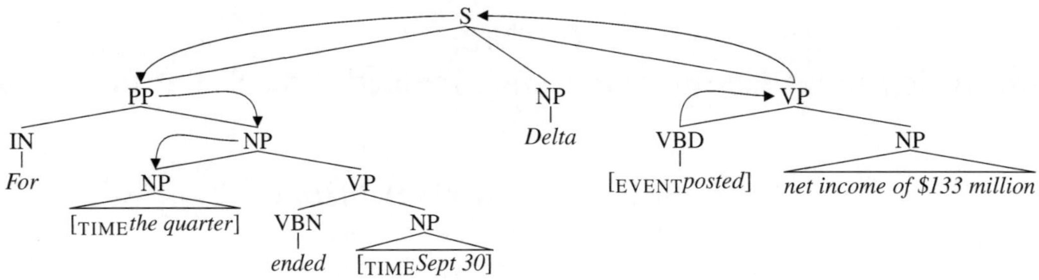

Figure 1: A syntactic tree. The path between *posted* and *the quarter* is VBD-VP-S-PP-NP-NP

pos The parts of speech[2] of the words, e.g. *this crucial moment* has the parts of speech DT-JJ-NN.

gov-prep Any prepositions governing the event or time, e.g. in *during the Iran-Iraq war*, the preposition *during* governs the event *war*, and in *after ten years*, the preposition *after* governs the time *ten years*.

gov-verb The verb that governs the event or time, e.g. in *rejected in peace talks*, the verb *rejected* governs the event *talks*, and in *withdrawing on Friday*, the verb *withdrawing* governs the time *Friday*. For events that are verbs, this feature is just the event itself.

gov-verb-pos The part of speech[2] of the governing verb, e.g. *withdrawing* has the part of speech VBG.

aux Any auxiliary verbs and adverbs modifying the governing verb, e.g. in *could not come*, the words *could* and *not* are considered auxiliaries for the event *come*, and in *will begin withdrawing on Friday*, the words *will* and *begin* are considered auxiliaries for the time *Friday*.

Events were further characterized using the features (the last six use gold-standard TempEval markup):

modal Whether or not the event has one of the auxiliaries, *can*, *will*, *shall*, *may*, or any of their variants (*could*, *would*, etc.).

gold-stem The stem, e.g. the stem of *fallen* is *fall*.

gold-pos The part-of-speech, e.g. NOUN or VERB.

gold-class The semantic class, e.g. REPORTING.

gold-tense The tense, e.g. PAST or PRESENT.

gold-aspect The aspect, e.g. PERFECTIVE.

gold-polarity The polarity, e.g. POS or NEG.

Times were further characterized using the following gold-standard TempEval features:

[2]From MXPOST (ftp.cis.upenn.edu/pub/adwait/jmx/)

gold-type The type, e.g. DATE or TIME.

gold-value The value, e.g. PAST_REF or 1990-09.

gold-func The temporal function, e.g. TRUE.

These gold-standard event and time features are similar to those used by Mani and colleagues (2006).

The features above don't capture much of the differences between the tasks, so we introduced some task-specific features. Task A included the features:

inter-time The count of time expressions between the event and time, e.g. in Figure 1, there is one time expression, *Sept 30*, between the event *posted* and the time *the quarter*.

inter-path The syntactic path between the event and the time, e.g. in Figure 1 the path between *posted* and *the quarter* is VBD>VP>S<PP<NP<NP.

inter-path-parts The path, broken into three parts: the tags from the event to the lowest common ancestor (LCA), the LCA, and the tags from the LCA to the time, e.g. in Figure 1 the parts are VBD>VP, S and PP<NP<NP.

inter-clause The number of clause nodes along the syntactic path, e.g. in Figure 1 there is one clause node along the path, the top S node.

Our syntactic features were derived from a syntactic tree, though Boguraev and Ando (2005) suggest that some could be derived from finite state grammars.

For Task C we included the following feature:

tense-rules The relation predicted by a set of tense rules, where past tense events come BEFORE present tense events, present tense events come BEFORE future tense events, etc. In the text:

(2) Finally today, we [EVENT *learned*] that the space agency has taken a giant leap forward. Collins will be [EVENT *named*] commander of Space Shuttle Columbia.

Since *learned* is in past tense and *named* is in future, the relation is (*learned* BEFORE *named*).

In preliminary experiments, the Task B system had the best performance, so we ran this system on the data for Tasks A and C, and used the output to add the following feature for both tasks:

task-b-rel The relation predicted by combining the output of the Task B system with temporal logic. For example, consider the text:

(3) [TIME *08-15-90 (=1990-08-15)*] Iraq's Saddam Hussein [TIME *today (=1990-08-15)*] sought peace on another front by promising to release soldiers captured during the Iran-Iraq [EVENT *war*].

If Task B said (*war* BEFORE *08–15–90*) then since *08–15–90=1990–08–15=today*, the relation (*war* BEFORE *today*) must hold.

3 Models

Using the features described in the previous section, each temporal relation — an event paired with a time or another event — was translated into a set of feature values. Pairing those feature values with the TempEval labels (BEFORE, AFTER, etc.) we trained a statistical classifier for each task. We chose support vector machines[3](SVMs) for our classifiers as they have shown good performance on a variety of natural language processing tasks (Kudo and Matsumoto, 2001; Pradhan et al., 2005).

Using cross-validations on the training data, we performed a simple feature selection where any feature whose removal improved the cross-validation F-score was discarded. The resulting features for each task are listed in Table 1. After feature selection, we set the SVM free parameters, e.g. the kernel degree and cost of misclassification, by performing additional cross-validations on the training data, and selecting the model parameters which yielded the highest F-score for each task[4].

[3]We used the TinySVM implementation from http://chasen.org/%7Etaku/software/TinySVM/ and trained one-vs-rest classifiers.

[4]We only experimented with polynomial kernels.

Feature	Task A	Task B	Task C
event-word			
event-pos	X		X
event-gov-prep	X		X
event-gov-verb	X		X
event-gov-verb-pos	X	X	2
event-aux	X	X	X
modal	X		X
gold-stem	X	X	1
gold-pos	X		X
gold-class	X	X	X
gold-tense	X	X	X
gold-aspect	X		X
gold-polarity	X		X
time-word	X		
time-pos	X		
time-gov-prep	X		
time-gov-verb	X		
time-gov-verb-pos	X		
time-aux	X		
gold-type			
gold-value	X	X	
gold-func	X		
inter-time	X		
inter-path	X		
inter-path-parts	X		
inter-clause	X		
tense-rules			X
task-b-rel	X		X

Table 1: Features used in each task. An X indicates that the feature was used for that task. For Task C, 1 indicates that the feature was used only for the first event and not the second, and 2 indicates the reverse.

	Strict			Relaxed		
Task	P	R	F	P	R	F
A	0.61	0.61	0.61	0.63	0.63	0.63
B	0.75	0.75	0.75	0.76	0.76	0.76
C	0.54	0.54	0.54	0.60	0.60	0.60

Table 2: (P)recision, (R)ecall and (F)-measure of the models on each task. Precision, recall and F-measure are all equivalent to classification accuracy.

4 Results

We evaluated our classifers on the TempEval test data. Because the Task A and C models derived features from the Task B temporal relations, we first ran the Task B classifer over all the data, and then ran the Task A and Task C classifiers over their individual data. The resulting temporal relation classifications were evalutated using the standard TempEval scoring script. Table 2 summarizes these results.

Our models achieved an accuracy of 61% on Task A, 75% on Task B and 54% on Task C, the second highest scores on all these tasks. The Temp-

Task	Feature Removed	Model Accuracy
A	-	0.663
	time-gov-prep	0.650
	gold-value	0.652
	polarity	0.655
	task-b-rel	0.656
B	-	0.809
	event-aux	0.780
	gold-stem	0.784
	gold-class	0.794
C	-	0.534
	event-gov-verb-2	0.522
	event-aux-2	0.525
	gold-class-1	0.526
	gold-class-2	0.527
	event-pos-2, task-b-rel	0.529

Table 3: Feature analysis. The '-' lines show the accuracy of the model with all features.

Eval scoring script also reported a relaxed measure where for example, systems could get partial credit for matching a gold standard label like OVERLAP-OR-AFTER with OVERLAP or AFTER. Under this measure, our models achieved an accuracy of 63% on Task A, 76% on Task B and 60% on Task C, again the second highest scores in the competition.

We performed a basic feature analysis where, for each feature in a task, a model was trained with that feature removed and all other features retained. We evaluated the performance of the resulting models using cross-validations on the training data[5]. Features whose removal resulted in the largest drops in model performance are listed in Table 3.

For Task A, the most important features were the preposition governing the time and the time's normalized value. For Task B, the most important features were the auxiliaries governing the event, and the event's stem. For Task C, the most important features were the verb and auxiliaries governing the second event. For both Tasks A and C, the features based on the Task B relations were one of the top six features. In general however, no single feature dominated any one task — the greatest drop in performance from removing a feature was only 2.9%.

5 Conclusions

TempEval 2007 introduced a common dataset for work on identifying temporal relations. We framed the TempEval tasks as pair-wise classification problems where pairs of events and times were assigned a temporal relation class. We introduced a variety of syntactic and semantic features, including paths between constituents in a syntactic tree, and temporal relations deduced by running our Task B system on the Task A and C data. Our models achieved an accuracy of 61% on Task A, 75% on Task B and 54% on Task C. Analysis of these models indicated that no single feature dominated any given task, and suggested that future work should focus on new features to better characterize temporal relations.

[5] We used cross-validations on the training data to preserve the validity of the TempEval test data for future research

6 Acknowledgments

This research was performed under an appointment of the first author to the DHS Scholarship and Fellowship Program, administered by the ORISE through an interagency agreement between DOE and DHS. ORISE is managed by ORAU under DOE contract number DE-AC05-06OR23100. All opinions expressed in this paper are the author's and do not necessarily reflect the policies and views of DHS, DOE, or ORAU/ORISE.

References

B. Boguraev and R. K. Ando. 2005. Timebank-driven timeml analysis. In Graham Katz, James Pustejovsky, and Frank Schilder, editors, *Annotating, Extracting and Reasoning about Time and Events*, Dagstuhl Seminars. German Research Foundation.

T. Kudo and Y. Matsumoto. 2001. Chunking with support vector machines. In *NAACL*.

I. Mani, M. Verhagen, B. Wellner, C. M. Lee, and J. Pustejovsky. 2006. Machine learning of temporal relations. In *COLING/ACL*.

S. Pradhan, K. Hacioglu, V. Krugler, W. Ward, J. H. Martin, and D. Jurafsky. 2005. Support vector learning for semantic argument classification. *Machine Learning*, 60(1):11–39.

J. Pustejovsky, P. Hanks, R. Saur, A. See, R. Gaizauskas, A. Setzer, D. Radev, B. Sundheim, D. Day, L. Ferro, and M. Lazo. 2003. The timebank corpus. In *Corpus Linguistics*, pages 647–656.

M. Verhagen, R. Gaizauskas, F. Schilder, M. Hepple, and J. Pustejovsky. 2007. Semeval-2007 task 15: Tempeval temporal relation identification. In *SemEval-2007: 4th International Workshop on Semantic Evaluations*.

CUNIT: A Semantic Role Labeling System for Modern Standard Arabic

Mona Diab
Columbia University
mdiab@cs.columbia.edu

Alessandro Moschitti
University of Trento, DIT
moschitti@dit.unitn.it

Daniele Pighin
FBK-irst; University of Trento, DIT
pighin@itc.it

Abstract

In this paper, we present a system for Arabic semantic role labeling (SRL) based on SVMs and standard features. The system is evaluated on the released SEMEVAL 2007 development and test data. The results show an $F_{\beta=1}$ score of 94.06 on argument boundary detection and an overall $F_{\beta=1}$ score of 81.43 on the complete semantic role labeling task using gold parse trees.

1 Introduction

There is a widely held belief in the computational linguistics field that identifying and defining the roles of predicate arguments, semantic role labeling (SRL), in a sentence has a lot of potential for and is a significant step towards the improvement of important applications such as document retrieval, machine translation, question answering and information extraction. However, effective ways for seeing this belief come to fruition require a lot more research investment.

Since most of the available data resources are for the English language, most of the reported SRL systems to date only deal with English. Nevertheless, we do see some headway for other languages, such as German and Chinese (Erk and Pado, 2006; Sun and Jurafsky, 2004; Xue and Palmer, 2005). The systems for non-English languages follow the successful models devised for English, e.g. (Gildea and Jurafsky, 2002; Xue and Palmer, 2004; Pradhan et al., 2003). However, no SRL system exists for Arabic.

In this paper, we present a system for semantic role labeling for modern standard Arabic. To our knowledge, it is the first SRL system for a semitic language in the literature. It is based on a supervised model that uses support vector machines (SVM) technology for argument boundary detection and argument classification. It is trained and tested using the pilot Arabic PropBank data released as part of the `SEMEVAL 2007` data. Given the lack of a reliable deep syntactic parser, in this research we use gold trees.

The system yields an F-score of 94.06 on the sub task of argument boundary detection and an F-score of 81.43 on the complete task, i.e. boundary plus classification.

2 SRL system for Arabic

The design of an optimal model for an Arabic SRL systems should take into account specific linguistic aspects of the language. However, a remarkable amount of research has already been done in SRL and we can capitalize from it to design a basic and effective SRL system. The idea is to use the technology developed for English and verify if it is suitable for Arabic.

Our adopted SRL models use Support Vector Machines (SVM) to implement a two steps classification approach, i.e. boundary detection and argument classification. Such models have already been investigated in (Pradhan et al., 2003; Moschitti et al., 2005) and their description is hereafter reported.

2.1 Predicate Argument Extraction

The extraction of predicative structures is carried out at the sentence level. Given a predicate within a natural language sentence, its arguments have to be properly labeled. This problem is usually divided in two subtasks: (a) the detection of the boundaries, i.e. the word spans of the arguments, and (b) the classification of their type, e.g. *Arg0* and *ArgM* in

Proceedings of the 4th International Workshop on Semantic Evaluations (SemEval-2007), pages 133–136,
Prague, June 2007.

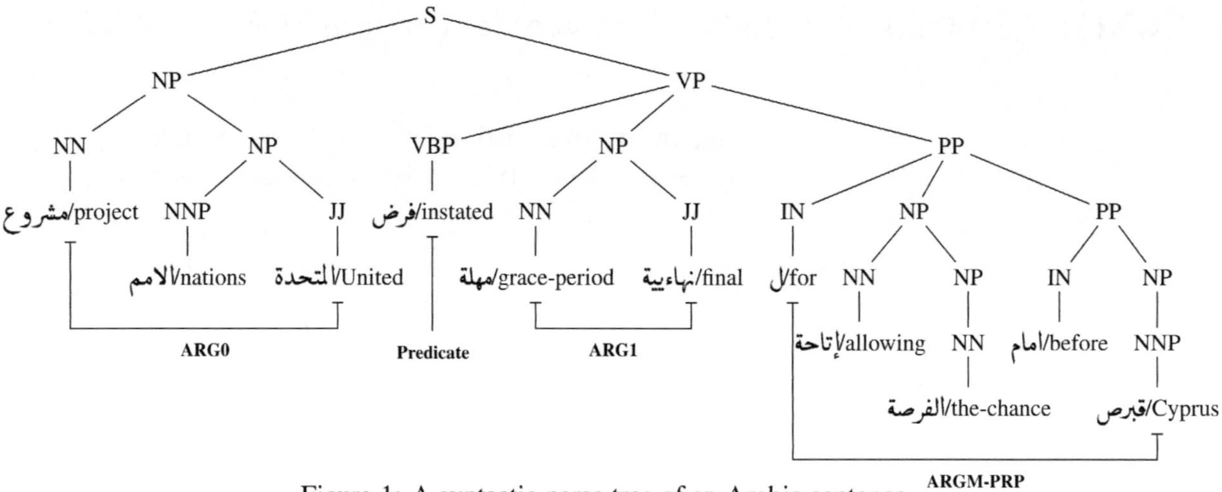

Figure 1: A syntactic parse tree of an Arabic sentence.

PropBank or *Agent* and *Goal* in FrameNet.

The standard approach to learn both the detection and the classification of predicate arguments is summarized by the following steps:

1. Given a sentence from the *training-set*, generate a full syntactic parse-tree;
2. let $\mathcal{P}$ and $\mathcal{A}$ be the set of predicates and the set of parse-tree nodes (i.e. the potential arguments), respectively;
3. for each pair $\langle p, a \rangle \in \mathcal{P} \times \mathcal{A}$:
   - extract the feature representation set, $F_{p,a}$;
   - if the subtree rooted in a covers exactly the words of one argument of p, put $F_{p,a}$ in T^+ (positive examples), otherwise put it in T^- (negative examples).

For instance, in Figure 1, for each combination of the predicate *instated* with the nodes `NP`, `S`, `VP`, `VPB`, `NNP`, `NN`, `PP`, `JJ` or `IN` the instances $F_{instated,a}$ are generated. In case the node a exactly covers "project nations United", "grace-period final" or "for allowing the chance before Cyprus", $F_{p,a}$ will be a positive instance otherwise it will be a negative one, e.g. $F_{instated,IN}$.

The T^+ and T^- sets are used to train the boundary classifier. To train the multi-class classifier, T^+ can be reorganized as positive $T^+_{arg_i}$ and negative $T^-_{arg_i}$ examples for each argument i. In this way, an individual ONE-vs-ALL classifier for each argument i can be trained. We adopted this solution, according to (Pradhan et al., 2003), since it is simple and effective. In the classification phase, given an unseen sentence, all its $F_{p,a}$ are generated and classified by each individual classifier C_i. The argument associated with the maximum among the scores provided by the individual classifiers is eventually selected.

The above approach assigns labels independently for the different arguments in the predicate argument structure. As a consequence the classifier output may generate overlapping arguments. Thus, to make the annotations globally consistent, we apply a disambiguating heuristic that selects only one argument among multiple overlapping arguments. The heuristic is based on the following steps:

- if more than two nodes are involved, i.e. a node d and two or more of its descendants n_i are classified as arguments, then assume that d is not an argument. This choice is justified by previous studies (Moschitti et al., 2005) showing that for lower nodes, the role classification is generally more accurate than for upper ones;
- if only two nodes are involved, i.e. they dominate each other, then keep the one with the higher SVM classification score.

2.2 Standard Features

The discovery of relevant features is, as usual, a complex task. However, there is a common consensus on the set of basic features that should be adopted. Among them, we select the following subset: (a) *Phrase Type*, *Predicate Word*, *Head Word*,

Position and *Voice* as defined in (Gildea and Jurafsky, 2002); (b) *Partial Path*, *No Direction Path*, *Head Word POS*, *First and Last Word/POS in Constituent* and *SubCategorization* as proposed in (Pradhan et al., 2003); and (c) *Syntactic Frame* as designed in (Xue and Palmer, 2004).

For example, *Phrase Type* indicates the syntactic type of the phrase labeled as a predicate argument, NP for *Arg1* in Figure 1 whereas the *Parse Tree Path* contains the path in the parse tree between the predicate and the argument phrase, expressed as a sequence of nonterminal labels linked by direction (up or down) symbols, VPB $\uparrow$ VP $\uparrow$ S $\downarrow$ NP for *Arg1* in Figure 1.

3 Experiments

In these experiments, we investigate if the technology proposed in previous work for automatic SRL of English texts is suitable for Arabic SRL systems. From this perspective, we tested each SRL phase, i.e. boundary detection and argument classification, separately.

The final labeling accuracy that we derive using the official CoNLL evaluator (Carreras and Màrquez, 2005) along with the official development and test data of SEMEVAL provides a reliable assessment of the accuracy achievable by our SRL model.

3.1 Experimental setup

We use the dataset released in the SEMEVAL 2007 Task 18 on Arabic Semantic Labeling, which is sampled from the Pilot Arabic PropBank. Such data covers the 95 most frequent verbs in the Arabic Treebank III ver. 2 (ATB) (Maamouri et al., 2004). The ATB consists of MSA newswire data from Annhar newspaper from the months of July through November 2002.

An important characteristic of the dataset is the use of unvowelized Arabic in the Buckwalter transliteration scheme. We used the gold standard parses in the ATB as a source for syntactic parses for the data. The data comprises a development set of 886 sentences, a test set of 902 sentences, and a training set of 8,402 sentences. The development set comprises 1,725 argument instances, the test data comprises 1,661 argument instances, and training data comprises 21,194 argument instances. These instances are distributed over 26 different role types.

	Precision	Recall	$F_{\beta=1}$
Dev	97.85%	89.86%	93.68
Test	97.85%	90.55%	94.06

Table 1: Boundary detection F1 results on the development and test sets.

The training instances for the boundary detection task relate to parse-tree nodes that do not correspond to correct boundaries. For efficiency reasons, we use only the first 350K training instances for the boundary classifier out of more than 700K available.

The experiments are carried out with the SVM-light-TK software available at http://ai-nlp.info.uniroma2.it/moschitti/ which encodes tree kernels in the SVM-light software. This allows us to design a system which can exploit tree kernels in future research. To implement the boundary classifier and the individual argument classifiers, we use a polynomial kernel with the default regularization parameter (of SVM-light), and a cost-factor equal to 1.

3.2 Official System Results

Our system is evaluated using the official CoNLL evaluator (Carreras and Màrquez, 2005), available at http://www.lsi.upc.es/~srlconll/soft.html.

Table 1 shows the F1 scores obtained on the development and test data. We note that the F1 on the development set, i.e. 93.68, is slightly lower than the result on the test set, i.e. 94.06. This suggests that the test data is *easier* than the development set.

Similar behavior can be observed for the role classification task in tables[1] 2 and 3.

Again, the overall F1 on the development set (77.85) is lower than the result on the test set (81.43). This confirms that the test data is, indeed, *easier* than the development set.

Regarding the F1 of individual arguments, we note that, as for English SRL, ARG0 shows high values, 95.42 and 96.69 on the development and test sets, respectively. Interestingly, ARG1 seems

[1] The arguments: ARG1-PRD, ARG2-STR, ARG4, ARGM, ARGM-BNF, ARGM-DIR, ARGM-DIS, ARGM-EXT and ARGM-REC have F1 equal to 0. To save space, we removed them from the tables, but their presence makes the classification task more complex than if they were removed from test data.

	Precision	Recall	$F_{\beta=1}$
Overall	81.31%	74.67%	77.85
ARG0	94.40%	96.48%	95.42
ARG1	91.69%	88.03%	89.83
ARG1-PRD	50.00%	50.00%	50.00
ARG1-STR	20.00%	4.35%	7.14
ARG2	60.51%	61.78%	61.14
ARG3	66.67%	15.38%	25.00
ARGM	100.00%	16.67%	28.57
ARGM-ADV	46.39%	43.69%	45.00
ARGM-CND	66.67%	33.33%	44.44
ARGM-DIS	60.00%	37.50%	46.15
ARGM-LOC	69.00%	84.15%	75.82
ARGM-MNR	63.08%	48.24%	54.67
ARGM-NEG	87.06%	97.37%	91.93
ARGM-PRD	25.00%	7.14%	11.11
ARGM-PRP	85.29%	69.05%	76.32
ARGM-TMP	82.05%	66.67%	73.56

Table 2: Argument classification results on the development set.

	Precision	Recall	$F_{\beta=1}$
Overall	84.71%	78.39%	81.43
ARG0	96.50%	96.88%	96.69
ARG0-STR	100.00%	20.00%	33.33
ARG1	92.06%	89.56%	90.79
ARG1-STR	33.33%	15.38%	21.05
ARG2	70.74%	73.89%	72.28
ARG3	50.00%	8.33%	14.29
ARGM-ADV	64.29%	54.78%	59.15
ARGM-CAU	100.00%	9.09%	16.67
ARGM-CND	25.00%	33.33%	28.57
ARGM-LOC	67.50%	88.52%	76.60
ARGM-MNR	54.17%	47.27%	50.49
ARGM-NEG	80.85%	97.44%	88.37
ARGM-PRD	20.00%	8.33%	11.76
ARGM-PRP	85.71%	66.67%	75.00
ARGM-TMP	90.82%	83.18%	86.83

Table 3: Argument classification results on the test set.

more difficult classify in Arabic than it is in English. In our current experiments, the F1 for ARG1 is only 89.83 (compared to 95.42 for ARG0). This may be attributed to two main factors. Arabic allows for different types of syntactic configurations, subject-verb-object, object-verb-subject, verb-subject-object, hence the logical object of a predicate is highly confusable with the logical subject. Moreover, around 30% of the ATB data is pro-dropped, where the subject is morphologically marked on the verb and its absence is marked in the gold trees with an empty trace. In the current version of the data, the traces are annotated with the ARG0 semantic role consistently allowing for the high relative performance yielded.

The F1 of the other arguments seems to follow the English SRL behavior as their lower value depends on the lower number of available training examples.

4 Conclusion

In this paper, we presented a first system for Arabic SRL system. The system yields results that are very promising, 94.06 for argument boundary detection and 81.43 on argument classification.

For future work, we would like to experiment with explicit morphological features and different POS tag sets that are tailored to Arabic. The results presented here are based on gold parses. We would like to experiment with automatic parses and shallower representations such as chunked data. Finally, we would like to experiment with more sophisticated kernels, the tree kernels described in (Moschitti, 2004), i.e. models that have shown a lot of promise for the English SRL process.

Acknowledgements

The first author is funded by DARPA Contract No. HR0011-06-C-0023.

References

Xavier Carreras and Lluís Màrquez. 2005. Introduction to the CoNLL-2005 shared task: Semantic role labeling. In *Proceedings of CoNLL-2005*, Ann Arbor, Michigan.

Katrin Erk and Sebastian Pado. 2006. Shalmaneser - a flexible toolbox for semantic role assignment. In *Proceedings of LREC-06*, Genoa, Italy.

Daniel Gildea and Daniel Jurafsky. 2002. Automatic labeling of semantic roles. *Computational Linguistics*, 28(3):245–288.

Mohamed Maamouri, Ann Bies, Tim Buckwalter, and Wig dan Mekki. 2004. The Penn-Arabic Treebank : Building a large-scale annotated Arabic corpus.

Alessandro Moschitti, Ana-Maria Giuglea, Bonaventura Coppola, and Roberto Basili. 2005. Hierarchical semantic role labeling. In *Proceedings of CoNLL-2005*, Ann Arbor, Michigan.

Alessandro Moschitti. 2004. A study on convolution kernels for shallow semantic parsing. In *proceedings of ACL-2004*, Barcelona, Spain.

Sameer Pradhan, Kadri Hacioglu, Wayne Ward, James H. Martin, and Daniel Jurafsky. 2003. Semantic role parsing: Adding semantic structure to unstructured text. In *Proceedings of ICDM-2003*, Melbourne, USA.

Honglin Sun and Daniel Jurafsky. 2004. Shallow semantic parsing of chinese. In *In Proceedings of NAACL 2004*, Boston, USA.

Nianwen Xue and Martha Palmer. 2004. Calibrating features for semantic role labeling. In *Proceedings of EMNLP 2004*, pages 88–94, Barcelona, Spain.

Nianwen Xue and Martha Palmer. 2005. Automatic semantic role labeling for chinese verbs. In *Proceedings of IJCAI*, Edinburgh, Scotland.

DFKI2: An Information Extraction Based Approach to People Disambiguation

Andrea Heyl
German Research Center for
Artificial Intelligence - DFKI,
Saarbrücken, Germany
andrea.heyl@dfki.de

Günter Neumann
German Research Center for
Artificial Intelligence - DFKI,
Saarbrücken, Germany
guenter.neumann@dfki.de

Abstract

We propose an IE based approach to people disambiguation. We assume the mentioning of NEs and the relational context of a person in the text to be important discriminating features in order to distinguish different people sharing a name.

1 Introduction

In this paper, we propose a system with a linguistic view on people disambiguation that exploits the relational and NE context of a person name as discriminating features.

Texts about different people differ from each other by the names of persons, places and organizations connected to these people and by the relations in which a person's name is connected to other entities. Therefore we had the hypothesis that the NEs in the documents for a person name should be a main distinctive criterion for disambiguating people.

Furthermore, the relational context of a person name should also be able to give good clues for disambiguation. Sentence patterns related to a name, i.e. patterns that contain the name as subject or object like "be(Person X, lawyer)" often convey uniquely identifying information about a person.

Our system was not built specifically for the web people search task WePS (Artiles et al., 2007), but is an early version of an IE system that has the more general goal to discover relations between NEs. We see the WePS task as a specific instance of the set of tasks our system should be able to handle. Therefore, we only adapted it slightly to work with the WePS data, but did not make any further customization w.r.t. the special requirements of people disambiguation. As our system was built to handle pure texts rather than structured web pages, we relied completely on linguistic information and did not exploit the html structure of the documents provided.

2 Related Work

Our system was inspired by the preemptive and on-demand IE approaches by Sekine and Shinyama (Sekine, 2006; Shinyama, 2006) that cluster newspaper articles into classes of articles that talk about the same type of event. They proposed a system to discover in advance all possible relations and to return them in form of tables.

We took the idea of distinctive personal attributes as a criterion for disambiguation from the work of Bollegala et al. (2006). They propose an unsupervised learning approach to extract phrases that uniquely identify a person from the web and use these discriminative features for clustering.

3 System Overview

The goal of the WePS task is to cluster the top 100 web pages returned by a web search engine for a certain name as search query and classify them w.r.t. the underlying different people they refer to.

The problem of clustering documents about people into different entities can be seen as two subproblems: The determination of the correct number of clusters and the clustering of the given documents into this number of entities. These problems could either be solved consecutively by first estimating the number of classes and then produce this pre-

Proceedings of the 4th International Workshop on Semantic Evaluations (SemEval-2007), pages 137–140,
Prague, June 2007.

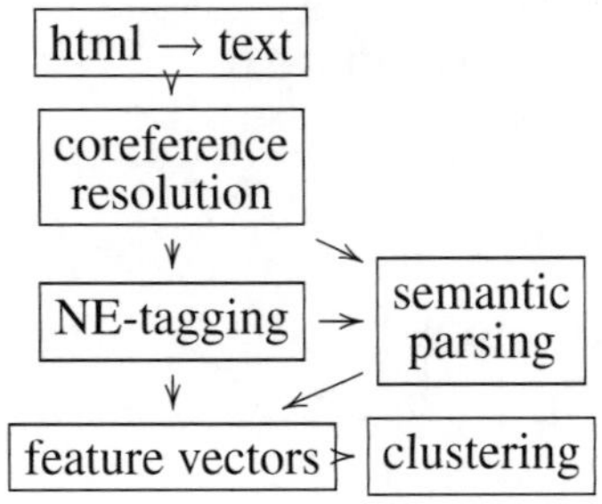

Figure 1: System Overview

set number of clusters or by determining the number of classes dynamically during the clustering process.

Figure 1 gives an overview of our system, that clusters web documents into a pre-defined number of classes, thereby being only concerned with the second problem and neglecting the estimation of different namesakes for now.

Every web page in the WePS training data is represented by the set of its files. As our system works on plain text only, we first needed to separate the textual parts of all files. Therefore, we extracted the text from the html pages. We merged the texts from all different html pages belonging to a single website into one document so that we obtained for every person's name 100 text files as the basis for further clustering.

These text files were processed by a coreference resolution tool. On the resulting texts, we ran both an NE tagger and an NLP tool for semantic parsing. This tool represents sentences containing the respective person name as predicate argument structures.

We constructed two feature vectors for each file based on the counts of the NEs and predicate argument structures that contain the specific person name. Those feature vectors were our basis for the clustering process.

The clustering unit of the system consecutively merged clusters, that at first contained a single file each, until the pre-set number of classes was reached and returned the clustering as an xml file.

4 System Components

4.1 Estimating the Number of Classes

In principle, the number of different people that are represented in the data cannot be known in advance. However, for the clustering process, either the number of classes has to be fixed before clustering, or some kind of termination criterion has to be found that tells the algorithm when to stop clustering.

A good estimation of the number of different entities is a necessary prerequisite for successful clustering. Clustering into too many classes would mean assigning documents to classes that have actually no own entity they refer to. Clustering into too few classes means merging two entities into one class.

Our initial intuition was to distinguish people by normally unique properties, like phone numbers or email addresses. So we assumed that the number of different email addresses and phone numbers occurring in all documents for one name would be a good means to estimate the number of different persons sharing this name, but we could not find any correlation between these features and the class number.

Therefore, we decided to estimate the average number of classes from the training data. The average number of different people for one name in the training data was about 18. Based on the observation that an underestimated number of classes leads to better results than assuming too many classes, we decided to guess 12 different persons for each name.

4.2 Preprocessing

For the extraction of plain text information from the web pages, we used the html2text [1] converter. In case that a web page consisted of more than one html document, we put all the output from the converter into one single file. By omitting any wrapping of the html pages, we obviously lost useful structural information but got the textual information for our linguistic analysis.

Afterward, we applied several linguistic preprocessing tools. We used coreference resolution to replace pronouns referring to a person, and variations of a name (like "Mr. Smith" after a mention of "John Smith" earlier in the text) with the person's name in the form of its first mention in the text.

For NE-tagging, we used the three NE types PERSON, LOCATION and ORGANIZATION. For both NE tagging and coreference resolution, we used the LingPipe toolkit [2]. We counted the occurrences of every NE in every file and replaced all instances by their specific NE type combined with a uniquely

[1] http://www.mbayer.de/html2text/index.shtml
[2] http://www.alias-i.com/lingpipe/

identifying number, e.g. we replaced all occurrences of "Paris" with "LOCATION27", in order to ensure that the predicate argument parser could work correctly and would not split up multi-word NEs into two or more arguments.

We passed all sentences with NEs that contained the specified persons family name (e.g. "Mr. Cooper" for the name "Alvin Cooper") to MontyLingua [3], that returns a semantic representation of the sentence like ("live" "PERSON2" "in LOCATION3"). These representations abstract from the actual surface form of a sentence as they represent every sentence in its underlying semantic form ("predicate" "semantic subject" "semantic object1"...) rather than just determining the syntactic subject and objects of a sentence. We called these structures "patterns" and kept only those that actually contained the respective NE.

4.3 Clustering

We decided on building two vectors for every text file, one for the NEs and one for sentence patterns connected to a person's name in order to give to the NEs a weight different from that for the patterns.

After tagging the documents for NEs, we counted the frequency of the different occurring NEs for one name. We built a first feature vector for each document that contained as entries the counts of the occurring NEs in this document. We set a threshold n to use only the n best NEs in the vectors, counted over all documents for one name. We then built for every document a second feature vector containing the counts of the MontyLingua patterns for the document.

For the actual clustering process, we used hierarchical clustering. We started with every file, represented by a pair of normalized feature vectors, constituting a single cluster. As distance measurement we used the weighted sum of the absolute distances between the centers of two clusters with regard to both feature vectors, respectively, i.e. we chose distance $= w \cdot \text{distance}_{NEs} + \text{distance}_{patterns}$. In every step, we made a pairwise comparison of all clusters and merged those with the lowest distance. The clustering terminated when the algorithm came down to the pre-set number of 12 clusters. So far we have not made any further use of the binary tree structure within each cluster.

We assigned every file to exactly one cluster. We had neither a "discarded" category nor did we handle the possibility that a page refers to more than one person and would hence belong to different clusters.

5 Experiments

5.1 Training of Parameters

We evaluated the system on the provided WePS training data to estimate the following parameters: number of classes, number of best NEs to be considered and weight of the NE vector compared to the pattern vector.

The relevant evaluation score is the F-measure ($\alpha = 0.5$) as the harmonic mean of purity and inverse purity as described by Hotho et al. (2003).

As our attempt to use distinctive features for the estimation of class numbers failed, we examined the influence of a wrongly estimated number of classes on the clustering results. Table 1 shows exemplarily for 2 person names how the F-measure varies if the correct number of classes is incorrectly assumed as a higher or lower value. We concluded that it is better to estimate the class number too low than too high.

name	A. Macomb	E. Fox
correct number of classes	21	16
10 classes assumed	0.76	0.80
12 classes assumed	0.75	0.75
14 classes assumed	0.72	0.76
16 classes assumed	0.69	0.60
18 classes assumed	0.60	0.58
20 classes assumed	0.48	0.72
22 classes assumed	0.56	0.55
24 classes assumed	0.59	0.58
26 classes assumed	0,52	0.56

Table 1: F-measure for different numbers of assumed classes

Primarily meant as a means to reduce computation time, we gave our system the possibility not to use all occurring NEs for clustering, but only a certain number of entities with maximal frequencies. Test runs did not confirm our hypothesis that considering a higher number of NEs leads to better results (cf. table 2). For both training of the number of NEs and the NE weight we assumed that we already knew the correct class number.

As the F-measure did not increase for more considered NEs, we believe that the most important NEs

[3] http://web.media.mit.edu/ hugo/montylingua/

are already covered within the best 100 and that adding more NEs rather adds coincidental information than any new important facts. Usually, the best 100 NEs already cover most of those which occur more than once in a text.

NEs	average. F-measure
100	0.66
200	0.68
500	0.68
1000	0.67

w	average F-measure
0.5	0.66
1.0	0.68
2.0	0.68
4.0	0.67

Table 2: varying the number of considered entities and weight of the feature vectors

The third parameter to estimate was the weight w given to the NE feature vector compared to the feature vector for sentence patterns. During training, this weight also appeared to have little influence on the clustering results (cf. 2). We have the hypothesis that sentence pattern detection is not very successful for the often unstructured web page texts.

5.2 Results for WePS Test Data

In the WePS evaluation, our system scored with a purity of 0.39, an inverse purity of 0.83 and a resulting overall F-measure ($\alpha = 0.5$) of 0.5.

One main reason for our test results to be worse than our training results is the fact that the test data had a much higher average number of classes (about 46 classes). Our F-measure was best for those names with the fewest number of referents. We had an average F-Measure ($\alpha = 0.5$) of 0.66 for those names with less than 30 instances compared to an overall average of 0.50. These numbers show the importance of a correct estimation of the assumed number of referents for a name.

Our purity was much lower than the inverse purity, i.e. there is too much noise in our clustering compared to the real partition, whereas the real clusters are well covered by our clustering. This is due to a too low estimation of the number of referents.

6 Conclusions and Future Work

One obvious improvement , that would accommodate the general relation extraction idea of our system, is to include the use of structural information from the html documents in addition to our purely linguistic view on web pages. Additionally, we should weight our NEs using e.g. a TF/IDF formula.

A promising direction for further research in people search will certainly include a better control of the number of classes. This could be done either by estimating this number in advance, or by setting the number of classes dynamically during clustering. The latter could include comparing the size of the current clusters to the overall feature space of all clusters or an approach of counting occurrences of uniquely identifying attributes within a cluster.

This second approach could match the original purpose of our system, namely to build tables that represent the most salient relations in a set of documents in the way Sekine and Shinyama did. If such a table, that represents the slots of a relation in its columns and every article in a row, is built for all documents in a cluster, we would expect the table to contain roughly the same information in every row. One could define a consistency measure for the resulting tables and stop clustering as soon as the tables are no longer consistent enough, i.e. when they contain too much contradictory information.

Acknowledgment

The work presented here was supported by a research grant from the Investitionsbank Berlin to the DFKI project IDEX (Interactive Dynamic IE).

References

Javier Artiles, Julio Gonzalo and Satoshi Sekine. 2007. *The SemEval-2007 WePS Evaluation: Establishing a Benchmark for the Web People Search Task.* Proceedings of Semeval 2007, ACL.

Danushka Bollegala, Yutaka Matsuo and Mitsuru Ishizuka. 2006. *Extracting Key Phrases to Disambiguate Personal Name Queries in Web Search.* Proceedings of the Workshop on How Can Computational Linguistics Improve Information Retrieval, p. 17–24.

Andreas Hotho, Steffen Staab and Gerd Stumme. 2003. *Wordnet Improves Text Document Clustering.* Proceedings of the Semantic Web Workshop at SIGIR-2003, 26th Annual International ACM SIGIR Conference, Toronto, Canada.

Satoshi Sekine. 2006. *On-Demand IE.* International Committee on Comp. Ling. and the ACL.

Yusuke Shinyama and Satoshi Sekine. 2006. *Preemptive Information Extraction using Unrestricted Relation Discovery.* Human Language Technology conference - North American chapter of the ACL annual meeting; New York City.

FBK-IRST: Kernel Methods for Semantic Relation Extraction

Claudio Giuliano and **Alberto Lavelli** and **Daniele Pighin** and **Lorenza Romano**
FBK-IRST, Istituto per la Ricerca Scientifica e Tecnologica
I-38050, Povo (TN), ITALY
{giuliano,lavelli,pighin,romano}@itc.it

Abstract

We present an approach for semantic relation extraction between nominals that combines shallow and deep syntactic processing and semantic information using kernel methods. Two information sources are considered: (i) the whole sentence where the relation appears, and (ii) WordNet synsets and hypernymy relations of the candidate nominals. Each source of information is represented by kernel functions. In particular, five basic kernel functions are linearly combined and weighted under different conditions. The experiments were carried out using support vector machines as classifier. The system achieves an overall F_1 of 71.8% on the Classification of Semantic Relations between Nominals task at SemEval-2007.

1 Introduction

The starting point of our research is an approach for identifying relations between named entities exploiting only shallow linguistic information, such as tokenization, sentence splitting, part-of-speech tagging and lemmatization (Giuliano et al., 2006). A combination of kernel functions is used to represent two distinct information sources: (i) the global context where entities appear and (ii) their local contexts. The whole sentence where the entities appear (*global context*) is used to discover the presence of a relation between two entities. Windows of limited size around the entities (*local contexts*) provide useful clues to identify the roles played by the entities within a relation (e.g., agent and target of a gene interaction). In the task of detecting *protein-protein* interactions, we obtained state-of-the-art results on two biomedical data sets. In addition, promising results have been recently obtained for relations such as *work for* and *org based in* in the news domain[1].

In this paper, we investigate the use of the above approach to discover semantic relations between nominals. In addition to the original feature representation, we have integrated deep syntactic processing of the global context and semantic information for each candidate nominals using WordNet as external knowledge source. Each source of information is represented by kernel functions. A tree kernel (Moschitti, 2004) is used to exploit the deep syntactic processing obtained using the Charniak parser (Charniak, 2000). On the other hand, bag of synonyms and hypernyms is used to enhance the representation of the candidate nominals. The final system is based on five basic kernel functions (bag-of-words kernel, global context kernel, tree kernel, supersense kernel, bag of synonyms and hypernyms kernel) linearly combined and weighted under different conditions. The experiments were carried out using support vector machines (Vapnik, 1998) as classifier.

We present results on the Classification of Semantic Relations between Nominals task at SemEval-2007, in which sentences containing ordered pairs of marked nominals, possibly semantically related, have to be classified. On this task, we achieve an overall F_1 of 71.8% (B category evaluation), largely outperforming all the baselines.

[1] These results appear in a paper currently under revision.

Proceedings of the 4th International Workshop on Semantic Evaluations (SemEval-2007), pages 141–144,
Prague, June 2007.

2 Kernel Methods for Relation Extraction

In order to implement the approach based on syntactic and semantic information, we employed a linear weighted combination of kernels, using support vector machines as classifier. We designed two families of basic kernels: syntactic kernels and semantic kernels. These basic kernels are combined by exploiting the closure properties of kernels. We define our composite kernel $K_C(x_1, x_2)$ as follows

$$\sum_{i=1}^{n} w_i \frac{K_i(x_1, x_2)}{\sqrt{K_i(x_1, x_1) K_i(x_2, x_2)}}, \quad (1)$$

where each basic kernel K_i is normalized and $w_i \in \{0, 1\}$ is the kernel weight. The normalization factor plays an important role in allowing us to integrate information from heterogeneous knowledge sources.

All basic kernels, but the tree kernel (see Section 2.1.3), are explicitly calculated as follows

$$K_i(x_1, x_2) = \langle \phi(x_1), \phi(x_2) \rangle, \quad (2)$$

where $\phi(\cdot)$ is the embedding vector. Even though the resulting feature space has high dimensionality, an efficient computation of Equation 2 can be carried out explicitly since the input representations defined below are extremely sparse.

2.1 Syntactic Kernels

Syntactic kernels are defined over the whole sentence where the candidate nominals appear.

2.1.1 Global Context Kernel

Bunescu and Mooney (2005) and Giuliano et al. (2006) successfully exploited the fact that relations between named entities are generally expressed using only words that appear simultaneously in one of the following three contexts.

Fore-Between Tokens before and between the two entities, e.g. *"the head of [ORG], Dr. [PER]"*.

Between Only tokens between the two entities, e.g. *"[ORG] spokesman [PER]"*.

Between-After Tokens between and after the two entities, e.g. *"[PER], a [ORG] professor"*.

Here, we investigate whether this assumption is also correct for semantic relations between nominals. Our global context kernel operates on the contexts defined above, where each context is represented using a *bag-of-words*. More formally, given

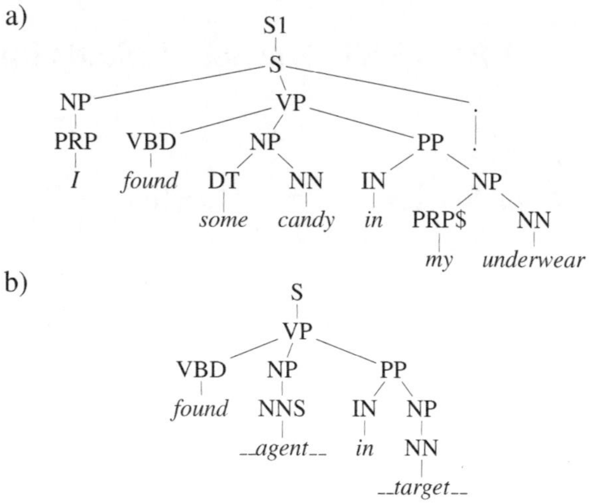

Figure 1: A *content-container* relation test sentence parse tree (a) and the corresponding RT structure (b).

a relation example R, we represent a context C as a row vector

$$\phi_C(R) = (tf(t_1, C), tf(t_2, C), \ldots, tf(t_l, C)) \in \mathbb{R}^l, \quad (3)$$

where the function $tf(t_i, C)$ records how many times a particular token t_i is used in C. Note that this approach differs from the standard bag-of-words as punctuation and stop words are included in ϕ_C, while the nominals are not. To improve the classification performance, we have further extended ϕ_C to embed n-grams of (contiguous) tokens (up to $n = 3$). By substituting ϕ_C into Equation 2, we obtain the n-gram kernel K_n, which counts uni-grams, bi-grams, ..., n-grams that two patterns have in common[2]. The *Global Context* kernel $K_{GC}(R_1, R_2)$ is then defined as

$$K_{FB}(R_1, R_2) + K_B(R_1, R_2) + K_{BA}(R_1, R_2), \quad (4)$$

where K_{FB}, K_B and K_{BA} are n-gram kernels that operate on the Fore-Between, Between and Between-After patterns respectively.

2.1.2 Bag-of-Words Kernel

The bag-of-words kernel is defined as the previous kernel but it operates on the whole sentence.

2.1.3 Tree Kernel

Tree kernels can trigger automatic feature selection and represent a viable alternative to the man-

[2] In the literature, it is also called *n-spectrum* kernel.

ual design of attribute-value syntactic features (Moschitti, 2004). A tree kernel $K_T(t_1, t_2)$ evaluates the similarity between two trees t_1 and t_2 in terms of the number of fragments they have in common. Let N_t be the set of nodes of a tree t and $\mathcal{F} = \{f_1, f_2, \ldots, f_{|\mathcal{F}|}\}$ be the fragment space of t_1 and t_2. Then

$$K_T(t_1, t_2) = \sum_{n_i \in N_{t_1}} \sum_{n_j \in N_{t_2}} \Delta(n_i, n_j) , \quad (5)$$

where $\Delta(n_i, n_j) = \sum_{k=1}^{|\mathcal{F}|} I_k(n_i) \times I_K(n_j)$ and $I_k(n) = 1$ if k is rooted in n, 0 otherwise.

For this task, we defined an *ad-hoc* class of structured features (Moschitti et al., 2006), the Reduced Tree (RT), which can be derived from a sentence parse tree t by the following steps: (1) remove all the terminal nodes but those labeled as relation entities and those POS tagged as verbs, auxiliaries, prepositions, modals or adverbs; (2) remove all the internal nodes not covering any remaining terminal; (3) replace the entity words with placeholders that indicate the direction in which the relation should hold. Figure 1 shows a parse tree and the resulting RT structure.

2.2 Semantic Kernels

In (Giuliano et al., 2006), we used the local context kernel to infer semantic information on the candidate entities (i.e., roles played by the entities). As the task organizers provide the WordNet sense and role for each nominal, we directly use this information to enrich the feature space and do not include the local context kernel in the combination.

2.2.1 Bag of Synonyms and Hypernyms Kernel

By using the WordNet sense key provided, each nominal is represented by the bag of its synonyms and hypernyms (direct and inherited hypernyms). Formally, given a relation example R, each nominal N is represented as a row vector

$$\phi_N(R) = (f(t_1, N), f(t_2, N), \ldots, f(t_l, N)) \in \mathbb{R}^l, \quad (6)$$

where the binary function $f(t_i, N)$ records if a particular lemma t_i is contained into the bag of synonyms and hypernyms of N. The *bag of synonyms and hypernyms* kernel $K_{S\&H}(R_1, R_2)$ is defined as

$$K_{target}(R_1, R_2) + K_{agent}(R_1, R_2), \quad (7)$$

where K_{target} and K_{agent} are defined by substituting the embedding of the target and agent nominals into Equation 2 respectively.

2.2.2 Supersense Kernel

WordNet synsets are organized into 45 lexicographer files, based on syntactic category and logical groupings. E.g., *noun.artifact* is for nouns denoting man-made objects, *noun.attribute* for nouns denoting attributes for people and objects etc. The *supersense* kernel $K_{SS}(R_1, R_2)$ is a variant of the previous kernel that uses the names of the lexicographer files (i.e., the supersense) to index the feature space.

3 Experimental Setup and Results

Sentences have been tokenized, lemmatized, and POS tagged with TextPro[3]. We considered each relation as a different binary classification task, and each sentence in the data set is a positive or negative example for the relation. The direction of the relation is considered labelling the first argument of the relation as agent and the second as target.

All the experiments were performed using the SVM package SVMLight-TK[4], customized to embed our own kernels. We optimized the linear combination weights w_i and regularization parameter c using 10-fold cross-validation on the training set. We set the cost-factor j to be the ratio between the number of negative and positive examples.

Table 1 shows the performance on the test set. We achieve an overall F_1 of 71.8% (B category evaluation), largely outperforming all the baselines, ranging from 48.5% to 57.0%. The average training plus test running time for a relation is about 10 seconds on a Intel Pentium M755 2.0 GHz. Figure 2 shows the learning curves on the test set. For all relations but *theme-tool*, accurate classifiers can be learned using a small fraction of training.

4 Discussion and Conclusion

Experimental results show that our kernel-based approach is appropriate also to detect semantic relations between nominals. However, differently from relation extraction between named entities, there is not a common kernel setup for all relations. E.g.,

[3] http://tcc.itc.it/projects/textpro/

[4] http://ai-nlp.info.uniroma2.it/moschitti/

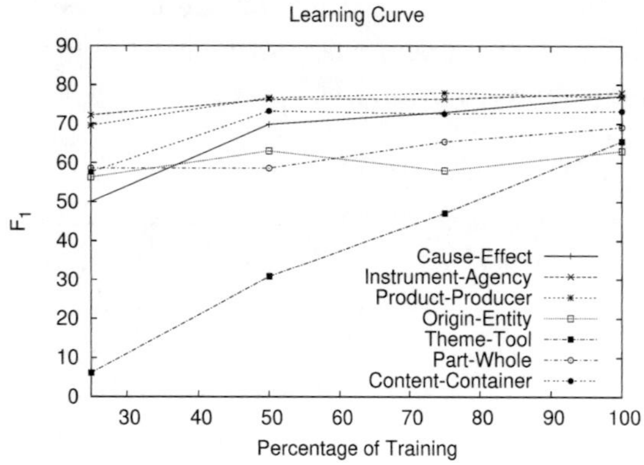

Figure 2: Learning curves on the test set.

Relation	P	R	F_1	Acc
Cause-Effect	67.3	90.2	77.1	72.5
Instrument-Agency	76.9	78.9	77.9	78.2
Product-Producer	76.2	77.4	76.8	68.8
Origin-Entity	62.2	63.9	63.0	66.7
Theme-Tool	69.2	62.1	65.5	73.2
Part-Whole	65.5	73.1	69.1	76.4
Content-Container	78.8	68.4	73.2	74.3
Avg	70.9	73.4	71.8	72.9

Table 1: Results on the test set.

for *content-container* we obtain the best performance combining the tree kernel and the bag of synonyms and hypernyms kernel; on the other hand, for *instrument-agency* the best performance is obtained by combining the global kernel and the supersense kernel. Surprisingly, the supersense kernel alone works quite well and obtains results comparable to the bag of synonyms and hypernyms kernel. This result is particularly interesting as a supersense tagger can easily provide a satisfactory accuracy (Ciaramita and Altun, 2006). On the other hand, obtaining an acceptable accuracy in word sense disambiguation (required for a realistic application of the bag of synonyms and hypernyms kernel) is impractical as a sufficient amount of training for at least all nouns is currently not available. Hence, the supersense could play a crucial role to improve the performance when approaching this task without the nominals disambiguated. To model the global context using the Fore-Between, Between and Between-After contexts did not produce a significant improvement with respect to the bag-of-words model. This is mainly due to the fact that examples have been collected from the Web using heuristic patterns/queries, most of which implying Between patterns/contexts (e.g., for the *cause-effect* relation "* comes from *", "* out of *" etc.).

5 Acknowledgements

Claudio Giuliano, Alberto Lavelli and Lorenza Romano are supported by the X-Media project (`http://www.x-media-project.org`), sponsored by the European Commission as part of the Information Society Technologies (IST) programme under EC grant number IST-FP6-026978.

References

Razvan Bunescu and Raymond J. Mooney. 2005. Subsequence kernels for relation extraction. In *Proceedings of the 19th Conference on Neural Information Processing Systems*, Vancouver, British Columbia.

Eugene Charniak. 2000. A maximum-entropy-inspired parser. In *Proceedings of the First Meeting of the North American Chapter of the Association for Computational Linguistics*, pages 132–139, San Francisco, CA, USA. Morgan Kaufmann Publishers Inc.

Massimiliano Ciaramita and Yasemin Altun. 2006. Broad-coverage sense disambiguation and information extraction with a supersense sequence tagger. In *Proceedings of the 2006 Conference on Empirical Methods in Natural Language Processing*, pages 594–602, Sydney, Australia, July.

Claudio Giuliano, Alberto Lavelli, and Lorenza Romano. 2006. Exploiting shallow linguistic information for relation extraction from biomedical literature. In *Proceedings of the Eleventh Conference of the European Chapter of the Association for Computational Linguistics (EACL-2006)*, Trento, Italy, 5-7 April.

Alessandro Moschitti, Daniele Pighin, and Roberto Basili. 2006. Semantic role labeling via tree kernel joint inference. In *Proceedings of the Tenth Conference on Computational Natural Language Learning, CoNLL-X.*

Alessandro Moschitti. 2004. A study on convolution kernels for shallow statistic parsing. In *Proceedings of the 42nd Meeting of the Association for Computational Linguistics (ACL'04), Main Volume*, pages 335–342, Barcelona, Spain, July.

Vladimir Vapnik. 1998. *Statistical Learning Theory*. John Wiley and Sons, New York, NY.

FBK-irst: Lexical Substitution Task Exploiting Domain and Syntagmatic Coherence

Claudio Giuliano and **Alfio Gliozzo** and **Carlo Strapparava**
FBK-irst, I-38050, Povo, Trento, ITALY
{giuliano, gliozzo, strappa}@itc.it

Abstract

This paper summarizes FBK-irst participation at the lexical substitution task of the SEMEVAL competition. We submitted two different systems, both exploiting synonym lists extracted from dictionaries. For each word to be substituted, the systems rank the associated synonym list according to a similarity metric based on Latent Semantic Analysis and to the occurrences in the Web 1T 5-gram corpus, respectively. In particular, the latter system achieves the state-of-the-art performance, largely surpassing the baseline proposed by the organizers.

1 Introduction

The lexical substitution (Glickman et al., 2006a) can be regarded as a subtask of the lexical entailment, in which for a given word in context the system is asked to select an alternative word that can be replaced in that context preserving the meaning. Lexical Entailment, and in particular lexical reference (Glickman et al., 2006b)[1], is in turn a subtask of textual entailment, which is formally defined as a relationship between a coherent text T and a language expression, the hypothesis H. T is said to entail H, denoted by $T \rightarrow H$, if the meaning of H can be inferred from the meaning of T (Dagan et al., 2005; Dagan and Glickman., 2004). Even though this notion has been only recently proposed in the computational linguistics literature, it attracts more and more attention due to the high generality of its settings and to the usefulness of its (potential) applications.

[1] In the literature, slight variations of this problem have been also referred to as *sense matching* (Dagan et al., 2006).

With respect to lexical entailment, the lexical substitution task has a more restrictive criterion. In fact, two words can be substituted when meaning is preserved, while the criterion for lexical entailment is that the meaning of the thesis is implied by the meaning of the hypothesis. The latter condition is in general ensured by substituting either hyperonyms or synonyms, while the former is more rigid because only synonyms are in principle accepted.

Formally, in a lexical entailment task a system is asked to decide whether the substitution of a particular term w with the term e in a coherent text $H_w = H^l w H^r$ generates a sentence $H_e = H^l e H^r$ such that $H_w \rightarrow H_e$, where H^l and H^r denote the left and the right context of w, respectively. For example, given the source word 'weapon' a system may substitute it with the target synonym 'arm', in order to identify relevant texts that denote the sought concept using the latter term.

A particular case of lexical entailment is recognizing synonymy, where both $H_w \rightarrow H_e$ and $H_e \rightarrow H_w$ hold. The lexical substitution task at SEMEVAL addresses exactly this problem. The task is not easy since lists of candidate entailed words are not provided by the organizers. Therefore the system is asked first to identify a set of candidate words, and then to select only those words that fit in a particular context. To promote unsupervised methods, the organizers did not provide neither labeled data for training nor dictionaries or list of synonyms explaining the meanings of the entailing words.

In this paper, we describe our approach to the Lexical Substitution task at SEMEVAL 2007. We developed two different systems (named IRST1-lsa and IRST2-syn in the official task ranking), both exploiting a common lists of synonyms extracted from dictionaries (i.e. WordNet and the Oxford Dictio-

Proceedings of the 4th International Workshop on Semantic Evaluations (SemEval-2007), pages 145–148,
Prague, June 2007.

nary) and ranking them according to two different criteria:

Domain Proximity: the similarity between each candidate entailed word and the context of the entailing word is estimated by means of a cosine between their corresponding vectors in the LSA space.

Syntagmatic Coherence: querying a large corpus, the system finds all occurrences of the target sentence, in which the entailing word is substituted with each synonym, and it assigns scores proportional to the occurrence frequencies.

Results show that both methods are effective. In particular, the second method achieved the best performance in the competition, defining the state-of-the-art for the lexical substitution task.

2 Lexical Substitution Systems

The lexical substitution task is a textual entailment subtask in which the system is asked to provide one or more terms $e \in E \subseteq syn(w)$ that can be substituted to w in a particular context $H_w = H^l w H^r$ generating a sentence $H_e = H^l e H^r$ such that both $H_w \rightarrow H_e$ and $H_e \rightarrow H_w$ hold, where $syn(w)$ is the set of synonyms lemmata obtained from all synset in which w appears in WordNet and H^l and H^r denote the left and the right context of w, respectively.

The first step, common to both systems, consists of determining the set of synonyms $syn(w)$ for each entailing word (see Section 2.1). Then, each system ranks the extracted lists according to the criteria described in Section 2.2 and 2.3.

2.1 Used Lexical Resources

For selecting the synonym candidates we used two lexical repositories: *WordNet 2.0* and the *Oxford American Writer Thesaurus* (1st Edition). For each target word, we simply collect all the synonyms for all the word senses in both these resources.

We exploited two corpora for our systems: the *British National Corpus* for acquiring the LSA space for ranking with domain proximity measure (Section 2.2) and the *Web 1T 5-gram Version 1* corpus from Google (distributed by Linguistic Data Consortium)[2] for ranking the proposed synonyms according to syntagmatic coherence (Section 2.3).

[2] Available from http://www.ldc.upenn.edu/Catalog/CatalogEntry.jsp?catalogId=LDC2006T13.

No other resources were used and the sense ranking in WordNet was not considered at all. Therefore our system is fully unsupervised.

2.2 Domain Proximity

Semantic Domains are common areas of human discussion, such as Economics, Politics, Law (Magnini et al., 2002). Semantic Domains can be described by DMs (Gliozzo, 2005), by defining a set of term clusters, each representing a Semantic Domain, i.e. a set of terms having similar topics. A DM is represented by a $k \times k'$ rectangular matrix $\mathbf{D}$, containing the domain relevance for each term with respect to each domain.

DMs can be acquired from texts by exploiting term clustering algorithms. The degree of association among terms and clusters, estimated by the learning algorithm, provides a domain relevance function. For our experiments we adopted a clustering strategy based on Latent Semantic Analysis (LSA) (Deerwester et al., 1990), following the methodology described in (Gliozzo, 2005).

The input of the LSA process is a Term by Document matrix $\mathbf{T}$ of the frequencies in the whole corpus for each term. In this work we indexed all lemmatized terms. The so obtained matrix is then decomposed by means of a Singular Value Decomposition, identifying the principal components of $\mathbf{T}$.

Once a DM has been defined by the matrix $\mathbf{D}$, the Domain Space is a k' dimensional space, in which both texts and terms are associated to Domain Vectors (DVs), i.e. vectors representing their domain relevance with respect to each domain. The DV $\vec{t'_i}$ for the term $t_i \in \mathcal{V}$ is the ith row of $\mathbf{D}$, where $\mathcal{V} = \{t_1, t_2, \ldots, t_k\}$ is the vocabulary of the corpus. The DVs for texts are obtained by mapping the document vectors $\vec{d_j}$, represented in the vector space model, into the vectors $\vec{d'_j}$ in the Domain Space, defined by

$$\mathcal{D}(\vec{d_j}) = \vec{d_j}(\mathbf{I^{IDF}}\mathbf{D}) = \vec{d'_j} \quad (1)$$

where $\mathbf{I^{IDF}}$ is a diagonal matrix such that $i^{IDF}_{i,i} = IDF(w_i)$ and $IDF(w_i)$ is the *Inverse Document Frequency* of w_i. The similarity among both texts and terms in the Domain Space is then estimated by the cosine operation.

To implement our lexical substitution criterion we ranked the candidate entailed words according to their domain proximity, following the intuition that if two words can be substituted in a particular context, then the entailed word should belong to the same semantic domain of the context in which the entailing word is located.

The intuition above can be modeled by estimating the similarity in the LSA space between the pseudo document, estimated by Equation 1, formed by all the words in the context of the entailing word (i.e. the union of H^l and H^r), and each candidate entailed word in $syn(w)$.

2.3 Syntagmatic Coherence

The syntagmatic coherence criterion is based on the following observation. If the entailing word w in its context $H_w = H^l w H^r$ is actually entailed by a word e, then there exist some occurrences on the WEB of the expression $H_e = H^l e H^r$, obtained by replacing the entailing word with the candidate entailed word. This intuition can be easily implemented by looking for occurrences of H_e in the Web 1T 5-gram Version 1 corpus.

Figure 1 presents pseudo-code for the synonym scoring procedure. The procedure takes as input the set of candidate entailed words $E = syn(w)$ for the entailing word w, the context H_w in which w occurs, the length of the n-gram ($2 \leqslant n \leqslant 5$) and the target word itself. For each candidate entailed word e_i, the procedure $ngrams(H_w, w, e_i, n)$ is invoked to substitute w with e_i in H_w, obtaining H_{e_i}, and returns the set Q of all n-grams containing e_i. For example, all 3-grams obtained replacing "bright" with the synonym "intelligent" in the sentence "He was *bright* and independent and proud." are "He was intelligent", "was intelligent and" and "intelligent and independent". The maximum number of n-grams generated is $\sum_{n=2}^{5} n$. Each candidate synonym is then assigned a score by summing all the frequencies in the Web 1T corpus of the so generated n-grams[3]. The set of synonyms is ranked according the so obtained scores. However, candidates which appear in longer n-grams are preferred to candidates appearing in shorter ones. Therefore, the ranked list contains first the candidate entailed words appearing in 5-grams, if any, then those appearing in 4-grams, and so on. For example, a candidate e_1 that appears only once in 5-grams is preferred to a candidate e_2 that appears 1000 times in 4-grams. Note that this strategy could lead to an output list with repetitions.

[3]Note that n-grams with frequency lower than 40 are not present in the corpus.

Given E, the set of candidate synonyms
Given H, the context in which w occurs
Given n, the length of the n-gram
Given w, the word to be substituted
$E' \leftarrow \emptyset$
for each e_i in E **do**
    $Q \leftarrow ngrams(H, w, e_i, n)$
    $score_i \leftarrow 0$
    for each q_j in Q **do**
        Get the frequency f_j of q_j
        $score_i \leftarrow score_i + f_j$
    end for
    if $score_i > 0$ **then** add the pair $\{score_i, e_i\}$ in E'
end for
Return E'

Figure 1: The synonym scoring procedure

3 Evaluation

There are basically two scoring methodologies: (i) BEST, which scores the best substitute for a given item, and (ii) OOT, which scores for the best 10 substitutes for a given item, and systems do not benefit from providing less responses[4].

BEST. Table 1 and 2 report the performance for the domain proximity and syntagmatic coherence ranking. Please note that in Table 2 we report both the official score and a score that takes into account just the *first* proposal of the systems, as the usual interpretation of BEST score methodology would suggest[5].

OOT. Table 4 and 5 report the performance for the domain proximity and syntagmatic coherence ranking, scoring for the 10 best substitutes. The results are quite good especially in the case of syntagmatic coherence ranking.

Baselines. Table 3 displays the baselines respectively for the BEST and OOT using WordNet 2.1 as calculated by the task organizers. They propose many baseline measures, but we report only the

[4]The task proposed a third scoring measure MW that scores precision and recall for detection and identification of multiwords in the input sentences. However our systems were not designed for this functionality. For the details of all scoring methodologies please refer to the task description documents.

[5]We misinterpreted that the official scorer divides anyway the figures by the number of proposals. So for the competition we submitted the oot result file without cutting the words after the first one.

	P	R	Mode P	Mode R
all	8.06	8.06	13.09	13.09

Table 1: BEST results for LSA ranking (IRST1-lsa)

	P	R	Mode P	Mode R
all	12.93	12.91	20.33	20.33
all (official)	*6.95*	*6.94*	*20.33*	*20.33*

Table 2: BEST results for Syntagmatic ranking (IRST2-syn)

WordNet one, as it is the higher scoring baseline. We can observe that globally our systems perform quite good with respect to the baselines.

4 Conclusion

In this paper we reported a detailed description of the FBK-irst systems submitted to the Lexical Entailment task at the SEMEVAL 2007 evaluation campaign. Our techniques are totally unsupervised, as they do not require neither the availability of sense tagged data nor an estimation of sense priors, not considering the WordNet sense order information. Results are quite good, as in general they significantly outperform all the baselines proposed by the organizers. In addition, the method based on syntagmatic coherence estimated on the WEB outperforms, to our knowledge, the other systems submitted to the competition. For the future, we plan to avoid the use of dictionaries by adopting term similarity techniques to select the candidate entailed words and to exploit this methodology in some specific applications such as taxonomy induction and ontology population.

Acknowledgments

Claudio Giuliano is supported by the X-Media project (`http://www.x-media-project.org`), sponsored by the European Commission as part of the Information Society Technologies (IST) programme under EC grant number IST-FP6-026978. Alfio Gliozzo is supported by FIRB-Israel research project N. RBIN045PXH.

	P	R	Mode P	Mode R
WN BEST	9.95	9.95	15.28	15.28
WN OOT	29.70	29.35	40.57	40.57

Table 3: WordNet Baselines

	P	R	Mode P	Mode R
all	41.23	41.20	55.28	55.28

Table 4: OOT results for LSA ranking (IRST1-lsa)

	P	R	Mode P	Mode R
all	69.03	68.90	58.54	58.54

Table 5: OOT results for Syntagmatic ranking (IRST2-syn)

References

I. Dagan and O. Glickman. 2004. Probabilistic textual entailment: Generic applied modeling of language variability. In *proceedings of the PASCAL Workshop on Learning Methods for Text Understanding and Mining*, Grenoble.

I. Dagan, O. Glickman, and B. Magnini. 2005. The pascal recognising textual entailment challenge. Proceedings of the PASCAL Challenges Workshop on Recognising Textual Entailment.

I. Dagan, O. Glickman, A. Gliozzo, E. Marmorshtein, and C. Strapparava. 2006. Direct word sense matching for lexical substitution. In *Proceedings ACL-2006*, pages 449–456, Sydney, Australia, July.

S. Deerwester, S. Dumais, G. Furnas, T. Landauer, and R. Harshman. 1990. Indexing by latent semantic analysis. *Journal of the American Society of Information Science*.

O. Glickman, I. Dagan, M. Keller, S. Bengio, and W. Daelemans. 2006a. Investigating lexical substitution scoring for subtitle generation tenth conference on computational natural language learning. In *Proceedings of CoNLL-2006*.

O. Glickman, E. Shnarch, and I. Dagan. 2006b. Lexical reference: a semantic matching subtask. In *proceedings of EMNLP 2006*.

A. Gliozzo. 2005. *Semantic Domains in Computational Linguistics*. Ph.D. thesis, ITC-irst/University of Trento.

B. Magnini, C. Strapparava, G. Pezzulo, and A. Gliozzo. 2002. The role of domain information in word sense disambiguation. *Natural Language Engineering*, 8(4):359–373.

FICO: Web Person Disambiguation Via Weighted Similarity of Entity Contexts

Paul Kalmar
Fair Isaac Corporation
3661 Valley Centre Dr.
San Diego, CA 92130 USA
PaulKalmar@FairIsaac.com

Matthias Blume
Fair Isaac Corporation
3661 Valley Centre Dr.
San Diego, CA 92130 USA
MatthiasBlume@FairIsaac.com

Abstract

Entity disambiguation resolves the many-to-many correspondence between mentions of entities in text and unique real-world entities. Fair Isaac's entity disambiguation uses language-independent entity context to agglomeratively resolve mentions with similar names to unique entities. This paper describes Fair Isaac's automatic entity disambiguation capability and assesses its performance on the SemEval 2007 Web People Search task.

1 Introduction

We use the term *entity* to mean a specific person or object. A *mention* is a reference to an entity such as a word or phrase in a document. Taken together, all mentions that refer to the same real-world object model that entity (Mitchell et al. 2004). Entity disambiguation inherently involves resolving many-to-many relationships. Multiple distinct strings may refer to the same entity. Simultaneously, multiple identical mentions refer to distinct entities (Bagga and Baldwin, 1998).

Fair Isaac's entity disambiguation software is based largely on language-independent algorithms that resolve mentions in the context of the entire corpus. The system utilizes multiple types of context as evidence for determining whether two mentions correspond to the same entity and it automatically learns the weight of evidence of each context item via corpus statistics.

The goal of the Web People Search task (Artiles et al. 2007) is to assign Web pages to groups, where each group contains all (and only those) pages that refer to one unique entity. A page is assigned to multiple groups if it mentions multiple entities, for example "John F. Kennedy" and the "John F. Kennedy Library". The pages were selected via a set of keyword queries, and the disambiguation is evaluated only on those query entities. This differs from Fair Isaac's system in a few key ways: our system deals with mentions rather than documents, our system does not require a filter on mentions, and our system is generally used for large collections of documents containing very many names rather than small sets of highly ambiguous documents dealing with one specific name. Nevertheless, it was possible to run the Fair Isaac entity disambiguation system on the Web People Search task data with almost no modifications and achieve accurate results.

The remaining sections of this paper describe Fair Isaac's automatic entity disambiguation methodology and report on the performance of the system on the WePS data.

2 Methodology

In unstructured text, each document provides a natural context for entity disambiguation. After cleaning up extraneous markup we carry out within-document co-reference resolution, aggregating information about each entity mentioned in each document. We then use these entity attributes as features in determining which documents deal with the same entity.

2.1 Dealing with Raw Web Data

The first challenge in dealing with data from the Web is to decide which documents are useful and

Proceedings of the 4th International Workshop on Semantic Evaluations (SemEval-2007), pages 149–152,
Prague, June 2007.

what text from those documents contains relevant information. As a first pass, the first HTML file in a folder which contained the query name was used as the main page. In retrospect, it might have been better to combine all portions of the page, or choose the longest page. We copied the title element and converted all text chunks to paragraphs, eliminating all other HTML and script. If no HTML was found in the directory for a page, the first text file which contained the query was used instead.

2.2 Within-Document Disambiguation

When dealing with unstructured text, a named entity recognition (NER) system provides the input to the entity disambiguation. Due to time constraints and that Persons are the entity type of primary interest, any mention that matches one of the query strings is automatically labeled as a Person, regardless of its actual type.

As described in Blume (2005), the system next carries out entity type-specific parsing in order to extract entity attributes such as titles, generate standardized names (e.g. p_abdul_khan_p for "Dr. Abdul Q. Khan"), and populate the data structures (token hashes) that are used to perform the within-document entity disambiguation.

We err on the side of not merging entities rather than incorrectly merging entities. Looking at multiple documents provides additional statistics. Thus, the cross-document disambiguation process described in the next section will still merge some entities even within individual documents.

2.3 Cross-Document Disambiguation

Our cross-document entity disambiguation relies on one key insight: an entity can be distinguished by the company it keeps. If Abdul Khan 1 associates with different people and organizations at different locations than Abdul Khan 2, then he is probably a different person. Furthermore, if it is possible to compare two entities based on one type of context, it is possible to compare them based on *every* type of context.

Within each domain, we require a finite set of context items. In the domains of co-occurring locations, organizations, and persons, these are the standardized names derived in the entity information extraction phase of within-document disambiguation. We use the logarithm of the inverse name frequency (the number of standard person names with which this context item appears), INF, as a weight indicating the salience of each context item. Co-occurrence with a common name provides less indication that two mentions correspond to the same entity than co-occurrence with an uncommon name. To reduce noise, only entities that occur within a given window of entities are included in this vector. In all test runs, this window is set to 10 entities on either side. Because of the effects that small corpora have on statistics, we added a large amount of newswire text to improve frequency counts. Many of the query names would have low frequency in a text corpus that is not about them specifically, but have high frequency in this task because each document contains at least one mention of them. This would cause the INF weight to incorrectly estimate the importance of any token; adding additional documents to the disambiguation run reduces this effect and brings frequency counts to more realistic levels.

We similarly count title tokens that occur with the entity and compute INF weights for the title tokens. Topic context, as described in Blume (2005), was used in some post-submission runs.

We define a separate distance measure per context domain. We are able to discount the co-occurrence with multiple items as well as quantify an unexpected *lack* of shared co-occurrence by engineering each distance measure for each specific domain. The score produced by each distance measure may be loosely interpreted as the log of the likelihood of two *randomly generated* contexts sharing the observed degree of similarity.

In addition to the context-based distance measures, we utilize a lexical (string) distance measure based on exactly the same transformations as used to compare strings for intra-document entity disambiguation plus the Soundex algorithm (Knuth 1998) to measure whether two name tokens sound the same. A large negative score indicates a great deal of similarity (log likelihood).

The process of cross-document entity disambiguation now boils down to repeatedly finding a pair of entities, comparing them (computing the sum of the above distance measures), and merging them if the score exceeds some threshold. We compute sets of keys based on lexical similarity and compare only entities that are likely to match. The WePS evaluation only deals with entities that match a query. Thus, we added a new step of key generation based on the query.

3 Performance

We have tested our entity disambiguation system on several semi-structured and unstructured text data sets. Here, we report the performance on the training data provided for the Web People Search task. This corpus consists of raw Web pages with substantial variation in capitalization, punctuation, grammar, and spelling – characteristics that make NER challenging. A few other issues also negatively impact our performance, including extraneous text, long lists of entities, and the issue of finding the correct document to parse.

The NER process identified a ratio of approximately 220 mentions per document across 3,359 documents. Within-document entity disambiguation reduced this to approximately 113 entities per document, which we refer to as *document-level entities*. Of these, 3,383 Persons (including those Organizations and Locations which were relabeled as Persons) contained a query name. Cross-document entity disambiguation reduced this to 976 distinct persons with 721 distinct standardized names. Thus, 2,407 merge operations were performed in this step. On average, there are 48 mentions per query name. Our system found an average of 14 unique entities per query name. In the gold standard, the average is 9 unique entities per query name.

Looking at the names that matched in the output, it is clear that NER is very important to the process. Post submission of our initial run, we used proper tokenization of punctuation and an additional NER system, which corrected many mistakes in the grouping of names. Also, many of the names that were incorrectly merged would not have been compared if not for the introduction of the additional key that compares all mentions that match a query name.

For the WePS evaluation submission, we converted our results to document-level entities by mapping each mention to the document that it was part of and removing duplicates. If we did not find a mention in a document, we labeled the document as a singleton entity.

We also used a number of standard metrics for our internal evaluation. Most of these operate on document-level entities rather than on documents. To convert the ground truth provided for the task to a form usable for these metrics, we assume that each entity contains all mentions in the corresponding document group. These metrics test the cross-document disambiguation rather than the NER and within-document disambiguation. These metrics should not be used to compare between different versions of NER and within-document disambiguation, since the ground truth used in the evaluation is generated by these processes.

In Table 1, we compare a run with the additional newswire data and the comparison key (our WePS submission), leaving out the additional newswire data and the additional comparison key, and leaving out only the additional comparison key.

In Table 2, we compare runs based on the improved NER (available only after the WePS submission deadline). The first uses the same parameters as our submission, the second uses an increased threshold, and the third utilizes the word vector-based clustering (document topics).

	Acc.	Prec.	Recall	Harm. Purity
WithExtraKey	0.670	0.545	0.906	0.818
NoAddedData	0.743	0.752	0.584	0.841
NoExtraKey	0.770	0.767	0.624	0.861

Table 1. Results of pairwise comparisons and clusterwise harmonic mean of purity and inverse purity on various disambiguation runs. Each metric is averaged across the individual results for every query name.

	Acc.	Prec.	Recall	Harm. Purity
WithExtraKey	0.690	0.618	0.552	0.815
1.25 Thresh	0.720	0.733	0.500	0.812
Topic Info	0.719	0.645	0.545	0.818

Table 2. Results based on improved named entity recognition. These should not be directly compared against those in Table 1, since the different NER yields different ground truth for these evaluation metrics.

Most of our metrics are based on pairwise comparisons – all document-level entities are compared against all other document-level entities that match the same query name, noting whether the pair was coreferent in the results and in the ground truth. With such comparison, we obtain measures including precision, recall, and accuracy. In this training data, depending on which NER is used, 35,000-50,000 pairwise comparisons are possible.

We also define a clusterwise measure of the harmonic mean between purity and inverse purity *with respect to mentions*. This is different from the metric provided by WePS, purity and inverse purity *at the document level.* Since some documents contain multiple entities, the latter metric does not perform correctly. Mentions, on the other hand, are always unique in our disambiguation. However, because the ground truth was specified at the document level, documents containing multiple entities that match a query yield ambiguous mentions. These decrease all purity-related scores equally and do not vary between runs.

The addition of the newswire data improved results. Inclusion of an extra comparison based on query name matches allowed for comparison of entities with names that do not match the format of person names, and only slightly reduced overall performance. The new NER run can only be compared on the last three runs. to the system performs better with topic context than without it.

In comparison, in the 2005 Knowledge Discovery and Dissemination (KD-D) Challenge Task ER-1a (the main entity disambiguation task), we achieved an accuracy of 94.5%. The margin of error in the evaluation was estimated at 3% due to errors in the "ground truth". This was a pure disambiguation task with no NER or name standardization required. The evaluation set contained 100 names, 9027 documents, and 583,152 pair-wise assertions.

4 Conclusions

Although the primary purposes of Fair Isaac's entity disambiguation system differ from the goal of the Web People Search task, we found that with little modification it was possible to fairly accurately cluster Web pages with a given query name according to the real-world entities mentioned on the page. Most of the errors that we encountered are related to information extraction from unstructured data as opposed to the cross-document entity disambiguation itself.

Acknowledgment

This material is based upon work supported by the Defense Advanced Research Projects Agency (DARPA) under Contract No. HR0011-06-C-0023.

Any opinions, findings and conclusions or recommendations expressed in this material are those of the author(s) and do not necessarily reflect the views of the Defense Advanced Research Projects Agency (DARPA).

References

Artiles, J., Gonzalo, J. and Sekine, S. (2007). The SemEval-2007 WePS Evaluation: Establishing a benchmark for the Web People Search Task. In Proceedings of Semeval 2007, Association for Computational Linguistics.

Bagga, A. and Baldwin, B. (1998). Entity-based Cross-document Coreferencing Using the Vector Space Model. 17th International Conference on Computational Linguistics (CoLing-ACL). Montreal, Canada. 10-14 August, 1998, 79-85.

Blume, M. (2005). Automatic Entity Disambiguation: Benefits to NER, Relation Extraction, Link Analysis, and Inference. 1st International Conference on Intelligence Analysis. McLean, Virginia. 2-5 May, 2005.

Gooi, C. H. and Allan, J. (2004). Cross-Document Coreference on a Large Scale Corpus. Human Language Technology Conference (HLT-NAACL). Boston, Massachusetts. 2-7 May, 2004, 9-16.

Kalashnikov, D. V. and Mehrotra, S. (2005). A Probabilistic Model for Entity Disambiguation Using Relationships. SIAM International Conference on Data Mining (SDM). Newport Beach, California. 21-23 April, 2005.

Knuth, D. E. (1998). *The Art of Computer Programming, Volume 3: Sorting and Searching.* Addison-Wesley Professional.

Mann, G. S. and Yarowsky, D. (2003). Unsupervised Personal Name Disambiguation. Conference on Computational Natural Language Learning (CoNLL). Edmonton, Canada. 31 May - 1 June, 2003, 33-40.

Mitchell, A.; Strassel, S.; Przybocki, P.; Davis, J. K.; Doddington, G.; Grishman, R.; Meyers, A.; Brunstein, A.; Ferro, L. and Sundheim, B. (2004). *Annotation Guidelines for Entity Detection and Tracking (EDT), Version 4.2.6.* http://www.ldc.upenn.edu/Projects/ACE/.

Ravin, Y. and Kazi, Z. (1999). Is Hillary Rodham Clinton the President? Disambiguating Names across Documents. ACL 1999 Workshop on Coreference and Its Applications. College Park, Maryland. 22 June, 1999, 9-16.

FUH (FernUniversität in Hagen): Metonymy Recognition Using Different Kinds of Context for a Memory-Based Learner

Johannes Leveling
Intelligent Information and Communication Systems (IICS)
FernUniversität in Hagen (University of Hagen)
johannes.leveling@fernuni-hagen.de

Abstract

For the metonymy resolution task at SemEval-2007, the use of a memory-based learner to train classifiers for the identification of metonymic location names is investigated. Metonymy is resolved on different levels of granularity, differentiating between literal and non-literal readings on the coarse level; literal, metonymic, and mixed readings on the medium level; and a number of classes covering regular cases of metonymy on a fine level. Different kinds of context are employed to obtain different features: 1) a sequence of n_1 synset IDs representing subordination information for nouns and for verbs, 2) n_2 prepositions, articles, modal, and main verbs in the same sentence, and 3) properties of n_3 tokens in a context window to the left and to the right of the location name.

Different classifiers were trained on the Mascara data set to determine which values for the context sizes n_1, n_2, and n_3 yield the highest accuracy ($n_1 = 4$, $n_2 = 3$, and $n_3 = 7$, determined with the leave-one-out method). Results from these classifiers served as features for a combined classifier. In the training phase, the combined classifier achieved a considerably higher precision for the Mascara data. In the SemEval submission, an accuracy of 79.8% on the coarse, 79.5% on the medium, and 78.5% on the fine level is achieved (the baseline accuracy is 79.4%).

1 Introduction

Metonymy is typically defined as a figure of speech in which a speaker uses *one entity to refer to another that is related to it* (Lakoff and Johnson, 1980). The identification of metonymy becomes important for NLP tasks such as question answering (Stallard, 1993) or geographic information retrieval (Leveling and Hartrumpf, 2006).

For regular cases of metonymy for locations and organizations, Markert and Nissim have proposed a set of metonymy classes. Annotating a subset of the BNC (British National Corpus), they extracted a set of metonymic proper nouns from two categories: country names (Markert and Nissim, 2002) and organization names (Nissim and Markert, 2003).

In the metonymy resolution task at SemEval-2007, the goal was to identify metonymic names in a subset of the BNC. The task consists of two subtasks for company and country names, which are further divided into classification on a coarse level (recognizing *literal* and *non-literal* readings), on a medium level (differentiating *non-literal* readings into *mixed* and *metonymic* readings), and on a fine level (identifying classes of regular metonymy, such as a name referring to the population, *place-for-people*). The task is described in more detail by Markert and Nissim (2007).

2 System Description

2.1 Tools and Resources

The following tools and resources are used for the metonymy classification:

- TiMBL 5.1 (Daelemans et al., 2004), a memory-based learner for classification is em-

Proceedings of the 4th International Workshop on Semantic Evaluations (SemEval-2007), pages 153–156,
Prague, June 2007.

ployed for training the classifiers (supervised learning).[1]

- Mascara 2.0 – Metonymy Annotation Scheme And Robust Analysis (Markert and Nissim, 2003; Nissim and Markert, 2003; Markert and Nissim, 2002) contains annotated data for metonymic names from a subset of the the BNC.

- WordNet 2.0 (Fellbaum, 1998) serves as a linguistic resource for assigning synset IDs and for looking up subordination information and frequency of readings.

- The TreeTagger (Schmid, 1994) is utilized for sentence boundary detection, lemmatization, and part-of-speech tagging. The English tagger was trained on the PENN treebank and uses the English morphological database from the XTAG project (Karp et al., 1992). The parameter files were obtained from the web site.[2]

2.2 Different Kinds of Context

Following the assumption that metonymic location names can be identified from the context, there are different kinds of context to consider. At most, the context comprises a single sentence in this setup. Three kinds of context were employed to extract features for the memory-based learner TiMBL:

- C_1: Subordination (hyponymy) information for nouns and verbs from the left and right context of the possibly metonymic name.

- C_2: The sentence context for modal verbs, main verbs, prepositions, and articles.

- C_3: A context window of tokens left and right of the location name.

The trial data provided (a subset of the Mascara data) contained 188 *non-literal* location names (of 925 samples total). For a supervised learning approach, this is too few data. Therefore, the full Mascara data was converted to form training data consisting of feature values for context C_1, C_2, and C_3. The training data contained 509 metonymic annotations (of 2797 samples total). Some cases in the Mascara corpus are filtered during processing, including cases annotated as homonyms and cases whose metonymy class could not be agreed upon. The test data had a majority baseline of 82.8% accuracy for country names.

2.3 Features

The Mascara data was processed to extract the following features (no hand-annotated data from Mascara was employed for feature values, i.e. no grammatical roles):

- For C_1 (WordNet context): From a context of n_1 verbs and nouns in the same sentence, their distance to the location name is calculated. A sequence of eight feature values of WordNet synset IDs is obtained by iteratively looking up the most frequent reading for a lemma in WordNet and determining its synset ID. Subordination information between synsets is used to find a parent synset. This process is repeated until a top-level parent synset is reached. No actual word sense disambiguation is employed.

- For C_2 (sentence context): Sentence boundaries, part-of-speech tags, and lemmatization are determined from the TreeTagger output. From a context window of n_2 tokens, lemma and distance are encoded as feature values for prepositions, articles, modal, and main verbs

- For C_3 (word context): From a context of n_3 tokens to the left and to the right, the distance between token and location name, three prefix characters, three suffix characters, part-of-speech tag, case information (U=upper case, L=lower case, N=numeric, O=other), and word length are used as feature values.

Table 1 and Table 2 show results for memory based learners trained with TiMBL. Performance measures were obtained with the leave-one-out method. The classifiers were trained on features for different context sizes (n_i ranging from 2 to 7) to determine the setting for which the highest accuracy is achieved (e.g. 1_c, 2_c, and 3_c). In the next step, classifiers with a combined context were

[1] Peirsman (2006) also employs TiMBL for metonymy resolution, but trains a single classifier.

[2] `http://www.ims.uni-stuttgart.de/projekte/corplex/TreeTagger/`

Table 1: Results for training the classifiers on the coarse location name classes (2797 instances, 509 *non-literal*, leave-one-out) for the Mascara data (P = precision, R = recall, F = F-score).

ID	n_1,n_2,n_3	coarse class	P	R	F
1_c	4,0,0	literal	0.850	0.893	0.871
1_c	4,0,0	non-literal	0.377	0.289	0.327
2_c	0,3,0	literal	0.848	0.874	0.860
2_c	0,3,0	non-literal	0.342	0.295	0.317
3_c	0,0,7	literal	0.880	0.889	0.885
3_c	0,0,7	non-literal	0.478	0.455	0.467
4_c	4,3,0	literal	0.848	0.892	0.896
4_c	4,3,0	non-literal	0.368	0.282	0.320
5_c	4,0,7	literal	0.860	0.913	0.885
5_c	4,0,7	non-literal	0.459	0.332	0.385
6_c	0,3,7	literal	0.875	0.905	0.889
6_c	0,3,7	non-literal	0.496	0.420	0.455
7_c	4,3,7	literal	0.860	0.918	0.888
7_c	4,3,7	non-literal	0.473	0.332	0.390
8_c	res. of 1_c–7_c	literal	0.852	0.968	0.907
8_c	res. of 1_c–7_c	non-literal	0.639	0.248	0.357

trained, selecting the setting with the highest accuracy for a single context for the combination (e.g. 4_c, 5_c, 6_c, and 7_c). As an additional experiment, a classifier was trained on classification results of the classifiers described above (combination of 1–7, e.g. 8_c). It was expected that the combination of features from different kinds of context would increase performance, and that the combination of classifier results would increase performance.

3 Evaluation Results

Table 3 shows results for the official submission. Compared to results from the training phase on the Mascara data (tested with the leave-one-out method), performance is considerably lower. For this data, the combined classifier achieved a considerably higher precision (63.9% for *non-literal* readings; 57.3% for the fine class *place-for-people* and even 83.3% for the rare class *place-for-event*).

Performance may be affected by several reasons: A number of problems were encountered while processing the data. The TreeTagger automatically tokenizes its input and applies sentence boundary detection. In some cases, the sentence boundary detection did not work well, returning sentences of more than 170 words. Furthermore, the tagger output had to be aligned with the test data again, as multi-word

Table 2: Excerpt from results for training the classifiers on the fine location name classes (2797 instances, leave-one-out) for the Mascara data.

ID	n_1,n_2,n_3	fine class	P	R	F
1_f	4,0,0	literal	0.851	0.895	0.873
1_f	4,0,0	pl.-for-p.	0.366	0.280	0.318
1_f	4,0,0	pl.-for-e.	0.370	0.270	0.312
2_f	0,3,0	literal	0.848	0.876	0.862
2_f	0,3,0	pl.-for-p.	0.332	0.276	0.301
2_f	0,3,0	pl.-for-e.	0.222	0.270	0.244
3_f	0,0,7	literal	0.878	0.892	0.885
3_f	0,0,7	pl.-for-p.	0.463	0.424	0.442
3_f	0,0,7	pl.-for-e.	0.279	0.324	0.300
4_f	4,3,0	literal	0.851	0.899	0.875
4_f	4,3,0	pl.-for-p.	0.358	0.269	0.307
4_f	4,3,0	pl.-for-e.	0.435	0.270	0.333
5_f	4,0,7	literal	0.861	0.914	0.887
5_f	4,0,7	pl.-for-p.	0.452	0.322	0.377
5_f	4,0,7	pl.-for-e.	0.550	0.297	0.386
6_f	0,3,7	literal	0.871	0.906	0.888
6_f	0,3,7	pl.-for-p.	0.468	0.383	0.422
6_f	0,3,7	pl.-for-e.	0.400	0.324	0.358
7_f	4,3,7	literal	0.861	0.918	0.889
7_f	4,3,7	pl.-for-p.	0.459	0.323	0.378
7_f	4,3,7	pl.-for-e.	0.500	0.297	0.373
8_f	res. of 1_f–7_f	literal	0.854	0.963	0.905
8_f	res. of 1_f–7_f	pl.-for-p.	0.573	0.262	0.360
8_f	res. of 1_f–7_f	pl.-for-e.	0.833	0.270	0.408

names (e.g. New York) were split into different tokens. In addition, the tag set of the tagger differs somewhat from the official PENN tag set and includes additional tags for verbs.

In earlier experiments on metonymy classification on a German corpus (Leveling and Hartrumpf, 2006), the data was nearly evenly distributed between literal and metonymic readings. This seems to make a classification task easier because there is no hidden bias in the classifier (i.e. the baseline of always selecting the literal readings is about 50%).

Features are obtained by shallow NLP methods only, not making use of a parser or chunker. Thus, important syntactic or semantic information to decide on metonymy might be missing in the features. However, semantic features are more difficult to determine, because reliable automatic tools for semantic annotation are still missing. This is also indicated by the fact that the grammatical roles (comprising syntactic features) in Mascara data are hand-annotated.

However, some linguistic phenomena are already implicitly represented by shallower features from

Table 3: Results for the coarse (908 samples: 721 *literal*, 187 *non-literal*), medium (721 *literal*, 167 *metonymic*, 20 *mixed*), and fine classification (721 *literal*, 141 *place-for-people*, 10 *place-for-event*, 1 *place-for-product*, 4 *object-for-name*, 11 *othermet*, 20 *mixed*) of location names.

class	P	R	F
FUH.location.coarse (0.798 accuracy)			
literal	0.812	0.971	0.884
non-literal	0.543	0.134	0.214
FUH.location.medium (0.795 accuracy)			
literal	0.810	0.970	0.883
metonymic	0.500	0.132	0.208
mixed	0.0	0.0	0.0
FUH.location.fine (0.785 accuracy)			
literal	0.808	0.965	0.880
place-for-people	0.386	0.120	0.183

the surface level (given enough training instances). For instance, active/passive voice may be encoded by a combination of features for main verb/modal verbs. If only a small training corpus is available, overall performance will be higher when utilizing explicit syntactic or semantic features.

Finally, the data may be too sparse for a supervised memory-based learning approach. The identification of rare classes of metonymy (e.g. *place-for-event*) would greatly benefit from a larger corpus covering these classes.

4 Conclusion

Evaluation results on the training data were very promising, indicating a boost of precision by combining classification results. In the training phase, an accuracy of 83.7% was achieved on the coarse level, compared to the majority baseline accuracy of 81.8%. For the submission for the metonymy resolution task at SemEval-2007, accuracy is close to the majority baseline (79.4%) on the coarse (79.8%), medium (79.5%), and fine (78.5%) level.

In summary, using different context sizes for different kinds of context and combining results of different classifiers for metonymy resolution increases performance. The general approach would profit from combining results of more diverse classifiers, i.e. classifiers employing features extracted from the surface, syntactic, and semantic context of a location name.

Acknowledgments

The research described was in part funded by the DFG (Deutsche Forschungsgemeinschaft) in the project IRSAW (Intelligent Information Retrieval on the Basis of a Semantically Annotated Web).

References

Walter Daelemans, Jakub Zavrel, Ko van der Sloot, and Antal van den Bosch. 2004. TiMBL: Tilburg memory based learner, version 5.1. TR 04-02, ILK.

Christiane Fellbaum, editor. 1998. *Wordnet. An Electronic Lexical Database*. MIT Press, Cambridge, Massachusetts.

Daniel Karp, Yves Schabes, Martin Zaidel, and Dania Egedi. 1992. A freely available wide coverage morphological analyzer for English. In *Proc. of COLING-92*, pages 950–955, Morristown, NJ.

George Lakoff and Mark Johnson. 1980. *Metaphors We Live By*. Chicago University Press.

Johannes Leveling and Sven Hartrumpf. 2006. On metonymy recognition for GIR. In *Proc. of GIR-2006, the 3rd Workshop on Geographical Information Retrieval (held at SIGIR 2006)*, Seattle, Washington.

Katja Markert and Malvina Nissim. 2002. Towards a corpus for annotated metonymies: The case of location names. In *Proc. of LREC 2002*, Las Palmas, Spain.

Katja Markert and Malvina Nissim. 2003. Corpus-based metonymy analysis. *Metaphor and symbol*, 18(3).

Katja Markert and Malvina Nissim. 2007. Task 08: Metonymy resolution at SemEval-07. In *Proc. of SemEval 2007*.

Malvina Nissim and Katja Markert. 2003. Syntactic features and word similarity for supervised metonymy resolution. In *Proc. of ACL-2003*, Sapporo, Japan.

Yves Peirsman. 2006. Example-based metonymy recognition for proper nouns. In *Proc. of the Student Research Workshop of EACL-2006*, pages 71–78, Trento, Italy.

Helmut Schmid. 1994. Probabilistic part-of-speech tagging using decision trees. In *International Conference on New Methods in Language Processing*, Manchester, UK.

David Stallard. 1993. Two kinds of metonymy. In *Proc. of ACL-93*, pages 87–94, Columbus, Ohio.

GPLSI: Word Coarse-grained Disambiguation aided by Basic Level Concepts*

Rubén Izquierdo **Armando Suárez**
GPLSI Group, DLSI
University of Alicante
Spain
{ruben, armando}@dlsi.ua.es

German Rigau
IXA NLP Group
EHU/UPV
Donostia, Basque Country
german.rigau@ehu.es

Abstract

We present a corpus-based supervised learning system for coarse-grained sense disambiguation. In addition to usual features for training in word sense disambiguation, our system also uses Base Level Concepts automatically obtained from WordNet. Base Level Concepts are some synsets that generalize a hyponymy sub–hierarchy, and provides an extra level of abstraction as well as relevant information about the context of a word to be disambiguated. Our experiments proved that using this type of features results on a significant improvement of precision. Our system has achieved almost 0.8 F1 (fifth place) in the coarse–grained English all-words task using a very simple set of features plus Base Level Concepts annotation.

1 Introduction

The GPLSI system in SemEval's task 7, *coarse–grained English all-words*, consists of a corpus-based supervised-learning method which uses local context information. The system uses Base Level Concepts (BLC) (Rosch, 1977) as features. In short, BLC are synsets of WordNet (WN) (Fellbaum, 1998) that are representative of a certain hyponymy sub–hierarchy. The synsets that are selected to be BLC must accomplish certain conditions that will be explained in next section. BLC are slightly different from Base Concepts of EuroWordNet[1] (EWN) (Vossen et al., 1998), Balkanet[2] or Meaning Project[3] because of the selection criteria but also because our method is capable to define them automatically. This type of features helps our system to achieve 0.79550 F1 (over the First–Sense baseline, 0.78889) while only four systems outperformed ours being the F1 of the best one 0.83208.

WordNet has been widely criticised for being a sense repository that often offers too fine–grained sense distinctions for higher level applications like Machine Translation or Question & Answering. In fact, WSD at this level of granularity, has resisted all attempts of inferring robust broad-coverage models. It seems that many word–sense distinctions are too subtle to be captured by automatic systems with the current small volumes of word–sense annotated examples. Possibly, building class-based classifiers would allow to avoid the data sparseness problem of the word-based approach.

Thus, some research has been focused on deriving different sense groupings to overcome the fine–grained distinctions of WN (Hearst and Schütze, 1993) (Peters et al., 1998) (Mihalcea and Moldovan, 2001) (Agirre et al., 2003) and on using predefined sets of sense-groupings for learning class-based classifiers for WSD (Segond et al., 1997) (Ciaramita and Johnson, 2003) (Villarejo et al., 2005) (Curran, 2005) (Ciaramita and Altun, 2006). However, most of the later approaches used the original Lexicographical Files of WN (more recently called Super-

*This paper has been supported by the European Union under the project QALL-ME (FP6 IST-033860) and the Spanish Government under the project Text-Mess (TIN2006-15265-C06-01) and KNOW (TIN2006-15049-C03-01)

[1] http://www.illc.uva.nl/EuroWordNet/
[2] http://www.ceid.upatras.gr/Balkanet
[3] http://www.lsi.upc.es/ nlp/meaning

Proceedings of the 4th International Workshop on Semantic Evaluations (SemEval-2007), pages 157–160,
Prague, June 2007.

senses) as very coarse–grained sense distinctions. However, not so much attention has been paid on learning class-based classifiers from other available sense–groupings such as WordNet Domains (Magnini and Cavaglia, 2000), SUMO labels (Niles and Pease, 2001), EuroWordNet Base Concepts or Top Concept Ontology labels (Atserias et al., 2004). Obviously, these resources relate senses at some level of abstraction using different semantic criteria and properties that could be of interest for WSD. Possibly, their combination could improve the overall results since they offer different semantic perspectives of the data. Furthermore, to our knowledge, to date no comparative evaluation have been performed exploring different sense–groupings.

This paper is organized as follows. In section 2, we present a method for deriving fully automatically a number of Base Level Concepts from any WN version. Section 3 shows the details of the whole system and finally, in section 4 some concluding remarks are provided.

2 Automatic Selection of Base Level Concepts

The notion of Base Concepts (hereinafter BC) was introduced in EWN. The BC are supposed to be the concepts that play the most important role in the various wordnets[4] (Fellbaum, 1998) of different languages. This role was measured in terms of two main criteria:

- A high position in the semantic hierarchy;
- Having many relations to other concepts;

Thus, the BC are the fundamental building blocks for establishing the relations in a wordnet and give information about the dominant lexicalization patterns in languages. BC are generalizations of features or semantic components and thus apply to a maximum number of concepts. Thus, the Lexicografic Files (or Supersenses) of WN could be considered the most basic set of BC.

Basic Level Concepts (Rosch, 1977) should not be confused with Base Concepts. BLC are the result of a compromise between two conflicting principles of characterization:

#rel.	**synset**
18	group_1,grouping_1
19	social_group_1
37	organisation_2,organization_1
10	establishment_2,institution_1
12	faith_3,religion_2
5	Christianity_2,**church_1**,Christian_church_1

#rel.	**synset**
14	entity_1,something_1
29	object_1,physical_object_1
39	artifact_1,artefact_1
63	construction_3,structure_1
79	building_1,edifice_1
11	place_of_worship_1, ...
19	**church_2**,church_building_1

#rel.	**synset**
20	act_2,human_action_1,human_activity_1
69	activity_1
5	ceremony_3
11	religious_ceremony_1,religious_ritual_1
7	service_3,religious_service_1,divine_service_1
1	**church_3**,church_service_1

Table 1: Possible Base Level Concepts for the noun *Church*

- Represent as many concepts as possible;
- Represent as many features as possible;

As a result of this, Basic Level Concepts typically occur in the middle of hierarchies and less than the maximum number of relations. BC mostly involve the first principle of the Basic Level Concepts only.

Our work focuses on devising simple methods for selecting automatically an accurate set of Basic Level Concepts from WN. In particular, our method selects the appropriate BLC of a particular synset considering the relative number of relations encoded in WN of their hypernyms.

The process follows a bottom-up approach using the chain of hypernym relations. For each synset in WN, the process selects as its Base Level Concept the first local maximum according to the relative number of relations. For synsets having multiple hypernyms, the path having the local maximum with higher number of relations is selected. Usually, this process finishes having a number of "fake" Base Level Concepts. That is, synsets having no descendants (or with a very small number) but being the first local maximum according to the number of relations considered. Thus, the process finishes checking if the number of concepts subsumed by the

[4]http://wordnet.princeton.edu

	Senses	BLC	SuperSenses
Nouns	4.92	4.10	3.01
Verbs	11.00	8.67	1.03
Nouns + Verbs	7.66	6.16	3.47

Table 2: Polysemy degree over SensEval–3

preliminary list of BLC is higher than a certain threshold. For those BLC not representing enough concepts according to a certain threshold, the process selects the next local maximum following the hypernym hierarchy.

An example is provided in table 1. This table shows the possible BLC for the noun "church" using WN1.6. The table presents the hypernym chain for each synset together with the number of relations encoded in WN for the synset. The local maxima along the hypernym chain of each synset appears in bold.

Table 2 presents the polysemy degree for nouns and verbs of the different words when grouping its senses with respect the different semantic classes on SensEval–3. Senses stand for the WN senses, BLC for the Automatic BLC derived using a threshold of 20 and SuperSenses for the Lexicographic Files of WN.

3 The GPLSI system

The GPLSI system uses a publicly available implementation of Support Vector Machines, SVMLight[5] (Joachims, 2002), and Semcor as learning corpus. Semcor has been properly mapped and labelled with both BLC[6] and sense-clusters.

Actually, the process of training-classification has two phases: first, one classifier is trained for each possible BLC class and then the SemEval test data is classified and enriched with them, and second, a classifier for each target word is built using as additional features the BLC tags in Semcor and SemEval's test.

Then, the features used for training the classifiers are: lemmas, word forms, PoS tags[7], BLC tags, and first sense class of target word (S1TW). All features were extracted from a window $[-3..+3]$ except for the last type (S1TW). The reason of using S1TW features is to assure the learning of the baseline. It is well known that Semcor presents a higher frequency on first senses (and it is also the baseline of the task finally provided by the organizers).

Besides, these are the same features for both first and second phases (obviously except for S1TW because of the different target set of classes). Nevertheless, the training in both cases are quite different: the first phase is class-based while the second is word-based. By word-based we mean that the learning is performed using just the examples in Semcor that contains the target word. We obtain one classifier per polysemous word are in the SemEval test corpus. The output of these classifiers is a sense-cluster. In class-based learning all the examples in Semcor are used, tagging those ones belonging to a specific class (BLC in our case) as positive examples while the rest are tagged as negatives. We obtain so many binary classifiers as BLC are in SemEval test corpus. The output of these classifiers is $true$ or $false$, "the example belongs to a class" or not. When dealing with a concrete target word, only those BLC classifiers that are related to it are "activated" (i.e, "animal" classifier will be not used to classify "church"), ensuring that the word will be tagged with coherent labels. In order to avoid statistical bias because of very large set of negative examples, the features are defined from positive examples only (although they are obviously used to characterize all the examples).

4 Conclusions and further work

The WSD task seems to have reached its maximum accuracy figures with the usual framework. Some of its limitations could come from the sense–granularity of WN. In particular, SemEval's coarse-grained English all-words task represents a solution in this direction.

Nevertheless, the task still remains oriented to words rather than classes. Then, other problems arise like data sparseness just because the lack of adequate and enough examples. Changing the set of classes could be a solution to enrich training corpora with many more examples Another option seems to be incorporating more semantic information.

[5] http://svmlight.joachims.org/

[6] Because BLC are automatically defined from WN, some tuning must be performed due to the nature of the task 7. We have not enough room to present the complete study but threshold 20 has been chosen, using SENSEVAL-3 English all-words as test data. Moreover, our tests showed roughly 5% of improvement against not using these features.

[7] TreeTagger (Schmid, 1994) was used

Base Level Concepts (BLC) are concepts that are representative for a set of other concepts. A simple method for automatically selecting BLC from WN based on the hypernym hierarchy and the number of stored relationships between synsets have been used to define features for training a supervised system.

Although in our system BLC play a simple role aiding to the disambiguation just as additional features, the good results achieved with such simple features confirm us that an appropriate set of BLC will be a better semantic discriminator than senses or even sense-clusters.

References

E. Agirre, I. Aldezabal, and E. Pociello. 2003. A pilot study of english selectional preferences and their cross-lingual compatibility with basque. In *Proceedings of the International Conference on Text Speech and Dialogue (TSD'2003)*, CeskBudojovice, Czech Republic.

J. Atserias, L. Villarejo, G. Rigau, E. Agirre, J. Carroll, B. Magnini, and P. Vossen. 2004. The meaning multilingual central repository. In *Proceedings of Global WordNet Conference (GWC'04)*, Brno, Czech Republic.

M. Ciaramita and Y. Altun. 2006. Broad-coverage sense disambiguation and information extraction with a supersense sequence tagger. In *Proceedings of the Conference on Empirical Methods in Natural Language Processing (EMNLP'06)*, pages 594–602, Sydney, Australia. ACL.

M. Ciaramita and M. Johnson. 2003. Supersense tagging of unknown nouns in wordnet. In *Proceedings of the Conference on Empirical methods in natural language processing (EMNLP'03)*, pages 168–175. ACL.

J. Curran. 2005. Supersense tagging of unknown nouns using semantic similarity. In *Proceedings of the 43rd Annual Meeting on Association for Computational Linguistics (ACL'05)*, pages 26–33. ACL.

C. Fellbaum, editor. 1998. *WordNet. An Electronic Lexical Database*. The MIT Press.

M. Hearst and H. Schütze. 1993. Customizing a lexicon to better suit a computational task. In *Proceedingns of the ACL SIGLEX Workshop on Lexical Acquisition*, Stuttgart, Germany.

Thorsten Joachims. 2002. *Learning to Classify Text Using Support Vector Machines*. Kluwer Academic Publishers.

B. Magnini and G. Cavaglia. 2000. Integrating subject fields codes into wordnet. In *Proceedings of the Second International Conference on Language Resources and Evaluation (LREC'00)*.

R. Mihalcea and D. Moldovan. 2001. Automatic generation of coarse grained wordnet. In *Proceding of the NAACL workshop on WordNet and Other Lexical Resources: Applications, Extensions and Customizations*, Pittsburg, USA.

I. Niles and A. Pease. 2001. Towards a standard upper ontology. In *Proceedings of the 2nd International Conference on Formal Ontology in Information Systems (FOIS-2001)*, pages 17–19. Chris Welty and Barry Smith, eds.

W. Peters, I. Peters, and P. Vossen. 1998. Automatic sense clustering in eurowordnet. In *First International Conference on Language Resources and Evaluation (LREC'98)*, Granada, Spain.

E. Rosch. 1977. Human categorisation. *Studies in Cross-Cultural Psychology*, I(1):1–49.

Helmut Schmid. 1994. Probabilistic part-of-speech tagging using decision trees. In *Proceedings of NemLap-94*, pages 44–49, Manchester, England.

F. Segond, A. Schiller, G. Greffenstette, and J. Chanod. 1997. An experiment in semantic tagging using hidden markov model tagging. In *ACL Workshop on Automatic Information Extraction and Building of Lexical Semantic Resources for NLP Applications*, pages 78–81. ACL, New Brunswick, New Jersey.

L. Villarejo, L. Màrquez, and G. Rigau. 2005. Exploring the construction of semantic class classifiers for wsd. In *Proceedings of the 21th Annual Meeting of Sociedad Espaola para el Procesamiento del Lenguaje Natural SEPLN'05*, pages 195–202, Granada, Spain, September. ISSN 1136-5948.

P. Vossen, L. Bloksma, H. Rodriguez, S. Climent, N. Calzolari, A. Roventini, F. Bertagna, A. Alonge, and W. Peters. 1998. The eurowordnet base concepts and top ontology. Technical report, Paris, France, France.

GYDER: maxent metonymy resolution

Richárd Farkas
University of Szeged
Department of Informatics
H-6720 Szeged, Árpád tér 2.
rfarkas@inf.u-szeged.hu

Eszter Simon
Budapest U. of Technology
Dept. of Cognitive Science
H-1111 Budapest, Stoczek u 2.
esimon@cogsci.bme.hu

György Szarvas
University of Szeged
Department of Informatics
H-6720 Szeged, Árpád tér 2.
szarvas@inf.u-szeged.hu

Dániel Varga
Budapest U. of Technology
MOKK Media Research
H-1111 Budapest, Stoczek u 2.
daniel@mokk.bme.hu

Abstract

Though the GYDER system has achieved the highest accuracy scores for the metonymy resolution shared task at SemEval-2007 in all six subtasks, we don't consider the results (72.80% accuracy for `org`, 84.36% for `loc`) particularly impressive, and argue that metonymy resolution needs more features.

1 Introduction

In linguistics *metonymy* means using one term, or one specific sense of a term, to refer to another, related term or sense. For example, in 'the pen is mightier than the sword' *pen* refers to writing, the force of ideas, while *sword* refers to military force. Named Entity Recognition (NER) is of key importance in numerous natural language processing applications ranging from information extraction to machine translation. Metonymic usage of named entities is frequent in natural language. On the basic NER categories `person`, `place`, `organisation` state-of-the-art systems generally perform in the mid to the high nineties. These systems typically do not distinguish between literal or metonymic usage of entity names, even though this would be helpful for most applications. Resolving metonymic usage of proper names would therefore directly benefit NER and indirectly all NLP tasks (such as anaphor resolution) that require NER.

Markert and Nissim (2002) outlined a corpus-based approach to proper name metonymy as a semantic classification problem that forms the basis of the 2007 SemEval metonymy resolution task. Instances like 'He was shocked by Vietnam' or 'Schengen boosted tourism' were assigned to broad categories like `place-for-event`, sometimes ignoring narrower distinctions, such as the fact that it wasn't the signing of the treaty at Schengen but rather its actual implementation (which didn't take place at Schengen) that boosted tourism. But the corpus makes clear that even with these (sometimes coarse) class distinctions, several metonymy types seem to appear extremely rarely in actual texts. The shared task focused on two broad named entity classes as metonymic sources, `location` and `org`, each having several target classes. For more details on the data sets, see the task description paper Markert and Nissim (2007).

Several categories (e.g. `place-for-event`, `organisation-for-index`) did not contain a sufficient number of examples for machine learning, and we decided early on to accept the fact that these categories will not be learned and to concentrate on those classes where learning seemed feasible. The shared task itself consisted of 3 subtasks of different granularity for both organisation and location names. The fine-grained evaluation aimed at distinguishing between all categories, while the medium-grained evaluation grouped different types of metonymic usage together and addressed literal / mixed / metonymic usage. The coarse-grained subtask was in fact a literal / nonliteral two-class classification task.

Though GYDER has obtained the highest accuracy for the metonymy shared task at SemEval-2007 in all six subtasks, we don't consider the results

Proceedings of the 4th International Workshop on Semantic Evaluations (SemEval-2007), pages 161–164,
Prague, June 2007.

(72.80% accuracy for `org`, 84.36% for `loc`) particularly impressive. In Section 3 we describe the feature engineering lessons learned from working on the task. In Section 5 we offer some speculative remarks on what it would take to improve the results.

2 Learning

GYDER (the acronym was formed from the initials of the author' first names) is a maximum entropy learner. It uses Zhang Le's [1] maximum entropy toolkit, setting the Gaussian prior to 1. We used random 5-fold cross-validation to determine the usefulness of a particular feature. Due to the small number of instances and features, the learning algorithm always converged before 30 iterations, so the cross-validation process took only seconds.

We also tested the classic C4.5 decision tree learning algorithm Quinlan (1993), but our early experiments showed that the maximum entropy learner was consistently superior to the decision tree classifier for this task, yielding about 2-5% higher accuracy scores on average on both tasks (on the training set, using cross-validation).

3 Feature Engineering

We tested several features describing orthographic, syntactic, or semantic characteristics of the Possibly Metonymic Words (PMWs). Here we follow Nissim and Markert (2005), who reported three classes of features to be the most relevant for metonymy resolution: the grammatical annotations provided for the corpus examples by the task organizers, the determiner, and the grammatical number of the PMW. We also report on some features that didn't work.

3.1 Grammatical annotations

We used the grammatical annotations provided for each PMW in several ways. First, we used as a feature the type of the grammatical relation and the word form of the related word. (If there was more than one related word, each became a feature.) To overcome data sparseness, it is useful to generalize from individual headwords Markert and Nissim (2003). We used three different methods to achieve this:

First, we used Levin's (1993) verb classification index to generalize the headwords of the most relevant grammatical relations (subject and object). The added feature was simply the class assigned to the verb by Levin.

We also used WordNet (Fellbaum 1998) to generalize headwords. First we gathered the hypernym path from WordNet for each headword's sense#1 in the train corpus. Based on these paths we collected synsets whose tree frequently indicated metonymic sense. We indicated with a feature if the headword in question was in one of such collected subtrees.

Third, we have manually built a very small verb classification 'Trigger' table for specific cases. E.g. *announce, say, declare* all trigger the same feature. This table is the only resource in our final system that was manually built by us, so we note that on the test corpus, disabling this 'Trigger' feature does not alter `org` accuracy, and decreases `loc` accuracy by 0.44%.

3.2 Determiners

Following Nissim and Markert (2005), we distinguished between definite, indefinite, demonstrative, possessive, wh and other determiners. We also marked if the PMW was sentence-initial, and thus necessarily determinerless. This feature was useful for the resolution of organisation PMWs so we used it only for the `org` tasks. It was not straightforward, however, to assign determiners to the PMWs without proper syntactic analysis. After some experiments, we linked the nearest determiner and the PMW together if we found only adjectives (or nothing) between them.

3.3 Number

This feature was particularly useful to separate metonymies of the `org-for-product` class. We assumed that only PMWs ending with letter *s* might be in plural form, and for them we compared the web search result numbers obtained by the Google API. We ran two queries for each PMWs, one for the full name, and one for the name without its last character. If we observed a significant increase in the number of hits returned by Google for the shorter phrase, we set this feature for plural.

[1] http://homepages.inf.ed.ac.uk/s0450736/maxent_toolkit.html

3.4 PMW word form

We included the surface form of the PMW as a feature, but only for the `org` domain. Cross-validation on the training corpus showed that the use of this feature causes an 1.5% accuracy improvement for organisations, and a slight degradation for locations. The improvement perfectly generalized to the test corpora. Some company names are indeed more likely to be used in a metonymic way, so we believe that this feature does more than just exploiting some specificity of the shared task corpora. We note that the ranking of our system would have been unaffected even if we didn't use this feature.

3.5 Unsuccessful features

Here we discuss those features where cross-validation didn't show improvements (and thus were not included in the submitted system).

Trigger words were automatically collected lists of word forms and phrases that more frequently appeared near metonymic PMWs.

Expert triggers were similar trigger words or phrases, but suggested by a linguist expert to be potentially indicative for metonymic usage. We experimented with sample-level, sentence-level and vicinity trigger phrases.

Named entity labels given by a state-of-the-art named entity recognizer (Szarvas et al. 2006).

POS tags around PMWs.

Ortographical features such as capitalisation and and other surface characteristics for the PMW and nearby words.

Individual tokens of the potentially metonymic phrase.

Main category of Levin's hierarchical classification.

Inflectional category of the verb nearest to the PMW in the sentence.

4 Results

Table 1. shows the accuracy scores of our submitted system on fine classification granularity. As a baseline, we also evalute the system without the WordNet, Levin, Trigger and PMW word form features. This baseline system is quite similar to the one described by Nissim and Markert (2005). We also publish the majority baseline scores.

run	majority	baseline	submitted
org train 5-fold	63.30	77.51	80.92
org test	61.76	70.55	**72.80**
loc train 5-fold	79.68	85.58	88.36
loc test	79.41	83.59	**84.36**

Table 1: Accuracy of the submitted system

We could not exploit the hierarchical structure of the fine-grained tag set, and ended up treating it as totally unstructured even for the mixed class, unlike Nissim and Markert, who apply complicated heuristics to exploit the special semantics of this class.

For the coarse and medium subtasks of the `loc` domain, we simply coarsened the fine-grained results. For the coarse and medium subtasks of the `org` domain, we coarsened the train corpus to medium coarseness before training. This idea was based on observations on training data, but was proven to be unjustified: it slightly decreased the system's accuracy on the medium subtask.

	coarse	medium	fine
location	85.24	84.80	84.36
organisation	76.72	73.28	72.80

Table 2: Accuracy of the GYDER system for each domain / granularity

In general, the coarser grained evaluation did not show a significantly higher accuracy (see Table 2.), proving that the main difficulty is to distinguish between literal and metonymic usage, rather than separating metonymy classes from each other (since different classes represent significantly different usage / context). Because of this, data sparseness remained a problem for coarse-grained classification as well.

Per-class results of the submitted system for both domains are shown on Table 3. Note that our system never predicted `loc` values from the four small classes `place-for-event and product`, `object-for-name` and `other` as these had only 26 instances altogether. Since we never had significant results for the `mixed` category, in effect the `loc` task ended up a binary classification task between `literal` and `place-for-people`.

loc class	#	prec	rec	f
literal	721	86.83	95.98	91.17
place-for-people	141	68.22	51.77	58.87
mixed	20	25.00	5.00	8.33
othermet	11	-	0.0	-
place-for-event	10	-	0.0	-
object-for-name	4	-	0.0	-
place-for-product	1	-	0.0	-
org class	#	prec	rec	f
literal	520	75.76	90.77	82.59
org-for-members	161	65.99	60.25	62.99
org-for-product	67	82.76	35.82	50.00
mixed	60	43.59	28.33	34.34
org-for-facility	16	100.0	12.50	22.22
othermet	8	-	0.0	-
object-for-name	6	50.00	16.67	25.00
org-for-index	3	-	0.0	-
org-for-event	1	-	0.0	-

Table 3: Per-class accuracies for both domains

While in the `org` set the system also ignores the smallest categories `othermet`, `org-for-index` and `event` (a total of 11 instances), the six major categories `literal`, `org-for-members`, `org-for-product`, `org-for-facility`, `object-for-name`, `mixed` all receive meaningful hypotheses.

5 Conclusions, Further Directions

The features we eventually selected performed well enough to actually achieve the best scores in all six subtasks of the shared task, and we think they are useful in general. But it is worth emphasizing that many of these features are based on the grammatical annotation provided by the task organizers, and as such, would require a better dependency parser than we currently have at our disposal to create a fully automatic system.

That said, there is clearly a great deal of merit to provide this level of annotation, and we would like to speculate what would happen if even more detailed annotation, not just grammatical, but also semantical, were provided manually. We hypothesize that the metonymy task would break down into the task of identifying several journalistic cliches such as "location for sports team", "capital city for government", and so on, which are not yet always distinguished by the depth of the annotation.

It would be a true challenge to create a data set of non-cliche metonymy cases, or a corpus large enough to represent rare metonymy types and challenging non-cliche metonymies better.

We feel that at least regarding the corpus used for the shared task, the potential of the grammatical annotation for PMWs was more or less well exploited. Future systems should exploit more semantic knowledge, or the power of a larger data set, or preferably both.

Acknowledgement

We wish to thank András Kornai for help and encouragement, and the anonymous reviewers for valuable comments.

References

Christiane Fellbaum ed. 1998. WordNet: An Electronic Lexical Database. MIT Press.

Beth Levin. 1993. English Verb Classes and Alternations. A Preliminary Investigation. The University of Chicago Press.

Katja Markert and Malvina Nissim. 2002. Metonymy resolution as a classification task. *Proceedings of the Conference on Empirical Methods in Natural Language Processing (EMNLP 2002)*. Philadelphia, USA.

Katja Markert and Malvina Nissim. 2003. Syntactic Features and Word Similarity for Supervised Metonymy Resolution. *Proceedings of the 41st Annual Meeting of the Association for Computational Linguistics (ACL2003)*. Sapporo, Japan.

Malvina Nissim and Katja Markert. 2005. Learning to buy a Renault and talk to BMW: A supervised approach to conventional metonymy. *International Workshop on Computational Semantics (IWCS2005)*. Tilburg, Netherlands.

Katja Markert and Malvina Nissim. 2007. SemEval-2007 Task 08: Metonymy Resolution at SemEval-2007. In Proceedings of SemEval-2007.

Ross Quinlan. 1993. C4.5: Programs for machine learning. Morgan Kaufmann.

György Szarvas, Richárd Farkas and András Kocsor. 2006. Multilingual Named Entity Recognition System Using Boosting and C4.5 Decision Tree Learning Algorithms. *Proceedings of Discovery Science 2006, DS2006, LNAI 4265 pp. 267-278*. Springer-Verlag.

HIT-IR-WSD: A WSD System for English Lexical Sample Task

Yuhang Guo, Wanxiang Che, Yuxuan Hu, Wei Zhang and Ting Liu
Information Retrieval Lab
Harbin Institute of technology
Harbin, China, 150001
{yhguo,wxche}@ir.hit.edu.cn

Abstract

HIT-IR-WSD is a word sense disambiguation (WSD) system developed for English lexical sample task (Task 11) of Semeval 2007 by Information Retrieval Lab, Harbin Institute of Technology. The system is based on a supervised method using an SVM classifier. Multi-resources including words in the surrounding context, the part-of-speech of neighboring words, collocations and syntactic relations are used. The final micro-avg raw score achieves 81.9% on the test set, the best one among participating runs.

1 Introduction

Lexical sample task is a kind of WSD evaluation task providing training and test data in which a small pre-selected set of target words is chosen and the target words are marked up. In the training data the target words' senses are given, but in the test data are not and need to be predicted by task participants.

HIT-IR-WSD regards the lexical sample task as a classification problem, and devotes to extract effective features from the instances. We didn't use any additional training data besides the official ones the task organizers provided. Section 2 gives the architecture of this system. As the task provides correct word sense for each instance, a supervised learning approach is used. In this system, we choose Support Vector Machine (SVM) as classifier. SVM is introduced in section 3. Knowledge sources are presented in section 4. The last section discusses the experimental results and present the main conclusion of the work performed.

2 The Architecture of the System

HIT-IR-WSD system consists of 2 parts: feature extraction and classification. Figure 1 portrays the architecture of the system.

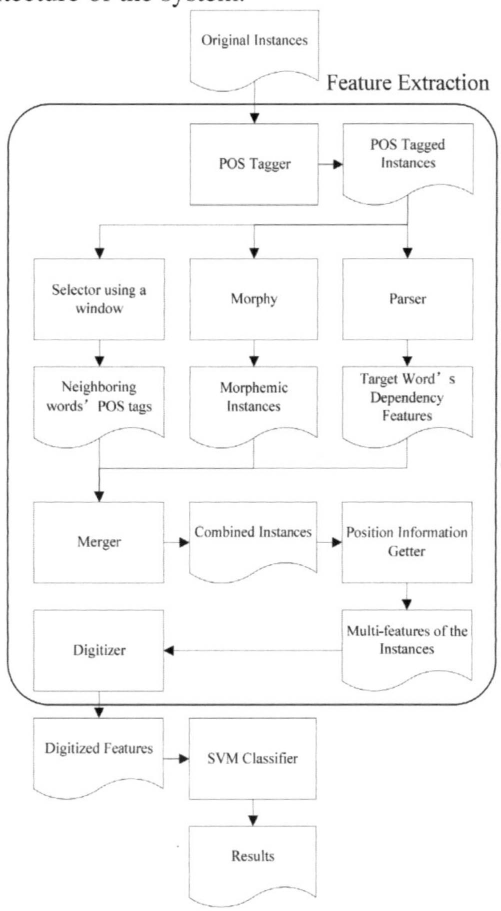

Figure 1: The architecture of HIT-IR-WSD

Proceedings of the 4th International Workshop on Semantic Evaluations (SemEval-2007), pages 165–168,
Prague, June 2007.

Features are extracted from original instances and are made into digitized features to feed the SVM classifier. The classifier gets the features of training data to make a model of the target word. Then it uses the model to predict the sense of target word in the test data.

3 Learning Algorithm

SVM is an effective learning algorithm to WSD (Lee and Ng, 2002). The SVM tries to find a hyperplane with the largest margin separating the training samples into two classes. The instances in the same side of the hyperplane have the same class label. A test instance's feature decides the position where the sample is in the feature space and which side of the hyperplane it is. In this way, it leads to get a prediction. SVM could be extended to tackle multi-classes problems by using one-against-one or one-against-rest strategy.

In the WSD problem, input of SVM is the feature vector of the instance. Features that appear in all the training samples are arranged as a vector space. Every instance is mapped to a feature vector. If the feature of a certain dimension exists in a sample, assign this dimension 1 to this sample, else assign it 0. For example, assume the feature vector space is *<x1, x2, x3, x4, x5, x6, x7>*; the instance is *"x2 x6 x5 x7"*. The feature vector of this sample should be *<0, 1, 0, 0, 1, 1, 1>*.

The implementation of SVM here is libsvm[1] (Chang and Lin, 2001) for multi-classes.

4 Knowledge Sources

We used 4 kinds of features of the target word and its context as shown in Table 1.

Part of the original text of an example is "... *This is the <head>age</head> of new media , the era of ...*".

Name	Extraction Tools	Example
Surrounding words	WordNet (morph)[2]	..., this, be, age, new, medium, ,, era, ...
Part-of-speech	SVMTool[3]	DT_0, VBZ_0, DT_0, NN_t, IN_1, JJ_1, NNS_1
Collocation		this_0, be_0, the_0, age_t, of_1, new_1, medium_1, ,_1, the_1
Syntactic relation	MaltParser[4]	SYN_HEAD_is SYN_HEADPOS_VBZ SYN_RELATION_PRD SYN_HEADRIGHT

Table 1: Features the system extracted

The next 4 subsections elaborate these features.

4.1 Words in the Surrounding Context

We take the neighboring words in the context of the target word as a kind of features ignoring their exact position information, which is called bag-of-words approach.

Mostly, a certain sense of a word is tend to appear in a certain kind of context, so the context words could contain some helpful information to disambiguate the sense of the target word.

Because there would be too many context words to be added into the feature vector space, data sparseness problem is inevitable. We need to reduce the sparseness as possible as we can. A simple way is to use the words' morphological root forms. In addition, we filter the tokens which contain no alphabet character (including punctuation symbols) and stop words. The stop words are tested separately, and only the effective ones would be added into the stop words list. All remaining words in the instance are gathered, converted to lower case and replaced by their morphological root forms. The implementation for getting the morphological root forms is WordNet (morph).

4.2 Part-of-Speechs of Neighboring Words

As mentioned above, the data sparseness is a serious problem in WSD. Besides changing tokens to their morphological root forms, part-of-speech is a good choice too. The size of POS tag set is much smaller than the size of surrounding words set. And the neighboring words' part-of-speeches also contain useful information for WSD. In this part, we use a POS tagger (Giménez and Márquez, 2004) to assign POS tags to those tokens.

We get the left and right 3 words' POS tags together with their position information in the target words' sentence.

For example, the word *age* is to be disambiguated in the sentence of "... *This is the*

[1] http://www.csie.ntu.edu.tw/~cjlin/libsvm/

[2] http://wordnet.princeton.edu/man/morph.3WN.html

[3] http://www.lsi.upc.es/~nlp/SVMTool/

[4] http://w3.msi.vxu.se/~nivre/research/MaltParser.html

<head>age</head> of new media , the era of …". The features then will be added to the feature vector are *"DT_0, VBZ_0, DT_0, NN_t, IN_1, JJ_1, NNS_1"*, in which *_0/_1* stands for the word with current POS tag is in the left/right side of the target word. The POS tag set in use here is Penn Treebank Tagset[5].

4.3 Collocations

Different from bag-of-words, collocation feature contains the position information of the target words' neighboring words. To make this feature in the same form with the bag-of-words, we appended a symbol to each of the neighboring words' morphological root forms to mark whether this word is in the left or in the right of the target word. Like POS feature, collocation was extracted in the sentence where the target word belongs to. The window size of this feature is 5 to the left and 5 to the right of the target word, which is attained by empirical value. In this part, punctuation symbol and stop words are not removed.

Take the same instance last subsection has mentioned as example. The features we extracted are *"this_0, be_0, the_0, age_t, of_1, new_1, medium_1"*. Like POS, *_0/_1* stands for the word is in the left/right side of the target word. Then the features were added to the feature vector space.

4.4 Syntactic Relations

Many effective context words are not in a short distance to the target word, but we shouldn't enlarge the window size too much in case of including too many noises. A solution to this problem is to use the syntactic relations of the target word and its parent head word.

We use Nivre et al., (2006)'s dependency parser. In this part, we get 4 features from every instance: head word of the target word, the head word's POS, the head word's dependency relation with the target word and the relative position of the head word to the target word.

Still take the same instance which has been mentioned in the las subsection as example. The features we extracted are *"SYN_HEAD_is, SYN_HEADPOS_VBZ, SYN_RELATION_PRD, SYN_HEADRIGHT"*, in which *SYN_HEAD_is* stands for *is* is the head word of *age*; *SYN_HEADPOS_VBZ* stands for the POS of the head word *is* is VBZ; *SYN_RELATION_PRD* stands for the relationship between the head word *is* and target word *age* is *PRD*; and *SYN_HEADRIGHT* stands for the target word *age* is in the right side of the head word *is*.

5 Data Set and Results

This English lexical sample task: Semeval 2007 task 11[6] provides two tracks of the data set for participants. The first one is from LDC and the second from web.

We took part in this evaluation in the second track. The corpus is from web. In this track the task organizers provide a training data and test data set for 20 nouns and 20 adjectives.

In order to develop our system, we divided the training data into 2 parts: training and development sets. The size of the training set is about 2 times of the development set. The development set contains 1,781 instances.

4 kinds of features were merged into 15 combinations. Here we use a vector (V) to express which features are used. The four dimensions stand for syntactic relations, POS, surrounding words and collocations, respectively. For example, *1010* means that the syntactic relations feature and the surrounding words feature are used.

V	Precision	V	Precision
0001	78.6%	1001	78.2%
0010	80.3%	1010	81.9%
0011	82.0%	1011	82.8%
0100	70.4%	1100	73.3%
0101	79.0%	1101	79.1%
0110	82.1%	1110	82.5%
0111	**82.9%**	1111	**82.9%**
1000	72.6%		

Table 2: Results of Combinations of Features

From Table 2, we can conclude that the surrounding words feature is the most useful kind of features. It obtains much better performance than other kinds of features individually. In other words, without it, the performance drops a lot. Among these features, syntactic relations feature is the most unstable one (the improvement with it is unstable), partly because the performance of the dependency parser is not good enough. As the ones with the vector 0111 and 1111 get the best perfor-

[5] http://www.lsi.upc.es/~nlp/SVMTool/PennTreebank.html

[6] http://nlp.cs.swarthmore.edu/semeval/tasks/task11/description.shtml

mance, we chose all of these kinds of features for our final system.

A trade-off parameter C in SVM is tuned, and the result is shown in Figure 2. We have also tried 4 types of kernels of the SVM classifier (parameters are set by default). The experimental results show that the linear kernel is the most effective as Table 3 shows.

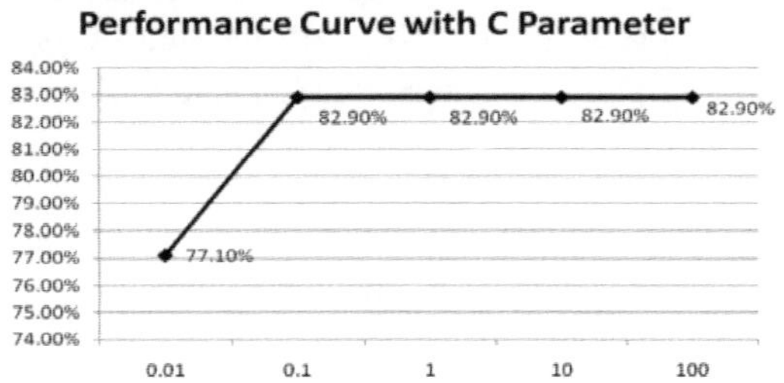

Figure 2: Accuracy with different C parameters

Kernel Function Type	Linear	Poly-nomial	RBF	Sig-moid
Accuracy	82.9%	68.3%	68.3%	68.3%

Table 3: Accuracy with different kernel function types

Another experiment (as shown in Figure 3) also validate that the linear kernel is the most suitable one. We tried using polynomial function. Unlike the parameters set by default above (g=1/k, d=3), here we set its Gama parameter as 1 (g=1) but other parameters excepting degree parameter are still set by default. The performance gets better when the degree parameter is tuned towards 1. That means the closer the kernel function to linear function the better the system performs.

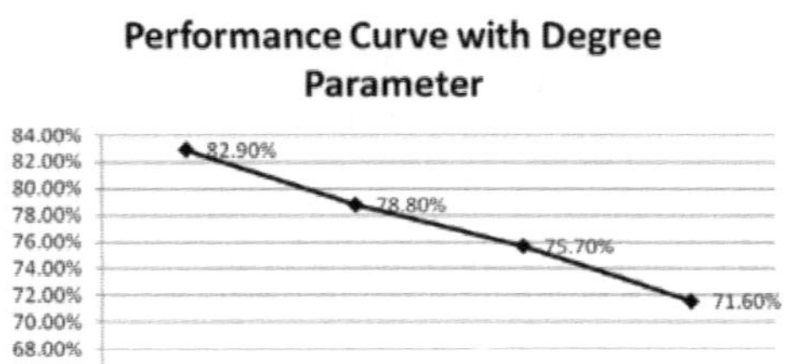

Figure 3: Accuracy with different degree in polynomial function

In order to get the relation between the system performance and the size of training data, we made several groups of training-test data set from the training data the organizers provided. Each of them has the same test data but different size of training data which are 2, 3, 4 and 5 times of the test data respectively. Figure 4 shows the performance curve with the training data size. Indicated in Figure 4, the accuracy increases as the size of training data enlarge, from which we can infer that we could raise the performance by using more training data potentially.

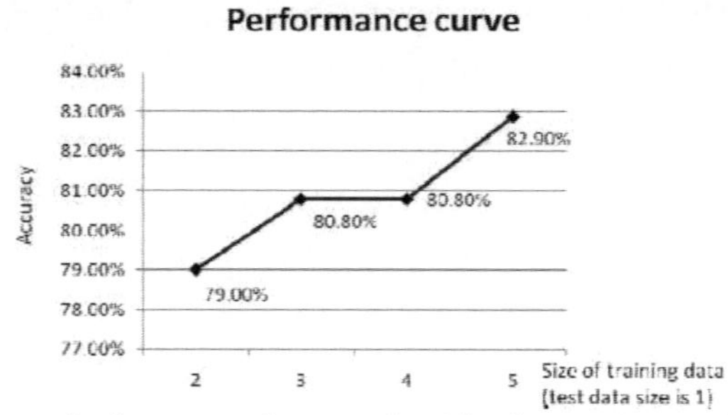

Figure 4: Accuracy's trend with the training data size

Feature extraction is the most time-consuming part of the system, especially POS tagging and parsing which take 2 hours approximately on the training and test data. The classification part (using libsvm) takes no more than 5 minutes on the training and test data. We did our experiment on a PC with 2.0GHz CPU and 960 MB system memory.

Our official result of HIT-IR-WSD is: micro-avg raw score 81.9% on the test set, the top one among the participating runs.

Acknowledgement

We gratefully acknowledge the support for this study provided by the National Natural Science Foundation of China (NSFC) via grant 60435020, 60575042, 60575042 and 60675034.

References

Lee, Y. K., and Ng, H. T. 2002. *An empirical evaluation of knowledge sources and learning algorithms for word sense disambiguation.* In *Proceedings of EMNLP02*, 41–48.

Chih-Chung Chang and Chih-Jen Lin, 2001. *LIBSVM: a library for support vector machines.*

Jesús Giménez and Lluís Márquez. 2004. *SVMTool: A general POS tagger generator based on Support Vector Machines.* Proceedings of the 4th International Conference on Language Resources and Evaluation (LREC'04). Lisbon, Portugal.

Nivre, J., Hall, J., Nilsson, J., Eryigit, G. and Marinov, S. 2006. *Labeled Pseudo-Projective Dependency Parsing with Support Vector Machines.* In *Proceedings of the Tenth Conference on Computational Natural Language Learning (CoNLL).*

HIT-WSD: Using Search Engine for Multilingual Chinese-English Lexical Sample Task

PengYuan Liu, TieJun Zhao, MuYun Yang
MOE-MS Key Laboratory of NLP & Speech, HIT, School of Computer Science and Technology, Harbin Institute of Technology, Harbin, Heilongjiang, China
{pyliu,tjzhao,ymy}@mtlab.hit.edu.cn

Abstract

We have participated in the Multilingual Chinese-English Lexical Sample Task of SemEval-2007. Our system disambiguates senses of Chinese words and finds the correct translation in English by using the web as WSD knowledge source. Since all the statistic data is obtained from search engine, the method is considered to be unsupervised and does not require any sense-tagged corpus.

1 Introduction

Due to the lack of sense tagged corpora (and the difficulty of manually creating them), the unsupervised method tries to avoid, or at least to reduce, the knowledge acquisition problem, which the supervised methods have to deal with. In order to tackle the problem of the knowledge acquisition bottleneck, we adopted an unsupervised approach based on search engine, which does not require any sense tagged corpus.

The majority of methods using the Web often try to automatically generate sense tagged corpora (Agirre and Martinez 2000;Agirre and Martinez 2004;Gonzalo et al. 2003; Mihalcea and Moldovan 1999;Santamaria et al. 2003). In this paper, we experiment with our initial attempt on another research trend that uses the Web not for extracting training samples but helping disambiguate directly during the translation selection process.

The approach we present here is inspired by (Mihalcea and Moldovan 1999;Brill 2003; Rosso et al. 2005; Dagan et al. 2006; McCarthy 2002). Suppose that source ambiguous words are apt to appear with its target translation on bilingual web pages either parallel or non-parallel. Instead of searching the source language or target language respectively on web, we try to let the search engine think in a bilingual style. First, our system gets the co-occurrence information of Chinese context and its corresponding English context. Then it computes association measurements of Chinese context and English context in 4 kinds of way. Finally, it selects the correct English translation by computing the association measurements.

In view that this is the first international standard evaluation to predict the correct English translation for ambiguous Chinese word, we built HIT-WSD system as our first attempt on disambiguation by using bilingual web search and just want to testify validity of our method.

2 HIT-WSD System

2.1 Disambiguation Process

HIT-WSD system disambiguates senses of Chinese target ambiguous word and finds the correct translation in English by searching bilingual information on the web. Figure 1 gives the flowchart of our proposed approach. Given an ambiguous word with a Chinese sentence, we easily create its Chinese context. English context can be acquired from a Chinese-English dictionary and the translation mapping set(offered by the Multilingual Chinese-English Lexical Sample Task). System puts Chinese context and English context as queries on search engine individually and collectively. After this step, frequency and co-occurrence frequency of Chinese context and English

Proceedings of the 4th International Workshop on Semantic Evaluations (SemEval-2007), pages 169–172,
Prague, June 2007.

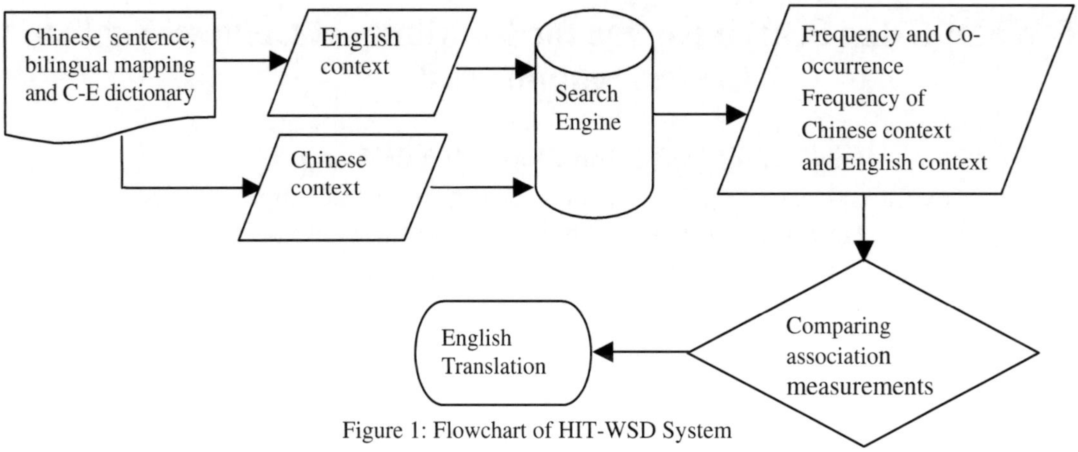

Figure 1: Flowchart of HIT-WSD System

context will be found. Finally, our system selects the most probable English translation by computing association measurements.

Figure 2 gives an example of how the proposed approach selects English translations of the Chinese ambiguous word "动摇/dongyao" given the sentence and its translation mapping set. This instance comes from the training data of Multilingual Chinese-English Lexical Sample Task of Semeval2007. According to the translation mapping set, Chinese target word "动摇/dongyao" has two English Translations: shake and vacillate.

English Context Candidates set is the translations set of the Chinese context. System uses translation mapping set to translate Chinese target ambiguous word and uses an Chinese-English dictionary to translate other words in Chinese context. English Context Candidates set could be any combination of translations and each combination could be selected as the English context.

After getting the Chinese context and English context, we put them as queries to search engine and extract page counts (which can be considered as frequency) which search engine returned. We not only search Chinese context and English context individually, but also put them together to search engine.

Association measurements: the Dice coefficient, point-wise mutual information, Log Likelihood score and χ^2 score are computed in the third phase while we got all kinds of statistic results from search engine. Finally, we determine the translation by simply computing the association measurements

Instance: 事实证明了邓小平同志对形势发展的判断，证明了坚持基本**路线不**<head>***动摇***</head>**是实现**中国现代化的根本保证。
Chinese Ambiguous Word: 动摇
Translation Mapping Set: 动摇-shake/动摇-vacillate
Translations of Chinese context in Chinese-English dictionary:不/not,是/is,路线/line,实现/ actualize

Chinese Context(CC): 路线不动摇是实现
English Context Candidates set:
Shake, shake is, not shake, line shake…/vacillate, not vacillate, vacillate is, line vacillate…
English Context(EC): shake/vacillate
Putting on Search Engine and getting counts:
$c(shake) = 1880000, c(vacillate) = 5450$

$c(CC) = 113000, c(CC, shake) = 77, c(CC, vacillate) = 12$

Computing association measurements:
$Dice(CC, shake) =$

$$\frac{2 \times c(CC, shake)}{((c(CC, shake) + c(shake)) \times (c(CC, shake) + c(CC}$$

$$= \frac{2 \times 77}{(77 + 1880000) \times (77 + 113000))} = 7.24e - 10$$

$Dice(CC, vacillate) =$

$$\frac{2 \times c(CC, vacillate)}{((c(CC, vacillate) + c(vacillate)) \times (c(CC, vacillate) + c(CC))}$$

$$= \frac{2 \times 12}{(12 + 5450) \times (12 + 11300)} = 3.89e - 8$$

Compare and Determine a Translation:
3.89e-8>7.24e-10, So the answer is **vacillate**.

Figure 2: Example of the Chinese ambiguous word "动摇/dongyao" selection process

2.2 Experiment Settings

Although the Chinese context can be represented with local features, topic features, parts of speech and so on, we use sentence segment as Chinese context in our experiment system. The sentence segment is a window size ± n segment of the sentence including the ambiguous words.

English Context Candidates set could be any combination of the translation of words appearing in Chinese context. In our experiment system, we just choose the translation of the Chinese target ambiguous words in the translation mapping set as English context.

We choose google[1] and baidu[2] as our search engine, for they are both most widely used for English and Chinese language respectively.

Putting Chinese context and English context as queries to the search engine, we will get corresponding page counts it returned as figure 2 shows.

Four statistical measurements were used in order to measure the degree of association of Chinese Context (CC) and English Context (EC). CC and EC can be seen as two random events occuring in the web pages:

1. Point-wise mutual information:

$$MI(CC,EC)=\log_2\frac{n\times a}{(a+b)\times(a+c)} \quad (1)$$

2. DICE coefficient:

$$DICE(CC,EC)=\frac{2\times a}{(a+b)\times(a+c)} \quad (2)$$

3. χ^2 score:

$$X^2(CC,EC)=\frac{n\times(a\times d-b\times c)^2}{(a+b)\times(a+c)\times(b+d)\times(c+d)} \quad (3)$$

4. Log Likelihood score:

$$LL(CC,EC)=2\times(a\times\log\frac{n\times a}{(a+b)\times(a+c)}$$
$$+b\times\log\frac{n\times b}{(a+b)\times(b+d)}+c\times\log\frac{n\times c}{(c+d)\times(a+c)}$$
$$+d\times\log\frac{n\times d}{(c+d)\times(b+d)}) \quad (4)$$

Here is the meaning of *a, b, c, d* and *n*.

a: all counts of the web pages which include Both CC and EC.

b: all counts of the web pages which include CC, do not include EC.

c: all counts of the web pages which include EC, do not include CC.

d: all counts of the web pages which include neither CC and EC.

$n=a+b+c+d$

We applied our method to the training data of Multilingual Chinese-English Lexical Sample Task. The results are as showed in Table 1.

Association Measurements	Precision(Micro-average) Context Window Size		
	-1,+1	-1,+2	-2,+2
MI(Baidu)	**0.349**	**0.349**	0.339
XX(Baidu)	0.338	0.344	0.314
LL(Baidu)	0.315	0.320	0.293
DICE(Baidu)	0.285	0.295	0.295
MI(google)	0.334	0.334	0.339
XX(google)	0.322	0.316	0.316
LL(google)	0.295	0.306	0.299
DICE(google)	0.281	0.278	0.272

Table 1:Training data results of Multilingual Chinese-English Lexical Sample Task

Since only one test result can be uploaded for one system, our system selects the settings of one of the best results. The final settings of our system is: window size is [-1, +2], the search engine is baidu and the association measurement is Point-wise mutual information.

3 Official Results

In multilingual Chinese-English lexical sample task of SemEval-2007, there are 2686 instances in training data for 40 Chinese ambiguous words. All these ambiguous words are either nouns or verbs. Test data consist of 935 untagged instances of the same target words.

The official result of our system in multilingual Chinese-English lexical sample task is reported as in Table 2.

	Micro-average	Macro-average
Our result	0.336898	0.395993
Baseline (MFS)	0.4053	0.4618

Table 2:Official results: Multilingual Chinese-English Lexical Sample Task

[1] www.google.com.

[2] www.baidu.com.

4 Conclusions

In SemEval-2007, we participated in Multilingual Chinese-English Lexical Sample Task with a fully unsupervised system based on bilingual web search. Our initial experiment result shows that our system fails to reach MFS (Most Familiar Sense) baseline due to our method is too simple where search queries are formed (just uses simple context window and English target translation). Our approach is the first attempt so far as we know on using bilingual web search for translation selection directly. The system is very simple but seemed to achieve a not bad performance when considered the performance of fully unsupervised systems in SENSEVAL-2, SENSEVAL -3 English tasks.

For future research, we will investigate the dependency of bilingual documents, optimize the search queries, filter out potential noises and combine the different results in order to devise an improved method that can utilize bilingual web search better.

References

Agirre, E.and Martinez, D. 2000. *Exploring Automatic Word Sense Disambiguation with Decision Lists and the Web.* Proc. of the COLING-2000.

Agirre, E.and Martinez, D. 2004. *Unsupervised word sense disambiguation based on automatically retrieved examples: The important of bias.* Proc. of the EMNLP 2004(Barcelona, Spain, July 2004).

Brill, E. 2003. *Processing Natural Language Processing without Natural Language Processing.* Lecture Notes in Computer Science, Vol. 2588. Springer-Verlag (2003) 360–369.

Dagan, I., Glickman, O., Gliozzo, A., Marmorshtein, E. and Strapparava, C. 2006. *Direct Word Sense Matching for lexical substitution.* Proceedings of ACL/COLING 2006.

Gonzalo, J., Verdejo, F. and Chugar, I. 2003. *The Web as a Resource for WSD.* 1st MEANING Workshop, Spain.

McCarthy, D. 2002. *Lexical Substitution as a Task for WSD Evaluation.* In Proceedings of the ACL Workshop on Word Sense Disambiguation: Recent Successes and Future Directions, Philadelphia, USA.

Mihalcea, R. and Moldovan, D.I. 1999. *An Automatic Method for Generating Sense Tagged Corpora.* Proc. of the 16th National Conf. on Artificial Intelligence. AAAI Press.

Rosso, P., Montes, M., Buscaldi, D., Pancardo, A., and Villase, A., 2005. *Two Web-based Approaches for Noun Sense Disambiguation.* Int. Conf. on Comput. Linguistics and Intelligent Text Processing, CICLing-2005, Springer Verlag, LNCS (3406), Mexico D.F., Mexico, pp. 261-273

Santamaria, C., Gonzalo, J. and Verdejo, F. 2003. *Automatic Association of WWW Directories to Word Senses.* Computational Linguistics (2003), Vol. 3, Issue 3 – Special Issue on the Web as Corpus, 485–502.

HIT: Web based Scoring Method for English Lexical Substitution

Shiqi Zhao, Lin Zhao, Yu Zhang, Ting Liu, Sheng Li
Information Retrieval Laboratory, School of Computer Science and Technology,
Box 321, Harbin Institute of Technology
Harbin, P.R. China, 150001
{ zhaosq, lzhao, zhangyu, tliu, lisheng }@ir.hit.edu.cn

Abstract

This paper describes the HIT system and its participation in SemEval-2007 English Lexical Substitution Task. Two main steps are included in our method: candidate substitute extraction and candidate scoring. In the first step, candidate substitutes for each target word in a given sentence are extracted from WordNet. In the second step, the extracted candidates are scored and ranked using a web-based scoring method. The substitute ranked first is selected as the best substitute. For the multiword subtask, a simple WordNet-based approach is employed.

1 Introduction

Lexical substitution aims to find alternative words that can occur in given contexts. It is important in many applications, such as query reformulation in question answering, sentence generation, and paraphrasing. There are two key problems in the lexical substitution task, the first of which is candidate substitute extraction. Generally speaking, synonyms can be regarded as candidate substitutes of words. However, some looser lexical relationships can also be considered, such as *Hypernyms* and *Hyponyms* defined in WordNet (Fellbaum, 1998). In addition, since lexical substitution is context dependent, some words which do not have similar meanings in general may also be substituted in some certain contexts (Zhao et al., 2007). As a result, finding a lexical knowledge base for substitute extraction is a challenging task.

The other problem is candidate scoring and ranking according to given contexts. In the lexical substitution task of SemEval-2007, context is constrained as a sentence. The system therefore has to score the candidate substitutes of each target word using the given sentence. The following questions should be considered here: (1) What words in the given sentence are "useful" context? (2) How to combine the context words and use them in ranking candidate substitutes? For the first question, we can use all words of the sentence, words in a window, or words having syntactic relations with the target word. For the second question, we can regard the context words as "bag of words", n-grams, or syntactic structures.

In HIT, we extract candidate substitutes from WordNet, in which both synonyms and hypernyms are investigated (Section 3.1). After that, we score the candidates using a web-based scoring method (Section 3.2). In this method, we first select fragments containing the target word from the given sentence. Then we construct queries by replacing the target word in the fragments with the candidate substitute. Finally, we search Google using the constructed queries and score each candidate based on the counts of retrieved snippets.

The rest of this paper is organized as follows: Section 2 reviews some related work on lexical substitution. Section 3 describes our system, especially the web-based scoring method. Section 4 presents the results and analysis.

2 Related Work

Synonyms defined in WordNet have been widely used in lexical substitution and expansion (Smeaton et al., 1994; Langkilde and Knight, 1998; Bol-

Proceedings of the 4th International Workshop on Semantic Evaluations (SemEval-2007), pages 173–176,
Prague, June 2007.

shakov and Gelbukh, 2004). In addition, a lot of methods have been proposed to automatically construct thesauri of synonyms. For example, Lin (1998) clustered words with similar meanings by calculating the dependency similarity. Barzilay and McKeown (2001) extracted paraphrases using multiple translations of literature works. Wu and Zhou (2003) extracted synonyms with multiple resources, including a monolingual dictionary, a bilingual corpus, and a monolingual corpus. Besides the handcrafted and automatic synonym resources, the web has been exploited as a resource for lexical substitute extraction (Zhao et al., 2007).

As for substitute scoring, various methods have been investigated, among which the classification method is the most widely used (Dagan et al., 2006; Kauchak and Barzilay, 2006). In detail, a binary classifier is trained for each candidate substitute, using the contexts of the substitute as features. Then a new contextual sentence containing the target word can be classified as 1 (the candidate is a correct substitute in the given sentence) or 0 (otherwise). The features used in the classification are usually similar with that in word sense disambiguation (WSD), including bag of word lemmas in the sentence, n-grams and parts of speech (POS) in a window, etc. There are other models presented for candidate substitute scoring. Glickman et al. (2006) proposed a Bayesian model and a Neural Network model, which estimate the probability of a word may occur in a given context.

3 HIT System

3.1 Candidate Substitute Extraction

In HIT, candidate substitutes are extracted from WordNet. Both synonyms and hypernyms defined in WordNet are investigated. Let *w* be a target word, *pos* the specified POS of *w*. *n* the number of *w*'s synsets defined in WordNet. Then the system extracts *w*'s candidate substitutes as follows:

- Extracts all the synonyms in each synset under *pos*[1] as candidate substitutes.
- If *w* has no synonym for the *i-th* synset ($1 \leq i \leq n$), then extracts the synonyms of its nearest hypernym.
- If *pos* is *r* (or *a*), and no candidate substitute can be extracted as described above, then extracts candidate substitutes under the POS *a* (or *r*).

[1] In this task, four kinds of POS are specified: *n* - noun, *v* - verb, *a* - adjective, *r* - adverb.

3.2 Candidate Substitute Scoring

As mentioned above, all words in the given sentence can be used as contextual information in the scoring of candidate substitutes. However, it is obvious that not all context words are really useful when determining a word's substitutes. An example can be seen from Figure 1.

> *She turns eyes <head>**bright**</head> with excitement towards Fiona , still tugging on the string of the minitiature airship-cum-dance card she has just received at the door .*

Figure 1. An example of a context sentence.

In the example above, words *turns*, *eyes*, *with*, and *excitement* are useful context words, while the others are not. The useless contexts may even be noise if they are used in the scoring. As a result, it is important to select context words carefully.

In HIT, we select context words based on the following assumption: useful context words for lexical substitute are those near the target word in the given sentence. In other words, the words that are far from the target word are not taken into consideration. Obviously, this assumption is not always true. However, considering only the neighboring words can reduce the risk of bringing in noise. Besides, Edmonds (1997) has also demonstrated in his paper that short-distance collocations with neighboring words are more useful in lexical choice than long ones.

Let *w* be the target word, *t* a candidate substitute, *S* the context sentence. Our basic idea is that: One can substitute *w* in *S* with *t*, which generates a new sentence *S'*. If *S'* can be found on the web, then the substitute is admissible. The more times *S'* occurs on the web, the more probable the substitute is. In practice, however, it is difficult to find a whole sentence *S'* on the web due to sparseness. Instead, we use fragments of *S'* which contains *t* and several neighboring context words (based on the assumption above). Then the question is how to obtain one (or more) fragment of *S'*.

A window with fixed size can be used here. Suppose *p* is the position of *t* in *S'*, for instance, we can construct a fragment using words from position *p-r* to *p+r*, where *r* is the radius of window.

However, a fixed *r* is difficult to set, since it may be too large for some sentences, which makes the fragments too specific, while too small for some other sentences, which makes the fragments too loose. An example can be seen in Table 1.

1(a) *But when Daniel turned <head>**blue**</head> one time and he totally stopped breathing.*
1(b) *Daniel turned **t** one time*
2(a) *We recommend that you <head>**check**</head> with us beforehand.*
2(b) *that you **t** with us*

Table 1. Examples of fragments with fixed size.

In Table1, 1(a) and 2(a) are two sentences from the test data of SemEval-2007Task10. 1(b) and 2(b) are fragments constructed according to 1(a) and 2(a), where the window radius is 2 and *t* denotes any candidate substitute of the target word. It is obvious that 1(b) is a rather strict fragment, which makes it difficult to find sentences containing it on the web, while 2(b) is quite loose, which can hardly constrain the semantics of *t*.

Having considered the problem above, we propose a rule-based method that constructs fragments with varied lengths. Let F_t be a fragment containing *t*, the construction rules are as follows:

Rule-1: F_t must contain at least two words besides *t*, at least one of which is non-stop word.

Rule-2: F_t does not cross sub-sentence boundary (“,”).

Rule-3: F_t should be the shortest fragment that satisfies Rule-1 and Rule-2.

According to the rules above, we construct at most three fragments for each *S'*: (1) *t* occurs at the beginning of F_t, (2) *t* occurs in the middle of F_t, and (3) *t* occurs at the end of F_t. Here we have another constraint: if one constructed fragment *F1* is the substring of *F2*, then *F2* is removed. Please note that the morphology is not taken into account when we construct queries.

For the sentence 1(a) and 2(a) in Table 1, the constructed fragments are as follows:

For 1(a): *Daniel turned **t**; **t** one time; turned **t** one*
For 2(a): *recommend that you **t**; **t** with us beforehand*

Table 2. Examples of the constructed fragments

To score a candidate substitute, we replace “*t*” in the fragments with each candidate substitute and use them as queries, which are then fed to Google. The score of *t* is computed according to the counts of retrieved snippets:

$$Score_{WebMining}(t) = \frac{1}{n}\sum_{i=1}^{n} count(Snippet(F_t i)) \quad (1)$$

where *n* is the number of constructed fragments, $F_t i$ is the *i-th* fragment (query) corresponding to *t*, and *count*($Snippet(F_t i)$) is the count of snippets retrieved by $F_t i$.

All candidate substitutes with scores larger than 0 are ranked and the first 10 substitutes are retained for the *oot* subtask. If the number of candidates whose scores are larger than 0 is less than 10, the system ranks the rest of the candidates by their frequencies using a word frequency list. The spare capacity is filled with those candidates with largest frequencies. For the *best* subtask, we simply output the substitute that ranks first in *oot*.

3.3 Detection of Multiwords

The method used to detect multiword in the HIT system is quite similar to that employed in the baseline system. We also use WordNet to detect if a multiword that includes the target word occurs within a window of 2 words before and 2 words after the target word.

A difference from the baseline system lies in that our system looks up WordNet using longer multiword candidates first. If a longer one is found in WordNet, then its substrings will be ignored. For example, if we find “*get along with*” in WordNet, we will output it as a multiword and will not check “*get along*” any more.

4 Results

Our system is the only one that participates all the three subtasks of Task10, i.e., *best*, *oot*, and *mw*. The evaluation results of our system can be found in Table 3 to Table 5. Our system ranks the fourth in the *best* subtask and seventh in the *oot* subtask.

We have analyzed the results from two aspects, i.e., the ability of the system to extract candidate substitutes and the ability to rank the correct substitutes in front. There are a total of 6,873 manual substitutes for all the 1,710 items in the gold standard, only 2,168 (31.54%) of which have been extracted as candidate substitutes by our system. This result suggests that WordNet is not an appropriate source for lexical substitute extraction. In the future work, we will try some other lexical resources, such as the Oxford American Writer Thesaurus and Encarta. In addition, we will also try the method that automatically constructs lexical resources, such as the automatic clustering method.

Further analysis shows that, 1,388 (64.02%) out of the 2,168 extracted correct candidates are ranked in the first 10 in the *oot* output of our system. This suggests that there is a big space for our system to improve the candidate scoring method. In the future work, we will consider more and richer features, such as the syntactic features, in candidate substitute scoring. Furthermore, A disadvantage of this method is that the web mining process is quite inefficient. Therefore, we will try to use the Web 1T 5-gram Version 1 from Google (LDC2006T13) in the future.

	P	R	ModeP	ModeR
OVERALL	11.35	11.35	18.86	18.86
Further Analysis				
NMWT	11.97	11.97	19.81	19.81
NMWS	12.55	12.38	19.93	19.65
RAND	11.81	11.81	20.03	20.03
MAN	10.81	10.81	17.53	17.53
Baselines				
WORDNET	9.95	9.95	15.58	15.58
LIN	8.84	8.53	14.69	14.23

Table 3. *best* results.

	P	R	ModeP	ModeR
OVERALL	33.88	33.88	46.91	46.91
Further Analysis				
NMWT	35.60	35.60	48.48	48.48
NMWS	36.63	36.63	49.33	49.33
RAND	33.95	33.95	47.25	47.25
MAN	33.81	33.81	46.53	46.53
Baselines				
WORDNET	29.70	29.35	40.57	40.57
LIN	27.70	26.72	40.47	39.19

Table 4. *oot* results.

	Our System		WordNet BL	
	P	R	P	R
detection	45.34	56.15	43.64	36.92
identification	41.61	51.54	40.00	33.85

Table 5. *mw* results.

Acknowledgements

This research was supported by National Natural Science Foundation of China (60575042, 60503072, 60675034).

References

Barzilay Regina and McKeown Kathleen R. 2001. Extracting paraphrases from a Parallel Corpus. In *Proceedings of ACL/EACL.*

Bolshakov Igor A. and Gelbukh Alexander. 2004. Synonymous Paraphrasing Using WordNet and Internet. In *Proceedings of NLDB.*

Dagan Ido, Glickman Oren, Gliozzo Alfio, Marmorshtein Efrat, Strapparava Carlo. 2006. Direct Word Sense Matching for Lexical Substitut*ion. In Proceedings of ACL.*

Edmonds Philip. 1997. Choosing the Word Most Typical in Context Using a Lexical Co-occurrence Network. In *Proceedings of ACL.*

Fellbaum Christiane. 1998. WordNet: An Electronic Lexical Database. MIT Press, Cambridge, MA.

Glickman Oren, Dagan Ido, Keller Mikaela, Bengio Samy. 2006. Investigating Lexical Substitution Scoring for Subtitle Generation. In *Proceedings of CoNLL.*

Kauchak David and Barzilay Regina. 2006. Paraphrasing for Automatic Evaluation. In *Proceedings of HLT-NAACL.*

Langkilde I. and Knight K. 1998. Generation that Exploits Corpus-based Statistical Knowledge. *In Proceedings of the COLING-ACL.*

Lin Dekang. 1998. Automatic Retrieval and Clustering of Similar Words. In *Proceedings of COLING-ACL.*

Smeaton Alan F., Kelledy Fergus, and O'Donell Ruari. 1994. TREC-4 Experiments at Dublin City University: Thresholding Posting Lists, Query Expansion with WordNet and POS Tagging of Spanish. *In Proceedings of TREC-4.*

Wu Hua and Zhou Ming. 2003. Optimizing Synonym Extraction Using Monolingual and Bilingual Resources. In *Proceedings of IWP.*

Zhao Shiqi, Liu Ting, Yuan Xincheng, Li Sheng, and Zhang Yu. 2007. Automatic Acquisition of Context-Specific Lexical Paraphrases. In *Proceedings of IJCAI-07.*

I2R: Three Systems for Word Sense Discrimination, Chinese Word Sense Disambiguation, and English Word Sense Disambiguation

Zheng-Yu Niu, Dong-Hong Ji
Institute for Infocomm Research
21 Heng Mui Keng Terrace
119613 Singapore
niu_zy@hotmail.com
dhji@i2r.a-star.edu.sg

Chew-Lim Tan
Department of Computer Science
National University of Singapore
3 Science Drive 2
117543 Singapore
tancl@comp.nus.edu.sg

Abstract

This paper describes the implementation of our three systems at SemEval-2007, for task 2 (word sense discrimination), task 5 (Chinese word sense disambiguation), and the first subtask in task 17 (English word sense disambiguation). For task 2, we applied a cluster validation method to estimate the number of senses of a target word in untagged data, and then grouped the instances of this target word into the estimated number of clusters. For both task 5 and task 17, We used the label propagation algorithm as the classifier for sense disambiguation. Our system at task 2 achieved 63.9% F-score under unsupervised evaluation, and 71.9% supervised recall with supervised evaluation. For task 5, our system obtained 71.2% micro-average precision and 74.7% macro-average precision. For the lexical sample subtask for task 17, our system achieved 86.4% coarse-grained precision and recall.

1 Introduction

SemEval-2007 launches totally 18 tasks for evaluation exercise, covering word sense disambiguation, word sense discrimination, semantic role labeling, and sense disambiguation for information retrieval, and other topics in NLP. We participated three tasks in SemEval-2007, which are task 2 (Evaluating Word Sense Induction and Discrimination Systems), task 5 (Multilingual Chinese-English Lexical Sample Task) and the first subtask at task 17 (English Lexical Sample, English Semantic Role Labeling and English All-Words Tasks).

The goal for SemEval-2007 task 2 (Evaluating Word Sense Induction and Discrimination Systems)(Agirre and Soroa, 2007) is to automatically discriminate the senses of English target words by the use of only untagged data. Here we address this word sense discrimination problem by (1) estimating the number of word senses of a target word in untagged data using a stability criterion, and then (2) grouping the instances of this target word into the estimated number of clusters according to the similarity of contexts of the instances. No sense-tagged data is used to help the clustering process.

The goal of task 5 (Chinese Word Sense Disambiguation) is to create a framework for the evaluation of word sense disambiguation in Chinese-English machine translation systems. Each participates of this task will be provided with sense tagged training data and untagged test data for 40 Chinese polysemous words. The "sense tags" for the ambiguous Chinese target words are given in the form of their English translations. Here we used a semi-supervised classification algorithm (label propagation algorithm) (Niu, et al., 2005) to address this Chinese word sense disambiguation problem.

The lexical sample subtask of task 17 (English Word Sense Disambiguation) provides sense-tagged training data and untagged test data for 35 nouns and 65 verbs. This data includes, for each target word: OntoNotes sense tags (these are groupings of WordNet senses that are more coarse-grained than tradi-

Proceedings of the 4th International Workshop on Semantic Evaluations (SemEval-2007), pages 177–182,
Prague, June 2007. ©2007 Association for Computational Linguistics

tional WN entries), as well as the sense inventory for these lemmas. Here we used only the training data supplied in this subtask for sense disambiguation in test set. The label propagation algorithm (Niu, et al., 2005) was used to perform sense disambiguation by the use of both training data and test data.

This paper will be organized as follows. First, we will provide the feature set used for task 2, task 5 and task 17 in section 2. Secondly, we will present the word sense discrimination method used for task 2 in section 3. Then, we will give the label propagation algorithm for task 5 and task 17 in section 4. Section 5 will provide the description of data sets at task 2, task 5 and task 17. Then, we will present the experimental results of our systems at the three tasks in section 6. Finally we will give a conclusion of our work in section 7.

2 Feature Set

In task 2, task 5 and task 17, we used three types of features to capture contextual information: part-of-speech of neighboring words (no more than three-word distance) with position information, unordered single words in topical context (all the contextual sentences), and local collocations (including 11 collocations). The feature set used here is as same as the feature set used in (Lee and Ng, 2002) except that we did not use syntactic relations.

3 The Word Sense Discrimination Method for Task 2

Word sense discrimination is to automatically discriminate the senses of target words by the use of only untagged data. So we can employ clustering algorithms to address this problem. Another problem is that there is no sense inventories for target words. So the clustering algorithms should have the ability to automatically estimate the sense number of a target word.

Here we used the sequential Information Bottleneck algorithm (sIB) (Slonim, et al., 2002) to estimate cluster structure, which measures the similarity of contexts of instances of target words according to the similarity of their contextual feature conditional distribution. But sIB requires the number of clusters as input. So we used a cluster validation method to automatically estimate the sense number of a target word before clustering analysis. Cluster validation (or stability based approach)is a commonly used method to the problem of model order identification (or cluster number estimation) (Lange, et al., 2002; Levine and Domany, 2001). The assumption of this method is that if the model order is identical with the true value, then the cluster structure estimated from the data is stable against resampling, otherwise, it is more likely to be the artifact of sampled data.

Table 1: Sense number estimation procedure for word sense discrimination.

1	Set lower bound K_{min} and upper bound K_{max} for sense number k;
2	Set $k = K_{min}$;
3	Conduct the cluster validation process presented in Table 2 to evaluate the merit of k;
4	Record k and the value of M_k;
5	Set $k = k + 1$. If $k \leq K_{max}$, go to step 3, otherwise go to step 6;
6	Choose the value $\hat{k}$ that maximizes M_k, where $\hat{k}$ is the estimated sense number.

3.1 The Sense Number Estimation Procedure

Table 1 presents the sense number estimation procedure. K_{min} was set as 2, and K_{max} was set as 5 in our system. The evaluation function M_k (described in Table 2) is relevant with the sense number k. q is set as 20 here. Clustering solution which is stable against resampling will give rise to a local optimum of M_k, which indicates the true value of sense number. In the cluster validation procedure, we used the sIB algorithm to perform clustering analysis (described in section 3.2).

The function $M(C^\mu, C)$ in Table 2 is given by (Levine and Domany, 2001):

$$M(C^\mu, C) = \frac{\sum_{i,j} 1\{C^\mu_{i,j} = C_{i,j} = 1, d_i \in D^\mu, d_j \in D^\mu\}}{\sum_{i,j} 1\{C_{i,j} = 1, d_i \in D^\mu, d_j \in D^\mu\}}, \quad (1)$$

where D^μ is a subset with size $\alpha|D|$ sampled from full data set D, C and C^μ are $|D| \times |D|$ connectivity matrixes based on clustering solutions computed on D and D^μ respectively, and $0 \leq \alpha \leq 1$. The connectivity matrix C is defined as: $C_{i,j} = 1$ if d_i and d_j belong to the same cluster, otherwise $C_{i,j} = 0$. C^μ is calculated in the same way. α is set as 0.90 in this paper.

Table 2: The cluster validation method for evaluation of values of sense number k.

	Function: Cluster_Validation(k, D, q)
	Input: cluster number k, data set D, and sampling frequency q;
	Output: the score of the merit of k;
1	Perform clustering analysis using sIB on data set D with k as input;
2	Construct connectivity matrix C_k based on above clustering solution on D;
3	Use a random predictor ρ_k to assign uniformly drawn labels to instances in D;
4	Construct connectivity matrix C_{ρ_k} using above clustering solution on D;
5	For $\mu = 1$ to q do
5.1	Randomly sample a subset (D^μ) with size $\alpha\|D\|$ from D, $0 \leq \alpha \leq 1$;
5.2	Perform clustering analysis using sIB on (D^μ) with k as input;
5.3	Construct connectivity matrix C_k^μ using above clustering solution on (D^μ);
5.4	Use ρ_k to assign uniformly drawn labels to instances in (D^μ);
5.5	Construct connectivity matrix $C_{\rho_k}^\mu$ using above clustering solution on (D^μ);
	Endfor
6	Evaluate the merit of k using following objective function: $M_k = \frac{1}{q}\sum_\mu M(C_k^\mu, C_k) - \frac{1}{q}\sum_\mu M(C_{\rho_k}^\mu, C_{\rho_k})$, where $M(C^\mu, C)$ is given by equation (1);
7	Return M_k;

$M(C^\mu, C)$ measures the proportion of document pairs in each cluster computed on D that are also assigned into the same cluster by clustering solution on D^μ. Clearly, $0 \leq M \leq 1$. Intuitively, if cluster number k is identical with the true value, then clustering results on different subsets generated by sampling should be similar with that on full data set, which gives rise to a local optimum of $M(C^\mu, C)$.

In our algorithm, we normalize $M(C_{F,k}^\mu, C_{F,k})$ using the equation in step 6 of Table 2, which makes our objective function different from the figure of merit (equation (1)) proposed in (Levine and Domany, 2001). The reason to normalize $M(C_{F,k}^\mu, C_{F,k})$ is that $M(C_{F,k}^\mu, C_{F,k})$ tends to decrease when increasing the value of k. Therefore for avoiding the bias that smaller value of k is to be selected as cluster number, we use the cluster validity of a random predictor to normalize $M(C_{F,k}^\mu, C_{F,k})$.

3.2 The sIB Clustering Algorithm

Here we used the sIB algorithm (Slonim, et al., 2002) to estimate cluster structure, which measures the similarity of contexts of instances according to the similarity of their feature conditional distribution. sIB is a simplified "hard" variant of information bottleneck method (Tishby, et al., 1999).

Let d represent a document, and w represent a feature word, $d \in D$, $w \in F$. Given the joint distribution $p(d, w)$, the document clustering problem is formulated as looking for a compact representation T for D, which preserves as much information as possible about F. T is the document clustering solution. For solving this optimization problem, sIB algorithm was proposed in (Slonim, et al., 2002), which found a local maximum of $I(T, F)$ by: given an initial partition T, iteratively drawing a $d \in D$ out of its cluster $t(d)$, $t \in T$, and merging it into t^{new} such that $t^{new} = argmax_{t \in T}\mathbf{d}(d, t)$. $\mathbf{d}(d, t)$ is the change of $I(T, F)$ due to merging d into cluster t^{new}, which is given by

$$\mathbf{d}(d, t) = (p(d) + p(t))JS(p(w|d), p(w|t)). \quad (2)$$

$JS(p, q)$ is the Jensen-Shannon divergence, which is defined as

$$JS(p, q) = \pi_p D_{KL}(p\|\overline{p}) + \pi_q D_{KL}(q\|\overline{p}), \quad (3)$$

$$D_{KL}(p\|\overline{p}) = \sum_y plog\frac{p}{\overline{p}}, \quad (4)$$

$$D_{KL}(q\|\overline{p}) = \sum_y qlog\frac{q}{\overline{p}}, \quad (5)$$

$$\{p, q\} \equiv \{p(w|d), p(w|t)\}, \quad (6)$$

$$\{\pi_p, \pi_q\} \equiv \{\frac{p(d)}{p(d) + p(t)}, \frac{p(t)}{p(d) + p(t)}\}, \quad (7)$$

$$\overline{p} = \pi_p p(w|d) + \pi_q p(w|t). \quad (8)$$

4 The Label Propagation Algorithm for Task 5 and Task 17

In the label propagation algorithm (LP) (Zhu and Ghahramani, 2002), label information of any vertex in a graph is propagated to nearby vertices through weighted edges until a global stable stage is achieved. Larger edge weights allow labels to travel through easier. Thus the closer the examples, more likely they have similar labels (the global consistency assumption).

In label propagation process, the soft label of each initial labeled example is clamped in each iteration to replenish label sources from these labeled data. Thus the labeled data act like sources to push out labels through unlabeled data. With this push from labeled examples, the class boundaries will be pushed through edges with large weights and settle in gaps along edges with small weights. If the data structure fits the classification goal, then LP algorithm can use these unlabeled data to help learning classification plane.

Let $Y^0 \in N^{n\times c}$ represent initial soft labels attached to vertices, where $Y^0_{ij} = 1$ if y_i is s_j and 0 otherwise. Let Y^0_L be the top l rows of Y^0 and Y^0_U be the remaining u rows. Y^0_L is consistent with the labeling in labeled data, and the initialization of Y^0_U can be arbitrary.

Optimally we expect that the value of W_{ij} across different classes is as small as possible and the value of W_{ij} within same class is as large as possible. This will make label propagation to stay within same class. In later experiments, we set σ as the average distance between labeled examples from different classes.

Define $n \times n$ probability transition matrix $T_{ij} = P(j \rightarrow i) = \frac{W_{ij}}{\sum_{k=1}^{n} W_{kj}}$, where T_{ij} is the probability to jump from example x_j to example x_i.

Compute the row-normalized matrix $\overline{T}$ by $\overline{T}_{ij} = T_{ij}/\sum_{k=1}^{n} T_{ik}$. This normalization is to maintain the class probability interpretation of Y.

Then LP algorithm is defined as follows:

1. Initially set t=0, where t is iteration index;

2. Propagate the label by $Y^{t+1} = \overline{T}Y^t$;

3. Clamp labeled data by replacing the top l row of Y^{t+1} with Y^0_L. Repeat from step 2 until Y^t converges;

4. Assign $x_h (l + 1 \leq h \leq n)$ with a label $s_{\hat{j}}$, where $\hat{j} = argmax_j Y_{hj}$.

This algorithm has been shown to converge to a unique solution, which is $\widehat{Y}_U = \lim_{t\rightarrow\infty} Y^t_U = (I - \overline{T}_{uu})^{-1}\overline{T}_{ul}Y^0_L$ (Zhu and Ghahramani, 2002). We can see that this solution can be obtained without iteration and the initialization of Y^0_U is not important, since Y^0_U does not affect the estimation of $\widehat{Y}_U$. I is $u \times u$ identity matrix. $\overline{T}_{uu}$ and $\overline{T}_{ul}$ are acquired by splitting matrix $\overline{T}$ after the l-th row and the l-th column into 4 sub-matrices.

For task 5 and 17, we constructed connected graphs as follows: two instances u, v will be connected by an edge if u is among v's k nearest neighbors, or if v is among u's k nearest neighbors as measured by cosine or JS distance measure. k is set 10 in our system implementation.

5 Data Sets of Task 2, Task 5 and Task 17

The test data for task 2 includes totally 27132 untagged instances for 100 ambiguous English words. There is no training data for task 2.

There are 40 ambiguous Chinese words in task 5. The training data for this task consists of 2686 instances, while the test data includes 935 instances.

There are 100 ambiguous English words in the first subtask of task 17. The training data for this task consists of 22281 instances, while the test data includes 4851 instances.

6 Experimental Results of Our Systems at Task 2, Task 5 and Task 17

Table 3: The best/worst/average F-score of all the systems at task 2 and the F-score of our system at task 2 for all target words, nouns and verbs with unsupervised evaluation.

	All words	Nouns	Verbs
Best	78.7%	80.8%	76.3%
Worst	56.1%	65.8%	45.1%
Average	65.4%	69.0%	61.4%
Our system	63.9%	68.0%	59.3%

Table 3 lists the best/worst/average F-score of all the systems at task 2 and the F-score of our system at task 2 for all target words, nouns and verbs with

Table 4: The best/worst/average supervised recall of all the systems at task 2 and the supervised recall of our system at task 2 for all target words, nouns and verbs with supervised evaluation.

	All words	Nouns	Verbs
Best	81.6%	86.8%	75.7%
Worst	78.5%	81.4%	75.2%
Average	79.6%	83.0%	75.7%
Our system	81.6%	86.8%	75.7%

Table 5: The best/worst/average micro-average precision and macro-average precision of all the systems at task 5 and the micro-average precision and macro-average precision of our system at task 5.

	Micro-average	Macro-average
Best	71.7%	74.9%
Worst	33.7%	39.6%
Average	58.5%	62.7%
Our system	71.2%	74.7%

unsupervised evaluation. Our system obtained the fourth place among six systems with unsupervised evaluation. Table 4 shows the best/worst/average supervised recall of all the systems at task 2 and the supervised recall of our system at task 2 for all target words, nouns and verbs with supervised evaluation. Our system is ranked as the first among six systems with supervised evaluation. Table 7 lists the estimated sense numbers by our system for all the words at task 2. The average of all the estimated sense numbers is 3.1, while the average of all the ground-truth sense numbers is 3.6 if we consider the sense inventories provided in task 17 as the answer. It seems that our estimated sense numbers are close to the ground-truth ones.

Table 5 provides the best/worst/average micro-average precision and macro-average precision of all the systems at task 5 and the micro-average precision and macro-average precision of our system at task 5. Our system obtained the second place among six systems for task 5.

Table 6 shows the best/worst/average coarse-grained score (precision) of all the systems the lexical sample subtask of task 17 and the coarse-grained score (precision) of our system at the lexical sample subtask of task 17. The attempted rate of all the systems is 100%. So the precision value is equal to the recall value for all the systems. Here we listed only the precision for the 13 systems at this subtask. Our system is ranked as the third one among 13 systems.

Table 6: The best/worst/average coarse-grained score (precision) of all the systems at the lexical sample subtask of task 17 and the coarse-grained score (precision) of our system at the lexical sample subtask of task 17.

	Coarse-grained score (precision)
Best	88.7%
Worst	52.1%
Average	70.0%
Our system	86.4%

7 Conclusion

In this paper, we described the implementation of our $I2R$ systems that participated in task 2, task 5, and task 17 at SemEval-2007. Our systems achieved 63.9% F-score and 81.6% supervised recall for task 2, 71.2% micro-average precision and 74.7% macro-average precision for task 5, and 86.4% coarse-grained precision and recall for the lexical sample subtask of task 17. The performance of our system is very good under supervised evaluation. It may be explained by that our system has the ability to find some minor senses so that it can outperforms the baseline system that always uses the most frequent sense as the answer.

References

Agirre E. , & Soroa A. 2007. SemEval-2007 Task 2: Evaluating Word Sense Induction and Discrimination Systems. *Proceedings of SemEval-2007, Association for Computational Linguistics.*

Lange, T., Braun, M., Roth, V., & Buhmann, J. M. 2002. Stability-Based Model Selection. *Advances in Neural Information Processing Systems 15.*

Lee, Y.K., & Ng, H.T. 2002. An Empirical Evaluation of Knowledge Sources and Learning Algorithms for Word Sense Disambiguation. *Proceedings of the 2002 Conference on Empirical Methods in Natural Language Processing*, (pp. 41-48).

Levine, E., & Domany, E. 2001. Resampling Method for Unsupervised Estimation of Cluster Validity. *Neural Computation*, Vol. 13, 2573–2593.

Niu, Z.Y., Ji, D.H., & Tan, C.L. 2005. Word Sense Disambiguation Using Label Propagation Based Semi-Supervised Learning. *Proceedings of the 43rd Annual Meeting of the Association for Computational Linguistics.*

Slonim, N., Friedman, N., & Tishby, N. 2002. Unsupervised Document Classification Using Sequential Information Maximization. *Proceedings of the 25th Annual International ACM SIGIR Conference on Research and Development in Information Retrieval.*

Tishby, N., Pereira, F., & Bialek, W. (1999) The Information Bottleneck Method. *Proc. of the 37th Allerton Conference on Communication, Control and Computing.*

Zhu, X. & Ghahramani, Z.. 2002. Learning from Labeled and Unlabeled Data with Label Propagation. *CMU CALD tech report CMU-CALD-02-107.*

Table 7: The estimated sense numbers by our system for all the words at task 2.

explain	2	move	3
position	3	express	4
buy	2	begin	2
hope	3	prepare	3
feel	5	policy	2
hold	2	attempt	2
work	5	recall	3
people	4	find	2
system	2	join	2
bill	2	build	2
hour	5	base	3
value	4	management	2
job	5	turn	4
rush	2	kill	2
ask	2	area	5
approve	4	affect	4
capital	4	keep	5
purchase	2	improve	2
propose	2	do	2
see	3	drug	5
president	3	come	5
power	3	disclose	4
effect	2	avoid	3
part	5	plant	2
exchange	4	share	2
state	2	carrier	2
care	5	complete	2
promise	3	maintain	3
estimate	2	development	4
rate	2	space	5
say	2	raise	3
remove	5	future	3
grant	4	network	3
remember	3	announce	5
cause	2	start	3
point	5	order	2
occur	4	defense	5
authority	3	set	3
regard	2	chance	2
go	3	produce	2
allow	4	negotiate	2
describe	2	enjoy	4
prove	3	exist	4
claim	4	replace	3
fix	2	examine	3
end	5	lead	3
receive	3	source	2
complain	3	report	2
need	2	believe	2
condition	2	contribute	3

ILK2: Semantic Role Labelling for Catalan and Spanish using TiMBL

Roser Morante, Bertjan Busser
ILK, Dept. of Language and Information Sciences
Tilburg University, P.O.Box 90153
NL-5000 LE Tilburg, The Netherlands
{R.Morante,G.J.Busser}@uvt.nl

Abstract

In this paper we present a semantic role labeling system submitted to the task *Multilevel Semantic Annotation of Catalan and Spanish* in the context of SemEval–2007. The core of the system is a memory–based classifier that makes use of full syntactic information. Building on standard features, we train two classifiers to predict separately the semantic class of the verb and the semantic roles.

1 Introduction

Semantic role labelling (SRL) has been addressed in the CoNLL–2004 and CoNLL–2005 Shared Tasks (Carreras and Màrquez, 2004; Carreras and Màrquez, 2005) for English. In the task *Multilevel Semantic Annotation of Catalan and Spanish* of the SemEval competition 2007, the target are two different languages. The general SRL task consists of two tasks: prediction of semantic roles (SR) and prediction of the semantic class of the verb (SC).

The data provided in the task (Màrquez et al., 2007) are sentences annotated with lemma, POS tags, syntactic information, semantic roles, and the semantic classes of the verb. A training corpus for Catalan (ca.3LB) and another for Spanish (sp.3LB) are provided. Although the setting is similar to the CoNLL–Shared Task 2005, three relevant differences are that the corpora are significantly smaller, that the syntactic information is based on a manually corrected treebank, which contains also syntactic functions (i.e. direct object, indirect object, etc.), and that the set of semantic roles is larger, especially for core arguments.

Our goal is to check whether simple individual systems could produce competitive results in both subtasks, and whether they would be robust enough when applied to two languages and to the held–out test sets provided.

2 System description

We approach the SRL task as two classification problems: prediction of SR and prediction of SC. We hypothesize that the two problems can be solved in the same way for both languages. We build two very similar systems that differ only in some of the features used, as we explain below.

The task is solved in three phases: 1) A pre–processing phase that is very similar to the sequentialization in (Màrquez et al., 2005). We call it *focus selection*. It consists of identifying the potential candidates to be assigned a semantic role or a semantic verb class. 2) The classification. 3) Some limited postprocessing.

2.1 Focus selection

The system starts by finding the target verb (which is marked in the corpus as such). Then, it finds the complete form of the verb (that in the corpus is tagged as verb group, infinitive, gerund, etc.) and the clause boundaries in order to look for the siblings of the verb that are under the same clause. Our assumption is that all siblings of the verb are potential candidates for semantic roles. The focus selection process produces two groups of focus tokens: on the one hand, the verbs and, on the other, the siblings of

Proceedings of the 4th International Workshop on Semantic Evaluations (SemEval-2007), pages 183–186,
Prague, June 2007.

the verbs. These tokens will be the instances in each training set. Table 1 shows the number of training and test instances for each subtask.

	Training 3LB		Test 3LB		Test CESS	
	Ca.	Sp.	Ca.	Sp.	Ca.	Sp.
SR	23202	24668	1335	1451	1241	1186
SC	8932	9707	510	615	463	465

Table 1: Number of instances per corpus for each task ('Ca' stands for Catalan, 'Sp' stands for Spanish).

2.2 Classification

In both systems we approach the classification task in one step, predicting directly the SR and the SC class. This means that in the SR task we do not perform a previous classification to select the tokens that might be assigned a role. We assume that all verbs belong to a class. As for the SR, we assume that most siblings of the verb will have a class, except for those that have syntactic functions AO, ET, MOD, NEG, IMPERS, PASS, and VOC. The siblings that do not have a semantic role are assigned the NONE tag. Because the corpus is small and because the amount of instances with a NONE class is proportionally low, we do not consider it necessary to filter these cases.

Regarding the **learning algorithm**, we use the IB1 classifier as implemented in TiMBL (version 5.1) (Daelemans et al., 2004), a supervised inductive algorithm for learning classification tasks based on the k nearest neighbor (k-nn) algorithm. In IB1, similarity is defined by a feature–level distance metric between a test instance and a memorized training instance. The metric combines a per–feature value–based distance metric with global feature weights that account for relative differences in importance of the features.

The TiMBL parameters used in the systems are the IB1 algorithm, the Jeffrey Divergence as feature metric, MVDM threshold at level 1, weighting using GainRatio, k=11, and weighting neighbors as function of their Inverse Linear Distance (for details we refer the reader to the TiMBL reference guide (Daelemans et al., 2004)).

As for the **features**, we started by using the same feature set for both classifiers and then, after some experimentation, we decided to use slightly different feature sets for the two sub-tasks. Most of the features we designed are features that have become standard for the SRL task (Gildea and Jurafsky, 2002; Xue and Palmer, 2004; Carreras and Màrquez, 2004; Carreras and Màrquez, 2005). In our system, the features relate to the verb, the verb siblings, what we take to be the content word of the siblings, the clause, and the relation verb–arguments. Additionally, we added lexical features extracted from the verb lexicon provided for the task, and from WordNet.

After experimenting with 323 features, we selected 98 for the SR task and 77 for the SC subclass. In order to select the features, we started with a basic system, the results of which were used as a baseline. Every new feature that was added to the basic system was evaluated in terms of average accuracy in 10-fold cross-validation experiments; if it improved the performance on held-out data, it was added to the selection. One problem with this hill-climbing method is that the selection of features is determined by the order in which the features have been introduced. We also performed experiments applying the feature selection process reported in (Tjong Kim Sang et al., 2005), a bi-directional hill climbing process. However, experiments with this advanced method did not produce a better selection of features.

The features for the SR prediction subtask are the following:

• Features on the verb (6). They are shared by all the instances that represent phrases belonging to the same clause:

VForm; **VLemma**; **VCau**: binary feature that indicate if the verb is in a causative construction with *hacer, fer* or if the main verb is *causar*; **VPron**, **VImp**, **VPass**: binary features that indicate if the verb is pronominal, impersonal, and in passive form respectively.

• Features on the sibling in focus (12):

SibSynCat: syntactic category; **SibSynFunc**: syntactic function; **SibPrep**: preposition; **SibLemW1, SibPOSW1, SibLemW2, SibPOSW2, SibLemW3, SibPOSW3**: lemma and POS tag of the first, second and third words of the sibling; **SibRelPos**: position of the sibling in relation to the verb (PRE or POST); **Sib+1RelPos**: position of the sibling next to the current phrase in relation to the verb (PRE or POST); **SibAbsPos**: absolute position of the sibling in the clause.

• Features that describe the properties of the content word (CW) of the focus sibling (13): in the case of prepositional phrases the CW is the head of the first noun phrase; in cases of coordination, we only take the first element of the coordination.

CWord; **CWLemma**; **CWPOS**: we take only the first character of the POS tags provided; **CWPOSType**: the type of POS, second character of the POS tags provided; **CWGender**; **CWne**: binary feature that indicates if the CW is a named entity; **CWtmp, CWloc**: binary features that indicate if the CW is a temporal or a locative adverb respectively; **CW+2POS, CW+3POS**: POS of the second and third words after CW.

CWwnsc1, CWwnsc2, CWwnsc3: additionally, if the CW is a noun, we extract information from WordNet (Fellbaum, 1998) about the first, second, and third more frequent semantic classes of the CW in WordNet. We cannot decide on a single one because the corpus is not disambiguated. The semantic class corresponds to the lexicographer files in WN3.0. For nouns there are 25 file numbers.

• Features on the clause (24):

CCtot: total number of siblings with function CC (circumstancial complement); **SUJRelPos, CAGRelPos, CDRelPos, CIRelPos, ATRRelPos, CPREDRelPos, CREGRelPos**: relative positions of siblings with functions SUJ, CAG, CD, CI,ATR, CPRED, and CREG in relation to verb (PRE or POST); **SEsib**: binary feature that indicates if the clause contains a verbal *se*; **SIBtot**: total number of verb siblings in the clause; **SynFuncSib8, SynCatSib8, PrepSib8,W1Sib8, W2Sib8, W3Sib8, W4Sib8, SynFuncSib9, SynCatSib9, PrepSib9, W1Sib9, W2Sib9, W3Sib9, W4Sib9**: syntactic function, syntactic category, preposition, and first to fourth word of siblings 8 and 9.

• Features extracted from the lexicon of verbal frames (43) that the task organizers provided. We access the lexicon to check if it is possible for a verb to have a certain semantic role. We check it for all semantic role classes, except for ArgX-Ag, ArgX-Cau, ArgX-Pat, ArgX-Tem because they proved not to be informative. The features are binary.

For the SC prediction task the features are similar, but not exactly the same. Both systems contain some features about all candidate arguments. We point out the differences:

• Features that are in the SR system and that are not in the SC system:

Verb form (**VForm**), verb lemma (**VLemma**), absolute position of the sibling in the clause (**SibAbsPos**), function of the sibling (**SibSynFunc**), preposition of the sibling (**SibPrep**), POS tag of the second and third words after CW (**CW+2POS, CW+3POS**), information about the WN classes of the CW (**CWwnsc1, CWwnsc2, CWwnsc3**), feature about the CW being a named entity (**CWne**, **SIBtot**), syntactic function, syntactic category, preposition and first to fourth word of siblings 8 and 9 (**SynFuncSib8, SynCatSib8, PrepSib8,W1Sib8, W2Sib8, W3Sib8, W4Sib8, SynFuncSib9, SynCatSib9, PrepSib9, W1Sib9, W2Sib9, W3Sib9, W4Sib9**).

• Features that are only in the SC system:

AllCats: vector of the syntactic categories of the siblings in the order that they appear in the clause; **AllFuncs**: vector of the functions of the siblings in the order that they appear; **AllFuncsBin** vector with eight binary values that represent if a sibling with that function is present or not; **Sib+1Prep, Sib+2Prep**: prepositions of the two siblings after the verb.

2.3 Postprocessing

As for the **postprocessing phase**, it consists of six simple rules to correct some basic errors in predicting some types of ArgM arguments. It only applies to the SR task. The rules are the following ones:

1. If prediction = ArgM–LOC, ArgM–MNR or ArgM–ADV, and either {**SibPrep** = 'durante' or 'durant'}, or {**SibSynCat** = sn and one of the WN semantic classes = 28}, then prediction = ArgM-TMP.

2. If prediction = ArgM–LOC, ArgM–MNR or ArgM–ADV, and **CWLemma** is a temporal adverb, then prediction = ArgM–TMP.

3. If prediction = ArgM–TMP and one of the WN classes = 15, then prediction = ArgM–LOC.

4. If prediction = ArgM–TMP, ArgM-MNR or ArgM-ADV, and **CWLemma** = locative adverb, then prediction = ArgM-LOC.

5. If prediction = ArgM-TMP or ArgM-ADV, and **CWwnsc1** = 15, and **SibPrep** = 'en' or 'desde' or 'hacia' or 'a' or 'des_de' or 'cap_a', then prediction = ArgM–LOC.

6. If prediction = ArgM–ADV and **CWLemma** = causal conjunction, then prediction = ArgM–CAU.

We are aware of the fact that these are very simple rules and that more elaborate postprocessing techniques can be applied, like the ones used in (Tjong Kim Sang et al., 2005) in order to make sure that the same role was not predicted more than once in the same clause.

SR TASK	Perf.Props	Precision	Recall	$F_{\beta=1}$
Test ca.3LB	73.35%	86.59%	85.91%	86.25
Test ca.CESS	60.55%	82.60%	78.03%	80.25
Overall ca	67.24%	84.72%	82.12%	83.40
Test sp.3LB	68.07%	83.05%	82.54%	82.80
Test sp.CESS	73.76%	85.88%	85.80%	85.84
Overall sp	70.52%	84.30%	83.98%	84.14
Overall SR	68.96%	84.50%	83.07%	83.78

SC TASK	Perf.Props	Precision	Recall	$F_{\beta=1}$
Test ca.3LB	90.86%	90.30%	88.72%	89.50
Test ca.CESS	90.41%	90.20%	88.27%	89.22
Overall ca	90.64%	90.25%	88.50%	89.37
Test sp.3LB	84.12%	80.00%	78.44%	79.21
Test sp.CESS	90.54%	89.89%	89.89%	89.89
Overall sp	86.88%	84.30%	83.36%	83.83
Overall SC	88.67%	87.12%	85.81%	86.46

SRL TASK	Perf.Props	Precision	Recall	$F_{\beta=1}$
Overall ca	–	86.44%	84.08 %	85.24
Overall sp	–	84.30%	83.78 %	84.04
Overall SRL	–	85.32%	83.93 %	84.62

Table 2: Overall results in the SR (above), SC (middle), and general SRL tasks ('Perf.Props': perfect propositions; 'ca': Catalan; 'sp': Spanish).

3 Results

The overall official results of the system are shown in Table 2. The SC system performs better (overall F_1 = 86.46) than the SR system (overall F_1 = 83.78). In global, the systems perform better for Catalan (overall F_1 = 85.24) than for Spanish (overall F_1 = 84.04), although the SC system performs better for Catalan (89.37 vs. 86.46), and the SR system performs better for Spanish (84.14 vs 83.40).

Striking results are that the SR system gets significantly better results with the held–out test for Spanish, and that both of the complete SRL systems get significantly better results with the held–out test for Spanish. This might be due to differences in the process of gathering and annotation of the corpus.

SP–CESS	F	Precision	Recall	$F_{\beta=1}$
Overall		85.88%	85.80%	85.84
Arg0–AGT	16.19%	92.83%	92.41%	92.62
Arg0–CAU	1.23%	100%	50%	66.67
Arg1	1.79%	88.46%	82.14%	85.19
Arg1–LOC	0.11%	0.00%	0.00%	0.00
Arg1–PAT	20.09%	93.82%	94.19%	94.00
Arg1–TEM	14.08%	86.54%	91.84%	89.11
Arg2	2.05%	68.00%	77.27%	72.34
Arg2–ATR	9.88%	91.67%	90.41%	91.03
Arg2–BEN	2.40%	96.30%	100.00%	98.11
Arg2–EFI	0.19%	0.00%	0.00%	0.00
Arg2–EXT	0.19%	0.00%	0.00%	0.00
Arg2–LOC	1.13%	0.00%	0.00%	0.00
Arg2–PAT	0.01%	0.00%	0.00%	0.00
Arg3–ATR	0.05%	0.00%	0.00%	0.00
Arg3–BEN	0.16%	100.00%	100.00%	100.00
Arg3–EIN	0.08%	0.00%	0.00%	0.00
Arg3–FIN	0.04%	100.00%	33.33%	50.00
Arg3–ORI	0.29%	0.00%	0.00%	0.00
Arg4–DES	0.60%	83.33%	83.33%	83.33
ArgL	0.71%	16.67%	20.00%	18.18
ArgM–ADV	10.67%	68.12%	68.12%	68.12
ArgM–CAU	1.50%	55.56%	45.45%	50.00
ArgM–FIN	1.30%	64.71%	84.62%	73.33
ArgM–LOC	4.94%	78.21%	77.22%	77.71
ArgM–MNR	2.28%	36.36%	57.14%	44.44
ArgM–TMP	7.19%	88.75%	81.61%	85.03
V	–	100.00%	100.00%	100.00

Table 3: Detailed results on the Spanish CESS–ECE test corpus for the SR subtask. F: frequency of the semantic roles in the training corpus, without counting V.

Table 3 shows detailed results on the Spanish CESS–ECE corpus for the SR task. Low scores are generally related to low frequency of the SR in the training corpus, and high scores are related to high frequency or to overt marking of the SR.

4 Conclusions

We have presented two memory–based SRL systems that make use of full syntactic information and approach the tasks in three steps. Results show that rather simple individual systems can produce competitive results in both tasks, and that they are robust enough to be applied to two languages and to the held–out test sets provided. Improvements of the systems would consist in improving the focus selection step, and applying more elaborate techniques for feature selection and postprocessing.

Acknowledgements

This research has been funded by the postdoctoral grant EX2005–1145 awarded by the Ministerio de Educación y Ciencia of Spain to the project *Técnicas semiautomáticas para el etiquetado de roles semánticos en corpus del español.* We would like to thank Martin Reynaert, Caroline Sporleder, Antal van den Bosch, and the anonymous reviewers for their comments and suggestions.

References

X. Carreras and Ll. Màrquez. 2004. Introduction to the CoNLL-2004 shared task: Semantic role labeling. In *Proceedings of CoNLL–2004*, Boston MA, USA.

X. Carreras and Ll. Màrquez. 2005. Introduction to the CoNLL-2005 shared task: Semantic role labeling. In *Proceedings of CoNLL–2005*, Ann Arbor, Michigan, June.

W. Daelemans, J. Zavrel, K. Van der Sloot, and A. Van den Bosch. 2004. TiMBL: Tilburg memory based learner, version 5.1, reference guide. Technical Report Series 04-02, ILK, Tilburg, The Netherlands.

Christiane Fellbaum, editor. 1998. *WordNet: An Electronic Database*. MIT Press, Cambridge, MA.

D. Gildea and D. Jurafsky. 2002. Automatic labeling of semantic roles. *Computational Linguistics*, 28(3):245–288.

LL. Màrquez, P. Comas, J. Giménez, and N. Català. 2005. Semantic role labeling as sequential tagging. In *Proceedings of CoNLL–2005*, Ann Arbor, Michigan.

Ll. Màrquez, M.A. Martí, M. Taulé, and L. Villarejo. 2007. SemEval-2007 Task 09: Multilevel semantic annotation of catalan and spanish. In *Proceedings of SemEval-2007, the 4th Workshop on Semantic Evaluations*, Prague, Czech Republic.

E. Tjong Kim Sang, S. Canisius, A. van den Bosch, and T. Bogers. 2005. Applying spelling error correction techniques for improving semantic role labelling. In *Proceedings of CoNLL-2005*, pages 229–232, Ann Arbor, Michigan.

N. Xue and M. Palmer. 2004. Calibrating features for semantic role labeling. In *Proceedings of 2004 Conference on Empirical Methods in Natural Language Processing*, Barcelona, Spain.

ILK: Machine learning of semantic relations with shallow features and almost no data

Iris Hendrickx
CNTS / Language Technology Group
Uversity of Antwerp,
Universiteitsplein 1
2610 Wilrijk, Belgium
iris.hendrickx@ua.ac.be

Roser Morante, Caroline Sporleder, Antal van den Bosch
ILK / Communication and Information Sciences
Tilburg University, P.O. Box 90153,
5000 LE Tilburg, The Netherlands
{R.Morante,C.Sporleder, Antal.vdnBosch}@uvt.nl

Abstract

This paper summarizes our approach to the Semeval 2007 shared task on "Classification of Semantic Relations between Nominals". Our overall strategy is to develop machine-learning classifiers making use of a few easily computable and effective features, selected independently for each classifier in wrapper experiments. We train two types of classifiers for each of the seven relations: with and without WordNet information.

1 Introduction

We interpret the task of determining semantic relations between nominals as a classification problem that can be solved, per relation, by machine learning algorithms. We aim at using straightforward features that are easy to compute and relevant to preferably all of the seven relations central to the task.

The starting conditions of the task provide us with a very small amount of training data, which further stresses the need for robust, generalizable features, that generalize beyond surface words. We therefore hypothesize that generic information on the lexical semantics of the entities involved in the relation is crucial. We developed two systems, based on two sources of semantic information. Since the entities in the provided data were word-sense disambiguated, an obvious way to model their lexical semantics was by utilizing WordNet3.0 (Fellbaum, 1998) (WN). One of the systems followed this route.

We also entered a second system, which did not rely on WN but instead made use of automatically generated semantic clusters (Decadt and Daelemans, 2004) to model the semantic classes of the entities.

For both systems we trained seven binary classifiers; one for each relation. From a pool of easily computable features, we selected feature subsets for each classifier in a number of wrapper experiments, i.e. repeated cross-validation experiments on the training set to test out subset selections systematically. Along with feature subsets we also chose the machine-learning method independently for each classifier.

Section 2 presents the system description, Section 3, the results, and Section 4, the conclusions.

2 System Description

The development of the system consists of a preprocessing phase to extract the features, and the classification phase.

2.1 Preprocessing

Each sentence is preprocessed automatically in the following steps. First, the sentence is tokenized with a rule-based tokenizer. Next a part-of-speech tagger and text chunker that use the memory-based tagger MBT (Daelemans et al., 1996) produces part-of-speech tags and NP chunk labels for each token. Then a memory-based shallow parser predicts grammatical relations between verbs and NP chunks such as subject, object or modifier (Buchholz, 2002). The tagger, chunker and parser were all trained on the WSJ Corpus (Marcus et al., 1993). We also use a memory-based lemmatizer (Van den Bosch et al., 1996) trained on Celex (Baayen et al., 1993) to predict the lemma of each word.

Proceedings of the 4th International Workshop on Semantic Evaluations (SemEval-2007), pages 187–190,
Prague, June 2007.

The features extracted are of three types: semantic, lexical, and morpho-syntactic. The features that apply to the entities in a relation (e1,e2) are extracted for term 1 (t1) and term 2 (t2) of the relation, where t1 is the first term in the relation name, and t2 is the second term. For example, in the relation CAUSE–EFFECT, t1 is CAUSE and t2 is EFFECT.

The semantic features are the following:

WN semantic class of t1 and t2. The WN semantic class of each entity in the relation. For the WN-based system, we determined the semantic class of the entities on the basis of the lexicographer file numbers (LFN) in WN3.0. The LFN are encoded in the synset number provided in the annotation of the data. For nouns there are 25 file numbers that correspond to suitably abstract semantic classes, namely:

noun.Tops(top concepts for nouns), act, animal, artifact, attribute, body, cognition, communication event, feeling, food, group, location, motive, object, person, phenomenon, plant, possession, process, quantity, relation, shape, state, substance, time.

Is_container (is_C). Exclusively for the CONTENT–CONTAINER relation we furthermore included two binary features that test whether the two entities in the relation are hyponyms of the synset *container* in WN. For the PART–WHOLE relation we also experimented with binary features expressing whether the two entities in the relation have some type of meronym and holonym relation, but these features did not prove to be predictive.

Cluster class of t1 and t2. A cluster class identifier for each entity in the relation. This information is drawn from automatically generated clusters of semantically similar nouns (Decadt and Daelemans, 2004) generated on the British National Corpus (Clear, 1993). The corpus was first preprocessed by a lemmatizer and the memory-based shallow parser, and the found verb–object relations were used to cluster nouns in groups. We used the top-5000 lemmatized nouns, that are clustered into 250 groups. This is an example of two of these clusters:

- {can pot basin tray glass container bottle tin pan mug cup jar bowl bucket plate jug vase kettle}
- {booth restaurant bath kitchen hallway toilet bedroom hall suite bathroom interior lounge shower compartment oven lavatory room}

The lexical features are the following:

Lemma of t1 and t2 (lem1, lem2). The lemmas of the entities involved in the relation. In case an entity consisted of multiple words (e.g. *storage room*) we use the lemma of the head noun (i.e. *room*).

Main verb (verb). The main verb of the sentence in which the entities involved in the relation appear, as predicted by the shallow parser.

The morpho-syntactic features are:

GramRel (gr1, gr2). The grammatical relation tags of the entities.

Suffixes of t1 and t2 (suf1, suf2). The suffixes of the entity lemmas. We implemented a rule-based suffix guesser, which determines whether the nouns involved in the relation end in a derivational suffix, such as *-ee*, *-ment* etc. Suffixes often provide cues for semantic properties of the entities. For example, the suffix *-ee* usually indicates animate (and typically human) referents (e.g. *detainee* etc.), whereas (*-ment*) points at abstract entities (e.g. *statement*).

While the features were selected independently for all relations, the seven classifiers in the WN-based system all make use of the WN semantic class features; in the system that did not use WN, the seven classifiers make use of the cluster class features instead.

2.2 Classification

We experimented with several machine learning frameworks and different feature (sub-)sets. For rapid testing of different learners and feature sets, and given the size of the training data (140 examples for each relation), we made use of the Weka machine learning software[1] (Witten and Frank, 1999). We systematically tested the following algorithms: NaiveBayes (NB) (Langley et al., 1992), BayesNet (BN) (Cooper and Herskovits, 1992), J48 (Quinlan, 1993), Jrip (Cohen, 1995), IB1 and IBk (Aha et al., 1991), LWL (Atkeson et al., 1997), and DecisionStumps (DS) (Iba and Langley, 1992), all with default algorithm settings.

The classifiers for all seven relations were optimized independently in a number of 10-fold cross-validation (CV) experiments on the provided train-

[1] `http://www.cs.waikato.ac.nz/ml/weka/`

ing sets. The feature sets and learning algorithms which were found to obtain the highest accuracies for each relation were then used when applying the classifiers to the unseen test data.

The classifiers of the cluster-based system (A) all use the two cluster class features. The other selected features and the chosen algorithms (CL) are displayed in Table 1. Knowledge of the identity of the lemmas was found to be beneficial for all classifiers. With respect to the machine learning framework, Naive Bayes was selected most frequently.

Relation	CL	lem1	lem2	verb	gr1	gr2	suf1	suf2
Cause-Effect	DS	+	+	+	+	+	+	+
Instr-Agency	LWL	+	+	+	+	+		
Product-Producer	NB	+	+	+	+	+	+	+
Origin-Entity	IBk	+	+		+	+	+	+
Theme-Tool	NB	+	+	+			+	+
Part-Whole	NB	+	+		+	+	+	+
Content-Container	NB	+	+		+	+	+	+

Table 1: The final selected algorithms and features for each relation by the cluster-based system (A).

The classifiers of the WN-based system (B) all use at least the WN semantic class features. Table 2 shows the other selected features and algorithm for each relation. None of the classifiers use all the features. For the part-whole relation no extra features besides the WN class are selected. Also the classifiers for the relations cause-effect and content-container only use two additional features. The list of best found algorithms shows that —like with the cluster-based system— a Bayesian approach is favorable, as it is selected in four of seven cases.

Relation	CL	lem1	lem2	verb	gr1	gr2	suf1	suf2	is_C
Cause-Effect	BN						+	+	
Instr-Agency	NB	+	+			+			
Product-Producer	IB1	+	+	+		+			
Origin-Entity	IBk	+	+		+	+	+		
Theme-Tool	NB	+	+	+	+		+	+	
Part-Whole	J48								
Content-Container	BN			+					+

Table 2: The final selected algorithms and features for each relation by the WN-based system (B). (*is_C* is the CONTENT-CONTAINER specific feature.)

3 Results

In Table 3 we first present the best results computed on the training set using 10-fold CV for the cluster-based system (A) and the WN-based system (B). These results are generally higher than the official test set results, shown in Tables 4 and 5, possibly showing a certain amount of overfitting on the training sets.

Relation	A	B
Cause-Effect	56.4	72.9
Instrument-Agency	71.4	75.7
Product-Producer	65.0	67.9
Origin-Entity	70.7	78.6
Theme-Tool	75.7	79.3
Part-Whole	65.7	73.6
Content-Container	70.0	75.4
Avg	67.9	74.8

Table 3: Average accuracy on the training set computed in 10-fold CV experiments of the cluster-based system (A) and the WN-based system (B).

The official scores on the test set are computed by the task organizers: accuracy, precision, recall and F_1 score. Table 4 presents the results of the cluster-based system. Table 5 presents the results of the WN-based system. (The column *Total* shows the number of instances in the test set.) Markable is the high accuracy for the PART-WHOLE relation as the classifier was only trained on two features coding the WN classes.

A4	Pre	Rec	F	Acc	Total
Cause–Effect	53.3	97.6	69.0	55.0	80
Instrument–Agency	56.1	60.5	58.2	57.7	78
Product–Producer	69.1	75.8	72.3	61.3	93
Origin–Entity	60.7	47.2	53.1	63.0	81
Theme–Tool	64.5	69.0	66.7	71.8	71
Part–Whole	48.4	57.7	52.6	62.5	72
Content–Container	71.4	78.9	75.0	73.0	74
Avg	60.5	69.5	63.8	63.5	78.4

Table 4: Test scores for the seven relations of the cluster-based system trained on 140 examples (A4).

The system using all training data with WordNet features, B4 (Table 5), performs better in terms of F-score on six out of the seven subtasks as compared to the system that does not use the WordNet features but the semantic cluster information instead, A4 (Table 4). This is largely due to a lower precision of the A4 system. The WordNet features appear to be directly responsible for a relatively higher precision.

In contrast, the semantic cluster features of system A sometimes boost recall. A4's recall on the

B4	Pre	Rec	F	Acc	Total
Cause–Effect	69.0	70.7	69.9	68.8	80
Instrument–Agency	69.8	78.9	74.1	73.1	78
Product–Producer	79.7	75.8	77.7	71.0	93
Origin–Entity	71.0	61.1	65.7	71.6	81
Theme–Tool	69.0	69.0	69.0	74.6	71
Part–Whole	73.1	73.1	73.1	80.6	72
Content–Container	78.1	65.8	71.4	73.0	74
Avg	72.8	70.6	71.5	73.2	78.4

Table 5: Test scores for the seven relations of the WN-based system trained on 140 examples (B4).

CAUSE–EFFECT relation is 97.6% (the classifier predicts the class 'true' for 75 of the 80 examples), and on CONTENT–CONTAINER the system attains 78.9%, markedly better than B4.

4 Conclusion

We have shown that a machine learning approach using shallow and easily computable features performs quite well on this task. The system using WordNet features based on the provided disambiguated word senses outperforms the cluster-based system. It would be interesting to compare both systems to a more realistic WN-based system that uses predicted word senses by a Word Sense Disambiguation system.

However we end by noting that the amount of training and test data in this shared task should be considered too small to base any reliable conclusions on. In a realistic scenario (e.g. when high-precision relation classification would be needed as a component of a question-answering system), more training material would have been gathered, and the examples would not have been seeded by a limited number of queries – especially the negative examples are very artificial now due to their similarity to the positive cases, and the fact that they are down-sampled very unrealistically. Rather, the focus of the task should be on detecting positive instances of the relations in vast amounts of text (i.e. vast amounts of implicit negative examples). Positive training examples should be as randomly sampled from raw text as possible. The seven relations are common enough to warrant a focused effort to annotate a reasonable amount of randomly selected text, gathering several hundreds of positive cases of each relation.

References

D. W. Aha, D. Kibler, M. Albert. 1991. Instance-based learning algorithms. *Machine Learning*, 6:37–66.

C. Atkeson, A. Moore, S. Schaal. 1997. Locally weighted learning. *Artificial Intelligence Review*, 11(1–5):11–73.

R. H. Baayen, R. Piepenbrock, H. van Rijn. 1993. *The CELEX lexical data base on CD-ROM*. Linguistic Data Consortium, Philadelphia, PA.

S. Buchholz. 2002. *Memory-Based Grammatical Relation Finding*. PhD thesis, University of Tilburg.

J. H. Clear. 1993. *The British national corpus*. MIT Press, Cambridge, MA, USA.

W. Cohen. 1995. Fast effective rule induction. In *Proceedings of the 12th International Conference on Machine Learning*, 115–123. Morgan Kaufmann.

G. F. Cooper, E. Herskovits. 1992. A bayesian method for the induction of probabilistic networks from data. *Machine Learning*, 9(4):309–347.

W. Daelemans, J. Zavrel, P. Berck, S. Gillis. 1996. Mbt: A memory-based part of speech tagger generator. In *Proceedings of the 4th ACL/SIGDAT Workshop on Very Large Corpora*, 14–27.

B. Decadt, W. Daelemans. 2004. Verb classification - machine learning experiments in classifying verbs into semantic classes. In *Proceedings of the LREC 2004 Workshop Beyond Named Entity Recognition: Semantic Labeling for NLP Tasks*, 25–30, Lisbon, Portugal.

C. Fellbaum, ed. 1998. *WordNet: An Electronic Database*. MIT Press, Cambridge, MA.

W. Iba, P. Langley. 1992. Induction of one-level decision trees. *Proceedings of the Ninth International Conference on Machine Learning*, 233–240.

P. Langley, W. Iba, K. Thompson. 1992. An analysis of Bayesian classifiers. In *Proceedings of the Tenth Annual Conference on Artificial Intelligence*, 223–228. AAAI Press and MIT Press.

M. Marcus, S. Santorini, M. Marcinkiewicz. 1993. Building a Large Annotated Corpus of English: the Penn Treebank. *Computational Linguistics*, 19(2):313–330.

J. Quinlan. 1993. *C4.5: Programs for Machine Learning*. Morgan Kaufmann, San Mateo, CA.

A. Van den Bosch, W. Daelemans, A. Weijters. 1996. Morphological analysis as classification: an inductive-learning approach. In K. Oflazer, H. Somers, eds., *Proceedings of the Second International Conference on New Methods in Natural Language Processing, NeMLaP-2, Ankara, Turkey*, 79–89.

I. H. Witten, E. Frank. 1999. *Data Mining: Practical Machine Learning Tools and Techniques with Java Implementations*. Morgan Kaufman, San Francisco, CA.

IRST-BP: Preposition Disambiguation based on Chain Clarifying Relationships Contexts

Octavian Popescu
FBK-IRST, Trento (Italy)
popescu@itc.it

Sara Tonelli
FBK-IRST, Trento (Italy)
satonelli@itc.it

Emanuele Pianta
FBK-IRST, Trento (Italy)
pianta@itc.it

Abstract

We are going to present a technique of preposition disambiguation based on sense discriminative patterns, which are acquired using a variant of Angluin's algorithm. They represent the essential information extracted from a particular type of local contexts we call Chain Clarifying Relationship contexts. The data set and the results we present are from the Semeval task, WSD of Preposition (Litkowski 2007).

1 Introduction

Word Sense Disambiguation (WSD) is a problem of finding the relevant clues in a surrounding context. Context is used with a wide scope in the NLP literature. However, there is a dichotomy among two types of contexts, local and topical contexts (Leacock et. all 1993), that is general enough to encompass the whole notion and at the same to represent a relevant distinction.

The local context is formed by information on word order, distance and syntactic structure and it is not restricted to open-class words. A topical context is formed by the list of those words that are likely to co-occur with a particular sense of a word. Generally, the WSD methods have a marked predilection for topical context, with the consequence that structural clues are rarely, if ever, taken into account. However, it has been suggested (Stetina&Nagao 1997, Dekang 1997) that structural words, especially prepositions and particles, play an important role in computing the lexical preferences considered to be the most important clues for disambiguation.

Closed class words, prepositions in particular, are ambiguous (Litkowski&Hargraves2006). Their disambiguation is essential for the correct processing of the meaning of a whole phrase. A wrong PP-attachment may render the sense of the whole sentence unintelligible. Consider for example:

(1) Joe heard the gossip about you and me.
(2) Bob rowed about his old car and his mother.

A probabilistic context free grammar most likely will parse both (1) and (2) wrongly[1]. It would attach "about" to "to hear" in (1) and would consider the "his old car and his mother" the object of "about" in (2).

The information needed for disambiguation of open class words is spread at all linguistics levels, from lexicon to pragmatics, and can be located within all discourse levels, from immediate collocation to paragraphs (Stevenson&Wilks 1999). Intuitively, prepositions have a different behavior. Most likely, their senses are determined within the government category of their

[1] Indeed, Charniak's parser, considered to be among the most accurate ones for English, parses wrongly both of them.

Proceedings of the 4th International Workshop on Semantic Evaluations (SemEval-2007), pages 191–194,
Prague, June 2007.

heads. We expect the local context to play the most important role in the disambiguation of prepositions.

We are going to present a technique of preposition disambiguation based on sense discriminative patterns, which are acquired using a variant of Angluin's algorithm. These patterns represent the essential information extracted from a particular type of local contexts we call Chain Clarifying Relationship contexts. The data set and the results we present are from the Semeval task, WSD of Preposition (Litkowski 2007).

In Section 2 we introduce the Chain Clarifying Relationships, which represent particular types of local contexts. In Section 3 we present the main ideas of the Angluin algorithm. We show in Section 4 how it can be adapted to accommodate the preposition disambiguation task. Section 5 is dedicated to further research.

2 Chain Clarifying Relationships

We think of ambiguity of natural language as a net - like relationship. Under certain circumstances, a string of words represents a unique collection of senses. If a different sense for one of these words is chosen, the result is an ungrammatical sentence. Consider (3) below:

> (3) Most people do not live in a state of high intellectual awareness about their every action.

Suppose one chooses the sense of "*to live*" to be "*to populate*". Then, its complement, "*state*", should be synonym with location. The analysis crashes when "*awareness*" is considered. There are two things we notice here: (a) the relationship between "*live*" and "*state*" – the only two acceptable sense combination out of four are (populate, location) and (experience, entity) – and (b) the chain like relationship between "*awareness*", "*state*", "*live*" where the sense of any of them determines the sense of all the others in a cascade effect, or results in ungrammaticality. A third thing, not directly observable in (3) is that the syntactic configuration is crucial in order for (a) and (b) to arise. Example (4) shows that in a different syntactic configuration the above sense relationship simply disappears:

(4) The awareness of people about the state institutions is arguably the first condition to live in a democratic state.

We call the relationship between "*live*", "*state*", "*awareness*" a Chain Clarifying Relationship (CCR). In that specific syntactic configuration their senses are interdependent and independent of the rest of the sentence. To each CCR corresponds a sense discriminative pattern. Our goal is to learn which local contexts are CCRs. Each CCR is a pattern of words on a syntactic configuration. Each slot can be filled only by words defined by certain lexical features. To learn a CCR means to discover the syntactic configuration and the respective features. For example consider (5) and (6) with their CCRs in (CCR5) and (CCR6) respectively:

> (5) Some people lived in the same state of disappointment/ optimism/ happiness.
> (CCR5) (vb=live_sense_2, prep1=in_1, prep1_obj=state_sense_1,prep2=of_sense_1a,prep2_obj=[State_of_Spirit])
> (6) Some people lived in the same state of Africa/ Latin America/ Asia.
> (CCR6) (vb=live_sense_1, prep1=in_1, prep1_obj=state_sense_1,prep2=of_1b,prep2_obj = [Location])

The lexical features of the open class words in a specific syntactic configuration trigger the senses of each word, if the context is a CCR. In (CCR5) any word that has the same lexical trait as the one required by prep2_obj slot will determine a unique sense for all the other words, including the preposition. The same holds for (CCR6). The difference between (CCR5) and (CCR6) is part of the linguistic knowledge (which can be clearly shown: "*how*" (5) vs. "*where*" (6)).

The CCR approach proposes a deterministic approach to WSD. There are two features of CCRs which are interesting from a strictly practical point of view. Firstly, CCR proposal is a way to determine the size of the window where the disambiguation clues are searched for (many WSD algorithms arbitrarily set it apriori). Secondly, within a CCR, by construction, the sense of one word determines the senses of all the others.

3 Angluin Learning Algorithm

Our working hypothesis is that we can learn the CCRs contexts by inferring differences via a regular language learning algorithm. What we want to learn is which features fulfil each syntactic slot. First we introduce the original Angluin's algorithm and then we mention a variant of it admitting unspecified values.

Angluin proved that a regular set can be learned in polynomial time by assuming the existence of an oracle which can gives "yes/no" answers and counterexamples to two types of queries: membership queries and conjecture queries (queries about the form of the regular language) (Angluin 1998).

The algorithm employs an observation table built on prefix /suffix closed classes. To each word a {1, 0} value is associated, "1" meaning that the word belongs to the target regular language. Initially the table is empty and is filled incrementally. The table is closed if all prefixes of the already seen examples are in the table and is consistent if two rows dominated by the same prefix have the same value, "0" or "1".

If the table is not consistent or closed then a set of membership queries is made. If the table is consistent and closed then a conjecture query is made. If the oracle responds "no", it has to provide a counterexample and the previous steps are cycled till "yes" is obtained.

The role of the oracle for conjecture questions can be substituted by a stochastic process. If strict equality is not requested, then a probably approximately correct identification of language can be obtained (PAC identification), which guarantees that the two languages (the identified one, L_i, and the target one, L_t) are equal up to a certain extent. The approximation is constrained by two parameters ε – accuracy and δ – confidence, and the constraint is $P(d(L_i, L_t) \leq \varepsilon) \geq \delta)$, where the distance between two languages is the probability to see a word in just one of them.

The algorithm can be further generalized to work with unspecified values. The examples may have three values ("yes", "no", "?"), as in many domains one has to deal with partial knowledge The main result is that a variant of the above algorithm successfully halts if the number of counterexamples provided by the oracle have O(log n) missing attributes, where n is the number of attributes (Goldmann et all 2003).

4 Preposition Disambiguation Task

The CCR extraction algorithm is supervised. Consider that you have a sense annotated corpora. Extract the dependency paths and filter out the ones which are not sense discriminative. Try to generalize each slot and retain the minimal ones. What is left are CCRs.

Unfortunately, for the preposition disambiguation task the training set is sense annotated only for prepositions. We have undertaken a different strategy. The training corpus can be used as an oracle. The main idea is to start with a set of few examples for each sense from the training set which are considered to be the most representative ones. We try to generalize each of them independently and to tackle down the border cases (the cases that may correspond to two different senses) which are considered unspecified examples. The process stops when the oracle does not bring any new information (the training cases have been learned). Below we explain this process step by step.

Step 1. Get the seed examples. For each preposition and sense get the seed examples. This operation is performed by a human expert. It may be the case that the glosses or the dictionary definition are a good starting point (with the advantage that the intervention of a human is no more required). However, we preferred do to it manually for better precision.

Besides the most frequent sense, we have considered, in average, another two senses. There is a practical reason for this limitation: the number of examples for the rest of the senses is insufficient. In total we have considered 149 senses out of the 241 senses present in the training set. For each an average of three examples has been chosen.

Step 2. Get the CCRs. For each example we read the lex units associated with its frame from FrameNet. Our goal is to identify the relevant syntactic and lexical features associated with each slot. We have undertaken two simplifying assumptions. Firstly, only the government category of the head of the PP is considered (which can be a verb, a noun or an adjective). Secondly, the lexical features are identified with synsets from WordNet.

We have used the Charniak's parser to extract the structure of the PP-phrases and further we have used Collin's algorithm to implement a head recogniser.

A head can have many synsets. In order to understand which sense the word has in the respective construction we look for the synset common to the elements extracted from lex. If the proposed synset uniquely identifies just one sense then it is considered a CCR. If not, we are looking for the next synset. This step corresponds to membership queries in Angluin's algorithm.

Step 3. Generalize the CCRs. At the end of step 2 we have a set of CCRs for each sense. We obtained 395 initial CCRs. We tried to extend the coverage by taking into account the hyperonyms of each synsets. Only approximately 10% of these new patterns have received an answer from the oracle. Consequently, for our approach ,a part of the training corpus has not been used. It serves only 15 examples in average to get a correct CCR. All the instances of the same CCR do not bring any new information to our approach.

Posteriori, we have noticed that the initial patterns have an almost 50% (48.57%) coverage in the test data. The generalized patterns obtained after the third step have 82% test corpus coverage. For the rest 18%, which are totally unknown cases, we have chosen the most frequent sense.

In table 1 we present the performances of our system. It achieves 0.65 (FF-score), which compares favourably against baseline – the most frequent -of 0.53. On the first column of Table 1 we write the FF score interval - more than 0.75, between 0.75 and 0.5, and less than 0.5 respectively, - on the second column we present the number of cases within that interval the system solved and on the third column we include the corresponding number for baseline.

Table 1

Interval	System	Baseline
1.00 - 0.75	18	8
0.75 - 0.50	15	6
0.00 – 0.50	2	20

5 Conclusion and Further Research

Our system did not perform very well (third position out of three). Analyzing the errors, we have noticed that our system systematically confound two senses in some cases (for example "*by*" 5(2) vs. 15(3), for "*on*" 4(1c) vs. 1(1) etc.). We would like to see whether these errors are due to a misclassification in training.

References

Angluin, D. (1987): "Learning Regular Sets from Queries and Counterexamples", Information and Computation Volume 75 , Issue 2

Goldman, S., Kwek, S., Scott, S. (2003): "Learning from examples with unspecified attribute values", Information and Computation, Volume 180

Leacock, C., Towell, G., Voorhes, E. (1993): "Towards Building Contextual Representations of Word Senses Using Statistical Models", In Proceedings, SIGLEX workshop: Acquisition of Lexical Knowledge from Text

Lin, D. (1997): "Using syntactic dependency as local context to resolve word sense ambiguity".ACL/EACL-97, Madrid

Litkowski, K. C. (2007):"Word Sense Disambiguation of Prepositions" , The Semeval 2007 WePS Track. In Proceedings of Semeval 2007, ACL

Litkowski, K. C., Hargraves O. (2006): "Coverage and Inheritance in the Preposition Project", Proceedings of the Third ACL-SIGSEM Workshop on Prepositions, Trento,

Stetina J, Nagao M (1997): "Corpus based PP attachment ambiguity resolution with a semantic dictionary.", Proc. of the 5th Workshop on very large corpora, Beijing and Hongkong, pp 66-80

Stevenson K., Wilks, Y.,(2001): "The interaction of knowledge sources in word sense disambiguation", Computational Linguistics, 27(3):321–349.

IRST-BP: Web People Search Using Name Entities

Octavian Popescu
FBK-irst, Trento (Italy)
popescu@itc.it

Bernardo Magnini
FBK-irst, Trento (Italy)
magnini@itc.it

Abstract

In this paper we describe a person clustering system for web pages and report the results we have obtained on the test set of the Semeval 2007 Web Person Search task. Deciding which particular person a name refers to within a text document depends mainly on the capacity to extract the relevant information out of texts when it is present. We consider "relevant" here to stand primarily for two properties: (1) uniqueness and (2) appropriateness. In order to address both (1) and (2) our method gives primary importance to Name Entities (NEs), defined according to the ACE specifications. The common nouns not referring to entities are considered further as coreference clues only if they are found within already coreferred documents.

1 Introduction

Names are ambiguous items (Artiles, Gonzalo and Sekine 2007). As reported on an experiment carried out on an Italian news corpus (Magnini et all 2006) within a 4 consecutive days from a local newspaper the perplexity is 56% and 14% for first and last name respectively. Deciding which particular person a name refers to within a text document depends mainly on the capacity to extract the relevant information out of texts when it is present[1]. We consider "relevant" here to stand primarily for two properties: (1) uniqueness and (2) appropriateness. A feature is unique as long as it appears only with one person. Consider a cluster of web pages that characterizes only one person. Many of the N-grams in this cluster are unique compared to other cluster. Yet the uniqueness may come simply from the sparseness. Appropriateness is the property of an N-gram to characterize that person.

Uniqueness may be assured by ontological properties (for example, "There is a unique president of a republic at a definite moment of time", "Alberta University is in Canada). However, the range of ontological information we are able to handle is quite restricted and we are not able to realize the coreference solely relying on them. Uniqueness may be assured by estimating a very unlike probability of the occurrence of certain N-grams for different persons (as, for example, "Dekang Lin professor Alberta Canada Google").

Appropriateness is a difficult issue because of two reasons: (a) it is a dynamic feature (b) it is hard to be localized and extracted from text. The greatest help comes from the name of the page, when it happens to be a suggestive name such as "homepage", "CV", "resume" or "about". Gene-

[1] It is very difficult to evaluate whether the information allowing the coreference of two instances of a (same) name is present in a web page or news. A crude estimation on our news corpus for the names occurring between 6-20 times, which represent 8% of the names inventory for the whole collection, is that in much more than 50% of the news, the relevant information is not present.

Proceedings of the 4th International Workshop on Semantic Evaluations (SemEval-2007), pages 195–198,
Prague, June 2007.

alogy pages are very useful, to the extent that the information could be accurately extracted and that the same information occurs in some other pages as well. However, in general, for plain web pages, we rely on paragraphs in which a single person is mentioned and consequently, the search space for similarity is also within this type of paragraphs.

Our proposal is to rely on special N-grams for coreference and it is a variant of agglomerative clustering based on social networks(Bagga&Baldwin 1998, Malin 2005) . The terms the N-grams contain are crucial. Suppose we have the same name shared by two different persons who happen to also have the same profession, let's say, "lawyer", and who also practice in the same state. While all three words – (name, profession, state) - might be rare words for the whole corpus, their probability computed as chance to be seen in the same document is low, their three-gram fails to cluster correctly the documents referring to the two persons[2]. Knowing that the "lawyer" is a profession that has different specializations, which are likely to be found as determiners, we may address this problem more accurately considering the same three-gram by changing "lawyer" with a word more specific denoting her specialization.

The present method for clustering people web pages containing names according addresses both uniqueness and appropiateness. We rely on a procedure that firstly identifies the surest cases of coreference and then recursively discover new cases. It is not necessarily the case that the latest found coreferences are more doubtful, but rather that the evidence required for their coreference is harder to achieve.

The cluster metrics gives a primary importance to words denoting entities which are defined according to ACE definitions: PER, LOC, ORG, GPE.

In Section 2 we present in detail the architecture of our system and in Section 3 we present its behavior and the results we obtained on the test set of Semeval 2007 Web Person Search task. In section 4 we present our conclusions and future directions for improvement.

[2] The traditional idf methods used in document clustering must be further refined in order to be effective in person coreference.

2 System Architecture

First, the text is split into paragraphs, based mainly on the html structure of the page. We have a Perl script which decides weather the name of interest is present within a paragraph. If the test is positive the paragraph is marked as a person-paragraph, and our initial assumption is that each person-paragraph refers to a different person.

The second step is considered the first procedure of the feature extraction module. To each paragraph person we associate a set of NEs, rare words and temporal expressions, each of them counting as independent items. For all of these items which are inside of the same dependency path we also consider the N-grams made out of the respective items preserving the order. For each person-paragraph we compute the list of above items and consider them as features for clustering. This set is called the association set.

The first step in making the coreference is the most important one and consists in two operations: (1) the most similar pages are clustered together and (2) for each cluster, we make a list of the pages which most likely do not refer to the same person. Starting with this initial estimation, the next steps are repeated till no new coreference is made.

For each cluster of pages, a new set of items is computed starting from the association sets. Only the ones which are specific to the respective cluster - comparing against all other clusters and against the list of pages not related (see (2) above) – are kept in the new association set. These are the features we use further for clustering. The clustering score of two person-paragraphs is given by summing up the individual score of common features in their association sets. The score of a feature is determined based on its type - (NE, distinctive words, temporal expressions) - , its length in terms of words compounding it, and the number of its occurrences inside the cluster and inside the whole corpus, considering only the web pages relative to that name and the absolute frequency of the words. The feature score is finally weighed with a factor which expresses the distance between the name and the respective feature. An empirical threshold has been chosen.

Each of the above paragraphs representing a module in our system is explained in one of the next subsections respectively.

2.1 Preprocessing

Web pages contain a lot of information outside the raw text. We wrote Perl scripts for identifying the e-mail addresses, phone and fax numbers and extract them if they were in the same paragraph with the name of interest. It seems that a lot can be gained considering the web addresses, the type of page, the links outside the pages and so on. However, we have not exploited up to now these extra clues for coreference. The whole corpus associated with a name is searched only once. If the respective items are found in two different pages, these two pages are clustered.

In web pages, the visual structure plays an important role, and many times the graphics design substitutes for linguistics features. Using a normal html parser, such as lynx, the text may lack its usual grammatical structure which may drastically decrease the performances of sentence splitters, Name Entity Recognizers and parsers. To alleviate this problem, the text is first tagged with PoS. If a paragraph, '\n', does not have a main verb, then it is treated separately. If the text contains only nouns and determiners and if the paragraph is within a paragraph containing the name of interest, the phrase "You are talking about" is added in front of it to make it a normal sentence.

The text is split into person-paragraphs, and each person-paragraph is split into sentences, lemmatized, the NEs are recognized[3] and the text is parsed using MiniPar (Dekang Lin 1998). We are interested only in dependency paths that are rooted in NEs – the NP which are included in bigger XP, or sister of NPs, or contain time expressions.

The person-paragraphs are checked for the interest names. We write rules for recognizing the valid names. If a page does not have a valid name of interest, it is discarded. A page is also discarded when a valid name of interest has its entity type "ORG".

[3] We thank to the Textec group at IRST for making it possible for everyone to pre process the text very easily with state of the art performances.

2.2 Feature Extraction

The association set contains a set of features. The features are NEs or part of NEs, because the closed class words, the very frequent words – computed on the set of all web pages for all persons – are deleted from the NEs[4]. When we refer to the length of a feature we mean the number of words it is made of, after deletion.

We consider words (phrases) which are not NEs as features but only if they are frequent in already coreferred person-paragraphs. That is, initially the coreference is determined solely on NEs. If there is enough evidence, i.e. when a word is frequent within the cluster and not present within other clusters, then the respective word (phrase) is taken into account for coreference.

Time expressions are relevant indicators for coreference if they are appropriately linked to a person. We consider them always, just like a NE, but when they appear in particular dependency trees they have a special value. If they are dominated by a name of interest and/or by the lemma "birth", "born" we consider them as a sure factor for coreference.

For all composed features we also consider the order preserved combinations of their parts obtaining new features.

The association sets increase their cardinality by coreference. At each step, the new added features are checked against the ones from the other clusters. The common features are kept in separate sets. The coreference is not decided on their basis, but these features are used to identify the paragraph persons that do not refer to a particular person, and therefore should not be included in the same cluster. We do not explicitly weigh differently the features (apart of the cases mentioned above) but they are actually weighed differently implicitly. The words within a composed feature are repeated, a feature of length n produces n(n-1) new features, n> 2. Besides, as we will see in the next section, the similarity score uses the length of a feature.

[4] Sometimes, correctly or not, the SVM base NER we use includes, especially inside of LOC and GPE name entities, common words. In order to remain as precise as possible, we choose not to consider these words when we compute the similarity score.

2.3 Similarity Measure

Our similarity score for two person-paragraphs is the sum of the individual scores of the common features which are weighed according to the maximum of distances between the name of interest and the feature.

There are three parameters on which we rely for computing similarity: the length, the number of occurrences, and the absolute frequency of a feature. The score considers the cube of the feature length (which means that the one word features do not score). We compute the ratio between the number of occurrences within the cluster and the number of occurrences in the web pages relative to that name. The third parameter is the absolute frequency of the words. As usually, if the word is a rare word it counts as more evidence for coreference. We regard these parameters as independent, in spite of their relative dependency, and we simply multiply them.

We define the distance between a feature and a name as a discrete measure. If the name and the feature are sisters of the same head then their distance is minimum, therefore their importance for similarity is the highest. The second lower distance value is given within the same sentence and the distance increases with the number of sentences. If there are no other names mentioned in the paragraph, the distance is divided by half.

We have established an empirical threshold which initially is very high, as the features are not checked among the clusters in the first run. After the first run, it is relaxed and the common and individual sets are computed as we have described in the previous section.

3 Evaluation

The system performance on the test set of Semeval 2007 Web Person Search task is $F_{\alpha=0.5}$ = 0.75, harmonic means of purity, and $F_{=0.2}$ = 0.80 - the inverse purity mean. The data set has been divided in three sets: SET1 ACL people, SET2 Wikipedia people, and SET3 census people. The results are presented in table 1. The fact that the system is less accurate on SET2 may be due to the fact that larger person paragraph are considered and therefore more inappropriate similarity are declared.

Test Set	Purity	Inverse Purity	$F_{\alpha=0.5}$
SET1	0,75	0,80	0,77
SET2	0,83	0,71	0,77
SET3	0,81	0,75	0,78

4 Conclusion and Further Research

Our method is greedy and it depends a lot on the accuracy of coreference as the system propagates the errors from step to step.

One of the big problems of our system is the preprocessing step and further improvement is required. That is because we rely on the performances of NER and parsers. We also hope that by the inclusion of extra textual information the html carries, we will have better results.

A second direction for us is to exactly understand the role of ontological information. For the moment, we recognized some of the words denoting professions and we tried to guess their determinators. We think that having hierarchical relationships among LOC, GPE and also for ORG may make a difference in results especially for massive corpora.

References

Artiles, J., Gonzalo, J. and Sekine, S. (2007). *Establishing a benchmark for the Web People Search Task: The Semeval 2007 WePS Track.* In Proceedings of Semeval 2007, Association for Computational Linguistics.

Bagga A., Baldwin B.,(1998) *Entity-Based cross-document-referencing using vector space model,* In proceedings of 17th International Conference on Computational Linguistics

Magnini B., Pianta E., Popescu O. and Speranza M. (2006). Ontology Population from Textual Mentions: *Task Definition and Benchmark. Proceedings of the OLP2 workshop on Ontology Population and Learning, Sidney, Australia,*. Joint with ACL/Coling

Malin. B., (2005): *Unsupervised Name Disambiguation via Network Similarity*, In proceedings SIAM Conference on Data Mining 2005

Zanolli R., Pianta E. (2006) *Technical report*, ITC IRST

JHU1 : An Unsupervised Approach to Person Name Disambiguation using Web Snippets

Delip Rao **Nikesh Garera** **David Yarowsky**
Dept. of Computer Science
Johns Hopkins University
Baltimore, MD 21218
{delip, ngarera, yarowsky}@cs.jhu.edu

Abstract

This paper presents an approach to person name disambiguation using K-means clustering on rich-feature-enhanced document vectors, augmented with additional web-extracted snippets surrounding the polysemous names to facilitate term bridging. This yields a significant F-measure improvement on the shared task training data set. The paper also illustrates the significant divergence between the properties of the training and test data in this shared task, substantially skewing results. Our system optimized on $F_{0.2}$ rather than $F_{0.5}$ would have achieved top performance in the shared task.

1 Introduction

Being able to automatically distinguish between John Doe, the musician, and John Doe, the actor, on the Web is a task of significant importance with applications in IR and other information management tasks. Mann and Yarowsky (2004) used bigographical data annotated with named entitities and perform fusion of extracted information across multiple documents. Bekkerman and McCallum (2005) studied the problem in a social network setting exploiting link topology to disambiguate namesakes. Al-Kamha and Embley (2004) used a combination of attributes (like zipcodes, state, etc.), links, and page similarity to derive the name clusters while Wan et. al. (2005) used lexical features and named entities.

2 Approaches

Our framework focuses on the K-means clustering model using both bag of words as features and various augumented feature sets. We experimented with several similarity functions and chose Pearson's correlation coefficient[1] as the distance measure for clustering. The weights for the features were set to the term frequency of their respective words in the document.[2]

2.1 Submitted system: Clustering using Web Snippets

We queried the Google search engine with the target person names and extracted up to the top one thousand results. For each result we also extracted the snippet associated with it. An example is shown below in Figure 2.1. As can be seen the

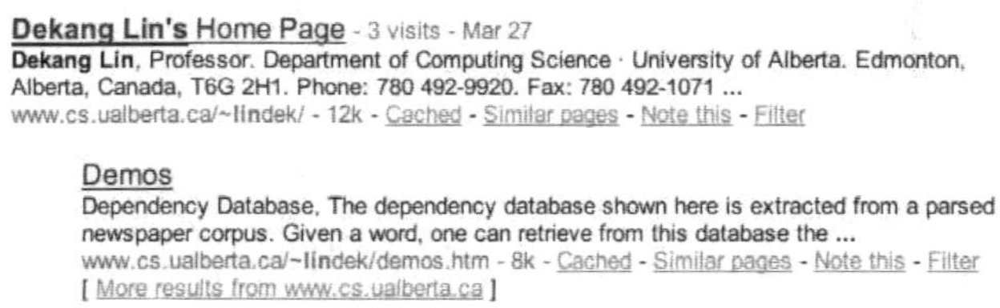

Figure 1: Google snippet for "Dekang Lin"

snippets contain high quality, low noise features that could be used to improve the performance of the system. Each snippet was treated as a document and

[1]This performs better than the standard measures like Euclidean and Cosine with K-means clustering on this data.

[2]We found that using TF weights instead of TF-IDF weights gives a better performance on this task.

Proceedings of the 4th International Workshop on Semantic Evaluations (SemEval-2007), pages 199–202,
Prague, June 2007.

clustered along with the supplied documents. This process is illustrated in Figure 2. The following example illustrates how these web snippets can improve performance by lexical transitivity. In this hypothetical example, a short test document contains a Canadian postal code (T6G 2H1) not found in any of the training documents. However, there may exist an additional web page not in the training or test data which contains both this term and also overlap with other terms in the training data (e.g. 492-9920), serving as an effective transitive bridge between the two.

Training Document 1	492-9920, not(T6G 2H1)
Web Snippet 2	both 492-9920, T6G 2H1
Test Document 3	T6G 2H1, not(492-9920)

Thus K-means clustering is likely to cluster the three documents above together while without this transitive bridge the association between training and test documents is much less strong. The final clustering of the test data is simply a projection with the training documents and web snippets removed.

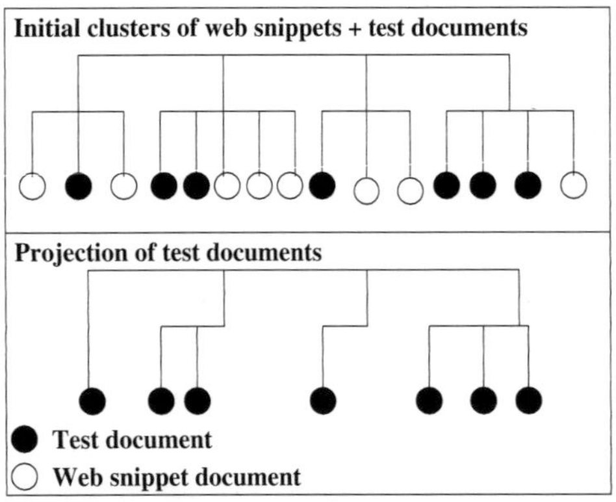

Figure 2: Clustering using Web Snippets

2.2 Baselines

In this section we describe several trivial baselines:

1. **Singletons:** A clustering where each cluster has only one document hence number of clusters is same as the number of documents.

2. **One Cluster:** A clustering with only one cluster containing all documents.

3. **Random:** A clustering scheme which partitions the documents uniformly at random into K clusters, where the value of K were the optimal K on the training and test data.

These results are summarized in Table 1. Note that all average F-scores mentioned in this table and the rest of the paper are microaverages obtained by averaging the purity and invese purity over all names and then calculating the F-score.

	Train		Test	
Baseline	$F_{0.2}$	$F_{0.5}$	$F_{0.2}$	$F_{0.5}$
Singletons	.676	.511	.843	.730
One Cluster	.688	.638	.378	.327
Random	.556	.493	.801	.668

Table 1: Baseline performance

2.3 K-means on Bag of Words model

The standard unaugumented Bag of Words model achieves $F_{0.5}$ of 0.666 on training data, as shown in Table 2.

2.4 Part of speech tag features

We then consider only terms that are nouns (NN, NNP) and adjectives (JJ) with the intuition that most of the content bearing words and descriptive words that disambiguate a person would fall in these classes. The result then improves to 0.67 on the training data.

2.5 Rich features

Another variant of this system, that we call RichFeats, gives preferential weighting to terms that are immediately around all variants of the person name in question, place names, occupation names, and titles. For marking up place names, occupation names, and titles we used gazetteer[3] lookup without explicit named entity disambiguation. The keywords that appeared in the HTML tag `<META ..>` were also given higher weights. This resulted in an $F_{0.5}$ of 0.664.

2.6 Snippets from the Web

The addition of web snippets as described in Section 2.1 yeilds a significant $F_{0.5}$ improvement to 0.72.

[3]Totalling 19646 terms, gathered from publicly available resources on the web. Further details are available on request.

2.7 Snippets and Rich features

This is a combination of the models mentioned in Sections 2.5 and 2.6. This model combination resulted in a slight degradation of performance over snippets by themselves on the training data but a slight improvement on test data.

Model	K	$F_{0.2}$	$F_{0.5}$
Vanilla BOW	10%	0.702	0.666
BOW + PoS	10%	0.706	0.670
BOW + RichFeats	10%	0.700	0.664
Snippets	10	**0.721**	**0.718**
Snippets + RichFeats	10	0.714	0.712

Table 2: Performance on Training Data

3 Selection of Parameters

The main parameter for K-means clustering is choosing the number of clusters, K. We optimized K over the training data varying K from 10%, 20%,$\cdots$,100% of the number of documents as well as varying absolute K values from 10, 20, $\cdots$ to 100 documents.[4] The evaluation score of F-measure can be highly sensitive to this parameter K, as shown in Table 3. The value of K that gives the best F-measure on training set using vanilla bag of words (BOW) model is K = 10%, however we see in Table 3 that this value of K actually performs much worse on the test data as compared to other K values.

4 Training/Test discrepancy and re-evaluation using cross validation on test data

Table 4 compares cluster statistics between the training and test data. This data was derived from Artiles et. al (2007). The large difference between average number of clusters in training and test sets indicates that the parameter K, optimized on training set cannot be transferred to test set as these two sets belong to a very different distribution. This can be emprically seen in Table 3 where applying the best K on training results in a significant performance drop on test set given this divergence when parameters are optimized for $F_{0.5}$ (although performance does transfer well when parameters are optimized on $F_{0.2}$). This was observed in our primary evaluation system which was optimized for $F_{0.5}$ and resulted in a low official score of $F_{0.5} = .53$ and $F_{0.2} = .65$.

	Train		Test	
K	$F_{0.2}$	$F_{0.5}$	$F_{0.2}$	$F_{0.5}$
10%	.702	**.666**	***.527***	***.600***
20%	.716	.644	.617	.630
30%	.724	.631	.683	.676
40%	.724	.618	.728	.705
50%	.732	.614	.762	.724
60%	.731	.601	.798	.747
70%	.730	.593	.832	.766
80%	**.732**	.586	***.855***	***.773***
90%	.714	.558	.861	.764
100%	.670	.502	.843	.730

Table 3: Selecting the optimal parameter on training data and application to test data

Thus an interesting question is to measure performance when parameters are chosen on data sharing the distributional character of the test data rather than the highly divergent training set. To do this, we used a standard 2-fold cross validation to estimate clustering parameters from a held-out, alternate-half portion of the test data[5], which more fairly represents the character of the other half of the test data than does the very different training data. We divide the test set into two equal halves (taking first fifteen names alphabetically in one set and the rest in another). We optimize K on the first half, test on the other half and vice versa. We report the two K-values and their corresponding F-measures in Table 5 and we also report the average in order to compare it with the results on the test set obtained using K optimized on training. Further, we also report what would be oracle best K, that is, if we optimize K on the entire test data [6]. We can see in Table 5 that how optimizing K on a devlopment set with

[4]We discard the training and test documents that have no text content, thus the absolute value K = 10 and percentage value K = 10% can result in different K's, even if name had originally 100 documents to begin with.

[5]This also prevents overfitting as the two halves for training and testing are disjoint.

[6]By *oracle best* K we mean the K obtained by optimizing over the entire test data. Note that, the oracle best K is just for comparison because it would be unfair to claim results by optimizing K on the entire test set, all our claimed results for different models are based on 2-fold cross validation.

same distribution as test set can give us F-measure in the range of 77%, a significant increase as compared to the F-measure obtained by optimizing K on given training data. Further, Table 5, also indicates results by a custom clustering method, that takes the best K-means clustering using vanilla bag of words model, retains the largest cluster and splits all the other clusters into singleton clusters. This method gives an improved 2-fold F-measure score over the simple bag of words model, implying that most of the namesakes in test data have one (or few) dominant cluster and a lot of singleton clusters. Table 6 shows a full enumeration of model variance under this cross validated test evaluation. POS and RichFeats yield small gains, and a best $F_{0.5}$ performance of .776.

Data set	cluster size		# of clusters	
	Mean	Variance	Mean	Variance
Train	5.4	144.0	10.8	146.3
Test	3.1	26.5	45.9	574.1

Table 4: Cluster statistics from the test and training data

Data set	K	$F_{0.2}$	$F_{0.5}$
$F_{0.5}$ Best K on train	10%	.702	.666
$F_{0.2}$ Best K on train	10	.707	.663
Best K on train	10%	.527	.560
applied to test	10	.540	.571
2Fold on Test	80	.847	.748
	80%	.862	.793
		*.854**	*.771**
2Fold on Single	80	.847	.749
Largest Cluster	80	.866	.795
		.856*	**.772***
Oracle on Test	80	.858	.774

Table 5: Comparision of training and test results using Vanilla Bag-of-words model. The values indicated with * represent the average value.

5 Conclusion

We presented a K-means clustering approach for the task of person name disambiguation using several augmented feature sets including HTML meta features, part-of-speech-filtered features, and inclusion of additional web snippets extracted from Google to facilitate term bridging. The latter showed significant empirical gains on the training data. Best performance on test data, when parameters are optimized for $F_{0.2}$ on training (Table 3), yielded a top performing $F_{0.2}$ of .855 on test data (and $F_{0.5}$=.773 on test data). We also explored the striking discrepancy between training and test data characteristics and showed how optimizing the clustering parameters on given training data does not transfer well to the divergent test data. To control for similar training and test distributional characteristics, we re-evaluated our test results estimating clustering parameters from alternate held-out portions of the test set. Our models achieved cross validated $F_{0.5}$ of .77-.78 on test data for all feature combinations, further showing the broad strong performance of these techniques.

Model	K	$F_{0.2}$	$F_{0.5}$
Vanilla BOW	80/	.847/.862	.749/.793
	80%	Avg = .854	Avg = .771
BOW + PoS	80%/	.844/.865	.749/.795
	80%	Avg = .854	Avg = .772
BOW	80%/	.847/.868	.754/.798
RichFeats	80%	Avg = .858	Avg = **.776**
Snippets	50%/	.842/.875	.746/.800
	50%	Avg = **.859**	Avg = .773
Snippets +	40%/	.836/.874	.750/.798
RichFeats	50%	Avg = .855	Avg = .774

Table 6: Performance on 2Fold Test Data

References

Reema Al-Kamha and David W. Embley. 2004. Grouping search-engine returned citations for person-name queries. In *Proceedings of the 6th annual ACM international workshop on Web information and data management*, pages 96–103.

Javier Artiles, Julio Gonzalo, and Felisa Verdejo. 2007. Evaluation: Establishing a benchmark for the web people search task. In *Proceedings of Semeval 2007, Association for Computational Linguistics*.

Ron Bekkerman and Andrew McCallum. 2005. Disambiguating web appearances of people in a social network. In *Proceedings of the 14th international conference on World Wide Web*, pages 463–470.

Gideon S. Mann and David Yarowsky. 2004. Unsupervised personal name disambiguation. In *Proceedings of the seventh conference on Natural language learning (CONLL)*, pages 33–40.

Xiaojun Wan, Jianfeng Gao, Mu Li, and Binggong Ding. 2005. Person resolution in person search results: Webhawk. In *Proceedings of the 14th ACM international conference on Information and knowledge management*, pages 163–170.

JU-SKNSB: Extended WordNet Based WSD on the English All-Words Task at SemEval-1

Sudip Kumar Naskar
Computer Sc. & Engg. Dept.,
Jadavpur University,
Kolkata, India
sudip.naskar@gmail.com

Sivaji Bandyopadhyay
Computer Sc. & Engg. Dept.,
Jadavpur University,
Kolkata, India
sivaji_cse_ju@yahoo.com

Abstract

This paper presents an Extended WordNet based word sense disambiguation system using a major modification to the Lesk algorithm. The algorithm tries to disambiguate nouns, verbs and adjectives. The algorithm relies on the POS-sense tagged synset glosses provided by the Extended WordNet. The basic unit of disambiguation of our algorithm is the entire sentence under consideration. It takes a global approach where all the words in the target sentence are simultaneously disambiguated. The context includes previous and next sentence. The system assigns the default WordNet first sense to a word when the algorithm fails to predict the sense of the word. The system produces a precision and recall of .402 on the SemEval-2007 English All-Words test data.

1 Introduction

In Senseval 1, most of the systems disambiguating English words, were outperformed by a Lesk variant serving as baseline(Kilgariff & Rosenzweig, 2000). On the other hand, during Senseval 2 and Senseval 3, Lesk baselines were outperformed by most of the systems in the lexical sample track (Edmonds, 2002).

In this paper, we explore variants of the Lesk algorithm on the English All Words SemEval 2007 test data (465 instances), as well as on the first 10 Semcor 2.0 files (9642 instances). The proposed WSD algorithm is POS-sense-tagged gloss (from Extended WordNet) based and is a major modification of the original Lesk algorithm.

2 Extended WordNet

The *eXtended WordNet* (Harabagiu et al., 1999) project aims to transform the WordNet glosses into a format that allows the derivation of additional semantic and logic relations. It intends to syntactically parse the glosses, transform glosses into logical forms and tag semantically the nouns, verbs, adjectives and adverbs of the glosses automatically. The last release of the Extended WordNet is based on WordNet 2.0 and has three stages: POS tagging and parsing, logic form transformation, and semantic disambiguation.

3 Related Works

Banerjee and Pedersen (2002) reports an adaptation of Lesk's dictionary-based WSD algorithm which makes use of WordNet glosses and tests on English lexical sample from SENSEVAL-2. They define *overlap* as the longest sequence of one or more consecutive *content* words that occurs in both glosses. Each overlap contributes a score equal to the square of the number of words in the overlap.

A version of Lesk algorithm in combination with WordNet has been reported for achieving good results in (Ramakrishnan et al., 2004).

Vasilescu et al. (2004) carried on a series of experiments on the Lesk algorithm, adapted to WordNet, and on some variants. They studied the effect of varying the number of words in the contexts, centered around the target word.

But till now no work has been reported which makes use of Extended WordNet for Lesk-like gloss-oriented approach.

Proceedings of the 4th International Workshop on Semantic Evaluations (SemEval-2007), pages 203–206,
Prague, June 2007.

4 Proposed Sense Disambiguation Algorithm

The proposed sense disambiguation algorithm is a major modification of the Lesk algorithm (Lesk, 1986). WordNet and Extended WordNet are the main resources.

4.1 Modifications to the Lesk Algorithm

We modify the Lesk algorithm (Lesk, 1986) in several ways to create our baseline algorithm. The Lesk algorithm relies on glosses found in traditional dictionaries which often do not have enough words for the algorithm to work well. We choose the lexical database *WordNet*, to take advantage of the highly inter–connected set of relations among different words that WordNet offers, and Extended WordNet to capitalize on its (POS and sense) tagged glosses.

The Lesk algorithm takes a *local approach* for sense disambiguation. The disambiguation of the various words in a sentence is a series of independent problems and has no effect on each other. We propose a *global* approach where all the words (we mean by *word*, an open-class lemma) in the context window are *simultaneously* disambiguated in a bid to get the best *combination* of senses for all the words in the window instead of only the target word. The process can be thought of as sense disambiguation of the whole context, instead of a word.

The Lesk algorithm disambiguates words in short phrases. But, the basic unit of disambiguation of our algorithm is the entire sentence under consideration. We later modify the context to include the previous and next sentence.

Another major change is that the dictionary definition or gloss of each of its senses is compared to the glosses of every other word in the context by the Lesk algorithm. But in the present work, the words themselves are compared with the glosses of every other word in the context.

4.2 Choice of Which Glosses to Use

While Lesk's algorithm restricts its comparisons to the dictionary meanings of the words being disambiguated, our choice of dictionary allows us to also compare the meanings (i.e., glosses) of the words, as well as the words that are related to them through various relationships defined in WordNet. For each POS we choose a relation if links of its kind form at least 5% of the total number of links for that part of speech, with two exceptions. We use the *attribute* relation although there are not many links of its kind. But this relation links adjectives, which are not well developed in WordNet, to nouns which have a lot of data about them. This potential to tap into the rich noun data prompted us to use this relation. Another exception is the *antonymy* relationship. Although there are sufficient antonymy links for adjectives and adverbs, we have not utilized these relations.

Noun	Verb	Adjective
Hypernym	Hyponym	Attribute
Hyponym	Troponym	Also see
Holonym	Also see	Similar to
Meronym		Pertainym of
Attribute		

Table 1. WordNet relations chosen for the disambiguation algorithm

4.3 The Algorithm

The gloss bag is constructed for every sense of every word in the sentence. The gloss-bag is constructed from the POS and sense tagged glosses of synsets, obtained from the Extended WordNet. For any synset, the words forming the synset and the gloss definition contribute to the gloss-bag. The non-content words are left out. Example sentences do not contribute to the gloss bag since they are not (POS and sense) tagged. Each word along with its POS and sense-tag are stored in the gloss bag. For words with different POS, different relations are taken into account (according to Table 1) for building the corresponding gloss-bag.

This gloss-bag creation process can be performed offline or online. It can be performed dynamically on a as-when-needed basis. Or, gloss-bags can be created for all WordNet entries only once and stored in a data file in prior. The issue is time versus space.

Once, this gloss-bag creation process is over, the comparison process starts. Each word (say W_i) in the context is compared with each word in the gloss-bag for every sense (say S_k) of every other word (say W_j) in the context. If a match is found, they are checked further for part-of-speech match. If the words match in part-of-speech as well, a score is assigned to both the words: the word being matched (W_i) and the word whose gloss-bag contains the match (W_j). This matching event indicates mutual confidence towards each other, so both words are rewarded for this event. Two two-dimensional (one for word index and the other for sense index) vectors are maintained: *sense_vote* for the word in context, and *sense_score* for the word in gloss-bag. Say, for example, the context word (W_i# *noun*) matches with gloss word (W_n# *noun* # *m*) (i.e., $W_i = W_n$) in the gloss bag for k^{th} sense of W_j. Then, a score of 1/(gloss bag size of (W_{jk})) is assigned to both *sense_vote*[i][m] and *sense_score*[j][k]. Scores are normalized before assigning because of huge discrepancy in gloss-bag sizes. This process continues until each context word is matched against all gloss-bag words for each sense of every other context words.

Once all the comparisons have been made, we add *sense_vote* value with the *sense_score* linearly value for each sense of every word to arrive at the combination score for this word-sense pair.

The algorithm assigns a word the nth sense for which the corresponding *sense_vote* and *sense_score* produces the maximum sum, and it does not assign a word any sense when the corresponding *sense_vote* and *sense_score* values are 0, even if the word has only one sense. In the event of a tie, we choose the one that is more frequent, as specified by WordNet.

Assuming that there are *N* words in the window of context (i.e. the sentence), and that, on an average there are *S* senses per word, and *G* number of gloss words in each gloss bag per sense, $N * S$ gloss bags need to be constructed, giving rise to a total of $N * S * G$ gloss words. Now these many gloss words are compared against each of the *N* context words. Thus, $N^2 * S * G$ pairs of word comparisons need to be performed. Both, *S* and *G* vary heavily.

5 Variants of the Algorithm

The algorithm discussed thus far is our baseline algorithm. We made some changes, as described in the following two subsections, to investigate whether the performance of the algorithm can be improved.

5.1 Increasing the Context Size

The poor performance of the algorithm perhaps suggests that sentential context is not enough for this algorithm to work. So we went for a larger context: a context window containing the current sentence under consideration (target sentence), its preceding sentence and the succeeding sentence. This increment in context size indeed performed better than the baseline algorithm.

5.2 Assigning Different Scores

When constructing the gloss-bags for a word-sense pair, some words may appear in more than one gloss (by gloss we mean to say synonyms as well as gloss). So, we added another parameter with every (word#pos#sense) in a gloss bag: *noc* - the number of occurrence of this (word#pos#sense) combination in this gloss-bag.

And, in case of a match of context word (say W_i) with a gloss-bag word (of say k^{th} sense of word W_j), we scored the words in four ways to see if this phenomenon has any effect on the sense disambiguation process. Say, for example, the context word (W_i # *noun*) matches with gloss word (W_n # *noun* # *m* # *noc*) in the gloss bag for k^{th} sense of W_j (i.e., the particular word appears *noc* times in the said gloss-bag) and the gloss bag size is *gbs*. Then, we reward W_i and W_j for this event in four ways given below.

1. Assign 1/*gbs* to *sense_vote*[i][m] and 1/*gbs* to *sense_score*[j][k].
2. Assign 1/*gbs* to *sense_vote*[i][m] and *noc*/*gbs* to *sense_score*[j][k].
3. Assign *noc*/*gbs* to *sense_vote*[i][m] and 1/*gbs* to *sense_score*[j][k].
4. Assign *noc*/*gbs* to *sense_vote*[i][m] and *noc*/*gbs* to *sense_score*[j][k].

The results of this four-way scoring proved that this indeed has influence on the disambiguation process.

The WSD system is based on Extended WordNet version 2.0-1.1 (the latest release), which is in turn based on WordNet version 2.0. So, the system returns WordNet 2.0 sense indexes. These WordNet sense indexes are then mapped to WordNet 2.1 sense indexes using sensemap 2.0 to 2.1.

6 Evaluations

The system has been evaluated on the SemEval-2007 English All-Words Tasks (465 test instances), as well as on the first 10 Semcor 2.0 files, which are manually disambiguated text corpora using WordNet senses.

We compute *F-Score as 2*P*R / (P+R)*. Table 2 shows the performance of the four variants of the system (with a context size of 3 sentences) on the first 10 Semcor 2.0 files. From table 2, it is clearly evident that model C produces the best result (precision - .621, recall - .533) among the 4 scoring schemes. POS-wise evaluation results for model C on Semcor 2.0 data is given in table 3.

	Model			
	A	B	C	D
Precision	.618	.602	.621	.604
Recall	.531	.517	.533	.519
F-Score	.571	.556	.574	.558

Table 2. Evaluation of the four models on Semcor Data

	Noun	Verb	Adj	Overall
Precision	.6977	.4272	.6694	.6211
Recall	.6179	.3947	.4602	.5335
F-Score	.6554	.4103	.5454	.574

Table 3. POS-wise Evaluation for model C on Semcor Data

Model C produced a precision of .393 and a recall of .359 on the SemEval-2007 English All-Words test data (465 test instances). Table 4 shows POS-wise evaluation results for this test data.

	Noun	Verb	Overall
Precision	.507	.331	.393
Recall	.472	.299	.359
F-Score	.489	.314	.375

Table 3. POS-wise Evaluation on SemEval-2007 English All-Words test data

When default WordNet first senses were assigned to the (40) words for which the algorithm failed to predict senses, both the precision and recall values went up to .402 (this result has been submitted in SemEval-2007). The WSD system stood 10th in the SemEval-2007 English All-Words task.

7 Discussions

We believe that this somewhat poor showing can be partially attributed to the brevity of definitions in WordNet in particular and dictionaries in general. The Lesk algorithm is crucially dependent on the lengths of glosses. However lexicographers aim to create short and precise definitions which, though a desirable quality in dictionaries, is disadvantageous to this algorithm. Nouns have the longest average glosses in WordNet, and indeed the highest recall obtained is on nouns. The characteristics of the gloss bags need to be further investigated. Again many of the sense tagged gloss words in Extended WordNet, which are determinant factors in this algorithm, are of "silver" or "normal" quality. And finally, since the system returns WordNet 2.0 sense indexes which are mapped to WordNet 2.1 indexes with certain amount of confidence using sensemap 2.0 to 2.1, there may be some loss of information during this mapping process.

References

A. Kilgarriff, and J. Rosenzweig. 2000. Framework and Results for English SENSEVAL. *Computers and the Humanities*, 34, 15-48.

Florentina Vasilescu, Philippe Langlais, and Guy Lapalme. 2004. Evaluating Variants of the Lesk Approach for Disambiguating Words. *LREC*, Portugal.

G. Ramakrishnan, B. Prithviraj, and P. Bhattacharyya. 2004. A Gloss Centered Algorithm for Word Sense Disambiguation. *Proceedings of the ACL SENSEVAL 2004*, Barcelona, Spain, 217-221.

M. Lesk. 1986. Automatic sense disambiguation using machine readable dictionaries: How to tell a pine cone from a ice cream cone. *Proceedings of SIGDOC '86.*

P. Edmonds. 2002. SENSEVAL : The Evaluation of Word Sense Disambiguation Systems, *ELRA Newsletter*, Vol. 7, No. 3.

S. Banerjee. 2002. Adapting the Lesk Algorithm for Word Sense Disambiguation to WordNet. *MS Thesis*, University of Minnesota.

S. Banerjee, and T. Pedersen. 2002. An Adapted Lesk Algorithm for Word Sense Disambiguation Using WordNet. *CICLing*, Mexico.

S. Harabagiu, G. Miller, and D. Moldovan. 1999. WordNet2 - a morphologically and semantically enhanced resource. *Proceedings of SIGLEX-99*, Univ of Mariland. 1-8.

KU: Word Sense Disambiguation by Substitution

Deniz Yuret
Koç University
Istanbul, Turkey
dyuret@ku.edu.tr

Abstract

Data sparsity is one of the main factors that make word sense disambiguation (WSD) difficult. To overcome this problem we need to find effective ways to use resources other than sense labeled data. In this paper I describe a WSD system that uses a statistical language model based on a large unannotated corpus. The model is used to evaluate the likelihood of various substitutes for a word in a given context. These likelihoods are then used to determine the best sense for the word in novel contexts. The resulting system participated in three tasks in the SemEval 2007 workshop. The WSD of prepositions task proved to be challenging for the system, possibly illustrating some of its limitations: e.g. not all words have good substitutes. The system achieved promising results for the English lexical sample and English lexical substitution tasks.

1 Introduction

A typical word sense disambiguation system is trained on a corpus of manually sense tagged text. Machine learning algorithms are then employed to find the best sense for a word in a novel context by generalizing from the training examples. The training data is costly to generate and inter-annotator agreement is difficult to achieve. Thus there is very little training data available: the largest single corpus of sense tagged text, SemCor, has 41,497 sense tagged words. (Yuret, 2004) observed that approximately half of the test instances do not match any of the contextual features learned from the training data for an all words disambiguation task. (Yarowsky and Florian, 2002) found that each successive doubling of the training data only leads to a 3-4% error reduction within their experimental range.

Humans do not seem to be cursed with an exponential training data requirement to become proficient with the use of a word. Dictionaries typically contain a definition and one or two examples of usage for each sense. This seems to be sufficient for a human to use the word correctly in contexts that share no surface features with the dictionary examples. The 10^8 waking seconds it takes a person to become proficient in a language does not seem sufficient to master all the words and their different senses. We need models that do not require large amounts of annotated text to perform WSD.

What possible process can explain our proficiency without relying on a lot of labeled data? Let us look at a concrete example: The two most frequent senses of the word "board" according to WordNet 3.0 (Fellbaum, 1998) are the "committee" sense, and the "plank" sense. When we hear a sentence like "There was a board meeting", it is immediately obvious that the first sense is intended. One hypothesis is that a common sense inference engine in your brain rules out the second sense. Maybe you visualize pieces of timber sitting around a meeting table and decide that it is absurd. Another hypothesis is that the plank sense does not even occur to you because you hear this sentence in the middle of a conversation about corporate matters. Therefore the plank sense is not psychologically "primed". Finally, maybe you subconsciously perform a substitution and the sentence

Proceedings of the 4th International Workshop on Semantic Evaluations (SemEval-2007), pages 207–214,
Prague, June 2007.

"There was a plank meeting" just sounds bad to your linguistic "ear".

In this paper I will describe a system that judges potential substitutions in a given context using a statistical language model as a surrogate for the linguistic "ear". The likelihoods of the various substitutes are used to select the best sense for a target word.

The use of substitutes for WSD is not new. (Leacock et al., 1998) demonstrated the use of related monosemous words (monosemous relatives) to collect examples for a given sense from the Internet. (Mihalcea, 2002) used the monosemous relatives technique for bootstrapping the automatic acquisition of large sense tagged corpora. In both cases, the focus was on collecting more labeled examples to be subsequently used with supervised machine learning techniques. (Martinez et al., 2006) extended the method to make use of polysemous relatives. More importantly, their method places these relatives in the context of the target word to query a search engine and uses the search results to predict the best sense in an unsupervised manner.

There are three areas that distinguish my system from the previous work: (i) The probabilities for substitutes in context are determined using a statistical language model rather than search hits on heuristically constructed queries, (ii) The set of substitutes are derived from multiple sources and optimized using WSD performance as the objective function, and (iii) A probabilistic generative model is used to select the best sense rather than typical machine learning algorithms or heuristics. Each of these areas is explained further below.

Probabilities for substitutes: Statistical language modeling is the art of determining the probability of a sequence of words. According to the model used in this study, the sentence "There was a committee meeting" is 17,629 times more likely than the sentence "There was a plank meeting". Thus, a statistical language model can be used as a surrogate for your inner ear that decides what sounds good and what sounds bad. I used a language model based on the Web 1T 5-gram dataset (Brants and Franz, 2006) which gives the counts of 1 to 5-grams in a web corpus of 10^{12} words. The details of the Web1T model are given in the Appendix.

Given that I criticize existing WSD algorithms for using too much data, it might seem hypocritical to employ a data source with 10^{12} words. In my defense, from an engineering perspective, an unannotated 10^{12} word corpus exists, whereas large sense tagged corpora do not. From a scientific perspective, it is clear that no human ever comes close to experiencing 10^{12} words, but they do outperform simple n-gram language models based on that much data in predicting the likelihood of words in novel contexts (Shannon, 1951). So, even though we do not know how humans do it, we do know that they have the equivalent of a powerful statistical language model in their heads.

Selecting the best substitutes: Perhaps more important for the performance of the system is the decision of which substitutes to try. We never thought of using "monkey" as a potential substitute for "board". One possibility is to use the synonyms in WordNet which were selected such that they can be interchanged in at least some contexts. However 54% of WordNet synsets do not have any synonyms. Besides, synonymous words would not always help if they share similar ambiguities in meaning. Substitutes that are not synonyms, on the other hand, may be very useful such as "hot" vs. "cold" or "car" vs. "truck". In general we are looking for potential substitutes that have a high likelihood of appearing in contexts that are associated with a specific sense of the target word. The substitute selection method used in this work is described in Section 3.

Selecting the best sense: Once we have a language model and a set of substitutes to try, we need a decision procedure that picks the best sense of a word in a given context. An unsupervised system can be designed to keep track of the sense associated with each substitute based on the lexical resource used. However since I used multiple lexical resources, and had training data available, I chose a supervised approach. For each instance in the training set, the likelihood of each substitute is determined. Then instances of a single sense are grouped together to yield a probability distribution over the substitutes for that sense. When a test instance is encountered its substitute distribution is compared to that of each sense to select the most appropriate one. Section 2 describes the sense selection procedure in detail.

We could say each context is represented with the likelihood it assigns to various substitutes rather than its surface features. That way contexts that do not share any surface features can be related to each other.

Results: To summarize the results, in the Word Sense Disambiguation of Prepositions Task, the system achieved 54.7% accuracy[1]. This is 15.1% above the baseline of picking the most frequent sense but 14.6% below the best system. In the Coarse Grained English Lexical Sample WSD Task, the system achieved 85.1% accuracy, which is 6.4% above the baseline of picking the most frequent sense and 3.6% below the best system. Finally, in the English Lexical Substitution Task, the system achieved the top result for picking the best substitute for each word.

2 Sense Selection Procedure

Consider a target word w_0 with n senses $S = \{s_1, \ldots, s_n\}$. Let $C_j = \{c_{j1}, c_{j2}, \ldots\}$ be the set of contexts in the training data where w_0 has been tagged with sense s_j. The prior probability of a sense s_j will be defined as:

$$P(s_j) = \frac{|C_j|}{\sum_{k=1}^{n} |C_k|}$$

Suppose we decide to use m substitutes $W = \{w_1, \ldots, w_m\}$. The selection of the possible substitutes is discussed in Section 3. Let $P(w_i, c)$ denote the probability of the context c where the target word has been replaced with w_i. This probability is obtained from the Web1T language model. The conditional probability of a substitute w_i in a particular context c is defined as:

$$P(w_i|c) = \frac{P(w_i, c)}{\sum_{w \in W} P(w, c)}$$

The conditional probability of a substitute w_i for a particular sense s_j is defined as:

$$P(w_i|s_j) = \frac{1}{|C_j|} \sum_{c \in C_j} P(w_i|c)$$

[1]In all the tasks participated, the system submitted a unique answer for each instance. Therefore precision, recall, F-measure, and accuracy have the same value. I will use the term accuracy to represent them all.

Given a test context c_t, we would like to find out which sense s_j it is most likely to represent:

$$\text{argmax}_j\ P(s_j|c_t) \propto P(c_t|s_j)P(s_j)$$

To calculate the likelihood of the test context $P(c_t|s_j)$, we first find the conditional probability distribution of the substitutes $P(w_i|c_t)$, as described above. Treating these probabilities as fractional counts we can express the likelihood as:

$$P(c_t|s_j) \propto \prod_{w \in W} P(w|s_j)^{P(w|c_t)}$$

Thus we choose the sense that maximizes the posterior probability:

$$\text{argmax}_j P(s_j) \prod_{w \in W} P(w|s_j)^{P(w|c_t)}$$

3 Substitute Selection Procedure

Potential substitutes for a word were selected from WordNet 3.0 (Fellbaum, 1998), and the Roget Thesaurus (Thesaurus.com, 2007).

When selecting the WordNet substitutes, the program considered all synsets of the target word and neighboring synsets accessible following a single link. All words contained within these synsets and their glosses were considered as potential substitutes.

When selecting the Roget substitutes, the program considered all entries that included the target word. By default, the entries that included the target word as part of a multi word phrase and entries that had the wrong part of speech were excluded.

I observed that the particular set of substitutes used had a large impact on the disambiguation performance in cross validation. Therefore I spent a considerable amount of effort trying to optimize the substitute sets. The union of the WordNet and Roget substitutes were first sorted based on their discriminative power measured by the likelihood ratio of their best sense:

$$\text{LR}(w_i) = \max_j \frac{P(w_i|s_j)}{P(w_i|\bar{s}_j)}$$

The following optimization algorithms were then run to maximize the leave-one-out cross validation (loocv) accuracy on the lexical sample WSD training data.

1. Each substitute was temporarily deleted and the resulting gain in loocv was noted. The substitute that led to the highest gain was permanently deleted. The procedure was repeated until no further loocv gain was possible.

2. Each pair of substitutes were tried alone and the pair that gave the highest loocv score was chosen as the initial list. Other substitutes were then greedily added to this list until no further loocv gain was possible.

3. Golden section search was used to find the ideal cutoff point in the list of substitutes sorted by likelihood ratio. Substitutes below the cutoff point were deleted.

None of these algorithms consistently gave the best result. Thus, each algorithm was run for each target word and the substitute set that gave the best loocv result was used for the final testing. The loocv gain from using the optimized substitute sets instead of the initial union of WordNet and Roget substitutes was significant. For example the average gain was 9.4% and the maximum was 38% for the English Lexical Sample WSD task.

4 English Lexical Substitution

The *English Lexical Substitution Task* (McCarthy and Navigli, 2007), for both human annotators and systems is to replace a target word in a sentence with as close a word as possible. It is different from the standard WSD tasks in that there is no sense repository used, and even the identification of a discrete sense is not necessary.

The task used a lexical sample of 171 words with 10 instances each. For each instance the human annotators selected several substitutes. There were three subtasks: **best:** scoring the best substitute for a given item, **oot:** scoring the best ten substitutes for a given item, and **mw:** detection and identification of multi-words. The details of the subtasks and scoring can be found in (McCarthy and Navigli, 2007). My system participated in the first two subtasks.

Because there is no training set, the supervised optimization of the substitute set using the algorithms described in Section 3 is not applicable. Based on the trial data, I found that the Roget substitutes work better than the WordNet substitutes most of the time. The antonyms in each entry and the entries that did not have the target word as the head were filtered out to improve the accuracy. Antonyms happen to be good substitutes for WSD, but not so good for lexical substitution.

BEST	P	R	Mode P	Mode R
all	12.90	12.90	20.65	20.65
Further Analysis				
NMWT	13.39	13.39	21.20	21.20
NMWS	14.33	13.98	21.88	21.42
RAND	12.67	12.67	20.34	20.34
MAN	13.16	13.16	21.01	21.01

OOT	P	R	Mode P	Mode R
all	46.15	46.15	61.30	61.30
Further Analysis				
NMWT	48.43	48.43	63.42	63.42
NMWS	49.72	49.72	63.74	63.74
RAND	47.80	47.80	62.84	62.84
MAN	44.23	44.23	59.55	59.55

Table 1: BEST and OOT results: P is precision, R is recall, Mode indicates accuracy selecting the single preferred substitute when there is one, NMWT is the score without items identified as multi-words, NMWS is the score using only single word substitutes, RAND is the score for the items selected randomly, and MAN is the score for the items selected manually.

For the final output of the system, the substitutes w_i in a context c were simply sorted by $P(w_i, c)$ which is calculated based on the Web1T language model.

In the **best** subtask the system achieved 12.9% accuracy, which is the top score and 2.95% above the baseline. The system was able to find the mode (a single substitute preferred to the others by the annotators) in 20.65% of the cases when there was one, which is 5.37% above the baseline and 0.08% below the top score. The top part of Table 1 gives the breakdown of the **best** score, see (McCarthy and Navigli, 2007) for details.

The low numbers here are partly a consequence of the scoring formula used. Specifically, the score for a single item is bounded by the frequency of the best substitute in the gold standard file. Therefore, the

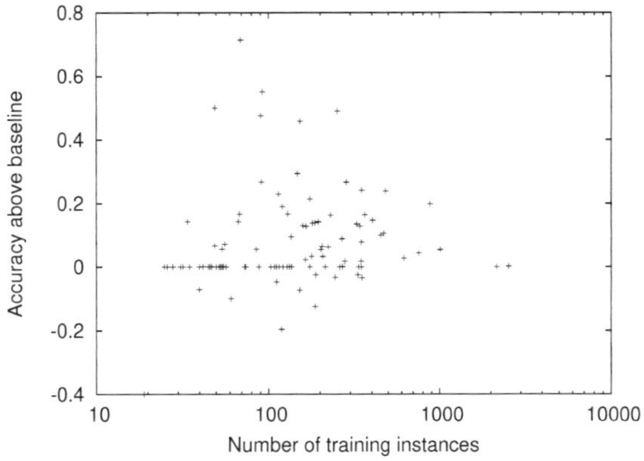

Figure 1: Training set size vs. accuracy above baseline for the English lexical sample task.

highest achievable score was not 100%, but 45.76%. A more intuitive way to look at the result may be the following: Human annotators assigned 4.04 distinct substitutes for each instance on average, and my system was able to guess one of these as the best in 33.73% of the cases.

In the **oot** subtask the system achieved 46.15% accuracy, which is 16.45% above the baseline and 22.88% below the top result. The system was able to find the mode as one of its 10 guesses in 61.30% of the cases when there was a mode, which is 20.73% above the best baseline and 4.96% below the top score. Unlike the **best** scores, 100% accuracy is possible for **oot**. Each item had 1 to 9 distinct substitutes in the gold standard, so an ideal system could potentially cover them all with 10 guesses. The second part of Table 1 gives the breakdown of the **oot** score.

In conclusion, selecting substitutes based on a standard repository like Roget and ranking them using the ngram language model gives a good baseline for this task. To improve the performance along these lines we need better language models, and better substitute selection procedures. Even the best language model will only tell us which words are most likely to replace our target word, not which ones preserve the meaning. Relying on repositories like Roget for the purpose of substitute selection seems ad-hoc and better methods are needed.

5 English Lexical Sample WSD

The *Coarse-Grained English Lexical Sample WSD Task* (Palmer et al., 2007), provided training and test data for sense disambiguation of 65 verbs and 35 nouns. On average there were 223 training and 49 testing instances for each word tagged with an OntoNote sense tag (Hovy et al., 2006). OntoNote sense tags are groupings of WordNet senses that are more coarse-grained than traditional WN entries, and which have achieved on average 90% inter-annotator agreement. The number of senses for a word ranged from 1 to 13 with an average of 3.6.

I used substitute sets optimized for each word as described in Section 3. Then a single best sense for each test instance was selected based on the model given in Section 2. The system achieved 85.05% accuracy, which is 6.39% above the baseline of picking the most frequent sense and 3.65% below the top score.

These numbers seem higher than previous Senseval lexical sample tasks. The best system in Senseval-3 (Mihalcea et al., 2004; Grozea, 2004) achieved 72.9% fine grained, 79.3% coarse grained accuracy. Many factors may have played a role but the most important one is probably the sense inventory. The nouns and verbs in Senseval-3 had 6.1 fine grained and 4.5 coarse grained senses on average.

The leave-one-out cross-validation result of my system on the training set was 83.21% with the unfiltered union of Roget and WordNet substitutes, and 90.69% with the optimized subset. Clearly there is some over-fitting in the substitute optimization process which needs to be improved.

Table 2 details the performance on individual words. The accuracy is 88.67% on the nouns and 81.02% on the verbs. One can clearly see the relation of the performance with the number of senses (decreasing) and the frequency of the first sense (increasing). Interestingly no clear relation exists between the training set size and the accuracy above the baseline. Figure 1 plots the relationship between training set size vs. the accuracy gain above the most frequent sense baseline. This could indicate that the system peaks at a low training set size and generalizes well because of the language model. However, it should be noted that each point in the plot represents a different word, not experiments with the same word at different training set sizes. Thus the difficulty of each word may be the overriding factor in determining performance. A more detailed study similar to (Yarowsky and Florian, 2002) is needed to explore the relationship in more detail.

6 WSD of Prepositions

The *Word Sense Disambiguation of Prepositions Task* (Litkowski and Hargraves, 2007), provided training and test data for sense disambiguation of 34 prepositions. On average there were 486 training and 234 test instances for each preposition. The number of senses for a word ranged from 1 to 20 with an average of 7.4.

The system described in Sections 2 and 3 were applied to this task as well. WordNet does not have information about prepositions, so most of the candidate substitutes were obtained from Roget and The Preposition Project (Litkowski, 2005). After optimizing the substitute sets the system achieved 54.7% accuracy which is 15.1% above the most frequent sense baseline and 14.6% below the top result. Unfortunately there were only three teams that participated in this task. The detailed breakdown of the results can be seen in the second part of Table 2.

The loocv result on the training data with the initial unfiltered set of substitutes was 51.70%. Optimizations described in Section 3 increased this to 59.71%. This increase is comparable to the one in the lexical substitution task. The final result of 54.7% shows signs of overfitting in the substitute selection process.

The average gain above the baseline for prepositions (39.6% to 54.7%) is significantly higher than the English lexical sample task (78.7% to 85.1%). However the preposition numbers are generally lower compared to the nouns and verbs because they are more ambiguous: the number of senses is higher and the first sense frequency is lower.

Good quality substitutes are difficult to find for prepositions. Unlike common nouns and verbs, common prepositions play unique roles in language and are difficult to replace. Open class words have synonyms, hypernyms, antonyms etc. that provide good substitutes: it is easy to come up with "I ate halibut" when you see "I ate fish". It is not as easy to replace "of" in the phrase "the president of the company". Even when there is a good substitute, e.g. "over" vs. "under", the two prepositions usually share the exact same ambiguities: they can both express a physical direction or a quantity comparison. Therefore the substitution based model presented in this work may not be a good match for preposition disambiguation.

7 Contributions and Future Work

A WSD method employing a statistical language model was introduced. The language model is used to evaluate the likelihood of possible substitutes for the target word in a given context. Each context is represented with its preferences for possible substitutes, thus contexts with no surface features in common can nevertheless be related to each other.

The set of substitutes used for a word had a large effect on the performance of the resulting system. A substitute selection procedure that uses the language model itself rather than external lexical resources may work better.

I hypothesize that the model would be advantageous on tasks like "all words" WSD, where data sparseness is paramount, because it is able to link contexts with no surface features in common. It can be used in an unsupervised manner where the substitutes and their associated senses can be obtained from a lexical resource. Work along these lines was not completed due to time limitations.

Finally, there are two failure modes for the algorithm: either there are no good substitutes that differentiate the various senses (as I suspect is the case for some prepositions), or the language model does not yield accurate preferences among the substitutes that correspond to our intuition. In the first case we have to fall back on other methods, as the substitutes obviously are of limited value. The correspondence between the language model and our intuition requires further study.

Appendix: Web1T Language Model

The Web 1T 5-gram dataset (Brants and Franz, 2006) that was used to build a language model for this work consists of the counts of word sequences up to length 5 in a 10^{12} word corpus derived from the Web. The data consists of mostly English words that have been tokenized and sentence tagged. Tokens that appear less than 200 times and ngrams that appear less than 40 times have been filtered out.

I used a smoothing method loosely based on the *one-count* method given in (Chen and Goodman, 1996). Because ngrams with low counts are not included in the data I used ngrams with missing counts instead of ngrams with one counts. The missing count is defined as:

$$m(w_{i-n+1}^{i-1}) = c(w_{i-n+1}^{i-1}) - \sum_{w_i} c(w_{i-n+1}^{i})$$

where w_{i-n+1}^{i} indicates the n-word sequence ending with w_i, and $c(w_{i-n+1}^{i})$ is the count of this sequence. The corresponding smoothing formula is:

$$P(w_i|w_{i-n+1}^{i-1}) = \frac{c(w_{i-n+1}^{i}) + (1+\alpha_n)m(w_{i-n+1}^{i-1})P(w_i|w_{i-n+2}^{i-1})}{c(w_{i-n+1}^{i-1}) + \alpha_n m(w_{i-n+1}^{i-1})}$$

The parameters $\alpha_n > 0$ for $n = 2 \dots 5$ was optimized on the Brown corpus to yield a cross entropy of 8.06 bits per token. The optimized parameters are given below:

$$\alpha_2 = 6.71, \ \alpha_3 = 5.94, \ \alpha_4 = 6.55, \ \alpha_5 = 5.71$$

References

Thorsten Brants and Alex Franz. 2006. Web 1T 5-gram version 1. Linguistic Data Consortium, Philadelphia. LDC2006T13.

Stanley F. Chen and Joshua Goodman. 1996. An empirical study of smoothing techniques for language modeling. In *Proceedings of the 34th Annual Meeting of the ACL.*

Christiane Fellbaum, editor. 1998. *Wordnet: An Electronic Lexical Database*. MIT Press.

Cristian Grozea. 2004. Finding optimal parameter settings for high performance word sense disambiguation. In *Proceedings of Senseval-3: The Third International Workshop on the Evaluation of Systems for the Semantic Analysis of Text.*

Eduard H. Hovy, M. Marcus, M. Palmer, S. Pradhan, L. Ramshaw, and R. Weischedel. 2006. Ontonotes: The 90% solution. In *Proceedings of the Human Language Technology / North American Association of Computational Linguistics conference (HLT-NAACL 2006)*, New York, NY. Short paper.

Claudia Leacock, Martin Chodorow, and George A. Miller. 1998. Using corpus statistics and wordnet relations for sense identifi cation. *Computational Linguistics*, 24(1):147–166, March.

Ken Litkowski and Orin Hargraves. 2007. SemEval-2007 Task 06: Word sense disambiguation of prepositions. In *SemEval-2007: 4th International Workshop on Semantic Evaluations.*

K. C. Litkowski. 2005. The preposition project. In *Proceedings of the Second ACL-SIGSEM Workshop on The Linguistic Dimensions of Prepositions and their Use in Computational Linguistics Formalisms and Applications*, Colchester, England, April. University of Essex.

David Martinez, Eneko Agirre, and Xinglong Wang. 2006. Word relatives in context for word sense disambiguation. In *Proceedings of the 2006 Australasian Language Technology Workshop (ALTW 2006)*, pages 42–50.

Diana McCarthy and Roberto Navigli. 2007. Semeval-2007 Task 10: English lexical substitution task. In *SemEval-2007: 4th International Workshop on Semantic Evaluations.*

Rada Mihalcea, Timothy Chklovski, and Adam Kilgarriff. 2004. The Senseval-3 English lexical sample task. In *Proceedings of Senseval-3: The Third International Workshop on the Evaluation of Systems for the Semantic Analysis of Text.*

Rada Mihalcea. 2002. Bootstrapping large sense tagged corpora. In *Proceedings of the 3rd International Conference on Languages Resources and Evaluations LREC 2002*, Las Palmas, Spain, May.

Martha Palmer, Sameer Pradhan, and Edward Loper. 2007. SemEval-2007 Task 17: English lexical sample, English SRL and English all-words tasks. In *SemEval-2007: 4th International Workshop on Semantic Evaluations.*

Claude Elwood Shannon. 1951. Prediction and entropy of printed English. *The Bell System Technical Journal*, 30:50–64.

Thesaurus.com. 2007. *Roget's New Millennium™ Thesaurus, First Edition (v 1.3.1).* Lexico Publishing Group, LLC. http://thesaurus.reference.com.

David Yarowsky and Radu Florian. 2002. Evaluating sense disambiguation across diverse parameter spaces. *Natural Language Engineering*, 8(4):293–310.

Deniz Yuret. 2004. Some experiments with a Naive Bayes WSD system. In *ACL 2004 Senseval-3 Workshop*, Barcelona, Spain, July.

English Lexical Sample WSD

lexelt	trn/tst	s	mfs	acc	lexelt	trn/tst	s	mfs	acc
affect.v	45/19	1	1.000	1.000	allow.v	108/35	2	0.971	0.971
announce.v	88/20	2	1.000	1.000	approve.v	53/12	2	0.917	0.917
area.n	326/37	3	0.703	0.838	ask.v	348/58	6	0.517	0.759
attempt.v	40/10	1	1.000	1.000	authority.n	90/21	4	0.238	0.714
avoid.v	55/16	1	1.000	1.000	base.n	92/20	5	0.100	0.650
begin.v	114/48	4	0.562	0.792	believe.v	202/55	2	0.782	0.836
bill.n	404/102	3	0.755	0.902	build.v	119/46	3	0.739	0.543
buy.v	164/46	5	0.761	0.783	capital.n	278/57	4	0.965	0.982
care.v	69/7	3	0.286	1.000	carrier.n	111/21	7	0.714	0.667
cause.v	73/47	1	1.000	1.000	chance.n	91/15	4	0.400	0.667
claim.v	54/15	3	0.800	0.800	come.v	186/43	10	0.233	0.372
complain.v	32/14	2	0.857	0.857	complete.v	42/16	2	0.938	0.938
condition.n	132/34	2	0.765	0.765	contribute.v	35/18	2	0.500	0.500
defense.n	120/21	7	0.286	0.476	describe.v	57/19	3	1.000	1.000
development.n	180/29	3	0.621	0.759	disclose.v	55/14	1	0.929	0.929
do.v	207/61	4	0.902	0.934	drug.n	205/46	2	0.870	0.935
effect.n	178/30	3	0.767	0.800	end.v	135/21	4	0.524	0.619
enjoy.v	56/14	2	0.571	0.643	estimate.v	74/16	1	1.000	1.000
examine.v	26/3	3	1.000	1.000	exchange.n	363/61	5	0.738	0.902
exist.v	52/22	2	1.000	1.000	explain.v	85/18	2	0.889	0.944
express.v	47/10	1	1.000	1.000	feel.v	347/51	3	0.686	0.765
find.v	174/28	5	0.821	0.821	fix.v	32/2	5	0.500	0.500
future.n	350/146	3	0.863	0.829	go.v	244/61	12	0.459	0.426
grant.v	19/5	2	0.800	0.400	hold.v	129/24	8	0.375	0.542
hope.v	103/33	1	1.000	1.000	hour.n	187/48	4	0.896	0.771
improve.v	31/16	1	1.000	1.000	job.n	188/39	3	0.821	0.795
join.v	68/18	4	0.389	0.556	keep.v	260/80	7	0.562	0.562
kill.v	111/16	4	0.875	0.875	lead.v	165/39	6	0.385	0.513
maintain.v	61/10	2	0.900	0.800	management.n	284/45	2	0.711	0.978
move.n	270/47	4	0.979	0.979	need.v	195/56	2	0.714	0.857
negotiate.v	25/9	1	1.000	1.000	network.n	152/55	3	0.909	0.836
occur.v	47/22	2	0.864	0.864	order.n	346/57	7	0.912	0.930
part.n	481/71	4	0.662	0.901	people.n	754/115	4	0.904	0.948
plant.n	347/64	2	0.984	0.984	point.n	469/150	9	0.813	0.920
policy.n	331/39	2	0.974	0.949	position.n	268/45	7	0.467	0.556
power.n	251/47	3	0.277	0.766	prepare.v	54/18	2	0.778	0.833
president.n	879/177	3	0.729	0.927	produce.v	115/44	2	0.750	0.750
promise.v	50/8	2	0.750	0.750	propose.v	34/14	2	0.857	1.000
prove.v	49/22	3	0.318	0.818	purchase.v	35/15	1	1.000	1.000
raise.v	147/34	7	0.147	0.441	rate.n	1009/145	2	0.862	0.917
recall.v	49/15	3	0.867	0.933	receive.v	136/48	2	0.958	0.958
regard.v	40/14	3	0.714	0.643	remember.v	121/13	2	1.000	1.000
remove.v	47/17	1	1.000	1.000	replace.v	46/15	2	1.000	1.000
report.v	128/35	3	0.914	0.914	rush.v	28/7	2	1.000	1.000
say.v	2161/541	5	0.987	0.987	see.v	158/54	6	0.444	0.574
set.v	174/42	9	0.286	0.500	share.n	2536/525	2	0.971	0.973
source.n	152/35	5	0.371	0.829	space.n	67/14	5	0.786	0.929
start.v	214/38	6	0.447	0.447	state.n	617/72	3	0.792	0.819
system.n	450/70	5	0.486	0.586	turn.v	340/62	13	0.387	0.516
value.n	335/59	3	0.983	0.983	work.v	230/43	7	0.558	0.721
AVG	222.8/48.5	3.6	0.787	0.851					

Preposition WSD

lexelt	trn/tst	s	mfs	acc	lexelt	trn/tst	s	mfs	acc
about.p	710/364	6	0.885	0.934	above.p	48/23	5	0.609	0.522
across.p	319/151	2	0.960	0.960	after.p	103/53	6	0.434	0.585
against.p	195/92	6	0.435	0.793	along.p	364/173	3	0.954	0.954
among.p	100/50	3	0.300	0.680	around.p	334/155	6	0.452	0.535
as.p	173/84	1	1.000	1.000	at.p	715/367	12	0.425	0.662
before.p	47/20	3	0.450	0.850	behind.p	138/68	4	0.662	0.676
beneath.p	57/28	3	0.571	0.679	beside.p	62/29	1	1.000	1.000
between.p	211/102	7	0.422	0.765	by.p	509/248	10	0.371	0.556
down.p	332/153	3	0.438	0.647	during.p	81/39	2	0.385	0.564
for.p	950/478	13	0.238	0.395	from.p	1204/578	16	0.279	0.415
in.p	1391/688	13	0.362	0.436	inside.p	67/38	4	0.526	0.579
into.p	604/297	8	0.451	0.539	like.p	266/125	7	0.768	0.808
of.p	3000/1478	17	0.205	0.374	off.p	161/76	4	0.763	0.776
on.p	872/441	20	0.206	0.469	onto.p	117/58	3	0.879	0.879
over.p	200/98	12	0.327	0.510	round.p	181/82	7	0.378	0.512
through.p	440/208	15	0.495	0.538	to.p	1182/572	10	0.322	0.579
towards.p	214/102	4	0.873	0.873	with.p	1187/578	15	0.249	0.455
AVG	486.3/238.1	7.4	0.397	0.547					

Table 2: English Lexical Sample and Preposition WSD Results: lexelt is the lexical item, trn/tst is the number of training and testing instances, s is the number of senses in the training set, mfs is the most frequent sense baseline, and acc is the final accuracy.

LCC-SRN: LCC's SRN System for SemEval 2007 Task 4

Adriana Badulescu
Language Computer Corporation
1701 N Collins Blvd #2000
Richardson, TX, 75080
adriana@languagecomputer.com

Munirathnam Srikanth
Language Computer Corporation
1701 N Collins Blvd #2000
Richardson, TX, 75080
srikanth@languagecomputer.com

Abstract

This document provides a description of the Language Computer Corporation (LCC) SRN System that participated in the SemEval 2007 Semantic Relation between Nominals task. The system combines the outputs of different binary and multi-class classifiers build using machine learning algorithms like Decision Trees, Semantic Scattering, Iterative Semantic Specialization, and Support Vector Machines.

1 Introduction

The Semantic Relations between Nominals task from SemEval 2007 focuses on identifying the semantic relations that hold between two arguments manually annotated with word senses (Girju et al, 2007).

The previous work in identifying semantic relations between nominals focuses on finding one or more relations in text for specific syntactic patterns or constructions (like genitives and noun compounds) using semi-automated and automated systems. An overview of some of these methods can be found in (Badulescu, 2004).

The LCC SRN system, developed during the SRN training period, was for us, the beginning of a different approach to semantic relations detection: detecting semantic relations in text without using a syntactic pattern. Our existing work on semantic relation detection was on detecting semantic relations in text (one or more at a time) at different levels in the sentence using different syntactic patterns like genitives, noun compounds, verb-arguments, etc.

For SRN, we built a new system that combines the output of the pattern dependent classifiers with the new pattern-independent classifiers for better results.

The remainder of this paper is organized as follows: Section 2 describes our system, Section 3 details the experimental results, and Section 4 summarizes the conclusions.

2 System description

The system consists of two types of classifiers: classifiers that do not use the syntactic parsed tree and that were built specifically for the SemEval 2007 Task 4(SRN) and classifiers that use specific syntactic pattern to determine the semantic relations and there were previously developed at LCC and then adapted to the SRN task (SRNPAT).

The classifiers for each type were built from annotated examples using supervised **machine learning algorithms** like Decision Trees (***DT***)[1], Support Vector Machines (***SVM***)[2], Semantic Scattering (***SS***) (Moldovan and Badulescu, 2005) , Iterative Semantic Specialization (***ISS***) (Girju, Badulescu, and Moldovan, 2006), Naïve Bayes (***NB***)[3] and Maximum Entropy (***ME***)[4].

The outputs of different classifiers (built using different types of machine learning algorithms were **combined** and ranked using predefined rules.

Figure 1 shows the **architecture** of our SRN system.

---

[1] C5.0., http://www.rulequest.com/see5-info.html
[2] LIBSVM, www.csie.ntu.edu.tw/~cjlin/libsvm/
[3] jBNC, http://jbnc.sourceforge.net
[4] http://homepages.inf.ed.ac.uk/s0450736/maxent_toolkit.html

Proceedings of the 4th International Workshop on Semantic Evaluations (SemEval-2007), pages 215–218,
Prague, June 2007.

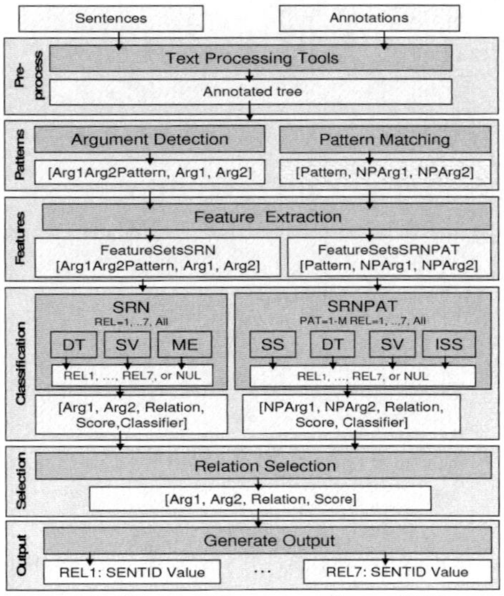

Figure 1. The architecture of our SRN system.

2.1 Text Preprocessing

The sentences were processed using an in-house text tokenizer, Brill's part-of-speech tagger, an in-house WordNet–based concept detector, an in-house Named Entity Recognizer, and an in-house syntactic parser.

Then, the syntactic and semantic information obtained using these tools (concepts, part of speech, named entities, etc) or obtained from the sensekeys for the arguments as provided by the Task 4 organizers (e.g. word senses, lemmas, etc) were mapped into the syntactic trees. If an argument corresponds to more than one tree node, the annotation was mapped to the phrase containing the two nodes.

2.2 Learning and Classification Methods

The core of our system is the learning and classification module.

We used two types of methods: pattern-dependent that uses the syntactic parsed trees for extracting and assigning a label to the arguments and pattern-independent that creates classifiers form all the examples disregarding the pattern in the tree.

2.2.1 Pattern-independent Methods (SRN)

Considering the limited number of examples for each pattern, we developed pattern-independent methods for classifying the semantic relations using the provided argument annotations and the context from the sentence.

We built two types of **classifiers**: **binary** that focuses on building a classifier for a specific relation (SRNREL) and **multi-class** methods that build classifiers for all the SRN relations (SRN). Table 1 presents the accuracy of the classifiers built using different machine learning algorithms.

Relation	DT	SVM	ME
1	52.10	46.15	46.67
2	41.40	30.76	60.00
3	61.70	51.61	63.33
4	59.30	52.17	53.33
5	58.60	39.99	50.00
6	71.70	24.99	73.33
7	50.00	57.13	43.33
Avg	56.40	43.26	55.71

Table 1. The accuracy of the SRNREL classifiers built using different machine learning algorithms.

The classifiers were built using lexical, semantic, and syntactic features of the arguments, their phrases, their clauses, their common phrase/clause, and their modifier or head phrase. The system uses WordNet, an in-house Named Entity Recognizer, and an in-house Syntactic Parser for determining the values of some of these features. Table 2 presents the list of features used by the SRN classifiers.

Argument's lexical, semantic, and syntactic features: the surface form, the label (POS tag or phrase label), the named entity (human, group, location, etc), the WordNet hierarchy (entity, group, abstraction, etc), the Semantic Scattering class (e.g. object, substance, etc), the grammatical role (subject or object of the clause), the syntactic parser structure, the POS Pattern (the sequence of POS of the words from the argument), and the phrase pattern (the sequence of labels of the phrases, words from the argument);
Argument's phrase features: surface form, label, grammatical role, named entity, POS pattern, Phrase patterns;
Argument's Modifier/Head features: the label, surface forms, NE, and WN Hierarchy for the first modifier, post modifier, pre-modifier, and head;
Arguments' common tree node features: label, named entity, grammatical role, POS pattern, and phrase pattern, the tree path between arguments, and their order in tree;
Arguments' clause: label, verb, voice, POS pattern, phrase pattern.

Table 2. The list of features used for the SRN classifiers.

2.2.2 Pattern-dependent Methods (SRNPAT)

The second type of methods we used, were for particular patterns frequent in the training corpus. Table 3 shows the list of most frequent **patterns** in the training corpus. For having general pattern and covering the arguments that correspond to more than one node in a tree, we considered as argument the noun phrase that contains the nominal instead of the node for the nominal.

Pattern name	Example
Noun compounds: NN_1 NN_2	If you are cleaning a *<e1>coffee</e1> <e2>maker</e2>* that hasn't been cleaned regularl271076ad y, repeat this step again with a fresh vinegar and water mixture.
Of-genitives: NP_1 of NP_2	The incoming *<e1>chairman</e1>* of *the <e2>committee</e2>* is promising an array of oversight investigations that could provoke sharp disagreement with Republicans and the White House.
S-genitives: NP_1 ‘s NP_2	This is the *<e1>government</e1>*'s *<e2>effort</e2>* to encourage more employers to open up childcare centres at the respective ministries and government departments.
Prepositional constructions: NP_1 IN NP_2	I believe that unless we take this issue seriously, the red squirrel is facing eventual *<e1>extinction</e1>* from *the <e2>woods</e2> of Scotland.*
Verbal constructions: NP_1 VB NP_2	On both of my systems, *the <e1>reboot</e1>* produced *the ominous <e2>message</e2> 'Missing operating system'.*
Verbal prepositional constructions: NP_1 VB IN NP_2	Manila radio station DZMM quoted survivors as saying that *the <e1>fire</e1>* started with *an <e2>explosion</e2>* in the cargo hold and spread across the ship within minutes.

Table 3. The most frequent patterns found in the training corpus.

For the pattern-dependent methods we adapted some of our existing binary and multi-class **classifiers** to work with the SRN relations.

For the SRN system we used only one **binary** classifier built for the Part-Whole relation (relation 6) using the ISS learning algorithm and trained/tested on the examples used in (Girju, Badulescu, and Moldovan, 2006) and different **multi-class** classifiers for the first 4 patterns from Table 3 built using DT, SVM, SS, and NB learning algorithms trained on a corpus annotated with 40 semantic relations (extracted from Wall Street Journal articles from the TreeBank collection and LATimes articles from TREC 9 collection) that includes the 7 SRN relations (or equivalents). (Badulescu, 2004) gives more details on this list of relations (definitions, examples, distribution on corpus, etc). Table 4 shows the **accuracy** of these classifiers on other WSJ and LAT articles for the 40 LCC relations and respectively Part-Whole relation for the most frequent patterns from the SRN corpus (Table 3).

Pattern cluster	SS	DT	NB	SVM	ISS
Noun compounds	52.54	47.8	53.45	74.79	73.59
S-genitives	62.27	56.2	58.27	72.66	87.26
Of-genitives	67.55	53.1	54.63	72	87.26
Prepositional constructions	43.48	43.3	41.92	64.52	75.97

Table 4. The accuracy of the SRNPAT classifiers for the list of 40 LCC relations and the Part-Whole Relation.

2.3 Relation Selection

Any of the SRN or SRNPAT classifiers can return a relation for a pair of arguments. The best relation is selected by weighting them using the following predefined rules:

- The relations returned by the SRN classifiers weight more than the ones returned by SRNPAT classifiers because they were trained on the task annotated examples
- The relations returned by the binary classifiers weight more than the ones returned by multi-class classifiers because they focus on one relation and therefore are more precise.

3 Experimental Results

3.1 Experiments on Testing

During the competition we performed several experiments to assess the correct combination of classifiers that leads to the best results.

The organizer provided 140 examples for each of the 7 relations. For testing the classifiers we trained the system on the first 110 examples and tested it on the last 30 of them.

We performed different sets of experiments.

- **Experiments with one type of classifiers**. These experiments showed that ME has a best performance (55.1) 10.05 more than DT and 8.05 more than SV. ME also got the highest score for Cause-Effect, while DT obtained the best score for Product-Producer.
- **Experiments with multiple classifiers**. These experiments showed that DT+SV+SS+ISS has the best score (66.72) followed by DT+SS+ISS with 55.66. Also by adding the SS and ISS classifiers the DT score increased with 10.51, the SV score with 5.81 and the DT+SV with 20.57.

▪ **Experiments with types of methods**. These experiments showed that the SRN methods (with a score 0.44) are better than the SRNPAT methods (with a score of 0.41) with 0.03 which was expected since SRN were trained on provided examples.

Table 5 shows the results of our SRN system when using specific classifiers or a combination of classifiers. The time did not permit us to do any experiments with the ME and NB classifiers.

Classifier Combination	Average F-measure
DT	45.05
SV	47.05
ME	55.10
DT+SV	46.15
DT+SS+ISS	*55.66*
SV+SS+ISS	52.96
DT+SV+SS+ISS	66.72
SRN	44.31
SRNPAT	41.15

Table 5. The results of some of our experiments with the different classifiers on the testing corpus.

We submitted the DT+SS+ISS version because of its closeness to the normal distribution rather than DT+SV+SS+ISS that had a better f-measure but it was closer to All-True. The evaluation results showed that the testing examples we used were representative and the DT+SV+SS+ISS produce better results.

3.2 Results

Table 6 shows the results obtained by our system on the evaluation corpus for the B4 case (using WordNet but not the query and all the training examples.

Relation	Precision	Recall	F-measure	Accuracy
1	50.8	73.2	60.0	50.0
2	54.5	31.6	40.0	53.8
3	66.7	100.0	80.0	66.7
4	80.0	22.2	34.8	63.0
5	42.2	65.5	51.4	42.3
6	39.6	80.8	53.2	48.6
7	57.1	31.6	40.7	51.4
Avg	55.9	57.8	51.4	53.7

Table 6. The results of our system on the evaluation corpus.

Table 7 shows a comparison of our results with the following baseline systems: *All-True*, a system that always returns true, *Majority*, a system that always returns the majority value from the training, and *Prob-Match*, a system that randomly generate the value. We have obtained a larger precision and accuracy than the All-True and the Prob-Match systems. However, we obtained a lower recall and therefore an F-measure.

System	Precision	Recall	F-measure	Accuracy
All-True	48.5	100.0	64.8	48.5
Majority	81.3	42.9	30.8	57.0
Prob-Match	48.5	48.5	48.5	51.7
LCC-SRN	55.9	57.8	51.4	53.7

Table 7. Comparison with the baselines.

3.3 Discussions

The results are promising. However, there is still room for improvement. The system was developed in a limited time, and therefore it could have been benefited from more features, feature selection, more experiments, a more complex relation selection scheme (using learning), more patterns, and more types of machine learning algorithms (especially unsupervised ones).

4 Conclusion

We presented a system for classifying the semantic relations between nominals that combines the results of different methods (pattern-dependent or pattern-independent) and machine learning algorithms (decision tree, support vector machines, semantic scattering, maximum entropy, naïve bayes, etc). The classifiers use lexical, semantic, and syntactic features and external resources like WordNet and an in-house Named Entity dictionary.

References

Adriana Badulescu. 2004. Classification of Semantic Relations between Nouns. PhD Dissertation. University of Texas at Dallas.

Dan Moldovan and Adriana Badulescu. 2005. A Semantic Scattering Model for the Automatic Interpretation of Genitives. In *Proceedings of HLT/EMNLP 2005*.

Roxana Girju, Adriana Badulescu, and Dan Moldovan. 2006. Automatic Discovery of Part-Whole Relations. *Computation Linguistics*, 32:1.

Roxana Girju et al. 2007. Classification of Semantic Relations between Nominals: Description of Task 4 in SemEval-1, In *Proceedings of ACL-2007, SemEval-1 Workshop*.

LCC-TE: A Hybrid Approach to Temporal Relation Identification in News Text

Congmin Min
Language Computer Corporation
1701 N. Collins Blvd. Suite 2000
Richardson, TX 75080
cmin@languagecomputer.com

Munirathnam Srikanth
Language Computer Corporation
1701 N. Collins Blvd, Suite 2000
Richardson, TX 75080
Srikanth.munirathnam
@languagecomputer.com

Abraham Fowler
Language Computer Corporation
1701 N. Collins Blvd, Suite 2000
Richardson, TX 75080
abraham@languagecomputer.com

Abstract

This paper explores a hybrid approach to temporal information extraction within the TimeML framework. Particularly, we focus on our initial efforts to apply machine learning techniques to identify temporal relations as defined in a constrained manner by the TempEval-2007 task. We explored several machine learning models and human rules to infer temporal relations based on the features available in TimeBank, as well as a number of other features extracted by our in-house tools. We participated in all three sub-tasks of the TempEval task in SemEval-2007 workshop and the evaluation shows that we achieved comparable results in Task A & B and competitive results in Task C.

1 Introduction

There has been a growing interest in temporal information extraction in recent years, as more and more operational NLP systems demands dealing with time-related issues in natural languages. In this paper, we report on an end-to-end system that is capable of automating identification of temporal referring expressions, events and temporal relations in text by leveraging various NLP tools and linguistic resources at LCC.

It has to be noted that the system we report here is not only intended for TempEval 2007 evaluation, but will also be used as a NLP tool for our other applications (e.g. temporal Question Answering). That is why we experimented to use our own temporal and event extraction capabilities in this work, although time and event tags have already been provided in the testing/training data. Another reason we use our own temporal tagging is that our temporal tagger extracts more information than that available in the training/testing data. For instance, temporal signals are removed from the data that the task organizers provide, but our temporal tagger detects that, as part of the tagging procedure. The following is an example for the tagged expression "on this coming Sunday".

```
<ArgStructure id="65" type="timex">
  <argRef type="determiner" tokStr="this"/>
  <argRef type="directionIndicator" tokStr="coming"/>
  <argRef type="focus" tokStr="Sunday"/>
  <argRef type="prepSignal" tokStr="on"/>
  <argRef type="head" tokStr="this coming Sunday"/>
  <argRef type="root" tokStr="on this coming Sunday"/>
  <argValue type="focusType" value="weekOfDay"/>
  <argValue type="subType" value="Fuzzy"/>
  <argValue type="type" value="Date"/>
</ArgStructure>
```

Our data structure allows us to easily access and manipulate any part of the tagged chunk of text, which leaves the interpretation of whether the temporal signal *on* in the example is part of the temporal expression to users of temporal tagger. Taking as input this data structure, the normalization, including relative date resolution, is a straightforward process, provided that the reference time can be computed from the context.

For temporal relation identification, by leveraging the capabilities of our temporal tagger, event tagger and several other in-house NLP tools, we derive a rich set of syntactic and semantic features for use by machine learning. We also explored the possibility of combining the rule-based approach with machine learning in an integrated manner so that our system can take advantage of these two approaches for temporal relation identification.

2 System Architecture

The overall architecture of our end-to-end system is illustrated in Figure 1 (Page 2).

Proceedings of the 4th International Workshop on Semantic Evaluations (SemEval-2007), pages 219–222,
Prague, June 2007.

In addition to several common NLP tools, e.g. Named Entity Recognizer, we use syntactic and semantic parsers to identify syntactic and semantic roles (e.g. AGENT or SUBJECT) of event terms and a context detector to detect linguistic contexts in a discourse. We use such information as extended features for machine learning. The Temporal Tagger tags and normalizes temporal expressions conforming to the TimeML guideline. The Temporal Merger compares our own temporal and event tagging with those supplied in training/testing data. If there is any inconsistency, it will replace the former with the latter, which guarantees that our temporal and event tagging are the same as those in training/testing data. Feature Extractor extracts and composes features from documents processed by the NLP tools. Machine Learner and Human Rule Predictor take as input the feature vector for each instance to predict temporal relation. The Human Rule Predictor is a rule interpreter that read hand-crafted rules from plain text file to match each event instance represented by a feature vector.

Note that in Figure 1, *Syntactic Parsing* is done by a probabilistic chart parser, which generates full parse tree for each sentence. *Syntactic Pattern Matching* is performed by a syntactic pattern matcher, which operates on parse trees produced by chart parser and used by Temporal Tagger to tag and normalize temporal expressions.

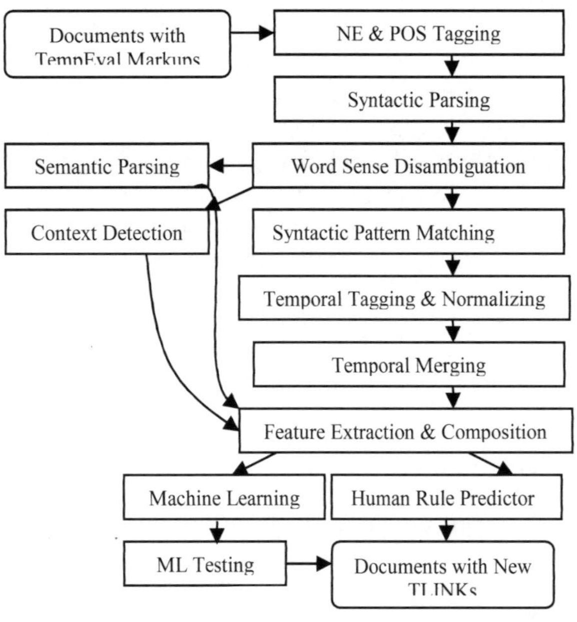

Figure 1. Overall System Architecture

3 Feature Engineering

While temporal tagging and normalization is rule-based in our system, temporal relation identification is a combination of machine learning and rule-based approaches. For machine learning, the feature set for the three tasks A, B and C we engineered consist of what we call 1) *first-class* features; 2) *derived* features; 3) *extended* features, and 4) *merged* features. The way we name the type of features is primarily for illustrating purpose.

3.1 First-class Features

The first-class features consist of:

- Event Class
- Event Stem
- Event and time strings
- Part of Speech of event terms
- Event Polarity
- Event Tense
- Event Aspect
- Type of temporal expression
- Value of temporal expression

The set of first-class features, which are directly obtained from the markups of training/testing data, are important, because most of them, including Event Class, Event Stem, POS, Tense and Type of Temporal Expression, have a great impact on performance of machine learning classifiers, compared with effects of other features.

3.2.2 Derived Features

From the first-class features, we derive and compute a number of other features:

- Tense and aspect shifts[1]
- Temporal Signal
- Whether an event is enclosed in quotes
- Whether an event has modals prior to it
- Temporal relation between the Document Creation Time and temporal expression in the target sentence.

The way we compute tense and aspect shifts is taking pair of contiguous events and assign a true/false value to each relation instance based on whether tense or shift change in this pair. Our experiments show that these two features didn't contribute to the overall score, probably because they are redundant with the Tense and Aspect features of each event term. Temporal Signal

[1] Initially used in (Mani, et. al. 2003)

represents temporal prepositions and they slightly contribute to the overall score of classifiers.

The last feature in this category is the Temporal Relation between the Document Creation Time and the Temporal Expression in the target sentence. The value of this feature could be "greater than", "less than", "equal", or "none". Experiments show that this is an important feature for Task A and B, because it contributes several points to the overall score. This value may be approximate for a number of reasons. For example, we can't directly compare a temporal expression of type Date with another expression of type Duration. However, even if we apply a simple algorithm to compute this relationship, it results in a noticeably positive effect on the performance of the classifier.

3.2.3 Extended Features

Features in the third category are extracted by our in-house tools, including:

- Whether an event term plays primary semantic or syntactic roles in a sentence
- Whether an event and a temporal expression are situated within the same linguistic context
- Whether two event terms co-refer in a discourse (This feature is only used for Task C)

Investigation reveals that different types of events defined in TimeML may or may not have specific semantic or syntactic roles (e.g. THM or OBJECT) in a particular context, therefore having an impact on their ways to convey temporal meanings. Experiments show that use of semantic and syntactic roles as binary features slightly increases performance.

The second feature in this category is *Context feature*. We use a context detection tool, which detects typical linguistic contexts, such as Reporting, Belief, Modal, etc. to decide whether an event and a temporal expression are within one context. For example[2],

- The company has **reported** ***declines*** *in operating profit in each of the past three years*, despite steady sales growth.

In this example, we identify a Reporting context with its signal *reported*. The temporal expression *each of the past three years* and the event *declines* are within the same context (the feature value would be *TRUE*). We intend this feature can help solve the problem of anchoring an event to its actual temporal expressions. In fact, we don't benefit from the use of this feature, probably because detecting those linguistic contexts is a problem in itself.

The third feature in this category is co-referential feature, which is only used for Task C. This feature indicates if two event terms within or outside one sentence are referring to the same event. Experiments show that this global feature produces a positive effect on the overall performance of the classifier.

3.2.4 Merged Features

The last type of feature we engineered is the *merged* feature. Due to time constraint, as well as the fact that the system for Task B produces better results than Task A and C, we only experimented merging the output of the system for Task B into the feature set of Task C and we achieved noticeable improvements because of adding this feature.

Most of the features introduced above are experimented in all three tasks A, B and C, except that the co-referential feature and the merged feature are only used in Task C. Also, in Task C since for each relation there are two events and possibly two temporal expressions, the number of features used is much more than that in Task A and B. The total number of features for Task C's training is 35 and 33 for testing.

3.1 Combination of Machine Learning and Human Rule

The design of our system allows both human rule-based and machine learning-based decision making. However, we have not decided exactly in what situations machine learning and human rule prediction should be used given a particular instance. The basic idea here is that we want to have the option to call either component on the fly in different situations so that we can take advantage of the two empirical approaches in an integrated way. We did some initial experiments on dynamically applying Human Rule Predictor and Machine Learner on Task B and we were able to obtain comparable results with or without using hand-crafted rules. As pointed out in (Li, et, al. 2006), Support Vector Machine, as well as other classifiers, makes most mistakes near the decision plane in feature space. We will investigate the

[2] This sentence is taken from the file *wsj_0027.tml* in TempEval 2007's training data.

possibility of applying human rule prediction to those relation instances where Machine Learning makes most mistakes.

3.2 Experiments and Results

Based on the features discussed in Section 3.3, we did a series of experiments for each task on four models: Naive-Bayes, Decision Tree (C5.0), Maximum Entropy and Support Vector Machine. Due to space constraint, we only report results from SVM model [3], which produces best performance in our case.

We here report two sets of performance numbers. The first set is based on our evaluation against a set of held-out data, 20 documents for each task, which were taken from the training data. The second set of performance numbers is based on evaluation against the final testing data provided by task organizers.

	strict			relaxed		
	P	R	F	P	R	F
Task A	0.68	0.68	0.68	0.69	0.69	0.69
Task B	0.80	0.80	0.80	0.82	0.82	0.82
Task C	0.63	0.63	0.63	0.67	0.67	0.67

Table 1. Performance figures evaluated against held-out data

	strict			relaxed		
	P	R	F	P	R	F
Task A	0.59	0.57	0.58	0.61	0.60	0.60
Task B	0.75	0.71	0.73	0.75	0.72	0.74
Task C	0.55	0.55	0.55	0.60	0.60	0.60

Table 2. Performance figures evaluated against testing data

Team	strict			relax		
	P	R	F	P	R	F
Ours	0.59	0.57	0.58	0.61	0.60	0.60
Average	0.59	0.54	0.56	0.62	0.57	0.59
Best	0.62	0.62	0.62	0.64	0.64	0.64

Table 3. Performance figures in Comparison for Task A

Team	strict			relax		
	P	R	F	P	R	F
Ours	0.75	0.71	0.73	0.76	0.72	0.74
Average	0.76	0.72	0.74	0.78	0.74	0.75
Best	0.80	0.80	0.80	0.84	0.81	0.81

Table 4. Performance figures in comparison for Task B

Team	strict			relax		
	P	R	F	P	R	F
Ours	0.55	0.55	0.55	0.60	0.60	0.60
Average	0.51	0.51	0.51	0.60	0.60	0.60
Best	0.55	0.55	0.55	0.66	0.66	0.66

Table 5. Performance figures in comparison for Task C

According to Table 1 and 2, it appears that there are significant differences between the TLINK patterns in the held-out data and the final testing data, since the performance of the classifier shows an apparent discrepancy in two cases.

Table 3, 4 and 5 show performance numbers of our system, the average and the best system in comparison. There are six teams in total participating in the TempEval 2007 evaluation this year.

4 Conclusion

We participated in the SemEval2007 workshop and achieved encouraging results by devoting our initial efforts in this area. In next step, we plan to seek ways to expand the training data, implement quality human rules by performing rigorous data analysis, and explore use of more features for machine learning through feature engineering.

References

B. Boguraev and R.K. Ando. 2005. TimeML-compliant Text Analysis for Temporal Reasoning. *Proceedings of IJCAI, UK.*

D. Ahn, S.F. Adafre and M.D. Rijke. 2005. Towards Task-based Temporal Extraction and Recognition. *Dagstuhl Seminar Proceedings 05151.*

Inderjeet Mani and George Wilson. 2000. Robust Temporal Processing of News. *Proceedings of ACL'2000.*

Inderjeet Mani, Barry Schiffman, and Jianping Zhang. 2003. Inferring Temporal Ordering of Events in News. *Proceedings of HLT-NAACL'03*, 55-57.

K. Hacioglu, Y. Chen and B. Douglas. 2005. Automatic Time Expression Labeling for English and Chinese Text, *Proceedings of CICLing-2005.*

L. Li, T. Mao, D. Huang and Y. Yang. 2006. Hybrid Models for Chinese Named Entity Recognition. *Proceedings of the Fifth SIGHAN Workshop on Chinese Language Processing.*

The TimeML Working Group. 2005. The TimeML 1.2 Specification. *http://www.timeml.org/site/publications/specs.html*

[3] We use the LIBSVM implementation of SVM, available at http://www.csie.ntu.edu.tw/cjlin/libsvm

LCC-WSD: System Description for English Coarse Grained All Words Task at SemEval 2007

Adrian Novischi, Munirathnam Srikanth and Andrew Bennett
Language Computer Corp.
Richardson, TX
{adrian,srikanth,abennet}@languagecomputer.com

Abstract

This document describes the Word Sense Disambiguation system used by Language Computer Corporation at English Coarse Grained All Word Task at SemEval 2007. The system is based on two supervised machine learning algorithms: Maximum Entropy and Support Vector Machines. These algorithms were trained on a corpus created from SemCor, Senseval 2 and 3 all words and lexical sample corpora and Open Mind Word Expert 1.0 corpus. We used topical, syntactic and semantic features. Some semantic features were created using WordNet glosses with semantic relations tagged manually and automatically as part of eXtended WordNet project. We also tried to create more training instances from the disambiguated WordNet glosses found in XWN project (XWN, 2003). For words for which we could not build a sense classifier, we used First Sense in WordNet as a back-off strategy in order to have coverage of 100%. The precision and recall of the overall system is 81.446% placing it in the top 5 systems.

1 Introduction

The performance of a Word Sense Disambiguation (WSD) system using a finite set of senses depends greatly on the definition of the word senses. Fine grained senses are hard to distinguish while coarse grained senses tend to be more clear. Word Sense Disambiguation is not a final goal, but it is an intermediary step used in other Natural Processing applications like detection of Semantic Relations, Information Retrieval or Machine Translation. Word Sense Disambiguation is not useful if it is not performed with high accuracy (Sanderson, 1994). A coarse grained set of sense gives the opportunity to make more precise sense distinction and to make a Word Sense Disambiguation system more useful to other tasks.

Our goal at SemEval 2007 was to measure the performance of known supervised machine learning algorithm using coarse grained senses. The idea of using supervised machine learning for WSD is not new and was used for example in (Ng and Lee, 1996). We made experiments with two supervised methods: Maximum Entropy (ME) and Support Vector Machines (SVM). These supervised algorithms were used with topical, syntactic and semantic features. We trained a classifier for each word using both supervised algorithms. New features were added in 3 incremental steps. After an initial set of experiments the algorithm performance was enhanced using a greedy feature selection algorithm similar to one in (Mihalcea, 2002). In order to increase the number of training instances, we tried to use the disambiguated WordNet glosses from XWN project (XWN, 2003). Combining other corpora with disambiguated glosses from XWN did not provide any improvement so we used XWN as a fall back strategy for 70 words that did not have any training examples in other corpora but XWN.

Section 2 describes the supervised methods used by our WSD system, the pre-processing module and the set of features. Section 3 presents the experiments we performed and their results. Section 4 draws the conclusions.

Proceedings of the 4th International Workshop on Semantic Evaluations (SemEval-2007), pages 223–226,
Prague, June 2007.

2 System Description

The system contains a preprocessing module used before computing the values of the features needed by the machine learning classifiers. The preprocessing module perform the following steps:

- Tokenization: using an in house text tokenizer
- Named Entity Recognition: using an in house system
- Part of Speech Tagging: normally we use the Brill tagger, but we took advantage of the part of speech tags given in the test file
- WordNet look-up to check if the word exists in WordNet and to get its lemma, possible part of speech for that lemma and if the word has a single sense or not. For SemEval English Coarse All Words task we took advantage by the lemma provided in the test file.
- Compound concept detection: using a classifier based on WordNet
- Syntactic Parsing: using an in-house implementation of Collin's parser (Glaysher and Moldovan, 2006)

The Maximum Entropy classifier is a C++ implementation found on web (Le, 2006). The classifier was adapted to accept symbolic features for classification tasks in Natural Language Processing.

For training SVM classifiers we used LIBSVM package (Chang and Lin, 2001). Each symbolic feature can have a single value from a finite set of values or can be assigned a subset of values from the set of all possible values. For each value we created a mapping between the feature value and a dimension in the N-dimensional classification space and we assigned the number 1.0 to that dimension if the feature had the corresponding value or 0.0 otherwise.

We first performed experiments with our existing set of features used at Senseval 3 All Words task. We call this set FS_1. Then we made three incremental changes to improve the performance.

The initial set contains the following features: current word form (CRT_WORD) and part of speech (CRT_POS), contextual features (CTX_WORD) in a window (-3,3) words, collocations in a window of (-3,3) words (COL_WORD), keywords (KEYWORDS) and bigrams (BIGRAMS) in a window of (-3,3) sentences, verb mode (VERB_MODE) which can take 4 values: ACTIVE, INFINITIVE, PAST, GERUND, verb voice (VERB_VOICE) which can take 2 values ACTIVE, PASSIVE, the parent of the current verb in the parse tree (CRT_PARENT) (ex: VP, NP), the first ancestor that is not VP in the parse tree (RAND_PARENT) (like S, NP, PP, SBAR) and a boolean flag indicating if the current verb belongs to the main clause or not (MAIN_CLAUSE).

We added new features to the initial set. We call this set FS_2.

- The lemmas of the contextual words in the window of (-3, 3) words around the target word (CTX_LEMMA).
- Collocations formed with the lemma of surrounding words in a window of (-3, 3) (COL_LEMMA)
- The parent of the contextual words in the parse tree in the window of (-3, 3) words around target word.
- Collocations formed with the parents of the surrounding words in the window (-3, 3) words around the target word (COL_PARENT).
- Occurrences in the current sentence of the words that are linked to the current word with a semantic relation of AGENT or THEME in WordNet 2.0 glosses (XWN_LEMMA).
  We used files from XWN project (XWN, 2003) containing WordNet 2.0 glosses that were sense disambiguated and tagged with semantic relations both manually and automatically. For each word to be disambiguated we created a signature consisting of the set of words that are linked with a semantic relation of THEME or AGENT in all WordNet glosses. For every word in this set we created a feature showing if that word appears in the current sentence containing the target word.

Then we added a new feature consisting of all the named entities in a window of (-5,5) sentences around the target word. We called this feature NAMED_ENTITIES. We created the feature set FS_3 by adding this new feature to FS_2.

In the end we applied a greedy feature selection algorithm to features in FS_3 inspired by (Mihalcea, 2002). Because feature selection was running very slow, the feature selection algorithm was run

CTX_WORD_1	CTX_WORD_-2	CTX_LEMMA_1	COL_POS_-2_0
CTX_POS_1	CTX_WORD_-1	CTX_LEMMA_2	COL_LEMMA_0_1
CTX_WORD_2	COL_PARENT_-3_-1	CTX_LEMMA_3	COL_PARENT_-2_2
CRT_WORD	COL_PARENT_-3_2	NAMED_ENTITIES	CTX_POS_3
CTX_WORD_-3	CTX_WORD_3	COL_PARENT_-1_1	COL_WORD_-1_1

Table 1: The feature set FS_4 obtained from the features most selected by the greedy selection algorithm applied to all the words in Senseval 2

only for words in Senseval 2 English lexical sample task and the top 20 features appearing the most often (at least 5 times) in the selected feature set for each word were used to create feature set FS_4 presented in table 1.

3 Experiments and results

For SemEval 2007 we performed several experiments: we tested ME and SVM classifiers on the 4 feature sets described in the previous section and then we tried to improve the performance using disambiguated glosses from XWN project. Each set of experiments together with the final submission is described in detail below.

3.1 Experiments with different feature sets

Initially we made experiments with the set of features used at Senseval 3 All Words task. For training the ME and SVM classifiers, we used a combined corpus made from SemCor, Senseval 3 All Words corpus, Senseval 3 Lexical Sample testing and training corpora and Senseval 2 Lexical sample training corpus. For testing we used Senseval 2 Lexical Sample corpus. We made 3 experiments for the first three feature sets FS_1, FS_2, FS_3. Both algorithms attempted to disambiguate all the words (coverage=100%) so the precision is equal with recall. The precision of each algorithm on each feature set is presented in table 2.

Algorithm	FS_1	FS_2	FS_3	FS_4
ME	76.03%	75.86%	76.03%	77.56%
SVM	73.30%	71.36%	71.46%	71.90%

Table 2: The precision of ME and SVM classifiers using 4 sets of features.

After the first 3 experiments we noticed that both ME and SVM classifiers had good results using the first set of features FS_1. This seemed odd since we expected an increase in performance with the additional features. This led us to the idea that not all the features are useful for all words. So we created a greedy feature selection algorithm based on the performance of the SVM classifier (Mihalcea, 2002). The feature selection algorithm starts with an empty set of features S, and iteratively adds one feature from the set of unused features U. Initially the set U contains all the features. The algorithm iterates as long as the overall performance increase. At each step the algorithm adds tentatively one feature from the set U to the existing feature list S and measures the performance of the classifier on a 10 fold cross validation on the training corpus. The feature providing the greatest increase in performance is finally added to S and removed from U.

The feature selection algorithm turned out to be very slow, so we could not use it to train all the words. Therefore we used it to train only the words from Senseval 2 Lexical Sample task and then we computed a global set of features by selecting the first 20 features that were selected the most (at least 5 times).

This list of features was named FS_4. Table 2 that SVM classifier with FS_4 did not get a better performance than FS_1 while ME surprisingly did get 1.53% increase in performance. Given the higher precision of ME classifier, it was selected for creating the submission file.

Corpus	Precision
SemCor	79.61%
XWN	57.21%
SemCor+XWN	79.44%

Table 3: The precision using SemCor and disambiguated glosses from XWN project

3.2 Experiments using disambiguated glosses from XWN project

The ME classifier works well for words with enough training examples. However we found many words for which the number of training examples was too small. We tried to increase the number of training examples using the disambiguated WordNet glosses from XWN project. Not all the senses in the disambiguated glosses were assigned manually and the text of the glosses is different than normal running text. However we were curious if we could improve the overall performance by adding more training examples. We made 3 experiments showed in table 3. For all three experiments we used Senseval 2 English All Words corpus for testing. On the first experiment we used SemCor for training, on the second we used disambiguated glosses from XWN project and on the third we used both. XWN did not bring an improvement to the overall precision, so we decided to use XWN as a fall back strategy only for 70 words that did not have training examples is other corpora.

3.3 Final Submission

For final submission we used trained ME models using feature set FS_4 for 852 words, representing 1715 instances using SemCor, Senseval 2 and 3 English All Words and Lexical Sample testing and training and OMWE 1.0. For 50 words representing 70 instances, we used disambiguated WordNet glosses from XWN project to train ME classifiers using feature set FS_4. For the rest of 484 words for which we could not find training examples we used the First Sense in WordNet strategy. The submitted answer had a 100% coverage and a 81.446% precision presented in table 4.

LCC-WSD	81.446%
Best submission	83.208%

Table 4: The LCC-WSD and the best submission at SemEval 2007 Coarse All Words Task

4 Conclusions

LCC-WSD team used two supervised approaches for performing experiments using coarse grained senses: Maximum Entropy and Support Vector Machines. We used 4 feature sets: the first one was the feature set used in Senseval 3 and next two representing incremental additions. The fourth feature set represents a global set of features obtained from the individual feature sets for each word resulted from the greedy feature selection algorithm used to improve the performance of SVM classifiers. In addition we used disambiguated WordNet glosses from XWN to measure the improvement made by adding additional training examples. The submitted answer has a coverage of 100% and a precision of 81.446%.

References

Chih-Chung Chang and Chih-Jen Lin, 2001. *LIBSVM: a library for support vector machines*. Software available at http://www.csie.ntu.edu.tw/ cjlin/libsvm.

Elliot Glaysher and Dan I. Moldovan. 2006. Speeding up full syntactic parsing by leveraging partial parsing decisions. In *Proceedings of the 21st International Conference on Computational Linguistics and 44th Annual Meeting of the Association for Computational Linguistics*, pages 295–300, Sydney, Australia. Association for Computational Linguistics.

Zhang Le, 2006. *Maximum Entropy Modeling Toolkit for Python and C++*. Software available at http://homepages.inf.ed.ac.uk/s0450736/maxent_toolkit.html.

Rada Mihalcea. 2002. Instance based learning with automatic feature selection applied to word sense disambiguation. In *Proceedings of the 19th International Conference on Computational Linguistics COLING 2002*, Taiwan.

Hwee Tou Ng and Hian Beng Lee. 1996. Integrating multiple knowledge sources to disambiguate word sense: an exemplar-based approach. In *Proceedings of the 34th annual meeting on Association for Computational Linguistics*, pages 40–47, Morristown, NJ, USA. Association for Computational Linguistics.

Mark Sanderson. 1994. Word sense disambiguation and information retrieval. In *Proceedings of SIGIR-94, 17th ACM International Conference on Research and Development in Information Retrieval*, pages 49–57, Dublin, IE.

XWN, 2003. *eXtended WordNet*. Software available at http://xwn.hlt.utdallas.edu.

LTH: Semantic Structure Extraction using Nonprojective Dependency Trees

Richard Johansson and **Pierre Nugues**
Department of Computer Science, Lund University, Sweden
{richard, pierre}@cs.lth.se

Abstract

We describe our contribution to the SemEval task on Frame-Semantic Structure Extraction. Unlike most previous systems described in literature, ours is based on dependency syntax. We also describe a fully automatic method to add words to the FrameNet lexical database, which gives an improvement in the recall of frame detection.

1 Introduction

The existence of links between grammatical relations and various forms of semantic interpretation has long been observed; grammatical relations play a crucial role in theories of *linking*, i.e. the realization of the semantic arguments of predicates as syntactic units (Manning, 1994; Mel'čuk, 1988). Grammatical relations may be covered by many definitions but it is probably easier to use them as an extension of dependency grammars, where relations take the form of arc labels. In addition, some linguistic phenomena such as *wh*-movement and discontinuous structures are conveniently described using dependency syntax by allowing *nonprojective* dependency arcs. It has also been claimed that dependency syntax is easier to understand and to teach to people without a linguistic background.

Despite these advantages, dependency syntax has relatively rarely been used in semantic structure extraction, with a few exceptions. Ahn et al. (2004) used a post-processing step to convert constituent trees into labeled dependency trees that were then used as input to a semantic role labeler. Pradhan et al. (2005) used a rule-based dependency parser, but the results were significantly worse than when using a constituent parser.

This paper describes a system for frame-semantic structure extraction that is based on a dependency parser. The next section presents the dependency grammar that we rely on. We then give the details on the frame detection and disambiguation, the frame element (FE) identification and classification, and dictionary extension, after which the results and conclusions are given.

2 Dependency Parsing with the Penn Treebank

The last few years have seen an increasing interest in dependency parsing (Buchholz and Marsi, 2006) with significant improvements of the state of the art, and dependency treebanks are now available for a wide range of languages. The parsing algorithms are comparatively easy to implement and efficient: some of the algorithms parse sentences in linear time (Yamada and Matsumoto, 2003; Nivre et al., 2006).

In the semantic structure extraction system, we used the Stanford part-of-speech tagger (Toutanova et al., 2003) to tag the training and test sentences and MaltParser, a statistical dependency parser (Nivre et al., 2006), to parse them.

We trained the parser on the Penn Treebank (Marcus et al., 1993). The dependency trees used to train the parser were created from the constituent trees using a conversion program (Johansson and Nugues, 2007)[1]. The converter handles most of the secondary edges in the Treebank and encodes those edges as (generally) nonprojective dependency arcs. Such information is available in the Penn Treebank in the form of empty categories and secondary edges, it is however not available in the output of traditional constituent parsers, although there have been some attempts to apply a post-processing step to predict it, see Ahn et al. (2004), *inter alia*.

Figures 1 and 2 show a constituent tree from the Treebank and its corresponding dependency tree. Note that the secondary edge from the *wh*-trace to *Why* is converted into a nonprojective `PRP` link.

3 Semantic Structure Extraction

This section describes how the dependency trees are used to create the semantic structure. The system

[1] Available at `http://nlp.cs.lth.se/pennconverter`

Proceedings of the 4th International Workshop on Semantic Evaluations (SemEval-2007), pages 227–230,
Prague, June 2007.

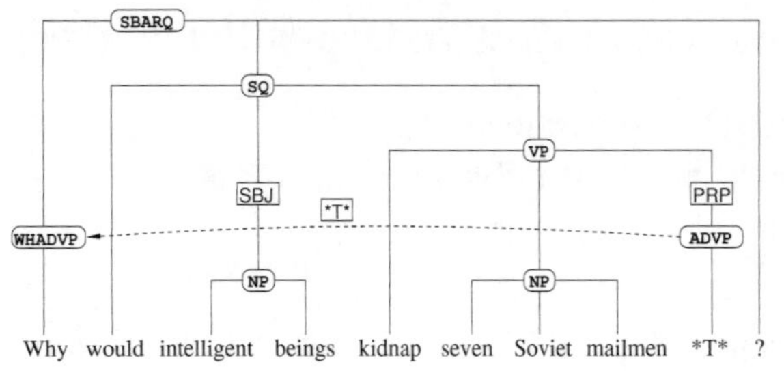

Figure 1: A constituent tree from the Penn Treebank.

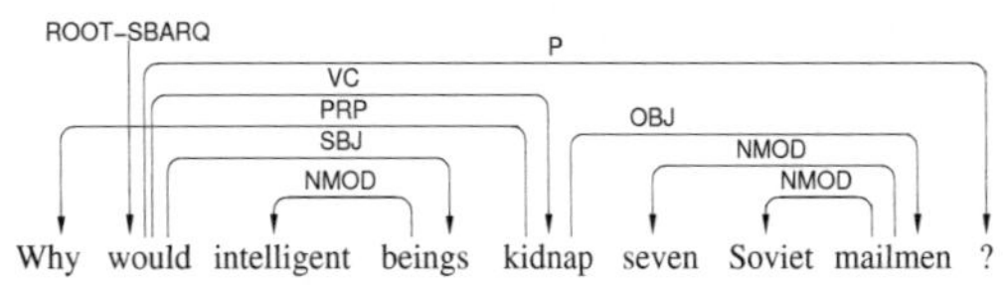

Figure 2: Converted dependency tree.

is divided into two main components: frame detection and disambiguation, and frame element detection and classification.

3.1 Frame Detection and Disambiguation

3.1.1 Filtering Rules

Since many potential target words appear in senses that should not be tagged with a frame, we use a filtering component as a first step in the frame detection. We also removed some words (especially prepositions) that caused significant performance degradation because of lack of training data. With the increasing availability of tagged running text, we expect that we will be able to replace the filtering rules with a classifier in the future.

- *have* was retained only if it had an object,
- *be* only if it was preceded by *there*,
- *will* was removed in its modal sense,
- *of course* and *in particular* were removed,
- the prepositions *above*, *against*, *at*, *below*, *beside*, *by*, *in*, *on*, *over*, and *under* were removed unless their head was marked as locative,
- *after* and *before* were removed unless their head was marked as temporal,
- *into*, *to*, and *through* were removed unless their head was marked as direction,
- *as*, *for*, *so*, and *with* were always removed,
- since the only sense of *of* was PARTITIVE, we removed it unless it was preceded by *only*, *member*, *one*, *most*, *many*, *some*, *few*, *part*, *majority*, *minority*, *proportion*, *half*, *third*, *quarter*, *all*, or *none*, or if it was followed by *all*, *group*, *them*, or *us*.

We also removed all targets that had been tagged as support verbs for some other target.

3.1.2 Sense Disambiguation

For the target words left after the filtering, we used a classifier to assign a frame, following Erk (2005). We trained a disambiguating SVM classifier on all ambiguous words listed in FrameNet. Its accuracy was 84% on the ambiguous words, compared to a first-sense baseline score of 74%.

The classifier used the following features: target lemma, target word, subcategorization frame (for verb targets only), the set of dependencies of the target, the set of words of the child nodes, and the parent word of the target.

The subcategorization frame feature was formed by concatenating the dependency labels of the children, excluding subject, parentheticals, punctuation and coordinations. For instance, for *kidnap* in Figure 2, the feature is `PRP+OBJ`.

3.1.3 Extending the Lexical Database

Coverage is one of the main weaknesses of the current FrameNet lexical database – it lists only 10,197 lexical units, compared to 207,016 word–sense pairs in WordNet 3.0 (Fellbaum, 1998). We tried to remedy this problem by training classifiers to find words that are related to the words in a frame.

We designed a feature representation for each lemma in WordNet, which uses a sequence of identifiers for each synset in its hypernym tree. All senses of the lemma were used, and the features were weighted with respect to the relative frequency of the sense. Using this feature representation, we trained an SVM classifier for each frame that tells whether a lemma belongs to that frame or not.

The FrameNet dictionary could thus be extended by 18,372 lexical units. If we assume a Zipf distribution and that the lexical units already in FrameNet are the most common ones, this would increase the coverage by up to 9%. In the test set, the new lexical units account for 53 out of the 808 target words our system detected (6.5%). We roughly estimated the precision to 70% by manually inspecting 100 randomly selected words in the extended dictionary.

This strategy is most successful when the frame is equivalent to one or a few synsets (and their subtrees). For instance, for the frame MEDICAL_CONDITION, we can add the complete subtree of the synset *pathological state*, resulting in 641 new lemmas referring to all sorts of diseases. On the other hand, the strategy also works well for motion verbs (which often exhibit complex patterns of polysemy): 137 lemmas could be added to the SELF_MOTION frame. Examples of frames with frequent errors are LEADERSHIP, which includes many insects (probably because the most frequent sense of *queen* in SemCor is the queen bee), and FOOD, which included many chemical substances as well as inedible plants and animals.

3.2 Frame Element Extraction

Following convention, we divided the FE extraction into two subtasks: argument identification and argument classification. We did not try to assign multiple labels to arguments. Figure 3 shows an overview. In addition to detecing the FEs, the argument identification classifier detects the dependency nodes that should be tagged on the layers other than the frame element layer: SUPP, COP, NULL, EXIST, and ASP. The ANT and REL labels could be inserted using simple rules. Similarly to Xue and Palmer (2004),

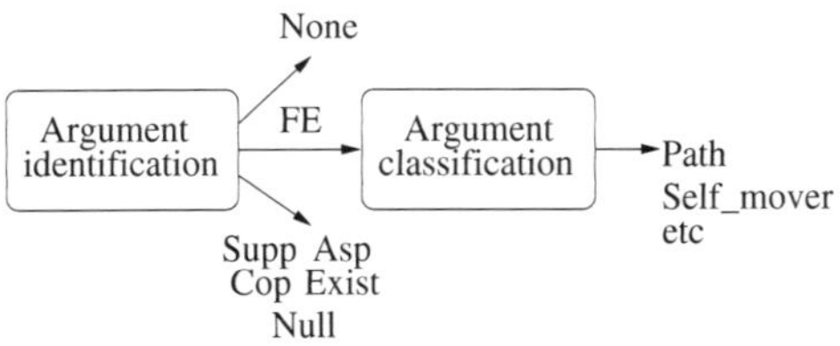

Figure 3: FE extraction steps.

we could filter away many nodes before the argument identification step by assuming that the arguments for a given predicate correspond to a subset of the dependents of the target or of its transitive heads.

Both classifiers were implemented using SVMs and use the following features: target lemma, voice (for verb targets only), subcategorization frame (for verb targets only), the set of dependencies of the target, part of speech of the target node, path through the dependency tree from the target to the node, position (before, after, or on), word and part of speech for the head, word and part of speech for leftmost and rightmost descendent.

In the path feature, we removed steps through verb chains and coordination. For instance, in the sentece *I have seen and heard it*, the path from *heard* to *I* is only `SBJ↓` and to *it* `OBJ↓`.

3.3 Named Entity Recognition

In addition to the frame-semantic information, the SemEval task also scores named entities. We used YamCha (Kudo and Matsumoto, 2003) to detect named entities, and we trained it on the SemEval full-text training sets. Apart from the word and part of speech, we used suffixes up to length 5 as features. We think that results could be improved further by using an external NE tagger.

4 Results

The system was evaluated on three texts. Table 1 shows the results for frame detection averaged over the test texts. In the Setting colums, the first shows whether Exact or Partial frame matching was used by the evaluation script, and the second whether Labels or Dependencies were used. Table 2 compares the results of the system using the extended dictionary with one using the orignal FrameNet dictionary, using the Partial matching and Labels scoring. The extended dictionary introduces some noise and thus lowers the precision slightly, but the effects on the recall are positive. Table 3 shows the aver-

Table 1: Results for frame detection.

Setting		Recall	Precision	$F1$
E	L	0.528	0.688	0.597
P	L	0.581	0.758	0.657
E	D	0.549	0.715	0.621
P	D	0.601	0.784	0.681

Table 2: Comparison of dictionaries.

Dictionary	Recall	Precision	$F1$
Original	0.550	0.767	0.634
Extended	0.581	0.758	0.657

aged precision, recall, and $F1$ measures for different evaluation parameters. The third column shows whether named entities were used (Y) or not (N). Interestingly, the scores are higher for the semantic dependency graphs than for flat labels, while the two other teams generally had higher scores for flat labels. We believe that the reason for this is that we used a dependency parser, and that the rules that we used to convert dependency nodes into spans may have produced some errors. It is possible that the figures would have been slightly higher if our program produced semantic dependency graphs directly.

Table 3: Results for frame and FE detection.

Setting			Recall	Precision	$F1$
E	L	Y	0.372	0.532	0.438
P	L	Y	0.398	0.570	0.468
E	D	Y	0.389	0.557	0.458
P	D	Y	0.414	0.594	0.488
E	L	N	0.364	0.530	0.432
P	L	N	0.391	0.570	0.464
E	D	N	0.384	0.561	0.456
P	D	N	0.411	0.600	0.488

5 Conclusion and Future Work

We have presented a system for frame-semantic structure extraction that achieves promising results. While most previous systems have been based on constituents, our system relies on a dependency parser. We also described an automatic method to add new units to the FrameNet lexical database.

To improve labeling quality, we would like to apply constraints to the semantic output so that semantic type and coreness rules are obeyed. In addition, while the system described here is based on pipelined classification, recent research on semantic role labeling has shown that significant performance improvements can be gained by exploiting interdependencies between arguments (Toutanova et al., 2005). With an increasing amount of running text annotated with frame semantics, we believe that this insight can be extended to model interdependencies between frames as well.

Our motivation for using dependency grammar is that we hope that it will eventually make semantic structure extraction easier to implement and more theoretically well-founded. How to best design the dependency syntax is also still an open question. Ideally, all arguments would be direct dependents of the predicate node and we could get rid of the sparse and brittle *Path* feature in the classifier.

References

David Ahn, Sisay Fissaha, Valentin Jijkoun, and Maarten de Rijke. 2004. The university of Amsterdam at Senseval-3: Semantic roles and logic forms. In *Proceedings of SENSEVAL-3*.

Sabine Buchholz and Erwin Marsi. 2006. CoNLL-X shared task on multilingual dependency parsing. In *Proceedings of the CoNLL-X*.

Katrin Erk. 2005. Frame assignment as word sense disambiguation. In *Proceedings of IWCS 6*.

Christiane Fellbaum, editor. 1998. *WordNet: An electronic lexical database*. MIT Press.

Richard Johansson and Pierre Nugues. 2007. Extended constituent-to-dependency conversion for English. In *Proceedings of NODALIDA 2007*. To appear.

Taku Kudo and Yuji Matsumoto. 2003. Fast methods for kernel-based text analysis. In *ACL-2003*.

Chistopher Manning. 1994. Ergativity: Argument structure and grammatical relations.

Mitchell P. Marcus, Beatrice Santorini, and Mary Ann Marcinkiewicz. 1993. Building a large annotated corpus of English: the Penn Treebank. *Computational Linguistics*, 19(2):313–330.

Igor A. Mel'čuk. 1988. *Dependency Syntax: Theory and Practice*. State University Press of New York, Albany.

Joakim Nivre, Johan Hall, and Jens Nilsson. 2006. MaltParser: A data-driven parser generator for dependency parsing. In *Proceedings of LREC*.

Sameer Pradhan, Wayne Ward, Kadri Hacioglu, James Martin, and Daniel Jurafsky. 2005. Semantic role labeling using different syntactic views. In *ACL-2005*.

Kristina Toutanova, Dan Klein, Christopher Manning, and Yoram Singer. 2003. Feature-rich part-of-speech tagging with a cyclic dependency network. In *Proceedings of HLT-NAACL*.

Kristina Toutanova, Aria Haghighi, and Christopher D. Manning. 2005. Joint learning improves semantic role labeling. In *Proceedings of ACL 2005*.

Nianwen Xue and Martha Palmer. 2004. Calibrating features for semantic role labeling. In *Proc. of EMNLP*.

Hiroyasu Yamada and Yuji Matsumoto. 2003. Statistical dependency analysis with support vector machines. In *Proceedings of IWPT-03*.

MELB-KB: Nominal Classification as Noun Compound Interpretation

Su Nam Kim and Timothy Baldwin
Computer Science and Software Engineering
University of Melbourne, Australia
{snkim,tim}@csse.unimelb.edu.au

Abstract

In this paper, we outline our approach to interpreting semantic relations in nominal pairs in SemEval-2007 task #4: Classification of Semantic Relations between Nominals. We build on two baseline approaches to interpreting noun compounds: sense collocation, and constituent similarity. These are consolidated into an overall system in combination with co-training, to expand the training data. Our two systems attained an average F-score over the test data of 58.7% and 57.8%, respectively.

1 Introduction

This paper describes two systems entered in SemEval-2007 task #4: Classification of Semantic Relations between Nominals. A key contribution of this research is that we examine the compatibility of noun compound (NC) interpretation methods over the extended task of nominal classification, to gain empirical insight into the relative complexity of the two tasks.

The goal of the nominal classification task is to identify the compatibility of a given semantic relation with each of a set of test nominal pairs, e.g. between *climate* and *forest* in the fragment *the climate in the forest* with respect to the CONTENT-CONTAINER relation. Semantic relations (or SRs) in nominals represent the underlying interpretation of the nominal, in the form of the directed relation between the two nominals.

The proposed task is a generalisation of the more conventional task of interpreting noun compounds (NCs), in which we take a NC such as *cookie jar* and interpret it according to a pre-defined inventory of semantic relations (Levi, 1979; Vanderwende, 1994; Barker and Szpakowicz, 1998). Examples of semantic relations are MAKE,[1], as exemplified in *apple pie* where the *pie* is made from *apple(s)*, and POSSESSOR, as exemplified in *family car* where the *car* is possessed by a *family*.

In the SemEval-2007 task, SR interpretation takes the form of a binary decision for a given nominal pair in context and a given SR, in judging whether that nominal pair conforms to the SR. Seven relations were used in the task: CAUSE-EFFECT, INSTRUMENT-AGENCY, PRODUCT-PRODUCER, ORIGIN-ENTITY, THEME-TOOL, PART-WHOLE and CONTENT-CONTAINER.

Our approach to the task was to: (1) naively treat all nominal pairs as NCs (e.g. *the climate in the forest* is treated as an instance of *climate forest*); and (2) translate the individual binary classification tasks into a single multiclass classification task, in the interests of benchmarking existing SR interpretation methods over a common dataset. That is, we take all positive training instances for each SR and pool them together into a single training dataset. For each test instance, we make a prediction according to one of the seven relations in the task, which we then map onto a binary classification for final evaluation purposes. This mapping is achieved by determining which binary SR classification the test instance was sourced from, and returning a positive classification if the predicted SR coincides with the target SR, and a negative classification if not.

We make three (deliberately naive) assumptions in our approach to the nominal interpretation task. First, we assume that all the positive training in-

[1] For direct comparability with our earlier research, semantic relations used in our examples are taken from (Barker and Szpakowicz, 1998), and differ slightly from those used in the SemEval-2007 task.

Proceedings of the 4th International Workshop on Semantic Evaluations (SemEval-2007), pages 231–236,
Prague, June 2007.

stances correspond uniquely to the SR in question, despite the task organisers making it plain that there is semantic overlap between the SRs. As a machine learning task, this makes the task considerably more difficult, as the performance for the standard baselines drops considerably from that for the binary tasks. Second, we assume that each nominal pair maps onto a NC. This is clearly a misconstrual of the task, and intended to empirically validate whether such an approach is viable. In line with this assumption, we will refer to nominal pairs as NCs for the remainder of the paper. Third and finally, we assume that the SR annotation of each training and test instance is insensitive to the original context, and use only the constituent words in the NC to make our prediction. This is for direct comparability with earlier research, and we acknowledge that the context (and word sense) is a strong determinant of the SR in practice.

Our aim in this paper is to demonstrate the effectiveness of general-purpose SR interpretation over the nominal classification task, and establish a new baseline for the task.

The remainder of this paper is structured as follows. We present our methods in Section 2 and depict the system architectures in Section 4. We then describe and discuss the performance of our methods in Section 5 and conclude the paper in Section 6.

2 Approach

We used two basic NC interpretation methods. The first method uses sense collocations as proposed by Moldovan et al. (2004), and the second method uses the lexical similarity of the component words in the NC as proposed by Kim and Baldwin (2005). Note that neither method uses the context of usage of the NC, i.e. the only features are the words contained in the NC.

2.1 Sense Collocation Method

Moldovan et al. (2004) proposed a method called semantic scattering for interpreting NCs. The intuition behind this method is that when the sense collocation of NCs is the same, their SR is most likely the same. For example, the sense collocation of *automobile factory* is the same as that of *car factory*, because the senses of *automobile* and *car*, and *factory* in the two instances, are identical. As a result, the two NCs have the semantic relation MAKE.

The semantic scattering model is outlined below.

The probability $P(r|f_i f_j)$ (simplified to $P(r|f_{ij})$) of a semantic relation r for word senses f_i and f_j is calculated based on simple maximum likelihood estimation:

$$P(r|f_{ij}) = \frac{n(r, f_{ij})}{n(f_{ij})} \quad (1)$$

and the preferred SR r^* for the given word sense combination is that which maximises the probability:

$$\begin{aligned} r^* &= \text{argmax}_{r \in R} P(r|f_{ij}) \\ &= \text{argmax}_{r \in R} P(f_{ij}|r) P(r) \end{aligned} \quad (2)$$

Note that in limited cases, the same sense collocation can lead to multiple SRs. However, since we do not take context into account in our method, we make the simplifying assumption that a given sense collocation leads to a unique SR.

2.2 Constituent Similarity Method

In earlier work (Kim and Baldwin, 2005), we proposed a simplistic general-purpose method based on the lexical similarity of unseen NCs with training instances. That is, the semantic relation of a test instance is derived from the train instance which has the highest similarity with the test instance, in the form of a 1-nearest neighbour classifier. For example, assuming the test instance *chocolate milk* and training instances *apple juice* and *morning milk*, we would calculate the similarity between modifier *chocolate* and each of *apple* and *morning*, and head noun *milk* and each of *juice* and *milk*, and find, e.g., the similarities .71 and .27, and .83 and 1.00 respectively. We would then add these up to derive the overall similarity for a given NC and find that *apple juice* is a better match. From this, we would assign the SR of MAKE from *apple juice* to *chocolate milk*.

Formally, S_A is the similarity between NCs $(N_{i,1}, N_{i,2})$ and $(B_{j,1}, B_{j,2})$:

$$\begin{aligned} &S_A((N_{i,1}, N_{i,2}), (B_{j,1}, B_{j,2})) = \\ &\frac{((\alpha S1 + S1) \times ((1-\alpha) S2 + S2))}{2} \end{aligned} \quad (3)$$

where $S1$ is the modifier similarity (i.e. $S(N_{i,1}, B_{j1})$) and $S2$ is head noun similarity (i.e. $S(N_{i,2}, B_{j2})$); $\alpha \in [0, 1]$ is a weighting factor. The similarity scores are calculated using the method of Wu and Palmer (1994) as implemented in `WordNet::Similarity` (Patwardhan et al., 2003). This is done for each pairing of WordNet senses of each of the two words in question, and the overall lexical similarity is calculated as the average across the pairwise sense similarities.

The final classification is derived from the training instance which has the highest lexical similarity with the test instance in question.

3 Co-Training

As with many semantic annotation tasks, SR tagging is a time-consuming and expensive process. At the same time, due to the inherent complexity of the SR interpretation task, we require large amounts of training data in order for our methods to perform well. In order to generate additional training data to train our methods over, we experiment with different co-training methodologies for each of our two basic methods.

3.1 Co-Training for the Sense Collocation Method

For the sense collocation method, we experiment with a substitution method whereby we replace one constituent in a training NC instance by a similar word, and annotate the new instance with the same SR as the original NC. For example, *car* in *car factory* (SR = MAKE) has similar words *automobile, vehicle, truck* from the synonym, hypernym and sister word taxonomic relations, respectively. When *car* is replaced by a similar word, the new noun compound(s) (i.e. *automobile/vehicle/truck factory*) share the same SR as the original *car factory*. Note that each constituent in our original example is tagged for word sense, which we use both in accessing sense-specific substitution candidates (via WordNet), and sense-annotating the newly generated NCs.

Substitution is restricted to one constituent at a time in order to avoid extreme semantic variation. This procedure can be repeated to generate more training data. However, as the procedure goes further, we introduce increasingly more noise.

In our experiments, we use this co-training method with the sense collocation method to expand the size and variation of training data, using synonym, hypernym and sister word relations. For our experiment, we ran the expansion procedure for only one iteration in order to avoid generating excessive amounts of incorrectly-tagged NCs.

3.2 Co-Training for the Constituent Similarity Method

Our experiments with the constituent similarity method over the trial data showed, encouragingly, that there is a strong correlation between the strength of overall similarity with the best-matching training NC, and the accuracy of the prediction. From this, we experimented with implementing the constituent similarity method in a cascading architecture. That is, we batch evaluate all test instances on each iteration, and tag those test instances for which the best match with a training instance is above a preset threshold, which we decrease on each iteration. In subsequent iterations, all tagged test instances are included in the training data. Hence, on each iteration, the number of training instances is increasing. As our threshold, we used a starting value of 0.85, which was decreased down to 0.65 in increments of 0.05.

4 Architectures

In Section 4.1 and Section 4.2, we describe the architecture of our two systems.

4.1 Architecture (I)

Figure 1 presents the architecture of our first system, which interleaves sense collocation and constituent similarity, and includes co-training for each. There are five steps in this system.

First, we apply the basic sense collocation method relative to the original training data. If the sense collocation between the test and training instances is the same, we judge the predicted SR to be correct.

Second, we apply the similarity method described in Section 2.2 over the original training data. However, we only classify test instances where the final similarity is above a threshold of 0.8.

Third, we apply the sense collocation co-training method and re-run the sense collocation method over the expanded training data from the first two steps. Since the sense collocations in the expanded

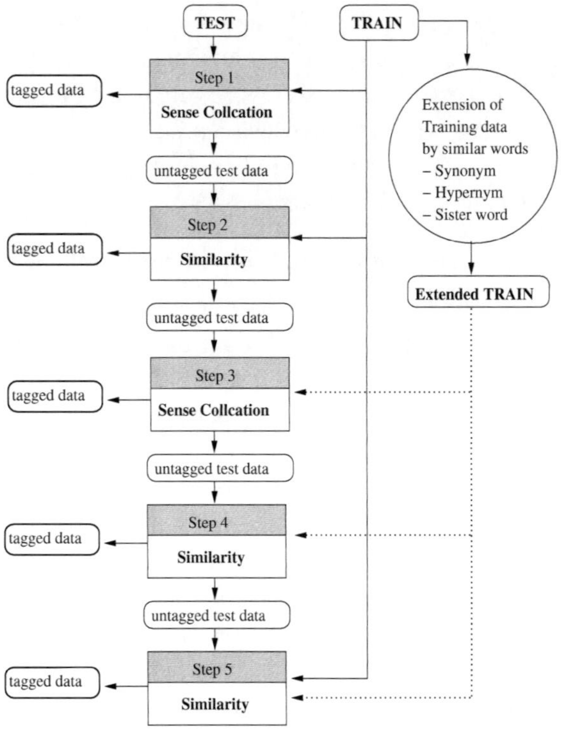

Figure 1: System Architecture (I)

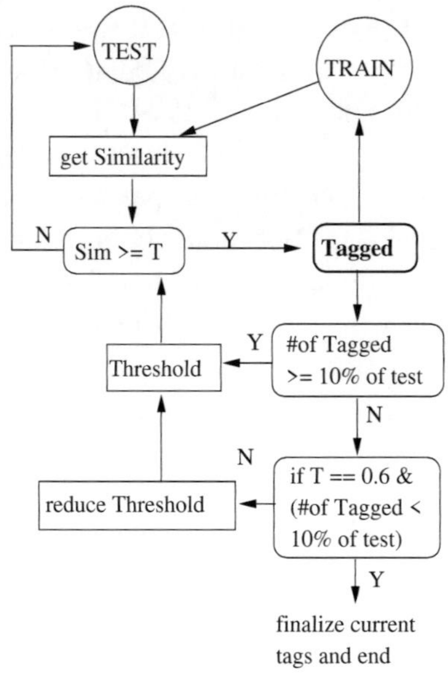

Figure 2: System Architecture (II)

training data have been varied through the advent of hypernyms and sister words, the number of sense collocations in the expanded training data is much greater than that of the original training data (937 vs. 16,676).

Fourth, we apply the constituent similarity co-training method over the consolidated training data (from both sense collocation and constituent similarity co-training) with the threshold unchanged at 0.8.

Finally, we apply the constituent similarity method over the combined training data, without any threshold (to guarantee a SR prediction for every test instance). However, since the generated training instances are more likely to contain errors, we decrement the similarity values for generated training instances by 0.2, to prefer predictions based on the original training instances.

4.2 Architecture (II)

Figure 2 depicts our second system, which is based solely on the constituent similarity method, with co-training.

We perform iterative co-training as described in Section 3.2, with the slight variation that we hold off reducing the threshold if more than 10% of the test instances are tagged on a given iteration, giving other test instances a chance to be tagged at a higher threshold level relative to newly generated training instances. The residue of test instances on completion of the final iteration (threshold = 0.6) are tagged according to the best-matching training instance, irrespective of the magnitude of the similarity.

5 Evaluation

We group our evaluation into two categories: (`A`) doesn't use `WordNet 2.1` or the query context; and (`B`) uses `WordNet 2.1` only (again without the query context). Of our two basic methods the sense collocation method and co-training method are based on `WordNet 2.1` only, while the constituent similarity method is based indirectly on `WordNet 2.1`, but doesn't preserve `WordNet 2.1` sense information. Hence, our first system is category `B` while our second system is (arguably) category `A`.

Table 1 presents the three baselines for the task, and the results for our two systems (System I and System II). The performance for both systems exceeded all three baselines in terms of accuracy, and all but the All True baseline (i.e. every instance is judged to be compatible with the given SR) in terms

Method	P	R	F	A
All True	48.5	100.0	64.8	48.5
Probability	48.5	48.5	48.5	51.7
Majority	81.3	42.9	30.8	57.0
System I	61.7	56.8	58.7	62.5
System II	61.5	55.7	57.8	62.7

Table 1: System results (*P* = precision, *R* = recall, *F* = F-score, and *A* = accuracy)

Team	P	R	F	A
759	66.1	66.7	64.8	66.0
281	60.5	69.5	63.8	63.5
633	62.7	63.0	62.7	65.4
220	**61.5**	**55.7**	**57.8**	**62.7**
161	56.1	57.1	55.9	58.8
538	48.2	40.3	43.1	49.9

Table 2: Results of category A systems

of F-score and recall.

Tables 2 and 3 show the performance of the teams which performed in the task, in categories A and B. Team 220 in Table 2 is our second system, and team 220 in Table 3 is our first system.

In Figures 3 and 4, we present a breakdown of the performance our first and second system, respectively, over the individual semantic relations. Our approaches performed best for the PRODUCT-PRODUCER SR, and worst for the PART-WHOLE SR. In general, our systems achieved similar performance on most SRs, with only PART-WHOLE being notably worse. The lower performance of PART-WHOLE pulls down our overall performance considerably.

Tables 4 and 5 show the number of tagged and untagged instances for each step of System I and System II, respectively. The first system tagged more than half of the data in the fifth (and final) step, where it weighs up predictions from the original and expanded training data. Hence, the performance of this approach relies heavily on the similarity method and expanded training data. Additionally, the difference in quality between the original and expanded training data will influence the performance of the approach appreciably. On the other hand, the number of instances tagged by the second system is well distributed across each iteration. However, since we accumulate generated training instances on each step, the relative noise level in the training data will

Team	P	R	F	A
901	79.7	69.8	72.4	76.3
777	70.9	73.4	71.8	72.9
281	72.8	70.6	71.5	73.2
129	69.9	64.6	66.8	71.4
333	62.0	71.7	65.4	67.0
538	66.7	62.8	64.3	67.2
571	55.7	66.7	60.4	59.1
759	66.4	58.1	60.3	63.6
220	**61.7**	**56.8**	**58.7**	**62.5**
371	56.8	56.3	56.1	57.7
495	55.9	57.8	51.4	53.7

Table 3: Results of category B systems

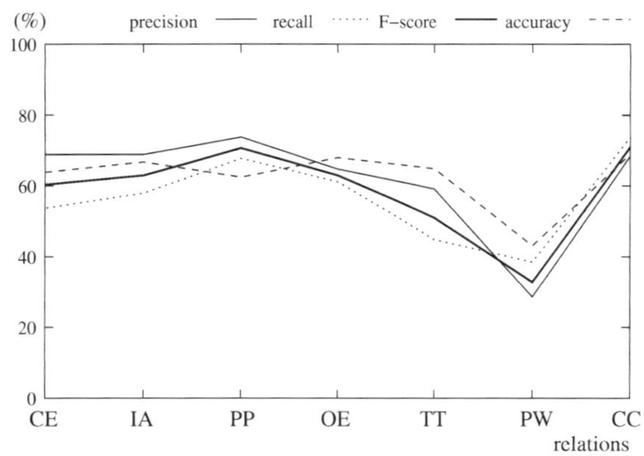

Figure 3: System I performance for each relation (CC=CAUSE-EFFECT, IA=INSTRUMENT-AGENCY, PP=PRODUCT-PRODUCER, OE=ORIGIN-ENTITY, TT=THEME-TOOL, PW=PART-WHOLE, CC=CONTENT-CONTAINER)

increase across iterations, impacting on the final performance of the system.

Over the trial data, we noticed that the system predictions are appreciably worse when the similarity value is low. In future work, we intend to analyse what is happening in terms of the overall system performance at each step. This analysis is key to improving the performance of our systems.

Recall that we are generalising from the set of binary classification tasks in the original task, to a multiclass classification task. As such, a direct comparison with the binary classification baselines is perhaps unfair (particularly All True, which has no correlate in a multiclass setting), and it is if anything remarkable that our system compares favourably compared to the baselines. Similarly, while we clearly lag behind other systems participating in the

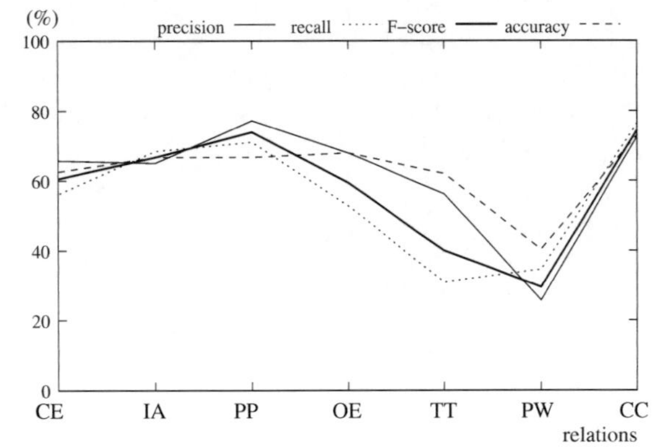

Figure 4: System II performance for each relation (CC=CAUSE-EFFECT, IA=INSTRUMENT-AGENCY, PP=PRODUCT-PRODUCER, OE=ORIGIN-ENTITY, TT=THEME-TOOL, PW=PART-WHOLE, CC=CONTENT-CONTAINER)

step	method	tagged	accumulated	untagged
s1	SC	21	3.8%	528
s2	Sim	106	23.1%	422
s3	extSC	0	23.1%	422
s4	extSim	61	34.2%	361
s5	SvsExtS	359	99.6%	2

Table 4: System I: Tagged data from each step (*SC*= sense collocation; *Sim* = the similarity method; *extSC* = SC over the expanded training data; *extSim* = similarity over the expanded training data; *SvsExtS* = the final step over both the original and expanded training data)

task, we believe we have demonstrated that NC interpretation methods can be successfully deployed over the more general task of nominal pair classification.

6 Conclusion

In this paper, we presented two systems entered in the SemEval-2007 Classification of Semantic Relations between Nominals task. Both systems are based on baseline NC interpretation methods, and the naive assumption that the nominal classification task is analogous to a conventional multiclass NC interpretation task. Our results compare favourably with the established baselines, and demonstrate that NC interpretation methods are compatible with the more general task of nominal classification.

I	T	tagged	accumulated	untagged
i1	.85	73	13.3%	476
i2	.80	56	23.5%	420
i3	.75	74	37.0%	346
i4	.70	101	55.4%	245
i5	.65	222	95.8%	23
–	<.65	21	99.6%	2

Table 5: System II: data tagged on each iteration (T = the threshold; iX = the iteration number)

Acknowledgments

This research was carried out with support from Australian Research Council grant no. DP0663879.

References

Ken Barker and Stan Szpakowicz. 1998. Semi-automatic recognition of noun modifier relationships. In *Proc. of the 17th International Conference on Computational Linguistics*, pages 96–102, Montreal, Canada.

Christiane Fellbaum, editor. 1998. *WordNet: An Electronic Lexical Database*. MIT Press, Cambridge, USA.

Timothy W. Finin. 1980. *The Semantic Interpretation of Compound Nominals*. Ph.D. thesis, University of Illinois.

Su Nam Kim and Timothy Baldwin. 2005. Automatic interpretation of Noun Compounds using WordNet similarity. In *Proc. of the 2nd International Joint Conference On Natural Language Processing*, pages 945–956, JeJu, Korea.

Judith Levi. 1979. The syntax and semantics of complex nominals. In *The Syntax and Semantics of Complex Nominals*. New York:Academic Press.

Dan Moldovan, Adriana Badulescu, Marta Tatu, Daniel Antohe, and Roxana Girju. 2004. Models for the semantic classification of noun phrases. In *Proc. of the HLT-NAACL 2004 Workshop on Computational Lexical Semantics*, pages 60–67, Boston, USA.

Siddharth Patwardhan, Satanjeev Banerjee, and Ted Pedersen. 2003. Using measures of semantic relatedness for word sense disambiguation. In *Proc. of the Fourth International Conference on Intelligent Text Processing and Computational Linguistics*, pages 241–57, Mexico City, Mexico.

Lucy Vanderwende. 1994. Algorithm for automatic interpretation of noun sequences. In *Proc. of the 15th conference on Computational linguistics*, pages 782–788, Kyoto, Japan.

Zhibiao Wu and Martha Palmer. 1994. Verb semantics and lexical selection. In *Proc. of the 32nd Annual Meeting of the Association for Computational Linguistics*, pages 133–138, Las Cruces, USA.

MELB-MKB: Lexical Substitution System based on Relatives in Context

David Martinez, Su Nam Kim and Timothy Baldwin
LT Group, CSSE
University of Melbourne
Victoria 3010 Australia
{davidm,snkim,tim}@csse.unimelb.edu.au

Abstract

In this paper we describe the MELB-MKB system, as entered in the SemEval-2007 lexical substitution task. The core of our system was the "Relatives in Context" unsupervised approach, which ranked the candidate substitutes by web-lookup of the word sequences built combining the target context and each substitute. Our system ranked third in the final evaluation, performing close to the top-ranked system.

1 Introduction

This paper describes the system we developed for the SemEval lexical substitution task, a new task in SemEval-2007. Although we tested different configurations on the trial data, our basic system relied on WordNet relatives (Fellbaum, 1998) and Google queries in order to identify the most plausible substitutes in the context.

The main goal when building our system was to study the following factors: (i) substitution candidate set, (ii) settings of the relative-based algorithm, and (iii) syntactic filtering. We analysed these factors over the trial data provided by the organisation, and used the BEST metric to tune our system. This metric accepts multiple answers, and averages the score across the answers. We did not experiment with the OOT (top 10 answers) and MULTIWORD metrics.

In the remainder of this paper we briefly introduce the basic Relatives in Context algorithm in Section 2. Next we describe our experiments on the trial data in Section 3. Our final system and its results are described in Section 4. Finally, our conclusions are outlined in Section 5.

2 Algorithm

Our basic algorithm is an unsupervised method presented in Martinez et al. (2006). This technique makes use of the WordNet relatives of the target word for disambiguation, by way of the following steps: (i) obtain a set of close relatives from WordNet for each sense of the target word; (ii) for each test instance define all possible word sequences that include the target word; (iii) for each word sequence, substitute the target word with each relative, and then query Google; (iv) rank queries according to the following factors: length of the query, distance of the relative to the target word, and number of hits; and (v) select the relative from the highest ranked query.[1]

For the querying step, first we tokenise each target sentence, and then we apply sliding windows of different sizes (up to 6 tokens) that include the target word. For each window and each relative in the pool, we substitute the target word for the relative, and query Google. The algorithm stops augmenting the window for the relative when one of its substrings returns zero hits. The length of the query is measured as the number of words, and the distance of the relative to the target words gives preference to synonyms over hypernyms, and immediate hypernyms over further ones.

One important parameter in this method is the candidate set. We performed different experiments to measure the expected score we could achieve

[1] In the case of WSD we would use the relative to chose the sense it relates to.

Proceedings of the 4th International Workshop on Semantic Evaluations (SemEval-2007), pages 237–240,
Prague, June 2007.

from WordNet relatives, and the contribution of different types of filters (syntactic, frequency-based, etc.) to the overall result. We also explored other settings of the algorithm, such as the ranking criteria, and the number of answers to return. These experiments and some other modifications of the basic algorithm are covered in Section 3.

3 Development on Trial data

In this section we analyse the coverage of WordNet over the data, the basic parameter exploration process, a syntactic filter, and finally the extra experiments we carried out before submission. The trial data consisted on 300 instances of 34 words with gold-standard annotations.

3.1 WordNet coverage

The most obvious resource for selecting substitution candidates was WordNet, due to its size and availability. We used version 2.0 throughout this work. In our first experiment, we tried to determine which kind of relationships to use, and the coverage of the gold-standard annotations that we could expect from WordNet relations only. As a basic set of relations, we used the following: SYNONYMY, SIMILAR-TO, ENTAILMENT, CAUSE, ALSO-SEE, and INSTANCE. We created two extended candidate sets using immediate and 2-step hypernyms (hype and hype2, respectively, in Table 1).

Given that we are committed to using WordNet, we set out to measure the percentage of gold-standard substitutes that were "reachable" using different WordNet relations. Table 1 shows the coverage for the three sets of candidates. Instance-coverage indicates the percentage of instances that have at least one of the gold-standard instances covered from the candidate set. We can see that the percentage is surprisingly low.

Any shortcoming in coverage will have a direct impact on performance, suggesting the need for alternate means to obtain substitution candidates. One possibility is to extend the candidates from WordNet by following links from the relatives (e.g. collect all synonyms of the synonymous words), but this could add many noisy candidates. We can also use other lexical repositories built by hand or automatically, such as the distributional theusauri built in Lin (1998). A different approach that we are testing for future work is to adapt the algorithm to work with wildcards instead of explicit candidates. Due to time constraints, we only relied on WordNet for our submission.

Candidate Set	Subs. Cov.	Inst. Cov.
basic	344/1152 (30%)	197 / 300 (66%)
hype	404/1152 (35%)	229/300 (76%)
hype2	419/1152 (36%)	229/300 (76%)

Table 1: WordNet coverage for different candidate sets, based on substitute (Subs.) and instance (Inst.) coverage.

3.2 Parameter Tuning

In this experiment we tuned different parameters of the basic algorithm. First, we observed the data in order to identify the most relevant variables for this task. We tried to avoid including too many parameters and overfitting the system to the trial dataset. At this point, we separated the instances by PoS, and studied the following parameters:

Candidate set: From WordNet, we tested four possible datasets for each target word: basic-set, 1st-sense (basic relations from the first sense only), hype (basic set and immediate hypernyms), and hype2 (basic set and up to two-step hypernyms).

Semcor-based filters: Semcor provides frequency information for WordNet senses, and can be used to identify rare senses. As each candidate is obtained via WordNet semantic relations with the target word, we can filter out those candidates that are related with unfrequent senses in Semcor. We tested three configurations: (1) no filter, (2) filter out candidates when the *candidate*-sense in the relation does not occur in Semcor, (3) and filter out candidates when the *target*-sense in the relation does not occur in Semcor. The filters can potentially lead to the removal of all candidates, in which case a back-off is applied (see below).

Relative-ranking criteria: Our algorithm ranks relatives according to the length in words of their context-match. In the case of ties, the number of returned hits from Google is applied. The length can be different depending on whether we count punctuation marks as separate tokens, and whether the word-length of substitute multiwords is included.

We tested three options: including the target word, not including the target word (multiwords count as a single word), and not counting punctuation marks.

Back-off: We need a back-off method in case the basic algorithm does not find any matches. We tested the following: sense-ordered synonyms from WordNet (highest sense first, randomly breaking ties), and most frequent synonyms from the first system (using two corpora: Semcor and BNC).

Number of answers: We also measured the performance for different numbers of system outputs (1, 2, or 3).

All in all, we performed 324 (4x3x3x3x3) runs for each PoS, based on the different combinations. The best scores for each PoS are shown in Table 2, together with the baselines. We can see that the precision is above the official WordNet baseline, but is still very low. The results illustrate the difficulty of the task. In error analysis, we observed that the performance and settings varied greatly depending on the PoS of the target word. Adverbs produced the best performance, followed by nouns. The scores were very low for adjectives and verbs (the baseline score for verbs was only 2%).

We will now explain the main conclusions extracted from the parameter analysis. Regarding the candidate set, we observed that using synonyms only was the best approach for all PoS, except for verbs, where hypernyms helped. The option of limiting the candidates to the first sense only helped for adjectives, but not for other PoS.

For the Semcor-based filter, our results showed that the target-sense filter improved the performance for verbs and adverbs. For nouns and adjectives, the candidate-sense filter worked best. All in all, applying the Semcor filters was effective in removing rare senses and improving performance.

The length criteria did not affect the results significantly, and only made a difference in some extreme cases. Not counting the length of the target word helped slightly for nouns and adverbs, and removing punctuation improved results for adjectives. Regarding the back-off method, we observed that the count of frequencies in Semcor was the best approach for all PoS except verbs, which reached their best performance with BNC frequencies.

PoS	Relatives in Context	WordNet Baseline
Nouns	18.4	14.9
Verbs	6.7	2.0
Adjectives	9.6	7.5
Adverbs	31.1	29.9
Overall	14.4	10.4

Table 2: Experiments to tune parameters on the trial data, based on the BEST metric. Scores correspond to precision (which is the same as recall).

Finally, we observed that the performance for the BEST score decreased significantly when more than one answer was returned, probably due to the difficulty of the task.

3.3 Syntactic Filter

After the basic parameter analysis, we studied the contribution of a syntactic filter to remove those candidates that, when substituted, generate an ungrammatical sentence. Intuitively, we would expect this to have a high impact for verbs, which vary considerably in their subcategorisation properties. For example, in the case of the (reduced) target *If we **order** our lives well ...*, the syntactic filter should ideally disallow candidates such as *If we **range** our lives well ...*

In order to apply this filter, we require a parser which has an explicit notion of grammaticality, ruling out the standard treebank parsers. We experimented briefly with RASP, but found that the English Resource Grammar (ERG: Flickinger (2002)), combined with the PET run-time engine, was the best fit for out needs. Unfortunately we could not get unknown word handling working within the ERG for our submission, such that we get a meaningful output for a given input string only in the case that the ERG has full lexical coverage over that string (we will never get a spanning parse for an input where we are missing lexical entries). As such, the syntactic filter is limited in coverage only to strings where the ERG has lexical coverage.

Ideally, we would have tested this filter on trial data, but unfortunately we ran out of time. Thus, we simply eyeballed a sample of examples, and we decided to include this filter in our final submission. As we will see in Section 4, its effect was minimal. We plan to perform a complete evaluation of this module in the near future.

3.4 Extra experiments

One of the limitations of the "Relatives in Context" algorithm is that it only relies on the local context. We wanted to explore the contribution of other words in the context for the task, and we performed an experiment including the Topical Signatures resource (Agirre and Lopez de Lacalle, 2004). We simply counted the overlapping of words shared between the context and the different candidates. We only tested this for nouns, for which the results were below baseline. We then tried to integrate the topic-signature scores with the "Relatives in Context" algorithm, but we did not improve our basic system's results on the trial data. Thus, this approach was not included in our final submission.

Another problem we observed in error analysis was that the Semcor-based filters were too strict in some cases, and it was desirable to have a way of penalising low frequency senses without removing them completely. Thus, we weighted senses by the inverse of their sense-rank. As we did not have time to test this intuition properly, we opted for applying the sense-weighting only when the candidates had the same context-match length, instead of using the number of hits. We will see the effect of this method in the next section.

4 Final system

The test data consisted of 1,710 instances. For our final system we applied the best configuration for each PoS as observed in the development experiments, and the syntactic filter. We also incorporated the sense-weighting to solve ties. The results of our system, the best competing system, and the best baseline (WordNet) are shown in Table 3 for the BEST metric. Precision and recall are provided for all the instances, and also for the "Mode" instances (those that have a single preferred candidate).

Our method outperforms the baseline in all cases, and performs very close to the top system, ranking third out of eight systems. This result is consistent in the "further analysis" tables provided by the task organisers for subsets of data, where our system always performs close to the top score. The overall scores are below 13% recall for all systems when targeting all instances. This illustrates the difficulty of the task, and the similarity of the top-3 scores suggests that similar resources (i.e. WordNet) have been used in the development of the systems.

	All instances		Mode	
System	**P**	**R**	**P**	**R**
Best	12.90	12.90	20.65	20.65
Relat. in Context	**12.68**	**12.68**	**20.41**	**20.41**
WordNet baseline	9.95	9.95	15.28	15.28

Table 3: Official results based on the BEST metric.

After the release of the gold-standard data, we tested two extra settings to measure the effect of the syntactic filter and the sense-weighting in the final score. We observed that our application of the syntactic filter had almost no effect in the performance, but sense-weighting increased the overall recall by 0.4% (from 12.3% to 12.7%).

5 Conclusions

Although the task was difficult and the scores were low, we showed that by using WordNet and the local context we are able to outperform the baselines and achieve close to top performance. For future work, we would like to integrate a parser with unknown word handling in our system. We also aim to adapt the algorithm to match the target context with wildcards, in order to avoid explicitly defining the candidate set.

Acknowledgments

This research was carried out with support from Australian Research Council grant no. DP0663879.

References

Eneko Agirre and Oier Lopez de Lacalle. 2004. Publicly available topic signatures for all WordNet nominal senses. In *Proc. of the 4rd International Conference on Languages Resources and Evaluations (LREC 2004)*, pages 1123–6, Lisbon, Portugal.

Christiane Fellbaum, editor. 1998. *WordNet: An Electronic Lexical Database*. MIT Press, Cambridge, USA.

Dan Flickinger. 2002. On building a more efficient grammar by exploiting types. In Stephan Oepen, Dan Flickinger, Jun'ichi Tsujii, and Hans Uszkoreit, editors, *Collaborative Language Engineering*. CSLI Publications, Stanford, USA.

Dekang Lin. 1998. Automatic retrieval and clustering of similar words. In *Proceedings of COLING-ACL*, pages 768–74, Montreal, Canada.

David Martinez, Eneko Agirre, and Xinglong Wang. 2006. Word relatives in context for word sense disambiguation. In *Proc. of the 2006 Australasian Language Technology Workshop*, pages 42–50, Sydney, Australia.

MELB-YB: Preposition Sense Disambiguation Using Rich Semantic Features

Patrick Ye and Timothy Baldwin
Computer Science and Software Engineering
University of Melbourne, Australia
{jingy,tim}@csse.unimelb.edu.au

Abstract

This paper describes a maxent-based preposition sense disambiguation system entry to the preposition sense disambiguation task of the SemEval 2007. This system uses a wide variety of semantic and syntactic features to perform the disambiguation task and achieves a precision of 69.3% over the test data.

1 Introduction

Prepositional phrases (PPs) are both common and semantically varied in open English text. While the conventional view on prepositions from the computational linguistics community has been that they are semantically transient at best, and semantically-vacuous at worst, a robust account of the semantics of prepositions and disambiguation method can be helpful in a range of NLP tasks including machine translation, parsing (prepositional phrase attachment) and semantic role labelling (Durand, 1993; O'Hara and Wiebe, 2003; Ye and Baldwin, 2006a).

The SemEval 2007 preposition sense disambiguation task provides a common test bed for the evaluation of preposition sense disambiguation systems.

Our proposed method is maximum entropy based, and combines features developed in the context of preposition sense disambiguation for semantic role labelling (Ye and Baldwin, 2006a), and verb sense disambiguation (Ye and Baldwin, 2006b).

The remainder of this paper is structured as follows. We first discuss the pre-processing steps used in our system (Section 2), and outline the features our preposition disambiguation method uses (Section 3) and our parameter tuning method (Section 4). We then discuss and analyse the results of our method (Section 5) and conclude the paper (Section 6).

2 Pre-processing

The following list shows the pre-processing steps that our system goes through and the tools used:

Part of speech tagging SVMTool version 1.2 (Giménez and Màrquez, 2004).

Chunking An in-house chunker implemented with fnTBL, a transformation based learner (Ngai and Florian, 2001), and trained on the British National Corpus (BNC).[1]

Parsing Charniak's re-ranking parser, version August, 2006 (Charniak and Johnson, 2005).

Named entity extraction A statistical NER system described in Cohn et al. (2005).

Supersense tagging A WordNet-based supersense tagger (Ciaramita and Altun, 2006).

Semantic role labeling ASSERT version 1.4 (Pradhan et al., 2004).

3 Features

The disambiguation features used by our system can be divided into three categories: collocation features, syntactic features and semantic-role based features. We discuss each in turn below.

3.1 Collocation Features

The collocation features were inspired by the one-sense-per-collocation heuristic proposed by Yarowsky (1995). These features were designed to capture open class words that exhibit strong collocation properties with respect to the different senses of the target preposition. Details of the features in this category are listed below.

[1]This chunker is not exactly the same as Ngai and Florian's system, however it does use the default transformation templates supplied by fnTBL.

Proceedings of the 4th International Workshop on Semantic Evaluations (SemEval-2007), pages 241–244,
Prague, June 2007.

Bag of open class words The part-of-speech (POS) tags and lemmas of all the open class words that occur in the same sentence as the target preposition.

Bag of WordNet synsets The WordNet (Miller, 1993) synonym sets and their hypernyms of all the open class words that occur in the same sentence as the target preposition.

Bag of named entities Each named entity in the same sentence as the target preposition is treated as a separate feature.

Surrounding words These features are the combinations of the lemma, POS tag and relative position of the words surrounding the target preposition within a window of 7 words.

Surrounding super senses These features are the combinations of super-sense tag, POS tag and relative position of the words surrounding the target preposition within a window of 7 words.

3.2 Syntactic Features

The syntactic features were designed to capture both the flat and recursive syntactic properties of the target preposition. The flat syntactic features were derived from the surrounding POS tags and chunk tags of the target preposition; the recursive syntactic features were derived from the parse trees. The details of these feature are given below.

Surrounding POS tags These features are the combination of POS tag and relative position of the words surrounding the target preposition within a window of 7 words.

Surrounding chunk tags These features are the combination of IOB style chunk tag and relative position of the words surrounding the target preposition within a window of 5 words.

Surrounding chunk types Instead of using only the chunk tags themselves, we also extracted the actual chunk types (NP, VP, ADJP, etc) of the words surrounding the target preposition within a window of 5 words. Each chunk type is also combined with its relative position to the target preposition as a separate feature.

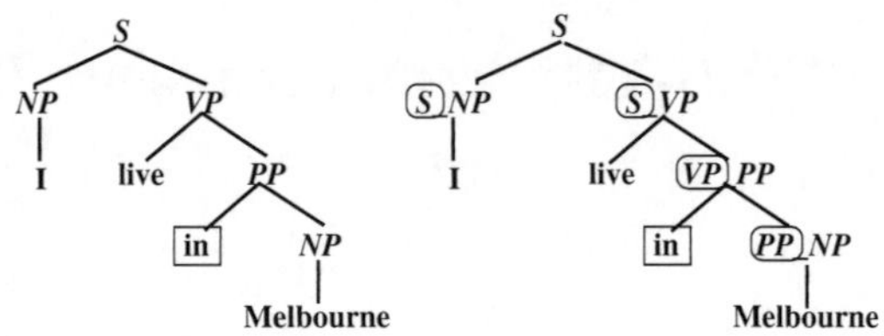

Figure 1: Parse tree examples

Parse tree features Given the position of the target preposition p in the parse tree, the basic form of the corresponding parse tree feature is just the list of nodes of p's siblings in the tree (the POS tags are treated as part of the terminal). For example, suppose the original parse tree for the sentence *I live in Melbourne* is the left tree in Figure 1, for the target preposition *in*, the basic form of the parse tree feature would be (1, NP). In order to gain more syntactic information, we further annotated each non-terminal of the parse tree with its parent node, and used the new non-terminals as our features. The right tree in Figure 1 shows the result of applying this annotation once to the original parse tree. Two levels of additional annotation were performed on the original parse trees in our feature extraction.

3.3 Semantic-Role Based Features

Finally, since prepositional phrases can often function as the temporal, location, and manner modifiers for verbs, we designed semantic-role-based features to specifically capture this type of verb-preposition semantic information. The details of these features are as follows:

Surrounding semantic role tags The semantic role tags of the words surrounding the target preposition within a window of 5 words are combined with their relative positions to the target preposition and treated as separate features. For example, consider the preposition *on* in the sentence *The man who stole my car on Sunday has apologised to me*, the semantic roles for the two verbs (*stole* and *apologised*) are shown in Table 1. The semantic roles for *stole* would generate the following features: (-5, I-A0), (-4, R-A0), (-3, TARGET), (-2, B-A1), (-1, I-A1), (0, B-AM-TMP), (1, I-AM-TMP), (2, O), (3, O), (4, O and (5, O).

Attached verbs This feature was designed to capture the verb-particle and verb-preposition-

	The	man	who	stole	my	car	on	Sunday	has	apologised	to	me
stole	B-A0	I-A0	R-A0	TARGET	B-A1	I-A1	B-AM-TMP	I-AM-TMP	O	O	O	O
apologised	B-A0	I-A0	I-A0	I-A0	I-A0	I-A0	I-A0	I-A0	O	TARGET	B-A2	I-A2

Table 1: Example semantic-role-labelled sentence

attachment relationships between verbs and prepositions. There are two situations in which a preposition p is deemed to be attached to a verb v: (1) p has a semantic role tag relative to v and this tag is a 'B' tag, (2) p has no semantic role tag relative to v, but the first token to the right of p has a 'B' tag relative to v. In the sentence shown in Table 1, *stole* would be considered as the governor of *on*.

Verb's relative position The lemma of each verb in the same sentence as the target preposition is combined with its relative position to the target preposition and treated as a separate feature. For example, the sentence shown in Table 1 would generate the two features: (-1, steal) and (1, apologize).

More detailed descriptions and examples for these features may be found in Ye and Baldwin (2006b).

4 Parameter Tuning

We used the ranking-based feature selection method from Ye and Baldwin (2006b) to select the most relevant feature based on our training data. This method works in two steps. Firstly, we calculated the information gain, gain ratio and Chi-squared statistics for each feature, and used these values to generate 3 sets of rankings for the features. We then summed up the individual ranks, and used the sums to create a set of final rankings for the features.

The feature selection process is based on 10-fold cross validation: we divided our training data into 10 pairs of training-test datasets; then for each fold, we extracted the top $N\%$ ranked features using our feature selection heuristic from the cv-training set (where N was set to values 5, 10, .., 100), and used these features to test the held-out test set. The best N as determined by the cross validation was then applied to the entire training data set.

Additionally, since we used a maximum entropy-based machine learning package,[2] it was important to determine the best Gaussian smoothing parameter g for the probability distribution. The tuning of g was incorporated into the cross validation process of feature selection.

[2]http://homepages.inf.ed.ac.uk/s0450736/maxent_toolkit.html

Given the possible combinations of parameter tuning, we trained the following three classifiers for the preposition sense disambiguation task:

Non-tuned Using all the original features and 10.0 for the Gaussian smoothing parameter.

Smoothing-tuned Using all the original features but automatically tuned Gaussian smoothing parameter.

Fully-tuned Using both automatically tuned features and Gaussian smoothing parameter.

5 Results and Analysis

The overall precision (%) obtained by the three classifiers for the fine-grained senses are as follows:

Non-tuned	Smoothing-tuned	Fully tuned
67.9	68.0	69.3

The best overall results were achieved when both the features and the Gaussian smoothing parameters were automatically tuned, achieving a 1.4% absolute precision gain over the non-tuned system. However, such parameter tuning may not always be useful: the same tuning process was found to be detrimental in a Senseval-2 verb sense disambiguation task (Ye and Baldwin, 2006b). Consistent with the findings of Ye and Baldwin (2006b), the improvement caused by the tuning of the Gaussian smoothing parameter is only marginal compared with the improvement caused by the tuning of the features.

We also evaluated our features based on their categories and types. Collocation features performed the best among the three feature categories. Without any parameter tuning, the collocation-feature-only classifier achieved an overall precision of 67.4% on the test set; the semantic-role-feature-only classifier and the syntactic-feature-only classifier achieved precision of 46.9% and 50.5% respectively.

The best-performing individual features are the bag-of-words features and bag-of-synsets features.

Feature type	Feature type % in top $N\%$ features			Overall % of the feature type
	10	20	30	
Bag of Words	13.46	13.43	12.94	13.37
Bag of Synsets	57.83	58.38	59.53	58.29
Verb's rel. positions	3.97	3.95	3.76	4.02
Surrounding POS tags	1.36	1.33	1.43	1.27

Table 2: Percentages of top-performing feature types in the top $N\%$ ranked features

On the test set, the bag-of-words-only classifier and the bag-of-synsets-only classifier achieved overall precision of 63.2% and 61.9% respectively.

We also analysed the top ranking features as calculated by our feature selection algorithm, as presented in Table 2. The results show the percentages of the top-performing feature types of each feature category in the top $N\%$ ranked features. It can be observed that none of the top-performing features seem to have a significantly disproportional representation in the top-ranked features. This indicates that the disambiguation power of a particular type of features is determined mostly by the number of features of that type.

On the other hand, the bag-of-words features appear to be the most effective, considering that they account for only 13.4% of the total features, but out-performed the bag-of-synsets features which account for nearly 60% of the total features.

It is also disappointing to see that the syntactic and semantic-role based features had little positive influence in the disambiguation process. However, this is perhaps caused by the sparseness of these features since they together only account for less than 10% of all the extracted features.

The overall finding from all this is that, similar to nouns and verbs, preposition sense is determined primarily by word context, and that syntactic and semantic role-based features play only a minor role.

6 Conclusions

In this paper, we have described a maximum entropy based preposition sense disambiguation system that uses a rich set of features. We have shown that this system performed well above the majority class baseline of 39.6% precision. Our analysis showed that the most important disambiguation features are collocation-based features. This indicates that the semantics of prepositions can be learnt mostly from their surrounding context, and not syntactic properties or verb-preposition semantics.

Acknowledgements

The research in this paper has been supported by the Australian Research Council through Discovery Project grant number DP0663879.

References

Eugene Charniak and Mark Johnson. 2005. Coarse-to-fine n-best parsing and maxent discriminative reranking. In *Proceedings of the 43rd Annual Meeting of the Association for Computational Linguistics (ACL'05)*, pages 173–180, Ann Arbor, USA.

Massimiliano Ciaramita and Yasemin Altun. 2006. Broad-coverage sense disambiguation and information extraction with a supersense sequence tagger. In *Proceedings of the 2006 Conference on Empirical Methods in Natural Language Processing*, pages 594–602, Sydney, Australia.

Trevor Cohn, Andrew Smith, and Miles Osborne. 2005. Scaling conditional random fields using error-correcting codes. In *Proceedings of the 43rd Annual Meeting of the Association for Computational Linguistics (ACL'05)*, pages 10–17, Ann Arbor, USA.

Jacques Durand. 1993. On the translation of prepositions in multilingual MT. In Frank Van Eynde, editor, *Linguistic Issues in Machine Translation*, pages 138–159. Pinter Publishers, London, UK.

Jesús Giménez and Lluís Màrquez. 2004. Svmtool: A general pos tagger generator based on support vector machines. In *Proceedings of the 4th International Conference on Language Resources and Evaluation*, pages 43–46, Lisbon, Portugal.

George A. Miller. 1993. Wordnet: a lexical database for english. In *HLT '93: Proceedings of the workshop on Human Language Technology*, pages 409–409, Princeton, USA.

Grace Ngai and Radu Florian. 2001. Transformation-based learning in the fast lane. In *Proc. of the 2nd Annual Meeting of the North American Chapter of Association for Computational Linguistics (NAACL2001)*, pages 40–7, Pittsburgh, USA.

Tom O'Hara and Janyce Wiebe. 2003. Preposition semantic classification via Treebank and FrameNet. In *Proc. of the 7th Conference on Natural Language Learning (CoNLL-2003)*, pages 79–86, Edmonton, Canada.

Sameer Pradhan, Kadri Hacioglu, Valerie Krugler, Wayne Ward, James H. Martin, and Daniel Jurafsky. 2004. Support vector learning for semantic argument classification. *Machine Learning*, 60(1–3):11–39.

David Yarowsky. 1995. Unsupervised word sense disambiguation rivaling supervised methods. In *Meeting of the Association for Computational Linguistics*, pages 189–196, Cambridge, USA.

Patrick Ye and Timothy Baldwin. 2006a. Semantic role labeling of prepositional phrases. *ACM Transactions on Asian Language Information Processing (TALIP)*, 5(3):228–244.

Patrick Ye and Timothy Baldwin. 2006b. Verb sense disambiguation using selectional preferences extracted with a state-of-the-art semantic role labeler. In *Proceedings of the Australasian Language Technology Workshop*, pages 141–148, Sydney, Australia.

NAIST.Japan: Temporal Relation Identification Using Dependency Parsed Tree

Yuchang Cheng, Masayuki Asahara and Yuji Matsumoto
Graduate School of Informatino Science,
Nara Institute of Science and Technology
8916-5 Takayama, Ikoma, Nara, 630-0192, Japan
{yuchan-c, masayu-a, matsu}@is.naist.jp

Abstract

In this paper, we attempt to use a sequence labeling model with features from dependency parsed tree for temporal relation identification. In the sequence labeling model, the relations of contextual pairs can be used as features for relation identification of the current pair. Head-modifier relations between pairs of words within one sentence can be also used as the features. In our preliminary experiments, these features are effective for the temporal relation identification tasks.

1 Overview of our system

This paper presents a temporal relation identifier by the team NAIST.Japan. Our identifier has two charactaristics: sequence labeling model and use of dependency parsed tree.

Firstly, we treated each problem a sequence labeling problem, such that event/time pairs were ordered by the position of the events and times in the document. This idea is for task B and C. In task B, the neighbouring relations between an EVENT and DCT-TIMEX3 tend to interact. In task C, when EVENT-a, EVENT-b, and EVENT-c are linearly ordered, the relation between EVENT-a and EVENT-b tends to affect the one between EVENT-b and EVENT-c.

Secondly, we introduced dependency features where each word was annotated with a label indicating its tree position to the event and the time, e.g. "descendant" of the event and "ancestor" of the time. The dependency features are introduced for our machine learning-based relation identifier. In task A, we need to label several different event-time pairs within the same sentence. We can use information from TIMEX3, which is a descendent of the target EVENT in the dependency tree.

Section 2 shows how to use a sequence labeling model for the task. Section 3 shows how to use the dependency parsed tree for the model. Section 4 presents the results and discussions.

2 Temporal Relation Identification by Sequence Labeling

Our approach to identify temporal relation is based on a sequence labeling model. The target pairs are linearly ordered in the texts.

Sequence labeling model can be defined as a method to estimate an optimal label sequence $y = \langle y_1, y_2, \ldots, y_n \rangle$ over an observed sequence $x = \langle x_1, x_2, \ldots, x_n \rangle$. We consider, w-parameterized function

$$f(x) = arg \max_{y \in \mathcal{Y}} F(x, y; w) = arg \max_{y \in \mathcal{Y}} \langle w, \Phi(x, y) \rangle.$$

Here, $\mathcal{Y}$ denotes all possible label combinations over y; $\Phi(x, y)$ denotes a feature expression over x, y. Introducing a kernel function:

$$K((x, y), (\bar{x}, \bar{y})) = \langle \Phi(x, y), \Phi(\bar{x}, \bar{y}) \rangle,$$

we have a dual representation:

$$F(x, y) = \sum_{i=1}^{m} \alpha_i K((\tilde{x}^{(i)}, \tilde{y}^{(i)}), (x, y)),$$

Proceedings of the 4th International Workshop on Semantic Evaluations (SemEval-2007), pages 245–248,
Prague, June 2007.

given a training data set $\{(\tilde{x}^{(1)}, \tilde{y}^{(1)}), \ldots, (\tilde{x}^{(m)}, \tilde{y}^{(m)})\}$. We use HMM_SVM (Altun et al., 2003) as the sequence labeling model, in which the training is performed to maximize a margin

$$\gamma_j = F(\tilde{x}^{(k)}, \tilde{y}^{(k)}) - \max_{y \neq \tilde{y}^{(k)}} F(\tilde{x}^{(k)}, y).$$

The sequence labeling approach is natural for task B and C. In task B, if a document is about affairs in the past, the relations between events and a document creation time tend to be "BEFORE". All relations in task B depend on each other. In task C, if a relation between the preceding event and the current one is "AFTER", the current one is in the past. The information helps to determine the relation between the current and succeeding one. Whereas we have reasonable explanation to introduce sequence labeling for task B and C, we cannot for task A. However, in our preliminary experiments with trial data, the sequence labeling model outperformed point-wise models for task A. Thus, we introduce the sequence labeling model for task A.

Now, we present the sequence labeling approach for each task in detail by figure 1, 2 and 3. The left parts of figures are the graphical models of the sequence labeling. The right parts are the tagged corpus: ⟨S⟩ and ⟨/S⟩ are sentence boundaries; a EVENT-*nn* denotes an EVENT; a TIME-*nn* denotes a TIMEX3; a TIME-DCT in figure 2 denotes a TIMEX3 with document creation time; a boxed EVENT-*nn* in figure 3 denotes a matrix verb EVENT.

For task A (figure 1), x is a sequence of pairs between an EVENT and a TIMEX3 within the same sentence. y is a sequence of corresponding relations. Event-time pairs are ordered first by sentence position, then by event position and finally by time position. For task B (figure 2), x is a sequence of pairs between an EVENT and a DCT-TIMEX3. y is a sequence of corresponding relations. All pairs in the same text are linearly ordered and connected. For task C (figure 3), x is a sequence of pairs between two matrix verb EVENTs in the neighboring sentences. y is a sequence of corresponding relations. All pairs in the same text are linearly ordered and connected, even if the two relations are not in the adjacent sentences.

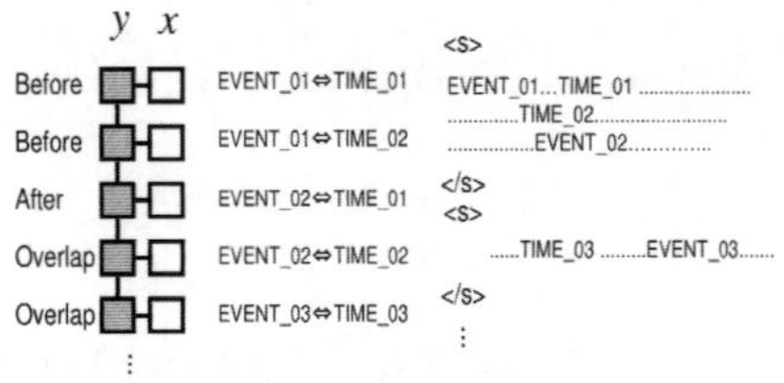

Figure 1: Sequence Labeling Model for Task A

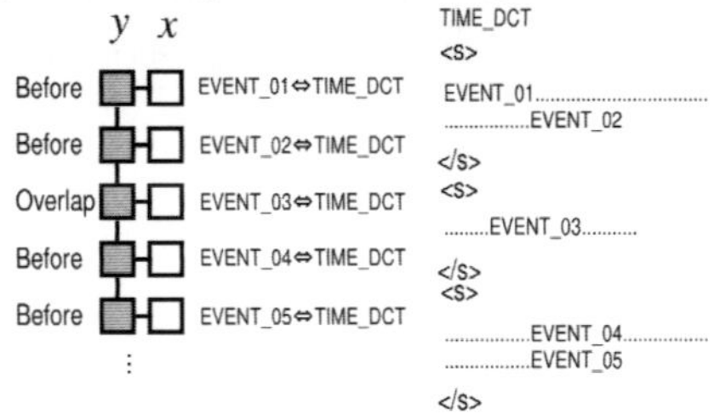

Figure 2: Sequence Labeling Model for Task B

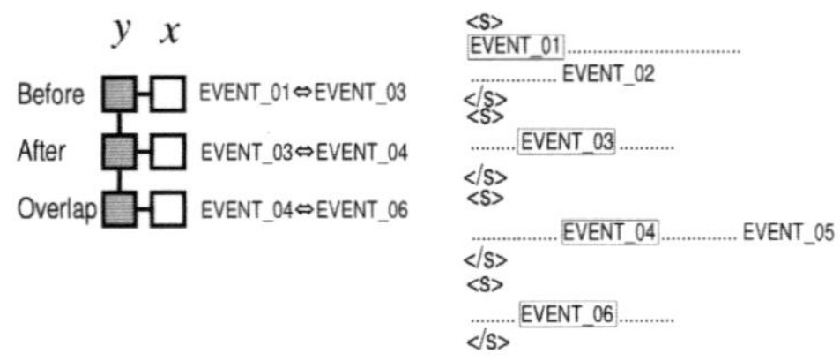

Figure 3: Sequence Labeling Model for Task C

3 Features from Dependency Parsed Tree

A dependency relation is a head-modifier relation on a syntactic tree. Figure 4 shows an example dependency parsed tree of the following sentence – "*The warrants may be exercised until 90 days after their issue date*". We parsed the TimeEval data using MSTParser v0.2 (McDonald and Pereira, 2006), which is trained with all Penn Treebank (Marcus et al., 1993) without dependency label.

We introduce **tree position** labels between an target node and another node on the dependency parsed tree: ANC (ancestor), DES (descendant), SIB (sibling), and TARGET (target word). Figure 5 shows the labels, in which the box with double lines is the target node. The tree position between the target EVENT and a word in the target TIMEX3 is used as a feature for our machine learning-based relation identifier.

We also use the words in the sentence including the target entities as features. Each word is anno-

Figure 4: An example of dependency parsed tree

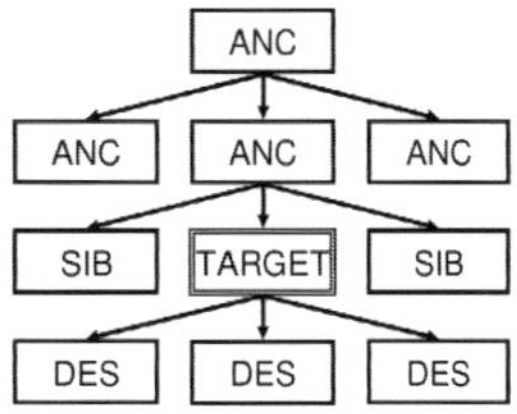

Figure 5: Tree position labels

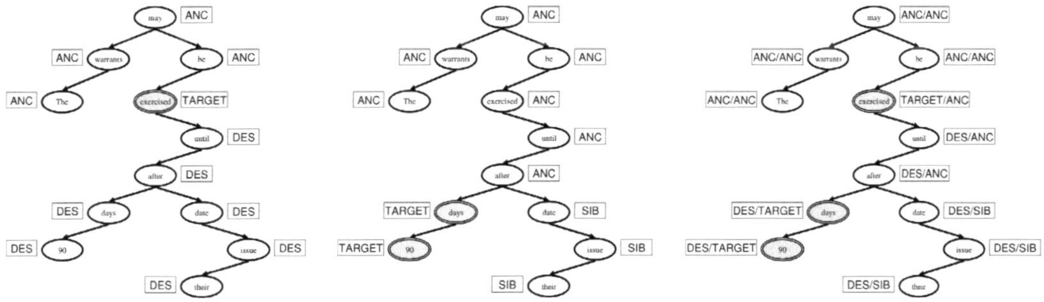

TARGET node: "*exercised*"

(1) EVENT-based

TARGET nodes: "*90*" and "*days*"

(2) TIMEX3-based

TARGET-A node: "*exercised*"
TARGET-B nodes: "*90*" and "*days*"

(3) JOINT

Figure 6: Tree position labels on the example dependency parsed tree

tated with (1) its tree position to the EVENT, (2) its tree position to the TIMEX3, and (3) the combination of the labels from (1) and (2). Fig. 6 shows the labels of tree positions. The left picture shows (1) EVENT-based labels of the tree position with the target EVENT "*exercised*". The center picture shows (2) TIMEX3-based ones with the target TIMEX3 "*90 days*". The right picture shows (3) JOINT ones which are combinations of the relation label with the EVENT and with the TIMEX3. We perform feature selection on the words in the current sentence according to the tree position labels. Note that, when MSTparser outputs more than one trees for a sentence, we introduce a meta-root node to bundle the ones in a tree.

4 Results and Discussions

We use HMM_SVM [1]as a sequence labeling model with features in Table 1, 2 and 3 for task A, B and C, respectively. The attributes *value* in TIMEX3 is encoded as the relation with DCT-TIMEX3: {BEFORE, OVERLAP, AFTER, VAGUE}. In task A, only words in the current sentence with JOINT relation labels "TARGET/∗" or "ANC/∗" or "*/DES"[2] were used. In task C, attributes in the TIMEX3 are annotated with the flag whether the TIMEX3 entity is the highest (namely the nearest to the root node) in the tree. Some adverbs and conjunctions in the succeeding sentence help to determine the adjacent two relations. Thus, we introduce all words in the succeeding sentence for Task A and B. These features are determined by our preliminary experiments with the trial data .

Table 4 is our results on the test data. Whereas, our system is average rank in task A and B, it is worst mark in task C. The features from dependency parsed trees are effective for task A and B. However, these are not for task C.

Now, we focus on what went wrong instead of what went right in our preliminary experiments in trial data. We tried point-wise methods with other

[1]http://svmlight.joachims.org/svm_struct.html

[2]'∗' stands for wild cards.

Table 1: Features for Task A

all attributes in the target EVENT
all attributes in the target TIMEX3 −the attributes *value* is encoded as the relation with DCT-TIMEX3
all words in the current sentence with TIMEX3-based label (2) of tree position
words in the current sentence with JOINT label (3) of tree position – only relation label with "TARGET/∗" or "ANC/∗" or "∗/DES" (∗ stands for wild cards)
label (1) of tree position from the EVENT to the TIMEX3
all words in the succeeding sentence

Table 2: Features for Task B

all attributes in the target EVENT
all attributes in the target TIMEX3 of in the current sentence with EVENT-based label (1) of tree position
all attributes in the target TIMEX3 of in the preceding and succeeding sentence
all words in the current sentence with EVENT-based label (1) of tree position
all words in the succeeding sentence

Table 3: Features for Task C

all attributes in the target two EVENTs (EVENT-1 and EVENT-2)
all attributes in the TIMEX3 in the sentence including EVENT-1 with the label (1) of tree position to EVENT-1
all attributes in the TIMEX3 in the sentence including EVENT-2 with the label (1) of tree position to EVENT-2
all words in the sentence including EVENT-1 with the label (1) of tree position to EVENT-1
all words in the sentence including EVENT-2 with the label (1) of tree position to EVENT-2

machine learners such as maximum entropy and multi-class support vector machines. However, sequence labeling method with HMM_SVM outperformed other point-wise methods in the trial data.

We have dependency parsed trees of the sentences. Naturally, it would be effective to introduce point-wise tree-based classifiers such as Tree Kernels in SVM (Collins and Duffy, 2002; Vishwanathan and Smola, 2002) and boosting for classification of trees (Kudo and Matsumoto, 2004). We tried a boosting learner[3] which enables us to perform subtree feature selection for the tasks. However, the boosting learner selected only one-node subtrees as useful features. Thus, we perform simple vector-based feature engineering on HMM_SVM.

[3]`http://chasen.org/~taku/software/bact/`

Table 4: Results

Task	P	R	F	Rank
Task A (strict)	0.61	0.61	0.61	2/6
Task A (relaxed)	0.63	0.63	0.63	2/6
Task B (strict)	0.75	0.75	0.75	2/6
Task B (relaxed)	0.76	0.76	0.76	2/6
Task C (strict)	0.49	0.49	0.49	5/6
Task C (relaxed)	0.56	0.56	0.56	6/6

We believe that it is necessary for solving task C to incorporate knowledge of verb-verb relation. We also tried to use features in verb ontology such as VERBOCEAN (Chklovsky and Pantel, 2004) which is used in (Mani et al., 2006). It did not improved performance in our preliminary experiments with trial data.

References

Y. Altun, I. Tsochantaridis, and T. Hofmann. 2003. Hidden markov support vector machines. In *Proc. of ICML-2003.*

T. Chklovsky and P. Pantel. 2004. Verbocean: Mining the web for fine-grained semantiv verb relations. In *Proc. of EMNLP-2004.*

M. Collins and N. Duffy. 2002. New ranking algorithms for parsing and tagging: Kernels over discrete structures, and the voted perceptron. In *Proc. of ACL-2002.*

T. Kudo and Y. Matsumoto. 2004. A boosting algorithm for classification of semi-structured text. In *Proc. of EMNLP-2004.*

I. Mani, M. Verhagen, B. Wellner, C. M. Lee, and J. Pustejovsky. 2006. Machine learning of temporal relations. In *Proc. of ACL-2006.*

M. Marcus, B. Santorini, and M. Marcinkiewicz. 1993. Building a large annotated corpus of English: the Penn Treebank. 19(2):313–330.

R. McDonald and F. Pereira. 2006. Online learning of approximate dependency parsing algorithms. In *Proc. of EACL-2006.*

M. Verhagen, R. Gaizauskas, F. Schilder, M. Hepple, and J. Pustejovsky. 2007. Semeval-2007 task 15: Tempeval temporal relation identification. In *Proc. of SemEval-2007.*

S. V. N. Vishwanathan and A. J. Smola. 2002. Fast kernels on strings and trees. In *Proc. of NIPS-2002.*

NUS-ML: Improving Word Sense Disambiguation Using Topic Features

Jun Fu Cai, Wee Sun Lee
Department of Computer Science
National University of Singapore
3 Science Drive 2, Singapore 117543
{caijunfu, leews}@comp.nus.edu.sg

Yee Whye Teh
Gatsby Computational Neuroscience Unit
University College London
17 Queen Square, London WC1N 3AR, UK
ywteh@gatsby.ucl.ac.uk

Abstract

We participated in SemEval-1 English coarse-grained all-words task (task 7), English fine-grained all-words task (task 17, subtask 3) and English coarse-grained lexical sample task (task 17, subtask 1). The same method with different labeled data is used for the tasks; SemCor is the labeled corpus used to train our system for the all-words tasks while the labeled corpus that is provided is used for the lexical sample task. The knowledge sources include part-of-speech of neighboring words, single words in the surrounding context, local collocations, and syntactic patterns. In addition, we constructed a topic feature, targeted to capture the global context information, using the latent dirichlet allocation (LDA) algorithm with unlabeled corpus. A modified naïve Bayes classifier is constructed to incorporate all the features. We achieved 81.6%, 57.6%, 88.7% for coarse-grained all-words task, fine-grained all-words task and coarse-grained lexical sample task respectively.

1 Introduction

Supervised corpus-based approach has been the most successful in WSD to date. However, this approach faces severe data scarcity problem, resulting features being sparsely represented in the training data. This problem is especially prominent for the bag-of-words feature. A direct consequence is that the global context information, which the bag-of-words feature is supposed to capture, may be poorly represented.

Our system tries to address this problem by clustering features to relieve the scarcity problem, specifically on the bag-of-words feature. In the process, we construct topic features, trained using the latent dirichlet allocation (LDA) algorithm. We train the topic model (Blei et al., 2003) on unlabeled data, clustering the words occurring in the corpus to a predefined number of topics. We then use the resulting topic model to tag the bag-of-words in the labeled corpus with topic distributions.

We incorporate the distributions, called the topic features, using a simple Bayesian network, modified from naïve Bayes model, alongside other features and train the model on the labeled corpus.

2 Feature Construction

2.1 Baseline Features

For both the lexical sample and all-words tasks, we use the following standard *baseline features*.

POS Tags For each word instance w, we include POS tags for P words prior to as well as after w within the same sentence boundary. We also include the POS tag of w. If there are fewer than P words prior or after w in the same sentence, we denote the corresponding feature as NIL.

Local Collocations We adopt the same 11 collocation features as (Lee and Ng, 2002), namely $C_{-1,-1}$, $C_{1,1}$, $C_{-2,-2}$, $C_{2,2}$, $C_{-2,-1}$, $C_{-1,1}$, $C_{1,2}$, $C_{-3,-1}$, $C_{-2,1}$, $C_{-1,2}$, and $C_{1,3}$.

Proceedings of the 4th International Workshop on Semantic Evaluations (SemEval-2007), pages 249–252,
Prague, June 2007.

Bag-of-Words For each training or testing word, w, we get G words prior to as well as after w, within the same document. These features are position insensitive. The words we extract are converted back to their morphological root forms.

Syntactic Relations We adopt the same syntactic relations as (Lee and Ng, 2002). For easy reference, we summarize the features into Table 1.

POS of w	Features
Noun	Parent headword h
	POS of h
	Relative position of h to w
Verb	Left nearest child word of w, l
	Right nearest child word of w, r
	POS of l
	POS of r
	POS of w
	Voice of w
Adjective	Parent headword h
	POS of h

Table 1: Syntactic Relations Features

The exact values of P and G for each task are set according to validation result.

2.2 Latent Dirichlet Allocation

We present here the latent dirichlet allocation algorithm and its inference procedures, adapted from the original paper (Blei et al., 2003).

LDA is a probabilistic model for collections of discrete data and has been used in document modeling and text classification. It can be represented as a three level hierarchical Bayesian model, shown graphically in Figure 1. Given a corpus consisting of M documents, LDA models each document using a mixture over K topics, which are in turn characterized as distributions over words.

In the generative process of LDA, for each document d we first draw the mixing proportion over topics θ_d from a Dirichlet prior with parameters α. Next, for each of the N_d words w_{dn} in document d, a topic z_{dn} is first drawn from a multinomial distribution with parameters θ_d. Finally w_{dn} is drawn from the topic specific distribution over words. The probability of a word token w taking on value i given that topic $z = j$ was chosen is parameterized using

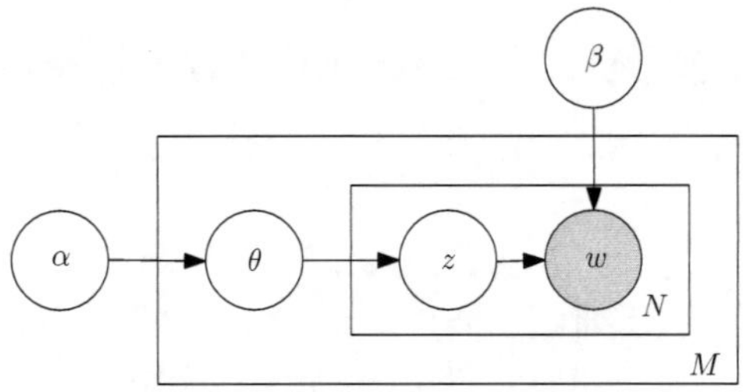

Figure 1: Graphical Model for LDA

a matrix β with $\beta_{ij} = p(w = i|z = j)$. Integrating out θ_d's and z_{dn}'s, the probability $p(D|\alpha, \beta)$ of the corpus is thus:

$$\prod_{d=1}^{M} \int p(\theta_d|\alpha) \left(\prod_{n=1}^{N_d} \sum_{z_{dn}} p(z_{dn}|\theta_d) p(w_{dn}|z_{dn}, \beta) \right) d\theta_d$$

In variational inference, the latent variables θ_d and z_{dn} are assumed independent and updates to the variational posteriors for θ_d and z_{dn} are derived (Blei et al., 2003). It can be shown that the variational posterior for θ_d is a Dirichlet distribution, say with variational parameters γ_d, which we shall use in the following to construct topic features.

2.3 Topic Features

We first select an unlabeled corpus, such as 20 Newsgroups, and extract individual words from it (excluding stopwords). We choose the number of topics, K, for the unlabeled corpus and we apply the LDA algorithm to obtain the β parameters, where β represents the probability of a word $w = i$ given a topic $z = j$, $p(w = i|z = j) = \beta_{ij}$.

The model essentially clusters words that occurred in the unlabeled corpus according to K topics. The conditional probability $p(w = i|z = j) = \beta_{ij}$ is later used to tag the words in the unseen test example with the probability of each topic.

We also use the document-specific γ_d parameters. Specifically, we need to run the inference algorithm on the labeled corpus to get γ_d for each document d in the corpus. The γ_d parameter provides an approximation to the probability of selecting topic i in the document:

$$p(z_i|\gamma_d) = \frac{\gamma_{di}}{\sum_K \gamma_{dk}}. \quad (1)$$

3 Classifier Construction

We construct a variant of the naïve Bayes network as shown in Figure 2. Here, w refers to the word. s refers to the sense of the word. In training, s is observed while in testing, it is not. The features f_1 to f_n are baseline features mentioned in Section 2.1 (including bag-of-words) while z refers to the latent topic that we set for clustering unlabeled corpus. The bag-of-words b are extracted from the neighbours of w and there are L of them. Note that L can be different from G, which is the number of bag-of-words in baseline features. Both will be determined by the validation result.

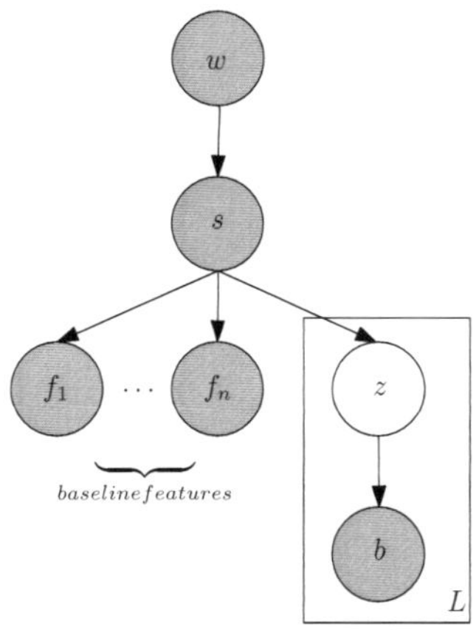

Figure 2: Graphical Model with LDA feature

The log-likelihood of an instance, $\ell(w, s, F, b)$ where F denotes the set of baseline features, can be written as

$$= \log p(w) + \log p(s|w) + \sum_F \log(p(f|s))$$

$$+ \sum_L \log \left(\sum_K p(z_k|s) p(b_l|z_k) \right).$$

The $\log p(w)$ term is constant and thus can be ignored. The first portion is normal naïve Bayes. And second portion represents the additional LDA plate. We decouple the training process into separate stages. We first extract baseline features from the task training data, and estimate, using normal naïve Bayes, $p(s|w)$ and $p(f|s)$ for all w, s and f.

Next, the parameters associated with $p(b|z)$ are estimated using LDA from unlabeled data, which is β. To estimate $p(z|s)$, we perform LDA inference on the training corpus in order to obtain γ_d for each document d. We then use the γ_d and β to obtain $p(z|b)$ for each word using

$$p(z_i|b_l, \gamma_d) = \frac{p(b_l|z_i)p(z_i|\gamma_d)}{\sum_K p(b_l|z_k)p(z_k|\gamma_d)},$$

where equation (1) is used for estimation of $p(z_i|\gamma_d)$.

This effectively transforms b to a topical distribution which we call a soft tag where each soft tag is probability distribution $t_1, \ldots, t_K$ on topics. We then use this topical distribution for estimating $p(z|s)$. Let s^i be the observed sense of instance i and $t_1^{ij}, \ldots, t_K^{ij}$ be the soft tag of the j-th bag-of-word feature of instance i. We estimate $p(z|s)$ as

$$p(z_{jk}|s) = \frac{\sum_{s^i=s} t_k^{ij}}{\sum_{s^i=s} \sum_{k'} t_{k'}^{ij}} \tag{2}$$

This approach requires us to do LDA inference on the corpus formed by the labeled training data, but not the testing data. This is because we need γ to get transformed topical distribution in order to learn $p(z|s)$ in the training. In the testing, we only apply the learnt parameters to the model.

4 Experimental Setup

We describe here the experimental setup on the English lexical sample task and all-words task. Note that we do not distinguish the two all-words tasks as the same parameters will be applied.

For lexical sample task, we use 5-fold cross validation on the training data provided to determine our parameters. For all-words task, we use SemCor as our training data and validate on Senseval-2 and Senseval-3 all-words test data.

We use MXPOST tagger (Adwait, 1996) for POS tagging, Charniak parser (Charniak, 2000) for extracting syntactic relations, and David Blei's version of LDA[1] for LDA training and inference. All default parameters are used unless mentioned otherwise.

For the all-word tasks, we use sense 1 as back-off for words that have not appeared in SemCor. We use the same fine-grained system for both the coarse and fine-grained all-words tasks. We make predictions

[1] http://www.cs.princeton.edu/~blei/lda-c/

for all words for all the systems - precision, recall and accuracy scores are all the same.

Baseline features For lexical sample task, we choose $P = 3$ and $G = 3$. For all-words task, we choose $P = 3$ and $G = 1$. ($G = 1$ means only the nearest word prior and after the test word.)

Smoothing For all standard baseline features, we use Laplace smoothing but for the soft tag (equation (2)), we use a smoothing parameter value of 2 for all-words task and 0.1 for lexical sample task.

Unlabeled Corpus Selection The unlabeled corpus we select from for LDA training include 20 Newsgroups, Reuters, SemCor, Senseval-2 lexical sample data, Senseval-3 lexical sample data and SemEval-1 lexical sample data. Although the last four are labeled corpora, we only need the words from these corpora and thus they can be regarded as unlabeled too. For lexical sample data, we define the whole passage for each training and testing instance as one document.

For lexical sample task, we use all the unlabeled corpus mentioned with $K = 60$ and $L = 18$. For all-words task, we use a corpora consisting only 20 Newsgroups and SemCor with $K = 40$ and $L = 14$.

Validation Result Table 2 shows the results we get on the validation sets. We give both the system accuracy (named as Soft Tag) and the naïve Bayes result with only standard features as baseline.

Validation Set	Soft Tag	NB baseline
SE-2 All-words	66.3	63.7
SE-3 All-words	66.1	64.6
Lexical Sample	89.3	87.9

Table 2: Validation set results (best configuration).

5 Official Results

We now present the official results on all three tasks we participated in, summarized in Table 3.

The system ranked first, fourth and second in the lexical sample task, fine-grained all-words task and coarse-grained all-words task respectively. For coarse-grained all-words task, we obtained 86.1, 88.3, 81.4, 76.7 and 79.1 for each document, from d001 to d005.

Task	Precision/Recall
Lexical sample(Task 17)	88.7
Fine-grained all-words(Task 17)	57.6
Course-grained all-words(Task 7)	81.6

Table 3: Official Results

5.1 Analysis of Results

For the lexical sample task, we compare the results to that of our naïve Bayes baseline and Support Vector Machine (SVM) (Vapnik, 1995) baseline. Our SVM classifier (using SVMlight) follows that of (Lee and Ng, 2002), which ranked the third in Senseval-3 English lexical sample task. We also analyse the result according to the test instance's part-of-speech and find that the improvements are consistent for both noun and verb.

System	Noun	Verb	Total
Soft Tag	92.7	84.2	88.7
NB baseline	91.7	83.5	87.8
SVM baseline	91.6	83.1	87.6

Table 4: Analysis on different POS on English lexical sample task

Our coarse-grained all-words task result outperformed the first sense baseline score of 0.7889 by about 2.7%.

References

Y. K. Lee and H. T. Ng. 2002. An Empirical Evaluation of Knowledge Sources and Learning Algorithms for Word Sense Disambiguation. In *Proc. of EMNLP*.

D. M. Blei and A. Y. Ng and M. I. Jordan. 2003. Latent Dirichlet Allocation. *Journal of Machine Learning Research*.

A. Ratnaparkhi 1996. A Maximum Entropy Model for Part-of-Speech Tagging. In *Proc. of EMNLP*.

E. Charniak 2000. A Maximum-Entropy-Inspired Parser. In *Proc. of the 1st Meeting of the North American Chapter of the Association for Computational Linguistics*.

V. N. Vapnik 1995. The Nature of Statistical Learning Theory. Springer-Verlag, New York.

NUS-PT: Exploiting Parallel Texts for Word Sense Disambiguation in the English All-Words Tasks

Yee Seng Chan and **Hwee Tou Ng** and **Zhi Zhong**
Department of Computer Science, National University of Singapore
3 Science Drive 2, Singapore 117543
{chanys, nght, zhongzhi}@comp.nus.edu.sg

Abstract

We participated in the SemEval-2007 coarse-grained English all-words task and fine-grained English all-words task. We used a supervised learning approach with SVM as the learning algorithm. The knowledge sources used include local collocations, parts-of-speech, and surrounding words. We gathered training examples from English-Chinese parallel corpora, SEMCOR, and DSO corpus. While the fine-grained sense inventory of WordNet was used to train our system employed for the fine-grained English all-words task, our system employed for the coarse-grained English all-words task was trained with the coarse-grained sense inventory released by the task organizers. Our scores (for both recall and precision) are 0.825 and 0.587 for the coarse-grained English all-words task and fine-grained English all-words task respectively. These scores put our systems in the first place for the coarse-grained English all-words task[1] and the second place for the fine-grained English all-words task.

1 Introduction

In this paper, we describe the systems we developed for the coarse-grained English all-words task and fine-grained English all-words task of SemEval-2007. In the coarse-grained English all-words task, systems have to perform word sense disambiguation (WSD) of all content words (noun, adjective, verb, and adverb) occurring in five documents, using a coarse-grained version of the WordNet sense inventory. In the fine-grained English all-words task, systems have to predict the correct sense of verbs and head nouns of the verb arguments occurring in three documents, according to the fine-grained sense inventory of WordNet.

Results from previous SENSEVAL English all-words task have shown that supervised learning gives the best performance. Further, the best performing system in SENSEVAL-3 English all-words task (Decadt et al., 2004) used training data gathered from multiple sources, highlighting the importance of having a large amount of training data. Hence, besides gathering examples from the widely used SEMCOR corpus, we also gathered training examples from 6 English-Chinese parallel corpora and the DSO corpus (Ng and Lee, 1996).

We developed 2 separate systems; one for each task. For both systems, we performed supervised word sense disambiguation based on the approach of (Lee and Ng, 2002) and using Support Vector Machines (SVM) as our learning algorithm. The knowledge sources used include local collocations, parts-of-speech (POS), and surrounding words. Our system employed for the coarse-grained English all-words task was trained with the coarse-grained sense inventory released by the task organizers, while our system employed for the fine-grained English all-words task was trained with the fine-grained sense

[1]A system developed by one of the task organizers of the coarse-grained English all-words task gave the highest overall score for the coarse-grained English all-words task, but this score is not considered part of the official scores.

Proceedings of the 4th International Workshop on Semantic Evaluations (SemEval-2007), pages 253–256,
Prague, June 2007.

inventory of WordNet.

In the next section, we describe the different sources of training data used. In Section 3, we describe the knowledge sources used by the learning algorithm. In Section 4, we present our official evaluation results, before concluding in Section 5.

2 Training Corpora

We gathered training examples from parallel corpora, SEMCOR (Miller et al., 1994), and the DSO corpus. In this section, we describe these corpora and how examples gathered from them are combined to form the training data used by our systems. As these data sources use an earlier version of the WordNet sense inventory as compared to the test data of the two tasks we participated in, we also discuss the need to map between different versions of WordNet.

2.1 Parallel Text

Research in (Ng et al., 2003; Chan and Ng, 2005) has shown that examples gathered from parallel texts are useful for WSD. In this evaluation, we gathered training data from 6 English-Chinese parallel corpora (Hong Kong Hansards, Hong Kong News, Hong Kong Laws, Sinorama, Xinhua News, and English translation of Chinese Treebank), available from the Linguistic Data Consortium (LDC). To gather examples from these parallel corpora, we followed the approach in (Ng et al., 2003). Briefly, after ensuring the corpora were sentence-aligned, we tokenized the English texts and performed word segmentation on the Chinese texts (Low et al., 2005). We then made use of the GIZA++ software (Och and Ney, 2000) to perform word alignment on the parallel corpora. Then, we assigned some possible Chinese translations to each sense of an English word w. From the word alignment output of GIZA++, we selected those occurrences of w which were aligned to one of the Chinese translations chosen. The English side of these occurrences served as training data for w, as they were considered to have been disambiguated and "sense-tagged" by the appropriate Chinese translations.

We note that frequently occurring words are usually highly polysemous and hard to disambiguate. To maximize the benefits of using parallel texts, we gathered training data from parallel texts for the set of most frequently occurring noun, adjective, and verb types in the Brown Corpus (BC). These word types (730 nouns, 326 adjectives, and 190 verbs) represent 60% of the noun, adjective, and verb tokens in BC.

2.2 SEMCOR

The SEMCOR corpus (Miller et al., 1994) is one of the few currently available, manually sense-annotated corpora for WSD. It is widely used by various systems which participated in the English all-words task of SENSEVAL-2 and SENSEVAL-3, including one of the top performing teams (Hoste et al., 2001; Decadt et al., 2004) which had performed consistently well in both SENSEVAL all-words tasks. Hence, we also gathered examples from SEMCOR as part of our training data.

2.3 DSO Corpus

Besides SEMCOR, the DSO corpus (Ng and Lee, 1996) also contains manually annotated examples for WSD. As part of our training data, we gathered training examples for each of the 70 verb types present in the DSO corpus.

2.4 Combination of Training Data

Similar to the top performing supervised systems of previous SENSEVAL all-words tasks, we used the annotated examples available from the SEMCOR corpus as part of our training data. In gathering examples from parallel texts, a maximum of 1,000 examples were gathered for each of the frequently occurring noun and adjective types, while a maximum of 500 examples were gathered for each of the frequently occurring verb types. In addition, a maximum of 500 examples were gathered for each of the verb types present in the DSO corpus. For each word, the examples from the parallel corpora and DSO corpus were randomly chosen but adhering to the sense distribution (proportion of each sense) of that word in the SEMCOR corpus.

2.5 Sense Inventory

The test data of the two SemEval-2007 tasks we participated in are based on the WordNet-2.1 sense inventory. However, the examples we gathered from the parallel texts and the SEMCOR corpus are based on the WordNet-1.7.1 sense inventory. Hence, there is a need to map these examples from WordNet-1.7.1 to WordNet-2.1 sense inventory. For this, we rely primarily on the WordNet sense mappings automatically generated by the work of (Daude et al., 2000). To ensure the accuracy of the mappings, we performed some manual corrections of our own, focusing on the set of most frequently occurring nouns, adjectives, and verbs. For the verb examples from the DSO corpus which are based on the WordNet-1.5 sense inventory, we manually mapped them to WordNet-2.1 senses.

3 WSD System

Following the approach of (Lee and Ng, 2002), we train an SVM classifier for each word using the knowledge sources of local collocations, parts-of-speech (POS), and surrounding words. We omit the syntactic relation features for efficiency reasons. For local collocations, we use 11 features: $C_{-1,-1}$, $C_{1,1}$, $C_{-2,-2}$, $C_{2,2}$, $C_{-2,-1}$, $C_{-1,1}$, $C_{1,2}$, $C_{-3,-1}$, $C_{-2,1}$, $C_{-1,2}$, and $C_{1,3}$, where $C_{i,j}$ refers to the ordered sequence of tokens in the local context of an ambiguous word w. Offsets *i* and *j* denote the starting and ending position (relative to *w*) of the sequence, where a negative (positive) offset refers to a token to its left (right). For parts-of-speech, we use 7 features: P_{-3}, P_{-2}, P_{-1}, P_0, P_1, P_2, P_3, where P_0 is the POS of *w*, and P_{-i} (P_i) is the POS of the *i*th token to the left (right) of *w*. For surrounding words, we consider all unigrams (single words) in the surrounding context of *w*. These words can be in a different sentence from *w*.

4 Evaluation

We participated in two tasks of SemEval-2007: the coarse-grained English all-words task and the fine-grained English all-words task. In both tasks, when there is no training data at all for a particular word, we tag all test examples of the word with its first sense in WordNet. Since our systems give exactly one answer for each test example, recall is the same as precision. Hence we will just report the micro-average recall in this section.

4.1 Coarse-Grained English All-Words Task

Our system employed for the coarse-grained English all-words task was trained with the coarse-grained WordNet-2.1 sense inventory released by the task organizers. We obtained a score of 0.825 in this task, as shown in Table 1 under the column $SC + DSO + PT$. It turns out that among the 16 participants of this task, the system which returned the best score was developed by one of the task organizers. Since the score of this system is not considered part of the official scores, our score puts our system in the first position among the participants of this task. For comparison, the WordNet first sense baseline score as calculated by the task organizers is 0.789. To gauge the contribution of parallel text examples, we retrained our system using only examples gathered from the SEMCOR and DSO corpus. As shown in Table 1 under the column $SC + DSO$, this gives a score of 0.817 when scored against the answer keys released by the task organizers. Although adding examples from parallel texts gives only a modest improvement in the scores, we note that this improvement is achieved from a relatively small set of word types which are found to be frequently occurring in BC. Future work can explore expanding the set of word types by automating the process of assigning Chinese translations to each sense of an English word, with the use of suit-

English all-words task	Training data	
	SC+DSO	SC+DSO+PT
Coarse-grained	0.817	0.825
Fine-grained	0.578	0.587

Table 1: Scores for the coarse-grained English all-words task and fine-grained English all-words task, using different sets of training data. SC+DSO refers to using examples gathered from SEMCOR and DSO corpus. Similarly, SC+DSO+PT refers to using examples gathered from SEMCOR, DSO corpus, and parallel texts.

Doc-ID	Recall	No. of test instances
d001	0.883	368
d002	0.881	379
d003	0.834	500
d004	0.761	677
d005	0.814	345

Table 2: Score of each individual test document, for the coarse-grained English all-words task.

able bilingual lexicons.

As part of the evaluation results, the task organizers also released the scores of our system on each of the 5 test documents. We show in Table 2 the score we obtained for each document, along with the total number of test instances in each document. We note that our system obtained a relatively low score on the fourth document, which is a Wikipedia entry on computer programming. To determine the reason for the low score, we looked through the list of test words in that document. We noticed that the noun *program* has 20 test instances occurring in that fourth document. From the answer keys released by the task organizers, all 20 test instances belong to the sense of "a sequence of instructions that a computer can interpret and execute", which we do not have any training examples for. Similarly, we noticed that another noun *programming* has 27 test instances occurring in the fourth document which belong to the sense of "creating a sequence of instructions to enable the computer to do something", which we do not have any training examples for. Thus, these two words alone account for 47 of the errors made by our system in this task, representing 2.1% of the 2,269 test instances of this task.

4.2 Fine-Grained English All-Words Task

Our system employed for the fine-grained English all-words task was trained on examples tagged with fine-grained WordNet-2.1 senses (mapped from WordNet-1.7.1 senses and 1.5 senses as described earlier). Unlike the coarse-grained English all-words task, the correct POS tag and lemma of each test instance are not given in the fine-grained task. Hence, we used the POS tag from the mrg parse files released as part of the test data and performed lemmatization using WordNet. We obtained a score of 0.587 in this task, as shown in Table 1. This ranks our system in second position among the 14 participants of this task. If we exclude parallel text examples and train only on examples gathered from the SEMCOR and DSO corpus, we obtain a score of 0.578.

5 Conclusion

In this paper, we describe the approach taken by our systems which participated in the coarse-grained English all-words task and fine-grained English all-words task of SemEval-2007. Using training examples gathered from parallel texts, SEMCOR, and the DSO corpus, we trained supervised WSD systems with SVM as the learning algorithm. Evaluation results show that this approach achieves good performance in both tasks.

6 Acknowledgements

Yee Seng Chan is supported by a Singapore Millennium Foundation Scholarship (ref no. SMF-2004-1076).

References

Yee Seng Chan and Hwee Tou Ng. 2005. Scaling up word sense disambiguation via parallel texts. In *Proc. of AAAI05*, pages 1037–1042.

Jordi Daude, Lluis Padro, and German Rigau. 2000. Mapping WordNets using structural information. In *Proc. of ACL00*, pages 504–511.

Bart Decadt, Veronique Hoste, Walter Daelemans, and Antal van den Bosch. 2004. GAMBL, genetic algorithm optimization of memory-based WSD. In *Proc. of SENSEVAL-3*, pages 108–112.

Veronique Hoste, Anne Kool, and Walter Daelemans. 2001. Classifi er optimization and combination in the English all words task. In *Proc. of SENSEVAL-2*, pages 83–86.

Yoong Keok Lee and Hwee Tou Ng. 2002. An empirical evaluation of knowledge sources and learning algorithms for word sense disambiguation. In *Proc. of EMNLP02*, pages 41–48.

Jin Kiat Low, Hwee Tou Ng, and Wenyuan Guo. 2005. A maximum entropy approach to Chinese word segmentation. In *Proc. of the Fourth SIGHAN Workshop on Chinese Language Processing*, pages 161–164.

George A. Miller, Martin Chodorow, Shari Landes, Claudia Leacock, and Robert G. Thomas. 1994. Using a semantic concordance for sense identifi cation. In *Proc. of HLT94 Workshop on Human Language Technology*, pages 240–243.

Hwee Tou Ng and Hian Beng Lee. 1996. Integrating multiple knowledge sources to disambiguate word sense: An exemplar-based approach. In *Proc. of ACL96*, pages 40–47.

Hwee Tou Ng, Bin Wang, and Yee Seng Chan. 2003. Exploiting parallel texts for word sense disambiguation: An empirical study. In *Proc. of ACL03*, pages 455–462.

Franz Josef Och and Hermann Ney. 2000. Improved statistical alignment models. In *Proc. of ACL00*, pages 440–447.

OE: WSD Using Optimal Ensembling (OE) Method

Harri M. T. Saarikoski
Helsinki University
Language Technology PhD Programme
F-00014 Helsinki, Finland
harri.saarikoski@helsinki.fi

Abstract

Optimal ensembling (OE) is a word sense disambiguation (WSD) method using word-specific training factors (average positive vs negative training per sense, *posex* and *negex*) to predict best system (classifier algorithm / applicable feature set) for given target word. Our official entry (OE1) in Senseval-4 Task 17 (coarse-grained English lexical sample task) contained many design flaws and thus failed to show the whole potential of the method, finishing -4.9% behind top system (+0.5 gain over best base system). A fixed system (OE2) finished only -3.4% behind (+2.0% net gain). All our systems were 'closed', i.e. used the official training data only (average 56 training examples per each sense). We also show that the official evaluation measure tends to favor systems that do well with high-trained words.

1 Introduction

Optimal ensembling is a novel method for combining WSD systems and obtaining higher classification accuracy (presented more fully in Saarikoski et al. 2007). The essential difference from other ensembling methods (such as various types of voting ensembles and cross-validation based best machine selection) is that best machine is predicted using factors calculated from words (e.g. number of senses) and their training data (e.g. number of training examples per sense). The method is loosely based on findings of system performance differences in both WSD (different machines by Yarowsky et al., 2002 and different feature sets by Mihalcea, 2002) and other classification tasks such as text categorization (Forman et al., 2004, Bay et al., 2002).

2 Method

We first describe in detail the two selection routines in OE as deployed in this experiment.

2.1 Machine (Mach) Selection

We selected support vector machine (SVM) (Vapnik, 1995) and Naive Bayes (NB) (John et al. 1995) as classifiers for our base systems to be optimally ensembled. This was mainly because of their attested strength at earlier Senseval evaluations (Edmonds et al. 2002, Mihalcea et al. 2004) and mutual complementarity discovered by us (Saarikoski et al., 2007). Original batch of candidate machines that we tested for OE using Senseval-2 dataset included the following classifiers: Decision Stump, Decision Tree with various values of confidence (c) parameter 0.05, 0.15, 0.25 and instance-based classifier with k values ranging from 1..15 at intervals of two [1]. After cross-validation runs against current dataset (see below), however, SVM and NB proved again to be overall strongest regardless of training input, so we built OE around those two classifiers.

2.2 Feature Set (Fset) Selection

We extracted three contextual feature sets from training data for all words to train the machines: 1-grams (1g) and sequential 2-grams both from whole instance (2g) as well as part-of-speech tags from local 1-word window around and including target word (pos3). We also used three 'multifsets' (1g-2g, 1g-pos3, 2g-pos3).

[1] We used Weka implementations (J48, Ibk, SMO, Decision Stump, NaiveBayes) of these algorithms (Witten, 2005).

Proceedings of the 4th International Workshop on Semantic Evaluations (SemEval-2007), pages 257–260,
Prague, June 2007.

2.3 Best-System Prediction Factors

In Figure 1, we quote prediction factors used for predicting best system for some test words.

word	posex	negex	OE1
ask.v	58	290	0,52
work.v	26	204	0,67
area.n	65	261	0,7
carrier.n	9	102	0,71
chance.n	30	61	0,73
prove.v	8	41	0,73
build.v	40	79	0,74
promise.v	25	25	0,75
produce.v	38	77	0,75
buy.v	23	141	0,76
believe.v	101	101	0,78
condition.n	33	99	0,78
state.n	154	463	0,79
claim.v	14	40	0,8
regard.v	13	27	0,86
complain.v	16	16	0,86
recall.v	12	37	0,87
rate.n	505	504	0,89
report.v	43	85	0,91
approve.v	27	26	0,92
propose.v	11	23	0,93
complete.v	14	28	0,94
capital.n	56	222	0,96
bill.n	51	353	0,96
receive.v	68	68	0,96
allow.v	54	54	0,97
value.n	67	268	0,98

Figure 1. Prediction factors and OE1 accuracy for some test words in Senseval-4 Task 17 (sorted by OE1 accuracy at the word).

3 System Descriptions

We designed and ran two systems:

OE1 (official): For OE1, we used two machines in three configurations (SVMc=0.1, SVMc=1.0, NB) trained on 3 feature sets, totalling at 3*3 = 9 base systems (number of machines * number of fsets for each). Selection of *c(omplexity)* parameter for SVM was based on previous knowledge of performance differences of c=0.1 and c=1.0 based systems as reported in Saarikoski et al. (2007). This is based on accounts by e.g. Vapnik (1995) that lower *c* value makes the classifier generate a more complex training model which is more suitable for tougher words (lower posex, higher negex).

We learned the best-system predictor model using performance data from Senseval-4 10CV runs only. For 70 words where two fsets performed within +/-5% of each other, we added the next best fset into a 'multifset'.

OE2 (unofficial): This system incorporated the following fixes to OE1 (see Discussion below for motivations for these fixes): First, we significantly reduced the base system grain. We only used two machines strongest in 10CV runs (SVMc=0.1 and NB) and these machines were trained with fsets found best for those machines in 10CV runs: pos3 for both machines, SVMc=0.1 was additionally trained with 1g and NB with 2g respectively. This resulted in a 2 * 2 = 4-system ensemble. Best fset was still selected on the basis of 10CV runs.

As training data for the best-machine predictor, we used the performance profiles of about 50 systems (both our own and Senseval systems) run mainly against Senseval-2 English lexical sample dataset. We decided to use only two prediction factors (posex and negex, see Figure 1) to predict best machine for each word. This was because previously we had found these two machines (SVM and NB) particularly differing with regard to the combination or cross-section of these two factors. (For illustration of the predictor model with posex and negex as the two axes and discussion of other possible factors, see Saarikoski et. al, 2007. As to reasons for such a performance difference between any two classification machines, see also Yarowsky et al., 2002).

Difference in the best-system predictions of these two systems (OE1 vs OE2) was substantial: 33 words fully changed machine (from SVM to NB or vice versa), 40 words partially changed the system (change of SVM configuration or change of fset from multifset to single fset). Only 27 words kept the same machine in same configuration and fset. We can therefore call OE2 a substantial revision of OE1 (in effect a rather total departure from CV-based selection toward actual word factor based optimal ensembling).

In both OEs, the mach-fset combination predicted to be the best for a word was run against the test instances of that word [2]. In case of 'multifsets', each single fset had equal probability-based vote in disambiguating the test instances of

[2] SyntaLex code (Mohammad and Pedersen, 2002, http://www.d.umn.edu/~tpederse/syntalex.html) was used for extracting n-grams and carrying out disambiguation. Brill Tagger (Brill, 1995) was used for extracting PoS tags. Weka library of classifiers (Witten, 2005) was used to run cross-validations and best-system predictors.

that word. As usual, the sense with highest probability was chosen as answer for each instance.

4 Test Results

Here are the results:

system name	gross gain	net gain	accuracy[3]
OE1	**+3.0 (+7.8)**	**+0.5 (+4.4)**	**83.8**
OE2	**+2.3 (+7.0)**	**+2.0 (+5.8)**	**85.3**

Table 1. Results of OE systems. In columns 2-3, macro (micro) averaged per-word gross and net gains calculated from actual test runs (not 10CV runs) are reported. Column 4 reports the official macro-averaged accuracy for all words of our systems. (Differences of the respective benefits of these evaluation measures are outlined in Discussion below and more generally in Sebastiani (2002). Terms 'gross (or potential) gain' and 'net (realized) gain' are defined in Saarikoski et al. (2007).).

5 Discussion

We now turn to analyze these results. We can first note that results are largely in line with our previous findings with OEs and other types of ensembles (see Saarikoski et al., 2007). In what follows we attempt to account for the results: why OE1 finished as much behind top system and also why OE2 performed that much better than OE1. This first 'known issue' concerns both OEs:

(1) Base system accuracy was low because we did not use strong fsets: Our official entry finished at 7th place in the evaluation, -4.9% behind top system while the inofficial entry would have finished in 5th place (-3.4% behind). We attribute this mainly to the absence of more advanced feature sets. For example, we did not employ syntactic parse features (such as predicate-object pairs) from which Yarowsky et al. (2002) showed +2% gain. We would also naturally lose to any systems using extra training or lexical knowledge (e.g. 2nd place finisher UBC-ALM, at 86.9 accuracy, used both semantic domains and SemCor corpus). But without knowing how much extra knowledge such 'open' systems used, we cannot say by how much.

Specifically in OE1 entry, there were two basic design flaws which we address next.

(2) Base system grain was too high to produce enough net gain: The base system grain (18 base systems) we attempted to predict in OE1 was far too great since prediction accuracy rapidly decreases when adding new systems. The grain was also unnecessarily great, since the 4-grain we used for OE2 could harvest most of the gross gain (cf. gross gains of the two systems in Table 1).

(3) Using 10CV runs uncritically for best fset selection: This was ill-advised because of many reasons. First, selecting best fset for WSD based on CV runs is known to be a difficult task (Mihalcea, 2002). Prediction accuracy for the three fsets we used for OE1 was 0.74, i.e. for 26 words out of 100 best fset was mispredicted. About half of these were cases where machine was mispredicted as well and average loss tended to be even greater. Second, multifsets could not be 10CV-tested with the Weka machine-learning toolkit we used (Witten, 2005). Our custom resolution to this multifset selection task was to select best and next best fset. This turned out to produce many false predictions, some of which were quite substantial (> 10% loss to best fset). For instance, at *system.n* we lost > 30% from selecting NB-2g instead of actual best system (NB-pos3). Third, only after submitting the entry, we also realized two strongest fsets are not necessarily complementary (i.e. that each would contain relevant clues for *different* test instances) and that learning machines might be confused (i.e. could not effectively carry out feature selection and weighting) by the profusion and heterogeneity of features in multifsets. In fact, we found that omitting multifsets from OE1 (i.e. having 3 single fsets with the same 3 machines = 6-system OE) would have worked slightly better than OE1 (3*3=9): the accuracy rose from 83.8 to 84.1. Fourth, it was found previously (Saarikoski et al., 2007) that CV-based best system prediction scheme tends to produce less gain than OE (cf. accuracy of OE1 < OE2 in Table 1).

The remaining argument discusses Senseval evaluation measure (applies to all OE systems):

(4) Official evaluation measure is particularly unfavorable to OE systems: Senseval scoring scheme[4] is calculated as the number of instances disambiguated correctly divided by number of all

[3] Best base system in both OEs was NB-pos3 (83.3).

[4] Documentation for scoring scheme can be found at: http://www.cse.unt.edu/~rada/senseval/senseval3/scoring/

instances in test dataset. This measure (termed 'macro-averaged accuracy' in Sebastiani, 2002) is known to upweigh classification cases (words) that have more test instances. While we recognize the usefulness of this measure, we calculated in Table 1 the alternative measure (termed 'micro-averaged accuracy' in Sebastiani, 2002). It differs from the former (defined by e.g. Sebastiani, 2002) in that *all words are treated equally* (i.e. 'normalized') regardless of number of test instances. In addition, it has been Senseval practice (Edmonds et al. 2002, Mihalcea et al. 2004) that words with great number of test instances tend to have an equally great number of training instances. At such 'easier' words, system performance differences (sysdiff) occur much less and since OE is based on locating and making use of sysdiff, it cannot perform well. Therefore, it is liable to lose to single-machine systems with inherently stronger fsets (see point 1 above). For these reasons, the measures are very different with the latter revealing the OE potential more appropriately.

In fact, we estimate that only 40 out of the 100 test words in this dataset show any kind of sysdiff between most participating systems (> 5% macro-averaged sysdiff per word). Furthermore, only 20 of them only are likely to produce substantial sysdiff (> 10%). For example, in our 10CV runs, we got 0.99 accuracies by all base systems for the very highly trained word *say.v* with posex > 500. If there was a participating system that achieved 1.00 in such a single high-train word (*say.v*), the huge number of test instances of that word raised its macro-averaged accuracy, winning considerably over systems performing well with low-train words (e.g. *propose.v* with posex=11 and negex=24 and grain=3 where both OE1 and OE2 performed at 0.93 accuracy owing to correct best system choice). In other words, the official measure does not account for the finding (Yarowsky et al., 2002 and Saarikoski et al., 2007) that systems considerably differ precisely in terms of their ability to disambiguate high/low-train words (measured by posex/negex factors). Therefore, it can be said that the official measure fails to treat all systems equally.

6 Conclusion and Further Work

Since OE is a generic method that can be applied to any base systems, we believe it has a place in WSD methodology. With remaining open questions resolved (optimizing system grain to feasible prediction accuracy, discovering more predictive factors for both machines and fsets, understanding how the evaluation measures complete each other), it is probable that OE can improve current state of the art WSD systems (especially if provided with stronger while still complementary base systems). Though OE systems run the risk that OE may in fact be inferior to its best base system, we would like to note that thus far no OE of ours (around 10-15 different tests) has failed to produce net gain.

References

Bay, S. D., and Pazzani, M. J. Characterizing model errors and differences. In 17th International Conference on Machine Learning (2000)

Brill, E. Transformation-Based Error-Driven Learning and Natural Language Processing: A Case Study in Part of Speech Tagging Computational Linguistics (1995)

Edmonds, P., and Kilgarriff, A. Introduction to the Special Issue on evaluating word sense disambiguation programs. Journal of Natural Language Engineering 8(4) (2002)

Forman, G., and Cohen, I. Learning from Little: Comparison of Classifiers Given Little Training. In ECML, 15th European Conference on Machine Learning and the 8th European Conference on Principles and Practice of Knowledge Discovery in Databases (2004)

John, G. and Langley, P. Estimating Continuous Distributions in Bayesian Classifiers. Proceedings of the Eleventh Conference on Uncertainty in Artificial Intelligence. Morgan Kaufmann, San Mateo (1995)

Mihalcea, R. Word sense disambiguation with pattern learning and automatic feature selection. Journal of Natural Language Engineering, 8(4) (2002)

Mihalcea, R., Kilgarriff, A. and Chklovski, T. The SENSEVAL-3 English lexical sample task. Proceedings of SENSEVAL-3 Workshop at ACL (2004)

Mohammad, S. and Pedersen, T (2004). Complementarity of Lexical and Simple Syntactic Features: The Syntalex Approach to Senseval-3. Proceedings of Senseval-3

Saarikoski, H., Legrand, S., Gelbukh, A. (2007) Case-Sensitivity of Classifiers for WSD: Complex Systems Disambiguate Tough Words Better. In CICLING 2007 and Lecture Notes in Computer Science, Springer

Sebastiani, F. Machine learning in automated text categorization, ACM Computing Surveys (CSUR), Vol. 34 Issue 1 (2002) ACM Press, New York, NY, USA.

Vapnik, V. N. The Nature of Statistical Learning Theory. Springer (1995)

Witten, I., Frank, E. Data Mining: Practical Machine Learning Tools and Techniques (Second Edition). Morgan Kaufmann (2005).

Yarowsky, D. and Florian, R. Evaluating sense disambiguation across diverse parameter spaces. Journal of Natural Language Engineering, 8(4) (2002) 293-311.

PKU: Combining Supervised Classifiers with Features Selection

Peng Jin, Danqing Zhu, *Fuxin Li and Yunfang Wu
Institute of Computational Linguistics
Peking University, Beijing, China
*Institute of Automation Chinese Academy of Sciences
Beijing, China
{jandp,zhudanqing,wuyf}@pku.edu.cn *Fuxin.li@ia.ac.cn

Abstract

This paper presents the word sense disambiguation system of Peking University which was designed for the SemEval-2007 competition. The system participated in the Web track of task 11 "English Lexical Sample Task via English-Chinese Parallel Text". The system is a hybrid model by combining two supervised learning algorithms SVM and ME. And the method of entropy-based feature chosen was experimented. We obtained precision (and recall) of 81.5%.

1 Introduction

The PKU system participated in the web track of task 11. In this task, the organizers propose an English lexical sample task for word sense disambiguation (WSD), where the sense-annotated examples are (semi)-automatically gathered from word-aligned English-Chinese parallel texts. After assigning appropriate Chinese translations to each sense of an English word, the English side of the parallel texts can then serve as the training data, as they are considered to have been disambiguated and "sense-annotated" by the appropriate Chinese translations. This proposed task is thus similar to the multilingual lexical sample task in Senseval3, except that the training and test examples are collected without manually annotating each individual ambiguous word occurrence.

The system consists of two supervised learning classifiers, support vector machines (SVM) and maximum entropy (ME). A method of entropy-based feature chosen was experimented to reduce the feature dimensions. The training data was limited to the labeled data provided by the task, and a PoS-tagger (tree-tagger) was used to get more features.

2 Features Selection

We used tree-tagger to PoS-tag the texts before the feature extractor. No other resource is used in the system. The window size of the context is set to 5 around the ambiguous word. Only the following features are used in the system:

Local words
Local PoSs
Bag-of-words
Local collocations

Here local collocation means any two words which fall into the context window to form collocation pair.

Two methods are used to reduce the dimensions of feature space. One comes from the linguistic knowledge, some words whose PoSs are IN, DT, SYM, POS, CC or "``" are not included as the features.

The second method is based on entropy. To each word, the training data was split to two parts for parameter estimation. One (usually consist of 30 – 50 instances) as the simultaneous test and the rest instances form the other part.

First the entropy of each feature was calculated. For example, the target word 'work', it has two senses and the dimensions of its feature space is N. For feature f_i, if it appears in m instances belonging to sense A and n instances in sense B. So the

Proceedings of the 4th International Workshop on Semantic Evaluations (SemEval-2007), pages 261–263,
Prague, June 2007. ©2007 Association for Computational Linguistics

probability distributions are: $p_1 = {}^{m}\!/_{m+n}$ and $p_2 = {}^{n}\!/_{m+n}$. The entropy of f_i is:

$$H(f_i) = \sum_{j=1}^{2} p_j \log \frac{1}{p_j}$$

We rank all the features according to their entropy from small to big. And then first percent lambda features are chosen as the final feature set. Using this smaller feature set, we use the classifier to make a new prediction.

The parameter λ is estimated by comparing the system performance on the simultaneous test. In our system, .68 is chosen. It means that 68% original features used to form the new feature space.

The same classifier was tried on different feature sets to get different outputs and then were combined.

3 Classifiers

The Support Vector Machines (SVM) are a group of supervised learning methods that can be applied to classification or regression. It is developed by Vapnik and has been applied into WSD (Lee et al., 2004). Since most of the target words have more than two senses, we used the implementation of SVM that includes lib-svm (Chang and Lin, 2001) and svm-multiclass (Joachims, 2004). To lib-svm, the parameter of "b" which is used to obtain probability information after training is set 0 or 1 individually to form different classifiers. The default linear kernel is used.

Each vector dimension represents a feature. The numerical value of a vector entry is the numerical value of the corresponding feature. In our system, we use binary features. If the context of an instance has a particular feature, then the feature value is set to 1, otherwise the value is set to 0.

ME modeling provides a framework for integrating information for classification from many heterogeneous information sources. The intuition behind the maximum entropy principle is: given a set of training data, model what is known and assume no further knowledge about the unknown by assigning them equal probability (entropy is maximum). There are also some researchers using ME to WSD (Chao and Dyer, 2002). Dekang Lin's implementation of ME was used. He used Generalized Iterative Scaling (GIS) algorithm.

4 Development

Because of time constraints, we could not experiment all the training data by cross-validation. To each target word, we extract first 50 training instances as the test.

Target Word	Svm-Multi-class	ME	Lib-svm		
			Prob. Output		Non-prob. Output
			Orig. F.S.	Red. FS	
Age	.68	.70	.70	.70	.66
Area	.80	.70	.80	.74	.82
Body	.84	.84	.90	.92	.16
Change	.48	.42	.66	.42	.58
Director	.96	.94	.96	.96	.96
Experience	.90	.88	.88	.90	.88
Future	.94	.94	.94	.98	.94
interest	.84	.82	.82	.88	.84
issue	.88	.88	.84	.90	.88
Life	.92	.94	.98	1.0	.94
Material	.88	.92	.94	.94	.88
Need	.86	.86	.86	.86	.86
performance	.78	.82	.80	.82	.80
Program	.70	.74	.72	.72	.72
Report	.94	.94	.94	.94	.94
System	.76	.70	.76	.76	.70
Time	.70	.64	.68	.60	.76
today	.72	.70	.74	.68	.76
Water	.90	.92	.88	.82	.90
Work	.90	.86	.90	.92	.90

Table 1: The Performance on Nouns

For some adjectives, we just extract first 30 because the training data is small. For ten of adjectives, the training data is too small, we directly use the lib-svm (with probability output) as the final classifier.

Both SVM and ME could output the probability for each instance to each class. So we try to combine them to improve the performance. Several methods of combining classifiers have been investigated (Radu et al., 2002). The enhanced Counted-based Voting (CBV) and Rank-Based Voting, Probability Mixture Model, and best single Classifier are experimented in the training data. Table 1 and Table 2 indicate the results of nouns and adjectives individually, which were achieved with each of the different methods. In these tables, "Orig F.S." and "Red. F.S." mean original feature set and reduced feature set. "Prob. output" and "Non Prob.

output" are two implementation of lib-svm. The former output the probability of each instance belonging to each class, otherwise the latter not. Different from the results of Radu, choosing the best single classifier get the better performance than any kinds of combination. In this paper, we did not list the performances of combining.

According to Table 1 and Table 2, the particular classifier chosen for that word was the one with the highest score in the training data.

Target Word	Svm-Multi-class	ME	Lib-svm		
			Prob. Output		Non-prob. output
			Orig. F.S.	Red. F.S.	
Early	.77	.80	.77	.80	.77
Educational	.87	.87	.87	.83	.87
Free	.74	.80	.84	.90	82
Human	.96	.92	.96	.90	.96
Long	.70	.70	.73	.87	.70
Major	.78	.78	.78	.80	.78
Medical	.76	.86	.78	.84	.78
New	.73	.77	.63	.43	.63
Simple	.73	.77	.77	.77	.80
Third	.98	.94	.98	1.0	.96

Table 2: The performance on Adjectives

Two parameters are different from these two SVMs. One is the "-c", which is the tradeoff between training error and margin. In lib-svm the value of "-c" is set 1; but in svm-multiclass is 0.01. The other is the strategy of how to utility binary-classification to resolve multi-class. In svm-multiclass, no strategy is needed since the algorithm in (Crammer and Singer, 2001) solves the multi-class problem directly. In lib-svm, we use the one-against-all approach which is the default in lib-svm. Down-sampling is used if some result is trivial classification. The reason is that the unbalanced distribution of training data. We compared selecting support vectors and down-sampling. The latter is better.

5 Results

We participated in the subtask of SemEval-2007 English lexical sample task via English-Chinese parallel text. The organizers make use of English-Chinese documents gathered from the URL pairs given by the STRAND Bilingual Databases. They used this corpus for the evaluation of 40 English words (20 nouns and 20 adjectives).

Our system gives exactly one sense for each test example. So the recall is always the same as precision. Micro-average precision is 81.5%. According to the task organizers, the recall of the best participating in this subtask is 81.9%. So the performance of our system compares favorably with the best participating system.

6 Acknowledgements

This research is supported by Humanity and Social Science Research Project of China State Education Ministry (No. 06JC740001) and National Basic Research Program of China (No. 2004CB318102).

We are indebted to Helmut Schmid, IMS, University of Stuttgart, for making Tree-Tagger available free of charge.

Finally, the authors thank the organizers Hwee Tou Ng and Yee Seng Chan, for their hard work to collect the training and test data.

References

Chih-Chung Chang and Chih-Jen Lin. 2001. *LIBSVM : a library for support vector machines.* www.csie.ntu.edu.tw/~cjlin/libsvm

Gerald Chao and Michael G. Dyer. 2002. Maximum entropy models for word sense disambiguation. *Proceedings of the 19th international conference on Computational linguistics.* Vol (1):1-7

Koby Crammer and Yoram Singer. 2001. On the Algorithmic Implementation of Multiclass Kernel-based Vector Machines. *Journal of Machine Learning Research*, 2, 265-292

Radu Florian, Silviu Cucerzan, Charles Schafer and David Yarowsky. 2002. Combining Classifiers for Word Sense Disambiguation. *Natural Language Engineering*, 8(4): 327 – 341.

Thorsten Joachims. *SVM-Multiclass.* http://svmlight.joachims.org/svm-multiclass.html,2004.

Yoong Keok Lee, Hwee Tou Ng and Tee Kiah Chia, Supervised Word Sense Disambiguation with Support Vector Machines and Multiple Knowledge Sources. *Proceedings of SENSEVAL-3.* 137 - 140

PNNL: A Supervised Maximum Entropy Approach to Word Sense Disambiguation

Stephen Tratz, Antonio Sanfilippo, Michelle Gregory, Alan Chappell, Christian Posse, Paul Whitney
Pacific Northwest National Laboratory
902 Battelle Blvd, PO Box 999
Richland, WA 99352, USA
{stephen.tratz, antonio.sanfilippo, michelle, alan.chappell, christian.posse, paul.whitney}@pnl.gov

Abstract

In this paper, we described the PNNL Word Sense Disambiguation system as applied to the English all-word task in SemEval 2007. We use a supervised learning approach, employing a large number of features and using Information Gain for dimension reduction. The rich feature set combined with a Maximum Entropy classifier produces results that are significantly better than baseline and are the highest F-score for the fined-grained English all-words subtask of SemEval.

1 Introduction

Accurate word sense disambiguation (WSD) can support many natural language processing and knowledge management tasks. The main goal of the PNNL WSD system is to support Semantic Web applications, such as semantic-driven search and navigation, through a reliable mapping of words in naturally occurring text to ontological classes. As described in Sanfilippo et al. (2006), this goal is achieved by defining a WordNet-based (Fellbaum, 1998) ontology that offers a manageable set of concept classes, provides an extensive characterization of concept class in terms of lexical instances, and integrates an automated class recognition algorithm. We found that the same features that are useful for predicting word classes are also useful in distinguishing individual word senses.

Our main objective in this paper is to predict individual word senses using a large combination of features including contextual, semantic, and syntactic information. In our earlier paper (Sanfilippo et al., 2006), we reported that the PNNL WSD system exceeded the performance of the best performers for verbs in the SENSEVAL-3 English all-words task dataset. SemEval 2007 is our first opportunity to enter a word sense disambiguation competition.

2 Approach

While many unsupervised word sense disambiguation systems have been created, supervised systems have generally produced superior results (Snyder and Palmer, 2004; Mihalcea et al., 2004). Our system is based on a supervised WSD approach that uses a Maximum Entropy classifier to predict WordNet senses.

We use SemCor[1], OMWE 1.0 (Chklovski and Mihalcea, 2002), and example sentences in WordNet as the training corpus. We utilize the OpenNLP MaxEnt implementation[2] of the maximum entropy classification algorithm (Berger et al., 1996) to train classification models for each lemma and part-of-speech combination in the training corpus. These models are used to predict WordNet senses for words found in natural text. For lemma and part-of-speech combinations that are not present in the training corpus, the PNNL WSD system defaults to the most frequent WordNet sense.

2.1 Features

We use a rich set of features to predict individual word senses. A large number of features are extracted for each word sense instance in the training data. Following Dang & Palmer (2005) and Kohomban & Lee (2005), we use contextual, syntactic and semantic information to inform our word

[1] http://www.cs.unt.edu/~rada/downloads.html.
[2] http://maxent.sourceforge.net/.

Proceedings of the 4th International Workshop on Semantic Evaluations (SemEval-2007), pages 264–267,
Prague, June 2007.

sense disambiguation system. However, there are significant differences between the specific types of contextual, syntactic and semantic information we use in our system and those proposed by Dang & Palmer (2005) and Kohomban & Lee (2005). More specifically, we employ novel features and feature combinations, as described below.

- *Contextual information.* The contextual information we use includes the word under analysis plus the three tokens found on each side of the word, within sentence boundaries. Tokens include both words and punctuation.
- *Syntactic information.* We include grammatical dependencies (e.g. subject, object) and morpho-syntactic features such as part of speech, case, number and tense. We use the Connexor parser[3] (Tapanainen and Järvinen, 1997) to extract lemma information, parts of speech, syntactic dependencies, tense, case, and number information. A sample output of a Connexor parse is given in Table 1. Features are extracted for all tokens that are related through no more than 3 levels of dependency to the word to be disambiguated.
- *Semantic information.* The semantic information we incorporate includes named entity types (e.g. PERSON, LOCATION, ORGANIZATION) and hypernyms. We use OpenNLP[4] and LingPipe[5] to identify named entities, replacing the strings identified as named entities (e.g., Joe Smith) with the corresponding entity type (PERSON). We also substitute personal pronouns that unambiguously denote people with the entity type PERSON. Numbers in the text are replaced with type label NUMBER. Hypernyms are retrieved from WordNet and added to the feature set for all noun tokens selected by the contextual and syntactic rules. In contrast to Dang & Palmer (2005), we only include the hypernyms of the most frequent sense, and we include the entire hypernym chain (e.g. motor, machine, device, instrumentality, artifact, object, whole, entity).

To address feature extraction processes specific to noun and verbs, we add the following conditions.

- *Syntactic information for verbs.* If the verb does not have a subject, the subject of the closest ancestor verb in the syntax tree is used instead.
- *Syntactic information for nouns.* The first verb ancestor in the syntax tree is also used to generate features.
- *Semantic information for nouns.* A feature indicating whether a token is capitalized for each of the tokens used to generate features.

A sample of the resulting feature vectors that are used by the PNNL word sense disambiguation system is presented in Table 2.

ID	Word	Lemma	Grammatical Dependencies	Morphosyntactic Features
1	the	the	det:>2	@DN> %>N DET
2	engine	engine	subj:>3	@SUBJ %NH N NOM SG
3	throbbed	throb	main:>0	@+FMAINV %VA V PAST
4	into	into	goa:>3	@ADVL %EH PREP
5	life	life	pcomp:>4	@<P %NH N NOM SG
6	.	.		

Table 1. Connexor sample output for the sentence *"The engine throbbed into life"*.

the	pre:2:the, pre:2:pos:DET, det:the, det:pos:DET, hassubj:det:
engine	pre:1:instrumentality, pre:1:object, pre:1:artifact, pre:1:device, pre:1:engine, pre:1:motor, pre:1:whole, pre:1:entity, pre:1:machine, pre:1:pos:N, pre:1:case:NOM, pre:1:num:SG,subj:instrumentality,subj:object, subj:artifact, subj:device, subj:engine, subj:motor, subj:whole, subj:entity, subj:machine, subj:pos:N, hassubj:, subj:case:NOM, subj:num:SG,
throbbed	haspre:1:,haspre:2:,haspost:1:, haspost:2:, haspost:3:, self:throb, self:pos:V, main:,throbbed, self:tense:PAST
into	post:1:into, post:1:pos:PREP, goa:into, goa:pos:PREP,
life	post:2:life, post:2:state, post:2:being, post:2:pos:N, post:2:case:NOM, post:2:num:SG, hasgoa:, pcomp:life, pcomp:state, pcomp:being, pcomp:pos:N, hasgoa:pcomp:, goa:pcomp:case:NOM, goa:pcomp:num:SG
.	post:3:.

Table 2. Feature vector for *throbbed* in the sentence *"The engine throbbed into life"*.

As the example in Table 2 indicates, the combination of contextual, syntactic, and semantic information types results in a large number of features. Inspection of the training data reveals that some features may be more important than others in establishing word sense assignment for each choice of word lemma. We use a feature selection proce-

[3] http://www.connexor.com/.

[4] http://opennlp.sourceforge.nt/.

[5] http://www.alias-i.com/lingpipe/.

dure to reduce the full set of features to the feature subset that is most relevant to word sense assignment for each lemma. This practice improves the efficiency of our word sense disambiguation algorithm. The feature selection procedure we adopted consists of scoring each potential feature according to a particular feature selection metric, and then taking the best *k* features.

We choose Information Gain as our feature selection metric. Information Gain measures the decrease in entropy when the feature is given versus when it is absent. Yang and Pederson (1997) report that Information Gain outperformed other feature selection approaches in their multi-class benchmarks, and Foreman (2003) showed that it performed amongst the best for his 2-class problems.

3 Evaluation

To evaluate our approach and feature set, we ran our model on the SENSEVAL-3 English all-words task test data. Using data provided by the SENSEVAL website[6], we were able to compare our results for verbs to the top performers on verbs alone. Upali S. Kohomban and Wee Sun Lee provided us with the results file for the Simil-Prime system (Kohomban and Lee, 2005). As reported in Sanfilippo et al. (2006) and shown in table 3, our results for verbs rival those of top performers. We had a significant improvement (p-value<0.05) over the baseline of 52.9%, a marginal improvement over the second best performer (SenseLearner) (Mihalcea and Faruque, 2004), and we were as good as the top performer (GAMBL) (Decadt et al., 2004).[7]

System	Precision	Fraction of Recall
Our system	61%	22%
GAMBL	59.0%	21.3%
SenseLearner	56.1%	20.2%
Baseline	52.9%	19.1%

Table 3. Results for verb sense disambiguation on SENSEVAL-3 data, adapted from Sanfilippo et al. (2006).

Since then, we have expanded our evaluation to all parts of speech. Table 4 provides the evaluation of our system as compared to the three top performers on the SENSEVAL-3 data and the baseline. The baseline of 0.631 F-score[8] was computed using the most frequent WordNet sense. The PNNL WSD system performs significantly better than the baseline (p-value<0.05) and rivals the top performers. The performance of the PNNL WSD system relative to the other three systems and the baseline remains unchanged when the unknown sense answers (denoted by a 'U') are excluded from the evaluation.

System	Precision	Recall
PNNL	0.670	0.670
Simil-Prime	0.661	0.663
GAMBL	0.652	0.652
SenseLearner	0.646	0.646
Baseline	0.631	0.631

Table 4. SENSEVAL-3 English all-words.

System	Recall	Precision
PNNL	0.669	0.671
GAMBL	0.651	0.651
Simil-Prime	0.644	0.657
SenseLearner	0.642	0.651
Baseline	0.631	0.631

Table 5. SENSEVAL-3 English all-words, No "U".

4 Experimental results on SemEval all-words subtask

This was our first opportunity to test our model in a WSD competition. For this competition, we focused our efforts on the fine-grained English all-words task because our system was set up to perform fine-grained WordNet sense prediction. We are pleased that our system achieved the highest score for this subtask. Our results for the SemEval dataset as compared to baseline are reported in Table 6. The PNNL WSD system did not assign the unknown sense, 'U', to any word instances in the SemEval dataset.

[6] http://www.senseval.org/.

[7] The 2% improvement in precision which our system showed as compared to GAMBL was not statistically significant (p=0.21).

[8] This baseline is slightly higher than that reported by others (Snyder and Palmer 2004).

System	F-score
PNNL	0.591
Baseline	0.514
p-value	<0.01

Table 6. SemEval Results.

5 Discussion

Although these results are promising, there is still much work to be done. For example, we need to investigate the contribution of each feature to the overall performance of the system in terms of precision and recall. Such a feature sensitivity analysis will provide us with a better understanding of how the algorithm can be further improved and/or made more efficient by leaving out features whose contribution is negligible.

Another important point to make is that, while our system shows the best precision/recall results overall, we can only claim statistical relevance with reference to the baseline and results worse than baseline. The size of the SemEval data set (N=465) is too small to establish whether the difference in precision/recall results with the other top systems is statistically significant.

Acknowledgements

We would like to thank Upali S. Kohomban and Wee Sun Lee for providing us with their SENSEVAL-3 English all-words task results file for SimilPrime. Many thanks also to Patrick Paulson, Bob Baddeley, Ryan Hohimer, and Amanda White for their help in developing the word class disambiguation system on which the work presented in this paper is based.

References

Berger, A., S. Della Pietra and V. Della Pietra (1996) A Maximum Entropy Approach to Natural Language Processing. *Computational Linguistics,* volume 22, number 1, pages 39-71.

Chklovski, T. and R. Mihalcea (2002) Building a sense tagged corpus with open mind word expert. In *Proceedings of the ACL-02 workshop on Word sense disambiguation: recent successes and future directions.*

Dang, H. T. and M. Palmer (2005) The Role of Semantic Roles in Disambiguating Verb Senses. In *Proceedings of the 43rd Annual Meeting of the Association for Computational Linguistics*, Ann Arbor MI, June 26-28, 2005.

Decadt, B., V. Hoste, W. Daelemans and A. Van den Bosch (2004) GAMBL, genetic algorithm optimization of memory-based WSD. *SENSEVAL-3: Third International Workshop on the Evaluation of Systems for the Semantic Analysis of Text.* Barcelona, Spain.

Fellbaum, C., editor. (1998) WordNet: An Electronic Lexical Database. MIT Press, Cambridge, MA.

Foreman, G. (2003) An Extensive Empirical Study of Feature Selection Metrics for Text Classification. *Journal of Machine Learning Research*, 3, pages 1289-1305.

Kohomban, U. and W. Lee (2005) Learning semantic classes for word sense disambiguation. In *Proceedings of the 43rd Annual meeting of the Association for Computational Linguistics*, Ann Arbor, MI.

Mihalcea, R., T. Chklovski, and A. Kilgarriff (2004) The SENSEVAL-3 English Lexical Sample Task, *SENSEVAL-3: Third International Workshop on the Evaluation of Systems for the Semantic Analysis of Text.* Barcelonna, Span.

Mihalcea, R. and E. Faruque (2004) SenseLearner: Minimally supervised word sense disambiguation for all words in open text. *SENSEVAL-3: Third International Workshop on the Evaluation of Systems for the Semantic Analysis of Text.* Barcelona, Spain.

Sanfilippo, A., S. Tratz, M. Gregory, A. Chappell, P. Whitney, C. Posse, P. Paulson, B. Baddeley, R. Hohimer, A. White (2006) Automating Ontological Annotation with WordNet. *Proceedings to the Third International WordNet Conference*, Jan 22-26, Jeju Island, Korea.

Snyder, B. and M. Palmer. 2004. The English All-Words Task. *SENSEVAL-3: Third International Workshop on the Evaluation of Systems for the Semantic Analysis of Text.* Barcelona, Spain.

Tapanainen, P. and Timo Järvinen (1997) A nonprojective dependency parser. In *Proceedings of the 5th Conference on Applied Natural Language Processing*, pages 64–71, Washington D.C. Association for Computational Linguistics.

Yang, Y. and J. O. Pedersen (1997) A Comparative Study on Feature Selection in Text Categorization. In *Proceedings of the 14th International Conference on Machine Learning* (ICML), pages 412-420, 1997.

PSNUS: Web People Name Disambiguation by Simple Clustering with Rich Features

Ergin Elmacioglu[1] **Yee Fan Tan**[2] **Su Yan**[1] **Min-Yen Kan**[2] **Dongwon Lee**[1]
[1]The Pennsylvania State University, USA
[2]National University of Singapore, Singapore
{ergin,syan,dongwon}@psu.edu, {tanyeefa,kanmy}@comp.nus.edu.sg

Abstract

We describe about the system description of the PSNUS team for the SemEval-2007 Web People Search Task. The system is based on the clustering of the web pages by using a variety of features extracted and generated from the data provided. This system achieves $F_{\alpha=0.5} = 0.75$ and $F_{\alpha=0.2} = 0.78$ for the final test data set of the task.

1 Introduction

We consider the problem of disambiguating person names in a Web searching scenario as described by the Web People Search Task in SemEval 2007 (Artiles et al., 2007). Here, the system receives as input a set of web pages retrieved from a search engine using a given person name as a query. The goal is to determine how many different people are represented for that name in the input web pages, and correctly assign each namesake to its corresponding subset of web pages.

There are many challenges towards an effective solution. We are to correctly estimate the number of namesakes for a given person name and group documents referring to the same individual. Moreover, the information sources to be processed are unstructured web pages and there is no certain way of correctly establishing a relation between any two web pages belonging to the same or different individuals.

We have taken several approaches to analyze different sources of information provided with the input data, and also compared strategies to combine these individual features together. The configuration that achieved the best performance (which were submitted for our run) used a single named entity feature as input to clustering. In the remainder of this paper, we first describe our system in terms of the clustering approach used and alternative features investigated. We then analyze the results on the training set before concluding the paper.

2 Clustering Algorithm

Clustering is the key part for such a task. We have chosen to view the problem as an unsupervised hard clustering problem. First, we view the problem as *unsupervised*, using the training data for parameter validation, to optimally tune the parameters in the clustering algorithm. Secondly, we observed that the majority of the input pages reference a single individual, although there are a few that reference multiple individuals sharing the same name. Hence, we view the problem as *hard* clustering, assigning input pages to exactly one individual, so that the produced clusters do not overlap.

Hard clustering algorithms can be classified as either partitive or hierarchical. Agglomerative hierarchical clustering generates a series of nested clusters by merging simple clusters into larger ones, while partitive methods try to find a pre-specified number of clusters that best capture the data. As the correct number of clusters is not given *a priori*, we chose a method from the second group. We use the *Hierarchical Agglomerative Clustering* (HAC) algorithm (Jain et al., 1999) for all experiments reported in this paper. HAC views each input web page as a separate cluster and iteratively combines the most similar pair of clusters to form a new cluster that re-

Proceedings of the 4th International Workshop on Semantic Evaluations (SemEval-2007), pages 268–271,
Prague, June 2007.

places the pair.

3 Features

As input to the clustering, we consider several different representations of the input documents. Each representation views the input web pages as a vector of features. HAC then computes the cosine similarity between the feature vectors for each pair of clusters to determine which clusters to merge. We now review the inventory of features studied in our work.

Tokens (T). Identical to the task baseline by (Artiles et al., 2005), we stemmed the words in the web pages using the Porter stemmer (Porter, 1980), to conflate semantically similar English words with the stem. Each stemmed word is considered to be a feature and weighted by its Term Frequency $\times$ Inverse Document Frequency (TF$\times$IDF).

Named Entities (NE). We extract the named entities from the web pages using the Stanford Named Entity Recognizer (Finkel et al., 2005). This tagger identifies and labels names of places, organizations and people in the input. Each named entity token is treated as a separate feature, again weighted by TF$\times$IDF. We do not perform stemming for NE features.

We also consider a more target-centric form of the NE feature, motivated by the observation that person names can be differentiated using their middle names or titles. We first discard all named entities that do not contain any token of the search target, and then discard any token from the remaining named entities that appears in the search target. The remaining tokens are then used as features, and weighted by their TF$\times$IDF. For example, for the search target "Edward Fox", the features generated from the name "Edward Charles Morrice Fox" are "Charles" and "Morrice". We call this variation NE targeted (NE-T).

Hostnames and domains (H and D). If two web pages have links pointing to the exact same URL, then there is a good chance that these two web pages refer the same person. However, we find such exact matches of URLs are rare, so we relax the condition and consider their hostnames or domain names instead. For example, the URL http://portal.acm.org/guide.cfm has hostname portal.acm.org and domain name acm.org. As such, for each web page, we can extract the list of hostnames from the links in this page.

We observe that some host/domain names serve as more discriminative evidence than others (e.g., a link to a university homepage is more telling than a link to the list of publications page of Google Scholar when disambiguating computer science scholars). To model this, we weight each host/domain name by its IDF. Note that we do not use TF as web pages often contain multiple internal links in the form of menus or navigation bars. Using IDF and cosine similarity has been proven effective for disambiguating bibliographic citation records sharing a common author name (Tan et al., 2006).

We also considered a variant where we include the URL of the input web page itself as a "link". We tried this variation only with hostnames, calling this Host with Self URL (H-S).

Page URLs (U). Uniform resource locations (URLs) themselves contain a rich amount of information. For example, the URL http://www.cs.ualberta.ca/~lindek/ itself suggests a home page of "lindek" in the Computer Science department, University of Alberta, Canada.

We used the MeURLin system (Kan and Nguyen Thi, 2005) to segment the URL of each web page into tokens as well as to generate additional features. These features include (a) segmentation of tokens such as "www.allposters.com" to "www", "all", "posters" and "com"; (b) the parts in the URL where the tokens occur, e.g., protocol, domain name, and directory paths; (c) length of the tokens; (d) orthographic features; (e) sequential n-grams; and (f) sequential bigrams. As each of these features can be seen as a "token", the output of the MeURLin segmenter for a web page can be seen as a "document", and hence it is possible to compute the TF$\times$IDF cosine similarity between two such documents.

3.1 Feature Combination

The features described above represent largely orthogonal sources of information in the input: input content, hyperlinks, and source location. We hypothesize that by combining these different features we can obtain better performance. To combine these features for use with HAC, we consider simply concatenating individual feature vectors together to create a single feature vector, and compute cosine similarity. We used this method in two configurations: namely, (T + NE + H-S), (T + D + NE + NE-T + U).

We also tried using the maximum and average component-wise similarities of individual features. (*max*(NE, H-S)) uses the maximum value of the Named Entity and Host with Self features. For the (*avg*(T, H-S)) and (*avg*(T, D, NE, NE-T, U)) runs, we compute the average similarity over the two and five sets of individual features, respectively.

4 Results

We present the clustering performances of the various methods in our system based on the different features that we extracted. Each experiment uses HAC with single linkage clustering. Since the number of clusters is not known, when to terminate the agglomeration process is a crucial point and significantly affects the quality of the clustering result. We empirically determine the best similarity thresholds to be 0.1 and 0.2 for all the experiments on the three different data sets provided. We found that larger values for these data sets do not allow the HAC algorithm to create enough clustering hierarchy by causing it to terminate early, and therefore result in many small clusters increasing purity but dramatically suffering from inverse purity performance.

Table 1 shows the results of our experiments on the training data sets (ECDL, Wikipedia and Census). Two different evaluation measures are reported as described by the task: $F_{\alpha=0.5}$ is a harmonic mean of purity and inverse purity of the clustering result, and $F_{\alpha=0.2}$ is a version of F that gives more importance to inverse purity (Artiles et al., 2007).

Among the individual features, Tokens and Named Entity features consistently show close to best performance for all training data sets. In most cases, NE is better than Tokens because some web pages contain lots of irrelevant text for this task (e.g., headers and footers, menus etc). Also, we found that the NEs have far more discriminative power than most other tokens in determining similarity between web pages. The NE variation, NE targeted, performs worse among the token based methods. Although NE targeted aims for highly precise disambiguation, it seems that it throws away too much information so that inverse purity is very much reduced. The other NEs, such as locations and organizations are also very helpful for this task. For example, the organization may indicate the affiliation of a particular name. This explains the superiority of NE over NE targeted for all three data sets.

Among the link based features, Domain gives better performance over Host as it leads to better inverse purity. The reason is that there are usually many pages on different hosts from a single domain for a given name (e.g., the web pages belonging to a researcher from university domain). This greatly helps in resolving the name while results in a slight drop in purity. Using a web page's URL itself in the features Host+Self and Domain+Self shows a larger increase in inverse purity at a smaller decrease in purity, hence these have improved F-measure in comparison to Domain and Host. Not surprisingly, these link based features perform very well for the ECDL data set, compared to the other two. A significant portion of the people in the ECDL data set are most likely present-day computer scientists, likely having extensive an web presence, which makes the task much easier. Although the other two data sets may have popular people with many web pages, their web presence are usually created by others and often scatter across many domains with little hyperlinkage between them. This explains why our link based methods are not very effective for such data sets.

Our final individual feature URL performs worst among all. Although highly precise, its resulting inverse purity is poor. While the features generated by MeURLin do improve the performance over pure host name and domain on the page URLs, its incorporation in a richer feature set does not lead to better results, as the other features which have richer information to process.

Each of the individual features has different degree of discriminative power in many different cases. By combining them, we expect to get better performance than individually. However, we do not obtain significant improvement in any of the data sets. Furthermore, in the Census data set, the combined features fail to outperform the individual NE and Tokens features. The relatively poor performance of the remaining features also degrades the performance of Tokens and NE when combined.

Considering the performances using the harmonic mean, we do not see any clear winner in all of three

Feature	ECDL		Wikipedia		Census	
	$F_{\alpha=0.5}$	$F_{\alpha=0.2}$	$F_{\alpha=0.5}$	$F_{\alpha=0.2}$	$F_{\alpha=0.5}$	$F_{\alpha=0.2}$
Tokens (T)	.72 / .77	.83 / .84	.72 / **.76**	.85 / .84	**.82** / **.84**	.88 / .86
Named Entities (NE)	.75 / **.80**	.84 / .79	.75 / **.77**	.85 / .78	**.89** / **.78**	.89 / .73
NE targeted (NE-T)	.54 / .55	.49 / .47	.66 / .64	.60 / .57	.64 / .64	.57 / .58
Host (H)	.72 / .57	.64 / .48	.67 / .51	.58 / .41	.67 / .63	.59 / .55
Host + Self (H-S)	.73 / .59	.66 / .49	.68 / .54	.60 / .43	.68 / .63	.60 / .56
Domain (D)	**.78** / .69	.72 / .60	.71 / .59	.66 / .50	.69 / .65	.61 / .58
Domain + Self (D-S)	**.79** / .70	.74 / .61	.72 / .62	.67 / .52	.70 / .66	.62 / .59
URL (U)	.50 / .43	.43 / .35	.56 / .42	.50 / .33	.64 / .58	.56 / .51
(T + NE + H-S)	.71 / .77	.83 / .83	.72 / **.76**	.85 / .83	.65 / .67	.78 / .76
(T + D + NE + NE-T + U)	.72 / .76	.83 / .80	.72 / **.77**	.84 / .83	.66 / .66	.78 / .74
(*max*(NE, H-S))	.74 / **.80**	.84 / .82	.74 / **.77**	.86 / .82	.71 / .66	.80 / .70
(*avg*(T, H-S))	.77 / **.81**	.86 / .76	.75 / **.77**	.86 / .76	.70 / .64	.80 / .67
(*avg*(T, D, NE, NE-T, U))	**.78** / .77	.86 / .73	.75 / **.78**	.86 / .76	.69 / .61	.77 / .62

Table 1: Experimental results for each training data set of the task: ECDL, Wikipedia and Census. Each experiment uses single link HAC with the similarity threshold values of 0.1 / 0.2. Best $F_{\alpha=0.5}$ performances are shown in bold.

training data sets. In addition, the method showing the best performance does not result in a win with a large margin in each data set. Relatively complicated methods do not always perform better over simpler, single featured based methods on all training data sets. Considering the results and Occam's razor (Thorburn, 1915), we conclude that a simple method should most likely work relatively well in many other different settings as well. Therefore, we selected the method based on the individual NE feature with the similarity threshold value of 0.2 for the final test submission run. We are able to achieve the following results for this submission run: purity = 0.73, inverse purity = 0.82, $F_{\alpha=0.5} = 0.75$, $F_{\alpha=0.2} = 0.78$.

5 Conclusion

We described our PSNUS system that disambiguates people mentions in web pages returned by a web search scenario, as defined in the inaugural Web People Search Task. As such, we mainly focus on extracting various kinds of information from web pages and utilizing them in the similarity computation of the clustering algorithm. The experimental results show that a simple Hierarchical Agglomerative Clustering approach using a single named entity feature seems promising as a robust solution for the various datasets.

References

Javier Artiles, Julio Gonzalo, and Felisa Verdejo. 2005. A testbed for people searching strategies in the WWW. In *ACM SIGIR*, pages 569–570, August.

Javier Artiles, Julio Gonzalo, and Satoshi Sekine. 2007. The SemEval-2007 WePS evaluation: Establishing a benchmark for the Web People Search Task. In *SemEval 2007, ACL*, June.

Jenny R. Finkel, Trond Grenager, and Christopher Manning. 2005. Incorporating non-local information into information extraction systems by Gibbs sampling. In *ACL*, pages 363–370, June.

Anil K. Jain, M. Narasimha Murty, and Patrick J. Flynn. 1999. Data clustering: A review. *ACM Computing Surveys*, 31(3):264–323, September.

Min-Yen Kan and Hoang Oanh Nguyen Thi. 2005. Fast webpage classification using URL features. In *CIKM*, pages 325–326, October/November.

Martin F. Porter. 1980. An algorithm for suffix stripping. *Program*, 14(3):130–137, July.

Yee Fan Tan, Min-Yen Kan, and Dongwon Lee. 2006. Search engine driven author disambiguation. In *ACM/IEEE JCDL*, pages 314–315, June.

William M. Thorburn. 1915. Occam's razor. *Mind*, 24:287–288.

PU-BCD: Exponential Family Models for the Coarse- and Fine-Grained All-Words Tasks

Jonathan Chang
Princeton University
Department of Electrical Engineering
jcone@princeton.edu

Miroslav Dudík, David M. Blei
Princeton University
Department of Computer Science
{mdudik,blei}@cs.princeton.edu

Abstract

This paper describes an exponential family model of word sense which captures both occurrences and co-occurrences of words and senses in a joint probability distribution. This statistical framework lends itself to the task of word sense disambiguation. We evaluate the performance of the model in its participation on the SemEval-2007 coarse- and fine-grained all-words tasks under a variety of parameters.

1 Introduction

This paper describes an *exponential family model* suited to performing word sense disambiguation. Exponential family models are a mainstay of modern statistical modeling (Brown, 1986) and they are widely and successfully used for example in text classification (Berger et al., 1996). In statistical machine learning research, a general methodology and many algorithms were developed for *undirected graphical model* representation of exponential families (Jordan, 2004), providing a solid basis for efficient inference.

Our model differs from other probabilistic models used for word sense disambiguation in that it captures not only word-sense co-occurrences but also contextual sense-sense co-occurrences, thereby breaking the naïve Bayes assumption. Although spare in the types of features, the model is extremely expressive. Our model has parameters that control for word-sense interaction and sense-sense similarity, allowing us to capture many of the salient features of word and sense use. After fitting the parameters of our model from a labeled corpus, the task of word sense disambiguation immediately follows by considering the *posterior distribution* of senses given words.

We used this model to participate in SemEval-2007 on the coarse- and fine-grained all-words tasks. In both of these tasks, a series of sentences are given with certain words tagged. Each competing system must assign a sense from a sense inventory to the tagged words. In both tasks, performance was gauged by comparing the output of each system to human-tagged senses. In the fine-grained task, precision and recall were simply and directly computed against the golden annotations. However, in the coarse-grained task, the sense inventory was first clustered semi-automatically with each cluster representing an equivalence class over senses (Navigli, 2006). Precision and recall were computed against equivalence classes.

This paper briefly derives the model and then explores its properties for WSD. We show how common algorithms, such as "dominant sense" and "most frequent sense," can be expressed in the exponential family framework. We then proceed to present an evaluation of the developed techniques on the SemEval-2007 tasks in which we participated.

2 The model

We describe an exponential family model for word sense disambiguation. We posit a joint distribution over words $\mathbf{w}$ and senses $\mathbf{s}$.

2.1 Notation

We define a *document* d to be a sequence of words from some lexicon $\mathcal{W}$; for the participation in this contest, a document consists of a sentence. Associated with each word is a *sense* from a lexicon $\mathcal{S}$. In

Proceedings of the 4th International Workshop on Semantic Evaluations (SemEval-2007), pages 272–276,
Prague, June 2007.

this work, our sense lexicon is the synsets of WordNet (Fellbaum and Miller, 2003), but our methods easily generalize to other sense lexicons, such as VerbNet (Kipper et al., 2000).

Formally, we denote the sequence of words in a document d by $\mathbf{w}_d = (w_{d,1}, \ldots, w_{d,n_d})$ and the sequence of synsets by $\mathbf{s}_d = (s_{d,1}, s_{d,2}, \ldots, s_{d,n_d})$, where n_d denotes the number of words in the document. A *corpus* $\mathcal{D}$ is defined as a collection of documents. We also write $w \in s$ if w can be used to represent sense s.

2.2 An exponential family of words and senses

We turn our attention to an exponential family of words and senses. The vector of parameters $\boldsymbol{\eta} = (\boldsymbol{\kappa}, \boldsymbol{\lambda})$ consists of two blocks capturing dependence on word-synset co-occurrences, and synset co-occurrences.

$$p_{\boldsymbol{\eta},n}(\mathbf{s}, \mathbf{w}) = \exp\{\textstyle\sum_i \kappa_{w_i,s_i} + \sum_{i,j} \lambda_{s_i,s_j}\}/Z_{\boldsymbol{\eta},n} \ . \tag{1}$$

The summations are first over all positions in the document, $1 \leq i \leq n$, and then over all pairs of positions in the document, $1 \leq i, j \leq n$. We discuss parameters of our exponential model in turn.

Word-sense parameters $\boldsymbol{\kappa}$ Using parameters $\boldsymbol{\kappa}$ alone, it is possible to describe an arbitrary context independent distribution between a word and its assigned synset.

Sense co-occurrence parameters $\boldsymbol{\lambda}$ Parameters $\boldsymbol{\lambda}$ are the only parameters that establish the dependence of sense on its context. More specifically, they capture co-occurrences of synset pairs within a context. Larger values favor, whereas smaller values disfavor each pair of synsets.

3 Parameter estimation

With the model in hand, we need to address two problems in order to use it for problems such as WSD. First, in *parameter estimation*, we find values of the parameters that explain a labeled corpus, such as SemCor (Miller et al., 1993). Once the parameters are fit, we use *posterior inference* to compute the posterior probability distribution of a set of senses given a set of unlabeled words in a context, $p(\mathbf{s} \mid \mathbf{w})$. This distribution is used to predict the senses of the words.

In this section, it will be useful to introduce the notation $\tilde{p}(s, w)$ to denote the empirical probabilities of observing the word-sense pair s, w in the entire corpus:

$$\tilde{p}(s, w) = \textstyle\sum_{d,i} \delta(s_{d,i}, s)\delta(w_{d,i}, w)/\sum_d n_d \ ,$$

where $\delta(x, y) = 1$ if $x = y$ and 0 otherwise. Similarly, we will define $\tilde{p}(s)$ to denote the empirical probability of observing a sense s over the entire corpus:

$$\tilde{p}(s) = \textstyle\sum_{d,i} \delta(s_{d,i}, s)/\sum_d n_d \ .$$

3.1 Word-sense parameters $\boldsymbol{\kappa}$

Fallback Let $\kappa^{\mathrm{WN}}_{w,s} = 0$ if $w \in s$ and $\kappa^{\mathrm{WN}}_{w,s} = -\infty$ otherwise. This simply sets to zero the probability of assigning a word w to a synset s when $w \notin s$ while making all $w \in s$ equally likely as an assignment to s. This forces the model to rely entirely on $\boldsymbol{\lambda}$ for inference. If $\boldsymbol{\lambda}$ is also set to $\mathbf{0}$, this then forces the system to fall back onto its arbitrary tie-breaking mechanism such as choosing randomly or choosing the first sense.

Most-frequent synset One approach to disambiguation is the technique of choosing the most frequently occurring synset which the word may express. This can be implemented within the model by setting $\kappa_{w,s} = \kappa^{\mathrm{MFS}}_{w,s} \equiv \ln \tilde{p}(s)$ if $w \in s$ and $-\infty$ otherwise.

MLE Given a labeled corpus, we would like to find the corresponding parameters that maximize likelihood of the data. Equivalently, we would like to maximize the log likelihood

$$\mathcal{L}(\boldsymbol{\eta}) = \textstyle\sum_d \left[\sum_i \kappa_{w_{d,i},s_{d,i}} + \sum_{i,j} \lambda_{s_{d,i},s_{d,j}} - \ln Z_{\boldsymbol{\eta},n_d}\right] \ . \tag{2}$$

In this section, we consider a simple case when it is possible to estimate parameters maximizing the likelihood exactly, i.e., the case where our model depends only on word-synset co-occurrences and is parametrized solely by $\boldsymbol{\kappa}$ (setting $\boldsymbol{\lambda} = \mathbf{0}$).

Using Eq. (1), with $\boldsymbol{\lambda} = \mathbf{0}$, we obtain

$$p_{\boldsymbol{\kappa}}(\mathbf{s}_{\mathcal{D}}, \mathbf{w}_{\mathcal{D}}) = \frac{\exp\{\sum_{d,i} \kappa_{w_{d,i},s_{d,i}}\}}{\prod_d Z_{\boldsymbol{\kappa},n_d}} \ .$$

Thus, $p_\kappa(\mathbf{s}_\mathcal{D}, \mathbf{w}_\mathcal{D})$ can be viewed as a multinomial model with $\sum_d n_d$ trials and $|\mathcal{S}|$ outcomes, parametrized by $\kappa_{w,s}$. The maximum likelihood estimates in this model are $\hat{\kappa}_{w,s} \equiv \ln \tilde{p}(s, w)$.

This setting of the parameters corresponds precisely to the *dominant-sense* model (McCarthy et al., 2004). The resulting model is thus

$$p_{\kappa,n}(\mathbf{s}, \mathbf{w}) = \prod_i \tilde{p}(s_i, w_i) \ . \qquad (3)$$

3.2 Sense co-occurrence parameters $\boldsymbol{\lambda}$

Unlike $\boldsymbol{\kappa}$, it is impossible to find a closed-form solution for the maximum-likelihood settings of $\boldsymbol{\lambda}$. Therefore, we turn to intuitive methods.

Observed synset co-occurrence One natural ad hoc statistic to use to compute the parameters λ are the empirical sense co-occurrences. In particular, we may set

$$\lambda_{s_i,s_j} = \lambda^{\text{SF}}_{s_i,s_j} \equiv \ln \tilde{p}(s_i, s_j) \ . \qquad (4)$$

We will observe in section 5 that the performance of $\boldsymbol{\lambda} = \boldsymbol{\lambda}^{\text{SF}}$ actually degrades the performance of the system, especially when combined with $\boldsymbol{\kappa} = \hat{\boldsymbol{\kappa}}$. This can be understood as a by-product of an unsympathetic interaction between $\boldsymbol{\kappa}$ and $\boldsymbol{\lambda}$. In other words, $\boldsymbol{\kappa}$ and $\boldsymbol{\lambda}$ overlap; by favoring a sense pair the model will also implicitly favor each of the senses in the pair.

Discounted observed synset co-occurrence As we noted earlier, the combination $\boldsymbol{\kappa} = \hat{\boldsymbol{\kappa}}, \boldsymbol{\lambda} = \boldsymbol{\lambda}^{\text{SF}}$ actually performs worse than $\boldsymbol{\kappa} = \hat{\boldsymbol{\kappa}}, \boldsymbol{\lambda} = \mathbf{0}$. In order to cancel out the aforementioned overlap effect, we attempt to compute the number of co-occurrences beyond what the *occurrences* themselves would imply. To do so, we set

$$\boldsymbol{\lambda} = \boldsymbol{\lambda}^{\text{DSF}} \equiv \ln \frac{\tilde{p}(s_i, s_j)}{\tilde{p}(s_i)\tilde{p}(s_j)} \ , \qquad (5)$$

a quantity which finds an analogue in the notion of *mutual information*. We will see shortly that such a setting of $\boldsymbol{\lambda}$ will allow sense co-occurrence to improve disambiguation performance.

4 Word Sense Disambiguation

Finally, we describe how to perform WSD using the exponential family model. Our goal is to assign a synset s_i to every word w_i in an unlabeled document d of length n. In this setting, the synsets are hidden variables. Thus, we assign synsets according to their posterior probability given the observed words:

$$\hat{\mathbf{s}} = \operatorname*{argmax}_{\mathbf{s} \in \mathcal{S}^n} \frac{p_{\boldsymbol{\eta},n}(\mathbf{s}, \mathbf{w})}{\sum_{\mathbf{s}'} p_{\boldsymbol{\eta},n}(\mathbf{s}', \mathbf{w})} \ ,$$

where the sum is over all possible sequences of synsets. This combinatorial sum renders exact inference computationally intractable. We discuss how to obtain the sense assignment using approximate inference.

4.1 Variational Inference

To approximate the posterior over senses, we use *variational inference* (Jordan et al., 1999). In variational inference, one first chooses a family of distributions for which inference is computationlly tractable. Then the distribution in that family which best approximates the posterior distribution of interest is found.

For our purposes, it is convenient to select q from the family of factorized multinomial distributions:

$$q(\mathbf{s}) = \prod_i q_i(s_i) \ ,$$

where each $q_i(s_i)$ is a multinomial distribution over all possible senses. Observe that finding $\hat{\mathbf{s}}$ is much simpler using $q(\mathbf{s})$: one can find the argmax of each individual q_i independently.

It can be shown that the multinomial which minimizes the KL-divergence must satisfy:

$$q_i(s_i) \propto \exp\left\{ \kappa_{w_i,s_i} + \sum_{j \neq i} \sum_{s_j} q_j(s_j) \lambda_{s_i,s_j} \right\} \qquad (6)$$

a system of transcendental equations which can be solved iteratively to find q. This q is then used to efficiently perform inference and hence disambiguation.

5 Evaluation

This section evaluates the performance of the model and the techniques described in the previous sections with respect to the coarse- and fine-grained all-words tasks at SemEval-2007.

In order to train the parameters, we trained our model in a supervised fashion on SemCor (Miller et

	$\kappa = \kappa^{\text{WN}}$	$\kappa = \kappa^{\text{MFS}}$	$\kappa = \hat{\kappa}$
$\lambda = 0$	52.0%	45.8%	51.2%
$\lambda = \lambda^{\text{SF}}$	48.8%	45.3%	52.5%
$\lambda = \lambda^{\text{DSF}}$	47.0%	44.6%	**54.2%**

Table 1: Precision for the fine-grained all-words task. The results corresponding to the bolded value was submitted to the competition.

al., 1993) with Laplace smoothing for parameter estimates. We utilized the POS tagging and lemmatization given in the coarse-grained all-words test set. Wherever a headword was tagged differently between the two test sets, we produced an answer only for the coarse-grained test and not for the fine-grained one. This led to responses on only 93.9% of the fine-grained test words. Of the 6.1% over which no response was given, 5.3% were tagged as "U" in the answer key.

In order to break ties between equally likely senses, for the fine-grained test, the system returned the first one returned in WordNet's sense inventory for that lemma. For the coarse-grained test, an arbitrary sense was returned in case of ties.

The precision results given in this section are over polysemous words (of all parts of speech) for which our system gave an answer and for which the answer key was not tagged with "U."

5.1 Fine-grained results (Task 17)

The fine-grained results over all permutations of the parameters mentioned in Section 3 are given in Table 1. Note here that the baseline number of $\lambda = 0, \kappa = \kappa^{\text{WN}}$ given in the upper-left is equivalent to simply choosing the first WordNet sense. Notably, such a simple configuration of the model outperforms all but two other of the other parameter settings.

When any sort of nonzero sense co-occurrence parameter is used with $\kappa = \kappa^{\text{WN}}$, the performance degrades dramatically, to 48.8% and 47.0% for λ^{SF} and λ^{DSF} respectively. Since the discounting scheme was devised to positively interact with $\kappa = \hat{\kappa}$, it is no surprise that it does poorly when κ is not set in such a way. And as mentioned previously, naïvely setting λ to λ^{SF} improperly conflates λ and κ, yielding a poor result.

When $\kappa = \kappa^{\text{MFS}}$ is used, the precision is even lower, dropping to 45.8% when no sense co-occurrence information is used. And similarly to $\kappa = \kappa^{\text{WN}}$, any nonzero λ significantly degrades performance. This seems to indicate the most-frequent synset, as predicted by our earlier analysis, is an inferior technique.

Finally, when $\kappa = \hat{\kappa}$ is used (i.e. dominant sense), the precision is 51.2%, slightly lower than but nearly on par with that of the baseline. When sense co-occurrence parameters are added, the performance increases. For λ^{SF}, a precision of 52.5% is achieved; a precision above the baseline. But again, because of the interaction between κ and λ, here we expect it to be possible to improve upon this performance.

And indeed, when $\lambda = \lambda^{\text{DSF}}$, the highest value of the entire table, 54.2% is achieved. This is a significant improvement over the baseline and demonstrates that our intuitively appealing mutual information discounting mechanism allows for κ and λ to work cooperatively.

5.2 Coarse-grained results (Task 7)

In order to perform the coarse-grained task, our system first determined the set of sense equivalence classes. We denote a sense equivalence class by $\overline{k}$, where k is some sense key member of the class. The equivalence classes were created according to the following constraints:

- Each sense key k may only belong to one equivalence class $\overline{k}$.
- All sense keys referring to the same sense s must belong in the same class.
- All sense keys clustered together must belong in the same class.

Once the clustering is complete, we can proceed exactly as we did in the previous sections, while replacing all instances of s with $\overline{k}$. Thus, training in this case was performed on a SemCor where all the senses were mapped back to their corresponding sense equivalence classes.

The model fared considerably worse on the coarse-grained all-words task. The precision of the system as given by the scorer was 69.7% and the recall 62.8%. These results, while naturally much higher than those for the fine-grained test, are low by coarse-grained standards. While the gold standard was not available for comparison for these results, there are two likely causes of the lower performance on this task.

The first is that ties were not adjudicated by choosing the first WordNet sense. Instead, an arbitrary sense was chosen thereby pushing cases in which the model is unsure from the baseline to the much lower random precision rate. The second is the same number of documents are mapped to a smaller number of "senses" (i.e. sense equivalence classes), the number of parameters is greatly reduced. Therefore, the expressive power of each parameter is diluted because it must be spread out across all senses within the equivalence class.

We believe that both of these issues can be easily overcome and we hope to do so in future work. Furthermore, while the model currently captures the most salient features for word sense disambiguation, namely word-sense occurrence and sense-sense cooccurrence, it would be simple to extend the model to include a larger number of features (e.g. syntactic features).

6 Conclusion

In summary, this paper described our participation in the the SemEval-2007 coarse- and fine-grained all-words tasks. In particular, we described an exponential family model of word sense amenable to the task of word sense disambiguation. The performance of the model under a variety of parameter settings was evaluated on both tasks and the model was shown to be particularly effective on the fine-grained task.

7 Acknowledgments

The authors would like to thank Christiane Fellbaum, Daniel Osherson, and the members of the CIMPL group for their helpful contributions. This research was supported by a grant from Google Inc. and by NSF grant CCR-0325463.

References

Adam L. Berger, Vincent J. Della Pietra, and Stephen A. Della Pietra. 1996. A maximum entropy approach to natural language processing. *Computational Linguistics*, 22(1):39–71.

Lawrence D. Brown. 1986. *Fundamentals of Statistical Exponential Families*. Institute of Mathematical Statistics, Hayward, CA.

Christiane Fellbaum and George A. Miller. 2003. Morphosemantic links in WordNet. *Traitement automatique de langue*.

Michael I. Jordan, Zoubin Ghahramani, Tommi Jaakkola, and Lawrence K. Saul. 1999. An introduction to variational methods for graphical models. *Machine Learning*, 37(2):183–233.

Michael I. Jordan. 2004. Graphical models. *Statistical Science*, 19(1):140–155.

Karin Kipper, Hoa Trang Dang, and Martha Palmer. 2000. Class-Based Construction of a Verb Lexicon. *Proceedings of the Seventeenth National Conference on Artificial Intelligence and Twelfth Conference on Innovative Applications of Artificial Intelligence table of contents*, pages 691–696.

Diana McCarthy, Rob Koeling, Julie Weeds, and John Carroll. 2004. Finding predominant senses in untagged text. In *Proceedings of the 42nd Annual Meeting of the Association for Computational Linguistics*, pages 280–287, Barcelona, Spain.

George A. Miller, Claudia Leacock, Randee Tengi, and Ross T. Bunker. 1993. A semantic concordance. In *3rd DARPA Workshop on Human Language Technology*.

Roberto Navigli. 2006. Meaningful clustering of senses helps boost word sense disambiguation performance. In *COLING-ACL 2006*, pages 105–112, July.

PUTOP: Turning Predominant Senses into a Topic Model for Word Sense Disambiguation

Jordan Boyd-Graber
Computer Science
Princeton University
Princeton, NJ 08540
jbg@princeton.edu

David Blei
Computer Science
Princeton University
Princeton, NJ 08540
blei@cs.princeton.edu

Abstract

We extend on McCarthy et al.'s predominant sense method to create an unsupervised method of word sense disambiguation that uses automatically derived topics using Latent Dirichlet allocation. Using topic-specific synset similarity measures, we create predictions for each word in each document using only word frequency information. It is hoped that this procedure can improve upon the method for larger numbers of topics by providing more relevant training corpora for the individual topics. This method is evaluated on SemEval-2007 Task 1 and Task 17.

1 Generative Model of WSD

Word Sense Disambiguation (WSD) is the problem of labeling text with the appropriate semantic labels automatically. Although WSD is claimed to be an essential step in information retrieval and machine translation, it has not seen effective practical application because the dearth of labeled data has prevented the use of established supervised statistical methods that have been successfully applied to other natural language problems.

Unsupervised methods have been developed for WSD, but despite modest success have not always been well understood statistically (Abney, 2004). Unsupervised methods are particularly appealing because they do not require expensive sense-annotated data and can use the ever-increasing amount of raw text freely available. This paper expands on an effective unsupervised method for WSD and embeds it into a topic model, thus allowing an algorithm trained on a single, monolithic corpora to instead hand-pick relevant documents in choosing a disambiguation. After developing this generative statistical model, we present its performance on a number of tasks.

1.1 The Intersection of Syntactic and Semantic Similarity

McCarthy et al. (2004) outlined a method for learning a word's most-used sense given an untagged corpus that ranks each sense ws_i using a distributional syntactic similarity γ and a WORDNET-derived semantic similarity α. This process for a word w uses its distributional neighbors N_w, the possible senses of not only the word in question, S_w, and also those of the distributionally similar words, S_{n_j}. Thus, $P(ws_i) =$

$$\sum_{n_j \in N_w} \gamma(w, n_j) \frac{wnss(ws_i, n_j)}{\sum_{ws_j \in S_w} wnss(ws_j, n_j)}, \quad (1)$$

where $wnss(s, c) =$

$$\max_{a \in S_c} \alpha(a, s). \quad (2)$$

One can view finding the appropriate sense as a search in two types of space. In determining how good a particular synset ws_i is, α guides the search in the semantic space and γ drives the search in the syntactic space. We consider all of the words used in syntactically similar contexts, which we call "corroborators," and for each of them we find the closest meaning to ws_i using a measure of semantic similarity α, for instance a WORDNET-based similarity measure such as Jiang-Conrath (1997). Each of the neighboring words' contributions is weighted by the syntactic probability, as provided by Lin's distributional similarity measure (1998), which rates two words to be similar if they enter into similar syntactic constructions.

Proceedings of the 4th International Workshop on Semantic Evaluations (SemEval-2007), pages 277–281,
Prague, June 2007.

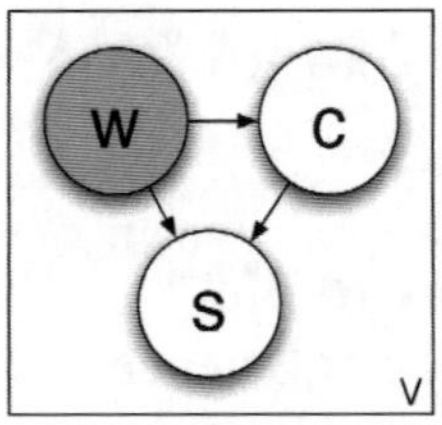

Figure 1: A reinterpretation of McCarthy et al.'s predominant sense method as a generative model. Note that this model has no notion of context; a synset is assigned in an identical manner for all of the words in a vocabulary.

One can think of this process as a generative model, even though it was not originally posed in such a manner. For each word w in the vocabulary, we generate one of the neighbor corroborators according to the Lin similarity, $\gamma(c, w)$, between the two words. We then generate a synset s for that word proportional to the maximum semantic similarity between s and any synset that contains the corroborator c (see Figure 1).

Our aim in this paper is to extend the method of McCarthy et al. using topic models. It is hoped that allowing the method to in effect "choose" the contexts that it uses will improve its ability to disambiguate sentences.

1.2 Using Topic Models to Partition a Document's Words

Topic models like Latent Dirichlet allocation (LDA) (Blei et al., 2003) assume a model of text generation where each document has a multinomial distribution over topics and each word comes from one of these topics. In LDA, each topic is a multinomial distribution, and each document has a multinomial distribution over topics drawn from a Dirichlet prior that selects the topic for each word in a document. Previous work has shown that such a model improves WSD over using a single corpus (Boyd-Graber et al., 2007), and we use this insight to develop an extension of McCarthy's method for multiple topics.

Although describing the statistical background and motivations behind topic models are beyond the scope of this paper, it suffices to note that the topics induced from a corpus provide a statistical grouping of words that often occur together and a probabilistic assignment of each word in a corpus to topics. Thus, one topic might have terms like "government," "president," "govern," and "regal," while another topic might have terms like "finance," "high-yield," "investor," and "market." This paper assumes that the machinery for learning these distributions can, given a corpus and a specified number of topics, return the topic distributions most likely to have generated the corpus.

1.3 Defining the Model

While the original predominant senses method used Lin's thesaurus similarity method alone in generating the corroborator, we will also use the probability of that word being part of the same topic as the word to be disambiguated. Thus the process of choosing the "corroborator" is no longer identical for each word; it is affected by its topic, which changes for every document. This new generative process can be thought of as a modified LDA system that, after selecting the word generated by the topic, continues on by generating a corroborator and a sense for the original word:

For each document $d \in \{1 \dots D\}$:

1. Select a topic distribution $\theta_d \sim \text{Dir}(\tau)$
2. For each word in the document $n \in \{1 \dots N\}$:
   (a) Select a topic $z_n \sim \text{Mult}(1, \theta_d)$
   (b) Select a word from that topic $w_n \sim \text{Mult}(1, \beta_z)$
   (c) Select a "corroborator" c_n also proportional to how important it is to the topic and its similarity to w
   (d) Now, select a synset s_n for that word based on a distribution $p(s_n|w_n, c_n, z_n)$

The conditional dependencies for generating a synset are shown in Figure 2. Our goal, like McCarthy et al.'s, is to determine the most likely sense for each word. This amounts to posterior inference, which we address by marginalizing over the unobserved variables (the topics and the corroborators), where $p(ws_i) =$

$$p(s|w) = \int_{\theta} \sum_{z} \sum_{c} p(s|w, c, z) p(c|z, w) p(z|w, \theta). \quad (3)$$

In order to fully specify this, we must determine the distribution from which the corroborator is drawn and the distribution from which the synset is drawn.

Ideally, we would want a distribution that for a single topic would be identical to McCarthy et al.'s

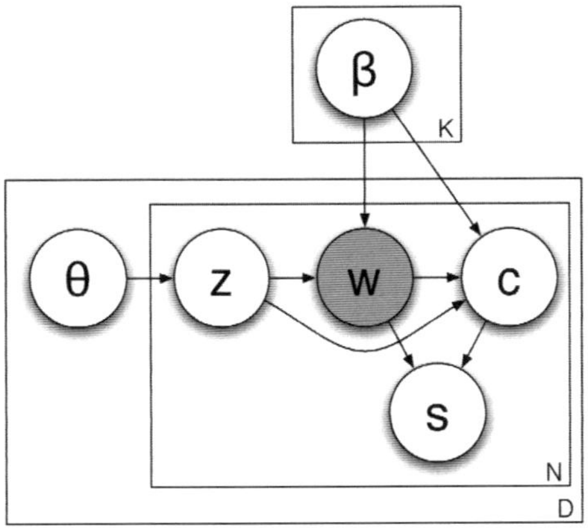

Figure 2: Our generative model assumes that documents are divided into topics and that these topics generate both the observed word and a "corroborator," a term similar in usage to the word. Next, a sense that minimizes the semantic distance between the corroborator and the word is generated.

method but would, as more topics are added, favor corroborators in the same topic as the number of topics increases. In McCarthy et al.'s method, the probability of the corroborator given a word w is proportional to the Lin similarity $\gamma(w, c)$ between the word and the corroborator. Here, the probability of a corroborator c is

$$p(c|z, w) \propto \frac{\beta_{z,c}}{\beta_c^0}\gamma(w, c), \quad (4)$$

where $\beta_{z,c}$ is the multinomial probability of word c in the zth topic, and β_c^0 is the multinomial probability of the word with a single topic (i.e. background word probability).

Before, the corroborator was weighted simply based on its syntactic similarity to the word w, now we also weight that contribution by how important (or unimportant) that word is to the topic that w has been assigned to. This has the effect of increasing the probability of words pertinent to the topic that also have high syntactic similarity. Thus, whenever the syntactic similarity captures polysemous usage, we hope to be able to separate the different usages. Note, however, that since for a single topic the β term cancels out and the procedure is equivalent to McCarthy et al.

We adapt the semantic similarity in much the same way to make it topic specific. Because the Jiang-Conrath similarity measure uses an underlying term frequency to generate a similarity score, we use the topic term frequency instead of the undivided term frequency. Thus, the probability of a sense is proportional to semantic similarity between it and the closest sense among the senses of a corroborator with respect to this topic-specific similarity (c.f. the global similarity in Equation 2). The probability of selecting a synset s given the corroborator c and a topic z then becomes

$$p(s|w, c, z) \propto \max_{s' \in S(c)} \alpha_z(s, s'). \quad (5)$$

This new dependence on the topic happens because we recompute the information content used by Jiang-Conrath with the distribution over words implied by each topic. We then use the similarity implied by that similarity for α_z. Following the lead of McCarthy, for notational ease, this becomes defined as $wnss$ in Equation 8.

1.4 Choosing a Synset

The problem of choosing a synset then is reduced to finding the synset with the highest probability under this model. The model is also designed so that the task of learning the assignment of topics to words and documents is not affected by this new machinery for corroborators and senses that we've added onto the model. Thus, we can use the variational inference method described in (Blei et al., 2003) as a foundation for the problem of synset inference.

Taking $p(z|w)$ as a given (i.e. determined by running LDA on the corpus), the probability for a synset s given a word w then becomes

$$p(s|w, z) = \sum_z \sum_c p(s|w, c, z)p(c|z)p(z|w), \quad (6)$$

whose terms have been described in the previous section. With all of the normalization terms, we now see that $p(s|w, z)$ becomes

$$\sum_z \sum_c \frac{\frac{\beta_{z,c}}{\beta_c^0}\gamma(w, c)}{\sum_{c'} \frac{\beta_{z,c}}{\beta_c^0}\gamma(w, c')} \frac{wnss(s, c, z)}{\sum_{s' \in S_w} wnss(s', c, z)}. \quad (7)$$

and $wnss(s, c, z)$ now becomes, for the zth topic,

$$\max_{a \in S(c)} \alpha_z(a, s). \quad (8)$$

Thus, we've now assigned a probability to each of the possible senses a word can take in a document.

1.5 Intuition

For example, consider the word "fly," which has two other words that have high syntactic similarity (in our formulation, γ) with the terms "fly_ball" and "insect." Both of these words would, given the semantic similarity provided by WORDNET, point to a single sense of "fly;" one of them would give a higher value, however, and thus all senses of the word "fly" would be assigned that sense. By separately weighting these words by the topic frequencies, we would hope to choose the sports sense in topics that have a higher probability of the terms like "foul_ball," "pop_fly," and "grounder" and the other sense in the contexts where insect has a higher probability in the topic.

2 Evaluations

This section describes three experiments to determine the effectiveness of this unsupervised system. The first was used to help understand the system, and the second two were part of the SemEval 2007 competition.

2.1 SemCor

As an initial evaluation, we learned LDA topics on the British National corpus with paragraphs as the underlying "document" (this allowed for a more uniform document length). These documents were then used to infer topic probabilities for each of the words in SemCor (Miller et al., 1993), and the model described in the previous section was run to determine the most likely synset. The results of this procedure are shown in Table 1. Accuracy is determined as the percentage of words for which the most likely sense was the one tagged in the corpus.

While the method does roughly recreate McCarthy et al.'s result for a single topic, it only offers a one percent improvement over McCarthy et al. on five topics and then falls below McCarthy for all greater numbers of topics tried. Thus, for all subsequent experiments we used a five topic model trained on the BNC.

2.2 SemEval-2007 Task 1: CLIR

Using IR metrics, this disambiguation scheme was evaluated against another competing platform and an algorithm provided by the Task 1 (Agirre et al., 2007) organizers. Our system had the best results of any expansion scheme considered (0.30) , although none of the expansion schemes did better than using no expansion (0.36). Although our technique also yielded a better score than the other competing platform for cross-language queries (0.17), it did not surpass the first sense-heuristic (0.26), but this is not surprising given that our algorithm does not assume the existence of such information. For an overview of Task 1 results, see Table 2.

Topics	All	Nouns
1	.393	.467
5	.397	.478
25	.387	.456
200	.359	.420

Table 1: Accuracy on disambiguating words in SemCor

Task	PUTOP
Topic Expansion	0.30
Document Expansion	0.15
English Translation	0.17
SensEval 2	0.39
SensEval 3	0.33

Table 2: Performance results on Task 1

2.3 SemEval-2007 Task 17: All-Words

Task 17 (Pradhan et al., 2007) asked participants to submit results as probability distributions over senses. Because this is also the output of this algorithm, we submitted the probabilities to the contest before realizing that the distributions are very close to uniform over all senses and thus yielded a precision of 0.12, very close to the random baseline. Placing a point distribution on the argmax with our original submission to the task, however, (consistent with our methodology for evaluation on SemCor), gives a precision of 0.39.

3 Conclusion

While the small improvement over the single topic suggests that topic techniques might have traction in determining the best sense, the addition is not appreciable. In a way the failure of the technique is encouraging in that it affirms the original methodology of McCarthy et al. in finding a single predominant sense for each word. While the syntactic similarity measure indeed usually offers high values of similarity for words related to a single sense of a word, the similarity for words related to other senses, which we had hoped to strengthen by using topic features, are on par with words observed because of noise.

Thus, for a word like "bank," words like "firm," "commercial_bank," "company," and "financial_institution" are the closest in terms of the syntactic similarity, and this allows the financial senses to be selected without any difficulty. Even if we had corroborating words for another sense in some topic, these words are absent from the syntactically similar words. If we want the meaning similar to that of "riverbank," the word with the most similar meaning, "side," had a syntactic similarity on par with the unrelated words "individual" and "group." Thus, interpretations other than the dominant sense as determined by the baseline method of McCarthy et al. are hard to find.

Because one topic is equivalent to McCarthy et al.'s method, this means that we do no worse on disambiguation. However, contrary to our hope, increasing the number of topics does not lead to significantly better sense predictions. This work has not investigated using a topic-based procedure for determining the syntactic similarity, but we feel that this extension could provide real improvement to the unsupervised techniques that can make use of the copious amounts of available unlabeled data.

References

Steven Abney. 2004. Understanding the yarowsky algorithm. *Comput. Linguist.*, 30(3):365–395.

Eneko Agirre, Oier Lopez de Lacalle, Arantxa Otegi, German Rigau, and Piek Vossen. 2007. The Senseval-2007 Task 1: Evaluating WSD on cross-language information retrieval. In *Proceedings of SemEval-2007*. Association for Computational Linguistics.

David Blei, Andrew Ng, and Michael Jordan. 2003. Latent Dirichlet allocation. *Journal of Machine Learning Research*, 3:993–1022, January.

Jordan L. Boyd-Graber, David M. Blei, and Jerry Zhu. 2007. Probabalistic walks in semantic hierarchies as a topic model for WSD. In *Proc. EMNLP 2007*.

Jay J. Jiang and David W. Conrath. 1997. Semantic similarity based on corpus statistics and lexical taxonomy. In *Proceedings on International Conference on Research in Computational Linguistics*, Taiwan.

Dekang Lin. 1998. An information-theoretic definition of similarity. In *Proc. 15th International Conf. on Machine Learning*, pages 296–304. Morgan Kaufmann, San Francisco, CA.

Diana McCarthy, Rob Koeling, Julie Weeds, and John Carroll. 2004. Finding predominant word senses in untagged text. In *In 42nd Annual Meeting of the Association for Computational Linguistics*, pages 280–287.

George Miller, Claudia Leacock, Randee Tengi, and Ross Bunker. 1993. A semantic concordance. In *3rd DARPA Workshop on Human Language Technology*, pages 303–308.

Sameer Pradhan, Martha Palmer, and Edward Loper. 2007. The Senseval-2007 Task 17: English fine-grained all-words. In *Proceedings of SemEval-2007*. Association for Computational Linguistics.

RACAI: Meaning Affinity Models

Radu Ion
Institute for Artificial Intelligence
13, "13 Septembrie",
050711, Bucharest 5,
Romania
radu@racai.ro

Dan Tufiş
Institute for Artificial Intelligence
13, "13 Septembrie",
050711, Bucharest 5,
Romania
tufis@racai.ro

Abstract

This article introduces an unsupervised word sense disambiguation algorithm that is inspired by the lexical attraction models of Yuret (1998). It is based on the assumption that the meanings of the words that form a sentence can be best assigned by constructing an interpretation of the whole sentence. This interpretation is facilitated by a dependency-like context specification of a content word within the sentence. Thus, finding the context words of a target word is a matter of finding a pseudo-syntactic dependency analysis of the sentence, called a linkage.

1 Introduction

Word Sense Disambiguation (WSD) is a difficult Natural Language Processing task which requires that for every content word (noun, adjective, verb or adverb) the appropriate meaning is automatically selected from the available sense inventory[1]. Traditionally, the WSD algorithms are divided into two rough classes: supervised and unsupervised. The supervised paradigm relies on sense annotated corpora, with the assumption that neighbouring disambiguate words provide a strongly discriminating and generalizable context representation for the meaning of a target word. Obviously, this approach suffers from the *knowledge acquisition bottleneck* in that there will never be enough training data to ensure a scalable result of such algorithms. The unsupervised alternative to WSD tries to alleviate the burden of manually sense tagging the corpora, by employing algorithms that use different knowledge sources to determine the correct meaning in context. In fact, the "knowledge source usage" is another way to distinguish among the WSD methods. Such methods call upon further processing of the text to be disambiguated such as parsing and/or use handcrafted, semantically rich sense inventories such as WordNet (Fellbaum, 1998). WSD methods in this category range from the very simple ranking based on counting the number of words occurring in both the target word's context and its sense definitions in a reference dictionary (Lesk, 1986) to the more elaborated approaches using the semantic lexicon's taxonomies, (shallow) parsing, collocation discovery etc. (Stevenson and Wilks, 2001).

One of the central issues of any WSD implementation is given by the *context representation*. The standard principle that is applied when trying to disambiguate the meaning of a word is that the same word in similar contexts should have the same meaning. By and large, the context of a target word is materialized by a collection of features among which are: the collocates of the target word, the part-of-speech (POS) of the target word, $\pm k$ words surrounding the target word and/or their POSes and so on. More often than not, the contexts similarity is estimated by the distance in the feature vector space. Lin (1997) defines the local context of a target word by the collection of syntactic dependencies in which the word takes part. According to this notion of con-

[1]In principle, one can select meanings for any part of speech that is represented into the semantic lexicon (prepositions for instance) but the content words disambiguation is the de facto standard.

Proceedings of the 4th International Workshop on Semantic Evaluations (SemEval-2007), pages 282–287,
Prague, June 2007. ©2007 Association for Computational Linguistics

text, Lin assumes that two different words are likely to have similar meanings if they occur in identical local contexts.

What we will attempt here is to combine the two views of context similarity/identity versus meaning similarity/identity by using a dependency-like representation of the context as a lexical attraction model. More specifically, we will not consider any feature of the context and will try to maximize a meaning attraction function over all linked words of a sentence. In section 2 we will describe **SynWSD**, an unsupervised, knowledge-based WSD algorithm and in sections 3 and 4 we will present the application of SynWSD to two of SEMEVAL-2007 "all words" tasks: English Coarse-Grained and English Fine-Grained. Finally, with section 5 we will conclude the article.

2 SynWSD

The syntactic context representation is not new in the realm of WSD algorithms. For instance, Lin (1997) used the dependency relations of the target word to specify its context and Stetina (1998) extracted head-modifier relations to obtain the context pairs for each word of interest from a constituents tree. The syntactic representation of the context of a target word has one main advantage over the collection of features method: the target word is related only with the relevant word(s) in its window and not with all the words and thus, many noisy cooccurrences are eliminated. Mel'čuk (1988) further strengthens the intuition of a syntactic context representation with his Meaning Text Model in which there is a deterministic translation from the surface syntactic dependency realization of the sentence to its deep syntactic one and therefore to the semantic representation.

To use a syntactic analysis as a context representation, one needs a parser which will supply the WSD algorithm with the required analysis. Because we have intended to develop a language independent WSD algorithm and because there is no available, reliable dependency parser for Romanian, we have backed off to a simpler, easier to obtain dependency-like representation of a sentence: a slightly modified version of the lexical attraction models of (Yuret, 1998).

2.1 LexPar

Lexical attraction is viewed as the likelihood of a syntactic dependency relation between two words of a sentence and is measured by the pointwise mutual information between them. Yuret (1998) shows that the search for the lowest entropy lexical attraction model leads to the unsupervised discovery of undirected dependency relations or links.

LexPar (Ion and Barbu Mititelu, 2006) is a link analyzer (a linker) which generates a connected, undirected, acyclic and planar graph of an input sentence in which the nodes are the words of the sentence and the edges are the highest lexical attracted dependency-like relations. This program is similar to the suboptimal one presented in (Yuret, 1998) with the following main differences:

- the policy of checking pairs of words to be related is based on the assumption that most of the syntactic relations[2] are formed between adjacent words and then between adjacent groups of linked words;
- it operates on POS-tagged and lemmatized corpora and attempts to improve parameter estimation by using both lemmas and POS tags. The score of a link is defined as the weighted sum of the pointwise mutual information of the lemmas and of the POS tags, thus coping even with the unknown lemmas;
- it uses a rule filter that will deny the formation of certain links based on the POSes of the candidate words. For instance, neither the relation between a determiner and an adverb nor the relation between a singular determiner and a plural noun should be permitted;

In Figure 1 we have an example of a XML encoded, LexPar processed sentence. The `head` attribute of the `w` tag specifies the position of the head word of the tagged word. Because LexPar considers non-directed dependency relations, for the purposes of XML encoding[3], the first word of every sentence

[2] At least for our languages of interest, namely English and Romanian.

[3] The encoding of the morpho-syntactic descriptors (MSD) is MULTEXT-East compliant (`http://nl.ijs.si/ME/V3/msd/00README.txt`).

```xml
- <tu id="3">
  - <seg lang="en">
    - <s id="d001.s003.en">
        <w lemma="we" ana="Pp1-pn">We</w>
        <w lemma="have" ana="Vaip1p" head="2">have</w>
        <w lemma="make" ana="Vmps" head="0">made</w>
        <w lemma="no" ana="Dz3" head="5">no</w>
        <w lemma="such" ana="Afp" head="5">such</w>
        <w lemma="statement" ana="Ncns" head="2">statement</w>
        <c>.</c>
      </s>
    </seg>
  </tu>
```

Figure 1: The XML representation of a LexPar processed sentence.

(position 0) is always the root of the syntactic dependency tree, its dependents are its children nodes, and so on while we recursively build the tree from the LexPar result.

We have chosen not to give a detailed presentation of LexPar here (the reader is directed towards (Yuret, 1998; Ion and Barbu Mititelu, 2006)) and instead, to briefly explain how the linkage in Figure 1 was obtained. The processor begins by inspecting a list G of groups of linked words which initially contains the positions of each of the words in the sentence:

$$G_0 = \{(0), (1), (2), (3), (4), (5)\}$$

The linking policy is trying to link words in the groups (0) and (1) or (1) and (2). The syntactic rule filter says that auxiliary verbs (`Va`) can only be linked with main verbs (`Vm`) and so one link is formed and the list of groups becomes:

$$G_1 = \{(0), (\langle 1, 2\rangle), (3), (4), (5)\}$$

Next, the processor must decide linking the groups $(\langle 1, 2\rangle)$ and (3) or (3) and (4) but the syntactic rule filter is denying any link from positions 1 or 2 to 3 (no links from any kind of verb `V` to any kind of a determiner `D`) or from 3 to 4 (no link from a negative determiner `Dz3` to a qualificative adjective `Af`). Continuing this way, the progress of G list is as follows:

$$\begin{aligned} G_1 &= \{(0), (\langle 1, 2\rangle), (3), (\langle 4, 5\rangle)\} \\ G_2 &= \{(\langle 0, 2\rangle, \langle 1, 2\rangle), (\langle 3, 5\rangle, \langle 4, 5\rangle)\} \\ G_3 &= \{(\langle 0, 2\rangle, \langle 1, 2\rangle, \langle 2, 5\rangle, \langle 3, 5\rangle, \langle 4, 5\rangle)\} \end{aligned}$$

So in 3 steps G_3 contains a single group of linked words namely the linkage of the sentence.

2.2 Meaning Affinity Models

If the lexical attraction models are geared towards the discovery of the most probable syntactic relations of a sentence, we can naturally generalize this idea to construct a class of models that will find a combination of meanings that maximizes a certain meaning attraction function over a linkage of a sentence. We call this class of models the *meaning affinity models*.

Optimizing meaning affinity over a syntactic representation of a sentence has been tried in (Stetina et al., 1998; Horbovanu, 2002). SynWSD (Ion, 2007) is an implementation with two phases of the meaning affinity concept: **training** which takes as input a corpus with LexPar linked sentences (of the type shown in Figure 1) and outputs a table M of meaning co-occurrence frequencies and **disambiguation** of a LexPar linked sentence S, based on the counts in table M from the previous phase.

Before continuing with the descriptions of these phases, we will introduce the notations that we will use throughout this section:

- A n-word sentence is represented by a vector S of n elements, each of them containing a triple $\langle \text{wordform}, \text{lemma}, \text{POS}\rangle$. For instance, the first element from S in Figure 1 is $S[0] = \langle \text{We}, \text{we}, \texttt{Pp1-pn}\rangle$;
- L is the LexPar linkage of S, and is also a vector containing pairs of positions $\langle i, j\rangle$ in S that are related, where $0 \leq i < j < n$;
- $\texttt{lem}(S, i)$ and $\texttt{pos}(S, i)$ are two functions that give the lemma and the POS of the position i in $S, 0 \leq i < n$.

The **training phase** is responsible for collecting meaning co-occurrence counts. It simply iterates over each sentence S of the training corpus and for every link $L[k]$ of the form $\langle a, b\rangle$ from its linkage, does the following (K stores the total number of recorded meaning pairs):

1. extracts the sets of meanings I_a and I_b corresponding to the lemma $\texttt{lem}(S, a)$ with the POS $\texttt{pos}(S, a)$ and to the lemma $\texttt{lem}(S, b)$ with the POS $\texttt{pos}(S, b)$ from the sense inventory[4];

[4]If the lemma does not appear in the sense inventory or its

2. increases by 1 the M table frequencies for every pair of the cartesian product $I_a \times I_b$. For every meaning $m \in I_a$, the frequency of the special pair $\langle m, * \rangle$ is increased with $|I_b|$. Similarly, the pair $\langle *, m \rangle$ frequency is also increased with $|I_a|$ for $m \in I_b$);

3. $K \leftarrow K + |I_a \times I_b|$.

We have used the Princeton WordNet (Fellbaum, 1998), version 2.0 (PWN20) as our sense inventory and the mappings from its synsets to the SUMO ontology concepts (Niles and Pease, 2003) and to the IRST domains (Magnini and Cavaglia, 2000). Thus we have tree different sense inventories each with a different granularity. For instance, the noun **homeless** has 2 senses in PWN20, its first sense ("*someone with no housing*") being mapped onto the more general `Human` SUMO concept and onto the `person` IRST domain. The second sense of the same noun is "*people who are homeless*" which corresponds to the same SUMO concept and to a different IRST domain (`factotum`).

In order to reduce the number of recorded pairs in the case of PWN20 meanings (the finest granularity available) and to obtain reliable counts, we have modified the step 1 of the training phase in the following manner:

- if we are dealing with nouns or verbs, for every meaning m_i of the lemma, extract the uppermost hypernym meaning which does not subsume any other meaning of the same lemma;
- if we are dealing with adjectives, for every meaning m_i of the lemma, extract the meaning of the head adjective if m_i is part of a cluster;
- if we are dealing with adverbs, for every meaning m_i of the lemma, return m_i (no generalization is made available by the sense inventory in this case).

This generalization procedure will be reversed at the time of disambiguation as will be explained shortly.

POS does not give a noun, verb, adjective or adverb, the lemma itself is returned as the sole meaning because in the disambiguation phase we need a meaning for every word of the sentence, be it content word or otherwise.

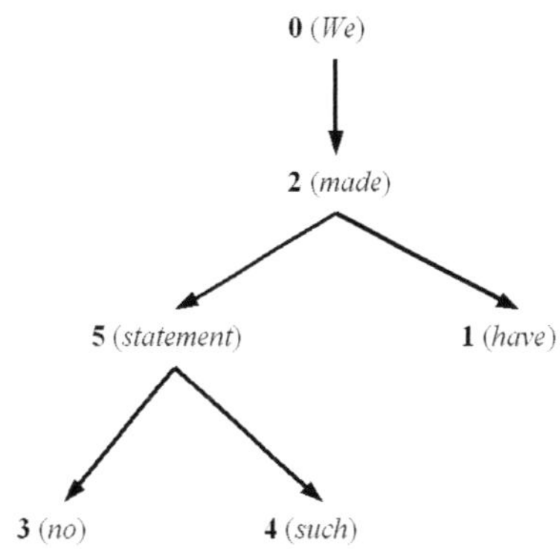

Figure 2: The tree representation of the sentence in Figure 1.

The **disambiguation phase** takes care of finding the best interpretation of a linked sentence based on the frequency table M. For a test sentence S, with the linkage L, the procedure goes as follows:

1. produce a proper tree T of positions from L by taking position 0 as the root of the tree. Then, for every link that contains 0 make the other position in the link a child of 0 and then, in a recursive manner, apply the same process for all children of 0. For instance, the tree for Figure 1 if depicted in Figure 2;

2. construct a vector P of sentence positions visited during a depth-first traversal of the T tree. The vector of sentence positions for Figure 2 is

$$P = (0, 2, 5, 3, 5, 4, 5, 2, 1, 2, 0)$$

3. construct a meaning vector V of the same length as P. $V[i]$ contains the list of meanings of the lemma $\texttt{lem}(S, P[i])$ with the POS $\texttt{pos}(S, P[i])$. If the sense inventory is PWN20, every meaning from the list is generalized as described above;

4. finally, apply the Viterbi algorithm ((Viterbi, 1967)) on the V vector and extract the path (sequence of meanings) which maximizes meaning affinity.

Each state transition is scored according to a meaning affinity function. In our experiments we have considered three meaning affinity functions. If K is the total number of meaning pairs and if m_1

and m_2 are two meanings from adjacent V positions for which $f(m_1, m_2)$ is the pair frequency extracted from M, the functions are:

1. DICE:

$$\texttt{dice}(m_1, m_2) = \frac{2f(m_1,m_2)+2f(m_2,m_1)}{f(m_1,*)+f(*,m_1)+f(m_2,*)+f(*,m_2)}$$

2. Pointwise mutual information:

$$\texttt{mi}(m_1, m_2) = log\frac{Kf(m_1,m_2)+Kf(m_2,m_1)}{(f(m_1,*)+f(*,m_1))(f(m_2,*)+f(*,m_2))}$$

3. Log-Likelihood, $\texttt{ll}(m_1, m_2)$ which is computed as in (Moore, 2004).

After the Viterbi path (best path) has been calculated, every state (meaning) from $V[i]$ $(0 \leq i < |V|)$ along this path is added to a final D vector. When the PWN20 sense inventory is used, the reverse of the generalization procedure is applied to each meaning recorded in D, thus coming back to the meanings of the words of S. Please note that an entry in D may contain more than one meaning especially in the case of PWN20 meanings for which there was not enough training data.

3 SEMEVAL-2007 Task #7: Coarse-grained English All-Words

LexPar and SynWSD were trained on an 1 million words corpus comprising the George Orwell's 1984 novel and the SemCor corpus (Miller et al., 1993). Both texts have been POS-tagged (with MULTEXT-East compliant POS tags) and lemmatized and the result was carefully checked by human judges to ensure a correct annotation.

SynWSD was run with all the meaning attraction functions (`dice`, `mi` and `ll`) for all the sense inventories (PWN20, SUMO categories and IRST domains) and a combined result was submitted to the task organizers. The combined result was prepared in the following way:

1. for each sense inventory and for each token identifier, get the union of the meanings for each run (`dice`, `mi` and `ll`);
2. for each token identifier with its three union sets of PWN20 meanings, SUMO categories and IRST domains:
   (a) for each PWN20 meaning m_i in the union, if there is a SUMO category that maps onto it, increase m_i's weight by 1;
   (b) for each PWN20 meaning m_i in the union, if there is a IRST domain that maps onto it, increase m_i's weight by 1;
   (c) from the set of weighted PWN20 meanings, select the subset C that best overlaps with a cluster. That is, the intersection between the subset and the cluster has a maximal number of meanings for which the sum of weights is also the greatest;
   (d) output the lowest numbered meaning in C.

With this combination, the official F-measure of SynWSD is 0.65712 which places it into the 11th position out of 16 competing systems[5].

Another possible combination is that of the intersection which is obtained with the exact same steps as above, replacing the union operation with the intersection. When the PWN20 meanings set is void, we can make use of the most frequent sense (MFS) backoff strategy thus selecting the MFS of the current test word from PWN20. Working with the official key file and scoring software, the intersection combination with MFS backoff gives an F-measure of 0.78713 corresponding to the 6th best result. The same combination method but without MFS backoff achieves a precision of 0.80559 but at the cost of a very low F-measure (0.41492).

4 SEMEVAL-2007 Task #17: English All-Words

For this task, LexPar and SynWSD were further trained on a 12 million POS tagged and lemmatized balanced corpus[6]. The run that was submitted was the intersection combination with the MFS backoff strategy which obtained an F-measure of 0.527. This score puts our algorithm on the 8th position out of 14 competing systems. For the union combinator

[5]Precision = Recall = F-measure. In what follows, mentioning only the F-measure means that this equality holds.

[6]A random subset of the BNC (`http://www.natcorp.ox.ac.uk/`).

(the MFS backoff strategy is not applicable), the F-measure decreases to 0.445 (10th place). Finally, if we train SynWSD only on corpora from task#7, the union combinator leads to an F-measure of 0.344.

5 Conclusions

SynWSD is a knowledge-based, unsupervised WSD algorithm that uses a dependency-like analysis of a sentence as a uniform context representation. It is a language independent algorithm that doesn't require any feature selection.

Our system can be improved in several ways. First, one can modify the generalization procedure in the case of PWN20 meanings in the sense of selecting a fixed set of top level hypernyms. The size of this set will directly affect the quality of meaning co-occurrence frequencies. Second, one may study the effect of a proper dependency parsing on the results of the disambiguation process including here making use of the syntactic relations names and orientation.

Even if SynWSD rankings are not the best available, we believe that the unsupervised approach to the WSD problem combined with different knowledge sources represents the future of these systems even if, at least during the last semantic evaluation exercise SENSEVAL-3, the supervised systems achieved top rankings.

References

Christiane Fellbaum, editor. 1998. *WordNet. An Electronic Lexical Database*. MIT Press, May.

Vladimir Horbovanu. 2002. Word Sense Disambiguation using WordNet. "Alexandru Ioan Cuza" University, Faculty of Computer Science, Iaşi, Romania. In Romanian.

Radu Ion and Verginica Barbu Mititelu. 2006. Constrained lexical attraction models. In *Proceedings of the Nineteenth International Florida Artificial Intelligence Research Society Conference*, pages 297–302, Menlo Park, Calif., USA. AAAI Press.

Radu Ion. 2007. *Word Sense Disambiguation methods applied to English and Romanian*. Ph.D. thesis, Research Institute for Artificial Intelligence (RACAI), Romanian Academy, January. In Romanian, to be defended.

Michael Lesk. 1986. Automatic sense disambiguation : How to tell a pine cone from an ice cream cone. In *Proceedings of the 1986 SIGDOC Conference, Association for Computing Machinery*, pages 24–26, New York.

Dekang Lin. 1997. Using syntactic dependency as local context to resolve word sense ambiguity. In *Proceedings of the 35th Annual Meeting of the Association for Computational Linguistics*, pages 64–71, Madrid, Spain, July.

Bernardo Magnini and Gabriela Cavaglia. 2000. Integrating Subject Field Codes into WordNet. In Gavrilidou M., Crayannis G., Markantonatu S., Piperidis S., and Stainhaouer G., editors, *Proceedings of LREC-2000, Second International Conference on Language Resources and Evaluation*, pages 1413–1418, Athens, Greece, June.

Igor Mel'čuk. 1988. *Dependency Syntax: theory and practice*. State University of New York Press, Albany, NY.

George A. Miller, Claudia Leacock, Randee Tengi, and Ross T. Bunker. 1993. A semantic concordance. In *Proceedings of the 3rd DARPA Workshop on Human Language Technology*, pages 303–308, Plainsboro, New Jersey.

Robert C. Moore. 2004. On Log-Likelihood Ratios and the Significance of Rare Events. In *Proceedings of the 2004 Conference on Empirical Methods in Natural Language Processing*, pages 333–340, Barcelona, Spain.

Ian Niles and Adam Pease. 2003. Linking Lexicons and Ontologies: Mapping WordNet to the Suggested Upper Merged Ontology. In *Proceedings of the 2003 International Conference on Information and Knowledge Engineering (IKE 03)*, Las Vegas, Nevada, June.

Jiri Stetina, Sadao Kurohashi, and Makoto Nagao. 1998. General word sense disambiguation method based on a full sentential context. In *Proceedings of the Coling-ACL'98 Workshop "Usage of WordNet in Natural Language Processing Systems"*, pages 1–8, Montreal.

Mark Stevenson and Yorick Wilks. 2001. The interaction of knowledge sources in word sense disambiguation. *Computational Linguistics*, 27(3):321–349.

Andrew J. Viterbi. 1967. Error bounds for convolutional codes and an asymptotically optimum decoding algorithm. *IEEE Transactions on Information Theory*, IT(13):260–269, April.

Deniz Yuret. 1998. *Discovery of linguistic relations using lexical attraction*. Ph.D. thesis, Department of Computer Science and Electrical Engineering, MIT, May.

RTV: Tree Kernels for Thematic Role Classification

Daniele Pighin
FBK-irst; University of Trento, DIT
pighin@itc.it

Alessandro Moschitti
University of Trento, DIT
moschitti@dit.unitn.it

Roberto Basili
University of Rome *Tor Vergata*, DISP
basili@info.uniroma2.it

Abstract

We present a simple, two-steps supervised strategy for the identification and classification of thematic roles in natural language texts. We employ no external source of information but automatic parse trees of the input sentences. We use a few attribute-value features and tree kernel functions applied to specialized structured features. The resulting system has an F_1 of 75.44 on the SemEval2007 closed task on semantic role labeling.

1 Introduction

In this paper we present a system for the labeling of semantic roles that produces VerbNet (Kipper et al., 2000) like annotations of free text sentences using only full syntactic parses of the input sentences. The labeling process is modeled as a cascade of two distinct classification steps: (1) boundary detection (BD), in which the word sequences that encode a thematic role for a given predicate are recognized, and (2) role classification (RC), in which the type of thematic role with respect to the predicate is assigned. After role classification, a set of simple heuristics are applied in order to ensure that only well formed annotations are output.

We designed our system on a per-predicate basis, training one boundary classifier and a battery of role classifiers for each predicate word. We clustered all the senses of the same verb together and ended up with 50 distinct boundary classifiers (one for each target predicate word) and 619 role classifiers to recognize the 47 distinct role labels that appear in the training set.

The remainder of this paper is structured as follows: Section 2 describes in some detail the architecture of our labeling system; Section 3 describes the features that we use to represent the classifier examples; Section 4 describes the experimental setting and reports the accuracy of the system on the SemEval2007 semantic role labeling closed task; finally, Section 5 discusses the results and presents our conclusions.

2 System Description

Given a target predicate word in a natural language sentence, a SRL system is meant to correctly identify all the arguments of the predicate. This problem is usually divided in two sub-tasks: (a) the detection of the boundaries (i. e. the word span) of each argument and (b) the classification of the argument type, e.g. *Arg0* or *ArgM* in PropBank or *Agent* and *Goal* in FrameNet or VerbNet.

The standard approach to learn both the detection and the classification of predicate arguments is summarized by the following steps:

1 Given a sentence from the *training-set*, generate a full syntactic parse-tree;

2 let $\mathcal{P}$ and $\mathcal{A}$ be the set of predicates and the set of parse-tree nodes (i.e. the potential arguments), respectively;

3 for each pair $\langle p, a\rangle \in \mathcal{P} \times \mathcal{A}$:

3.1 extract the feature representation set, $F_{p,a}$;

3.2 if the sub-tree rooted in a covers exactly the words of one argument of p, put $F_{p,a}$ in T^+ (positive examples), otherwise put it in T^- (negative examples).

For instance, in Figure 1.a, for each combination of the predicate *approve* with any other tree node a

Proceedings of the 4th International Workshop on Semantic Evaluations (SemEval-2007), pages 288–291,
Prague, June 2007.

that does not overlap with the predicate, a classifier example $F_{\text{approve},a}$ is generated. If a exactly covers one of the predicate arguments (in this case: "The charter", "by the EC Commission" or "on Sept. 21") it is regarded as a positive instance, otherwise it will be a negative one, e. g. $F_{\text{approve,(NN charter)}}$.

The T^+ and T^- sets are used to train the boundary classifier. To train the role multi-class classifier, T^+ can be reorganized as positive $T^+_{\text{arg}_i}$ and negative $T^-_{\text{arg}_i}$ examples for each argument i. In this way, an individual ONE-vs-ALL classifier for each argument i can be trained. We adopted this solution, according to (Pradhan et al., 2005), since it is simple and effective. In the classification phase, given an unseen sentence, all its $F_{p,a}$ are generated and classified by each individual role classifier. The role label associated with the maximum among the scores provided by the individual classifiers is eventually selected.

To make the annotations consistent with the underlying linguistic model, we employ a few simple heuristics to resolve the overlap situations that may occur, e. g. both "charter" and "the charter" in Figure 1 may be assigned a role:

- if more than two nodes are involved, i. e. a node d and two or more of its descendants n_i are classified as arguments, then assume that d is not an argument. This choice is justified by previous studies (Moschitti et al., 2006b) showing that the accuracy of classification is higher for lower nodes;

- if only two nodes are involved, i. e. they dominate each other, then keep the one with the highest classification score.

3 Features for Semantic Role Labeling

We explicitly represent as attribute-value pairs the following features of each $F_{p,a}$ pair:

- *Phrase Type*, *Predicate Word*, *Head Word*, *Position* and *Voice* as defined in (Gildea and Jurasfky, 2002);

- *Partial Path, No Direction Path, Head Word POS, First and Last Word/POS in Constituent* and *SubCategorization* as proposed in (Pradhan et al., 2005);

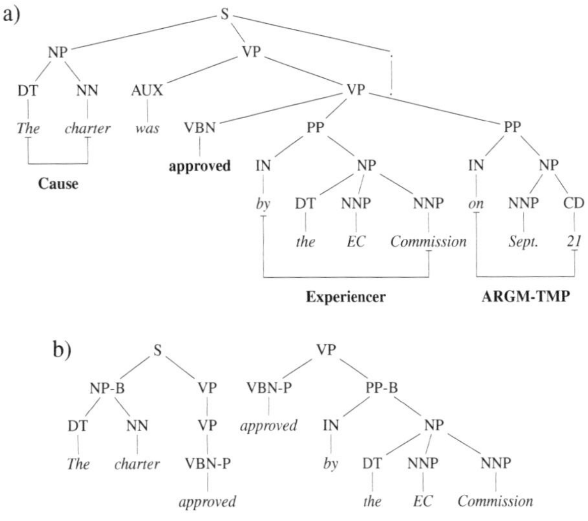

Figure 1: A sentence parse tree (a) and two example AST_1^m structures relative to the predicate *approve* (b).

Set	Props	T	T$^+$	T$^-$
Train	15,838	793,104	45,157	747,947
Dev	1,606	75,302	4,291	71,011
Train - Dev	14,232	717,802	40,866	676,936

Table 1: Composition of the dataset in terms of: number of annotations (Props); number of candidate argument nodes (T); positive (T^+) and negative (T^-) boundary classifier examples.

- *Syntactic Frame* as designed in (Xue and Palmer, 2004).

We also employ structured features derived by the full parses in an attempt to capture relevant aspects that may not be emphasized by the explicit feature representation. (Moschitti et al., 2006a) and (Moschitti et al., 2006b) defined several classes of structured features that were successfully employed with tree kernels for the different stages of an SRL process. Figure 1 shows an example of the AST_1^m structures that we used for both the boundary detection and the role classification stages.

4 Experiments

In this section we discuss the setup and the results of the experiments carried out on the dataset of the SemEval2007 closed task on SRL.

Task	Kernel(s)	Precision	Recall	$F_{\beta=1}$
BD	poly	94.34%	71.26%	81.19
	poly + TK	92.89%	76.09%	83.65
BD + RC	poly	88.72%	68.76%	77.47
	poly + TK	86.60%	72.40%	78.86

Table 2: SRL accuracy on the development test for the boundary detection (BD) and the complete SRL task (BD+RC) using the polynomial kernel alone (poly) or combined with a tree kernel function (poly + TK).

4.1 Setup

The training set comprises 15,838[1] training annotations organized on a per-verb basis. In order to build a development set (Dev), we sampled about one tenth, i. e. 1,606 annotations, of the original training set. For the final evaluation on the test set (Test), consisting of 3,094 annotations, we trained our classifiers on the whole training data. Statistics on the dataset composition are shown in Table 1.

The evaluations were carried out with the SVM-Light-TK[2] software (Moschitti, 2004) which extends the SVM-Light package (Joachims, 1999) with tree kernel functions. We used the default polynomial kernel (degree=3) for the linear features and a SubSet Tree (SST) kernel (Collins and Duffy, 2002) for the comparison of AST_1^m structured features. The kernels are normalized and summed by assigning a weight of 0.3 to the TK contribution.

Training all the 50 boundary classifiers and the 619 role classifiers on the whole dataset took about 4 hours on a 64 bits machine (2.2GHz, 1GB RAM)[3].

4.2 Evaluation

All the evaluations were carried out using the CoNLL2005 evaluator tool available at `http://www.lsi.upc.es/~srlconll/soft.html`.

Table 2 shows the aggregate results on boundary detection (BD) and the complete SRL task (BD+RC) on the development set using the polynomial kernel alone (poly) or in conjunction with the tree kernels and structured features (poly+TK). For both tasks, tree kernel functions do trigger automatic feature selection and improve the polynomial kernel by 2.46 and 1.39 F_1 points, respectively.

Role	#TI	Precision	Recall	$F_{\beta=1}$
Ov(BD)	6931	87.09%	72.96%	79.40
Ov(BD+RC)		81.58%	70.16%	75.44
ARG2	4	100.00%	25.00%	40.00
ARG3	17	61.11%	64.71%	62.86
ARG4	4	0.00%	0.00%	0.00
ARGM-ADV	188	55.14%	31.38%	40.00
ARGM-CAU	13	50.00%	23.08%	31.58
ARGM-DIR	4	100.00%	25.00%	40.00
ARGM-EXT	3	0.00%	0.00%	0.00
ARGM-LOC	151	51.66%	51.66%	51.66
ARGM-MNR	85	41.94%	15.29%	22.41
ARGM-PNC	28	38.46%	17.86%	24.39
ARGM-PRD	9	83.33%	55.56%	66.67
ARGM-REC	1	0.00%	0.00%	0.00
ARGM-TMP	386	55.65%	35.75%	43.53
Actor1	12	85.71%	50.00%	63.16
Actor2	1	100.00%	100.00%	100.00
Agent	2551	91.38%	77.34%	83.78
Asset	21	42.42%	66.67%	51.85
Attribute	17	60.00%	70.59%	64.86
Beneficiary	24	65.00%	54.17%	59.09
Cause	48	75.56%	70.83%	73.12
Experiencer	132	86.49%	72.73%	79.01
Location	12	83.33%	41.67%	55.56
Material	7	100.00%	14.29%	25.00
Patient	37	76.67%	62.16%	68.66
Patient1	20	72.73%	40.00%	51.61
Predicate	181	63.75%	56.35%	59.82
Product	106	70.79%	59.43%	64.62
R-ARGM-LOC	2	0.00%	0.00%	0.00
R-ARGM-MNR	2	0.00%	0.00%	0.00
R-ARGM-TMP	4	0.00%	0.00%	0.00
R-Agent	74	70.15%	63.51%	66.67
R-Experiencer	5	100.00%	20.00%	33.33
R-Patient	2	0.00%	0.00%	0.00
R-Predicate	1	0.00%	0.00%	0.00
R-Product	2	0.00%	0.00%	0.00
R-Recipient	8	100.00%	87.50%	93.33
R-Theme	7	75.00%	42.86%	54.55
R-Theme1	7	100.00%	85.71%	92.31
R-Theme2	1	50.00%	100.00%	66.67
R-Topic	14	66.67%	42.86%	52.17
Recipient	48	75.51%	77.08%	76.29
Source	25	65.22%	60.00%	62.50
Stimulus	21	33.33%	19.05%	24.24
Theme	650	79.22%	68.62%	73.54
Theme1	69	77.42%	69.57%	73.28
Theme2	60	74.55%	68.33%	71.30
Topic	1867	84.26%	82.27%	83.25

Table 3: Evaluation of the semantic role labeling accuracy on the SemEval2007 - Task 17 test set using the poly + TK kernel. Column *#TI* reports the number of instances of each role label in the test set. Rows *Ov(BD)* and *Ov(BD + RC)* show the overall accuracy on the boundary detection and the complete SRL task, respectively.

The SRL accuracy for each one of the 47 distinct role labels is shown in Table 3. Column 2 lists

[1] A bunch of unaligned annotations were removed from the dataset.

[2] `http://ai-nlp.info.uniroma2.it/moschitti/`

[3] In order to have a faster development cycle, we only used 60k training examples to train the boundary classifier of the verb *say*. The accuracy on this relation is still very high, as we measured an overall F_1 of 87.18 on the development set and of 85.13 on the test set.

the number of instances of each role in the test set. Many roles have very few positive examples both in the training and the test sets, and therefore have little or no impact on the overall accuracy which is dominated by the few roles which are very frequent, such as *Theme*, *Agent*, *Topic* and *ARGM-TMP* which account for almost 80% of all the test roles.

5 Final Remarks

In this paper we presented a system that employs tree kernels and a basic set of flat features for the classification of thematic roles.

We adopted a very simple approach that is meant to be as general and fast as possible. The issue of generality is addressed by training the boundary and role classifiers on a per-predicate basis and by employing tree kernel and structured features in the learning algorithm. The resulting architecture can indeed be used to learn the classification of roles of non-verbal predicates as well, and the automatic feature selection triggered by the tree kernel should compensate for the lack of *ad-hoc*, well established explicit features for some classes of non-verbal predicates, e. g. adverbs or prepositions.

Splitting the learning problem also has the clear advantage of noticeably improving the efficiency of the classifiers, thus reducing training and classification time. On the other hand, this split results in some classifiers having too few training instances and therefore being very inaccurate. This is especially true for the boundary classifiers, which conversely need to be very accurate in order to positively support the following stages of the SRL process. The solution of a monolithic boundary classifier that we previously employed (Moschitti et al., 2006b) is noticeably more accurate though much less efficient, especially for training. Indeed, after the SemEval2007 evaluation period was over, we ran another experiment using a monolithic boundary classifier. On the test set, we measured F1 values of 82.09 vs 79.40 and 77.17 vs 75.44 for the boundary detection and the complete SRL tasks, respectively.

Although it was provided as part of both the training and test data, we chose not to use the verb sense information. This choice is motivated by our intention to depend on as less external resources as possible in order to be able to port our SRL system to other linguistic models and languages, for which such resources may not exist. Still, identifying the predicate sense is a key issue especially for role classification, as the argument structure of a predicate is largely determined by its sense. In the near feature we plan to use larger structured features, i. e. spanning all the potential arguments of a predicate, to improve the accuracy of our role classifiers.

Acknowledgments

The development of the SRL system was carried out at the University of Rome *Tor Vergata* and financed by the EU project PrestoSpace[4] (FP6-507336).

References

Michael Collins and Nigel Duffy. 2002. New ranking algorithms for parsing and tagging: Kernels over discrete structures, and the voted perceptron. In *ACL02*.

Daniel Gildea and Daniel Jurasfky. 2002. Automatic labeling of semantic roles. *Computational Linguistic*, 28(3):496–530.

T. Joachims. 1999. Making large-scale SVM learning practical. In B. Schölkopf, C. Burges, and A. Smola, editors, *Advances in Kernel Methods - Support Vector Learning*.

Karin Kipper, Hoa Trang Dang, and Martha Palmer. 2000. Class-based construction of a verb lexicon. In *Proceedings of AAAI-2000 Seventeenth National Conference on Artificial Intelligence, Austin, TX*.

Alessandro Moschitti, Daniele Pighin, and Roberto Basili. 2006a. Semantic role labeling via tree kernel joint inference. In *Proceedings of the Tenth Conference on Computational Natural Language Learning, CoNLL-X*.

Alessandro Moschitti, Daniele Pighin, and Roberto Basili. 2006b. Tree kernel engineering in semantic role labeling systems. In *Proceedings of the Workshop on Learning Structured Information in Natural Language Applications, EACL 2006*, pages 49–56, Trento, Italy, April. European Chapter of the Association for Computational Linguistics.

Alessandro Moschitti. 2004. A study on convolution kernel for shallow semantic parsing. In *proceedings of ACL-2004*, Barcelona, Spain.

Sameer Pradhan, Kadri Hacioglu, Valeri Krugler, Wayne Ward, James H. Martin, and Daniel Jurafsky. 2005. Support vector learning for semantic argument classification. *to appear in Machine Learning Journal*.

Nianwen Xue and Martha Palmer. 2004. Calibrating features for semantic role labeling. In *Proceedings of EMNLP 2004*, pages 88–94, Barcelona, Spain, July.

[4] `http://www.prestospace.org`

SHEF: Semantic Tagging and Summarization Techniques Applied to Cross-document Coreference

Horacio Saggion
Department of Computer Science
University of Sheffield
211 Portobello Street - Sheffield, England, UK, S1 4DP
Tel: +44-114-222-1947
Fax: +44-114-222-1810
saggion@dcs.shef.ac.uk

Abstract

We describe experiments for the cross-document coreference task in SemEval 2007. Our cross-document coreference system uses an in-house agglomerative clustering implementation to group documents referring to the same entity. Clustering uses vector representations created by summarization and semantic tagging analysis components. We present evaluation results for four system configurations demonstrating the potential of the applied techniques.

1 Introduction

Cross-document coreference resolution is the task of identifying if two mentions of the same (or similar) name in different sources refer to the same individual. Deciding if two documents refer to the same individual is a difficult problem because names are highly ambiguous. Automatic techniques for solving this problem are required not only for better access to information but also in natural language processing applications such as multidocument summarization and information extraction. Here, we concentrate on the following SemEval 2007 Web People Search Task (Artiles et al., 2007): a search engine user types in a person name as a query. Instead of ranking web pages, an ideal system should organize search results in as many clusters as there are different people sharing the same name in the documents returned by the search engine. The input is, therefore, the results given by a web search engine using a person name as query. The output is a number of sets, each containing documents referring to the same individual.

As past and recent research (Bagga and Baldwin, 1998; Phan et al., 2006), we have addressed the problem as a document clustering problem. For our first participation in SemEval 2007, we use two approaches: a lexical or bag-of-words approach and a semantic based approach. We have implemented our own clustering algorithms but rely on available extraction and summarization technology developed in our laboratory to produce document representations used as input for the clustering procedure.

2 Clustering Algorithm

We have implemented an agglomerative clustering algorithm. The input to the algorithm is a set of document representations implemented as vectors of terms and weights. Initially, there are as many clusters as input documents; as the algorithm proceeds clusters are merged until a certain termination condition is reached. The algorithm computes the similarity between vector representations in order to decide whether or not to merge two clusters. The similarity metric we use is the cosine of the angle between two vectors. This metric gives value one for identical vectors and zero for vectors which are orthogonal (non related). Various options have been implemented in order to measure how close two clusters are, but for the experiments reported here we have used the following approach: the similarity between two clusters (sim_C) is equivalent to the "document" similarity (sim_D) between the two more similar documents in the two clusters; the following formula is used:

Proceedings of the 4th International Workshop on Semantic Evaluations (SemEval-2007), pages 292–295,
Prague, June 2007.

$$\text{sim}_C(\text{C}_1,\text{C}_2) =$$

$$\max_{d_i \in C_1; d_j \in C_2} \text{sim}_D(\text{d}_i,\text{d}_j)$$

Where C_k are clusters, d_l are document representations (e.g., vectors), and sim_D is the cosine metric.

If this similarity is greater than a threshold – experimentally obtained – the two clusters are merged together. At each iteration the most similar pair of clusters is merged. If this similarity is less than a certain threshold the algorithm stops.

3 Extraction and Summarization

The input for analysis is a set of documents and a person name (first name and last name). The documents are analysed by the default GATE[1] ANNIE system (Cunningham et al., 2002) and single document summarization modules (Saggion and Gaizauskas, 2004b) from our summarization toolkit[2]. No attempt is made to analyse or use contextual information given with the input document. The processing elements include:

- Document tokenisation
- Sentence splitting
- Parts-of-speech tagging
- Named Entity Recognition using a gazetteer lookup module and regular expressions
- Named entity coreference using an orthographic name matcher

Named entities of type *person*, *organization*, *address*, *date*, and *location* are considered relevant document terms and stored in a special named entity called *Mention*.

Coreference chains are created and analysed and if they contain an entity matching the target person's surname, all elements of the chain are marked. Extractive summaries are created for each document, a sentence belongs to the summary if it contains a mention which is coreferent with the target entity.

Using language resources creation modules from the summarization tool, two frequency tables are created for each document set (or person): (i) an inverted document frequency table for *words* (no normalisation is applied); and (ii) an inverted frequency table for *Mentions* (the full entity string is used, no normalisation is applied).

Statistics (term frequencies and *tf*idf*) are computed over tokens and *Mentions* using the appropriate tables (these tools are part of the summarization toolkit) and vector representations created for each document (same as in (Bagga and Baldwin, 1998)). Two types of representations were considered for these experiments: (i) full document or summary (terms in the summary are considered for vector creation); and (ii) words or *Mentions*.

4 System Configurations

Four system configurations were prepared for SemEval:

- System I: vector representations were created for full documents. Words were used as terms and local inverted document frequencies used (word frequencies) for weighting.
- System II: vector representations were created for full documents. *Mentions* were used as terms and local inverted document frequencies used (Mentions frequencies) for weighting.
- System III: vector representations were created for person summaries. Words were used as terms and local inverted document frequencies used (word frequencies) for weighting.
- System IV: vector representations were created for person summaries. *Mentions* were used as terms and local inverted document frequencies used (Mentions frequencies) for weighting.

Because only one system configuration was allowed per participant team, we decided to select System II for official evaluation interested in evaluating the effect of semantic information in the clustering process.

5 Parameter Setting and Results

Evaluation of the task was carried out using standard clustering evaluation measures of "purity" and "inverse purity" (Hotho et al., 2003), and the harmonic

[1] http://gate.ac.uk

[2] http://www.dcs.shef.ac.uk/~saggion

Configuration	Purity	Inv.Purity	F-Score
System I	0.68	0.85	0.74
System II	0.62	0.85	0.68
System III	0.84	0.70	0.74
System IV	0.65	0.75	0.64

Table 1: Results for our configurations omitting one set. System II was the system we evaluated in SemEval 2007.

mean of purity and inverse purity: F-score. We estimated the threshold for the clustering algorithm using the ECDL subset of the training data provided by SemEval. We applied the clustering algorithm to each document set and computed purity, inverse purity, and F-score at each iteration of the algorithm, recording the similarity value of each newly created cluster. The similarity values for the best clustering results (best F-score) were recorded, and the maximum and minimum values discarded. The rest of the values were averaged to obtain an estimate of the optimal threshold. Two different thresholds were obtained: 0.10 for word vectors and 0.12 for named entity vectors.

Results for the test set in SemEval are presented in Table 1 (One set – "Jerry Hobbs" – was ignored when computing these numbers: due to a failure during document analysis this set could not be clustered. The error was identified too close to the submission's date to allow us to re-process the cluster). Our official submission System II (SHEF in the official results) obtained an F-score of 0.66 positioning itself in 5th place (out of 16 systems). Our best configuration obtained 0.74 F-score, so a fourth place would be in theory possible.

Our system obtained an F-score greater than the average of 0.60 of all participant systems. Our optimal configurations (System I and System II) both perform similarly with respect to F-score. While System I favours "inverse purity", System III favours "purity". Results for every individual set are reported in the Appendix.

6 Conclusions and Future Work

We have presented a system used to participate in the SemEval 2007 Web People Search task. The system uses an in-house clustering algorithm and available extraction and summarization techniques to produce representations needed by the clustering algorithm. Although the configuration we submitted was suboptimal, we have obtained good results; in fact all our system configurations produce results well above the average of all participants. Our future work will explore how the use of contextual information available on the web can lead to better performance. We will explore if a similar approach to our method for creating profiles or answering definition questions (Saggion and Gaizauskas, 2004a) which uses co-occurence information to identify pieces of information related to a given entity can be applied here.

Acknowledgements

This work was partially supported by the EU-funded MUSING project (IST-2004-027097) and the EU-funded LIRICS project (eContent project 22236).

References

J. Artiles, J. Gonzalo, and S. Sekine. 2007. The SemEval-2007 WePS Evaluation: Establishing a benchmark for Web People Search Task. In *Proceedings of Semeval 2007, Association for Computational Linguistics*.

A. Bagga and B. Baldwin. 1998. Entity-Based Cross-Document Coreferencing Using the Vector Space Model. In *Proceedings of the 36th Annual Meeting of the Association for Computational Linguistics and the 17th International Conference on Computational Linguistics (COLING-ACL'98)*, pages 79–85.

H. Cunningham, D. Maynard, K. Bontcheva, and V. Tablan. 2002. GATE: A Framework and Graphical Development Environment for Robust NLP Tools and Applications. In *Proceedings of the 40th Anniversary Meeting of the Association for Computational Linguistics (ACL'02)*.

A. Hotho, S. Staab, and G. Stumme. 2003. WordNet improves text document clustering. In *Proc. of the SIGIR 2003 Semantic Web Workshop*.

X.-H. Phan, L.-M. Nguyen, and S. Horiguchi. 2006. Personal name resolution crossover documents by a semantics-based approach. *IEICE Trans. Inf. & Syst.*, Feb 2006.

H. Saggion and R. Gaizauskas. 2004a. Mining on-line sources for definition knowledge. In *Proceedings of the 17th FLAIRS 2004*, Miami Bearch, Florida, USA, May 17-19. AAAI.

H. Saggion and R. Gaizauskas. 2004b. Multi-document summarization by cluster/profile relevance and redundancy removal. In *Proceedings of the Document Understanding Conference 2004*. NIST.

Appendix I: Detailed Results

The following tables present purity, inverse purity, and F-score results for all sets and systems. These results were computed after re-processing the "Jerry Hobbs" missing set.

	System I			System II		
Person	**Pur.**	**I-Pur.**	**F**	**Pur.**	**I-Pur.**	**F**
Alvin Cooper	0.72	0.87	0.79	0.86	0.70	0.77
Arthur Morgan	0.90	0.83	0.86	0.75	0.92	0.83
Chris Brockett	0.87	0.85	0.86	0.94	0.67	0.78
Dekang Lin	1.00	0.63	0.77	1.00	0.66	0.79
Frank Keller	0.68	0.81	0.74	0.65	0.66	0.66
George Foster	0.61	0.83	0.71	0.45	0.88	0.60
Harry Hughes	0.82	0.80	0.81	0.71	0.93	0.80
James Curran	0.76	0.74	0.75	0.53	0.84	0.65
James Davidson	0.74	0.91	0.82	0.59	0.90	0.71
James Hamilton	0.52	0.90	0.66	0.25	0.97	0.39
James Morehead	0.38	0.91	0.54	0.39	0.92	0.55
Jerry Hobbs	0.67	0.86	0.75	0.61	0.85	0.71
John Nelson	0.64	0.93	0.76	0.56	0.90	0.69
Jonathan Brooks	0.70	0.89	0.78	0.54	0.89	0.67
Jude Brown	0.75	0.80	0.78	0.74	0.77	0.75
Karen Peterson	0.60	0.92	0.72	0.19	1.00	0.32
Leon Barrett	0.75	0.84	0.80	0.43	0.96	0.59
Marcy Jackson	0.60	0.91	0.72	0.87	0.85	0.86
Mark Johnson	0.57	0.86	0.68	0.33	0.94	0.49
Martha Edwards	0.49	0.96	0.65	0.43	0.91	0.58
Neil Clark	0.74	0.83	0.78	0.60	0.76	0.67
Patrick Killen	0.83	0.77	0.80	0.82	0.77	0.79
Robert Moore	0.64	0.78	0.71	0.44	0.91	0.60
Sharon Goldwater	1.00	0.80	0.89	1.00	0.80	0.89
Stephan Johnson	0.84	0.87	0.85	0.97	0.69	0.81
Stephen Clark	0.63	0.87	0.73	0.57	0.83	0.67
Thomas Fraser	0.51	0.94	0.66	0.44	0.94	0.60
Thomas Kirk	0.66	0.94	0.78	0.87	0.92	0.90
Violet Howard	0.34	0.96	0.51	0.71	0.90	0.80
William Dickson	0.55	0.94	0.70	0.38	0.95	0.54
AVERAGES	0.68	0.86	0.74	0.62	0.85	0.68

	System III			System VI		
Person	**Pur.**	**I-Pur.**	**F**	**Pur.**	**I-Pur.**	**F**
Alvin Cooper	0.98	0.58	0.73	0.93	0.52	0.67
Arthur Morgan	0.98	0.64	0.78	0.71	0.79	0.75
Chris Brockett	1.00	0.32	0.49	0.95	0.31	0.47
Dekang Lin	1.00	0.40	0.58	1.00	0.34	0.51
Frank Keller	0.85	0.65	0.74	0.50	0.71	0.59
George Foster	0.80	0.80	0.80	0.48	0.86	0.61
Harry Hughes	0.91	0.65	0.76	0.76	0.77	0.77
James Curran	0.92	0.69	0.79	0.64	0.77	0.70
James Davidson	0.82	0.85	0.83	0.48	0.93	0.63
James Hamilton	0.65	0.87	0.74	0.26	0.96	0.41
James Morehead	0.66	0.73	0.70	0.57	0.70	0.63
Jerry Hobbs	0.67	0.82	0.74	0.63	0.86	0.73
John Nelson	0.80	0.78	0.79	0.52	0.92	0.66
Jonathan Brooks	0.84	0.85	0.85	0.55	0.86	0.67
Jude Brown	0.75	0.72	0.74	0.80	0.69	0.74
Karen Peterson	0.80	0.86	0.83	0.26	0.94	0.41
Leon Barrett	0.91	0.52	0.66	0.79	0.62	0.69
Marcy Jackson	0.95	0.58	0.72	0.98	0.57	0.72
Mark Johnson	0.76	0.84	0.80	0.44	0.90	0.60
Martha Edwards	0.78	0.85	0.81	0.57	0.87	0.69
Neil Clark	0.85	0.53	0.65	0.60	0.75	0.67
Patrick Killen	0.99	0.57	0.73	0.90	0.61	0.73
Robert Moore	0.74	0.67	0.71	0.49	0.85	0.62
Sharon Goldwater	1.00	0.15	0.26	1.00	0.23	0.37
Stephan Johnson	0.94	0.71	0.81	0.95	0.71	0.81
Stephen Clark	0.87	0.80	0.83	0.55	0.82	0.66
Thomas Fraser	0.62	0.89	0.73	0.47	0.92	0.62
Thomas Kirk	0.81	0.87	0.84	0.84	0.86	0.85
Violet Howard	0.89	0.78	0.83	0.87	0.75	0.81
William Dickson	0.68	0.88	0.77	0.52	0.88	0.66
AVERAGES	0.84	0.70	0.73	0.67	0.74	0.65

SICS: Valence annotation based on seeds in word space

Magnus Sahlgren
SICS
Box 1263
SE-164 29 Kista
Sweden
`mange@sics.se`

Jussi Karlgren
SICS
Box 1263
SE-164 29 Kista
Sweden
`jussi@sics.se`

Gunnar Eriksson
SICS
Box 1263
SE-164 29 Kista
Sweden
`guer@sics.se`

Abstract

This paper reports on a experiment to identify the emotional loading (the "valence") of news headlines. The experiment reported is based on a resource-thrifty approach for valence annotation based on a word-space model and a set of seed words. The model was trained on newsprint, and valence was computed using proximity to one of two manually defined points in a high-dimensional word space — one representing positive valence, the other representing negative valence. By projecting each headline into this space, choosing as valence the similarity score to the point that was closer to the headline, the experiment provided results with high recall of negative or positive headlines. These results show that working without a high-coverage lexicon is a viable approach to content analysis of textual data.

1 The Semeval task

This a report of an experiment proposed as the "Affective Text" task of the 4th international Workshop on Semantic Evaluation (SemEval) to determine whether news headlines are loaded with preeminently positive or negative emotion or *valence*. An example of a test headline can be:

DISCOVERED BOYS BRING SHOCK, JOY

2 Working without a lexicon

Our approach takes as its starting point the observation that lexical resources always are noisy, out of date, and most often suffer simultaneously from being both too specific and too general. For our experiments, our only lexical resource consists of a list of eight positive words and eight negative words, as shown below in Table 1. We use a medium-sized corpus of general newsprint to build a general *word space*, and use our minimal lexical resource to orient ourselves in it.

3 Word space

A word space is a high-dimensional vector space built from distributional statistics (Schütze, 1993; Sahlgren, 2006), in which each word in the vocabulary is represented as a *context vector* $\vec{v}$ of occurrence frequencies: $\vec{v_i} = [f_j, \cdots, f_n]$ where f is the frequency of word i in some context j.

The point of this representation is that semantic similarity between words can be computed using vector similarity measures. Thus, the similarity in meaning between the words w_1 and w_2 can be quantified by computing the similarity between their respective context vectors: $\text{sim}(w_1, w_2) \approx \text{sim}(\vec{v_1}, \vec{v_2})$.

The semantics of such a word space are determined by the data from which the occurrence information has been collected. Since the data set in the SemEval Affective Text task consists of news headlines, a relevant word space should be produced from topically and stylistically similar texts, such as newswire documents. For this reason, we trained our model on a corpus of English-language newsprint which is available for experimentation for participants in the Cross Language Evaluation Fo-

Proceedings of the 4th International Workshop on Semantic Evaluations (SemEval-2007), pages 296–299,
Prague, June 2007.

rum (CLEF).[1] The corpus consists of some 100 000 newswire documents from Los Angeles Times for the year 1994. We presume any similarly sized collection of newsprint would produce similar results. We lemmatized the data using tools from Connexor,[2] and removed stop words, leaving some 28 million words with a vocabulary of approximately 300 000 words. Since the data for the affective task only consisted of news headlines, we treated each headline in the LA times corpus as a separate document, thus doubling the number of documents in the data.

For harvesting occurrence information, we used documents as contexts and standard tfidf-weighting of frequencies, resulting in a 220 220-dimensional word space. No dimensionality reduction was used.

4 Seeds

In order to construct valence vectors, we used a set of manually selected seed words (8 positive and 8 negative words), shown in Table 1. These words were chosen (subjectively) to represent typical expression of positive or negative attitude in news texts. The size of the seed set was determined by a number of initial experiments on the development data, where we varied the size of the seed sets from these 8 words to some 700 words in each set (using the WordNet Affect hierarchy (Strapparava and Valitutti, 2004)).

As comparison, Turney and Littman (2003) used seed sets consisting of 7 words in their word valence annotation experiments, while Turney (2002) used minimal seed sets consisting of only one positive and one negative word ("excellent" and "poor") in his experiments on review classification. Such minimal seed sets of antonym pairs are not possible to use in the present experiment because they are often nearest neighbors to each other in the word space. Also, it is difficult to find such clear paradigm words for the newswire domain.

The seed words were used to postulate one positive and one negative point (i.e. vector) in the word space by simply taking the centroid of the seed word points: $\vec{v}_S = \sum \vec{v}_{w \in S}$ where S is one of the seed sets, and w is a word in this set.

[1] http://www.clef-campaign.org/

[2] http://www.conexor.fi/

Positive	Negative
positive	negative
good	bad
win	defeat
success	disaster
peace	war
happy	sad
healthy	sick
safe	dangerous

Table 1: The seed words used to create valence vectors.

5 Syntagmatic vs paradigmatic relations

Our hypothesis is that words carrying most of the valence in news headlines in the experimental test set are *syntagmatically* rather than paradigmatically related to the kind of very general words used in our seed set.[3] As an example, consider test headline 501:

TWO HUSSEIN ALLIES ARE HANGED, IRAQI OFFICIAL SAYS.

It seems reasonable to believe that this headline should be annotated with a negative valence, and that the desicive word in this case is "hanged." Obviously, "hanged" has no paradigmatic neighbors (e.g. synonyms, antonyms or other 'nyms) among the seed words. However, it is likely that "hanged" will co-occur with (and therefore have a syntagmatic relation to) general negative terms such as "dangerous" and maybe "war." In fact, in this example headline, the most negatively associated words are probably "Hussein" and "Iraqi," which often co-occur with general negative terms such as "war" and "dangerous" in newswire text.

To produce a word space that contains predominantely syntagmatic relations, we built the distributional relations using entire documents as contexts (i.e. each dimension in the word space corresponds to a document in the data). If we would have used words as contexts instead, we would have ended up with a paradigmatic word space.[4]

[3] Syntagmatic relations hold between co-occurring words, while paradigmatic relations hold between words that do not co-occur, but that occur with the same *other* words.

[4] See Sahlgren (2006) for an explanation of how the choice of contexts determines the semantic content of the word space.

6 Compositionality and semantic relations

The relations between words in headlines were modeled using the most simple operation conceivable: we simply add all words' context vectors to a compound headline vector and use that as the representation of the headline: $\vec{v}_H = \sum \vec{v}_{w \in H}$ where H is a test headline, and w is a word in this headline.

This is obviously a daring, if not foolhardy, approach to modelling syntactic structure, compositional semantics, and all types of intra-sentential semantic dependencies. It can fairly be expected to be improved upon through an appropriate finer-grained analysis of word presence, adjacency and syntactic relationships. However, this approach is similar to that taken by most search engines in use today, is a useful first baseline, and as can be seen from our results below, does deliver acceptable results.

7 Valence annotation

To perform the valence annotation, we first lemmatized the headlines and removed stop words and words with frequency above 10 000 in the LA times corpus. For each headline, we then summed — as discussed above — the context vectors of the remaining words, thus producing a 220 220-dimensional vector for each headline. This vector was then compared to each of the postulated valence vectors by computing the cosine of the angles between the vectors.

We thus have for each headline two cosines, one between the headline and the positive vector and one between the headline and the negative vector. The valence vector with highest cosine score (and thus the smallest spatial angle) was chosen to annotate the headline. For the negative valence vector we assigned a negative valence value, and for the positive vector a positive value. In 11 cases, a value of -0.0 was ascribed, either because all headline words were removed by frequency and stop word filtering, or because none of the remaining words occurred in our newsprint corpus.

Our method thus only delivers a binary valence decision — either positive or negative valence. Granted, we could have assigned a neutral valence to very low cosine scores, but as any threshold for deciding on a neutral score would be completely arbitrary, we decided to only give fully positive or negative scores to the test headlines. Also, since our aim was to provide a high-recall result, we did not wish to leave any headline with an equivocal score. We scaled the scores to fit the requirements of the coarse-grained evaluation: for each headline with a non-zero score, we multiplied the value with 100 and boosted each value with 50.[5] By this scaling operation we guaranteed a positive or a negative score for each headline (apart from the 11 exceptions, in effect unanalyzed by our algorithm, as mentioned above).

8 Results

The results from the fine-grained and coarse-grained evaluations are shown in Table 2. They show, much as we anticipated, that the coarse-grained evaluation was appropriate for our purposes.

Fine-grained	Coarse-grained		
	Accuracy	Precision	Recall
20.68	29.00	28.41	60.17

Table 2: The results of the valence annotation.

8.1 Correlation coefficients, normality assumptions, and validity of results

The fine-grained evaluation as given by the organisers and as shown in Table 2 was computed using Pearson's product-moment coefficient. Pearson's correlation coefficient is a parametric statistic and assumes normal distribution of the data it is testing for correlation. While we have no idea of neither the other contributions' score distribution, nor that of the given test set, we certainly do know that our data are not normally distributed. We would much prefer to evaluate our results using a non-parametric correlation test, such as Spearman's ρ, and suggest that the all results would be rescored using some non-parametric method instead — this would reduce the risk of inadvertent false positives stemming from divergence from the normal distribution rather than divergence from the test set.

[5]The coarse-grained evaluation collapsed values in the ranges $[-100, -50]$ as negative, $[-50, 50]$ as neutral, and $[50, 100]$ as positive.

8.2 Use cases

Evaluation of abstract features such as emotional valence can be done within a system oriented framework such as the one used in this experiment. Alternatively, one could evaluate the results using a parametrized use case scenario. A simple example might be to aim for either high recall or high precision, rather than using an average which folds in both scenarios into one numeric score — easy to compare between systems but dubious in its relevance to any imaginable real life task. There are metrics, as formal as the simple recall-precision-framework in traditional adhoc retrieval, that could be adapted for this purpose (Järvelin and Kekäläinen, 2002, e.g.).

9 Related research

Our approach to valence annotation is similar to the second method described by Turney and Littman (2003). In short, their method uses singular value decomposition to produce a reduced-dimensional word space, in which word valence is computed by subtracting the cosine between the word and a set of negative seed words from the cosine between the word and a set of positive seed words.

The difference between our approach and theirs is that our approach does not require any computationally expensive matrix decomposition, as we do not see any reason to restructure our word space. Turney and Littman (2003) hypothesize that singular value decomposition is beneficial for the results in valency annotation because it infers paradigmatic relations between words in the reduced space. However, as we argued in Section 5, we believe that the headline valency annotation task calls for syntagmatic rather than paradigmatic relations. Furthermore, we fail to see the motivation for using singular value decomposition, since if paradigmatic relations are what is needed, then why not simply use words as dimensions of the word space?

10 Concluding remarks

Our results show that a resource-poor but data-rich method can deliver sensible results. This is in keeping with our overall approach, which aims for as little pre-computed resources as possible.

At almost every juncture in our processing we made risky and simplistic assumptions — using simple frequencies of word occurrence as a semantic model; using a small seed set of positive and negative terms as a target; postulating one semantic locus each for positive and negative emotion; modelling syntactic and semantic relations between terms by vector addition — and yet we find that the semantic structure of distributional statistics yields a signal good enough for distinguishing positive from negative headlines with a non-random accuracy. Despite its simplicity, out method produces very good recall (60.17) in the coarse-grained evaluation (the median recall for all systems is 29.59). This speaks to the power of distributional semantics and gives promise of improvement if some of the choice points during the process are returned to: some decisions can well benefit from being made on principled and informed grounds rather than searching under the street lamp, as it were.

References

Kalervo Järvelin and Jaana Kekäläinen. 2002. Cumulated gain-based evaluation of IR techniques. *ACM Transactions on Information Systems*, 20(4):422–446.

Magnus Sahlgren. 2006. *The Word-Space Model: Using distributional analysis to represent syntagmatic and paradigmatic relations between words in high-dimensional vector spaces.* PhD Dissertation, Department of Linguistics, Stockholm University.

Hinrich Schütze. 1993. Word space. In *Proceedings of the 1993 Conference on Advances in Neural Information Processing Systems, NIPS'93*, pages 895–902, San Francisco, CA, USA. Morgan Kaufmann Publishers Inc.

Carlo Strapparava and Alessandro Valitutti. 2004. Wordnet-affect: an affective extension of wordnet. In *Proceedings of the 4th International Conference on Language Resources and Evaluation, LREC'04*, pages 1083–1086.

Peter D. Turney and Michael L. Littman. 2003. Measuring praise and criticism: Inference of semantic orientation from association. *ACM Transactions on Information Systems*, 21(4):315–346.

Peter D. Turney. 2002. Thumbs up or thumbs down? semantic orientation applied to unsupervised classification of reviews. In *Proceedings of the 40th Conference of the Association for Computational Linguistics, ACL'02*, pages 417–424.

SRCB-WSD: Supervised Chinese Word Sense Disambiguation with Key Features

Yun Xing
Ricoh Software Research Center Beijing Co., Ltd
Beijing, China
yun.xing@srcb.ricoh.com

Abstract

This article describes the implementation of Word Sense Disambiguation system that participated in the SemEval-2007 multilingual Chinese-English lexical sample task. We adopted a supervised learning approach with Maximum Entropy classifier. The features used were neighboring words and their part-of-speech, as well as single words in the context, and other syntactic features based on shallow parsing. In addition, we used word category information of a Chinese thesaurus as features for verb disambiguation. For the task we participated in, we obtained precision of 0.716 in micro-average, which is the best among all participated systems.

1 Introduction

Word Sense Disambiguation(WSD) is the process of assigning a meaning to a word based on the context in which it occurs. It is very important to many research fields such as Machine Translation, Information Retrieval. The goal of the multilingual Chinese-English lexical sample task in SemEval-2007 is to predict the correct English translation for an ambiguous Chinese word w.

We considered this task as a classification problem, and our system adopted a supervised learning approach with Maximum Entropy classifier, which is widely used in natural language processing(NLP). Within the Maximum Entropy framework, evidence from different features can be combined with no assumptions of feature independence. The used features include neighboring words and their part-of-speech(POS), single words in the context, and other syntactic features based on shallow parsing. In addition, we used word category information of a Chinese thesaurus for verb disambiguation. Note that we did not do any feature selection in this work.

Next, we will describe the Maximum Entropy framework and detail the features used in our WSD system.

2 Maximum Entropy

Maximum entropy modelling is a framework for integrating information from many heterogeneous information sources for classification (Manning and Schütze, 1999). It has been successfully applied to a wide range of NLP tasks, including sentence boundary detection, POS tagging, and parsing (Ratnaparkhi, 1998) . The system estimates the conditional probability that an ambiguous word has sense x given that it occurs in context y, where y is a conjunction of features. The estimated probability is derived from feature weights which are determined automatically from training data so as to produce a probability distribution that has maximum entropy, under the constraint that it is consistent with observed evidence (Dang et al., 2002). We used the implementation of Maximum Entropy framework with OpenNLP MAXENT[1], where each nominal feature was represented as "feature_code=value". Based on this framework, we defined the feature set and implemented the interface of feature extraction. For the convenient of evaluation, the default parameters

[1]http://maxent.sourceforge.net/

Proceedings of the 4th International Workshop on Semantic Evaluations (SemEval-2007), pages 300–303,
Prague, June 2007.

of training model were used.

3 Used Features

Many research (Stevenson and Wilks, 2001; Lee and Ng, 2002) have indicated that a combination of knowledge sources improves WSD accuracy, but not any kind of knowledge source contributes the improvement of Chinese WSD (Dang et al., 2002). For multilingual Chinese-English lexical sample task, some basic features can be obtained directly. Also, we extracted other syntactic features through shallow parsing. In addition, we used word category information for verb disambiguation.

3.1 Basic Features

Since the data of multilingual Chinese-English lexical sample task are word-segmented and POS-tagged, we can get the following features directly.

- $W_{-1(+1)}$: the words (if any) immediately preceding and following w
- $P_{-1(+1)}$: the POS of the words(if any) immediately preceding and following w
- SW: single words in the context. We did not consider all words in the context as features for WSD, because our experiment shows that it will bring some noise in small scale supervised learning if we add all words in the context to feature set(See Section 4.1 for details). After carefully analyzing the POS set specification which is provided by task organizers, we only picked out words of POS listed in Table 1 as features.

3.2 Syntactic Features based on Shallow Parsing

To get further syntactic features from context, we implemented a simple rule-based parser to do shallow parsing on each instance. The parser only identifies phrases such as noun phrase, verb phrase, adjectival phrase, time phrase, position phrase and quantity phrase. These phrases are considered as constituents of context, as well as words and punctuations which do not belong to any phrase. Table 2 lists the constituent types and relative tags.

POS Tag	Specification
Ng	Nominal morpheme
n	Noun
nr	Personal name
ns	Place name
nt	Institution and Group
nz	Any other proper names
Vg	Verbal morpheme
v	Verb
vd	Verb with the attribute of adverb
vn	Verb with the attribute of noun
r	Pronoun
j	Abbreviation

Table 1: POS of single words in the context to be considered in our WSD system

For example, a word-segmented and POS-tagged instance in Figure 1 would be processed as a constituent list in Figure 2 after shallow parsing.

他/r 没有/d 说明/v 事情/n 的/u 真相/n 。/w

Figure 1: A word-segmented and POS-tagged instance. Note that the instance is not illustrated in XML format as data of multilingual Chinese-English lexical sample task, instead, it is illustrated in the form of "word/pos" for convenient.

他/entity 没有说明/action 事情的真相/entity 。/w

Figure 2: After shallow parsing, instance is organized in the form of "constituent/tag", that is, the word "他" is identified as an entity, and words "没有" and "说明" are merged together as an action.

Suppose C_0 is the constituent which the target word w belongs to , then we add following information to feature set:

- CT_0: the constituent tag of C_0
- $CT_{-i(+i)}, 0 < i \leq 3$: the tag of ith constituent to the left(right) of C_0
- $KCT_{-i(+i)}, 0 < i \leq 3$: the tag of ith constituent to the left(right) of C_0, and the type must be entity or action

Constituent type	Tag
noun phrase	entity
verb phrase	action
adjective phrase	adjective
time phrase	time
place phrase	place
quantity phrase	quantity
non-phrase	same as POS tag

Table 2: Constituent type and relative tag

- $LPOS_{-i(+i)}$: the POS of ith word in the same constituent of w.

3.3 Word Category Information

We considered word category information as an important knowledge source for verb disambiguation. The word category information comes from a Chinese thesaurus (Mei et al., 1983). If w is a verb, then the word category information of nouns in the right side of w is added into feature set. Figure 3 shows an example of how to use word category information for verb disambiguation.

他/r 坐/v 飞机/n 回/v 北京/ns

Figure 3: A word-segmented and POS-tagged instance of ambiguous verb "坐". The word category information of noun "飞机" has to be added into feature set.

Note that some nouns can belong to more than two categories, in this case, we do not use the word category information of this kind of noun for disambiguation.

Our experiment showed that this extra knowledge source did improve the accuracy of WSD (See 4.1 for detail).

4 Evaluation

Since the multilingual Chinese-English lexical sample task of SemEval-2007 is quite similar to the Chinese lexical sample task of SENSEVAL-3, we firstly evaluated feature set on the data of SENSEVAL-3 Chinese lexical sample task, and then gave the official SemEval-2007 scores of our system based on the best feature set.

Feature Set	Micro-average precision
FS1	0.630
FS2	0.635
FS3	0.654

Table 3: Result of feature set evaluation on SENSEVAL-3 test data

System	Micro-average precision	Macro-average precision
SRCB-WSD	0.716	0.749

Table 4: Official result on SemEval-2007 test data

4.1 Evaluation on SENSEVAL-3 Data

We did three experiments on the data of SENSEVAL-3 Chinese lexical sample task to evaluate if all the single words in the context should be included in feature set, and if the word category information of Chinese thesaurus is helpful for WSD. The first experiment used feature set (FS1) included almost the same features listed in Section 3.1 and 3.2, the only difference is that all single words in the context were considered. The second experiment used feature set (FS2) included all the features listed in Section 3.1 and 3.2. The third experiment used feature set (FS3) included all the features listed in Section 3.1, 3.2 and 3.3. The experimental result is given in Table 3. It shows that considering all single words in the context as features did not improve the performance of WSD, while word category information of Chinese thesaurus improved the accuracy obviously.

4.2 Official SemEval-2007 Scores

In multilingual Chinese-English lexical sample task, there are 2686 instances in training data for 40 Chinese ambiguous words. All these ambiguous words are noun or verb. Test data consist of 935 untagged instances of the same target words. The official result of our system in multilingual Chinese-English lexical sample task is reported in Table 4.

According to the task organizers, our system achieved the best performance out of all the participated systems.

5 Conclusion

In this paper, we described our participating system in the SemEval-2007 multilingual Chinese-English lexical sample task. We adopted Maximum Entropy method, and collected features not only from context provided by task organizers, but also from extra knowledge source. Evaluation results show that this feature set is much effective for supervised Chinese WSD.

Acknowledgements

We would like to thank the anonymous reviewers for their constructive comments and suggestions.

References

Manning, C. and Schütze, H. 1999. *Foundations of Statistical Natural Language Processing.*. The MIT Press, Cambridge, Massachusetts.

Ratnaparkhi, A. 1998. *Maximum Entropy Models for Natural Language Ambiguity Resolution.* Ph.D. thesis University of Pennsylvania.

Dang, H.T., Chia, C.Y., Palmer, M. and Chiou, F.D. 2002. *Simple Features for Chinese Word Sense Disambiguation.* In Proc. of COLING.

Mei, J.J., Li, Y.M., Gao, Y.Q. and et al. 1983. *Chinese thesaurus(Tongyici Cilin).* Shanghai thesaurus Press.

Stevenson, M. and Wilks, Y. 2001. *The interaction of knowledge sources in word sense disambiguation.* Computational Linguistics, 27(3):321-349.

Lee, Y.K. and Ng, H.T. 2002. *An empirical evaluation of knowledge sources and learning algorithms for word sense disambiguation.* In Proceedings of the Conference on Empirical Methods in Natural Language Processing(EMNLP), pages 41-48.

SW-AG: Local Context Matching for English Lexical Substitution

George Dahl, Anne-Marie Frassica, Richard Wicentowski
Department of Computer Science
Swarthmore College
Swarthmore, PA 19081 USA
{george.dahl, afrassi1}@gmail.com, richardw@cs.swarthmore.edu

Abstract

We present two systems that pick the ten most appropriate substitutes for a marked word in a test sentence. The first system scores candidates based on how frequently their local contexts match that of the marked word. The second system, an enhancement to the first, incorporates cosine similarity using unigram features. The core of both systems bypasses intermediate sense selection. Our results show that a knowledge-light, direct method for scoring potential replacements is viable.

1 Introduction

An obvious way to view the problem of lexical substitution is as a sense disambiguation task. For example, one possible approach is to identify the sense of the target word and then to pick a synonym based on the identified sense. Following Dagan et al. (2006), we refer to this as an *indirect* approach. A system using an indirect approach must have access to a list of senses for each target word, and each sense must have a corresponding list of synonyms. Though one can use a predefined sense inventory, such as WordNet, the granularity of the sense inventory may not be appropriate for the task. If the sense inventory is too fine-grained, then picking the correct sense may be needlessly difficult. Conversely, if it is too coarse, picking the correct sense may not narrow down the list of potential substitutions sufficiently.

To avoid these problems, we propose a *direct* approach, which will break the problem into two steps: for each target word, generate a list of candidate synonyms; then rank each synonym for its quality as a replacement. Although our second system makes use of some sense information, it is used only to rerank candidates generated using a direct approach.

We describe two systems: the first is a purely direct method based on local context matching, and the second is a hybrid of local context matching and wider context bag-of-words matching. Both are knowledge-light and unsupervised.

2 Methods

As mentioned above, we divide the task into two steps: compiling a list of synonyms and then, for each test instance, ranking the list of appropriate synonyms. Both of our systems create lists of candidate synonyms in the same way and only differ in the way they arrive at a ranking for these candidates.

2.1 Compiling a substitution lexicon

We begin by compiling a list of candidate synonyms for each target word. Following Dagan et al. (2006), we will refer to this list of synonyms as our *substitution lexicon*. The performance of our system is limited by the substitution lexicon because it can only pick the correct replacements if they are in the lexicon. The substitution lexicon available to our scoring system therefore determines both the maximum attainable recall and the baseline probability of randomly guessing a correct replacement.

One approach to generating a substitution lexicon is to query WordNet for lists of synonyms grouped by the senses of each word. While WordNet has its advantages, we aimed to create a knowledge-light

Proceedings of the 4th International Workshop on Semantic Evaluations (SemEval-2007), pages 304–307,
Prague, June 2007.

system. A more knowledge-free system would have used a machine readable dictionary or a large natural language sample to retrieve its synonyms (see, for example, Lin (1998)), but our system falls short of this, relying on Roget's New Millennium Thesaurus[1] (henceforth RT) as a source of synonyms. Though this thesaurus is similar to WordNet in some ways, it does not contain semantic relationships beyond synonyms and antonyms. One important advantage of a thesaurus over WordNet is that it is easier to obtain for languages other than English.

We used the trial data to ensure that the quality of the list compiled from RT would be satisfactory for this task. We found that by using the synonyms in WordNet synsets[2] as our substitution lexicon, we could achieve a maximum recall of 53% when using an oracle to select the correct synonyms. However, using the synonyms from RT as the substitution lexicon led to a maximum recall of 85%.

Querying RT for the synonyms of a word returns multiple entries. For our purposes, each entry consists of a Main Entry, a part of speech, a definition, and a list of synonyms. Many of the returned entries do not list the query word as the Main Entry. For instance, given the query *"tell"*, RT returns 115 entries: 7 whose Main Entry is *"tell"*, an additional 3 that contain *"tell"* (e.g. *"show and tell"*), and the remaining 105 entries are other words (e.g. *"gossip"*) that list *"tell"* as a synonym. Where the Main Entry matches the query, RT entries roughly correspond to the traditional notion of "sense".

In order to reduce the number of potentially spurious synonyms that could be picked, we created a simple automatic filtering system. For each RT query, we kept only those entries whose Main Entry and part of speech matched the target word exactly[3]. In addition, we removed obscure words which we believed human annotators would be unlikely to pick. We used the unigram counts from the Web 1T 5-gram corpus (Brants and Franz, 2006) to determine the frequency of use of each candidate synonym. We experimented with discarding the least frequent third of the candidates. Although this filtering reduced our maximum attainable recall from 85% to 75% on the trial data, it significantly raised our precision.

2.2 Ranking substitutions

We created two systems (and submitted two sets of results) for this task. The first system is fully described in Section 2.2.1. The second system includes the first system and is fully described in the remainder of Section 2.2.

2.2.1 Local context matching (LCM)

Our first system matches the context of target words to the context of candidate synonyms in a large, unannotated corpus. If the context of a candidate synonym exactly matches the context of a target word, it is considered a good replacement synonym. Context matches are made against the Web 1T corpus' list of trigrams. Though this corpus provides us with a very large amount of data[4], to increase the likelihood of finding an appropriate match, we mapped inflected words to their roots in both the corpus and the test data (Baayen et al., 1996).

The context of a target word consists of a set of up to 3 trigrams, specifically those trigrams in the test sentence that contain the target word. For example, the context of *"bright"* in the sentence[5] "... who was a *bright* boy only ..." is the set {"was a *bright*", "a *bright* boy", "*bright* boy only"}.

Once we identified the set of context trigrams, we filtered this set by removing all trigrams which did not include content words. To identify content words, we used the NLTK-Lite tagger to assign a part of speech to each word (Loper and Bird, 2002). We considered open class words (with the exception of the verb *to be*) and pronouns to be content words. We call the filtered set of trigrams the test trigrams. From the above example, we would remove the trigram "was a *bright*" since it does not contain a content word other than the target word.

We match the test trigrams against trigrams in the Web 1T corpus. A corpus trigram is said to match one of the test trigrams if the only difference between them is that the target word is replaced with a candidate synonym.

A scoring algorithm is then applied to each candidate. The scoring algorithm relies on the test tri-

[1] `http://thesaurus.reference.com`

[2] excluding the extended relations such as hyponyms, etc.

[3] Since RT was not always consistent in labeling adjectives and adverbs, we conflated these in filtering.

[4] There are over 967 million unique trigrams in this corpus

[5] Excerpted from trial instance 1.

grams, denoted by T, the set of candidate synonyms, C, and the frequencies of the trigrams in the corpus. Let $m(t, c)$ be the frequency of the corpus trigram that matches test trigram t, where the target word in t is replaced with candidate c. The score of a candidate c is given by:

$$\text{score}(c) = \sum_{t \in T} \frac{m(t, c)}{\sum_{x \in C} m(t, x)}.$$

The normalization factor prevents high frequency test trigrams from dominating the score of candidates. The candidates are ranked by score, and the top ten candidates are returned as substitutions.

2.2.2 Nearest "synonym" neighbor

In some cases, the words in the local context did not help identify a replacement synonym. For example, in test instance 391 the trigrams used in the local context model were: "by a *coach*", "a *coach* and", and "*coach* and five". The first two trigrams were removed because they did not contain content words. The final trigram does not provide conclusive evidence: the correct synonym in this case can be determined by knowing whether the next word is "players" (*coach = instructor*) or "horses" (*coach = vehicle)*. Without backoff, extending the local context model to 5-grams led to sparse data problems.

Rather than match exact n-grams, we use a nearest neighbor cosine model with unigram (bag of words) features for all words in the target sentence. For each instance, an "instance vector" was created by counting the unigrams in the target sentence.

Since the Web 1T corpus does not contain full sentences, we matched each of the instance vectors against vectors derived from the British National Corpus[6]. For each candidate synonym, we created a single vector by summing the unigram counts in all sentences containing the candidate synonym (or one of its morphological variants). We ranked each candidate by the cosine similarity between the candidate vector and the instance vector.

2.2.3 Nearest "sense" neighbor

Manual inspection of the trial data key revealed that, for many instances, a large majority (if not all) of the human-selected synonyms in that instance were found in just one or two RT entries. This not altogether unexpected insight led to the creation of a second nearest neighbor cosine model.

We first created instance vectors, following the method described above. However, instead of creating a single vector for each candidate synonym, we created a single vector for each "sense" (RT entry): for each RT entry, we created a single vector by summing the unigram counts in all BNC sentences containing any of that entry's candidate synonyms (or morphological variants). We ranked each candidate sense by the cosine similarity between the sense vector and the instance vector.

This method is not used on its own but rather to filter the results (Section 2.2.4) of the nearest "synonym" neighbor method. Also note that while we used the "senses" provided by RT for this method, we could have used an automatic method, e.g. Lin and Pantel (2001), to achieve the same goal.

2.2.4 Filtering by sense

The nearest synonym neighbor method underperformed the local context matching method on the trial data. This result led us to filter the nearest neighbor results by keeping only those words listed as synonyms of the highest ranked senses, as determined by the nearest sense neighbor model. This proved successful, increasing accuracy from .41 to .44 (for instances which had a mode) when we kept only those synonyms found in the top half of the senses returned by the nearest sense model.[7]

We attempted the sense filtering method on the local context model but found that it was less successful. No matter what threshold we set for filtering, we always did best by not doing the filtering at all. However, applying the filtering to only *noun* instances, keeping only those synonyms belonging to the single most highly ranked sense, increased our accuracy on nouns from .51 to .57 (for instances which had a mode). This surprising result, used in the following section, requires further investigation which was not possible in the limited time provided.

2.2.5 Model Combination

A straightforward model combination using the relative ranking of synonyms by the filtered local

[6] `http://www.natcorp.ox.ac.uk/`

[7] We rounded up if there were an odd number of senses, and we always kept a minimum of two senses.

	P	R	Mode P	Mode R
all	35.53	32.83	47.41	43.82
Further Analysis				
NMWT	37.49	34.64	49.11	45.35
NMWS	38.36	35.67	49.41	45.70
RAND	36.94	34.52	48.94	45.72
MAN	33.83	30.85	45.63	41.67

Table 1: SWAG1:OOT results

	P	R	Mode P	Mode R
all	37.80	34.66	50.18	46.02
Further Analysis				
NMWT	39.95	36.51	52.28	47.78
NMWS	40.97	37.75	52.25	47.98
RAND	39.74	36.36	53.61	48.78
MAN	35.56	32.79	46.34	42.88

Table 2: SWAG2:OOT results

context matching (FLCM) model[8] and the filtered nearest neighbor (FNN) model yielded results which were inferior to those provided by the FLCM model on its own. Examination of the results of each model showed that the FLCM model was best on nouns and adjectives, the FNN model was best on adverbs, and the combination model was best on verbs. Though limited time prohibited us from doing a more thorough evaluation, we decided to use this unorthodox combination as the basis for our second system.

3 Results

We submitted two sets of results to this task: the first was our local context matching system (SWAG1) and the second was the combined FLCM and FNN hybrid system (SWAG2).

Our systems consistently perform better when a mode exists, which makes sense because those are instances in which the annotators are in agreement (McCarthy and Navigli, 2007). In these cases it is more likely that the most appropriate synonym is clear from the context and therefore easier to pick.

It is hard to say exactly why SWAG2 outperforms SWAG1 because we haven't had enough time to fully analyze our results. Our decision to choose different systems for each part of speech may have been partially responsible. For example, both LCM (used in SWAG1 and SWAG2) and the nearest neighbor cosine comparison algorithm (used in SWAG2) performed poorly on verbs on the trial data. The voter described in the SWAG2 discussion always performed better on verbs than either system did individually, so this may account for part of the higher precision and recall.

[8] Filtering was done only on nouns as described above.

4 Conclusions

Our results show that direct methods of lexical substitution deserve more investigation. It does indeed seem possible to successfully do lexical substitution without doing sense disambiguation. Furthermore, this task can be accomplished in a knowledge-light way. Further investigation of this method could include generating the list of synonyms using a completely knowledge-free approach.

References

R.H. Baayen, R. Piepenbrock, and L. Gulikers. 1996. CELEX2. LDC96L14, Linguistic Data Consortium, Philadelphia.

T. Brants and A. Franz. 2006. Web 1T 5-gram, ver. 1. LDC2006T13, Linguistic Data Consortium, Philadelphia.

I. Dagan, O. Glickman, A. Gliozzo, E. Marmorshtein, and C. Strapparava. 2006. Direct word sense matching for lexical substitution. In Proceedings of the 44th Annual Meeting of the Association for Computational Linguistics.

D. Lin and P. Pantel. 2001. Induction of semantic classes from natural language text. In Proceedings of the 7th ACM SIGKDD International Conference on Knowledge Discovery and Data Mining.

D. Lin. 1998. Automatic retrieval and clustering of similar words. In Proceedings of the 36th Annual Meeting of the Association for Computational Linguistics.

E. Loper and S. Bird. 2002. NLTK: The Natural Language Toolkit. In Proceedings of the ACL-02 Workshop on Effective Tools and Methodologies for Teaching Natural Language Processing and Computational Linguistics.

D. McCarthy and R. Navigli. 2007. SemEval-2007 Task 10: English lexical substitution task. In Proceedings of SemEval-2007.

SWAT-MP: The SemEval-2007 Systems for Task 5 and Task 14

Phil Katz, Matthew Singleton, Richard Wicentowski
Department of Computer Science
Swarthmore College
Swarthmore, PA
{katz,msingle1,richardw}@cs.swarthmore.edu

Abstract

In this paper, we describe our two SemEval-2007 entries. Our first entry, for Task 5: Multilingual Chinese-English Lexical Sample Task, is a supervised system that decides the most appropriate English translation of a Chinese target word. This system uses a combination of Naïve Bayes, nearest neighbor cosine, decision lists, and latent semantic analysis. Our second entry, for Task 14: Affective Text, is a supervised system that annotates headlines using a predefined list of emotions. This system uses synonym expansion and matches lemmatized unigrams in the test headlines against a corpus of hand-annotated headlines.

1 Introduction

This paper describes our two entries in SemEval-2007. The first entry, a supervised system used in the Multilingual Chinese-English Lexical Sample task (Task 5), is an extension of the system described in (Wicentowski et al., 2004). We implement five different classifiers: a Naïve Bayes classifier, a decision list classifier, two different nearest neighbor cosine classifiers, and a classifier based on Latent Semantic Analysis. Section 2.2 describes each of the individual classifiers, Section 2.3 describes our classifier combination system, and Section 2.4 presents our results.

The second entry, a supervised system used in the Affective Text task (Task 14), uses a corpus of headlines hand-annotated by non-experts. It also uses an online thesaurus to match synonyms and antonyms of the sense labels (Thesaurus.com, 2007). Section 3.1 describes the creation of the annotated training corpus, Section 3.2 describes our method for assigning scores to the headlines, and Section 3.3 presents our results.

2 Task 5: Multilingual Chinese-English LS

This task presents a single Chinese word in context which must be disambiguated. Rather than asking participants to provide a sense label corresponding to a pre-defined sense inventory, the goal here is to label each ambiguous word with its correct English translation. Since the task is quite similar to more traditional lexical sample tasks, we extend an approach used successfully in multiple Senseval-3 lexical sample tasks (Wicentowski et al., 2004).

2.1 Features

Each of our classifiers uses the same set of context features, taken directly from the data provided by the task organizers. The features we used included:

- Bag-of-words (unigrams)
- Bigrams and trigrams around the target word
- Weighted unigrams surrounding the target word

The weighted unigram features increased the frequencies of the ten words before and after the target word by inserting them multiple times into the bag-of-words.

Proceedings of the 4th International Workshop on Semantic Evaluations (SemEval-2007), pages 308–313,
Prague, June 2007.

Many words in the Chinese data were broken up into "subwords": since we were unsure how to handle these and since their appearance seemed inconsistent, we decided to simply treat each subword as a word for the purposes of creating bigrams, trigrams, and weighted unigrams.

2.2 Classifiers

Our system consists of five unique classifiers. Three of the classifiers were selected by our combination system, while the other two were found to be detrimental to its performance. We describe the contributing classifiers first. Table 1 shows the results of each classifier, as well as our classifier combination system.

2.2.1 Naïve Bayes

The Naïve Bayes classifier is based on Bayes' theorem, which allows us to define the similarity between an instance, *I*, and a sense class, S_j, as:

$$Sim(I, S_j) = Pr(I, S_j) = Pr(S_j) * Pr(I|S_j)$$

We then choose the sense with the maximum similarity to the test instance.

Additive Smoothing

Additive smoothing is a technique that is used to attempt to improve the information gained from low-frequency words, in tasks such as speech pattern recognition (Chen and Goodman, 1998). We used additive smoothing in the Naïve Bayes classifier. To implement additive smoothing, we added a very small number, δ, to the frequency count of each feature (and divided the final product by this δ value times the size of the feature set to maintain accurate probabilities). This small number has almost no effect on more frequent words, but boosts the score of less common, yet potentially equally informative, words.

2.2.2 Decision List

The decision list classifier uses the log-likelihood of correspondence between each context feature and each sense, using additive smoothing (Yarowsky, 1994). The decision list was created by ordering the correspondences from strongest to weakest. Instances that did not match any rule in the decision list were assigned the most frequent sense, as calculated from the training data.

2.2.3 Nearest Neighbor Cosine

The nearest neighbor cosine classifier required the creation of a *term-document matrix*, which contains a row for each training instance of an ambiguous word, and a column for each feature that can occur in the context of an ambiguous word. The rows of this matrix are referred to as *sense vectors* because each row represents a combination of the features of all ambiguous words that share the same sense.

The nearest neighbor cosine classifier compares each of the training vectors to each ambiguous instance vector. The cosine between the ambiguous vector and each of the sense vectors is calculated, and the sense that is the "nearest" (largest cosine, or smallest angle) is selected by the classifier.

TF-IDF

TF-IDF (Term Frequency-Inverse Document Frequency) is a method for automatically adjusting the frequency of words based on their semantic importance to a document in a corpus. TF-IDF decreases the value of words that occur in more different documents. The equation we used for TF-IDF is:

$$tf_i \cdot idf_i = n_i \cdot \log\left(\frac{|D|}{|D : t_i \epsilon D|}\right)$$

where n_i is the number of occurrences of a term t_i, and *D* is the set of all training documents.

TF-IDF is used in an attempt to minimize the noise from words such as "*and*" that are extremely common, but, since they are common across all training instances, carry little semantic content.

2.2.4 Non-contributing Classifiers

We implemented a classifier based on Latent Semantic Analysis (Landauer et al., 1998). To do the calculations required for LSA, we used the SVDLIBC library[1]. Because this classifier actually weakened our combination system (in cross-validation), our classifier combination (Section 2.3) does not include it.

We also implemented a *k*-Nearest Neighbors classifier, which treats each individual training instance

[1] `http://tedlab.mit.edu/~dr/SVDLIBC/`

as a separate vector (instead of treating each set of training instances that makes up a given sense as a single vector), and finds the *k*-nearest training instances to the test instance. The most frequent sense among the *k*-nearest to the test instance is the selected sense. Unfortunately, the *k*-NN classifier did not improve the results of our combined system and so it is not included in our classifier combination.

2.3 Classifier Combination

The classifier combination algorithm that we implement is based on a simple voting system. Each classifier returns a score for each sense: the Naïve Bayes classifier returns a probability, the cosine-based classifiers (including LSA) return a cosine distance, and the decision list classifier returns the weight associated with the chosen feature (if no feature is selected, the frequency of the most frequent sense is used). The scores from each classifier are normalized to the range [0,1], multiplied by an empirically determined weight for that classifier, and summed for each sense. The combiner then chooses the sense with the highest score. We used cross validation to determine the weight for each classifier, and it was during that test that we discovered that the best constant for the LSA and *k*-NN classifiers was zero. The most likely explanation for this is that the LSA and k-NN are doing similar, only less accurate, classifications as the nearest neighbor classifier, and so have little new knowledge to add to the combiner. We also implemented a simple majority voting system, where the chosen sense is the sense chosen by the most classifiers, but found it to be less accurate.

2.4 Evaluation

To increase the accuracy of our system, we needed to optimize various parameters by running the training data through 10-way cross-validation and averaging the scores from each set. Table 2 shows the results of this cross-validation in determining the δ value used in the additive smoothing for both the Naïve Bayes classifier and for the decision list classifier.

We also experimented with different feature sets. The results of these experiments are shown in Table 3.

Classifier	Cross-Validation Score
MFS	34.99%
LSA	38.61%
k-NN Cosine	61.54%
Naïve Bayes	58.60%
Decision List	64.37%
NN Cosine	65.56%
Simple Combined	65.89%
Weighted Combined	67.38%
Classifier	**Competition Score**
SWAT-MP	65.78%

Table 1: The (micro-averaged) precision of each of our classifiers in cross-validation, plus the actual results from our entry in SemEval-2007.

Naïve Bayes	
δ	precision
10^{-1}	53.01%
10^{-2}	58.60%
10^{-3}	60.80%
$\mathbf{10^{-4}}$	**61.09%**
10^{-5}	60.95%
10^{-6}	61.06%
10^{-7}	61.08%

Decision List	
δ	precision
1.0	64.14%
0.5	64.37%
0.1	**64.59%**
0.05	64.48%
0.005	64.37%
0.001	64.37%

Table 2: On cross-validated training data, system precision when using different smoothing parameters in the Naïve Bayes and decision list classifiers.

2.5 Conclusion

We presented a supervised system that used simple *n*-gram features and a combination of five different classifiers. The methods used are applicable to any lexical sample task, and have been applied to lexical sample tasks in previous Senseval competitions.

3 Task 14

The goal of Task 14: Affective Text is to take a list of headlines and meaningfully annotate their emotional content. Each headline was scored along seven axes: six predefined emotions (Anger, Disgust, Fear, Joy, Sadness, and Surprise) on a scale from 0 to 100, and the negative/positive polarity (valence) of the headline on a scale from -100 to $+100$.

Naïve Bayes	Feature	Dec. List
55.36%	word trigrams	59.98%
55.55%	word bigrams	59.98%
58.50%	weighted unigrams	62.77%
58.60%	all features	**64.37%**

NN-Cosine	Feature	Combined
60.39%	word trigrams	62.03%
60.42%	word bigrams	62.66%
65.56%	weighted unigrams	64.56%
62.92%	all features	**67.38%**

Table 3: On cross-validated training data, the precision when using different features with each classifier, and with the combination of all classifiers. All feature sets include a simple, unweighted bag-of-words in addition to the feature listed.

3.1 Training Data Collection

Our system is trained on a set of pre-annotated headlines, building up a knowledge-base of individual words and their emotional significance.

We were initially provided with a trial-set of 250 annotated headlines. We ran 5-way cross-validation with a preliminary version of our system, and found that a dataset of that size was too sparse to effectively tag new headlines. In order to generate a more meaningful knowledge-base, we created a simple web interface for human annotation of headlines. We used untrained, non-experts to annotate an additional 1,000 headlines for use as a training set. The headlines were taken from a randomized collection of headlines from the Associated Press.

We included a subset of the original test set in the set that we put online so that we could get a rough estimate of the consistency of human annotation. We found that consistency varied greatly across the emotions. As can be seen in Table 4, our annotators were very consistent with the trial data annotators on some emotions, while inconsistent on others.

In ad-hoc, post-annotation interviews, our annotators commented that the task was very difficult. What we had initially expected to be a tedious but mindless exercise turned out to be rather involved. They also reported that some emotions were consistently harder to annotate than others. The results in Table 4 seem to bear this out as well.

Emotion	Correlation
Valence	0.83
Sadness	0.81
Joy	0.79
Disgust	0.38
Anger	0.32
Fear	0.19
Surprise	0.19

Table 4: Pearson correlations between trial data annotators and our human annotators.

One difficulty reported by our annotators was determining whether to label the emotion experienced by the reader or by the subject of the headline. For example, the headline "White House surprised at reaction to attorney firings" clearly states that the White House was surprised, but the reader might not have been.

Another of the major difficulties in properly annotating headlines is that many headlines can be annotated in vastly different ways depending on the viewpoint of the annotator. For example, while the headline "Hundreds killed in earthquake" would be universally accepted as negative, the headline "Italy defeats France in World Cup Final," can be seen as positive, negative, or even neutral depending on the viewpoint of the reader. These types of problems made it very difficult for our annotators to provide consistent labels.

3.2 Data Processing

Before we can process a headline and determine its emotions and valence, we convert our list of tagged headlines into a useful knowledge base. To this end, we create a word-emotion mapping.

3.2.1 Pre-processing

The first step is to lemmatize every word in every headline, in an attempt to reduce the sparseness of our data. We use the CELEX2 (Baayen et al., 1996) data to perform this lemmatization. There are unfortunate cases where lemmatizing actually changes the emotional content of a word (*unfortunate* becomes *fortunate*), but without lemmatization, our data is simply too sparse to be of any use. Once we have our list of lemmatized words, we score the emotions and valence of each word as the average of the emotions and valence of every headline, *H*, in which that word, *w*, appears, ignoring non-content words:

$$Score(Em, w) = \sum_{H:\, w \,\epsilon\, H} Score(Em, H)$$

In the final step of pre-processing, we add the synonyms and antonyms of the sense labels themselves to our word-emotion mapping. We queried the web interface for Roget's New Millennium Thesaurus (Thesaurus.com, 2007) and added every word in the first 8 entries for each sense label to our map, with a score of 100 (the maximum possible score) for that sense. We also added every word in the first 4 antonym entries with a score of -40. For example, for the emotion Joy, we added *alleviation* and *amusement* with a score of 100, and we added *despair* and *misery* with a score of -40.

3.2.2 Processing

After creating our word-emotion mapping, predicting the emotions and valence of a given headline is straightforward. We treat each headline as a bag-of-words and lemmatize each word. Then we look up each word in the headline in our word-emotion map, and average the emotion and valence scores of each word in our map that occurs in the headline. We ignore words that were not present in the training data.

3.3 Evaluation

Emotion	Training Size (Headlines)		
	100	250	1000
Valence	19.07	32.07	35.25
Anger	8.42	13.38	24.51
Disgust	11.22	23.45	18.55
Fear	14.43	18.56	32.52
Joy	31.87	46.03	26.11
Sadness	16.32	35.09	38.98
Surprise	1.15	11.12	11.82

Table 5: A comparison of results on the provided trial data as headlines are added to the training set. The scores are given as Pearson correlations of scores for training sets of size 100, 250, and 1000 headlines.

As can be seen in Table 5, four out of six emotions and the valence increase along with training set size. This leads us to believe that further increases in the size of the training set would continue to improve results. Lack of time prevents a full analysis that can explain the sudden drop of Disgust and Joy.

Table 6 shows our full results from this task. Our system finished third out of five in the valence sub-task and second out of three in the emotion sub-task.

Emotion	Fine	Coarse-Grained		
		A	P	R
Valence	35.25	53.20	45.71	3.42
Anger	24.51	92.10	12.00	5.00
Disgust	18.55	97.20	0.00	0.00
Fear	32.52	84.80	25.00	14.40
Joy	26.11	80.60	35.41	9.44
Sadness	38.98	87.70	32.50	11.92
Surprise	11.82	89.10	11.86	10.93

Table 6: Our full results from SemEval-2007, Task 14, as reported by the task organizers. Fine-grained scores are given as Pearson correlations. Coarse-grained scores are given as accuracy (A), precision (P), and recall (R).

3.4 Conclusion

We presented a supervised system that used a unigram model to annotate the emotional content of headlines. We also used synonym expansion on the emotion label words. Our annotators encountered significant difficulty while tagging training data, due to ambiguity in definition of the task.

References

R.H. Baayen, R. Piepenbrock, and L. Gulikers. 1996. CELEX2. LDC96L14, Linguistic Data Consortium, Philadelphia.

S. F. Chen and J. Goodman. 1998. An empirical study of smoothing techniques for language modeling. Technical Report TR-10-98, Harvard University.

T.K. Landauer, Foltz P.W, and D. Laham. 1998. Introduction to latent semantic analysis. *Discourse Processes*, 25:259–284.

Thesaurus.com. 2007. Roget's New Millennium Thesaurus, 1st ed. (v 1.3.1). Lexico Publishing Group, LLC, `http://thesaurus.reference.com`.

Richard Wicentowski, Emily Thomforde, and Adrian Packel. 2004. The Swarthmore College SENSEVAL-3 System. In *Proceedings of Senseval-3, Third International Workshop on Evaluating Word Sense Disambiguation Systems.*

David Yarowsky. 1994. Decision lists for lexical ambiguity resolution: Application to accent restoration in Spanish and French. In *Proceedings of the 32nd Annual Meeting of the Association for Computational Linguistics*, pages 88–95.

Sussx: WSD using Automatically Acquired Predominant Senses

Rob Koeling and Diana McCarthy
Department of Informatics
University of Sussex
Brighton BN1 9QJ, UK
robk,dianam@sussex.ac.uk

1 Introduction

We introduced a method for discovering the predominant sense of words automatically using raw (unlabelled) text in (McCarthy et al., 2004) and participated with this system in SENSEVAL3. Since then, we worked on further developing ideas to improve upon the base method. In the current paper we target two areas where we believe there is potential for improvement. In the first one we address the fine-grained structure of WordNet's (WN) sense inventory (i.e. the topic of the task in this particular track). The second issue we address here, deals with topic domain specilisation of the base method.

Error analysis tought us that the method is sensitive to the fine-grained nature of WN. When two distinct senses in the WN sense inventory are closely related, the method often has difficulties discriminating between the two senses. If, for example, sense 1 and sense 7 for a word are closely related, choosing sense 7 in stead of sense 1 has serious consequences if you are using a first-sense heuristic (considering the highly skewed distribution of word senses). We expect that applying our method on a coarser grained sense inventory might help us resolve some of the more unfortunate errors.

(Magnini et al., 2002) have shown that information about the domain of a document is very useful for WSD. This is because many concepts are specific to particular domains, and for many words their most likely meaning in context is strongly correlated to the domain of the document they appear in. Thus, since word sense distributions are skewed and depend on the domain at hand we would like to explore if we can estimate the most likely sense of a word *for each domain of application* and exploit this in a WSD system.

2 Predominant Sense Acquisition

We use the method described in (McCarthy et al., 2004) for finding predominant senses from raw text. The method uses a thesaurus obtained from the text by parsing, extracting grammatical relations and then listing each word (w) with its top k nearest neighbours, where k is a constant. Like (McCarthy et al., 2004) we use $k = 50$ and obtain our thesaurus using the distributional similarity metric described by (Lin, 1998) and we use WordNet (WN) as our sense inventory. The senses of a word w are each assigned a ranking score which sums over the distributional similarity scores of the neighbours and weights each neighbour's score by a WN Similarity score (Patwardhan and Pedersen, 2003) between the sense of w and the sense of the neighbour that maximises the WN Similarity score. This weight is normalised by the sum of such WN similarity scores between all senses of w and the senses of the neighbour that maximises this score. We use the WN Similarity **jcn** score (Jiang and Conrath, 1997) since this gave reasonable results for (McCarthy et al., 2004) and it is efficient at run time given precompilation of frequency information. The **jcn** measure needs word frequency information, which we obtained from the British National Corpus (BNC) (Leech, 1992). The distributional thesaurus was constructed using subject, direct object adjective modifier and noun modifier relations.

Proceedings of the 4th International Workshop on Semantic Evaluations (SemEval-2007), pages 314–317,
Prague, June 2007. ©2007 Association for Computational Linguistics

3 Coarse Sense Inventory Adaptation

We contrasted ranking of the original WordNet senses with ranking produced using the coarse grained mapping between WordNet senses and the clusters provided for this task. In the first, which we refer to as fine-grained training (SUSSX-FR), we use the original method as described in section 2 using WordNet 2.1 as our sense inventory. For the second method which we refer to as coarse-grained training (SUSSX-CR), we use the clusters of the target word as our senses. The distributional similarity of each neighbour is apportioned to these clusters using the maximum WordNet similarity between any of the WordNet senses in the cluster and any of the senses of the neighbour. This WordNet similarity is normalised as in the original method, but for the denominator we use the sum of the WordNet similarity scores between this neighbour and all clusters of the target word.

4 Domain Adaptation

The topic domain of a document has a strong influence on the sense distribution of words. Unfortunately, it is not feasible to produce large manually sense-annotated corpora for every domain of interest. Since the method described in section 2 works with raw text, we can specialize our sense rankings for a particular topic domain, simply by feeding a domain specific corpus to the algorithm. Previous experiments have shown that unsupervised estimation of the predominant sense of certain words using corpora whose domain has been determined by hand outperforms estimates based on domain-independent text for a subset of words and even outperforms the estimates based on counting occurrences in an annotated corpus (Koeling et al., 2005). A later experiment (using SENSEVAL2 and 3 data) showed that using domain specific predominant senses can slightly improve the results for some domains (Koeling et al., 2007). However, a firm idea of when domain specilisation should be considered could not (yet) be given.

4.1 Creating the Domain Corpora

In order to estimate topic domain specific sense rankings, we need to specify what we consider 'domains' and we need to collect corpora of texts for these domains. We decided to use text classification for determining the topic domain and adopted the domain hierarchy as defined for the topic domain extension for WN (Subject Field Codes or WordNet Domains (WN-DOMAINS) (Magnini et al., 2002)).

Domains In WN-DOMAINS the Princeton English WordNet is augmented with domain labels. Every synset in WN's sense inventory is annotated with at least one domain label, selected from a set of about 200 labels hierarchically organized (based on the Dewey Decimal Classification (Diekema,)). Each synset of Wordnet 1.6 was labeled with one or more labels. The label 'factotum' was assigned if any other was inadequate. The first level consists of 5 main categories (e.g. 'doctrines' and 'social_science') and 'factotum'. 'doctrines', for example, has subcategories such as 'art', 'religion' and 'psychology'. Some subcategories are divided in sub-subcategories, e.g. 'dance', 'music' or 'theatre' are subcategories of 'art'.

Classifier We extracted bags of domain-specific words from WordNet for all the defined domains by collecting all the word senses (synsets) and corresponding glosses associated with a certain domain label. These bags of words define the domains and we used them to train a Support Vector Machine (SVM) text classifier using 'TwentyOne'[1].

The classifier distinguishes between 48 classes (first and second level of the WN-DOMAINS hierarchy). When a document is evaluated by the classifier, it returns a list of all the classes (domains) it recognizes and an associated *confidence score* reflecting the certainty that the document belongs to that particular domain.

Corpora We used the Gigaword English Corpus as our data source. This corpus is a comprehensive archive of newswire text data that has been acquired over several years by the Linguistic Data Consortium, at the University of Pennsylvania. For the experiments described in this paper, we use the first 20 months worth of data of all four sources (Agence France Press English Service, Associated Press Worldstream English Service, The New York Times Newswire Service and The Xinhua News Agency English Service). There are 4 different types

[1]TwentyOne Classifier is an Irion Technologies product: www.irion.ml/products/english/products_classify.html

Doc.Id.	Class	Conf. Score
d001	Medicine (Economy)	0.75 (0.75)
d002	Economy (Politics)	0.76 (0.74)
d003	Transport (Biology)	0.75 (0.68)
d004	Comp-Sci (Architecture)	0.81 (0.68)
d005	Psychology (Art)	0.78 (0.74)

Table 1: Output of the classifier for the 5 documents. The classifiers second choice is given between brackets.

of documents identified in the corpus. The vast majority of the documents are of type 'story'. We are using all the data.

The five documents were fed to the classifier. The results are given in table 1. Unfortunately, only one document (d004) was considered to be a clear-cut example of a particular domain by the classifier (i.e. a high score is given to the first class and a much lower score to the following classes).

4.2 Domain rankings

We created domain corpora by feeding the GigaWord documents to the classifier and adding each document to the domain corpus corresponding to the classifier's first choice. The five corpora we needed for these documents were parsed using RASP (Briscoe and Carroll, 2002) and the resulting grammatical relations were used to create a distributional similarity thesaurus, which in turn was used for computing the predominant senses (see section 2). The only pre-processing we performed was stripping the XML codes from the documents. No other filtering was undertaken. This resulted in five sets of sense inventories with domain-dependent sense rankings. Each of them has a slightly different set of words. The words they have in common do have the same senses, but not necessarily the same estimated most frequently used sense.

5 Results from Semeval

Coarse Disambiguation of coarse-grained senses is obviously an easier task than fine grained training. We had hoped that the coarse-grained training might show superior performance by removing the noise created by related but less frequent senses. Since the mapping between fine-grained senses and clusters is used anyway in the scorer the noise from related senses does not seem to be an issue. Related senses are scored correctly. Indeed the performance of the fine-grained training is superior to that of the coarse-grained training. We believe this is because predominant meanings have more related senses. There are therefore more chances that the distributional similarity of the neighbours will get apportioned to one of the related senses when there are more related senses. The coarse grained ranking would have an advantage on occasions when in the fine-grained ranking the credit between related senses is split and an unrelated sense ends up with a higher ranking score. Since the coarse-grained ranker lumps the credit for related sense together it would be at an advantage. Clearly this doesn't happen enough in the data to outweigh the beneficial effect of the number of related senses compensating for other noise in the data.

Doc.Id.	Class	SUSSX-FR	SUSSX-C-WD
d001	Medicine	0.556	0.560
d002	Economy	0.508	0.515
d003	Transport	0.487	0.454
d004	Comp-Sci	0.407	0.424
d005	Psychology	0.356	0.372

Table 2: Impact of domain specialisation for each of the five documents (F_1 scores).

Domain Unfortuately, the system specialised for domain (SUSSX-C-WD) did not improve the results over the 5 documents significantly. However, if we look at the contributions made by each document, we might learn something about the relation beteen the output of the classifier and the impact on the WSDresults. Table 2 shows the per-document results for the systems SUSSX-FR and SUSSX-C-WD. The first two documents show very little difference with the domain independent results. The documents 'd004' and 'd005' show a small but clear improved performance for the domain results. Unfortunately, document 'd003' displays a very disappointing drop of more than 3% in performance, and cancels out all the gains made by the last two documents.

The output of the classifier seems to be indicative of the results for all documents except 'd003'. The classifier doesn't seem to find enough evidence for a marked preference for a particular domain for documents 'd001' and 'd002'. This could be an indication that there is no strong domain effect to be expected. The strong preference for the 'computer_science' domain for 'd004' is reflected in good performance of SUSSX-C-WD and even though the confidence scores for the first 2 alternatives of 'd005' are fairly close, there is a clear drop in confidence score for the third alternative, which might indicate that the topic of this document is related to both first choices of the classifier. It will be interesting to evaluate the results for 'd005' using the 'Art' sense rankings. One would expect those results to be similar to the results found here. Finally, the results for 'd003' are hard to explain. We will need to do an extensive error analysis as soon as the gold-standard is available.

6 Conclusions

In this paper we investigated two directions where we expect potential for improving the performance of our method for acquiring predominant senses. In order to fully appreciate what the effects of the coarse grained sense inventory are (i.e. whether some of the more unfortunate errors are resolved), we will have to do an extensive error analysis as soon as the gold standard becomes available. Considering the fairly low number of attempted tokens (only 72.8% of the tokens are attempted), we are at a disadvantage compared to systems that back-off to (for example) the first sense in WN. However, we are well pleased with the high precision (71.7%) of the method SUSSX-FR, considering this is a completely unsupervised method. There seems to be potential gains for domain adaptation, but applying it to each document does not seem to be advisable. More research needs to be done to identify in which cases a performance boost can be expected. Five documents is not enough to fully investigate the matter. At the moment we are performing a larger scale experiment with the documents in SemCor. These documents seem to cover a fairly wide range of domains (according to our text classifier) and many domains are represented by several documents.

Acknowledgements

This work was funded by UK EPSRC project EP/C537262 "Ranking Word Senses for Disambiguation: Models and Applications", and by a UK Royal Society Dorothy Hodgkin Fellowship to the second author. We would also like to thank Piek Vossen for giving us access to the Irion Technologies text categoriser.

References

Ted Briscoe and John Carroll. 2002. Robust accurate statistical annotation of general text. In *Proceedings of LREC-2002*, pages 1499–1504, Las Palmas de Gran Canaria.

Anne Diekema. http://www.oclc.org/dewey/.

Jay Jiang and David Conrath. 1997. Semantic similarity based on corpus statistics and lexical taxonomy. In *International Conference on Research in Computational Linguistics*, Taiwan.

Rob Koeling, Diana McCarthy, and John Carroll. 2005. Domain-specific sense distributions and predominant sense acquisition. In *Proceedings of the Human Language Technology Conference and Conference on Empirical Methods in Natural Language Processing.*, pages 419–426, Vancouver, Canada.

Rob Koeling, Diana McCarthy, and John Carroll. 2007. Text categorization for improved priors of word meaning. In *Proceedings of the Eighth International Conference on Intelligent Text Processing and Computational Linguistics (Cicling 2007)*, pages 241–252, Mexico City, Mexico.

Geoffrey Leech. 1992. 100 million words of English: the British National Corpus. *Language Research*, 28(1):1–13.

Dekang Lin. 1998. Automatic retrieval and clustering of similar words. In *Proceedings of COLING-ACL 98*, Montreal, Canada.

Bernardo Magnini, Carlo Strapparava, Giovanni Pezzulo, and Alfio Gliozzo. 2002. The role of domain information in word sense disambiguation. *Natural Language Engineering*, 8(4):359–373.

Diana McCarthy, Rob Koeling, Julie Weeds, and John Carroll. 2004. Finding predominant senses in untagged text. In *Proceedings of the 42nd Annual Meeting of the Association for Computational Linguistics*, pages 280–287, Barcelona, Spain.

Siddharth Patwardhan and Ted Pedersen. 2003. The cpan wordnet::similarity package. http://search.cpan.org/s̃id/WordNet-Similarity/.

TITPI: Web People Search Task Using Semi-Supervised Clustering Approach

Kazunari Sugiyama
Precision and Intelligence Laboratory
Tokyo Institute of Technology
4259 Nagatsuta, Midori, Yokohama,
Kanagawa 226-8503, Japan
sugiyama@lr.pi.titech.ac.jp

Manabu Okumura
Precision and Intelligence Laboratory
Tokyo Institute of Technology
4259 Nagatsuta, Midori, Yokohama,
Kanagawa 226-8503, Japan
oku@pi.titech.ac.jp

Abstract

Most of the previous works that disambiguate personal names in Web search results employ agglomerative clustering approaches. However, these approaches tend to generate clusters that contain a single element depending on a certain criterion of merging similar clusters. In contrast to such previous works, we have adopted a semi-supervised clustering approach to integrate similar documents into a labeled document. Moreover, our proposed approach is characterized by controlling the fluctuation of the centroid of a cluster in order to generate more accurate clusters.

1 Introduction

Personal names are often submitted to search engines as query keywords, as described in a report[1] indicating that about 10% of the English queries from the search engine *ALLTheWeb*[2] contain personal names. However, in response to a personal name query, search engines return a long list of search results containing that contains Web pages about several namesakes. For example, when a user submits a personal name like "William Cohen" as a query to the search engine Google[3], the returned results represent more than one person named "William Cohen." In the results, a computer science professor, an American politician, a surgeon, and others are not classified into separate clusters but mixed together.

Most of the previous works on disambiguating personal names in Web search results employ several kinds of agglomerative clustering approach as described in Section 2. However, in these approaches, a lot of clusters that contain only one element tend to be generated, depending on a certain criterion for merging similar clusters. In addition, in person search results from the World Wide Web (WWW), we can often observe that a small number of entities have a lot of search-result Web pages, while others have only one or two. In light of these facts, if a labeled Web page that describes a person is introduced, clustering for personal name disambiguation would be much more accurate. In the following, we refer to such a labeled Web page as the "*seed page*." Then, in order to disambiguate personal names in Web search results, we introduce semi-supervised clustering that uses the seed page to aid the clustering of unlabeled search-result Web pages. Our semi-supervised clustering approach is characterized by controlling the fluctuation of the centroid of a cluster.

2 Related Work

(Mann and Yarowsky, 2003) first extract biographical information, such as birthdates, birthplaces, occupations, and so on. Then, for each document, they generate a feature vector composed of the extracted biographical information, proper nouns, and the TF-IDF score computed from the documents in the search results. Finally, using this feature vector, they disambiguate personal names by generating clusters based on a bottom-up centroid agglomera-

[1] http://tap.stanford.edu/PeopleSearch.pdf
[2] http://www.alltheweb.com/
[3] http://www.google.com/

Proceedings of the 4th International Workshop on Semantic Evaluations (SemEval-2007), pages 318–321,
Prague, June 2007.

tive clustering algorithm. (Wan et al., 2005) employ an approach similar to that of (Mann and Yarowsky, 2003), and have developed a system called *Web-Hawk*.

(Pedersen et al., 2005) recently proposed a method for discriminating names by clustering the instances of a given name into groups. They extract the context of each instance of an ambiguous name and generate second-order context vectors using significant bigrams. The vectors are then clustered such that instances that are similar to each other are grouped into the same cluster.

(Bekkerman and McCallum, 2005) propose the following three unsupervised approaches: (1) an approach based on the hyperlink structures of Web pages; (2) an approach based on agglomerative/conglomerative double clustering (Bekkerman et al., 2005); and (3) a hybrid approach combining the first two.

(Bollegala et al., 2006) first agglomeratively cluster a set of documents and then select key phrases from the resulting clusters to distinguish different namesakes. They extract key phrases from the documents and merge the clusters according to the similarity between the extracted phrases.

3 Our Proposed Approach

In this section, we first review the pure agglomerative clustering approach that most of the previous related works employ and then describe our proposed semi-supervised clustering approach.

In the following discussion, we denote the feature vector $\boldsymbol{w}^p$ of a search-result Web page p in a set of search results as follows:

$$\boldsymbol{w}^p = (w^p_{t_1}, w^p_{t_2}, \cdots, w^p_{t_m}), \quad (1)$$

where m is the number of distinct terms in the Web page p, and t_k $(k = 1, 2, \cdots, m)$ denotes each term. Stop words were eliminated from all Web pages in the search results based on the stopword list[4], and stemming was performed using Porter stemmer[5]. In our preliminary experiments, we found that gain (Papineni, 2001) is the most effective term weighting scheme for generating feature vectors for clustering in this kind of task. Using the gain scheme, we also define each element $w^p_{t_k}$ of $\boldsymbol{w}^p$ as follows:

[4]ftp://ftp.cs.cornell.edu/pub/smart/english.stop

[5]http://www.tartarus.org/~martin/PorterStemmer/

Algorithm: Agglomerative clustering
Input: Set of search-result Web page $p_i (i = 1, 2, \cdots n)$,
$P = \{p_1, p_2, \cdots p_n\}$.
Output: Clusters that contain the Web pages that refer to the same person.
Method:
1. Set the each element in P as initial clusters.
2. Repeat the following steps for all p_i $(i = 1, 2, \cdots, n)$ in P
until all of the similarities between two clusters are less than the predefi ned threshold.
2.1 Compute the similarity between p_i and p_{i+1}
if the similarity is greater than the predefi ned threshold,
then merge p_i and p_{i+1}, and recompute the centroid of the cluster using Equation (3),
else p_i is an independent cluster.
2.2 Compute all of the similarities between two clusters.

Figure 1: Agglomerative clustering algorithm.

$$w^p_{t_k} = \frac{df(t_k)}{N}\left(\frac{df(t_k)}{N} - 1 - \log\frac{df(t_k)}{N}\right),$$

where $df(t_k)$ is the document frequency of term t_k, and N is the total number of search-result Web pages.

We also define the centroid vector of a cluster $\boldsymbol{G}$ as follows:

$$\boldsymbol{G} = (g_{t_1}, g_{t_2}, \cdots, g_{t_m}), \quad (2)$$

where g_{t_k} is the weight of the centroid vector of a cluster, and t_k $(k = 1, 2, \cdots, m)$ denotes each term.

3.1 Agglomerative Clustering

In pure agglomerative clustering, initially, each Web page is an individual cluster, and then two clusters with the largest similarity are iteratively merged to generate a new cluster until this similarity is less than a predefined threshold. The detailed algorithm is shown in Figure 1. In this algorithm, the new centroid vector of cluster $\boldsymbol{G}^{new}$ after merging a cluster into its most similar cluster is defined as follows:

$$\boldsymbol{G}^{new} = \frac{\left(\sum^n_{\boldsymbol{w}^{p(G)} \in \boldsymbol{G}} \boldsymbol{w}^{p^{(G)}} + \boldsymbol{w}^p\right)}{n+1}, \quad (3)$$

where $\boldsymbol{w}^{p^{(G)}}$ and n represent the feature vector $\boldsymbol{w}^p$ of a search-result Web page and the number of search-result Web pages in the centroid cluster, respectively.

3.2 Our Proposed Semi-supervised Clustering

As described in Section 1, if a seed page that describes a person is introduced, the clustering for personal name disambiguation would be much more accurate. Therefore, we apply semi-supervised clustering to disambiguate personal names in Web

Algorithm: Semi-supervised clustering
Input: Set of search-result Web page $p_i (i = 1, 2, \cdots n)$,
and a seed page p_{seed}, $P = \{p_1, p_2, \cdots p_n, p_{seed}\}$.
Output: Clusters that contain the Web pages that refer to the same person.
Method:
1. Set the each element in P as initial clusters.
2. Repeat the following steps for all p_i $(i = 1, 2, \cdots, n)$ in P.
   2.1 Compute the similarity between p_i and p_{seed}.
   if the similarity is greater than the predefi ned threshold,
   then merge p_i into p_{seed} and recompute the centroid of the cluster using Equation (4),
   else p_i is stored as other clusters Oth, namely, $Oth = \{p_i\}$.
3. Repeat the following steps for all p_j $(j = 1, 2, \cdots, m, (m < n))$ in Oth until all of the similarities between two clusters are less than the predefi ned threshold.
   3.1 Compute the similarity between p_j and p_{j+1}
   if the similarity is greater than the predefi ned threshold,
   then merge p_j and p_{j+1}, and recompute the centroid of the cluster using Equation (3),
   else p_j is an independent cluster.
   3.2 Compute all of the similarities between two clusters.

Figure 2: Semi-supervised clustering algorithm.

search results. Our proposed approach is novel in that it controls the fluctuation of the centroid of a cluster when a new cluster is merged into it. In this process, when we merge the feature vector $\boldsymbol{w}^p$ of a search-result Web page into a particular centroid $\boldsymbol{G}$, we weight each element of $\boldsymbol{w}^p$ by the distance between $\boldsymbol{G}$ and $\boldsymbol{w}^p$. As a measure of the distance, we employ the Mahalanobis distance (Hand et al., 2001) that takes into account the correlations of the data set in the clusters. Using Equations (1) and (2), we define the new centroid vector of cluster $\boldsymbol{G}^{new}$ after merging a cluster into its most similar cluster as follows:

$$\boldsymbol{G}^{new} = \frac{\left(\sum^{n}_{\boldsymbol{w}^{p(G)} \in \boldsymbol{G}} \boldsymbol{w}^{p^{(G)}} + \frac{\boldsymbol{w}^p}{D_{mhl}(\boldsymbol{G}, \boldsymbol{w}^p)}\right)}{n+1}, \quad (4)$$

where $\boldsymbol{w}^{p^{(G)}}$ and n are the feature vector $\boldsymbol{w}^p$ of a search-result Web page and the number of search-result Web pages in the centroid cluster, respectively. In Equation (4), the Mahalanobis distance $D_{mhl}(\boldsymbol{G}, \boldsymbol{w}^p)$ between the centroid vector of cluster $\boldsymbol{G}$ and the feature vector $\boldsymbol{w}^p$ of search-result Web page p is defined as follows:

$$D_{mhl}(\boldsymbol{G}, \boldsymbol{w}^p) = \sqrt{(\boldsymbol{w}^p - \boldsymbol{G})^T \boldsymbol{\Sigma}^{-1} (\boldsymbol{w}^p - \boldsymbol{G})},$$

where $\boldsymbol{\Sigma}$ is the covariance matrix defined by the members in the centroid of a cluster. Figure 2 shows the detailed algorithm of our proposed semi-supervised clustering.

In our semi-supervised clustering approach, we use the following two kinds of seed page: (a) the article on each person in Wikipedia, and (b) the top ranked Web page in the Web search results. However, not every personal name in the test data of Web People Search Task has an corresponding article in Wikipedia. Therefore, if a personal name has an article in Wikipedia, we used it as the seed page. Otherwise, we used the top ranked Web pages in the Web search results as the seed page. Table 1 shows personal names classified based on each seed page used in our experiment.

Table 1: Personal names and two kinds of seed page.

Seed page	Personal name
(a) Wikipedia article	Arthur Morgan, George Foster, Harry Hughes, James Davidson, James Hamilton, James Morehead, Jerry Hobbs, John Nelson, Mark Johnson, Neil Clark, Patrick Killen, Robert Moore, Stephen Clark, Thomas Fraser, Thomas Kirk, William Dickson (16 names)
(b) The top ranked Web page	Alvin Cooper, Chris Brockett, Dekang Lin, Frank Keller, James Curran, Jonathan Brooks, Jude Brown, Karen Peterson, Leon Barrett, Marcy Jackson, Martha Edwards, Sharon Goldwater, Stephan Johnson, Violet Howard (14 names)

4 Evaluation Results & Discussion

Tables 2 and 3 show evaluation results in each document set obtained using pure agglomerative clustering and our proposed semi-supervised clustering, respectively. "Set 1," "Set 2," and "Set 3" contain the names from participants in the ACL conference, from biographical articles in the English Wikipedia, and from the US Census, respectively. According to these tables, we found that, although agglomerative clustering outperforms our proposed semi-supervised clustering by 0.21 in the value of purity, our proposed semi-supervised clustering outperforms agglomerative clustering by 0.4 and 0.06 in the values of inverse purity and F-measure, respectively. This indicates that our proposed method tends to integrate search-result Web pages into a seed page and a small number of clusters are generated compared with agglomerative clustering. In terms of these facts, it is easier for a user to browse Web pages clustered based on each personal entity. On the other hand, the small values of purity indicate that irrelevant search-result Web pages are often contained in the generated clusters. Therefore, we can guess that irrelevant search-result Web pages are integrated into a seed page. In fact, we observed that more than 50 search-result Web pages could be grouped together with a seed page.

Table 2: Evaluation results in each document set obtained using agglomerative clustering.

Document set	Purity	Inverse purity	F-measure (alpha=0.5)
Set 1	0.58	0.51	0.45
Set 2	0.67	0.47	0.53
Set 3	0.72	0.47	0.55
Global average	0.66	0.49	0.51

Table 3: Evaluation results in each document set obtained using our proposed semi-supervised clustering.

Document set	Purity	Inverse purity	F-measure (alpha=0.5)
Set 1	0.53	0.86	0.62
Set 2	0.42	0.89	0.55
Set 3	0.41	0.92	0.55
Global average	0.45	0.89	0.57

Table 4: Evaluation results based on each seed page obtained using our proposed semi-supervised clustering.

Seed page	Purity	Inverse purity	F-measure (alpha=0.5)
(a) Wikipedia article	0.44	0.96	0.55
(b) The top ranked Web page	0.47	0.81	0.60

Table 4 shows the evaluation results obtained using each seed page. The value of F-measure obtained using seed page (a) (0.55) is comparable to that obtained using seed page (b) (0.60). In addition, we could observe that some Wikipedia articles are under updating. Therefore, if the Wikipedia articles are continuously updated, the reliability of Wikipedia as a source of seed pages will be promising in the future. Moreover, observing the results of each person in detail, we found that the purity values are improved when we use a seed page that describes the person using more than about 200 words. On the other hand, in the case where a seed page describes a person with less than 150 words, or describes not only the target person but also some other persons, we could not obtain high purity values.

5 Conclusion

In this paper, we described our participating system in the SemEval-2007 Web People Search Task (Artiles et al., 2007). Our system used a semi-supervised clustering which controls the fluctuation of the centroid of a cluster. The evaluation results showed that our proposed method achieves high scores in inverse purity, with the lower scores in purity. This fact indicates that our proposed method tends to integrate search-result Web pages into a seed page. This clustering result makes it easier for a user to browse the results of a person Web search. However, in the generated cluster with a seed page, irrelevant search-result Web pages are also contained. This problem can be solved by introducing multiple seed pages. In our experiment, we used the full contents of search-result Web pages and a seed page. We consider that this can cause lower scores in purity. Therefore, in future work, in order to improve the accuracy of clustering, we plan to conduct further experiments by introducing multiple seed pages and using parts of search-result Web pages and seed pages such as words around an ambiguous name.

References

Javier Artiles, Julio Gonzalo, and Satoshi Sekine. 2007. The SemEval-2007 WePS Evaluation: Establishing a Benchmark for the Web People Search Task. In *Proceedings of Semeval 2007, Association for Computational Linguistics*.

Ron Bekkerman, Ran El-Yaniv, and Andrew McCallum. 2005. Multi-way Distributional Clustering via Pairwise Interactions. In *Proceedings of the 22nd International Conference on Machine Learning (ICML2005)*, pages 41-48.

Ron Bekkerman and Andrew McCallum. 2005. Disambiguating Web Appearances of People in a Social Network. In *Proceedings of the 14th International World Wide Web Conference (WWW2005)*, pages 463-470.

Danushka Bollegala, Yutaka Matsuo and Mitsuru Ishizuka. 2006. Extracting Key Phrases to Disambiguate Personal Names on the Web. In *Proceedings of the 7th International Conference on Computational Linguistics and Intelligent Text Processing (CICLing2006)*, pages 223-234.

David J. Hand, Heikki Mannila and Padhraic Smyth. 2001. Principles of Data Mining. MIT Press, 2001.

Gideon. S. Mann and David Yarowsky. 2003. Unsupervised Personal Name Disambiguation. In *Proceedings of the 7th Conference on Natural Language Learning (CoNLL-2003)*, pages 33-40.

Kishore Papineni. 2001. Why Inverse Document Frequency? In *Proceedings of the 2nd Meeting of the North American Chapter of the Association for Computational Linguistics (NAACL 2001)*, pages 25-32.

Ted Pedersen, Amruta Purandare, and Anagha Kulkarni. 2005. Name Discrimination by Clustering Similar Contexts. In *Proceedings of the 6th International Conference on Computational Linguistics and Intelligent Text Processing (CICLing2005)*, pages 226-237.

Xiaojun Wan, Jianfeng Gao, Mu Li, and Binggong Ding. 2005. Person Resolution in Person Search Results: WebHawk. In *Proceedings of the 14th International Conference on Information and Knowledge Management (CIKM 2005)*, pages 163-170.

TKB-UO: Using Sense Clustering for WSD

Henry Anaya-Sánchez[1], **Aurora Pons-Porrata**[1], **Rafael Berlanga-Llavori**[2]
[1] Center of Pattern Recognition and Data Mining, Universidad de Oriente, Cuba
[2] Computer Science, Universitat Jaume I, Spain
[1] {henry,aurora}@csd.uo.edu.cu
[2] berlanga@lsi.uji.es

Abstract

This paper describes the clustering-based approach to Word Sense Disambiguation that is followed by the TKB-UO system at SemEval-2007. The underlying disambiguation method only uses WordNet as external resource, and does not use training data. Results obtained in both Coarse-grained English all-words task (task 7) and English fine-grained all-words subtask (task 17) are presented.

1 Introduction

The TKB-UO system relies on the knowledge-driven approach to Word Sense Disambiguation (WSD) presented in (Anaya-Sánchez et al., 2006). Regarding that meaningful senses of words in a textual unit must be coherently related, our proposal uses sense clustering with the aim of determining cohesive groups of senses that reflect the connectivity of the disambiguating words.

The way this proposal uses clustering for disambiguation purposes is different from those usages reported in other works of the WSD area. For example, in (Pedersen et al., 2005) textual contexts are clustered in order to represent senses for Word Sense Discrimination. Other works like (Agirre and López, 2003), cluster fine-grained word senses into coarse-grained ones for polysemy reduction. Instead, our method clusters all possible senses corresponding to all words in a disambiguating textual unit. Thus, our system implements a novel clustering approach for the contextual disambiguation of words.

We use the lexical resource WordNet (version 2.1) as the repository of word senses, and also as the provider of sense representations. It is worth mentioning that our proposal does not require the use of training data.

2 The disambiguation algorithm

Our method starts with a clustering of all possible senses of the disambiguating words. Such a clustering tries to identify cohesive groups of word senses, which are assumed to represent the different meanings for the set of disambiguating words. Then, clusters that match the best with the context are selected via a filtering process. If the selected clusters disambiguate all words, the process is stopped and the senses belonging to the selected clusters are interpreted as the disambiguating ones. Otherwise, the clustering and filtering steps are performed again (regarding the remaining senses) until the disambiguation is achieved.

Algorithm 1 shows the general steps of our proposal for the disambiguation of a set of words W. In the algorithm, *clustering* represents the basic clustering method, *filter* is the function that selects the clusters, and T denotes the intended textual context from which words in W are disambiguated (typically, a broader bag of words than W). Next subsections describe in detail each component of the whole process.

2.1 Sense Representation

For clustering purposes, word senses are represented as topic signatures (Lin and Hovy, 2000). Thus, for each word sense s we define a vector

Proceedings of the 4th International Workshop on Semantic Evaluations (SemEval-2007), pages 322–325,
Prague, June 2007.

Algorithm 1 Clustering-based approach for the disambiguation of the set of words W in the textual context T

Input: The finite set of words W and the textual context T.
Output: The disambiguated word senses.
Let S be the set of all senses of words in W, and $i = 0$;
repeat
  $i = i + 1$
  $G = clustering(S, \beta_0(i))$
  $G' = filter(G, W, T)$
  $S = \bigcup_{g \in G'} \{s | s \in g\}$
until $|S| = |W|$ or $\beta_0(i+1) = 1$
return S

$\langle t_1 : \sigma_1, \ldots, t_m : \sigma_m \rangle$, where each t_i is a WordNet term highly correlated to s with an association weight σ_i. The set of signature terms for a word sense includes all its WordNet hyponyms, its directly related terms (including coordinated terms) and their filtered and lemmatized glosses. To weight signature terms, the *tf-idf* statistics is used, considering each word as a collection and its senses as its of documents. Topic signatures of senses form a Vector Space Model similar to those defined in Information Retrieval Systems. In this way, they can be compared with measures such as cosine, Dice and Jaccard (Salton et al., 1975).

In (Anaya-Sánchez et al., 2006), it is shown that this kind of WordNet-based signatures outperform those Web-based ones developed by the Ixa Research Group [1] in the disambiguation of nouns.

2.2 Clustering Algorithm

Sense clustering is carried out by the Extended Star Clustering Algorithm (Gil et al., 2003), which builds star-shaped and overlapped clusters. Each cluster consists of a star and its satellites, where the star is the sense with the highest connectivity of the cluster, and the satellites are those senses connected with the star. The connectivity is defined in terms of the β_0-similarity graph, which is obtained using the cosine similarity measure between topic signatures and the minimum similarity threshold β_0. The way this clustering algorithm relates word senses resembles the manner in which syntactic and discourse relation links textual elements.

[1] http://ixa.si.ehu.es/Ixa/

2.3 Filtering Process

Once clustering is performed over the senses of words in W, a set of sense clusters is obtained. As some clusters can be more appropriate to describe the semantics of W than others, they are ranked according to a measure w.r.t the textual context T.

As we represent the context T in the same vector space that the topic signatures of senses, the following function can be used to score a cluster of senses g regarding T:

$$\left(|words(g)|, \frac{\sum_i \min\{\bar{g}_i, T_i\}}{\min\{\sum_i \bar{g}_i, \sum_i T_i\}}, -\sum_{s \in g} number(s) \right)$$

where $words(g)$ denotes the set of words having senses in g, $\bar{g}$ is the centroid of g (computed as the barycenter of the cluster), and $number(s)$ is the WordNet number of sense s according to its corresponding word.

Then, we rank all clusters by using the lexicographic order of their scores w.r.t. the above function.

Once the clusters have been ranked, they are orderly processed to select clusters for covering the words in W. A cluster g is selected if it contains at least one sense of an uncovered word and other senses corresponding to covered words are included in the current selected clusters. If g does not contain any sense of uncovered words it is discarded. Otherwise, g is inserted into a queue Q. Finally, if the selected clusters do not cover W, clusters in Q adding senses of uncovered words are chosen until all words are covered.

2.4 β_0 Threshold and the Stopping Criterion

As a result of the filtering process, a set of senses for all the words in W is obtained (i.e. the union of all the selected clusters). Each word in W that has only a sense in such a set is considered disambiguated. If some word still remains ambiguous, we must refine the clustering process to get stronger cohesive clusters of senses. In this case, all the remaining senses must be clustered again but raising the β_0 threshold.

Notice that this process must be done iteratively until either all words are disambiguated or when it is impossible to raise β_0 again. Initially, β_0 is defined as:

$$\beta_0(1) = pth(90, sim(S))$$

and at the i-th iteration ($i > 1$) it is raised to:

$$\beta_0(i) = \min_{p \in \{90,95,100\}} \{\beta = pth(p, sim(S)) | \beta > \beta_0(i-1)\}$$

In these equations, S is the set of current senses, and $pth(p, sim(S))$ represents the p-th percentile value of the pairwise similarities between senses (i.e. $sim(S) = \{cos(s_i, s_j) | s_i, s_j \in S, i \neq j\} \cup \{1\}$).

2.5 A Disambiguation Example

In this subsection we illustrate the use of our proposal in the disambiguation of the content words appearing in the sentence *"The runner won the marathon"*. In this example, the set of disambiguating words W includes the nouns *runner* and *marathon*, and the verb *win* (lemma of the verbal form *won*). Also, we consider that the context is the vector $T = \langle runner : 1, win : 1, marathon : 1 \rangle$. The rest of words are not considered because they are meaningless. As we use WordNet 2.1, we regard that the correct senses for the context are $runner\#6$, $win\#1$ and $marathon\#2$.

Figure 1 graphically depicts the disambiguation process carried out by our method. The boxes in the figure represent the obtained clusters, which are sorted regarding the ranking function (scores are under the boxes).

Initially, all word senses are clustered using β_0=0.049 (the 90th-percentile of the pairwise similarities between the senses). It can be seen in the figure that the first cluster comprises the sense $runner\#6$ (the star), which is the sense refering to a trained athlete who competes in foot races, and $runner\#4$, which is the other sense of *runner* related with sports. Also, it includes the sense $win\#1$ that concerns to the victory in a race or competition, and $marathon\#2$ that refers to a footrace. It can be easily appreciated that this first cluster includes senses that cover the set of disambiguating words. Hence, it is selected by the filter and all other clusters are

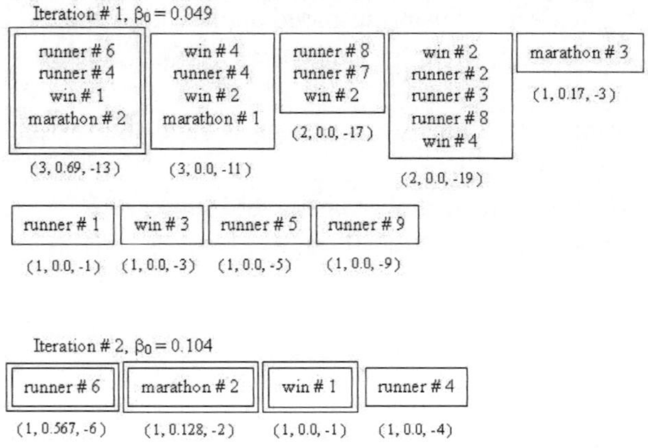

Figure 1: Disambiguation of words in *"The runner won the marathon"*.

discarded. After this step, S is updated with the set $\{runner\#6, runner\#4, win\#1, marathon\#2\}$.[2]

In this point of the process, the senses of S do not disambiguate W because the noun *runner* has two senses in S. Therefore, the sttoping criterion does not hold because neither $|S| \neq |W|$ and $\beta_0(2) = 0.104 \neq 1$. Consequently, a new cluster distribution must be obtained using the current set S.

The boxes in the bottom of Figure 1 represent the new clusters. In this case, all clusters are singles. Obviously, the cluster containing the sense $runner\#4$ is discarded because the cluster that includes the sense $runner\#6$ overlaps better with the context, and therefore precedes it in the order.

Then, the final set of selected senses is $S = \{runner\#6,\ win\#1,\ marathon\#2\}$, which includes only one sense for each word in W.

3 SemEval-2007 Results

Our system participated in the Coarse-grained English all-words task (task 7) and in the English fine-grained all-words subtask (task 17). In both cases, the disambiguation process was performed at the sentence level. Thus, we defined the intended textual context T for a sentence to be the bag of all its lemmatized content words. However, W was set up in a different manner for each task.

We present our results only in terms of the F1 measure. *Recall* and *Precision* values are omitted

[2]In the figure, doubly-boxed clusters depict the selected ones by the filter.

Test set	F1
d001	0.78804
d002	0.72559
d003	0.69400
d004	0.70753
d005	0.58551
Total	0.70207

Table 1: TKB-UO results in Coarse-grained English all-words task.

Category	Instances	F1
Noun	161	0.367
Verb	304	0.303
All	465	0.325

Table 2: TKB-UO results in English Fine-grained all-words subtask.

because our method achieves a 100 % of *Coverage*.

3.1 Coarse-grained English All-words Task

Firstly, it is worth mentioning that we do not use the coarse-grained inventory provided by the competition for this task. Indeed, our approach can be viewed as a method to build such a coarse-grained inventory as it clusters tightly related senses.

Each W was defined as the set of all tagged words belonging to the sentence under consideration. Table 3.1 shows the official results obtained by our system.

As it can be appreciated, the effectiveness of our method was around the 70 %, except in the fifth test document (d005), which is an excerpt of stories about Italian painters.

3.2 English Fine-grained All-words Subtask

Similar to previous task, we included into each W those tagged words of the disambiguating sentence. However, as the set of tagged words per sentence was verb-plentiful, with very few nouns, we expanded W with the rest of nouns and adjectives of the sentence.

Table 3.2 summarizes the results (split by word categories) obtained in this subtask. The second column of the table shows the number of disambiguating word occurrences.

As we can see, in this subtask only nouns and verbs were required to be disambiguated, and overall, verbs predominate over nouns. The poor performance obtained by verbs (w.r.t. nouns) can be explained by its high polysemy degree and its relatively small number of relations in WordNet.

4 Conclusions

In this paper, we have described the TKB-UO system for WSD at SemEval-2007. This knowledge-driven system relies on a novel way of using clustering in the WSD area. Also, it benefits from topic signatures built from WordNet, which in combination with the clustering algorithm overcomes the sparseness of WordNet relations for associating semantically related word senses. The system participated in both the Coarse-grained English all-words task (task 7) and the English fine-grained all-words subtask (task 17). Since we use sense clustering, we do not use the coarse-grained sense inventory provided by the competition for task 7. Further work will focus on improving the results of fine-grained WSD.

References

Eneko Agirre and Oier López. 2003. Clustering wordnet word senses. *Proceedings of the Conference on Recent Advances on Natural Language Processing*, pp. 121–130

Henry Anaya-Sánchez, Aurora Pons-Porrata, and Rafael Berlanga-Llavori. 2006. Word sense disambiguation based on word sense clustering. *Lecture Notes in Artificial Intelligence*, 4140:472–481.

Reynaldo Gil-García, José M. Badía-Contelles, and Aurora Pons-Porrata. 2003 Extended Star Clustering Algorithm. *Lecture Notes on Computer Sciences*, 2905:480–487

Chin-Yew Lin and Eduard Hovy. 2000. The Automated Acquisition of Topic Signatures for Text Summarization. *Proceedings of the COLING Conference*, pp. 495–501

Ted Pedersen, Amruta Purandare, and Anagha Kulkarni. 2005. Name Discrimination by Clustering Similar Contexts. *Lecture Notes in Computer Science*, 3406:226–237

Gerard Salton, A. Wong, and C.S. Yang. 1975. A Vector Space Model for Information Retrieval. *Journal of the American Society for Information Science*, 18(11):613–620

TOR, TORMD: Distributional Profiles of Concepts for Unsupervised Word Sense Disambiguation

Saif Mohammad
Dept. of Computer Science
University of Toronto
Toronto, ON M5S 3G4
Canada
smm@cs.toronto.edu

Graeme Hirst
Dept. of Computer Science
University of Toronto
Toronto, ON M5S 3G4
Canada
gh@cs.toronto.edu

Philip Resnik
Dept. of Linguistics and UMIACS
University of Maryland
College Park, MD 20742
USA
resnik@umiacs.umd.edu

Abstract

Words in the context of a target word have long been used as features by supervised word-sense classifiers. Mohammad and Hirst (2006a) proposed a way to determine the strength of association between a sense or concept and co-occurring words—the distributional profile of a concept (DPC)—without the use of manually annotated data. We implemented an unsupervised naïve Bayes word sense classifier using these DPCs that was best or within one percentage point of the best unsupervised systems in the Multilingual Chinese–English Lexical Sample Task (task #5) and the English Lexical Sample Task (task #17). We also created a simple PMI-based classifier to attempt the English Lexical Substitution Task (task #10); however, its performance was poor.

1 Introduction

Determining the intended sense of a word is potentially useful in many natural language tasks including machine translation and information retrieval. The best approaches for word sense disambiguation are supervised and they use words that co-occur with the target as features. These systems rely on sense-annotated data to identify words that are indicative of the use of the target in each of its senses.

However, only limited amounts of sense-annotated data exist and it is expensive to create. In our previous work (Mohammad and Hirst, 2006a), we proposed an unsupervised approach to determine the strength of association between a sense or concept and its co-occurring words—**the distributional profile of a concept (DPC)**—relying simply on raw text and a published thesaurus. The categories in a published thesaurus were used as coarse senses or concepts (Yarowsky, 1992). We now show how distributional profiles of concepts can be used to create an *unsupervised* naïve Bayes word-sense classifier. We also implemented a simple classifier that relies on the pointwise mutual information (PMI) between the senses of the target and co-occurring words. These DPC-based classifiers participated in three SemEval 2007 tasks: the English Lexical Sample Task (task #17), the English Lexical Substitution Task (task #10), and the Multilingual Chinese–English Lexical Sample Task (task #5).

The English Lexical Sample Task (Pradhan et al., 2007) is a traditional word sense disambiguation task wherein the intended (WordNet) sense of a target word is to be determined from its context. We manually mapped the WordNet senses to the categories in a thesaurus and the DPC-based naïve Bayes classifier was used to identify the intended sense (category) of the target words.

The object of the Lexical Substitution Task (McCarthy and Navigli, 2007) is to replace a target word in a sentence with a suitable substitute that preserves the meaning of the utterance. The list of possible substitutes for a given target word is usually contingent on its intended sense. Therefore, word sense disambiguation is expected to be useful in lexical substitution. We used the PMI-based classier to determine the intended sense.

Proceedings of the 4th International Workshop on Semantic Evaluations (SemEval-2007), pages 326–333,
Prague, June 2007.

The objective of the Multilingual Chinese–English Lexical Sample Task (Jin et al., 2007) is to select from a given list a suitable English translation of a Chinese target word in context. Mohammad et al. (2007) proposed a way to create **cross-lingual distributional profiles of a concepts (CL-DPCs)**—the strengths of association between the concepts of one language and words of another. For this task, we mapped the list of English translations to appropriate thesaurus categories and used an implementation of a CL-DPC–based unsupervised naïve Bayes classifier to identify the intended senses (and thereby the English translations) of target Chinese words.

2 Distributional profiles of concepts

In order to determine the strength of association between a sense of the target word and its co-occurring words, we need to determine their individual and joint occurrence counts in a corpus. Mohammad and Hirst (2006a) and Mohammad et al. (2007) proposed ways to determine these counts in a monolingual and cross-lingual framework without the use of sense-annotated data. We summarize the ideas in this section; the original papers give more details.

2.1 Word–category co-occurrence matrix

We create a **word–category co-occurrence matrix (WCCM)** having English word types w^{en} as one dimension and English thesaurus categories c^{en} as another. We used the *Macquarie Thesaurus* (Bernard, 1986) both as a very coarse-grained sense inventory and a source of words that together represent each category (concept). The WCCM is populated with co-occurrence counts from a large English corpus (we used the *British National Corpus (BNC)*). A particular cell m_{ij}, corresponding to word w_i^{en} and concept c_j^{en}, is populated with the number of times w_i^{en} co-occurs with any word that has c_j^{en} as one of its senses (i.e., w_i^{en} co-occurs with any word listed under concept c_j^{en} in the thesaurus).

	c_1^{en}	c_2^{en}	$\ldots$	c_j^{en}	$\ldots$
w_1^{en}	m_{11}	m_{12}	$\ldots$	m_{1j}	$\ldots$
w_2^{en}	m_{21}	m_{22}	$\ldots$	m_{2j}	$\ldots$
$\vdots$	$\vdots$	$\vdots$	$\ddots$	$\vdots$	$\vdots$
w_i^{en}	m_{i1}	m_{i2}	$\ldots$	m_{ij}	$\ldots$
$\vdots$	$\vdots$	$\vdots$	$\ldots$	$\vdots$	$\ddots$

A particular cell m_{ij}, corresponding to word w_i^{en} and concept c_j^{en}, is populated with the number of times w_i^{en} co-occurs with any word that has c_j^{en} as one of its senses (i.e., w_i^{en} co-occurs with any word listed under concept c_j^{en} in the thesaurus). This matrix, created after a first pass of the corpus, is the **base word–category co-occurrence matrix (base WCCM)** and it captures strong associations between a sense and co-occurring words (see discussion of the general principle in Resnik (1998)). From the base WCCM we can determine the number of times a word w and concept c co-occur, the number of times w co-occurs with any concept, and the number of times c co-occurs with any word. A statistic such as PMI can then give the strength of association between w and c. This is similar to how Yarowsky (1992) identifies words that are indicative of a particular sense of the target word.

Words that occur close to a target word tend to be good indicators of its intended sense. Therefore, we make a second pass of the corpus, using the base WCCM to roughly disambiguate the words in it. For each word, the strength of association of each of the words in its context (± 5 words) with each of its senses is summed. The sense that has the highest cumulative association is chosen as the intended sense. A new **bootstrapped WCCM** is created such that each cell m_{ij}, corresponding to word w_i^{en} and concept c_j^{en}, is populated with the number of times w_i^{en} co-occurs with any word *used in sense* c_j^{en}.

Mohammad and Hirst (2006a) used the DPCs created from the bootstrapped WCCM to attain near-upper-bound results in the task of determining word sense dominance. Unlike the McCarthy et al. (2004) dominance system, this approach can be applied to much smaller target texts (a few hundred sentences) without the need for a large similarly-sense-distributed text[1]. Mohammad and Hirst (2006b) used the DPC-based monolingual distributional measures of *concept-distance* to rank word pairs by their semantic similarity and to correct real-word spelling errors, attaining markedly better results than monolingual distributional measures of *word-distance*. In the spelling correction task, the

[1]The McCarthy et al. (2004) system needs to first generate a distributional thesaurus from the target text (if it is large enough—a few million words) or from another large text with a distribution of senses similar to the target text.

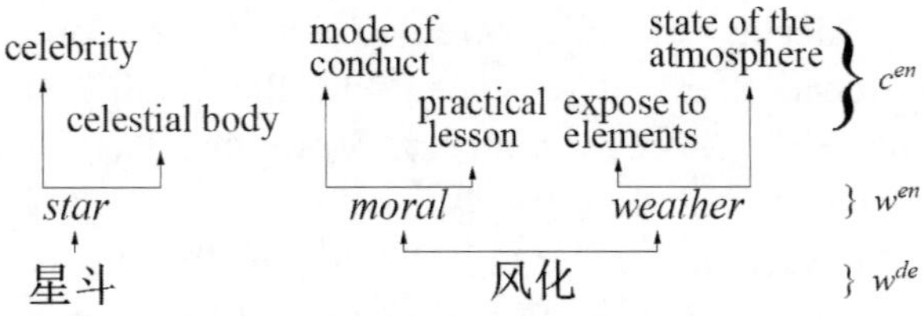

Figure 1: The cross-lingual candidate senses of Chinese words 星斗 and 风化.

distributional concept-distance measures performed better than all WordNet-based measures as well, except for the Jiang and Conrath (1997) measure.

2.2 Cross-lingual word–category co-occurrence matrix

Given a Chinese word wch in context, we use a Chinese–English bilingual lexicon to determine its different possible English translations. Each English translation w^{en} may have one or more possible coarse senses, as listed in an English thesaurus. These English thesaurus concepts (c^{en}) will be referred to as **cross-lingual candidate senses** of the Chinese word w^{ch}.[2] Figure 1 depicts examples.

We create a cross-lingual word–category co-occurrence matrix (CL-WCCM) with Chinese word types wch as one dimension and English thesaurus concepts c^{en} as another.

	c_1^{en}	c_2^{en}	$\ldots$	c_j^{en}	$\ldots$
w_1^{ch}	m_{11}	m_{12}	$\ldots$	m_{1j}	$\ldots$
w_2^{ch}	m_{21}	m_{22}	$\ldots$	m_{2j}	$\ldots$
$\vdots$	$\vdots$	$\vdots$	$\ddots$	$\vdots$	$\vdots$
w_i^{ch}	m_{i1}	m_{i2}	$\ldots$	m_{ij}	$\ldots$
$\vdots$	$\vdots$	$\vdots$	$\ldots$	$\vdots$	$\ddots$

The matrix is populated with co-occurrence counts from a large Chinese corpus; we used a collection of LDC-distributed corpora[3]—Chinese Treebank English Parallel Corpus, FBIS data, Xinhua Chinese–English Parallel News Text Version 1.0 beta 2, Chinese English News Magazine Parallel Text, Chinese News Translation Text Part 1, and Hong Kong Parallel Text. A particular cell m_{ij}, corresponding to word w_i^{ch} and concept c_j^{en}, is populated with the number of times the Chinese word w_i^{ch} co-occurs with any Chinese word having c_j^{en} as one of its *cross-lingual candidate senses*. For example, the cell for 太空 ('space') and 'celestial body' will have the sum of the number of times 太空 co-occurs with 天体, 日, 太阳, 星, 星斗, and so on (see Figure 2). We used the *Macquarie Thesaurus* (Bernard, 1986) (about 98,000 words). The possible Chinese translations of an English word were taken from the Chinese–English Translation Lexicon version 3.0 (Huang and Graff, 2002) (about 54,000 entries).

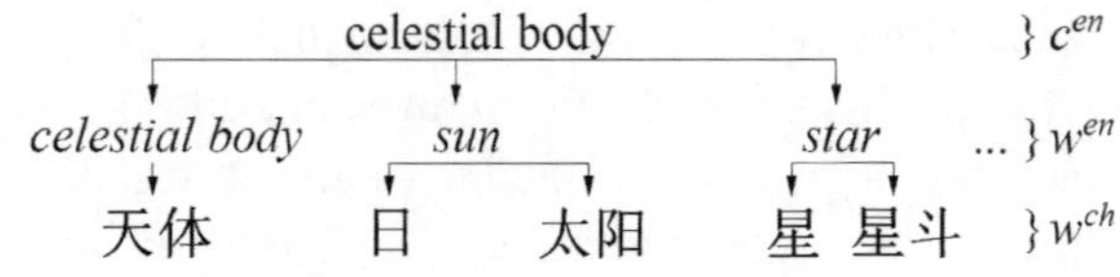

Figure 2: Chinese words having 'celestial body' as one of their cross-lingual candidate senses.

This base word–category co-occurrence matrix (base WCCM), created after a first pass of the corpus, captures strong associations between a category (concept) and co-occurring words. For example, even though we increment counts for both 太空–'celestial body' and 太空–'celebrity' for a particular instance where 太空 co-occurs with 星斗, 太空 will co-occur with a number of words such as 天体, 太阳, and 日 that each have the sense of *celestial body* in common (see Figure 2), whereas all their other senses are likely different and distributed across the set of concepts. Therefore, the co-occurrence count of 太空 and 'celestial body' will be relatively higher than that of 太空 and 'celebrity'.

As in the monolingual case, a second pass of the corpus is made to disambiguate the (Chinese) words in it. For each word, the strength of association of each of the words in its context (±5 words) with each of its cross-lingual candidate senses is summed. The sense that has the highest cumulative association with co-occurring words is chosen as the intended sense. A new bootstrapped WCCM is created by populating each cell m_{ij}, corresponding to word w_i^{ch} and concept c_j^{en}, with the number of times the Chinese word w_i^{ch} co-occurs with any Chi-

[2] Some of the cross-lingual candidate senses of wch might not really be senses of w^{ch} (e.g., 'celebrity', 'practical lesson', and 'state of the atmosphere' in Figure 1). However, as substantiated by experiments by Mohammad et al. (2007), our algorithm is able to handle the added ambiguity.

[3] http://www.ldc.upenn.edu

nese word *used in cross-lingual sense* c_j^{en}. A statistic such as PMI is then applied to these counts to determine the strengths of association between a target concept and co-occurring words, giving the distributional profile of the concept.

Mohammad et al. (2007) combined German text with an English thesaurus using a German–English bilingual lexicon to create German–English DPCs. These DPCs were used to determine semantic distance between German words, showing that state-of-the-art accuracies for one language can be achieved using a knowledge source (thesaurus) from another.

Given that a published thesaurus has about 1000 categories and the size of the vocabulary N is at least 100,000, the CL-WCCM and the WCCM are much smaller matrices (about $1000 \times N$) than the traditional word–word co-occurrence matrix ($N \times N$). Therefore the WCCMs are relatively inexpensive both in terms of memory and computation.

3 Classification

We implemented two unsupervised classifiers. The words in context were used as features.

3.1 Unsupervised Naïve Bayes Classifier

The naïve Bayes classifier has the following formula to determine the intended sense c_{nb}:

$$c_{nb} = \underset{c_j \in C}{\operatorname{argmax}} P(c_j) \prod_{w_i \in W} P(w_i|c_j) \qquad (1)$$

where C is the set of possible senses (as listed in the *Macquarie Thesaurus*) and W is the set of words that co-occur with the target (we used a window of ± 5 words).

Traditionally, prior probabilities of the senses ($P(c_j)$) and the conditional probabilities in the likelihood ($\prod_{w_i \in W} P(w_i|c_j)$) are determined by simple counts in sense-annotated data. We approximate these probabilities using counts from the word–category co-occurrence matrix (monolingual or cross-lingual), thereby obviating the need for manually-annotated data.

$$P(c_j) = \frac{\sum_i m_{ij}}{\sum_{i,j} m_{ij}} \qquad (2)$$

$$P(w_i|c_j) = \frac{m_{ij}}{\sum_i m_{ij}} \qquad (3)$$

For the English Lexical Task, m_{ij} is the number of times the English word w_i co-occurs with the English category c_j—as listed in the word–category co-occurrence matrix (WCCM). For the Multilingual Chinese–English Lexical Task, m_{ij} is the number of times the Chinese word w_i co-occurs with the English category c_j—as listed in the cross-lingual word–category co-occurrence matrix (CL-WCCM).

3.2 PMI-based classifier

We calculate the pointwise mutual information between a sense of the target word and a co-occurring word using the following formula:

$$PMI(w_i, c_j) = \log \frac{P(w_i, c_j)}{P(w_i) \times P(c_j)} \qquad (4)$$

$$\text{where } P(w_i, c_j) = \frac{m_{ij}}{\sum_{i,j} m_{ij}} \qquad (5)$$

$$\text{and } P(w_i) = \frac{\sum_j m_{ij}}{\sum_{i,j} m_{ij}} \qquad (6)$$

m_{ij} is the count in the WCCM or CL-WCCM (as described in the previous subsection). For each sense of the target, the sum of the strength of association (PMI) between it and each of the co-occurring words (in a window of ± 5 words) is calculated. The sense with the highest sum is chosen as the intended sense.

$$c_{pmi} = \underset{c_j \in C}{\operatorname{argmax}} \sum_{w_i \in W} PMI(w_i, c_j) \qquad (7)$$

Note that this PMI-based classifier does not capitalize on prior probabilities of the different senses.

4 Data

4.1 English Lexical Sample Task

The English Lexical Sample Task training and test data (Pradhan et al., 2007) have 22281 and 4851 instances respectively for 100 target words (50 nouns and 50 verbs). WordNet 2.1 is used as the sense inventory for most of the target words, but certain words have one or more senses from OntoNotes (Hovy et al., 2006). Many of the fine-grained senses are grouped into coarser senses.

Our approach relies on representing a sense with a number of near-synonymous words, for which a thesaurus is a natural source. Even though the approach can be ported to WordNet[4], there was no easy

[4]The synonyms within a synset, along with its one-hop neighbors and all its hyponyms, can represent that sense.

WORDS	BASELINE	PMI-BASED	NAÏVE BAYES	PRIOR	LIKELIHOOD	NAÏVE BAYES
	TRAINING DATA			TEST DATA		
all	27.8	41.4	50.8	37.4	49.4	52.1
nouns only	25.6	43.4	53.6	18.1	49.6	49.7
verbs only	29.2	38.4	44.5	58.9	49.1	54.7

Table 1: English Lexical Sample Task: Results obtained using the PMI-based classifier on the training data and the naïve Bayes classifier on both training and test data

way of representing OntoNotes senses with near-synonymous words. Therefore, we asked four native speakers of English to map the WordNet and OntoNotes senses of the 100 target words to the *Macquarie Thesaurus* and use it as our sense inventory. We also wanted to examine the effect of using a very coarse sense inventory such as the categories in a published thesaurus (811 in all).

The annotators were presented with a target word, its WordNet/OntoNotes senses, and the Macquarie senses. WordNet senses were represented by synonyms, gloss, and example usages. The OntoNotes senses were described through syntactic patterns and example usages (provided by the task organizers). The Macquarie senses (categories) were described by the category head (a representative word for the category) and five other words in the category. Specifically, words in the same semicolon group[5] as the target were chosen. Annotators 1 and 2 labeled each WordNet/OntoNotes sense of the first 50 target words with one or more appropriate Macquarie categories. Annotators 3 and 4 labeled the senses of the other 50 words. We combined all four annotations into a WordNet–Macquarie mapping file by taking, for each target word, the union of categories chosen by the two annotators.

4.2 English Lexical Substitution Task

The English Lexical Substitution Task has 1710 test instances for 171 target words (nouns, verbs, adjectives, and adverbs) (McCarthy and Navigli, 2007). Some instances were randomly extracted from an Internet corpus, whereas others were selected manually from it. The target word might or might not be part of a multiword expression. The task is not tied to any particular sense inventory.

[5]Words within a semicolon group of a thesaurus tend to be more closely related than words across groups.

4.3 Multilingual Chinese–English Lexical Sample Task

The Multilingual Chinese–English Lexical Sample Task training and test data (Jin et al., 2007) have 2686 and 935 instances respectively for 40 target words (19 nouns and 21 verbs). The instances are taken from a corpus of *People's Daily News*. The organizers used the *Chinese Semantic Dictionary (CSD)*, developed by the Institute of Computational Linguistics, Peking University, both as a sense inventory and bilingual lexicon (to extract a suitable English translation of the target word once the intended Chinese sense is determined).

In order to determine the English translations of Chinese words in context, our system relies on Chinese text and an English thesaurus. As the thesaurus is used as our sense inventory, the first author and a native speaker of Chinese mapped the English translations of the target to appropriate Macquarie categories. We used three examples (from the training data) per English translation for this purpose.

5 Evaluation

5.1 English Lexical Sample Task

Both the naïve Bayes classifier and the PMI-based one were applied to the training data. For each instance, the Macquarie category c that best captures the intended sense of the target was determined. The instance was labeled with all the WordNet senses that are mapped to c in the WordNet–Macquarie mapping file (described earlier in Section 4.1).

5.1.1 Results

Table 1 shows the performances of the two classifiers. The system attempted to label all instances and so we report accuracy values instead of precision and recall. The naïve Bayes classifier performed markedly better in training than the PMI-based one and so was applied to the test data. The table also lists baseline results obtained when a system randomly guesses one of the possible senses for each target word. Note that since this is a completely unsupervised system, it is not privy to the dominant sense of the target words. We do not rely on the ranking of senses in WordNet as that would be an implicit use of the sense-tagged SemCor corpus. Therefore, the most-frequent-sense baseline does not apply. Table 1 also shows results obtained using just the prior probability and likelihood components of the naïve Bayes formula. Note that the combined accuracy is higher than individual components for nouns but not for verbs.

5.1.2 Discussion

The naïve Bayes classifier's accuracy is only about one percentage point lower than that of the best unsupervised system taking part in the task (Pradhan et al., 2007). One reason that it does better than the PMI-based one is that it takes into account prior probabilities of the categories. However, using just the likelihood also outperforms the PMI classifier. This may be because of known problems of using PMI with low frequencies (Manning and Schütze, 1999). In case of verbs, lower combined accuracies compared to when using just prior probabilities suggests that the bag-of-words type features are not very useful. It is expected that more syntactically oriented features will give better results. Using window sizes ($\pm 1, \pm 2$, and ± 10) on the training data resulted in lower accuracies than that obtained using a window of ± 5 words. A smaller window size is probably missing useful co-occurring words, whereas a larger window size is adding words that are not indicative of the target's intended sense.

The use of a sense inventory (*Macquarie Thesaurus*) different from that used to label the data (WordNet) clearly will have a negative impact on the results. The mapping from WordNet/OntoNotes to Macquarie is likely to have some errors. Further, for 19 WordNet/OntoNotes senses, none of the annotators found a thesaurus category close enough in meaning. This meant that our system had no way of correctly disambiguating instances with these senses. Also impacting accuracy is the significantly fine-grained nature of WordNet compared to the thesaurus. For example, following are the three coarse senses for the noun *president* in WordNet: (1) executive officer of a firm or college, (2) the chief executive of a republic, and (3) President of the United States. The last two senses will fall into just one category for most, if not all, thesauri.

	BEST		OOT	
	Acc	Mode Acc	Acc	Mode Acc
all	2.98	4.72	11.19	14.63
Further Analysis				
NMWT	3.22	5.04	11.77	15.03
NMWS	3.32	4.90	12.22	15.26
RAND	3.10	5.20	9.98	13.00
MAN	2.84	4.17	12.61	16.49

Table 2: English Lexical Substitution Task: Results obtained using the PMI-based classifier

5.2 English Lexical Substitution Task

We used the PMI-based classifier[6] for the English Lexical Substitution Task. Once it identifies a suitable thesaurus category as the intended sense for a target, ten candidate substitutes are chosen from that category. Specifically, the category head word and up to nine words in the same semicolon group as the target are selected (words within a semicolon group are closer in meaning). Of the ten candidates, the single-word expression that is most frequent in the BNC is chosen as the best substitute; the motivation is that the annotators, who created the gold standard, were instructed to give preference to single words over multiword expressions as substitutes.

5.2.1 Results

The system was evaluated not only on the best substitute (BEST) but also on how good the top ten candidate substitutes are (OOT). Table 2 presents the results.[7] The system attempted all instances. The table also lists performances of the system on instances where the target is not part of a multiword expression (NMWT), on instances where the substitute is not a multiword expression (NMWS), on instances randomly extracted from the corpus (RAND), and on instances manually selected (MAN).

[6]Due to time constraints, we were able to upload results only with the PMI-based classifier by the task deadline.

[7]The formulae for accuracy and mode accuracy are as described by Pradhan et al. (2007).

Words	Training Data: Baseline micro	Baseline macro	PMI-based micro	PMI-based macro	Naïve Bayes micro	Naïve Bayes macro	Test Data: Prior micro	Prior macro	Likelihood micro	Likelihood macro	Naïve Bayes micro	Naïve Bayes macro
all	33.1	38.3	33.9	40.0	38.5	44.7	35.4	41.7	38.8	44.6	37.5	43.1
nouns only	41.9	43.5	43.6	45.0	49.4	50.5	45.3	47.1	48.1	50.8	50.0	51.6
verbs only	28.0	34.1	28.0	35.6	31.9	39.6	29.1	36.8	32.9	39.0	29.6	35.5

Table 3: Multilingual Chinese–English Lexical Sample Task: Results obtained using the PMI-based classifier on the training data and the naïve Bayes classifier on both training and test data

5.2.2 Discussion

Competitive performance of our DPC-based system on the English Lexical Sample Task and the Chinese–English Lexical Sample Task (see next subsection) suggests that DPCs are useful for sense disambiguation. Poor results on the substitution task can be ascribed to several factors. First, we used the PMI-based classifier that we found later to be markedly less accurate than the naïve Bayes classifier in the other two tasks. Second, the words in the thesaurus categories may not always be near-synonyms; they might just be strongly related. Such words will be poor substitutes for the target. Also, we chose as the best substitute simply the most frequent of the ten candidates. This simple technique is probably not accurate enough. On the other hand, because we chose the candidates without any regard to frequency in a corpus, the system chose certain infrequent words such as *wellnigh* and *ecchymosed*, which were not good candidate substitutes.

5.3 Multilingual Chinese–English Lexical Sample Task

In the Multilingual Chinese–English Lexical Sample Task, both the naïve Bayes classifier and the PMI-based classifier were applied to the training data. For each instance, the Macquarie category, say c, that best captures the intended sense of the target word is determined. Then the instance is labeled with all the English translations that are mapped to c in the English translations–Macquarie mapping file (described earlier in Section 4.3).

5.3.1 Results

Table 3 shows accuracies of the two classifiers. Macro average is the ratio of number of instances correctly disambiguated to the total, whereas micro average is the average of the accuracies achieved on each target word. As in the English Lexical Sample Task, both classifiers, especially the naïve Bayes classifier, perform well above the random baseline. Since the naïve Bayes classifier also performed markedly better than the PMI-based one in training, it was applied to the test data. Table 3 also shows results obtained using just the likelihood and prior probability components of the naïve Bayes classifier on the test data.

5.3.2 Discussion

Our naïve Bayes classifier scored highest of all unsupervised systems taking part in the task (Jin et al., 2007). As in the English Lexical Sample Task, using just the likelihood again outperforms the PMI classifier on the training data. The use of a sense inventory different from that used to label the data again will have a negative impact on the results as the mapping may have a few errors. The annotator believed none of the given Macquarie categories could be mapped to two Chinese Semantic Dictionary senses. This meant that our system had no way of correctly disambiguating instances with these senses.

There were also a number of cases where more than one CSD sense of a word was mapped to the same Macquarie category. This occurred for two reasons: First, the categories of the *Macquarie Thesaurus* act as very coarse senses. Second, for certain target words, the two CSD senses may be different in terms of their syntactic behavior, yet semantically very close (for example, the 'be shocked' and 'shocked' senses of 震惊). This many-to-one mapping meant that for a number of instances more than one English translation was chosen. Since the task required us to provide exactly one answer (and there was no partial credit in case of multiple answers), a category was chosen at random.

6 Conclusion

We implemented a system that uses distributional profiles of concepts (DPCs) for unsupervised word sense disambiguation. We used words in the context as features. Specifically, we used the DPCs to create a naïve Bayes word-sense classifier and a simple PMI-based classifier. Our system attempted three SemEval-2007 tasks. On the training data of the English Lexical Sample Task (task #17) and the Multilingual Chinese–English Lexical Sample Task (task #5), the naïve Bayes classifier achieved markedly better results than the PMI-based classifier and so was applied to the respective test data. On both test and training data of both tasks, the system achieved accuracies well above the random baseline. Further, our system placed best or close to one percentage point from the best among the unsupervised systems. In the English Lexical Substitution Task (task #10), for which there was no training data, we used the PMI-based classifier. The system performed poorly, which is probably a result of using the weaker classifier and a simple brute force method for identifying the substitute among the words in a thesaurus category. Markedly higher-than-baseline performance of the naïve Bayes classifier on task #17 and task #5 suggests that the DPCs are useful for word sense disambiguation.

Acknowledgments

We gratefully acknowledge Xiaodan Zhu, Michael Demko, Christopher Parisien, Frank Rudicz, and Timothy Fowler for mapping training-data labels to categories in the *Macquarie Thesaurus*. We thank Michael Demko, Siddharth Patwardhan, Xinglong Wang, Vivian Tsang, and Afra Alishahi for helpful discussions. This research is financially supported by the Natural Sciences and Engineering Research Council of Canada, the University of Toronto, ONR MURI Contract FCPO.810548265 and Department of Defense contract RD-02-5700.

References

J.R.L. Bernard, editor. 1986. *The Macquarie Thesaurus*. Macquarie Library, Sydney, Australia.

Eduard Hovy, Mitchell Marcus, Martha Palmer, Lance Ramshaw, and Ralph Weischedel. 2006. OntoNotes: The 90% Solution. In *Proceedings of the Human Language Technology Conference of the North American Chapter of the ACL*, pages 57–60, New York, NY.

Shudong Huang and David Graff. 2002. Chinese–english translation lexicon version 3.0. *Linguistic Data Consortium*.

Jay J. Jiang and David W. Conrath. 1997. Semantic similarity based on corpus statistics and lexical taxonomy. In *Proceedings of International Conference on Research on Computational Linguistics*, Taiwan.

Peng Jin, Yunfang Wu, and Shiwen Yu. 2007. SemEval-2007 task 05: Multilingual Chinese-English lexical sample task. In *Proceedings of the Fourth International Workshop on the Evaluation of Systems for the Semantic Analysis of Text*, Prague, Czech Republic.

Christopher D. Manning and Hinrich Schütze. 1999. *Foundations of Statistical Natural Language Processing*. MIT Press, Cambridge, Massachusetts.

Diana McCarthy and Roberto Navigli. 2007. SemEval-2007 task 10: English lexical substitution task. In *Proceedings of the Fourth International Workshop on the Evaluation of Systems for the Semantic Analysis of Text (SemEval-2007)*, Prague, Czech Republic.

Diana McCarthy, Rob Koeling, Julie Weeds, and John Carroll. 2004. Finding predominant senses in untagged text. In *Proceedings of the 42nd Annual Meeting of the Association for Computational Linguistics (ACL-04)*, pages 280–267, Barcelona, Spain.

Saif Mohammad and Graeme Hirst. 2006a. Determining word sense dominance using a thesaurus. In *Proceedings of the 11th Conference of the European Chapter of the Association for Computational Linguistics (EACL)*, Trento, Italy.

Saif Mohammad and Graeme Hirst. 2006b. Distributional measures of concept-distance: A task-oriented evaluation. In *Proceedings of the Conference on Empirical Methods in Natural Language Processing (EMNLP-2006)*, Sydney, Australia.

Saif Mohammad, Iryna Gurevych, Graeme Hirst, and Torsten Zesch. 2007. Cross-lingual distributional profiles of concepts for measuring semantic distance. In *Proceedings of the Joint Conference on Empirical Methods in Natural Language Processing and Computational Natural Language Learning (EMNLP/CoNLL-2007)*, Prague, Czech Republic.

Sameer Pradhan, Martha Palmer, and Edward Loper. 2007. SemEval-2007 task 17: English lexical sample, English SRL and English all-words tasks. In *Proceedings of the Fourth International Workshop on the Evaluation of Systems for the Semantic Analysis of Text (SemEval-2007)*, Prague, Czech Republic.

Philip Resnik. 1998. Wordnet and class-based probabilities. In Christiane Fellbaum, editor, *WordNet: An Electronic Lexical Database*, pages 239–263. The MIT Press, Cambridge, Massachusetts.

David Yarowsky. 1992. Word-sense disambiguation using statistical models of Roget's categories trained on large corpora. In *Proceedings of the 14th International Conference on Computational Linguistics (COLING-92)*, pages 454–460, Nantes, France.

UA-ZBSA: A Headline Emotion Classification through Web Information

Zornitsa Kozareva, Borja Navarro, Sonia Vázquez, Andrés Montoyo
DLSI, University of Alicante
Carretera de San Vicente S/N
Alicante, Spain
03080
zkozareva,borja,svazquez,montoyo@dlsi.ua.es

Abstract

This paper presents a headline emotion classification approach based on frequency and co-occurrence information collected from the World Wide Web. The content words of a headline (nouns, verbs, adverbs and adjectives) are extracted in order to form different bag of word pairs with the joy, disgust, fear, anger, sadness and surprise emotions. For each pair, we compute the Mutual Information Score which is obtained from the web occurrences of an emotion and the content words. Our approach is based on the hypothesis that group of words which co-occur together across many documents with a given emotion are highly probable to express the same emotion.

1 Introduction

The subjective analysis of a text is becoming important for many Natural Language Processing (NLP) applications such as Question Answering, Information Extraction, Text Categorization among others (Shanahan et al., 2006). The resolution of this problem can lead to a complete, realistic and coherent analysis of the natural language, therefore major attention is drawn to the opinion, sentiment and emotion analysis, and to the identification of beliefs, thoughts, feelings and judgments (Quirk et al., 1985), (Wilson and Wiebe, 2005).

The aim of the Affective Text task is to classify a set of news headlines into six types of emotions: "anger", "disgust", "fear", "joy", "sadness" and "surprise". In order to be able to conduct such multi-category analysis, we believe that first we need a comprehensive theory of what a human emotion is, and then we need to understand how the emotion is expressed and transmitted within the natural language. These aspects rise the need of syntactic, semantic, textual and pragmatic analysis of a text (Polanyi and Zaenen, 2006). However, some of the major drawbacks in this field are related to the manual or automatic acquisition of subjective expressions, as well as to the lack of resources in terms of coverage.

For this reason, our current emotion classification approach is based on frequency and co-occurrence bag of word counts collected from the World Wide Web. Our hypothesis is that words which tend to co-occur across many documents with a given emotion are highly probable to express this emotion.

The rest of the paper is organized as follows. In Section 2 we review some of the related work, in Section 3 we describe our web-based emotion classification approach for which we show a walk-through example in Section 4. A discussion of the obtained results can be found in Section 5 and finally we conclude in Section 6.

2 Related work

Our approach for emotion classification is based on the idea of (Hatzivassiloglou and McKeown, 1997) and is similar to those of (Turney, 2002) and (Turney and Littman, 2003). According to Hatzivassiloglou and McKeown (1997), adjectives with the same polarity tended to appear together. For example the negative adjectives "corrupt and brutal" co-

Proceedings of the 4th International Workshop on Semantic Evaluations (SemEval-2007), pages 334–337,
Prague, June 2007.

occur very often.

The idea of tracing polarity through adjective co-occurrence is adopted by Turney (2002) for the binary (positive and negative) classification of text reviews. They take two adjectives, for instance "excellent" and "poor" in a way that the first adjective expresses positive meaning, meanwhile the second one expresses negative. Then, they extract all adjectives from the review text and combine them with "excellent" and "poor". The co-occurrences of these words are searched on the web, and then the Mutual Information score for the two groups of adjectives is measured. When the adjective of the review appear more often with "excellent", then the review is classified as positive, and when the adjectives appear more often with "poor", then the review is classified as negative.

Following Hatzivassiloglou and McKeown (1997) and Turney (2002), we decided to observe how often the words from the headline co-occur with each one of the six emotions. This study helped us deduce information according to which "birthday" appears more often with "joy", while "war" appears more often with "fear".

Some of the differences between our approach and those of Turney (2002) are mentioned below:

- objectives: Turney (2002) aims at binary text classification, while our objective is six class classification of one-liner headlines. Moreover, we have to provide a score between 0 and 100 indicating the presence of an emotion, and not simply to identify what the emotion in the text is. Apart from the difficulty introduced by the multi-category classification, we have to deal with a small number of content words while Turney works with large list of adjectives.

- word class: Turney (2002) measures polarity using only adjectives, however in our approach we consider the noun, the verb, the adverb and the adjective content words. The motivation of our study comes from (Polanyi and Zaenen, 2006), according to which each content word can express sentiment and emotion. In addition to this issue we saw that most of the headlines contain only nouns and verbs, because they express objectivity.

- search engines: Turney (2002) uses the Altavista web browser, while we consider and combine the frequency information acquired from three web search engines.

- word proximity: For the web searches, Turney (2002) uses the NEAR operator and considers only those documents that contain the adjectives within a specific proximity. In our approach, as far as the majority of the query words appear in the documents, the frequency count is considered.

- queries: The queries of Turney (2002) are made up of a pair of adjectives, and in our approach the query contains the content words of the headline and an emotion.

There are other emotion classification approaches that use the web as a source of information. For instance, (Taboada et al., 2006) extracted from the web co-occurrences of adverbs, adjectives, nouns and verbs. Gamon and Aue (2005) were looking for adjectives that did not co-occur at sentence level. (Baroni and Vegnaduzzo, 2004) and (Grefenstette et al., 2004) gathered subjective adjectives from the web calculating the Mutual Information score.

Other important works on sentiment analysis are those of (Wilson et al., 2005) and (Wiebe et al., 2005; Wilson and Wiebe, 2005), who used linguistic information such as syntax and negations to determine polarity. Kim and Hovy (2006) integrated verb information from FrameNet and incorporated it into semantic role labeling.

3 Web co-occurrences

In order to determine the emotions of a headline, we measure the Pointwise Mutual Information (MI) of e_i and cw_j as $MI(e_i, cw_j) = \log_2 \frac{hits(e_i, cw_j)}{hits(e_i) hits(cw_j)}$, where $e_i \in \{anger, disgust, fear, joy, sadness, surprise\}$ and cw_j are the content words of the headline j. For each headline, we have six MI scores which indicate the presence of the emotion. MI is used in our experiments because it provides information about the independence of an emotion and a bag of words.

To collect the frequency and co-occurrence counts of the headline words, we need large and massive data repositories. To surmount the data sparsity problem, we used as corpus the World Wide Web which is constantly growing and daily updated.

Our statistical information is collected from three web search engines: MyWay[1], AlltheWeb[2] and Yahoo[3]. It is interesting to note that the emotion distribution provided by each one of the search engines for the same headline has different scores. For this reason, we decided to compute an intermediate MI score as $aMI = \frac{\sum_{s=1}^{n} MI(e_i, cw_j)}{s}$.

In the trail data, besides the MI score of an emotion and all headline content words, we have calculated the MI for an emotion and each one of the content words. This allowed us to determine the most sentiment oriented word in the headline and then we use this predominant emotion to weight the association sentiment score for the whole text. Unfortunately, we could not provide results for the test data set, due to the high number of emotion-content word pairs and the increment in processing time and returned responses of the search engines.

4 Example for Emotion Classification

As a walk through example, we use the *Mortar assault leaves at least 18 dead* headline which is taken from the trial data. The first step in our emotion classification approach consists in the determination of the part-of-speech tags for the one-liner. The non-content words are stripped away, and the rest of the words are taken for web queries. To calculate the MI score of a headline, we query the three search engines combining "mortar, assault, leave, dead" with the anger, joy, disgust, fear, sadness and surprise emotions. The obtained results are normalized in a range from 0 to 100 and are shown in Table 1.

	MyWay	AllWeb	Yahoo	Av.	G.Stand.
anger	19	22	24	22	22
disgust	5	6	7	6	2
fear	44	50	53	49	60
joy	15	19	20	18	0
sadness	28	36	36	33	64
surprise	4	5	6	5	0

Table 1: Performance of the web-based emotion classification for a trail data headline

[1]www.myway.com
[2]www.alltheweb.com
[3]www.yahoo.com

As can be seen from the table, the three search engines provide different sentiment distribution for the same headline, therefore in our final experiment we decided to calculate intermediate MI. Comparing our results to those of the gold standard, we can say that our approach detects significantly well the fear, sadness and angry emotions.

5 Results and Discussion

Table 2 shows the obtained results for the affective test data. The low performance of our approach is explainable by the minimal knowledge we have used. An interesting conclusion deduced from the trail and test emotion data is that the system detects better the negative feelings such as anger, disgust, fear and sadness, in comparison to the positive emotions such as joy and surprise. This makes us believe that according to the web most of the word-emotion combinations we queried are related to the expression of negative emotions.

UA-ZBSA	Fine-grained	Coarse-grained		
	Pearson	Acc.	P.	R.
Anger	23.20	86.40	12.74	21.66
Disgust	16.21	97.30	0.00	0.00
Fear	23.15	75.30	16.23	26.27
Joy	2.35	81.80	40.00	2.22
Sadness	12.28	88.90	25.00	0.91
Surprise	7.75	84.60	13.70	16.56

Table 2: Performance of the web-based emotion classification for the whole test data set

In the test run, we could not apply the emotion-word weighting, however we believe that it has a significant impact over the final performance. Presently, we were looking for the distribution of all content words and the emotions, but in the future we would like to transform all words into adjectives and then conduct web queries.

Furthermore, we would like to combine the results from the web emotion classification with the polarity information given by SentiWordNet[4]. A-priory we want to disambiguate the headline content words and to determine the polarities of the words and their corresponding senses. For instance, the adjective "new" has eleven senses, where new#a#3 and new#a#5 express negativism, new#a#4 and new#a#9 positivism and the rest of the senses are objective.

[4]http://sentiwordnet.isti.cnr.it/

So far we did not consider the impact of valence shifter (Polanyi and Zaenen, 2006) and we were unable to detect that a negative adverb or adjective transforms the emotion from positive into negative and vice versa. We are also interested in studying how to conduct queries not as a bag of words but bind by syntactic relations (Wilson et al., 2005).

6 Conclusion

Emotion classification is a challenging and difficult task in Natural Language Processing. For our first attempt to detect the amount of angry, fear, sadness, surprise, disgust and joy emotions, we have presented a simple web co-occurrence approach. We have combined the frequency count information of three search engines and we have measured the Mutual Information score between a bag of content words and emotion.

According to the yielded results, the presented approach can determine whether one sentiment is predominant or not, and most of the correct sentiment assignments correspond to the negative emotions. However, we need to improve the approach in many aspects and to incorporate more knowledge-rich resources, as well as to tune the 0-100 emotion scale.

Acknowledgements

This research has been funded by QALLME number FP6 IST-033860 and TEX-MESS number TIN2006-15265-C06-01.

References

Marco Baroni and Stefano Vegnaduzzo. 2004. Identifying subjective adjectives through web-based mutual information. In Ernst Buchberger, editor, *Proceedings of KONVENS 2004*, pages 17–24.

Michael Gamon and Anthony Aue. 2005. Automatic identification of sentiment vocabulary: exploiting low association with known sentiment terms. In *Proceedings of the Workshop on Feature Engineering for Machine Learning in Natural Language Processing (ACL 2005)*, pages 57–64.

Gregory Grefenstette, Yan Qu, James G. Shanahana, and David A. Evans. 2004. Coupling niche browsers and affect analysis for an opinion mining application. In *Proceeding of RIAO-04*.

Vasileios Hatzivassiloglou and Kathleen R. McKeown. 1997. Predicting the semantic orientation of adjectives. In *Proceedings of the eighth conference on European chapter of the Association for Computational Linguistics (EACL)*.

Soo-Min Kim and Eduard Hovy. 2006. Extracting opinions, opinion holders, and topics expressed in online news media text. In *Proceedings of the Workshop on Sentiment and Subjectivity in Text*, pages 1–8.

Livia Polanyi and Annie Zaenen. 2006. Contextual valence shifter. In James G. Shanahan, Yan Qu, and Janyce Wiebe, editors, *Computing Attitude and Affect in Text: Theory and Applications*, chapter 1, pages 1–10. Springer.

R. Quirk, S. Greenbaum, G. Leech, and J. Svartvik. 1985. *A Comprehensive Grammar of the English Language*. Longman.

James G. Shanahan, Yan Qu, and Janyce Wiebe. 2006. *Computing Attitude and Affect in Text: Theory and Applications*. Springer.

Maite Taboada, Caroline Anthony, and Kimberly Voll. 2006. Methods for creating semantic orientation databases. In *Proceeding of LREC-06, the 5th International Conference on Language Resources and Evaluation*, pages 427–432.

Peter D. Turney and Michael L. Littman. 2003. Measuring praise and criticism: Inference of semantic orientation from association. *ACM Transactions on Information Systems*, 21(4):315–346.

Peter D. Turney. 2002. Thumbs up or thumbs down? semantic orientation applied to unsupervised classification of reviews. In *Proceedings of the 40th Annual Meeting of the Association for Computational Linguistics (ACL)*, pages 417–424.

Janyce Wiebe, Theresa Wilson, and Claire Cardie. 2005. Annotating expressions of opinions and emotions in language. *Language Resources and Evaluation (formerly Computers and the Humanities)*, 39(2-3):165–210.

Theresa Wilson and Janyce Wiebe. 2005. Annotating attributions and private states. In Ann Arbor, editor, *Proceedings of the Workshop on Frontiers in Corpus Annotation II: Pie in the Sky*, pages 53–60.

Theresa Wilson, Janyce Wiebe, and Paul Hoffmann. 2005. Recognizing contextual polarity in phrase-level sentiment analysis. In *Proceedings of the conference on Human Language Technology and Empirical Methods in Natural Language Processing*, pages 347–354.

UA-ZSA: Web Page Clustering on the basis of Name Disambiguation

Zornitsa Kozareva, Sonia Vazquez, Andres Montoyo
DLSI, University of Alicante
Carretera de San Vicente S/N
Alicante, Spain
03080
zkozareva,svazquez,montoyo@dlsi.ua.es

Abstract

This paper presents an approach for web page clustering. The different underlying meanings of a name are discovered on the basis of the title of the web page, the body content, the common named entities across the documents and the sub-links. This information is feeded into a K-Means clustering algorithm which groups together the web pages that refer to the same individual.

1 Introduction

Ambiguity is the task of building up multiple alternative linguistic structures for a single input. Most of the approaches focus on word sense disambiguation (WSD), where the sense of a word has to be determined depending on the context in which it is used.

The same problem arises for named entities shared by different people or for grandsons named after their grandparents. For instance, querying the name "Michael Hammond" in the World Wide Web where there are huge quantities of massive and unstructured data, a search engine retrieves thousands of documents related to this name. However, there are several individuals sharing the name "Michael Hammon". One is a biology professor at the University of Arizona, another is at the University of Warwick, there is a mathematician from Toronto among others. The question is which one of these referents we are actually looking for and interested in. Presently, to be able to answer to this question, we have to skim the content of the documents and retrieve the correct answers on our own.

To automate this process, the named entities can be disambiguated and the different underlying meanings of the name can be found. On the basis of this information, the web pages can be clustered together and organized in a hierarchical structure which can ease the documents' browsing. This is also the objective of the Web People Search (WePS) task (Artiles et al., 2007). What makes the WePS task even more challenging is the fact that in contrast to WSD where the number of senses of a word are predefined, in WePS we do not know the exact number of different individuals.

For the resolution of the WePS task, we have developed a web page clustering approach using the title and the body content of the web pages. In addition, we group together the documents that share many location, person and organization names, as well as those that point out to the same sub-links.

The rest of the paper is organized as follows. In Section 2 we describe various approaches for name disambiguation and discrimination. Our approach is shown in Section 3, the obtained results and a discussion are provided in Section 4 and finally we conclude in Section 5.

2 Related Work

Early work in the field of name disambiguation is that of (Bagga and Baldwin, 1998) who proposed cross-document coreference resolution algorithm which uses vector space model to resolve the ambiguities between people sharing the same name. The approach is evaluated on 35 different mentions of John Smith and reaches 85% f-score.

Mann and Yarowski (2003) developed an unsu-

Proceedings of the 4th International Workshop on Semantic Evaluations (SemEval-2007), pages 338–341,
Prague, June 2007.

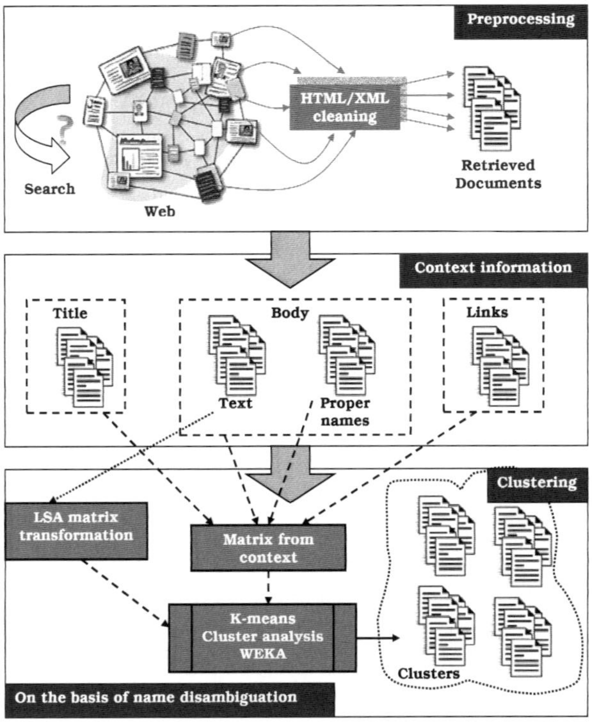

Figure 1: Architecture of the WePS System

pervised approach to name discrimination where biographical features (age, date of birth), familiar relationships (wife, son, daughter) and associations (country, company, organization) are considered. Therefore, in our approach we use person, organization and location names in order to construct a social similarity network between two documents.

Another unsupervised clustering technique for name discrimination of web pages is that of Pedersen and Kulkarni (2007). They used contextual vectors derived from bigrams, and measured the impact of several association measures. During the evaluation, some names were easily discriminable compared to others categories for which was even difficult to find and obtain discriminative feature. We worked with their unigram model (Purandare and Pedersen, 2004) to cluster the web pages using the text content between the title tags.

3 Web Person Disambiguation

Our web people clustering approach is presented in Figure 1 and consists of the following steps:

- HTML cleaning: all *html* tags are stripped away, the *javascript* code is eliminated, the non closed WePS tags are repaired, the missing begin/end body tags are included and then the content between the title, the body and the anchor tags is extracted.

- name matching: the location, person and organization names in the body texts are identified with the GATE[1] system (Cunningham, 2005). Each named entity of a document is matched with its corresponding named entity category from the rest of the web pages. This information is used to calculate the social semantic similarity of the person, the location and the organization names. Our hypothesis is that documents with similar names tend to refer to the same individual. The output of this module is a matrix with binary values, where 1 stands for the documents which share more than the half of their proper names, and 0 otherwise.

- links: for each document, we extract the links situated between the anchor tags. Since the links are too specific, we wrote an url function which transform a given web page d_1 with URL http://www.cs.ualberta.ca/~lindek/index.htm into www.cs.ualberta.ca/~lindek, and the web page d_2 with URL http://www.cs.ualberta.ca/~lindek/demos.htm into www.cs.ualberta.ca/~lindek. According to our approach, the two web pages d_1 and d_2 are linked to each other if their link structures (LS) intersect, that is $LS(d1) \bigcap LS(d2) \neq 0$. The output of this module is a matrix with binary values, where 1 stands for two web pages having more than 3 links in common and 0 otherwise.

- titles: for each document, we extract the text between the title tags. We create a unigram matrix which is feed into SenseClusters[2]. We use automatic cluster stopping criteria with the gap statistics which groups the web pages into several clusters according to the context of the titles. From the obtained clusters, we generate a new matrix with binary values, where 1 corresponds to the documents which were put in the

[1] http://sourceforge.net/projects/gate

[2] http://marimba.d.umn.edu/cgi-bin/SC-cgi/index.cgi

same cluster according to SenseClusters and 0 otherwise.

- bodies: the text between the body tags is extracted, tokenized and the part-of-speech (POS) tags [3] are determined. The original text is transformed by encoding the POS tag information as follows: "*water#v the#det flowers#n and#conj pass#v me#pron the#det glass#n of#prep water#n*". This corpus transformation is done, because we want the Latent Semantic Analysis (LSA) module to consider the syntactic categories of the words and to construct a more reliable semantic space. For instance, in the example above, there are two different representations of *water*: the noun and the verb, while without the corpus transformation LSA sees only the string *water*.

- LSA[4]: the semantic similarity score for the web-pages is calculated with Latent Semantic Analysis (LSA). From the encoded body texts, we build up a matrix, where the rows represent the words of the web-page collection, the columns stand for the web-pages we want to cluster and the cells show the number of times a word of the corpus occurs in a web page. In order to reduce the noise and the data sparsity, we apply the Singular Value Decomposition algorithm by reducing the original vector space into 300 dimensions. The output of the LSA module is a matrix, which represents the semantic similarity among the web pages.

- knowledge combination: the outputs of the name matching, link, title and body modules are combined into a new matrix 100×400 dimensional matrix. The rows correspond to the number of web pages and the columns represent the obtained values of the link, title, body and name modules. This matrix is fed into the K-means clustering algorithm which determines the final web page clustering.

- K-means[5]: the clustering of N web pages into K disjoint subsets S_j containing N_j data points is done by the minimization of the sum-of-squares criterion $J = \sum_{j=1}^{K} \sum_{n \in S_j} |x_n - mu_j|^2$, where x_n is a vector representing the nth data point and mu_j is the geometric centroid of the data points in S_j. The information matrix from which the web page clustering is performed includes the similarity information for the title, link, proper name and body. The current implementation of K-means (Witten and Frank, 2005) does not have an automatic cluster stopping criteria, therefore the number of clusters is set up manually.

[3] http://www.ims.uni-stuttgart.de/projekte/corplex/TreeTagger/

[4] infomap-nlp.sourceforge.net/

[5] http://www.cs.waikato.ac.nz/ml/weka/

4 Results and Discussion

Table 1 shows the obtained results for the test data set. The average performance of our system is 56% and we ranked on 10-th position from 16 participating teams. Although, we have used different sources of information and various approximations, in the future we have to surmount a number of obstacles.

One of the limitations comes from the usage of the text snippets situated between the body tags. There are a number of web pages which do not contain any text. The semantic space for these documents cannot be built with LSA and their similarity score is zero.

Despite the fact that we have eliminated the stop words from the documents and we have transformed the web pages by encoding the syntactic categories, the classification power of LSA was different for the ambiguous names and for the web pages. To some extend this is due to the varying number of words in the web pages. In the future, we want to conduct experiments with a fixed context windows for all documents.

In this task, the number of senses (e.g. number of different individuals that share the same name) is unknown, and one of the major drawbacks in our approach is related to the setting up of the number of clusters. The K-Means clustering algorithm we used, did not include an automatic cluster stopping criteria, and we had to set up the number of clusters manually. To be able to do that, we have observed the average number of clusters per name in the trial data. We have evaluated the performance of our approach with several different numbers of clusters. According to the obtained results, the best clusters are 25 and 50. We used the same number

Name	Purity	Inverse Purity	F α=0.5	F α=0.2
Mark Johnson	0,55	0,74	0,63	0,69
Sharon Goldwater	0,96	0,23	0,37	0,27
Robert Moore	0,36	0,67	0,47	0,57
Leon Barrett	0,62	0,51	0,56	0,52
Dekang Lin	0,99	0,43	0,60	0,49
Stephen Clark	0,52	0,75	0,62	0,69
Frank Keller	0,38	0,67	0,48	0,58
Jerry Hobbs	0,54	0,63	0,58	0,61
James Curran	0,53	0,61	0,57	0,59
Chris Brockett	0,73	0,40	0,51	0,44
Thomas Fraser	0,66	0,57	0,61	0,58
John Nelson	0,68	0,76	0,72	0,74
James Hamilton	0,56	0,60	0,58	0,59
William Dickson	0,59	0,78	0,67	0,73
James Morehead	0,36	0,64	0,46	0,56
Patrick Killen	0,56	0,69	0,62	0,66
George Foster	0,46	0,70	0,56	0,64
James Davidson	0,58	0,71	0,64	0,68
Arthur Morgan	0,77	0,47	0,59	0,51
Thomas Kirk	0,26	0,90	0,41	0,60
Patrick Killen	0,56	0,69	0,62	0,66
Harry Hughes	0,66	0,54	0,59	0,56
Jude Brown	0,64	0,63	0,64	0,63
Stephan Johnson	0,56	0,80	0,66	0,73
Marcy Jackson	0,40	0,73	0,52	0,63
Karen Peterson	0,56	0,72	0,63	0,68
Neil Clark	0,68	0,36	0,47	0,40
Jonathan Brooks	0,53	0,76	0,63	0,70
Violet Howard	0,58	0,75	0,65	0,71
Global average	0,58	0,64	0,58	0,60

Table 1: Evaluation results

of clusters for the test data, however this is a rough parameter estimation.

5 Conclusion

Person name disambiguation is a very important task whose resolution can improve the performance of the search engine by grouping together web pages which refer to different individuals that share the same name.

For our participation in the WePS task, we presented a name disambiguation approach which uses only the information extracted from the web pages. We conducted an experimental study with the trail data set, according to which the combination of the title, the body, the proper names and sub-links reaches the best performance. Our current approach can be improved with the incorporation of automatic cluster stopping criteria.

So far we did not take advantage of the document ranking and the returned snippets, but we want to incorporate this information by measuring the snippet similarity on the basis of relevant domain information (Kozareva et al., 2007).

Acknowledgements

Many thanks to Ted Pedersen for useful comments and suggestions. This work was partially funded by the European Union under the project QALLME number FP6 IST-033860 and by the Spanish Ministry of Science and Technology under the project TEX-MESS number TIN2006-15265-C06-01.

References

J. Artiles, J. Gonzalo, and S. Sekine. 2007. The semeval-2007 weps evaluation: Establishing a benchmark for the web people search task. In *Proceedings of Semeval 2007, Association for Computational Linguistics*.

A. Bagga and B. Baldwin. 1998. Entity-based cross-document coreferencing using the vector space model. In *Proceedings of ACL*, pages 79–85.

H. Cunningham. 2005. Information Extraction, Automatic. *Encyclopedia of Language and Linguistics, 2nd Edition*.

Z. Kozareva, S. Vazquez, and A. Montoyo. 2007. The usefulness of conceptual representation for the identification of semantic variability expressions. In *Proceedings of the Eighth International Conference on Intelligent Text Processing and Computational Linguistics, (CICLing-2007)*.

G. Mann and D. Yarowsky. 2003. Unsupervised personal name disambiguation. In *Proceedings of the seventh conference on Natural language learning at HLT-NAACL 2003*, pages 33–40.

T. Pedersen and A. Kulkarni. 2007. Discovering identities in web contexts with unsupervised clustering. In *Proceedings of the IJCAI-2007 Workshop on Analytics for Noisy Unstructured Text Data*.

A. Purandare and T. Pedersen. 2004. Senseclusters - finding clusters that represent word senses. In *AAAI*, pages 1030–1031.

I. Witten and E. Frank. 2005. *Data Mining: Practical machine learning tools and techniques*, volume 2. Morgan Kaufmann.

UBC-ALM: Combining k-NN with SVD for WSD

Eneko Agirre and Oier Lopez de Lacalle
IXA NLP Group
University of the Basque Country
Donostia, Basque Country
{e.agirre, jibloleo}@ehu.es

Abstract

This work describes the University of the Basque Country system (UBC-ALM) for lexical sample and all-words WSD subtasks of SemEval-2007 task 17, where it performed in the second and fifth positions respectively. The system is based on a combination of k-Nearest Neighbor classifiers, with each classifier learning from a distinct set of features: local features (syntactic, collocations features), topical features (bag-of-words, domain information) and latent features learned from a reduced space using Singular Value Decomposition.

1 Introduction

Our group (UBC-ALM) participated in the lexical sample and all-words WSD subtasks of SemEval-2007 task 17. We applied a combination of different k-Nearest Neighbor (k-NN) classifiers. Each classifier manages different information sources (features), making the combination a powerful solution. This algorithm was previously tested on the datasets from previous editions of Senseval (Agirre et al., 2005; Agirre et al., 2006). Before submission, the performance of the system was tested on the SemEval lexical sample training data. For learning we use a rich set of features, including latent features obtained from a reduced space using Singular Value Decomposition (SVD).

This paper is organized as follows. The learning features are presented in section 2, and the learning algorithm and the combinations of single k-NNs are given in section 3. Section 4 focuses on the tuning experiments. Finally, section 5 summarizes the official results and some conclusions.

2 Feature set

We relied on an extensive set of features of different types, obtained by means of different tools and resources. We defined two main groups: the **original features** extracted directly from the text, and the **SVD features** obtained after applying SVD decomposition and projecting the original features into the new semantic space (Agirre et al., 2005).

2.1 Original features

Local collocations: bigrams and trigrams formed with the words around the target. These features are constituted by lemmas, word-forms, or PoS tags[1]. Other local features are those formed with the previous/posterior lemma/word-form in the context.

Syntactic dependencies: syntactic dependencies were extracted using heuristic patterns, and regular expressions defined with the PoS tags around the target[2]. The following relations were used: object, subject, noun-modifier, preposition, and sibling.

Bag-of-words features: we extract the lemmas of the content words in the whole context, and in a $\pm$4-word window around the target. We also obtain salient bigrams in the context, with the methods and the software described in (Pedersen, 2001).

Domain features: The WordNet Domains resource was used to identify the most relevant domains in the context. Following the relevance formula presented in (Magnini and Cavagliá, 2000), we defined 2 feature types: (1) the most relevant domain, and (2) a list of domains above a predefined threshold[3].

[1]The PoS tagging was performed with the fnTBL toolkit (Ngai and Florian, 2001).

[2]This software was kindly provided by David Yarowsky's group, from Johns Hopkins University.

[3]The software to obtain the relevant domains was kindly provided by Gerard Escudero's group, from Universitat Politec-

Proceedings of the 4th International Workshop on Semantic Evaluations (SemEval-2007), pages 342–345,
Prague, June 2007.

2.2 SVD features

Singular Value Decomposition (SVD) is an interesting solution to the sparse data problem. This technique reduces the dimensions of the vectorial space finding correlations and collapsing features. It also gives the chance to use unlabeled data as an additional source of correlations.

$M \ni \mathbf{R}^{m \times n}$, a matrix of features-by-document is built from the training corpus and decomposed into three matrices, as shown in Eq. (1). U and V, row and column matrix, respectively, have orthonormal columns and Σ is a diagonal matrix which contains k eigenvalues in descending order.

$$M = U \Sigma V^T = \sum_{i=1}^{k=min\{m,n\}} \sigma_i u_i v i^T \quad (1)$$

We used the *singular value* matrix (Σ) and the *column* matrix (U) to create a projection matrix, which is used to project the data (represented in features vectors) from the original space to a reduced space. Prior to that we selected the first p columns from the Σ and U matrices ($p < k$): $\vec{t_p} = \vec{t}^T U_p \Sigma_p^{-1}$

We have explored two different variants in order to build a matrix, and obtain the SVD features:

SVD One Matrix per Target word (SVD-OMT). For each word (i) we extracted all the features from the given training (test) corpus, (ii) built the feature-by-document matrix from training corpus, (iii) decomposed it with SVD, and (iv) project all the training (test) data. Note that this variant has been only used in the lexical sample task due to its costly computational requirements.

SVD Single Matrix for All target words (SVD-SMA): (i) we extracted bag-of-words features from the British National Corpus (BNC) (Leech, 1992), (ii) built the feature-by-document matrix, (iii) decompose it with SVD, and (iv) project all the data (train/test).

3 Learning Algorithm

The machine learning (ML) algorithm presented in this section rely on the previously described features. Each occurrence or instance is represented by the features found in the context (f_i). Given an occurrence of a word, the ML method below returns a weight for each sense $(weight(s_k))$. The sense with maximum weight will be selected.

We use a set of combination of the k**-Nearest Neighbor** (k-NN) to tag the target words in both the lexical sample and all-words tasks.

3.1 k-Nearest Neighbor

k-NN is a memory-based learning method, where the neighbors are the k most similar contexts, represented by feature vectors ($\vec{c_i}$), of the test vector ($\vec{f}$). The similarity among instances is measured by the cosine of their vectors. The test instance is labeled with the sense obtaining the maximum sum of the weighted votes of the k most similar contexts. The vote is weighted depending on its (neighbor) position in the ordered rank, with the closest being first. Eq. (2) formalizes k-NN, where C_i corresponds to the sense label of the i-th closest neighbor.

$$\arg\max_{S_j} = \sum_{i=1}^{k} \begin{cases} \frac{1}{i} & \text{if } C_i = S_j \\ 0 & \text{otherwise} \end{cases} \quad (2)$$

3.2 k-NN combinations and feature splits

As seen in section 2 we use a variety of heterogeneous sets of features. Our previous experience has shown that splitting the problem up into more coherent spaces, training different classifiers in each feature space, and then combining them into a single classifier is a good way to improve the results (Agirre et al., 2005; Agirre et al., 2006). Depending on the feature type (original features or features extracted from SVD projection) we split different sets of feature spaces. In total we tried 10 features spaces.

For the **original features**:

- **all_feats**: Extracted all original features.
- **all_notdom**: All original features except domain features.
- **local**: All the original features except domain and bag-of-words features.
- **topic**: The sum of bag-of-words and domain features.
- **bow**: Bag-of-word features.
- **dom**: Domain features.

nica de Catalunya

Combination	accuracy
all_feats+topic+local+SVD-OMT[all_feats]+SVD-OMT[topic]+SVD-OMT[local]	88.8
all_feats+all_notdom+topic+local+SVD-SMA+SVD-OMT[all_feats]+SVD-OMT[topic]+SVD-OMT[local]	88.7
all_feats+topic+local+SVD-SMA+SVD-OMT[all_feats]+SVD-OMT[topic]+SVD-OMT[local]	88.5
all_notdom+topic+local+SVD-SMA+SVD-OMT[all_feats]+SVD-OMT[topic]+SVD-OMT[local]	88.5
all_feats+all_notdom+topic+local	88.4
all_notdom+local+SVD-SMA	88.3
all_feats+all_notdom+local+SVD-SMA	88.2
all_notdom+topic+local	88.1
all_feats+topic+local	88.1
word-by-word optimization	**89.5**

Table 1: Result for the best k-NN combinations in 3 fold cross-validation SemEval lexical sample.

For the **SVD features**:

- **SVD-OMT[all_feats]**: OMT matrix applied to all original features.
- **SVD-OMT[local]**: OMT matrix to the **local** original features.
- **SVD-OMT[topic]**: OMT matrix to the **topic** original features.
- **SVD-SMA**: Features obtained from the projection of **bow** features with the SMA matrix.

Depending on the ML method one can try different approaches to combine classifiers. In this work, we exploited the fact that a k-NN classifier can be seen as k points casting each one vote. The votes are weigthed by the inverse ratio of its position in the rank $(k - r_i + 1)/k$, where r_i is the rank. Each of the k-NN classifiers is trained on a different feature space and then combined.

4 Experiments on training data

We optimized and tuned the system differently for each kind of tasks. We will examine each in turn.

4.1 Optimization for the lexical sample task

For the lexical sample task we only use the training data provided. We tuned the classifiers using 3 fold cross-validation on the SemEval lexical sample training data. We tried to optimize several parameters: number of neighbors, SVD dimensions and best combination of the single k-NNs. We set k as one of $1, 3, 5$ and 7, and the SVD dimension (d) as one of $50, 100, 200$ and 300. We also fixed the best combination. This is the optimization procedure we followed:

1. For each single classifier and feature set (see section 2), check each parameter combination.
2. Fix the parameters for each single classifier. In our case, $k = 5$ and $k = 7$ had similar results, so we postponed the decision. $d = 200$ was the best dimension for all classifiers, except SVD-OMT[topic] which was $d = 50$.
3. For the best parameter settings ($k = 5; k = 7$ and $d = 200$; $d = 50$ when SVD-OMT[topic]) make *a priori* meaningful combinations (due to CPU requirements, not all combination were feasible).
4. Choose the x best combination overall, and optimize word by word among these combination. We set $x = 8$ for this work, k was fixed in 5, and $d = 200$ (except with SVD-OMT[topic] which was $d = 50$).

Table 1 shows the best results for 3 fold cross-validation in SemEval lexical sample training corpus. The figures show that optimizing each word the performance increases 0.7 percentage points over the best combination.

4.2 Optimization for the all-words task

To train the classifiers for the all-words task we just used Semcor (Miller et al., 1993). In (Agirre et al., 2006) we already tested our approach on the Senseval-3 all-words task. The best performance for the Senseval-3 all-words task was obtained with $k = 5$ and $d = 200$, but we decided to to perform further experiments to search for the best combination. We tested the performance of the combination of single k-NN training on Semcor and testing both on the Senseval-3 all-words data (cf. Table 2) and on the training data from SemEval-2007 lexical sample (cf. Table 3).

Note that tables 2 and 3 show contradictory results. Given that in SemEval-2007 lexical sample

Combination	rec.	prec.
all_feats+local+notbow	0.685	0.685
all_feats+local+SVD-SMA	0.679	0.679
all_feats+topic+local+SVD-SMA	0.689	0.689

Table 2: Results for the best k-NN combinations in Senseval-3 all-words, using Semcor as training corpus.

Combination	rec.	prec.
all_feats+SVD-SMA	0.666	0.666
all_feats+local+SVD-SMA	0.661	0.661
all_feats+topic+local+SVD-SMA	0.664	0.664

Table 3: Results for the best k-NN combinations in training part of SemEval lexical sample, using Semcor as training corpus.

Task	Method	Rank	rec.	prec.
LS	Best	1	0.887	0.887
LS	UBC-ALM	2	0.869	0.869
LS	Baseline	-	0.780	0.780
AW	Best	1	0.591	0.591
AW	k-NN combination	5	0.544	0.544
AW	Baseline	-	0.514	0.514

Table 4: Official results for SemEval-2007 task 17 lexical sample and all-words subtasks.

the senses are more coarse grained, we decided to take the best combination on Senseval-3 all-words for the final submission.

5 Results and conclusions

Table 4 shows the performance obtained by our system and the winning systems in the SemEval lexical sample and all-words evaluation. On the lexical sample evaluation our system is 2.6 lower than the cross-validation evaluation. This can be a sign of a slight overfitting on the training data. All in all we ranked second over 13 systems.

Our all-words system did not perform so well. Our system is around 4.7 points below the winning system, ranking 5th from a total of 14, and 3 points above the baseline given by the organizers. This is a disappointing result when compared to our previous work on Senseval-3 all-words where we were able to beat the best official results (Agirre et al., 2006). Note that the test set was rather small, with 465 occurrences only, which might indicate that the performance differences are not statistically significant. We plan to further investigate the reasons for our results.

Acknowledgments

We wish to thank to David Martínez for helping us extracting learning features. This work has been partially funded by the Spanish education ministry (project KNOW). Oier Lopez de Lacalle is supported by a PhD grant from the Basque Government.

References

E. Agirre, O.Lopez de Lacalle, and David Martínez. 2005. Exploring feature spaces with svd and unlabeled data for Word Sense Disambiguation. In *Proceedings of the Conference on Recent Advances on Natural Language Processing (RANLP'05)*, Borovets, Bulgaria.

E. Agirre, O. Lopez de Lacalle, and D. Martínez. 2006. Exploring feature spaces with svd and unlabeled data for Word Sense Disambiguation. In *Proceedings of the XXII Conference of Sociedad Espaola para el Procesamiento del Lenguaje Natural (SEPLN'06)*, Zaragoza, Spain.

G. Leech. 1992. 100 million words of English: the British National Corpus. *Language Research*, 28(1):1–13.

B. Magnini and G. Cavagliá. 2000. Integrating subject field codes into WordNet. In *Proceedings of the Second International LREC Conference*, Athens, Greece.

G.A. Miller, C. Leacock, R. Tengi, and R.Bunker. 1993. A Semantic Concordance. In *Proceedings of the ARPA Human Language Technology Workshop. Distributed as* Human Language Technology *by San Mateo, CA: Morgan Kaufmann Publishers.*, pages 303–308, Princeton, NJ.

G. Ngai and R. Florian. 2001. Transformation-Based Learning in the Fast Lane. *Proceedings of the Second Conference of the North American Chapter of the Association for Computational Linguistics, pages 40-47, Pittsburgh, PA, USA.*

T. Pedersen. 2001. A Decision Tree of Bigrams is an Accurate Predictor of Word Sense. In *Proceedings of the Second Meeting of the North American Chapter of the Association for Computational Linguistics (NAACL-01)*, Pittsburgh, PA.

UBC-AS: A Graph Based Unsupervised System for Induction and Classification

Eneko Agirre and Aitor Soroa
IXA NLP Group
UBC
Donostia, Basque Contry
{e.agirre,a.soroa}@si.ehu.es

Abstract

This paper describes a graph-based unsupervised system for induction and classification. The system performs a two stage graph based clustering where a co-occurrence graph is first clustered to compute similarities against contexts. The context similarity matrix is pruned and the resulting associated graph is clustered again by means of a random-walk type algorithm. The system relies on a set of parameters that have been tuned to fit the corpus data. The system has participated in tasks 2 and 13 of the SemEval-2007 competition, on word sense induction and Web people search, respectively, with mixed results.

1 Introduction

This paper describes a graph-based unsupervised system for induction and classification. Given a set of data to be classified, the system first induces the possible clusters and then clusters the data accordingly. The paper is organized as follows. Section 2 gives an description of the general framework of our system. Sections 3 and 4 presents in more detail the implementation of the framework for the Semeval-2007 WEPS task (Artiles et al., 2007) and Semeval-2007 sense induction task (Agirre and Soroa, 2007), respectively. Section 5 presents the results obtained in both tasks, and Section 6 draws some conclusions.

2 A graph based system for unsupervised classification

The system performs a two stage graph based clustering where a co-occurrence graph is first clustered to compute similarities against contexts. The context similarity matrix is pruned and the resulting associated graph is clustered again by means of a random-walk type algorithm. We will see both steps in turn.

First step: calculating hub score vectors

In a first step, and for each entity to be clustered, a graph consisting on context word co-occurrences is built. Vertices in the co-occurrence graph are words and two vertices share an edge whenever they co-occur in the same context. Besides, each edge receives a weight, which indicates how strong the incident vertices relate each other.

As shown in (Véronis, 2004), co-occurrence graphs exhibit the so called small world structure (Watts and Strogatz, 1998) and, thus, they contain highly dense subgraphs which will represent the different clusters the entity may have. For identifying these clusters we have implemented two algorithms based on the notion of centrality of the vertices, where some highly dense vertices, called "hubs", are chosen as representatives of each cluster. The algorithms are the HyperLex algorithm (Véronis, 2004) and the HITS algorithm (Kleinberg, 1999).

Once the hubs are identified, the minimum spanning tree (MST) of the co-occurrence graph is computed. The root elements of the MST are precisely the induced hubs and each vertex of the original graph —and, thus, each word of the corpus— is attached to exactly one of these hubs, at a certain distance. Note that the MST can be considered as a single link clustering over the co-occurrence graph.

The original contexts are then taken one by one and scored according to the MST in the following way: each word in the context receives a set of score vectors, with one score per hub, where all scores are

Proceedings of the 4th International Workshop on Semantic Evaluations (SemEval-2007), pages 346–349,
Prague, June 2007.

0 except for the one corresponding to the hub where it is placed[1], which will receive a socre $d(h_i, v)$, which is the distance between the hub h_i and the node representing the word v in the MST. Thus, $d(h_i, v)$ assigns a score of 1 to hubs and the score decreases as the nodes move away from the hub in the MST. As a consequence, each context receives a hub score vector, which is just the sum of the score vectors of all the words in the context.

At this point we can use the hub score vectors to create clusters of contexts, just assigning to each context the hub with maximum score. This process is thoroughly explained in (Agirre et al., 2006b). One of the problems of such an approach comes from the tendency of the system to produce a high number of hubs, somehow favouring small micro-clusters over coarse ones. Knowing in advance that the number of clusters in the tasks we will participate in would not be very high, we decided to perform a second stage and re-cluster again the results obtained in the first step, using a different graph-based technique. Re-clustering also gives us the opportunity to feed the system with additional data, as will be explained below.

Second step: clustering via MCL

In this second stage, we compute a square matrix with as many rows/columns as contexts, and where each element represents the relatedness between two contexts, just computing the cosine distance of its (normalized) hub score vectors obtained in the first step. We prune each row in the matrix and keep only the element with maximum values, so that the percentage of the kept elements' sum respect the total is below a given threshold. The resulting matrix M represents the adjacency matrix of a directed weighted graph, where vertices are contexts and edges represent the similarity between them. We can feed the matrix M with external information just by calculating another dissimilarity matrix between contexts and lineally interpolating the matrices with a factor.

Finally, we apply the Markov Clustering (MCL) algorithm (van Dongen, 2000) over the graph M for calculating the final clusters. MCL is a graph-clustering algorithm based on simulation of stochastic flows in graphs, its main idea being that random walks within the graph will tend to stay in the same cluster rather than jump between clusters. MCL has the remarkable property that there is no need to a-priori decide how many clusters it must find. However, it has some parameters which will influence the granularity of the clusters.

In fact, the behavior of the whole process relies on a number of parameters, which can be divided in several groups:

- Parameters for calculating the hubs
- Parameters for merging the hubs information with external information in the matrix M (α)
- The threshold for pruning the graph (δ)
- Parameters of the MCL algorithm (I, inflation parameter)

In sections 3 and 4 we describe the parameters we actually used for the final experiments, as well as how the tuning of these parameters has been performed for the two tasks.

3 Web People Search task

In this section we will explain in more detail how we implemented the general schema described in the previous section to the "Web People Search" task (Artiles et al., 2007). The task consist on disambiguating person names in a web searching scenario. The input consists on web pages retrieved from a web searching engine using person names as a query. The aim is to determine how many referents (people with the same name) exist for that person name, and classify each document with its corresponding referent. There is a train set consisting on 49 names and 100 documents per name. The test setting consist on 30 unrelated names, with 100 document per name. The evaluation is performed following the "purity" and "inverse purity" measures. Roughly speaking, purity measures how many classes they are in each cluster (like the precision measure). If a cluster fits into one class, the purity equals to 1. On the other side, inverse purity measures how many clusters they are in each class (recall). The final figure is obtained by combining purity and inverse purity by means of the standard F-Measure with $\alpha = 0.5$.

The parameters of the system were tuned using the train part of the corpus as a development set. As usual, the parameters that yielded best results were used on the test part.

[1] Note that each word will be attached to exactly one hub in the MST.

We first apply a home-made wrapper over the html files for retrieving the text chunks of the pages, which is usually mixed with html tags, javascript code, etc. The text is split into sentences and parsed using the FreeLing parser (Atserias et al., 2006). Only the lemmas of nouns are retained. We filter the nouns and keep only back those words whose frequency, according to the British National Corpus, is greater than 4. Next, we search for the person name across the sentences, and when such a sentence is found we build a context consisting on its four predecessor and four successors, i.e., contexts consists on 9 sentences. At the end, each document is represented as a set of contexts containing the person name. Finally, the person names are removed from the contexts.

For inducing the hubs we apply the HyperLex algorithm (Véronis, 2004). Then, the MST is calculated and every context is assigned with a hub score vector. We calculate the hub score vector of the whole document by averaging the score vectors of its contexts. The M matrix of pairwise similarities between documents is then computed and pruned with a threshold of 0.2, as described in section 2.

We feed the system with additional data about the topology of the pages over the web. For each document d_i to be classified we retrieve the set of documents P_i which link to d_i. We use the publicly available API for Microsoft Search. Then, for each pair of documents d_i and d_j we calculate the number of overlapping documents linking to them, i.e., $l_{ij} = \#\{P_i \cap P_j\}$ with the intuition that, the more pages point to the two documents, the more probably is that they both refer to the same person. The resulting matrix, M^L is combined with the original matrix M to give a final matrix M', by means of a linear interpolation with factor of 0.2, i.e. $M' = 0.2M + 0.8M_L$. Finally, the MCL algorithm is run over M' with an inflation parameter of 5.

4 Word Sense Induction and Discrimination task

The goal of this task is to allow for comparison across sense-induction and discrimination systems, and also to compare these systems to other supervised and knowledge-based systems. The input consist on 100 target words (65 verbs and 35 nouns), each target word having a set of contexts where the word appears. The goal is to automatically induce the senses each word has, and cluster the contexts accordingly. Two evaluation measures are provided: and unsupervised evaluation (FScore measure) and a supervised evaluation, where the organizers automatically map the induced clusters onto senses. See (Agirre and Soroa, 2007) for more details.

In order to improve the overall performance, we have clustered the 35 nouns and the 65 verbs separately. In the case of nouns, we have filtered the original contexts and kept only noun lemmas, whereas for verbs lemmas of nouns, verbs and adjectives were hold.

The algorithm for inducing the hubs is also different among nouns and verbs. Nouns hubs are induced with the usual HyperLex algorithm (just like in section 3) but for identifying verb hubs we used the HITS algorithm (Kleinberg, 1999), based on preliminary experiments.

The co-occurrence relatedness is also measured differently for verbs: instead of using the original conditional probabilities, the χ^2 measure between words is used. The reason behind is that conditional probabilities, as used in (Véronis, 2004), perform poorly in presence of words which occur in nearly all contexts, giving them an extraordinary high weight in the graph. Very few nouns happen to occur in many contexts, but they are verbs which certainly do (be, use, etc). On the other hand, χ^2 measures to what extent the observed co-occurrences diverge from those expected by chance, so weights of edges incident with very common, non-informant words will be low.

Parameter tuning for both nouns and verbs was performed over the senseval-3 testbed, and the best parameter combination were applied over the sense induction corpus. However, there is a factor we have taken into account in tuning directly over the sense induction corpus, i.e., that the granularity —and thus the number of classes— of senses in OntoNotes (the inventory used in the gold standard) is considerably coarser than in senseval-3. Therefore, we have manually tuned the inflation parameter of the MCL algorithm in order to achieve numbers of clusters between 1 and 4.

A threshold of 0.6 was used when pruning the dissimilarity matrix M for both nouns and verbs. We have tried to feed the system with additional data

System	All	Nouns	Verbs
Best	78.7	80.8	76.3
Worst	56.1	62.3	45.1
Average	65.4	69.0	61.4
UBC-AS	78.7	80.8	76.3

Table 1: Results of Semeval-2007 Task 2. Unsupervised evaluation (FScore).

System	All	Nouns	Verbs
Best	81.6	86.8	76.2
Worst	77.1	80.5	73.3
Average	79.1	82.8	75.0
UBC-AS	78.5	80.7	76.0

Table 2: Results of Semeval-2007 Task 2. Supervised evaluation as recall.

(mostly local and domain features of the context words) but, although the system performed slightly better, we decided that the little gain (which probably was not statistically significant) was no worth the effort.

5 Results

Table 1 shows the results of the unsupervised evaluation in task 2, where our system got the best results in this setting. Table 2 shows the supervised evaluation on the same task, where our system got a ranking of 4, performing slightly worse than the average of the systems.

In Table 3 we can see the results of Semeval-2007 Task 13. As can be seen, our system didn't manage to capture the structure of the corpus, and it got the worst result, far below the average of the systems.

6 Conclusions

We have presented graph-based unsupervised system for induction and classification. The system performs a two stage graph based clustering where a cooccurrence graph is first clustered to compute similarities against contexts. The context similarity matrix is pruned and the resulting associated graph is clustered again by means of a random-walk type algorithm. The system has participated in tasks 2 and 13 of the SemEval-2007 competition, on word sense induction and Web people search, respectively, with mixed results. We did not have time to perform an in-depth analysis of the reasons causing such a different performance. One of the reasons for the failure in the WePS task could be the fact that we were first-comers, with very little time to develop the system, and we used a very basic and coarse preprocessing of the HTML files. Another factor could be that we intentionally made our clustering algorithm return few clusters. We were mislead by the training data provided, as the final test data had more classes on average.

System	$F_{\alpha=0.5}$
Best	78.0
Worst	40.0
Average	60.0
UBC-AS	40.0

Table 3: Results of Semeval-2007 Task 13

Acknowledgements

This work has been partially funded by the Spanish education ministry (project KNOW) and by the regional government of Gipuzkoa (project DAHAD).

References

E. Agirre and A. Soroa. 2007. Semeval-2007 task 2:evaluating word sense induction and discrimination systems. In *Proceedings of Semeval 2007, Association for Computational Linguistics.*

E. Agirre, D. Martínez, O. López de Lacalle, and A. Soroa. 2006a. Evaluating and optimizing the parameters of an unsupervised graph-based wsd algorithm. In *Proceedings of TextGraphs Workshop. NAACL06.*, pages 89–96. Association for Computational Linguistics, June.

E. Agirre, D. Martínez, O. López de Lacalle, and A. Soroa. 2006b. Two graph-based algorithms for state-of-the-art wsd. In *Proceedings of the 2006 Conference on Empirical Methods in Natural Language Processing*, pages 585–593. Association for Computational Linguistics, July.

J. Artiles, J. Gonzalo, and S. Sekine. 2007. Establishing a benchmark for the web people search task: The semeval 2007 weps track. In *Proceedings of Semeval 2007, Association for Computational Linguistics.*

J. Atserias, B. Casas, E. Comelles, M. González, L. Padró, and M. Padró. 2006. Freeling 1.3: Syntactic and semantic services in an open-source NLP library. In *Proceedings of the 5th International Conference on Language Resources and Evaluation (LREC'06)*, pages 48–55.

Jon M. Kleinberg. 1999. Authoritative sources in a hyperlinked environment. *Journal of the ACM*, 46(5):604–632.

Stijn van Dongen. 2000. A cluster algorithm for graphs. Technical Report INS-R0010, National Research Institute for Mathematics and Computer Science in the Netherlands, Amsterdam, May.

J. Véronis. 2004. Hyperlex: lexical cartography for information retrieval. *Computer Speech & Language*, 18(3):223–252.

D. J. Watts and S. H. Strogatz. 1998. Collective dynamics of 'small-world' networks. *Nature*, 393(6684):440–442, June.

UBC-UMB: Combining unsupervised and supervised systems for all-words WSD

David Martinez,Timothy Baldwin
LT Group, CSSE
University of Melbourne
Victoria 3010 Australia
{davidm,tim}@csse.unimelb.edu.au

Eneko Agirre, Oier Lopez de Lacalle
IXA NLP Group
Univ. of the Basque Country
Donostia, Basque Country
{e.agirre,jibloleo}@ehu.es

Abstract

This paper describes the joint submission of two systems to the all-words WSD subtask of SemEval-2007 task 17. The main goal of this work was to build a competitive unsupervised system by combining heterogeneous algorithms. As a secondary goal, we explored the integration of unsupervised predictions into a supervised system by different means.

1 Introduction

This paper describes the joint submission of two systems to the all-words WSD subtask of SemEval-2007 task 17. The systems were developed by the University of the Basque Country (UBC), and the University of Melbourne (UMB). The main goal of this work was to build a competitive unsupervised system by combining heterogeneous algorithms. As a secondary goal, we explored the integration of this method into a supervised system by different means. Thus, this paper describes both the unsupervised system (UBC-UMB-1), and the combined supervised system (UBC-UMB-2) submitted to the all-words task.

Our motivation in building unsupervised systems comes from the difficulty of creating hand-tagged data for all words and all languages, which is colloquially known as the knowledge acquisition bottleneck. There have also been promising results in recent work on the combination of unsupervised approaches that suggest the gap with respect to supervised systems is narrowing (Brody et al., 2006).

The remainder of the paper is organized as follows. First we describe the disambiguation algorithms in Section 2. Next, the development experiments are presented in Section 3, and our final submissions and results in Section 4. Finally, we summarize our conclusions in Section 5.

2 Algorithms

In this section, we will describe the standalone algorithms (three unsupervised and one supervised) and the combination schemes we explored. The unsupervised methods are based on different intuitions for disambiguation (topical features, local context, and WordNet relations), which is a desirable characteristic for combining algorithms.

2.1 Topic Signatures (TS)

Topic signatures (Agirre and de Lacalle, 2004) are lists of words related to a particular sense. They can be built from a variety of sources, and be used directly to perform WSD. Cuadros and Rigau (2006) present a detailed evaluation of topic signatures built from a variety of knowledge sources. In this work we built those coming from the following:

- the relations in the Multilingual Central Repository (TS-MCR)
- the relations in the Extended WordNet (TS-XWN)

In order to apply this resource for WSD, we simply measured the word-overlap between the target context and each of the senses of the target word. The sense with highest overlap is chosen as the correct sense.

Proceedings of the 4th International Workshop on Semantic Evaluations (SemEval-2007), pages 350–353,
Prague, June 2007.

2.2 Relatives in Context (RIC)

This is an unsupervised method presented in Martinez et al. (2006). This algorithm makes use of the WordNet relatives of the target word for disambiguation. The process is carried out in these steps: (i) obtain a set of close relatives from WordNet for each sense (the relatives can be polysemous); (ii) for each test instance define all possible word sequences that include the target word; (iii) for each word sequence, substitute the target word with each relative and query a web search engine; (iv) rank queries according to the following factors: length of the query, distance of the relative to the target word, and number of hits; and (v) select the sense associated with the highest ranked query.

The intuition behind this system is that we can find related words that can be substituted for the target word in a given context, which are indicative of its sense. The close relatives that can form more common phrases from the target context determine the target sense.

2.3 Relative Number (RNB)

This heuristic has been motivated as a way of identifying rare senses of a word. An important disadvantage of unsupervised systems is that rare senses can be over-represented in the models, while supervised systems are able to discard them because they have access to token-level word sense distributions.

This simple algorithm relies on the number of close relatives found in WordNet for each sense of the word. The senses are ranked according to the number of synonyms, direct hypernyms, and direct hyponyms they have in WordNet. The highest ranked sense is taken to be the most important for the target word, and all occurrences of the target word are tagged with that sense.

2.4 k-Nearest Neighbours (kNN)

As our supervised system, we relied on kNN. This is a memory-based learning method where the neighbours are the k most similar contexts, represented by feature vectors ($\vec{c_i}$) of the test vector ($\vec{f}$). The similarity among instances is measured by the cosine of their vectors. The test instance is labeled with the sense that obtains the maximum sum of the weighted votes of the k most similar contexts. Each vote is weighted depending on its (neighbour) position in the ordered rank, with the closest being first. Equation 1 formalizes kNN, where C_i corresponds to the sense label of the i-th closest neighbour.

$$\arg\max_{S_j} = \sum_{i=1}^{k} \begin{cases} \frac{1}{i} & \text{if } C_i = S_j \\ 0 & \text{otherwise} \end{cases} \quad (1)$$

The UBC group used a combination of kNN classifiers trained over a large set of features, and enhanced this method using Singular Value Decomposition (SVD) for their supervised submission (UBC-ALM) to the lexical-sample and all-words subtasks (Agirre and Lopez de Lacalle, 2007). However, we only used the basic implementation in this work, due to time constraints.

2.5 Combination of systems

We explored two approaches to combine the standalone systems. The first consisted simply of adding up the normalized weights that each system would give to each sense. We tested this voting approach both for the unsupervised and supervised settings.

The second method could only be applied in combination with the supervised kNN system. The idea was to include the unsupervised predictions as weighted features for the supervised system. We refer to this method as "stacking", and it has been previously used to integrate heterogeneous knowledge sources for WSD (Stevenson and Wilks, 2001).

3 Development experiments

We tested the single algorithms and their combination over both Semcor and the training distribution of the SemEval-2007 lexical-sample subtask of task 17 (S07LS for short). The goal of these experiments was to obtain an estimate of the expected performance, and submit the most promising configuration. We present first the tests on the unsupervised setting, and then the supervised setting. It is important to note that the hand-tagged corpora was not used to fine-tune the parameters of the unsupervised algorithms.

3.1 Unsupervised systems

For the first evaluation of our unsupervised systems, we relied on Semcor, and tagged 43,063 instances of the 329 word types occurring in SemEval-2007

System	Recall
RNB	30.6
TS-MCR	**57.5**
TS-XWN	47.0
TS-MCR & TS-XWN	57.3
RBN & TS-MCR & TS-XWN	53.6

Table 1: Evaluation of standalone and combined unsupervised systems over 43,063 instances from Semcor

System	Recall
TS-MCR	60.1
TS-XWN	54.3
TS-MCR & TS-XWN	61.1
TS-MCR & TS-XWN & RIC*	**61.2**

Table 2: Evaluation of standalone and combined unsupervised systems over 8,518 instances from S07LS training

all-words. Due to time constraints, we were not able to test the RIC algorithm on this dataset. The results are shown in Table 1. We can see that the RNB heuristic performs poorly, and that the best configuration consists of applying the single TS-MCR algorithm. From this experiment, we decided to remove the RNB heuristic and focus on the topic signatures and RIC.

We also used S07LS for extra experiments in the unsupervised setting. From the training part of the S07LS dataset, we extracted 8,518 instances of words also occurring in SemEval-2007 all-words. As S07LS used senses from OntoNotes, we relied on the mapping provided by the task organisers to link them to WordNet senses. We left RNB out of this experiment due to its low performance in Semcor, and regarding RIC, we only evaluated a sample of 68 instances. Results are shown in Table 2. The best scores are achieved when combining both sets of topic signatures. The few cases that have been disambiguated with RIC improve the overall performance slightly.

3.2 Combined system

We could not rely on Semcor in the supervised setting (we used it for training), and therefore tried to use as much data as possible from the training component of S07LS, wherein all the instances available (22,281) were disambiguated. We tested first

System	Recall
kNN	**87.4**
kNN & TS-MCR	86.8
kNN & TS-XWN	86.4
kNN & TS-MCR & TS-XWN	86.0

Table 3: Evaluation of voting supervised systems in 22,281 instances from S07LS training

System	Recall
kNN	71.7
kNN & TS-MCR & TS-XWN	**71.8**

Table 4: Evaluation of "stacking" the unsupervised systems on kNN over 8,518 instances from S07LS training

the voting combination by adding the normalized weights from the output of each system. Due to time constraints we only evaluated the combination of kNN with TS-MCR and TS-XWN. Results are shown in Table 3, where we can see that combining the unsupervised systems with voting hurts the performance of the kNN method.

Finally, we applied the second combination approach, consisting of including the predictions of the unsupervised systems as features for kNN ("stacking"). We performed this experiment on the training part of S07LS, but only for the 8,518 instances of the words occurring on the all-words dataset. The results of this experiment are given in Table 4. We observed a slight improvement in this case.

4 Final systems

For our final submissions, we chose the combination "TS-MCR & TS-XWN & RIC" for the unsupervised system (UBC-UMB-1), and the combination "kNN & TS-MCR & TS-XWN" via "stacking" for our supervised system (UBC-UMB-2). The results of all the systems are given in Table 5.

We can see that our unsupervised system ranked 10th. Unfortunately, we do not know at the time of writing which other systems are unsupervised, and therefore are unable to compare to other unsupervised systems.

Our "stacking" supervised system performs slightly lower than the kNN supervised systems by UBC-ALM (which ranks 7th), showing that our system was not able to profit from information from

System	Precision	Recall
1.	0.537	0.537
2.	0.527	0.527
3.	0.524	0.524
4.	0.522	0.486
5.	0.518	0.518
6.	0.514	0.514
7.	0.493	0.492
8. UBC-UMB-2	**0.485**	**0.484**
9.	0.420	0.420
10. UBC-UMB-1	**0.362**	**0.362**
11.	0.355	0.355
12.	0.337	0.337
13.	0.298	0.298
14.	0.120	0.118

Table 5: Official results for all systems in task #17 of SemEval-2007. Our systems are shown in bold. UBC-UMB-1 stands for TS-MCR & TS-XWN & RIC, and UBC-UMB-2 for kNN & TS-MCR & TS-XWN.

System	Precision	Recall
TS-MCR	36.7	36.5
TS-XWN	33.1	32.9
RIC	30.6	30.4
TS-MCR & TS-XWN	37.5	37.3
TS-MCR & TS-XWN & RIC	36.2	36.2

Table 6: Our unsupervised systems in the SemEval-2007 all words test data

the unsupervised systems. However, we cannot attribute the decrease only to the unsupervised features, as the kNN implementations were different (UBC-ALM relied on SVD).

After the gold-standard data was released, we were able to test the contribution of each of the unsupervised systems in the ensemble, as well as two additional combinations. The results are given in Table 6. We can see that TS-MCR is the best performing method, confirming our development experiments (cf. Tables 1 and 2). In contrast, including RIC decreased the performance by 0.7 percent points, and had we used only TS-MCR and TS-XWN our results would have been better.

5 Conclusions

In this submission we combined heterogeneous unsupervised algorithms to obtain competitive performance without relying on training data. However, due to time constraints, we were only able to submit a preliminary system, and some of the unsupervised methods were not properly developed and tested.

For future work we plan to properly test these methods, and deploy other unsupervised algorithms. We also plan to explore more sophisticated combination strategies, using meta-learning to try to predict which features of each word make a certain WSD system succeed (or fail).

Acknowledgements

The first and second authors were supported by Australian Research Council grant no. DP0663879. We want to thank German Rigau from the University of the Basque Country for kindly providing access to the MCR.

References

Eneko Agirre and Oier Lopez de Lacalle. 2004. Publicly available topic signatures for all WordNet nominal senses. In *Proceedings of the 4rd International Conference on Language Resources and Evaluations (LREC)*, pages 1123–6, Lisbon, Portugal.

Eneko Agirre and Oier Lopez de Lacalle. 2007. UBC-ALM: Lexical-Sample and All-Words tasks. In *Proceedings of SemEval-2007 (forthcoming)*, Prague, Czech Republic.

Samuel Brody, Roberto Navigli, and Mirella Lapata. 2006. Ensemble methods for unsupervised WSD. In *Proceedings of the 21st International Conference on Computational Linguistics and the 44th annual meeting of the ACL*, pages 97–104, Sydney, Australia.

Montse Cuadros and German Rigau. 2006. Quality assessment of large scale knowledge resources. In *Proceedings of the International Conference on Empirical Methods in Natural Language Processing (EMNLP-06)*, pages 534–41, Sydney, Australia.

David Martinez, Eneko Agirre, and Xinglong Wang. 2006. Word relatives in context for word sense disambiguation. In *Proceedings of the 2006 Australasian Language Technology Workshop*, pages 42–50, Sydney, Australia.

Mark Stevenson and Yorick Wilks. 2001. The interaction of knowledge sources in word sense disambiguation. *Computational Linguistics*, 27(3):321–49.

UBC-UPC: Sequential SRL Using Selectional Preferences. An aproach with Maximum Entropy Markov Models

Beñat Zapirain, Eneko Agirre
IXA NLP Group
University of the Basque Country
Donostia, Basque Country
{benat.zapirain,e.agirre}@ehu.es

Lluís Màrquez
TALP Research Center
Technical University of Catalonia
Barcelona, Catalonia
lluism@lsi.upc.edu

Abstract

We present a sequential Semantic Role Labeling system that describes the tagging problem as a Maximum Entropy Markov Model. The system uses full syntactic information to select BIO-tokens from input data, and classifies them sequentially using state-of-the-art features, with the addition of Selectional Preference features. The system presented achieves competitive performance in the CoNLL-2005 shared task dataset and it ranks first in the SRL subtask of the Semeval-2007 task 17.

1 Introduction

In Semantic Role Labeling (SRL) the goal is to identify word sequences or arguments accompanying the predicate and assign them labels depending on their semantic relation. In this task we disambiguate argument structures in two ways: predicting VerbNet (Kipper et al., 2000) thematic roles and PropBank (Palmer et al., 2005) numbered arguments, as well as adjunct arguments.

In this paper we describe our system for the SRL subtask of the Semeval2007 task 17. It is based on the architecture and features of the system named 'model 2' of (Surdeanu et al., forthcoming), but it introduces two changes: we use Maximum Entropy for learning instead of AdaBoost and we enlarge the feature set with combined features and other semantic features.

Traditionally, most of the features used in SRL are extracted from automatically generated syntactic and lexical annotations. In this task, we also experiment with provided hand labeled semantic information for each verb occurrence such as the PropBank predicate sense and the Levin class. In addition, we use automatically learnt Selectional Preferences based on WordNet to generate a new kind of semantic based features.

We participated in both the "close" and the "open" tracks of Semeval2007 with the same system, making use, in the second case, of the larger CoNLL-2005 training set.

2 System Description

2.1 Data Representation

In order to make learning and labeling easier, we change the input data representation by navigating through provided syntactic structures and by extracting BIO-tokens from each of the propositions to be annotated as shown in (Surdeanu et al., forthcoming). These sequential tokens are selected by exploring the sentence spans or regions defined by the clause boundaries, and they are labeled with BIO tags depending on the location of the token: at the beginning, inside, or outside of a verb argument. After this data pre-processing step, we obtain a more compact and easier to process data representation, making also impossible overlapping and embedded argument predictions.

2.2 Feature Representation

Apart from Selectional Preferences (cf. Section 3) and those extracted from provided semantic information, most of the features we used are borrowed from the existing literature (Gildea and Jurafsky, 2002; Xue and Palmer, 2004; Surdeanu et al., forthcoming).

Proceedings of the 4th International Workshop on Semantic Evaluations (SemEval-2007), pages 354–357,
Prague, June 2007.

On the verb predicate:

- Form; Lemma; POS tag; Chunk type and Type of verb phrase; Verb voice; Binary flag indicating if the verb is a start/end of a clause.
- Subcategorization, i.e., the phrase structure rule expanding the verb parent node.
- VerbNet class of the verb (in the "close" track only).

On the focus constituent:

- Type; Head;
- First and last words and POS tags of the constituent.
- POS sequence.
- Bag-of-words of nouns, adjectives, and adverbs in the constituent.
- TOP sequence: right-hand side of the rule expanding the constituent node; 2/3/4-grams of the TOP sequence.
- Governing category as described in (Gildea and Jurafsky, 2002).

Context of the focus constituent:

- Previous and following words and POS tags of the constituent.
- The same features characterizing focus constituents are extracted for the two previous and following tokens, provided they are inside the clause boundaries of the codified region.

Relation between predicate and constituent:

- Relative position; Distance in words and chunks; Level of embedding with respect to the constituent: in number of clauses.
- Binary position; if the argument is after or before the predicate.
- Constituent path as described in (Gildea and Jurafsky, 2002); All 3/4/5-grams of path constituents beginning at the verb predicate or ending at the constituent.
- Partial parsing path as described in (Carreras et al., 2004)); All 3/4/5-grams of path elements beginning at the verb predicate or ending at the constituent.
- Syntactic frame as described by Xue and Palmer (2004)

Combination Features

- Predicate and Phrase Type
- Predicate and binary position
- Head Word and Predicate
- Predicate and PropBank frame sense
- Predicate, PropBank frame sense, VerbNet class (in the "close" track only)

2.3 Maximum Entropy Markov Models

Maximum Entropy Markov Models are a discriminative model for sequential tagging that models the local probability $P(s_n \mid s_{n-1}, o)$, where o is the context of the observation.

Given a MEMM, the most likely state sequence is the one that maximizes the following

$$S = argmax \prod_{i=1}^{n} P(s_i \mid s_{i-1}, o)$$

Translating the problem to SRL, we have role/argument labels connected to each state in the sequence (or proposition), and the observations are the features extracted in these points (token features). We get the most likely label sequence finding out the most likely state sequence (Viterbi).

All the conditional probabilities are given by the Maximum Entropy classifier with a tunable Gaussian prior from the Mallet Toolkit[1].

Some restrictions are considered when we search the most likely sequence[2]:

1. No duplicate argument classes for A0-A5 and thematic roles.
2. If there is a R-X argument (reference), then there has to be a X argument before (referenced).
3. If there is a C-X argument (continuation), then there has to be a X argument before.
4. Before a I-X token, there has to be a B-X or I-X token (because of the BIO encoding).
5. Given a predicate and its PropBank sense, only some arguments are allowed (e.g. not all the verbs support A2 argument).
6. Given a predicate and its Verbnet class, only some thematic roles are allowed.

3 Including Selectional Preferences

Selectional Preferences (SP) try to capture the fact that linguistic elements prefer arguments of a certain semantic class, e.g. a verb like 'eat' prefers as subject edible things, and as subject animate entities, as in "She was eating an apple" They can be learned from corpora, generalizing from the observed argument heads (e.g. 'apple', 'biscuit', etc.) into abstract classes (e.g. edible things). In our case we

[1] http://mallet.cs.umass.edu

[2] Restriction 5 applies to PropBank output. Restriction 6 applies to VerbNet output

follow (Agirre and Martinez, 2001) and use WordNet (Fellbaum, 1998) as the generalization classes (the concept `<food,nutrient>`).

The aim of using Selectional Preferences (SP) in SRL is to generalize from the argument heads in the training instances into general word classes. In theory, using word classes might overcome the data sparseness problem for the head-based features, but at the cost of introducing some noise.

More specifically, given a verb, we study the occurrences of the target verb in a training corpus (e.g. the PropBank corpus), and learn a set of SPs for each argument and adjunct of that verb. For instance, given the verb 'kill' we would have 2 SPs for each argument type, and 4 SPs for some of the observed adjuncts: `kill_A0`, `kill_A1`, `kill_AM-LOC`, `kill_AM-MNR`, `kill_AM-PNC` and `kill_AM-TMP`.

Rather than coding the SPs directly as features, we code the *predictions* instead, i.e. for each proposition in the training and testing set, we check the SPs for all the argument (and adjunct) headwords, and the SP which best fits the headword (see below) is the one that is selected. We codify the predicted argument (or adjunct) label as features, and we insert them among the corresponding argument features.

For instance, let's assume that the word 'railway' appears as the headword of a candidate argument of 'kill'. WordNet 1.6 yields the following hypernyms for 'railway' (from most general to most specific, we include the WordNet 1.6 concept numbers preceded by their specifity level);

```
1 00001740              1 00017954
2  00009457             2  05962976
3   00011937            3   05997592
4    03600463           4    06004580
5     03243979          5     06008236
6      03526208         6      06005839
7       03208595        7       02927599
                        8        03209020
```

Note that we do not care about the sense ambiguity and the explosion of concepts that it carries. Our algorithm will check each of the hypernyms of railway and match them with the concepts in the SPs of 'kill', giving preference to the most specific concept. In case that equally specific concepts match different SPs, we will choose the SP that has the concept that ranks highest in the SP, and code the SP feature with the label of the SP where the match succeeds. In the example, these are the most specific matches:

```
AM-LOC Con:03243979 Level:5 Ranking:32
A0     Con:06008236 Level:5 Ranking:209
```

There is a tie in the level, so we choose the one with the highest rank. All in all, this means that according to the learnt SPs we would predict that 'railway' is a location feature for 'kill', and we would therefore insert the 'SP:AM-LOC' feature among the argument features.

If 'railway' appears as the headword of other verbs, the predicted argument might be different. See for instance, the following verbs:

```
destroy:A1 Con:03243979 Level:5 Ranking:43
go:A0      Con:02927599 Level:7 Ranking:131
go:A2      Con:02927599 Level:7 Ranking:721
build:A1   Con:03209020 Level:8 Ranking:294
```

Note that our training examples did not contain 'railway' as an argument of any of these verbs, but due to the SPs we are able to code into a feature that 'railway' belongs to a concrete semantic class which contains conceptually similar headwords.

We decided to code the prediction of the SPs, rather than the SPs themselves, in order to be more robust to noise.

There is a further subtlety with our SP system. In order to label training and testing sets in similar conditions and avoid overfitting problems as much as possible, we split the training set into five folds and tagged each one with SPs learnt from the other four. For extracting SP features from test set examples, we use SPs learnt in the whole training set.

4 Experiments and Results

We participated in the "close" and the "open" tracks with the same classification model, but using different training sets in each one. In the close track we only use the provided training set, and in the open, the CoNLL-2005 training set (without VerbNet classes or thematic roles).

Before our participation, we tested the system in the CoNLL-2005 close track setting and it achieved competitive performance in comparison to the state-of-the-art results published in that challenge.

4.1 Semeval2007 setting

The data provided in the close track consists of the propositions of 50 different verb lemmas from PropBank (sections 02-21). The data for the CoNLL-2005 is also a subset of the PropBank data, but it

Track	Label	rank	prec.	rec.	F1
Close	VerbNet	1st	85.31	82.08	83.66
Close	PropBank	1st	85.04	82.07	83.52
Open	PropBank	1st	84.51	82.24	83.36

Table 1: Results in the SRL subtask of SemEval-2007 task 17

includes all the propositions in sections 02-21 and no VerbNet classes nor thematic roles for learning.

There is a total of 21 argument types for PropBank and 47 roles for VerbNet, which amounts to $21 * 2 + 1 = 43$ BIO-labels for PropBank predictions and $47 * 2 + 1 = 95$ for VerbNet. We filtered the less frequent (<5).

We trained the Maximum Entropy classifiers with 114,380 examples for the close track, and with 828,811 for the open track. We tuned the classifier by setting the Exponential Gaussian prior in 0.1

4.2 Results

In the close track we trained two classifiers, one to label PropBank numbered arguments and a second to label VerbNet thematic roles. Due to lack of time, we only trained the PropBank labels in the open track. Table 1 shows the results obtained in the SRL subtask. We ranked first in all of them, out of two participants.

4.3 Discussion

The results indicate that in the close track the system performs similarly on both PropBank arguments and VerbNet roles. The absence of VerbNet class-based features in the CoNLL-2005 training data could cause the loss of performance in the open track. We plan to perform the experiment on VerbNet roles for the open track to check the ability of the classifier to generalize across verbs.

Regarding the use of SP features, nowadays, we have not obtained relevant improvements in the predictions of the classifiers. It is our first approach to these kind of semantic features and there are more sophisticated but evident extraction variants which we are exploring.

Although the general performance is very similar without SP features, using them our system obtains better results in ARG3 core arguments and in the most frequent adjuncts such as location (*LOC*), general-purpose (*ADV*) and temporal (*TMP*).

We reproduced this improvements in experiments realized with CoNLL-2005 larger test sets. In that case, we improved ARG3-ARG4 core arguments as well as the mentioned adjuncts. There were more examples to be classified and we get better overall performance, but we need further experiments to be more conclusive.

5 Conclusions

We have presented a sequential semantic role labeling system for the Semeval-2007 task 17 (SRL). Based on Maximum Entropy Markov Models, it obtains competitive and promising results. We also have introduced semantic features extracted from Selectional Restrictions but we only have preliminary evidence of their usefulness.

Acknowledgements

We thank David Martinez for kindly providing the software that learnt the selectional preferences. This work has been partially funded by the Spanish education ministry (KNOW). Beñat is supported by a PhD grant from the University of the Basque Country.

References

E. Agirre and D. Martinez. 2001. Learning class-to-class selectional preferences. In *Proceedings of CoNLL-2001*, Toulouse, France.

X. Carreras, L. Màrquez, and G. Chrupała. 2004. Hierarchical recognition of propositional arguments with perceptrons. In *Proceedings of CoNLL 2004*.

C. Fellbaum. 1998. *WordNet: An Electronic Lexical Database*. MIT Press.

D. Gildea and D. Jurafsky. 2002. Automatic labeling of semantic roles. *Computational Linguistics*, 28(3).

K. Kipper, Hoa Trang Dang, and M. Palmer. 2000. Class-based construction of a verb lexicon. In *Proceedings of AAAI-2000 Seventeenth National Conference on Artificial Intellingence, Austin, TX*.

M. Palmer, D. Gildea, and P. Kingsbury. 2005. The proposition bank: An annotated corpus of semantic roles. *Computational Linguistics*, 31(1).

M. Surdeanu, L. Màrquez, X. Carreras, and P. Comas. (forthcoming). Combination strategies for semantic role labeling. In *Journal of Artificial Intelligence Research*.

N. Xue and M. Palmer. 2004. Calibrating features for semantic role labeling. In *Proceedings of EMNLP-2004*.

UBC-ZAS: A k-NN based Multiclassifier System to perform WSD in a Reduced Dimensional Vector Space

Ana Zelaia, Olatz Arregi and Basilio Sierra
Computer Science Faculty
University of the Basque Country
ana.zelaia@ehu.es

Abstract

In this article a multiclassifier approach for word sense disambiguation (WSD) problems is presented, where a set of k-NN classifiers is used to predict the category (sense) of each word. In order to combine the predictions generated by the multiclassifier, Bayesian voting is applied. Through all the classification process, a reduced dimensional vector representation obtained by Singular Value Decomposition (SVD) is used. Each word is considered an independent classification problem, and so different parameter setting, selected after a tuning phase, is applied to each word. The approach has been applied to the lexical sample WSD subtask of SemEval 2007 (task 17).

1 Introduction

Word Sense Disambiguation (WSD) is an important component in many information organization and management tasks. Both, word representation and classification method are crucial steps in the word sense disambiguation process. In this article both issues are considered. On the one hand, Latent Semantic Indexing (LSI) (Deerwester et al., 1990), which is a variant of the vector space model (VSM) (Salton and McGill, 1983), is used in order to obtain the vector representation of the corresponding word. This technique compresses vectors representing word related contexts into vectors of a lower-dimensional space. LSI, which is based on Singular Value Decomposition (SVD) (Berry and Browne, 1999) of matrices, has shown to have the ability to extract the relations among features representing words by means of their context of use, and has been successfully applied to Information Retrieval tasks.

On the other hand, a multiclassifier (Ho et al., 1994) which uses different training databases is constructed. These databases are obtained from the original training set by random subsampling. The implementation of this approach is made by a model inspired in bagging (Breiman, 1996), and the k-NN classification algorithm (Dasarathy, 1991) is used to make the sense predictions for testing words.

Our group (UBC-ZAS) has participated in the lexical sample subtask of SemEval-2007 for task 17, which consists on 100 different words for which a training and testing database have been provided.

The aim of this article is to give a brief description of our approach to deal with the WSD task and to show the results obtained. In Section 2, our approach is presented. In Section 3, the experimental setup is introduced. The experimental results are presented and discussed in Section 4, and finally, Section 5 contains some conclusions and comments on future work.

2 Proposed Approach

In this article a multiclassifier based WSD system which classifies word senses represented in a reduced dimensional vector space is proposed.

In Figure 1 an illustration of the experiment performed for each one of the 100 words can be seen. First, vectors in the VSM are projected to the reduced space by using SVD. Next, random subsampling is applied to the training database TD to obtain

Proceedings of the 4th International Workshop on Semantic Evaluations (SemEval-2007), pages 358–361,
Prague, June 2007.

different training databases TD_i. Afterwards the k-NN classifier is applied for each TD_i to make sense label predictions. Finally, Bayesian voting scheme is used to combine predictions, and c_j will be the final sense label prediction for testing word q.

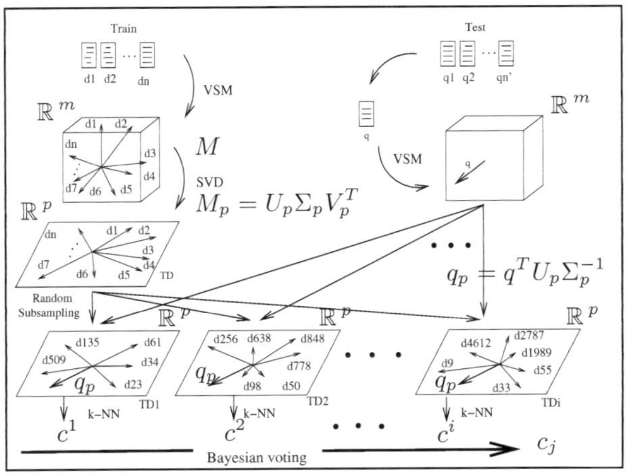

Figure 1: Proposed approach for WSD task

In the rest of this section, the preprocessing applied, the SVD dimensionality reduction technique, the k-NN algorithm and the combination of classifiers used are briefly reviewed.

2.1 Preprocessing

In order to obtain the vector representation for each of the word contexts (documents, cases) given by the organizers of the SemEval-2007 task, we used the features extracted by the UBC-ALM participating group (Agirre and Lopez de Lacalle, 2007). These features are local collocations (bigrams and trigrams formed with the words around the target), syntactic dependencies (object, subject, noun-modifier, preposition, and sibling) and Bag-of-words features (basically lemmas of the content words in the whole context, and in a $\pm$4-word window).

2.2 The SVD Dimensionality Reduction Technique

The classical Vector Space Model (VSM) has been successfully employed to represent documents in text categorization tasks. The newer method of Latent Semantic Indexing (LSI) [1] (Deerwester et al., 1990) is a variant of the VSM in which documents are represented in a lower dimensional space created from the input training dataset. The SVD technique used by LSI consists in factoring term-document matrix M into the product of three matrices, $M = U\Sigma V^T$ where Σ is a diagonal matrix of singular values, and U and V are orthogonal matrices of singular vectors (term and document vectors, respectively).

For classification purposes (Dumais, 2004), the training and testing documents are projected to the reduced dimensional space, $q_p = q^T U_p \Sigma_p^{-1}$, by using p singular values and the cosine is usually calculated to measure the similarity between training and testing document vectors.

2.3 The k-NN classification algorithm

k-NN is a distance based classification approach. According to this approach, given an arbitrary testing case, the k-NN classifier ranks its nearest neighbors among the training word senses, and uses the sense of the k top-ranking neighbors to predict the corresponding to the word which is being analyzed (Dasarathy, 1991).

2.4 Combination of classifiers

The combination of multiple classifiers has been intensively studied with the aim of improving the accuracy of individual components (Ho et al., 1994). A widely used technique to implement this approach is *bagging* (Breiman, 1996), where a set of training databases TD_i is generated by selecting n training cases drawn randomly with replacement from the original training database TD of n cases. When a set of $n_1 < n$ training cases is chosen from the original training collection, the bagging is said to be applied by random subsampling. In fact, this is the approach used in our work and the n_1 parameter has been selected via tuning.

According to the random subsampling, given a testing case q, the classifier will make a label prediction c^i based on each one of the training databases TD_i. One way to combine the predictions is by Bayesian voting (Dietterich, 1998), where a confidence value $cv^i_{c_j}$ is calculated for each training database TD_i and sense c_j to be predicted. These confidence values have been calculated based on the training collection. Confidence values are summed

[1] http://lsi.research.telcordia.com, http://www.cs.utk.edu/~lsi

by sense; the sense c_j that gets the highest value is finally proposed as a prediction for the testing examples.

3 Experimental Setup

In the approach proposed in this article there are some decisions that need to be taken, because it is not clear (1) how many examples should be selected from the TD of each word in order to create each one of the TD_i; (2) which is the appropriate dimension to be used in order to represent word related contexts (cases) for each word database; (3) which is the appropriate number of TD_i that should be created (number of classifiers to be used) and (4) which is the appropriate number of neighbors to be considered by the k-NN algorithm.

Therefore, a parameter tuning phase was carried out in order to fix the parameters. We decided to adjust them for each word independently.

In the following, the parameters are introduced and the tuning process carried out is explained. For two of the parameters (the number of classifiers and the number of neigbors for k-NN), the tuning phase was performed based on our previous experiments on document categorization tasks.

3.1 The size of each TD_i

As it was mentioned, the multiclassifier is implemented by random subsampling, where a set of $n_1 < n$ vectors is chosen from the original training collection of n examples for a given word (n is a different value for each one of the 100 words). Consequently, the size of each TD_i will vary depending on the value of n_1. The selection of different numbers of cases was experimented for each word in two different ways:

a) according to the following equation:

$$n_1 = \sum_{i=1}^{s}(2 + \lfloor\frac{t_i}{j}\rfloor), \qquad j = 1, \ldots, 10$$

where t_i is the total number of training cases in the sense c_i and s is the total number of senses for the given word. By dividing parameter t_i by j, the number of cases selected from each sense preserves the proportion of cases per sense in the original one. However, it has to be taken into account that some of the senses have a very low number of cases assigned to them. By summing 2, at least 2 cases will be selected from each sense. In order to decide the optimal value for parameter j, the classification experiment was carried out varying j from 1 to 10 for each word.

b) selecting a fixed number of cases for each of the senses which appeared for the word in the training database. Again, in the tuning phase, different numbers of cases (from 1 to 10) have been used for each of the 100 words in order to select a value for each of the words.

We optimized the size of each TD_i for each word by selecting the number of cases sometimes by procedure a) and sometimes by b).

3.2 The dimension of the reduced Vector Space Model

Taking into account the wide differences among the training case numbers for different words, we decided to project vectors representing them to different reduced dimensional spaces. The selection of those dimensions is based on the number of training cases available for each word, and limited to 500; the used dimensions vary from 19 (for the word *grant*) to 481 (for the word *part*).

3.3 The number of classifiers (TD_i)

Based on previous experiments carried out for document categorization (Zelaia et al., 2006), we decided to create 30 classifiers for some words and 50 for others, i.e. 30 or 50 individual k-NN algorithms will be used by the multiclassifier in order to combine opinions by Bayesian voting.

3.4 Number of neigbors for k-NN

Based on our previous experiments, we decided to use $k = 1$ and $k = 5$, and to select the best for each of the words. The cosine similarity measure is used in order to find the nearest or the 5 nearests.

4 Experimental Results

The experiment was conducted by considering the optimal values for parameters tuned by using the training case set.

Results published in this section were calculated by the SemEval-2007 organizers. Table 1 shows accuracy rates obtained by the 13 participants in the SemEval-2007, 17 task, lexical sample WSD subtask.

System	Accuracy	System	Accuracy
1.	0.887	8.	0.803
2.	0.869	**9.**	**0.799**
3.	0.864	10.	0.796
4.	0.857	11.	0.743
5.	0.851	12.	0.538
6.	0.851	13.	0.521
7.	0.838		

Table 1: Accuracy rates obtained by the 13 participants. SemEval-2007, 17 task (Lexical Sample)

The result obtained by our system is 0.799 (the 9th among 13 participants), 1 point over the mean accuracy (0.786).

5 Conclusions and Future Work

Results obtained show that the construction of a multiclassifier, together with the use of Bayesian voting to combine label predictions, plays an important role in the improvement of results. We also want to remark that we used the SVD dimensionality reduction technique in order to reduce the vector representation of cases.

The approach presented in this paper was already used in a document categorization task. However, we never used it for WSD task. Therefore, in order to adapt the method to the new task, we fixed some parameters based on our previous experiments (30-50 classifiers, $k = 1, 5$ for the k-NN algorithm) and tuned some other parameters by experimenting quite a high number of TD_i sizes and using different dimensions for each word. However, we noticed that the application of our approach to a different task is not straightforward. Greater effort will have to be made in order to tune the different parameters to this specific task of WSD.

One of the main difficulties we found was the difference in the number of training cases, comparing with the high number usually available in other tasks like text categorization.

As future work, we can think of applying a new preprocessing approach in order to extract better features from the training database which could help the SVD technique improving the accuracy after a dimensionality reduction is applied. The use of Wordnet may help.

6 Acknowledgements

This research was supported by the University of the Basque Country by the project "ANHITZ 2006: Language Technologies for Multilingual Interaction in Intelligent Environments", IE 06-185

We wish to thank to the UBC-ALM group for helping us extracting learning features.

References

E. Agirre and O. Lopez de Lacalle. 2007. Ubc-alm: Combining k-nn with svd for wsd. submited for publication to SemEval-2007.

M.W. Berry and M. Browne. 1999. *Understanding Search Engines: Mathematical Modeling and Text Retrieval.* SIAM Society for Industrial and Applied Mathematics, ISBN: 0-89871-437-0, Philadelphia.

L. Breiman. 1996. Bagging predictors. *Machine Learning*, 24(2):123–140.

B.V. Dasarathy. 1991. *Nearest Neighbor (NN) Norms: NN Pattern Recognition Classification Techniques.* IEEE Computer Society Press.

S. Deerwester, S.T. Dumais, G.W. Furnas, T.K. Landauer, and R. Harshman. 1990. Indexing by latent semantic analysis. *Journal of the American Society for Information Science*, 41:391–407.

T.G. Dietterich. 1998. Machine learning research: Four current directions. *The AI Magazine*, 18(4):97–136.

S. Dumais. 2004. Latent semantic analysis. In *ARIST (Annual Review of Information Science Technology)*, volume 38, pages 189–230.

T.K. Ho, J.J. Hull, and S.N. Srihari. 1994. Decision combination in multiple classifi er systems. *IEEE Transactions on Pattern Analysis and Machine Intelligence*, 16(1):66–75.

G. Salton and M. McGill. 1983. *Introduction to Modern Information Retrieval.* McGraw-Hill.

A. Zelaia, I. Alegria, O. Arregi, and B. Sierra. 2006. A multiclassifi er based document categorization system: profi ting from the singular value decomposition dimensionality reduction technique. In *Proceedings of the Workshop on Learning Structured Information in Natural Language Applications*, pages 25–32.

UC3M_13: Disambiguation of Person Names Based on the Composition of Simple Bags of Typed Terms

David del Valle-Agudo **César de Pablo-Sánchez** **María Teresa Vicente-Díez**
Universidad Carlos III de Madrid
Escuela Politécnica Superior
Av. de la Universidad, 30 – 28911
Leganés (Madrid) Spain
{dvalle, cdepablo, tvicente}@inf.uc3m.es

Abstract

This paper describes a system designed to disambiguate person names in a set of Web pages. In our approach Web documents are represented as different sets of features or terms of different types (bag of words, URLs, names and numbers). We apply Agglomerative Vector Space clustering that uses the similarity between pairs of analogous feature sets. This system achieved a value of 66% for $F_{\alpha=0.2}$ and a value of 48% for $F_{\alpha=0.5}$ in the Web People Search Task at SemEval-2007 (Artiles et al., 2007).

1 Introduction

Name queries account for a substantial part of Web queries in commercial search engines. Name queries often aim at retrieving information about particular persons. Nevertheless, the same query or mention name usually recalls several people and the user is unaware of the potential ambiguity and expects to find the related person after skimming some results.

Similar problems are also common for products, organizations and almost any other named object in real world. A related problem appears for different kinds of objects receiving the same name. For example, Firebird can refer to a car, a guitar, a fiction superhero or a database product among more than twenty different senses collected in Wikipedia. In all these cases, the user could benefit from a structured representation that facilitates browsing results. Other applications like Question Answering would also benefit from name disambiguation and person names disambiguation, in particular. In this work we focus on the task of disambiguating Web pages retrieved for a person name query as proposed in the Web People Search Task at SemEval-2007.

2 Background and Related Research

In recent work in named entity disambiguation, Malin (2005) identifies two different dimensions to classify approaches to the task depending on the information type that is used and whether the method to train the system is supervised or unsupervised. Regarding the information type, Malin (2006) identifies personal information like biographical facts (Bagga and Baldwin, 1998; Mann and Yarowsky, 2003) or relational information (Bekkerman and McCallum, 05), collocations with other entities.

Personal name disambiguation has been studied in relation with citation analysis and record linkage and their use to improve Web search results have attracted more interest recently (Guha and Garg 2004; Bollegala, 2006), but it is evaluated only at a small scale. In contrast Bekkerman and McCallum (2005) have focused on disambiguating complete social networks and not only results for one name.

3 System description

Web People Search proposes a task to find different people sharing the same name referred in a set of Web pages and associate each of these pages to these people. To solve the task we added two simplifying assumptions; each document refers only to one person, and every listed document refers to a person.

Proceedings of the 4th International Workshop on Semantic Evaluations (SemEval-2007), pages 362–365,
Prague, June 2007.

Our approach is an unsupervised personal name disambiguation system according to the classification proposed by Malin. In this system the method applied to solve ambiguity consists of extracting from each document a set of features, that we called *document context* and afterwards to cluster them according to their similarity

3.1 Document representation

In this task we do not have structured information to estimate similarity. For this reason, the first step of the system consists of extracting features from the documents. Since our goal is to develop techniques that work for large amounts of documents, most of the features are based simply on words, HTML structure and simple patterns that aim to substitute more elaborated features based on information extraction. Features might not have a direct correspondence with facts that help to identify a person like *date of birth* or *telephone* but, in some cases, dealing with them instead of with proper semantic information can be a good approach. On the other hand, some people features, as emails or related URLs, are detected through simple patterns. Other simple patterns like numbers can also provide information about some people features.

All terms identified by the same pattern are represented as a bag of terms. Document context is composed of a set of bags, each containing all the terms of the document that were captured with a fixed pattern.

3.2 Types of Contexts

The bags of terms used in document contexts are the following:

a) emails, b) URLs, c) proper names, d) long numbers (more than four figures), e) short numbers (up to four figures), f) title terms, g) terms of the titles of related documents, h) terms contained in the '*meta*' tag of the documents, i) terms of emphasized text fragments (bold, italic, etc.), j) terms of the document snippet, and k) terms of the related documents snippets.

The bags b, f, g, j, and k have been extracted from the data files provided (snippets, rank, etc.), whereas a, c, d, e, h and i have been directly extracted from result pages.

From all the bags of terms, we finally selected to compound the contexts b, c, d, e, f, g and j as in the training set they contributed to obtain the best result.

3.3 Term normalization and filtering

Each extracted term is normalized, filtered and weighted before being added to a bag of terms. A filter for stopwords is applied to every bag of words and they are represented in lowercase. Spurious HTML tags and terms under three characters are also considered stopwords. Bag of numbers are normalized by removing blanks, hyphens and parenthesis.

In addition to stopwords, terms with low frequency, lower than 0.2 times the frequency of the more frequent term of each bag of words, are not considered. Finally the *tf-idf* value of every term is associated.

Proper names are extracted with a robust rule based name recognizer based on surface feature and some trigger words. It should be emphasized that over the bag of proper names, a filtering is implemented to make the detection of co-referents proper names easier when comparing different arrays. In this way, a similarity measure among proper names is considered (Camps and Daudé, 2003) more flexible than the simple comparison of their strings of characters. This approach tolerates the omission, substitution or inclusion of words in the proper name, the alteration in the order of the words, or the substitution of words with initials, as well as the omission, substitution or inclusion of characters. First, all proper names that are in the set of documents are identified, and all similar proper names according to these relaxed rules are grouped by the same common term. In this way, arrays of proper names are rewritten, referencing each proper name through its common term and recalculating its frequency.

3.4 Clustering algorithm

Our system uses *Agglomerative Vector Space Clustering* to group and disambiguate pages. Given the nature of the problem, it does not need to indicate the number of classes to be obtained in advance. To determine if two documents should be assigned to the same cluster, we evaluate the similarity between each pair of bags of terms and, later, it is determined how many of these pairs have a similarity over a threshold. For a document to be in the same cluster we require a minimum number of similar pairs.

In order to allow finer adjustments in the number of similar pairs needed, instead of requiring N similar pairs, the pairs are arranged in a decreasing order according to the obtained similarity and it is checked if the similarity of the nth pair is above or below the threshold. In this case, interpolation can be applied, so the number of necessary similar pairs is not limited to the natural numbers. The developed system uses linear interpolation to calculate this function.

We use the cosine vector similarity as similarity measurement.

4 Results and Evaluation

For the evaluation the system has been adjusted with a threshold of similarity of 0.001, 2.5 pairs of bags of terms above the threshold required for including two documents in the same cluster and the following bags of terms: bags of URLs, proper names, long and short numbers, terms of titles, terms of the titles of the related documents and terms of the document snippets.

With this adjustment it is noticed that some problems affect the results of the evaluation. The most important of these problems is the small number of clusters in which pages are classified. For instance, Mark Johnson refers to 70 different people in key, but our system classified his pages in only 14 clusters. Due to this small number of clusters, each contains more than one person to search, but with a good recall of pages for each person. Table 1 shows the results obtained for the test set, where P is the purity, R is the inverse purity, $F_{\alpha=0.5}$ represents the harmonic mean of purity and inverse purity, and $F_{\alpha=0.2}$ is the measure of F that considers more important inverse purity than purity.

Although at a first sight set 1 shows better results than set 2 and 3, once we discard the people names 'Sharon Goldwater' and 'Dekang Lin' (whose results are above the mean), results are very similar for all groups. We consider that our system behaves in a homogenous way regardless of the proportion of the different types of names the sets are composed of: less frequent names (with lower ambiguity) and 'celebrity' names (with people that dominate the set of pages).

In the other hand, the assumptions considered to solve the problem (each page references at least one and only one person) were definitely too naïve, as there is a lot of discarded pages (in some cases more than 50% of the pages are not taken into account) and some pages refer to several people. These facts also contribute to make lower purity.

Table 1. Test results (in percentages)

		P	R	$F_{\alpha=.5}$	$F_{\alpha=.2}$
Set 1	**Mark Johnson**	20	98	33	54
	Sharon Goldwater	99	99	99	99
	Robert Moore	26	94	40	61
	Leon Barrett	34	97	50	70
	Dekang Lin	100	98	99	98
	Stephen Clark	21	98	34	56
	Frank Keller	25	90	39	59
	Jerry Hobbs	52	92	67	80
	James Curran	24	98	39	61
	Chris Brockett	68	97	80	89
Set 2	**Thomas Fraser**	33	96	49	70
	John Nelson	24	96	38	60
	James Hamilton	19	99	32	54
	William Dickson	20	99	33	55
	James Morehead	26	96	41	62
	Patrick Killen	55	99	71	86
	George Foster	35	94	51	70
	James Davidson	25	98	39	61
	Arthur Morgan	54	98	70	84
	Thomas Kirk	11	98	20	39
Set 3	**Harry Hughes**	36	79	50	64
	Jude Brown	25	91	39	59
	Stephan Johnson	57	92	70	82
	Marcy Jackson	32	95	48	68
	Karen Peterson	12	99	21	40
	Neil Clark	46	98	62	80
	Jonathan Brooks	21	95	35	56
	Violet Howard	15	88	26	45
	Martha Edwards	11	96	20	38
	Alvin Cooper	34	95	50	70
	Set 1 Average	47	96	58	73
	Set 2 Average	30	97	44	64
	Set 3 Average	29	93	42	60
	Global Average	**35**	**95**	**48**	**66**

5 Conclusions and future works

This system obtains a good result for inverse purity to the detriment of purity. This causes a difference of almost twenty points in the measures of $F_{\alpha=0.5}$ and $F_{\alpha=0.2}$. In order to correct this weakness, in the future we will consider that any person can be mentioned in different pages, and that not all pages reference to any of the people to search.

Also we will perform additional experiments regarding parameter tuning. Although the number of similar contexts considered in these experiments is 1.5 (value that maximizes the measure of F), results show that this value causes larger groups than those found in search results. Probably a smaller value for this parameter will divide pages in more clusters, improving the purity of the result.

Finally, we would like to consider different methods to select relevant terms.

References

A. Bagga and B. Baldwin. 1998. *Entity-based cross-document coreferencing using the vector space model.* In Proc 36th Annual Meeting of the Association for Computational Linguistics. San Francisco, CA.; 79-85.

Artiles, J., Gonzalo, J. and Sekine, S. (2007). *Establishing a benchmark for the Web People Search Task: The Semeval 2007 WePS Track.* In Proceedings of Semeval 2007, Association for Computational Linguistics.

Bradley Malin. 2005. *Unsupervised name disambiguation via social network similarity.* In Proceedings of the Workshop on Link Analysis, Counterterrorism, and Security, in conjunction with the SIAM International Conference on Data Mining. Newport Beach, CA; 93-102.

Camps, R., Daudé, J. 2003. *Improving the efficacy of aproximate personal name matching.* NLDB'03. 8th International Conference on Applications of Natural langage to Informations Systems.

Danushka Bollegala, Yutaka Matsuo and Mitsuru Ishizuka. 2006. *Disambiguating Personal Names on the Web using Automatically Extracted Key Phrases.* Proceedings of the European Community of Artificial Intelligence (ECAI 2006), Italy

G. Mann and D. Yarowsky. 2003. *Unsupervised personal name disambiguation.* In Proc 7th Conference on Computational Natural Language Learning. Edmonton, Canada.

Ramanathan V. Guha and A. Garg. 2004. *Disambiguating people in search.* In WWW2004.

Ron Bekkerman, Andrew McCallum. 2005. *Disambiguating Web appearances of people in a social network.* Proceedings of the 14th international conference on World Wide Web 2005. Pages 463 - 470.

UCB: System Description for SemEval Task #4

Preslav I. Nakov
EECS, CS division
University of California at Berkeley
Berkeley, CA 94720
nakov@cs.berkeley.edu

Marti A. Hearst
School of Information
University of California at Berkeley
Berkeley, CA 94720
hearst@ischool.berkeley.edu

Abstract

The UC Berkeley team participated in the SemEval 2007 Task #4, with an approach that leverages the vast size of the Web in order to build lexically-specific features. The idea is to determine which verbs, prepositions, and conjunctions are used in sentences containing a target word pair, and to compare those to features extracted for other word pairs in order to determine which are most similar. By combining these Web features with words from the sentence context, our team was able to achieve the best results for systems of category C and third best for systems of category A.

1 Introduction

Semantic relation classification is an important but understudied language problem arising in many NLP applications, including question answering, information retrieval, machine translation, word sense disambiguation, information extraction, etc. This year's *SemEval* (previously *SensEval*) competition has included a task targeting the important special case of *Classification of Semantic Relations between Nominals*. In the present paper we describe the UCB system which took part in that competition.

The *SemEval* dataset contains a total of 7 semantic relations (not exhaustive and possibly overlapping), with 140 training and about 70 testing sentences per relation. Sentence classes are approximately 50% negative and 50% positive ("near misses"). Table 1 lists the 7 relations together with some examples.

#	Relation Name	Examples
1	Cause-Effect	hormone-growth, laugh-wrinkle
2	Instrument-Agency	laser-printer, ax-murderer
3	Product-Producer	honey-bee, philosopher-theory
4	Origin-Entity	grain-alcohol, desert-storm
5	Theme-Tool	work-force, copyright-law
6	Part-Whole	leg-table, door-car
7	Content-Container	apple-basket, plane-cargo

Table 1: **SemEval dataset**: Relations with examples (context sentences are not shown).

Each example consists of a sentence, two nominals to be judged on whether they are in the target semantic relation, manually annotated WordNet 3.0 sense keys for these nominals, and the Web query used to obtain that example:

```
"Among the contents of the <e1>vessel</e1>
were a set of carpenters <e2>tools</e2>,
several large storage jars, ceramic
utensils, ropes and remnants of food, as
well as a heavy load of ballast stones."
WordNet(e1) = "vessel%1:06:00::",
WordNet(e2) = "tool%1:06:00::",
Content-Container(e2, e1) = "true",
Query = "contents of the * were a"
```

2 Related Work

Lauer (1995) proposes that eight prepositions are enough to characterize the relation between nouns in a noun-noun compound: *of*, *for*, *in*, *at*, *on*, *from*, *with* or *about*. Lapata and Keller (2005) improve on his results by using Web statistics. Rosario et al. (2002) use a "descent of hierarchy", which characterizes the relation based on the semantic category of the two nouns. Girju et al. (2005) apply SVM, decision trees, semantic scattering and iterative seman-

Proceedings of the 4th International Workshop on Semantic Evaluations (SemEval-2007), pages 366–369,
Prague, June 2007.

tic specialization, using WordNet, word sense disambiguation, and linguistic features. Barker and Szpakowicz (1998) propose a two-level hierarchy with 5 classes at the upper level and 30 at the lower level. Turney (2005) introduces latent relational analysis, which uses the Web, synonyms, patterns like "X for Y", "X such as Y", etc., and singular value decomposition to smooth the frequencies. Turney (2006) induces patterns from the Web, e.g. CAUSE is best characterized by "*Y * causes X*", and "*Y in * early X*" is the best pattern for TEMPORAL. Kim and Baldwin (2006) propose to use a *predefined* set of seed verbs and multiple resources: WordNet, CoreLex, and Moby's thesaurus. Finally, in a previous publication (Nakov and Hearst, 2006), we make the claim that the relation between the nouns in a noun-noun compound can be characterized by the set of intervening verbs extracted from the Web.

3 Method

Given an entity-annotated example sentence, we reduce the target entities e_1 and e_2 to single nouns $noun_1$ and $noun_2$, by keeping their last nouns only, which we assume to be the heads. We then mine the Web for sentences containing both $noun_1$ and $noun_2$, from which we extract features, consisting of word(s), part of speech (verb, preposition, verb+preposition, coordinating conjunction), and whether $noun_1$ precedes $noun_2$. Table 2 shows some example features and their frequencies.

We start with a set of exact phrase queries against Google: "$infl_1$ THAT $\star$ $infl_2$", "$infl_2$ THAT $\star$ $infl_1$", "$infl_1$ $\star$ $infl_2$", and "$infl_2$ $\star$ $infl_1$", where $infl_1$ and $infl_2$ are inflectional variants of $noun_1$ and $noun_2$, generated using WordNet (Fellbaum, 1998); THAT can be *that*, *which*, or *who*; and $\star$ stands for 0 or more (up to 8) stars separated by spaces, representing the Google $\star$ single-word wildcard match operator. For each query, we collect the text snippets from the result set (up to 1000 per query), split them into sentences, assign POS tags using the OpenNLP tagger[1], and extract features:

Verb: If one of the nouns is the subject, and the other one is a direct or indirect object of that verb, we extract it and we lemmatize it using WordNet (Fellbaum, 1998). We ignore modals and auxiliaries, but retain the passive *be*, verb particles and prepositions (in case of indirect object).

[1]OpenNLP: http://opennlp.sourceforge.net

Freq.	Feature	POS	Direction
2205	of	P	$2 \rightarrow 1$
1923	be	V	$1 \rightarrow 2$
771	include	V	$1 \rightarrow 2$
382	serve on	V	$2 \rightarrow 1$
189	chair	V	$2 \rightarrow 1$
189	have	V	$1 \rightarrow 2$
169	consist of	V	$1 \rightarrow 2$
148	comprise	V	$1 \rightarrow 2$
106	sit on	V	$2 \rightarrow 1$
81	be chaired by	V	$1 \rightarrow 2$
78	appoint	V	$1 \rightarrow 2$
77	on	P	$2 \rightarrow 1$
66	and	C	$1 \rightarrow 2$
...	...	...	...

Table 2: **Most frequent features for *committee member***. V stands for verb, P for preposition, and C for coordinating conjunction.

Preposition: If one of the nouns is the head of an NP which contains a PP, inside which there is an NP headed by the other noun (or an inflectional form thereof), we extract the preposition heading that PP.

Coordination: If the two nouns are the heads of two coordinated NPs, we extract the coordinating conjunction.

In addition, we include some non-Web features[2]:

Sentence word: We use as features the words from the context sentence, after stop words removal and stemming with the Porter stemmer.

Entity word: We also use the lemmas of the words that are part of e_i $(i = 1, 2)$.

Query word: Finally, we use the individual words that are part of the query string. This feature is used for category C runs only (see below).

Once extracted, the features are used to calculate the similarity between two noun pairs. Each feature triplet is assigned a weight. We wish to downweight very common features, such as "of" used as a preposition in the $2 \rightarrow 1$ direction, so we apply tf.idf weighting to each feature. We then use the following variant of the Dice coefficient to compare the weight vectors $A = (a_1, \ldots, a_n)$ and $B = (b_1, \ldots, b_n)$:

$$Dice(A, B) = \frac{2 \times \sum_{i=1}^{n} \min(a_i, b_i)}{\sum_{i=1}^{n} a_i + \sum_{i=1}^{n} b_i} \quad (1)$$

This vector representation is similar to that of

[2]Features have type prefix to prevent them from mixing.

System	Relation	P	R	F	Acc
UCB-A1	Cause-Effect	58.2	78.0	66.7	60.0
	Instrument-Agency	62.5	78.9	69.8	66.7
	Product-Producer	77.3	54.8	64.2	59.1
	Origin-Entity	67.9	52.8	59.4	67.9
	Theme-Tool	50.0	31.0	38.3	59.2
	Part-Whole	51.9	53.8	52.8	65.3
	Content-Container	62.2	60.5	61.3	60.8
	average	**61.4**	**58.6**	**58.9**	**62.7**
UCB-A2	Cause-Effect	58.0	70.7	63.7	58.8
	Instrument-Agency	65.9	71.1	68.4	67.9
	Product-Producer	80.0	77.4	78.7	72.0
	Origin-Entity	60.6	55.6	58.0	64.2
	Theme-Tool	45.0	31.0	36.7	56.3
	Part-Whole	41.7	38.5	40.0	58.3
	Content-Container	56.4	57.9	57.1	55.4
	average	**58.2**	**57.5**	**57.5**	**61.9**
UCB-A3	Cause-Effect	62.5	73.2	67.4	63.8
	Instrument-Agency	65.9	76.3	70.7	69.2
	Product-Producer	75.0	67.7	71.2	63.4
	Origin-Entity	48.4	41.7	44.8	54.3
	Theme-Tool	62.5	51.7	56.6	67.6
	Part-Whole	50.0	46.2	48.0	63.9
	Content-Container	64.9	63.2	64.0	63.5
	average	**61.3**	**60.0**	**60.4**	**63.7**
UCB-A4	Cause-Effect	63.5	80.5	71.0	66.2
	Instrument-Agency	70.0	73.7	71.8	71.8
	Product-Producer	76.3	72.6	74.4	66.7
	Origin-Entity	50.0	47.2	48.6	55.6
	Theme-Tool	61.5	55.2	58.2	67.6
	Part-Whole	52.2	46.2	49.0	65.3
	Content-Container	65.8	65.8	65.8	64.9
	average	**62.7**	**63.0**	**62.7**	**65.4**
	Baseline (majority)	81.3	42.9	30.8	57.0

Table 3: **Task 4 results.** UCB systems $A1$-$A4$.

System	Relation	P	R	F	Acc
UCB-C1	Cause-Effect	58.5	75.6	66.0	60.0
	Instrument-Agency	65.2	78.9	71.4	69.2
	Product-Producer	81.4	56.5	66.7	62.4
	Origin-Entity	67.9	52.8	59.4	67.9
	Theme-Tool	50.0	31.0	38.3	59.2
	Part-Whole	51.9	53.8	52.8	65.3
	Content-Container	62.2	60.5	61.3	60.8
	Average	**62.4**	**58.5**	**59.4**	**63.5**
UCB-C2	Cause-Effect	58.0	70.7	63.7	58.8
	Instrument-Agency	67.5	71.1	69.2	69.2
	Product-Producer	80.3	79.0	79.7	73.1
	Origin-Entity	60.6	55.6	58.0	64.2
	Theme-Tool	50.0	37.9	43.1	59.2
	Part-Whole	43.5	38.5	40.8	59.7
	Content-Container	56.4	57.9	57.1	55.4
	Average	**59.5**	**58.7**	**58.8**	**62.8**
UCB-C3	Cause-Effect	62.5	73.2	67.4	63.8
	Instrument-Agency	68.2	78.9	73.2	71.8
	Product-Producer	74.1	69.4	71.7	63.4
	Origin-Entity	56.8	58.3	57.5	61.7
	Theme-Tool	62.5	51.7	56.6	67.6
	Part-Whole	50.0	42.3	45.8	63.9
	Content-Container	64.9	63.2	64.0	63.5
	Average	**62.7**	**62.4**	**62.3**	**65.1**
UCB-C4	Cause-Effect	63.5	80.5	71.0	66.2
	Instrument-Agency	70.7	76.3	73.4	73.1
	Product-Producer	76.7	74.2	75.4	67.7
	Origin-Entity	59.0	63.9	61.3	64.2
	Theme-Tool	63.0	58.6	60.7	69.0
	Part-Whole	52.2	46.2	49.0	65.3
	Content-Container	64.1	65.8	64.9	63.5
	Average	**64.2**	**66.5**	**65.1**	**67.0**
	Baseline (majority)	81.3	42.9	30.8	57.0

Table 4: **Task 4 results.** UCB systems $C1$-$C4$.

Lin (1998), who measures word similarity by using triples extracted from a dependency parser. In particular, given a noun, he finds all verbs that have it as a subject or object, and all adjectives that modify it, together with the corresponding frequencies.

4 Experiments and Results

Participants were asked to classify their systems into categories depending on whether they used the WordNet sense (WN) and/or the Google query (GC). Our team submitted runs for categories A (WN=no, QC=no) and C (WN=no, QC=yes) only, since we believe that having the target entities annotated with the correct WordNet senses is an unrealistic assumption for a real-world application.

Following Turney and Littman (2005) and Barker and Szpakowicz (1998), we used a 1-nearest-neighbor classifier. Given a test example, we calculated the Dice coefficient between its feature vector and the vector of each of the training examples. If there was a single highest-scoring training example, we predicted its class for that test example. Otherwise, if there were ties for first, we assumed the class predicted by the majority of the tied examples. If there was no majority, we predicted the class that was most likely on the training data. Regardless of the classifier's prediction, if the head words of the two entities e_1 and e_2 had the same lemma, we classified that example as negative.

Table 3 and 4 show the results for our A and C runs for different amounts of training data: 45 ($A1$, $C1$), 90 ($A2$, $C2$), 105 ($A3$, $C3$) and 140 ($A4$, $C4$). All results are above the baseline: always propose the majority label ("true"/"false") in the test set. In fact, our category C system is the best-performing (in terms of F and Acc) among the participating systems, and we achieved the third best results for category A. Our category C results are slightly but consistently better than for A for all measures (P, R, F, Acc), which suggests that knowing the query is helpful. Interestingly, systems UCB-$A2$ and UCB-$C2$ performed worse than UCB-$A1$ and UCB-$C1$, which means that having more training data does not necessarily help with a 1NN classifier.

Table 5 shows additional analysis for $A4$ and $C4$. We study the effect of adding extra Google contexts (using up to 10 stars, rather than 8), and using different subsets of features. We show the results for: (a) leave-one-out cross-validation on the training data, (b) on the test data, and (c) our official UCB runs.

Acknowledgements: This work is supported in part by NSF DBI-0317510.

References

Ken Barker and Stan Szpakowicz. 1998. Semi-automatic recognition of noun modifier relationships. In *Proceedings of COLING-ACL'98*, pages 96–102.

Christiane Fellbaum, editor. 1998. *WordNet: An Electronic Lexical Database*. MIT Press.

Roxana Girju, Dan Moldovan, Marta Tatu, and Daniel Antohe. 2005. On the semantics of noun compounds. *Computer Speech and Language*, 19(4):479–496.

Su Nam Kim and Timothy Baldwin. 2006. Interpreting semantic relations in noun compounds via verb semantics. In *Proceedings of COLING/ACL 2006. (poster)*, pages 491–498.

Mirella Lapata and Frank Keller. 2005. Web-based models for natural language processing. *ACM Transactions on Speech and Language Processing*, 2:1–31.

Mark Lauer. 1995. *Designing Statistical Language Learners: Experiments on Noun Compounds*. Ph.D. thesis, Department of Computing Macquarie University NSW 2109 Australia.

Dekang Lin. 1998. An information-theoretic definition of similarity. In *Proceedings of International Conference on Machine Learning*, pages 296–304.

Preslav Nakov and Marti Hearst. 2006. Using verbs to characterize noun-noun relations. In *Proceedings of AIMSA*, pages 233–244.

Barbara Rosario, Marti Hearst, and Charles Fillmore. 2002. The descent of hierarchy, and selection in relational semantics. In *ACL*, pages 247–254.

Peter Turney and Michael Littman. 2005. Corpus-based learning of analogies and semantic relations. *Machine Learning Journal*, 60(1-3):251–278.

Peter Turney. 2005. Measuring semantic similarity by latent relational analysis. In *Proceedings IJCAI*, pages 1136–1141.

Peter Turney. 2006. Expressing implicit semantic relations without supervision. In *Proceedings of COLING-ACL*, pages 313–320.

Features Used	Leave-1-out	Test	UCB
Cause-Effect			
$sent$	45.7	50.0	
p	55.0	53.8	
v	59.3	68.8	
$v+p$	57.1	63.7	
$v+p+c$	70.5	67.5	
$v+p+c+sent$	58.5	66.2	66.2
$v+p+c+sent+query$	59.3	66.2	66.2
Instrument-Agency			
$sent$	63.6	59.0	
p	62.1	70.5	
v	71.4	69.2	
$v+p$	70.7	70.5	
$v+p+c$	70.0	70.5	
$v+p+c+sent$	68.6	71.8	71.8
$v+p+c+sent+query$	70.0	73.1	73.1
Product-Producer			
$sent$	47.9	59.1	
p	55.7	58.1	
v	70.0	61.3	
$v+p$	66.4	65.6	
$v+p+c$	67.1	65.6	
$v+p+c+sent$	66.4	69.9	66.7
$v+p+c+sent+query$	67.9	69.9	67.7
Origin-Entity			
$sent$	64.3	72.8	
p	63.6	56.8	
v	69.3	71.6	
$v+p$	67.9	69.1	
$v+p+c$	66.4	70.4	
$v+p+c+sent$	68.6	72.8	55.6
$v+p+c+sent+query$	67.9	72.8	64.2
Theme-Tool			
$sent$	66.4	69.0	
p	56.4	56.3	
v	61.4	70.4	
$v+p$	56.4	67.6	
$v+p+c$	57.1	69.0	
$v+p+c+sent$	52.1	62.0	67.6
$v+p+c+sent+query$	52.9	62.0	69.0
Part-Whole			
$sent$	47.1	51.4	
p	57.1	54.1	
v	60.0	66.7	
$v+p$	62.1	63.9	
$v+p+c$	61.4	63.9	
$v+p+c+sent$	60.0	61.1	65.3
$v+p+c+sent+query$	60.0	61.1	65.3
Content-Container			
$sent$	56.4	54.1	
p	57.9	59.5	
v	71.4	67.6	
$v+p$	72.1	67.6	
$v+p+c$	72.9	67.6	
$v+p+c+sent$	69.3	67.6	64.9
$v+p+c+sent+query$	71.4	71.6	63.5
Average A4		**67.3**	**65.4**
Average C4		**68.1**	**67.0**

Table 5: **Accuracy for different features and extra Web contexts:** on leave-one-out cross-validation, on testing data, and in the official UCB runs.

UCD-FC: Deducing semantic relations using WordNet senses that occur frequently in a database of noun-noun compounds *

Fintan J. Costello,
School of Computer Science and Informatics, University College Dublin,
Belfield, Dublin 6, Ireland.
fintan.costello@ucd.ie

Abstract

This paper describes a system for classifying semantic relations among nominals, as in SemEval task 4. This system uses a corpus of 2,500 compounds annotated with WordNet senses and covering 139 different semantic relations. Given a set of nominal pairs for training, as provided in the SemEval task 4 training data, this system constructs for each training pair a set of features made up of relations and WordNet sense pairs which occurred with those nominals in the corpus. A Naive Bayes learning algorithm learns associations between these features and relation membership categories. The identification of relations among nominals in test items takes place on the basis of these associations.

1 Introduction

This paper describes a system for deducing the correct semantic relation between a pair of nominals in a sentence, as in SemEval task 4 (Girju, Hearst, Nakov, Nastase, Szpakowicz, Turney, & Yuret, 2007). This system is an adaptation of an existing system for deducing the correct semantic relation between the pair of words in a noun-noun compound. This compound disambiguation system (named PRO, for Proportional Relation Occurrence; see Costello, Veale, & Dunne, 2006) makes use of a corpus of 2,500 compounds annotated with WordNet senses and covering 139 different semantic relations, with each noun and each relation annotated with its correct WordNet sense.[1] Section 2 of the paper will describe the format and structure of this corpus, Section 3 will describe the original PRO compound disambiguation system, and Section 4 will explain how the PRO system was adapted to deduce the correct semantic relation between a pair of nominals, as in SemEval task 4. Four different versions of the adapted system were produced (versions A,B, C and D), either using or not using the WordNet labels and the Query labels provided with training and test items in SemEval task 4. Section 5 discusses the performance of these different versions of the system. Finally, Section 6 finishes the paper with some discussion and ideas for future work.

2 A Corpus of Annotated Compounds

Using WordNet (Miller, 1995), version 2.0, a corpus of noun-noun compounds was constructed such that each compound was annotated with the correct WordNet noun senses for constituent words, the correct semantic relation between those words, and the correct WordNet verb sense for that relation, as described below.

2.1 Corpus Procedure

The compounds used in this corpus were selected from the set of noun-noun compounds defined in WordNet. Compounds from WordNet were used because each compound had an associated gloss or

* This research was supported by the FP6 NEST Programme of the European Commission (ANALOGY: Humans the Analogy-Making Species: STREP Contr. No 029088)

[1] A file containing this corpus is available for download from http://inismor.ucd.ie/~fintanc/wordnet_compounds

Proceedings of the 4th International Workshop on Semantic Evaluations (SemEval-2007), pages 370–373,
Prague, June 2007. ©2007 Association for Computational Linguistics

definition explaining the relation between the words in that compound (compounds from other sources would not have such associated definitions). Also, using compounds from WordNet guarantees that all constituent words of those compounds would also have entries in WordNet. An initial list of over 40,000 two-word noun-noun compounds was extracted from WordNet 2.0. From this list a random subset was selected. From that set all compounds using scientific latin (e.g. ocimum basilicum), idiomatic compounds (e.g. zero hour), compounds containing proper nouns (e.g. Yangtze river), non-english compounds (e.g. faux pas), and chemical terminology (e.g. carbon dioxide) were excluded.

The remaining compounds were placed in random order, and a research assistant annotated each with the WordNet noun senses of the constituent words, the semantic relation between those words, and the WordNet verb sense of that relation. A web page was created for this annotation task, showing the annotator the compound to be annotated and the WordNet gloss (meaning) for that compound. This page also showed the annotator the list of WordNet senses for the modifier noun and head noun in the compound, allowing the annotator to select the correct sense for each word. After word-sense selection another page was presented allowing the annotator to identify the correct semantic relation for that compound and to select the correct WordNet sense for the verb in that relation.

2.2 Corpus Results

Word sense, relation, and relation sense information was gathered for 2,500 compounds. Relation occurrence was well distributed across these compounds: there were 139 different relations used in the corpus. Note that in SemEval task 4, the number of relation categories available was much smaller than the set of relation categories available in our corpus (just 7 relation categories in the SemEval task).

3 Compound Disambiguation Algorithm

This section presents the 'Proportional Relation Occurrence' (PRO) algorithm which makes use of the corpus results described above to deduce semantic relations for noun-noun compounds. In Section 4 this algorithm is adapted to deduce relations between nominals in SemEval task 4.

Preconditions:
The entry for each compound C in corpus D contains:
$C_{modList}$ = sense + hypernym senses for modifier of C;
$C_{headList}$ = sense + hypernym senses for head of C;
C_{rel} = semantic relation of C;

Input:
X = compound for which a relation is required;
$modList$ = sense + hypernym senses for modifier of X;
$headList$ = sense + hypernym senses for head of X;
$finalRelationList$ = ();
$finalPairList$ = ();

Begin:
for each modifier sense $M \in modList$
  for each head sense $H \in headList$
    $relCount$ = ();
    $matchCount$ = 0;
    $P = (M, H)$;
    for each compound $C \in$ corpus D
      if $((M \in C_{modList})$ and $(H \in C_{headList}))$
        $relCount[C_{rel}] = relCount[C_{rel}] + 1$;
        $matchCount = matchCount + 1$;
    for each relation $R \in relCount$
      $score = relCount[R]/matchCount$;
      $prevScore = finalRelationList[R]$;
      if $(score > prevScore)$
        $finalRelationList[R] = score$;
      if $(score > pairScore)$
        $finalPairList[P] = score$;
sort $finalRelationList$ by score ;
sort $finalPairList$ by score ;
return $(finalRelationList, finalPairList)$;
End.

Figure 1: PRO disambiguation algorithm.

The approach to compound disambiguation taken here is similar to that taken by for example Kim & Baldwin (2005) and Girju, Moldovan, Tatu, & Antohe (2005), and works by finding other compounds containing words from the same semantic categories as the words in the compound to be disambiguated: if a particular relation occurs frequently in those other compounds, that relation is probably also the correct relation for the compound in question. We take WordNet senses to represent semantic categories. Once the correct WordNet sense for a word has been identified, that word can placed in a set of nested semantic categories: the category represented by that sense, by the parent sense (or hypernym) of that sense, the parent of that parent, and so on up to the (notional) root sense of WordNet.

Figure 1 shows the algorithm in pseudocode. The algorithm uses the corpus of annotated noun-noun compounds and, to disambiguate a compound, takes as input the correct WordNet sense for the modifier and head words of that compound (if known) plus all hypernyms of those senses. If modifier and head word senses are not known, the most frequent senses for those words are used, plus all hypernyms of those senses. The algorithm pairs each modifier sense with every head sense. For each sense-pair, the algorithm goes through the corpus of compounds and extracts every compound whose modifier sense (or a hypernym of that sense) is equal to the modifier sense in the current sense-pair, and whose head sense (or a hypernym of that sense) is equal to the head sense in that pair. The algorithm counts the number of times each relation occurs in that set of compounds, and assigns each relation a Proportional Relation Occurrence (PRO) score for that pair, equal to the conditional probability of relation R given sense-pair S.

If the PRO score for relation R in the current sense-pair is greater than the score obtained for R with some other pair, the current score is recorded for R. If the score for R for the current pair P is greater than any previous score obtained for P, that score is recorded for P. In this way the algorithm finds the maximum score for each relation R across all sense-pairs, and the maximum score for each pair P across all relations. The algorithm returns a list of relations and of sense-pairs for the compound, both sorted by score. The relations and sense-pairs with the highest scores are those most likely to be correct for that compound and to be most important for its relational meaning.

In Costello, Veale and Dunne (2006), this algorithm was tested by applying it to the annotated corpus using a leave-one-out approach. These tests showed a reliable relationship between PRO score and accuracy of response. At a PRO level of 1, the algorithm return a response (selects a relation) for just over 900 compounds, and approximately 850 of those responses are correct (the algorithm's precision at this level is 0.92).

4 Adapting to the SemEval 4 task

To apply the PRO algorithm to the training and test sentences in SemEval task 4 first required a mapping from the labels used to tag nominals in that task (labels *e1* and *e2*) to the modifier and head categories used by the PRO algorithm. To carry out this mapping the nominal whose label appeared in the first position in a relation tag was taken to be the modifier for that relation, and that in the second position was taken to be the head; for example, with the relation tag *CONTAINER-CONTENT(E1,E2)* the nominal *e1* would be taken to be the modifer and *e2* to be the head. Given this mapping the PRO algorithm could be applied to sentences from SemEval task 4, taking modifier and head nominals as input and producing as output lists of candidate relations and relevant sense pairs (sorted by PRO score).

The relations produced by the PRO algorithm do not correspond to the 7 relations in SemEval task 4. To make predictions about the 7 SemEval relations, the scored relation lists and sense-pair lists returned by the PRO algorithm were used as features for a straightforward Naive Bayes learning algorithm, as implemented in the Perl module *Algorithm::NaiveBayes*. For each sentence in a training set in SemEval task 4, the PRO algorithm was applied to produce a list of relations and sense pairs describing that sentence. Each relation and each sense pair in this list has an associated PRO score, and Naive Bayes was trained on these features of all members of the training set, and then applied to test set sentences to produce predictions about each sentence's membership or non-membership in the relation in question.

Version A of the system used neither the WordNet sense tags nor the Query labels provided with the 7 relation categories used. Instead of using WordNet senses for the input words the system simply used the first (most frequent) noun senses for those words, and proceeded as described above. Version B used WordNet sense tags. Versions C and D of the system used either the first WordNet sense or the provided sense tags, coupled with the query terms used in the SemEval task. An additional module in the system was intended to make use of these query terms in relation classification by comparing the query term of the sentence to be classified with query terms in positive or negative training examples of that relation, and making a decision based on that comparison. Unfortunately, due to an error this query term module was not activated in the submitted runs, so the results from versions C and D are the same as from A and B.

Table 1: F-Score results by relation and run.

relation	A4	B4	C4	D4
Cause-Effect	72.1	65.1	72.1	65.1
Instrument-Agency	69.8	58.1	69.8	58.1
Product-Producer	73.1	73	73.1	73
Origin-Entity	43.1	42.3	43.1	42.3
Theme-Tool	50	49.2	50	49.2
Part-Whole	71.7	75	71.7	75
Content-Container	73.8	59.4	73.8	59.4
Avg	64.8	60.3	64.8	60.3

5 SemEval 4 task results

Table 1 shows the results returned for the PRO system for training run 4 (using all 140 training items in each relation) for the four possible runs A, B, C and D. Due to the error in activating the query term module, columns C4 and D4 are identical to columns A4 and B4. There are two notable aspects of the results in Table 1. First, the system's performance was better for run A4 (that did not use WordNet senses) than for B4 (using WordNet senses). Indeed, the system came first out of 6 systems which took part in the A4 run. This was surprising: it had been expected that using the correct WordNet senses for nominals would improve the system's performance. Analysis revealed that A4 runs using most frequent WordNet senses provided more matches with entries in the compound corpus the B4 run using the correct WordNet senses. This may explain why the system gave a better performance for A4 than B4.

The second interesting aspect of Table 1 is the variation of the system's responses across the different relation categories. For the two relations 'Origin-Entity' and 'Theme-Tool' the system has an F-score of 50 or less, while for the other five relations the system's F-score is around 70. It is not as yet clear why the system performed so poorly for these relations: further investigation is needed to explain this curious pattern.

6 Conclusions

This paper has described a system for automatically seslecting relations between nominals which uses the PRO algorithm and compound corpus to form features for pairs of nominals (consisting of candidate relations and sense-pairs co-occurring with those relations), and uses a Naive Bayes algorithm to learn to identify relations between nominals from those features. The system performs best using the most frequent WordNet senses for those nominals, suggesting that the system may work usefully in deducing semantic relations between nominals without the need to deduce word senses. However, the system's performance does not seem particularly impressive or suitable for application to real-world tasks as yet. The system's best performance represents an accuracy of 66% across relations: in other words, the system gets 1 in three relations wrong in the SemEval task.

There is one very obvious area for improvement in the system described here. Currently the system uses a simple Naive Bayes algorithm for learning associations between features and relation categories. A more sophisticated approach (using Support Vector Machines, for example) would be likely to improve the systsem's performance noticably. The conversion of the system to use some form of SVM should not be difficult. A more difficult problem, however, is to address the system's poor performance on some relations. This is currently difficult to understand, and represents a serious flaw in the system. Resolving this problem may reveal some useful aspects of the structure of different sorts of semantic relations between nominals.

References

F. J. Costello, T. Veale and S. Dunne. 2006. Using WordNet to Automatically Deduce Relations between Words in Noun-Noun Compounds. In Proceedings of the COLING/ACL 2006 Main Conference, pp 160–167.

R. Girju, M. Hearst, P. Nakov, V. Nastase, S. Szpakowicz, P. Turney and D. Yuret. 2007. Classification of Semantic Relations between Nominals: Dataset for Task 4 in SemEval 2007. 4th International Workshop on Semantic Evaluations, June 23-24, Prague, Czech Republic.

R. Girju, D. Moldovan, M. Tatu, and D. Antohe. 2005. On the semantics of noun compounds. Computer Speech and Language 19, 4, 479–496.

S. N. Kim and T. Baldwin. Automatic Interpretation of Noun Compounds using WordNet::Similarity. 2nd Internationl Joint Conference on Natual Language Processing, Korea, 2005.

G. Miller. 1995. WordNet: A lexical database. Communication of the ACM, 38(11), 39–41.

UCD-PN: Classification of Semantic Relations Between Nominals using WordNet and Web Counts

Paul Nulty
School of Computer Science and Informatics
University College Dublin
Dublin, Ireland
paul.nulty@ucd.ie

Abstract

For our system we use the SMO implementation of a support vector machine provided with the WEKA machine learning toolkit. As with all machine learning approaches, the most important step is to choose a set of features which reliably help to predict the label of the example. We used 76 features drawn from two very different knowledge sources. The first 48 features are boolean values indicating whether or not each of the nominals in the sentence are linked to certain other words in the WordNet hypernym and meronym networks. The remaining 28 features are web frequency counts for the two nominals joined by certain common prepositions and verbs. Our system performed well on all but two of the relations; theme-tool and origin entity.

1 Introduction and Related Work

This paper describes a system for participating in SemEval 2007 task 4; "Classification of Semantic Relations Between Nominals". This SemEval task required systems to establish whether or not a particular semantic relation held between two nominals in a sentence. There were 7 semantic relations, with approximately 70 positive and 70 negative example sentences for each relation. There were approximately 70 examples in the test sets for each relation.

This task is similar to the problem of determining what semantic relation holds between the constituents of a noun-noun compound. Work in this area has used both statistical information about the frequencies of lexical patterns and hand-built knowledge databases such as WordNet and thesaura. In our system we combine these two knowledge sources and build a set of features to use as input to a Support Vector Machine learning algorithm.

The use of hit counts from web search engines to obtain lexical information was introduced by Turney (2001). The idea of searching a large corpus for specific lexico-syntactic phrases to indicate a semantic relation of interest was first described by Hearst (1992). A lexical pattern specific enough to indicate a particular semantic relation is usually not very frequent, and using the web as a corpus alleviates the data sparseness problem. However, it also introduces some problems. The number of results returned is unstable as pages are created and deleted all the time, and the major search engines return only rounded frequency estimates and do not allow a very sophisticated query interface. Nakov and Hearst (2005) examined the use of web-based n-gram frequencies for an NLP task and concluded that these issues do not greatly impact the interpretation of the results.

Turney and Littman (2005) use web queries to the AltaVista search engine as the basis for their system to assign semantic relations to modifier-noun phrases. They use a set of 64 short prepositional and conjunctive phrases (joining terms) to generate exact queries of the form "*noun joining term modifier*", and "*modifier joining term noun*". Using 64 joining terms and trying the noun and modifier in either order resulted in a vector of 128

Proceedings of the 4th International Workshop on Semantic Evaluations (SemEval-2007), pages 374–377,
Prague, June 2007.

hit counts for each noun-modifier pair. These hit counts were used with a supervised (nearest neighbor) algorithm to label the modifier-noun phrases.

Nakov and Hearst (2006) use queries of the form "*noun that * modifier*" where '*' is a wildcard operator. By retrieving the words that most commonly occurred in the place of the wildcard they were able to identify very specific predicates that are likely to represent the relation between noun and modifier.

There have also been several approaches which used hand built knowledge sources. Rosario and Hearst (2001) used MeSH, a lexical hierarchy of medical terms. They use this hierarchy to assign semantic properties to head and modifier words in the medical domain. They use a neural network trained on these attributes to assign the noun phrases a semantic relation.

Nastase and Szpakowicz (2003) use the position of the noun and modifier words within general semantic hierarchies (Roget's Thesaurus and WordNet) as attributes for their learning algorithms. They experiment with decision trees, a rule induction system, a relational learner and memory based learning. They conclude that the rule induction system is capable of generalizing to characterize the noun phrases.

Moldovan et al (2004) also use WordNet. They experiment with a Bayesian algorithm, decision trees, and their own algorithm; semantic scattering.

As far as we are aware ours is the first system to combine features derived from a hand-built lexical database with corpus frequencies of lexical patterns.

2 System Description

2.1 WordNet Features

Our system uses both features derived from WordNet and features obtained by collecting web frequencies for lexical patterns. We did not use any information from the sentence in which the two nominals appeared, nor did we use the query used to retrieve the examples. We did make use of the WordNet sense for the features we obtained from WordNet.

There are 48 features derived from WordNet. Most of these are boolean values indicating whether or not each of the nominals in the sentence appear below certain other high-level concepts in the hypernym hierarchy. We chose 22 high level concepts we believed may be good predictors of whether or not a nominal could be an argument of the semantic relations used in this task. These concepts are listed below in table 1.

physical_entity	physical_object
grouping	substance
attribute	matter
psychological_feature	process
quantity	causal_agent
container	tool
act	device
work	content
being	event
natural_object	unit
instrumentation	state

Table 1. Concepts in the WordNet hierarchy used to generate features.

For each of these WordNet entries we checked whether or not each of the nominals in the example sentence appeared below the entry in the WordNet hypernym tree. This gave us 44 features. We also checked whether the first nominal was a hypernym of the second; and vice-versa; and whether the first nominal was a meronym of the second; and vice versa. This gives us in total 48 boolean features derived from WordNet.

2.2 Web Frequencies

The remaining features were numerical values obtained by retrieving the frequencies of web searches for the two nominals joined by certain common prepositions and verbs. These joining terms are listed below in table 2.

of	produces
for	used for
in	has
on	contains
at	from
with	causes
about	made from

Table 2. Joining terms used to generate features.

To obtain the frequencies we used the API to the "MSN Live" search engine.

Choosing a set of joining terms in a principled manner is not an easy task, but there is certainly some correlation between a prepositional term or short linking verb and a semantic relation. For example, "*contains*" tends to indicate a spatial relation, while the preposition "*in*" indicates a locative relation, either temporal or spatial.

When collecting web frequencies we took advantage of the OR operator provided by the search engine. For each joining term, we wanted to sum the number of hits for the term on its own, the term followed by '*a*', and the term followed by '*the*'. Instead of conducting separate queries for each of these forms, we were able to sum the results with just one search. For example, if the two nominals in the sentence were "*battery*" and "*phone*"; one of the queries would be:

"battery in phone" OR "battery in *a phone" OR "battery in the phone"*

These features were numeric values; the raw number of documents returned by the query.

2.3 Learning Algorithm

All of the features were used as input to our learning algorithm, which was a Support Vector Machine (SVM). An SVM is a method for creating a classification function which works by trying to find a hypersurface in the space of possible inputs that splits the positive examples from the negative examples for each class. We did not normalize these values as normalization is handled by the WEKA implementation which we used.

WEKA is a machine learning toolkit written in Java (Witten and Frank, 1999). The algorithm we used was an SVM trained with the Sequential Minimal Optimization method provided by Weka.

3. Results

The average f-value obtained by our system using all of the training data was 65.4. There was a significant difference in performance across different relations. The results for each relation are below.

Relation	Pre	Rec	F	Acc
cause-effect	61.7	90.2	73.3	66.2
instrument-agency	59.3	84.2	69.6	64.1
product-producer	70.9	98.4	82.4	72.0
origin-entity	51.4	50.0	50.7	56.8
theme-tool	52.9	31.0	39.1	60.6
part-whole	66.7	69.2	67.9	76.4
content-container	71.4	78.9	75.0	73.0
Average	62.0	71.7	65.4	67.

The standard deviation of the f-values is 13.9. The average of the f-values is brought down by two of the relations; origin-entity and theme-tool. The poor performance of these relations was noted during early experimentation with the training data; and the list of WordNet concepts and joining terms was amended to try to improve classification, but no improvement was achieved. If the results for these relations are omitted the average f-score rises to 73.6

3.1 Information Gain

In order to evaluate which features were the most useful for each relation, we used the Information Gain feature ranking tool in WEKA. This tool measures the change in entropy attributed to each feature and ranks them accordingly. In some cases we found that the high ranking features for a relation were ones which were intuitively relevant to predicting that relation; however some features still had high Information Gain despite seeming unlikely to be predictive of the relation.

The eight most informative features for the Cause-Effect and Content-Container relations are shown below. WordNet features are in normal

Cause-Effect	Content-Container
quantity	Instrumentation2
at	Container2
used for2	*contains*
grouping	physical_object2
object2	physical_entity2
substance	psychological_feature
substance2	substance2
instrumentation2	device2

Table 3. The features with the highest information gain for cause-effect and content-container.

font; the joining terms for web searches in italics. The '2' after a feature indicates that the web search was of the form "N2 joining term N1"; or that the WordNet property holds for N2; where the relation is *relation*(N1,N2).

Most of these features make sense. For example, the search query "contains" and the Wordnet entry "Container" linked to the second noun are the second and third most informative for the content container class, and the query "N2 used for N1" ranks highly in the cause-effect relation. However, it is unclear why being a hyponym of "quantity" would provide information about the cause-effect relation.

4 Conclusion and Future Work

This paper describes a system for participating in SemEval 2007 task 4; "Classification of Semantic Relations Between Nominals". Our system combines features generated by analyzing the WordNet hypernym tree with features which indicate the frequencies of certain lexical patterns involving the nominals and common prepositions, using the web as a corpus.

The performance of the system was above the average score of other systems which used the WordNet sense of the training examples but not the query used to obtain them. The system was held back particularly by two relations, theme-tool and origin-entity.

There are many potential avenues for future work in this area. We chose 48 features based on WordNet and 28 lexical patterns to search the web for. These were chosen arbitrarily on the basis that they looked like they would be informative in general, over all seven relations. A more principled approach would be to begin with a much larger number of features and use information gain to select the most informative features for *each relation individually*. This should improve performance by ensuring that only the most relevant features for a specific relation are used to train the classifier for that relation.

Also, there is room for more investigation into how short prepositional joining phrases map onto underlying semantic relations (Girjiu 2006).

References

Roxana Girju. 2006. Out-of-context noun phrase semantic interpretation with cross-linguistic evidence. In *Proceedings of the 15th ACM international conference on Information and knowledge management*

Marti A. Hearst: 1992. Automatic Acquisition of Hyponyms from Large Text Corpora. *COLING:539-545*

Dan Moldovan, Adriana Badulescu, Marta Tatu, Daniel Antohe and Roxana Girju. 2004. Models for the Semantic Classification of Noun Phrases. *In Proceedings of the HLT/NAACL Workshop on Computational Lexical Semantics. Boston , MA.*

Preslav Nakov and Marti Hearst. 2006. Using Verbs to Characterize Noun-Noun Relations, *in the Proceedings of AIMSA 2006,*

Preslav Nakov and Marti Hearst. 2005. Using the Web as an Implicit Training Set: Application to Structural Ambiguity Resolution, *in HLT/EMNLP'05,*

Vivi Nastase and Stan Szpakowicz. 2003. Exploring Noun-Modifier Semantic Relations. *International Workshop on Computational Semantics, Tillburg, Netherlands, 2003*

Barbara Rosario and Marti A. Hearst. 2001. Classifying the semantic relations in noun compounds via a domain-specific lexical hierarchy. *In Proceedings of the 2001 Conference on Empirical Methods in Natural Language Processing. ACL*

Peter D. Turney. 2001. Mining the web for synonyms: PM-IR vs LSA on TOEFL, *Proceedings of the Twelth European Conference on machine learning,*

Peter D. Turney and Michael L. Littman. 2005. Corpus-based learning of analogies and semantic relations. *Machine Learning, 60(1–3):251–278*

Ian H. Witten and Eibe Frank. 1999. *Data Mining: Practical Machine Learning Tools and Techniques with Java Implementations*, Morgan Kaufmann (1999)

UCD-S1: A hybrid model for detecting semantic relations between noun pairs in text

Cristina Butnariu
School of Computer Science and Informatics
University College Dublin
Belfield, Dublin 4, Ireland.
ioana.butnariu@UCD.ie

Tony Veale
School of Computer Science and Informatics
University College Dublin
Belfield, Dublin 4, Ireland.
tony.veale@UCD.ie

Abstract

We describe a supervised learning approach to categorizing inter-noun relations, based on Support Vector Machines, that builds a different classifier for each of seven semantic relations. Each model uses the same learning strategy, while a simple voting procedure based on five trained discriminators with various blends of features determines the final categorization. The features that characterize each of the noun pairs are a blend of lexical-semantic categories extracted from WordNet and several flavors of syntactic patterns extracted from various corpora, including Wikipedia and the WMTS corpus.

1 Introduction

The SemEval task for classifying inter-noun semantic relations employs seven semantic relations that are not exhaustive: Cause-Effect, Instrument-Agency, Product-Producer Origin-Entity, Theme-Tool, Part-Whole and Content-Container. The task is to classify the relations between pairs of concepts that are part of the same syntactic structure in a given sentence. This approach employs a context-dependent classification, as opposed to usual out-of-context approaches in classifying semantic relations between noun pairs (e.g., (Turney, 2005), (Nastase *et. al.*, 2006)).

Our approach is based on the Support Vector Machines learning paradigm (Vapnik, 1995), in which supervised machine learning is used to find the most salient combination of features for each semantic relation. These features include semantic generalizations of the noun-senses as encoded as WordNet (WN) hyponyms, some manually selected linguistic features (e.g., *agentive*, *gerundive*, etc.) as well as the observed relational behaviour of the given nouns in three different corpora: the collected glosses of WordNet; the collected text of Wikipedia; and the WMTS corpus.

One can find similar approaches in the literature to the semantic classification of noun compounds. Turney (2005) uses automatically extracted paraphrases to build a similarity measure between pairs of concepts, while Nastase *et. al.* (2006) proposes separate models for two different word representations when determining the semantic relation in modifier-noun compounds: a model based on the lexico-semantic aspects of words and a model that uses contextual information from corpora. Our approach is different in that we use all the available features of word representations and concept interactions in a single hybrid model.

2 System description

Our system, named the Semantic Relation Discriminator (or SRD), takes as input a set of noun pairs that are manually classified as positive/negative for a given semantic relation and produces as output a discriminator for that semantic relation. We used SRD to learn different models for each of the seven semantic relations in the classification scheme for task 4 in the SemEval Workshop. The SRD system relies on several data-resources and tools: the WN noun-sense hierarchy, a corpus made up of the WordNet glosses, the complete text of Wikipedia (downloaded June, 2005), a search engine indexing a very large corpus of text, and the WEKA Data Mining software package (version 3.5).

SRD combines two types of features for each noun pair: semantic features extracted from WN noun-sense hierarchy, for which the WN synset-id

Proceedings of the 4th International Workshop on Semantic Evaluations (SemEval-2007), pages 378–381,
Prague, June 2007.

information of each noun is used and syntactic features extracted from the unlabeled and unstructured corpora mentioned above for which a shallow parsing approach is employed.

2.1 Feature acquisition

SRD follows four steps in acquiring features:

- *Select semantic generalizations.* For each noun-sense in a pair, SRD extracts all hypernyms at depth 8 or higher in the WordNet noun-sense hierarchy.
- *Extract syntactic phrases.* SRD looks for phrases in corpora that occur before or after each noun in a pair and which obey one of several syntactic templates. SRD also looks for joining phrases between each pair of nouns that contain 5 words or less.
- *Clean-up these phrases.* SRD lemmatizes the words in each phrase and removes function words such as articles, possessive pronouns, adjective and adverbs.
- *Record observed patterns.* For each noun pair, SRD records the following types of syntactic patterns together with their corpus frequencies: joining terms that comprise at least one verb; phrases that are composed of one verb and one preposition; and phrases that are composed of a simple verb or a phrasal verb.

2.2 Selecting the features

Due to the large number of features extracted in these steps, SRD employs five different models that use different combination of features and which pool their votes to determine a single prediction for each learning task. We describe below the feature sets used for each component. The features have binary values: 1 if the feature is present for a noun pair, and 0 otherwise.

Each model employs WordNet hypernyms (from the top 8 layers of the noun hierarchy) of both noun-senses as semantic features, while models 1 and 2 employ the following additional features for each noun pair (N1, N2):

1. The most frequent syntactic patterns that appear between N1 and N2 in corpora
2. The most frequent syntactic patterns that appear between N2 and N1 in corpora

Model 1 and Model 2 differ only in the syntactic templates used to validate inter-noun patterns. Model 1 fixates on patterns that contain a verb, while Model 2 accepts patterns that contain either a preposition or a verb, or both. This yields, on average, 5,000 binary features for Model 1 for each of the seven relation types, and an average of 10,000 binary features for Model 2.

In addition to WN-derived hypernymic-features, models 3 and 4 employ the following:

1. The most frequent syntactic patterns that immediately precede N1 in a corpus
2. The most frequent syntactic patterns that immediately follow N1 in a corpus
3. The most frequent syntactic patterns that immediately precede N2 in a corpus
4. The most frequent syntactic patterns that immediately follow N2 in a corpus

In Model 3 each syntactic pattern comprises a hyphenated verb, while the syntactic patterns in Model 4 each contain a preposition or a verb. SRD generates, on average, 1,500 binary features in Model 3 and 2,500 features in Model 4 for each relation-type.

In addition to WN-derived hypernymic-features, model 5 employs the following:

1. A set of linguistic features for N1, indicating whether this noun is a nominalized verb, or whether it frequently appears in a specific semantic case role (e.g., agent).
2. The same set of linguistic features as determined for N2.

SRD generates, on average, approximately 700 binary features for each relation-type in Model 5.

2.3 Building the models

The SVM learning paradigm seems particularly suitable to our task for a number of reasons. Firstly, it behaves robustly for all seven learning tasks, ignoring the noise in the training set. This is important, since e.g., some training pairs for the Instrument-Agency relation were labeled as both true and false. Secondly, SVM has an automated mechanism for parameter tuning, which reduces the overall computational effort.

SRD employs polynomial SVMs because they appear to perform better for this task compared with simple linear SVMs or radial-basis functions. We used the WEKA implementation of John Platt's Sequential Minimal Optimization method (Platt, 1998) to train the feature weights on all the available training data. Using SMO to train the polynomial SVM takes approx. 2.8 CPU sec. per model.

The motivation for a multiple model scheme approach comes from empirical results. SRD yields higher results relative to the five single models schemes that compose our system when evaluated using 10-fold cross validation on the training data.

3 Experiments and Results

The SemEval data-set for each of the seven semantic relations comprises 140 annotated instances for training and between 70 to 90 for testing. Each instance is manually labelled with the part of speech of each concept in a pair, as well as the WN synset-id of the intended word-sense and a sample sentential context. SRD's predictions fall into evaluation category B, as the system uses WN synset-id but not the query pattern used to originally populate the data-sets with instances. SRD also skips those training instances where WN sense-ids are not provided, so that the actual number of training instances used ranges from 129 to 138 manually labelled examples per relation-type.

SRD's precision, recall, F-score and accuracy for each relation is given by Table 1.

	P	*R*	*F1*	*Acc*	*#t inst.*
Cause-Effect	69.8	73.2	71.4	70.0	80
Instrument-Agency	72.5	76.3	74.4	74.4	78
Product-Producer	80.6	87.1	83.7	77.4	93
Origin-Entity	60.0	50.0	54.5	63.0	81
Theme-Tool	50.0	34.5	40.8	59.2	71
Part-Whole	71.4	57.7	63.8	76.4	72
Content-Container	84.8	73.7	78.9	79.7	74
Average	**69.9**	**64.6**	**66.8**	**71.4**	**78.4**

Table1. Results for SRD across the seven learning tasks

To assess the effect of varying quantities of training data, the model was tested on different fractions of the training data: dataset B1 comprises the first quarter of the training data, dataset B2 the first half, while B3 dataset comprises the first three quarters and B4 comprises the complete training dataset. We report the behavior of SRD in predicting the unseen test data when learning from these datasets in table 2. The measures of table 2 represent an average of SRD's performance across all relation-types.

	P	*R*	*F1*	*Acc*
Dataset B1	65.4	53.3	56.4	66.2
Dataset B2	67.8	63.8	63.5	69.6
Dataset B3	71.7	64.0	66.8	71.6
Dataset B4	69.9	64.6	66.8	71.4

Table2. Results for SRD on different training datasets

3.1 Error analysis

Three types of baseline values were proposed for this task. Baseline 1 ("majority baseline") is obtained by always guessing either "true" or "false", according to whichever is the majority category in the testing data-set for the given relation. Baseline 2 ("alltrue baseline") is achieved by always guessing "true". Baseline 3 ("probmatch baseline") is obtained by randomly guessing "true" or "false" with a probability matching the distribution of "true" or "false" in the testing dataset.

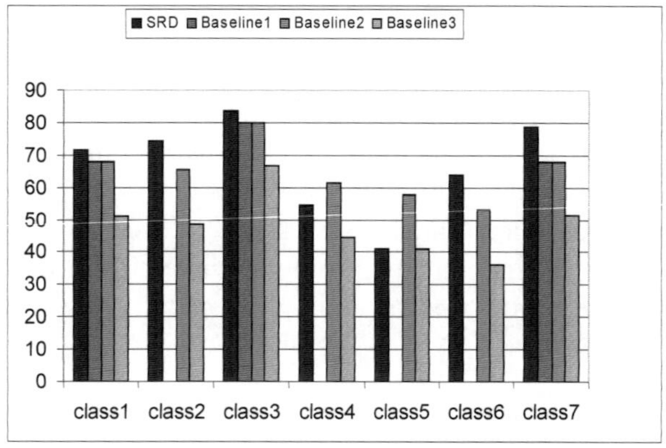

Figure1. Comparison of SRD's F-scores for each semantic relation and the corresponding baselines.

Figure 1 plots the F-scores obtained for each semantic relation. We observe that SRD has exhibits poor performance on two particular relations, Origin-Entity and Theme-Tool, denoted "class4" and "class5" in the plot of Figure 1. SRD achieves the same F-measure score as the random prediction baseline for Theme-Tool class, suggesting that the features used are simply not capable of building a discriminator for this semantic relation. SRD's F-score for Origin-Entity class is 10% higher than the random baseline, but still performs below the other two baselines. SRD's best performance is achieved for Product-Producer and Part-Whole, with an F-score 11% higher than the highest baseline.

	Feature Set1	Feature Set2	Feature Set3	Feature Set4
Cause-Effect	71.4	72.7	**75.7**	61.3
Instrument-Agency	74.4	74.6	**76.3**	72
Product-Producer	**83.7**	81.3	80.5	77
Origin-Entity	54.5	44.8	38	**61.5**
Theme-Tool	40.8	42.8	**53.8**	42.5
Part-Whole	63.8	**72.3**	62.7	60
Content-Container	**78.9**	75.6	77.1	73.2
Average	**66.8**	66.3	66.3	64

Table3. SRD F-measures using different feature sets

3.2 Improvements

One obvious problem with SRD is that we use a high-dimensional feature-space to train each model. Research in text categorization (e.g., Dumais *et al.,* 1998) shows that feature selection algorithms like information gain can identify the most productive dimensions of the feature space and simultaneously boost classification accuracy.

To explore this potential for improvement, we applied two types of feature selection filters (using WEKA): the *InfoGainAttrEval* filter that evaluates the utility of a feature by measuring information gain w.r.t. the class; and the *CfsSubsetEval* filter, which evaluates the utility of a subset of features by considering the individual predictive ability of each individually and the degree of redundancy between them collectively. Results of our experiments with SRD using different subsets of feature sets are displayed in Table 3. Set 1 is the complete set of all features. Set 2 is the subset obtained with the top n features as ranked by the *InfoGainAttrEval* filter (n is determined using 10-fold cross validation on the training data). Set 3 is a tailored feature-set created for each relation-type using the *CfsSubsetEval* filter. Set 4 is the subset of all features extracted from WN.

We find that feature-filtering boosts the performance of some learning tasks by up to 14 % (e.g., the Theme-Tool relation), but it can also decrease performance by the same amount (e.g., the Origin-Entity relation). SRD achieves its best performance -- an overall F-measure of 71.7% -- when using a feature set that is tailored to each of the semantic relation classification tasks (e.g., Set 4 (WN only) for Origin-Entity, Set 1 (all) for Product-Producer and Container-Content, Set 4 and Set 3 (relation-specific subsets) for everything else).

4 Conclusions

SRD is an SVM-based approach to classifying noun-pairs into categories that best reflect the semantic relationship underlying each pair. Without feature-filtering, SRD shows modest classification capability, performing better than the highest baselines for five of the seven relational classes. Experiments with feature filtering encourage us to try and refine SRD's feature space to focus on more discriminatory and semantically-revealing features of nouns. Feature-filtering can diminish as well as improve performance, and thus, should ideally be linked to an insightful theory of how particular features contribute to the human-understanding of noun-noun pairs. Filtering techniques provide a good basis for formulating feature-based hypotheses, but the most productive feature sets will come, we hope, from a cognitive and conceptual understanding of the processes of phrase construction, rather than from an exhaustive and largely theory-free exploration of different feature-sets.

Acknowledgments

We would like to thank Peter Turney for granting us access to the NRC copy of the WMTS.

References

Joachims, T. (1998) Text categorization with support vector machines: learning with many relevant features. *Proceedings of ECML-98, 10th European Conference on Machine Learning.*

Dumais, S. T., Platt, J., Heckerman D., Sahami M., (1998) Inductive learning algorithms and representations for text categorization, *Proceedings of ACM-CIKM98*

Nastase, V., Sayyad-Shirabad, J., Sokolova, M., and Szpakowicz, S. (2006). Learning noun-modifier semantic relations with corpus-based and WordNet-based features. *In Proceedings of the 21st National Conference on Artificial Intelligence*, Boston, MA.

Platt, J. (1998), Fast Training of SVMs Using Sequential Minimal Optimization, *Support Vector Machine Learning*, MIT Press, Cambridge.

Turney, P.D. (2005). Measuring semantic similarity by latent relational analysis. *In Proceedings of the Nineteenth International Joint Conference on Artificial Intelligence*, Edinburgh, Scotland.

Vapnik, V. (1995). The Nature of Statistical Learning Theory, *Springer-Verlag*, New York

UC3M: Classification of Semantic Relations between Nominals using Sequential Minimal Optimization

Isabel Segura Bedmar
Computer Science Department
University Carlos III of Madrid
isegura@inf.uc3m.es

Doaa Samy
Computer Science Department
University Carlos III of Madrid
dsamy@inf.uc3m.es

Jose L. Martinez
Computer Science Department
University Carlos III of Madrid
jlmartinez@inf.uc3m.es

Abstract

This paper presents a method for automatic classification of semantic relations between nominals using Sequential Minimal Optimization. We participated in the four categories of SEMEVAL task 4 (A: No Query, No Wordnet; B: WordNet, No Query; C: Query, No WordNet; D: WordNet and Query) and for all training datasets. Best scores were achieved in category B using a set of feature vectors including lexical file numbers of nominals obtained from WordNet and a new feature *WordNet Vector* designed for the task[1].

1 Introduction

The survey of the state-of-art reveals an increasing interest in automatically discovering the underlying semantics in natural language. In this interdisciplinary field, the growing interest is justified by the number of applications which can directly benefit from introducing semantic information. Question Answering, Information Retrieval and Text Summarization are examples of these applications (Turney and Littman, 2005; Girju et al., 2005).

In the present work and for the purpose of the SEMEVAL task 4, our scope is limited to the semantic relationships between nominals. By this definition, we understand it is the process of discovering the underlying relations between two concepts expressed by two nominals.

Within the framework of SEMEVAL, nominals can occur either on the phrase, clause or the sentence level. This fact constitutes the major challenge in this task since most of the previous research limited their approaches to certain types of nominals mainly the "compound nominals"(Girju et al. 2005).

The paper is divided as follows; section 2 is a brief introduction to SMO used as the classifier for the task. Section 3 is dedicated to the description of the set of features applied in our experiments. In section 4, we discuss the experiment's results compared to the baselines of the SEMEVAL task and the top scores. Finally, we summarize our approach, pointing out conclusions and future directions of our work.

2 Sequential Minimal Optimization

We decided to use Support Vector Machine (SVM), as one of the most successful Machine Learning techniques, achieving the best performances for many classification tasks. Algorithm performance and time efficiency are key issues in our task, considering that our final goal is to apply this classification in a Question Answering System.

Sequential Minimal Optimization (SMO) is a fast method to train SVM. SMO breaks the large quadratic programming (QP) optimization problem needed to be resolved in SVM into a series of smallest possible QP problems. These small QP problems are analytically solved, avoiding, in this way, a time-consuming numerical QP optimization as an inner loop. We used Weka (Witten and Frank, 2005) an implementation of the SMO (Platt, 1998).

[1] This work has been partially supported by the Regional Government of Madrid Ander the Research Network MAVIR (S-0505/TIC-0267)

Proceedings of the 4th International Workshop on Semantic Evaluations (SemEval-2007), pages 382–385,
Prague, June 2007.

3 Features

Prior to the classification of semantic relations, characteristics of each sentence are automatically extracted using GATE (Cunningham et al., 2002). GATE is an infrastructure for developing and deploying software components for Language Engineering. We used the following GATE components: English Tokenizer, Part-Of-Speech (POS) tagger and Morphological analyser.

The set of features used for the classification of semantic relations includes information from different levels: word tokens, POS tags, verb lemmas, semantic information from WordNet, etc. Semantic features are only applied in categories B and D.

On the lexical level, the set of word features include the two nominals, their heads in case one of the nominals in question or both are compound nominals (e.g. the relation between <e1>*tumor shrinkage*</e1> and <e2>*radiation therapy* </e2> is actually between the head of the first "*shrinkage*" and "*radiation_therapy*"). More features include: the two words before the first nominal, the two words after the second nominal, and the word list in-between (Wang et al., 2006).

On the POS level, we opted for using a set of POS features since word features are often too sparse. This set includes POS tags of the two words occurring before the first nominal and the two words occurring after the second nominal together with the tag list of the words in-between (Wang et al., 2006). POS tags of nominals are considered redundant information.

Information regarding verbs and prepositions, occurring in-between the two nominals, is highly considered. In case of the verb, the system takes into account the verb token and the information concerning the voice and lemma. In the same way, the system keeps track of the prepositions occurring between both nominals. In addition, a feature, called *numinter,* indicating the number of words between nominals is considered.

Other important feature is the path from the first nominal to the second nominal. This feature is built by the concatenation of the POS tags between both nominals.

The feature related to the query provided for each sentence is only considered in the categories C and D according to the SEMEVAL restrictions.

On the semantic level, we used features obtained from WordNet. In addition to the WordNet sense keys, provided for each nominal, we extracted its synset number and its lexical file number.

Based on the work of Rosario, Hearst and Fillmore (2002), we suppose that these lexical file numbers can help to determine if the nominals satisfy the restrictions for each relation. For example, in the relation Theme-Tool, the theme should be an object, an event, a state of being, an agent, or a substance. Else, it is possible to affirm that the relation is false.

For the Part-Whole relation and due to its relevance in this classification task, a feature indicating metonymy relation in WordNet was taken into account.

Furthermore, we designed a new feature, called *WordNet vector*. For constructing this vector, we selected the synsets of the third level of depth in WordNet and we detected if each is ancestor or not of the nominal. It is a binary vector, i.e. if the synset is ancestor of the nominal it is assigned the value 1, else it is assigned the value 0. In this way, we worked with two vectors, one for each nominal. Each vector has a dimension of 13 coordinates. Each coordinate represents one of the 13 nodes in the third level of depth in WordNet. Our initial hypothesis considers that this representation for the nominals could perform well on unseen data.

4 Experiment Results

Cross validation is a way to test the ability of the model to classify unseen examples. We trained the system using 10-fold cross-validation; the fold number recommended for small training datasets. For each relation and for each category (A, B, C, D) we selected the set of features that obtained the best results using the indicated cross validation.

We submitted 16 sets of results as we participated in the four categories (A, B, C, D). We also used all the possible sizes of the training dataset (1: 1 to 35, 2:1 to 70, 3:1 to 106, 4:1 to 140).

	A: No Query, No WordNet			B: No Query, WordNet			C: No Query, No WordNet			D: Query, WordNet		
	Prec	Rec	F	Prec	Rec	F	Prec	Rec	F	Prec	Rec	F
Cause-Effect	50.0	51.2	50.6	66.7	73.2	69.8	42.9	36.6	39.5	59.0	56.1	57.5
Instrument-Agency	47.5	50.0	48.7	73.7	73.7	73.7	51.4	50.0	50.7	67.5	71.1	69.2
Product-Producer	65.3	51.6	57.7	83.7	66.1	73.9	67.4	50.0	57.4	74.5	61.3	67.3
Origin-Entity	50.0	27.8	35.7	63.0	47.2	54.0	54.5	33.3	41.4	63.3	52.8	57.6
Theme-Tool	50.0	27.6	35.6	50.0	48.3	49.1	47.4	31.0	37.5	40.9	31.0	35.3
Part-Whole	26.5	34,6	30.0	72.4	80.8	76.4	34.0	61.5	43.8	57.1	76.9	65.6
Content-Container	48.4	39.5	43.5	57.6	50.0	53.5	48.6	44.7	46.6	63.6	55.3	59.2
Avg for UC3M	48.2	40.3	43.1	66.7	62.8	64.3	49.4	43.9	45.3	60.9	57.8	58.8
Avg for all systems	59.2	58.7	58.0	65.3	64.4	63.6	59.9	59.0	58.4	64.9	60.4	60.6
Max Avg F			64.8			72.4			65.1			62.6

Table 1 Scores for A4, B4, C4 and D4

For some learning algorithms such as decision trees and rule learning, appropriate selection of features is crucial. For the SVM model, this is not so important due to its learning mechanism, where irrelevant features are usually balanced between positive and negative examples for a given binary classification problem. However, in the experiments we observed that certain features have strong influence on the results, and its inclusion or elimination from the vector, influenced remarkably the outcomes.

In this section, we will briefly discuss the experiments in the four categories highlighting the most relevant observations.

In category A, we expected to obtain better results, but the overall performance of the system has decreased in the seven relations. This shows that our system has over-fitted the training set. The contrast between the F score values in the cross-validation and the final test results demonstrates this fact. For all the relations in the category A4, we obtained an average of F=43.1% [average score of all participating teams: F=58.0% and top average score: F=64.8%].

In Product-Producer relation, only two features were used: the two heads of the nominals. In training, we obtained an average F= 60% using cross-validation, while in the final test data, we achieved an average score F=57.7%. For the relation Theme-Tool, other set of features was employed: nominals, their heads, verb, preposition and the list of word between both nominals. Based on the results of the 10-fold cross validation, we expected to obtain an average of the F=70%. Nevertheless, the score obtained is F =30%.

In category B, our system has achieved better scores. Our average score F is 64.3% and it is above the average of participating teams (F=63.6%) and the baseline.

Best results in this category were achieved in the relations: Instrument-Agency (F=73.7%), Product-Producer (F=73.9%), Part-Whole (F=76.4%). However, for the relation Theme-Tool the system obtained lower scores (F=49.1%).

It is obvious that introducing WordNet information has improved notably the results compared with the results obtained in the category A.

In categories C and D, only three groups have participated. In category C (as in category A), the system results have decreased obviously (F=45.3%) with respect to the expected scores in the 10-fold cross validation. Moreover, the score obtained is lower than the average score of all participants (F=58.4%) and the best score (F=65.1%). For example, in training the Instrument-Agent relation, the system achieved an average F=78% using 10-fold cross-validation, while for the final score it only obtained F=50.7%.

Results reveal that the main reason behind the low scores in A and C, is the absence of information from WordNet. Hence, the vector design needs further consideration in case no semantic information is provided.

In category D, both WordNet senses and query were used, we achieved an average score F=58.8%. The average score for all participants is F=60.6% and the best system achieved F=62.6%. However, the slight difference shows that our system worked relatively well in this category.

Both run time and accuracy depend critically on the values given to two parameters: the upper bound on the coefficient's values in the equation for the hyperplane (-C), and the degree of the polynomials in the non-linear mapping (-E) (Witten and Frank, 2005). Both are set to 1 by default. The best settings for a particular dataset can be found only by experimentation.

We made numerous experiments to find the best value for the parameter C (C=1, C=10, C=100, C=1000, C=10000), but the results were not remarkably affected. Probably, this is due to the small size of the training set.

5 Conclusions and Future Work

In our first approach to automatic classification of semantic relations between nominals and as expected from the training phase, our system achieved its best performance using WordNet information. In general, we obtained better scores in category 4 (size of training: 1 to 140), i.e., when all the training examples are used.

On the other hand, overfitting the training data (most probably due to the small size of training dataset) is the main reason behind the low scores obtained by our system.

These facts lead us to the conclusion that semantic features from WordNet, in general, play a key role in the classification task. However, the relevance of WordNet-related features varies. For example, lexical file numbers proved to be highly effective, while the use of the *WordNet Vector* did not improve significantly the results. Thus, we consider that a level 3 *WordNet Vector* is rather abstract to represent each nominal. Developing a *WordNet Vector* with a deeper level (> 3) could be more effective as the representation of nouns is more descriptive.

Query features, on the other hand, did not improve the performance of the system. This is due to the fact that the same query could represent both positive and negative examples of the relation. However, to improve results in categories A and C, more features need to introduced, especially context and syntactic information such as chunks or dependency relations.

To improve results across the whole dataset, wider use of semantic information is necessary. For example, the immediate hypernym for each synset obtained from WordNet could help in improving the system performance (Nastase et al., 2006). Besides, information regarding the entity features could help in the classification of some relations like Origin-Entity or Product-Producer. Other semantic resources such as VerbNet, FrameNet, PropBank, etc. could also be used.

Furthermore, we consider introducing a Word Sense Disambiguation module to obtain the corresponding synsets of the nominals. Also, information concerning the synsets of the list of the context words could be of great value for the classification task (Wang et al., 2006).

References

Hamish Cunningham, Diana Maynard and Kalina Bontcheva, Valentin Tablan, Cristian Ursu. 2002. *The GATE User Guide.* http://gate.ac.uk/

Roxana Girju, Dan Moldovan, Marta Tatu and Daniel Antohe. 2005. On the semantics of noun compunds. *Computer Speech and Language 19* pp. 479-496.

Vivi Nastase, Jelber Sayyad-Shirbad, Marina Sokolova and Stan Szpakowicz. 2006. Learning noun-modifier semantic relations with corpus-based and WordNet-based features. In *Proc. of the 21st National Conference on Artificial Intelligence (AAAI 2006).* Boston, MA.

John C. Platt. 1998. Sequential Minimal Optimization: A Fast Algorithm for Training Support Vector Machines, *Microsoft Research Technical Report MSR-TR-98-14.*

Barbara Rosario, Marti A. Hearst, and Charles Fillmore. 2002. "The descent of hierarchy, and selection in relations semantics". In *Proceedings of the 40 th Annual Meeting of the Association for Computacional Linguistics (ACL'02),* Philadelphia, PA, pages 417-424.

Ian H. Witten, Eibe Frank. 2005. Data Mining: Practical machine learning tools and techniques. *Morgan Kaufmann.*

Peter D. Turney and Michael L. Littman. 2005. Corpus-based learning of analogies and semantic rela-tions. *Machine Learning, in press.*

Ting Wang, Yaoyong Li, Kalina Bontcheva, Hamish Cunningham and Ji Wang. 2006. Automatic Extraction of Hierarchical Relations from Text. In *Proceedings of the Third European Semantic Web Conference (ESWC 2006),* Lecture Notes in Computer Science 4011, Springer, 2006.

UIUC: A Knowledge-rich Approach to Identifying Semantic Relations between Nominals

Brandon Beamer,[1,4] Suma Bhat,[2,4] Brant Chee,[3,4] Andrew Fister,[1,4] Alla Rozovskaya,[1,4] Roxana Girju[1,4]

Department of Linguistics[1],
Department of Electrical and Computer Engineering[2],
Department of Library and Information Science[3],
Beckman Institute[4],
University of Illinois at Urbana-Champaign
{bbeamer, spbhat2, chee, afister2, rozovska, girju}@uiuc.edu

Abstract

This paper describes a supervised, knowledge-intensive approach to the automatic identification of semantic relations between nominals in English sentences. The system employs different sets of new and previously used lexical, syntactic, and semantic features extracted from various knowledge sources. At SemEval 2007 the system achieved an F-measure of 72.4% and an accuracy of 76.3%.

1 Introduction

The SemEval 2007 task on Semantic Relations between Nominals is to identify the underlying semantic relation between two nouns in the context of a sentence. The dataset provided consists of a definition file and 140 training and about 70 test sentences for each of the seven relations considered: *Cause-Effect, Instrument-Agency, Product-Producer, Origin-Entity, Theme-Tool, Part-Whole*, and *Content-Container*. The task is defined as a binary classification problem. Thus, given a pair of nouns and their sentential context, the classifier decides whether the nouns are linked by the target semantic relation. In each training and test example sentence, the nouns are identified and manually labeled with their corresponding WordNet 3.0 senses. Moreover, each example is accompanied by the heuristic pattern (query) the annotators used to extract the sentence from the web and the position of the arguments in the relation.

(1) 041 "He derives great joy and <e_1>happiness</e_1> from <e_2>cycling</e_2>." WordNet(e_1) = "happiness%1:12:00::", WordNet(e_2) = "cycling%1:04:00::", Cause-Effect(e_2,e_1) = "true", Query = "happiness from *"

Based on the information employed, systems can be classified in four types of classes: (A) systems that use neither the given WordNet synsets nor the queries, (B) systems that use only WordNet senses, (C) systems that use only the queries, and (D) systems that use both.

In this paper we present a type-B system that relies on various sets of new and previously used linguistic features employed in a supervised learning model.

2 Classification of Semantic Relations

Semantic relations between nominals can be encoded by different syntactic constructions. We extend here over previous work that has focused mainly on noun compounds and other noun phrases, and noun–verb–noun constructions.

We selected a list of 18 lexico-syntactic and semantic features split here into three sets: *feature set #1* (core features), *feature set #2* (context features), and the *feature set #3* (special features). Table 1 shows all three sets of features along with their definitions; a detailed description is presented next. For some features, we list previous works where they proved useful. While features F1 – F4 were selected from our previous experiments, all the other features are entirely the contribution of this research.

Feature set #1: Core features

This set contains six features that were employed in all seven relation classifiers. The features take into consideration only lexico-semantic information

Proceedings of the 4th International Workshop on Semantic Evaluations (SemEval-2007), pages 386–389, Prague, June 2007. ©2007 Association for Computational Linguistics

No.	Feature	Definition
Feature Set #1: Core features		
F1	**Argument position** (Girju et al., 2005; Girju et al., 2006)	indicates the position of the arguments in the semantic relation (e.g., Part-Whole(e_1, e_2), where e_1 is the *part* and e_2 is the *whole*).
F2	**Semantic specialization** (Girju et al., 2005; Girju et al., 2006)	this is the prediction returned by the automatic WordNet IS-A semantic specialization procedure.
F3, F4	**Nominalization** (Girju et al., 2004)	indicates whether the nouns e_1 (F3) and e_2 (F4) are nominalizations or not. Specifically, we distinguish here between *agential nouns*, *other nominalizations*, and *neither*.
F5, F6	**Spatio-Temporal features**	indicate if e_1 (F5) or e_2 (F6) encode time or location.
Feature Set #2: Context features		
F7, F8	**Grammatical role**	describes the grammatical role of e_1 (F7) and e_2 (F8). There are three possible values: *subject, direct object*, or *neither*.
F9	**PP Attachment**	applies to NP PP constructions and indicates if the prepositional phrase containing e_2 attaches to the NP containing e_1.
F10, F11	**Semantic Role**	is concerned with the semantic role of the phrase containing either e_1 (F10) or e_2 (F11). In particular, we focused on three semantic roles: *Time, Location, Manner*. The feature is set to 1 if the target noun is part of a phrase of that type and to 0 otherwise.
F12, F13, F14	**Inter-noun context sequence**	is a set of three features. F12 captures the sequence of stemmed words between e_1 and e_2, while F13 lists the part of speech sequence in between the target nouns. F14 is a scoring weight (with possible values 1, 0.5, 0.25, and 0.125) which measures the similarity of an unseen sequence to the set of sequence patterns associated with a relation.
Feature Set #3: Special features		
F15, F16	**Psychological feature**	is used in the *Theme-Tool* classifier; indicates if e_1 (F15) or e_2 (F16) belong or not to a predefined set of psychological features.
F17	**Instrument semantic role**	is used for the *Instrument-Agency* relation and indicates whether the phrase containing e_1 is labeled as em Instrument or not.
F18	**Syntactic attachment**	is used for the *Instrument-Agent* relation and indicates whether the phrase containing the *Instrument* role attaches to a noun or a verb

Table 1: The three sets of features used for the automatic semantic relation classification.

about the two target nouns.

Argument position (F1) indicates the position of the semantic arguments in the relation. This information is very valuable, since some relations have a particular argument arrangement depending on the lexico-syntactic construction in which they occur. For example, most of the noun compounds encoding Stuff-Object / Part-Whole relations have e_1 as the part and e_2 as the whole (e.g., *silk dress*).

Semantic specialization (F2) is a binary feature representing the prediction of a semantic specialization learning model. The method consists of a set of iterative procedures of specialization of the training examples on the WordNet IS-A hierarchy. Thus, after all the initial noun–noun pairs are mapped through generalization to *entity* – *entity* pairs in WordNet, a set of necessary specialization iterations is applied until it finds a boundary that separates positive and negative examples. This boundary is tested on new examples for relation prediction.

The *nominalization* features (F3, F4) indicate if the target noun is a nominalization and, if yes, of what type. We distinguish here between *agential nouns*, *other nominalizations*, and *neither*. The features were identified based on WordNet and NomLex-Plus[1] and were introduced to filter some of negative examples, such as *car owner*/THEME.

Spatio–Temporal features (F5, F6) were also introduced to recognize some near miss examples, such as Temporal and Location relations. For instance, *activation by summer* (near-miss for *Cause-Effect*) and *mouse in the field* (near-miss for *Content-Container*). Similarly, for *Theme-Tool*, a word acting as a Theme should not indicate a period of time, as in *<e_1>the appointment</e_1> was for more than one <e_2>year</e_2>*. For this we used the information provided by WordNet and special classes generated from the works of (Herskovits, 1987), (Linstromberg, 1997), and (Tyler and Evans, 2003).

[1]NomLex-Plus is a hand-coded database of 5,000 verb nominalizations, de-adjectival, and de-adverbial nouns. http://nlp.cs.nyu.edu/nomlex/index.html

Feature set #2: Context features
This set takes advantage of the sentence context to identify features at different linguistic levels.

The *grammatical role* features (F7, F8) determine if e_1 or e_2 is the *subject, direct object*, or *neither*. This feature helps filter out some instances with poor context, such as noun compounds and identify some near-miss examples. For example, a restriction imposed by the definition of *Theme-Tool* indicates that in constructions such as *Y*/Tool *is used for V-ing X*/Theme, neither X nor Y can be the subject of the sentence, and hence Theme-Tool(X, Y) would be false. This restriction is also captured by the nominalization feature in case X or Y is an agential noun.

PP attachment (F9) is defined for NP PP constructions, where the prepositional phrase containing the noun e_2 attaches or not to the NP (containing e_1). The rationale is to identify negative instances where the PP attaches to any other word before NP in the sentence. For example, *eat* <e_1>*pizza*</e_1> *with* <e_2>*a fork*</e_2>, where *with a fork* attaches to the verb *to eat* (cf. (Charniak, 2000)).

Furthermore, we implemented and used two *semantic role* features which identify the semantic role of the phrase in a verb–argument structure, phrase containing either e_1 (F10) or e_2 (F11). In particular, we focus on three semantic roles: *Time, Location, Manner*. The feature is set to 1 if the target noun is part of a semantic role phrase and to 0 otherwise. The idea is to filter out near-miss examples, expecially for the *Instrument-Agency* relation. For this, we used ASSERT, a semantic role labeler developed at the University of Colorado at Boulder[2] which was queried through a web interface.

Inter-noun context sequence features (F12, F13) encode the sequence of lexical and part of speech information between the two target nouns. Feature F14 is a weight feature on the values of F12 and F13 and indicates how similar a new sequence is to the already observed inter-noun context associated with the relation. If there is a direct match, then the weight is set to 1. If the part-of-speech pattern of the new substring matches that of an already seen substring, then the weight is set to 0.5. Weights 0.25 and 0.125 are given to those sequences that overlap entirely or partially with patterns encoding other semantic relations in the same contingency set (e.g., semantic relations that share syntactic pattern sequences). The value of the feature is the summation of the weights thus obtained. The rationale is that the greater the weight, the more representative is the context sequence for that relation.

Feature set #3: Special features
This set includes features that help identify specific information about some semantic relations.

Psychological feature was defined for the *Theme-Tool* relation and indicates if the target noun (F15, F16) belongs to a list of special concepts. This feature was obtained from the restrictions listed in the definition of *Theme-Tool*. In the example *need for money*, the noun *need* is a psychological feature, and thus the instance cannot encode a *Theme-Tool* relation. A list of synsets from WordNet subhierarchy of *motivation* and *cognition* constituted the psychological factors. This was augmented with preconditions such as *foundation* and *requirement* since they would not be allowed as tools for the theme.

The *Instrument semantic role* is used for the *Instrument-Agency* relation as a boolean feature (F17) indicating whether the argument identified as Instrument in the relation (e.g., e_1 if Instrument-Agency(e_1, e_2)) belongs to an instrument phrase as identified by a semantic role tool, such as ASSERT.

The *syntactic attachment* feature (F18) is a feature that indicates whether the argument identified as Instrument in the relation attaches to a verb or to a noun in the syntactically parsed sentence.

3 Learning Model and Experimental Setting

For our experiments we chose libSVM, an open source SVM package[3]. Since some of our features are nominal, we followed the standard practice of representing a nominal feature with n discrete values as n binary features. We used the RBF kernel.

We built a binary classifier for each of the seven relations. Since the size of the task training data per relation is small, we expanded it with new examples from various sources. We added a new corpus of 3,000 sentences of news articles from the TREC-9 text collection (Girju, 2003) encoding *Cause-Effect* (1,320) and *Product-Producer* (721). Another col-

[2]http://oak.colorado.edu/assert/

[3]http://www.csie.ntu.edu.tw/~cjlin/libsvm/

Relation	P	R	F	Acc	Total	Base-F	Base-Acc	Best features
Cause-Effect	69.5	100.0	82.0	77.5	80	67.8	51.2	F1, F2, F5, F6, F12–F14
Instrument-Agency	68.2	78.9	73.2	71.8	78	65.5	51.3	F7, F8, F10, F11, F15–F18
Product-Producer	84.5	79.0	81.7	76.3	93	80.0	66.7	F1–F4, F12–F14
Origin-Entity	86.4	52.8	65.5	75.3	81	61.5	55.6	F1, F2, F5, F6, F12–F14
Theme-Tool	85.7	41.4	55.8	73.2	71	58.0	59.2	F1–F6, F15, F16
Part-Whole	70.8	65.4	68.0	77.8	72	53.1	63.9	F1–F4
Content-Container	93.1	71.1	80.6	82.4	74	67.9	51.4	F1–F6, F12–F14
Average	79.7	69.8	72.4	76.3	78.4			

Table 2: Performance obtained per relation. Precision, Recall, F-measure, Accuracy, and Total (number of examples) are macro-averaged for system's performance on all 7 relations. Base-F shows the baseline F measure (all true), while Base-Acc shows the baseline accuracy score (majority).

lection of 3,129 sentences from Wall Street Journal (Moldovan et al., 2004; Girju et al., 2004) was considered for *Part-Whole* (1,003), *Origin-Entity* (167), *Product-Producer* (112), and *Theme-Tool* (91). We also extracted 552 *Product-Producer* instances from eXtended WordNet[4] (noun entries and their gloss definition). Moreover, for *Theme-Tool* and *Content-Container* we used special lists of constraints[5]. Besides the selectional restrictions imposed on the nouns by special features such as F15 and F16 (psychological feature), we created lists of containers from various thesauri[6] and identified selectional restrictions that differentiate between containers and locations relying on taxonomies of spatial entities discussed in detail in (Herskovits, 1987) and (Tyler and Evans, 2003).

Each instance in this text collection had the target nouns identified and annotated with WordNet senses. Since the annotations used different WordNet versions, senses were mapped to sense keys.

4 Experimental Results

Table 2 shows the performance of our system for each semantic relation. *Base-F* indicates the baseline F-measure (all true), while *Base-Acc* shows the baseline accuracy score (majority). The *Average* score of precision, recall, F-measure, and accuracy is macroaveraged over all seven relations. Overall, all features contributed to the performance, with a different contribution per relation (cf. Table 2).

5 Conclusions

This paper describes a method for the automatic identification of a set of seven semantic relations based on support vector machines (SVMs). The approach benefits from an extended dataset on which binary classifiers were trained for each relation. The feature sets fed into the SVMs produced very good results.

Acknowledgments

We would like to thank Brian Drexler for his valuable suggestions on the set of semantic relations.

References

E. Charniak. 2000. A Maximum-entropy-inspired Parser. In the Proceedings of *the 1st NAACL Conference*.

R. Girju, A. Giuglea, M. Olteanu, O. Fortu, O. Bolohan, and D. Moldovan. 2004. Support vector machines applied to the classification of semantic relations in nominalized noun phrases. In the Proceedings of *the HLT/NAACL Workshop on Computational Lexical Semantics.*

R. Girju, D. Moldovan, M. Tatu, and D. Antohe. 2005. On the semantics of noun compounds. *Computer Speech and Language*, 19(4):479–496.

R. Girju, A. Badulescu, and D. Moldovan. 2006. Automatic discovery of part-whole relations. *Computational Linguistics*, 32(1).

R. Girju. 2003. Automatic detection of causal relations for question answering. In the Proceedings of *the ACL Workshop on "Multilingual Summarization and Question Answering - Machine Learning and Beyond"*.

A. Herskovits. 1987. *Language and spatial cognition: An interdisciplinary study of the prepositions in English.* Cambridge University Press.

S. Linstromberg. 1997. *English Prepositions Explained.* John Benjamins Publishing Co., Amsterdam/Philaderphia.

D. Moldovan, A. Badulescu, M. Tatu, D. Antohe, and R. Girju. 2004. Models for the semantic classification of noun phrases. In the Proceedings of *the HLT/NAACL Workshop on Computational Lexical Semantics.*

A. Tyler and V. Evans. 2003. *The Semantics of English Prepositions: Spatial Sciences, Embodied Meaning, and Cognition.* Cambridge University Press.

[4]http://xwn.hlt.utdallas.edu/

[5]The *Instrument-Agency* classifier was trained only on the task dataset.

[6]Thesauri such as TheFreeDictionary.com.

UMND1: Unsupervised Word Sense Disambiguation Using Contextual Semantic Relatedness

Siddharth Patwardhan
School of Computing
University of Utah
Salt Lake City, UT 84112.
sidd@cs.utah.edu

Satanjeev Banerjee
Language Technologies Inst.
Carnegie Mellon University
Pittsburgh, PA 15217.
banerjee@cs.cmu.edu

Ted Pedersen
Dept. of Computer Science
University of Minnesota
Duluth, MN 55812.
tpederse@d.umn.edu

Abstract

In this paper we describe an unsupervised WordNet-based Word Sense Disambiguation system, which participated (as UMND1) in the SemEval-2007 Coarse-grained English Lexical Sample task. The system disambiguates a target word by using WordNet-based measures of semantic relatedness to find the sense of the word that is semantically most strongly related to the senses of the words in the context of the target word. We briefly describe this system, the configuration options used for the task, and present some analysis of the results.

1 Introduction

WordNet::SenseRelate::TargetWord[1] (Patwardhan et al., 2005; Patwardhan et al., 2003) is an unsupervised Word Sense Disambiguation (WSD) system, which is based on the hypothesis that the intended sense of an ambiguous word is related to the words in its context. For example, if the "financial institution" sense of *bank* is intended in a context, then it is highly likely the context would contain related words such as *money*, *transaction*, *interest rate*, etc. The algorithm, therefore, determines the intended sense of a word (*target word*) in a given context by measuring the relatedness of each sense of that word with the words in its context. The sense of the target word that is most related to its context is selected as the intended sense of the target word. The system uses WordNet-based measures of semantic relatedness[2] (Pedersen et al., 2004) to measure the relatedness between the different senses of the target word and the words in its context.

This system is completely unsupervised and requires no annotated data for training. The lexical database WordNet (Fellbaum, 1998) is the only resource that the system uses to measure the relatedness between words and concepts. Thus, our system is classified under the *closed track* of the task.

2 System Description

Our WSD system consists of a modular framework, which allows different algorithms for the different subtasks to be plugged into the system. We divide the disambiguation task into two primary subtasks: *context selection* and *sense selection*. The context selection module tries to select words from the context that are most likely to be indicative of the sense of the target word. The sense selection module then uses the set of selected context words to choose one of the senses of the target word as the answer.

Figure 1 shows a block schematic of the system, which takes SemEval-2007 English Lexical Sample instances as input. Each instance is a made up of a few English sentences, and one word from these sentences is marked as the target word to be disambiguated. The system processes each instance through multiple modules arranged in a sequential pipeline. The final output of the pipeline is the sense that is most appropriate for the target word in the given context.

[1] http://senserelate.sourceforge.net

[2] http://wn-similarity.sourceforge.net

Proceedings of the 4th International Workshop on Semantic Evaluations (SemEval-2007), pages 390–393,
Prague, June 2007.

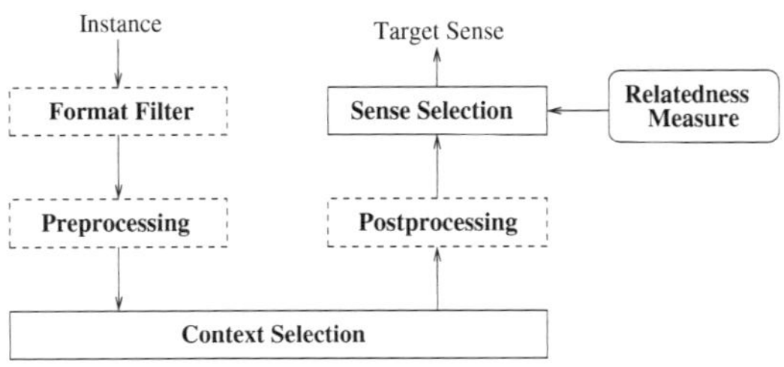

Figure 1: System Architecture

2.1 Data Preparation

The input text is first passed through a *format filter*, whose task is to parse the input XML file. This is followed by a *preprocessing* step. Each instance passed to the preprocessing stage is first segmented into words, and then all compound words are identified. Any sequence of words known to be a compound in WordNet is combined into a single entity.

2.2 Context Selection

Although each input instance consists of a large number of words, only a few of these are likely to be useful for disambiguating the target word. We use the context selection algorithm to select a subset of the context words to be used for sense selection. By removing the unimportant words, the computational complexity of the algorithm is reduced.

In this work, we use the *NearestWords* context selection algorithm. This algorithm algorithm selects $2n + 1$ content words surrounding the target word (including the target word) as the context. A stop list is used to identify closed-class non-content words. Additionally, any word not found in WordNet is also discarded. The algorithm then selects n content words before and n content words following the target word, and passes this unordered set of $2n + 1$ words to the Sense Selection module.

2.3 Sense Selection Algorithm

The sense selection module takes the set of words output by the context selection module, one of which is the target word to be disambiguated. For each of the words in this set, it retrieves a list of senses from WordNet, based on which it determines the intended sense of the target word.

The package provides two main algorithms for Sense Selection: the *local* and the *global* algorithms, as described in previous work (Banerjee and Pedersen, 2002; Patwardhan et al., 2003). In this work, we use the *local* algorithm, which is faster and was shown to perform as well as the *global* algorithm.

The *local* sense selection algorithm measures the semantic relatedness of each sense of the target word with the senses of the words in the context, and selects that sense of the target word which is most related to the context word-senses. Given the $2n + 1$ context words, the system scores each sense of the target word. Suppose the target word t has T senses, enumerated as $t_1, t_2, \ldots, t_T$. Also, suppose $w_1, w_2, \ldots, w_{2n}$ are the words in the context of t, each having $W_1, W_2, \ldots, W_{2n}$ senses, respectively. Then for each t_i a score is computed as

$$\mathrm{score}(t_i) = \sum_{j=1}^{2n} \max_{k=1\, to\, W_j} (\mathrm{relatedness}(t_i, w_{jk}))$$

where w_{jk} is the kth sense of word w_j. The sense t_i of target word t with the highest score is selected as the intended sense of the target word.

The relatedness between two word senses is computed using a measure of semantic relatedness defined in the WordNet::Similarity software package (Pedersen et al., 2004), which is a suite of Perl modules implementing a number WordNet-based measures of semantic relatedness. For this work, we used the Context Vector measure (Patwardhan and Pedersen, 2006). The relatedness of concepts is computed based on word co-occurrence statistics derived from WordNet glosses. Given two WordNet senses, this module returns a score between 0 and 1, indicating the relatedness of the two senses.

Our system relies on WordNet as its sense inventory. However, this task used OntoNotes (Hovy et al., 2006) as the sense inventory. OntoNotes word senses are groupings of similar WordNet senses. Thus, we used the training data answer key to generate a mapping between the OntoNotes senses of the given lexical elements and their corresponding WordNet senses. We had to manually create the mappings for some of the WordNet senses, which had no corresponding OntoNotes senses. The sense selection algorithm performed all of its computations with respect to the WordNet senses, and finally the OntoNotes sense corresponding to the selected WordNet sense of the target word was output as the answer for each instance.

3 Results and Analysis

For this task, we used the freely available WordNet::SenseRelate::TargetWord v0.10 and the WordNet::Similarity v1.04 packages. WordNet v2.1 was used as the underlying knowledge base for these. The context selection module used a window size of five (including the target word). The semantic relatedness of concepts was measured using the Context Vector measure, with configuration options as defined in previous research (Patwardhan and Pedersen, 2006). Since we always predict exactly one sense for each instance, the precision and recall values of all our experiments were always the same. Therefore, in this section we will use the name "accuracy" to mean both precision and recall.

3.1 Overall Results, and Baselines

The overall accuracy of our system on the test data is 0.538. This represents 2,609 correctly disambiguated instances, out of a total of 4,851 instances.

As baseline, we compare against the *random* algorithm where for each instance, we randomly pick one of the WordNet senses for the lexical element in that instance, and report the OntoNotes senseid it maps to as the answer. This algorithm gets an accuracy of 0.417. Thus, our algorithm gets an improvement of 12% absolute (29% relative) over this random baseline.

Additionally, we compare our algorithm against the *WordNet SenseOne* algorithm. In this algorithm, we pick the *first* sense among the WordNet senses of the lexical element in each instance, and report its corresponding OntoNotes sense as the answer for that instance. This algorithm leverages the fact that (in most cases) the WordNet senses for a particular word are listed in the database in descending order of their frequency of occurrence in the corpora from which the sense inventory was created. If the new test data has a similar distribution of senses, then this algorithm amounts to a "majority baseline". This algorithm achieves an accuracy of 0.681 which is 15% absolute (27% relative) better than our algorithm. Although this seemingly naïve algorithm outperforms our algorithm, we choose to avoid using this information in our algorithms because it represents a large amount of human supervision in the form of manual sense tagging of text, whereas our goal is to create a purely unsupervised algorithm. Additionally, our algorithms can, with little change, work with other sense inventories besides WordNet that may not have this information.

3.2 Results Disaggregated by Part of Speech

In our past experience, we have found that average disambiguation accuracy differs significantly between words of different parts of speech. For the given test data, we separately evaluated the noun and verb instances. We obtained an accuracy of 0.399 for the noun targets and 0.692 for the verb targets. Thus, we find that our algorithm performs much better on verbs than on nouns, when evaluated using the OntoNotes sense inventory. This is different from our experience with SENSEVAL data from previous years where performance on nouns was uniformly better than that on verbs. One possible reason for the better performance on verbs is that the OntoNotes sense inventory has, on average, fewer senses per verb word (4.41) than per noun word (5.71). However, additional experimentation is needed to more fully understand the difference in performance.

3.3 Results Disaggregated by Lexical Element

To gauge the accuracy of our algorithm on different words (lexical elements), we disaggregated the results by individual word. Table 1 lists the accuracy values over instances of individual verb lexical elements, and Table 2 lists the accuracy values for noun lexical elements. Our algorithm gets all instances correct for 13 verb lexical elements, and for none of the noun lexical elements. More generally, our algorithm gets an accuracy of 50% or more on 45 out of the 65 verb lexical elements, and on 15 out of the 35 noun lexical elements. For nouns, when the accuracy results are viewed in sorted order (as in Table 2), one can observe a sudden degradation of results between the accuracy of the word *system.n* – 0.443 – and the word *source.n* – 0.257. It is unclear why there is such a jump; there is no such sudden degradation in the results for the verb lexical elements.

4 Conclusions

This paper describes our system UMND1, which participated in the SemEval-2007 Coarse-grained

Word	Accuracy	Word	Accuracy
remove	1.000	purchase	1.000
negotiate	1.000	improve	1.000
hope	1.000	express	1.000
exist	1.000	estimate	1.000
describe	1.000	cause	1.000
avoid	1.000	attempt	1.000
affect	1.000	say	0.969
explain	0.944	complete	0.938
disclose	0.929	remember	0.923
allow	0.914	announce	0.900
kill	0.875	occur	0.864
do	0.836	replace	0.800
maintain	0.800	complain	0.786
believe	0.764	receive	0.750
approve	0.750	buy	0.739
produce	0.727	regard	0.714
propose	0.714	need	0.714
care	0.714	feel	0.706
recall	0.667	examine	0.667
claim	0.667	report	0.657
find	0.607	grant	0.600
work	0.558	begin	0.521
build	0.500	keep	0.463
go	0.459	contribute	0.444
rush	0.429	start	0.421
raise	0.382	end	0.381
prove	0.364	enjoy	0.357
see	0.296	set	0.262
promise	0.250	hold	0.250
lead	0.231	prepare	0.222
join	0.222	ask	0.207
come	0.186	turn	0.048
fix	0.000		

Table 1: Verb Lexical Element Accuracies

Word	Accuracy	Word	Accuracy
policy	0.949	people	0.904
future	0.870	drug	0.870
space	0.857	capital	0.789
effect	0.767	condition	0.765
job	0.692	bill	0.686
area	0.676	base	0.650
management	0.600	power	0.553
development	0.517	chance	0.467
exchange	0.459	order	0.456
part	0.451	president	0.446
system	0.443	source	0.257
network	0.218	state	0.208
share	0.192	rate	0.186
hour	0.167	plant	0.109
move	0.085	point	0.080
value	0.068	defense	0.048
position	0.044	carrier	0.000
authority	0.000		

Table 2: Noun Lexical Element Accuracies

English Lexical Sample task. The system is based on WordNet::SenseRelate::TargetWord, which is a freely available unsupervised Word Sense Disambiguation software package. The system uses WordNet-based measures of semantic relatedness to select the intended sense of an ambiguous word. The system required no training data and using WordNet as its only knowledge source achieved an accuracy of 54% on the blind test set.

Acknowledgments

This research was partially supported by a National Science Foundation Early CAREER Development award (#0092784).

References

S. Banerjee and T. Pedersen. 2002. An Adapted Lesk Algorithm for Word Sense Disambiguation Using WordNet. In *Proceedings of the Third International Conference on Intelligent Text Processing and Computational Linguistics*, pages 136–145, Mexico City, Mexico, February.

C. Fellbaum, editor. 1998. *WordNet: An electronic lexical database*. MIT Press.

E. Hovy, M. Marcus, M. Palmer, L. Ramshaw, and R. Weischedel. 2006. OntoNotes: The 90% Solution. In *Proceedings of the Human Language Technology Conference of the North American Chapter of the ACL*, pages 57–60, New York, NY, June.

S. Patwardhan and T. Pedersen. 2006. Using WordNet-based Context Vectors to Estimate the Semantic Relatedness of Concepts. In *Proceedings of the EACL 2006 Workshop on Making Sense of Sense: Bringing Computational Linguistics and Psycholinguistics Together*, pages 1–8, Trento, Italy, April.

S. Patwardhan, S. Banerjee, and T. Pedersen. 2003. Using Measures of Semantic Relatedness for Word Sense Disambiguation. In *Proceedings of the Fourth International Conference on Intelligent Text Processing and Computational Linguistics*, pages 241–257, Mexico City, Mexico, February.

S. Patwardhan, T. Pedersen, and S. Banerjee. 2005. SenseRelate::TargetWord - A Generalized Framework for Word Sense Disambiguation. In *Proceedings of the Twentieth National Conference on Artificial Intelligence (Intelligent Systems Demonstrations)*, pages 1692–1693, Pittsburgh, PA, July.

T. Pedersen, S. Patwardhan, and J. Michelizzi. 2004. WordNet::Similarity - Measuring the Relatedness of Concepts. In *Human Language Technology Conference of the North American Chapter of the Association for Computational Linguistics Demonstrations*, pages 38–41, Boston, MA, May.

UMND2 : SenseClusters Applied to the Sense Induction Task of SENSEVAL-4

Ted Pedersen
Department of Computer Science
University of Minnesota
Duluth, MN 55812
tpederse@d.umn.edu
http://senseclusters.sourceforge.net

Abstract

SenseClusters is a freely–available open–source system that served as the University of Minnesota, Duluth entry in the SENSEVAL-4 sense induction task. For this task SenseClusters was configured to construct representations of the instances to be clustered using the centroid of word co-occurrence vectors that replace the words in an instance. These instances are then clustered using k–means where the number of clusters is discovered automatically using the Adapted Gap Statistic. In these experiments SenseClusters did not use any information outside of the raw untagged text that was to be clustered, and no tuning of the system was performed using external corpora.

1 Introduction

The object of the sense induction task of SENSEVAL-4 (Agirre and Soroa, 2007) was to cluster 27,132 instances of 100 different words (35 nouns and 65 verbs) into senses or classes. The task data consisted of the combination of the test and training data (minus the sense tags) from the English lexical sample task. Each instance is a context of several sentences which contains an occurrence of a given word that serves as the target of sense induction.

SenseClusters is based on the presumption that words that occur in similar contexts will have similar meanings. This intuition has been presented as both the Distributional Hypothesis (Harris, 1968) and the Strong Contextual Hypothesis (Miller and Charles, 1991).

SenseClusters has been in active development at the University of Minnesota, Duluth since 2002. It is an open–source project that is freely–available from sourceforge, and has been been described in detail in numerous publications (e.g., (Purandare and Pedersen, 2004), (Pedersen et al., 2005), (Pedersen and Kulkarni, 2007)).

SenseClusters supports a variety of techniques for selecting lexical features, representing contexts to be clustered, determining the appropriate number of cluster automatically, clustering, labeling of clusters, and evaluating cluster quality. The configuration used in SENSEVAL-4 was just one possible combination of these techniques.

2 Methodology in Sense Induction Task

For this task, SenseClusters represents the instances to be clustered using second order co–occurrence vectors. These are constructed by first identifying word co–occurrences, and then replacing each word in an instance to be clustered with its co-occurrence vector. Then all the vectors that make up an instance are averaged together to represent that instance.

A co–occurrence matrix is constructed by identifying bigrams that occur in the contexts to be clustered two or more times and have a Pointwise Mutual Information (PMI) score greater than five. If the value of PMI is near 1.0, this means that the words in the bigram occur together approximately the number of times expected by chance, and they are not strongly associated. If this value is greater than 1, then the words in the bigram are occurring more of-

Proceedings of the 4th International Workshop on Semantic Evaluations (SemEval-2007), pages 394–397,
Prague, June 2007. ©2007 Association for Computational Linguistics

ten than expected by chance, and they are therefore associated.

The rows of the co–occurrence matrix represent the first word in the selected bigrams, and the columns represent the second word. A window size of 12 is allowed, which means that up to 10 intervening words can be observed between the pair of words in the bigram. This rather large window size was employed since the sample sizes for each word were relatively small, often no more than a few hundred instances.

A stop list was used to eliminate bigrams where either word is a high–frequency low–content word. The particular list used is distributed with the Ngram Statistics Package and is loosely based on the SMART stop list. It consists of 295 words; in addition, all punctuation, single letter words, and numbers (with the exception of years) were eliminated.

Each of the contexts that contain a particular target word is represented by a single vector that is the average (or the centroid) of all the co-occurrence vectors found for the words that make up the context. This results in a context by feature matrix, where the features are the words that occur with the words in the contexts (i.e., second order co–occurrences). The k–means algorithm is used for clustering the contexts, where the number of clusters is automatically discovered using the Adapted Gap Statistic (Pedersen and Kulkarni, 2006). The premise of this method is to create a randomized sample of data with the same characteristics of the observed data (i.e., the contexts to be clustered). This is done by fixing the marginal totals of the context by feature matrix and then generating randomized values that are consistent with those marginal totals. This creates a matrix that is can be viewed as being from the same population as the observed data, except that the data is essentially noise (because it is randomly generated).

The randomized data is clustered for successive values of k from 1 to some upper limit (the number of contexts or the point at which the criterion functions have plateaued). For each value of k the criterion function measures the quality of the clustering solution. The same is done for that observed data, and the difference between the criterion function for the observed data and the randomized data is determined, and the value of k where that difference is largest is selected as the best solution for k, since that is when the clustered data least resembles noise, and is therefore the most organized or best solution. In these experiments the criterion function was intra-cluster similarity.

3 Results and Discussion

There was an unsupervised and a supervised evaluation performed in the sense induction task. Official scores were reported for 6 participating systems, plus the most frequent sense (MFS) baseline, so rankings (when available) are provided from 1 (HIGH) to 7 (LOW). We also conducted an evaluation using the SenseClusters method.

3.1 Unsupervised Evaluation

The unsupervised evaluation was based on the traditional clustering measures of F-score, entropy, and purity. While the participating systems clustered the full 27,132 instances, only the 4,581 instance subset that corresponds to the English lexical sample evaluation data was scored in the evaluation. Table 1 shows the averaged F-scores over all 100 words, all 35 nouns, and all 65 verbs.

In this table the SenseClusters system (UMND2) is compared to the MFS baseline, which is attained by assigning all the instances of a word to a single cluster. We also include several random baselines, where randomX indicates that one of X possible clusters was randomly assigned to each instance of a word. Thus, approximately $100 * X$ distinct clusters are created across the 100 words. The random results are not ranked as they were not a part of the official evaluation. We also present the highest (HIGH, rank 1) and lowest (LOW, rank 7) scores from participating systems, to provide points of comparison.

The randomX baseline is useful in determining the sensitivity of the evaluation technique to the number of clusters discovered. The average number of classes in the gold standard test data is 2.9, so random3 approximates a system that randomly assigns the correct number of clusters. It attains an F-score of 50.0. Note that random2 performs somewhat better (59.7), suggesting that all other things being equal, the F-score is biased towards methods that find a smaller than expected number of clusters.

Table 1: Unsupervised F-Score (test)

	All	Nouns	Verbs	Rank
MFS/HIGH	78.9	80.7	76.8	1
UMND2	66.1	67.1	65.0	4
random2	59.7	60.9	58.4	
LOW	56.1	65.8	45.1	7
random3	50.0	49.9	50.1	
random4	44.9	44.2	45.7	
random10	29.7	28.0	31.7	
random50	17.9	14.9	21.1	

Table 2: Supervised Accuracy (test)

	All	Nouns	Verbs	Rank
HIGH	81.6	86.8	75.7	1
UMND2	80.6	84.5	76.2	2
random2	78.9	81.6	75.8	
MFS	78.7	80.9	76.2	4
LOW	78.5	81.4	75.2	7
random4	78.4	81.1	75.5	
random3	78.3	80.5	75.9	
random10	77.9	79.8	75.8	
random50	75.6	78.5	72.4	

As the number of random clusters increases the F-score declines sharply, showing that it is highly sensitive to the number of clusters discovered, and significantly penalizes systems that find more clusters than indicated in the gold standard data.

We observed for UMND2 that purity (81.7) is quite a bit higher than the F-score (66.1), and that it discovered a smaller number of clusters on average (1.4) than exists in the gold standard data (2.9). This shows that while SenseClusters was able to find relatively pure clusters, it errored in finding too few clusters, and was therefore penalized to some degree by the F-score.

3.2 Supervised Evaluation

A *supervised* evaluation was also carried out on the same clustering of the 27,132 instances as was used in the unsupervised evaluation, following the method defined in (Agirre et al., 2006). Here the train portion (22,281 instances) is used to learn a table of probabilities that is used to map discovered clusters in the test data to gold standard classes. The cluster assigned to each instance in the test portion (4,851 instances) is mapped (assigned) to the most probable class associated with that cluster as defined by this table.

After this transformation is performed, the newly mapped test results are scored using the scorer2 program, which is the official evaluation program of the English lexical sample task and reports the F-measure, which in these experiments is simply accuracy since precision and recall are the same.

In Table 2 we show the results of the supervised evaluation, which includes the highest and lowest score from participating systems, as well as UMND2, MFS, and the same randomX baselines as included in the unsupervised evaluation.

We observed that the difference between the score of the best performing system (HIGH) and the random50 baseline is six points (81.6 - 75.6). In the unsupervised evaluation of this same data this difference is 61 points (78.9 - 17.9) according to the F-score.

The smaller range of values for the supervised measure can be understood by noting that the mapping operation alters the number and distribution of clusters as discovered in the test data. For example, random3 results in an average of 2.9 clusters per word in the test data, but after mapping the average number of clusters is 1.1. The average number of clusters discovered by UMND2 is 1.4, but after mapping this average is reduced to 1.1. For random50, the average number of clusters per word is 24.1, but after mapping is 2.0. This shows that the supervised evaluation has a tendency to converge upon the MFS, which corresponds to assigning 1 cluster per word.

When looking at the randomX results in the supervised evaluation, it appears that this method does not penalize systems for getting the number of clusters incorrect (as the F-score does). This is shown by the very similar results for the randomX baselines, where the only difference in their results is the number of clusters. This lack of a penalty is due to the fact that the mapping operation takes a potentially large number of clusters and maps them to relatively few classes (e.g., random50) and then performs the evaluation.

3.3 SenseClusters Evaluation (F-Measure)

An evaluation was carried out on the full 27,132 instance train+test data set using the SenseClusters evaluation methodology, which was first defined in (Pedersen and Bruce, 1997). This corresponds to an unsupervised version of the F-measure, which in these experiments can be viewed as an accuracy measure since precision and recall are the same (as is the case for the supervised measure).

It aligns discovered clusters with classes such that their agreement is maximized. The clusters and classes must be aligned one to one, so a large penalty can result if the number of discovered clusters differs from the number of gold standard classes.[1]

For UMND2, there were 145 discovered clusters and 368 gold standard classes. Due to the one to one alignment that is required, the 145 discovered clusters were aligned with 145 gold standard classes such that there was agreement for 15,291 of 27,132 instances, leading to an F-measure (accuracy) of 56.36 percent. Note that this is significantly lower than the F-score of UMND2 for the train+test data, which was 63.1. This illustrates that the SenseClusters F-measure and the F-score are not equivalent.

4 Conclusions

One of the strengths of SenseClusters (UMND2) is that it is able to automatically identify the number of clusters without any manual intervention or setting of parameters. In these experiments the Adapted Gap statistic was quite conservative, only discovering on average 1.4 classs per word, where the actual number of classes in the gold standard data was 2.9. However, this is a reasonable result, since for many words there were just a few hundred instances. Also, the gold standard class distinctions were heavily skewed, with the majority sense occurring 80% of the time on average. Under such conditions, there may not be sufficient information available for an unsupervised clustering algorithm to make fine grained distinctions, and so discovering one cluster for a word may be a better course of action that making divisions that are not well supported by the data.

[1]An implementation of this measure is available in the SenseClusters system, or by contacting the author.

5 Acknowledgments

These experiments were conducted with version 0.95 of the SenseClusters system. Many thanks to Amruta Purandare and Anagha Kulkarni for their invaluable work on this and previous versions of SenseClusters.

This research was partially supported by the National Science Foundation Faculty Early Career Development (CAREER) Program (#0092784).

References

E. Agirre and A. Soroa. 2007. Semeval-2007 task 2: Evaluating word sense induction and discrimination systems. In *Proceedings of SemEval-2007: 4th International Workshop on Semantic Evaluations*, June.

E. Agirre, D. Martínez, O. López de Lacalle, and A. Soroa. 2006. Two graph-based algorithms for state-of-the-art wsd. In *Proceedings of the 2006 Conference on Empirical Methods in Natural Language Processing*, pages 585–593, Sydney, Australia, July.

Z. Harris. 1968. *Mathematical Structures of Language*. Wiley, New York.

G.A. Miller and W.G. Charles. 1991. Contextual correlates of semantic similarity. *Language and Cognitive Processes*, 6(1):1–28.

T. Pedersen and R. Bruce. 1997. Distinguishing word senses in untagged text. In *Proceedings of the Second Conference on Empirical Methods in Natural Language Processing*, pages 197–207, Providence, RI, August.

T. Pedersen and A. Kulkarni. 2006. Automatic cluster stopping with criterion functions and the Gap Statistic. In *Proceedings of the Demo Session of HLT/NAACL*, pages 276–279, New York City, June.

T. Pedersen and A. Kulkarni. 2007. Unsupervised discrimination of person names in web contexts. In *Proceedings of the Eighth International Conference on Intelligent Text Processing and Computational Linguistics*, pages 299–310, Mexico City, February.

T. Pedersen, A. Purandare, and A. Kulkarni. 2005. Name discrimination by clustering similar contexts. In *Proceedings of the Sixth International Conference on Intelligent Text Processing and Computational Linguistics*, pages 220–231, Mexico City, February.

A. Purandare and T. Pedersen. 2004. Word sense discrimination by clustering contexts in vector and similarity spaces. In *Proceedings of the Conference on Computational Natural Language Learning*, pages 41–48, Boston, MA.

UNIBA: JIGSAW algorithm for Word Sense Disambiguation

P. Basile and **M. de Gemmis** and **A.L. Gentile** and **P. Lops** and **G. Semeraro**
Department of Computer Science - University of Bari - Via E. Orabona, 4 70125 Bari ITALY
{basilepp, degemmis, al.gentile, lops, semeraro}@di.uniba.it

Abstract

Word Sense Disambiguation (WSD) is traditionally considered an AI-hard problem. A breakthrough in this field would have a significant impact on many relevant web-based applications, such as information retrieval and information extraction. This paper describes JIGSAW, a knowledge-based WSD system that attemps to disambiguate all words in a text by exploiting WordNet[1] senses. The main assumption is that a specific strategy for each Part-Of-Speech (POS) is better than a single strategy. We evaluated the accuracy of JIGSAW on SemEval-2007 task 1 competition[2]. This task is an application-driven one, where the application is a fixed cross-lingual information retrieval system. Participants disambiguate text by assigning WordNet synsets, then the system has to do the expansion to other languages, index the expanded documents and run the retrieval for all the languages in batch. The retrieval results are taken as a measure for the effectiveness of the disambiguation.

1 The JIGSAW algorithm

The goal of a WSD algorithm consists in assigning a word w_i occurring in a document d with its appropriate meaning or sense s, by exploiting the *context* C in where w_i is found. The context C for w_i is defined as a set of words that precede and follow w_i. The sense s is selected from a predefined set of possibilities, usually known as *sense inventory*. In the proposed algorithm, the sense inventory is obtained from WordNet 1.6, according to SemEval-2007 task 1 instructions. JIGSAW is a WSD algorithm based on the idea of combining three different strategies to disambiguate nouns, verbs, adjectives and adverbs. The main motivation behind our approach is that the effectiveness of a WSD algorithm is strongly influenced by the POS tag of the target word. An adaptation of Lesk dictionary-based WSD algorithm has been used to disambiguate adjectives and adverbs (Banerjee and Pedersen, 2002), an adaptation of the Resnik algorithm has been used to disambiguate nouns (Resnik, 1995), while the algorithm we developed for disambiguating verbs exploits the nouns in the *context* of the verb as well as the nouns both in the glosses and in the phrases that WordNet utilizes to describe the usage of a verb. JIGSAW takes as input a document $d = \{w_1, w_2, \dots, w_h\}$ and returns a list of WordNet synsets $X = \{s_1, s_2, \dots, s_k\}$ in which each element s_i is obtained by disambiguating the *target word* w_i based on the information obtained from WordNet about a few immediately surrounding words. We define the *context* C of the target word to be a window of n words to the left and another n words to the right, for a total of $2n$ surrounding words. The algorithm is based on three different procedures for nouns, verbs, adverbs and adjectives, called $JIGSAW_{nouns}$, $JIGSAW_{verbs}$, $JIGSAW_{others}$, respectively. More details for each one of the above mentioned procedures follow.

1.1 $JIGSAW_{nouns}$

The procedure is obtained by making some variations to the algorithm designed by Resnik (1995) for disambiguating noun groups. Given a set of nouns $W = \{w_1, w_2, \dots, w_n\}$, obtained from document d, with each w_i having an associated sense inventory $S_i = \{s_{i1}, s_{i2}, \dots, s_{ik}\}$ of possible senses, the goal is assigning each w_i with the most appropriate sense $s_{ih} \in S_i$, according to the *similarity* of w_i with the other words in W (the context for w_i). The idea is to define a function $\varphi(w_i, s_{ij})$, $w_i \in W$, $s_{ij} \in S_i$, that computes a value in $[0, 1]$ representing the confidence with which word w_i can be assigned with sense s_{ij}. The intuition behind this algorithm is essentially the same exploited by Lesk (1986) and other authors: The most plausible assignment of senses to multiple co-occurring words is the one that maximizes *relatedness* of meanings among the cho-

[1] http://wordnet.princeton.edu/
[2] http://www.senseval.org/

Proceedings of the 4th International Workshop on Semantic Evaluations (SemEval-2007), pages 398–401,
Prague, June 2007. ©2007 Association for Computational Linguistics

sen senses. $JIGSAW_{nouns}$ differs from the original algorithm by Resnik (1995) in the similarity measure used to compute relatedness of two senses. We adopted the Leacock-Chodorow measure (Leacock and Chodorow, 1998), which is based on the length of the path between concepts in an IS-A hierarchy. The idea behind this measure is that similarity between two synsets, s_1 and s_2, is inversely proportional to their distance in the WordNet IS-A hierarchy. The distance is computed by finding the *most specific subsumer* (MSS) between s_1 and s_2 (each ancestor of both s_1 and s_2 in the WordNet hierarchy is a subsumer, the MSS is the one at the lowest level) and counting the number of nodes in the path between s_1 and s_2 that traverse their MSS. We extended this measure by introducing a parameter k that limits the search for the MSS to k ancestors (i.e. that climbs the WordNet IS-A hierarchy until either it finds the MSS or $k + 1$ ancestors of both s_1 and s_2 have been explored). This guarantees that "too abstract" (i.e. "less informative") MSSs will be ignored. In addition to the semantic similarity function, $JIGSAW_{nouns}$ differs from the Resnik algorithm in the use of:

1. a Gaussian factor G, which takes into account the distance between the words in the text to be disambiguated;
2. a factor R, which gives more importance to the synsets that are more common than others, according to the frequency score in WordNet;
3. a *parametrized* search for the MSS between two concepts (the search is limited to a certain number of ancestors).

Algorithm 1 The procedure for disambiguating nouns derived from the algorithm by Resnik

procedure $JIGSAW_{nouns}(W, depth1, depth2)$ ▷ finds the proper synset for each polysemous noun in the set $W = \{w_1, w_2, \ldots, w_n\}$, $depth1$ and $depth2$ are used in the computation of MSS
    for all $w_i, w_j \in W$ **do**
        if $i < j$ **then**
            $sim \leftarrow sim(w_i, w_j, depth1) * G(pos(w_i), pos(w_j))$ ▷ $G(x, y)$ is a Gaussian function which takes into account the difference between the positions of w_i and w_j
            $MSS_{ij} \leftarrow MSS(w_i, w_j, depth2)$ ▷ MSS_{ij} is the most specific subsumer between w_i and w_j, search for MSS restricted to $depth2$ ancestors
            for all $s_{ik} \in S_i$ **do**
                if is-ancestor(MSS_{ij},s_{ik}) **then** ▷ if MSS_{ij} is an ancestor of s_{ik}
                    $sup_{ik} \leftarrow sup_{ik} + sim$
                end if
            end for
            for all $s_{jh} \in S_j$ **do**
                if is-ancestor(MSS_{ij},s_{jh}) **then**
                    $sup_{jh} \leftarrow sup_{jh} + sim$
                end if
            end for
            $norm_i \leftarrow norm_i + sim$
            $norm_j \leftarrow norm_j + sim$
        end if
    end for
    for all $w_i \in W$ **do**
        for all $s_{ik} \in S_i$ **do**
            if $norm_i > 0$ **then**
                $\varphi(i, k) \leftarrow \alpha * sup_{ik}/norm_i + \beta * R(k)$
            else
                $\varphi(i, k) \leftarrow \alpha/|S_i| + \beta * R(k)$
            end if
        end for
    end for
end procedure

Algorithm 1 describes the complete procedure for the disambiguation of nouns. This algorithm considers the words in W pairwise. For each pair (w_i,w_j), the most specific subsumer MSS_{ij} is identified, by reducing the search to $depth1$ ancestors at most. Then, the similarity $sim(w_i, w_j, depth2)$ between the two words is computed, by reducing the search for the MSS to $depth2$ ancestors at most. MSS_{ij} is considered *as supporting evidence* for those synsets s_{ik} in S_i and s_{jh} in S_j that are descendants of MSS_{ij}. The MSS search is computed choosing the nearest MSS in all pairs of synsets s_{ik},s_{jh}. Likewise, the similarity for (w_i,w_j) is the max similarity computed in all pairs of s_{ik},s_{jh} and is weighted by a gaussian factor that takes into account the position of w_i and w_j in W (the shorter is the distance between the words, the higher is the weight). The value $\varphi(i, k)$ assigned to each candidate synset s_{ik} for the word w_i is the sum of two elements. The first one is the proportion of support it received, out of the support possible, computed as $sup_{ik}/norm_i$ in Algorithm 1. The other element that contributes to $\varphi(i, k)$ is a factor $R(k)$ that takes into account the rank of s_{ik} in WordNet, i.e. how common is the sense s_{ik} for the word w_i. $R(k)$ is computed as:

$$R(k) = 1 - 0.8 * \frac{k}{n-1} \quad (1)$$

where n is the cardinality of the sense inventory S_i for w_i, and k is the rank of s_{ik} in S_i, starting from 0.

Finally, both elements are weighted by two parameters: α, which controls the contribution given to $\varphi(i,k)$ by the normalized support, and β, which controls the contribution given by the rank of s_{ik}. We set $\alpha = 0.7$ and $\beta = 0.3$. The synset assigned to each word in W is the one with the highest φ value. Notice that we used two different parameters, $depth1$ and $depth2$ for setting the maximum depth for the search of the MSS: $depth1$ limits the search for the MSS computed in the similarity function, while $depth2$ limits the computation of the MSS used for assigning support to candidate synsets. We set $depth1 = 6$ and $depth2 = 3$.

1.2 $JIGSAW_{verbs}$

Before describing the $JIGSAW_{verbs}$ procedure, the *description* of a synset must be defined. It is the string obtained by concatenating the gloss and the sentences that WordNet uses to explain the usage of a synset. First, $JIGSAW_{verbs}$ includes, in the context C for the target verb w_i, all the nouns in the window of $2n$ words surrounding w_i. For each candidate synset s_{ik} of w_i, the algorithm computes $nouns(i,k)$, that is the set of nouns in the description for s_{ik}.

$$max_{jk} = max_{w_l \in nouns(i,k)} \{\mathtt{sim}(w_j, w_l, depth)\} \quad (2)$$

where $\mathtt{sim}(w_j, w_l, depth)$ is defined as in $JIGSAWnouns$. In other words, max_{jk} is the highest similarity value for w_j wrt the nouns related to the k-th sense for w_i. Finally, an overall similarity score among s_{ik} and the whole context C is computed:

$$\varphi(i,k) = R(k) \cdot \frac{\sum_{w_j \in C} G(pos(w_i), pos(w_j)) \cdot max_{jk}}{\sum_h G(pos(w_i), pos(w_h))} \quad (3)$$

where $R(k)$ is defined as in Equation 1 with a different constant factor (0.9) and $G(pos(w_i), pos(w_j))$ is the same Gaussian factor used in $JIGSAWnouns$, that gives a higher weight to words closer to the target word. The synset assigned to w_i is the one with the highest φ value. Algorithm 2 provides a detailed description of the procedure.

Algorithm 2 The procedure for the disambiguation of verbs

procedure $JIGSAW_{verbs}(w_i, d, depth)$ ▷ finds the proper synset of a polysemous verb w_i in document d
  $C \leftarrow \{w_1, ..., w_n\}$ ▷ C is the context for w_i. For example, $C = \{w_1, w_2, w_4, w_5\}$, if the sequence of words $\{w_1, w_2, w_3, w_4, w_5\}$ occurs in d, w_3 being the target verb, w_j being nouns, $j \neq 3$
  $S_i \leftarrow \{s_{i1}, ...s_{im}\}$ ▷ S_i is the sense inventory for w_i, that is the set of all candidate synsets for w_i returned by WordNet
  $s \leftarrow null$ ▷ s is the synset to be returned
  $score \leftarrow -MAXDOUBLE$ ▷ $score$ is the similarity score assigned to s
  $p \leftarrow 1$ ▷ p is the position of the synsets for w_i
  for all $s_{ik} \in S_i$ **do**
    $max \leftarrow \{max_{1k}, ..., max_{nk}\}$
    $nouns(i,k) \leftarrow \{noun_1, ..., noun_z\}$ ▷ $nouns(i,k)$ is the set of all nouns in the description of s_{ik}
    $sumGauss \leftarrow 0$
    $sumTot \leftarrow 0$
    for all $w_j \in C$ **do** ▷ computation of the similarity between C and s_{ik}
      $max_{jk} \leftarrow 0$ ▷ max_{jk} is the highest similarity value for w_j, wrt the nouns related to the k-th sense for w_i.
      $sumGauss \leftarrow G(pos(w_i), pos(w_j))$ ▷ Gaussian function which takes into account the difference between the positions of the nouns in d
      for all $noun_l \in nouns(i,k)$ **do**
        $sim \leftarrow sim(w_j, noun_l, depth)$ ▷ sim is the similarity between the j-th noun in C and l-th noun in $nouns(i,k)$
        if $sim > max_{jk}$ **then**
          $max_{jk} \leftarrow sim$
        end if
      end for
    end for
    for all $w_j \in C$ **do**
      $sumTot \leftarrow sumTot + G(pos(w_i), pos(w_j)) * max_{jk}$
    end for
    $sumTot \leftarrow sumTot/sumGauss$
    $\varphi(i,k) \leftarrow R(k) * sumTot$ ▷ $R(k)$ is defined as in $JIGSAW_{nouns}$
    if $\varphi(i,k) > score$ **then**
      $score \leftarrow \varphi(i,k)$
      $p \leftarrow k$
    end if
  end for
  $s \leftarrow s_{ip}$
  return s
end procedure

1.3 $JIGSAW_{others}$

This procedure is based on the WSD algorithm proposed by Banerjee and Pedersen (2002). The idea is to compare the glosses of each candidate sense for the target word to the glosses of all the words in its context. Let W_i be the sense inventory for the target word w_i. For each $s_{ik} \in W_i$, $JIGSAW_{others}$ computes the string $targetGloss_{ik}$ that contains the words in the gloss of s_{ik}. Then, the procedure computes the string $contextGloss_i$, which contains the words in the glosses of all the synsets corresponding to each word in the context for w_i. Finally, the procedure computes the *overlap* between $contextGloss_i$ and $targetGloss_{ik}$, and assigns the synset with the highest overlap score to w_i. This score is computed by counting the words that occur both in $targetGloss_{ik}$ and in $contextGloss_i$. If ties occur, the most common synset in WordNet is chosen.

2 Experiment

We performed the experiment following the instructions for SemEval-2007 task 1 (Agirre et al., 2007). $JIGSAW$ is implemented in JAVA, by using JWNL library[3] in order to access WordNet 1.6 dictionary. We ran the experiment on a Linux-based PC with Intel Pentium D processor having a speed of 3 GHz and 2 GB of RAM. The dataset consists of 29,681 documents, including 300 topics. Results are reported in Table 1. Only two systems (PART-A and PART-B) partecipated to the competition, thus the organizers decided to add a third system (ORGANIZERS) developed by themselves. The systems were scored according to standard IR/CLIR measures as implemented in the TREC evaluation package[4]. Our system is labelled as PART-A.

system	*IR documents*	*IR topics*	*CLIR*
no expansion	0.3599		0.1446
full expansion	0.1610	0.1410	0.2676
1st sense	0.2862	0.1172	0.2637
ORGANIZERS	0.2886	0.1587	0.2664
PART-A	0.3030	0.1521	0.1373
PART-B	0.3036	0.1482	0.1734

Table 1: SemEval-2007 task 1 Results

All systems show similar results in IR tasks, while their behaviour is extremely different on CLIR task. WSD results are reported in Table 2. These results are encouraging as regard precision, considering that our system exploits only WordNet as kwnoledge-base, while ORGANIZERS uses a supervised method that exploits SemCor to train a kNN classifier.

3 Conclusions

In this paper we have presented a WSD algorithm that exploits WordNet as knowledge-base and uses three different methods for each part-of-speech. The algorithm has been evaluated by SemEval-2007 task 1. The system shows a good performance in all tasks, but low precision in CLIR evaluation. Probably, the negative result in CLIR task depends on complex interaction of WSD, expansion and indexing. Contrarily to other tasks, organizers do not plan to provide a ranking of systems on SemEval-2007 task 1. As a consequence, the goal of this task - what is the best WSD system in the context of a CLIR system? - is still open. This is why the organizers stressed in the call that this was *"a first try"*.

system	*precision*	*recall*	*attempted*
SENSEVAL-2			
ORGANIZERS	0.584	0.577	93.61%
PART-A	0.498	0.375	75.39%
PART-B	0.388	0.240	61.92%
SENSEVAL-3			
ORGANIZERS	0.591	0.566	95.76%
PART-A	0.484	0.338	69.98%
PART-B	0.334	0.186	55.68%

Table 2: WSD results on all-words task

[3]http://sourceforge.net/projects/jwordnet

[4]http://trec.nist.gov/

References

E. Agirre, B. Magnini, o. Lopez de Lacalle, A. Otegi, G. Rigau, and Vossen. 2007. Semeval-2007 task 1: Evaluating wsd on cross-language information retrieval. In *Proceedings of SemEval-2007*. Association for Computational Linguistics.

S. Banerjee and T. Pedersen. 2002. An adapted lesk algorithm for word sense disambiguation using wordnet. In *CICLing'02: Proc. 3rd Int'l Conf. on Computational Linguistics and Intelligent Text Processing*, pages 136–145, London, UK. Springer-Verlag.

C. Leacock and M. Chodorow. 1998. Combining local context and wordnet similarity for word sense identification. In *C. Fellbaum (Ed.), WordNet: An Electronic Lexical Database*, pages 305–332. MIT Press.

M. Lesk. 1986. Automatic sense disambiguation using machine readable dictionaries: how to tell a pine cone from an ice cream cone. In *Proceedings of the 1986 SIGDOC Conference*, pages 20–29. ACM Press.

P. Resnik. 1995. Disambiguating noun groupings with respect to WordNet senses. In *Proceedings of the Third Workshop on Very Large Corpora*, pages 54–68. Association for Computational Linguistics.

UNN-WePS: Web Person Search using co-Present Names and Lexical Chains

Jeremy Ellman
Northumbria University
Pandon Building
Newcastle upon Tyne
UK
Jeremy. Ellman @unn.ac.uk

Gary Emery
Northumbria University
Pandon Building
Newcastle upon Tyne
UK
Gary.Emery@unn.ac.uk

Abstract

We describe a system, UNN-WePS for identifying individuals from web pages using data from Semeval Task 13. Our system is based on using co-presence of person names to form seed clusters. These are then extended with pages that are deemed conceptually similar based on a lexical chaining analysis computed using Roget's thesaurus. Finally, a single link hierarchical agglomerative clustering algorithm merges the enhanced clusters for individual entity recognition. UNN-WePS achieved an average purity of 0.6, and inverse purity of 0.73.

1 Introduction

Guha and Garg (2004) report that approximately 4% of internet searches are to locate named individuals. Yet, many people share the same name with for example 157630 individuals in the UK sharing the most common name 'David Jones' (UK statistics cited by Ash 2006). Consequently identifying web pages on specific individuals is a significant problem that will grow as everyone acquires a web presence.

There are several proposed approaches to identifying which individuals correspond to which web pages. For example, Bollegala et al. (2007) propose augmenting queries in the style of relevance feedback (Salton and Buckley 1990), Kalashnikov (2007) treat Web Person Search (WePS) as a disambiguation problem whose objective is to distinguish individuals, whilst Wan et al. (2005) see WePS as a clustering problem.

WePS has both similarities and differences to word sense disambiguation (WSD). Both seek to classify instances of usage, but in WSD the sense inventory is fixed. WSD then is more amenable to a classification solution where a system can be effectively trained using learning algorithms. In WePS we do not know from the outset how many individuals our pages correspond to. Consequently we took the view that WePS is better seen as a clustering rather than a classification problem.

1.1 Ambiguity

Ambiguity is a common feature of WePS and WSD. There are multiple types of ambiguity in the relation between person names and entities that confound overly simple approaches. Firstly, note that some first names are also last names (Les Paul, Michael Howard), and that some last names also occur as given names (Woodrow Wilson Guthrie, Martin Luther King). Consequently, an overly simple name parser will easily be confused. Secondly many last names are also place names (Jack London, William Manchester). Thus, if a last name is not found in the names database, but is found in the gazetteer, a name can be confused with a location. Finally, we come to toponym ambiguity, where the name of a place may correspond to several locations. (For example, there are thirteen places called Manchester, multiple Londons, Washingtons etc.) Resolving toponyms is a research problem itself (Leidner, 2004).

1.2 Statistics

Statistics are a further relation between WePS and WSD. We expect Zipf's law (e.g. Adamic and Huberman 2002) to apply to the relation between

Proceedings of the 4th International Workshop on Semantic Evaluations (SemEval-2007), pages 402–405,
Prague, June 2007.

web pages and individuals, meaning that relative frequency and rank form a harmonic series. In other words some people will be associated with many pages and increasingly more will be linked to fewer. This has a strong link to disambiguation, where an inaccurate algorithm may give inferior performance to the strategy of always selecting the most frequent sense.

Now if we consider the types of data that distinguish individuals, we might find colleagues, friends, and family mentioned in web pages, in addition to locations, dates, and topics of interest. Of these, names are particularly useful, and we define co-present names as names found in a web page in addition to the name for which we are searching.

Names are statistically useful, even though many people share the same name. For example there are 7640 individuals in the UK (for example) that share the most popular female name "Margaret Smith". Given the population of the UK is approximately 60 million, the probability of even the most common female name in the UK occurring randomly is 1.27+10-4 (of course not all the individuals have web pages).

Now, Semeval WePS pages (Artiles 2007) have been retrieved in response to a search for one name. Often such web pages will contain additional names. The probability that a web page will contain two names corresponding to two different individuals is quite low (~ca 7x10-8). Consequently co-present names form indicators of an individual's identity. These give accurate seed points, which are critical to the success of many clustering algorithms such as k-means (Jain et al. 1999)

1.3 Lexical Chain Text Similarity

Not all WePS pages contain multiple names, or even content in any form. Consequently we need to distinguish between pages that are similar in meaning to a page already in a seed cluster, those that refer to separate entities, and those to be discarded

This was done by comparing the conceptual similarity of the WePS pages using Roget's thesaurus as the conceptual inventory. The approach was described in Ellman (2000), where lexical chains are identified from each document using Roget's thesaurus. These chains are then unrolled to yield an attribute value vector of concepts where the values are given by repetition, type of thesaural relation found, and textual cohesion. Thus, we are not simply indexing by thesaural categories.

Vectors corresponding to different documents can be compared to give a measure of conceptual similarity. Roget's thesaurus typically contains one thousand sense entries divided by part of speech usage, giving a total of 6400 entries. Such vectors may be compared using many algorithms, although a nearest neighbor algorithm was implemented in Ellman (2000).

1.4 One Sense Per Discourse

UNN-WePS was based on a deliberate strategy that the success of an active disambiguation method needed to exceed its overall error rate in order to improve baseline performance. As such, simple methods that improved overall success modestly were preferred to complex ones that did not. Consequently, to reduce the search space, we used the 'one sense per discourse' heuristic (Gale et al. 1992). This assumes that one web page would not refer to two different individuals that share a name.

2 System Description

UNN-WePS was made up of three components, comprising modules to:

1. Create seed clusters that associated files with person names other than those being searched for.
2. Match similarity of unallocated documents to micro clusters using lexical chains derived from Roget's thesaurus.
3. Identify entities using single link agglomerative clustering algorithm.

In detail, a part of speech tagger (Coburn et al. 2007) was used to identify sequences of proper nouns. Person names were identified from these sequences using the following simple names 'grammar' coupled with data from the US Census (1990).

Name = [Title*][Initials | 1st name]+[2nd name]+

Figure 1: Regular Expression Name Syntax

We also used a gazetteer to forms seed clusters using data from the World Gazetteer (2007). This did not form part of the submitted system.

In the second step, conceptual similarity was determined using the method and tool described in Ellman (2000). Documents not allocated to seed clusters, were compared for conceptual similarity to all other documents. If similar to a document in a seed cluster, the unallocated document was inserted into the seed cluster. If neither document nor one to which it was similar too were in a seed cluster, they were formed into a new seed cluster. Finally if document has 'meaningful' content, but is not conceptually similar to any other it is stored in a singleton seed cluster otherwise, it is discarded.

In the final step, seed clusters were sorted by size and merged using a single link hierarchical agglomerative clustering algorithm to identify entities (Jain et al. 1999). The use of a single link means that a document can only be associated with one entity, which conforms to the 'one sense per discourse' heuristic.

Further details of the UNN-WePS algorithm are given in figure 2 below.

```
FOREACH Person_Name
  1. TAG raw html Files with Part of Speech.
  2. IDENTIFY Generic Document Profiles using
       lexical chains in html Files.
  3. CONSTRUCT table T to associate person
       names with Files.
     a.  FOREACH File in Person_Name
           i. IDENTIFY Names in File
          ii. FOREACH Name in Names
                   IF Name ≠ Person_Name
                   STORE Name, File in T
  4. CREATE Seed clusters by inverting T to
       give files that are associated by co-
       present names
  5. MATCH Similarity of unallocated docu-
       ments to seed clusters
     a. FOREACH unallocated document D
         IF similar to a document in cluster C
           INSERT D into C
         ELSE IF similar to a non-clustered
         document D'
         CREATE  D, D' as new cluster C'
         ELSE IF CONTAINS D > 200 words
              CREATE D as new cluster C''
              ELSE DISCARD D
  6. IDENTIFY entities using single link ag-
       glomerative clustering algorithm over
       seed clusters.
```

Figure 2: UNN-WePS Algorithm

3 Results

UNN-WePS achieved an average purity of 0.6, and inverse purity of 0.73 in Semeval Task 13, achieving seventh position out of sixteen competing systems (Artiles et al. 2007). However there was considerable variance in UNN-WePS results as shown in graph 1 below.

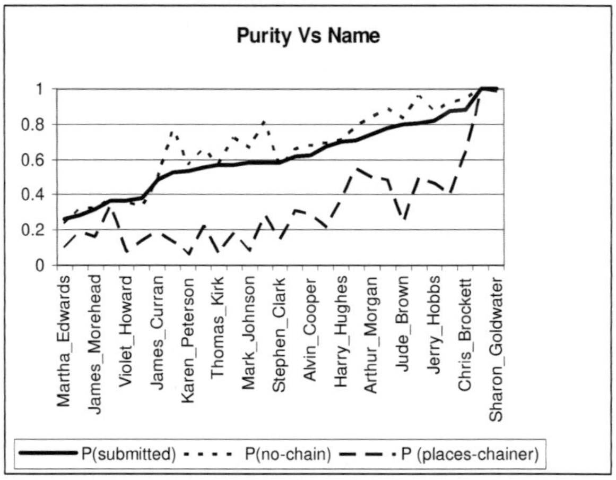

Graph 1: UNN-WePS purity performance

Graph 1 shows the purity scores for UNN-WePS on the Semeval 13 test data on three conditions: (1) as submitted (solid line), (2) using the gazetteer (dashed line), and (3) without the lexical chain based similarity matching (dotted line).

Note although the purity is lower when similarity matching is included the number of discarded documents is approximately halved.

An examination of the data suggests that where performance was especially poor it was due to genealogical data. Firstly this contains multiple individuals sharing the same name violating the 'one sense per discourse' heuristic. Secondly genealogical data includes birth and death information which was outside the scope of UNN-WePS. Furthermore, the large number of names confounds the statistical utility of co-present names.

4 Conclusion and Future Work

We have described a system, UNN-WePS that disambiguates individuals in web pages as required for Semeval task 13 (Artiles et al. 2007).

UNN-WePS was composed of three modules. The first formed seed clusters based on names present in web pages other than the individual for whom we are searching. The second used a lexical chain based similarity measure to associates remaining files with clusters, whilst the third joined the clusters to identify identities using a single link hierarchical algorithm.

UNN-WePS performed surprisingly well considering the simplicity of its basic seeding algorithm. The use however of the 'one sense per discourse' heuristic was flawed. Names do re-occur across generations in families.

Genealogy is a popular Internet pastime, and web pages containing genealogy data frequently refer to multiple individuals that share a name at different time periods. As UNN-WePS did not account for time, this could not be detected. Furthermore, the large number of names in on-line genealogical data does lead to spurious associations.

As WePS was time limited, several extensions and refinements were envisaged, but not executed. Firstly, as described, the world gazetteer (2007) did not lead to performance improvements. We speculate therefore the disambiguation effect from using place names was exceeded by the ambiguity introduced by using them blindly. We note especially the inference between unidentified names (or street names, or building names) being interpreted as place data.

A further system deficiency was the lack of recognition of date data. This is essential to differentiate between identically named individuals in genealogical data.

Finally, we are currently experimenting with different clustering algorithms using the CLUTO toolkit (Karypis 2002) to improve on UNN-WePS baseline performance.

References

Adamic L.A. and Huberman B.A., 2002 *Zipf's law and the Internet, Glottometrics* 3, 2002, 143-150

Artiles, J., Gonzalo, J. and Sekine, S. (2007). *The SemEval-2007 WePS Evaluation: Establishing a benchmark for the Web People Search Task.* In Proceedings of Semeval 2007, Association for Computational Linguistics.

Ash, Russell 2006 *The top 10 of Everything* Hamlyn, Palazzo Bath UK

Bollegala, Danushka, Matsuo Yutaka Ishizuka Mitsuru *Disambiguating Personal Names on the Web using Automatically Extracted Key Phrases* Proc. ECAI 2006, pp.553-557, Trento, Italy (2006.8)

Coburn A, Ceglowski M, and Cuadrado J 2007 *Lingua::EN::Tagger, a Perl part-of-speech tagger for English text.* http://search.cpan.org/~acoburn/ Lingua-EN-Tagger-0.13/

Ellman, Jeremy. 2000 *Using Roget's Thesaurus to Determine the Similarity of Texts.* PhD thesis, University of Sunderland [Available at http://citeseer.ist.psu.edu/ellman00using.html]

Gale, W., Church, K., and Yarowsky, D. (1992). *One sense per discourse.* In Proceedings of the Fourth DARPA Speech and Natural Language Workshop, pages 233--237.

Guha R. & Garg A. *Disambiguating People in Search.* Stanford University, 2004

Jain, A. K., Murty, M. N., and Flynn, P. J. 1999. *Data clustering: a review.* ACM Comput. Surv. 31, 3 (Sep. 1999), 264-323

Karypis G. 2002. *CLUTO: A clustering toolkit.* Technical Report 02-017, University of Minnesota. Available at: http://wwwusers.cs.umn.edu/~karypis/cluto/.

Leidner, Jochen L. (2004). *Toponym Resolution in Text: "Which Sheffield is it?"* in proc. 27th Annual International ACM SIGIR Conference (SIGIR 2004), Sheffield, UK.

Navigli, Roberto 2006. *Meaningful clustering of senses helps boost word sense disambiguation performance.* In *Proc. ACL* (Sydney, Australia, July 17 - 18, 2006).

Salton and Buckley 1990 *Improving Retrieval Performance by Relevance Feedback* JASIS 41(4) pp288-297

US Census 1990 http://www.census.gov/ genealogy/names/names_files.html accessed 17th April 2007

Wan, X., Gao, J., Li, M., and Ding, B. 2005. *Person resolution in person search results: WebHawk.* in Proc. CIKM '05. ACM Press, New York, NY

World Gazetteer 2007 http://world-gazetteer.com/ accessed 17th April 2007

UNT-Yahoo: SuperSenseLearner: Combining SenseLearner with SuperSense and other Coarse Semantic Features

Rada Mihalcea and **Andras Csomai**
University of North Texas
rada@cs.unt.edu,csomaia@unt.edu

Massimiliano Ciaramita
Yahoo! Research Barcelona
massi@yahoo-inc.com

Abstract

We describe the SUPERSENSELEARNER system that participated in the English all-words disambiguation task. The system relies on automatically-learned semantic models using collocational features coupled with features extracted from the annotations of coarse-grained semantic categories generated by an HMM tagger.

1 Introduction

The task of word sense disambiguation consists of assigning the most appropriate meaning to a polysemous word within a given context. Applications such as machine translation, knowledge acquisition, common sense reasoning, and others, require knowledge about word meanings, and word sense disambiguation is considered essential for all these tasks.

Most of the efforts in solving this problem were concentrated so far toward targeted supervised learning, where each sense tagged occurrence of a particular word is transformed into a feature vector, which is then used in an automatic learning process. The applicability of such supervised algorithms is however limited only to those few words for which sense tagged data is available, and their accuracy is strongly connected to the amount of labeled data available at hand.

Instead, methods that address all words in unrestricted text have received significantly less attention. While the performance of such methods is usually exceeded by their supervised lexical-sample alternatives, they have however the advantage of providing larger coverage.

In this paper, we describe SUPERSENSELEARNER – a system for solving the semantic ambiguity of all words in unrestricted text. SUPERSENSELEARNER brings together under one system the features previously used in the SENSELEARNER (Mihalcea and Csomai, 2005) and the SUPERSENSE (Ciaramita and Altun, 2006) all-words word sense disambiguation systems. The system is using a relatively small pre-existing sense-annotated data set for training purposes, and it learns global semantic models for general word categories.

2 Learning for All-Words Word Sense Disambiguation

Our goal is to use as little annotated data as possible, and at the same time make the algorithm *general* enough to be able to disambiguate as many content words as possible in a text, and *efficient* enough so that large amounts of text can be annotated in real time. SUPERSENSELEARNER is attempting to learn general semantic models for various word categories, starting with a relatively small sense-annotated corpus. We base our experiments on SemCor (Miller et al., 1993), a balanced, semantically annotated dataset, with all content words manually tagged by trained lexicographers.

The input to the disambiguation algorithm consists of raw text. The output is a text with word meaning annotations for all open-class words.

The algorithm starts with a preprocessing stage, where the text is tokenized and annotated with part-

Proceedings of the 4th International Workshop on Semantic Evaluations (SemEval-2007), pages 406–409,
Prague, June 2007. ©2007 Association for Computational Linguistics

of-speech tags; collocations are identified using a sliding window approach, where a collocation is defined as a sequence of words that forms a compound concept defined in WordNet (Miller, 1995).

Next, a semantic model is learned for all predefined word categories, where a word category is defined as a group of words that share some common syntactic or semantic properties. Word categories can be of various granularities. For instance, a model can be defined and trained to handle all the *nouns* in the test corpus. Similarly, using the same mechanism, a finer-grained model can be defined to handle all the verbs for which at least one of the meanings is of type e.g., "<move>". Finally, small coverage models that address one word at a time, for example a model for the adjective "small," can be also defined within the same framework. Once defined and trained, the models are used to annotate the ambiguous words in the test corpus with their corresponding meaning. Sections 3 and 4 below provide details on the features implemented by the various models.

Note that the semantic models are applicable only to: (1) words that are covered by the word category defined in the models; and (2) words that appeared at least once in the training corpus. The words that are not covered by these models (typically about 10-15% of the words in the test corpus) are assigned the most frequent sense in WordNet.

3 SenseLearner Semantic Models

Different semantic models can be defined and trained for the disambiguation of different word categories. Although more general than models that are built individually for each word in a test corpus (Decadt et al., 2004), the applicability of the semantic models built as part of SENSELEARNER is still limited to those words previously seen in the training corpus, and therefore their overall coverage is not 100%.

Starting with an annotated corpus consisting of all the annotated files in SemCor, augmented with the SENSEVAL-2 and SENSEVAL-3 all-words data sets, a separate training data set is built for each model. There are seven models provided with the current SENSELEARNER distribution, implementing the following features:

3.1 Noun Models

modelNN1: A contextual model that relies on the first noun, verb, or adjective before the target noun, and their corresponding part-of-speech tags.
modelNNColl: A collocation model that implements collocation-like features based on the first word to the left and the first word to the right of the target noun.

3.2 Verb Models

modelVB1 A contextual model that relies on the first word before and the first word after the target verb, and their part-of-speech tags.
modelVBColl A collocation model that implements collocation-like features based on the first word to the left and the first word to the right of the target verb.

3.3 Adjective Models

modelJJ1 A contextual model that relies on the first noun after the target adjective.
modelJJ2 A contextual model that relies on the first word before and the first word after the target adjective, and their part-of-speech tags.
modelJJColl A collocation model that implements collocation-like features using the first word to the left and the first word to the right of the target adjective.

Based on previous performance in the SENSEVAL-2 and SENSEVAL-3 evaluations, we selected the noun and verb collocational models for inclusion in the SUPERSENSELEARNER system participating in the SEMEVAL all-words task.

4 SuperSenses and other Coarse-Grained Semantic Features

A great deal of work has focused in recent years on shallow semantic annotation tasks such as named entity recognition and semantic role labeling. In the former task, systems analyze text to detect mentions of instances of coarse-grained semantic categories such as "person", "organization" and "location". It seems natural to ask if this type of shallow semantic information can be leveraged to improve lexical disambiguation. Particularly, since the best performing taggers typically implement sequential decoding schemes, e.g., Viterbi decoding, which have linear complexity and can be performed quite efficiently. In practice thus, this type of pre-processing resembles POS-tagging and could provide the WSD system with useful additional evidence.

4.1 Tagsets

We use three different tagsets. The first is the set of WordNet supersenses (Ciaramita and Altun, 2006): a mapping of WordNet's synsets to 45 broad lexicographers categories, 26 for nouns, 15 for verbs, 3 for adjectives and 1 for adverbs. The second tagset is based on the ACE 2007 English data for entity mention detection (EMD) (ACE, 2007). This tagset defines seven entity types: Facility, Geo-Political Entity, Location, Organization, Person, Vehicle, Weapon; further subdivided in 44 subtypes. The third tagset is derived from the BBN Entity Corpus (BBN, 2005) which complements the Wall Street Journal Penn Treebank with annotations of a large set of entities: 12 named entity types (Person, Facility, Organization, GPE, Location, Nationality, Product, Event, Work of Art, Law, Language, and Contact-Info), nine nominal entity types (Person, Facility, Organization, GPE, Product, Plant, Animal, Substance, Disease and Game), and seven numeric types (Date, Time, Percent, Money, Quantity, Ordinal and Cardinal). Several of these types are further divided into subtypes, for a total of 105 classes.[1]

4.2 Taggers

We annotate the training and evaluation data using three sequential taggers, one for each tagset. The tagger is a Hidden Markov Model trained with the perceptron algorithm introduced in (Collins, 2002), which applies Viterbi decoding and is regularized using averaging. Label to label dependencies are limited to the previous tag (first order HMM). We use a generic feature set for NER based on words, lemmas, POS tags, and word shape features, in addition we use as a feature of each token the supersense of a first (super)sense baseline. A detailed description of the features used and the tagger can be found in (Ciaramita and Altun, 2006). The supersense tagger is trained on the Brown sections one and two of SemCor. The BBN tagger is trained on sections 2-21 of the BBN corpus. The ACE tagger is trained on the 599 ACE 2007 training files. The accuracy of the tagger is, approximately, 78% F-score for supersenses and ACE, and 87% F-score for the BBN corpus.

[1]BBN Corpus documentation.

4.3 Features

The taggers disregard the lemmatization of the evaluation data. In practice, this means that multiword lemmas such as "take off", are split into their basic components. In fact, the goal of the tagger is to guess the elements of the instances of semantic categories by means of the usual BIO encoding. In other words, the tagger predicts a labeled bracketing of the tokens in each sentence. As an example, the supersense tagger annotates the tokens in the phrase "substance abuse" as "substance$_{B-noun.act}$" and "abuse$_{I-noun.act}$", although the gold standard segmentation of the data does not identify the phrase as one lemma. We use the labels generated in this way as features of each token to disambiguate.

5 Feature Combination

For the final system we create a combined feature set for each target word, consisting of the lemma, the part of speech, the collocational SENSELEARNER features, and the three coarse grained semantic tags of the target word. Note that the semantic features are represented as *lemma_TAG* to avoid overgeneralization.

In the training stage, a feature vector is constructed for each sense-annotated word covered by a semantic model. The features are model-specific, and feature vectors are added to the training set pertaining to the corresponding model. The label of each such feature vector consists of the target word and the corresponding sense, represented as *word#sense*. Table 1 shows the number of feature vectors constructed in this learning stage for each semantic model. To annotate new text, similar vectors are created for all the content-words in the raw text. Similar to the training stage, feature vectors are created and stored separately for each semantic model.

Next, word sense predictions are made for all the test examples, with a separate learning process run for each semantic model. For learning, we are using the Timbl memory based learning algorithm (Daele-

mode	Training size	RESULTS Precision	Recall
noun	89052	0.658	0.228
verb	48936	0.539	0.353
all	137988	0.583	0.583

Table 1: Precision and recall for the SUPERSENSELEARNER semantic models.

mode	Training size	RESULTS Precision	Recall
noun	89052	0.666	0.233
verb	48936	0.554	0.360
all	137988	0.593	0.593

Table 2: Precision and recall for the SUPERSENSELEARNER semantic models - without U labels.

mans et al., 2001), which was previously found useful for the task of word sense disambiguation (Hoste et al., 2002; Mihalcea, 2002).

Following the learning stage, each vector in the test data set is labeled with a *predicted* word and sense. If the word predicted by the learning algorithm coincides with the target word in the test feature vector, then the predicted sense is used to annotate the test instance. Otherwise, if the predicted word is different from the target word, no annotation is produced, and the word is left for annotation in a later stage (e.g., using the most frequent sense back-off method).

6 Results

The SUPERSENSELEARNER system participated in the SEMEVAL all-words word sense disambiguation task. Table 1 shows the results obtained for each part-of-speech (nouns and verbs), as well as the overall results. We have also ran a separate evaluation excluding the U (unknown) tag, which is shown in Table 2. SUPERSENSELEARNER was ranked the third among the fourteen participating systems, proving the validity of the approach.

Acknowledgments

We would like to thank Mihai Surdeanu for providing a pre-processed version of the ACE data.

References

2007. Automatic content extraction workshop. http://www.nist.gov/speech/tests/ace/ace07/index.htm.

2005. BBN pronoun coreference and entity type corpus. Linguistic Data Consortium (LDC) catalog number LDC2005T33.

M. Ciaramita and Y. Altun. 2006. Broad-coverage sense disambiguation and information extraction with a supersense sequence tagger. In *Proceedings of the Conference on Empirical Methods in Natural Language Processing*.

M. Collins. 2002. Discriminative training methods for hidden markov models: Theory and experiments with perceptron algorithms. In *Proceedings of the Conference on Empirical Methods in Natural Language Processing (EMNLP)*, Philadelphia, July. Association for Computational Linguistics.

W. Daelemans, J. Zavrel, K. van der Sloot, and A. van den Bosch. 2001. Timbl: Tilburg memory based learner, version 4.0, reference guide. Technical report, University of Antwerp.

B. Decadt, V. Hoste, W. Daelemans, and A. Van den Bosch. 2004. Gambl, genetic algorithm optimization of memory-based wsd. In *Senseval-3: Third International Workshop on the Evaluation of Systems for the Semantic Analysis of Text*, Barcelona, Spain, July.

V. Hoste, W. Daelemans, I. Hendrickx, and A. van den Bosch. 2002. Evaluating the results of a memory-based word-expert approach to unrestricted word sense disambiguation. In *Proceedings of the ACL Workshop on "Word Sense Disambiguatuion: Recent Successes and Future Directions"*, Philadelphia, July.

R. Mihalcea and A. Csomai. 2005. Senselearner: Word sense disambiguation for all words in unrestricted text. In *Proceedings of the 43nd Annual Meeting of the Association for Computational Linguistics*, Ann Arbor, MI.

R. Mihalcea. 2002. Instance based learning with automatic feature selection applied to Word Sense Disambiguation. In *Proceedings of the 19th International Conference on Computational Linguistics (COLING 2002)*, Taipei, Taiwan, August.

G. Miller, C. Leacock, T. Randee, and R. Bunker. 1993. A semantic concordance. In *Proceedings of the 3rd DARPA Workshop on Human Language Technology*, Plainsboro, New Jersey.

G. Miller. 1995. Wordnet: A lexical database. *Communication of the ACM*, 38(11):39–41.

UNT: SubFinder: Combining Knowledge Sources for Automatic Lexical Substitution

Samer Hassan, Andras Csomai, Carmen Banea, Ravi Sinha, Rada Mihalcea*
Department of Computer Science and Engineering
University of North Texas
samer@unt.edu, csomaia@unt.edu, carmenb@unt.edu, rss0089@unt.edu, rada@cs.unt.edu

Abstract

This paper describes the University of North Texas SUBFINDER system. The system is able to provide the most likely set of substitutes for a word in a given context, by combining several techniques and knowledge sources. SUBFINDER has successfully participated in the *best* and *out of ten (oot)* tracks in the SEMEVAL lexical substitution task, consistently ranking in the first or second place.

1 Introduction

Lexical substitution is defined as the task of identifying the most likely alternatives (substitutes) for a target word, given its context (McCarthy, 2002). Many natural language processing applications can benefit from the availability of such alternative words, including word sense disambiguation, lexical acquisition, machine translation, information retrieval, question answering, text simplification, and others.

The task is closely related to the problem of word sense disambiguation, with the substitutes acting as synonyms for the input word meaning. Unlike word sense disambiguation however, lexical substitution is not performed with respect to a given sense inventory, but instead candidate synonyms are generated "on the fly" for a given word occurrence. Thus, lexical substitution can be regarded in a way as a hybrid task that combines word sense disambiguation and distributional similarity, targeting the identification of *semantically similar* words that *fit the context*.

2 A system for lexical substitution

SUBFINDER is a system able to provide the most likely set of substitutes for a word in a given context. In SUBFINDER, the lexical substitution task is carried out as a sequence of two steps. First, candidates are extracted from a variety of knowledge sources; so far, we experimented with WordNet (Fellbaum, 1998), Microsoft Encarta encyclopedia, Roget, as well as synonym sets generated from bilingual dictionaries, but additional knowledge sources can be integrated as well. Second, provided a list of candidates, a number of ranking methods are applied in a weighted combination, resulting in a final list of lexical substitutes ranked by their semantic fit with both the input target word and the context.

3 Candidate Extraction

Candidates are extracted using several lexical resources, which are combined into a larger comprehensive resource.

WordNet: WordNet is a large lexical database of English, with words grouped into synonym sets called *synsets*. A problem we encountered with this resource is that often times the only candidate in the synset is the target word itself. Thus, to enlarge the set of candidates, we use both the synonyms and the hypernyms of the target word. We also remove the target word from the synset, to ensure that only viable candidates are considered.

Microsoft Encarta encyclopedia: The Microsoft Encarta is an online encyclopedia and thesaurus resource, which provides for each word the part of speech and a list of synonyms. Using the part of speech as identified in the context, we are able to extract synsets for the target word. An important feature in the Encarta Thesaurus is that the first word in the synset acts as a definition for the synset, and therefore disambiguates the target word. This definition is maintained as a separate entry in the com-

*Contact author.

Proceedings of the 4th International Workshop on Semantic Evaluations (SemEval-2007), pages 410–413,
Prague, June 2007.

prehensive resource, and it is also added to its corresponding synset.

Other Lexical Resources: We have also experimented with two other lexical resources, namely the Roget thesaurus and a thesaurus built using bilingual dictionaries. In evaluations carried out on the development data set, the best results were obtained using only WordNet and Encarta, and thus these are the resources used in the final SUBFINDER system.

All these resources entail different forms of synset clustering. In order to merge them, we use the largest overlap among them. It is important to note that the choice of the first resource considered has a bearing on the way the synsets are clustered. In experiments ran on the development data set, the best results were obtained using a lexical resource constructed starting with the Microsoft Encarta Thesaurus and then mapping the WordNet synsets to it.

4 Candidate Ranking

Several ranking methods are used to score the candidate substitutes, as described below.

Lexical Baseline (LB): In this approach we use the pre-existing lexical resources to provide a ranking over the candidate substitutes. We rank the candidates based on their occurrence in the two selected lexical resources WordNet and Encarta, with those occurring in both resources being assigned a higher ranking. This technique emphasizes the resources annotators' agreement that the candidates belong indeed to the same synset.

Machine Translation (MT): We use machine translation to translate the test sentences back-and-forth between English and a second language. From the resulting English translation, we extract the replacement that the machine translation engine provides for the target word. To locate the translated word we scan the translation for any of the candidates (and their inflections) as obtained from the comprehensive resource, and score the candidate synset accordingly.

We experimented with a range of languages such as French, Italian, Spanish, Simplified Chinese, and German, but the best results obtained on the development data were based on the French translations. This could be explained because French is part of the Romance languages family and synonyms to English words often find their roots in Latin. If we consider again the word *bright*, it was translated into French as *intelligent* and then translated back into English as *intelligent* for obvious reasons. In one instance, *intelligent* was the best replacement for *bright* in the trial data. Despite the fact that we also used Italian and Spanish (which are both Latin-based) we can only assume that French worked better because translation engines are better trained on French. From the resulting English translation, we extract the replacement that the machine translation engine provides for the target word. To locate the translated word we scan the translation for any of the candidates (and their inflections) as obtained from the comprehensive resource, and score the candidate synset accordingly. The translation process was carried out using Google and AltaVista translation engines resulting in two systems MTG and MTA respectively. The translation systems feature high precision when a candidate is found (about 20% of the time), at the cost of low recall. The lexical baseline method is therefore used when no candidates are returned by the translation method.

Most Common Sense (MCS): Another method we use for ranking candidates is to consider the first word appearing in the first synset returned by WordNet. When no words other than the target word are available in this synset, the method recursively searches the next synset available for the target word. In order to guarantee a sufficient number of candidates, we use the lexical baseline method as a baseline.

Language Model (LM): We model the semantic fit of a candidate substitute within the given context using a language model, expressed using the conditional probability:

$$P(c|g) = P(c,g)/P(g) \approx Count(c,g) \quad (1)$$

where c represents a possible candidate and g represents the context. The probability $P(g)$ of the context is the same for all the candidates, hence we can ignore it and estimate $P(c|g)$ as the N-gram frequency of the context where the target word is replaced by the proposed candidate. To avoid skewed counts that can arise from the different morphological inflections of the target word or the candidate and the bias that the context might have toward any specific inflection, we generalize $P(c|g)$ to take into account all the inflections of the selected candidate as shown in equation 2.

$$P^n(c|g) \approx \sum_{i=1}^{n} Count(c_i, g) \quad (2)$$

where n is the number of possible inflections for the candidate c.

We use the Google N-gram dataset to calculate the term $Count(c_i\ g)$. The Google N-gram corpus is a collection of English N-grams, ranging from one to five N-grams, and their respective frequency counts observed on the Web (Brants and Franz, 2006). In order for the model to give high preference to the longer N-grams, while maintaining the relative frequencies of the shorter N-grams (typically more frequent), we augment the counts of the higher order N-grams with the maximum counts of the lower order N-grams, hence guaranteeing that the score assigned to an N-gram of order N is higher than the the score of an N-gram of order $N - 1$.

Semantic Relatedness using Latent Semantic Analysis (LSA): We expect to find a strong semantic relationship between a good candidate and the target context. A relatively simple and efficient way to measure such a relatedness is the Latent Semantic Analysis (Landauer et al., 1998). Documents and terms are mapped into a 300 dimensional latent semantic space, providing the ability to measure the semantic relatedness between two words or a word and a context. We use the InfoMap package from Stanford University's Center for the Study of Language and Information, trained on a collection of approximately one million Wikipedia articles. The rank of a candidate is given by its semantic relatedness to the entire context sentence.

Information Retrieval (IR): Although the Language Model approach is successful in ranking the candidates, it suffers from the small N-gram size imposed by using the Google N-grams corpus. Such a restriction is obvious in the following 5-gram example *who was a bright boy* in which the context is not sufficient to disambiguate between *happy* and *smart* as possible candidates. As a result, we adapt an information retrieval approach which uses all the content words available in the given context. Similar to the previous models, the target word in the context is replaced by all the generated inflections of the selected candidate and then queried using a web search engine. The resulting rank represents the sum of the total number of pages in which the candidate or any of its inflections occur together with the context. This also reflects the semantic relatedness or the relevance of the candidate to the context.

Word Sense Disambiguation (WSD): Since previous work indicated the usefulness of word sense disambiguation systems in lexical substitution (Dagan et al., 2006), we use the SenseLearner word sense disambiguation tool (Mihalcea and Csomai, 2005) to disambiguate the target word and, accordingly, to propose its synonyms as candidates.

Final System: Our candidate ranking methods are aimed at different aspects of what constitutes a good candidate. On one hand, we measure the semantic relatedness of a candidate with the original context (the LSA and WSD methods fall under this category). On the other hand, we also want to ensure that the candidate fits the context and leads to a well formed English sentence (e.g., the language model method). Given that the methods described earlier aim at orthogonal aspects of the problem, it is expected that a combination of these will provide a better overall ranking.

We use a voting mechanism, where we consider the reciprocal of the rank of each candidates as given by one of the described methods. The final score of a candidate is given by the decreasing order of the weighted sum of the reciprocal ranks:

$$score\,(c_i) = \sum_{m \in rankings} \lambda_m \frac{1}{r^m_{c_i}}$$

To determine the weight λ of each individual ranking we run a genetic algorithm on the development data, optimized for the *mode* precision and recall. Separate sets of weights are obtained for the *best* and *oot* tasks. Table 1 shows the weights of the individual ranking methods. As expected, for the *best* task, the language model type of methods obtain higher weights, whereas for the *oot* task, the semantic methods seem to perform better.

5 Results and Discussion

The SUBFINDER system participated in the *best* and the *oot* tracks of the lexical substitution task. The *best* track calls for any number of best guesses, with the most promising one listed first. The credit for each correct guess is divided by the number of guesses. The *oot* track allows systems to make up to 10 guesses, without penalizing, and without being of any benefit if less than 10 substitutes are provided. The ordering of guesses in the *oot* metric is unimportant.

For both tracks, the evaluation is carried out using precision and recall, calculated based on the number of matching responses between the system and the human annotators, respectively. A "mode" evaluation is also conducted, which measures the ability of the systems to capture the most frequent response (the "mode") from the gold standard annotations. For details, please refer to the official task description document (McCarthy and Navigli, 2007).

Tables 2 and 3 show the results obtained by SUBFINDER in the *best* and *oot* tracks respectively. The tables also show a breakdown of the results based on: only target words that were not identified as multiwords (NMWT); only substitutes that were not identified as multiwords (NMWS); only items with sentences randomly selected from the Internet corpus (RAND); only items with sentences manually selected from the Internet corpus (MAN).

	WSD	LSA	IR	LB	MCS	MTA	MTG	LM
best	34	2	64	63	56	69	38	97
oot	6	82	7	28	46	14	32	68

Table 1: Weights of the individual ranking methods

	P	R	Mode P	Mode R
OVERALL	12.77	12.77	20.73	20.73
Further Analysis				
NMWT	13.46	13.46	21.63	21.63
NMWS	13.79	13.79	21.59	21.59
RAND	12.85	12.85	20.18	20.18
MAN	12.69	12.69	21.35	21.35
Baselines				
WORDNET	9.95	9.95	15.28	15.28
LIN	8.84	8.53	14.69	14.23

Table 2: BEST results

	P	R	Mode P	Mode R
OVERALL	49.19	49.19	66.26	66.26
Further Analysis				
NMWT	51.13	51.13	68.03	68.03
NMWS	54.01	54.01	70.15	70.15
RAND	51.71	51.71	68.04	68.04
MAN	46.26	46.26	64.24	64.24
Baselines				
WORDNET	29.70	29.35	40.57	40.57
LIN	27.70	26.72	40.47	39.19

Table 3: OOT results

Compared to other systems participating in this task, our system consistently ranks on the first or second place. SUBFINDER clearly outperforms all the other systems for the "mode" evaluation, showing the ability of the system to find the substitute most often preferred by the human annotators. In addition, the system exceeds by a large margin all the baselines calculated for the task, which select substitutes based on existing lexical resources (e.g., WordNet or Lin distributional similarity).

Separate from the "official" submission, we ran a second experiment where we optimized the combination weights targeting high precision and recall (rather than high *mode*). An evaluation of the system using this new set of weights yields a precision and recall of 13.34 with a *mode* of 21.71 for the *best* task, surpassing the best system according to the anonymous results report. For the *oot* task, the precision and recall increased to 50.30, still maintaining second place.

6 Conclusions

The lexical substitution task goes beyond simple word sense disambiguation. To approach such a task, we first need a good comprehensive and precise lexical resource for candidate extraction. Secondly, we need to semantically filter the highly diverse and ambiguous set of candidates, while taking into account their fitness in the context in order to form a proper linguistic expression. To accomplish this, we built a system that incorporates lexical, semantic, and probabilistic methods to capture both the semantic similarity with the target word and the semantic fit in the context. Compared to other systems participating in this task, our system consistently ranks on the first or second place. SUBFINDER clearly outperforms all the other systems for the "mode" evaluation, proving its ability to find the substitute most often preferred by the human annotators.

Acknowledgments

This work was supported in part by the Texas Advanced Research Program under Grant #003594. The authors are grateful to the Language and Information Technologies research group at the University of North Texas for many useful discussions and feedback on this work.

References

T. Brants and A. Franz. 2006. Web 1t 5-gram version 1. Linguistic Data Consortium.

I. Dagan, O. Glickman, A. Gliozzo, E. Marmorshtein, and C. Strapparava. 2006. Direct word sense matching for lexical substitution. In *Proceedings of the International Conference on Computational Linguistics ACL/COLING 2006*.

C. Fellbaum. 1998. *WordNet, An Electronic Lexical Database*. The MIT Press.

T. K. Landauer, P. Foltz, and D. Laham. 1998. Introduction to latent semantic analysis. *Discourse Processes*, 25.

D. McCarthy and R. Navigli. 2007. The semeval English lexical substitution task. In *Proceedings of the ACL Semeval workshop*.

D. McCarthy. 2002. Lexical substitution as a task for wsd evaluation. In *Proceedings of the ACL Workshop on Word Sense Disambiguation: Recent Successes and Future Directions*, Philadelphia.

R. Mihalcea and A. Csomai. 2005. Senselearner: Word sense disambiguation for all words in unrestricted text. In *Proceedings of the 43nd Annual Meeting of the Association for Computational Linguistics*, Ann Arbor, MI.

UOY: A Hypergraph Model For Word Sense Induction & Disambiguation

Ioannis P. Klapaftis
University of York
Department of Computer Science
giannis@cs.york.ac.uk

Suresh Manandhar
University of York
Department of Computer Science
suresh@cs.york.ac.uk

Abstract

This paper is an outcome of ongoing research and presents an unsupervised method for automatic word sense induction (WSI) and disambiguation (WSD). The induction algorithm is based on modeling the co-occurrences of two or more words using hypergraphs. WSI takes place by detecting high-density components in the co-occurrence hypergraphs. WSD assigns to each induced cluster a score equal to the sum of weights of its hyperedges found in the local context of the target word. Our system participates in SemEval-2007 word sense induction and discrimination task.

1 Introduction

The majority of both supervised and unsupervised approaches to WSD is based on the "fixed-list" of senses paradigm where the senses of a target word is a closed list of definitions coming from a standard dictionary (Agirre et al., 2006). Lexicographers have long warned about the problems of such an approach, since dictionaries are not suited to this task; they often contain general definitions, they suffer from the lack of explicit semantic and topical relations or interconnections, and they often do not reflect the exact content of the context, in which the target word appears (Veronis, 2004).

To overcome this limitation, unsupervised WSD has moved towards inducing the senses of a target word directly from a corpus, and then disambiguating each instance of it. Most of the work in WSI is based on the vector space model, where the context of each instance of a target word is represented as a vector of features (e.g second-order word co-occurrences) (Schutze, 1998; Purandare and Pedersen, 2004). These vectors are clustered and the resulting clusters represent the induced senses. However, as shown experimentally in (Veronis, 2004), vector-based techniques are unable to detect low-frequency senses of a target word.

Recently, graph-based methods were employed in WSI to isolate highly infrequent senses of a target word. HyperLex (Veronis, 2004) and the adaptation of PageRank (Brin and Page, 1998) in (Agirre et al., 2006) have been shown to outperform the most frequent sense (MFS) baseline in terms of supervised recall, but they still fall short of supervised WSD systems.

Graph-based approaches operate on a 2-dimensional space, assuming a one-to-one relationship between co-occurring words. However, this assumption is insufficient, taking into account the fact that two or more words are usually combined to form a relationship of concepts in the context. Additionally, graph-based approaches fail to model and exploit the existence of collocations or terms consisting of more than two words.

This paper proposes a method for WSI, which is based on a hypergraph model operating on a n-dimensional space. In such a model, co-occurrences of two or more words are represented using weighted hyperedges. A hyperedge is a more expressive representation than a simple edge, because it is able to capture the information shared by two or more words. Our system participates in

Proceedings of the 4th International Workshop on Semantic Evaluations (SemEval-2007), pages 414–417,
Prague, June 2007.

SemEval-2007 word sense induction and discrimination task (SWSID) (Agirre and Soroa, 2007).

2 Sense Induction & Disambiguation

This section presents the induction and disambiguation algorithms.

2.1 Sense Induction

2.1.1 The Hypergraph Model

A hypergraph $H = (V, F)$ is a generalization of a graph, which consists of a set of vertices V and a set of hyperedges F; each hyperedge is a subset of vertices. While an edge relates 2 vertices, a hyperedge relates n vertices (where $n \geq 1$). In our problem, we represent each word by a vertex and any set of co-occurring related words by a hyperedge. In our approach, we restrict hyperedges to 2, 3 or 4 words. Figure 1 shows an example of an abstract hypergraph model [1].

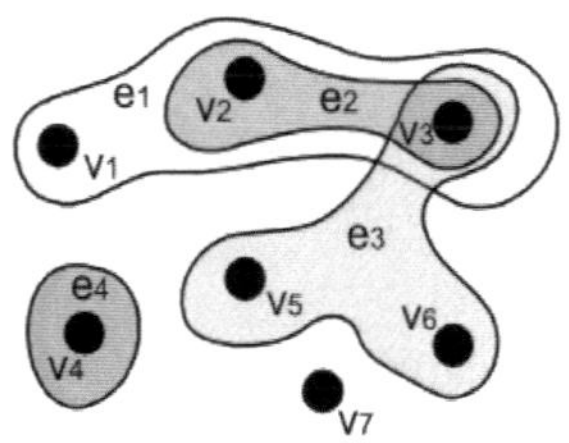

Figure 1: An example of a Hypergraph

The *degree* of a vertex is the number of hyperedges it belongs to, and the degree of a hyperedge is the number of vertices it contains. A path in the hypergraph model is a sequence of vertices and hyperedges such as $v_1, f_1, ..., v_{i-1}, f_{i-1}, v_i$, where v_k are vertices, f_k are hyperedges, each hyperedge f_k contains vertices to its left and right in the path and no hyperedge or vertex is repeated. The length of a path is the number of hyperedges it contains, the distance between two vertices is the shortest path between them and the distance between two hyperedges is the minimum distance of all the pairs of their vertices.

2.1.2 Building The Hypergraph

Let bp be the base corpus from which we induce the senses of a target word tw. Our bp consists of BNC and all the SWSID paragraphs containing the target word. The total size of bp is 2000 paragraphs. Note that if SWSID paragraphs of tw are more than 2000, BNC is not used.

In order to build the hypergraph, tw is removed from bp and each paragraph p_i is POS-tagged. Following the example in (Agirre et al., 2006), only nouns are kept and lemmatised. We apply two filtering heuristics. The first one is the minimum frequency of nouns (parameter p_1), and the second one is the minimum size of a paragraph (parameter p_2).

A key problem at this stage is the determination of related vertices (nouns), which can be grouped into hyperedges and the weighting of each such hyperedge. We deal with this problem by using association rules (Agrawal and Srikant, 1994). Frequent hyperedges are detected by calculating *support*, which should exceed a user-defined threshold (parameter p_3).

Let f be a candidate hyperedge and a, b, c its vertices. Then $freq(a, b, c)$ is the number of paragraphs in bp, which contain all the vertices of f, and n is the total size of bp. *Support* of f is shown in Equation 1.

$$support(f) = \frac{freq(a, b, c)}{n} \quad (1)$$

The weight assigned to each collected hyperedge, f, is the average of m calculated *confidences*, where m is the size of f. Let f be a hyperedge containing the vertices a, b, c. The *confidence* for the rule $r_0 = \{a, b\} => \{c\}$ is defined in Equation 2.

$$confidence(r_0) = \frac{freq(a, b, c)}{freq(a, b)} \quad (2)$$

Since there is a three-way relationship among a, b and c, we have two more rules $r_1 = \{a, c\} => \{b\}$ and $r_2 = \{b, c\} => \{a\}$. Hence, the weighting of f is the average of the 3 calculated *confidences*. We apply a filtering heuristic (parameter p_4) to remove hyperedges with low weights from the hypergraph. At the end of this stage, the constructed hypergraph is reduced, so that our hypergraph model agrees with the one described in subsection 2.1.1.

2.1.3 Extracting Senses

Preliminary experiments on 10 nouns of SensEval-3 English lexical-sample task (Mihalcea et al., 2004) (S3LS), suggested that our hypergraphs

[1] Image was taken from Wikipedia (Rocchini, 2006)

are small-world networks, since they exhibited a high clustering coefficient and a small average path length. Furthermore, the frequency of vertices with a given degree plotted against the degree showed that our hypergraphs satisfy a power-law distribution $P(d) = c * d^{-\alpha}$, where d is the vertex degree, $P(d)$ is the frequency of vertices with degree d. Figure 2 shows the log-log plot for the noun *difference* of S3LS.

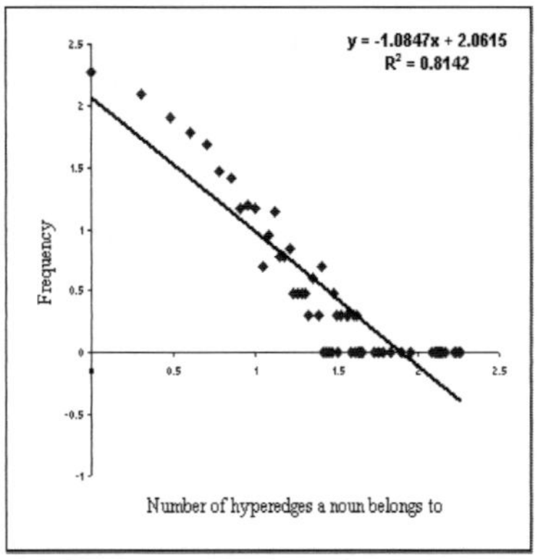

Figure 2: Log-log plot for the noun *difference*.

In order to extract the senses of the target word, we modify the HyperLex algorithm (Veronis, 2004) for selecting the root hubs of the hypergraph as follows. At each step, the algorithm finds the vertex v_i with the highest degree, which is selected as a root hub, according to two criteria.

The first one is the minimum number of hyperedges it belongs to (parameter p_5), and the second is the average weight of the first p_5 hyperedges (parameter p_6) [2]. If these criteria are satisfied, then hyperedges containing v_i are grouped to a single cluster c_j (new sense) with a 0 distance from v_i, and removed from the hypergraph. The process stops, when there is no vertex eligible to be a root hub.

Each remaining hyperedge, f_k, is assigned to the cluster, c_j, closest to it, by calculating the minimum distance between f_k and each hyperedge of c_j as defined in subsection 2.1.1. The weight assigned to f_k is inversely proportional to its distance from c_j.

2.2 Word Sense Disambiguation

Given an instance of the target word, tw, paragraph p_i containing tw is POS-tagged, nouns are kept and lemmatised. Next, each induced cluster c_j is assigned a score equal to the sum of weights of its hyperedges found in p_i.

3 Evaluation

3.1 Preliminary Experiments

This method is an outcome of ongoing research. Due to time restrictions we were able to test and tune (Table 1), but not optimize, our system only on a very small set of nouns of S3LS targeting at a high supervised recall. Our supervised recall on the 10 first nouns of S3LS was 66.8%, 9.8% points above the MFS baseline.

Parameter	Value
p_1:Minimum frequency of a noun	8
p_2:Minimum size of a paragraph	4
p_3:Support threshold	0.002
p_4:Average confidence threshold	0.2
p_5:Minimum number of hyperedges	6
p_6:Minimum average weight of hyperedges	0.25

Table 1: Chosen parameters for our system

3.2 SemEval-2007 Results

Tables 2 and 3 show the average supervised recall, FScore, entropy and purity of our system on nouns and verbs of the test data respectively. The submitted answer consisted only of the winning cluster per instance of a target word, in effect assigning it with weight 1 (default).

Entropy measures how well the various gold standard senses are distributed within each cluster, while purity measures how pure a cluster is, containing objects from primarily one class. In general, the lower the entropy and the larger the purity values, the better the clustering algorithm performs.

Measure	Proposed methodology	MFS
Entropy	**25.5**	46.3
Purity	**89.8**	82.4
FScore	65.8	**80.7**
Sup. Recall	**81.6**	80.9

Table 2: System performance for nouns.

For nouns our system achieves a low entropy and a high purity outperforming the MFS baseline, but a lower FScore. This can be explained by the fact that the average number of clusters we produce for nouns is 11, while the gold standard average of senses is around 2.8. For verbs the performance of our system

[2]Hyperedges are sorted in decreasing order of weight

is worse than for nouns, although entropy and purity still outperform the MFS baseline. FScore is very low, despite that the average number of clusters we produce for verbs (around 8) is less than the number of clusters we produce for nouns. This means that for verbs the senses of gold standard are much more spread among induced clusters than for nouns, causing a low unsupervised recall. Overall, FScore results are in accordance with the idea of microsenses mentioned in (Agirre et al., 2006). FScore is biased towards clusters similar to the gold standard senses and cannot capture that theory.

Measure	Proposed methodology	MFS
Entropy	**28.9**	44.4
Purity	**82.0**	77
F-score	45.1	**76.8**
Sup. Recall	73.3	**76.2**

Table 3: System performance for verbs.

Our supervised recall for verbs is 73.3%, and below the MFS baseline (76.2%), which no system managed to outperform. For nouns our supervised recall is 81.6%, which is around 0.7% above the MFS baseline. In order to fully examine the performance of our system we applied a second evaluation of our methodology using the SWSID official software.

The solution per target word instance included the entire set of clusters with their associated weights (Table 4). Results show that the submitted answer (*instance - winning_cluster*), was degrading seriously our performance both for verbs and nouns due to the loss of information in the mapping step.

POS	Proposed Methodology	MFS
Nouns	**84.3**	80.9
Verbs	75.6	**76.2**
Total	**80.2**	78.7

Table 4: Supervised recall in second evaluation.

Our supervised recall for nouns has outperformed the MFS baseline by 3.4% with the best system achieving 86.8%. Performance for verbs is 75.6%, 0.6% below the best system and MFS.

4 Conclusion

We have presented a hypergraph model for word sense induction and disambiguation. Preliminary experiments suggested that our reduced hypergraphs are small-world networks. WSI identifies the highly connected components (hubs) in the hypergraph, while WSD assigns to each cluster a score equal to the sum of weights of its hyperedges found in the local context of a target word.

Results show that our system achieves high entropy and purity performance outperforming the MFS baseline. Our methodology achieves a low FScore producing clusters that are dissimilar to the gold standard senses. Our supervised recall for nouns is 3.4% above the MFS baseline. For verbs, our supervised recall is below the MFS baseline, which no system managed to outperform.

References

Eneko Agirre and Aitor Soroa. 2007. Semeval-2007 task 2: Evaluating word sense induction and discrimination systems. In *Proceedings of SemEval-2007*. ACL.

Eneko Agirre, David Martínez, Oier López de Lacalle, and Aitor Soroa. 2006. Two graph-based algorithms for state-of-the-art wsd. In *Proceedings of the EMNLP Conference*, pages 585–593. ACL.

Rakesh Agrawal and Ramakrishnan Srikant. 1994. Fast algorithms for mining association rules in large databases. In *VLDB '94: Proceedings of the 20th International Conference on Very Large DataBases*, pages 487–499, USA. Morgan Kaufmann Publishers Inc.

Sergey Brin and Lawrence Page. 1998. The anatomy of a large-scale hypertextual Web search engine. *Computer Networks and ISDN Systems*, 30(1–7):107–117.

Rada Mihalcea, Timothy Chklovski, and Adam Kilgarriff. 2004. The senseval-3 english lexical sample task. In *R. Mihaleca and P. Edmonds, editors, SensEval-3 Proceedings*, pages 25–28, Spain, July. ACL.

Amruta Purandare and Ted Pedersen. 2004. Word sense discrimination by clustering contexts in vector and similarity spaces. In *Proceedings of CoNLL-2004*, pages 41–48. ACL.

Claudio Rocchini. 2006. Hypergraph sample image. *Wikipedia*.

Hinrich Schutze. 1998. Automatic word sense discrimination. *Computational Linguistics*, 24(1):97–123.

Jean Veronis. 2004. Hyperlex:lexical cartography for information retrieval. *Computer Speech & Language*, 18(3).

UP13: Knowledge-poor Methods (Sometimes) Perform Poorly

Thierry Poibeau
Laboratoire d'Informatique de Paris-Nord
CNRS UMR 7030 et université Paris 13
99, avenue J.-B. Clément F-93430 Villetaneuse
thierry.poibeau@lipn.univ-paris13.fr

Abstract

This short paper presents a system developed at the Université Paris 13 for the Semeval 2007 Metonymy Resolution Task (task #08, location name track; see Markert and Nissim, 2007). The system makes use of plain word forms only. In this paper, we evaluate the accuracy of this minimalist approach, compare it to a more complex one which uses both syntactic and semantic features, and discuss its usefulness for metonymy resolution in general.

1 Introduction

This short paper presents the system developed at the Université Paris 13 for the Metonymy resolution task, during Semeval 2007 (Markert and Nissim, 2007). Two sub-tasks were proposed, concerning 1) country names and 2) company names. We only participated in the first task (country names). We developed a simple approach which we present and thoroughly evaluate in this paper. We discuss the relevance of this approach and compare it to more complex ones.

2 Motivation

We participated in the metonymy task with a very basic system. The idea was to investigate the efficiency of a minimalist (though, not Chomskian) system. This system tags entities on the basis of discriminative (plain) word forms occurring in a given window only. Our aim was to find out which word forms are discriminative enough to be considered as parameters.

In the past, we developed a system for metonymy resolution for French, evaluated in the framework of the ESTER evaluation (Gravier, 2004). This system, described in Poibeau (2006), uses various kinds of information, among others: plain word forms, part-of-speech tags, and syntactic and semantic tags (conceptual word classes).

The usefulness of complex linguistic features (especially syntactic and semantic tags) is questionable: they may be hard to compute, error-prone and their contribution is not clear. We therefore developed a new version of the system mainly based on 1) a distributional analysis (on surface word forms) along with 2) a filtering process. The latter restricted metonymic readings to country and capital names (as opposed to other location names), since they include a vast majority of the metonymic readings (this proved to be efficient but is of course a harsh pragmatic over-simplification without real linguistic basis). We nevertheless obtained a highly versatile system, performing reasonably well, compared to our previous, much more complex implementation (F-score was .58 instead of .63; we computed F-score with β=1).

In the framework of the Semeval evaluation, the filtering process is irrelevant since only country names are considered as entities. However, we thought that it would be interesting to develop a very basic system, to evaluate the performance one can obtain using plain word forms only.

3 A (too) Lazy Approach

We chose not to use any part-of-speech tagger or syntactic or semantic analyzer; we did not use any external knowledge or any other annotated corpus than the one provided for the training phase. Since no NLP tool was used, we had to duplicate most of the words in order to get the singular and the plural form. Our system is thus very simple compared to

Proceedings of the 4th International Workshop on Semantic Evaluations (SemEval-2007), pages 418–421,
Prague, June 2007.

the state-of-art in this domain (e.g. Nissim and Markert, 2003).

We used discriminative plain words only. These are gathered as follows: all the words in a given window (here we use a 7 word window, before and after the target entity since it gave the best results on the training data) are extracted and associated with two classes (literal *vs.* non literal). We thus consider the most discriminative words, *i.e.* words that appear frequently in some contexts but not in others (literal *vs.* non-literal readings). Discriminative words are elements that are abnormally frequent or rare in one corpus compared to another one.

Characteristic features are selected based on their probabilities. Probability levels measure the significance of the differences between the relative frequency of an expression or a feature within a group (or a category) with its global relative frequency calculated over the entire corpus (Lafon, 1980). They are calculated under the hypothesis of a random distribution of the forms. The smaller the probability levels, the more characteristic the corresponding forms (Lebart and Salem, 1997).

We thus obtained 4 lists of discriminative words (literal *vs.* non-literal × before *vs.* after the target entity). As the result, some semantic families emerged, especially for words appearing before literal readings: lists of prepositions (*in*, *at*, *within…*) and geographical items (*east*, *west*, *western…*). Some lists were manually completed, when a "natural" series appeared to be incomplete (for example, if we got *east*, *west*, *north*, we completed the word series with *south*).

3.1 Reducing the Size of the Search Space

The approach described so far may seems a bit simplistic (and, indeed, it is!), but nevertheless it yielded highly discriminative features. For example, if we only tag country names immediately preceded by the preposition *in* as 'literal', we obtain the results presented in table 1 (in the following tables, precision is the most relevant issue; coverage gives an idea of the percentage of tagged entities by the considered feature, compared to the total number of entities to be tagged). Figure 1 shows that detecting the preposition *in* in front of a location name discriminates almost perfectly 23% of the literal readings.

	Training	Test
Precision	1	.98
Coverage	.23	.23

Table 1. Results for the pattern `in + LOC` (result tag = literal)

A simple discriminative analysis of the training corpus produces the following list of prepositions and geographical discriminative features: `"at"`, `"within"`, `"in"`, `"into"`, `"from"`, `"coast"`, `"land"`, `"area"`, `"southern"`, `"south"`, `"east"`, `"north"`, `"west"`, `"western"`, `"eastern"`, etc[1]. Table 2 presents the results obtained from this list of words (occurring in a 7 word window, on the left of the target word):

	Training	Test
Precision	.91	.88
Coverage	.60	.55

Table 2. Results for the pattern `<at+within+…> + LOC` (note that table 1 is contained in table 2)

Another typical feature was the use of the entity in a genitive construction (e.g. in *Iran's official commitment*, *Iran* is considered as a literal reading). The presence of *'s* on the right side of the target entity is highly discriminative (table 3):

	Training	Test
Precision	.87	.89
Coverage	.15	.17

Table 3. Results for the pattern `LOC's` (result tag = literal)

This strategy may seem strange, since the task is to find metonymic readings rather than literal ones (the baseline is to tag all the target entities as literal). However, it is useful in reducing the size of the search space by approximately 50%. This means that more than 70% of the entities with a literal meaning can be tagged with a confidence around 90% using this technique, thus reducing the number of problematic cases. The resulting file is relatively balanced: it contains about 50-60% of literal meaning and 40-50% of metaphorical meaning (instead of a classical ratio 80% *vs.* 20%).

[1] The list also contains nouns and verbs like: `"enter"`, `"entered"`, `"fly"`, `"flown"`, `"went"`, `"go"`, `"come"`, `"land"`, `"country"`, `"mountain"`…

3.2 Looking for Metonymy, Desperately …

We used the same strategy for metonymic readings. We have observed in the past that word forms are much more efficient for literal readings than for metonymic readings. However, the fact that the location name is followed by a verb like `"has"`, `"should"`, `"was"`, `"would"`, `"will"` seemed to be discriminative on the training corpus. Unfortunately, this feature did not work well on the test corpus (table 4).

	Training	Test
Precision	.6	.3
Coverage	.1	.04

Table 4. Results for the pattern `LOC + <was, should…>` (result tag = metonymic)

This simply means that a syntactic analysis would be useful to discriminate between the sentences where the target entity is the subject of the following verb (in this context, the entity is most of the time used with a metaphoric reading; to go further, one needs to filter the verb according to semantic classes).

Another point that was clear from the task guidelines was that sport's teams correspond to metonymic readings. The list of characteristic words for this class, obtained from the training corpus was the following: `"player"`, `"team"`, `"defender"`, `"plays"`, `"role"`, `"score"`, `"scores"`, `"scored"`, `"win"`, `"won"`, `"cup"`, `"v"`[2], `"against"`, `"penalty"`, `"goal"`, `"goals"`, `"champion"`, `"champions"`, *etc.* But, bad luck! This list did not work well on the test corpus either:

	Training	Test
Precision	.64	.32
Coverage	.13	.05

Table 5. Results for the pattern `LOC + <player, team…>` (result tag = metonymic)

Table 5 shows that coverage as well as precision are very low.

Yet another category included words related to the political role of countries, which entails a metonymic reading: `"role"`, `"institution"`, `"preoccupation"`, `"attitude"`, `"ally"`, `"allies"`, `"institutions"`, `"initiative"`, `"according"`, `"authority"`… All these categories had low coverage on the test corpus. This is not so surprising and is related to our knowledge-poor strategy: the training corpus is relatively small and it was foreseeable that we would miss most of the relevant contexts. However, we wanted to maintain precision above .5 (*i.e.* relevant contexts should remain relevant), but failed in this, as one can see from the overall results.

4 Overall Evaluation

We mainly discuss here the results of the *coarse* evaluation, where only `literal` *vs* `non-literal` meanings were targeted. We did not develop any specific strategy for the other tracks (*medium* and *fine*) since there were too few examples in the training data. We just transferred non-literal readings to the most probable class according to the training corpus (`metonymic` for *medium*, `place-for-people` for *fine*). However, the performance of our system (*i.e.* accuracy) is relatively stable between these three tracks, since the distribution of examples between the different classes is very unequally distributed.

Before giving the results, recall that our purpose was to investigate a knowledge-poor strategy, in order to establish how far one can get using only surface indicators. Thus, unsurprisingly, our results for the training corpus were already lower than those obtained using a more sophisticated system (Nissim and Markert, 2003). They are however a good indicator of performance when one uses only surface features.

The accuracy on the training corpus was .815. Precision and recall are presented in the table 6.

	Literal	Non-lit.
Precision	.88	.54
Recall	.88	.57
P&R	.88	.55

Table 6. Overall results on the training corpus

Accuracy on the test corpus is .754 only. Table 7 shows the results obtained for the different kinds of location names. The result is obvious: there is a significant drop in both recall and precision, compared to the results on the training corpus.

[2] *v* for *versus*, especially in sports: *Arsenal-MU 3 v 2*.

	Literal	Non lit.
Precision	.83	.38
Recall	.86	.31
P&R	.84	.34

Table 7. Overall results on the test corpus

5 Discussion

Metonymy is a complex linguistic phenomenon and it is thus no surprise that such a basic system performed badly, even if the drop in precision between training and test set was disappointing. The main conclusion of this approach is that surface forms can be used to reduce the size of the search space with a relatively good accuracy. A large part of the literal readings can be tagged using surface forms only. For the remaining cases, the use of more sophisticated linguistic information (both syntactic and semantic) is necessary.

During this work, we discovered some problematic target entities whose annotation is challenging. For instance, we tagged the following example as metonymic (because of the keywords "role" and "above"), whereas it is tagged as literal in the gold standard:

```
This two-track approach was seen (…) as
reflecting continued manoeuvring over
the role of the <annot> <location
reading="literal"> United States
</location> </annot> in the alliance, …
```

See also the following example (tagged by our system as metonymic because of the keyword "relations", but assumed to be literal in the gold standard):

```
Relations with China and <annot>
<location reading="literal"> Singapore
</location></annot> …
```

On the other hand, the following example was tagged as literal by our system (due to the preposition *in*) instead of metonymic.

```
After their European Championship
victory (…), Holland will be expected
to do well in <annot> <location
reading="metonymic" metotype="place-
for-event"> Italy </location></annot>.
```

If *Italy* is assumed to refer to the World Cup occurring in Italy, we think that the literal reading is not completely irrelevant (a paraphrase could be: *"…to do well during their stay in Italy"* which is clearly literal).

Metonymy is a form of figurative speech "in which one expression is used to refer to the referent of a related one" (Markert and Nissim, 2007). The phenomenon corresponds to a semantic shift in interpretation ("a profile shift") that appears to be a function of salience (Cruse and Croft, 2004). We assume that this semantic shift does not completely erase the original referent: it rather puts the focus on a specific feature of the content ("the profile") of the standard referent. If we adopt this theory, we can explain why it may be difficult to tag some examples, since both readings may co-exist.

6 Conclusion

In this paper, we presented a (minimalist) system for metonymy resolution and evaluated its usefulness for the task. The system worked well for reducing the size of the search space but performed badly for the recognition of metonymic readings themselves. It should be used in combination with more complex features, especially syntactic and semantic information.

References

A. Cruse and W. Croft. 2004. *Meaning in language, an introduction to semantics and pragmatics*. Oxford University Press, Oxford.

G. Gravier, J.-F. Bonastre, E. Geoffrois, S. Galliano, K. Mc Tait and K. Choukri. 2004. The ESTER evaluation campaign for the rich transcription of French broadcast news". *Proceedings of LREC'04*. Lisbon, Portugal. pp. 885–888.

P. Lafon. 1980. Sur la variabilité de la fréquence des formes dans un corpus. *Mots*. 1. pp. 127–165.

L. Lebart and A. Salem. 1997. *Exploring Textual Data*. Springer. Berlin.

K. Markert and M. Nissim. 2007. Task08: Metonymy Resolution at Semeval 2007. *Proceedings of Semeval 2007*. Prague, Czech Rep.

M. Nissim and K. Markert. 2003. Syntactic Features and Word Similarity for supervised Metonymy Resolution. *Proceedings of ACL'03*. Sapporo, Japan. pp. 56–63.

T. Poibeau. 2006. Dealing with Metonymic Readings of Named Entities. *Proceedings of COGSCI'06*. Vancouver, Canada. pp. 1962–1968.

UPAR7: A knowledge-based system for headline sentiment tagging

François-Régis Chaumartin
Lattice/Talana – Université Paris 7
30, rue du château des rentiers - 75013 Paris - France
fchaumartin@linguist.jussieu.fr / frc@proxem.com

Abstract

For the Affective Text task at SemEval-2007, University Paris 7's system first evaluates emotion and valence on all words of a news headline (using enriched versions of SentiWordNet and a subset of WordNet-Affect). We use a parser to find the head word, considering that it has a major importance. We also detect contrasts (between positive and negative words) that shift valence. Our knowledge-based system achieves high accuracy on emotion and valence annotation. These results show that working with linguistic techniques and a broad-coverage lexicon is a viable approach to sentiment analysis of headlines.

1 Introduction

1.1 Objectives

The detection of emotional connotations in texts is a recent task in computational linguistics. Its economic stakes are promising; for example, a company could detect, by analyzing the blogosphere, people's opinion on its products.

The goal of the SemEval task is to annotate news headlines for emotions (using a predefined list: anger, disgust, fear, joy, sadness & surprise), and for valence (positive or negative). A specific difficulty here is related to the small number of words available for the analysis.

1.2 Overall architecture

Our system is mainly rule-based and uses a linguistic approach. From a macroscopic point of view, we follow the hypothesis that, in a news title, all the words potentially carry emotions. If linguistic resources make it possible to detect these emotions individually, how can we deal with headlines where bad and good emotions appear at once?

Our objective is to identify the expression which carries the main topic of the title. One can consider that this expression has a primary importance.

We also seek to lay down rules for detecting specific emotions. For instance, surprise sometimes comes from the contrast between good and bad news. And sometimes, simple lexical elements are characteristic of an emotion; a negation or a modal auxiliary in a title may be a relevant indicator of surprise.

We describe here the techniques we implemented to address all these points.

2 Components & resources used

The system we employed for the Affective Text evaluation consists of the following components[1]:

- The SS-Tagger (a Part-of-Speech tagger)[2],
- The Stanford Parser.

We also used several lexical resources:

- WordNet version 2.1,
- A subset of WordNet-Affect,
- SentiWordNet.

As the SS-Tagger is straightforward, we will not say more about it here. We will, however, discuss the remaining components and resources below.

[1] We used them through the Antelope NLP framework (www.proxem.com), which makes them easy to use.

[2] This fast PoS tagger uses an extension of Maximum Entropy Markov Models. See (Tsuruoka, Tsujii, 2005).

Proceedings of the 4th International Workshop on Semantic Evaluations (SemEval-2007), pages 422–425,
Prague, June 2007.

2.1 Choice of the Stanford Parser

We wished to use a syntactic parser for this task. We hesitated between two parsers producing a dependency graph, the *Link Grammar Parser* (Sleator, Temperley, 1991) and the *Stanford Parser* (Manning, Klein, 2002).

As a news title is sometimes reduced to a nominal group, without a verb, our experiments showed that we should modify the title to make it "grammatically correct". Such a step is essential to obtain accurate results with a rule-based analyzer such as the Link Grammar Parser. On the other hand, a statistical analyzer like the Stanford Parser is more tolerant with constructions which are not grammatically correct. That is why we chose it.

2.2 WordNet

We used WordNet (Miller, 1995) as a semantic lexicon. This well-known project, started in 1985 at Princeton, offers a broad-coverage semantic network of the English language, and is probably one of the most popular NLP resources.

In WordNet, words are grouped into sets of synonyms. Various semantic relations exist between these synsets (for example, hypernymy and hyponymy, antonymy, derivation…).

2.3 WordNet-Affect

WordNet-Affect (Strapparava, Valitutti, 2004) is a hierarchy of "affective domain labels", with which the synsets representing affective concepts are further annotated. We used the subset of WordNet-Affect provided as emotions lists by the SemEval organizers. To improve it, we manually added to the emotion lists new words that we found important on the task trial data.

	Nouns	Verbs	Adjectives	Adverbs
Anger	37	26	16	0
Disgust	35	19	9	0
Fear	71	26	20	4
Joy	50	22	14	1
Sadness	88	37	29	4
Surprise	16	29	13	2

Table 1: Counting of new words for each emotion.

Nouns	Verbs	Adjectives	Adverbs
cancer danger poverty	demolish injure kidnap	comatose nuclear violent	bloody dead worse

Table 2: Some words added for "fear" emotion.

The synsets of emotions lists were considered as seeds; our system recursively propagated their emotions to their neighbor synsets[3].

SentiWordNet

SentiWordNet (Esuli, Sebastiani, 2006) describes itself as a lexical resource for opinion mining. SentiWordNet assigns to each synset of WordNet three sentiment scores[4]: positivity, negativity, objectivity, the sum of which always equals 1.0.

This resource has been created with a mix of linguistics and statistics (using classifiers). The advantage of this approach is to allow the automatic generation of emotion values for all the synsets of WordNet. The disadvantage is that, as all the results are not manually validated, some resulting classifications can appear incorrect[5].

We recursively propagate the positivity and negativity values throughout neighbor synsets[6].

3 UPAR7 Affective Text system

3.1 "De-capitalization" of common words

A preliminary problem that we had to solve was related to the Anglo-Saxon habit of putting initial capital letters in all the words of a title.

The first pass of our system thus detected news titles that were "improperly" capitalized, and "de-capitalizes" their common words.

For that, we used the SS-Tagger on the title; according to the part of speech of each word, information found in WordNet, and some hand-crafted rules[7], the system chooses or not to keep the initial.

The impact of this processing step is far from negligible, from the point of view of the Stanford Parser. Indeed, let us have a look at the difference between the parsing of the title, before (figure 1) and after (figure 2) this processing.

[3] Following relations such as Hyponym, Derivation, Adjective Similar, Adjective Participle, Derivation and Pertainym.

[4] For instance, the synset ESTIMABLE#1 (*deserving of respect or high regard*) has: Positivity = 0.75, Negativity = 0.00, Objectivity = 0.25.

[5] For example, RAPE#3 (*the crime of forcing a woman to submit to sexual intercourse against her will*) is classified with Positivity=0.25 and Negativity=0.0 despite the presence of the word "crime" in its gloss.

[6] Using WordNet's relations such as Hyponym (for noun and verb), Antonym and Derivation. For antonyms, positivity and negativity values are exchanged.

[7] For instance, a word that cannot be any form of a WordNet lemma is probably a proper noun, and then we keep its initial.

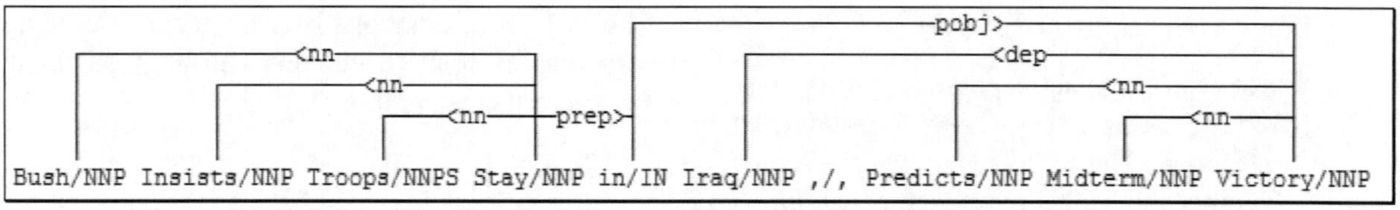

Figure 1 : Output of the Stanford Parser with a title that is **"improperly"** capitalized.

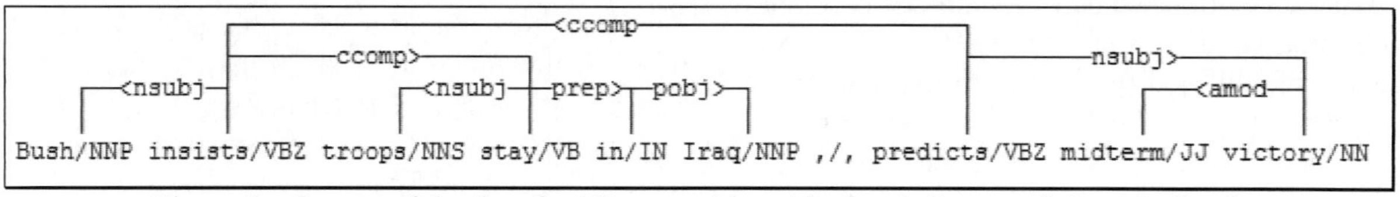

Figure 2 : Output of the Stanford Parser with a title that is "**properly**" capitalized.
(Words are tagged with the right part-of-speech, and dependencies are now correct.)

3.2 Individual words rating

For the moment, we consider the output of the Stanford Parser as an array of PoS-tagged words. We use WordNet's morphology functions to find the possible base form of each word.

At this stage, an important question arose: was lexical disambiguation possible? We thought not, because with short sentences, few relevant heuristics apply. We chose another solution, by considering that the emotion and valence values of a word were the linear combination of that of all its possible meanings, balanced by the frequency of each lemma.

We detected emotion and valence values for each word, by using our enriched version of WordNet-Affect and SentiWordNet.

In fact, we also detected some extra information:

- An additional 7th emotion, that looks like "compassion for people needing protection". Our assumption is that certain words express a subjacent need for protection. For example, there is "student" behind "school", and "child" behind "adoption". So, we built a list of words designating something that needs protection; we also include in this list words such as "troops", "shoppers"…
- We tried to detect acronyms relating to technology; for this, we defined a list of high-tech companies and a very basic regular expression rule saying that a word (not in WordNet) containing numbers, or capitals not in first position, should be something high-tech. (This very basic rule seems to work nicely on PS3, iPod, NASA…). We use these high-tech indications to increase the "joy" emotion.
- We counted lexical elements that we think are good indicators of surprise: negations, modal auxiliaries, question marks.

At this stage, we begin some post-processing on individual words. Which factors cause anger rather that sadness? We believe that human intention (to harm) causes the former emotion, while natural factors such as disease or climatic catastrophes cause the latter. So, we used a few rules related to the WordNet noun hierarchy, based on the fact that when a noun is a hyponym of a given synset, we boost some emotions:

Does noun inherit from?	Emotions to boost
UNHEALTHINESS	Fear, sadness
ATMOSPHERIC PHENOMENON	Fear, sadness
AGGRESSION, HOSTILITY, WRONGFUL CONDUCT	Anger, fear, sadness, disgust
WEAPONRY, WEAPON SYSTEM	Anger, fear, sadness
UNFORTUNATE PERSON	Sadness, "compassion"
HUMAN WILL	Anger

Table 3: Hypernyms triggering an emotion boost.

Then, the emotions found serve to update the valence, by increasing positivity or negativity:

Emotion	Positivity	Negativity
Joy	++	--
Anger, disgust, sadness, fear, "compassion"	--	++

Table 4: Emotions that change valence.

3.3 Global sentence rating

At this stage, our system tries to find the main subject of the news title. Again, we use the output of the Stanford Parser, but this time, we make use of the dependency graph. We consider that the main word is the root of the dependency graph, i.e. the word that is never a dependant word. (For instance, in figure 2, the main word is "predicts".)

We think that the contribution of this main word is much more important than that of the other words of the title[8]. So, we multiply its individual valence and emotion by 6.

The last important part of linguistic processing is the detection of contrasts and accentuations between "good" or "bad" things. We search patterns like [noun→subject→verb] or [verb→direct object→noun] in the dependency graph, with verbs that increase or decrease a quantity[9]. Using the valence of the given noun, this gives our system the ability to detect very good news ("boosts (brain) power") or good news where something bad gets less important ("reduces risk", "slows decline", "hurricane weakens"...).

4 Results

	Fine-grained	Coase-grained		
	Pearson	Accuracy	Precision	Recall
Anger	32.33	93.60	16.67	1.66
Disgust	12.85	95.30	0.00	0.00
Fear	44.92	87.90	33.33	2.54
Joy	22.49	82.20	54.54	6.66
Sadness	40.98	89.00	48.97	22.02
Surprise	16.71	88.60	12.12	1.25

Table 5: Results of the emotion annotation.

Our rule-based system detects the six emotions in news headlines with an average accuracy reaching 89.43% (coarse-grained evaluation). However, recall is low.

	Fine-grained	Coase-grained		
	Pearson	Accuracy	Precision	Recall
Valence	36.96	55.00	57.54	8.78

Table 6: Results of the valence annotation.

The valence detection accuracy (55% in coarse-grained evaluation) is lower than in emotion annotation. We attribute this difference to the fact that it is easier to detect emotions (that are given by individual words) rather than valence, which needs a global understanding of the sentence.

5 Conclusion

Emotion and valence tagging is a complex and interesting task. For our first attempt, we designed and developed a linguistic rule-based system, using WordNet, SentiWordNet and WordNet-Affect lexical resources, that delivers high accuracy results. In our future work, we will explore the potential of simultaneously using a statistical approach, in order to improve recall of sentiment annotation.

References

Andrea Esuli, Fabrizio Sebastiani. 2006. *SentiWordNet: A Publicly Available Lexical Resource for Opinion Mining.* Proceedings of LREC 2006, fifth international conference on Language Resources and Evaluation, pp. 417-422.

Christopher Manning, Dan Klein. 2002. *Fast Exact Inference with a Factored Model for Natural Language Parsing.* Advances in Neural Information Processing Systems 15 (NIPS 2002).

George Miller. 1995. *WordNet: A lexical database.* Acts of ACM 38, 39-41.

Livia Polanyi, Annie Zaenen. 2006. Contextual Valence Shifters. In J. G. Shanahan, Y. Qu, and J. Wiebe, editors, *Computing Attitude and Affect in Text: Theory and Application.* Springer Verlag.

Daniel Sleator, Davy Temperley. 1991. *Parsing English with a Link Grammar.* Acts of Third International Workshop on Parsing Technologies.

Carlo Strapparava, Alessandro Valitutti. 2004. *WordNet-Affect: an affective extension of WordNet.* Proceedings of the 4th International Conference on Language Resources and Evaluation (LREC 2004), pp. 1083-1086.

Yoshimasa Tsuruoka, Jun'ichi Tsujii. 2005. *Bidirectional Inference with the Easiest-First Strategy for Tagging Sequence Data.* Proceedings of HLT/EMNLP 2005, pp. 467-474.

[8] In sentences like "study says...", "scientists say...", "police affirm...", the main head word is the verb of the relative.

[9] We "rediscovered" valence shifters (words that modify the sentiment expressed by a sentiment-bearing word, see (Polanyi and Zaenen, 2006)).

UPC: Experiments with Joint Learning within SemEval Task 9

Lluís Màrquez, Lluís Padró, Mihai Surdeanu, Luis Villarejo
Technical University of Catalonia
{lluism,padro,surdeanu,luisv}@lsi.upc.edu

1 Introduction

This paper describes UPC's participation in the SemEval-2007 task 9 (Màrquez et al., 2007).[1] We addressed all four subtasks using supervised learning. The paper introduces several novel issues: (a) for the SRL task, we propose a novel re-ranking algorithm based on the re-ranking Perceptron of Collins and Duffy (2002); and (b) for the same task we introduce a new set of global features that extract information not only at proposition level but also from the complete set of frame candidates. We show that in the SemEval setting, i.e., small training corpora, this approach outperforms previous work. Additionally, we added NSD and NER information in the global SRL model but this experiment was unsuccessful.

2 Named Entity Recognition

For the NER subtask we recognize first strong NEs, followed by weak NE identification. Any single token with the `np0000`, `W`, or `Z` PoS tag is considered a strong entity and is classified using the (Atserias et al., 2006) implementation of a multi-label AdaBoost.MH algorithm, with a configuration similar to the NE classification module of Carreras et al. (2003). The classifier yields predictions for four classes (person, location, organization, misc). Entities with NUM and DAT are detected separately solely based on POS tags.

The features used by the strong NE classifier model a [-3,+3] context around the focus word, and include bag-of-words, positional lexical features, PoS tags, orthographic features, as well as features indicating whether the focus word, some of its components, or some word in the context are included in external gazetteers or *trigger words* files.

The second step starts by selecting all noun phrases (`np`) that cover a span of more than one token and include a strong NE as weak entity candidates. This strategy covers more than 95% of the weak NEs. A second AdaBoost.MH classifier is then applied to decide the right class for the noun phrase among the possible six (person, location, organization, misc, number, date) plus a *NONE* class indicating that the noun phrase is not a weak NE.

The features used for weak NE classification are: (1) *simple features* – length in tokens, head word, lemma, and POS of the `np`, syntactic function of the `np` (if any), minimum and maximum number of `np` nodes in the path from the candidate noun phrase to any of the strong NEs included in it, and number and type of the strong NEs predicted by the first–level classifier that fall inside the candidate; (2) *bag of content words* inside the candidate; and (3) *pattern-based features*, consisting in codifying the sequence of lexical tokens spanned by the candidate according to some generalizations. When matching, tokens are generalized to: the POS tag (in case of `np0000`, `W`, `Z`, and punctuation marks), *trigger-word* of class X, *word-in-gazetteer* of class X, and *strong-NE* of type X, predicted by the first level classifier. The rest of words are abstracted to a common form ("w" standing for a single word and "w+" standing for a sequence of $n > 1$ words). Beginning and end of the span are also codified explicitly in the pattern–based features. Finally, to avoid sparsity, only paths of up

[1]Two of the authors of this paper, Lluís Màrquez and Luis Villarejo, are organizers of the SemEval-2007 task 9.

Proceedings of the 4th International Workshop on Semantic Evaluations (SemEval-2007), pages 426–429,
Prague, June 2007.

to length 6 are codified as features. Also, for each path, n–grams of length 2, 3 and 4 are considered. We filter out features that occur less than 10 times.

3 Noun Sense Disambiguation

We have approached the NSD subtask using supervised learning. In particular, we used SVM^{light} (Joachims, 1999), which is a freely available implementation of Support Vector Machines (SVM).

We trained binary SVM classifiers for every sense of words with more than 15 examples in the training set and a probability distribution over its senses in which no sense is above 90%. The words not covered by the SVM classifiers are disambiguated using the most frequent sense (MFS) heuristic. The MFS was calculated from the relative frequencies in the training corpus. To the words that do not appear in the training corpus we assigned the first WordNet sense.

We used a fairly regular set of features from the WSD literature. We included: (1) a bag of content words appearing in a ±10-word window; (2) a bag of content words appearing in the clause of the target word; (3) $\{1,\ldots,n\}$–grams of POS tags and lemmas in a $\pm n$-word window (n is 3 for POS and 2 for lemmas); (4) unigrams and bigrams of (POS-tag,lemma) pairs in a ±2-word window; and (5) syntactic features, i.e., label of the syntactic constituent from which the target noun is the head, syntactic function of that constituent (if any), and the verb.

Regarding the empirical setting, we filtered out features occurring less than 3 times, we used linear SVMs with a 0.5 value for the C regularization parameter (trade-off between training error and margin), and we applied one-vs-all binarization.

4 Semantic Role Labeling

The SRL approach deployed here implements a re-ranking strategy that selects the best argument frame for each predicate from the top N frames generated by a base model. We describe the two models next.

4.1 The Local Model

The local (i.e., base) model is an adaption of Model 3 of Màrquez et al. (2005). This SRL approach maps each frame argument to one syntactic constituent and trains one-vs-all AdaBoost (Schapire and Singer, 1999) classifiers to jointly identify and classify constituents in the full syntactic tree of the sentence as arguments. The model was adapted to the languages and corpora used in the SemEval evaluations by removing the features that were specific either to English or PropBank (governing category, content word, and temporal cue words) and adding several new features: (a) *syntactic function* features – the syntactic functions available in the data often point to specific argument labels (e.g., `SUJ` usually indicates an `Arg0`); and (b) *back-off* features for syntactic labels and POS tags – for the features that include POS tags or syntactic labels we add a back-off version of the feature where the POS tags and syntactic labels are reduced to a small set.

In addition to feature changes we modified the candidate filtering heuristic: we select as candidates only syntactic constituents that are immediate descendents of `S` phrases that include the corresponding predicate (for both languages, over 99.6% of the candidates match this constraint).

4.2 The Global Model

We base our re-ranking approach on a variant of the re-ranking Perceptron of Collins and Duffy (2002). We modify the original algorithm in two ways to make it more robust to the small training set available: (a) instead of comparing the score of the correct frame only with that of the best candidate for each frame, we sequentially compare it with the score of *each* candidate in order to acquire more information, and (b) we learn not only when the prediction is incorrect but also when the prediction is not confident enough.

The algorithm is listed in Algorithm 1: $\mathbf{w}$ is the vector of model parameters, $\mathbf{h}$ generates the feature vector for one example, and $\mathbf{x_{ij}}$ denotes the jth candidate for the ith frame in the training data. $\mathbf{x_{i1}}$, which denotes the "correct" candidate for frame i, is selected to maximize the F_1 score for each frame. The algorithm sequentially inspects all candidates for each frame and learns when the difference between the scores of the correct and the current candidate is less than a threshold τ. During testing we use the average of all acquired model vectors, weighted by the number of iterations they survived in training. We tuned all system parameters through cross-validation on the training data. For both languages we set $\tau = 10$ (we do not normalize feature vectors)

Algorithm 1: Re-ranking Perceptron

$\mathbf{w} = \vec{0}$
for $i = 1$ **to** n **do**
  for $j = 2$ **to** n_i **do**
    if $\mathbf{w} \cdot \mathbf{h}(\mathbf{x_{ij}}) > \mathbf{w} \cdot \mathbf{h}(\mathbf{x_{i1}}) - \tau$ **then**
      $\mathbf{w} \leftarrow \mathbf{w} + \mathbf{h}(\mathbf{x_{i1}}) - \mathbf{h}(\mathbf{x_{ij}})$

and the number of training epochs to 2.

With respect to the features used, we focus only on global features that can be extracted independently of the local models. We show in Section 6 that this approach performs better on the small SemEval corpora than approaches that include features from the local models. We group the features into two sets: (a) features that extract information from the whole candidate set, and (b) features that model the structure of each candidate frame:

Features from the whole candidate set:
(1) Position of the current candidate in the whole set. Frame candidates are generated using the dynamic programming algorithm of Toutanova et al. (2005), and then sorted in descending order of the log probability of the whole frame (i.e., the sum of all argument log probabilities as reported by the local model). Hence, smaller positions indicate candidates that the local model considers better.
(2) For each argument in the current frame, we store its number of repetitions in the whole candidate set. The intuition is that an argument that appears in many candidate frames is most likely correct.

Features from each candidate frame:
(3) The complete sequence of argument labels, extended with the predicate lemma and voice, similar to Toutanova et al. (2005).
(4) Maximal overlap with a frame from the verb lexicon. Both the Spanish and Catalan TreeBanks contain a static lexicon that lists the accepted sequences of arguments for the most common verbs. For each candidate frame, we measure the maximal overlap with the lexicon frames for the given verb and use the precision, recall, and F_1 scores as features.
(5) Average probability (from the local model) of all arguments in the current frame.
(6) For each argument label that repeats in the current frame, we add combinations of the predicate lemma, voice, argument label, and the number of label repetitions as features. The intuition is that argument repetitions typically indicate an error (even if allowed by the domain constraints).

5 Semantic Class Detection

The semantic class detection subtask has been performed using a naive cascade of heuristics: (1) the predicted frame for each verb is compared with the frames present in the provided verbal lexicon, and the class of the lexicon frame with the largest number of matching arguments is chosen; (2) if there is more than one verb with the maximum score, the first one in the lexicon (i.e., the most frequent) is used; (3) if the focus verb is not found in the lexicon, its most frequent class in the training corpus is used; (4) if the verb does not appear in the training data, the most frequent class overall (D2) is assigned. The results obtained on the training corpus are 81.1% F_1 for Spanish and 86.6% for Catalan. As a baseline, assigning the most frequent class for each verb (or D2 if not seen in training), yields F_1 values of 48.1% for Spanish and 64.0% for Catalan.

6 Results and Discussion

Table 1 lists the results of our system on the SemEval test data. Our results are encouraging considering the size of the training corpus (e.g., the English PropBank is 10 times larger than the corpus used here) and the complexity of the problem (e.g., the NER task includes both weak and strong entities; the SRL task contains 33 core arguments for Spanish vs. 6 for English). We analyze the behavior of our system next.

The first issue that deserves further analysis is the contribution of our global SRL model. We list the results of this analysis in Table 2 as improvements over the local SRL model. We report results for 6 corpora: the 4 test corpora and the 2 training corpora, where the results are generated through 5-fold cross validation. The first block in the table shows the contribution of our best re-ranking model. The second block shows the results of a re-ranking model using our best feature set but the original re-ranking Perceptron of Collins and Duffy (2002). The third block shows the performance of our re-ranking algorithm configured with the features proposed by Toutanova et al. (2005). We draw several conclusions from this experiment: (a) our re-ranking model

	NER			NSD			SRL			SC
	P	R	F_1	P	R	F_1	P	R	F_1	F_1
ca.CESS-ECE	79.92%	76.63%	78.24	87.47%	87.47%	87.47	82.16%	70.05%	75.62	85.71
es.CESS-ECE	72.53%	68.48%	70.45	83.30%	83.30%	83.30	86.24%	75.58%	80.56	87.74
ca.3LB	82.04%	79.42%	80.71	85.69%	85.53%	85.61	86.36%	85.30%	85.83	87.35
es.3LB	62.03%	53.85%	57.65	88.14%	88.14%	88.14	82.23%	80.78%	81.50	76.01

Table 1: Official results on the test data. Due to space constraints, we show only the F_1 score for SC.

	Re-ranking			Collins			Toutanova		
	P	R	F_1	P	R	F_1	P	R	F_1
ca.train	**+1.87**	**+1.79**	**+1.83**	+1.56	+1.48	+1.52	-6.81	-6.67	-6.73
es.train	**+3.16**	**+3.12**	**+3.14**	+2.96	+2.93	+2.95	-6.51	-6.96	-6.75
ca.CESS-ECE	+0.77	+0.66	+0.71	**+0.99**	**+0.84**	**+0.91**	-8.11	-6.29	-7.10
es.CESS-ECE	**+1.85**	**+1.94**	**+1.91**	+1.45	+1.85	+1.68	-10.84	-8.46	-9.54
ca.3LB	**+1.58**	**+1.47**	**+1.53**	+1.48	+1.39	+1.44	-7.71	-7.57	-7.64
es.3LB	+2.57	+2.83	+2.71	**+2.71**	**+2.91**	**+2.82**	-10.53	-11.95	-11.26

Table 2: Analysis of the re-ranking model for SRL.

using only global information always outperforms the local model, with F_1 score improvements ranging from 0.71 to 3.14 points; (b) the re-ranking Perceptron proposed here performs better than the original algorithm, but the improvement is minimal; and (c) the feature set proposed here achieve significant better performance on the SemEval corpora than the set proposed by Toutanova et al., which never improves over the local model. The model configured with the Toutanova et al. feature set performs modestly because the features are too sparse for the small SemEval corpora (e.g., all features from the local model are included, concatenated with the label of the corresponding argument). On the other hand, we replicate the behavior of the local model just with feature (1), and furthermore, all the other 5 global features proposed have a positive contribution.

In a second experiment we investigated simple strategies for model combination. We incorporated NER and NSD information in the re-ranking model for SRL as follows: for each frame argument, we add features that concatenate the predicate lemma, the argument label, and the NER or NSD labels for the argument head word (we add features both with and without the predicate lemma). We used only the best NER/NSD labels from the local models. To reduce sparsity, we converted word senses to coarser classes based on the corresponding WordNet semantic files. This new model boosts the F_1 score of our best re-ranking SRL model with an average of 0.13 points on two corpora (es.3LB and ca.CESS-ECE), but it reduces the F_1 of our best SRL model with an average of 0.17 points on the other 4 corpora. We can conclude that, in the current setting, NSD and NER do not bring useful information to the SRL problem. However, it is soon to state that problem combination is not useful. To have a conclusive answer one will have to investigate true joint learning of the three subtasks.

References

J. Atserias, B. Casas, E. Comelles, M. Gonzàlez, L. Padró, and M. Padró. 2006. Freeling 1.3: Syntactic and semantic services in an open-source NLP library. In *Proc. of LREC*.

X. Carreras, L. Màrquez, and L. Padró. 2003. A simple named entity extractor using AdaBoost. In *CoNLL 2003 Shared Task Contribution*.

M. Collins and N. Duffy. 2002. New ranking algorithms for parsing and tagging: Kernels over discrete structures, and the voted perceptron. In *Proc. of ACL*.

T. Joachims. 1999. *Making large-scale SVM learning practical, Advances in Kernel Methods - Support Vector Learning*. MIT Press, Cambridge, MA.

L. Màrquez, M. Surdeanu, P. Comas, and J. Turmo. 2005. A robust combination strategy for semantic role labeling. In *Proc. of EMNLP*.

L. Màrquez, M.A. Martí, M. Taulé, and L. Villarejo. 2007. SemEval-2007 task 09: Multilevel semantic annotation of Catalan and Spanish. In *Proc. of SemEval-2007, the 4th Workshop on Semantic Evaluations. Association for Computational Linguistics*.

R.E. Schapire and Y. Singer. 1999. Improved boosting algorithms using confidence-rated predictions. *Machine Learning*, 37(3).

K. Toutanova, A. Haghighi, and C. Manning. 2005. Joint learning improves semantic role labeling. In *Proc. of ACL*.

UPV-SI: Word Sense Induction using Self Term Expansion*

David Pinto[(1,2)] and **Paolo Rosso**[1]
[1]Polytechnic University of Valencia
DSIC, Valencia, Spain, 46022
[2]B. Autonomous University of Puebla
FCC, Puebla, Mexico, 72570
{dpinto, prosso}@dsic.upv.es

Héctor Jiménez-Salazar
Autonomous Metropolitan University
Department of Information Technologies
Cuajimalpa, DF, Mexico, 11850
hgimenezs@gmail.com

Abstract

In this paper we are reporting the results obtained participating in the "Evaluating Word Sense Induction and Discrimination Systems" task of Semeval 2007. Our totally unsupervised system performed an automatic self-term expansion process by mean of co-ocurrence terms and, thereafter, it executed the unsupervised KStar clustering method. Two ranking tables with different evaluation measures were calculated by the task organizers, every table with two baselines and six runs submitted by different teams. We were ranked third place in both ranking tables obtaining a better performance than three different baselines, and outperforming the average score.

1 Introduction

Word Sense Disambiguation (WSD) is a particular problem of computational linguistics which consists in determining the correct sense for a given ambiguous word. It is well-known that supervised algorithms have obtained the best results in public evaluations, but their accuracy is close related with the amount of hand-tagged data available. The construction of that kind of training data is difficult for real applications. The unsupervised WSD overcomes this drawback by using clustering algorithms which do not need training data in order to determine the possible sense for a given ambiguous word.

This paper describes a simple technique for unsupervised sense induction for ambiguous words. The approach is based on a self term expansion technique which constructs a set of co-ocurrence terms and, thereafter, it uses this set to expand the target dataset. The implemented system was performed in the task "SemEval-2007 Task 2: Evaluating Word Sense Induction and Discrimination Systems"(Agirre and A., 2007). The aim of the task was to permit a comparison across sense-induction and discrimination systems. Moreover, the comparison with other supervised and knowledge-based systems may be also done, since the test corpus was borrowed from the well known "English lexical-sample" task in SemEval-2007, with the usual training + test split.

The self term expansion method consists in replacing terms of a document by a set of co-related terms. The goal is to improve natural language processing tasks such as clustering narrow-domain short texts. This process may be done by mean of different ways, often just by using a knowledge database. In information retrieval, for instance, the expansion of query terms is a very investigated topic which has shown to improve results with respect to when query expansion is not employed (Qiu and Frei, 1993; Ruge, 1992; R.Baeza-Yates and Ribeiro-Neto, 1999; Grefenstette, 1994; Rijsbergen, 1979).

The availability of Machine Readable Resources (MRR) like "Dictionaries", "Thesauri" and "Lexicons" has allowed to apply term ex-

*This work has been partially supported by the MCyT TIN2006-15265-C06-04 project, as well as by the BUAP-701 PROMEP/103.5/05/1536 grant

Proceedings of the 4th International Workshop on Semantic Evaluations (SemEval-2007), pages 430–433,
Prague, June 2007.

pansion to other fields of natural language processing like WSD. In (Banerjee and Pedersen, 2002) we may see the typical example of using a external knowledge database for determining the correct sense of a word given in some context. In this approach, every word close to the one we would like to determine its correct sense is expanded with its different senses by using the WordNet lexicon (Fellbaum, 1998). Then, an overlapping factor is calculated in order to determine the correct sense of the ambiguous word. Different other approaches have made use of a similar procedure. By using dictionaries, the proposals presented in (Lesk, 1986; Wilks et al., 1990; Nancy and Véronis, 1990) are the most sucessful in WSD. Yarowsky (Yarowsky, 1992) used instead thesauri for their experiments. Finally, in (Sussna, 1993; Resnik, 1995; Banerjee and Pedersen, 2002) the use of lexicons in WSD has been investigated. Although in some cases the knowledge resource seems not to be used strictly for term expansion, the aplication of co-occurrence terms is included in their algorithms. Like in information retrieval, the application of term expansion in WSD by using co-related terms has shown to improve the baseline results if we carefully select the external resource to use, with a priori knowledge of the domain and the broadness of the corpus (wide or narrow domain). Evenmore, we have to be sure that the Lexical Data Base (LDB) has been suitable constructed. Due to the last facts, we consider that the use of a self automatically constructed LDB (using the same test corpora), may be of high benefit. This assumption is based on the intrinsic properties extracted from the corpus itself. Our proposal is related somehow with the investigations presented in (Schütze, 1998) and (Purandare and Pedersen, 2004), where words are also expanded with co-ocurrence terms for word sense discrimination. The main difference consists in the use of the same corpora for constructing the co-ocurrence list.

Following we describe the self term expansion method used and, thereafter, the results obtained in the task #2 of Semeval 2007 competition.

2 The Self Term Expansion Method

In literature, co-ocurrence terms is the most common technique used for automatic construction of LDBs (Grefenstette, 1994; Frakes and Baeza-Yates, 1992). A simple approach may use n-grams, which allows to predict a word from previous words in a sample of text. The frequency of each n-gram is calculated and then filtered according to some threshold. The resulting n-grams constitutes a LDB which may be used as an "expansion dictionary" for each term.

On the other hand, an information theory-based co-ocurrence measure is discussed in (Manning and Schütze, 2003). This measure is named pointwise Mutual Information (MI), and its applications for finding collocations are analysed by determining the co-ocurrence degree among two terms. This may be done by calculating the ratio between the number of times that both terms appear together (in the same context and not necessarily in the same order) and the product of the number of times that each term ocurrs alone. Given two terms X_1 and X_2, the pointwise mutual information between X_1 and X_2 can be calculated as follows:

$$MI(X_1, X_2) = \log_2 \frac{P(X_1X_2)}{P(X_1) \times P(X_2)}$$

The numerator could be modified in order to take into account only bigrams, as presented in (Pinto et al., 2006), where an improvement of clustering short texts in narrow domains has been obtained.

We have used the pointwise MI for obtaining a co-ocurrence list from the same target dataset. This list is then used to expand every term of the original data. Since the co-ocurrence formula captures relations between related terms, it is possible to see that the self term expansion magnifies less the noisy than the meaninful information. Therefore, the execution of the clustering algorithm in the expanded corpus should outperform the one executed over the non-expanded data.

In order to fully appreciate the self term expansion method, in Table 1 we show the co-ocurrence list for some words related with the verb "kill" of the test corpus. Since the MI is calculated after preprocessing the corpus, we present the stemmed version of the terms.

Word	Co-ocurrence terms
soldier	kill
rape	women think shoot peopl old man kill death beat
grenad	todai live guerrilla fight explod
death	shoot run rape person peopl outsid murder life lebanon kill convict...
temblor	tuesdai peopl least kill earthquak

Table 1: An example of co-ocurrence terms

For the task #2 of Semeval 2007, a set of 100 ambiguous words (35 nouns and 65 verbs) were provided. We preprocessed this original dataset by eliminating stopwords and then applying the Porter stemmer (Porter, 1980). Thereafter, when we used the pointwise MI, we determined that the single ocurrence of each term should be at least three (see (Manning and Schütze, 2003)), whereas the maximum separation among the two terms was five. Finally, we selected the unsupervised KStar clustering method (Shin and Han, 2003) for our experiments, defining the average of similarities among all the sentences for a given ambiguous word as the stop criterion for this clustering method. The input similarity matrix for the clustering method was calculated by using the Jaccard coefficient.

3 Evaluation

The task organizers decided to use two different measures for evaluating the runs submitted to the task. The first measure is called unsupervised one, and it is based on the Fscore measure. Whereas the second measure is called supervised recall. For further information on how these measures are calculated refer to (Agirre et al., 2006a; Agirre et al., 2006b). Since these measures give conflicting information, two different evaluation results are reported in this paper.

In Table 2 we may see our ranking and the Fscore measure obtained (UPV-SI). We also show the best and worst team Fscores; as well as the total average and two baselines proposed by the task organizers. The first baseline (Baseline1) assumes that each ambiguous word has only one sense, whereas the second baseline (Baseline2) is a random assignation of senses. We are ranked as third place and our results are better scored than the other teams except for the best team score. However, given the similar values with the "Baseline1", we may assume that that team presented one cluster per ambiguous word as its result as the Baseline1 did; whereas we obtained 9.03 senses per ambiguous word in average.

Name	Rank	All	Nouns	Verbs
Baseline1	1	78.9	80.7	76.8
Best Team	2	78.7	80.8	76.3
UPV-SI	3	66.3	69.9	62.2
Average	-	63.6	66.5	60.3
Worst Team	7	56.1	65.8	45.1
Baseline2	8	37.8	38.0	37.6

Table 2: Unsupervised evaluation (Fscore performance).

In Table 3 we show our ranking and the supervised recall obtained (UPV-SI). We again show the best and worst team recalls. The total average and one baseline is also presented (the other baseline obtained the same Fscore). In this case, the baseline tags each test instance with the most frequent sense obtained in a train split. We are ranked again in third place and our score is slightly above the baseline.

Name	Rank	All	Nouns	Verbs
Best Team	1	81.6	86.8	76.2
UPV-SI	3	79.1	82.5	75.3
Average	-	79.1	82.8	75.0
Baseline	4	78.7	80.9	76.2
Worst Team	6a	78.5	81.8	74.9
Worst Team	6b	78.5	81.4	75.2

Table 3: Supervised evaluation (Recall).

The results show that the technique employed have learned, since our simple approach obtained a better performance than the baselines, especially the one that have chosen the most frequent sense as baseline.

4 Conclusions

We have reported the performance of a single approach based on self term expansion. The technique uses the pointwise mutual information for calculating a set of co-ocurrence terms which then are used to expand the original dataset. Once the expansion has been done, the unsupervised KStar clustering method was used to induce the sense for the different ocurrences of each ambiguous word. We obtained the third place in the two measures proposed in the task. We will further investigate whether an improvement may be obtained by applying term selection methods to the expanded corpus.

References

E. Agirre and Soroa A. 2007. SemEval-2007 Task 2: Evaluating Word Sense Induction and Discrimination Systems. In *SemEval-2007*. Association for Computational Linguistics.

E. Agirre, O. Lopez de Lacalle Lekuona, D. Martinez, and A. Soroa. 2006a. Evaluating and optimizing the parameters of an unsupervised graph-based WSD algorithm. In *Textgraphs 2006 workshop, NAACL06*, pages 89–96.

E. Agirre, O. Lopez de Lacalle Lekuona, D. Martinez, and A. Soroa. 2006b. Two graph-based algorithms for state-of-the-art WSD. In *EMNLP*, pages 585–593. ACL.

S. Banerjee and T. Pedersen. 2002. An Adapted Lesk Algorithm for Word Sense Disambiguation Using WordNet. In *CICLing 2002 Conference*, volume 3878 of *LNCS*, pages 136–145. Springer-Verlang.

C. Fellbaum. 1998. *WordNet: An Electronic Lexical Database*. MIT Press.

W. B. Frakes and R. A. Baeza-Yates. 1992. *Information Retrieval: Data Structures & Algorithms*. Prentice-Hall.

G. Grefenstette. 1994. *Explorations in Automatic Thesaurus Discovery*. Kluwer Academic.

M. Lesk. 1986. Automatic sense disambiguation: How to tell a pine cone from an ice cream cone. In *ACM SIGDOC Conference*, pages 24–26. ACM Press.

D. C. Manning and H. Schütze. 2003. *Foundations of Statistical Natural Language Processing*. MIT Press. Revised version May 1999.

I. Nancy and J. Véronis. 1990. Mapping dictionaries: A spreading activation approach. In *6th Annual Conference of the Centre for the New Oxford English Dictionary*, pages 52–64.

D. Pinto, H. Jiménez-Salazar, and P. Rosso. 2006. Clustering abstracts of scientific texts using the transition point technique. In *CICLing*, volume 3878 of *LNCS*, pages 536–546. Springer-Verlang.

M. F. Porter. 1980. An algorithm for suffix stripping. *Program*, 14(3).

A. Purandare and T. Pedersen. 2004. Word sense discrimination by clustering contexts in vector and similarity spaces. In *Proceedings of the Conference on Computational Natural Language Learning*, pages 41–48, Boston, MA.

Y. Qiu and H. P. Frei. 1993. Concept based Query Expansion. In *ACM SIGIR on R&D in information retrieval*, pages 160–169. ACM Press.

R.Baeza-Yates and B. Ribeiro-Neto. 1999. *Modern information retrieval*. New York: ACM Press; Addison-Wesley.

P. Resnik. 1995. Disambiguating Noun Groupings with Respect to WordNet Senses. In *3rd Workshop on Very Large Corpora*, pages 54–68. ACL.

C. J. Van Rijsbergen. 1979. *Information Retrieval, 2nd edition*. Dept. of Computer Science, University of Glasgow.

G. Ruge. 1992. Experiments on linguistically-based term associations. *Information Processing & Management*, 28(3):317–332.

H. Schütze. 1998. Automatic word sense discrimination. *Computational Linguistics*, 24(1):97–123.

K. Shin and S. Y. Han. 2003. Fast clustering algorithm for information organization. In *CICLing*, volume 2588 of *LNCS*, pages 619–622. Springer-Verlang.

M. Sussna. 1993. Word sense disambiguation for free-test indexing using a massive semantic network. In *2nd International Conference on Information and Knowledge Management*, pages 67–74.

Y. Wilks, D. Fass, C. Guo, J. McDonald, T. Plate, and B. Slator. 1990. Providing machine tractable dictionary tools. *Machine Translation*, 5(2):99–154.

D. Yarowsky. 1992. Word-sense disambiguation using statistical models of Rogets categories trained on large corpora. In *14th Conference on Computational Linguistics*, pages 454–460. ACL.

UPV-WSD : Combining different WSD Methods by means of Fuzzy Borda Voting

Davide Buscaldi and **Paolo Rosso**
DSIC, Dpto. Sistemas Informáticos y Computación
Universidad Politécnica de Valencia
Valencia, Spain
{dbuscaldi,prosso}@dsic.upv.es

Abstract

This paper describes the WSD system developed for our participation to the SemEval-1. It combines various methods by means of a fuzzy Borda voting. The fuzzy Borda vote-counting scheme is one of the best known methods in the field of collective decision making. In our system the different disambiguation methods are considered as experts that give a preference ranking for the senses a word can be assigned. Then the preferences are evaluated using the fuzzy Borda scheme in order to select the best sense. The methods we considered are the sense frequency probability calculated over SemCor, the Conceptual Density calculated over both hyperonyms and meronyms hyerarchies in WordNet, the extended Lesk by Banerjee and Pedersen, and finally a method based on WordNet domains.

1 Introduction

One of the lessons learned from our previous experience at Senseval-3[1] (Buscaldi et al., 2004; Vazquez et al., 2004) is that the integration of different systems usually works better than a standalone system. In our opinion this reflects the reality where humans do not apply always the same rule in order to disambiguate the same ambigue word; for instance, if we consider the sentences "*He hit a home run*" and "*The thermometer hit 100 degrees*", in the first case the sport domain helps in determining the right sense for *hit*, whereas in the latter the disambiguation is carried out mostly depending on the fact that the subject of the sentence is an object.

The combination of distinct methods represents itself a major problem. If the methods return different answers, how can we select the best one? In this sense the available choices are the following:

- *Rule-based* selection: a set of rules that can be both hand-made or automatically learned from examples;
- *Probability-based*: the output of the methods is normalized in the range $[0, 1]$ and is considered as a probability. Then the values are multiplied in order to obtain the sense with a maximum probability.
- *Vote-based*: the output of the methods is considered as a weighted vote. Then a voting scheme is used in order to obtain the most voted sense.

In our previous participation with the R2D2 project (Vazquez et al., 2004) the selection was rule-based, with hand-made rules that attempted to take into account the reliability of the various method. We subsequently attempted to learn automatically the rules, but the results of these experiments did not allow to determine clearly which method was to be used in each context.

Working with probabilities can be problematic due to the null probabilities that make necessary the adoption of smoothing techniques. Therefore, we opted for a voting scheme, in this case the fuzzy Borda (Nurmi, 2001; García Lapresta and Martínez

[1] http://www.senseval.org

Proceedings of the 4th International Workshop on Semantic Evaluations (SemEval-2007), pages 434–437,
Prague, June 2007.

Panero, 2002), one of the best known methods in the field of collective decision making. With this scheme the disambiguation methods are considered as experts providing a preference ranking over the sense of the word.

The methods we choose as experts are the sense probability calculated over SemCor, the Conceptual Density algorithm by (Rosso et al., 2003), the extended Lesk by (Banerjee and Pedersen, 2002), and an algorithm that takes into account the domains of the word to be disambiguated and the context words. In the following sections we describe in detail the fuzzy Borda scheme and each WSD expert.

2 The Fuzzy Borda voting scheme

The original Borda vote-counting scheme was introduced in 1770 by Jean Charles de Borda, and adopted by the French Academy of Sciences with the purpose of selecting its members. In the classical Borda count each expert gives a mark to each alternative, according to the number of alternatives worse than it. The fuzzy variant (Nurmi, 2001; García Lapresta and Martínez Panero, 2002) is a natural extension that allows the experts to show numerically how much some alternatives are preferred to the others, evaluating their preference intensities from 0 to 1.

Let $R^1, R^2, \ldots, R^m$ be the fuzzy preference relations of m experts over n alternatives $x_1, x_2, \ldots, x_n$. For each expert k we obtain a matrix of preference intensities:

$$\begin{pmatrix} r^k_{11} & r^k_{12} & \ldots & r^k_{1n} \\ r^k_{21} & r^k_{22} & \ldots & r^k_{2n} \\ \ldots & \ldots & \ldots & \ldots \\ r^k_{n1} & r^k_{n2} & \ldots & r^k_{nn} \end{pmatrix}$$

where each $r^k_{ij} = \mu_{R^k}(x_i, x_j)$, with $\mu_{R^k} : X \times X \rightarrow [0, 1]$ being the membership function of R^k. The number $r^k_{ij} \in [0, 1]$ is considered as the degree of confidence with which the expert k prefers x_i to x_j. The final value assigned by the expert k to each alternative x_i is:

$$r_k(x_i) = \sum_{j=1, r^k_{ij}>0.5}^{n} r^k_{ij} \tag{1}$$

which coincides with the sum of the entries greater than 0.5 in the i-th row in the preference matrix. The threshold 0.5 ensure the relation $R^k$to be an ordinary preference relation (García Lapresta and Martínez Panero, 2002).

Therefore, the definitive fuzzy Borda count for an alternative x_i is obtained as the sum of the values assigned by each expert:

$$\mathbf{r}(x_i) = \sum_{k=1}^{m} r_k(x_i) \tag{2}$$

In order to fill the preference matrix with the correct confidence values, the output weights $w_1, w_2, \ldots, w_n$ of each expert k are transformed to fuzzy confidence values by means of the following transformation:

$$r^k_{ij} = \frac{w_i}{w_i + w_j} \tag{3}$$

An example of how fuzzy Borda is used to combine the votes in order to obtain the right sense of the target word is shown in Section 4.

3 WSD Experts

We considered five experts in order to carry out the disambiguation process. Sense probability and the extended lesk were available for every word, while the Conceptual Density was calculated only for nouns. Therefore, all the experts were available only for the nouns. For each expert different contexts were taken into account, depending on the specific characteristics of each expert.

3.1 Sense Probability

This expert is the simplest one: its votes are calculated using only the frequency count in SemCor of the WordNet senses of the word. The transformation of the frequency counts to the preference ranking is done according to Formula (3). Zero frequency are normalized to 1.

3.2 Conceptual Density

Conceptual Density (CD) was originally introduced by (Agirre and Rigau, 1996). It is computed on WordNet subhierarchies, determined by the *hypernymy* (or *is-a*) relationship. Our formulation (Rosso et al., 2003) of the Conceptual Density of a WordNet subhierarchy s is:

$$CD(m, f, n) = m^{\alpha} \left(\frac{m}{n}\right) \tag{4}$$

Where m are the *relevant* synsets in the subhierarchy, n is the total number of synsets in the subhierarchy.The relevant synsets are both the synsets of the word to be disambiguated and those of the context words.

The WSD system based on this formula participated at the Senseval-3 competition as the CIAOSENSO system (Buscaldi et al., 2004), obtaining 75.3% in precision over nouns in the all-words task (baseline: 70.1%). These results were obtained with a context window of two nouns, the one preceding and the one following the word. In Senseval-3 the WSD system took also into account the frequency of senses depending on their rank. In SemEval-1 we do not, because of the presence of the Sense Probability expert.

The CD-based expert uses a context of two nouns for the disambiguation process too. The weights from Formula (4) are used for computing the fuzzy confidence values that are used to fill the preference matrix after they are transformed according to Formula (3).

A second CD-based expert exploits the *holonymy*, or *part-of* relationship instead of *hyperonymy*. This expert uses as context all the nouns in the sentence of the word to be disambiguated.

3.3 Extended Lesk

This expert is based on the algorithm by (Banerjee and Pedersen, 2002), a WordNet-enhanced version of the well-known dictionary-based algorithm proposed by (Lesk, 1986). The original Lesk was based on the comparison of the gloss of the word to be disambiguated with the context words and their glosses. This enhancement consists in taking into account also the glosses of concepts related to the word to be disambiguated by means of various WordNet relationships. Then similarity between a sense of the word and the context is calculated by means of *overlaps*. The word is assigned the sense obtaining the best overlap match with the glosses of the context words and their related synsets.

The weights used as input for Formula (3) are the similarity values between the senses of the world and the context words. The context for this expert consists of 4 WordNet words (disregarding their Part-Of-Speech) located in the same sentence of the word to be disambiguated, i.e., words with POS noun, verb, adjective or adverb that can be found in WordNet.

3.4 WordNet Domains

This expert uses WordNet Domains (Magnini and Cavaglià, 2000) in order to provide the system with domain-awareness. All WordNet words in the same sentence of the target word are used as context. The weight for each sense is obtained by counting the number of times the same domain of the sense appears in the context (all senses of context words are considered). We decided to not take into account the "factotum" domain.

4 Example

In this example we will consider only the sense probability and extended Lesk experts for simplicity.

Let us consider the following phrase: "*And he has kept mum on how his decision might affect a bid for United Airlines , which includes a big stake by British Airways PLC.*" with *affect* as target word. We can observe that in WordNet the verb *affect* has 5 senses. The sense count values are 43 for the first sense, 11 for the second, 4 for both the third and the fourth one, and 0 for the last one. We decided to normalize the cases with 0 occurrences to 1. After applying the transformation (3) to the sense counts, we obtain the following preference matrix for the sense probability expert:

$$\begin{pmatrix} 0.5 & 0.80 & 0.91 & 0.91 & 0.98 \\ 0.20 & 0.5 & 0.73 & 0.73 & 0.92 \\ 0.09 & 0.27 & 0.5 & 0.5 & 0.8 \\ 0.09 & 0.27 & 0.5 & 0.5 & 0.8 \\ 0.02 & 0.08 & 0.2 & 0.2 & 0.5 \end{pmatrix}$$

Therefore, the final fuzzy Borda counts by the sense probability expert are 3.60 for `affect(1)`, 2.38 for `affect(2)`, 0.8 for `affect(3)` and `affect(4)`, and 0 for `affect(5)`, obtained from the sum of the rows where the value is greater than 0.5.

The extended Lesk expert calculates the following similarity scores for thesenses of *affect*, with context words *decision*, *might*, *bid* and *include*: respectively 107, 70, 35, 63 and 71 for senses 1 to 5. After applying the transformation (3) to the weights, we obtain the preference matrix for this expert:

$$\begin{pmatrix} 0.5 & 0.60 & 0.75 & 0.63 & 0.60 \\ 0.40 & 0.5 & 0.67 & 0.53 & 0.49 \\ 0.25 & 0.33 & 0.5 & 0.36 & 0.33 \\ 0.37 & 0.47 & 0.64 & 0.5 & 0.47 \\ 0.40 & 0.51 & 0.67 & 0.53 & 0.5 \end{pmatrix}$$

In this case the final fuzzy Borda counts are 2.58 for the first sense, 1.2 for sense 2, 0 for sense 3, 0.64 and 1.71 for senses 4 and 5 respectively.

Finally, the sum of Borda counts of every expert for each sense (see Table 4) are used to disambiguate the word.

sense no:	1	2	3	4	5
expert 1	3.60	2.38	0.80	0.80	0
expert 2	2.58	1.20	0	0.64	1.71
total:	**6.18**	3.58	0.80	1.44	1.71

Table 1: Borda Count for the verb *affect* in the example phrase.

5 Results

The system was not tested before SemEval. Our participation was limited to the All-Word and Coarse-Grained tasks (without the sense inventory provided by the organizers). The results are compared to the best system and the MFS (Most Frequent Sense) baseline. We calculated also the partial results over nouns in the all word task, obtaining that the MFS baseline in this case is about 0.633, whereas our system obtains 0.520.

task	upv-wsd	MFS	best system
coarse-grained	0.786	0.789	0.832
awt	0.420	0.471	0.537

Table 2: Recall obtained by our system (upv-wsd) in each task we participated in, compared with the most frequent sense baseline and the best system in the task.

6 Conclusions

The combination of different systems allowed us to attain higher recall than with our previous system used in Senseval-3. However, overall results were not as good as expected. Partial results over the nouns show that the CD expert did not perform as in the Senseval-3 and that the CD formula needs to include sense frequency ranking in order to achieve a good performance. As a further work we plan to add a weight reflecting the reliability of each expert.

Acknowledgements

We would like to thank the TIN2006-15265-C06-04 research project for partially supporting this work. We would also like to thank Prof. Eugene Levner of the Holon Institute of Technology for inspiring us to use the fuzzy Borda voting scheme.

References

Eneko Agirre and German Rigau. 1996. Word sense disambiguation using conceptual density. In *COLING*, pages 16–22.

Satanjeev Banerjee and Ted Pedersen. 2002. An adapted lesk algorithm for word sense disambiguation using wordnet. In *Proceedings of CICLing 2002*, pages 136–145, London, UK. Springer-Verlag.

Davide Buscaldi, Paolo Rosso, and Francesco Masulli. 2004. The upv-unige-CIAOSENSO WSD System. In *Proc. of Senseval-3 Workshop*, Barcelona (Spain), July. ACL.

José Luis García Lapresta and Miguel Martínez Panero. 2002. Borda Count Versus Approval Voting: A Fuzzy Approach. *Public Choice*, 112(1-2):167–184.

Michael Lesk. 1986. Automatic sense disambiguation using machine readable dictionaries: how to tell a pine cone from an ice cream cone. In *Proc. of SIGDOC '86*, pages 24–26.

Bernardo Magnini and Gabriela Cavaglià. 2000. Integrating Subject Field Codes into WordNet. In *Proc. of the 2nd LREC Conference*, pages 1413–1418, Athens, Greece.

Hannu Nurmi. 2001. Resolving Group Choice Paradoxes Using Probabilistic and Fuzzy Concepts. *Group Decision and Negotiation*, 10(2):177–199.

Paolo Rosso, Francesco Masulli, Davide Buscaldi, Ferran Pla, and Antonio Molina. 2003. Automatic noun sense disambiguation. In *Proc. of CICLing 2003*, pages 273–276.

Sonia Vazquez, Rafael Romero, Armando Suarez, Andres Montoyo, Manuel García, M. Teresa Martin, M. Angel García, Alfonso Ureña, Davide Buscaldi, Paolo Rosso, Antonio Molina, Ferran Pla, and Encarna Segarra. 2004. The R2D2 Team at SENSEVAL-3. In *Proc. of Senseval-3 Workshop*.

USFD: Preliminary Exploration of Features and Classifiers for the TempEval-2007 Tasks

Mark Hepple
Dept of Computer Science
University of Sheffield
Regent Court
211 Portobello Street
Sheffield S1 4DP, UK
hepple@dcs.shef.ac.uk

Andrea Setzer
Dept of Computer Science
University of Sheffield
Regent Court
211 Portobello Street
Sheffield S1 4DP, UK
andrea@dcs.shef.ac.uk

Rob Gaizauskas
Dept of Computer Science
University of Sheffield
Regent Court
211 Portobello Street
Sheffield S1 4DP, UK
robertg@dcs.shef.ac.uk

Abstract

We describe the Sheffield system used in TempEval-2007. Our system takes a machine-learning (ML) based approach, treating temporal relation assignment as a simple classification task and using features easily derived from the TempEval data, i.e. which do not require 'deeper' NLP analysis. We aimed to explore three questions: (1) How well would a 'lite' approach of this kind perform? (2) Which features contribute positively to system performance? (3) Which ML algorithm is better suited for the TempEval tasks? We used the Weka ML workbench to facilitate experimenting with different ML algorithms. The paper describes our system and supplies preliminary answers to the above questions.

1 Introduction

The Sheffield team were involved in TempEval as co-proposers/co-organisers of the task.[1] For our participation in the task, we decided to pursue an ML-based approach, the benefits of which have been explored elsewhere (Boguraev and Ando, 2005; Mani et al., 2006). For the TempEval tasks, this is easily done by treating the assignment of temporal relation types as a simple classification task, using readily available information for the instance features. More specifically, the features used were ones provided as attributes in the TempEval data annotation for the events/times being related, plus some additional features that could be straightforwardly computed from documents, i.e. without the use of more heavily 'engineered' NLP components. The aims of this work were three-fold. First, we wanted to see whether a 'lite' approach of this kind could yield reasonable performance, before pursuing possibilities that relied on using 'deeper' NLP analysis methods. Secondly, we were interested to see which of the features considered would contribute positively to system performance. Thirdly, rather than selecting a single ML approach (e.g. one of those currently in vogue within NLP), we wanted to look across ML algorithms to see if any approach was better suited to the TempEval tasks than any other, and consequently we used the Weka workbench (Witten and Frank, 2005) in our ML experiments.

In what follows, we will first describe how our system was constructed, before going on to discuss our main observations around the key aims mentioned above. For example, in regard to our 'lite' approach, we would observe (c.f. the results reported in the Task Description paper) that although some other systems scored more highly, the score differences were relatively small. Regarding features, we found for example that the system performed better for Task A when, surprisingly, the `tense` attribute of EVENTs was *excluded*. Regarding ML algorithms, we found not only that there was substantial variation between the effectiveness of different algorithms for assigning relations (as one might expect), but also that there was considerable differences in the relative effectiveness of algorithms *across* tasks,

[1] We maintained a strict separation between persons assisting in annotation of the test corpus and those involved in system development.

Proceedings of the 4th International Workshop on Semantic Evaluations (SemEval-2007), pages 438–441,
Prague, June 2007.

i.e. so that an algorithm performing well on one task (compared to the alternatives), might perform rather poorly on another task. The paper closes with some comments about future research directions.

2 System Description

The TempEval training and test data is marked up to identify all event and time expressions occurring within documents, and also to record the TLINK relations that are relevant for each task (except that TLINK relation types are absent in the test data). These annotations provide additional information about these entities in the form of XML attributes, e.g. for EVENT annotations we find attributes such as tense, aspect, part-of-speech and so on.

Our system consists of a suite of Perl scripts that create the input files required for Weka, and handle its output. These include firstly an 'extraction' script, which extracts information about EVENT, TIMEXs and TLINKs from the data files, and secondly a 'feature selection/reformatting' script, which allows the information that is to be supplied to Weka to be selected, and recasts it into the format that Weka requires for its training/test files. A final script takes Weka's output over the test files and connects it back to the original test documents to produce the final output files required for scoring.

The information that the first extraction script extracts for each EVENT, TIMEX and TLINK largely corresponds to attributes/values associated with the annotations of these items in the initial data files (although not all such attributes are of use for machine learning purposes). In addition, the script determines for each EVENT expression whether it is one deemed relevant by the Event Target List (ETL) for Tasks A and B. This script also maps EVENTs and TIMEXs into sequential order – intra-sentential order for task A and inter-sentential order for task C. This information can be used to compute various 'order' features, such as:

`event-first`: do a related EVENT and TIMEX (for Task A) appear with the EVENT before or after the TIMEX?

`adjacent`: do a related EVENT and TIMEX (again for Task A) appear adjacently in the sequence of temporal entities or not? (Note that this allows an EVENT and TIMEX to be adjacent if there tokens that intervene, but not any other temporal entities.)

`event-between`: for a related EVENT/TIMEX pair, do any other events appear between them?

`timex-between`: for a related EVENT/TIMEX pair, do any other timexes appear between them?

		Task		
Type	Attribute	A	B	C
EVENT	aspect	✓	✓	✓
EVENT	polarity	✓	✓	×
EVENT	POS	✓	✓	✓
EVENT	stem	✓	×	×
EVENT	string	×	×	×
EVENT	class	×	✓	✓
EVENT	tense	×	✓	✓
ORDER	adjacent	✓	N/A	N/A
ORDER	event-first	✓	N/A	N/A
ORDER	event-between	×	N/A	N/A
ORDER	timex-between	×	N/A	N/A
TIMEX3	mod	✓	×	N/A
TIMEX3	type	✓	×	N/A
TLINK	reltype	✓	✓	✓

Table 1: Features

Table 1 lists all the features that we tried using for any of the three tasks. Aside from the ORDER features (as designated in the leftmost column), which were computed as just described, and the EVENT `string` feature (which is the literal tagged expression from the text), all other features correspond to annotation attributes. Note that the TLINK `reltype` is extracted from the training data to provide the target attribute for training (a dummy value is provided for this in test data).

The output of the extraction script is converted to a format suitable for use by Weka by a second script. This script also allows a manual selection to be made as to the features that are included. For each of the three tasks, a rough-and-ready process was followed to find a 'good' set of features for use with that task, which proceeded as follows. Firstly, the maximal set of features considered for the task was tried with a few ML algorithms in Weka (using a 10-fold cross-validation over the training data) to find one that seemed to work quite well for the task. Then using only that algorithm, we checked whether the `string` feature could be dropped (since this feature's value set was always of quite high cardinality), i.e. if its omission improved performance, which for all three tasks was the case. Next, we tried dropping each of the remaining features in turn, to identify those whose exclusion improved performance, and then for those features so identified, tried dropping them in combination to arrive at a final 'optimal' feature set. Table 1 shows for each of the tasks which of the features were considered for inclusion (those marked N/A were *not*), and which of these remained in the final optimal feature set (✓).

Having determined the set of features for use with each task, we tried out a range of ML algorithms (again with a 10-fold cross-validation over the training data), to arrive at the final feature-set/ML algorithm combination that was used for the task in the competitive evaluation. This was trained over the entire training data and applied to the test data to produce the final submitted results.

3 Discussion

Looking to Table 1, and the features that were considered for each task and then included in the final set, various observations can be made. First, note that the `string` feature was omitted for all tasks, which is perhaps not surprising, since its values will be sparsely distributed, so that there will be very few training instances for most of its individual values. However, the `stem` feature was found to be useful for Task A, which can be interpreted as evidence for a 'lexical effect' on local event-timex relations, e.g. perhaps with different verbs displaying different trends in how they relate to timexes. No corresponding effects were observed for Tasks B and C.

The use of ORDER features for Task A *was* found to be useful – specifically the features indicating whether the event or timex appeared linearly first in the sentence and whether the two were adjacent or not. The more elaborate ORDER features, addressing more specific cases of what might intervene between the related timex and event expression, were not found to be helpful.

Perhaps the most striking observation to be made regarding the table is that it was found beneficial to exclude the feature `tense` for Task A, whilst the feature `aspect` was retained. We have no explanation to offer for this result. Likewise, the event `class` feature, which distinguishes e.g. perception vs. reporting vs. aspectual etc verbs, was excluded for Task A, although it was retained for Task B.

	Task		
Algorithm	A	B	C
`baseline`	49.8	62.1	42.0
`lazy.KStar`	**58.2**	76.7	54.0
`rules.DecisionTable`	53.3	**79.0**	52.9
`functions.SMO`(svm)	55.1	78.1	**55.5**
`rules.JRip`	50.7	78.6	53.4
`bayes.NaiveBayes`	56.3	76.2	50.7

Table 2: Comparing different algorithms (%-acc. scores, from cross-validation over training data)

In regard to the use of different ML algorithms for the classification tasks addressed in TempEval, we observed considerable variation between algorithms as to their performance, and this was not unexpected. However, given the seemingly high similarity of the three tasks, we were rather more surprised to see that there was considerable variation between the performance of algorithms *across* tasks, i.e. so that an algorithm performing well on one task (compared to the alternatives), might perform rather poorly on another task. This is illustrated by the results in Table 2 for a selected subset of the algorithms considered, which shows %-accuracy scores that were computed by cross-validation over the training data, using the feature set chosen as 'optimal' for each task.[2] The algorithm names in the left-hand column are the ones used in WEKA (of which `functions.SMO` is the WEKA implementation of support-vector machines or SVM). The first row of results give a 'baseline' for performance, corresponding to the assignment of the most common label for the task. (These were produced using WEKA's `rules.ZeroR` algorithm, which does exactly that.)

The best results observed for each task are shown in bold in the table. These best performing algorithms were used for the corresponding tasks in the competition. Observe that the `lazy.KStar`

[2]These scores are computed under the 'strict' requirement that key and response labels should be identical. The TempEval competition also uses a 'relaxed' metric which gives partial credit when one (or both) label is disjunctive and there is a partial match, e.g. between labels AFTER and OVERLAP-OR-AFTER. See (Verhagen et al., 2007) for details.

	Task A		Task B		Task C	
	F_S	F_R	F_S	F_R	F_S	F_R
USFD	0.59	0.60	0.73	0.74	0.54	0.59
ave.	0.56	0.59	0.74	0.75	0.51	0.60
max.	0.62	0.64	0.80	0.81	0.55	0.66

Table 3: Competition task scores for Sheffield system (USFD), plus average/max scores across all competing systems

method, which gives the best performance for Task A, gives a rather 'middling' performance for Task B. Similarly, the SVM method that gives the best results for Task C falls quite a way below the performance of `KStar` on Task A. A more extreme case is seen with the results for `rules.JRip` (Weka's implementation of the RIPPER algorithm), whose score for Task B is close to that of the best-performing system, but which scores only slightly above baseline on Task A.

The competition scores for our system are given in Table 3, shown as (harmonic) F-measures under both strict (F_S) and relaxed (F_R) metrics (see footnote 2). The table also shows the average score for each task/metric across all systems taking part in the competition, as well as the maximum score returned by any system. See (Verhagen et al., 2007) for a full tabulation of results for all systems.[3]

4 Future Directions

SIGNALs and SLINKs are possible candidates as additional features – signals obviously so, whereas the benefits of exploiting subordination information are less clear. Our initial exploratory efforts in this direction involved pulling information regarding SIGNALs and SLINKs across from TimeBank[4] (Pustejovsky et al., 2003) so as to make this available for use with the TempEval tasks, in the hope that this would allow us to determine if this information would be useful without first facing the cost of developing SIGNAL and SLINK recognisers. Regarding SIGNALs, however, we ran into the problem that there are many TLINKs in the TempEval data for which no corresponding TLINK appears in TimeBank, and hence for which SIGNAL information could not be imported. We were unable to progress this work sufficiently in the time available for there to be any useful results to report here.

5 Conclusion

We have explored using a ML-based approach to the TempEval tasks, which does not rely on the use of deeper NLP-analysis components. We observe that although some other systems in the competition have produced higher scores for the tasks, the score differences are relatively small. In the course of this work, we have made some interesting observations regarding the performance variability of different ML algorithms when applied to the diffent TempEval tasks, and regarding the features that contribute to the system's performance.

[3]The TempEval test data identifies precisely the temporal entity pairs to which a relation label must be assigned. When a fixed set of items is classified, the scores for precision, recall and F-measure will be identical, being the same as the score for simple accuracy. However, not all the participating systems follow this pattern of assigning labels to 'all and only' the entity pairs identified in the test data, i.e. some systems decide which entity pairs to label, as well as which label to assign. Accordingly, the performance results given in (Verhagen et al., 2007) are reported using metrics of precision, recall and F-measure.

[4]This was possible because both the trial and training data were derived from TimeBank.

References

B. Boguraev and R. Kubota Ando. 2005. TimeML-Compliant Text Analysis for Temporal Reasoning. In *Proceedings of IJCAI-05*, pages 997–1003.

Inderjeet Mani, Marc Verhagen, Ben Wellner, Chong Min Lee, and James Pustejovsky. 2006. Machine Learning of Temporal Relations. In *ACL '06: Proceedings of the 21st International Conference on Computational Linguistics and the 44th annual meeting of the ACL*, pages 753–760, Morristown, NJ, USA. Association for Computational Linguistics.

J. Pustejovsky, D. Day, L. Ferro, R. Gaizauskas, P. Hanks, M. Lazo, D. Radev, R. Saurí, A. See, A. Setzer, and B. Sundheim. 2003. The TIMEBANK Corpus. In *Proceedings of Corpus Linguistics 2003*, pages 647–656, Lancaster, March.

M. Verhagen, R. Gaizauskas, F. Schilder, M. Hepple, G. Katz, and J. Pustejovsky. 2007. SemEval-2007 Task 15: TempEval Temporal Relation Identification. In *Proceedings of SemEval-2007: 4th International Workshop on Semantic Evaluations*.

I.H. Witten and E. Frank, editors. 2005. *Data Mining: Practical Machine Learning Tools and Techniques*. Morgan Kaufmann, San Francisco, second edition.

USP-IBM-1 and USP-IBM-2: The ILP-based Systems for Lexical Sample WSD in SemEval-2007

Lucia Specia, Maria das Graças Volpe Nunes
ICMC - University of São Paulo
Trabalhador São-Carlense, 400, São Carlos, 13560-970, Brazil
{lspecia, gracan}@icmc.usp.br

Ashwin Srinivasan, Ganesh Ramakrishnan
IBM India Research Laboratory
Block 1, Indian Institute of Technology, New Delhi 110016, India
{ashwin.srinivasan, ganramkr}@in.ibm.com

Abstract

We describe two systems participating of the English Lexical Sample task in SemEval-2007. The systems make use of Inductive Logic Programming for supervised learning in two different ways: (a) to build Word Sense Disambiguation (WSD) models from a rich set of background knowledge sources; and (b) to build interesting features from the same knowledge sources, which are then used by a standard model-builder for WSD, namely, Support Vector Machines. Both systems achieved comparable accuracy (0.851 and 0.857), which outperforms considerably the most frequent sense baseline (0.787).

1 Introduction

Word Sense Disambiguation (WSD) aims to identify the correct sense of ambiguous words in context. Results from the last edition of the Senseval competition (Mihalcea et al., 2004) have shown that, for supervised learning, the best accuracies are obtained with a combination of various types of features, together with traditional machine learning algorithms based on feature-value vectors, such as Support Vector Machines (SVMs) and Naive Bayes. While the features employed by these approaches are mostly considered to be "shallow", that is, extracted from corpus or provided by shallow syntactic tools like part-of-speech taggers, it is generally thought that significant progress in automatic WSD would require a "deep" approach in which access to substantial body of linguistic and world knowledge could assist in resolving ambiguities. Although the access to large amounts of knowledge is now possible due to the availability of lexicons like WordNet, parsers, etc., the incorporation of such knowledge has been hampered by the limitations of the modelling techniques usually employed for WSD. Using certain sources of information, mainly relational information, is beyond the capabilities of such techniques, which are based on feature-value vectors. Arguably, Inductive Logic Programming (ILP) systems provide an appropriate framework for dealing with such data: they make explicit provisions for the inclusion of background knowledge of any form; the richer representation language used, based on first-order logic, is powerful enough to capture contextual relationships; and the modelling is not restricted to being of a particular form (e.g., classification).

We describe the investigation of the use of ILP for WSD in the Lexical Sample task of SemEval-2007 in two different ways: (a) the construction of models that can be used directly to disambiguate words; and (b) the construction of interesting features to be used by a standard feature-based algorithm, namely, SVMs, to build disambiguation models. We call the systems resulting of the two different approaches "USP-IBM-1" and "USP-IBM-2", respectively. The background knowledge is from 10 different sources of information extracted from corpus, lexical resources and NLP tools.

In the rest of this paper we first present the specification of ILP implementations that construct ILP models and features (Section 2) and then describe the experimental evaluation on the SemEval-2007 Lexical Sample task data (Section 3).

Proceedings of the 4th International Workshop on Semantic Evaluations (SemEval-2007), pages 442–445,
Prague, June 2007.

2 Inductive Logic Programming

Inductive Logic Programming (ILP) (Muggleton, 1991) employs techniques from Machine Learning and Logic Programming to build first-order theories or descriptions from examples and background knowledge, which are also represented by first-order clauses. Functionally, ILP can be characterised by two classes of programs. The first, predictive ILP, is concerned with constructing models (in this case, sets of rules) for discriminating accurately amongst positive and negative examples. The partial specifications provided by (Muggleton, 1994) form the basis for deriving programs in this class:

- B is background knowledge consisting of a finite set of clauses $= \{C_1, C_2, \ldots\}$
- E is a finite set of examples $= E^+ \cup E^-$ where:
  - *Positive Examples.* $E^+ = \{e_1, e_2, \ldots\}$ is a non-empty set of definite clauses
  - *Negative Examples.* $E^- = \{\overline{f_1}, \overline{f_2} \ldots\}$ is a set of Horn clauses (this may be empty)
- H, the output of the algorithm given B and E, is acceptable if these conditions are met:
  - *Prior Satisfiability.* $B \cup E^- \not\models \square$
  - *Posterior Satisfiability.* $B \cup H \cup E^- \not\models \square$
  - *Prior Necessity.* $B \not\models E^+$
  - *Posterior Sufficiency.* $B \cup H \models e_1 \wedge e_2 \wedge \ldots$

The second category of ILP programs, descriptive ILP, is concerned with identifying relationships that hold amongst the background knowledge and examples, without a view of discrimination. The partial specifications for programs in this class are based on the description in (Muggleton and Raedt, 1994):

- B is background knowledge
- E is a finite set of examples (this may be empty)
- H, the output of the algorithm given B and E is acceptable if the following condition is met:
  - *Posterior Sufficiency.* $B \cup H \cup E \not\models \square$

The intuition behind the idea of exploiting a feature-based model constructor that uses first-order features is that certain sources of structured information that cannot be represented by feature vectors can, by a process of "propositionalization", be identified and converted in a way that they can be accommodated in such vectors, allowing for traditional learning techniques to be employed. Essentially, this involve two steps: (1) a feature-construction step that identifies all the features, that is, a set of clauses H, that are consistent with the constraints provided by the background knowledge B (descriptive ILP); and (2) a feature-selection step that retains some of the features based on their utility in classifying the examples, for example, each clause must entail at least one positive example (predictive ILP). In order to be used by SVMs, each clause h_i in H is converted into a boolean feature f_i that takes the value 1 (or 0) for any individual for which the body of the clause is true (if the body is false). Thus, the set of clauses H gives rise to a boolean vector for each individual in the set of examples. The features constructed may express conjunctions on different knowledge sources. For example, the following boolean feature built from a clause for the verb "ask" tests whether the sentence contains the expression "ask out" and the word "dinner". More details on the specifications of predictive and descriptive ILP for WSD can be found in (Specia et al., 2007):

$$f_1(X) = \begin{cases} 1 & expr(X, \text{'ask out'}) \wedge bag(X, dinner) \; = \; 1 \\ 0 & \text{otherwise} \end{cases}$$

3 Experiments

We investigate the performance of two kinds of ILP-based models for WSD:

1. *ILP models* (USP-IBM-1 system): models constructed by an ILP system for predicting the correct sense of a word.
2. *ILP-assisted models* (USP-IBM-2 system): models constructed by SVMs for predicting the correct sense of a word that, in addition to existing shallow features, use features built by an ILP system according to the specification for feature construction in Section 2.

The data for the English Lexical Sample task in SemEval-2007 consists of 65 verbs and 35 nouns. Examples containing those words were extracted from the WSJ Penn Treebank II and Brown corpus. The number of training / test examples varies from 19 / 2 to 2,536 / 541 (average = 222.8 / 48.5). The senses of the examples were annotated according to OntoNotes tags, which are groupings of WordNet senses, and therefore are more coarse-grained. The number of senses used in the training examples for a given word varies from 1 to 13 (average = 3.6).

First-order clauses representing the following background knowledge sources, which were automatically extracted from corpus and lexical resources or provided by NLP tools, were used to describe the target words in both systems:

B1. Unigrams consisting of the 5 words to the right and left of the target word.

B2. 5 content words to the right and left of the target word.

B3. Part-of-speech tags of 5 words to the right and left of the target word.

B4. Syntactic relations with respect to the target word. If that word is a verb, subject and object syntactic relations are represented. If it is a noun, the representation includes the verb of which it is a subject or object, and the verb / noun it modifies.

B5. 12 collocations with respect to the target word: the target word itself, 1st preposition to the right, 1st and 2nd words to the left and right, 1st noun, 1st adjective, and 1st verb to the left and right.

B6. A relative count of the overlapping words in the sense inventory definitions of each of the possible senses of the target word and the words surrounding that target word in the sentence, according to the sense inventories provided.

B7. If the target word is a verb, its selectional restrictions, defined in terms of the semantic features of its arguments in the sentence, as given by LDOCE. WordNet relations are used to make the verification more generic and a hierarchy of feature types is used to account for different levels of specificity in the restrictions.

B8. If the target word is a verb, the phrasal verbs possibly occurring in a sentence, according to the list of phrasal verbs given by dictionaries.

B9. Pairs of words in the sentence that occur frequently in the corpus related by verb-subject/object or subject/verb/object-modifier relations.

B10. Bigrams consisting of adjacent words in a sentence occurring frequently in the corpus.

Of these 10 sources, B1–B6 correspond to the so called "shallow features", in the sense that they can be straightforwardly represented by feature vectors. A feature vector representation of these sources is built to be used by the feature-based model constructor. Clausal definitions for B1–B10 are directly used by the ILP system.

We use the Aleph ILP system (Srinivasan, 1999) to construct disambiguation models in USP-IBM-1 and to construct features to be used in USP-IBM-2. Feature-based model construction in USP-IBM-2 system is performed by a linear SVM (the SMO implementation in WEKA).

In the USP-IBM-1 system, for each target word, equipped with examples and background knowledge definitions (B1–B10), Aleph constructs a set of clauses in line with the specifications for predictive ILP described in Section 2. Positive examples are provided by the correct sense of the target word. Negative examples are generated automatically using all the other senses. 3-fold cross-validation on the training data was used to obtain unbiased estimates of the predictive accuracy of the models for a set of relevant parameters. The best average accuracies were obtained with the greedy induction strategy, in conjunction with a minimal clause accuracy of 2. The constructed clauses were used to predict the senses in the test data following the order of their production, in a decision-list like manner, with the addition to the end of a default rule assigning the majority sense for those cases which are not covered by any other rule.

In the USP-IBM-2 system, for constructing the "good" features for each target word from B1–B10 (the "ILP-based features"), we first selected, in Aleph, the clauses covering at least 1 positive example. 3-fold cross-validation on the training data was performed in order to obtain the best model possible using SVM with features in B1–B6 and the ILP-based features. A feature selection method based on information gain with various percentages of features to be selected ($1/64$, ..., $1/2$) was used, which resulted in different numbers of features for each target word.

	Baseline	USP-IBM-1	USP-IBM-2
Nouns	0.809	0.882	0.882
Verbs	0.762	0.817	0.828
All	0.787	0.851	0.857

Table 1: Average accuracies of the ILP-based models for different part-of-speeches

```
sense(X, 3) :-
expr(X, 'come to').
sense(X, 1) :-
satisfy_restrictions(X, [animate], nil);
(relation(X, subj, B), pos(X, B, nnp)).
```

Figure 1: Examples of rules learned for "come"

Table 1 shows the average accuracy of a baseline classifier that simply votes for the most frequent sense of each word in the training data against the accuracy of our ILP-based systems, USP-IBM-1 and USP-IBM-2, according to the part-of-speech of the target word, and for all words. Clearly, the "majority class" classifier performs poorest, on average. The difference between both ILP-based systems and the baseline is statistically significant according to a paired t-test with $p < 0.01$. The two ILP-based models appear to be comparable in their average accuracy. Discarding ties, IBM-USP-2 outperforms IBM-USP-1 for 31 of the words, but the advantage is not statistically significant (cf. paired t-test).

The low accuracy of the ILP-based systems for certain words may be consequence of some characteristics of the data. In particular, the sense distributions are very skewed in many cases, with different distributions in the training and test data. For example, in the case of "care" (accuracy = 0.428), the majority sense in the training data is 1 (78.3%), while in the test data the majority sense is 2 (71%). In cases like this, many of the test examples remain uncovered by the rules produced by the ILP system and backing off to the majority sense also results in a mistake, since the majority sense in the training data does not apply for most of the test examples. The same goes for the feature-based system: features which are relevant for the test examples will not be built or selected.

One relevant feature of ILP is its ability to produce expressive symbolic models. These models can reproduce any kind of background knowledge using sets of rules testing conjunctions of different types of knowledge, which may include variables (intensional clauses). This is valid both for the construction of predictive models and for the construction of features (which are derived from the clauses). Examples of rules induced for the verb "come" are given in Figure 1. The first rule states that the sense of the verb in a sentence X will be 3 (progress to a state) if that sentence contains the expression "come to". The second rule states that the sense of the verb will be 1 (move, travel, arrive) if its subject is "animate" and there is no object, or if it has has a subject B that is a proper noun (nnp).

4 Concluding Remarks

We have investigated the use of ILP as a mechanism for incorporating shallow and deep knowledge sources into the construction of WSD models for the Semeval-2007 Lexical Sample Task data. Results consistently outperform the most frequent sense baseline. It is worth noticing that the knowledge sources used here were initially designed for the disambiguation of verbs (Specia et al., 2007) and therefore we believe that further improvements could be achieved with the identification and specification of other sources which are more appropriate for the disambiguation of nouns.

References

R. Mihalcea, T. Chklovski, A. Kilgariff. 2004. The SENSEVAL-3 English Lexical Sample Task. *SENSEVAL-3: 3rd Int. Workshop on the Evaluation of Systems for Semantic Analysis of Text*, 25–28.

S. Muggleton. 1991. Inductive Logic Program-ming. *New Generation Computing*, 8(4):29-5-318.

S. Muggleton. 1994. Inductive Logic Programming: derivations, successes and shortcomings. *SIGART Bulletin*, 5(1):5–11.

S. Muggleton and L. D. Raedt. 1994. Inductive logic programming: Theory and methods. *Journal of Logic Programming*, 19,20:629–679.

L. Specia, M.G.V. Nunes, A. Srinivasan, G. Ramakrishnan. 2007. Word Sense Disambiguation using Inductive Logic Programming. *Proceedings of the 16th International Conference on ILP*, Springer-Verlag.

A. Srinivasan. 1999. *The Aleph Manual*. Computing Laboratory, Oxford University.

USYD: WSD and Lexical Substitution using the Web1T Corpus

Tobias Hawker
School of Information Technologies
University of Sydney
NSW 2006, Australia
toby@it.usyd.edu.au

Abstract

This paper describes the University of Sydney's WSD and Lexical Substitution systems for SemEval-2007. These systems are principally based on evaluating the substitutability of potential synonyms in the context of the target word. Substitutability is measured using Pointwise Mutual Information as obtained from the Web1T corpus.

The WSD systems are supervised, while the Lexical Substitution system is unsupervised. The lexical sample sub-task also used syntactic category information given from a CCG-based parse to assist in verb disambiguation, while both WSD tasks also make use of more traditional features.

These related systems participated in the Coarse-Grained English All-Words WSD task (task 7), the Lexical Substitution Task (task 10) and the English Lexical Sample WSD sub-task (task 17).

1 Introduction

This paper describes closely related systems that were applied to three tasks of the SemEval-2007 workshop. The unifying characteristic of these systems is that they use the same measure of 'substitutability' for a given word and a surrounding context to perform the tasks. This measure is based on frequencies involving the word and the context from n-gram counts derived from one trillion words of Web text.

These systems participated in the English Coarse-Grained All Words and English Lexical Sample Word Sense Disambiguation (WSD) tasks, and in the Lexical Substitution task.

The Lexical Substitution system relies entirely on the substitutability measure to rank potential synonyms, and only uses manual sense inventories to preferentially select words which have been identified by lexicographers as being synonyms for the original word in some contexts. It does not make use of any machine learning, and is thus unsupervised.

The WSD systems are supervised, using a Support Vector Machine (SVM) to learn from sense-tagged examples of ambiguous words and predict the class of the test instances. Classifiers for both systems use a small number of additional feature types beyond those derived from the n-gram counts, including Bag of Words (BOW) and local context features. A single separate model was trained for each ambiguous lemma.

For verbs in the lexical sample, the classifier also uses the syntactic category assigned to the target verb by a parser as additional information for disambiguation.

The remainder of this paper is organised as follows. Relevant background for the ideas employed is briefly discussed, as is the nature of the Web1T corpus. Descriptions of the particular systems used for each of the tasks are described in ascending order of task number. Details of particular sources of information and the methods used to capture them are introduced along with the task they are used in. A presentation of results and discussion follows the description of each system, and overall conclusions

Proceedings of the 4th International Workshop on Semantic Evaluations (SemEval-2007), pages 446–453,
Prague, June 2007.

are presented at the end of the paper.

2 Background

Algorithms making use of unannotated data for WSD and similar tasks are not particularly new. One strategy which resembles the substitutability technique employed by our systems is relatives-in-context (Martinez et al., 2006), an unsupervised approach which uses a web search engine to find the 'best' match for the current context, according to heuristic criteria. Monosemous relatives (Leacock et al., 1998) increase the amount of training data for supervised learners by recruiting the contexts of synonyms in unannotated data, with the caveat that those synonyms are not themselves ambiguous. As substantial gold-standard data sets for lexical substitution have not previously been available, the SemEval data presents a promising opportunity to examine the behaviour of our method.

Gomez (2001) argues that the syntactic roles of ambiguous verbs in particular are interlinked with their semantic class, and thus knowledge about the syntactic function of a verb can provide information to help identify its sense. Syntactic relationships have been used to resolve ambiguity (Lin, 1997) and a reduction of ambiguity has been shown to assist in the acquisition of verb subcategorization frames (Korhonen and Preiss, 2003).

3 The Substitutability Measure

As an example to demonstrate the basic mechanism underlying the measure of substitutability, consider the sentence fragments around the verb *ruled* in:

the court ruled it was clear that

and

a republic ruled by the people

Two possible synonyms, pertaining to different senses for the verb *ruled*, are *found* and *governed*. It is clear that in a sufficiently large quantity of text, the fragments:

the court found it was clear that

and

a republic governed by the people

would be substantially more common than the sequences:

the court governed it was clear that

or

a republic found by the people

and thus *found* should be considered more substitutable in the context of the first fragment, and *governed* in the second.

Church et al. (1994) show that Pointwise Mutual Information (PMI) is a suitable measure to capture the degree to which a given word may substitute for another; we have adopted PMI as the quantified measure of substitutability in the systems used for these tasks.

While previous WSD systems have made use of counts obtained from Internet search engines, for example Martinez et al. (2006), to our knowledge WSD using *corpus* data at the scale of the Web1T resource has not previously been published. Our WSD systems combine our novel PMI-Web1T features and CCG category features with additional features described in the literature. While the Web1T corpus consists only of counts, and thus is somewhat similar to the direct use of counts from Internet search engines, it is also of a known size and thus it is straightforward to determine useful quantities such as PMI, and to exhaustively catalog potential matches as for the lexical substitution task.

3.1 Web1T Corpus

The Web1T corpus (Brants and Franz, 2006) is a dataset consisting of the counts for n-grams obtained from 1 trillion (10^{12}) words of English Web text, subject to a minimum occurrence threshold (200 instances for unigrams, 40 for others). The Web1T corpus contains counts for 1, 2, 3, 4 and 5-grams, and is large enough to present serious processing difficulties: it is 25GB in compressed form.

The systems presented here thus use custom high-performance software to extract only the n-gram counts of interest from the Web1T data, including simple wildcard pattern-matching. The scale of the data rules out attempting to perform arbitrary queries — even though the counts are lexicographically ordered, disk access times and decompression overheads are severe, and case-insensitive queries are not possible. This software will be released for community use. A limitation in the implementation is that the number of tokens that can be matched in a wildcard expression is fixed at one. This limitation precluded the testing of substitutability of multi-word-expressions (MWEs) in the systems applied to the SemEval tasks.

4 Task 7: Coarse Grained-English All-Words WSD

The system for Coarse-Grained All-Words WSD was supervised, but only attempted classification for a subset of words. These words were chosen according to the amount of sense-tagged training data available, drawn from SemCor (Miller et al., 1993) and the SenseEval-3 lexical sample (Mihalcea et al., 2004) task. Features were extracted and a classifier trained for each ambiguous content word that was either present in the SenseEval-3 lexical sample, or occurred at least 100 times in SemCor. These criteria yielded classifiers for 183 words.

For ambiguous words without sufficient available training data, the first sense baseline (determined from WordNet version 2.1 (Fellbaum, 1998)) was assigned to every instance. No manual augmentation of the information from WordNet was performed. For those words where models were being trained, the sense clusterings provided by the task organisers were used to completely unify all senses belonging to a cluster, thus attempting disambiguation at the level of the coarse senses. As the system does not attempt to disambiguate words not selected for modeling, the exclusion of the most frequent sense (MFS) baseline would be likely to have a severe adverse impact on this type of supervised approach. Extension of the substitutability measure to directly select a sense related to good substitutes, similar to the approach outlined in Lin (1997) would be one possible approach to resolve this consistently.

The classifier used for the system was an SVM (libsvm) (Chang and Lin, 2001). Linear kernels were used, as previous experiments using similar features with other data sets for WSD had shown that these kernels outperformed radial basis function and polynomial kernels; this disparity became particularly pronounced with larger number of features compared to training instances, and with the combination of different feature types. The number of unique features for each lemma was, on average, more than an order of magnitude higher than the number of training instances: 4475 compared to 289.

The features used to train the selected lemmas included the substitutability measurement, all content words within 3 sentences of the target, and immediate local context features. These are detailed below. There is no in-principle reason why CCG category features used for the Lexical Sample task (see Section 6.2) could not also be used for verbs in the all-words task. Sentences containing target verbs could have been selectively parsed and redundancy among disambiguated running text in SemCor exploited. However, the system architecture was not amenable to small modifications along these lines, and time constraints prevented implementation before the close of the evaluation period. The impact of this additional useful feature would be an interesting subject for future study.

4.1 Features

4.1.1 Substitutability: Pointwise Mutual Information

To transform the notion of substitutability into a set of features suitable for WSD, a set of potential substitute words was chosen for each modeled lemma. These words were taken from WordNet 2.1 (Fellbaum, 1998). For nouns, all synonyms, immediate hypernyms and immediate hyponyms for all senses were included. For verbs, synonyms for all senses were used. The selection of potential substitutes was stricter for verbs as the number of synonyms tended to be greater than for nouns, and these criteria kept the number of substitutes manageable.

A sliding window was used to maximise the information extracted from the Web1T corpus. All windows at all sizes covered by the Web1T corpus that included the target word were used to determine the overall substitutability.

The counts of interest for determining the PMI for a single substitute in a single window position include the unigram frequency of the substitute itself the overall frequency of the context, irrespective of the word in the target position; and crucially, the frequency of the substitute in that context. For a given substitute and context, an overall PMI is determined as a single quantity, obtained by simply adding the PMI together from each window position of each size covered in the data:

$$PMI = \sum_{n=2}^{5}\sum_{i=1}^{n} \log_2 \frac{\text{observation}_{n,i}}{\text{expectation}_{n,i}}$$

$$= \sum_{n=2}^{5}\sum_{i=1}^{n} \log_2 \frac{\#(\text{sub} + \text{context}_{n,i})}{p(\text{sub}) \cdot p(\text{context}_{n,i}) \cdot N_n}$$

Here n represents the window size (varying from 2 to 5), i is the position within the window, and N_n indicates the total number of n-grams present in the corpus for a given value of n. Following Church et al. (1994) the Maximum Likelihood Estimate (MLE) is used for both probabilities in the denominator. $p(\text{sub})$ is estimated from the unigram frequency of the substitute word, while $p(\text{context})$ is derived from the counts of the context ignoring the token in the target location.

Features were also created that harnessed the idea that it is not only the level of substitutability for each candidate word that is useful, but also that it may be informative to recognise that some words are better substitutes than others. This information was captured by adding additional features consisting of the pairwise differences between PMI values for all candidate substitute words. To further draw the differing levels of substitutability into relief, features representing the rank of each pair's PMI difference were also included.

Finally, each of the above feature types yields real-valued features. Before being used in classification, these features were converted to binary features using supervised Entropy-Based Discretisation (Fayyad and Irani, 1993). This process characterises the partition selection as a message coding problem: the class labels in the training data are a message to be encoded given that the value of the feature is known for each instance, and the process aims to minimise the length of that message. This is achieved by recursively bifurcating each feature's values at the partition point that would result in the shortest message. Useful boundaries are those where knowing which side of the partition the feature value falls on can be used to reduce the message length beyond any increase required to specify the partition. The algorithm terminates when the existing partitions cannot be divided further and still satisfy this condition. If this occurs when attempting to find the first partition, the feature is dropped altogether.

4.1.2 Bag of Words in broad context

Bag of words (BOW) features were introduced to represent the presence or absence of almost all words within a window of three sentences of the target word. A small stop list (approximately 50 words) was used to remove common closed-class words such as prepositions and conjunctions. The words were lemmatised before being transformed into features, and were not weighted for their distance from the target word. No attribute subset selection was performed on the BOW features.

4.1.3 Local Context Features

The sentence containing the target word was tagged for Part of Speech (POS) using the POS tagger in the C&C parser tools. For four tokens either side of the target lemma, features were formed from the displacement of the token concatenated with:

- The POS tag
- The lemmatised word
- The POS and lemma together

Also included were features combining the above information for pairs of tokens before, after, and either side of the target word. Finally, a feature representing the POS tag of the target word was added, providing such information as number and tense.

The portion of the context used to form these features is identical with that used to determine substitutability of potential synonyms using the Web1T-based features. Combining the abstract substitutability features with features that use the particular tokens in the local context helps to maximise the utility of information present near the target word by approaching it from multiple perspectives.

4.2 Results and Discussion

The results of the system are shown in Table 1

The first-sense baseline achieves scores of 0.788 for precision, recall and F1, and thus outperforms our system for all documents.

Unfortunately we are currently unable to explain this relatively poor performance. It is possible that an error of a similar nature to the one which affected the initial results for the lexical sample system

Doc.	Attempted	Precision	Recall	F1
d001	0.986	0.625	0.617	0.621
d002	0.958	0.598	0.573	0.585
d003	0.948	0.610	0.578	0.593
d004	0.929	0.606	0.563	0.583
d005	0.965	0.471	0.455	0.463
Total	0.953	0.588	0.560	0.574

Table 1: Coarse-Grained WSD results

(see Section 6.3) was also present in this system, although we have not yet been unable to identify such a problem. It is also possible that the current highly supervised and lexicalised approach employed is not well-suited to the all-words task, and may require extension to achieve broad coverage.

5 Task 10: English Lexical Substitution

5.1 Methodology

As for the WSD systems, the Lexical Substitution system concentrated on words whose occurrence in local contexts similar to that of the target was more frequent than expected in the Web1T corpus.

Aside from preferring sets of potential synonyms obtained from lexical resources, the system is entirely unsupervised. Consequently, no sense-annotated corpus resources were used.

The lexical resources used were WordNet version 2.1 (Fellbaum, 1998) and the Macquarie Thesaurus (Bernard, 1985), a pre-defined, manually constructed Thesaurus. The only information used from these resources was a list of potential synonyms for all listed senses that matched the target word's part-of-speech. These synonyms were used to preferentially choose potential substitutes obtained from the corpus data, as described below. The union of potential synonyms from both resources was used, although MWEs were not included due to limitations with the corpus. Although these lexical resources were not augmented, the system was capable of producing substitutes not present in these resources by using high-scoring words found in the corpus. The ordering of synonyms in these resources was not used directly, nor was their association with particular senses.

The PMI for potential substitutes that occurred in the target position of each local context window was determined using the Web1T corpus, as for coarse WSD above. The strategy differed slightly from the supervised process employed for WSD however, in that rather than testing a fixed set of potential substitutes, every word that occurred in the correct location in a matching context was considered as a substitute. This introduced an additional computational burden which restricted the set of n-grams used to 4 and 5 grams. In particular, this is because the set of words occurring in the target position grew prohibitively large for 2 and 3 grams.

As for WSD, the PMI for each potential substitute was combined by summing the individual PMIs over all locations and size of n-gram where it occurred. This sum was used to rank the substitutes. After the production of the ranked list, the set of synonyms obtained from the lexical resources was used for preferential selection. Substitutes in the ranked list that also occurred in the synonym pool were chosen first. The exact manner of the preferential selection differed for the two evaluation measures the system participated in.

For the BEST measure, the highest PMI-ranked substitute that occurred in the synonym pool was given as the only substitute. If no substitutes from the synonym pool were present in the ranked list, the top three substitutes from the list were given.

For the out-of-ten (OOT) measure, the ten highest-ranked substitutes that were in the synonym pool were given. If fewer than 10 substitutes were present in the list, the remaining best ranked substitutes not in the synonym pool were used to make up the ten answers.

As with the Coarse-Grained All Word WSD, limitations in the current implementation of the Web1T processing software meant that it was not possible to examine MWEs, and there was thus no provision to detect or handle MWEs in the system. For this reason, the MW measure was not produced by the system.

5.2 Results and Discussion

The results for the BEST and OOT measures are given in tables 2 and 3 respectively. While the results for the other tasks are reported as a decimal fraction of 1, the results here are percentage scores, in line with the results provided by the task organisers.

	P	R	Mode P	Mode R
all	11.23	10.88	18.22	17.64
Further Analysis				
NMWT	11.68	11.34	18.46	17.90
NMWS	12.48	12.10	19.25	18.63
RAND	11.47	11.01	19.14	18.35
MAN	10.95	10.73	17.20	16.84

Table 2: BEST results

	P	R	Mode P	Mode R
all	36.07	34.96	43.66	42.28
Further Analysis				
NMWT	37.62	36.17	44.71	43.35
NMWS	40.13	38.89	46.25	44.77
RAND	35.67	34.26	42.90	41.13
MAN	36.52	35.78	44.50	43.58

Table 3: OOT results

Notably, recall is always lower than precision. If no substitutes were found to have finite PMI at any position, no substitute was rendered by the system. This meant a small number of examples in the submitted system had no answer provided. The system's design meant that no attempt was made to provide any answer when counts were zero for all Web1T queries. This was the case for around 3% of the evaluation set. As the query retrieval software was limited to single word substitutions, this should be expected to occur for MWEs more frequently than for single word substitutions. The results for both BEST and OOT confirm this, showing that the system's performance is uniformly better when MWEs are excluded.

As a consequence of the properties of the Web1T corpus, the system chooses substitutes on the basis of information that is derived from at most four words either side of the target word. It is thus encouraging that it is able to outperform the baselines on each evaluation measure.

Interestingly, for the BEST evaluation the performance on the randomly selected (RAND) examples outperforms that on the manually selected (MAN) examples. For the OOT evaluation the situation is reversed. This could indicate that, depending on the motivation for the manual selections, the system is not particularly well-suited to selecting an obvious singular substitution, but is quite capable of ranking reasonably acceptable ones near the top of the list.

6 Task 17: Coarse Grained English Lexical Sample sub-task

6.1 Approach

The Lexical Sample system used features identical to those described for the Coarse-Grained All-Words task, with the addition of the CCG supertag feature, discussed below. Labeled data used for training the classifier models in this system consisted of only the instances in the training data supplied for the task, although the Web1T corpus was of course used to provide extensive information in the form of features for those instances. As for the All-Words system, an individual SVM model was trained using linear kernels for each lemma being disambiguated. The contextual BOW features were not selected from within a window as for the All-Words system; instead the entire context provided in the training and test data was used.

Unlike the other systems, the Lexical Sample system produced a prediction for every instance in the test data, as the MWE limitation of the Web1T processing software did not present an impediment.

6.2 CCG Verb Categories

The Lexical sample data was parsed using the Clark and Curran CCG parser (Clark and Curran, 2004). Existing tagging and parsing models, derived from CCGBank are included with the parser package, and were used without adjustment. Gold-standard parses available for the source data were not used.

The syntactic combination category ("supertags") assigned to target verbs by the parser were used as features. This category label encodes information about the types of the other sentential components used when building a parse. A forward slash indicates that the current token requires a component of the specified type to the right; a backwards slash requires one to the left. The C&C parser includes a supertagger, but this supertagger assigns multiple labels with varying degrees of confidence, and when the parse is performed, the supertag labels are subject to revision in determining the most likely parse. The feature used for the Lexical Sample system uses the final, parser-determined supertag.

As an example, consider the occurrence of the verb *find* in the following two fragments where it has different senses:

managers did not find out about questionable billing

and

or new revenues are found by Congress

In the first fragment *find* has a (simplified) supertag of (S\NP)/PP, while in the second it is playing a different grammatical role, and hence has a different supertag: S\NP. While these supertags are generally not exclusively associated with a single sense in particular, their distribution is sufficiently distinct over different senses that features derived from them are informative for the WSD task. To form features, the system uses the supertags obtained from the parser as binary features, with a slight simplification: by removing distinctions between the argument types of the main S component, generalisation is facilitated among instances of verbs which differ slightly on a local level but combine with other parts of the sentence similarly.

6.3 Results and Discussion

Unfortunately, the component of the lexical sample system responsible for assigning identifiers for evaluation contained a systematic error, resulting in a mismatch between the predictions of the system and the correct labels as used in evaluation. The system assumed that for each lemma in the test set, the instances in the test data file would have lexicographically ascending identifiers, and matched predictions to identifiers using this assumption. This was not the case in the task data, and yielded a result for the submission that severely underestimated the performance of the system. We calculated a baseline of 0.788 for the Lexical Sample sub-task, using the Most Frequent Sense for each lemma in the training data. The result for the systems initial submission was 0.743 (precision, recall, accuracy and F1 are all identical, as the system provides an answer for every instance).

However, as the mismatch is systematic, and only occurred after the classifier had made its predictions, it was possible to correct almost all of the alignment by post-processing the erroneous answer file. By holding the order of predictions constant, but lexicographically sorting instance identifiers within each lemma, predictions were re-matched with their intended identifiers. Using the test labels provided by the task organisers, the accuracy of the system after repairing the mismatch was 0.891.

As the parser does not have 100% coverage, the parse of the test sentence did not succeed in every instance. This in turn caused some supertag features to be misaligned with other feature types before the error was rectified. This meant that a small fraction of instances were given predictions in the submitted data that differed from those produced by the corrected system. When the already-trained models were used to re-predict the classes of the correctly aligned test instances, a further small improvement to a result of 0.893 was achieved.

It is encouraging that the results (after correcting the misaligned identifiers) for the patched system are approaching the Inter Tagger Agreement (ITA) level reported for OntoNotes sense tags by the task organisers – 90%. This could be seen as an positive outcome of the movement towards coarser-grained sense inventories for the WSD tasks, it is difficult for automated systems to agree with humans more often than they agree with each other.

7 Conclusion

Substantially similar information in the form of a PMI-based substitutability measure from the Web1T corpus was used in all USYD systems. That this information yielded positive results in different semantic-ambiguity related tasks, both supervised and unsupervised, demonstrates the usefulness of the data at the scale of the Web1T corpus, either alone or in concert with other information sources, and there are still many more approaches to using this resource for semantic processing that could be explored.

The systems demonstrated outstanding performance on the Lexical Sample WSD task – nearly at the level of the reported ITA. Good unsupervised performance above the baseline was also achieved on the Lexical Substitution task.

8 Acknowledgements

Many thanks to Jon Patrick, James Curran, and Matthew Honnibal for their invaluable assistance, insights and advice.

References

J. R. L. Bernard, editor. 1985. *The Macquarie Thesaurus*. The Macquarie Library, Sydney.

Thorsten Brants and Alex Franz. 2006. Web 1T 5-gram corpus version 1.1. Technical report, Google Research.

Chih-Chung Chang and Chih-Jen Lin. 2001. *LIBSVM: A Library for Support Vector Machines*. Software available at http://www.csie.ntu.edu.tw/~cjlin/libsvm.

Kenneth Ward Church, Willam Gale, Patrick Hanks, Donald Hindle, and Rosamund Moon. 1994. Lexical substitutability. In B. T. S. Atkins and A. Zampolli, editors, *Computational Approaches to the Lexicon*, pages 153–177. Oxford University Press.

Stephen Clark and James R. Curran. 2004. Parsing the WSJ using CCG and log-linear models. In *Proceedings of the 42nd Annual Meeting of the Association for Computational Linguistics (ACL-04)*, pages 104–111. Barcelona, Spain.

Usama M. Fayyad and Keki. B. Irani. 1993. Multi-interval discretization of continuous-valued attributes for classification learning. In *Proceedings of the Thirteenth International Joint Conference on Artificial Intelligence*, pages 1022–1029. Chambery, France.

Christiane Fellbaum, editor. 1998. *Wordnet: An Electronic Lexical Database*. MIT Press.

Fernando Gomez. 2001. An algorithm for aspects of semantic interpretation using an enhanced wordnet. In *Proceedings of NAACL-2001*, pages 1–8.

Anna Korhonen and Judita Preiss. 2003. Improving subcategorization acquisition using word sense disambiguation. In *ACL '03: Proceedings of the 41st Annual Meeting on Association for Computational Linguistics*, pages 48–55.

Claudia Leacock, Martin Chodorow, and George A. Miller. 1998. Using corpus statistics and WordNet relations for sense identification. *Computational Linguistics*, 24:147–165.

Dekang Lin. 1997. Using syntactic dependency as local context to resolve word sense ambiguity. In *Proceedings of the 35th Annual Meeting of the Association for Computational Linguistics*.

David Martinez, Eneko Agirre, and Xinglong Wang. 2006. Word relatives in context for word sense disambiguation. In *Proceedings of the 2006 2006 Australasian Language Technology Workshop (ALTW 2006)*, pages 42–50.

Rada Mihalcea, Timothy Chklovski, and Adam Kilgarriff. 2004. The senseval-3 english lexical sample task. In Rada Mihalcea and Phil Edmonds, editors, *Senseval-3: Third International Workshop on the Evaluation of Systems for the Semantic Analysis of Text*, pages 25–28. Association for Computational Linguistics.

George. A. Miller, Claudia. Leacock, Tengi Randee, and Ross Bunker. 1993. A semantic concordance. In *Proceedings of the 3rd DARPA Workshop on Human Language Technology*, pages 303–308.

UTD-HLT-CG: Semantic Architecture for Metonymy Resolution and Classification of Nominal Relations

Cristina Nicolae, Gabriel Nicolae and Sanda Harabagiu
Human Language Technology Research Institute
The University of Texas at Dallas
Richardson, Texas
{cristina, gabriel, sanda}@hlt.utdallas.edu

Abstract

In this paper we present a semantic architecture that was employed for processing two different SemEval 2007 tasks: Task 4 (Classification of Semantic Relations between Nominals) and Task 8 (Metonymy Resolution). The architecture uses multiple forms of syntactic, lexical, and semantic information to inform a classification-based approach that generates a different model for each machine learning algorithm that implements the classification. We used decision trees, decision rules, logistic regression and lazy classifiers. A voting module selects the best performing module for each task evaluated in SemEval 2007. The paper details the results obtained when using the semantic architecture.

1 Introduction

Automatic semantic interpretations of natural language text rely on (1) semantic theories that capture the subtleties employed by human communications; (2) lexico-semantic resources that encode various forms of semantic knowledge; and (3) computational methods that model the selection of the optimal interpretation derived from the textual data. Two of the SemEval 2007 tasks, namely Task 4 (Classification of Semantic Relations between Nominals)and Task 8 (Metonymy Resolution) employed distinct theories for the interpretation of their corresponding semantic phenomena, but, nevertheless, they also shared several lexico-semantic resources, and, furthermore, both these tasks could have been cast as classification problems, in vein with most of the recent work in computational semantic processing. Based on this observation, we have designed and implemented a semantic architecture that was used in both tasks. In Section 2 of this paper we give a brief description of the semantic theories corresponding to each of the two tasks, while in Section 3 we detail the semantic architecture. Section 4 describes the experimental results and evaluation.

We have used three lexico-semantic resources: (i) the WordNet lexico-semantic database; (ii) VerbNet; and (iii) the Lexical Conceptual Structure (LCS) database. Used only by Task 4, WordNet is a lexico-semantic database created at Princeton University[1] (Fellbaum, 1998), which encodes a vast majority of the English nouns, verbs, adjectives and adverbs, and groups synonym words into synsets. VerbNet[2] is a broad-coverage, comprehensive verb lexicon created at University of Pennsylvania, compatible with WordNet, but with explicitly stated syntactic and semantic information, using Levin verb classes (Levin, 1993) to systematically construct lexical entities. Classes are hierarchically organized and each class in the hierarchy has its corresponding syntactic frames, semantic predicates and a list of typical verb arguments. The Lexical Conceptual Structure (Traum and Habash, 2000) is a compositional abstraction with language-independent properties. An LCS is a directed graph with a root. Each node is associated with certain information, including a type, a primitive and a field. An LCS captures the semantics

[1] http://wordnet.princeton.edu
[2] http://verbs.colorado.edu/verb-index/verbnet-2.1.tar.gz

Proceedings of the 4th International Workshop on Semantic Evaluations (SemEval-2007), pages 454–459,
Prague, June 2007.

Relation	*Positive example*
1. CAUSE-EFFECT	Earplugs relieve the *discomfort* from *traveling* with a cold allergy or sinus condition.
2. INSTRUMENT-AGENCY	The *judge* hesitates, *gavel* poised, shooting them a warning look.
3. PRODUCT-PRODUCER	The *boy* who made the *threat* was arrested, charged, and had items confiscated from his home.
4. ORIGIN-ENTITY	*Cinnamon oil* is distilled from *bark chips* and used to alleviate stomach upsets.
5. THEME-TOOL	The *port scanner* is a utility to scan a system to get the status of the TCP.
6. PART-WHOLE	The *granite benches* are former windowsills from the Hearst Memorial Mining Building.
7. CONTENT-CONTAINER	The *kitchen* holds patient *drinks* and snacks.

Table 1: Examples of semantic relations.

of a lexical item through a combination of semantic structure and semantic content.

2 Semantic Tasks

The two semantic tasks addressed in this paper are: **Classification of Semantic Relations between Nominals (Task 4)**, defined in (Girju et al., 2007) and **Metonymy Resolution (Task 8)**, defined in (Markert and Nissim, 2007). Please refer to these task description papers for more details. Both are cast as classification tasks: given an unlabeled instance, a system must label it according to one class of a set specific to each task.

The training and testing datasets for the metonymy resolution task are annotated in an XML format. There are 1090 training and 842 testing instances for companies, and 941 training and 908 testing instances for locations. Each training instance corresponds to a context in which a single name is annotated with its reading (*metonymic/literal/mixed*) and, in case of metonymy, its type (*metotype*). The testing dataset for this task is annotated in a similar manner, only the reading of the name is left unknown and must be decided by the system.

For the classification of semantic relations between nominals, there exist seven training sets of 140 instances each for the seven semantic relations, and seven corresponding testing sets of around 70 instances each. A training instance is annotated with information about the boundaries of the two nominals whose relation must be determined, the truth value of their relation, the WordNet sense of each nominal, and the query that was employed by the annotators to retrieve this example from the Web. The testing instances are similar, with the only difference being that the truth value of the relations is unknown and must be determined.

3 Semantic Architecture

The semantic architecture that we have designed is illustrated in Figure 1, which contains the basic modules and resources used in the various phases of processing the input data towards the final submission format. The grayed-out modules are all used only for the semantic relations classification task, while the part of the figure represented by dotted lines appears only in the metonymy resolution algorithm. The input to the system, for both tasks, comprises the annotated instances, either from the training or the testing dataset. Before any feature is extracted, the data passes through a pipeline of preprocessing modules. The text is first split into tokens in a heuristic manner. The resulting tokenized text is given as input to Brill's part of speech tagger[3], which associates each word with its part of speech (e.g., *NN*, *PRP*). The data further goes through Collins' syntactic parser[4], which builds the syntactic trees for all the sentences in the text.

Additionally, for semantic relations classification, the system creates the dependency structures for all the sentences, using the dependency parser built at Stanford[5] and described in (de Marneffe et al., 2006). The dependency parser extracts some of 48 grammatical relations for each pair of words in a sentence. A second module that is specific only to this task is (Surdeanu and Turmo, 2005)'s semantic role labeler, which extracts the shallow semantic structure for each sentence, that is, the predicates and their arguments.

In order to extract the features for the machine learning algorithm, the modules described above are used, and, in addition, information from WordNet, VerbNet and the LCS Database is incorporated,

[3] http://www.cs.jhu.edu/~brill/

[4] http://people.csail.mit.edu/mcollins/code.html

[5] http://nlp.stanford.edu/downloads/lex-parser.shtml

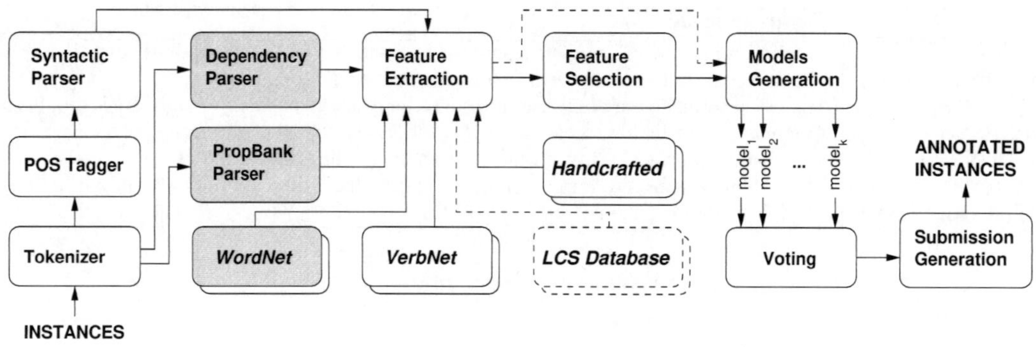

Figure 1: Semantic architecture.

Category	*Feature name*	*Feature description*
syntactic	*prevpos*	part of speech of previous word in the sentence
	nextpos	part of speech of next word in the sentence
	determiner	if the word has a determiner
	prepgoverning	if the word is governed by a prepositional phrase (PP), we extract the preposition
	insidequotes	if the word is inside quotes
	lemmapost	if the word is postmodifier for a noun, take the lemma of the noun
	lemmapre	if the word is premodifier for a noun, take the lemma of the noun
	possession	if the word is a possessor, and what it possesses
semantic	*role*	the role(s) of the name in the sentence: subject, object, under PP
	rolelemma	the combination between the role and the lemma of the verb whose argument the word is
	rolevn	same as above, but using the VerbNet class instead of the verb's lemma
	rolelevin	same as above, but using the Levin class instead of the verb's lemma
	rolelcs	same as above, but using LCS primitives from the LCS database instead of the verb's lemma

Table 2: Features for metonymy resolution.

along with other features, based on the manual annotations for both the training and testing datasets by the task organizers. These other features use the grammatical annotations for the possibly metonymic name, in the case of metonymy resolution, and the query that was used to retrieve that particular instance and the disambiguated WordNet sense for the two nominals, in the case of semantic relations classification.

The features implemented for the two tasks are described in Tables 2 and 3. Their types are: syntactic, semantic, lexical and other. The *syntactic features* express the relationships between the target words and words from the rest of the sentence (e.g., the part of speech of the previous word in the sentence, or the dependency relations between two words). The *semantic features* make use of the information given by the resources used by the system (e.g., the VerbNet class of the verb whose argument the word is, or the lexicographic category of a word in WordNet). The *lexical feature* is the lemma of the word. The *other feature* is the query provided by Task 4.

Using these sets of features, a number of models were generated by different machine learning techniques included with the Weka data mining software (Witten and Frank, 2005). The machine learning classifiers comprise decision trees, decision rules, logistic regression, and "lazy" classifiers like k-nearest-neighbor. Because of too many features generated for a relatively small training dataset, feature selection is performed by Weka before creating the models. Metonymy resolution uses in addition the entire set of features, since the dataset has seven times more instances than the other task. For the classification of semantic relations, the initial total and the number of features that remain after the selection are printed in Table 4.

For metonymy resolution, there are six subtasks to be resolved, which result from all combinations between *organization/location* and *coarse/medium/fine* granularity of the label. For the classification of nominal relations, there are 28 subtasks, resulting from the processing of the seven se-

Category	*Feature name*	*Feature description*
syntactic	*dependency*	the dependency relations between the two words
	modifier	if one word is a modifier of the other
	prepositions	the prepositions immediately before and after both words
	determiners	the determiners of the two words
	pattern	the simplified pattern that exists in the sentence between the two words
lexical	*lemmas*	the lemmas of the words
semantic	*predicates*	the predicates whose arguments the two words are
	predtypes	the predicate types of the predicates above
	samepred	if the two words are arguments of the same predicate, which one that is
	lexname	the lexicographic category of each word in WordNet
	hyponym	if one word is a hyponym of the other in WordNet
	partof	if one word is a part of the other in WordNet
	shareholonym	if the two words share a holonym in WordNet
	shareparent	if the two words share a parent in WordNet
other	*query*	the query that was used by the annotators to retrieve the training example from the Web

Table 3: Features for classification of semantic relations between nominals.

	R1	*R2*	*R3*	*R4*	*R5*	*R6*	*R7*
before	682	1200	913	898	861	849	677
after	13	19	10	15	15	8	16

Table 4: The number of features before and after Weka selection, for each semantic relation dataset: R1 CAUSE-EFFECT, R2 INSTRUMENT-AGENCY, R3 PRODUCT-PRODUCER, R4 ORIGIN-ENTITY, R5 THEME-TOOL, R6 PART-WHOLE, and R7 CONTENT-CONTAINER.

Base type	*Coarse*	*Medium*	*Fine*	*BA*
Locations	84.1	84.0	82.2	79.4
Organizations	73.9	71.1	71.1	61.8

Table 5: Accuracy for the metonymy resolution system at three granularity levels.

Base type	*Reading*	*P*	*R*	*F*	*BA*
Locations	literal	88.2	92.4	90.2	79.4
	non-literal	64.1	52.4	57.6	20.6
Organizations	literal	75.8	84.8	80.0	61.8
	non-literal	69.6	56.2	62.2	38.2

Table 6: Performance for the metonymy resolution system for the coarse level.

mantic relations, in which four experiments are conducted, each with an increasing number of training instances. We treated each subtask as a separate classification problem. Its training set and features are fed into Weka to create several models. Each classification algorithm mentioned before is employed to obtain one model. For each subtask, the voting module selects the best performing model on 10-fold crossvalidation, which is used to classify the test instances. These annotated instances make up the submission dataset for that particular subtask. To note is that the coarse metonymic level and the semantic relations classification are binary classifications, while the rest of the metonymic subtasks are multi-class classifications, performed in a single stage.

4 Experimental Results and Evaluation

Both the metonymy resolution system and the system for classification of semantic relations performed well in the SemEval 2007 competition. The experiments presented in this paper were done on the training and testing datasets for each subtask. To note is that no other training data was collected or used than the one provided by the organizers.

4.1 Results for Metonymy Resolution

This system was scored by measuring its accuracy at three granularity levels (*coarse, medium,* and *fine*) and the precision, recall and F score for all combinations of *locations/organizations* and *literal/non-literal*. These results are tabulated in Tables 5, 6, 7 and 8.

All results are compared with the baseline accuracy values (BA). In Table 5, the baselines are computed by taking all readings to be literal; for the rest, the baseline is the percentage in the gold test data of each reading. As can be observed, the readings

Base type	*Reading*	*P*	*R*	*F*	*BA*
Locations	literal	87.8	93.5	90.5	79.4
	mixed	0.0	0.0	0.0	2.2
	metonymic	63.6	52.3	58.0	18.4
Organizations	literal	74.3	90.0	81.4	61.8
	mixed	28.6	13.1	18.0	7.2
	metonymic	66.8	47.1	55.3	31.0

Table 7: Performance for the metonymy resolution system for the medium level.

Base type	*Reading*	*P*	*R*	*F*	*BA*
Loc	literal	85.7	94.6	89.9	79.4
	mixed	0.0	0.0	0.0	2.2
	othermet	0.0	0.0	0.0	1.2
	obj-for-name	0.0	0.0	0.0	0.0
	obj-for-repr	0.0	0.0	0.0	0.0
	place-for-people	57.1	45.4	50.6	15.5
	place-for-event	0.0	0.0	0.0	1.1
	place-for-prod	0.0	0.0	0.0	0.1
Org	literal	74.4	90.4	81.6	61.8
	mixed	50.0	3.33	6.25	7.1
	othermet	0.0	0.0	0.0	1.0
	obj-for-name	80.0	66.7	72.7	0.7
	obj-for-repr	0.0	0.0	0.0	0.0
	org-for-members	61.3	64.0	62.6	19.1
	org-for-event	0.0	0.0	0.0	0.1
	org-for-prod	60.6	29.9	40.0	8.0
	org-for-fac	0.0	0.0	0.0	1.9
	org-for-index	0.0	0.0	0.0	0.4

Table 8: Performance for the metonymy resolution system for the fine level.

for locations were more reliably identified than the ones for companies. An explanation for this difference in performance lies in the fact that locations, in their literal readings, are inactive entities, whereas in their non-literal readings they are very often active, especially in the annotated instances of the training dataset. This cannot be said for organizations– they can be active in their literal readings. The active vs. inactive criterion, therefore, functions better for locations. Furthermore, since the training set contains a ratio *literals/non-literals* of 1.7 for organizations and 3.9 for locations, the models were skewed, identifying literal readings more easily than non-literal ones, as shown in Table 6.

4.2 Results for Classification of Semantic Relations between Nominals

This task's performance was measured by accuracy, precision, recall and F-measure, the latter constituting the score for ranking the systems in the competition. Table 9 presents these scores by semantic relation. The column entitled "Inst" contains the number of instances in the testing sets corresponding to each relation. The average baseline values were computed by guessing the label to be the majority in the dataset for each relation. From this table it can be observed that the PRODUCT-PRODUCER, INSTRUMENT-AGENCY, and CAUSE-EFFECT relations were detected with a relatively very high performance score, whereas the THEME-TOOL relation classification yielded a relatively small score. This can be explained as the effect of their specifications; the three best-ranked relations are well-defined by human standards, while the THEME-TOOL relation is more ambiguous.

Semantic relation	*P*	*R*	*F*	*Acc*	*Inst*
Cause-Effect	65.5	87.8	75.0	70.0	80
Instrument-Agency	68.3	73.7	70.9	70.5	78
Product-Producer	66.7	96.8	78.9	65.6	93
Origin-Entity	62.9	61.1	62.0	66.7	81
Theme-Tool	70.0	24.1	35.9	64.8	71
Part-Whole	55.6	76.9	64.5	69.4	72
Content-Container	82.4	36.8	50.9	63.5	74
Average	67.3	65.3	**62.6**	67.2	78.4
Avg baseline	81.3	42.9	56.2	57.0	78.4

Table 9: Performance of the semantic relations classification system for each semantic relation.

Table 10 contains the scores of the 10-fold cross-validation experiments that were performed on the training dataset in order to select the best classification algorithm. The classifiers used in these experiments were, in the order of appearance in the table: JRip, Random Forest, ADTree, Logistic Regression, IBk, and Random Tree. The Logistic Regression classifier was chosen in the vast majority of cases, because it achieved the highest score for six out of the seven relations. For R6, PART-WHOLE, Random Forest was preferred. This ranking between the scores of classifying relations, done considering training accuracy only, does not however anticipate the final F score ranking in Table 9. In particular, the crossvalidation accuracy of R5, THEME-TOOL, is better than the accuracy for R3, PRODUCT-PRODUCER, which came first in the final results, whereas R5 came last and at a large distance from the others. These lower-than-expected results in the

Alg	*R1*	*R2*	*R3*	*R4*	*R5*	*R6*	*R7*
JRip	72.1	76.4	68.6	66.4	68.6	66.4	73.6
RandF	78.6	85.0	72.1	77.1	74.3	**70.7**	73.6
ADTree	72.9	79.3	70.0	70.7	70.7	68.6	69.3
LogReg	**79.3**	**85.7**	**72.1**	**80.0**	**76.4**	70.0	**75.7**
IBk	78.6	83.6	70.7	75.7	74.3	70.0	72.1
RandT	79.3	85.7	71.4	77.1	75.0	70.0	72.1

Table 10: Results on 10-fold crossvalidation for each relation and each classifier.

evaluation were caused in part by the drastic feature selection module that was applied before generating the models. In experiments performed on the development data, the accuracy on 10-fold crossvalidation was increased with an average of 7% by feature selection, but the same feature set on the testing data obtained a final score 4.7% less than the one obtained by using all the features (F=67.3%). The results submitted in the evaluation were based on feature selection because of this misleading performance shift observed on the development set.

The task of classification of semantic relations between nominals required data to be separated into four training sets: the first 35 instances (D1), the first 70 instances (D2), the first 105 instances (D3), and the entire set, 140 instances (D4). The letter "D" stands for systems that use both the WordNet and the query information provided by the organizers. The results on the four sets are illustrated in Figure 2. The results generally increase with the size of training data, and tend to be the same on D3 and D4, which means that the D4 set does not bring significant new information compared to D3.

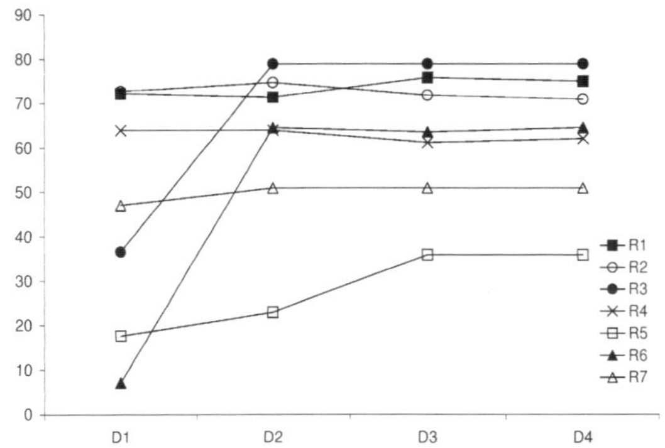

Figure 2: Results of training on different portions of the training dataset.

5 Conclusions

This paper has presented a semantic architecture that participated in the SemEval 2007 competition to evaluate two tasks, one for metonymy resolution, and the other for the classification of semantic relations between nominals. Although the tasks were very different, the architecture produced competitive results. The experimental results are reported in this paper in a detailed manner, and some interesting observations can be drawn from them.

References

Marie-Catherine de Marneffe, Bill MacCartney, and Christopher D. Manning. 2006. Generating typed dependency parses from phrase structure parses. In *5th International Conference on Language Resources and Evaluation (LREC 2006)*.

C. Fellbaum, editor. 1998. *WordNet: An Electronic Lexical Database and Some of its Applications*. MIT Press.

Roxana Girju, Dan Moldovan, Marta Tatu, and Daniel Antohe. 2005. On the semantics of noun compounds. In *Computer Speech and Language*, volume 19, pages 479–496.

Roxana Girju, Marti Hearst, Preslav Nakov, Vivi Nastase, Stan Szpakowicz, Peter Turney, and Deniz Yuret. 2007. Task 04: Classification of semantic relations between nominal at semeval 2007. In *SemEval 2007*.

Beth Levin. 1993. *English Verb Classes and Alternations*. The University of Chicago Press, Chicago and London.

Katja Markert and Malvina Nissim. 2002. Metonymy resolution as a classification task. In *the 2002 Conference on Empirical Methods in Natural LAnguage Processing (EMNLP2002)*.

Katja Markert and Malvina Nissim. 2007. Task 08: Metonymy resolution at semeval 2007. In *SemEval 2007*.

Mihai Surdeanu and Jordi Turmo. 2005. Semantic role labeling using complete syntactic analysis. In *CoNLL 2005, Shared Task*.

David Traum and Nizar Habash. 2000. Generation from lexical conceptual structure. In *Workshop on Applied Interlinguas, ANLP-2000*.

Ian H. Witten and Eibe Frank. 2005. *Data Mining: Practical machine learning tools and techniques*. Morgan Kaufmann, 2nd edition.

UTD-SRL: A Pipeline Architecture for Extracting Frame Semantic Structures

Cosmin Adrian Bejan and **Chris Hathaway**
Human Language Technology Research Institute
The University of Texas at Dallas
Richardson, TX 75083-0688, USA
{ady,chris}@hlt.utdallas.edu

Abstract

This paper describes our system for the task of extracting frame semantic structures in SemEval–2007. The system architecture uses two types of learning models in each part of the task: Support Vector Machines (SVM) and Maximum Entropy (ME). Designed as a pipeline of classifiers, the semantic parsing system obtained competitive precision scores on the test data.

1 Introduction

The SemEval–2007 task for extracting frame semantic structures relies on the human annotated data available in the FrameNet (FN) database. The Berkeley FrameNet project (Baker et al., 1998) is an ongoing effort of building a semantic lexicon for English based on the theory of *frame semantics*. In frame semantics, the meaning of words or word expressions, also called *target words* (TW), comprises aspects of conceptual structures, or *frames*, that describe specific situations. The semantic roles, or *frame elements* (FE), associated with a target word are locally defined in the frame evoked by the target word. Currently, the FN lexicon includes more than 135,000 sentences extracted from the British National Corpus containing more than 6,100 target words that evoke more than 825 semantic frames.

For this task, we extended our previous work at Senseval-3 (Bejan et al., 2004) by (1) experimenting with additional features, (2) adding new classification sub-tasks to accomplish all the requirements, and (3) integrating these sub-tasks into a pipeline architecture.

2 System Description

Given a sentence, the frame semantic structure extraction task consists of recognizing the word expressions that evoke semantic frames, assigning the correct frame to them and, for each target word, detecting and labeling the corresponding frame elements properly. The task also requires the determination of syntactic realizations associated to a frame element, such as *grammatical function* (GF) and *phrase type* (PT). The following illustrates a sentence example annotated with frame elements together with their corresponding grammatical functions and phrase types for the target word *"tie"*:

To extract semantic structures similar to those illustrated in the example we divide the SemEval–2007 task into four sub-tasks: (1) target word frame disambiguation (TWFD); (2) FE boundary detection (FEBD); (3) GF label classification (GFLC) and (4) FE label classification (FELC). The sub-tasks TWFD and GFLC are natural extensions of the approach described in (Bejan et al., 2004) for the task of semantic role labeling at Senseval-03. We design machine learning classifiers specific for each of the four sub-tasks and arrange them in a pipeline architecture such that a classifier can use information predicted by its previous classifiers. The system architecture is illustrated in Figure 1. In the data processing step, we parse each sentence into a syntactic tree using the Collins parser and extract named entities using an in

Proceedings of the 4th International Workshop on Semantic Evaluations (SemEval-2007), pages 460–463,
Prague, June 2007. ©2007 Association for Computational Linguistics

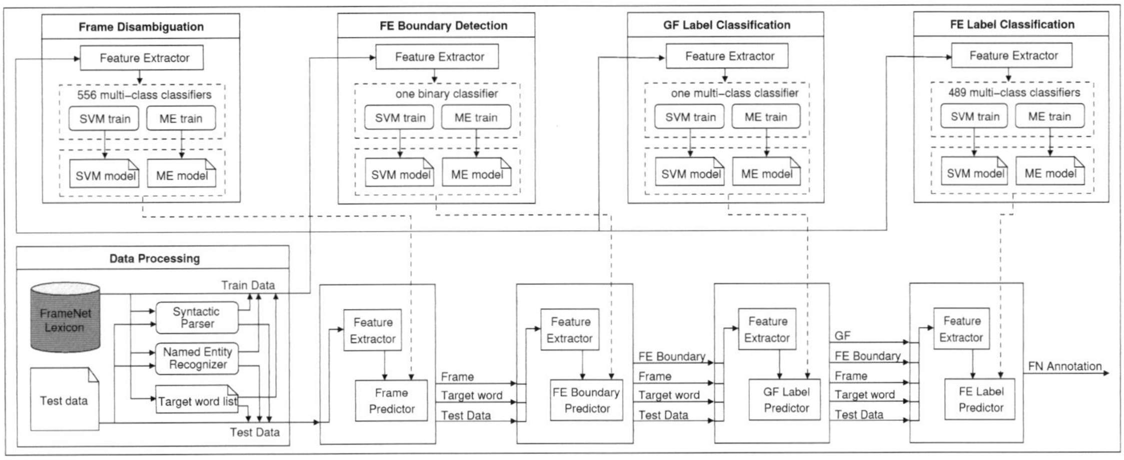

Figure 1: System architecture.

house implementation of a named entity recognizer. We also extract from the FN lexicon mappings of target words and the semantic frames they evoke.

Various features corresponding to constituents were extracted and passed to SVM and ME classifiers. For example, in Figure 2, the frame dis-

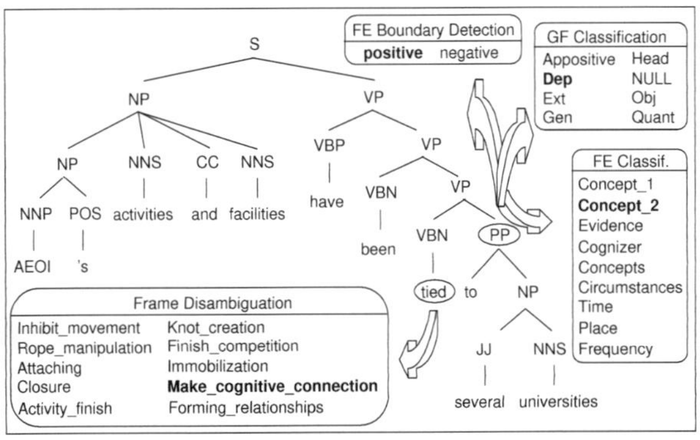

Figure 2: Classification examples for each sub-task.

ambiguation sub-task extracts features corresponding to the constituent *tied* in order to predict the right frame between the semantic frames that can be evoked by this target word. In this figure, the correct categories for each sub-task are shown in boldface.

The complete set of features extracted for all the classification sub-tasks is illustrated in Figure 3. These represent a subset of features used in previous works (Gildea and Jurafsky, 2002; Florian et al., 2002; Surdeanu et al., 2003; Xue and Palmer, 2004; Bejan et al., 2004; Pradhan et al., 2005) for automatic semantic role labeling and word sense disambiguation. Figure 3 also indicates whether or not a feature is selected for a specific classification task.

In the remaining part of this section we describe in detail each classification sub-task and the features that have the most salient effect on improving the corresponding classifiers.

2.1 Frame Disambiguation

In FrameNet, some target words can evoke multiple semantic frames. In order to extract the semantic structure of an ambiguous target word, the first step is to assign the correct frame to the target word in a given context. This task is similar with the word sense disambiguation task.

We select from the FN lexicon 556 target words that evoke at least two semantic frames and have at least five sentences annotated for each frame, and assemble a multi-class classifier for each ambiguous target word. As described in Figure 3, for this task we extract features used in word sense disambiguation (Florian et al., 2002), lexical features of the target word, and NAMED ENTITY FLAGS associated with the root node in a syntactic parse tree. For the rest of the ambiguous target words that have less than five sentences annotated we randomly choose a frame as being the correct frame in a given context.

2.2 Frame Element Identification

The idea of splitting the automatic semantic role labeling task into FE boundary detection and FE label classification was first proposed in (Gildea and Jurafsky, 2002) and then adopted by other works in this task. The problem of detecting the FE boundaries is cast as the problem of deciding whether or not a constituent is a valid candidate for a FE.

NO	TWFD	FEBD	GFLC	FELC	Feature Description
01	v				TW UNIGRAMS: The words, stem words and part of speech (POS) unigrams that are adjacent to target word expressions;
02	v				TW BIGRAMS: The words, stem words and POS bigrams that are adjacent to target word expressions;
03	v				TW WORD: The target word expression;
04			v	v	TW STEM: The stem word(s) of the target word expression;
05	v				TW POS: The POS of the target word;
06			v	v	TW CLASS: The lexical class of the target word, e.g. verb, noun, adjective;
07	v			v	NAMED ENTITY FLAGS: Set of binary features indicating whether a constituent contains, is contained or exactly identifies a named entity;
08	v				VERB WSD: If the target word is a verb, extract the head noun of the direct object and the prepositional object included in the verbal phrase;
09	v				NOUN WSD: If the target word is a noun, extract the head word of the verbal phrase that is in a verb–subject or verb–object relation with the noun;
10	v				ADJECTIVE WSD: If the target word is an adjective, extract the head noun that is modified by the adjective;
11			v	v	PHRASE TYPE: The syntactic category of the constituent;
12		v	v	v	DIRECTED PATH: Path in the syntactic parse tree between the constituent and the target word preserving the movement direction;
13				v	UNDIRECTED PATH: Same syntactic path as DIRECTED PATH without preserving the movement direction;
14		v			PARTIAL PATH: Path from the constituent to the earlier common ancestor of the target word and the constituent;
15		v	v	v	POSITION: Test whether the constituent contains the target word, or appears before or after the target word;
16			v	v	VOICE: Test if the verbal target word has active or passive construction;
17		v	v	v	HW: The head word of the constituent;
18			v	v	HW POS: The syntactic head POS of the constituent;
19				v	HW STEM: The stem word of the constituent's head word;
20				v	CW: The content word of the constituent computed as described in (Surdeanu et al., 2003);
21				v	CW POS: The POS corresponding to the content word;
22				v	CW STEM: Stemmed content word;
23			v	v	GOVERNING CATEGORY: Test whether the noun phrase constituents are dominated by verbal phrases or sentence phrases;
24		v			SYNTACTIC DISTANCE: The length of the syntactic path;
25				v	PP FIRST WORD: If the constituent is a prepositional phrase, return the first word in the phrase;
26				v	HUMAN: Test whether the constituent phrase is either a personal pronoun or a hyponym of first sense of PERSON synset in WordNet;
27				v	CONSTITUENTS NUMBER: The number of candidate FEs;
28				v	CONSTITUENTS LIST: Constituents labels list of the candidate FEs;
29				v	SAME CLAUSE: Test whether the constituent is in the same clause with the target word;
30				v	GF: The grammatical function of a candidate frame element;
31				v	GF LIST: The list of grammatical functions associated to the candidate FEs;
32		v	v	v	FRAME: The name of the semantic frame that is evoked by the target word;
33				v	NP SISTER: Determine whether the constituent has a noun phrase sister;
34				v	FIRST/LAST WORD: Return the first/last word of the constituent phrase;
35		v		v	FIRST/LAST POS: Return the first/last POS in the constituent;
36				v	LEFT/RIGHT SISTER LABEL: Return the left/right sibling constituent label;
37				v	LEFT/RIGHT SISTER HEAD: Return the left/right sibling head word;
38				v	LEFT/RIGHT SISTER STEM HEAD: Return the left/right sibling stemmed head word;
39				v	LEFT/RIGHT SISTER POS HEAD: Return the left/right sibling head POS;
40				v	TW STEM & HW STEM: Join of TW STEM and HW STEM;
41				v	TW STEM & PHRASE TYPE: Join of TW STEM and PHRASE TYPE;
42				v	VOICE & POSITION: Join of VOICE and POSITION.

Figure 3: Feature set for extracting frame semantic structures.

We consider a binary classifier over the entire FN data and extract features for each constituent from a syntactic parse tree. Because this experimental setup allows training the binary classifier on a large set of examples, the best feature combination consists of a restrained number of features. Most of these features are from the set proposed by (Gildea and Jurafsky, 2002). Another feature that improved the prediction of FE boundaries in every feature selection experiment is the FRAME feature. Since the frame disambiguation is executed before the FE boundary detection in the pipeline architecture, we can use the FRAME feature at this step. This feature helps the binary classifier distinguish between frame element structures from different semantic frames.

2.3 Grammatical Function Classification

Once we identify the candidate boundaries for frame elements, the next step is to assign the grammatical functions to these boundaries. In FrameNet, the grammatical functions represent the manner in which the frame elements satisfy grammatical constraints with respect to the target word.

For this task we train a multi-class classifier over the entire lexicon to predict seven categories of GFs that exist in FN. In addition, we assign the NULL category for those FEs that double as target words. The features are extracted only for the constituents that are identified as FEs in the previous FE boundary identification sub-task. The best feature set in this phase includes the features proposed by (Gildea and Jurafsky, 2002) and the FRAME feature.

2.4 Frame Element Classification

The task of FE classification is to assign FE labels to every constituent identified as FE. In order to predict the frame elements, which are locally defined for each semantic frame, we built 489 multi-class classifiers, where each classifier corresponds to a frame in FrameNet. This partitioning of the FN lexicon has the advantage of increasing the overall classification performance and efficiently learning the frame elements labels. On the other hand, this approach suffers from the lack of annotated data in some frames and hence it requires using a large set of features.

The advantage of designing the classifiers in a pipeline architecture is best illustrated in this subtask. Some of the most effective features for FE classification are extracted using information from previous sub-tasks: FRAME feature is made available by the TWFD sub-task, CONSTITUENTS NUMBER and CONSTITUENTS LIST are made available by the FEBD sub-task, and GF and GF LIST are made available by the GFLC sub-task.

3 Experimental Results

We report experimental results on all four classification sub-tasks. In our experiments we trained two types of classification models for each sub-task: SVM and ME. In order to optimize the performance measure of each sub-task and to find the best configuration of classification models we used 20% of the sub-tasks training data as validation data. Table 1 lists the best configuration of classification models as well as the best sub-task results when running the experiments on the validation data. For frame disambiguation, we obtained 76.71% accuracy compared to a baseline of 60.72% accuracy that always predicts the most annotated frame for each of the 556 target words. The results for GFLC and FELC sub-tasks listed in Table 1 were achieved by using gold FE boundaries.

Task	*Best Model*	*Accuracy*		
Frame Disambiguation	SVM	76.71		
GF Label Classification	ME	96.00		
FE Label Classification	ME	88.93		
		Precision	*Recall*	*F1–measure*
FE Boundary Detection	SVM	73.65	87.08	79.80

Table 1: Task results on the validation set.

The SemEval–2007 organizers provided fully annotated training files, a scorer to evaluate these training files, and testing files containing flat sentences. In the evaluation process, a semantic dependency graph corresponding to a fully system annotated sentence is created and then matched with its gold dependency graph. The matching process not only evaluates every semantic structure of a target word, but also considers frame-to-frame and FE-to-FE graph relations between the semantic structures. In addition, various scoring options were considered: exact or partial frame matching, partial credit for evaluating the named entities, evaluation of the flat frame elements labels, and an option for matching only the frames in evaluation. The evaluation for flat frame elements labels is similar with the evaluation performed at Senseval-3. The only difference is that for this scorer the FE boundaries must match exactly.

In Table 2, we present the averaged precision, recall and F1 measures for evaluating the semantic dependency graphs and detecting the semantic frames on the testing files. The *"Options"* column represents the configuration parameters of the scorer: (E)xact/(P)artial frame matching, semantic (D)ependency or (L)abels only evaluation, and (Y)es/(N)o named entity evaluation.

Options	*Semantic Dependency Evaluation*			*Frame Detection Evaluation*		
	Precision	*Recall*	*F1–measure*	*Precision*	*Recall*	*F1–measure*
E L Y	51.10	27.74	35.88	69.16	42.73	52.71
	55.56	30.19	39.04	77.82	48.09	59.32
	50.29	27.05	35.11	71.69	44.43	54.74
	54.78	29.48	38.26	80.35	49.79	61.35
	51.85	27.59	35.94	69.16	42.73	52.71
	56.59	30.14	39.25	77.82	48.09	59.32
E D N	51.38	26.95	35.29	71.69	44.43	54.74
P D N	56.13	29.45	38.57	80.35	49.79	61.35

Table 2: System results on the test set.

Although the system achieved good precision scores on the test data, the recall values caused the system to obtain unsatisfactory F1-measure values. We expect that the recall will increase by considering various heuristics for a better mapping of the frame elements to constituents in parse trees.

4 Conclusions

We described a system that participated in SemEval–2007 for the task of extracting frame semantic structures. We showed that a pipeline architecture of the SVM and ME classifiers as well as an adequate selection of the classification models can improve the performance measures of each sub-task.

References

Collin F. Baker, Charles J. Fillmore, and John B. Lowe. 1998. The Berkeley FrameNet project. In *Proceedings of the COLING-ACL*, Montreal, Canada.

Cosmin Adrian Bejan, Alessandro Moschitti, Paul Morărescu, Gabriel Nicolae, and Sanda Harabagiu. 2004. Semantic Parsing Based on FrameNet. In *Senseval-3: Workshop on the Evaluation of Systems for the Semantic Analysis of Text*.

Radu Florian, Silviu Cucerzan, Charles Schafer, and David Yarowsky. 2002. Combining classifiers for word sense disambiguation. *Natural Language Engineering*.

Daniel Gildea and Daniel Jurafsky. 2002. Automatic Labeling of Semantic Roles. *Computational Linguistic*.

Sameer Pradhan, Kadri Hacioglu, Valeri Krugler, Wayne Ward, James H. Martin, and Daniel Jurafsky. 2005. Support vector learning for semantic argument classification. *Journal of Machine Learning Research*.

Mihai Surdeanu, Sanda M. Harabagiu, John Williams, and Paul Aarseth. 2003. Using predicate-argument structures for information extraction. In *Proceedings of ACL*.

Nianwen Xue and Marta Palmer. 2004. Calibrating features for semantic role labeling. In *Proceedings of EMNLP*.

UTH: Semantic Relation Classification using Physical Sizes

Eiji ARAMAKI **Takeshi IMAI** **Kengo MIYO** **Kazuhiko OHE**
The University of Tokyo Hospital department
7-3-1 Hongo, Bunkyo-ku, Tokyo 113-8656, Japan
aramaki@hcc.h.u-tokyo.ac.jp

Abstract

Although researchers have shown increasing interest in extracting/classifying semantic relations, most previous studies have basically relied on lexical patterns between terms. This paper proposes a novel way to accomplish the task: a system that captures a physical size of an entity. Experimental results revealed that our proposed method is feasible and prevents the problems inherent in other methods.

1 Introduction

Classification of semantic relations is important to NLP as it would benefit many NLP applications, such as machine translation and information retrieval.

Researchers have already proposed various schemes. For example, Hearst (1992) manually designed lexico-syntactic patterns for extracting is-a relations. Berland and Charniak (1999) proposed a similar method for part-whole relations. Brin (1998) employed a bootstrapping algorithm for more specific relations (author-book relations). Kim and Baldwin (2006) and Moldovan et al.(2004) focused on nominal relations in compound nouns. Turney (2005) measured relation similarity between two words. While these methods differ, they all utilize lexical patterns between two entities.

Within this context, our goal was to utilize information specific to an entity. Although entities contain many types of information, we focused on the **physical size** of an entity. Here, **physical size** refers to the typical width/height of an entity. For example, we consider *book* to have a physical size of 20×25 cm, and *book* to have a size of 10×10 m, etc.

We chose to use physical size for the following reasons:

1. Most entities (except abstract entities) have a physical size.

2. Several semantic relations are sensitive to physical size. For example, a content-container relation ($e1$ content-container $e2$) naturally means that $e1$ has a smaller size than $e2$. A *book* is also smaller than its container, *library*. A part-whole relation has a similar constraint.

Our next problem was how to determine physical sizes. First, we used Google to conduct Web searches using queries such as "*book (*cm x*cm)*" and "*library (*m x*m)*". Next, we extracted numeric expressions from the search results and used the average value as the physical size.

Experimental results revealed that our proposed approach is feasible and prevents the problems inherent in other methods.

2 Corpus

We used a corpus provided by SemEval2007 Task #4 training set. This corpus consisted of 980 annotated sentences (140 sentences×7 relations). Table 1 presents an example.

Although the corpus contained a large quantity of information such as WordNet sense keys, comments, etc., we used only the most pertinent information: entity1 ($e1$), entity2 ($e2$), and its relation (true/false)

Proceedings of the 4th International Workshop on Semantic Evaluations (SemEval-2007), pages 464–467,
Prague, June 2007.

```
The <e1>library</e1> contained <e2>books
</e2> of guidance on the processes.
WordNet(e1) = "library\%1:14:00::",
WordNet(e2) = "book\%1:10:00::",
Content-Container(e2, e1) = "true",
Query = "the * contained books"
```

Table 1: An Example of Task#4 Corpus.

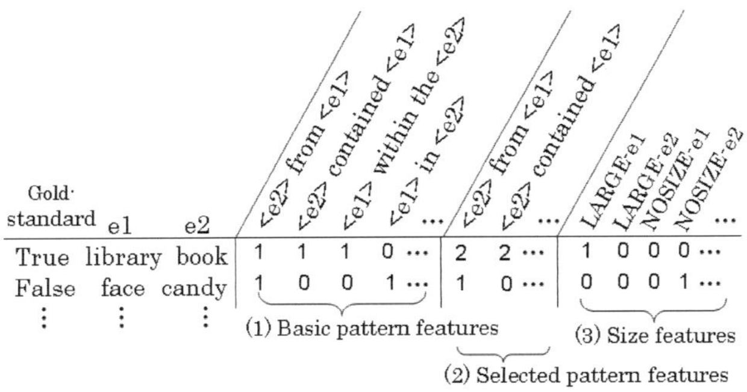

Figure 1: Three types of Features.

[1]. For example, we extracted a triple example (*library*, *book*, *true* from Table 1.

3 Method

We applied support vector machine (SVM)-based learning (Vapnik, 1999) using three types of features: (1) basic pattern features (Section 3.1), (2) selected pattern features (Section 3.2), and (3) physical size features (Section 3.3). Figure 1 presents some examples of these features.

3.1 Basic Pattern Features

First, the system finds lexical patterns that co-occur with semantic relations between two entities ($e1$ and $e2$). It does so by conducting searches using two queries "*e1 * e2*" and "*e2 * e1*". For example, two queries, "*library * book*" and "*book * library*", are generated from Table 1.

Then, the system extracts the word (or word sequences) between two entities from the snippets in the top 1,000 search results. We considered the extracted word sequences to be basic patterns. For example, given "*...library contains the book...*", the basic pattern is "*(e1) contains the (e2)*"[2].

We gathered basic patterns for each relation, and identified if each pattern had been obtained as a SVM feature or not (1 or 0). We refer to these features as **basic pattern features**.

3.2 Selected Pattern Features

Because basic pattern features are generated only from snippets, precise co-occurrence statistics are not available. Therefore, the system searches again with more specific queries, such as "*library contains the book*". However, this second search is a heavy burden for a search engine, requiring huge numbers of queries (# of samples $\times$ # of basic patterns).

We thus selected the most informative n patterns (STEP1) and conducted specific searches (# of samples $\times$ n basic patterns)(STEP2) as follows:

STEP1: To select the most informative patterns, we applied a decision tree (C4.5)(Quinlan, 1987) and selected the basic patterns located in the top n branches [3].

STEP2: Then, the system searched again using the selected patterns. We considered log weighted hits ($\log_{10}|hits|$) to be selected pattern features. For example, if "*library contains the book*" produced 120,000 hits in Google, it yields the value $\log_{10}(12,000) = 5$.

3.3 Physical Size Features

As noted in Section 1, we theorized that an entity's size could be a strong clue for some semantic relations.

We estimated entity size using the following queries:

1. "$< entity >$ (* cm x * cm)",
2. "$< entity >$ (* x * cm)",
3. "$< entity >$ (* m x * m)",
4. "$< entity >$ (* x * m)".

In these queries, $< entity >$ indicates a slot for each entity, such as "*book*", "*library*", etc. Then, the system examines the search results for the numerous expressions located in "*" and considers the average value to be the size.

[1]Our system is classified as an A4 system, and therefore does not use WordNet or Query.

[2]This operation does not handle any stop-words. Therefore, "*(e1) contains THE (e2)*" and "*(e1) contains (e2)*" are different patterns.

[3]In the experiments in Section 4, we set $n = 10$.

	Precision	Recall	$F_{\beta=1}$
PROPOSED	**0.57 (=284/497)**	**0.60 (=284/471)**	**0.58**
+SEL	0.56 (=281/496)	0.59 (=281/471)	0.57
+SIZE	0.53 (=269/507)	0.57 (=269/471)	0.54
BASELINE	0.53 (=259/487)	0.54 (=259/471)	0.53

Table 2: Results.

When results of size expressions were insufficient (numbers < 10), we considered the entity to be non-physical, i.e., to have no size.

By applying the obtained sizes, the system generates a size feature, consisting of six flags:

1. **LARGE-e1**: ($e1$'s X $>$ $e2$'s X) and ($e1$'s Y $>$ $e2$'s Y)
2. **LARGE-e2**: ($e1$'s X $<$ $e2$'s X) and ($e1$'s Y $<$ $e2$'s Y)
3. **NOSIZE-e1**: only $e1$ has no size.
4. **NOSIZE-e2**: only $e2$ has no size.
5. **NOSIZE-BOTH**: Both $e1$ and $e2$ have no size.
6. **OTHER**: Other.

4 Experiments

4.1 Experimental Set-up

To evaluate the performance of our system, we used a SemEval-Task No#4 training set. We compared the following methods using a ten-fold cross-validation test:

1. **BASELINE**: with only basic pattern features.
2. **+SIZE**: BASELINE with size features.
3. **+SEL**: BASELINE with selected pattern features.
4. **PROPOSED**: BASELINE with both size and selected pattern features.

For SVM learning, we used TinySVM with a linear kernel[4].

4.2 Results

Table 2 presents the results. PROPOSED was the most accurate, demonstrating the basic feasibility of our approach.

Table 3 presents more detailed results. +SIZE made a contribution to some relations (REL2 and REL4). Particularly for REL4, +SIZE significantly boosted accuracy (using McNemar tests (Gillick and Cox, 1989); $p = 0.05$). However, contrary to our expectations, size features were disappointing for part-whole relations (REL6) and content-container relations (REL7).

[4]http://chasen.org/ taku/software/TinySVM/

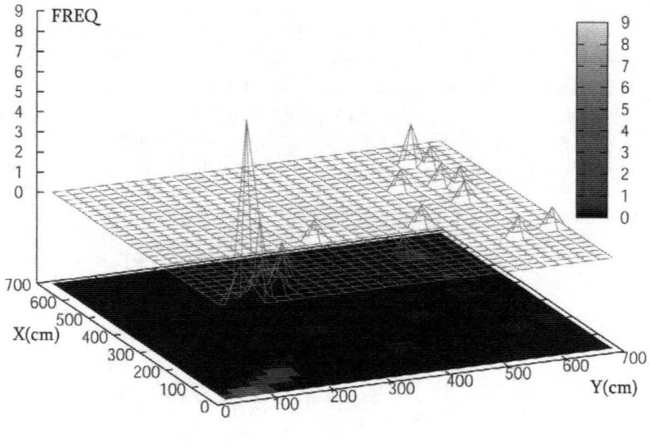

Figure 2: The Size of a "Car".

The reason for this was mainly the difficulty in estimating size. Table 4 lists the sizes of several entities, revealing some strange results, such as a *library* sized 12.1×8.4 cm, a *house* sized 53×38 cm, and a *car* sized 39×25 cm. These sizes are unusually small for the following reasons:

1. Some entities (e.g."*car*") rarely appear with their size,
2. In contrast, entities such as "*toy car*" or "*mini car*" frequently appear with a size.

Figure 2 presents the size distribution of "*car*." Few instances appeared of real cars sized approximately 500×400 cm, while very small cars smaller than 100×100 cm appeared frequently. Our current method of calculating average size is ineffective under this type of situation.

In the future, using physical size as a clue for determining a semantic relation will require resolving this problem.

5 Conclusion

We briefly presented a method for obtaining the size of an entity and proposed a method for classifying semantic relations using entity size. Experimental results revealed that the proposed approach yielded slightly higher performance than a baseline, demonstrating its feasibility. If we are able to estimate en-

Relation		PROPOSED	+SEL	+SIZE	BASELINE
	Precision	**0.60 (=50/83)**	0.56 (=53/93)	0.54 (=53/98)	0.50 (=53/106)
REL1	Recall	0.68 (=50/73)	**0.72 (=53/73)**	**0.72 (=53/73)**	**0.72 (=53/73)**
(Cause-Effect)	$F_{\beta=1}$	**0.64**	0.63	0.59	0.61
	Precision	0.59 (=43/72)	**0.60 (=44/73)**	0.56 (=45/79)	0.55 (=44/79)
REL2	Recall	0.60 (=43/71)	0.61 (=44/71)	**0.63 (=45/71)**	0.61 (=44/71)
(Instrument-Agency)	$F_{\beta=1}$	0.60	**0.61**	0.59	0.58
	Precision	0.70 (=56/80)	**0.73 (=55/75)**	0.65 (=54/82)	0.68 (=51/74)
REL3	Recall	**0.65 (=56/85)**	0.64 (=55/85)	0.63 (=54/85)	0.60 (=51/85)
(Product-Producer)	$F_{\beta=1}$	0.67	**0.68**	0.64	0.64
	Precision	0.41 (=23/56)	0.35 (=18/51)	0.48 (=24/49)	**0.52 (=13/25)**
REL4	Recall	0.42 (=23/54)	0.33 (=18/54)	**0.44 (=24/54)**	0.24 (=13/54)
(Origin-Entity)	$F_{\beta=1}$	0.41	0.34	**0.46**	0.32
	Precision	**0.62 (=40/64)**	0.61 (=40/65)	0.56 (=28/50)	0.56 (=29/51)
REL5	Recall	**0.68 (=40/58)**	**0.68 (=40/58)**	0.48 (=28/58)	0.50 (=29/58)
(Theme-Tool)	$F_{\beta=1}$	**0.65**	**0.65**	0.51	0.53
	Precision	0.45 (=46/101)	**0.46 (=46/100)**	0.41 (=49/118)	0.43 (=53/123)
REL6	Recall	0.70 (=46/65)	0.70 (=46/65)	0.75 (=49/65)	**0.81 (=53/65)**
(Part-Whole)	$F_{\beta=1}$	0.55	0.55	0.53	**0.56**
	Precision	0.63 (26/41)	**0.64 (=25/39)**	0.51 (=16/31)	0.55 (=16/29)
REL7	Recall	**0.40 (26/65)**	0.38 (=25/65)	0.24 (=16/65)	0.24 (=16/65)
(Content-Container)	$F_{\beta=1}$	**0.49**	0.48	0.33	0.34

Table 3: Detailed Results.

entity	#	size
library	51	12.1×8.4 m
room	204	5.4×3.5 m
man	75	1.5×0.5 m
benches	33	93×42 cm
granite	68	76×48 cm
sink	34	57×25 cm
house	86	53×38 cm
books	50	46×24 cm
car	91	39×25 cm
turtles	15	38×23 cm
food	38	35×26 cm
oats	16	24×13 cm
tumor shrinkage	6	-
habitat degradation	5	-

Table 4: Some Examples of Entity Sizes.

"#" indicates the number of obtained size expressions.

"-" indicates a "NO-SIZE" entity.

tity sizes more precisely in the future, the system will become much more accurate.

References

Matthew Berland and Eugene Charniak. 1999. Finding parts in very large corpora. In *Proceedings of the Annual Conference of the Association for Computational Linguistics (ACL1999)*, pages 57–64.

Sergey Brin. 1998. Extracting patterns and relations from the world wide web. In *WebDB Workshop at 6th International Conference on Extending Database Technology, EDBT'98*, pages 172–183.

L. Gillick and SJ Cox. 1989. Some statistical issues in the comparison of speech recognition algorithms. In *Proceedings of IEEE International Conference on Acoustics, Speech, and Signal Processing*, pages 532–535.

M. Hearst. 1992. Automatic acquisition of hyponyms from large text corpora. In *Proceedings of International Conference on Computational Linguistics (COLING1992)*, pages 539–545.

Su Nam Kim and Timothy Baldwin. 2006. Interpreting semantic relations in noun compounds via verb semantics. In *Proceedings of the COLING/ACL 2006 Main Conference Poster Sessions*, pages 491–498.

D. Moldovan, A. Badulescu, M. Tatu, D. Antohe, and R. Girju. 2004. Models for the semantic classification of noun phrases. *Proceedings of HLT/NAACL-2004 Workshop on Computational Lexical Semantics*.

J.R. Quinlan. 1987. Simplifying decision trees. *International Journal of Man-Machine Studies*, 27(1):221–234.

Peter D. Turney. 2005. Measuring semantic similarity by latent relational analysis. In *Proceedings of the Nineteenth International Joint Conference on Artificial Intelligence (IJCAI-05)*, pages 1136–1141.

Vladimir Vapnik. 1999. *The Nature of Statistical Learning Theory*. Springer-Verlag.

UVA: Language Modeling Techniques for Web People Search

Krisztian Balog
ISLA, University of Amsterdam
kbalog@science.uva.nl

Leif Azzopardi
University of Glasgow
leif@dcs.gla.ac.uk

Maarten de Rijke
ISLA, University of Amsterdam
mdr@science.uva.nl

Abstract

In this paper we describe our participation in the SemEval 2007 Web People Search task. Our main aim in participating was to adapt language modeling tools for the task, and to experiment with various document representations. Our main finding is that single pass clustering, using title, snippet and body to represent documents, is the most effective setting.

1 Introduction

The goal of the Web People Search task at SemEval 2007 was to disambiguate person names in a web searching scenario (Artiles et al., 2007). Participants were presented with the following setting: given a list of documents retrieved from a web search engine using a person's name as a query, group documents that refer to the same individual.

Our aim with the participation was to adapt language modeling techniques to this task. To this end, we employed two methods: *single pass clustering* (SPC) and *probabilistic latent semantic analysis* (PLSA). Our main finding is that the former leads to high purity, while the latter leads to high inverse purity scores. Furthermore, we experimented with various document representations, based on the snippets and body text. Highest overall performance was achieved with the combination of both.

The remainder of the paper is organized as follows. In Section 2 we present the two approaches we employed for clustering documents. Next, in Section 3 we discuss document representation and preprocessing. Section 4 reports on our experiments. We conclude in Section 5.

2 Modeling

2.1 Single Pass Clustering

We employed single pass clustering (Hill., 1968) to automatically assign pages to clusters, where we assume that each cluster is a set of pages related to one particular sense of the person.

The process for assignment was performed as follows: The first document was taken and assigned to the first cluster. Then each subsequent document was compared against each cluster with a similarity measure based on the log odds ratio (initially, there was only the initial one created). A document was assigned to the most likely cluster, as long as the similarity score was higher than a threshold α; otherwise, the document was assigned to a new cluster, unless the maximum number of desired clusters η had been reached; in that case the document was assigned to the last cluster (i.e., the left overs).

The similarity measure we employed was the log odds ratio to decide whether the document was more likely to be generated from that cluster or not. This approach follows Kalt (1996)'s work on document classification using the document likelihood by representing the cluster as a multinomial term distribution (i.e., a cluster language model) and predicting the probability of a document D, given the cluster language model, i.e., $p(D|\theta_C)$. It is assumed that the terms t in a document are sampled *independently and identically*, so the log odds ratio is calculated as

Proceedings of the 4th International Workshop on Semantic Evaluations (SemEval-2007), pages 468–471,
Prague, June 2007.

follows:

$$\log O(D,C) = \log \frac{p(D|\theta_C)}{p(D|\theta_{\bar{C}})} \quad (1)$$
$$= \log \frac{\prod_{t \in D} p(t|\theta_C)^{n(t,D)}}{\prod_{t \in D} p(t|\theta_{\bar{C}})^{n(t,D)}},$$

where $n(t,D)$ is the number of times a term appears in a document, and the $\theta_{\overline{C}}$ represents the language model that represents not being in the cluster. Note this is similar to a well-known relevance modeling approach, where the clusters are relevance and non-relevance, except, here, it is applied in the context of classification as done by Kalt (1996).

The cluster language model was estimated by performing a linear interpolation between the empirical probability of a term occurring in the cluster $p(t|C)$ and the background model $p(t)$, the probability of a term occurring at random in the collection, i.e., $p(t|\theta_C) = \lambda \cdot p(t|C) + (1-\lambda) \cdot p(t)$, where λ was set to 0.5.[1] The "not in the cluster" language model was approximated by using the background model $p(t)$. The similarity threshold above (used for deciding whether to assign a document to an existing cluster) was set to $\alpha = 1$, and η was set to 100.

2.2 Probabilistic Latent Semantic Analysis

The second method for disambiguation we employed was probabilistic latent semantic analysis (PLSA) (Hofmann, 1999). PLSA clusters documents based on the term-document co-occurrence which results in semantic decomposition of the term document matrix into a lower dimensional latent space. Formally, PLSA can be defined as:

$$p(t,d) = p(d) \sum_z p(t|z)p(z|d), \quad (2)$$

where $p(t,d)$ is the probability of term t and document d co-occurring, $p(t|z)$ is the probability of a term given a latent topic z and $p(z|d)$ is the probability of a latent topic in a document. The prior probability of the document, $p(d)$, was assumed to be uniform. This decomposition can be obtained automatically using the EM algorithm (Hofmann, 1999). Once estimated, we assumed that each latent topic represents one of the different senses of the person, so the document is assigned to one of the person-topics. Here, we made the assignment based on the maximum $p(z|d)$, so if $p(z|d) = \max p(z|d)$, then d was assigned to z.

In order to automatically select the number of person-topics, we performed the following process to decide when the appropriate number of person-topics (defined by k) have been identified: (1) we set $k = 2$ and computed the log-likelihood of the decomposition on a held out sample of data; (2) we incremented k and computed the log-likelihood; if the log-likelihood had increased over a given threshold (0.001) then we repeated step 2, else (3) we stopped as we have maximized the log-likelihood of the decompositions, with respect to the number person-topics. This point was assumed to be the optimal with respect to the number of person senses. Since, we are focusing on identifying the true number of classes, this should result in higher inverse purity, whereas with the single pass clustering the number of clusters is not restricted, and so we would expect single pass clustering to produce more clusters but with a higher purity.

We used Lemur[2] and the PennAspect implementation of PLSA (Schein et al., 2002) for our experiments, where the parameters for PLSA where set as follows. For each k we performed 10 initializations where the best initialization in terms of log-likelihood was selected. The EM algorithm was run using tempering with up to 100 EM Steps. For tempering the setting suggested in (Hofmann, 1999) were used. The models were estimated on 90% of the data and 10% of the data was held out in order to compute the log-likelihood of the decompositions.

3 Document Representation

This section describes the various document representations we considered, and preprocessing steps we applied.

For each document, we considered the *title*, *snippet*, and *body* text. Title and snippet were provided by the output of the search engine results (`person_name.xml` files), while the body text was extracted from the crawled `index.html` files.

[1]This value was not tuned but selected based on best performing range suggested by Lavrenko and Croft (2001).

[2]`http://www.lemurproject.org`

Method	Title+Snippet				Body				Title+Snippet+Body			
	Pur	InvP	$F_{0.5}$	$F_{0.2}$	Pur	InvP	$F_{0.5}$	$F_{0.2}$	Pur	InvP	$F_{0.5}$	$F_{0.2}$
Train data												
SPC	0.903	0.298	0.422	0.336	0.776	0.416	0.482	0.434	0.768	0.438	0.506	0.456
PLSA	0.589	0.833	0.636	0.716	0.591	0.656	0.563	0.592	0.579	0.724	0.588	0.641
Test data												
SPC	0.867	0.541	0.640	0.575	0.818	0.570	0.647	0.596	0.810	0.607	0.669	0.628
PLSA	0.292	0.892	0.383	0.533	0.311	0.869	0.413	0.563	0.305	0.923	0.405	0.566

Table 1: Results of the clustering methods using various document representations.

3.1 Acquiring Plain-Text Content from HTML

Our aim is to extract the plain-text content from HTML pages and to leave out blocks or segments that contain little or no useful textual information (headers, footers, navigation menus, adverts, etc.). To this end, we exploit the fact that most webpages consist of blocks of text content with relatively little markup, interspersed with navigation links, images with captions, etc. These segments of a page are usually separated by block-level HTML tags. Our extractor first generates a syntax tree from the HTML document. We then traverse this tree while bookkeeping the stretch of uninterrupted non-HTML text we have seen. Each time we encounter a block-level HTML tag we examine the buffer of text we have collected, and if it is longer than a threshold, we output it. The threshold for the minimal length of buffer text was empirically set to 10. In other words, we only consider segments of the page, separated by block-level HTML tags, that contain 10 or more words.

3.2 Indexing

We used a standard (English) stopword list but we did not apply stemming. A separate index was built for each person, using the Lemur toolkit. We created three index variations: `title+snippet`, `body`, and `title+snippet+body`.

In our official run we used the `title+snippet+body` index; however, in the next section we report on all three variations.

4 Results

Table 1 reports on the results of our experiments using the Single Pass Clustering (SPC) and Probabilistic Latent Semantic Analysis (PLSA) methods with various document representations. The measures (purity, inverse purity, and F-score with $\alpha = 0.5$ and $\alpha = 0.2$) are presented for both the train and test data sets.

The results clearly demonstrate the difference in the behaviors of the two clustering methods. SPC assigns people to the same cluster with high precision, as is reflected by the high purity scores. However, it is overly restrictive, and documents that belong to the same person are distributed into a number of clusters, which should be further merged. This explains the low inverse purity scores. Further experiments should be performed to evaluate to which extent this restrictive behavior could be controlled by the α parameter of the method.

In contrast with SPC, the PLSA method produces far fewer clusters per person. These clusters may cover multiple referents of a name, as is witnessed by the low purity scores. On the other hand, inverse purity scores are very high, which means referents are usually not dispersed among clusters.

As to the various document representations, we found that highest overall performance was achieved with the combination of title, snippet, and body text.

Since the data was not homogenous, it would be interesting to see how performance varies on the different names. We leave this analysis to further work.

Our official run employed the SPC method, using the `title+snippet+body` index. The results of our official submission are presented in Table 2. Our purity score was the highest of all submissions, and our system was ranked overall 4th, based on the $F_{\alpha=0.5}$ measure.

	Pur	InvP	$F_{0.5}$	$F_{0.2}$
Lowest	0.30	0.60	0.40	0.55
Highest	0.81	0.95	0.78	0.83
Average	0.54	0.82	0.60	0.69
UVA	0.81	0.60	0.67	0.62

Table 2: Official submission results and statistics.

5 Conclusions

We have described our participation in the SemEval 2007 Web People Search task. Our main aim in participating was to adapt language modeling tools for the task, and to experiment with various document representations. Our main finding is that single pass clustering, using title, snippet and body to represent documents, is the most effective setting.
We explored the two very different clustering schemes with contrasting characteristics. Looking forward, possible improvements might be pursued by combining the two approaches into a more robust system.

6 Acknowledgments

Krisztian Balog was supported by the Netherlands Organization for Scientific Research (NWO) under project number 220-80-001. Maarten de Rijke was supported by NWO under project numbers 017.001.190, 220-80-001, 264-70-050, 354-20-005, 600.065.120, 612-13-001, 612.000.106, 612.066.-302, 612.069.006, 640.001.501, 640.002.501, and by the E.U. IST programme of the 6th FP for RTD under project MultiMATCH contract IST-033104.

References

J. Artiles, J. Gonzalo, and S. Sekine. 2007. The SemEval-2007 WePS Evaluation: Establishing a benchmark for the Web People Search Task. In *Proceedings of Semeval 2007, Association for Computational Linguistics.*

D. R. Hill. 1968. A vector clustering technique. In Samuelson, editor, *Mechanised Information Storage, Retrieval and Dissemination*, North-Holland, Amsterdam.

Thomas Hofmann. 1999. Probabilistic latent semantic analysis. In *Proc. of Uncertainty in Artificial Intelligence, UAI'99*, Stockholm.

T. Kalt. 1996. A new probabilistic model of text classification and retrieval. Technical Report CIIR TR98-18, University of Massachusetts, January 25, 1996.

V. Lavrenko and W. B. Croft. 2001. Relevance-based language models. In *Proceedings of the 24th annual international ACM SIGIR conference*, pages 120–127, New Orleans, LA. ACM Press.

Andrew I. Schein, Alexandrin Popescul, Lyle H. Ungar, and David M. Pennock. 2002. Methods and metrics for cold-start recommendations. In *SIGIR '02: Proceedings of the 25th annual international ACM SIGIR conference on Research and development in information retrieval*, pages 253–260, New York, NY, USA. ACM Press. See http://www.cis.upenn.edu/datamining/software_dist/PennAspect/.

UVAVU: WordNet Similarity and Lexical Patterns for Semantic Relation Classification

Willem Robert van Hage
TNO Science & Industry
Stieltjesweg 1, 2628CK Delft
the Netherlands
wrvhage@few.vu.nl

Sophia Katrenko
HCSL, University of Amsterdam
Kruislaan 419, 1098VA Amsterdam
the Netherlands
katrenko@science.uva.nl

Abstract

The system we propose to learning semantic relations consists of two parallel components. For our final submission we used components based on the similarity measures defined over WordNet and the patterns extracted from the Web and WMTS. Other components using syntactic structures were explored but not used for the final run.

1 Experimental Set-up

The system we used to classify the semantic relations consists of two parallel binary classifiers. We ran this system for each of the seven semantic relations separately. Each classifier predicts for each instance of the relation whether it holds or not. The predictions of all the classifiers are aggregated for each instance by disjunction. That is to say, each instance is predicted to be false by default unless any of the classifiers gives evidence against this.

To generate the submitted predictions we used two parallel classifiers: (1) a classifier that combines eleven WordNet-based similarity measures, see Sec. 2.1, and (2) a classifier that learns lexical patterns from Google and the Waterloo Multi-Text System (WMTS)(Turney, 2004) snippets and applies these on the same corpora, see Sec. 2.2.

Three other classifiers we experimented with, but that were not used to generate the submitted predictions: (3) a classifier that uses string kernel methods on the dependency paths of the training sentences, see Sec. 3.1, (4) a classifier that uses string kernels on the local context of the subject and object nominals in the training sentences, see Sec. 3.2 and (5) a classifier that uses hand-made lexical patterns on Google and WMTS, see Sec. 3.3.

2 Submitted Run

2.1 WordNet-based Similarity Measures

WordNet 3.0 (Fellbaum, 1998) is the most frequently used lexical database of English. As this resource consists of lexical and semantic relations, its use constitutes an appealing option to learning relations. In particular, we believe that given two mentions of the same semantic relation, their arguments should also be similar. Or, in analogy learning terms, if $R_1(X_1,Y_1)$ and $R_2(X_2,Y_2)$ are relation mentions of the same type, then $X_1 :: Y_1$ as $X_2 :: Y_2$. Our preliminary experiments with WordNet suggested that few arguments of each relation are connected by immediate hyperonymy or meronymy relations. As a result, we decided to use similarity measures defined over WordNet (Pedersen et al., 2004). The WordNet::Similarity package (Pedersen et al., 2004) includes 11 different measures, which mostly use either the WordNet glosses (*lesk* or *vector* measures) or the paths between a pair of concepts (*lch*; *wup*) to determine their relatedness.

To be able to use WordNet::Similarity, we mapped all WordNet sense keys from the training and test sets to the earlier WordNet version (2.1). Given a relation $R(X,Y)$, we computed the relatedness scores for each pair of arguments X and Y. The scores together with the sense keys of arguments were further used as features for the machine learning method. As there is no a priori knowledge on what measures are the most important for each rela-

Proceedings of the 4th International Workshop on Semantic Evaluations (SemEval-2007), pages 472–475,
Prague, June 2007.

tion, all of them were used and no feature selection step has been taken.

We experimented with a number of machine learning methods such as k-nearest neighbour algorithm, logistic regression, bayesian networks and others. For each relation a method performing best on the training set was selected (using 5-fold cross-validation).

2.2 Learnt Lexical Patterns

This classifier models the intuition that when a pair of nominals is used in similar phrases as another pair they share at least one relation, and when no such phrases can be found they do not share any relation. Applied to the semantic relation classification problem this means that when a pair in the test set can be found in the same patterns as pairs from the training set, the classification for the pair will be true.

To find the patterns we followed step 1 to 6 described in (Turney, 2006), with the exception that we used both Google and the WMTS to compute pattern frequency.

First we extracted the pairs of nominals $\langle X,Y \rangle$ from the training sentences and created one Google query and a set of WMTS queries for each pair. The Google queries were of the form `"X * Y" OR "Y * X"`. Currently, Google performs morphological normalization on every query, so we did not make separate queries for various endings of the nominals. For the WMTS we did make separate queries for various morphological variations. We used the following set of suffixes: '-tion(s|al)', '-ly', '-ist', '-ical', '-y', '-ing', '-ed', '-ies', and '-s'. For this we used Peter Turney's `pairs` Perl package. The WMTS queries looked like `[n]>([5].."X"..[i].."Y"..[5])` and `[n]>([5].."Y"..[i].."X"..[5])` for $i = 1,2,3$ and $n = i+12$, and for each variation of X and Y. Then we extracted sentences from the Google snippets and cut out a context of size 5, so that we were left with similar text segments as those returned by the WMTS queries. We merged the lists of text segments and counted all n-grams that contained both nominals for $n = 1$ to 6. We substituted the nominals by variables in the n-grams with a count greater than 10 and used these as patterns for the classifier. An example of such a pattern for the Cause-Effect relation is `"generation of Y by X"`. After this we followed step 3 to 6 of (Turney, 2006), which left us with a matrix for each of the seven semantic relations, where each row represented a pair of nominals and each column represented the frequency of a pattern, and where each pair was classified as either true or false. The straightforward way to find pattern frequencies for the pairs in the test set would be to fill in these patterns with the pairs of nominals from the test set. This was not feasible given the time limitation on the task. So instead, for each pair of nominals in the test set we gathered the top-1000 snippets and computed pattern frequencies by counting how often the nominals occur in every pattern on this set text segments. We constructed a matrix from these frequencies in the same way as for the training set, but without classifications for the pairs. We experimented with various machine learning algorithms to predict the classes of the pairs. We chose to use k-nearest neighbors, because it was the only algorithm that gave more subtle predictions than true for every pair or false for every pair. For each semantic relation we used the value of k that produced the highest F_1 score on 5-fold cross validation on the training data.

3 Additional Runs

3.1 String Kernels on Dependency Paths

It has been a long tradition to use syntactic structures for relation extraction task. Some of the methods as in (Katrenko and Adriaans, 2004) have used information extracted from the dependency trees. We followed similar approach by considering the paths between each pair of arguments X and Y. Ideally, if each syntactic structure is a tree, there is only one path from one node to the other. After we have extracted paths, we used them as input for the string kernel methods (Hal Daumé III, 2004). The advantage of using string kernels is that they can handle sequences of different lengths and already proved to be efficient for a number of tasks.

All sentences in the training data were parsed using MINIPAR (Lin, 1998). From each dependency tree we extracted a dependency path (if any) between the arguments by collecting all lemmas (nodes) and syntactic functions (edges). The sequences we obtained were fed into string kernel.

To assess the results, we carried out 5-fold cross-validation. Even by optimizing the parameters of the kernel (such as the length of subsequences) for each relation, the highest accuracy we obtained was equal 61,54% (on Origin-Entity relation) and the lowest was accuracy for the Instrument-Agency relation (50,48%).

3.2 String Kernels on Local Context

Alternatively to syntactic information, we also extracted the snippets of the fixed length from each sentence. For each relation mention of $R(X,Y)$, all tokens between the relation arguments X and Y were collected along with at most three tokens to the left and to the right. Unfortunately, the results we obtained on the training set were comparable to those obtained by string kernels on dependency paths and less accurate than the results provided by WordNet similarity measures or patterns extracted from the Web and WMTS. As a consequence, string kernel methods were not used for the final submission.

3.3 Manually-created Lexical Patterns

The results of the method described in Sec. 2.2 are quite far below what we expected given earlier results in the literature (Turney, 2006; van Hage, Katrenko, and Schreiber, 2005; van Hage, Kolb, and Schreiber, 2006; Berland and Charniak, 2006; Etzioni et al., 2004). We think this is caused by the fact that many pairs in the training set are non-stereotypical examples. So often the most commonly described relation of such a pair is not the relation we try to classify with the pair. For example, common associations with the pair ⟨body,parents⟩ are that it is the parents' body, or that the parents are member of some organizing body, while it is a positive example for the Product-Producer relation. We wanted to see if this could be the case by testing whether more intuitive patterns give better results on the test set. The patterns we manually created for each relation are shown in Table 1. If a pair gives any results for these patterns on Google or WMTS, we classify the pair as true, otherwise we classify it as false. The results are shown in Table 2. We did not use these results for the submitted run, because only automatic runs were permitted. The manual patterns did not yield many useful results at all. Apparently intuitive patterns do not capture what is required to classify the relations in the test set. The patterns we used for the Part-Whole (6) relation had an average Precision of .50, which is much lower than the average Precision found in (van Hage, Kolb, and Schreiber, 2006), which was around 0.88. We conclude that both the sets of training and test examples capture different semantics of the relations than the intuitive ones, which causes common sense background knowledge, such as Google to produce bad results.

rel.	patterns
1.	X causes Y, X caused by Y, X * cause Y
2.	X used Y, X uses Y, X * with a Y
3.	X made by Y, X produced by Y, Y makes X, Y produces X
4.	Y comes from X, X * source of Y, Y * from * X
5.	Y * to * X, Y * for * X, used Y for * X
6.	X in Y, Y contains X, X from Y
7.	Y contains X, X in Y, X containing Y, X into Y

Table 1: Hand-written patterns.

relation	N	Prec.	Recall	F_1	Acc.
1. Cause-Effect	6	1	0.15	0.25	0.56
2. Instr.-Agency	2	1	0.05	0.10	0.54
3. Prod.-Prod.	4	0.75	0.05	0.09	0.35
4. Origin-Ent.	6	0.33	0.05	0.09	0.35
5. Theme-Tool	2	0	0	0	0.56
6. Part-Whole	16	0.50	0.31	0.38	0.64
7. Cont.-Cont.	11	0.54	0.16	0.24	0.50

Table 2: Results for hand-written lexical patterns on Google and WMTS.

4 Results

4.1 WordNet-based Similarity Measures

Table 3 shows the results of the WordNet-based similarity measure method. In the 'methods' column, the abbreviation LR stands for logistic regression, K-NN stands for k-nearest neighbour, and DT stands for decision trees.

relation	method	Prec.	Recall	F_1	Acc.
1. Cause-Effect	LR	0.48	0.51	0.49	0.45
2. Instr.-Agency	DT	0.65	0.63	0.64	0.62
3. Prod.-Prod.	DT	0.67	0.50	0.57	0.46
4. Origin-Ent.	LR	0.50	0.47	0.49	0.49
5. Theme-Tool	LR	0.54	0.52	0.53	0.62
6. Part-Whole	DT	0.54	0.73	0.62	0.67
7. Cont.-Cont.	2-NN	0.66	0.55	0.60	0.62

Table 3: Results for similarity-measure methods.

4.2 Learnt Lexical Patterns

Table 4 shows the results of the learnt lexical patterns method. For all relations we used the k-nearest neighbour method.

relation	method	Prec.	Recall	F_1	Acc.
1. Cause-Effect	3-NN	0.53	0.76	0.63	0.54
2. Instr.-Agency	2-NN	0.47	0.89	0.62	0.46
3. Prod.-Prod.	2-NN	0	0	0	0.33
4. Origin-Ent.	2-NN	0.47	0.22	0.30	0.54
5. Theme-Tool	3-NN	0.39	0.93	0.55	0.38
6. Part-Whole	2-NN	0.36	1	0.53	0.36
7. Cont.-Cont.	2-NN	0.51	0.97	0.67	0.51

Table 4: Results for learnt lexical patterns on Google and WMTS.

5 Discussion

Our methods had the most difficulty with classifying relation 1, 3 and 4. We wanted to see if human assessors perform less consistent for those relations. If so, then those relations would simply be harder to classify. Otherwise, our system performed worse for those relations. We manually assessed ten sample sentences from the test set, five of which were positive examples and five were false examples. The result of a comparison with the test set is shown in Table 5. The numbers listed there represent the fraction of examples on which we agreed with the judges of the test set. There was quite a

relation	inter-judge agreement judge 1	judge 2
1. Cause-Effect	0.93	0.93
2. Instrument-Agency	0.77	0.77
3. Product-Producer	0.87	0.80
4. Origin-Entity	0.80	0.77
5. Theme-Tool	0.80	0.77
6. Part-Whole	0.97	1.00
7. Content-Container	0.77	0.77

Table 5: Inter-judge agreement.

large variation in the inter-judge agreement, but for relation 1 and 3 the consensus was high. We conclude that the reason for our low performance on those relations are not caused by the difficulty of the sentences, but due to other reasons. Our intuition is that the sentences, especially those of relation 1 and 3, are easily decidable by humans, but that they are non-stereotypical examples of the relation, and thus hard to learn. The following example sentence breaks common-sense domain and range restrictions: Product-Producer #142 *"And, of course, everyone wants to prove the truth of their beliefs through experience, but the <e1>belief</e1> begets the <e2>experience</e2>."* The common-sense domain and range restriction of the Product-Producer relation are respectively something like 'Entity' and 'Agent'. However, 'belief' is generally not considered to be an entity, and 'experience' not an agent. The definition of Product-Producer relation used for the Challenge is more flexible and allows therefore many examples which are difficult to find by such common-sense resources as Google or WordNet.

References

Matthew Berland and Eugene Charniak. 1999. Finding Parts in Very Large Corpora. *In Proceedings of ACL 1999.*

Christiane Fellbaum (ed.). 1998. WordNet: An Electronic Lexical Database. *MIT Press.*

Hal Daumé III. 2004. SVMsequel Tutorial Manual. *Available at* `http://www.cs.utah.edu/~hal/SVMsequel/svmsequel.pdf`

Oren Etzioni et al. 2004. Methods for Domain-Independent Information Extraction from the Web: An Experimental Comparison. *In Proceedings of AAAI 2004.*

Willem Robert van Hage, Sophia Katrenko, and Guus Schreiber. 2005. A Method to Combine Linguistic Ontology-Mapping Techniques. *In Proceedings of ISWC 2005.*

Willem Robert van Hage, Hap Kolb, and Guus Schreiber. 2006. A Method for Learning Part-Whole Relations. *In Proceedings of ISWC 2006.*

Sophia Katrenko and Pieter Adriaans. 2007. Learning Relations from Biomedical Corpora Using Dependency Trees. *In KDECB, LNBI, vol. 4366.*

Dekang Lin. 1998. Dependency-based Evaluation of MINIPAR. *In Workshop on the Evaluation of Parsing Systems, Granada, Spain.*

Ted Pedersen, Patwardhan, and Michelizzi. 2004. WordNet::Similarity - Measuring the Relatedness of Concepts. *In the Proceedings of AAAI-04, San Jose, CA.*

Peter Turney. 2006. Expressing Implicit Semantic Relations without Supervision. *In Proceedings of COLING-ACL 2006.*

Peter Turney. 2004. The MultiText Project Home Page, University of Waterloo, School of Computer Science, `http://www.multitext.uwaterloo.ca`

UofL: Word Sense Disambiguation Using Lexical Cohesion

Yllias Chali
Department of Computer Science
University of Lethbridge
Lethbridge, Alberta, Canada, T1K 3M4
chali@cs.uleth.ca

Shafiq R. Joty
Department of Computer Science
University of Lethbridge
Lethbridge, Alberta, Canada, T1K 3M4
jotys@cs.uleth.ca

Abstract

One of the main challenges in the applications (i.e.: text summarization, question answering, information retrieval, etc.) of Natural Language Processing is to determine which of the several senses of a word is used in a given context. The problem is phrased as "Word Sense Disambiguation (WSD)" in the NLP community. This paper presents the dictionary based disambiguation technique that adopts the assumption of one sense per discourse in the context of SemEval-2007 Task 7: "Coarse-grained English all-words".

1 Introduction

Cohesion can be defined as the way certain words or grammatical features of a sentence can connect it to its predecessors (and successors) in a text. (Halliday and Hasan, 1976) defined cohesion as "the set of possibilities that exist in the language for making text hang together". Cohesion occurs where the interpretation of some element in the discourse is dependent on that of another. For example, an understanding of the reference of a pronoun (i.e.: he, she, it, etc.) requires to look back to something that has been said before. Through this cohesion relation, two text clauses are linked together.

Cohesion is achieved through the use in the text of semantically related terms, reference, ellipse and conjunctions (Barzilay and Elhadad, 1997). Among the different cohesion-building devices, the most easily identifiable and the most frequent type is lexical cohesion. Lexical cohesion is created by using semantically related words (repetitions, synonyms, hypernyms, hyponyms, meronyms and holonyms, glosses, etc.)

Our technique used WordNet (Miller, 1990) as the knowledge source to find the semantic relations among the words in a text. We assign weights to the semantic relations. The technique can be decomposed into two steps: (1) building a representation of all possible senses of the words and (2) disambiguating the words based on the highest score. The remainder of this paper is organized as follows. In the next section, we review previous work. In Section 3, we define the semantic relations and their weights. Section 4 presents our two step procedure for WSD. We conclude with the evaluation.

2 Previous Work

Lexical Chaining is the process of connecting semantically related words, creating a set of chains that represent different threads of cohesion through the text (Galley and McKeown, 2003). This intermediate representation of text has been used in many natural language processing applications, including automatic summarization (Barzilay and Elhadad, 1997; Silber and McCoy, 2003), information retrieval (Al-Halimi and Kazman, 1998), and intelligent spell checking (Hirst and St-Onge, 1998).

Morris and Hirst (1991) at first proposed a manual method for computing lexical chains and first computational model of lexical chains was introduced by Hirst and St-Onge (1997). This linear-time algorithm, however, suffers from inaccurate WSD, since their greedy strategy immediately disambiguates a word as it is first encountered. Later

Proceedings of the 4th International Workshop on Semantic Evaluations (SemEval-2007), pages 476–479,
Prague, June 2007.

research (Barzilay and Elhadad, 1997) significantly alleviated this problem at the cost of a worse running time (quadratic); computational inefficiency is due to their processing of many possible combinations of word senses in the text in order to decide which assignment is the most likely. Silber and McCoy (2003) presented an efficient linear-time algorithm to compute lexical chains, which models Barzilay's approach, but nonetheless has inaccuracies in WSD.

More recently, Galley and McKeown (2003) suggested an efficient chaining method that separated WSD from the actual chaining. It performs the WSD before the construction of the chains. They showed that it could achieve more accuracy than the earlier ones. Our method follows the similar technique with some new semantic relations (i.e.: gloss, holonym, meronym).

3 Semantic Relations

We used WordNet2.1[1] (Miller, 1990) and eXtended WordNet (Moldovan and Mihalcea, 2001) as our knowledge source to find the semantic relations among the words in a context. We assigned a weight to each semantic relation. The relations and their scores are summarized in the table 1.

4 System Overview

The global architecture of our system is shown in Figure 1. Each of the modules of the system is described below.

4.1 Context Processing

Context-processing involves preprocessing the contexts using several tools. We have used the following tools:

Extracting the main text: This module extracts the context of the target word from the source xml document removing the unnecessary tags and makes the context ready for further processing.

Sentence Splitting, Text Stemming and Chunking: This module splits the context into sentences, then stems out the words and chunks those. We used OAK systems[2] (Sekine, 2002) for this purpose.

Candidate Words Extraction: This module extracts the candidate words (for task 7: noun, verb, adjective and adverb) from the chunked text.

4.2 All Sense Representation

Each candidate word is expanded to all of its senses. We created a hash representation to identify all possible word representations, motivated from Galley and McKeown (2003). Each word sense is inserted into the hash entry having the index value equal to its synsetID. For example, athlete and jock are inserted into the same hash entry (Figure 2).

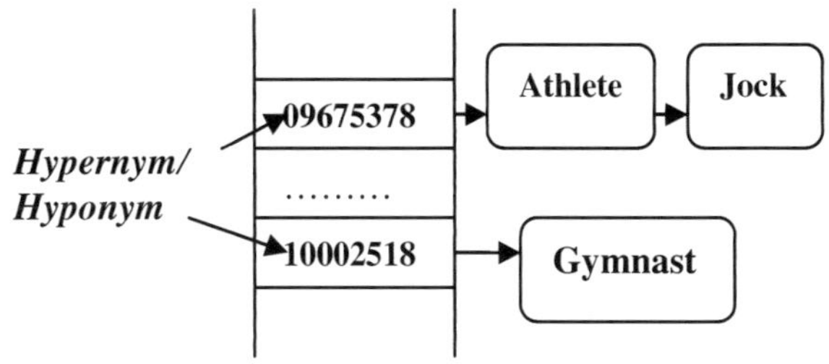

Figure 2. Hash indexed by synsetID

On insertion of the candidate sense into the hash we check to see if there exists an entry into the index value, with which the current word sense has one of the above mentioned relations. No disambiguation is done at this point; the only purpose is to build a representation used in the next stage of the algorithm. This representation can be shown as a disambiguation graph (Galley and McKeown, 2003) where the nodes represent word instances with their WordNet senses and weighted edges connecting the senses of two different words represent semantic relations (Figure: 3).

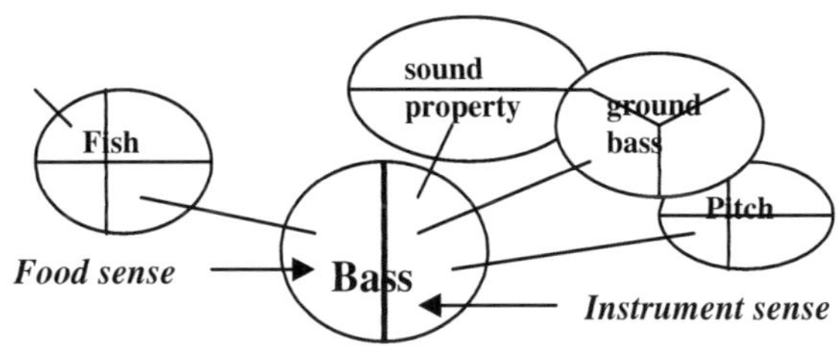

Figure 3. Partial Disambiguation graph, Bass has two senses, 1. Food related 2. Music instrument related sense. The instrument sense dominates over the fish sense as it has more relations (score) with the other words in the context.

[1] http://wordnet.princeton.edu/

[2] http://nlp.cs.nyu.edu/oak/

4.3 Sense Disambiguation

We use the intermediate representation (disambiguation graph) to perform the WSD. We sum the weight of all edges leaving the nodes under their different senses. The one sense with the highest score is considered the most probable sense. For example in fig: 3 Bass is connected with three words: Pitch, ground bass and sound property by its instrument sense and with one word: Fish by its Food sense. For this specific example all the semantic relations are of Hyponym/Hypernym type (score 0.33). So we get the score as in table 2.

In case of tie between two or more senses, we select the one sense that comes first in WordNet, since WordNet orders the senses of a word by decreasing order of frequency.

Sense	**Mnemonic**	**Score**	**Disambiguated Sense**
4928349	Musical Instrument	3*0.33 =0.99	Musical Instrument (4928349)
7672239	Fish or Food	0.33	

Table 2. Score of the senses of word "Bass"

Relation	**Definition**	**Example**	**Weight**
Repetition	Same occurrences of the word	***Weather*** is great in Atlanta. Florida is having a really bad ***weather***.	1
Synonym	Words belonging to the same synset in WordNet	Not all ***criminals*** are ***outlaws***.	1
Hypernym and Hyponym	*Y* is a hypernym of *X* if *X* is a (kind of) *Y* ***And*** *X* is a hyponym of *Y* if *X* is a (kind of) *Y*.	Peter bought a ***computer***. It was a Dell ***machine***.	0.33
Holonym And Meronym	*Y* is a holonym of *X* if *X* is a part of *Y* ***And*** *X* is a meronym of *Y* if *X* is a part of *Y*	The ***keyboard*** of this ***computer*** is not working.	0.33
Gloss	Definition and/or example sentences for a synset.	Gloss of word ***"dormitory"*** is {a college or ***university*** building containing living quarters for students}	0.33

Table 1: The relations and their associated weights

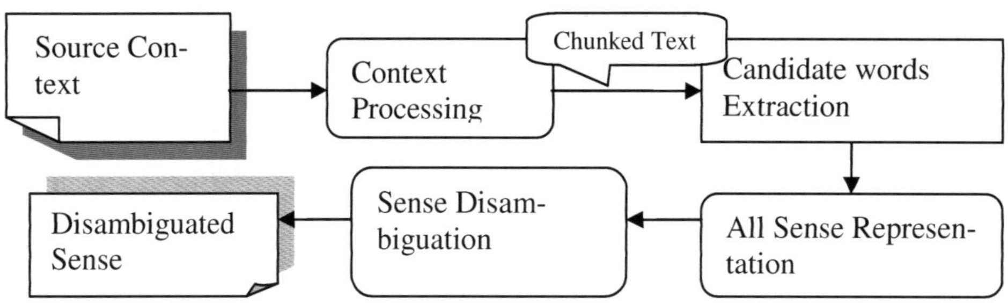

Figure 1: Overview of WSD System

5 Evaluation

In SemEval-2007, we participated in Task 7: "Coarse-grained English all-words". The evaluation of our system is given below:

Cases	Precision	Recall	F1-measure
Average	0.52592	0.48744	0.50595
Best	0.61408	0.59239	0.60304
Worst	0.44375	0.41159	0.42707

6 Conclusion

In this paper, we presented briefly our WSD system in the context of SemEval 2007 Task 7. Along with normal WordNet relations, our method also included additional relations such as repetition and gloss using semantically enhanced tool, eXtended WordNet. After disambiguation, the intermediate representation (disambiguation graph) can be used to build the lexical chains which in tern can be used as an intermediate representation for other NLP applications such as text summarization, question answering, text clustering. This method (summing edge weights in selecting the right sense) of WSD before constructing the chain (Gallery and McKeown, 2003) outperforms the earlier methods of Barzilay and Elhadad (1997) and Silber and McCoy (2003) but this method is highly dependent on the lexical cohesion among words in a context. So the length of context is an important factor for our system to achieve good performance. For the task the context given for a tagged word was not so large to capture the semantic relations among words. This may be the one of the reasons for which our system could not achieve one of the best results.

References

Barzilay, R. and Elhadad, M. 1997. Using Lexical Chains for Text Summarization. In *Proceedings of the 35th Annual Meeting of the Association for Computational Linguistics and the 8th European Chapter Meeting of the Association for Computational Linguistics*, Workshop on Intelligent Scalable Test Summarization, pages 10-17, Madrid.

Chali, Y. and Kolla, M. 2004. Summarization techniques at DUC 2004. In *Proceedings of the Document Understanding Conference,* pages 105 -111, Boston. NIST.

Galley, M. and McKeown, K. 2003. Improving Word Sense Disambiguation in Lexical Chaining. In *Proceedings of the 18th International Joint Conference on Artificial Intelligence (IJCAI'03)*, pages 1486-1488, Acapulco, Mexico.

Halliday M. and Hasan R. 1976. Cohesion in English. *Longman*, London.

Harabagiu S. and Moldovan D. 1998. WordNet: An Electronic Lexical Database, chapter Knowledge Processing on an Extended WordNet. *MIT press.*

Hirst G. and St-Onge D. 1997. Lexical Chains as representation of context for the detection and correction of malapropisms. In *Christiane Fellbaum, editor, WordNet: An Electronic Lexical Database and Some of its Applications. MIT Press,* pages 305-332.

Morris J. and Hirst. G. 1991, Lexical Cohesion Computed by Thesaural Relations as an Indicator of the Structure of Text .*Computational Linguistics*, 17(1):21-48.

Silber H.G. and McCoy K.F. 2002. Efficiently Computed Lexical Chains As an Intermediate Representation for Automatic Text Summarization. *Computational Linguistics,* 28(4):487-496.

WIT: Web People Search Disambiguation using Random Walks

José Iria, Lei Xia, Ziqi Zhang
The University of Sheffield
211 Portobello Street
Sheffield S1 4DP, United Kingdom
{j.iria, l.xia, z.zhang}@sheffield.ac.uk

Abstract

In this paper, we describe our work on a random walks-based approach to disambiguating people in web search results, and the implementation of a system that supports such approach, which we used to participate at Semeval'07 Web People Search task.

1 Introduction

Finding information about people on the Web using a search engine is far from being a quick and easy process. There is very often a many-to-many mapping of person names to the actual persons, that is, several persons may share the same name, and several names may refer to the same person. In fact, person names are highly ambiguous: (Guha and Garg, 2004) reports that only 90.000 thousand different names are shared by 100 million people according to the U.S. Census Bureau. This creates the need to disambiguate the several referents typically found in the web pages returned by a query for a given person name.

The Semeval'07 Web People Search challenge (Artiles et al., 2007) formally evaluated systems on this task. In this paper, we describe our work on a random walks-based approach to disambiguating people in web search results, heavily influenced by (Minkov et al., 2006). This particular model was chosen due to its elegance in seamlessly combining lexico-syntactic features local to a given webpage with topological features derived from its place in the network formed by the hyperlinked web pages returned by the query, to arrive at one single measure of similarity between any two pages.

2 Proposed Method

In a nutshell, our approach 1) uses a graph to model the web pages returned by the search engine query, 2) discards irrelevant web pages using a few simple hand-crafted heuristics, 3) computes a similarity matrix for web pages using random walks over the graph, and 4) finally clusters the web pages given the similarity matrix. The next subsections detail these steps.

2.1 Web People Search Graph

We build a directed weighted typed graph from the corpus. The graph is a 5-tuple $G = (V, E, t, l, w)$, where V is the set of nodes, $E : V \times V$ is the ordered set of edges, $t : V \rightarrow T$ is the *node type function* ($T = \{t_1, \ldots, t_{|T|}\}$ is a set of types), $l : E \rightarrow L$ is the *edge label function* ($L = \{l_1, \ldots, l_{|L|}\}$ is a set of labels), and $w : L \rightarrow \mathbb{R}$ is the *label weight function*. We structure our problem domain with the types and labels presented in Figure 1.

In order to transform the text into a graph that conforms to the model shown, we take the output of standard NLP tools and input it as nodes and edges into the graph, indexing nodes by string value to ensure that identical contents for any given node type are merged into a single node in the graph. To process the corpus, we run a standard NLP pipeline seperately over the metadata, title and body of the HTML pages, but not before having transformed its contents as much into plain text as possible, by removing HTML tags, javascript code, etc. The pipeline used is composed of tokenization, removal of stop words and infrequent words, and stemming with Porter's algorithm. The resulting graph at this

Proceedings of the 4th International Workshop on Semantic Evaluations (SemEval-2007), pages 480–483,
Prague, June 2007.

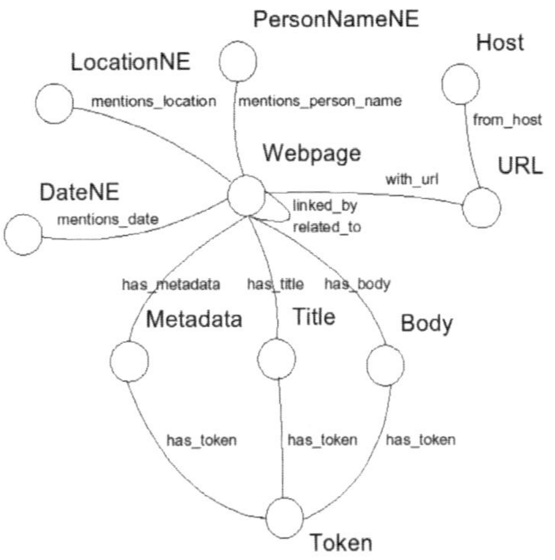

Figure 1: The data representation model adopted

stage consists of the nodes of type *Token*, *Webpage*, *Metadata*, *Title* and *Body*, properly interconnected. We then run a named entity recognizer to associate NE tags to the respective documents, via the constituent words of the NE. The information about the original *URL* of page is given by the corpus, while *Host* is trivially obtained from it. We finalise the graph by inserting an edge of type *linked_by* between any web page linked by another in the corpus, and an edge of type *related_to* between any web page related to another in the corpus, as given by Google's *related:* operator.

For the named entity recognition task, we have compared GATE and OpenNLP toolkits. Although both toolkits show comparable results, OpenNLP demonstrated faster performance. Moreover, some documents in the corpus consisted of very extensive lists of names (e.g. phonebook records) which slowed the NER to a halt in practice. To compensate for this, we applied a chunking window at the beginning and end of each body content and around each occurrence of the person name being considered (and its variants determined heuristically). The window size used was 3000 characters in length, and an overlap between windows results in a merged window.

2.2 Discarding using heuristics

To discard irrelevant documents within the corpus, we manually devised two heuristics rules for classification by observing the training data at hand. The heuristics are 1) whether the page has content at all, 2) whether the page contains at least one appearance of mentioned person name with its variants. This simple classification showed high precision and low recall on the training data. We also tried a SVM-based classifier trained on a typical bag-of-words feature vector space obtained from the training data, but found the such classifier not to be sufficiently reliable.

2.3 Random Walks Model

We aim to determine the similarity between any two nodes of type *Webpage* in the graph. In our work, similarity between two nodes in the graph is obtained by employing a random walks model. A random walk, sometimes called a "drunkard's walk," is a formalization of the intuitive idea of taking successive steps in a graph, each in a random direction (Lovász, 2004). Intuitively, the "harder" it is for a drunkard to arrive at a given webpage starting from another, the less similar the two pages are.

Our model defines weights for each edge type, which, informally, determine the relevance of each feature type to establish a similarity between any two pages. Let $L_{t_d} = \{l(x, y) : (x, y) \in E \wedge T(x) = t_d\}$ be the set of possible labels for edges leaving nodes of type t_d. We require that the weights form a probability distribution over L_{t_d}, i.e.

$$\sum_{l \in L_{t_d}} w(l) = 1 \tag{1}$$

We build an adjacency matrix of locally appropriate similarity between nodes as

$$W_{ij} = \begin{cases} \sum_{l_k \in L} \frac{w(l_k)}{|(i,\cdot) \in E : l(i,\cdot) = l_k|}, & (i,j) \in E \\ 0, & otherwise \end{cases} \tag{2}$$

where W_{ij} is the ith-line and jth-column entry of W, indexed by V. Equation 2 distributes uniformly the weight of edges of the same type leaving a given node. We could choose to distribute them otherwise, e.g. we could distribute the weights according to some string similarity function or language model (Erkan, 2006), depending on the label.

We associate the state of a Markov chain to every node of the graph, that is, to each node i we associate the one-step probability $P^{(0)}(j|i)$ of a random walker traversing to an adjacent node j. These probabilities are expressed by the row stochastic matrix $D^{-1}W$, where D is the diagonal degree matrix given by $D_{ii} = \sum_k W_{ik}$. The "reinforced" similarity between two nodes in the graph is given by the t-step transition probability $P^{(t)}(j|i)$, which can be simply computed by a matrix power, i.e., $P^{(t)}(j|i) = [(D^{-1}W)^t]_{ij}$.

Note that t should not be very large in our case. The probability distribution of an infinite random walk over the nodes, called the stationary distribution of the graph, is uninteresting to us for clustering purposes since it gives an information related to the global structure of the graph. It is often used as a measure to rank the structural importance of the nodes in a graph (Page et al., 1998). For clustering, we are more interested in the local similarities inside a cluster of nodes that separate them from the rest of the graph. Also, in practice, using $t > 2$ leads to high computational cost requirements, as the matrix becomes more dense as t grows.

Equation 2 introduces the need to learn the function w. In other words, we need to tune the model to use the most relevant features for this particular task. Tuning is performed on the training set by comparing the standard purity and inverse purity measures of the clusters against the gold standard, and using a simulated annealing optimization method as described in (Nie et al., 2005).

2.4 Commute Time Distance

The algorithm takes as input a symmetric similarity matrix S, which we derive from the random walk model of the previous section as follows. We compute the Euclidean Commute Time (ECT) distance (Saerens et al., 2004) of any two nodes of type *Webpage* in the graph. The ECT distance is (also) based on a random walk model, and presents the interesting property of decreasing when the number of paths connecting two nodes increases or when the length of any path decreases, which makes it well-suited for clustering tasks. Another nice property of ECT is that it is non-parametric, so no tuning is required here. ECT has connections with principal component analysis and spectral theory (Saerens et al., 2004).

In particular, we are interested in the *average commute time* quantity, $n(i,j)$, which is defined as the average number of steps a random walker, starting in state i, will take before entering a given state j for the first time, and go back to i. That is, $n(i,j) = m(j|i) + m(i|j)$, where the quantity $m(j|i)$, called the *average first-passage time*, is defined as the average number of steps a random walker, starting in state i, will take to enter state j for the first time. We compute the average first-passage time iteratively by means of the following recurrence:

$$\begin{cases} m(i|j) = 1 + \sum_{k=1,k\neq i}^{|V|} P^{(t)}(k|j)m(i|k), & j \neq i \\ m(i|i) = 0 \end{cases} \tag{3}$$

where $P^{(t)}(\cdot|\cdot)$ is the t-step transition probability of the random walk model over G presented in the previous section.

Informally, we may regard the random walk model presented in the previous section as a "refined" document similarity measure, replacing, e.g., the typical TF-IDF measure with a measure that works in a similar way but over all features represented in the graph, whereas we can regard the ECT measure presented in this section as a "booster" to a basic clustering techniques (cf. next section), achieved by means of coupling clustering with a random walk-based distance which has been shown to be competitive with state-of-the-art algorithms such as spectral clustering (Luh Yen et al., 2007).

2.5 Clustering

Clustering aims at partitioning n given data points into k clusters, such that points within a cluster are more similar to each other than ones taken from different clusters. An important feature of the clustering algorithm that we require for the problem at hand is its ability to determine the number k of natural clusters, since any number of referents may be present in the web search results. However, most clustering algorithms require this number to be an input, which means that they may break up or combine natural clusters, or even create clusters when no natural ones exist in the data.

We use a form of group-average agglomerative clustering as described in (Fleischman and Hovy, 2004), shown in Table 1, which works fast for this problem. A difficult problem (with any clustering approach) has to do with the number of initial clusters or, alternatively, with setting a threshold for when to stop clustering. This threshold could po-

Input: symmetric similarity matrix S, threshold θ
Output: a set of clusters C
1. $(i, j) \leftarrow$ find min score in S
2. if $S_{ij} > \theta$ then exit
3. place i and j in the same cluster in C (merging existing clusters of i and j if needed)
4. (average pairs of edges connecting to nodes i,j from any node k)
4a. $S_{ik} \leftarrow (S_{ik} + S_{jk})/2, k \neq i, j$
4b. $S_{ki} \leftarrow (S_{ki} + S_{kj})/2, k \neq i, j$
5. remove j-th column and j-th line from S (effectively merging nodes i,j into a single node)
6. goto 1
7. return clusters C

Table 1: The simple group-average agglomerative clustering algorithm used

tentially also be optimized using the training data; however, we have opted for unsupervised heuristics to do that, e.g. the well-known Calinski&Harabasz stopping rule (Calinski&Harabasz, 1974).

3 Results Obtained

The results obtained by the system are presented in the following table. The evaluation measures used were f-measure, purity and inverse purity - for a detailed description refer to the task description (Artiles et al., 2007).

aver_f05	aver_f02	aver_pur	aver_inv_pur
0,49	0,66	0,36	0,93

The results are below average for this Semeval task, and should not be regarded as representative of the approach adopted, since the authors have had limited time available to ensure a pristine implementation of the whole approach.

References

Artiles, J., Gonzalo, J., & Sekine, S. (2007). The SemEval-2007 WePS Evaluation: Establishing a benchmark for the Web People Search Task. *In Proceedings of Semeval 2007, Association for Computational Linguistics.*

Calinski and Harabasz (1974). A Dendrite Method for Cluster Analysis *Communications in Statistics, 3(1), 1974, 1-27.*

Erkan, G. (2006). Language model-based document clustering using random walks. *Proceedings of the main conference on Human Language Technology Conference of the North American Chapter of the Association of Computational Linguistics* (pp. 479–486). Association for Computational Linguistics.

Fleischman, M. B., & Hovy, E. (2004). Multi-document person name resolution. *Proceedings of the ACL 2004.* Association for Computational Linguistics.

Guha, R. V., & Garg, A. (2003). Disambiguating People in Search. *TAP: Building the Semantic Web..* ACM Press.

Luh Yen, Francois Fouss, C. D., Francq, P., & Saerens, M. (2007). Graph nodes clustering based on the commute-time kernel. *To appear in the proceedings of the 11th Pacific-Asia Conference on Knowledge Discovery and Data Mining (PAKDD 2007).* Lecture Notes in Computer Science (LNCS).

Minkov, E., Cohen, W. W., & Ng, A. Y. (2006). Contextual search and name disambiguation in email using graphs. *SIGIR '06: Proceedings of the 29th annual international ACM SIGIR conference on Research and development in information retrieval* (pp. 27–34). ACM Press.

Nie, Z., Zhang, Y., Wen, J. R., & Ma, W. Y. (2005). Object-level ranking: Bringing order to web objects. *Proceedings of WWW'05.*

Page, L., Brin, S., Motwani, R., & Winograd, T. (1998). *The pagerank citation ranking: Bringing order to the web* (Technical Report). Stanford Digital Library Technologies Project.

Saerens, M., Fouss, F., Yen, L., & Dupont, P. (2004). The principal components analysis of a graph, and its relationships to spectral clustering. *Proceedings of the 15th European Conference on Machine Learning.*

László Lovász (1993). Random Walks on Graphs: A Survey. *Combinatorics, Paul Erdos is Eighty (Volume 2), Keszthely (Hungary), 1993, p 1-46..*

WVALI: Temporal Relation Identification by Syntactico-Semantic Analysis

Georgiana Puşcaşu[†§]
[†]Research Group in Computational Linguistics
University of Wolverhampton, UK
[§]Department of Software and Computing Systems
University of Alicante, Spain
georgie@wlv.ac.uk

Abstract

This paper reports on the participation of University of Wolverhampton and University of Alicante at the SemEval-2007 TempEval evaluation exercise. TempEval consisted of three tasks involving the identification of event-time and event-event temporal relations. We participated in all three tasks with TICTAC (Syntactico-Semantic Temporal Annotation Cluster), a system comprising both knowledge based and statistical techniques. Our system achieved the highest strict and relaxed scores for tasks A and B, and the highest relaxed score for task C.

1 Introduction

TempEval comprises novel tasks concerned with the identification of temporal relations between events and temporal expressions (TEs). The evaluation exercise includes three tasks testing the capability of participating systems to relate an event and a TE located in the same sentence (task A), an event and the TE representing the Document Creation Time (DCT) (task B), and two events located in neighbouring sentences (task C). We tackle all tasks with a mix of knowledge based and statistical techniques incorporated in our system TICTAC.

Our approach for discovering intrasentential temporal relations relies on sentence-level syntactic trees and on a bottom-up propagation of the temporal relations between syntactic constituents, by employing syntactical and lexical properties of the constituents and the relations between them. A temporal reasoning mechanism is afterwards employed to relate the two targeted temporal entities to their closest ancestor and then to each other. Conflict resolution heuristics are also applied.

In establishing a temporal relation between an event and the Document Creation Time (DCT), the temporal expressions directly or indirectly linked to that event are first analysed and, if no relation is detected, the temporal relation with the DCT is propagated top-down in the syntactic tree.

Inter-sentence temporal relations are discovered by first applying several heuristics that involve the temporal expressions and the tensed verbs of the two clauses containing the main events to be temporally related, and then by using statistical data extracted from the training corpus that revealed the most frequent temporal relation between two tensed verbs characterised by the tense information.

This paper presents the techniques employed for the three TempEval tasks (Sections 2, 3 and 4 correspond to the tasks A, B and C). The evaluation results are presented and discussed in Section 5. Conclusions are drawn in the last section.

2 Task A

Task A at TempEval involved the automatic identification of the temporal relations holding between events and all temporal expressions appearing in the same sentence. The events and TEs were annotated in the source in accordance with the TimeML standard (Pustejovsky et al., 2003a).

For all tasks, the set of temporal relations to be predicted includes: OVERLAP, BEFORE, AFTER,

Proceedings of the 4th International Workshop on Semantic Evaluations (SemEval-2007), pages 484–487,
Prague, June 2007.

BEFORE-OR-OVERLAP, OVERLAP-OR-AFTER and VAGUE.

Figure 1 depicts the processing stages involved in the identification of the temporal relation given the event, the TE and the sentence they are in. The sentence is first annotated with morpho-syntactic and functional dependency information by employing Conexor's FDG Parser (Tapanainen and Jaervinen, 1997).

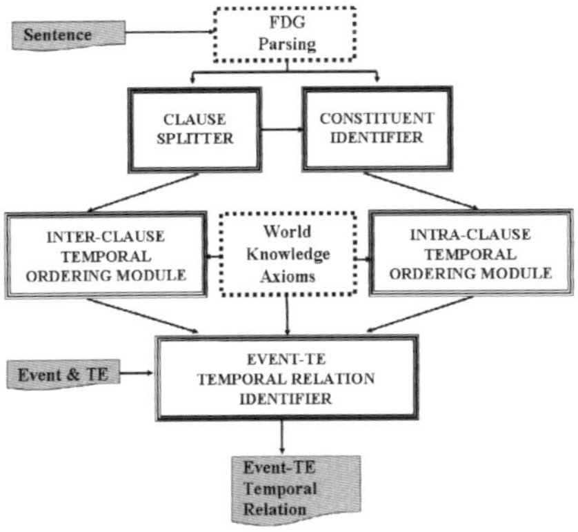

Figure 1: Task A processing stages

A clause splitter previously developed by the author is then used to detect clause boundaries and to establish the dependencies between the resulting clauses by relying on formal indicators of coordination and subordination and, in their absence, on the functional dependency relation predicted by the FDG parser. On the basis of the morpho-syntactic information we identify in each clause a set of temporally-relevant constituents (verb phrase VP, noun phrases NPs, prepositional phrases PPs, non-finite verbs and adverbial TEs).

The identified constituents and the syntactic tree of the corresponding clause are afterwards employed in a recursive bottom-up process of finding the temporal order between directly linked constituents. Each constituent is linked only with the constituent it syntactically depends on with one of the predefined temporal relations. The temporal relation is decided on the basis of heuristics that involve parameters such as: semantic properties of the two constituents' heads (whether their root forms denote reporting or aspectual start/end events), the type of the two constituents, the syntactic relation holding between them, presence of temporal signals (e.g. prepositions like *before*, *after*, *until*), the tense of the clause VP and the temporal relation between any clause TE and the DCT. This process will result in a path of temporal relations connecting every clause constituent with the clause VP.

Each pair of clauses involved in a dependency relation are then temporally related by means of their VPs' tenses, of the dependency relation between them and of their property of being reporting events or not. The underlying hypothesis is that the clause binding elements and the tenses of the two VPs provide a natural way to establish temporal relations between two syntactically related clauses. For example, in the case of an *if*-clause, its temporal relation with the superordinate clause is BEFORE. In this way, each syntactic tree branch connecting a non-root node with its father gets tagged with a temporal relation (Figure 2).

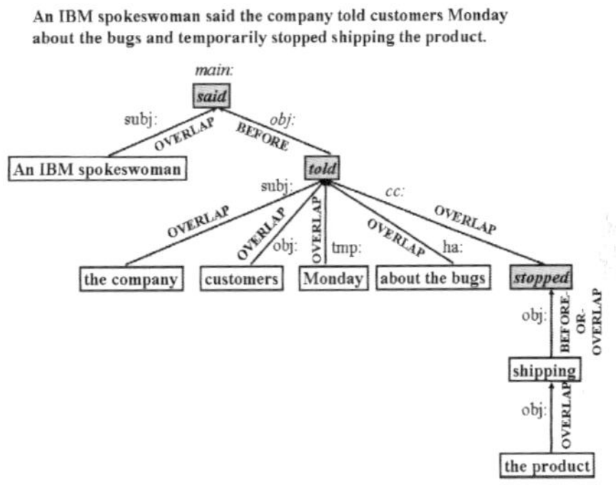

Figure 2: Temporally tagged parse tree

The final stage involves the detection of the temporal relation between a certain event and a certain TE, both situated in the sentence processed as above. The two entities are first tested to determine if they comply with world knowledge axioms that would predict their temporal relation. For example if the TE refers to a date that is previous to the DCT, and the event is a Future tensed verb, then the event-TE temporal relation is obviously AFTER. If no axiom applies to the two entities, a temporal reasoning mechanism is employed to relate the two targeted temporal entities to their closest ancestor and then to each other. If conflicts occur in relating one entity to the ancestor, priority is given to the relation linked to the entity, but if the conflict is between the event-ancestor and the TE-ancestor temporal relations, the TE-ancestor relation wins.

3 Task B

Task B consisted of the identification of temporal relations between events and the DCT. The processing stages for solving task B follow the course of the ones involved in task A, with the only difference that the inter-clause and intra-clause temporal ordering modules no longer order clauses/constituents with respect to each other and in a bottom-up manner, but with respect to the DCT going top-down through the syntactic tree and employing the knowledge gained at task A about the relative ordering between same clause constituents.

Whenever establishing a temporal relation between a constituent and the DCT, the TEs directly linked to it or situated in the same clause with it are first analysed and, if no relation can be detected, the temporal relation with the DCT is propagated top-down in the syntactic tree using the father node's temporal relation with the DCT and the temporal relation between the two constituents. For clause VPs, the relation with the DCT is found on the basis of the VP tense, the superordinate clause's VP tense, the syntactic relation connecting the clause with its superordinate and the relation between the superordinate clause's VP and the DCT.

4 Task C

For task C each pair of events signalled by the main verbs of two consecutive sentences needs to be temporally linked. This time, besides the events and TEs, the main verb in the matrix clause (matrix verb) of each sentence is also annotated in the documents.

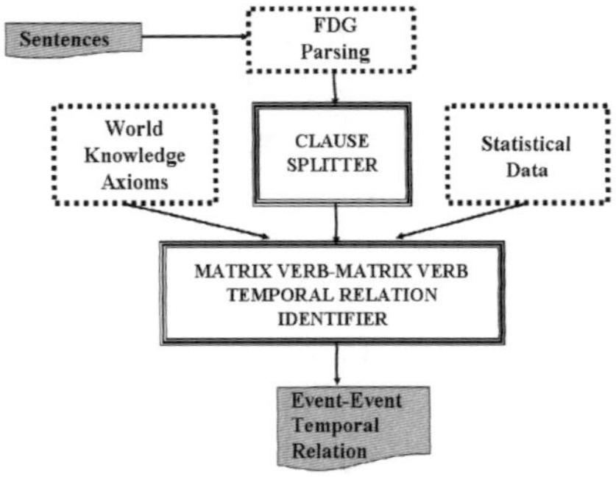

Figure 3: Task C processing stages

Figure 3 illustrates the task C processing flow. The two sentences are first parsed using Conexor's FDG Parser and then clause boundaries are identified. Due to the fact that we have noticed cases when the annotated matrix verb was not the central verb of the main clause, we have considered as matrix verb the tensed verb of the clause including the annotated matrix verb.

All TEs situated in the same clause with each matrix verb are investigated and if through these TEs and the relations between them and the matrix verbs we are able to predict a temporal relation then this relation represents the system output.

At the next stage the semantic properties of the two matrix verbs are checked to detect whether they denote reporting events or not.

If both matrix verbs are reporting events then their tense information is used to predict a relation.

If only one matrix verb is a reporting event, then we look at the TEs linked to the other matrix verb to see if we can predict the relation to the DCT. The assumption is that a reporting event is located temporally simultaneous with the DCT and, if a relation between the other event and the DCT can be established by means of surrounding TEs, then this is the relation providing us the output. If the non-reporting event can not be positioned in time with respect to the DCT by analysing surrounding TEs, then its relation with the DCT will be the one established by solving task B.

The most complicated case is the one in which both matrix verbs are non-reporting events. This case is solved by extracting statistics from the training documents, statistics involving the number of occurrences of a certain pair of verb tenses with a certain predicted temporal relation. The extracted statistics are then reconciled for tense pairs with more possible temporal relations, in the sense that if the first two most frequent possibilities have very similar frequencies, then the reconciliation is performed according to Table 1. In this manner a temporal relation is associated to each tense pair and, consequently, the temporal relation between the two matrix verbs is identified.

5 Results

The test corpus consists of 20 articles from TimeBank (Pustejovsky et al., 2003b). The performance is assessed with three evaluation

Temporal Relation	Temporal Relation	Reconciled Relation
OVERLAP	BEFORE-OR-OVERLAP	BEFORE-OR-OVERLAP
OVERLAP	BEFORE	BEFORE-OR-OVERLAP
OVERLAP	OVERLAP-OR-AFTER	OVERLAP-OR-AFTER
OVERLAP	AFTER	OVERLAP-OR-AFTER
BEFORE	BEFORE-OR-OVERLAP	BEFORE-OR-OVERLAP
AFTER	OVERLAP-OR-AFTER	OVERLAP-OR-AFTER
VAGUE	any relation	any relation

Table 1: Reconciliation between temporal relations

metrics (precision, recall, f-measure) and two scoring schemes (strict, relaxed). The strict scoring scheme counts only exact matches, while the relaxed one gives credit to partial semantic matches too.

The following three tables illustrate for each task the results our team obtained at TempEval, the baseline, the minimum and maximum values achieved by participating systems.

For each of the three tasks, the baseline is established by the most frequent temporal relation encountered in that task's training data. In the case of task A the most frequent temporal relation present in the training data is OVERLAP, in the case of task B BEFORE and for task C OVERLAP.

TASK A	STRICT SCORE			RELAXED SCORE		
	P	R	F	P	R	F
WVALI	*0.62*	*0.62*	***0.62***	*0.64*	*0.64*	***0.64***
BASELINE	0.49	0.49	**0.49**	0.51	0.51	**0.51**
MIN	0.53	0.25	**0.34**	0.60	0.30	**0.41**
MAX	0.62	0.62	**0.62**	0.64	0.64	**0.64**

Table 2: Results for task A

Our system achieved the highest strict and relaxed f-measure scores in tasks A and B, with the task B results substantially above the baseline (18%).

TASK B	STRICT SCORE			RELAXED SCORE		
	P	R	F	P	R	F
WVALI	*0.80*	*0.80*	***0.80***	*0.81*	*0.81*	***0.81***
BASELINE	0.62	0.62	**0.62**	0.62	0.62	**0.62**
MIN	0.73	0.57	**0.66**	0.74	0.62	**0.71**
MAX	0.80	0.80	**0.80**	0.84	0.81	**0.81**

Table 3: Results for task B

TASK C	STRICT SCORE			RELAXED SCORE		
	P	R	F	P	R	F
WVALI	*0.54*	*0.54*	***0.54***	*0.66*	*0.66*	***0.66***
BASELINE	0.42	0.42	**0.42**	0.46	0.46	**0.46**
MIN	0.42	0.42	**0.42**	0.56	0.56	**0.56**
MAX	0.55	0.55	**0.55**	0.66	0.66	**0.66**

Table 4: Results for task C

Despite the challenges posed by task C, our system achieved the best relaxed score among all participants, as well as a high strict score.

6 Conclusion

This paper presented our approach and participation in the TempEval evaluation exercise involving the identification of event-time and event-event temporal relations. We propose an approach mainly based on syntactical properties, combining knowledge-based and statistical techniques, all included in our automatic temporal annotation system TICTAC. Our system participated in all three TempEval tasks.

When compared to the other systems participating in this competition, we have obtained the highest results both in the strict and relaxed scoring schemes in the case of tasks A and B, as well as in the relaxed scoring scheme for task C. Therefore, we conclude that the proposed approach is appropriate for the TempEval tasks and we plan to find ways of improving the system's performance.

Several future work directions emerge naturally from a first look and shallow analysis of the results. Firstly, we would like to carry out an in-depth study of other possible correlations between syntax and temporality. Secondly, we aim at exploiting apart from the syntax of the analysed text, more of its semantics.

Acknowledgments

The author would like to thank Patricio Martinez Barco, Andres Montoyo and Constantin Orasan for their advice and support.

References

J. Pustejovsky, J. Castano, R. Ingria, R. Sauri, R. Gaizauskas, A. Setzer, and G. Katz. 2003a. TimeML: Robust Specification of Event and Temporal Expressions in Text. In *Proceedings of the Fifth International Workshop on Computational Semantics (IWCS-5)*.

J. Pustejovsky, P. Hanks, R. Sauri, A. See, R. Gaizuaskas, A. Setzer, D. Radev, B. Sundheim, D. Day, L. Ferro, and M. Lazo. 2003b. The TIMEBANK Corpus. In *Proceedings of Corpus Linguistics 2003*.

P. Tapanainen and T. Jaervinen. 1997. A non–projective dependency parser. In *Proceedings of the 5th Conference of Applied Natural Language Processing, ACL*.

XRCE-M: A Hybrid System for Named Entity Metonymy Resolution

***Caroline Brun** ***Maud Ehrmann** ***Guillaume Jacquet**

* Xerox Research Centre Europe
6, chemin de Maupertuis
38240 Meylan France

*{Caroline.Brun, Maud.Ehrmann, Guillaume.Jacquet}@xrce.xerox.com

Abstract

This paper describes our participation to the Metonymy resolution at SemEval 2007 (task #8). In order to perform named entity metonymy resolution, we developed a hybrid system based on a robust parser that extracts deep syntactic relations combined with a non-supervised distributional approach, also relying on the relations extracted by the parser.

1 Description of our System

SemEval 2007 introduces a task aiming at resolving metonymy for named entities, for location and organization names (Markert and Nissim 2007). Our system addresses this task by combining a symbolic approach based on robust deep parsing and lexical semantic information, with a distributional method using syntactic context similarities calculated on large corpora. Our system is completely unsupervised, as opposed to state-of-the-art systems (see (Market and Nissim, 2005)).

1.1 Robust and Deep Parsing Using XIP

We use the Xerox Incremental Parser (XIP, (Aït et al., 2002)) to perform robust and deep syntactic analysis. Deep syntactic analysis consists here in the construction of a set of syntactic relations[1] from an input text. These relations, labeled with deep syntactic functions, link lexical units of the input text and/or more complex syntactic domains that are constructed during the processing (mainly chunks, see (Abney, 1991)).

Moreover, together with surface syntactic relations, the parser calculates more sophisticated relations using derivational morphologic properties, deep syntactic properties[2], and some limited lexical semantic coding (Levin's verb class alternations, see (Levin, 1993)), and some elements of the Framenet[3] classification, (Ruppenhofer et al., 2006)). These deep syntactic relations correspond roughly to the agent-experiencer roles that is subsumed by the SUBJ-N relation and to the patient-theme role subsumed by the OBJ-N relation, see (Brun and Hagège, 2003). Not only verbs bear these relations but also deverbal nouns with their corresponding arguments.

Here is an example of an output (chunks and deep syntactic relations):

Lebanon still wanted to see the implementation of a UN resolution

TOP{SC{NP{Lebanon} FV{still wanted}} IV{to see} NP{the implementation} PP{of NP{a UN resolution}} .}

MOD_PRE(wanted,still)
MOD_PRE(resolution,UN)
MOD_POST(implementation,resolution)
COUNTRY(Lebanon)
ORGANISATION(UN)
EXPERIENCER_PRE(wanted,Lebanon)
EXPERIENCER(see,Lebanon)
CONTENT(see,implementation)
EMBED_INFINIT(see,wanted)
OBJ-N(implement,resolution)

1.2 Adaptation to the Task

Our parser includes a module for "standard" named entity recognition, but needs to be adapted to handle named entity metonymy. Following the guidelines of the SemEval task #8, we performed a

[1] inspired from dependency grammars, see (Mel'čuk, 1998), and (Tesnière, 1959).

[2] Subject and object of infinitives in the context of control verbs.

[3] http://framenet.icsi.berkeley.edu/

Proceedings of the 4th International Workshop on Semantic Evaluations (SemEval-2007), pages 488–491,
Prague, June 2007.

corpus study on the trial data in order to detect lexical and syntactic regularities triggering a metonymy, for both location names and organization names. For example, we examined the subject relation between organizations or locations and verbs and we then classify the verbs accordingly: we draw hypothesis like "if a location name is the subject of a verb referring to an economic action, like *import*, *provide*, *refund*, *repay*, etc., then it is a place-for-people". We adapted our parser by adding dedicated lexicons that encode the information collected from the corpus and develop rules modifying the interpretation of the entity, for example:

If (LOCATION(#1) & SUBJ-N(#2[v_econ],#1))[4]
➔ PLACE-FOR-PEOPLE(#1)

We focus our study on relations like subject, object, experiencer, content, modifiers (nominal and prepositional) and attributes. We also capitalize on the already-encoded lexical information attached to verbs by the parser, like communication verbs like *say*, *deny*, *comment*, or categories of the FrameNet Experiencer subject frame, i.e. verbs like *feel*, *sense*, *see*. This information was very useful since experiencers denote persons, therefore all organizations or locations having an experiencer role can be considered as organization-for-members or place-for-people. Here is an example of output[5], when applying the modified parser on the following sentence:

*"It was the largest **Fiat** everyone had ever seen".*

ORG-FOR-PRODUCT(Fiat)
MOD_PRE(seen,ever)
SUBJ-N_PRE(was,It)
EXPERIENCER_PRE(seen,everyone)
SUBJATTR(It,Fiat)
QUALIF(Fiat,largest)

Here, the relation QUALIF(Fiat, largest) triggers the metonymical interpretation of "Fiat" as org-for-product.

This first development step is the starting point of our methodology, which is completed by a non-supervised distributional approach described in the next section.

[4] Which read as "if the parser has detected a location name (#1), which is the subject of a verb (#2) bearing the feature "v-econ", then create a PLACE-FOR-PEOPLE unary predicate on #1.

[5] Only dependencies are shown.

1.3 Hybridizing with a Distributional Approach

The distributional approach proposes to establish a distance between words depending on there syntactic distribution.

The distributional hypothesis is that words that appear in similar contexts are semantically similar (Harris, 1951): the more two words have the same distribution, i.e. are found in the same syntactic contexts, the more they are semantically close.

We propose to apply this principle for metonymy resolution. Traditionally, the distributional approach groups words like *USA*, *Britain*, *France*, *Germany* because there are in the same syntactical contexts:

(1) Someone live in Germany.
(2) Someone works in Germany.
(3) Germany declares something.
(4) Germany signs something.

The metonymy resolution task implies to distinguish the literal cases, (1) & (2), from the metonymic ones, (3) & (4). Our method establishes these distinctions using the syntactic context distribution. We group contexts occurring with the same words: the syntactic contexts *live in* and *work in* are occurring with *Germany*, *France*, *country*, *city*, *place*, when syntactic contexts *subject-of-declare* and subject-of-*sign* are occurring with *Germany*, *France*, *someone*, *government*, *president*.

For each Named Entity annotation, the hybrid method consists in using symbolic annotation if there is (§1.2), else using distributional annotation (§1.3) as presented below.

Method: We constructed a distributional space with the 100M-word BNC. We prepared the corpus by lemmatizing and then parsing with the same robust parser than for the symbolic approach (XIP, see section 3.1). It allows us to identify triple instances. Each triple have the form w1.R.w2 where w1 and w2 are lexical units and R is a syntactic relation (Lin, 1998; Kilgarriff & *al.* 2004).

Our approach can be distinguished from classical distributional approach by different points.

First, we use triple occurrences to build a distributional space (one triple implies two contexts and two lexical units), but we use the transpose of the classical space: each point x_i of this space is a syntactical context (with the form R.w.), each dimension j is a lexical units, and each value $x_i(j)$ is the frequency of corresponding triple occurrences. Second, our lexical units are words but also complex nominal groups or verbal groups. Third, contexts can be simple contexts or composed contexts[6].

We illustrate these three points on the phrase *provide Albania with food aid*. The XIP parser gives the following triples where for example, *food aid* is considered as a lexical unit:

OBJ-N('VERB:provide','NOUN: Albania').
PREP_WITH('VERB: provide ','NOUN:aid').
PREP_WITH('VERB: provide ','NP:food aid').

From these triples, we create the following lexical units and contexts (in the context *1.VERB: provide. OBJ-N*, *"1"* mean that the verb *provide* is the governor of the relation OBJ-N):

Words:	Contexts:
VERB:provide	1.VERB: provide. OBJ-N
NOUN:Albania	1.VERB: provide.PREP_WITH
NOUN:aid	2.NOUN: Albania.OBJ-N
NP:food aid	2.NOUN: aid. PREP_WITH
	2.NP: food aid. PREP_WITH
	1.VERB:provide.OBJ-N+2.NOUN:aid. PREP_WITH
	1.VERB:provide.OBJ-N+2.NP:food aid. PREP_WITH
	1.VERB:provide.PREP_WITH +2.NO:Albania.OBJ-N

We use a heuristic to control the high productivity of these lexical units and contexts. Each lexical unit and each context should appear more than 100 times in the corpus. From the 100M-word BNC we obtained 60,849 lexical units and 140,634 contexts. Then, our distributional space has 140,634 units and 60,849 dimensions.

Using the global space to compute distances between each context is too consuming and would induce artificial ambiguity (Jacquet, Venant, 2005). If any named entity can be used in a metonymic reading, in a given corpus each named entity has not the same distribution of metonymic readings. The country *Vietnam* is more frequently used as an event than *France* or *Germany*, so, knowing that a context is employed with *Vietnam* allow to reduce the metonymic ambiguity.

For this, we construct a singular sub-space depending to the context and to the lexical unit (the ambiguous named entity):

For a given couple context *i* + lexical unit *j* we construct a subspace as follows:

Sub_contexts = list of contexts which are occurring with the word *i*. If there are more than k contexts, we take only the *k* more frequents.

Sub_dimension = list of lexical units which are occurring with at least one of the contexts from the Sub_contexts list. If there are more than *n* words, we take only the *n* more frequents (relative frequency) with the Sub_contexts list (for this application, $k = 100$ and $n = 1{,}000$).

We reduce dimensions of this sub-space to 10 dimensions with a PCA (Principal Components Analysis).

In this new reduced space (k*10), we compute the closest context of the context *j* with the Euclidian distance.

At this point, we use the results of the symbolic approach described before as starting point. We attribute to each context of the Sub_contexts list, the annotation, if there is, attributed by symbolic rules. Each kind of annotation (literal, place-for-people, place-for-event, etc) is attributed a score corresponding to the sum of the scores obtained by each context annotated with this category. The score of a context *i* decreases in inverse proportion to its distance from the context *j*: score(context *i*) = 1/d(context *i*, context *j*) where d(*i,j*) is the Euclidian distance between *i* and *j*.

We illustrate this process with the sentence *provide Albania with food aid.* The unit *Albania* is found in 384 different contexts (|Sub_contexts| = 384) and 54,183 lexical units are occurring with at least one of the contexts from the Sub_contexts list (|Sub_dimension| = 54,183).

After reducing dimension with PCA, we obtain the context list below ordered by closeness with the given context (1.VERB:provide.OBJ-N):

Contexts	**d**	**symb. annot.**
1.VERB:provide.OBJ-N	0.00	
1.VERB:allow.OBJ-N	0.76	place-for-people
1.VERB:include.OBJ-N	0.96	
2.ADJ:new.MOD_PRE	1.02	
1.VERB:be.SUBJ-N	1.43	
1.VERB:supply.SUBJ-N_PRE	1.47	literal
1.VERB:become.SUBJ-N_PRE	1.64	
1.VERB:come.SUBJ-N_PRE	1.69	
1.VERB:support.SUBJ-N_PRE	1.70	place-for-people
etc.		

Score for each metonymic annotation of *Albania*:

→	**place-for-people**	**3.11**
	literal	1.23
	place-for-event	0.00
	...	0.00

The score obtained by each annotation type allows annotating this occurrence of *Albania* as a *place-for-people* metonymic reading. If we can't choose only one annotation (all score = 0 or equality between two annotations) we do not annotate.

[6] For our application, one context can be composed by two simple contexts.

2 Evaluation and Results

The following tables show the results on the **test** corpus:

type	Nb. samp	accuracy	coverage	Baseline accuracy	Baseline coverage
Loc/coarse	908	0.851	1	0.794	1
Loc/medium	908	0.848	1	0.794	1
Loc /fine	908	0.841	1	0.794	1
Org/coarse	842	0.732	1	0.618	1
Org/medium	842	0.711	1	0.618	1
Org/fine	842	0.700	1	0.618	1

Table 1: Global Results

	Nb occ.	Prec.	Recall	F-score
Literal	721	0.867	0.960	0.911
Place-for-people	141	0.651	0.490	0.559
Place-for-event	10	0.5	0.1	0.166
Place-for-product	1	_	0	0
Object-for-name	4	1	0.5	0.666
Object-for-representation	0	_	_	_
Othermet	11	_	0	0
mixed	20	_	0	0

Table 2: Detailed Results for Locations

	Nb occ.	Prec.	Recall	F-score
Literal	520	0.730	0.906	0.808
Organization-for-members	161	0.622	0.522	0.568
Organization-for-event	1	_	0	0
Organization-for-product	67	0.550	0.418	0.475
Organization-for-facility	16	0.5	0.125	0.2
Organization-for-index	3	_	0	0
Object-for-name	6	1	0.666	0.8
Othermet	8	_	0	0
Mixed	60	_	0	0

Table 3: Detailed Results for Organizations

The results obtained on the test corpora are above the baseline for both location and organization names and therefore are very encouraging for the method we developed. However, our results on the test corpora are below the ones we get on the train corpora, which indicates that there is room for improvement for our methodology.

Identified errors are of different nature:

Parsing errors: For example in the sentence "*Many galleries in the States, England and France declined the invitation.*", because the analysis of the coordination is not correct, *France* is calculated as subject of *declined*, a context triggering a place-for-people interpretation, which is wrong here.

Mixed cases: These phenomena, while relatively frequent in the corpora, are not properly treated.

Uncovered contexts: some of the syntactico-semantic contexts triggering a metonymy are not covered by the system at the moment.

3 Conclusion

This paper describes a system combining a symbolic and a non-supervised distributional approach, developed for resolving location and organization names metonymy. We plan to pursue this work in order to improve the system on the already-covered phenomenon as well as on different names entities.

References

Abney S. 1991. *Parsing by Chunks.* In Robert Berwick, Steven Abney and Carol Teny (eds.). Principle-based Parsing, Kluwer Academics Publishers.

Aït-Mokhtar S., Chanod, J.P., Roux, C. 2002. *Robustness beyond Shallowness: Incremental Dependency Parsing.* Special issue of NLE journal.

Brun, C., Hagège C., 2003. *Normalization and Paraphrasing Using Symbolic Methods*, Proceeding of the Second International Workshop on Paraphrasing. ACL 2003, Vol. 16, Sapporo, Japan.

Harris Z. 1951. *Structural Linguistics*, University of Chicago Press.

Jacquet G.,Venant F. 2003. *Construction automatique de classes de sélection distributionnelle,* In Proc. TALN 2003, Dourdan.

Kilgarriff A., Rychly P., Smrz P., Tugwell D. 2004. *The sketch engine.* In Proc. EURALEX, pages 105-116.

Levin, B. 1993. *English Verb Classes and Alternations – A preliminary Investigation.* The University of Chicago Press.

Nissim, M. and Markert, K. 2005. *Learning to buy a Renault and to talk to a BMW: A supervised approach to conventional metonymy.* Proceedings of the 6th International Workshop on Computational Semantics, Tilburg.

Nissim, M. and Markert, K. 2007. *SemEval-2007 Task 08: Metonymy Resolution at SemEval-2007.* In Proceedings of SemEval-2007.

Lin D. 1998. *Automatic retrieval and clustering of similar words.* In COLING-ACL, pages 768-774.

Mel'čuk I. 1988. *Dependency Syntax.* State University of New York, Albany.

Ruppenhofer, J. Michael Ellsworth, Miriam R. L. Petruck, Christopher R Johnson and Jan Scheffczyk. 2006. *Framenet II: Extended Theory and Practice.*

Tesnière L. 1959. *Eléments de Syntaxe Structurale.* Klincksiek Eds. (Corrected edition Paris 1969).

XRCE-T: XIP temporal module for TempEval campaign

Caroline Hagège
XEROX Research Centre Europe
6, chemin de Maupertuis
38240 MEYLAN, FRANCE
Caroline.Hagege@xrce.xerox.com

Xavier Tannier
XEROX Research Centre Europe
6, chemin de Maupertuis
38240 MEYLAN, FRANCE
Xavier.Tannier@xrce.xerox.com

Abstract

We present the system we used for the TempEval competition. This system relies on a deep syntactic analyzer that has been extended for the treatment of temporal expressions, thus making temporal processing a complement to a better general purpose text understanding system.

1 General presentation and system overview

Although interest in temporal and aspectual phenomena is not new in NLP and AI, temporal processing of real texts is a topic that has been of growing interest in the last years (Mani et al. 2005).

The work we have done concerning temporal processing of texts is part of a more general process in text understanding, integrated into a more generic tool.

In this article, we present briefly our general purpose analyzer XIP and explain how we perform our three-level temporal processing. TempEval experiments of our system are finally described and results we obtained are discussed.

1.1 XIP – a general purpose deep syntactic analyzer

Our temporal processor, called XTM, is an extension of XIP (Xerox Incremental Parser (Aït Mokhtar et al., 2002). XIP extracts basic grammatical relations and also thematic roles in the form of dependency links. See (Brun and Hagège 2003) for details on deep linguistic processing using XIP.
XIP is rule-based and its architecture can roughly be divided into the three following parts:

- A pre-processing stage handling tokenization, morphological analysis and POS tagging.
- A surface syntactic analysis stage consisting in chunking the input and dealing with Named Entity Recognition (NER).
- A deep syntactic analysis

1.2 Intertwining temporal processing and linguistic processing

The underlying idea is that temporal processing is one of the necessary steps in a more general task of text understanding. All temporal processing at the sentence level is performed together with other tasks of linguistic analysis. Association between temporal expressions and events is considered as a particular case of the more general task of attaching thematic roles to predicates (the TIME and DURATION roles). We will detail in sections 3.1 and 3.2 how low-level temporal processing is combined with the rest of the linguistic processing.

2 Three levels of temporal processing

Temporal processing has the following purposes:
1) Recognizing and interpreting temporal expressions, 2) Attaching these expressions to the corresponding events[1] they modify, 3) Ordering these events using a set of temporal expressions we present above.

We deliberately decided not to change our system's output in order to match TempEval goldstandard EVENTs and TIMEX3s. This would have

[1] We consider as events: verbs, deverbal nouns or any kind of non-deverbal nouns from a pre-defined list (e.g.: "sunrise" or "war").

Proceedings of the 4th International Workshop on Semantic Evaluations (SemEval-2007), pages 492–495,
Prague, June 2007. ©2007 Association for Computational Linguistics

implied to change our parser's behavior. As linking events and temporal expressions is only a part of a general syntactico-semantic process, changing this part would have had bad consequences for the other aspects of the parsing.

2.1 Local level

Recognition of temporal expressions is performed by local rules that can make use of left and/or right context. Together with contextual rules, some actions are associated. These actions are meant to attribute a value to the resulting temporal expression. Figure 1 illustrates this stage for a simple anchor date. An ADV (adverbial) node with associated Boolean features is built from linguistic expressions such as "4 years ago". Note that there is a call to a Python function (Roux, 2006) "merge_anchor_and_dur" whose parameters are three linguistic nodes (`#0` represents the resulting left-hand expression). The representation of the values is close to TimeML format (Saurí et al, 2006).

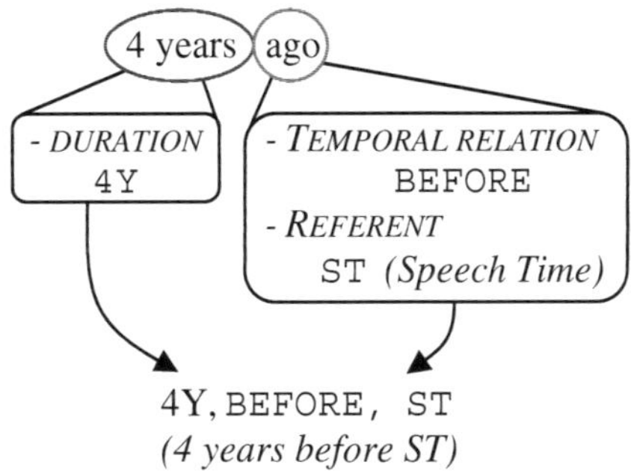


```
ADV[tempexpr:+,anchor:+] =
  #1[dur], adv#2[temp_rel,temp_ref],
where(merge anchor and dur(#2,#1,#0))
```

Figure 1: Local level processing, anchor date.

2.2 Sentence level

The sentence level is the place where some links between temporal expressions and the events they modify are established, as well as temporal relations between events in a same sentence.

Attaching temporal expressions to events

As a XIP grammar is developed in an incremental way, at a first stage, any prepositional phrase (PP, included temporal PP) is attached to the predicate it modifies through a very general MOD (modifier) dependency link. Then, in a later stage, these dependency links are refined considering the nature and the linguistic properties of the linked constituents.

In the case of temporal expressions, a specific relation TEMP links the temporal expression and the predicate it is attached to.

For instance, in the following sentence (extracted from trial data):

```
People began gathering in Abuja
Tuesday for the two day rally.
```

The following dependencies are extracted

```
TEMP(began, Tuesday)
TEMP(rally, two day)
```

"Tuesday"is recognized as a date and "two day" as a duration.

Temporal relations between events in the same sentence

Using the temporal relations presented above, the system can detect in certain syntactic configurations if predicates in the sentence are temporally related and what kind of relations exist between them. When it is explicit in the text, a temporal distance between the two events is also calculated.

The following example illustrates these temporal dependencies:

```
This move comes a month after
Qantas suspended a number of
services.
```

In this sentence, the clause containing the verb "suspended" is embedded into the main clause headed by "comes". These two events have a temporal distance of one month, which is expressed by the expression "a month after". We obtain the following dependencies:

```
ORDER[before](suspended, comes)
DELTA(suspended, comes, a month)
```

Verbal tenses and aspect

Morphological analysis gives some information about tenses. But the final tense of a complex verbal chain is calculated considering not only morphological clues, but also aspectual information. Tenses of complex verbal chains may be underspecified when there is insufficient context.

For instance, for the chain “has been taken”, we extract “take” as the semantic head of the verbal chain. The aspect is perfective and the tense of the auxiliary “has” is present.
From this information, we deduce that this form is either in present or in past. This is expressed the following way:

```
PRES-OR-PAST(taken).
```

2.3 Document level

Beyond sentence-level, the system is at the first stage of development. We are only able to complete relative dates when it refers to the document creation time, and to infer new relations with the help of composition rules, by saturating the graph of temporal relations (Muller and Tannier, 2004).

3 Adapting XTM to TempEval specifications

The TempEval track consists of three different tasks described in (Verhagen et al. 2007). TempEval guidelines present several differences with respect to our own methodology. These differences concern definitions of relations and events, as well as choices about linking.

3.1 TIMEX3 definition

TimeML definition of a temporal expression (TIMEX3) is slightly different from what we consider to be a temporal expression in XTM:

- First, we incorporate signals (in, at…) into temporal expressions boundaries. But, as TIMEX3s are provided in the test collection, a simple mapping is quite easy to perform.
- We also have a different tokenization for complex temporal expressions. This tokenization is based on syntactic and semantic properties of the whole expression.

For example, our criteria make that we consider “ten days ago yesterday" as a single temporal expression, while "during 10 days in December" should be split into "during 10 days" and "in December".

3.2 TIMEX3 linking

XTM does not handle temporal relations between events and durations. In our temporal model, an event can have duration. However, this is not represented by a temporal relation, but by an attribute of the event. Durations included in a larger temporal expression (like in “two days later”) introduce an interval for the temporal relation: AFTER(A, B, interval: two days). Here again no temporal relation is attributed with respect to the duration.

Therefore, we had to adapt our system so that it is able to infer at least some relations between events and durations. We used two ways to do so:

- An event having an explicit duration attributed by XTM gets the relation OVERLAP with this duration.
- An event occurring, for example, “two days after another one” (resp. “two days before”) gets the relation AFTER (resp. BEFORE) with this duration.

Other relations are found (or not) by composition rules.

3.3 TIMEX3 values

TempEval test collection provides a "value" attribute for each TIMEX3. However we did not use this value, because we wanted to obtain an evaluation as close as possible to a real world application. The only value we used was the given Document Creation Time.

3.4 EVENTs mapping

Event lists do not match either between TempEval corpus and our system analysis. Unfortunately, when a TempEval EVENT is not considered as an event by XTM, we did not find any successful way to map this EVENT to another event of the sentence.

3.5 Temporal relation mapping

The set of temporal relations we use is the following: AFTER, BEFORE, DURING, INCLUDES, OVERLAPS, IS_OVERLAPPED AND EQUALS.

This choice is explained in more details in (Muller and Tannier, 2004).

Obtaining TempEval relations from our own relations is straightforward: AFTER and BEFORE are kept just as they are. The other relations or disjunctions of these relations are turned into OVERLAP. Disjunctions of relations containing AFTER (resp. BEFORE) and OVERLAP-like relations are turned into OVERLAP-OR-AFTER (resp. BEFORE-OR-OVERLAP).

4 Results

The trial, training and test sets of document provided were all subsets of the annotated TimeBank corpus. For each task, two metrics are used, the strict measure and the relaxed measure (see also (Muller and Tannier, 2004)).

Our rule-based analyzer is designed to favor precision. As our system is intended for use in information extraction, finding correct relations is more important than finding a large number of relations. That is why, at least for tasks A and B, we do not assign a temporal relation when the parser does not find any link. For the same reason, in our opinion, the strict measure is not as valuable as the relaxed one. We would argue that it does not really make sense to use a strict metric in combination with disjunctive relations.

Tasks A and B were evaluated together. We obtained the best precision for relaxed matching (0.79), but with a low recall (respectively 0.50). Strict matching is not very different. Another interesting figure is that less than 10% of the relations are totally incorrect (e.g.: BEFORE instead of AFTER). As we said, this was our main aim.

Note that if we choose a default behavior (OVERLAP for task A, BEFORE for task B, which are respectively the most frequent relations) for every undefined relation, we obtain precision and recall of 0.69, which is lower than but not far from the best team results.

Task C was more exploratory. Even more than for task AB, the fact that we chose not to use the provided TIMEX3 values makes the problem harder. Our gross results are quite low. We used a default OVERLAP for each unfound relation[2] and finally got equal precision and recall of 0.57.

However, assigning OVERLAP to all 258 links led to precision and recall of 0.508; no team managed to bring a satisfying trade-off in this task.

5 Conclusion

We described in this paper the system that we adapted in order to participate to TempEval 2007 evaluation campaign. We obtained a good precision score and a very low rate of incorrect relations, which makes the tool robust enough for information extraction applications. Errors and low recall are mostly due to parsing errors or underspecification and to the fact that we gave priority to our own theoretical choices concerning event and temporal expression definitions and event-temporal expression linking.

References

James Allen, 1984. Toward a general theory of action and time. *Artificial Intelligence*, 23:123-154.

Salah Aït-Mokhtar, Jean-Pierre Chanod and Claude Roux. 2002. *Robustness beyond Shallowness: Incremental Deep Parsing*. Natural Language Engineering, 8 :121-144

Caroline Brun and Caroline Hagege, 2003. *Normalization and Paraphrasing using Symbolic Methods*, 2nd Workshop on Paraphrasing, ACL 2003.

Inderjeet Mani, James Pustejovsky and Robert Gaizauskas (ed.) 2005. *The Language of Time A reader.*

Philippe Muller and Xavier Tannier 2004. *Annotating and measuring temporal relations in texts.* In Proceedings of COLING 2004.

James Pustejovsky, Patrick Hanks, Roser Saurí, Andrew See, Robert Gaizauskas, Andrea Setzer and Beth Sundheim. 2003. The TIMEBANK Corpus. *Corpus Linguistics.* Lancaster, U.K.

Claude Roux. 2006. *Coupling a linguistic formalism and a script language.* CSLP-06, Coling-ACL.

Roser Saurí, Jessica Littman, Bob Knippen, Robert Gaizauskas, Andrea Setzer and James Pustejovsky. TimeML Annotation Guidelines. 2006.

Marc Verhagen, Robert Gaizauskas, Frank Schilder, Mark Hepple, Graham Katz and James Pustejovsky. 2007. *SemEval-2007 – Task 15: TempEval Temporal Relation Identification.* SemEval workshop in ACL 2007.

[2] The OVERLAP relation is the most frequent for task C training data.

Author Index

Task and System Index

Association for Computational Linguistics
209 N. Eighth Street
Stroudsburg, Pennsylvania 18360

Constraint Grammar - Methods, Tools, and Applications (CG-MTA 2023)

Thorshavn, Faroe Islands
22 May 2023